7250
85E

A Bookman's Guide to the Indians of the Americas:

a compilation of over
10,000 catalogue entries
with prices and annotations,
both bibliographical
and descriptive

by
RICHARD A. HAND

The Scarecrow Press, Inc.
Metuchen, N.J., & London
1989

British Library Cataloguing-in-Publication data available

Library of Congress Cataloging-in-Publication Data

Hand, Richard A., 1941-
    A bookman's guide to the Indians of the Americas :
a compilation of over 10,000 catalogue entries with
prices and annotations, both bibliographical and descriptive / by Richard A. Hand
        p.   cm.
    Includes index.
    ISBN 0-8108-2182-6
    1. Indians--Bibliography--Catalogs. I. Title.
Z1209.H24   1989
[E58]
016.97000497--dc19   88-38642

I Dedicate This Book

To My Wife

JEANNETTE ELAINE HAND

Who Knew I Could

Encouraged Me To

And Made Sure I Did

PREFACE

This "Bookman's Guide to the Indians of the Americas" is intended to provide a reference tool for the bookperson, whether he or she is a collector, dealer, or librarian.

In putting this book together, my tasks were to gather and arrange supplied information in some semblance of order. The credit for all other crucial talents, such as research, pricing and annotations, belongs to the book dealers whose catalogues are represented in this work.

I have tried to make this compilation as comprehensive as space limitations will permit, listing the following stable, permanent features of each book listed: author, title, size and number of volumes, pagination, place and date of publication, number of plates, maps, tables and charts, when available. Approximately 200 catalogues were used in this compilation. My goal for this book was to provide 10,000 listings with up-to-date prices and annotations, both bibliographical and descriptive, of books retailing for $10.00 or more.

Information as to book descriptions was kept as it appeared in the catalogue; the only liberty taken by me was to rewrite the entries to maintain a continuity of format. Minor injuries or blemishes are passed over without comment, because second-hand books are expected to display some indications of prior ownership. The reader should understand that most cataloguers only describe damage of a rather serious nature in their descriptions. I have listed without comment only items in "very good" condition. If less than very good condition, appropriate descriptions are given.

In some cases wide divergence in prices exists in identical books. These wide variances in prices in most cases can be attributed to the type of dealer, i.e., specialty dealers in American Indians or general line dealers. The specialty dealer usually has a customer base which allows him to charge a higher price. General line dealers usually do not have this customer base, and the resulting prices are lower. Other factors to be considered are the region where the book is offered for sale, supply and demand, and the overall condition of the book.

v

There are undoubtedly errors in this work. Cross-checking and proofreading have helped to eliminate most errors, but in a work consisting of so much transcription, it is inevitable that others remain. Contradictions of page numbers in book descriptions appear quite frequently. This is not so much due to erroneous information, but in the method the individual cataloguer uses in counting the pages. Some dealers disregard all preliminary pages when counting; others combine them with text pages and subsequent pages for a total count; others count only text pages, and still others differentiate between preliminary, text and remaining pages. This results in the possibility that the same book may be described with at least four different totals for the number of pages.

It should be kept in mind that price quotations listed in this book represent retail prices. Private book owners offering items for sale to dealers should quote far enough below prevailing prices to permit dealers to resell at a reasonable profit.

In closing, I wish to express my appreciation to Richard M. Weatherford for advice and assistance freely given; to Arnold M. Rogoff, of Ethnographic Arts Publications, for the use of his copyrighted material, and to my good friend Robert H. Richardson, whose sympathetic ear and biweekly luncheons helped keep me on course and preserve my sanity, and most importantly, to all the dealers whose catalogues were used in this work. After the hundreds of hours spent working with their catalogues, I must admit my admiration for their attention to detail, research, long hours spent in putting them together and their not infrequent good sense of humor.

Richard A. Hand
Antiquarian Bookseller
Wheeling, West Virginia

DIRECTORY OF BOOK DEALERS

Listed alphabetically below are the book dealers whose catalogues were used in this compilation. The identifying initials following each dealer's name are used throughout, giving intellectual credit in reference to annotations.

Argosy Book Store, Inc. (ABS), 116 East 59th Street, New York, NY, 10022

The Arthur H. Clark, Co. (AHC), P.O. Box 230, Glendale, CA, 91209

Bob Fein Books (BF), 150 Fifth Avenue, Room 623, New York, NY, 10011

Cedric L. Robinson (CLR), 597 Palisado Avenue, Windsor, CT, 06095

Christine Young Books (CY), 955 Park Avenue, New York, NY, 10028

Dean W. Hand-Books (DWH), P.O. Box 628, Sterling, CO, 80751

Ethnographic Arts Publications (EAP), 1040 Erica Road, Mill Valley, CA, 94941

G. F. Hollingsworth (GFH), P.O. Box 3725, Manhattan Beach, CA, 90266

High Latitude (HL), P.O. Box 11254, Bainbridge Island, WA, 98110

J. Parmer, Booksellers (JP), 7644 Forrestal Rd., San Diego, CA, 92120

Louis Collins Books (LC), 1211 East Denny Way, Seattle, WA, 98122

Magnum Opus Rare Books (Mag. Op.), P.O. Box 1301, Charlottesville, VA, 22902

Oregon Territorial Books (OTB), P.O. Box 22, Sublimity, OR, 97385

Pa-Has-Ka Books (PHK), 8436 Samra Drive, Canoga Park, CA, 91304

R. M. Weatherford, Inc. (RMW), P.O. Box 5, Southworth, WA, 98386

The Sagebrush Press (SP), P.O. Box 87, Morongo Valley, CA, 92256

T. N. Luther, Books (TNL), P.O. Box 429, Taos, NM, 87571

Trans-Allegheny Books, Inc. (TA), 8th and Green Streets, Parkersburg, WV, 26101

Territorial Editions, Inc. (TE), P.O. Box 8394, Santa Fe, NM, 87504

Wm. Reese Co. (WR), 409 Temple Street, New Haven, CT, 06511

Wm. Sutfin-Books (WS), P.O. Box 16144, Indianapolis, IN, 46216

ABBREVIATIONS

The abbreviations listed below are used in this compilation.

All edges gilt	a.e.g.
Boards	bds
Circa	c.
Cover(s)	cvr (cvrs)
Dust jacket	d.j.
Edition	ed.
Frontispiece	frontis
Hinge	hnge
Large	lrge or lrg
Leaf	lf
Leaves	lvs
No date	n.d.
No place	n.p.
Near	nr
Page(s)	p. (pp)
Plate(s)	pl (pls)
Printing	print.
Small	sml
Title page	t.p.
Top edge gilt	t.e.g.
Worn (wear)	wrn (wr)

REFERENCES

Adams. Six-Guns and Saddle Leather. A Bibliography of Books and Pamphlets on Western Outlaws and Gunmen. Norman, 1969.

Anderson. Southwestern American Literature. A Bibliography. 1980.

Arctic Institute. Arctic Bibliography. Washington, 1953.

Berlo. Art of Pre-Hispanic Mesoamerica. An Annotated Bibliography. Boston, 1985.

Bernal. Bibliografia de Arqueologia y Etnografia. Mexico, 1962.

Bureau of American Ethnology, Bulletin No. 200. List of Publications ... With Index to Authors and Titles. R. M. Weatherford, 1978.

Bureau of Indian Affairs. Annotated Bibliography of Alaska. Juneau, 1968.

Cowan. A Bibliography of the History of California and the Pacific West, 1510-1906. Columbus, 1962.

Cox. Reference Guide to Literature of Travel. Seattle, 1935.

Crotty. Zamorano 80. A Selection of Distinguished California Books. 1969.

Cuthbertson and Ewers. A Preliminary Bibliography on the American Fur Trade. St. Louis, 1939.

De Moraes. Bibliografia Brasiliana. Rio de Janeiro, 1958.

Dobie. Guide to Life and Literature of the Southwest. Dallas: 1965 (revised).

Dustin. Bibliography of the Battle of the Little Big Horn, in Colonel W. A. Graham's "The Custer Myth. A Source Book of Custeriana." Harrisburg, 1953.

Eberstadt. Catalogue #119. The Northwest Coast, A Century of Personal Narratives of Discovery, Conquest and Exploration from Bering's Landfall to Wilke's Surveys, 1741-1841. New York, (1941).

Field. An Essay Towards an Indian Bibliography. Columbus, 1951.

Harding and Bolling. Bibliography of Articles and Papers on North American Indian Art. New York, 1969.

Hargrett. The Gilcrease-Hargrett Catalogue of Imprints. Norman, 1972.

Haskell. United States Exploring Expeditions, its Publications. New York, 1968.

Howes. U.S.iana 1650-1950; A Selective Bibliography in which are Described 11,620 Uncommon and Significant Books Relating to the Continental Portion of the United States. New York, 1962.

Jennewein. Black Hills Booktrails. South Dakota, 1962.

Kendall. Art and Archaeology of Pre-Columbia Middle America. An Annotated Bibliography of Works in English. Boston, 1977.

Lada-Mocarski. Books on Alaska. New Haven, 1969.

Lande. A Bibliography of Canadiana. Montreal, 1965.

Larned. Literature of American History. Columbus, 1953.

Luther. Custer High Spots. (Ft. Collins), 1972.

McVicker. Writings of J. Frank Dobie. A Bibliography. Lawton, OK, 1968.

Newberry Library. (Ayer) Narratives of Captivity Among the Indians of North America ... in the Edward E. Ayer Collection. Chicago, 1912, and Supplement I, Chicago, 1926.

Peel. Bibliography of the Prairie Provinces. Toronto, 1956.

Pilling. Bibliography of the Algonquian Languages. BAE Bulletin No. 13, (1892).

_____. Bibliography of the Athapascan Languages. BAE Bulletin No. 14, 1892.

_____. Bibliography of the Chinookan Languages. BAE Bulletin No. 15, 1893.

_____. Bibliography of the Eskimo Language. BAE Bulletin No. 1, 1887.

_____. Bibliography of the Iroquoian Languages. BAE Bulletin No. 6, (1889).

_____. Bibliography of the Muskhogean Languages. BAE Bulletin No. 9, 1889.

_____. Bibliography of the Salishan Languages. BAE Bulletin No. 16, 1893.

_____. Bibliography of the Siouan Languages. BAE Bulletin No. 5, 1887.

_____. Bibliography of the Wakashan Languages. BAE Bulletin No. 19, 1894.

_____. Catalogue of Linguistic Manuscripts in the Library of the Bureau of Ethnology. BAE Annual Report No. 1, 1887.

Rader. South of Forty. From the Mississippi to the Rio Grande. A Bibliography. Norman, 1947.

Rittenhouse. The Santa Fe Trail. A Historical Bibliography. Albuquerque, (1971).

Rocq. California Local History, A Bibliography. 1970 (2nd revised ed.).

Sabin. Dictionary of Books Relating to America. New York, 1936.

Saunders. A Guide to Materials Bearing on Cultural Relations in New Mexico. Albuquerque, 1944.

Schoenberg. Jesuit Mission Presses in the Pacific Northwest. A History and Bibliography of Imprints, 1876-1899. Portland, 1957.

Smith. Pacific Northwest Americana. A Check List of Books and Pamphlets Relating to the History of the Pacific Northwest. 3rd edition revised and extended by Isabel Mayhew. Portland, 1950.

Smith and Wilder. Guide to the Art of Latin America. New York, 1948.

Storm. Catalogue of the Everett D. Graff Collection of Western Americana. Chicago, 1968.

Streeter. The T. W. Streeter Sale at Parke Bernet. 7 Volumes plus index volume, New York, 1969.

Wagner-Camp. The Plains and the Rockies. A Bibliography of Original Narratives of Travel and Adventure. 1800-1865. Columbus, 1953.

Wickersham. Bibliography of Alaskan Literature. Cordova, 1927.

Note: An additional 98 bibliographical references are listed in the index.

A1. ABBATE (Francesco) (Editor). Precolumbian Art of North
America and Mexico. 159pp, 98 full-color pls, bibliography, mostly devoted to Mexico, but some coverage of
Eskimo and North American Indian art. London, 1972.
d.j. $20.00

A2. ABBOTT (Charles C.) et al. Paleolithic Implements of the
Valley of the Delaware. pp124-149, wrappers, reprinted
from Peabody Museum, Proc. Vol. 21, Cambridge, 1881.
                                                        $10.00

A3. ABBOTT (D. N.) (Editor). The World Is as Sharp as a
Knife. An Anthology in Honor of Wilson Duff. 343pp,
187 photographs, 10pp color drawings, 75 b/w drawings,
2 maps. Victoria, 1981. $40.00
     In honor of Wilson Duff--anthropologist, teacher, writer,
admirer and lover of Northwest Coast art, and one of the
most influential persons in the field of the culture of Northwest Coast peoples--a number of friends, colleagues, and
former students contributed the papers in this anthology.
The 37 papers (which include several by Duff)--scientific,
literary and artistic--focus, not surprisingly, on Northwest
Coast art and include more than 200 illustrations many
previously unpublished. (EAP)

A4. ABBOTT (Jacob). American History. Volume I. Aboriginal
America. 288pp, map, pls, 12mo. New York, Sheldon,
1860 (1st ed.). $35.00
     Sabin: 31. Field: 3. History written for young peo-
ple. Charming illustrations.
     ___Another Copy. Same.

A5. ABEL (Annie H.) (Editor). Chardon's Journal at Fort Clark
1834-1839 ... A Fur Trader's Experiences Among Mandans,
Gross Ventres ... Ravages of Small Pox Epidemic of 1837.
xlvi, 457pp, 3 pls, notes, index. Pierre, SD, 1932 (1st
ed.). $75.00
     Descriptive of life on the Upper Missouri--of a fur
trader's experiences among the tribes and relating the
devastating small pox epidemic of 1837.
     ___Another Copy. Same. $75.00

A6. ABEL (Annie H.). (Annual Report of the American Historical
Assn. for 1906, Part I, Washington, 1908) The History of

Events Resulting in Indian Consolidation West of the Mississippi River. pp235-450, 3/4 leather. $75.00

A7. ABEL (Annie H.) (Editor). Tabeau's Narrative of Loisel's Expedition to the Upper Missouri. 272pp, index, folding chart. Norman, 1968, d.j. $25.00

One of the most important fur trade and Indian accounts extant. Tabeau's narrative covers a fur trading expedition during 1803 and 1804 with the Mandan and Arikara Indians.

A8. ABEL-VIDOR (Suzanne) et al. Between Continents, Between Seas: Pre-Columbian Art of Costa Rica. 240pp, 333 illus, including 100 color pls. New York, Abrams, 1981.
$25.00

A9. ABERLE (D. F.). (In Journal of American Folklore, Vol. 55, No. 217, 1942) Mythology of the Navaho Game Stick-Dice. pp144-155. $17.00

A10. ABERLE (D. F.). (University of Colorado, Series in Anthropology, No. 6, 1957) Navaho and Ute Peyotism: A Chronological and Distributional Study. ix, 129pp, 9 tables. $24.00
___Another Copy. Same. $20.00

A11. ABERLE (D. F.). (Viking Fund Publications in Anthropology, No. 42, 1966) The Peyote Religion Among the Navaho. 490pp, 26 photographs, 50 tables, 13 charts, 7 maps, diagrams and graphs, cloth. $48.00
___Another Copy. Same. Wrappers $38.00
___Another Copy. Same. $35.00
___Another Copy. Same. $35.00

A12. ABERLE (D. F.). (American Anthropologist, Vol. 50, No. 4, Part 2, 1948) The Pueblo Indians of New Mexico, Their Land, Economy and Civil Organizations. 93pp, 13 tables, 1 fold-out map. $14.00

A13. ABERT (Lt. J. W.). (GALVIN, John, Editor). Through the Country of the Comanche Indians in the Fall of the Year 1845. 77pp, color pls, 2 folding maps, 4to. San Francisco, 1970. $50.00

A14. ABRAHAM (Eli). (Sioux Indian Language) Yewicasipi Taanpetupi En: Wotatin Waste Ayapi. 62pp, 5 maps, 12 mo, an outline of the life of St. Paul, wrappers. Santee, NE, 1925. $75.00

A15. ABRAMS (George H. J.). The Seneca People. 106pp, photographs, b/w and color drawings, maps, wrappers, part of the Indian Tribal Series. Phoenix, 1976 (1st ed.).
$15.00

A16. ACEVEDO (G. R.). Apuntes para la Interpretacion de los Datos Cronologicos Expresados en los Jeroglificos Mayas del Codice de Dresden, 69pp, illus (7 facsimile pls) in rear pocket. Mexico, 1979. $35.00

ACKERKNECHT (Erwin H.). See BAE Bulletin No. 143.

A17. ACKERMAN (Robert E.). The Kenaitze People. 106pp, b/w and color photographs, drawings, maps, wrappers, part of the Indian Tribal Series. Phoenix, 1975 (1st ed.).
$15.00

A18. ACOSTA (J. R.). (Instituto Nacional de Antropologia e Historia, Memorias, Mexico City, 1964) El Palacio del Quetzalpapalotl. 85pp of text containing 6pp of color pls, 10pp of b/w pls, plus 50pp of photographs and 22pp of drawings, cloth. $30.00

A19. ACOSTA (Jorge). Esplendor del Mexico Antiguo. (2 Volumes.) Vol. I: xxvi, 478pp approx 1,250 b/w and color photographs, drawings and maps. Vol. II: xiii, pp479-1281, approx 2,000 b/w and color photographs, drawings and maps, leather cvrd bds in original d.j., inner hinges Vol. I have been reinforced. Centro de Investigaciones Anthropologicas de Mexico, Mexico City, 1959. $275.00
  Both volumes considered to be among the most notable and comprehensive publications in the past three decades on Mexican archaeology.
  ___Another Copy. Same. $175.00
  ___ Another Copy. Same, some wear to d.j. $85.00

A20. ACUNA (Rene). (Centro de Estudio Mayas Cuaderno 15, Mexico, 1978) Farsas y Representaciones Escenicas de los Mayas Antiguos. 75pp, illus, wrappers. $15.00

A21. ACUNA (Rene). (Centro de Estudio Mayas Cuaderno 12, Mexico, 1975) Introduccion al Estudio del Rabinal Achi. 216pp, folded charts, wrappers. $25.00

A22. ADAIR (James). History of the American Indians, Particularly Those Nations Adjoining to the Mississippi. xxviii, 508pp, folding map, limited to 750 copies, cloth. Nashville, 1953. $30.00
  Howes: A-38. Larned: "A work of great value, showing the relations of the English traders to the Indians, and is of much importance to the student of Indian customs." (GFH)
  ___Another Copy. New York, Johnson Reprints, 1968, facsimile reprint of 1775 1st ed., ... East and West Florida, Georgia, South and North Carolina and Virginia. 464pp, folding map, review copy. $65.00
  ___Another Copy. New York, 1973, d.j. 508pp, map endpapers, index. $30.00
  ___Another Copy. New York, 1980, d.j. $25.00
  ___ Another Copy. New York, 1986, edited with introduction by S. C. Williams. $30.00

A23. ADAIR (J.). The Navajo and Pueblo Silversmiths. 237pp, 24pp photographs, 11 tables, 2 maps, cloth. Norman, 1944 (1st ed.). $25.00
  Authoritative account of the Indian silver jewelry fashioned in the Southwest by the Navajo, Zuni, Hopi, etc., illustrated with 24 full-page plates.
  ___Another Copy. Norman, 1966, d.j., 220pp, illus, index, bibliography, map. $20.00
  ___Another Copy. Norman, 1970, d.j. $10.00

A24. ADAM (Leonhard). Nordwestamerikanische Indianerkunst. 44pp, 48pls, text figures, original bds. Orbis Pictus

Band 17, Berlin, n.d. (c. 1920). $25.00

___Another Copy. Same. Berlin, 1923. $50.00

A25. ADAMIC (Louis). The House in Antigua. 300pp, decorated
cloth. New York, 1937 (1st ed.). $35.00

A26. ADAMS (Alexander). Geronimo, a Bibliography. 381pp,
frontis, 18pp photographs, notes, bibliography, index,
endpaper maps. New York, Putnam, 1971 (1st ed.).
                                             $20.00

___Another Copy. Same. $25.00

___Another Copy. Same. $20.00

A27. ADAMS (Alexander B.). Sitting Bull. An Epic of the
Plains. 431pp, index, photographs, notes, bibliography.
New York, 1973 (1st ed.). $10.00

A28. ADAMS (Arthur) (Editor). The Explorations of Pierre Esprit
Radisson. 342pp, map, index. Minneapolis, 1961, d.j.
                                             $25.00

Originally published in 1885, this edition is taken from
the manuscript in the British Museum and includes all six
"voyages" plus a new biographical sketch and an informative foreword. Firsthand material on the Indians of the
Great Lakes region during the 17th Century. (GFH)

A29. ADAMS (C.). Fritz Scholder: Lithographs. 192pp, 78
b/w and 25 color illus. Boston, 1976. $22.00

A30. ADAMS (Evelyn C.). American Indian Education. 122pp,
maps, bibliography, index, from the 1600s to the present.
New York, 1946 (1st ed.). $15.00

A31. ADAMS (Richard C.). The Ancient Religion of the Delaware
Indians and Observations and Reflections. 45pp, photographic frontis, wrappers. Rader: 51. Washington,
1904 (1st ed.). $15.00

A32. ADAMS (R. E.) and HAVILAND (W. A.) et al. Tikal Reports. (Numbers 5-10) 225pp, 73 figures. University
Museum, Philadelphia, 1961.

A33. ADAMS (Robert M.). (Transactions of Academy of Sciences
St. Louis, Vol. XXX, No. 5, 1941) Archaeological Investigations in Jefferson County, Missouri, 1939-40. pp151-221,
pls, map, bibliography, wrappers. $15.00

A34. ADAMS (R. N.). (American Ethnological Society, Seattle,
1959) A Community in the Andes, Problems and Progress
in Muquiyauauyo. 251pp, 2 figures, 3 maps, cloth.
                                             $20.00

A35. ADAMS (R. W.). (Peabody Museum, Papers, Vol. 63, No.
1, 1971) The Ceramics of Altar de Sacrificios. x, 177pp
of text containing 26 tables, plus 107pp of photographs
and drawings of approx 1500 artifacts, 11 charts in a rear
pocket. $65.00

A36. ADAMS (Spencer L.). The Long House of the Iroquois.
175pp, 125 photographs. Illinois, 1944 (1st ed.) $60.00

A37. ADAMS (William H.) et al. (Washington State University
Reports, Investigations, No. 53, 1975) Archaeological

Excavations at Silcott, WA: The Data Inventory. xi,
280pp, figures, bibliography, lrg 8vo, wrappers. $15.00
ADAMS (William Y.). See BAE Bulletin No. 188.

A38. ADAMSON (Thelma) (Editor). (Memoirs of American Folk
Lore Society, Vol. XXVII, New York, 1934, 1st ed.)
Folk-Tales of the Coast Salish. xv, 430pp, map, upper
Chehalis, Cowlitz, Humptulip, Wynoochee, Satsop and
other tribal stories, tales refer to time "when all the
animals were people," i.e., most participants are animals.
$55.00

A39. ADELSON (L.) and TRACT (A.). Aymara Weavings, Ceremonial Textiles of Colonial and 19th Century Bolivia.
159pp, 101 photographs, 1 map, 1 chart. Washington,
1983. $28.00
This history of the weaving tradition of the Aymara
Indians of Bolivia was published to accompany a traveling
exhibition of some of the finest--and most beautiful--of
these textiles. Never before had such a rare and comprehensive collection--ponchos, tunics, skirts, mantles,
coca bags, coca cloth and belts--been assembled, and it
is documented in color photographs. (EAP)

A40. ADNEY (E. T.) and CHAPELLE (H. I.). (Smithsonian Museum of History and Technology, Washington, 1964)
The Bark Canoes and Skin Boats of North America.
242pp, 224 figures, 4to. $60.00
___Another Copy. Same. $25.00

A41. ADOVASIO (J. M.). (University of Pittsburgh, Ethnology
Monograph No. 7, 1985) Basketry and Miscellaneous
Perishable Artifacts from Walpi Pueblo, Arizona. xiii,
121pp, 59 figures. $28.00

A42. ADOVASIO (J. M.). The Origin, Development and Distribution of Western Archaic Textiles. xi, 106pp, doctoral
dissertation, 8pp of figures, 5 tables, cloth. Provo,
privately printed, 1970. $60.00

A43. AGASSIZ (Prof. and Mrs. Louis). A Journey in Brazil.
569pp, illus, original cloth, handsome cuts and pls showing native costumes, arts and crafts, native types, much
history and anthropology. Boston, 1868 (2d ed.). $85.00

A44. (AGENCIES). (House of Representatives Document 56,
18:1, Washington, 1824, 1st print.) Indian Agencies.
7pp, removed, review of agencies and plans for moving
tribes. $10.00

A45. (AGENCIES). (Senate Executive Document 75, 53:2, Washington, 1894, 1st print.) Indian Agencies of the United
States. 6pp, removed, letter from Secretary of Interior,
lists agents, agencies, tribes and locations. $10.00

A46. (AGENTS). (Doc. No. 1, Washington, 1850) Report of
the Commissioner of Indian Affairs for 1850. 141pp,
removed, wrappers. This document contains 38 reports
of Indian agents mostly from Western agencies including
a lengthy report from Thomas Fitzpatrick and several

from J. S. Calhoun at Sante Fe. Wagner-Camp: 149n.
$45.00

A47. AGNEW (Brad). Fort Gibson, Terminal on the Trail of Tears. 261pp plus index, photographs, drawings, maps, bibliography, established in 1824, Ft. Gibson served as a means of control for the removed eastern tribes. Norman, 1981 (2d print), d.j. $15.00

A48. AGRINIER (P.). (New World Archaeological Foundation, Brigham Young University Paper No. 16, 1964) The Archaeological Burials at Chiapa De Corzo and Their Furniture. 76pp, 131 figures. $12.00

A49. AGRINIER (P.). (New World Archaeological Foundation, Brigham Young University Paper No. 6, 1960) The Carved Human Femurs from Tomb 1, Chiapa De Corzo, Chiapas, Mexico. 43pp, 49 figures. $20.00

A50. AGRINIER (P.). (New World Archaeological Foundation, Brigham Young University, Paper No. 24, 1969) Excavations at San Antonio, Chiapas, Mexico. 63pp, 96 figures. $10.00

A51. AGRINIER (P.). (New World Archaeological Foundation, Brigham Young University, Paper No. 39, 1975) Mounds 9 and 10 at Mirador, Chiapas, Mexico. 104pp, 89 figures. $15.00

A52. AGRINIER (P.). (New World Archaeological Foundation, Brigham Young University, Paper No. 28, 1969) Mound 20, Mirador, Chiapas, Mexico. 84pp, 107 figures. $10.00

A53. AGRINIER (P.). (New World Archaeological Foundation, Brigham Young University, Paper No. 42, 1978) A Sacrificial Mass Burial at Miramar, Chiapas, Mexico. 52pp, 39 figures. $10.00

A54. AGUILERA (Carmen). Codices del Mexico Antiguo: Una Seleccion. 137pp, 18 illus, several in color, wrappers. Exhibition catalogue, Instituto Nacional de Antropologia e Historia, Mexico, 1979. $20.00
___Another Copy. Same. $18.00

A55. AGUIRRE BELTRAN (Gonzalo). Cuijla: Esbozo Ethnografico de un Pueblo Negro Mexico. 241pp, illus, folded map. Mexico. 1958, 1974 (reprint). $25.00

A56. AHENAKEW (Edward). (BUCK, Ruth, Editor). Voices of the Plains Cree. 204pp, illus, bibliography, cloth, Ahenakew transcribed Cree legends told to him by a Cree Chief and added some of his own stories. Toronto, 1973, d.j. $15.00

A57. AIELLO (Constantine) (Editor). OO-OOnah Art. 6pp, 40pp, 31 color pls, introduction by Frank Waters, pictorial cloth, autographed by editor, limited to 1200 copies, Taos Indian children's art. Tanner: B6. Taos, 1970 (1st ed.). $35.00

A58. Akten Des 34 Internationale Amerikanistenkongress. Wein, 18-25, Juli 1960. viii, 874pp, approx 125 figures. Vienna, 1962. $55.00

A59. (ALASKA). Annotated Bibliography on Alaska. 58pp.
      U.S. Department of Interior, Bureau of Indian Affairs,
      Juneau, 1968 (revised). $14.00
A60. (ALASKA). (Anthropological Papers of the University of
      Alaska, Vol. 12, No. 2, Summer, 1964) 135pp, 36 illus,
      articles include: Origin of the "Chief's Copper." $10.00
A61. (ALASKA). (Senate Executive Document 14, 51:2, Wash-
      ington, 1890, 1st print.) Condition of the Natives of
      Alaska. 5pp, removed, plea by Sheldon Jackson for
      methods of making Indians self-sufficient again. $12.00
A62. (ALASKA). (Peabody Foundation Papers, Vol. 6, Nos.
      1 and 2, 1964) Investigations in Southwest Yukon.
      488pp, illus, folding map. $60.00
A63. (ALASKA). (University Museum, Philadelphia, Bulletin
      Vol. 4, No. 2, 1933) Three Carvings from Cook Inlet,
      Alaska. pp56-58, 1 full-page photograph. $10.00
A64. ALBERS (Anni). Pre-Columbian Mexican Miniatures. Pro-
      fusely illus, lrg 4to. New York, 1970, d.j. $65.00
A65. ALCINA (J.). L'Art Precolombien. 613pp, 177 color
      photographs--mostly full page--and 875 b/w photographs
      and drawings, plus 124 drawings of Maya divinities,
      glyphs and hieroglyphs, cloth. Paris, 1978. $195.00
          An absolutely sumptuous volume that covers the entire
      panorama of pre-Columbian art, this thick, picture-filled
      book is very ambitious in its scope--and it comes as close
      to achieving that ambition as any volume. Examples of
      virtually every culture/period/type of pre-Columbian art
      --principally from great European museum collections--are
      illustrated. Text in French. (EAP)
      ___Another Copy. New York, 1983, Pre-Columbian Art.
      The English language edition to the above title, identical
      to the French edition, though the color plates in the
      French seem to be a bit stronger. $125.00
A66. ALDAN (John Richard). John Stuart and the Southern
      Colonial Frontier. A Study of Indian Relations, War,
      Trade, and Land Problems in the Southern Wilderness,
      1754-1775. 384, (1)pp, frontis, illus with 4 maps, ap-
      pendix, bibliography, index, cloth. New York, Gordian
      Press, 1966, reprint of University of MI Press 1944 ed.
                                                           $25.00
A67. ALDEN (Timothy). An Account of Sundry Missions Per-
      formed Among the Senecas and Munsees. frontis, por-
      trait, 180pp, 12mo, original leather backed bds. New
      York, J. Seymour, 1827 (1st ed.) $70.00
          This little volume contains many valuable historical and
      biographical sketches, particularly one of Cornplanter.
      Also contains a short vocabulary of the dialect of the
      Seneca Indians. Howes: A-106. Field: 20. (RMW)
A68. ALEKSEENKO (E. A.). Ketv, Istorinko-Ethnograficheskic
      Ocherki. 262pp, (papers dealing with the shelter,
      rituals, masks and carved figures of Arctic peoples)

54 b/w photographs and drawings, color pl, cloth. Museum of Anthropology, Moscow, 1967. $40.00

A69. ALEXANDER (H.). Manito Masks: American Indian Spirit Legends. 209pp, 12 woodcuts by Anders J. Haugseth, cloth. New York, 1925. $65.00

___Another Copy. Same. Cvr scuffed, spine repaired. $50.00

A70. ALEXANDER (Harley Burr). L'Art et la Philosophie des Indiens de l'Amerique du Nord. iii, 116pp, 26 pls, 5 in color, 1/2 linen, marbled bds. Paris, E. Leroux, 1926. $65.00

A71. ALEXANDER (H. B.). North American Mythology. 323pp, color frontis, 33 pls of which 13 are in color. Boston, 1937. $40.00

A72. ALEXANDER (H. B.) and HIGHWATER (J.) (intro.). Pueblo Indian Painting. 28pp, 50 loose color lithographs in a tied linen portfolio case. C. Szwedzicki, Nice, 1932; Bell Editions, Santa Fe, 1979 (facsimile reprint) $395.00
Limited edition facsimile reprint of the rare 1932 folio is almost faithful to the original. Color lithographs are $22\frac{1}{2}"x15\frac{1}{4}"$ in size, signed by Jamake Highwater. (EAP)

A73. ALEXANDER (H. B.). Sioux Indian Painting. (In Two Parts). Part I: Painting of the Sioux and Other Tribes of the Great Plains. 15pp of text, 20 color and 5 b/w lithographs. Nice, C. Szwedzicki, 1938. Part II: The Art of Amos Bad Heart Buffalo. 10pp text, 22 color and 3 b/w lithographs. Nice, C. Szwedzicki, 1938. Both parts. $2,500.00
One of the earliest and most important publications on Plains Indian painting, these two rare folios ($19\frac{1}{2}"x15\frac{1}{4}"$) contain stunning lithographs done by Sioux, Mandan, Shoshone, and Kiowa artists in Part I, and in Part II by Amos Bad Heart Buffalo, quite probably the most notable Plains Indian artist whose work is known. The texts, in English and French, provide an overview of the folios and give detailed information on each lithograph. Each of these publications was limited to an edition of 400 and was signed by the publisher. (EAP)

A74. ALEXANDER (H. B.). The World's Rim. Great Mysteries of the North American Indians. 243pp plus index, foreword by Clyde Kluckhohn, the rituals of the American Indians. Lincoln, 1953 (1st ed.), d.j. $25.00

A75. ALEXANDER (R. K.). (University of Texas Archeological Survey Papers, No. 19, Austin, 1970, 1st ed.) Archeological Investigations of Parida Cave Val Verde County, Texas. 103pp, maps, pls, bibliography, lrg 8vo, wrappers. $10.00

A76. (ALGONKIANS). Researches and Transactions of the New York State Archaeological Association, Rochester, 1923. (2 parts.) Part I: The Algonkian Occupation in New York, by A. Skinner. 48pp, 5 pls. Part II: Outline

of the Algonkian Occupation in New York, by A. C.
Parker. pp49-80, pls 6-20, wrappers. $35.00

A77. ALLA (Ogal). Blue Eye, A Story of the People of the
Plains by Ogal Alla (pseud. of F. G. Mock). 245pp, pictorial cloth. Portland, Irwin Hodson, 1905 (1st ed.).
$25.00
___Another Copy. Same. ALLA (Ogal) or (Blue Eye).
A Story of the People of the Plains. $20.00

A78. ALLEN (Charles). Report on the Stockbridge Indians, to
the Legislature. pp23, wrappers. Boston, Wright and
Potter, 1870 (1st ed.). $50.00

A79. ALLEN (E. A.). The Prehistoric World: Or, Vanished
Races. 820pp, pictorial cloth, about Indian races of the
world, contains a long section on the Pueblo country of
Arizona and New Mexico. Cincinnati, 1885 (1st ed.).
$40.00

A80. ALLEN (L. G.). (Museum of Northern Arizona, 1984)
Contemporary Hopi Pottery. 127pp, 144 b/w and 84 color
photographs. $15.00

A81. ALLEN (L. L.). A Thrilling Sketch of the Life of the Distinguished Chief Okah Tubbee of Choctaw Nation of Indians. 43pp, wrappers, 12mo. New York, 1848 (1st
ed.). $100.00

A82. ALLEN (Philippa). Whispering Wind. Folktales of the
Navaho Indians. 63pp, frontis, cloth. Chicago, 1930
(1st ed.). $25.00
___Another Copy. Same. d.j. $12.00

A83. ALLEN (T. D.). Navahos Have Five Fingers. 241pp plus
index, illus, map endpapers, bibliography, thorough
account of the Navaho of today, compared to their background. Norman, 1963 (1st ed.), d.j. $25.00
___Another Copy. Norman, 1982, d.j. 249pp. $17.00

A84. ALLEN (Wilkes). The History of Chelmsford: A Memoir of
the Pawtuckett Tribe of Indians. 192pp, 8vo, original
bds, limited to 400 copies. Howes: A-161. Sabin: 883.
Field: 26. Haverhill, P. N. Green, 1820 (1st ed.).
$135.00

A85. ALLEN (Dr. William A.). Adventures with Indians and Game,
or, Twenty Years in the Rocky Mountains. 302pp, illus,
decorated leather, Time-Life reprint of the 1903 ed.
1983. $25.00

A86. (ALLOTMENTS). (Senate Bill S5973, 62:2, Washington,
1912) A Bill authorizing the Secretary of the Interior to
cause allotments to be made to the Indians of the Morongo
Indian Reservation in California. 1pp, removed. $10.00

A87. (ALLOTMENTS). (House of Representatives House Bill 8359,
64:1, Washington, 1916) A Bill authorizing the Secretary
of the Interior to cause allotments to be made on Mission
Indian Reservations in California. 1pp, removed. $10.00

A88. ALMSTEDT (Ruth F.). Bibliography of the Diegueno Indians. 52pp, 4to, wrappers, lists 500 works of ethnographic, historical, linguistic and anthropological nature with map showing Diegueno territory in upper and lower California. Ramona, 1974 (1st ed.). $18.00

ALPHONSE (Ephraim S.). See also BAE Bulletin No. 162.

A89. ALSBERG (John L.) and PETSCHEK (Rodolfo). Ancient Sculpture from Western Mexico: The Evolution of Artistic Form. lrg 4to, illus with photographs. Berkeley, 1968, d.j. $65.00

A90. ALSOP (George). A Character of the Province of Maryland; A Treatise on the Wild and Naked Indians (Susquehanokes). A New Edition. 125pp, (4 advs.), 40 (Gowan Catalogue), portrait, map, cloth, reprint of the very rare London 1666 edition, contains valuable introduction and notes by John G. Shea. Howes: A-188. Sabin: 963. Field: 28. New York, W. Gowans, 1869. $65.00

A91. ALVA (Ixtlilxochitl), Bartolome de. Confessionario Mayor, y Menor en Lengua Mexicana ... Nuevamente Compuesto por ... Bartholome de Alva .... Quarto, contemporary limp vellum with title hand-lettered on spine, title page and first leaf of text defective, with pieces torn away and replaced, with some loss. Imprenta de Francisco Salbago, Mexico, 1634. $4,800.00

Vinaza: 167. Garcia Icazbalceta Lenguas: 83. Medina (Mexico) P 444. Palau: 9049. Alva, a son of Fernando Alva Ixtlilxochitl (the author of "La Historia Chicimeca" and other ethnohistorical works in Nahuatl), was a native of Mexico, a descendent of the Kings of Tezcuco, and an ecclesiastical judge in Chiapa de Mota and a Nahuatl expert. An early confessional in Nahuatl, the language of the Aztecs, and Spanish in double-column format, with the Credo, Paternoster, Ave Maria and Salve in Nahuatl only. Included are discourses against the superstitions of idolatry. The importance of this and other confessionals as sources for social history of the New World should not be underestimated. They provide researchers with a view into the confessional box where they can observe the European moral training of the natives. The scheme in which degrees of culpability are attached to various kinds of sins, indicated by amounts and types of penances required, is very refined and supplies significant material for study of the interaction of European and non-European values. (WR)

A92. ALVARDO TEZOZOMOC (Hernando De). Cronica Mexicana: Escrita Hacia el Ano de 1598. Notas de Manuel Orozco y Berra. 545pp, wrappers. Mexico, 1944. $35.00

A93. ALVAREZ (Carlos) and CASASOLA (Luis). Las Figurillas de Jonuta, Tabasco. 117pp, 36 pls of multiple artifacts. Mexico, 1935. $25.00
_____Another Copy. Same. $20.00

A94. ALVAREZ (Maria Cristina). (Seminarion de Estudios de la Escritura Maya Cuaderno 1, Mexico, 1969) Description

Estructural Del Maya De Chilam Balam De Chunmayel.
87pp, wrappers. $15.00

A95.   ALVAREZ (M. C.). Diccionario Ethnolinguistico del Idioma
Maya Yucateco Colonial. 377pp, wrappers, Mexico, UNAM,
1965. $30.00

A96.   (AMAZON INDIANS) Indiens D'Amazone Bresil. 96pp,
22pp photographs, 12 drawings, exhibition catalogue,
Musee d'Ethnogrpahie, Geneva, 1971) $12.00

A97.   AMBLER (J. Richard). (Texas Historical Commission, Report No. 8, Austin, 1967, 1st ed.) Three Prehistoric
Sites Near Cedar Bayou, Galveston Bay Area. 83pp,
illus, pls, maps, bibliography, lrg 8vo, wrappers.
$10.00
_____Another Copy. Same. $10.00

A98.   AMBLER (J. R.). (University of Texas, Archeological Survey Report, No. 6, Austin, 1968, 1st ed.) Wallisville
Reservoir Area, Southeast Texas. 33pp, maps, pls, bibliography, lrg 8vo, wrappers. $10.00

A99.   AMSDEN (C. A.). Prehistoric Southwesterners from Bas-
ketmaker to Pueblo. 177pp, 39 full-page photographs.
Southwest Museum, Los Angeles, 1949. $23.00
_____Another Copy. Los Angeles, 1976. $10.00
_____Another Copy. Same. $12.00

A100.   AMSDEN (C. A.). Navaho Weaving, Its Technic and History. xviii, 261pp of text, 123pp of illus, 108pp b/w
photographs, 6pp color photographs, 9pp drawings, lrg
fold-out color frontis of Saxony serape, drawn by Tom
Lea, foreword by F. W. Hodge, color linen cvr done in
a 3rd phase chief design. Santa Ana, Fine Arts Press,
1934. $495.00
     Still the most comprehensive volume ever published on
Navaho weaving, this rare first edition of Amsden's major
opus contains more illustrations and information than any
other text on the subject. This edition was limited to
1,000 copies. (EAP)
_____Another Copy. Albuquerque, 1949 (2d ed.), xx,
263pp. $195.00
_____Another Copy. Chicago, 1964, First Rio Grande
Press Edition, xviii, 261pp, red cloth. $40.00

A101.   AMSDEN (Monroe). (Southwest Museum Papers No. 1, Los
Angeles, 1970) Archaeological Reconnaissance in Sonora.
51pp, illus, map, wrappers. $10.00

A102.   (ANALES). Anales del Instituto Nacional de Antropologia
e Historia. Tomo II. 1941-1946. 472pp, many photographs, drawings and maps, heavily illus sections on
friezes in Teotihuacan and the temples of Quetzacoatl.
Mexico City, 1947. $45.00

A103.   (ANALES). Anales del Instituto Nacional de Antropologia
e Historia. Tomo III, 1947-1948. 218pp, many photographs, drawings and maps. Mexico City, 1949. $25.00

A104.   (ANALES). Anales Instituto Nacional de Antropologia e

Historia. Tomo XVII-1964. XLV de la Coleccion. 483pp, many photographs. Mexico City, 1965. $25.00

A105. (ANALES). Anales Instituto Nacional de Antropologia e Historia. Volume 1. 248pp. Mexico City, 1965. $15.00

A106. (ANALES). Anales Instituto Nacional de Antropologia e Historia. Volume 2. 265pp. Mexico City, 1965. $15.00

A107. (ANALES). Anales Instituto Nacional de Antropologia e Historia, Epoca 7a, Tomo II. 395pp, approx 150 photographs, drawings and maps. Mexico City, 1969. $20.00

A108. (ANALES). Anales Instituto Nacional de Antropologia e Historia, Epoca 7a, Tomo III. 224pp, approx 150 photographs, drawings and maps. Mexico City, 1973. $15.00

A109. (ANALES). Anales Instituto Nacional de Antropologia e Historia, Epoca 7a, Tomo IV. 376pp, several hundred photographs and drawings. Mexico City, 1975. $20.00

A110. (ANALES). Anales Instituto Nacional de Antropologia e Historia, Epoca 7a, Tomo V. 304pp, several hundred photographs and drawings. Mexico City, 1976. $20.00

A111. (ANALES). Anales Instituto Nacional de Antropologia e Historia, Primer Centenario 1877-1976, Epoca 7a, Tomo VI. 287pp, approx 100 photographs and drawings, maps. Mexico City, 1976. $20.00

A112. (ANALES). Anales Instituto Nacional de Antropologia e Historia, Epoca 8a, Tomo I. 139pp, 32 photographs, 6pp of maps. Mexico City, 1977. $10.00

A113. ANAWALT (P. R.). Indian Clothing Before Cortes: MesoAmerican Costumes from the Codices. xx, 232pp, 16 color pls, 64 figures, 4to. Norman, 1981 (1st ed.), d.j. $45.00

A114. Ancient Images on Stone, Rock Art of the Californias. 128pp, 21 full-page photographs, 21 drawings, 2 maps. Institute of Archaeology, Los Angeles, 1983. $45.00

A115. (ANCIENT MEXICO). (Instituto Nacional de Antropologia e Historia, Memorias XI, Mexico City, 1964) Colegios de Tepotzotlan, Restauraciones y Museologia. 132pp of text containing 64 photographs, 31pp of plans, most of which are fold-out, 5 fold-out color drawings, decorated cloth cvr. $45.00

A116. ANDERS (F.). Das Pantheon der Maya. viii, 433pp, 30pp of color and b/w photographs, 144 drawings, cloth. Graz, 1963. $75.00

A117. ANDERSON (Arthur J. O.) and DIBBLE (Charles E.) (Editors). The War of Conquest. How it Was Waged Here in Mexico. The Aztecs' Own Story as Given to Fr. Bernardino de Sahagun, Rendered into Modern English. 94pp, mainly double column, drawings, review copy. Salt Lake City, 1978 (1st ed.). $10.00

A118. ANDERSON (Bernice G.) Trickster Tales from Prairie Lodgefires. 94pp, illus, Kiowa and Ponca legends. Nashville, 1979 (1st ed.), d.j. $10.00

A119. ANDERSON (Eugene N.). (Anthropological Papers 11,

Socorro, Ballena Press, 1978) A Revised, Annotated Bibliography of the Chumash and Their Predecessors. 82pp, wrappers. $18.00

___Another Copy. Same. $12.00

A120. ANDERSON (Eva Greenslit). Chief Seattle. 386pp plus index, b/w and color illus, map endpapers. Caldwell, 1950 (3rd print.) $10.00

A121. ANDERSON (George E.). Treaty Making and Treaty Rejection By The Federal Government in California, 1850-1852. 124pp, 4to, wrappers, full study of the treaties between the U.S. Government and the California Indians. Socorro, 1978 (1st ed.). $13.00

A122. ANDERSON (Keith M.) et al. (Southern Methodist University Contributions to Anthropology, No. 11, Dallas, 1974) Archaeological Investigations at Lake Palestine, Texas. 203pp, photographs, drawings, maps, wrappers. $10.00

A123. ANDERSON (Rufus). Memoir of Catherine Brown. A Christian Indian of the Cherokee Nation. 143pp, frontis. full leather. Cincinnati, 1827 (3rd ed.). $100.00

Howes: A-235. Field: 32. Born in 1800 in present-day Alabama, Catherine Brown was one of the first Cherokees to be educated by the White Missionaries at Chic-a-mau-gah. (TA)

A124. ANDERSON (R. W.) and EHRENBERG (F.). A Celebration of Masks from Chicago Collections. 36pp, 109 photographs. Chicago, 1984. $12.00

A125. ANDREWS (C. L.). The Eskimo and His Reindeer in Alaska. 253pp, 8vo, photographic pls, frontis map. Caldwell, 1939 (1st ed.), d.j. $55.00

___Another Copy. Same. $75.00

A126. ANDREWS (E. W.) and ROVNER (I.). (Middle American Research, Tulane University, Publication 31, No. 4, 1973) Archaeological Evidence on Social Stratification and Commerce in the North Maya Lowlands: Two Masons' Tool Kits from Muna and Dzibilchaltun, Yucatan. 21pp, 11 figures. $10.00

A127. ANDREWS (E. W.). (Middle American Research, Tulane University Publication 34, 1969) The Archaeological Use and Distribution of Mullusca in the Maya Lowlands. 115pp, 6 figures, 21 pls. $55.00

A128. ANDREWS (E. W.). (Middle American Research, Tulane University Publication 32, 1970) Galankanche, Throne of the Tiger Priest. Archaeological Discoveries in a Yucatan Cave, with Transcription and Translation of Modern Maya Ritual Celebrated Therein. 196pp, 60 figures, 2 color pls, 33 1/3 record included, cloth. $65.00

A129. ANDREWS (E. W.). (Middle American Research, Tulane University Publication 31, No. 1, 1965) Explorations in the Gruta de Chac, Yucatan, Mexico. 30pp, illus. $20.00

A130. ANDREWS (E. W.). (Middle American Research, Tulane

University Publication 31, No. 2, 1965) Progress Report
on the 1960-64 Field Seasons, National Geographic Society,
Tulae University Dzibilchaltun Program. 44pp, 11 figures,
5 tables. $15.00

A131. ANDREWS (E. W.) and STUART (G. E.). (Middle American Research, Tulane University, Publication 31, No. 3,
1968) The Ruins of Ikil, Yucatan, Mexico. 12pp, 8
figures. $10.00

A132. ANDREWS (Ralph W.). Indian Primitive: Northwest Coast
Indians of the Former Days. 175pp, numerous illus,
sml 4to. New York, Bonanza Reprint of 1960 ed. $35.00
_____Another Copy. New York, 1960, d.j. $14.00

A133. ANDREWS (R. W.). Indians as the Westerners Saw Them.
176pp, 200 photographs, includes work by Curtis, Jackson and others. Seattle, 1963 (1st ed.), d.j. $35.00

A134. ANDRIST (Ralph K.). The Long Death. The Last Days
of the Plains Indian. 371pp, illus, bibliography, index.
New York, 1964, (1st print.), d.j. $23.00
_____Another Copy. Same. lacks d.j. $18.00
_____Another Copy. 1964 (2d print.), cloth. $17.00

A135. ANDRUDE (M. J.). (Columbia University Contributions to
Anthropology, Vol. XII, 1931) Quileute Texts. 221pp,
cloth. New York. $47.00

A136. (ANECDOTES). Anecdotes of the American Indians, Illustrating Their Eccentricities of Character. 252pp, frontis,
vignette on title page, woodcut illus, pages browned.
New York, Alexander V. Blake, 1844. $100.00

A137. ANGEL (J. Lawrence). (Smithsonian Contributions to
Anthropology, Vol. 2, No. 1, Washington, 1966) Early
Skeletons from Tranquility, California. 19pp, photo-
graphs, bibliography, wrappers. $10.00

A138. ANGULO (Jorge). (Instituto Nacional de Antropologia e
Historia) Una Vison del Museo Cuauhnahuac, Palacio de
Cortes. 250pp, 53 illus, 3 folding maps, wrappers.
Mexico City, 1979. $30.00

A139. ANGULO (Jorge.). (Instituto Nacional de Antropologia e
Historia, Mexico, 1979) Una Vision del Museo Cuauhnahuac Palacio de Cortes: Recopilacion Historico-Arqueologia
del Proceso de Cambio en el Edo de Morelos. 350pp,
numerous illus, 2 maps, some color illus, wrappers.
                                                    $30.00

A140. ANNEQUIN (Guy). The Civilization of the Maya. 234pp,
photographs. Geneva, 1978. $10.00

A141. ANSON (Bert). The Miami Indians. xvii, 329pp, 20pp of
photographs, bibliography, index. Norman, 1970 (1st
ed.), d.j. $25.00
_____Another Copy. Same. lacks d.j. $18.00

A142. (ANTHROPOLOGY). (American Museum of Natural History
Anthropological Papers Vol. XIII, 1900) x, 330pp (some
uncut), approx 200 photographs and drawings, articles
include: Symbolism of the Arapaho Indians, by A. L.

Kroeber, 18pp of text, 138 figures; two papers by M. H. Saville--A Shell Gorget from Huastaec, Mexico; and An Onyx Jar from Mexico, in Process of Manufacture. $95.00

A143. (ANTHROPOLOGY). (University of California, Publications in Anthropology, Vol. 1, 1964) Animal Husbandry in Navajo Society and Culture. 104pp, wrappers. $15.00

A144. (ANTHROPOLOGY). (American Museum of Natural History, Vol. XIV, 1901) A Bronze Figurine from British Columbia; also: A. J. Stone's Measurements of the Northwest Territories, both by F. Boas. pp53-68, 6pp photographs, contains other articles. $57.00

A145. (ANTHROPOLOGY). (Fieldiana Anthropology, Vol. 65, 1975) Chapters in the Prehistory of Eastern Arizona, IV. 186pp, 40 photographs, 3 figures, 11 tables. $24.00

A146. (ANTHROPOLOGY). (National Museum of Canada, Bulletin 194, Ottawa, 1964) Contributions to Anthropology 1961-62, Part II. 280pp, 62 illus. $13.00

A147. (ANTHROPOLOGY). (Contributions of University of California Archaeological Research Facility, No. 21, 1974) Four Papers on Great Basin Anthropology. 70pp, 4to, illus, maps, bibliography, wrappers. $10.00

A148. (ANTHROPOLOGY). (Anthropological Society of Washington, 75th Anniversary Volume, 1955) New Interpretations of Aboriginal American Culture History. 135pp (9 monographs). $22.00

A149. (ANTHROPOLOGY). (University of California, Archaeological Research Facility Contribution No. 7, 1970) Papers on Anthropology of the Great Basin. 78pp, wrappers, illus. $25.00

A150. (ANTHROPOLOGY). (University of California Archaeological Research Facility Contribution No. 35, 1977) Great Basin Anthropological Papers. 150pp, wrappers, illus. $22.00

A151. (ANTHROPOLOGY). Papers on the Physical Anthropology of the American Indian. 202pp, studies by Birdsell, Newman, Laughlin, Boyd, Dahlberg and others, wrappers. Viking Fund, New York, 1949. $25.00

A152. (ANTHROPOLOGY). Smithsonian Institution, Annual Report for the Year Ending June 30, 1895. Articles include "The Social Organization and the Secret Societies of the Kwakiutl Indians," by F. Boas. 429pp, 317 illus. Also: "The Graphic Art of the Eskimo Based Upon the Collections in the National Museum," by W. J. Hoffman. 210pp, 82pls, 152 figures, cloth. $295.00

These works are the major papers in this classic 1,080-page report for 1895. The Boas study provides a detailed description of Kwakiutl life and is heavily illustrated with photographs and drawings of objects in the National Museum and from the Jacobsen Collection at the Royal Ethnographical Museum. Also illustrated are a number of Nootka, Haida, and Tsimshian masks. Hoffman's paper examines Nelson's collection of Eskimo art drawn on ivory, horn, bone, wood, metal and skin, and deals not only with the materials, but also with the designs, creatures and objects that were drawn. (EAP)

A153. (ANTHROPOLOGY). Smithsonian Institution Annual Report for the Year Ending June 10, 1939. Articles include "The Use of Soapstone by the Indians of the Eastern United States," by D. I. Bushnell, and "The Modern Growth of the Totem Pole on the Northwest Coast," by M. Barbeau. xii, 567pp, 7 figures, 15pp photographs.
$30.00

A154. (ANTHROPOLOGY). (University of California Archaeological Research Facility, Contribution No. 22, 1974) Two Papers on the Physical Anthropology of California Indians. 57pp, wrappers. $10.00

A155. (ANTHROPOLOGY). (University of Utah, Anthropology Papers, Vol. 1, 1950, through Volume 87, 1967) $875.00
This important journal, among the most respected in its field, concentrates on the archaeology, ethnology and material culture of Native Americans in the Southwest / Great Basin area--Utah, Arizona and New Mexico. The average number of pages per volume is approx 150; the average number of figures per volume is approx 65. This run, complete except for volumes 9 and 26, covers the first eighteen years of publication. (EAP)

A156. (ANTHROPOLOGY). (Yale University, Publications in Anthropology, Nos. 1-7) 154pp, 3 figures, contains Wissler (on Plains Indians); C. Osgood (on the Northern Athapaskan); W. W. Hill (on Navajo Warfare) and E. Beaglehold (on Hopi Hunting Rituals). $48.00
_____ Another Copy. 1970 reprint. $35.00

A157. (ANTHROPOLOGY). (Yale University, Publications in Anthropology, Nos. 8-13) 171pp, 5 maps, contains Murdock (on Potlatch Among the Haida); Morgan (on Navaho) and Fenton (on Seneca Ceremonies). $35.00

A158. (ANTHROPOLOGY). (Yale University, Publications in Anthropology, Nos. 35 and 36, 1946) 149pp, 30 figures, 16 tables, contains W. C. Bennett (on Excavation in Cuenca Region); C. Osgood (on Archaeology in British Guiana) $45.00
_____ Another Copy. No. 35 (Bennett) only, 86pp. $15.00

A159. (ANTHROPOLOGY). (Yale University, Publications in Anthropology, Nos. 49 and 50, 1953) 240pp, 13 figures, 8 tables, 12pp photographs, contains W. C. Bennett (on excavations at Wari) and J. A. Bullbrook (on excavations of a shell mound in Trinidad). $45.00

A160. ANTON (Ferdinand). Ancient Mexican Art. 303pp plus index, 314 illus (40 in color), notes, bibliography. New York, 1969 (1st American ed.). $25.00

A161. ANTON (F.). Art of the Maya. 344pp, 365 illus, (37 in color). New York, 1970 (1st ed.). $60.00

A162. ANTON (F.) and DOCKSTADER (F.). Pre-Columbian Art

and Later Tribal Arts. 264pp, profusely illus (many in color). New York, Abrams, 1968. $40.00

A163. ANTON (F.). Women in Pre-Columbian America. B/w and color illus, d.j. New York, Abner Schram, 1973. $75.00

A164. ANYON (R.) and LeBLANC (S. A.). (Maxwell Museum of Anthropology, 1984) The Galaz Ruin, A Prehistoric Mimbres Village in Southwestern New Mexico. xi, 612pp, 148pp of photographs of Mimbres ceramics. $50.00

The Galaz ruin has yielded over 800 classic Mimbres bowls and was excavated in the 1920s and 1970s. This account, one of the most complete studies on Mimbres culture, brings together all information on the site and reproduces the entire collection. (EAP)

A165. AOKI (Haruo). (University of California Publications in Linguistics, Vol. 62, Berkeley, 1973) Nez Perce Grammar. 168pp, map, 4to, phonology, morphology, verbs, particles, syntax, etc. $29.00

A166. (APACHE INDIANS). Memorial and Affidavits Showing Outrages Perpetrated by the Apache Indians in the Territory of Arizona During 1869 and 1870. 32pp, wrappers, complete facsimile reprint of the original 1871 ed. Tucson, 1964. $12.00

_____ Another Copy. Same. $10.00

A167. (APACHE INDIANS). The People Called Apache. Written and Illustrated by Thomas Mails. Includes over 300 previously unpublished photographs. New York, Promontory Press, 1981 (reprint of 1974 ed.). $45.00

APARICIO (Francisco de). See BAE Bulletin No. 143.

A168. APES (William). Eulogy on King Philip, as Pronounced at the Odeon, in Federal Street, Boston, by the Rev. William Apes, an Indian, January 8, 1836. 48pp, frontis, 1 pl of death of King Philip, self wrappers. Boston, by the author, 1837 (2d ed.). $95.00

King Philip, whose Indian name was Metacomet, died in 1676. He was the son of the equally famous Indian Chief Massasoit, sachem of the Wampanoags. King Philip declared war on the English settlers on Indian lands when the English killed three of his warriors in 1675. The bloody war lasted a year, until King Philip was tracked down and killed. (RMW)

A169. APES (W.). Indian Nullification of the Unconstitutional Laws of Massachusetts, Relative to the Marshpee Tribe: Or the Pretended Riot Explained. Frontis, 168pp, 12mo, later wraps with frontis mounted on frnt wrapper. Boston, J. Howe, 1835 (1st ed.). $75.00

A170. APES (W.). A Son of the Forest. The Experiences of William Apes, A Native of the Forest. 215pp, portrait, 18mo, 1/2 leather bds, very worn, foxing, some stains, the author, a Pequot Indian, served in the War of 1812 and became a Methodist minister. New York, 1831 (2d ed, revised and corrected). $70.00

A171.   APPLEGATE (Frank G.).   Indian Stories from the Pueblos.
        178pp, 7 color illus from original Pueblo Indian paintings,
        forword by Witter Bynner, cloth.   Philadelphia, 1929
        (1st ed.). $50.00
            Saunders: 1426.   Lindsay: F6.   Major: p.136-37.
        Campbell: p.241.   A collection of Indian tales from vari-
        ous Pueblos throughout New Mexico and a few Hopi stories.
        The author was a friend and trader to the Pueblos and
        recorded what he had learned.   (TE)
        ___ Another Copy.   Same. $40.00
        ___ Another Copy.   Same. $40.00

A172.   APPLEGATE (Richard).   (Anthropological Papers 13, Socor-
        ro, Ballena Press, 1978)   Atishwin: The Dream Helper
        in South-Central California.   98pp, wrappers. $18.00

A173.   APPLETON (L. H.).   Indian Art of the Americas.   xii,
        279pp, 79pp of full color drawings of over 700 objects
        and designs, cloth.   New York, 1950. $150.00
            Often referred to as, "... a virtual encyclopedia of
        American Indian design," this long out of print study is
        particularly sought after in this original edition, with its
        very rich color plates.   The 79 full-page color plates rep-
        resent the designs of more than 100 tribes and groups,
        ranging from the Arctic Circle to Cape Horn.   (EAP)
        ___ Another Copy.   Same.   d.j. $75.00
        ___ Another Copy.   Same.   Tape marking across spine
        and number blocked out, no internal marks but evidently
        ex-library. $30.00

A174.   (APPORTIONMENT).   (House of Representatives House Bill
        10542, 63:2, Washington, 1913).   A Bill providing for
        the segregation and apportionment of Indian tribal proper-
        ty....   3pp, removed, folded, this act did not apply to
        the Five Civilized tribes or the Osages and calls for a
        final roll for each tribe by 1915. $10.00

A175.   (APPROPRIATIONS).   (House of Representatives Miscellane-
        ous Document 38, 33:1, Washington, 1854)   Indian Ap-
        propriations.   16pp, removed, expenses for Washington
        Territory, Apache, Navajo, Utah, New Mexico Territory
        Pueblo Indians. $10.00

A176.   (ARAUCANIAN INDIANS).   The Araucanians; or, Notes of
        a Tour Among the Indian Tribes of Southern Chile.
        355pp, 17 engravings, frontis, newly rebound.   New
        York, 1855 (1st ed.). $75.00

A177.   (ARCHAEOLOGY).   (Logan Museum Bulletin No. 4, Wiscon-
        sin, 1931)   The Ancient Mimbrenos (Mattock Ruin).
        105pp, 43 pls, some in color, 4to, wrappers. $50.00

A178.   (ARCHAEOLOGY).   (Anthropological Society of Washington,
        1968)   Anthropological Archaeology in the Americas.   xi,
        151pp, 10 figures, cloth. $25.00

A179.   (ARCHAEOLOGY).   (University of California Archaeological
        Research Facility, Contribution No. 12, 1971)   The Appli-
        cation of the Physical Sciences to Archaeology.   62pp,
        wrappers. $12.00

A180. (ARCHAEOLOGY). (Southwest Museum Papers No. 4, Los
Angeles, 1970) Archaeological Explorations in Southern
Nevada. 126pp, illus, map, wrappers. $12.00
A181. (ARCHAEOLOGY). (Smithsonian Miscellaneous Collections
Vol. 65, No. 6, 1915) Explorations and Field-Work of
the Smithsonian Institution in 1914. 95pp, 89 photo-
graphs. $17.00
A182. (ARCHAEOLOGY). (Gobierno del Estado de Veracruz,
Dept. de Antropologia, Jalapa, 1955) Exploraciones en
la Isla de Sacrificios. 107pp, 65 color and 7 b/w photo-
graphs, 10 drawings, map, fold-out plate of drawings,
photographs and drawings are of artifacts, wrappers.
$40.00
A183. (ARCHAEOLOGY). (Museo Nacional de Arqueologia, His-
toria y Ethnografia. Tomo I, Mexico, 1934) Articles
include "Carta del Arzobispo de Mexico al Consejo de
Indias" (1556). pp339-360; also "Las Razas Indigenas de
Mexico" (Ponton). pp361-422, 30 pls of pre-Columbian
sites. $75.00
A184. (ARCHAEOLOGY). (University of California Archaeological
Research Facility Contribution No. 13, 1971) Papers on
Olmec and Maya Archaeology. 166pp, illus, wrappers.
$35.00
A185. (ARCHAEOLOGY). (National Research Council, Bulletin
No. 74, Washington, 1929) Report of the Conference on
Midwestern Archaeology, Held in St. Louis, 1929. 120pp,
illus, printed wrappers. $10.00
A186. (ARCHAEOLOGY). Teotihuacan 80-82, Primeros Resultados.
155pp (13 papers), approx 60 photographs and drawings,
11 fold-out figures. Instituto Nacional de Antropologia
e Historia, Mexico City, 1982. $20.00
A187. (ARCTIC). Arctic Anthropology, Vol. VIII, No. 1, Madison,
1971. 170pp, 13pp photographs, 34 figures. $17.00
A188. (ARCTIC). Arctic Anthropology, Vol. XIII, No. 2, Madison, 1976. 134pp, all are of papers from a 1972 symposium on Aleutian archaeology. $14.00
A189. (ARCTIC). (Studia Ethnographica Upsaliensia, XI, 1956)
Arctica. 296pp, 21 illus papers by noted Arctic scholars
dealing with peoples of the North Sea, 150 illus. $40.00
A190. (ARGENTINA). Los Aborigenes de la Republica Argentina.
149pp, 146 figures, lacks color pl, cloth. Buenos Aires,
n.d. $45.00
A191. ARIMA (E. Y.). (National Museum of Canada, Bulletin
189, 1963) Report on an Eskimo Umiak Built at Ivuyivik,
P.G., in the Summer of 1960. vi, 83pp, 32 photographs,
10 figures. $33.00
A192. ARIMA (E. Y.). (British Columbia Provincial Museum Special Publication 6, 1983) The West Coast People, the
Nootka of Vancouver Island and Cape Flattery. vii,
205pp, 53 lrg photographs, 7pp drawings, map. $12.00
A193. (ARIZONA). (House of Representatives Executive Document

139, 41:3, Washington, 1871, 1st print.) Survey of
Pima and Maricopa Reservation in Arizona. 17pp, removed. $15.00

A194. (ARIZONA). (Executive Document 20, 48:2, Washington,
1885) Report Upon the Coal on the White Mountain
Reservation in Arizona. 7pp, folding chart. $10.00

A195. (ARIZONA). Arizona Highways, January, 1974. All articles in this issue deal with Indian turquoise. $17.00

A196. (ARIZONA). Arizona Highways, August, 1974. All articles in this issue deal with Indian jewelry. $17.00

A197. (ARIZONA). Arizona Highways, July, 1975. Special edition: American Indian Basketry. $17.00

A198. ARMBRUSTER (Eugene L.). The Indians of New England
and New Netherland. 11pp, map, wrappers, limited to
100 copies. Brooklyn, New York, 1918, (2d ed.). $10.00

A199. ARMER (Laura A.). Dark Circle of Branches. ix, 212pp,
pls, decorative cloth, endpapers, illus by Sidney Armer,
a tale of the Navaho people written for younger readers.
New York, 1933 (1st ed.). $30.00

ARMSTRONG (John M.). See also BAE Bulletin No. 143.

A200. ARMSTRONG (P. A.). The Piasa, or, the Devil Among the
Indians. 48pp, illus, decorated wrappers. Morris, IL,
E. B. Fletcher, 1887. $55.00

A201. ARMSTRONG (Virginia Irving) (Editor). I Have Spoken.
American History through the Voices of the Indians.
200pp, bibliography, index. Chicago, 1971 (1st ed.).
$10.00

A202. ARNOLD (Elliott). Blood Brother. 553pp, signed by author, cloth, historical novel set in Arizona and New
Mexico during 1856-1872. New York, 1947 (1st ed.).
$20.00

A203. (ART). The American Indian: The American Flag.
148pp, b/w and color illus, photographs, map, bibliography, wrappers. Exhibition catalog of Indian Art with
a patriotic theme. Flint Institute of Art, Flint, MI,
1975 (1st ed.). $35.00

A204. (ART). American Indian Art Magazine. Volume 1, No. 1,
through Volume 12, No. 2. Complete run of this beautifully illus and informative magazine, which covers many
aspects of Indian art, past and present. 46 issues, lrg
8 vo. Scottsdale, AZ, 1975-1987. $400.00

A205. (ART). American Primitive. 64pp, 54 color photographs,
hard bd cvrs. Lausanne, 1967, New York, 1974. $10.00

A206. (ART). Introduction to American Indian Art; To Accompany the First Exhibition of American Indian Art Selected
Entirely With Consideration of Esthetic Value. Parts I
and II. Part I: 58pp, 33 pls (9 color pls tipped in),
stiff pictorial wrappers. Part II: 146pp, illus, stiff
printed wrappers. New York, 1931, (1st ed.). $150.00
Saunders: 2367. Articles by different authors pagi-
nated separately. Artist John Sloan was the president

of the Exposition with an editorial board made up of
Frederick Webb Hodge, Herbert J. Spinden and Oliver
LaFarge. The second part has separate illustrated arti-
cles by illustrious writers as May Austin, Alice Corgin
Henderson, Laura Adams Armer and others. An excellent
overview of Indian Art with much on the Southwest.
(TE)

A207. (ART). Ke Mo Ha. 65pp, 214 color photographs of Indian
and Western Art, map, cloth. Woolaroc Museum, Bartles-
ville, 1964. $19.00

A208. (ART). Exhibition catalogue, Le Musee de L'Or de Bogota.
68pp, 32 b/w and 9 color photographs, 7 drawings, mostly
full page. Petit Palais, Paris, 1973. $15.00

A209. (ART) Sacred Circles: 2,000 Years of North American
Indian Art. 252pp, 732 illus, 20 color pls. Exhibition
catalogue, Nelson Gallery of Art, Kansas City, 1977.
$20.00

A210. (ART). Twenty Centuries of Mexican Art. 199pp, b/w
and color illus, end paper map and chart, decorative
cloth, printed in English and Spanish, in addition to the
art represented, this work is a valuable reference for
the brief biographies of the artists. Museum of Modern
Art in collaboration with the Mexican Government, New
York, 1940, d.j. $35.00

A211. (ARTIFACTS). Catalogue and Price Guide. 96pp, illus,
wrappers, Vol. 1, No. 1, Fall, 1974. $15.00

A212. (ARTIFACTS). (Museum of the American Indian Contributions, Vol. XIII, 1944) Inlaid Stone and Bone Artifacts
from Southern California. 202pp, 71 full-page photographs containing several hundred objects. $27.00

A213. (ARTIFACTS). Native American Artifacts of California
and the Southwest, from the Collection of Austen D.
Warburton. 38pp, 18 b/w and 4 color photographs, folio.
Triton Art Museum, Santa Clara, 1980. $12.00

A214. (ARTIFACTS). Northwest Coast Artifacts from the H. R.
MacMillan Collections. 48pp, 19pp of color photographs,
wrappers. Museum of Anthropology, Vancouver, 1976.
$10.00

A215. (ARTS AND CRAFTS). Indian Arts and Crafts Catalogue.
116pp, photographs, wrappers, items for sale made by
Indians and Eskimos. Ottawa, 1974. $15.00

A216. ASHTON (R.). Images of American Indian Art. 72pp,
62 color and 64 lrg b/w photographs. New York, 1977.
$13.00

A217. ASHWELL (R.). Indian Tribes of the Northwest. 74pp,
70 photographs. Saanichton, 1977. $10.00

A218. ASSAD (C.). (University of Texas at San Antonio, Center for Archeological Research, Survey Report No. 54,
1978, 1st ed.) Archeological Testing South of Olmos
Dam.... 14pp. $10.00

A219. ASSAD (C.). (University of Texas at San Antonio, Center

for Archeological Research, Survey Report No. 50, 1978,
1st ed.) Evaluation of Archeological Sites ... Dry Comal
Creek.... 26pp. $10.00

A220. (ASSINIBOINES). The Assiniboines, from the Accounts
of the Old Ones Told to First Boy (James Larpenteur
Long). Edited and with an Introduction by Michael S.
Kennedy. 209pp, illus with drawings. Norman, 1961
(1st print.), d.j. $35.00

A221. ASTROV (Margot) (Editor). The Winged Serpent: An
Anthology of American Indian Prose and Poetry. 366pp,
decorative cloth. New York, 1946 (1st ed.). $25.00
Campbell: p. 220. Dobie: p. 28: "Here are singu-
lar expressions of beauty and dignity." (TE)

A222. ASTURIA de BARRIOS (L.). Comalapa: El Traje y Su
Significado. viii, 124pp, 26 full and half-page color
photographs and 25 b/w photographs, 10 drawings, 1
map. Museo Ixchel del Traje Indigena de Guatemala,
1985. $38.00
The indigenous dress of the peoples of Comalapa,
Chimaltenango is the subject of this publication that examines the antecedents of this tradition and the textiles
woven in the middle and latter parts of this century.
The garments illustrated--in remarkably fine photographs
--are from the collections of the Museo Ixchel and from
private collections in the area. None have been previously published. The text is extremely detailed and is in
Spanish. (EAP)

A223. ATHERTON (William). Narrative of the Suffering and Defeat of the Northwestern Army, Under General Winchester.... 152pp, sml 8vo, half calf, marbled bds, rebacked. Frankfort, KY, 1842. $325.00
Graff: 103. Field: 52. Howes: A-366. Jones:
1058. Sabin: 2273. Atherton's first hand account of the
Raisin River Massacre and its preface, followed by his
experiences as prisoner of war at the hands of the British. Atherton's group traveled from Kentucky through
Michigan and into Canada. Included are observations of
Indian customs. (WR)

A224. ATKINSON (Mary J.). Indians of the Southwest. 333pp,
illus endpapers, bibliography. San Antonio, 1958.
                                                        $22.00

A225. ATKINSON (M. J.). The Texas Indians. 345pp. San
Antonio, 1935 (1st ed.). $30.00

A226. (ATLAS). Atlas Arqueologico de la Republica Mexicana I:
Quintana Roo. 74pp, 4to, illus, wrappers. Mexico,
1959. $30.00

A227. ATWATER (Caleb). Description of the Antiquities Discovered in the State of Ohio and Other Western States.
From Archaeologia Americana, Trans. Amer. Antiquarian
Society, Vol. I, Worcester, Mass., 1829 (removed).
pp105-267, 10 (of 11) maps and plans, 3 pls, text illus,

wrappers. According to Field: 53, lacks map of Ohio.
$35.00

A228. ATWATER (C.). Remarks Made on a Tour to Prairie Du Chien; Thence to Washington City, in 1829. viii, 296pp, original leather backed bds. Columbus, Jenkins and Glover, 1831 (1st ed.). $100.00
Howes: A-380. Field: 53. Account of a visit to the Winnebagos, Pottawatomies, Chippewas and Ottawas.

A229. ATWATER (Caleb). The Writings of Caleb Atwater. 408pp, 11 pls, some folding, original cloth. Columbus, by the author, 1833. $115.00
Reprints, with some additions, "Remarks on a Tour to Prairie du Chien" and "A Description of the Antiquities Discovered in the Western Country." Howes: A-380. Field: 53. (RMW)

A230. AUSTIN (Mary). The American Rhythm: Studies and Re-Expressions of Amerindian Songs. x, 174pp, cloth with printed labels, enlarged reprint of 1923 edition. Boston, 1930, d.j. $25.00
Pearce: p.145. Saunders: 2072. Weigle: p.197. Campbell: p.111: "Her thesis here is that old Indian and modern American song and poetry derive their rhythm from climate and environment, which she thinks determines everything from religion to language." (TE)
___Another Copy. New York, Harcourt Brace & Co., 1923 (1st ed.) 155pp, frontis, decorated brown cloth, sml 8vo, appendix. $45.00

A231. AUSTIN (Mary). Indian Pottery of the Rio Grande. 16 unnumbered pp, printed wrappers, two-color pictorial title page. Pearce: p.145. Pasadena, 1934 (1st ed.).
$35.00

A232. AVENI (Anthony F.). In Pre-Columbian America. 463pp, illus. Austin, 1977. $32.00

A233. AVERKIEVA (Ju. P.). Indeiskoe Kochevoe Obstchestvo XVIII-XIX BB. (Indian Nomadic Society in the 18th and 19th Centuries) 176pp, 11pp of photographs and drawings, mainly of artifacts, 14 sml drawings, 2 maps. USSR Academy of Sciences, Moscow, 1970. $24.00

A234. (AZTEC). The Badianus Manuscript. (Codex Barberini, Latin 241) Vatican Library. An Aztec Herbal of 1552 presented with the Introduction, Translations and Annotations by Emily W. Emmart. 341pp, 118 color pls, 4to. Baltimore, The John Hopkins Pr., 1940, d.j. $250.00

A235. (AZTEC). Centeola and Other Tales. 312pp, rebound. Wright II: 2473. New York, 1864 (1st ed.). $20.00

A236. (AZTEC). Codex Mendoza: Aztec Manuscript. 123pp, color illus. Fribourg, 1978. $35.00

A237. (AZTEC). The de la Cruz-Badiano Aztec Herbal of 1552. Translation and Commentary by William Gates. xxii, 144pp, over 100 pls. The Maya Society, Baltimore, 1939 (1st ed.). $150.00

A238. (AZTEC). (Instituto Nacional Antropologia e Historia)
Rescate Arquelogico del Monolito Coyolxauhqui: Informe
Preliminar. 94pp, 66 illus, wrappers. Mexico, 1978.
$25.00

-B-

B1. BABB (T. A.). In the Bosom of the Comanches. 146pp,
illus, Amarillo, 1923 (2nd ed.). $40.00
B2. BABINGTON (S. H.). Navajos, Gods, Tom-Toms. 242pp,
plus index, illus. bibliography, map endpapers, the
result of 20 years of studying Navajo Medicine men by
a doctor, New York, 1950 (1st ed.), d.j. $20.00
___Another Copy. Lacks d.j. $15.00
B3. BACK (Capt. George). Narrative of the Arctic Land Expedition to the Mouth of the Great Fish River, and Along
the Shores of the Arctic Ocean, in the Years 1833, 1834,
and 1835. 2 advs pp, text, 456pp, folding map, bds,
rebacked, Philadelphia, E. L. Carey and A. Hart, 1836
(1st Amer. ed.). $150.00
    Hill, p. 12: "In search of Capt. John Ross. Narra-
tive is full of details about the Cree, Chippewa, Copper-
mine Indians, and other tribes, upon whom the members
of the expedition were obliged to depend on during a
terrible winter." Field: "None have produced a more
complete, interesting, and evidently faithful narration of
the character of the savage tribes of the frozen regions
of North America."
BAE (Bureau of American Ethnology).
B4. ...First Annual Report, 1879-1880. Washington, DC, 1881.
xxxv, 638pp, 347 figures (including 54 plates), Map.
Includes "Sketch of the Mythology of the North American
Indians," and "A Further Contribution to the Study of
the Mortuary Customs of the North American Indians."
$145.00
___Another Copy. Original cloth. $145.00
___Another Copy. Rebound in later cloth. $135.00
___Another Copy. Special morocco binding. $165.00
___Another Copy. Ex-lib. $60.00
___Another Copy. Original cloth (Good). $80.00
B5. ...Second Annual Report, 1880-1881. Washington, DC,
1883. xxxvii, 477pp, 77 plates, 402 figures, 2 maps.
Includes "Zuni Fetiches," "Myths of the Iroquois," "Ani-
mal Carvings from Mounds of the Mississippi Valley,"
"Navajo Silversmiths," "Art in Shell of the Ancient Amer-
icans," and "Illustrated Catalogue of the Collections Ob-
tained from the Indians of New Mexico and Arizona in
1879." $165.00

   ___Another Copy. Ex-lib. $55.00
   ___Another Copy. (Good.) $80.00
   ___Another Copy. Damp stain bottom edge. $50.00

B6. ...Third Annual Report, 1881-1882. Washington, DC, 1884.
lxxiv, 606pp, 44 plates, 200 (plus 2 unnumbered) figures.
Includes "On Masks, Labrets, and Certain Aboriginal Customs, with an Inquiry into the Bearing of Their Geographical Distribution," "Omaha Sociology," "Navajo Weavers,"
and "Prehistoric Textile Fabrics of the United States, Derived from Impressions on Pottery." $160.00
   ___Another Copy. (Good.) $80.00
   ___Another Copy. Ex-lib. $50.00
   ___Another Copy. Original cloth, edge wr. $115.00

B7. ...Fourth Annual Report, 1882-1883. Washington, DC, 1886.
lxiii, 532pp, 83 plates, 565 figures. Includes "Pictographs
of the North American Indians; a Preliminary Paper,"
"Pottery of the Ancient Pueblos," "Ancient Pottery of the
Mississippi Valley," and "A Study of Pueblo Pottery as Il-
lustrative of Zuni Culture Growth." $165.00
   ___Another Copy. Rebound in later cloth. $155.00
   ___Another Copy. Ex-lib. $50.00
   ___Another Copy. Rebound in linen cloth. $125.00
   ___Another Copy. Spine tear, soil. $95.00

B8. ...Fifth Annual Report, 1883-1884. Washington, DC, 1887.
617pp, 23 plates, 2 pocket maps, 77 figures. Includes
"Burial Mounds of the Northern Sections of the United
States," and "The Mountain Chant: A Navajo Ceremony."
             $135.00
   ___Another Copy. (Good.) $80.00
   ___Another Copy. Rebound, ex-lib. $50.00
   ___Another Copy. Ex-lib. $45.00

B9. ...Sixth Annual Report, 1884-1885. Washington, DC, 1888.
733pp (including 6pp of music), 10 plates, 2 pocket maps,
546 figures, 44 sml unnumbered cuts. Includes "Ancient
Art of the Province of Chiriqui, Colombia," "Aids to the
Study of the Maya Codices," and "The Central Eskimo."
             $140.00
   ___Another Copy. Rebound in later cloth. $130.00
   ___Another Copy. Ex-lib. $50.00
   ___Another Copy. Damp stain top edge. $80.00

B10. ...Seventh Annual Report, 1885-1886. Washington, DC, 1891.
xliii, 409pp, 27 plates, pocket map, 39 figures. Includes
"Indian Linguistic Families of America North of Mexico,"
"The Midewiwin or 'Grand Medicine Society' of the Ojibwa,"
and "The Sacred Formulas of the Cherokees." $110.00
   ___Another Copy. Red morocco, marbled bds. $145.00
   ___Another Copy. Ex-lib. $45.00
   ___Another Copy. (Good.) $80.00

B11. ...Eighth Annual Report, 1886-1887. Washington, DC, 1891.
xxxvi, 298pp, 123 plates, 118 figures. Includes "A Study
of Pueblo Architecture: Tusayan and Cibola," and

"Ceremonial of Hasjelti Dailijis and Mythical Sand Paintings
of the Navajo Indians." $130.00
___Another Copy. Rebound in later cloth. $120.00
___Another Copy. Ex-lib. $40.00
___Another Copy. Hinges started. $65.00

B12. ...Ninth Annual Report, 1887-1888. Washington, DC, 1892.
xlvi, 617pp, 8 plates, 448 figures. Includes "Ethnological
Results of the Point Barrow Expedition," and "The Medi-
cine-Men of the Apaches." $175.00
___Another Copy. Original cloth (stained). $155.00
___Another Copy. Rebound in later cloth. $165.00
___Another Copy. Original cloth (worn). $90.00
___Another Copy. Ex-lib. $60.00

B13. ...Tenth Annual Report, 1888-1889. Washington, DC, 1893.
xxx, 822pp, 54 plates, 1,291 figures, 116 unnumbered
cuts. Includes "Picture Writing of the American Indians."
$170.00
___Another Copy. some wr at edges, cvrs soiled.
$90.00
___Another Copy. Inner hinge broken. $75.00
___Another Copy. Ex-lib. $50.00
___Another Copy. (Good.) $80.00

B14. ...Eleventh Annual Report, 1889-1890. Washington, DC,
1894. 600pp, 50 plates, 200 figures. Includes "Ethnology
of the Ungava District, Hudson Bay Territory," and "A
Study of Siouan Cults." $125.00
___Another Copy. Ex-lib. $55.00
___Another Copy. (Good.) $80.00
___Another Copy. Rebound in library cloth. $45.00

B15. ...Twelfth Annual Report, 1890-1891. Washington, DC,
1894. 790pp, 42 plates, 344 figures. Includes "Report
on the Mound Exploration of the Bureau of Ethnology."
$120.00
___Another Copy. Ex-lib. $60.00
___Another Copy. Shaken, cracked hinge. $40.00
___Another Copy. Original cloth (stained). $45.00

B16. ...Thirteenth Annual Report, 1891-1892. Washington, DC,
1896. 521pp, 60 plates, 330 figures. Includes "Prehis-
toric Textile Art of Eastern United States," "Stone Art,"
"Aboriginal Remains in Verde Valley, Arizona," "Omaha
Dwellings, Furniture, and Implements," "Casa Grande
Ruin," and "Outlines of Zuni Creation Myths." $120.00
___Another Copy. (Good.) $80.00
___Another Copy. Sml water spot back cvr. $45.00
___Another Copy. Hinge cracked. $55.00

B17. ...Fourteenth Annual Report, 1892-1893 (in two parts).
Washington, DC, 1896.
Part 1: ixi, 637pp, 94 pls, 55 figures.
Includes "The Menomini Indians." $110.00
Part 2: 499pp, 28 pls, 48 figures. Includes
"The Ghost-Dance Religion and the
Sioux Outbreak of 1890." $110.00

    ____Another Copy. Part 1: rebound in later
                                cloth. $95.00
                     Part 2: bound with special
                                leather for U.S.
                                Congress. $110.00
    ____Another Copy. Part 1: ex-lib. $50.00
                     Part 2: ex-lib. $55.00

B18. ...Fifteenth Annual Report, 1893-1894. Washington, DC, 1897. cxxi, 366pp, 125 plates, 49 figures. Includes "Stone Implements of the Potomac-Chesapeake Tidewater Province," "The Siouan Indians: A Preliminary Sketch," "Siouan Sociology: A Posthumous Paper," "Tusayan Katcinas," and "The Repair of Casa Grande Ruin, Arizona, in 1891." $135.00
    ____Another Copy. (Good.) $70.00
    ____Another Copy. Rebound in later cloth. $125.00
    ____Another Copy. Original cloth, spine weak. $60.00

B19. ...Sixteenth Annual Report, 1894-1895. Washington, DC, 1897. 445pp, 81 plates, 83 figures. Includes "The Cliff Ruins of Canyon de Chelly, Arizona," "Day Symbols of the Maya Year," and "Tusayan Snake Ceremonies." $125.00
    ____Another Copy. (Good.) $75.00
    ____Another Copy. 3/4 red leather. $50.00
    ____Another Copy. Ex-lib. $40.00

B20. ...Seventeenth Annual Report, 1895-1896 (in 2 parts). Washington, DC, 1898. 847pp, 182 plates, 357 figures.
    Part 1: 563pp. Includes "The Seri Indians,"
              and "Calendar History of the Kiowa
              Indians." $110.00
    Part 2: 284pp. Includes "Navajo Houses," and
              "Archaeological Expedition to Arizona
              in 1895." $95.00
    ____Another Copy. Part 1: original cloth, some
                                soil. $90.00
                     Part 2: original cloth, some
                                soil, edge wr. $75.00
    ____Another Copy. Part 1 only. Ex-lib. $35.00

B21. ...Eighteenth Annual Report, 1896-1897 (in 2 parts). Washington, DC, 1899. 1,054pp, 174 plates, 165 figures.
    Part 1: 575pp. Includes "The Eskimo About
              Bering Strait." $225.00
    Part 2: 479pp. Includes "Indian Land Cessions
              in the United States." $85.00
    ____Another Copy. Part 1 only. $135.00
    ____Another Copy. Part 1 only. Shaken,
                              binding loose, ex-lib. $125.00
    ____Another Copy. Part 1: cover soil. $95.00
    ____Another Copy. Part 2: soil, hinge cracked. $50.00

B22. ...Nineteenth Annual Report, 1897-1898 (in 2 parts). Washington, DC, 1900. 1,252pp, frontis, 80 plates, 49 figures.

Part 1: 668pp, 20 pls, 2 figures. Includes
"Myths of the Cherokees." $100.00
Part 2: 584pp, 79 pls, 47 figures. Includes
"Mounds in Northern Honduras,"
"Mayan Calendar Systems," "Numeral
Systems of Mexico and Central Amer-
ica," and three papers on the Tusayan. $125.00

    ___Another Copy. Part 1: ex-lib. $35.00
    Part 2: ex-lib. $35.00
    ___Another Copy. Part 1. $80.00
    Part 2. $100.00
    ___Another Copy. Part 1. $45.00
    Part 2: soil, hinge weak. $40.00

B23. ...Twentieth Annual Report, 1898-1899. Washington, DC,
1903. ccxxiv, 237pp, 180 plates, 79 figures. Includes
"Aboriginal Pottery of the Eastern United States." $130.00
    ___Another Copy. VG. $100.00
    ___Another Copy. hinge weak, cvr soil. $65.00
    ___Another Copy. ex-lib. $55.00

B24. ...Twenty-First Annual Report, 1899-1900. Washington, DC,
1903. xl, 360pp, 69 plates, some in color. Includes
"Hopi Katcinas: Drawn by Native Artists," and "Iroquoian
Cosmology." $250.00
    ___Another Copy. Leather binding for U.S.
    Congress. $220.00
    ___Another Copy. Cover soil. $125.00
    ___Another Copy. Ex-lib. $130.00
    ___Another Copy. Tear in spine, edge wr. $95.00

B25. ...Twenty-Second Annual Report, 1900-1901 (in 2 parts).
Washington, DC, 1904. 738pp, 91 plates, 178 figures.
Part 1: "Two Summers Work in Pueblo Ruins,"
and "Mayan Calendar Systems." $110.00
Part 2: 373pp, 8 pls, 10 figures. Includes
"The Hako: A Pawnee Ceremony." $110.00
    ___Another Copy. Ex-lib. (Parts 1 and 2.) $60.00
    ___Another Copy. Part 2 only. $75.00
    ___Another Copy. Part 1. $60.00
    Part 2. $65.00

B26. ...Twenty-Third Annual Report, 1901-1902. Washington,
DC, 1904 (1905). xlv, 634pp, 139 plates, 34 figures.
Includes "The Zuni Indians: Their Mythology, Esoteric
Fraternities, and Ceremonies." $180.00
    ___Another Copy. Ex-lib. $130.00
    ___Another Copy. Rebound in library cloth. $100.00
    ___Another Copy. Rebound, hinge weak. $95.00

B27. ...Twenty-Fourth Annual Report, 1902-1903. Washington,
DC, 1907. xl, 846pp, 21 plates, 1,112 figures. Includes
"Games of the North American Indians." $175.00
    ___Another Copy. Rebound in later cloth. $155.00
    ___Another Copy. Ex-lib. $60.00
    ___Another Copy. Cvr soil. $90.00
    ___Another Copy. (Good.) $85.00

B28.   ...Twenty-Fifth Annual Report, 1903-1904. Washington, DC,
       1907.   325pp, 129 plates, 70 figures.   Includes "Certain
       Antiquities of Eastern Mexico," and "The Aborigines of
       Porto Rico and Neighboring Islands." $115.00
       ___Another Copy.   Leather (worn). $100.00
       ___Another Copy.   (Good.) $75.00
       ___Another Copy.   Few faded spots. $40.00
B29.   ...Twenty-Sixth Annual Report, 1904-1905. Washington, DC,
       1908.   xxxi, 512pp, 58 plates, 117 figures.   Includes "The
       Pima Indians," and "Social Condition, Beliefs and Linguistic
       Relationship of the Tlingit Indians." $155.00
       ___Another Copy.   VG. $100.00
       ___Another Copy.   Back cvr stained. $60.00
       ___Another Copy.   Ex-lib. $50.00
B 30. ...Twenty-Seventh Annual Report, 1905-1906. Washington,
       DC, 1911.   672pp, 65 plates, 132 figures.   Includes "The
       Omaha Tribe." $120.00
       ___Another Copy.   Original cloth, spine repairs. $95.00
       ___Another Copy.   Sml tear top of spine. $85.00
       ___Another Copy.   VG. $75.00
B 31. ...Twenty-Eighth Annual Report, 1906-1907. Washington,
       DC, 1912.   xxxv, 308pp, 103 plates, 68 figures.   Includes
       "Casa Grande, Arizona," "Antiquities of the Upper Verde
       River and Walnut Creek Valleys, Arizona," and "Preliminary
       Report on the Linguistic Classification of Algonquian
       Tribes." $110.00
       ___Another Copy.   Light shelf wr. $85.00
       ___Another Copy.   VG. $75.00
       ___Another Copy.   Faded spine. $45.00
B 32. ...Twenty-Ninth Annual Report, 1907-1908. Washington,
       DC, 1916.   636pp, 21 plates, 31 maps.   Includes "The
       Ethnogeography of the Tewa Indians." $110.00
       ___Another Copy.   VG. $40.00
       ___Another Copy.   Nice ex-lib copy. $45.00
       ___Another Copy.   Stains and soil. $25.00
B 33. ...Thirtieth Annual Report, 1908-1909. Washington, DC,
       1915.   450pp, 7 plates, 6 figures.   Includes "An Inquiry
       into the Animism and Folklore of the Guiana Indians," and
       "Ethnobotany of the Zuni Indians." $90.00
       ___Another Copy.   Ex-lib. $30.00
       ___Another Copy.   VG. $40.00
B 34. ...Thirty-First Annual Report, 1909-1910. Washington, DC,
       1916.   1,037pp, 3 plates, 24 figures.   Includes "Tsimshian
       Mythology." $135.00
       ___Another Copy.   Original cloth, stained, tear
                          in spine. $110.00
       ___Another Copy.   Original cloth, ex-lib. $45.00
       ___Another Copy.   VG. $65.00
B 35. ...Thirty-Second Annual Report, 1910-1911. Washington,
       DC, 1918.   819pp.   Includes "Seneca Fiction, Legends,
       and Myths." $85.00

    ____Another Copy. VG. $40.00
    ____Another Copy. Original cloth, 2 stains back
            cvr. $45.00
    ____Another Copy. Ex-lib. $45.00

B36. ...Thirty-Third Annual Report, 1911-1912. Washington, DC, 1919. 667pp, 97 plates, 112 figures. Includes "Prelimininary Account of the Antiquities of the Region Between the Mancos and La Plata Rivers in Southwestern Colorado," and "Designed on Prehistoric Hopi Pottery." $150.00
    ____Another Copy. Original cloth, ex-lib. $55.00
    ____Another Copy. VG. $75.00
    ____Another Copy. Soiled original cloth. $60.00

B37. ...Thirty-Fourth Annual Report, 1912-1913. Washington, DC, 1922. 281pp, 120 plates, 69 figures. Includes "A Prehistoric Culture Area of America." $120.00
    ____Another Copy. VG. $75.00
    ____Another Copy. Water stain to bottom edge. $40.00
    ____Another Copy. Ex-lib. $45.00

B38. ...Thirty-Fifth Annual Report, 1913-1914 (in 2 parts). Washington, DC, 1921.
    Part 1: xi, 794pp. Includes "Ethnology of the Kwakiutl." $110.00
    Part 2: viii, 795pp. "Ethnology of the Kwakiutl." (Continued.) $85.00
    ____Another Copy. Original cloth, ex-lib (Parts 1 and 2). $80.00
    ____Another Copy. VG (Parts 1 and 2). $75.00

B39. ...Thirty-Sixth Annual Report, 1914-1915. Washington, DC, 1921. 604pp, 23 plates, 15 figures. Includes "The Osage Tribe: Rite of the Chiefs; Sayings of the Ancient Men." $110.00
    ____Another Copy. Original cloth, ex-lib. $40.00
    ____Another Copy. (Fine.) $75.00

B40. ...Thirty-Seventh Annual Report, 1915-1916. Washington, DC, 1923. 567pp, 58 plates, 38 figures. Includes "The Winnebago Tribe." $135.00
    ____Another Copy. (Fine.) $75.00
    ____Another Copy. Ex-lib. $50.00
    ____Another Copy. Faded spine, ex-lib. $40.00

B41. ...Thirty-Eighth Annual Report, 1916-1917. Washington, DC, 1924. vii, 745pp, 183 plates, 341 figures. Includes "An Introductory Study of the Arts, Crafts, and Customs of the Guiana Indians." $135.00
    ____Another Copy. Original cloth, ex-lib. $35.00
    ____Another Copy. Lightly soiled. $86.00

B42. ...Thirty-Ninth Annual Report, 1916-1917. Washington, DC, 1925. 636pp, 17 plates, 4 figures. Includes "The Osage Tribe: The Rite of Vigil." $95.00
    ____Another Copy. Original cloth, ex-lib. $45.00
    ____Another Copy. (Fine.) $75.00

B43. ...Fortieth Annual Report, 1917-1918. Washington, DC,

vii, 664pp, 2 plates, 2 figures. Includes "The Mythical Origin of the White Buffalo Dance of the Fox Indians," and "Notes on Fox Mortuary Customs and Beliefs."
$135.00
___Another Copy. (Fine.) $75.00
___Another Copy. Ex-lib. $40.00
___Another Copy. Original cloth, VG. $60.00

B 44. ...Forty-First Annual Report, 1919-1924. Washington, DC, 1928. ix, 626pp, 137 plates, 201 figures, frontis, map in pocket. Includes "Coiled Basketry in British Columbia and Surrounding Region," and "Two Prehistoric Villages in Middle Tennessee." $265.00
___Another Copy. Original cloth, tear in spine. $200.00
___Another Copy. Original cloth, ex-lib. $150.00
___Another Copy. Inner hinge broken. $200.00

B 45. ...Forty-Second Annual Report, 1924-1925. Washington, DC, 1928. vii, 900pp, 17 plates, 108 figures. Includes "Religious Beliefs and Medical Practices of the Creek Indians," and "Aboriginal Culture of the Southeast." $135.00
___Another Copy. Ex-lib. $80.00
___Another Copy. VG. $100.00
___Another Copy. Soiled original cloth. $80.00

B 46. ...Forty-Third Annual Report, 1925-1926. Washington, DC, 1928. vii, 828pp, 44 plates, 9 figures. Includes "The Osage Tribe: Two Versions of the Child Naming Rite," "Native Tribes and Dialects of Connecticut: A Mohegan-Pequot Diary," "Picuris Children's Stories, with Texts and Songs," and "Iroquoian Cosmology. Part II."
$135.00
___Another Copy. Ex-lib. $75.00
___Another Copy. VG. $75.00

B 47. ...Forty-Fourth Annual Report, 1926-1927. Washington, DC, 1928. vii, 555pp, 98 plates, 16 figures. Includes "Exploration of the Burton Mound at Santa Barbara, California," "Uses of Plants by the Chippewa Indians," and "Archaeological Investigations II." $110.00
___Another Copy. Original cloth, spotted. $60.00
___Another Copy. VG. $75.00

B 48. ...Forty-Fifth Annual Report, 1927-1928. Washington, DC, 1930. vii, 857pp, 29 plates, 49 figures. Includes "The Salishan Tribes of the Western Plateaus," "Tattooing and Face and Body Painting of the Thompson Indians, British Columbia," and "The Osage Tribe: Rite of Teh-Wa-Xo-Be." $140.00
___Another Copy. Original wraps, torn along spine edge, but intact. $100.00
___Another Copy. Wraps, slight cvr wr. $75.00

B 49. ...Forty-Sixth Annual Report, 1928-1929. Washington, DC, 1930. vii, 654pp, 80 plates, 35 figures. Includes "Anthropological Survey in Alaska," and "Indian Tribes of the Upper Missouri." $140.00

_____Another Copy. Rebound in cloth, neat ex-lib.
                                                    $125.00
_____Another Copy. Wrappers, edges curled. $75.00
_____Another Copy. Damp stain in upper margin. $60.00

B50. ...Forty-Seventh Annual Report, 1929-1930. Washington,
        DC, 1932. vii, 1,108pp, 61 plates, 32 figures, map.
        Includes "The Acoma Indians," "Isleta, New Mexico," "In-
        troduction to Zuni Ceremonialism," "Zuni Origin Myths,"
        and "Zuni Katcinas: An Analytical Study." $195.00
_____Another Copy. (Fine.) $225.00
_____Another Copy. Water-damaged wraps. $50.00
_____Another Copy. Chipping at head and foot
                        of spine. $85.00

B51. ...Forty-Eighth Annual Report, 1930-1931. Washington,
        DC, 1933. v, 1,221pp. Includes General Index, Annual
        Reports of the Bureau of American Ethnology, Vols. 1-48
        (1879-1931). $120.00
_____Another Copy. Rebound, ex-lib. $65.00
_____Another Copy. Cvr wr to wrappers. $50.00

B52. ...Annual Reports, Complete Run, Volumes 1-48, 1879-1933,
        54 volumes total, uniform color and condition throughout
        with the last few volumes in slightly worn wrappers.
                                                          $5,000.00

NOTE: The Forty-eighth Annual Report is the last of this series
published in royal octavo size with accompanying scientific papers.
Subsequent annual reports of the Bureau consist only of the ad-
ministrative report, which were to be issued in octavo form.

B53. ...Bulletin No. 1. PILLING (J. C.). Bibliography of the
        Eskimo Language. v, 116pp, 8pp facsimiles, 8pp have
        creases, rebound in library cloth, Washington, DC, 1887.
                                                            $35.00
_____Another Copy. In worn wraps. $25.00
_____Another Copy. Rebacked. $25.00

B54. ...Bulletin No. 2. HENSHAW (Henry W.). Perforated
        Stones from California. 34pp, 16 figures, wrappers,
        Washington, DC, 1887. $40.00
_____Another Copy. Rebacked. $28.00
_____Another Copy. Back wrapper missing. $15.00

B55. ...Bulletin No. 3. HOLMES (William H.). The Use of Gold
        and Other Metals Among the Ancient Inhabitants of Chiri-
        qui, Isthmus of Darien. 27pp, 22 figures, bound in grey
        linen, collection stamp on title page, Washington, DC,
        1887. $40.00
_____Another Copy. Wrappers. $22.00
_____Another Copy. Rebacked. $15.00
_____Another Copy. Wrappers, slightly soiled. $35.00

B56. ...Bulletin No. 4. THOMAS (Cyrus). Work in Mound Ex-
        ploration of the Bureau of Ethnology. 15pp, 1 figure,
        Washington, DC, 1887. $65.00
_____Another Copy. Back cvr missing. $15.00
_____Another Copy. VG. $40.00

B57. ...Bulletin No. 5. PILLING (James C.). Bibliography of
the Siouan Languages. v, 87pp, Washington, DC, 1887.
$80.00
___Another Copy. Edges curled on wraps, soil. $30.00
___Another Copy. Rebacked. $35.00
___Another Copy. Wraps soiled. $35.00

B58. ...Bulletin No. 6. PILLING (James C.). Bibliography of
the Iroquoian Languages. vi, 208pp (including 4pp of
facsimiles), 5 unnumbered facsimiles, Washington, DC,
1888 (1889). $80.00
___Another Copy. Wrappers, cvrs loose. $30.00
___Another Copy. Rebacked, back wrap some
water stain, signed by author. $30.00
___Another Copy. Wraps, VG. $40.00

B59. ...Bulletin No. 7. HOLMES (William H.). Textile Fabrics
of Ancient Peru. 16pp, 11 figures, wraps, Washington,
DC, 1889. $45.00
___Another Copy. Head and foot of spine
chipped. $25.00
___Another Copy. Wrapper edges curled. $15.00

B60. ...Bulletin No. 8. THOMAS (Cyrus). The Problem of the
Ohio Mounds. 54pp, 8 figures, Washington, DC, 1889.
$55.00
___Another Copy. VG. $25.00
___Another Copy. Rebacked in cloth. $40.00

B61. ...Bulletin No. 9. PILLING (J. C.). Bibliography of the
Muskhogean Languages. v, 114pp, Washington, DC,
1889. $50.00
___Another Copy. Worn wrappers. $30.00
___Another Copy. Chipping of backstrip. $25.00

B62. ...Bulletin No. 10. THOMAS (Cyrus). The Circular,
Square and Octagonal Earthworks of Ohio. 35pp, 11
plates, 5 figures, bound in later stiff wrapper with front
wrap superimposed, ex-lib, Washington, DC, 1889. $25.00
___Another Copy. Original wraps. $35.00

B63. ...Bulletin No. 11. DORSEY (James O.). Omaha and Ponka
Letters. 127pp, rebound in red library cloth, Washing-
ton, DC, 1891. $30.00
___Another Copy. Backstrip nearly all chipped
away. $15.00
___Another Copy. VG. $45.00

B64. ...Bulletin No. 12. THOMAS (Cyrus). Catalogue of Prehistoric Works East of the Rocky Mountains. 246pp, 17
plates (all maps), Washington, DC, 1891. $75.00
___Another Copy. Original wrappers, worn. $45.00
___Another Copy. Lacks half title page. $20.00

B65. ...Bulletin No. 13. PILLING (James C.). Bibliography of
the Algonquian Languages. x, 614pp, 82 facsimiles,
(Bibliographic notes on Eliot's Indian Bible and other
works, pp 127-184, 21 pls), rebound in 3/4 leather with
marbled bds, Washington, DC, 1891 (1892). $140.00

B66. ...Bulletin No. 14. PILLING (James C.). Bibliography of the Athapascan Languages. xiii, 125pp (including 4pp of facsimiles), Washington, DC, 1892. $45.00
    ___Another Copy. Original wraps, chipped and soiled. $60.00
    ___Another Copy. VG. $30.00

B67. ...Bulletin No. 15. PILLING (James C.). Bibliography of Chinookan Languages (including the Chinook Jargon). xiii, 81pp (including 3 facsimiles), Washington, DC, 1893. $60.00
    ___Another Copy. Rebacked. $30.00
    ___Another Copy. Wraps, spine chipped. $35.00

B68. ...Bulletin No. 16. PILLING (James C.). Bibliography of the Salishan Languages. xiii, 86pp (including 4pp of facsimiles), wrappers, Washington, DC, 1893. $40.00
    ___Another Copy. VG. $60.00
    ___Another Copy. Rebacked, repaired tear frnt wrap. $25.00

B69. ...Bulletin No. 17. POLLARD (J. G.). The Pamunkey Indians of Virginia. Preface by W. J. McGee. 19pp, Washington, DC, 1894. $35.00
    ___Another Copy. Rebacked, soil. $15.00

B70. ...Bulletin No. 18. THOMAS (Cyrus). The Maya Year. Prefatory note by W. J. McGee. 64pp, 1 plate, Washington, DC, 1894. $50.00
    ___Another Copy. VG. $45.00
    ___Another Copy. Rebound in half linen. $60.00

B71. ...Bulletin No. 19. PILLING (James C.). Bibliography of the Wakashan Languages. xi, 70pp (including 2pp of facsimiles), Washington, DC, 1894. $60.00
    ___Another Copy. Wraps, G-VG. $25.00
    ___Another Copy. Cvrs chipped, spine tear. $40.00

B72. ...Bulletin No. 20. BOAS (Franz). Chinook Texts. 278pp, 1 plate, Washington, DC, 1894. $40.00
    ___Another Copy. Rebound in red library cloth. $30.00
    ___Another Copy. Wrappers, cvrs loose. $25.00

B73. ...Bulletin No. 21. HOLMES (W. H.). An Ancient Quarry in Indian Territory. 19pp, 12 plates, 7 figures, Washington, DC, 1894. $22.00
    ___Another Copy. VG. $25.00

B74. ...Bulletin No. 22. MOONEY (James). The Siouan Tribes of the East. 101pp, map, Washington, DC, 1894. $60.00
    ___Another Copy. Rebound in cloth. $35.00

B75. ...Bulletin No. 23. FOWKE (Gerard). Archaeologic Investigations in James and Potomac Valleys. 80pp, 17 figures, Washington, DC, 1894 (1895). $60.00
    ___Another Copy. Wrappers, good. $25.00
    ___Another Copy. Wraps, head and foot of spine chipped. $30.00

B76. ...Bulletin No. 24. HODGE (Frederick W.). List of the Publications of the Bureau of Ethnology with Index to

Authors and Subjects. 25pp, Washington, DC, 1894.
$15.00
___Another Copy. Wrappers, soiled. $25.00
B77. ...Bulletin No. 25. TRUMBULL (James Hammond). Natick
Dictionary. Introduction by Edward Everett Hale.
pp-(ix-xiii) xxviii, 349pp, Washington, DC, 1903. $45.00
___Another Copy. Soiled wrappers. $25.00
___Another Copy. Rebound in cloth. $20.00
B78. ...Bulletin No. 26. BOAS (Franz). Kathlamet Texts.
261pp, 1 plate, Washington, DC, 1901. $35.00
___Another Copy. 4to, rebound. $20.00
B79. ...Bulletin No. 27. BOAS (Franz). Tsimshian Texts.
244pp, 4to, Washington, DC, 1902. $25.00
___Another Copy. 3/4 leather, VG. $40.00
___Another Copy. Rebound in half linen. $65.00
B80. ...Bulletin No. 28. BOWDITCH (Charles). Translated and
Edited by. Mexican and Central American Antiquities,
Calendar Systems, and History: Twenty-four Papers by
Eduard Seler, E. Forstemann, Paul Schellhas, Carl Sap-
per, and E. P. Dieseldorff. 682pp, 49 plates, 134 figures,
Washington, DC, 1904. $65.00
___Another Copy. Some illus in color, many are
folding, VG. $75.00
___Another Copy. VG. $65.00
___Another Copy. Rebound in cloth. $30.00
B81. ...Bulletin No. 29. SWANTON (John R.). Haida Texts--
Skidegate Dialect. 448pp, 5 figures, Washington, DC,
1905. $35.00
___Another Copy. VG. $50.00
___Another Copy. G-VG. $35.00
___Another Copy. Rebound, VG. $40.00
B82. ...Bulletin No. 30. HODGE (Frederick Webb). Handbook
of American Indians North of Mexico. (in 2 parts).
Part 1: ix, 972pp, many figures, map, 1907. Part 2:
iv, 1,221pp, many figures, 1910. Washington, DC, 1907,
1910. $150.00
___Another Copy. Parts 1 and 2. $75.00
Note: Reprinted, January 1913, by Concurrent Resolution of Au-
gust 12, 1912; 6,000 copies for the use of Congress and 500 copies
for distribution by the Bureau.
B83. ...Bulletin No. 31. (Bibliography). List of Publications
of the Bureau of American Ethnology, with Index to Au-
thors and Titles. 31pp, Washington, DC, 1906. $15.00
___Another Copy. VG. $20.00
B84. ...Bulletin No. 32. HEWETT (Edgar L.). Antiquities of
the Jemez Plateau, New Mexico. 55pp, 17 plates (includ-
ing 1 map), 31 figures, Washington, DC, 1906. $45.00
___Another Copy. Wraps, slightly chipped. $20.00
___Another Copy. G-VG. $15.00
B85. ...Bulletin No. 33. HRDLICKA (Ales). Skeletal Remains
Suggesting or Attributed to Early Man in North America.

113pp, 21 plates, 16 figures, Washington, DC, 1907.
$25.00
___Another Copy. Rebound in library cloth. $30.00
___Another Copy. G-VG. $15.00
___Another Copy. Wrappers, VG. $20.00

B86. ...Bulletin No. 34. HRDLICKA (Ales). Physiological and Medical Observations Among the Indians of Southwestern United States and Northern Mexico. ix, 460pp, 28 plates, 2 figures, Washington, DC, 1908. $25.00
___Another Copy. (Nr Fine). $65.00
___Another Copy. G-VG. $15.00
___Another Copy. Rebound. $30.00

B87. ...Bulletin No. 35. HOUGH (Walter). Antiquities of the Upper Gila and Salt River Valleys in Arizona and New Mexico. 96pp, 11 plates (including 1 map), 51 figures, Washington, DC, 1907. $35.00
___Another Copy. Rebound in linen cloth. $40.00
___Another Copy. 3/4 leather, inscribed. $45.00
___Another Copy. VG. $22.00

B88. ...Bulletin No. 36. (bibliography) List of Publications of the Bureau of Ethnology, with Index to Authors and Titles. 31pp, Washington, DC, 1907. $18.00
___Another Copy. VG. $15.00

B89. ...Bulletin No. 37. FOWKE (Gerard). Antiquities of Central and Southeastern Missouri. vii, 116pp, 19 plates, 20 figures, Washington, DC, 1910. $45.00
___Another Copy. Original cloth. $20.00
___Another Copy. G-VG. $15.00
___Another Copy. VG. $20.00

B90. ...Bulletin No. 38. EMERSON (N. B.). Unwritten Literature of Hawaii: The Sacred Songs of the Hula. Frontis, 288pp, 24 pls, numbered label on spine, some shelf wear, Washington, DC, 1909. $45.00
___Another Copy. Cvrs dark. $20.00
___Another Copy. Ex-lib. $25.00

B91. ...Bulletin No. 39. SWANTON (John R.). Tlingit Myths and Texts. viii, 451pp, Washington, DC, 1909. $15.00
___Another Copy. G-VG. $35.00
___Another Copy. Original cloth, VG. $40.00
___Another Copy. Original cloth, edge wr. $35.00

B92. ...Bulletin No. 40. BOAS (Franz). Handbook of American Indian Languages (in 2 parts). Part 1: vii, 1,069pp, 1911. Part 2: v, 903pp, 1922. Washington, DC, 1911, 1922. $95.00
___Another Copy. Original cloth, ex-lib, Parts 1 and 2. $125.00
___Another Copy. Parts 1 and 2. VG. $60.00
___Another Copy. Parts 1 and 2. Ex-lib. $65.00

B93. ...Bulletin No. 41. FEWKES (J. Walter). Antiquities of the Mesa Verde National Park: Spruce-Tree House. viii, 57pp, 21 plates, 37 figures, Washington, DC, 1909. $35.00

      ____Another Copy. Rebound in red library cloth. $15.00
      ____Another Copy. Ex-lib. $20.00
      ____Another Copy. VG. $50.00

B94. ...Bulletin No. 42. HRDLICKA (Ales). Tuberculosis Among Certain Indian Tribes of the United States. vii, 48pp, 22 plates, Washington, DC, 1909. $28.00
      ____Another Copy. Ex-lib. $10.00
      ____Another Copy. VG. $12.00
      ____Another Copy. Two spots back cvr. $10.00

B95. ...Bulletin No. 43. SWANTON (John R.). Indian Tribes of the Lower Mississippi Valley and Adjacent Coast of the Gulf of Mexico. vii, 387pp, 32 plates (including 1 map), 2 figures, Washington, DC, 1911. $85.00
      ____Another Copy. G-VG. $30.00
      ____Another Copy. Folding color map, original cloth, overall VG. $45.00
      ____Another Copy. VG. $40.00

B96. ...Bulletin No. 44. THOMAS (Cyrus). Indian Languages of Mexico and Central America, and Their Geographical Distribution. Assisted by John R. Swanton. vii, 108pp, linguistic map, Washington, DC, 1911. $20.00
      ____Another Copy. VG. $22.00
      ____Another Copy. Folding color map, VG. $17.00
      ____Another Copy. G-VG. $22.00

B97. ...Bulletin No. 45. DENSMORE (Frances). Chippewa Music. xix, 216pp, 12 plates, 8 figures, 200 songs, Washington, DC, 1910. $25.00
      ____Another Copy. G-VG. $17.00

B98. ...Bulletin No. 46. BYINGTON (Cyrus). A Dictionary of the Choctaw Language. xi, 611pp, 1 plate, Washington, DC, 1915. $45.00
      ____Another Copy. Ex-lib. $25.00
      ____Another Copy. G-VG. $25.00

B99. ...Bulletin No. 47. DORSEY (James Owen) and SWANTON (John R.). A Dictionary of the Biloxi and Ofo Languages, Accompanied with Thirty-One Biloxi Texts and Numerous Biloxi Phrases. v, 340pp, Washington, DC, 1912. $20.00
      ____Another Copy. Ex-lib. $10.00
      ____Another Copy. G-VG. $12.00

B100. ...Bulletin No. 48. BUSHNELL (David I.). The Choctaw of Bayou Lacomb, St. Tammany Parish, Louisiana. ix, 37pp, 22 plates, 1 figure, 1909. $25.00
      ____Another Copy. G-VG. $12.00
      ____Another Copy. VG. $17.00

B101. ...Bulletin No. 49. (Bibliography). List of Publications of the Bureau of American Ethnology, with Index to Authors and Titles. 32pp, Washington, DC, 1910. $25.00
      ____Another Copy. Ex-lib. $12.00
      ____Another Copy. 2nd printing, 34pp, 1911. $22.00

B102. ...Bulletin No. 50. FEWKES (Jesse Walter). Preliminary Report on a Visit to the Navaho National Monument,

Arizona. vii, 35pp, 22 plates, 3 figures, Washington,
DC, 1911. $40.00
   Another Copy. G-VG. $10.00
   Another Copy. VG. $25.00
   Another Copy. Ex-lib. $12.00

B103. ...Bulletin No. 51. FEWKES (J. W.). Antiquities of the
Mesa Verde National Park: Cliff Palace. 82pp, 35 plates,
4 figures, Washington, DC, 1911. $40.00
   Another Copy. Rebacked. $20.00
   Another Copy. G-VG. $15.00

B104. ...Bulletin No. 52. HRDLICKA (Ales). Early Man in South
America. xv, 405pp, 68 plates, 51 figures, Washington,
DC, 1912. $45.00
   Another Copy. G-VG. $22.00
   Another Copy. VG. $37.00
   Another Copy. Ex-lib. $22.00

B105. ...Bulletin No. 53. DENSMORE (Frances). Chippewa
Music-II. xxi, 341pp, 45 plates, 6 figures, 180 songs,
Washington, DC, 1913. $65.00
   Another Copy. Numerous pls of beadwork and
            costumes, G-VG. $25.00
   Another Copy. VG. $30.00
   Another Copy. Ex-lib. $15.00

B106. ...Bulletin No. 54. HEWETT (E. L.), HENDERSON (J.),
and ROBBINS (Wilfred W.). The Physiography of the
Rio Grande Valley, New Mexico, in Relation to Pueblo
Culture. 76pp, 11 plates, 2 figures, Washington, DC,
1913. $27.00
   Another Copy. G-VG. $15.00
   Another Copy. Wrappers, VG. $20.00
   Another Copy. Ex-lib. $15.00

B107. ...Bulletin No. 55. ROBBINS (W. R.), HARRINGTON (J.),
and FREIRE-MARRECO (Barbara). Ethnobotany of the
Tewa Indians. xii, 124pp, 9 plates, 7 figures, Washing-
ton, DC, 1916. $25.00
   Another Copy. Ex-lib. $17.00
   Another Copy. VG. $32.00
   Another Copy. Rebound, ex-lib. $12.00

B108. ...Bulletin No. 56. HENDERSON (J.) and HARRINGTON
(J. P.). Ethnozoology of the Tewa Indians. x, 76pp,
Washington, DC, 1914. $25.00
   Another Copy. Rebound. $10.00
   Another Copy. VG. $35.00
   Another Copy. G-VG. $17.00

B109. ...Bulletin No. 57. MORLEY (Sylvanus Griswold). An
Introduction to the Study of the Maya Hieroglyphs.
xvi, 284pp, 32 plates, 85 figures, some photos and
drawings in color, Washington, DC, 1915. $22.00
   Another Copy. (Nr fine.) $30.00
   Another Copy. Ex-lib. $22.00

B110. ...Bulletin No. 58. (Bibliography). List of Publications

of the Bureau of American Ethnology, with Index to Authors and Titles. 39pp, Washington, DC, 1914. $18.00
    ___Another Copy. VG. $10.00

B111. ...Bulletin No. 59. BOAS (Franz). Kutenai Tales. Together with Texts Collected by Alexander Chamberlain.
xii, 387pp, Washington, DC, 1918. $45.00
    ___Another Copy. VG. $30.00
    ___Another Copy. Ex-lib. $10.00
    ___Another Copy. G-VG. $25.00

B112. ...Bulletin No. 60. HOLMES (W. H.). Handbook of Aboriginal American Antiquities. Part I. Introductory:
The Lithic Industries. xvii, 380pp, 223 figures, Washington, DC, 1919. $45.00
    ___Another Copy. G-VG. $35.00
    ___Another Copy. VG. $50.00
    ___Another Copy. Rebound in linen cloth. $45.00

B113. ...Bulletin No. 61. DENSMORE (Frances). Teton Sioux
Music. xxviii, 561pp, 82 plates, 43 figures, 240 songs,
Washington, DC, 1918. $50.00
    ___Another Copy. (Nr fine). $60.00
    ___Another Copy. Ex-lib. $50.00
    ___Another Copy. G-VG. $30.00
    ___Another Copy. 3/4 leather, hinges broken. $50.00

B114. ...Bulletin No. 62. HRDLICKA (Ales). Physical Anthropology of the Lenape or Delawares, and of the Eastern
Indians in General. 130pp, 29 plates, 1 figure, Washington, DC, 1916. $25.00
    ___Another Copy. G-VG. $12.00
    ___Another Copy. About fine. $15.00
    ___Another Copy. Ex-lib. $12.00

B115. ...Bulletin No. 63. COOPER (John M.). Analytical and
Critical Bibliography of the Tribes of Tierra Del Fuego
and Adjacent Territory. ix, 233pp, map, Washington,
DC, 1917. $20.00
    ___Another Copy. G-VG. $10.00
    ___Another Copy. VG. $12.00

B116. ...Bulletin No. 64. GANN (Thomas W. F.). The Maya
Indians of Southern Yucatan and Northern British Honduras. 146pp, 28 plates, 84 figures, Washington, DC,
1918. $35.00
    ___Another Copy. G-VG. $18.00
    ___Another Copy. About fine. $25.00

B117. ...Bulletin No. 65. KIDDER (Alfred Vincent). Archaeological Explorations in Northeastern Arizona. 228pp, 97
plates, 102 figures, Washington, DC, 1919. $65.00
    ___Another Copy. VG. $38.00
    ___Another Copy. Ex-lib. $15.00
    ___Another Copy. G-VG. $18.00

B118. ...Bulletin No. 66. HRDLICKA (Ales). Recent Discoveries Attributed to Early Man in America. 67pp, 14
plates, 8 figures, Washington, DC, 1918. $30.00

    ___Another Copy. Ex-lib. $12.00

    ___Another Copy. G-VG. $12.00

    ___Another Copy. VG. $17.00

B119. ...Bulletin No. 67. FRACHTENBERG (Leo J.). Alsea Text and Myths. 304pp, Washington, DC, 1920. $45.00

    ___Another Copy. VG. $35.00

    ___Another Copy. G-VG. $20.00

    ___Another Copy. G-VG. $20.00

    ___Another Copy. Rebound in library cloth. $22.00

B120. ...Bulletin No. 68. SWANTON (John R.). A Structural and Lexical Comparison of the Tunica, Chitimacha and Atakapa Languages. 56pp, Washington, DC, 1919. $25.00

    ___Another Copy. G-VG. $20.00

    ___Another Copy. VG. $22.00

    ___Another Copy. Ex-lib with markings. $17.00

B121. ...Bulletin No. 69. BUSHNELL (David I.). Native Villages and Village Sites East of the Mississippi. 111pp, 17 plates, 12 figures, Washington, DC, 1919. $27.00

    ___Another Copy. Rebound in red cloth. $30.00

    ___Another Copy. VG. $20.00

    ___Another Copy. Ex-lib. $17.00

B122. ...Bulletin No. 70. FEWKES (Jesse W.). Prehistoric Villages, Castles, and Towers of Southwestern Colorado. 79pp, 33 plates, 18 figures, Washington, DC, 1919. $40.00

    ___Another Copy. G-VG. $20.00

    ___Another Copy. (Nr fine.) $30.00

    ___Another Copy. Ex-lib. $20.00

    ___Another Copy. Rebound in red library cloth, few spots frnt cvr. $17.00

B123. ...Bulletin No. 71. BUSHNELL (David I.). Native Cemeteries and Forms of Burial East of the Mississippi. 160pp, 17 plates, 17 figures, Washington, DC, 1920. $20.00

    ___Another Copy. VG. $28.00

    ___Another Copy. (Nr fine.) $35.00

    ___Another Copy. Rebound, ex-lib. $20.00

B124. ...Bulletin No. 72. MICHELSON (Truman). The Owl Sacred Pack of the Fox Indians. 83pp, 4 plates, Washington, DC, 1921. $25.00

    ___Another Copy. Ex-lib. $10.00

    ___Another Copy. VG. $15.00

B125. ...Bulletin No. 73. SWANTON (John R.). Early History of the Creek Indians and Their Neighbors. 492pp, 10 plates (all pocket maps), Washington, DC, 1922. $50.00

    ___Another Copy. VG. $40.00

    ___Another Copy. Rebound in cloth. $25.00

B126. ...Bulletin No. 74. TOZZER (Alfred M.). Excavation of a Site at Santiago Ahuitzotla, D. F. Mexico. 56pp, 19 plates, 9 figures, Washington, DC, 1921. $12.00

    ___Another Copy. VG. $15.00

    ___Another Copy. G-VG. $10.00

B127. ...Bulletin No. 75. DENSMORE (Frances). Northern Ute
Music. 213pp, 16 plates, 21 figures, 110 songs, Wash-
ington, DC, 1922. $37.00
___Another Copy. VG. $35.00
___Another Copy. Ex-lib. $12.00
___Another Copy. G-VG. $25.00
___Another Copy. Rebound in 3/4 leather with
marbled bds, edge wr. $30.00

B128. ...Bulletin No. 76. FOWKE (Gerald). Archaeological In-
vestigations. I. Caves in the Ozark Region. II. Caves
in Other States. III. Explorations Along Missouri River
Bluffs in Kansas and Nebraska. IV. Aboriginal House
Mounds. V. Archaeological Work in Hawaii. 204pp, 45
plates, 37 figures, Washington, DC, 1922. $45.00
___Another Copy. VG. $47.00
___Another Copy. Rebound, ex-lib. $15.00

B129. ...Bulletin No. 77. BUSHNELL (David I.). Villages of
the Algonquian, Siouan, and Caddoan Tribes West of the
Mississippi. x, 211pp, 55 plates, 12 figures, Washington,
DC, 1922. $40.00
___Another Copy. VG. $45.00
___Another Copy. G-VG. $20.00
___Another Copy. Cvrs spotted. $20.00

B130. ...Bulletin No. 78. KROEBER (A. L.). Handbook of the
Indians of California. xviii, 995pp, 83 plates (including
1 pocket map), 78 figures, Washington, DC, 1925.
$150.00
___Another Copy. Ex-lib, fair. $100.00
___Another Copy. G-VG. $80.00
___Another Copy. 1953 reprint, VG. $45.00

B131. ...Bulletin No. 79. KARSTEN (Rafael). Blood Revenge,
War, and Victory Feasts Among the Jivaro Indians of
Eastern Ecuador. vii, 94pp, 10 plates, Washington,
DC, 1923. $25.00
___Another Copy. VG. $20.00
___Another Copy. G-VG. $15.00
___Another Copy. Rebound in red library cloth,
spots back cvr, ex-lib. $22.00

B132. ...Bulletin No. 80. DENSMORE (Frances). Mandan and
Hidatsa Music. xx, 192pp, 19 plates, 6 figures, 110
songs, Washington, DC, 1923. $35.00
___Another Copy. G-VG. $20.00

B133. ...Bulletin No. 81. JEANCON (J. A.). Excavations in
the Chama Valley, New Mexico. ix, 80pp, 65 plates, 38
figures, Washington, DC, 1923. $47.00
___Another Copy. VG. $27.00
___Another Copy. G-VG. $20.00
___Another Copy. Ex-lib. $22.00

B134. ...Bulletin No. 82. JUDD (Neil M.). Archaeological Observations North of the Rio Grande. ix, 171pp, 61
plates, 46 figures, Washington, DC, 1926. $42.00

    ___Another Copy. GD. $20.00

    ___Another Copy. G-VG. $40.00

    ___Another Copy. Ex-lib. $18.00

    ___Another Copy. About fine. $45.00

B135. ...Bulletin No. 83. BUSHNELL (David I.). Burials of the Algonquian, Siouan, and Caddoan Tribes West of the Mississippi. x, 103pp, 37 plates, 3 figures, Washington, DC, 1927. $47.00

    ___Another Copy. G-VG. $22.00

    ___Another Copy. VG. $18.00

    ___Another Copy. Ex-lib. $12.00

B136. ...Bulletin No. 84. HARRINGTON (John P.). Vocabulary of the Kiowa Language. v, 255pp, 1 figure, Washington, DC, 1928. $38.00

    ___Another Copy. Rebound. $25.00

    ___Another Copy. G-VG. $15.00

    ___Another Copy. VG. $30.00

B137. ...Bulletin No. 85. MICHELSON (Truman). Contributions to Fox Ethnology: Notes on the Ceremonial Runners of the Fox Indians; a Sauk and Fox Sacred Pack; a Sacred Pack Called A'penäwänä'a Belonging to the Thunder Gens of the Fox Indians; a Sacred Pack Called Sāgimā'kwäwa Belonging to the Bear Gens of the Fox Indians. vii, 168pp, 2 pls, 2 figures, Washington, DC, 1927. $25.00

    ___Another Copy. VG. $45.00

B138. ...Bulletin No. 86. DENSMORE (Frances). Chippewa Customs. xii, 204pp, 90 plates, 27 figures, Washington, DC, 1929. $35.00

    ___Another Copy. G-VG. $20.00

    ___Another Copy. VG. $57.00

    ___Another Copy. Ex-lib. $20.00

B139. ...Bulletin No. 87. MICHELSON (Truman). Notes on the Buffalo-Head Dance of the Thunder Gens of the Fox Indians. v, 94pp, 1 figure, Washington, DC, 1928. $25.00

    ___Another Copy. VG. $25.00

    ___Another Copy. Ex-lib. $10.00

    ___Another Copy. Ex-lib, fair. $12.00

B140. ...Bulletin No. 88. SWANTON (John R.). Myths and Tales of the Southwestern Indians. x, 275pp, Washington, DC, 1929. $47.00

    ___Another Copy. VG. $30.00

    ___Another Copy. G-VG. $25.00

    ___Another Copy. Ex-lib. $10.00

B141. ...Bulletin No. 89. MICHELSON (Truman). Observations on the Thunder Dance of the Bear Gens of the Fox Indians. v, 73pp, 1 figure, Washington, DC, 1929. $30.00

    ___Another Copy. VG. $25.00

    ___Another Copy. G-VG. $12.00

    ___Another Copy. Ex-lib. $10.00

B142. ...Bulletin No. 90. DENSMORE (Frances). Papago Music. xx, 229pp, 19 plates, 4 figures, 167 songs, Washington,

DC, 1929. $40.00
___Another Copy. VG. $25.00
___Another Copy. Ex-lib. $12.00

B143. ...Bulletin No. 91. ROTH (Walter E.). Additional Studies of the Arts, Crafts, and Customs of the Guiana Indians, with Special Reference to Those of Southern British Guiana. xvii, 110pp, 34 plates, 90 figures, Washington, DC, 1929. $25.00
___Another Copy. Ex-lib. $15.00

B144. ...Bulletin No. 92. ROBERTS (Frank H. H. Jr.). Shabik'eshchee Village: A Late Basket Maker Site in the Chaco Canyon, New Mexico. viii, 164pp, 31 plates, 32 figures, Washington, DC, 1929. $50.00
___Another Copy. Original cloth, fine copy. $35.00
___Another Copy. VG. $20.00
___Another Copy. Ex-lib. $18.00

B145. ...Bulletin No. 93. DENSMORE (Frances). Pawnee Music. xviii, 129pp, 8 plates, 86 songs, Washington, DC, 1929. $30.00
___Another Copy. Ex-lib. $12.00
___Another Copy. G-VG. $20.00
___Another Copy. VG. $25.00
___Another Copy. Rebound. $20.00

B146. ...Bulletin No. 94. HARRINGTON (J. P.). Tobacco Among the Karuk Indians of California. xxxvi, 284pp, 36 plates, 2 figures, Washington, DC, 1932. $50.00
___Another Copy. Wraps, a bit frayed. $12.00
___Another Copy. VG. $50.00
___Another Copy. G-VG. $20.00

B147. ...Bulletin No. 95. MICHELSON (Truman). Contributions to Fox Ethnology II. vii, 183pp, 1 figure, Washington, DC, 1930. $30.00
___Another Copy. Wrappers, VG. $17.00
___Another Copy. Ex-lib. $10.00
___Another Copy. G-VG. $12.00

B148. ...Bulletin No. 96. ROBERTS (Frank H. H. Jr.). Early Pueblo Ruins in the Piedra District, Southwestern Colorado. ix, 190pp, 55 plates, 40 figures, Washington, DC, 1930. $45.00
___Another Copy. Wrappers, VG. $20.00
___Another Copy. Rebound in cloth. $25.00
___Another Copy. G-VG. $20.00

B149. ...Bulletin No. 97. GIFFORD (E. W.). The Kamia of Imperial Valley. vii, 94pp, 2 plates, 4 figures, Washington, DC, 1931. $30.00
___Another Copy. Wraps, VG. $30.00
___Another Copy. VG. $17.00
___Another Copy. Ex-lib. $12.00

B150. ...Bulletin No. 98. BENEDICT (Ruth). Tales of the Cochiti Indians. x, 256pp, Washington, DC, 1931. $35.00

    ____Another Copy. Wraps, fine. $35.00
    ____Another Copy. G-VG. $15.00
    ____Another Copy. Ex-lib. $12.00

B151. ...Bulletin No. 99. MOONEY (James). The Swimmer Manuscript: Cherokee Sacred Formulas and Medicinal Prescriptions. Revised, Completed, and Edited by Frans Olbrechts. xvii, 319pp, 13 plates, Washington, DC, 1932. $50.00
    ____Another Copy. Wraps, VG+. $45.00
    ____Another Copy. Wraps, about fine. $30.00
    ____Another Copy. Rebound in cloth, ex-lib. $25.00

B152. ...Bulletin No. 100. ROBERTS (Frank H. H. Jr.). The Ruins at Kiatuthlanna, Eastern Arizona. viii, 195pp, 47 plates, 31 figures, Washington, DC, 1931. $50.00
    ____Another Copy. G-VG. $20.00
    ____Another Copy. Ex-lib, Good. $17.00

B153. ...Bulletin No. 101. LA FLESCHE (Francis). War Ceremony and Peace Ceremony of the Osage Indians. vii, 280pp, 13 plates, 1 figure, Washington, DC, 1939. $40.00
    ____Another Copy. Wrappers, VG. $28.00
    ____Another Copy. Head of spine has tape
            repair. $20.00
    ____Another Copy. Ex-lib. $17.00

B154. ...Bulletin No. 102. DENSMORE (Frances). Menominee Music. xxii, 230pp, 27 plates, 3 figures, 140 songs, Washington, DC, 1932. $40.00
    ____Another Copy. Wrappers, VG. $25.00
    ____Another Copy. Ex-lib. $15.00

B155. ...Bulletin No. 103. SWANTON (John R.). Source Material for the Social and Ceremonial Life of the Choctaw Indians. vii, 282pp, 6 plates, 1 figure, Washington, DC, 1931. $35.00
    ____Another Copy. G-VG. $18.00
    ____Another Copy. Wraps, VG. $20.00
    ____Another Copy. Wraps, about fine. $35.00

B156. ...Bulletin No. 104. COLTON (Harold S.). A Survey of Prehistoric Sites in the Region of Flagstaff, Arizona. vii, 69pp, 10 plates (including 4 maps), 21 figures, Washington DC, 1932. $25.00
    ____Another Copy. Wraps, VG. $20.00
    ____Another Copy. Ex-lib. $15.00

B157. ...Bulletin No. 105. MICHELSON (Truman). Notes on the Fox Wapanowiweni. v, 195pp, 1 figure, Washington, DC, 1932. $30.00
    ____Another Copy. Wraps, cvrs loose. $15.00
    ____Another Copy. About fine. $10.00
    ____Another Copy. Ex-lib. $15.00

B158. ...Bulletin No. 106. CONZEMIUS (Eduard). Ethnographical Survey of the Miskito and Sumu Indians of Honduras and Nicaragua. vii, 191pp, 10 plates, 1 figure, Washington, DC, 1932. $35.00

    ___Another Copy. VG. $22.00
    ___Another Copy. G-VG. $20.00
    ___Another Copy. Rebound. $15.00
    ___Another Copy. 3/4 leather, marbled bds,
                    edges scuffed, hinge weak. $25.00

B159. ...Bulletin No. 107. HARRINGTON (J. P.). Karuk Indian
       Myths. v, 34pp, Washington, DC, 1932. $20.00
    ___Another Copy. Rebound, VG. $15.00
    ___Another Copy. G-VG. $12.00

B160. ...Bulletin No. 108. GATSCHET (Albert S.) and SWANTON
       (John R.). A Dictionary of the Atakapa Language, Ac-
       companied by Text Material. v, 181pp, 1 plate, Washing-
       ton, DC, 1932. $30.00
    ___Another Copy. G-VG. $18.00
    ___Another Copy. Ex-lib. $18.00

B161. ...Bulletin No. 109. LA FLESCHE (Francis). A Dictionary
       of the Osage Language. v, 406, Washington, DC, 1932.
                                                      $35.00
    ___Another Copy. Ex-lib. $12.00
    ___Another Copy. G-VG. $18.00
    ___Another Copy. Wrappers, VG. $25.00

B162. ...Bulletin No. 110. DENSMORE (Frances). Yuman and
       Yaqui Music. xviii, 216pp, 31 plates, 7 figures, 130
       songs, Washington, DC, 1932. $40.00
    ___Another Copy. G-VG. $20.00
    ___Another Copy. Wrappers, VG. $27.00
    ___Another Copy. Ex-lib. $20.00

B163. ...Bulletin No. 111. ROBERTS (Frank H. H. Jr.). The
       Village of the Great Kivas on the Zuni Reservation, New
       Mexico. ix, 197pp, 64 plates, 34 figures, Washington,
       DC, 1932. $45.00
    ___Another Copy. G-VG. $22.00
    ___Another Copy. VG. $30.00
    ___Another Copy. Rebound in red library
                    cloth, ex-lib. $15.00

B164. ...Bulletin No. 112. WEDEL (Waldo Rudolph). An Intro-
       duction to Pawnee Archaeology. xi, 122pp, 12 plates,
       10 maps, 12 figures, Washington, DC, 1936. $35.00
    ___Another Copy. Wraps, fine. $40.00
    ___Another Copy. Wraps, VG. $25.00
    ___Another Copy. Ex-lib. $20.00

B165. ...Bulletin No. 113. WALKER (Winslow M.). The Troy-
       ville Mounds, Catahoula Parish, Louisiana. vii, 73pp,
       16 plates, 15 figures, Washington, DC, 1936. $30.00
    ___Another Copy. Wrappers, VG. $25.00
    ___Another Copy. Ex-lib. $12.00

B166. ...Bulletin No. 114. MICHELSON (Truman). Fox Miscel-
       lany. v, 124pp, 9 figures, Washington, DC, 1937.
                                                      $25.00
    ___Another Copy. Wraps, VG. $17.00
    ___Another Copy. G-VG. $10.00

B167. ...Bulletin No. 115. Journal of Friederich Kurz. Trans-
lated by Myrtis Jarrell. Edited by J. N. B. Hewitt.
ix, 382pp, 48 plates, Washington, DC, 1937. $50.00
____Another Copy. Wraps, plates water stained,
                  cvr taped, contents sound. $50.00
____Another Copy. Wraps, about fine. $75.00
____Another Copy. Wraps, VG. $65.00

B168. ...Bulletin No. 116. STEWARD (Julian H.). Ancient
Caves of the Great Salt Lake Region. xiv, 131pp, 9
plates, map, 48 figures, Washington, DC, 1938. $37.00
____Another Copy. Wraps, VG. $20.00
____Another Copy. Ex-lib. $15.00
____Another Copy. Rebound in red library
                  cloth, ex-lib. $20.00
____Another Copy. Tape repaired wraps, title
                  on spine in ink. $17.00

B169. ...Bulletin No. 117. STIRLING (M. W.). Historical and
Ethnographical Material on the Jivaro Indians. xi, 148pp,
37 plates, map, 6 figures, Washington, DC, 1938. $25.00
____Another Copy. G-VG. $15.00
____Another Copy. VG. $20.00

B170. ...Bulletin No. 118. WEBB (William S.). An Archaeologi-
cal Survey of the Norris Basin in Eastern Tennessee.
xv, 398pp, 152 plates, 2 maps, 79 figures, Washington,
DC, 1938. $50.00
____Another Copy. VG. $50.00
____Another Copy. G-VG. $35.00
____Another Copy. Rebound in red library
                  cloth, ex-lib. $22.00

Note: With Bulletin No. 119, the Bureau of American Ethnology
inaugurated a new series of Anthropological Papers, designed as
an outlet for brief articles. These papers are numbered consecu-
tively, a bulletin being devoted to them from time to time as they
accumulate. A limited edition of Anthropological Papers is issued
in separate form.

B171. ...Bulletin No. 119. Anthropological Papers, Nos. 1-6.
Paper No. 1: KELLY (A. R.). A Preliminary Report on
Archaeological Explorations at Macon, Georgia. v-ix,
68pp, plates 1-12, figures 1-7. Paper No. 2: CARTER
(John G.). The Northern Arapaho Flat Pipe and the
Ceremony of Covering the Pipe. pp 69-102, figures 8-10.
Paper No. 3: TAYLOR (D.). The Caribs of Dominica.
pp 103-159, plates 13-18, figures 11-37. Paper No. 4:
MICHELSON (T.). What Happened to Green Bear Who
Was Blessed with a Sacred Pack. pp 161-176. Paper
No. 5: STEWARD (J. H.). Lemhi Shoshoni Physical
Therapy. pp 177-181. Paper No. 6: STEWARD (J. H.).
Panatubiji, an Owens Valley Paiute. pp 183-195. Wash-
ington, DC, 1938. $37.00
____Another Copy. Wraps, VG. $37.00
____Another Copy. G-VG. $30.00
____Another Copy. Ex-lib. $18.00

B172. ...Bulletin No. 120. STEWARD (Julian H.). Basin-Plateau
Aboriginal Sociopolitical Groups. xii, 346pp, 3 plates,
13 figures, Washington, DC, 1938. $40.00
____Another Copy. G-VG. $20.00
____Another Copy. Wrappers, VG. $37.00
____Another Copy. Ex-lib, fair. $15.00

B173. ...Bulletin No. 121. ROBERTS (Frank H. H. Jr.).
Archaeological Remains in the Whitewater District, Eastern
Arizona. Part I: House Types. xii, 276pp, 30 plates,
53 figures, Washington, DC, 1939. $45.00
____Another Copy. Wraps, VG. $30.00
____Another Copy. G-VG. $25.00
____Another Copy. Ex-lib. $15.00

B174. ...Bulletin No. 122. WEBB (William S.). An Archaeologi-
cal Survey of Wheeler Basin on the Tennessee River in
Northern Alabama. xv, 214pp, 122 plates, 2 maps, 25
figures, Washington, DC, 1939. $42.00
____Another Copy. G-VG. $35.00
____Another Copy. VG. $35.00
____Another Copy. Wraps, VG. $37.00
____Another Copy. Ex-lib. $22.00

B175. ...Bulletin No. 123. Anthropological Papers 7-12. Paper
No. 7: GANN (Thomas and Mary). Archaeological Investigations in the Corozal District of British Honduras.
vii-viii, 66p, plates 1-10, figures 1-11. Paper No. 8:
MICHELSON (T.). Linguistic Classification of Cree and
Montagnais-Naskapi Dialects. pp 67-95, figure 12. Paper No. 9: Sedelmayr's Relacion of 1746. Translated
and Edited by Ronald L. Ives. pp. 97-117. Paper No.
10: HEWITT (J. N. B.). Notes on the Creek Indians.
Edited by John R. Swanton. pp 119-159, figures 13-14.
Paper No. 11: PETRULLO (Vincenzo). The Yaruros of
the Capanaparo River, Venezuela. pp 161-290, plates
11-25, figures 15-27. Paper No. 12: PETRULLO (Vincenzo). Archaeology of Arauquin. pp 291-295, plates
26-32. Washington, DC, 1939. $25.00
____Another Copy. G-VG. $20.00
____Another Copy. VG. $25.00

B176. ...Bulletin No. 124. DENSMORE (Frances). Nootka and
Quileute Music. xxvi, 358pp, 24 plates, 7 figures, 210
songs, Washington, DC, 1939. $47.00
____Another Copy. VG. $40.00
____Another Copy. (Nr fine). $55.00
____Another Copy. Rebound in red library
cloth, ex-lib. $25.00

B177. ...Bulletin No. 125. JONES (William). Ethnography of
the Fox Indians. Edited by Margaret W. Fisher. ix,
156pp, Washington, DC, 1939. $37.00
____Another Copy. Wraps, VG. $20.00
____Another Copy. Some internal water stain. $10.00
____Another Copy. G-VG. $25.00

B178.   ...Bulletin No. 126.   ROBERTS (Frank H. H. Jr.).
Archaeological Remains in the Whitewater District,
Eastern Arizona. Part II: Artifacts and Burials. xi,
170pp, 57 plates, 44 figures, Washington, DC, 1940.

                 $40.00

  ___ Another Copy. Wraps, fine. $40.00
  ___ Another Copy. G-VG. $20.00
  ___ Another Copy. Rebound in library cloth,
         ex-lib. $17.00

B179.   ...Bulletin No. 127.   SWANTON (John R.).   Linguistic
Material from the Tribes of Southern Texas and Northeastern Mexico. v, 145pp, Washington, DC, 1940.

                 $35.00

  ___ Another Copy. G-VG. $25.00
  ___ Another Copy. Wrappers, paper label on
         frnt cvr. $30.00

B180.   ...Bulletin No. 128.   Anthropological Papers, Nos. 13-18.
Paper No. 13: BALL (Sydney H.). The Mining of Gems
and Ornamental Stones by American Indians. ix-xii, 77pp,
plates 1-5. Paper No. 14: FENTON (William N.). Iroquois Suicide: A Study in the Stability of a Culture Pattern. pp 79-137, plates 6-8. Paper No. 15: FENTON
(W. N.). Tonawanda Longhouse Ceremonies: Ninety
Years After Lewis Henry Morgan. pp 139-165, plates
9-18. Paper No. 16: GILLIN (John). The Quichua-
Speaking Indians of the Province of Imbabura (Ecuador)
and Their Anthropometric Relations with the Living Populations of the Andean Area. pp 167-228, plates 19-29,
figures 1-2. Paper No. 17: SPECK (Frank G.). Art
Processes in Birchbark of the River Desert Algonquin, a
Circumboreal Trait. pp 229-274, plates 30-42, figures
3-25. Paper No. 18: STEWARD (Julian H.). Archaeological Reconnaissance of Southern Utah. pp 275-356,
plates 43-52, figures 26-77. Washington, DC, 1941.

                 $45.00

  ___ Another Copy. G-VG. $25.00
  ___ Another Copy. Wraps, VG. $30.00
  ___ Another Copy. Ex-lib. $25.00
  ___ Another Copy. Rebound in red library cloth,
         ex-lib. $22.00

B181.   ...Bulletin No. 129.   JONES (W. B.) et al.   An Archaeo-
logical Survey of Pickwick Basin in the Adjacent Portions
of the States of Alabama, Mississippi, and Tennessee.
xxii, 536pp, 316 plates, 2 maps, 99 figures, Washington,
DC, 1942. $70.00
  ___ Another Copy. G-VG. $20.00
  ___ Another Copy. Library spine label, else VG. $35.00
  ___ Another Copy. VG. $60.00

B182.   ...Bulletin No. 130.   WEDEL (Waldo R.).   Archaeological
Investigations at Buena Vista Lake, Kern County, Cali-
fornia. viii, 194pp, 57 plates, 19 figures, Washington,
DC, 1941. $35.00

	___Another Copy. Wrappers, VG.	$25.00
	___Another Copy. GVG.	$20.00
B183.	...Bulletin No. 131. SETZLER (Frank M.) and JENNINGS (Jesse D.). Peachtree Mound and Village Site, Cherokee County, North Carolina. ix, 103pp, 50 plates, 12 figures, Washington, DC, 1941.	$48.00
	___Another Copy. Wrappers, VG.	$25.00
	___Another Copy. G-VG.	$20.00
	___Another Copy. (Nr fine).	$50.00
	___Another Copy. Ex-lib.	$18.00
B184.	...Bulletin No. 132. SWANTON (John R.). Source Material on the History and Ethnology of the Caddo Indians. vii, 332pp, 19 plates, 5 figures, Washington, DC, 1942.	$55.00
	___Another Copy. Wraps, about fine.	$40.00
	___Another Copy. G-VG.	$32.00
	___Another Copy. Wraps, VG.	$30.00
	___Another Copy. Rebound in red library cloth, ex-lib.	$20.00

B185. ...Bulletin No. 133. Anthropological Papers, Nos. 19-26. Paper No. 19: DENSMORE (Frances). A Search for Songs Among the Chitimacha Indians in Louisiana. pp 1-15, plates 1-4. Paper No. 20: DRUCKER (Philip). Archaeological Survey on the Northern Northwest Coast. pp 17-142, Plates 5-9, figures 1-33. Paper No. 21: FLANNERY (Regina). Some Notes on a Few Sites in Beaufort County, South Carolina. pp 143-153, figures 34-35. Paper No. 22: GRIFFIN (James B.). An Analysis and Interpretation of the Ceramic Remains from Two Sites Near Beaufort, South Carolina. pp 155-168, plates 10-12. Paper No. 23: GILBERT (William Harlen Jr.). The Eastern Cherokees. pp 169-413, plates 13-17, figures 36-55. Paper No. 24: HEIZER (Robert F.). Aconite Poison Whaling in Asia and America: An Aleutian Transfer to the New World. pp 415-468, plates 18-23a, figures 56-60. Paper No. 25: JENNESS (Diamond). The Carrier Indians of the Bulkley River: Their Social and Religious Life. pp 469-586, plates 24-34, figures 61-62. Paper No. 26: SWANTON (John R.). The Quipu and Peruvian Civilization. pp 587-596. Washington, DC, 1943 (1944).

		$60.00
	___Another Copy. Wrappers, VG.	$25.00
	___Another Copy. Wrappers, about fine.	$50.00
	___Another Copy. Rebound.	$30.00
B186.	...Bulletin No. 134. METRAUX (Alfred). The Native Tribes of Eastern Bolivia and Western Matto Grosso. ix, 182pp, 5 plates, 1 figure, Washington, DC, 1942.	$25.00
	___Another Copy. G-VG.	$20.00
	___Another Copy. VG.	$25.00
	___Another Copy. Ex-lib.	$17.00

    ____Another Copy. Rebound in red library cloth,
                ex-lib. $15.00

B187. ...Bulletin No. 135. STIRLING (Matthew W.). Origin
    Myth of Acoma and Other Records. viii, 123pp, 17
    plates, 8 figures, Washington, DC, 1942. $48.00
    ____Another Copy. Wrappers, VG. $40.00
    ____Another Copy. G-VG. $35.00
    ____Another Copy. Ex-lib. $22.00

B188. ...Bulletin No. 136. Anthropological Papers, Nos. 27-32.
    Paper No. 27: DENSMORE (Frances). Music of the In-
    dians of British Columbia. pp 1-99, plates, 1-9, figures
    1-2, 98 songs. Paper No. 28: DENSMORE (Frances).
    Choctaw Music. pp 101-188, plates 10-21, figures 3-4,
    65 songs. Paper No. 29: STEGGERDA (Morris). Some
    Ethnological Data Concerning One Hundred Yucatan
    Plants. pp 189-226, plates 22-24. Paper No. 30:
    STEGGERDA (Morris). A Description of Thirty Towns
    in Yucatan, Mexico. pp 227-248, plates 25-28. Paper
    No. 31: STEWARD (Julian H.). Some Western Shoshoni
    Myths. pp 249-299. Paper No. 32: WHITE (Leslie A.).
    New Material from Acoma. pp 301-359, plates 29-32,
    figure 5. Washington, DC, 1943 (1944). $50.00
    ____Another Copy. Wraps, VG. $25.00
    ____Another Copy. Wraps, about fine. $48.00
    ____Another Copy. Rebound, ex-lib. $25.00

B189. ...Bulletin No. 137. SWANTON (John R.). The Indians
    of the Southeastern United States. xiii, 943pp, 107
    plates, 5 figures, 13 maps, Washington, DC, 1946.
                                      $125.00
    ____Another Copy. G-VG. $65.00
    ____Another Copy. Rebound in 3/4 leather,
                 marbled bds, hinge started. $100.00
    ____Another Copy. VG. $65.00
    ____Another Copy. Rebound in red library cloth,
                 ex-lib. $40.00

B190. ...Bulletin No. 138. STIRLING (Matthew W.). Stone
    Monuments of Southern Mexico. vii, 84pp, 62 plates, 14
    figures, Washington, DC, 1943 (1944). $40.00
    ____Another Copy. Wrappers, GD. $30.00
    ____Another Copy. G-VG. $20.00
    ____Another Copy. VG. $32.00

B191. ...Bulletin No. 139. WEIANT (C. W.). An Introduction to
    the Ceramics of Tres Zapotes, Veracruz, Mexico. xiv,
    144pp, 78 plates, 54 figures, 10 maps, Washington, DC,
    1943. $38.00
    ____Another Copy. Wrappers, about fine. $35.00
    ____Another Copy. G-VG. $22.00
    ____Another Copy. Rebound. $17.00

B192. ...Bulletin No. 140. DRUCKER (Philip). Ceramic Se-
    quences at Tres Zapotes, Veracruz, Mexico. ix, 155pp,
    65 plates, 46 figures, Washington, DC, 1943. $45.00

___Another Copy. Wrappers, VG.		$20.00
___Another Copy. G-VG.		$25.00
___Another Copy. Ex-lib.		$15.00

B193. ...Bulletin No. 141. DRUCKER (Philip). Ceramic Stratigraphy at Cerro de las Mesas, Veracruz, Mexico. viii,
95pp, 58 plates, 210 figures, Washington, DC, 1943
(1944). $38.00
   ___Another Copy. G-VG. $25.00
   ___Another Copy. Ex-lib. $18.00

B194. ...Bulletin No. 142. BEALS (Ralph L.). The Contemporary Culture of the Cahita Indians. xii, 244pp, 20
plates, 33 figures, 1 map, Washington, DC, 1945. $20.00
   ___Another Copy. G-VG. $22.00
   ___Another Copy. Wrappers, about fine. $30.00
   ___Another Copy. Rebound in red library
cloth, ex-lib. $12.00

B195. ...Bulletin No. 143. STEWARD (Julian H.) (Editor).
Handbook of South American Indians. (7 Volumes).
Volume 1. The Marginal Tribes. xix, 624pp, 112 plates,
69 figures, 7 maps, 1946.
Volume 2. The Andean Civilizations. xxxiv, 1,035pp,
192 plates, 100 figures, 11 maps, 1946.
Volume 3. The Tropical Forest Tribes. xxvi, 986pp,
126 plates, 134 figures, 8 maps, 1948.
Volume 4. The Circum-Caribbean Tribes. xx, 609pp,
98 plates, 79 figures, 11 maps, 1948.
Volume 5. The Comparative Ethnology of South American
Indians. xxvi, 818pp, 56 plates, 190 figures, 22 maps,
1949.
Volume 6. Physical Anthropology, Linguistics, and Cultural Geography of South American Indians. xiii, 715pp,
47 plates, 3 figures, 18 maps, 1950.
Volume 7. Index (to the 6 volumes of the Handbook).
vi, 286pp, 1959.
7 Volumes issued 1946-1959. Washington, DC, original
cloth set in VG condition. $350.00
   ___Another Set. 7 volumes, cloth, fine. $300.00

___Individual Volumes.	Vol. 1.	$60.00
		$40.00
	Vol. 2.	$85.00
	Vol. 3.	$60.00
		$40.00
	Vol. 4.	$60.00
		$40.00
	Vol. 6.	$60.00
	Vol. 7. (index)	$35.00

   ___Another Set. 7 volumes, cloth, VG. $275.00

B196. ...Bulletin No. 144. DRUCKER (Philip). The Northern
and Central Nootkan Tribes. ix, 480pp, 5 plates, 28
figures, 8 maps, Washington, DC, 1951. $35.00
   ___Another Copy. About fine. $50.00
   ___Another Copy. VG. $35.00

B197. ...Bulletin No. 145. SWANTON (John R.). The Indian
Tribes of North America. vi, 726pp, 5 maps, Washington,
DC, 1952. $125.00
    This classic handbook provides basic information (loca-
tion, history, population, language connection, tribal
subdivisions--if any, and any distinction for which the
tribe is noted) for all North American Indian tribes.
The bulk of the work deals with the tribes of the 49
states and Canada; the tribes of Mexico, Central America,
and the West Indies are also covered, though with less
detail.
____Another Copy. G-VG. $65.00
____Another Copy. Shaken, overall good. $50.00
____Another Copy. VG. $75.00
____Another Copy. Reprint, 1977. $55.00

B198. ...Bulletin No. 146. HILGER (Sister M. I.). Chippewa
Child Life and Its Cultural Background. xiv, 204pp,
31 plates, 1 figure, Washington, DC, 1951. $40.00
____Another Copy. G-VG. $20.00
____Another Copy. VG. $25.00
____Another Copy. Ex-lib. $15.00

B199. ...Bulletin No. 147. CULBERTSON (Thaddeus A.). Jour-
nal of an Expedition to the Mauvaises Terres and the
Upper Missouri in 1850. Edited by John F. McDermott.
viii, 164pp, 2 maps, Washington, DC, 1952. $30.00
____Another Copy. Wrappers, VG. $25.00
____Another Copy. About fine. $35.00

B200. ...Bulletin No. 148. HILGER (Sister M. Inez). Arapaho
Child Life and Its Cultural Background. xv, 253pp, 40
plates, 1 figure, Washington, DC, 1952. $42.00
____Another Copy. Wraps, VG. $40.00
____Another Copy. G-VG. $20.00

B201. ...Bulletin No. 149. FENTON (William N.) Editor. Symposium on Local Diversity in Iroquois Culture. v, 187pp,
21 figures, Washington, DC, 1951. $35.00
____Another Copy. Wrappers, VG. $35.00
____Another Copy. G-VG. $17.00

B202. ...Bulletin No. 150. WALLACE (Anthony F. C.). The
Modal Personality Structure of the Tuscarora Indians as
Revealed by the Rorschach Test. viii, 120pp, 1 plate,
8 figures, Washington, DC, 1952. $25.00
____Another Copy. VG. $25.00
____Another Copy. G-VG. $12.00
____Another Copy. VG. $25.00

B203. ...Bulletin No. 151. Anthropological Papers, Nos. 33-42.
Paper No. 33: DENIG (Edwin Thompson). Of the Crow
Nation. Edited with Biographical Sketch and Footnotes
by John C. Ewers. pp 1-74, plates 1-6, map. Paper
No. 34: RANDS (Robert L.). The Water Lily in Maya
Art: A Complex of Alleged Asiatic Origin. pp 75-153,
figures 1-6. Paper No. 35: CAPRON (Louis). The

Medicine Bundles of the Florida Seminole and the Green
Corn Dance. pp 155-210, plates 7-15, figures 7-10.
Paper No. 36: DENSMORE (Frances). Technique in the
Music of the American Indian. pp 213-216. Paper No.
37: DENSMORE (Frances). The Belief of the Indian in
a Connection Between Song and the Supernatural. pp
217-223. Paper No. 38: HEIZER (Robert F.). Aborig-
inal Fish Poisons. pp 225-283, plates 16-19, maps 2-4.
Paper No. 39: HEIZER (Robert F.) and MASSEY (William
C.). Aboriginal Navigation off the Coasts of Upper and
Baja California. pp 285-311, plates 20-23, figures 11 and
12, maps 5-7. Paper No. 40: SOLECKI (Ralph S.).
Exploration of an Adena Mound at Natrium, West Virginia.
pp 313-395, plates 24-29, figures 13-19. Paper No. 41:
SHIMKIN (D. B.). The Wind River Shoshone Sun Dance.
pp 397-484, plates 30-37, figures 20-25. Paper No. 42:
VOGET (Fred W.). Current Trends in the Wind River
Shoshone Sun Dance. pp 485-499. Washington, DC,
1953. $50.00
___Another Copy. Bottom of spine frayed. $25.00
___Another Copy. G-VG. $25.00
___Another Copy. VG. $30.00

B204.   ...Bulletin No. 152. NICHOLS (Frances S.) Compiler.
Index to Schoolcraft's "Indian Tribes of the United
States." vi, 257pp, Washington, DC, 1954. $25.00
___Another Copy. Wrappers, VG. $15.00
___Another Copy. G-VG. $15.00
___Another Copy. VG. $20.00

B205.   ...Bulletin No. 153. DRUCKER (Philip). La Venta, Tab-
asco: A Study of Olmec Ceramics and Art. With a
Chapter on Structural Investigations in 1943, by Waldo
R. Wedel, and Appendix on Technological Analyses by
Anna O. Shepard. x, 257pp, 66 plates, 64 figures,
Washington, DC, 1952. $25.00
___Another Copy. About fine. $30.00
___Another Copy. VG. $25.00

Note: Another subseries, River Basin Surveys Papers, was inaugurated with Bulletin No. 154 (1953). These papers reported on the
results of the Inter-Agency Archaeological Salvage Program. A
limited edition of each River Basin Surveys Paper was issued in
separate form.

B206.   ...Bulletin No. 154. River Basin Surveys Papers, Nos.
1-6. Papers Nos. 1 and 2: WEDEL (Waldo R.). Prehistory and the Missouri Valley Development Program:
Summary Report on the Missouri River Basin Archaeological Surveys in 1948 and 1949. pp xv-xviii, 1-101, plates
1-15, figure 1. Paper No. 3: KIVETT (Marvin F.).
The Woodruff Ossuary, a Prehistoric Burial Site in Phillips County, Kansas. pp 103-141, plates 16-28, figures
2-3. Paper No. 4 (in two parts): The Addicks Dam
Site: Part I: WHEAT (Joe Ben). An Archaeological

Survey of the Addicks Dam Basin, Southeast Texas. pp
143-252, plates 29-47, figures 4-23. Part II: NEWMAN
(Marshall T.). Indian Skeletal Remains from the Doering
and Kobs Sites, Addicks Reservoir, Texas. pp 253-266,
figures 24-28. Paper No. 5 (in two parts): The Hodges
Site: Part I: DICK (Herbert W.). Two Rock Shelters
Near Tucumcari, New Mexico. pp 267-284, plates 48-54,
figures 29-30. Part II: JUDSON (Sheldon). Geology of
the Hodges Site, Quay County, New Mexico. pp 285-302,
figures 31-35. Paper No. 6: CALDWELL (Joseph R.).
The Rembert Mounds, Elbert County, Georgia. pp 303-
320, plates 55-56, figures 36-40. Washington, DC,
1953. $35.00
___Another Copy. Wraps, VG. $25.00
___Another Copy. About fine. $38.00
___Another Copy. Ex-lib. $15.00
B207. ...Bulletin No. 155. WILLEY (Gordon R.). Prehistoric
Settlement Patterns in the Viru Valley, Peru. xxii,
453pp, 60 plates, 88 figures, Washington, DC, 1953.
                                                             $45.00
___Another Copy. VG. $40.00
___Another Copy. G-VG. $25.00
___Another Copy. Ex-lib. $17.00
B208. ...Bulletin No. 156. FENTON (William N.). The Iroquois
Eagle Dance, an Offshoot of the Calumet Dance. With an
Analysis of the Iroquois Eagle Dance and Songs by Gert-
rude Prokosch Kurath. vi, 324pp, 28 plates, 36 figures,
Washington, DC, 1953. $40.00
___Another Copy. G-VG. $20.00
___Another Copy. VG. $32.00
___Another Copy. Rebound. $30.00
B209. ...Bulletin No. 157. Anthropological Papers, Nos. 43-48.
Paper No. 43: STIRLING (Matthew W.). Stone Monuments
of the Rio Chiquito, Veracruz, Mexico. pp 1-23, plates
1-26, figure 1. Paper No. 44: DRUCKER (Philip).
The Cerro de las Mesas Offering of Jade and Other Materials. pp 25-68, plates 27-54, figures 2-9. Paper No.
45: WEDEL (Waldo R.). Archaeological Materials from
the Vicinity of Mobridge, South Dakota. pp 69-188,
plates 55-71, figures 10-12. Paper No. 46: HARRINGTON
(John P.). The Original Strachey Vocabulary of the Virginia Indian Language. pp 189-202, 16 sheets of vocabulary with 16 keys. Paper No. 47: JONES (J.A.). The
Sun Dance of the Northern Ute. pp 203-263, figure 13.
Paper No. 48: RANDS (Robert L.). Some Manifestations
of Water in Mesoamerican Art. pp 265-393, plates 72-76,
figures 14-23. Washington, DC, 1955. $35.00
___Another Copy. Wraps, VG. $30.00
___Another Copy. G-VG. $25.00
B210. ...Bulletin No. 158. River Basin Surveys Papers, No. 7.
LEHMER (D. J.) et al. Archaeological Investigations in

the Oahe Dam Area, South Dakota. xi, 190pp, 22 plates,
56 figures, 6 maps, Washington, DC, 1954. $35.00
___Another Copy. Wrappers, VG. $20.00
___Another Copy. Ex-lib. $15.00
___Another Copy. VG. $25.00
B211. ...Bulletin No. 159. EWERS (John C.). The Horse in
Blackfoot Culture, with Comparative Material from Other
Western Tribes. xv, 374pp, 17 plates, 33 figures,
Washington, DC, 1955. $65.00
___Another Copy. About fine. $48.00
___Another Copy. G-VG. $35.00
___Another Copy. Rebound. $30.00
B212. ...Bulletin No. 160. EVANS (Clifford). A Ceramic Study
of Virginia Archaeology. With Appendix, An Analysis
of Projectile Points and Large Blades, by C. G. Holland.
viii, 195pp, 30 plates, 23 figures, Washington, DC,
1955. $38.00
___Another Copy. Wrappers, VG. $25.00
___Another Copy. About fine. $40.00
___Another Copy. G-VG. $25.00
B213. ...Bulletin No. 161. DENSMORE (Frances). Seminole Mu-
sic. xxviii, 224pp, 18 plates, 1 figure, 243 music
scores, Washington, DC, 1956. $30.00
___Another Copy. Fine. $35.00
___Another Copy. Cloth, about fine. $25.00
___Another Copy. Shaken, ex-lib. $12.00
___Another Copy. Rebound in 3/4 leather,
    marbled bds, scuffed. $40.00
B214. ...Bulletin No. 162. ALPHONSE (Ephraim S.). Guaymi
Grammar and Dictionary, with Some Ethnological Notes.
ix, 128pp, Washington, DC, 1956. $18.00
___Another Copy. Wrappers, VG. $15.00
___Another Copy. G-VG. $12.00
B215. ...Bulletin No. 163. O'BRYAN (Aileen). The Dine:
Origin Myths of the Navaho Indians. vii, 194pp, Wash-
ington, DC, 1956. $40.00
___Another Copy. About fine. $38.00
___Another Copy. VG. $28.00
___Another Copy. G-VG. $30.00
B216. ...Bulletin No. 164. Anthropological Papers, Nos. 49-56.
Paper No. 49: JENNINGS (Jesse D.) et al. The Ormond
Beach Mound, East Central Florida. v-x, 1-28pp, plates
1-12, figures 1-4. Paper No. 50: EWERS (John C.).
Hair Pipes in Plains Indian Adornment, a Study in Indian
and White Ingenuity. pp 29-85, plates 13-37, maps 1-6.
Paper No. 51: WEDEL (Waldo R.) Observations on Some
Nineteenth-Century Pottery Vessels from the Upper Mis-
souri. pp 87-114, plates 38-45, map 7. Paper No. 52:
MILLER (Carl F.). Revaluation of the Eastern Siouan
Problem, with Particular Emphasis on the Virginia
Branches; the Occaneechi, the Saponi, and the Tutelo.

pp 115-212, maps 8-14. Paper No. 53: STIRLING
(M. W.). An Archaeological Reconnaissance in South-
eastern Mexico. pp 213-240, plates 46-73, figure 5,
map 15. Paper No. 54: HARRINGTON (John P.).
Valladolid Maya Enumeration. pp 241-278. Paper No.
55: Letters to Jack Wilson, the Paiute Prophet, Written
Between 1908-1911, Edited and With an Introduction by
Grace M. Dangberg. pp 279-296. Paper No. 56:
FENTON (William N.). Factionalism at Taos Pueblo, New
Mexico. pp 297-344, plates 74-75. Washington, DC,
1957. $40.00
____Another Copy. VG. $30.00
____Another Copy. Rebound, ex-lib. $20.00

B217. ...Bulletin No. 165. DENSMORE (Frances). Music of Aco-
ma, Isleta, Cochiti, and Zuni Pueblos. xii, 117pp, 6
plates, 82 music transcriptions, Washington, DC, 1957.
                                                            $30.00
____Another Copy. G-VG. $25.00
____Another Copy. Wraps, fine. $30.00
____Another Copy. Rebound, ex-lib. $18.00
____Another Copy. Rebound in red library
                  cloth, ex-lib. $15.00

B218. ...Bulletin No. 166. River Basin Surveys Papers, No. 8.
OSBORNE (Douglas). Excavations in the McNary Reser-
voir Basin Near Umatilla, Oregon. With Appendixes by
M. T. Newman, A. Woodward, W. J. Kroll, and B. H.
McLeod. ix, 258pp, 40 plates, 6 figures, 19 maps,
Washington, DC, 1957. $35.00
____Another Copy. G-VG. $15.00
____Another Copy. About fine. $38.00
____Another Copy. Ex-lib. $15.00

B219. ...Bulletin No. 167. MEGGERS (Betty J.) and EVANS
(Clifford). Archaeological Investigations at the Mouth
of the Amazon. xxviii, 664pp, 112 plates, 206 figures,
71 tables, Washington, DC, 1957. $65.00
____Another Copy. G-VG. $30.00
____Another Copy. VG. $45.00
____Another Copy. Rebound. $30.00

B220. ...Bulletin No. 168. DRUCKER (Philip). The Native
Brotherhoods: Modern Intertribal Organizations on the
Northwest Coast. iv, 194pp, Washington, DC, 1958.
                                                            $35.00
____Another Copy. G-VG. $35.00
____Another Copy. Fine. $38.00

B221. ...Bulletin No. 169. River Basin Surveys Papers, Nos.
9-14. Paper No. 9: COOPER (Paul L.). Archaeological
Investigations in the Heart Butte Reservoir Area, North
Dakota. pp 1-40, plates 1-12, figures 1 and 2, maps 1
and 2. Paper No. 10: CUMMING (Robert B. Jr.).
Archaeological Investigations at the Tuttle Creek Dam,
Kansas. pp 41-78, plates 13-24, maps 3 and 4. Paper

No. 11: SMITH (Carlye S.) and GRANGE (Roger T.
Jr.). The Spain Site (36LM301), a Winter Village in
Fort Randall Reservoir, South Dakota. pp 79-128, plates
25-36, figures 3 and 4, maps 5 and 6. River Basin Surveys Papers. Paper No. 12: SEARS (William H.). The
Wilbanks Site (9CK-5), Georgia. pp 129-194, plates 37-
45, figures 5-9, map 7. Paper No. 13: BOYD (Mark F.).
Historic Sites in and Around the Jim Woodruff Reservoir
Area, Florida-Georgia. pp 195-314, plates 46-55, figures
10 and 11, map 8. Paper No. 14: BULLEN (Ripley P.).
Six Sites Near the Chattahoochee River in the Jim Woodruff Reservoir Area, Florida. pp 315-357, plates 56-73,
figures 12 and 13, map 9. Washington, DC, 1958.

		$40.00
___Another Copy.	G-VG.	$18.00
___Another Copy.	Fine.	$35.00
___Another Copy.	Ex-lib.	$15.00

B222. ...Bulletin No. 170. DRUCKER (Philip). Excavations at
La Venta, Tabasco, 1955. With Appendixes by J. E.
Gullberg, G. H. Curtis, and A. S. Leopold. viii, 312pp,
63 plates, 82 figures, Washington, DC, 1959. $45.00
    ___Another Copy. G-VG. $18.00
    ___Another Copy. VG. $38.00
    ___Another Copy. Rebound in red library cloth,
                     ex-lib. $18.00

B223. ...Bulletin No. 171. SPENCER (Robert F.). The North
Alaskan Eskimo: A Study in Ecology and Society. vi,
490pp, 9 plates, 2 figures, 4 maps, Washington, DC,
1959. $58.00
    ___Another Copy. About fine. $50.00
    ___Another Copy. VG. $50.00
    ___Another Copy. G-VG. $35.00
    ___Another Copy. Rebound in red library cloth,
                     ex-lib. $20.00

B224. ...Bulletin No. 172: DE LAGUNA (Frederica). The Story
of a Tlingit Community: A Problem in the Relationship
Between Archaeological, Ethnological, and Historical
Methods. x, 254pp, 11 plates, 18 figures, Washington,
DC, 1960. $45.00
    ___Another Copy. VG, signed. $35.00
    ___Another Copy. G-VG. $25.00

B225. ...Bulletin No. 173. Anthropological Papers, Nos. 57-62.
Paper No. 57: HOLLAND (C. G.). Preceramic and
Ceramic Cultural Patterns in Northwest Virginia. pp
1-129, figures 1-12. Paper No. 58: GUNNERSON (James
H.). An Introduction to Plains Apache Archaeology; the
Dismal River Aspect. pp 131-260, plates 1-38, figures
13-24. Paper No. 59: STIRLING (M. W.). The Use of
the Atlatl on Lake Patzcuaro, Michoacan. pp 261-268,
plates 39-41. Paper No. 60: RIESENBERG (Saul H.)
and KANESHIRO (S.). A Caroline Islands Script. pp

269-333, plates 42-44, figures 25-28, map 1. Paper No. 61: HOWARD (James H.). Dakota Winter Counts as a Source of Plains History. pp 335-416, plates 45-47. Paper No. 62: KEHOE (Thomas F.). Stone Tipi Rings in North-Central Montana and the Adjacent Portion of Alberta, Canada: Their Historical, Ethnological, and Archaeological Aspects. pp 417-473, plates 48-61, figures 29-37, map 2. Washington, DC, 1960. $40.00
  ___Another Copy. Wraps, VG. $25.00
  ___Another Copy. G-VG. $18.00
  ___Another Copy. Ex-lib. $20.00

B226. ...Bulletin No. 174. WEDEL (Waldo R.). An Introduction to Kansas Archaeology. With Description of the Skeletal Remains from Doniphan and Scott Counties, Kansas. xvii, 723pp, 97 plates, 109 figures, Washington, DC, 1959. $58.00
  ___Another Copy. VG. $75.00

B227. ...Bulletin No. 175. DEVEREUX (George). Mohave Ethnopsychiatry and Suicide: The Psychiatric Knowledge and the Psychic Disturbances of an Indian Tribe. vi, 586pp, 10 plates, Washington, DC, 1961. $50.00
  ___Another Copy. Fine. $65.00
  ___Another Copy. G-VG. $30.00
  ___Another Copy. 1969, reprint. $25.00

B228. ...Bulletin No. 176. Inter-Agency Archaeological Salvage Program. Frank H. H. Roberts, Jr., Editor. River Basin Surveys Papers, Numbers 15-20. Paper No. 15: MATTES (Merrill J.). Historic Sites Archaeology on the Upper Missouri. pp 1-23. Paper No. 16: MILLS (John E.). Historic Sites Archaeology in the Fort Randall Reservoir, South Dakota. pp 25-48, plates 1-9, figures 1-2, map 1. Paper No. 17: MILLER (Carl F.). The Excavation and Investigation of Fort Lookout Trading Post II (39LM57) in the Fort Randall Reservoir, South Dakota. pp 49-82, plates 10-18, figures 3-14, map 2. Paper No. 18: SMITH (G. H.). Fort Pierre II (39ST217), a Historic Trading Post in the Oahe Dam Area, South Dakota. pp 83-158, plates 19-30, maps 3 and 4. Paper No. 19: SMITH (G. H.). Archaeological Investigations at the Site of Fort Stevenson (32ML1), Garrison Reservoir, North Dakota. With Appendix by Carlyle S. Smith. pp 159-238, plates 31-54, figures 15-20, maps 5 and 6. Paper No. 20: WOOLWORTH (A. R.) and WOOD (W. R.). The Archaeology of a Small Trading Post Kipp's Post (32MN1) in the Garrison Reservoir, North Dakota. pp 239-305, plates 55-65, figures 21-25, map 7. Washington, DC, 1960. $35.00
  ___Another Copy. Wraps, fine. $25.00
  ___Another Copy. G-VG. $20.00
  ___Another Copy. Wraps, VG. $25.00

B229. ...Bulletin No. 177. EVANS (Clifford) and MEGGERS

(Betty J.). Archaeological Investigations in British
Guiana, South America. xxi, 418pp, 68 plates, 127 fig-
ures, Washington, DC, 1960. $45.00
___Another Copy. G-VG. $22.00
___Another Copy. Fine. $38.00
___Another Copy. Rebound in red library cloth,
ex-lib. $20.00

B230. ...Bulletin No. 178. BONNERJEA (Biren). Index to Bul-
letins 1-100 of the Bureau of American Ethnology, with
Index to Contributions to North American Ethnology, In-
troductions, and Miscellaneous Publications. vi, 726pp,
Washington, DC, 1963. $30.00
___Another Copy. G-VG. $15.00
___Another Copy. Cloth, fine. $25.00

B231. ...Bulletin No. 179. River Basin Surveys Papers, Nos.
21-24. Paper No. 21: JELKS (Edward B.). Excavations at Texarkana Reservoir, Sulphur River, Texas.
xiii-xviii, 1-78pp, plates 1-17, figures 1-9. Paper No.
22: CALDWELL (Warren W.). Archaeological Investigations
at the Coralville Reservoir, Iowa. pp 79-148, plates 18-
29, figures 10-20. Paper No. 23: SHINER (Joel L.).
The McNary Reservoir: A Study in Plateau Archaeology.
pp 149-226, plates 30-46, figures 25-40, maps 1-7.
Paper No. 24: OSBORNE (Douglas) et al. The Sheep
Island Site and the Mid-Columbia Valley. pp 267-306,
plates 45-56, figures 41-43. Washington, DC, 1961.
$35.00
___Another Copy. Wraps, VG. $25.00
___Another Copy. G-VG. $20.00
___Another Copy. Rebound in red library cloth,
ex-lib. $22.00
___Another Copy. About fine. $38.00

B232. ...Bulletin No. 180. FENTON (William N.) and GULICK
(John). Symposium on Cherokee and Iroquois Culture.
Papers, Nos. 1-25. vi, 292pp, Washington, DC, 1961.
$35.00
___Another Copy. G-VG. $15.00
___Another Copy. Fine. $30.00
___Another Copy. Ex-lib. $15.00

B233. ...Bulletin No. 181. GOLDFRANK (Esther S.) Editor.
Isleta Paintings. Introduction and Commentary by Elsie
Clews Parsons. Annotated Glossary of Isleta Terms by
George L. Trager. xvi, 299pp, 142 plates (including 12
in color), Washington, DC, 1962. $70.00
___Another Copy. VG. $50.00
___Another Copy. Fine. $55.00
___Another Copy. G-VG. $50.00
___Another Copy. Rebound. $38.00
___Another Copy. 1970, reprint. $40.00

B234. ...Bulletin No. 182. ROBERTS (Frank H. H. Jr.) Editor.
Inter-Agency Archaeological Salvage Program. River

Basin Surveys Papers, No. 25. Archaeology of the John
H. Kerr Reservoir Basin, Roanoke River, Virginia-North
Carolina, by Carl F. Miller. With Appendix: Human
Skeletal Remains from the Tollifero (He6) and Clarksville
(Mc14) Sites, John H. Kerr Reservoir Basin, Virginia,
by Lucile E. Hoyme and W. M. Bass. xvi, 447pp, 110
plates, 65 figures, 20 maps, Washington, DC, 1962.
$40.00

    ____Another Copy. G-VG. $20.00
    ____Another Copy. Fine. $28.00
    ____Another Copy. About fine. $25.00
    ____Another Copy. Rebound in red library cloth,
                        ex-lib. $18.00

B235. ...Bulletin No. 183. CHAFE (Wallace L.). Seneca Thanks-
giving Rituals. iii, 302pp, Washington, DC, 1961. $25.00
    ____Another Copy. G-VG. $15.00
    ____Another Copy. Fine. $25.00
    ____Another Copy. Ex-lib. $15.00

B236. ...Bulletin No. 184. WHITE (Leslie A.). The Pueblo of
Sia, New Mexico. xii, 358pp, 12 plates, 55 figures,
Washington, DC, 1962. $50.00
    ____Another Copy. VG. $38.00
    ____Another Copy. Cloth, fine. $35.00

B237. ...Bulletin No. 185. ROBERTS (Frank H. H. Jr.) Editor.
Inter-Agency Archaeological Salvage Program. River
Basin Surveys Papers, Nos. 26-32. Paper No. 26:
METCALF (George). Small Sites in and About Fort
Berthold Indian Reservation, Garrison Reservoir. Pa-
per No. 27: METCALF (George). Star Village: A Forti-
fied Historic Arikara Site in Mercer County, North Dakota.
Paper No. 28: HARTLE (Donald D.). The Dance Hall
of the Santee Bottoms on the Fort Berthold Reservation,
Garrison Reservoir, North Dakota. Paper No. 29:
MALOUF (Carling). Crow-Flies-High (32MZ1), a Historic
Hidatsa Village in the Garrison Reservoir Area, North
Dakota. Paper No. 30: WHEELER (R. P.). The Stuts-
man Focus: An Aboriginal Culture Complex in the Jamestown Reservoir Area. Paper No. 31: MILLER (Carl F.).
Archaeological Manifestations in the Toole County Section
of the Tiber Reservoir Basin, Montana. Paper No. 32:
NEUMAN (Robert W.). Archaeological Salvage Investigations in the Lovewell Reservoir Area, Kansas. xii,
344pp, 57 plates, 43 figures, 5 maps, Washington, DC,
1963. $30.00
    ____Another Copy. Wraps, fine. $25.00
    ____Another Copy. G-VG. $25.00

B238. ...Bulletin No. 186. Anthropological Papers, Nos. 63-67.
Paper No. 63: STIRLING (Matthew and Marion). Tar-
qui, an Early Site in Manabi Province, Ecuador. Paper
No. 64: EWERS (John C.). Blackfoot Indian Pipes and
Pipe Making. Paper No. 65: GENTRY (Howard Scott).

The Warihio Indians of Sonora-Chihuahua: An Ethno-
graphic Survey. Paper No. 66: WILDER (Carleton S.).
The Yaqui Deer Dance: A Study in Cultural Change.
Paper No. 67: PETERSON (Karen Daniels). Chippewa
Mat-Weaving Techniques. iv, 310pp, 60 plates, 35
figures, 2 maps, Washington, DC, 1963. $50.00
  ___Another Copy. Wraps, VG. $35.00
  ___Another Copy. G-VG. $20.00
  ___Another Copy. Ex-lib. $18.00

B239. ...Bulletin No. 187. KURATH (Gertrude P.). Iroquois
Music and Dance: Ceremonial Arts of Two Seneca Long-
houses. xvi, 268pp, 3 plates, 164 figures, Washington,
DC, 1964. $40.00
  ___Another Copy. G-VG. $25.00
  ___Another Copy. Fine. $30.00
  ___Another Copy. Rebound in red library cloth,
          ex-lib. $20.00

B240. ...Bulletin No. 188. ADAMS (William Y.). Shonto: A
Study of the Role of the Trader in a Modern Navaho
Community. xi, 329pp, 10 plates, 3 figures, 3 maps,
12 charts, Washington, DC, 1963. $35.00
  ___Another Copy. About fine. $45.00
  ___Another Copy. Fine. $35.00
  ___Another Copy. G-VG. $25.00
  ___Another Copy. Ex-lib. $22.00
  ___Another Copy. Rebound in red library cloth,
          ex-lib. $25.00

B241. ...Bulletin No. 189. ROBERTS (Frank H. H. Jr.) Editor.
Inter-Agency Archaeological Salvage Program. River
Basin Surveys Papers, Nos. 33-38. Paper No. 33:
WOOD (W. R.) and WOOLWORTH (A. R.). The Paul
Brave Site (32S14), Oahe Reservoir Area, North Dakota.
Paper No. 34: WOOLWORTH (A. R.) and WOOD (W. R.).
The Demery Site (39CO1), Oahe Reservoir Area, South
Dakota. Paper No. 35: MILLER (Carl F.). Archaeologi-
cal Investigations at the Hosterman Site (39PO7), Oahe
Reservoir Area, Potter County, South Dakota, 1956.
Paper No. 36: CALDWELL (W. W.) et al. Archaeological
Investigations at the Hickey Brothers Site (39LM4), Big
Bend Reservoir, Lyman County, South Dakota. Paper
No. 37: NEUMAN (Robert W.). The Good Soldier Site
(39LM238), Big Bend Reservoir, Lyman County, South
Dakota. Paper No. 38: HOWARD (J. H.). Archaeologi-
cal Investigations in the Toronto Reservoir Area, Kansas.
xiv, 405pp, 58 plates, 66 figures, 13 maps, Washington,
DC, 1964. $28.00
  ___Another Copy. Wrappers, VG. $25.00
  ___Another Copy. G-VG. $18.00
  ___Another Copy. Ex-lib. $15.00

B242. ...Bulletin No. 190. TOOKER (Elisabeth). An Ethnography
of the Huron Indians, 1615-1649. iv, 183pp, Washington,
DC, 1964. $35.00

    ___Another Copy. G-VG. $20.00
    ___Another Copy. Fine. $25.00
    ___Another Copy. VG. $25.00
    ___Another Copy. Rebound in library cloth,
                        ex-lib. $15.00

B243. ...Bulletin No. 191. Anthropological Papers, Nos. 68-74. Paper No. 68: BIESE (Leo P.). The Prehistory of Panama Viejo. Paper No. 69: DAVIS (Irvine). The Language of Santa Ana Pueblo. Paper No. 70: HOFF-MAN (B. G.). Observations on Certain Ancient Tribes of the Northern Appalachian Province. Paper No. 71: STIRLING (Matthew and Marion). El Limon, an Early Tomb Site in Cocle Province, Panama. Paper No. 72: STIRLING (Matthew and Marion). Archaeological Notes on Almirante Bay, Bocas del Toro, Panama. Paper No. 73: STIRLING (Matthew and Marion). The Archaeology of Taboga, Uraba, and Taboguilla Islands, Panama. Paper No. 74: HENDRY (Jean). Iroquois Masks and Maskmaking at Onondaga. iii, 425pp, 104 plates, 55 figures, 13 maps, Washington, DC, 1964. $50.00
    ___Another Copy. Wraps, VG. $25.00
    ___Another Copy. G-VG. $18.00

B244. ...Bulletin No. 192. DE LAGUNA (Fredrica) et al. Archaeology of the Yakutat Bay Area, Alaska. xi, 245pp, 19 plates, 25 figures, 7 maps, Washington, DC, 1964.
                               $38.00
    ___Another Copy. G-VG. $25.00
    ___Another Copy. Wraps, VG. $25.00
    ___Another Copy. About fine. $40.00
    ___Another Copy. Ex-lib. $18.00

B245. ...Bulletin No. 193. LADD (John). Archaeological Investigations in the Parita and Santa Maria Zones of Panama. xii, 291pp, 25 plates, 68 figures, 2 maps, 14 charts, Washington, DC, 1964. $15.00
    ___Another Copy. Fine. $25.00
    ___Another Copy. G-VG. $15.00

B246. ...Bulletin No. 194. BOWERS (Alfred W.). Hidatsa Social and Ceremonial Organization. xii, 528pp, 12 plates, 12 figures, 5 maps, 14 charts, 4 tables, Washington, DC, 1965. $50.00
    ___Another Copy. G-VG. $25.00
    ___Another Copy. Fine. $50.00
    ___Another Copy. VG. $35.00

B247. ...Bulletin No. 195. HOWARD (James H.). The Ponca Tribe. xii, 191pp, 24 plates, 8 figures, 1 map, Washington, DC, 1965. $40.00
    ___Another Copy. G-VG. $22.00
    ___Another Copy. Fine. $30.00

B248. ...Bulletin No. 196. Anthropological Papers, Nos. 75-80. Paper No. 75: KILPATRICK (Anna G. and Jack F.). Chronicles of Wolftown: Social Documents of the North

Carolina Cherokees, 1850-1862. Paper No. 76: BASSO (Keith H.). The Gift of Changing Woman. Paper No. 77: KILPATRICK (Jack F.) Editor. The Wahnenauhi Manuscript: Historical Sketches of the Cherokees, Together with Some of Their Customs, Traditions, and Superstitions. Paper No. 78: KUPFERER (Harriet J.). The "Principal People," 1960: A Study of Cultural and Social Groups of the Eastern Cherokee. Paper No. 79: KLUCKHOHN (Clyde). The Ramah Navaho. Paper No. 80: KILPATRICK (Jack F. and Anna G.). Eastern Cherokee Folktales: Reconstructed from the Field Notes of Fran M. Olbrechts. iii, 470pp, 4 plates, 14 figures, 2 maps, 26 tables, Washington, DC, 1966. $35.00
    ___Another Copy. Wraps, fine. $25.00
    ___Another Copy. G-VG. $18.00

B249. ...Bulletin No. 197. JOHNSTON (Denis Foster). An Analysis of Sources of Information on the Population of the Navaho. v, 220pp, 7 maps, 36 tables, Washington, DC, 1966. $35.00
    ___Another Copy. G-VG. $15.00
    ___Another Copy. Fine. $18.00
    ___Another Copy. VG. $25.00
    ___Another Copy. Rebound in red library cloth, ex-lib. $18.00

B250. ...Bulletin No. 198. STEPHENSON (Robert L.) Editor. Inter-Agency Archaeological Salvage Program. River Basin Surveys Papers, No. 39. An Interpretation of Mandan Culture History, by W. Raymond Wood. xiv, 232pp, 17 figures, 9 plates, 20 maps, 15 tables, Washington, DC, 1967. $38.00
    ___Another Copy. Fine. $25.00
    ___Another Copy. G-VG. $18.00
    ___Another Copy. Rebound in red library cloth, ex-lib. $12.00

B251. ...Bulletin No. 199. OSWALT (Wendell H.) and VAN STONE (James W.). The Ethnoarchaeology of Crow Village, Alaska. viii, 136 figures, 16 plates, 1 map, Washington, DC, 1967. $25.00
    ___Another Copy. About fine. $35.00
    ___Another Copy. Cloth, fine. $38.00
    ___Another Copy. G-VG. $22.00
    ___Another Copy. Ex-lib. $12.00

B252. ...Bulletin No. 200. List of Publications of the Bureau of American Ethnology, with Index to Authors and Titles. vi, 134pp, Washington, DC, 1970. $35.00
    ___Another Copy. Wraps, fine. $22.00
    ___Another Copy. G-VG. $12.00
    ___Another Copy. Reprinted in 1978 by R. M. Weatherford. $10.00

Note: The appearance of Bulletin 200 brings to an end all publications under the Bureau name, the Bulletin series having been superseded by the new series "Smithsonian Contributions to Anthropology," initiated in 1965.

B253. BAER (Joshua). Collecting the Navajo's Child's Blanket.
vi, 44pp of full color illus, 5pp explanatory text, wrappers, Santa Fe, 1986 (1st ed). $22.00

B254. BAERREIS (David Albert). (Museum of Anthropology, Univ. of Michigan, Anthropological Paper, No. 6, Ann Arbor, 1951) The Pre-Ceramic Horizons of Northeastern Oklahoma. 125pp, illus with stone artifacts, map, bibliography, wrappers. $12.00

B255. BAHTI (Tom). Southwestern Indian Arts and Crafts.
32pp, 26 b/w and 37 color illus, cloth, Las Vegas, 1977.
$12.00

B256. BAHTI (Tom). Southwestern Indian Ceremonials. 66pp, illus with full color photographs and paintings, 4to, map, good accounts of the ceremonials of the Navaho, Zuni, Hopi, etc., Las Vegas, 1974. $12.00

B257. BAHTI (Tom). Southwestern Indian Tribes. 74pp, illus, 4to, map, wrappers, Las Vegas, 1973. $12.00

B258. BAILEY (Flora). (Peabody Museum Papers, Vol. 40, No. 2, Cambridge, 1950) Some Sex Beliefs and Practices in a Navaho Community with Comparative Material from Other Navaho Areas. xii, 108pp, stiff printed wrappers.
$50.00
____Another Copy. Same. $35.00

B259. BAILEY (G.) and GLENN (R.). A History of the Navajos: The Reservations. 360pp, illus, Santa Fe, 1986. $30.00

B260. BAILEY (G. A.). (Univ. of Oregon Anthropological Papers, No. 5, 1973) Changes in Osage Social Organization, 1673-1906. vi, 122pp, 4 figures, 7 maps, wraps. $12.00

B261. BAILEY (George W.). (Senate Executive Document 132, 46:2, Washington, 1880, 1st printing) Report ... Upon the Number, Occupation, and Condition of the People of Alaska. 48pp, 1pp, removed. $20.00

B262. BAILEY (Helen M.). Santa Cruz of the Etla Hills (Oaxaca). illus, Univ. of Florida Press, 1958, d.j. $18.00

B263. BAILEY (Lynn R.). If You Take My Sheep: The Evolution and Conflicts of Navajo Pastoralism, 1630-1868. 300pp, illus, index, map, bibliography. Pasadena, 1980 (1st ed.), d.j. $15.00

B264. BAILEY (L. R.). Indian Slave Trade in the Southwest. 236pp, illus, index, bibliography, endpaper maps. Los Angeles, 1973, d.j. $20.00
____Another Copy. Same. $15.00

B265. BAILEY (L. R.). The Long Walk, A History of the Navaho Wars, 1846-1868. xiii, 252pp, 16pp photographs, 3 maps, endpaper maps, bibliography, index, pictorial cloth. Los Angeles, Westernlore Press, 1964 (1st ed.), d.j.
$25.00
____Another Copy. Los Angeles, 1978, 3rd printing, d.j. $15.00

B266. BAILEY (L. R.) Editor. The Navajo Reconnaissance. A
Military Exploration of the Navajo Country in 1859, by
Capt. J. G. Walker and Major O. L. Shepherd. 106pp,
plus index, illus, endpaper maps, limited to 600 copies.
Los Angeles, 1964 (1st ed.), d.j. $25.00

B267. BAILEY (M. Thomas). Reconstruction in Indian Territory:
A Story of Avarice, Discrimination, and Opportunism.
225pp, index, bibliography. Port Washington, 1972.
$15.00

B268. BAILEY (Paul). The Claws of the Hawk. The Incredible
Life of Walker the Ute. 358pp. Los Angeles, 1966
(1st ed.), d.j. $25.00

B269. BAILEY (Paul). Ghost Dance Messiah. 206pp. Los Angeles, 1970 (1st ed.). $25.00
The story of Wovoka and his dramatic life in Western
Nevada where his Ghost Dance Religion inspired the Indians to dreams of power, freedom and peace, but also
led to war.

B270. BAILEY (Paul). Jacob Hamblin: Buckskin Apostle. xi,
408pp, illus, cloth. Hamblin was a Mormon peacemaker
among the tribes. Los Angeles, 1961 (2nd ed.). $15.00

B271. BAILEY (Paul). Wovoka, The Indian Messiah. 217pp, plus
index, illus. Los Angeles, 1957 (1st ed.), d.j. $27.00
___Another Copy. Same. $25.00
___Another Copy. Same. $24.00

B272. BAIRD (W. David). Peter Pitchlynn: Chief of the Choctaws. 238pp, illus, index, bibliography, maps. Norman,
1972 (1st ed.), d.j. $25.00
Well-documented biography of Pitchlynn, who was born
in 1806 and assumed an important role in tribal affairs
early in life. His leadership was especially apparent during negotiations of the 1830 treaty of removal process itself. In the west he took an even larger role in the recreation of Indian society, helping to build a national
tribal government and education system.
___Another Copy. Same. $20.00
___Another Copy. Same. $20.00

B273. BAIRD (W. D.). The Quapaw People. 104pp, photographs
(some in color), maps, cloth. Phoenix, 1975 (1st ed.).
$17.00

B274. BAIRD (G.). Northwest Indian Basketry. 40pp, 22
photographs, 14 drawings, 2 maps. Tacoma, 1976.
$10.00

B275. BAKER (Charlotte). Sunrise Island. A Story of the
Northwest Coast Indians Before the Coming of the White
Man. 158pp, pictorial cloth, juvenile novel, New York,
1952 (1st ed.), d.j. $12.00

B276. BAKER (Paul E.). The Forgotten Kutenai. 64pp, illus,
map, bibliography, decorated wraps. Boise, 1955 (1st
ed.). $10.00

B277. BAKER (S. G.). (Bureau of Land Management: Utah,

Cultural Series, No. 13, Salt Lake City, 1982) Contributions to the Prehistory of Southeastern Utah. 118pp, illus, maps, bibliography, lrge 8vo, wraps. $15.00

B278. BALDWIN (Dr. Gordon C.). The Warrior Apaches: A Story of the Chiricahua and Western Apache. 144pp, illus, cloth. Tucson, 1965 (1st ed.). $18.00
___Another Copy. Wrappers, 1965, 1st. $15.00

B279. BALDWIN (Gordon C.). Games of the American Indian. 147pp, plus index, drawings, photographs, map, New York, 1969 (1st ed.). $17.00

B280. BALDWIN (John D.). Ancient America, In Notes on American Archaeology. 299pp, 70 illus, original decorated cloth, New York, Harpers, 1871. $55.00
Includes sections on the Mound-Builders, Mexico, Central America, Aztec civilization, and Peru.
___Another Copy. New York, 1872. $80.00
___Another Copy. New York, 1872. $35.00

B281. BALL (Eve) et al. An Apache Odyssey--Indeh. 334pp, illus with photographs, maps. Provo, 1980 (1st ed.), d.j. $18.00

B282. BALL (Eve). In the Days of Victorio, Recollections of a Warm Springs Apache. xv, 222pp, illus with photographs, map, notes, bibliography, index. Apache version of events of the late 1800's as narrated by James Kaywaykla. Tucson, Univ. of Arizona, 1970 (1st ed.), d.j. $25.00

BALL (Sydney H.). See also BAE Bulletins, Nos. 92, 120, 128, 143, Vols. 5 and 6.

B283. BALL (Sydney H.). The Mining of Gems and Ornamental Stones by American Indians. Offprint, Smithsonian Anthropological Papers, Washington, 1941. pp 1-77, 3 pls, folding table, folding map, bibliography, printed wraps. $10.00

B284. BALLANTYNE (Robert M.). Hudson's Bay; or, Every-Day Life in the Wilds of North America. (2 advs), xii, 328pp, illus, blank section of half title removed, gilt decorated cloth, Edinburgh, London, W. Blackwood & Sons, 1848 (2nd ed.). $135.00
Sabin: 2952. Field: 69. From Mr. Ballantyne's diaries of 6 years work trading with the Crees and Chippewayans. Field: "None have produced a more complete, interesting, and evidently faithful narration of the various phases of a fur trader's life among the Indians, than Mr. Ballantyne. (RMW)

B285. BALLARD (Arthur). (Univ. of Washington, Publications in Anthropology, Vol. 3, No. 2, Seattle, 1919) Mythology of Southern Puget Sound. 119pp, wrappers. $35.00
___Another Copy. Same. $30.00

B286. BALLOU (M. M.). Aztec Land. 355pp, some wear to backstrip, Boston, 1890 (1st ed.). $10.00

B287. BANCROFT (Hubert H.) Central America. (3 Volumes). pp 704; 766; 776, original brown cloth. San Francisco, 1882-1887. $150.00

B288. BANCROFT (Hubert H.). The Native Races. (5 Volumes).
Vol. 1: Wild Tribes. xlvii, 797pp. Vol. 2: Civilized
Nations. xii, 805pp. Vol. 3: Myths and Languages.
xii, 796pp. Vol. 4: Antiquities. ix, 807pp. Vol. 5:
Primitive History. xi, 796pp, index. 11 folding maps,
one folding chart, numerous illus in Vol. 4, 33pp of au-
thorities quoted, full calf, hinges started on all volumes,
San Francisco, 1886. $150.00
_____Another Copy. 3/4 leather, marbled bds,
San Francisco, 1883. $270.00
_____Another Copy. First 3 volumes only, half
calf, San Francisco, 1883-
88. $75.00

B289. BANDELIER (Adolf F.). (Hemenway Southwestern Archaeological Expedition, Papers, Archaeological Institute of
America, Cambridge, 1890) Contributions to the Southwestern Portion of the United States. 206pp, folding
map, stiff wraps. $125.00

B290. BANDELIER (Adolf F.). The Delight Makers (Pueblo Indians). 490pp, pictorial orange cloth. New York, 1890
(1st ed.). $150.00
    The first edition of one of the classics of Southwestern
literature. Powell, Heart of the Southwest: "This first
of a long line of Southwest Indian documentary novels has
never been surpassed in its faithfulness to the facts of
Pueblo Indian Culture...." (WR)
_____Another Copy. Same. $70.00
_____Another Copy. New York, 1916, d.j. $15.00
_____Another Copy. New York, 1916, lacks d.j. $12.00
_____Another Copy. New York, 1949. $25.00

B291. BANDELIER (Adolf F.). (Papers of the School of American
Archaeology, No. 13, New York, 1910) Documentary History of the Rio Grande Pueblos of New Mexico. 28pp,
bibliographic introduction, wrappers. $25.00
_____Another Copy. n.p., 1910, printed wraps. $75.00

B292. BANDELIER (Adolf F.). A History of the Southwest. (2
Volumes). Vol. I: A Catalogue of the Bandelier Collection in the Vatican Library. 233pp. Vol. II: Supplement to Volume I with Reproduction in Color of 30
Sketches and 10 Maps. Wrappers. Jesuit Historical Institute, 1969. $125.00

B293. BANDELIER (Adolf F.). (Reprinted from Vol. III, Journal
of American Ethnology and Archaeology, n.d.) History
of the Zuni Tribe. 115pp, wrappers. $100.00

B294. BANDELIER (Adolf F.). Indians of the Rio Grande Valley.
E. L. Hewett, Co-Author. 274pp, 8 full page color draw-
ings, 26pp photographs, map, cloth, Univ. of New
Mexico, 1937. $135.00

B295. BANDELIER (Adolf F.). The Islands of Titicaca and Koati.
(Bolivia) 358pp, frontis, 85 pls, 2 are in color, folding
map, illus include multiple artifacts excavated, original
cloth. New York, 1910. $175.00

B296. BANDELIER (Adolf F.). (Peabody Museum Report, No. 10, Cambridge, n.d., c.1880) On the Art of War and Mode of Warfare of the Ancient Mexicans. pp 95-161, wrappers.
$30.00

B297. BANDELIER (Adolf F.). Peabody Museum Report, No. 12, Cambridge, n.d., c.1880) On the Distribution and Tenure of Lands ... Among the Ancient Mexicans. pp 385-448, wrappers.
$30.00

B298. BANDELIER (Adolf F.). (Journals of American Ethnology and Archaeology, Hemenway SW Archaeological Expedition, Vol. III, Boston, 1892, 1st ed.) An Outline of the Documentary History of the Zuni Tribe. 144pp, map, original frnt wrapper bound into later cloth.
$100.00

___Another Copy. n.p., n.d., 115pp, quarto, original printed wraps.
$150.00

Note: First separate edition, reprinted, with new pagination, from (The Journal of American Ethnology and Archaeology, Vol. III), and issued as (Hemenway Southwestern Archaeological Expedition Publication I). A particularly important and uncommon work by the most noted southwestern anthropologist of the period. (WR)

B299. BANDELIER (Adolf F.). Report of an Archaeological Tour in Mexico in 1881. 326pp, illus, 13 photographic pls, map, Boston, 1885.
$100.00

B300. BANDELIER (Adolf F.). (Peabody Annual Reports, 12th and 13th, Vol. 2, Nos. 3, 4, Cambridge, 1880) Social Organization and Mode of Government of the Ancient Mexicans. pp 557-699, wrappers.
$35.00

___Another Copy. Same.
$30.00

B301. (Adolf F. Bandelier). The Southwestern Journals of Adolf F. Bandelier, 1885-1888. Edited by C. E. Lange and C. Riley. 702pp, illus. Santa Fe, 1975 (1st ed.).
$75.00

B302. BANKES (G.). Moche Pottery from Peru. 55pp, 33 photographs, 4 drawings, map. British Museum, 1980.
$12.00

B303. BANKES (G.). Peru Before Pizarro. 208pp, 33 drawings, 100 b/w and 17 color photographs, cloth. London, 1978.
$17.00

B304. BAPTISTA (Juan). ...Sermonario en Lengua Mexicana ... Primera Parte. pp (26)ff., pp 1-559 (repeating page numbers 335 and 472, skipping 430-439), ff. 560-599, pp 600-639, ff. 640-647, pp 648-655, 664-709 (repeating page number 708), (1)pp, (24)ff. Octavo, 19th century quarter morocco with gilt ruling and center panel ornaments on spine. The first two leaves and the final leaf are supplied in facsimile. En Mexico: En Casa de Diego Lopez Davalos, 1606.
$4,750.00

Medina (Mexico): 227. Puttick & Simpson: 154. Garcia Icazbalceta Lenguas: 13. Vinaza: 114. Palau: 23467. A Collection of sermons in Nahuatl, the most widely spoken language of native Mexican Indians, by

one of the most important Nahuatl writers of the time.
Not only is this, like Baptista's other works, an extremely scarce Mexicanum, but its desirability is enhanced by
its five woodcut illustrations. (WR)

B305. BARAGA (Bishop Frederic). A Dictionary of the Otchipwe
Language, Explained in English. Part I. vi, 301pp,
modern quarter red morocco, raised bands. Montreal,
Beauchemin & Valois, 1878. $70.00

B306. BARAGA (Bishop F.). A Theoretical and Practical Grammar of the Otchipwe Language for the Use of Missionaries and Other Persons Living Among the Indians. A
Second Edition, by a Missionary of the Oblates. xi,
422pp, modern quarter red morocco. Montreal, 1878.
$95.00

B307. BARBA DE PINA CHAN (Beatriz). (Acta Antropologica,
Epoca 2, Vol. 1, No. 1, Mexico, 1956) "Tlapacoya" un
Sitio Preclasico de Transicion. 204pp, illus, wraps.
$35.00

B308. BARBER (Edwin A.). U.S. Geological Survey Bulletin,
n.d.) Comparative Vocabulary of Utah Dialects. pp
533-545, wrappers. $20.00

B309. BARBER (John Warner). History and Antiquities of New
England, New York, and New Jersey. 576pp, engraved
frontis, woodcut pls, sml woodcuts in text, modern cloth.
Worcester, Mass., 1841. $40.00

B310. BARBEAU (C. M.). (Canada Dept. of Mines, Memoir 46,
No. 7, Ottawa, 1915) Classification of Iroquoian Radi-
cals with Subjective Pronominal Prefixes. 30pp, wraps.
$15.00

B311. BARBEAU (Marius). (National Museum of Canada, Bulletin
No. 93, c.1939) Assomption Sash. color frontis, 37pp,
plus 18 pls, includes Iroquois, Osage, Winnebago, Sauk
and Fox, Menominee and Shawnee Indians, ex-lib, wrappers. $35.00

B312. BARBEAU (M.). (National Museum of Canada, Bulletin No.
139, Anthropology Series No. 38, Ottawa, 1957) Haida
Carvers in Argillite. viii, 214pp, 216 photographs, 13
drawings, wrappers. $125.00
___Another Copy. Same. $65.00
___Another Copy. Facsimile edition, Ottawa,
1974. $45.00

B313. BARBEAU (M.). (National Museum of Canada, Bulletin
No. 27, Anthropology Series, No. 32, Ottawa, 1953)
Haida Myths, Illustrated in Argillite Carvings. ix,
417pp, 328 photographs, wrappers. $125.00
___Another Copy. Same. $75.00
___Another Copy. Same. $85.00
___Another Copy. Same. $75.00

B314. BARBEAU (Marius). (National Museum of Canada Bulletin
165, Ottawa, 1960, 1st ed.) Huron-Wyandot Traditional
Narratives in Translation and Native Texts. 388pp, 14
photographic pls, map, wrappers. $18.00

B315. BARBEAU (M.). Indian Days in the Canadian Rockies.
207, (1)pp, frontis, illus by Langdon Kihn, 1/2 cloth,
Toronto, 1923 (1st ed.), d.j. $70.00

B316. BARBEAU (M.). (National Museum of Canada Bulletin No.
163, Ottawa, 1960) Indian Days on the Western Prairies.
v, 234pp, 165 photographs, wraps. $38.00
_____Another Copy. Same. $20.00

B317. BARBEAU (M.) and MELVIN (G.). The Indian Speaks.
117pp, interpretive illus by G. Melvin, Caldwell, 1943
(1st ed.). $30.00

B318. BARBEAU (M.). (National Museum of Canada Bulletin No.
152, Ottawa, 1958) Medicine Men of the North Pacific
Coast. 95pp, 90 photographs, wrappers. $50.00

B319. BARBEAU (M.). The Modern Growth of the Totem Pole
on the Northwest Coast. pp 491-498. From, Smithsonian
Annual Report for 1939. Illustrated with photographs,
wraps. $12.00

B320. BARBEAU (M.). (National Museum of Canada Bulletin No.
119, Anthropology Series No. 30, Ottawa, 1950) Totem
Poles. (2 Volumes). Vol. I: Totem Poles According
to Crests and Topics. 433pp. Vol. II: Totem Poles
According to Location. pp 434-880. Illus with photographs and drawings, map endpapers, wraps.
                                                      $150.00
_____Another Copy. Same. $100.00

B321. BARBEAU (M.). Totem Poles: A Recent Native Art of
the Northwest Coast of America. Extracted from Smithsonian Institution Annual Report for the Year Ending
June 30, 1931. pp 559-570, 6pp of photographs, map,
cloth. $25.00

B322. BARBEAU (M.). Totem Poles of the Gitskan, Upper Skeena
River, British Columbia. 275pp, 33 pls, map, wrappers,
Ottawa, 1973. $17.00

B323. BARBEAU (M.). (National Museum of Canada Bulletin No.
174, Anthropology Series No. 51, Ottawa, 1961) Tsim-
syan Myths Illustrated. v, 97pp, 21 photographs, wrappers. $40.00

B324. BARBOUR (Philip L.). Pocahontas and Her World. 299pp,
plus index, drawings, notes, bibliography, appendices,
Rolfe genealogy, photographs, map, Boston, 1970 (1st
printing), d.j. $10.00

B325. BARCO (Miguel Del). (Baja California Travel Series,
No. 44, Los Angeles, 1981) Ethnology and Linguistics
of Baja California. 112pp, wraps. $30.00
_____Another Copy. Same. $22.00

B326. BARDIN (P.). Artesanias Argentinas Tradicionales. (Argentine Traditional Artifacts.) 107pp, text in Spanish
and English. 29pp of color photographs and 18pp of
b/w photographs, map, cloth, Buenos Aires, 1981.
                                                       $40.00

The traditional artifacts of Argentina's indigenous peoples are treated to an extensive photographic introduction. The text is quite brief, but the large, excellent photographs of artifacts are the main purpose of the book. Included are textiles, basketry, pottery, dance masks, wooden containers, etc. (EAP)

B327. BARKER (M. A. R.). (Univ. of California Publications in Linguistics, Vol. 32, Berkeley, 1964) Klamath Grammar. 364pp, 4to, wrappers. $25.00
_____Another Copy. Same. $18.00

B328. BARKER (M. A. R.). (Univ. of California Publications in Linguistics, Vol. 30, Berkeley, 1963) Klamath Texts. 197pp, pls, map, wrappers. $20.00
_____Another Copy. Same. $12.00

B329. BARNARD (Thomas). A Discourse Before the Society for Propagating the Gospel Among the Indians and Others in North America, November 6, 1806. 39pp, removed, Charlestown, S. Etheridge, 1806. $75.00

B330. BARNES (Annie Maria). How A-Chon-Ho-Ah Found the Light. 266pp, cloth, foxing throughout, shaken, Richmond, 1894. $12.00

B331. BARNES (Nellie). American Indian Love Lyrics and Other Verse: From the Songs of the North American Indians, Foreword by Mary Austin. 189pp, cloth, New York, 1925 (1st ed.). $30.00

B332. BARNETT (F.). Dictionary of Prehistoric Indian Artifacts of the American Southwest. 148pp, 249 b/w and 3 color photographs of artifacts, Flagstaff, 1973, 1977 (reprint in wraps). $12.00

B333. BARNETT (Franklin). Excavation of Main Pueblo at Fitzmaurice Ruin: Prescott Culture in Yavapai County, Arizona. 138pp, 95 figures, wrappers, Museum of Northern Arizona, 1974. $22.00
_____Another Copy. Same. $14.00

B334. BARNETT (Franklin). (Museum of Northern Arizona, Bulletin No. 51, Flagstaff, 1978) Las Vegas Ranch Ruin-East and Las Vegas Ranch Ruin-West: Two Small Prehistoric Prescott Indian Culture Ruins in West Central Arizona. 107pp, illus, wrappers. $20.00

B335. BARNETT (Franklin). (Museum of Northern Arizona, Tech. Series, No. 10, Flagstaff, 1970) Matli Ranch Ruins: A Report of Excavation of Five Small Prehistoric Indian Ruins of the Prescott Culture of Arizona. 90pp, illus, wrappers. $15.00

B336. BARNETT (Homer G.). The Coast Salish of British Columbia. xiii, 320pp, illus, folding map, figures, bibliography, index, Univ. of Oregon, 1955 (1st ed.), d.j.
                                                    $40.00
_____Another Copy. Wrappers, ex-lib. $25.00
_____Another Copy. 1955, worn d.j. $75.00

B337. BARNETT (H. G.). (Univ. of California Anthropological

Records, Vol. 1, No. 5, Berkeley, 1939) Culture Element Distributions: IX. Gulf of Georgia Salish. 79pp, 51 drawings, map, wrappers. $40.00

B338. BARNETT (H. G.). Indian Shakers, a Messianic Cult of the Pacific Northwest. 378pp, 4 pls, notes, bibliography, index, Carbondale, Southern Illinois Univ., 1957 (1st ed.), d.j. $40.00

___Another Copy. Same. $28.00
___Another Copy. Same. $25.00

B339. BARNETT (H. G.). The Nature and Function of the Potlatch. 132pp. Reproduced in 1968 by the Dept. of Anthropology, Univ. of Oregon from the author's 1938 doctoral dissertation, wrappers. $30.00

B340. BARNOUW (Victor). (American Anthropological Assoc., Memoir No. 72, Menasha, 1950) Acculturation and Personality Among the Wisconsin Chippewa. 152pp, wrappers. $15.00

___Another Copy. Same. $12.00

B341. BARRADAS (J. P. de). Arqueologia Agustiniana. x, 169pp of text containing 173 figures, plus 189 lves of photographs, Biblioteca de Cultura Colombiana, Bogota, 1943. $135.00

B342. BARRATT (Joseph) Editor. The Indian of New England, Derived from Nicola Tenesles. 24pp, printed wraps, Middletown, CT., C. H. Pelton, 1851 (1st ed.). $150.00

___Another Copy. Same. $75.00

B343. BARRENCHEA (Raul P.). Fuentes Historicas Peruanas. 601pp, wrappers, Lima, 1955. $60.00

B344. BARRERE (Pierre). Nouvelle Relation de la France Equinoxiale.... 3 leaves, 251pp, 3 folding maps, 16 folding pls, original wrappers laid in a folding box, Paris, 1743. $350.00

Sabin: 3604. LeClerc: 119. The author, a doctor, spent three years in French Guiana. This work is mainly devoted to describing the Carib Indians, and is illustrated with the finest plates of Caribs extant, showing native ornaments, boats, weapons, methods of fishing, etc. Remarkably detailed and accurate, they are of great ethnological interest. (WR)

B345. BARRETT (S. A.). (Univ. of California Publications in American Archaeology and Ethnology, Vol. 12, No. 10, Berkeley, 1917) Ceremonies of the Pomo Indians. pp 397-441, 8 text figures, wrappers. $25.00

___Another Copy. Same. $28.00

B346. BARRETT (S. A.). (Univ. of California Publications in American Archaeology and Ethnology, Vol. 6, No. 1, Berkeley, 1908) The Ethnography of the Pomo and Neighboring Indians. 332pp, 2 folding maps, one map is in color, wrappers. $40.00

___Another Copy. Same. $85.00

B347. BARRETT (S. A.) and HAWKES (E. W.). (Milwaukee

Public Museum Bulletin, Vol. III, No. 1, 1919) The
Kratz Creek Mound Group, A Study in Wisconsin Indian
Mounds. 138pp, 19 figures, 19pp of photographs, wraps.
$30.00

B348. BARRETT (S. A.). (Milwaukee Public Museum Bulletin
Vol. 20, Part 1, 1952) Material Aspects of Pomo Culture.
Part One. 260pp, 30 photographic pls, drawings, wraps.
$25.00

B349. BARRETT (S. A.). (Milwaukee Public Museum Bulletin
Vol. 20, Part 2, 1952) Material Aspects of Pomo Culture.
Part Two. pp 261-508, 32pp photographs, 4 figures,
wraps. $95.00

B350. BARRETT (S. A.). (Univ. of California Publications in
American Archaeology and Ethnology, Vol. 5, No. 4,
Berkeley, 1910) The Material Culture of the Klamath
Lake and Modoc Indians of Northeastern California and
Southern Oregon. 53pp, 16pp of photographs, wrappers.
$85.00
____Another Copy. Same. $67.00

B351. BARRETT (S. A.) and GIFFORD (E. W.). (Milwaukee
Public Museum Bulletin, Vol. II, No. 4, 1933) Miwok
Material Culture. 229pp, 64 figures, 48pp of photo-
graphs, half leather, linen cvrd bds. $90.00
____Another Copy. Same. $80.00
____Another Copy. Same. $75.00
____Another Copy. Yosemite, 1933, reprint. $12.00

B352. BARRETT (S. A.). (Univ. of California Publications in
American Archaeology and Ethnology, Vol. 12, No. 11,
Berkeley, 1917) Pomo Bear Doctors. 22pp, illus, wraps.
$18.00

B353. BARRETT (S. A.). (Univ. of California Publications in
American Archaeology and Ethnology, Vol. 7, No. 3,
Berkeley, 1908) Pomo Indian Basketry. 174pp, 13pp of
photographs, 3pp drawings, 231 figures, 1 fold-out page
of drawings of designs, wrappers. $98.00
____Another Copy. Same. $75.00
____Another Copy. Same. $40.00
____Another Copy. Glorita, 1976, reprint. $30.00

B354. BARRETT (S. A.). (Milwaukee Public Museum Bulletin,
Vol. 15, 1933) Pomo Myths. 353pp, plus index, bibliography, wrappers. $35.00

B355. BARRETT (S. A.). (Milwaukee Public Museum Bulletin,
Vol. 2, No. 1, 1917) The Washo Indians. 52pp, 22 fig-
ures, map, 13pp photographs (most of baskets), wraps.
$40.00
____Another Copy. Same. $35.00
____Another Copy. New York, 1978, reprint. $12.00

B356. BARRETT (S. A.). (Univ. of California Publications in
American Archaeology and Ethnology, Vol. 14, No. 4,
Berkeley, 1919) The Wintun Hesi Ceremony. 56pp,
2pp of photographs, 3 figures, wrappers. $38.00
____Another Copy. Same. $30.00

B357. BARRETT (S. M.) Editor. Geronimo's Story of His Life.
216pp, illus with photographs, New York, 1906 (1st
ed.). $45.00
____Another Copy. New York, 1907. $25.00
____Another Copy. New York, 1970, d.j. $10.00

B358. BARROW (S.) et al. Arts of a Vanished Era. 64pp, 73
photographs of northwest coast and Eskimo objects,
wrappers, Exhibition Catalogue, Whatcom Museum, 1975.
                                                              $10.00

B359. BARROWS (David Prescott). The Ethno-Botany of the
Coahuilla Indians of Southern California. Including a
Coahuilla Bibliography and Introductory Essays by
Harry W. Lawton, Lowell John Bean and William Bright,
82pp, Banning, 1967. $25.00

B360. BARRY (J.). American Indian Pottery, An Identification
and Value Guide. 214pp, 414 color photographs, 248
b/w photographs, 5 tables, cloth, Florence, 1981, 1984
(2nd ed.). $50.00
A veritable mini-Encyclopedia of pottery types and
prices. This volume with its over 600 photographs provides prototypes of Indian pottery; prehistoric, historic
and contemporary, not only from the southwest, but from
the less familiar sections in the Southwest, Midwest, New
England, and Canada. (EAP)

B361. BARTHEL (Thomas). Intentos de Lectura de los Afijos de
los Jeroglificos en los Codices Mayas. 47pp, wraps,
Cuaderno 2, Mexico, 1969. $10.00

B362. BARLETT (K.). (Museum of Northern Arizona, Bulletin
No. 7, Flagstaff, 1934) The Material Culture of Pueblo
II in the San Francisco Mountains, Arizona. 76pp, 48
illus, wrappers. $20.00

B363. BARTON (Edwin). Physician to the Mayas: The Story of
Dr. Carroll Behrhorst. 208pp, illus, about the Cakchi-
kels of Guatemala, Philadelphia, 1970 (1st ed.). $20.00

B364. BARTRAM (William). (Transactions of American Ethnography
Society, Vol. III, Part I, New York, 1853) Observations
on the Creek and Cherokee Indians, 1789. Prefatory and
Supplementary notes by E. G. Squier. 81pp drawings;
(76pp), drawings; (5pp) of 202pp. Also contains:
Observations on the Archaeology and Ethnology of Nica-
ragua by E. G. Squier. A Choctaw Tradition.... by
C. C. Copeland. Newly rebound in modern cloth. $45.00

B365. (BASKETRY). Anthropological Studies in California. Extracted from U.S. National Museum Report for Year 1900,
Washington, DC, 1902. pp 161-187, 50 pls, wrappers.
                                                              $30.00

B366. (BASKETRY). The Art and Romance of Indian Basketry.
118 unnumbered pp, 21pp of photographs showing 80
baskets from the Clark Field Collection, wraps, Tulsa,
1957 (1st ed.). $10.00

B367. (BASKETRY). Illustrated History of Indian Baskets Made by California Indians and Many Other Tribes. 34 pls, wrappers. Original edition 1915, reprinted California, 1967. (Panama-Pacific International Exposition). $35.00

B368. (BASKETRY). Indian Basket Weaving by the Navajo School of Indian Basketry. frontis, 104pp, illus, imprinted burlap (tied). Los Angeles, CA, 1903 (1st ed.). $100.00

B369. (BASKETRY). (Museum Journal, Philadelphia, December, 1918) The Patty Stuart Dewett Collection. pp 225-243, 4 color and 11 b/w photographs (all full-page) of baskets made by California Indians, wrappers. $30.00

B370. BASS (Althea). The Arapaho Way: A Memoir of an Indian Boyhood. Introduction by Frank Waters. 22 illus in full color by Carl Sweezy, New York, 1966, d.j. $30.00
____Another Copy. New York, 1967, d.j. $15.00
____Another Copy. New York, 1966, 1st, lacks d.j. $12.00

B371. BASS (Althea). Cherokee Messenger. 348pp, illus, index, Norman, 1968, d.j. $20.00
Biography of Samuel Austin Worcester, a New England missionary who worked for the Cherokees from the 1820's until his death in 1859.

B372. BASS (Althea). The Thankful People. Illus by Walter R. West, Caldwell, Caxton, 1950, d.j. $18.00

BASSO (Keith H.). See also BAE Bulletin No. 196.

B373. BASSO (Keith H.). Gift of Changing Woman. Offprint, Smithsonian Anthropological Papers, Washington, 1966. pp 113-173, figures, map, bibliography, printed wraps. $12.00

B374. BASSO (Keith H.). Meaning in Anthropology. 247pp, plus index, bibliography, edited by Henry A. Selby, nine scholars present different approaches to the investigation of symbolic forms. One chapter deals with the Western Apache. Albuquerque, 1976 (1st ed.), d.j. $18.00

B375. BASSO (Keith H.). (Univ. of Arizona, Anthropology Papers No. 15, Tucson, 1969) Western Apache Witchcraft. 73pp, wrappers. $22.00
____Another Copy. Same. $18.00

BASSO (William M.). See BAE Bulletin No. 182.

BASTOS d'AVILA (Jose). See BAE Bulletin No. 143.

B376. BATES (Craig). (Museum of Man, Paper No. 15, San Diego, 1982) Coiled Basketry of the Sierra Miwok. 41pp, 4to, illus, wrappers. $12.00

B377. BATRES (Leopoldo). Falsificacion y Falsificadores, Antiquedades Mejicanas Falsificadas. 30pp of text, plus 63 leaves, each with a full-page photograph with tissue guard between each leaf, 1 fold-out photograph, fold-out map, decorated frontispiece, the text is printed on especially fine paper and was possibly hand printed, S. Soria, Mexico City, n.d., c.1940. $175.00

B378. BATRES (L.). Exploraciones Arqueologicas en la Calle

de la Escalerillas. 59pp, 17 photographs, 10 drawings,
2pp of color pls, 2 fold-out site plans, cloth, Mexico
City, 1902. $125.00

B379. BATRES (L.). Visita a los Monumentos Arqueologicos de
       "La Quemada," Zacatecas. 43pp, 10 figures, 27 pls,
       wrappers. Mexico, 1903. $90.00

B380. BATTEY (Thomas C.). The Life and Adventures of a
       Quaker Among the Indians. 339pp, illus, Boston, 1875
       (1st ed.). $130.00
           Extracts from the author's diary kept while operating
       a school in the Kiowa and Comanche country from 1871
       to 1874. Much on Satanta and Kicking Bird and other
       prominent Indians on the Texas frontier.
       ____Another Copy. Same. $75.00
       ____Another Copy. Boston, 1889. $75.00

B381. BAUDEZ (C. F.). America Central. 258pp, 106 b/w and
       54 color photographs, mostly full-page, cloth, Geneva,
       1970, Barcelona, 1976. $40.00

B382. BAUDEZ (C.) and BECQUELIN (P.). Arqueologie de los
       Naranjos. 432pp, 152 pls, 16 tables, folding map in
       rear pocket, Mission Archeologie et Ethnologie, 1973,
       d.j. $125.00
       ____Another Copy. Lacks d.j. $90.00

B383. BAYLOR (Byrd). Before You Came This Way. A Poetic
       and Visual Presentation of Prehistoric Indian Petro-
       glyphs. 32 unnumbered pages, illus by Tom Bahti, pic-
       torial bds, New York, 1969 (1st ed.). $20.00

B384. BEACH (W. W.) Editor. The Indian Miscellany: Papers
       on the History, Antiquities, Arts, Languages, Religions,
       Traditions and Superstitions of the American Aborigines.
       490pp, includes: (Squier) Bark Record of the Lenape.
       (Dorr) Apaches. (Packard) Esquimaux of Labrador.
       (Hallam) Sioux. (Ray) Aboriginal Inhabitants of Con-
       necticut. (Dall) Alaskan Mummies. 2pp in facsimile,
       Albany, 1877. $90.00

B385. BEAGLEHOLE (Ernest and Pearl). (American Anthropology
       Assoc., Memoir No. 44, Menasha, 1935) Hopi of the
       Second Mesa. 65pp, wrappers. $15.00

B386. BEAL (Merrill). I Will Fight No More Forever. Chief
       Joseph and the Nez Perce War. xvii, 366pp, 8pp of
       photographs, 2 maps, notes, bibliography, index,
       Seattle, Univ. of Washington, 1963 (1st ed.), d.j.
                                                               $35.00

B387. BEAL (Merrill D.). The Story of Man in Yellowstone
       Park. 309pp, illus, maps, bibliography, index, Cald-
       well, 1949 (1st ed.). $20.00

B388. BEALS (Carleton). Nomads and Empire Builders. Native
       Peoples and Cultures of South America. illus, Phila.,
       1961, d.j. $20.00

BEALS (Ralph L.). See also BAE Bulletin No. 142.

B389. BEALS (Ralph). (Univ. of California, Ibero-Americana:

19, Berkeley, 1943) The Aboriginal Culture of the
Cahita Indians. x, 94pp, map, figures, pls, bibliography, tribe located in Sonora and Sinaloa Mexico, wraps.
$20.00

B390. BEALS (R. L.). (Smithsonian Institute of Social Anthropology, Publication No. 2, Washington, 1946) Cheran:
A Sierra Tarascan Village. 244pp, 8pp of photographs,
19 figures, wraps. $25.00
___Another Copy. Same. $15.00

B391. BEALS (R. L.). The Comparative Ethnology of Northern
Mexico Before 1750. 132pp, folded map, Univ. of California, Berkeley, 1932. $35.00

B392. BEALS (R. L.). (Univ. of California Publications in American Archaeology and Ethnology, Vol. 42, No. 1, Berkeley, 1945) Ethnology of the Western Mixe. 176pp, illus,
wrappers. $35.00

B393. BEALS (R. L.). (Univ. of California Publications in American Archaeology and Ethnology, Vol. 31, No. 6, Berkeley, 1933) Ethnology of the Nisenan. 82pp, 2pp of
photographs, 3 figures, map, wraps. $35.00

B394. BEALS (R. L.) et al. (Smithsonian Institute of Social
Anthropology, Publication No. 1, Washington, 1944)
Houses and House Use of the Sierra Tarascans. x, 37pp,
20 figures, 8 pp of photographs, wrappers. $20.00
___Another Copy. Same. $10.00

B395. BEALS (R. L.). Material Culture of the Pima, Papago
and Western Apache. 44pp, lrge 8vo, bibliography,
wraps, National Park Service, Berkeley, 1934. $15.00

B396. BEALS (R. L.). Preliminary Report on the Ethnography
of the Southwest. iii, 36pp, 2 full-page maps, wrappers,
National Park Service, Berkeley, 1935. $35.00

B397. BEAN (Lowell). The Cahuilla Indians of Southern California; Their History and Culture. 13pp, illus with photographs, wraps, Banning, 1965. $12.00

B398. BEAN (Lowell). Mukat's People: The Cahuilla Indians of
Southern California. 201pp, maps, bibliography, Berkeley, 1974. $20.00

B399. BEAN (Lowell) et al. Persistence and Power: A Study of
Native American Peoples in the Sonoran Desert, and the
Devers-Palo Verde High Voltage Transmission Line.
406pp, 4to, maps, tables, Menlo Park, 1978. $65.00
This environmental report contains a wealth of mate-
rial on the Indians of southeastern Arizona and south-
western California. The report was prepared by the
Cultural Systems Research, Inc. for Southern California
Edison Co. and was never offered for general sale.
(GFH)

B400. BEATTY (Charles). The Journal of a Two Months Tour:
With a View of Promoting Religion Among the Frontier
Inhabitants of Pennsylvania, and of Introducing Chris-
tianity Among the Indians to the Westward of the

Alegheny Mountains.... viii, (9)-110pp, one leaf of ads, three quarter crushed morocco and cloth, spine gilt extra, marginal water stain to a few leaves, ex-lib, London, 1768. $1,250.00

Howes: 281. Thomson: 72. Field: 102. Sabin: 4149. Pilling: 324. The rare first edition, "quite difficult to procure complete" (Field). The Irish-born missionary was one of the most popular preachers of his day, traveling extensively in Europe as well as in America. In 1760 he was sent with Duffield to observe and investigate the condition of the Indian tribes. This account, one of only a few pieces by Beatty to ever see publication, includes "the first account of Indian towns in Southeast Ohio" (Howes). Includes interviews with Indian chiefs and encounters with Delaware Indians, whom Beatty conjectures to be descended from the ten tribes. (WR)

B401. BEAUCHAMP (W. M.). (New York State Museum Bulletin, Vol. 4, No. 6, October, 1897) Aboriginal Chipped Stone Implements of New York. 84pp of text, 23pp of illus, wraps. $65.00
___Another Copy. Same. $45.00

B402. BEAUCHAMP (W. M.). (New York State Museum Archaeology Bulletins, Vol. 7, No. 32, Albany, 1900) Aboriginal Occupation of New York. 187pp, 91 plans, pocket map, index, wrappers. $35.00
___Another Copy. Same. $42.00

B403. BEAUCHAMP (W. M.). (New York State Museum Archaeology Bulletin No. 108, Albany, 1907) Aboriginal Place Names of New York. 333pp, index, listing and explanation by county, original wrappers. $50.00

B404. BEAUCHAMP (W. M.). (New York State Museum Archaeology Bulletin, No. 89, Albany, 1905) Aboriginal Use of Wood in New York. 186pp of text, plus 35pp of drawings of artifacts, masks, etc., wrappers. $85.00

B405. BEAUCHAMP (W. M.). (New York State Museum Archaeology Bulletin, No. 113, Albany, 1907) Civil, Religious and Mourning Councils and Ceremonies of Adoption of the New York Indians. pp 341-451, 3 pls showing types of wampum, 4 folding pls of music, self wraps. $30.00

B406. BEAUCHAMP (W. M.). (New York State Museum Archaeology Bulletin, Vol. 5, No. 22, Albany, 1898) Earthenware of the New York Aborigines. 146pp, illus of 245 pots, pipes, and other artifacts, index, wraps. $55.00
___Another Copy. Same. $65.00

B407. BEAUCHAMP (W. M.). (New York State Museum Archaeology Bulletin, No. 78, Albany, 1905) A History of the New York Iroquois. 461pp, 18 pls, folding map in frnt pocket, original cloth. $90.00
___Another Copy. New York, 1962, 3rd printing. $20.00

B408. BEAUCHAMP (W. M.). Iroquois Folk-Lore: Gathered from

the Six Nations of New York. 247pp, rebound in half
leather, Syracuse, 1922. $100.00

B409. BEAUCHAMP (W. M.). (New York State Museum Archaeology Bulletin, No. 55, Albany, 1902) Metallic Implements
of the New York Indians. 92pp, 37 pls, 8vo, original
wrappers. $45.00
___Another Copy. Same. $55.00

B410. BEAUCHAMP (W. M.). (New York State Museum Archaeology Bulletin, Vol. 2, Appendices 6-7, Albany, 1905)
Metallic Ornaments of the New York Indians. 120pp,
19 pls, index, cloth; with ... A History of the New York
Iroquois. pp 123-461, 17 pls, maps, index. $70.00

B411. BEAUCHAMP (W. M.). (New York State Museum Archaeology Bulletin, No. 87, Albany, 1905) Perch Lake Mounds.
82pp, 12 pls, index, 8vo, original maps. $45.00
___Another Copy. Same. $30.00

B412. BEAUCHAMP (W. M.). (New York State Museum Archaeology Bulletin, Vol. 4, No. 18, Albany, 1897) Polished
Stone Articles Used by the New York Aborigines Before
and During European Occupation. 102pp, 245 illus, index, wrappers. $55.00
___Another Copy. Same. $65.00
___Another Copy. Same. $85.00

B413. BEAVER (Herbert). Reports and Letters of ... 1836-1838.
Chaplain to Hudson's Bay Company and Missionary to
Indians at Fort Vancouver. xxiv, 153pp, edition of 750
copies, by Lawton Kennedy, index, Champoeg Press,
1959 (1st ed.). $60.00

B414. BECKER-DONNER (Etta). Prakolumbische Malerei. 14pp,
plus 24 color pls, wraps, Vienna, 1962. $15.00

B415. BECKHAM (Stephen Dow). Requiem for a People; The
Rogue Indians and the Frontiersmen. 214pp, illus, map,
bibliography, index, Norman, 1971, d.j. $17.00
___Another Copy. Same. $15.00

B416. BECKWITH (Martha). Myths and Hunting Stories of the
Mandan and Hidatsa Sioux. 116pp, New York, American
Museum Society (reprint of 1930 edition). $15.00

B417. BECKWITH (Thomas). The Indian or Mound Builder: The
Indian's Mode of Living, Manners, Customs, Dress, Orna-
ments, Etc., Before the White Man Came to the Country,
Together With a List of Relics Gathered by the Author.
Illus, Cape Girardeau, Naeter Bros., 1911. $55.00

B418. BECQUELIN (P.). (Memoires de L'Institut d'Ethnologie-II,
Paris, 1969) Archeologie de la Region de Nebaj, Guatemala. 324pp, 102pp of photographs and drawings,
wrappers. $25.00

B419. BECQUELIN (P.) and BAUDEZ (C. F.). Tonina, Una Cite
Maya du Chiapas. (3 Volumes). Vol. I: 538pp, 206pp
of Photographs, drawings and plans, cloth, Paris, 1979.
Vol. II: pp 549-1192, Paris, 1982. Vol. III: pp 1199-
1456, these 258pp consist of photographs, drawings, maps
or plans. Paris, 1982. $165.00

The results of the 1972, 1973 and 1977 excavations at Tonina and in the Ocosingo Valley are presented in this highly detailed three volume work. Because it was situated at the western boundary of the Maya region, Tonina was a city of considerable importance due to both the Maya and non-Maya features found in its institutions and customs and in its archaeology. The excavations also provided valuable information on the final period of the city--the last stele was inaugurated in 909 AD, the latest known date in Maya culture. Text in French. (EAP)

B420. BEDFORD (Clay P.). Western North American Indian Baskets from the Collection of Clay P. Bedford. 68pp, many photographs in color, map, bibliography, wrappers, n. p., n. d., San Francisco, c.1980. $15.00

B421. BEDFORD (Denton R.). Tsali. 252pp, 4pp of drawings by Dan B. Timmons. An account of the Cherokee removal from the standpoint of the Indians, by an Indian author. wrappers, San Francisco, 1972 (1st ed.). $12.00

B422. BEDFORD (J.) et al. Mohawk Micmac Malisett, and Other Indian Souvenir Art from Victorian Canada. 26pp, 21pp insert, 4pp color and 9 b/w photographs, 3 drawings, wraps, London, 1985. $15.00

B423. BEDINGER (Margery). Indian Silver. Navajo and Pueblo Jewelers. 255pp, plus index, photographs (some in color), map, bibliography, Albuquerque, 1973 (1st ed.), d.j. $35.00
        Another Copy. Same, lacks d.j. $22.00

B424. BEEDE (A. McG.). Toward the Sun. 199pp, appendix, notes on Indians by Melvin R. Gilmore, Bismark, 1916 (1st ed.). $20.00

B425. BEEDE (A. M.). Sitting Bull--Custer. 14pp, 50pp, illus, embossed suede, Bismark, 1913 (1st ed.). $75.00

B426. BEESON (John). Plea for the Indians, with Facts and Features of the Late War in Oregon. 143pp, original tan printed wraps, 12.5x19cm, New York, 1858. $250.00
        Howes: B-314. Streeter: 3376. This pamphlet's value lies not in its account of the overland journey ... but in description of harsh treatment of Indians ... and in giving the Indian point of view of the war of 1855-56 in Oregon. (OTB)

B427. BEGAY (Harrison). The Sacred Mountains of the Navajo. 24 unnumbered pp, 5 pls (4 in color), text by Leland C. Wyman, printed wrappers, Flagstaff, 1967. $15.00

B428. BEGG (Alexander). History of British Columbia from Its Earliest Discovery to the Present Time. 568pp, photographs, lrge folding map in back cvr, Toronto, 1894 (1st ed.). $60.00

B429. BEHN (Harry). The Painted Cave. 63pp, illus, pictorial cloth, Indian myths as seen through the eyes of a boy based upon cave pictures in the Grand Canyon area, New York, 1957 (1st ed.). $20.00

B430. BEIDLER (Peter G.). Fig Tree John. An Indian in Fact
       and Fiction. 147pp, plus index, photographs, map,
       bibliography, Tucson, 1977 (1st ed.), d.j. $15.00

BELAIEFF (Juan). See BAE Bulletin No. 143, Vol. 1, and No. 151.

B431. BELDEN (B. L.). Indian Peace Medals Issued in the United
       States. 46pp, plus 22 pls, edition limited to 350 copies
       (numbered), wrappers, New York, American Numismatic
       Society, 1927. $75.00

B432. BELL (Ed, Barbara and Steve). Zuni. The Art and the
       People. (3 Volumes). pp 80; 64; 72, beautiful illus of
       the works of the Zuni Silversmiths, cloth, Dallas, 1975,
       1976, 1977. $55.00

B433. BELL (R. E.). (Oklahoma Anthropological Society, Spe-
       cial Bulletin No. 1, 1958) Guide to the Identification of
       Certain American Indian Projectile Points. 104pp, 50
       pls, wraps. $12.00

B434. BELL (William A.). New Tracks in North America. A
       Journal of Travel and Adventure. lxix, 565pp, 20 color
       lithographs, illus, folding map, gilt decorated cloth,
       London, Chapman and Hall, 1870 (2nd ed.). $115.00
          Field: "Traces the migration northward of the Aztec
       race, driven by Spanish cruelty ... by the ruins of
       their peculiar architecture.

B435. BELT (Thomas). The Naturalist in Nicaragua. 306pp,
       illus, includes a search for Indian antiquities, New York,
       n.d. (reprint of 1874 edition). $30.00

B436. BELTRAMI (J. C.). A Pilgrimage in Europe and America,
       Leading to the Discovery of the Sources of the Mississippi
       and Bloody River.... (2 Volumes). lxxxvi, 472; 555
       pp, (1), errata slip, portrait, 3 pls, 2 engraved folding
       plans, folding map, later half leather, bds, London,
       Hunt and Clarke, 1828 (1st English ed.). $300.00
          Field: "Volume II is almost entirely devoted to the
       author's travels among the northwestern Indians, of whom
       he gives some novel particulars." (RMW)

B437. BEMISTER (M.). Indian Legends. Stories of America Be-
       fore Columbus. viii, 187pp, 17 drawings, pictorial frnt
       cvr, juvenile, New York, 1914, 1915. $30.00

B438. (Benavides, Alonzo Fray). The Memorial of.... 309pp,
       cloth, Chicago, 1916. $300.00
          Translated by Mrs. Edward Ayer, and issued in an
       edition of 300 copies. A basic New Mexico book recount-
       ing a visit there in 1630, and particularly the Indians of
       the province at the time.

B439. BENDER (Norman J.) Editor. Missionaries, Outlaws and
       Indians: Taylor F. Ealy at Lincoln and Zuni. xxi,
       234pp, illus, map, cloth, Albuquerque, 1984 (1st ed.),
       d.j. $35.00

B440. BENDOR-SAMUEL (D.). Hierarchical Structures in Guajara
       (Brazil). 214pp, wrappers, Norman, Summer Institute
       of Linguistics, 1972. $15.00

BENEDICT (Ruth). See also BAE Bulletin No. 98.

B441. BENEDICT (Ruth). Introduction to Zuni Mythology. pp
xi-xliii, stiff wrappers. Reprinted from Zuni Mythology,
Vol. I, New York, 1935. $25.00

B442. BENHAM (B. L.) et al. (Southern Methodist Univ.,
Archaeology Research Program, 1973) Archaeological Research Toledo Bend Reservoir. 91pp, plus pls, maps,
bibliography, lrge 8vo, wrappers. $15.00

B443. BENITEZ (Fernando). In the Footsteps of Cortes. 256pp,
a personal journey with comments about the conquest,
New York, 1952 (1st ed.), d.j. $20.00

B444. BENITEZ (Fernando). Ki El Drama de un Pueblo y de Una
Planta. 243pp, illus, wrappers, Mexico, 1962, 1973
(2nd ed.). $25.00

B445. BENNETT (Edna M. and John F.). Turquoise Jewelry of
the Indians of the Southwest. 148pp, 40 color illus and
numerous b/w illus, 4to, wraps, Colorado Springs, 1974.
$35.00
___Another Copy. Same. $15.00

B446. BENNETT (Kay). Kaibah. Recollection of a Navajo Girl-
hood. 253pp, illus by author, Los Angeles, 1964 (1st
ed.), d.j. $20.00
___Another Copy. Same. $22.00
___Another Copy. Same, lacks d.j. $12.00

B447. BENNETT (Kay and Russ). A Navaho Saga. 239pp, draw-
ings, map endpapers, San Antonio, 1969 (1st ed.), d.j.
$15.00
___Another Copy. Same. $25.00
___Another Copy. Same, lacks d.j. $12.00

B448. BENNETT (Kenneth). (Univ. of Arizona, Anthropology
Papers, No. 23, Tucson, 1973) The Indians of Point of
Pines, Arizona. 75pp, 4to, illus, wraps. $15.00

B449. BENNETT (Noel). Designing with the Wool. 118pp, drawings, photographs, advanced techniques in Navajo weaving, wrappers, Flagstaff, 1979 (1st ed.). $10.00

B450. BENNETT (Noel). The Weaver's Pathway; A Clarification
of the "Spirit Trail" in Navajo Weaving. 64pp, illus,
Flagstaff, 1974 (1st ed.), d.j. $18.00
First definitive study of the small line--commonly called
the Spirit Trail--which passes from the background to
the selvage in some bordered Navajo rugs. This line
appears at first glance to be a mistake, but it is the result of an old Navajo superstitution.
___Another Copy. Same. $25.00

BENNETT (Wendell C.). See also BAE Bulletin 143, Vols. 2, 4,
and 5. (EAP)

B451. BENNETT (Wendell C.). Ancient Arts of the Andes. 186pp,
1pp, illus with photographs (some in color), maps, bibliography, endpaper maps, New York, 1954 (1st ed.).
$35.00

B452. BENNETT (W. C.) and BIRD (J. B.) (American Museum

of Natural History, Handbook Series, No. 15, New York,
1949) Andean Culture History. 319pp, 53 photographs,
4 maps, cloth. $35.00
___Another Copy. Same. $40.00
___Another Copy. 2nd revised ed., 1960. $30.00

B453. BENNETT (W. C.). (Yale Univ. Publications in Anthropology, No. 30, 1944) Archaeological Regions of Colombia:
A Ceramic Survey. 115pp, 12 pls of multiple artifacts,
wrappers. $25.00

B454. BENNETT (W. C.). (American Museum of Natural History,
Anthropological Papers, Vol. XXXVII, Part I, New York,
1939) Archaeology of the North Coast of Peru, An Account of Explorations and Excavations in Viru and Lam-
bayeque Valleys. 153pp, 23pp of figures. $50.00

B455. BENNETT (W. C.). (Yale Univ. Publications in Anthropology, Nos. 30 and 31, 1947) Archaeological Regions of
Colombia: A Ceramic Survey. and FORD (J. A.).
Excavations in the Vicinity of Cali, Colombia, 202pp of
text containing 45 figures and 16pp of photographs, 9
tables, rebound in cloth. $70.00

B456. BENNETT (W. C.). (Yale Univ. Anthropological Studies,
Vol. III, 1942) Chavin Sonte Carving. 40pp, 30 full-
page figures, wrappers. $15.00

B457. BENNETT (W. C.). (American Museum of Natural History
Papers, Vol. XXXIV, Part III, New York, 1934) Excavations at Tiahuanaco. pp 359-515, 35 figures, wraps.
$60.00

B458. BENNETT (W. C.). (American Museum of Natural History
Anthropological Papers, Vol. 30, Part 4, New York,
1936) Excavations in Bolivia. 76pp, 48 figures, wraps.
$45.00

B459. BENNETT (W. C.) et al. (Yale Univ. Publications in
Anthropology, Nos. 38 and 39, New Haven, 1948) Northwest Argentine Archaeology and Lowland Argentine
Archaeology. 224pp, 39 full-pages of photographs and
drawings of hundreds of artifacts, wrappers. $60.00

B460. BENNETT (W. C.). (American Museum of Natural History
Papers, Vol. 39, Part 1, New York, 1944) The North
Highlands of Peru, Excavations in the Callejon de Huay-
las and at Chavin de Huantar. 114pp of text containing
33 figures, plus 8pp of photographs, wrappers. $40.00
___Another Copy. Same. $35.00

B461. BENNETT (W. C.). (Memoirs of the Society for American
Archaeology, American Antiquity, Vol. 4, Menasha and
Salt Lake City, 1948) Reappraisal of Peruvian Archaeol-
ogy. x, 128pp, illus, figures, bibliography, wraps.
$17.00

B462. BENNETT (W. C.) and ZINGG (R. M.). The Tarahumara,
an Indian Tribe of Northern Mexico. xix, 412pp, 14pp
of photographs, 7 figures, fold-out table, cloth, Chicago, 1935 (1st ed.). $70.00

  ___Another Copy. Same. $35.00

  ___Another Copy. Same. $35.00

  ___Another Copy. Same. $30.00

B463. BENSON (E.). Cult of the Feline, A Conference in Pre-
Columbian Iconography. vii, 166pp, numerous pls and
figures, Dumbarton Oaks, Washington, DC, 1972.

                  $20.00

B464. BENSON (E. P.). The Maya World. 176pp, 60 illus, New
York, 1977 (new revised ed.). $25.00

  ___Another Copy. Same. $15.00

B465. BENSON (E. P.) Editor. Mesoamerican Sites and World-
Views. 245pp, 109 illus, cloth, Dumbarton Oaks, 1981.

                  $50.00

    In October of 1976, a conference was held at Dumbar-
ton Oaks to explore the questions of the placement and
arrangement of Mesoamerican sites. Seven of the more
important papers (all illustrated) read at the conference
are presented in this volume. Among the general topics
addressed were the Cosmology and world view of the
people who constructed the sites and their physical environment and belief systems. (EAP)

B466. BENSON (E. P.). Mesoamerican Writing Systems. 226pp,
illus, wraps, Washington, 1973. $20.00

B467. BENSON (E. P.). Mochica: A Culture of Peru. 164pp,
137 b/w and 7 color photographs, 2 maps, cloth, New
York, 1972. $20.00

B468. BENSON (E. P.). (Studies in Pre-Columbian Art and
Archaeology, No. 8, Dumbarton Oaks, Washington, 1970)
An Olmec Figure at Dumbarton Oaks. 39pp, illus, wraps.

                  $10.00

B469. BENSON (Henry C.). Life Among the Choctaw Indians,
and Sketches of the Southwest. 314pp, 12mo, original
cloth, Cincinnati, L. Swormstedt & A. Poe, 1860 (1st
ed.). $175.00

  ___Another Copy. Same. $175.00

B470. BENNYHOFF (J. A.). (Univ. of California Anthropological
Records, Vol. 9, No. 4, Berkeley, 1950) Çalifornian
Spears and Harpoons. iv, 43pp, 7pp of drawings, 3
maps, wrappers.

B471. BERG (Lillie Clara). Early Pioneers and Indians of Minnesota and Rice County. 207pp, photographs, maps,
printed in a limited edition of 100 copies by Lawton Kennedy, index, San Leandro, 1959 (1st ed.). $25.00

B472. BERG (W. A.) The White Gods of the Aztecs. 416pp,
index of names, Boston, 1961 (1st ed.), d.j. $20.00

B473. BERGHOLD (Alexander). The Indians' revenge; or, Days
of Horror; Some Appalling Events in the History of the
Sioux. 240pp, illus, San Francisco, 1891. $75.00

    The first English language edition of this history of
the Indian troubles in and around New Ulm in 1862. This
copy has been bound in 3/4 dark green morocco with

raised bands and gilt lettering. (GFH)

___Another Copy. Cloth. $125.00

B474. BERGSLAND (Knut). (Transactions, American Philosophical Society, Vol. 49, Part 3, Philadelphia, 1959) Aleut Dialects of Atka and Attu. 128pp, illus, lrge 4to, wraps. $25.00

B475. BERGSOE (P.). (Ingeniorvidenskabelige Skrifter, Nr. A 46, Copenhagen, 1938) The Gilding Process and the Metallurgy of Copper and Lead Among the Pre-Columbian Indians. 58pp of text, plus 6pp of photographs of Ecuadorian objects, wrappers. $35.00

B476. BERJON-NEAU (J. L.) and SONNERY (M. D.). Rediscovered Masterpieces of Mesoamerica: Mexico, Guatemala. 228pp, 212 color and 218 b/w photographs, 5 maps, cloth, Boulogne, 1985. $85.00

___Another Copy. Deluxe edition, limited to 500 copies, leather. $175.00

B477. BERKHOFER (Robert F. Jr.). The White Man's Indians. Images of the American Indian from Columbus to the Present. 250pp, plus index, illus, notes, New York, 1978 (1st ed.), d.j. $15.00

B478. BERLANDIER (Jean Louis). The Indians of Texas in 1830. Edited by John C. Ewers. 209pp, 4to, illus, index, map, Smithsonian Institution Press, Washington, DC, 1969 (1st ed.), d.j. $40.00

Berlandier traveled from Mexico into present-day Texas in 1828 as a member of a Mexican boundary and scientific expedition. He carefully recorded what he learned of the native tribes; their origins, languages, beliefs, dwellings, clothing, hunting, war tactics, etc. This is the first English edition of his manuscript. Illustrated with full-page plates, reproducing watercolors executed under Berlandier's supervision. An important work on Texas Indians of the 19th century. (GFH)

___Another Copy. Same. $55.00

B479. BERLIN (H.). (Carnegie Institution Contributions to American Anthropology and History, No. 59, 1956) Late Pottery Horizons of Tabasco, Mexico. pp 97-152, 7pp of photographs, 4pp of drawings, plans, fold-out map, wrappers. $30.00

B480. BERLO (J. C.). The Art of Pre-Hispanic Mesoamerica, An Annotated Bibliography. xiii, 272pp, 1,533 entries, cloth, Boston, 1985. $50.00

This fully annotated bibliography cites works on ancient Mesoamerican art during the 3,000 years before the coming of the Spanish. Each of the entries has a descriptive and evaluative annotation, and includes publications in five languages--English, French, German, Spanish and Italian. Also included are a subject index and an important 27 page historiographic review of over four and one-half centuries of Pre-Columbian art publications. (EAP)

___Another Copy. Same. $35.00

B481. BERNAL (Ignacio). (Instituto Nacional de Antropologia e
Historia, Corpus Antiquitatum Americanensium, Mexico
City, 1974) Mexico VII. Bajorrelieves en el Museum de
Arte Zapoteco de Mitla, Oaxaca. 101pp of text in Span-
ish and English, 35pp of drawings, wraps.
$42.00

B482. BERNAL (I.) and MENDEZ (R.). (Instituto Nacional de
Antropologia e Historia, Mexico, 1974) Bajorrelieves en
el Museum de Arte Zapoteco de Mitla. 31pp, 35 pls, in
original wrappers. $25.00

B483. BERNAL (I.). (Instituto Nacional de Antropologia e Historia, Mexico, 1962) Bibliographia de Arqueologia y
Ethnographia Mesoamerica y Norte de Mexico, 1514-1960.
634pp, folding maps, original wraps.
$50.00

An absolutely essential reference volume, this thick,
12 1/2" x 9" bibliography contains 13,990 entries dealing
with the archaeology and ethnography of Mesoamerica.
Quite probably the most comprehensive bibliography ever
published on the archaeology and ethnology of this area,
this volume includes books, journals, and articles published from 1514 to 1960. Arranged by geographic area
and then by subject within the area, this bibliography
was limited to a printing of 3,000 copies. (EAP)
____Another Copy. Same. $40.00

B484. BERNAL (I.). (Instituto Nacional de Antropologia e Historia, Corpus Antiquitatum Americanensium, Mexico
City, 1973) Mexico VI. Esculturas Asociadas del Valle
de Oaxaca. 108pp (in a folio), text in Spanish and
English, 38pp of photographs, wraps.
$30.00

B485. BERNAL (I.) and SEUFFERT (A.). (Instituto Nacional
de Antropologia e Historia, Mexico, 1973) Esculturas
Asociadas del Valle de Oaxaca. 29pp, 19 pls loose in
folio with ties, text in Spanish and English.
$25.00

B486. BERNAL (I.). Exploraciones en Cuilapan de Guerrero,
1902-1954. 92pp, 45pp of photographs, 10pp of drawings, 11pp of maps, wraps, Mexico City, 1957.
$35.00

B487. BERNAL (Ignacio). 100 Great Masterpieces of the Mexican
National Museum of Anthropology. 100 color pls, 35pp
of descriptive text, Abrams, New York, 1969, d.j.
$50.00

B488. BERNAL (I.). Great Sculpture of Ancient Mexico. 191pp,
text pages are double and tirple column, index, many
color and b/w photographs, New York, 1979 (1st American ed.), d.j. $30.00
____Another Copy. Same, lacks d.j. $25.00

B489. BERNAL (I.) and HURTADO (E. D.). Huastecos Totanacos

y Sus Vecinos. 567pp, illus, wrappers, Mexico, 1953.
$45.00

B490. BERNAL (I.). The Olmec World. Translated by Doris Heyden and Fernando Horcasitas. 208pp, plus 103 photographic pls, index, drawings, bibliography, Berkeley, 1969 (1st English ed.), d.j.
$25.00

B491. BERNAL (I.). Teotihuacan: Descubrimientos; Reconstrucciones. 52pp with numerous photographs and folding charts, 4to, wrappers, INAH, Mexico, 1963.
$25.00

B492. BERNAL (I.). 3,000 Years of Art and Life in Mexico, As Seen in the National Museum of Anthropology, Mexico City. 216pp, 147 b/w and 24 color photographs, cloth, New York, n.d., c.1970.
$40.00

B493. BERNAL (I.) and SEUFFERT (A.). (Instituto Nacional de Antropologia e Historia, Mexico, 1970) Yugos de la Coleccion del Museo Nacional de Antropologia. 51pp, 42 illus on 27 pls, loose in folio with ties, text in English and Spanish.
$35.00

B494. BERREMAN (J. V.). (American Anthropological Assn., Memoirs, No. 47, 1937) Tribal Distribution in Oregon. 67pp, 2 figures, wraps.
$18.00
___Another Copy. Same, Menasha.
$15.00
___Another Copy. Same.
$10.00

B495. BERRIN (K.) Editor. Art of the Huichol Indians. 212pp, 4to, approx. 100 photographs, many in color, includes 8 studies, exhibition catalogue for San Francisco Fine Arts Museum, New York, 1978.
$45.00

B496. BERTHRONG (Donald G.). The Cheyenne and Arapaho Ordeal: Reservation and Agency Life in the Indian Territory, 1875-1907. 402pp, illus, index, bibliography, maps, Norman, 1976 (1st ed.), d.j.
$30.00
___Another Copy. Same.
$22.00
___Another Copy. Same, lacks d.j.
$16.00

B497. BERTHRONG (Donald G.). The Southern Cheyenne. 446pp, 3 maps, pl illus, index, bibliography, Norman, 1963 (1st ed.), d.j.
$24.00
___Another Copy. Same.
$27.00
___Another Copy. 1972.
$18.00

B498. BERTON (Pierre). The Mysterious North. 345pp, plus index, photographs, map, covers Canadian northland, Yukon, Indians, Eskimos, etc., New York, 1964 (5th printing), d.j.
$10.00

B499. BETETA (Ramon). Camino a Tlaxcalantongo. 126pp, illus, wrappers, Mexico, 1961.
$15.00

B500. BETZINEZ (Jason) and NYE (W. Sturtevant). I Fought with Geronimo. 224pp, illus, endpaper maps, other maps, index, Harrisburg, 1959 (1st ed.), d.j.
$40.00

      ___Another Copy. Same. $35.00
      ___Another Copy. Same. $30.00

B501. BEUCHAT (H.). Manuel D'Archeologie Americaine (Amerique Prehistorique-Civilisations Dispaves). xvi, 773pp, 262 illus, a scholarly, comprehensive treatment of Pre-Columbian cultures, includes North and South America, Paris, 1912.
                                                            $85.00

B502. BEUF (Ann H.). Red Children in White America. 149pp, plus index, appendix, bibliography, Philadelphia, 1977 (1st ed.), d.j. $10.00

B503. BEYER (H.). (Middle American Research Series, No. 4, Publication 5, New Orleans, 1933) Shell Ornament Sets from the Huasteca, Mexico. pp 169-213, 8 pls, wraps.
                                                            $20.00

B504. BIART (Lucien). The Aztecs, Their History, Manners and Customs. Translation by J. L. Garner. ix, 333pp, 20 illus, decorated cloth, inner hinges repaired, Chicago, 1887. $165.00
      ___Another Copy. Same, cvr wear. $95.00

B505. BIBAUD (F. M. Maximilein). Biographie Des Sagamos Illustres de l'Amerique Septentrionale. 309pp, errata slip, 1/2 leather, marbled bds, Montreal, Lovell and Gibson, 1848 (1st ed.).
      Title translates: "Biography of Illustrious Indian Chiefs of North America." Field: "Gives a resume of discovery and wars with the natives, as a frame in which to hang his portraits." Howes: B-418. Sabin: 5145. (RMW)

B506. (BIBLIOGRAPHY). (Instituto Nacional de Antropologia e Historia, Mexico City, 1962) Bibliografia, 1827-1962. 338pp, wraps. $20.00

B507. (BIBLIOGRAPHY). (Univ. of California, Archaeological Research Facility, Contribution No. 6, 1970) A Bibliography of California Archaeology. 78pp, wrappers.
                                                            $25.00

B508. (BIBLIOGRAPHY). Dictionary Catalogue of the Library of the Provincial Archives of British Columbia. (8 Volumes). 5,505pp, 176,000 cards, cloth, Boston, 1971.
                                                   $975.00
      The Provincial Archives of British Columbia is the oldest archival institution in western Canada. Its library includes books, pamphlets, reports, and official publications, as well as periodical literature relating to British Columbia and adjacent States of Washington, Oregon, Idaho, Montana, and Alaska; Canada west of the Great Lakes, Yukon Territory; and Arctic exploration. (EAP)

B509. (BIBLIOGRPAHY). (Yale Anthropological Studies, Vol. 1, 1960) Ethnographic Bibliography of North America. xxiii, 393pp, 16 maps, wraps (3rd ed.). $50.00
      ___Another Copy. 1972, cloth. $60.00

B510. BIBOLOTTI (B.). Moseteno Vocabulary and Treatises. From an Unpublished Manuscript in Possession of the Northwestern University Library. cxii, 141pp. At the time of publication, this was the most complete work on the language and vocabulary of this Bolivian Indian Group. Cloth, Evanston, 1917. $65.00
    ___Another Copy. Same. $85.00

B511. BICKLEY (George W. L.). History of the Settlement and Indian Wars of Tazewell County, Virginia. 267, (16)-pp, illus, cloth, facsimile reprint of 1852 edition with added material compiled by U. Allen Neal; an account of the early Indians in Tazewell County is included, Parsons, 1974. $35.00

B512. BIERHORST (John) Editor. The Girl Who Married a Ghost, and Other Tales from the North American Indian. 115pp, photographs by Edward S. Curtis, New York, 1978, d.j. $12.00

BIESE (Leo P.). See also BAE Bulletin No. 191.

B513. BIESE (Leo P.). The Prehistory of Panama Viejo. Offprint, Smithsonian Anthropological Papers, Washington, 1964. pp 1-50, 20 photographs, figures, bibliography, printed wrappers. $10.00

B514. BIGELOW (Lt. John Jr.). On the Bloody Trial of Geronimo. Foreword and Introduction by Arthur Woodward. 264pp, illus, endpaper maps, notes, index, limited to 750 copies signed by Woodward, Los Angeles, 1958 (1st ed.), d.j. $50.00

B515. BILBY (Julian W.). Among Unknown Eskimo. An Account of Twelve Years Intimate Relations with the Primitive Eskimos of Ice-Bound Baffin Land, With a Description of Their Ways of Living, Hunting, etc., 280pp, 15 pls, folding map, original cloth, London, 1923. $40.00

B516. BILLARD (Jules B.) Editor. The World of the American Indian. 400pp, square 4to, 1/2 leather, illus, index, maps, issued by the National Geographic Society, 1974, d.j. $20.00

B517. BINFORD (L. R.) et al. (Memoirs of the Society for American Archaeology, American Antiquity, Vol. 24, Menasha, Salt Lake City, 1970) Archaeology at Hatchery West. vii, 91pp, illus, figures, bibliography, wraps. $15.00
    ___Another Copy. Same. $12.00

B518. BINGHAM (Hiram). Across South America: An Account of a Journey from Buenos Aires to Lima by Way of Potosi. illus, maps, Boston, 1911. $110.00

B519. BINGHAM (Hiram). Inca Land: Explorations in the Highlands of Peru. 365pp, illus, Boston, 1922. $60.00
    ___Another Copy. Same. $65.00
    ___Another Copy. Same. $45.00

B520. BINGHAM (Hiram). Journal of an Expedition Across

Venezuela and Colombia, 1906-1907. 287pp, 133 illus, folding map, cloth, New Haven, 1909.
$60.00

B521. BINGHAM (Hiram). Lost City of the Incas: The Story of Machu Picchu and Its Builders. 263pp, illus, numerous figures, New York, 1948 (1st ed.). $40.00
___Another Copy. Same. $25.00

B522. BINGHAM (Hiram). Machu Picchu, A Citadel of the Incas. 244pp, folding map, 219 photographs, diagrams, sketches, decorated cloth, New York 1979 (reprint of 1930 edition).
$40.00

B523. BINNEY (G.). The Eskimo Book of Knowledge. Rendered Into the Labrador Dialect by W. W. Barrett. 237pp, illus with photographs, facing pages in English and Eskimo, pictorial cvr, London, 1931.
$45.00

B524. BIRD (Henry). Narrative of Henry Bird, Who Was Carried Away by the Indians After the Murder of His Whole Family in 1811. 14pp, facsimile title page from the original edition, limited to 120 copies, Ye Galleon Press, Fairfield, Washington, 1973. $12.00

BIRD (Junius B.). See also BAE Bulletin No. 143; Vol. 1.

B525. BIRD (J. B.). (American Museum of Natural History Papers, Vol. XXXVIII, Part V, 1944) Excavations at Tampico and Panuco in the Huasteca, Mexico. pp 321-512, 57pp of figures, wrappers. $60.00

B526. BIRD (J. B.). (American Museum of Natural History Papers, Vol. XXXVIII, Part IV, 1943) Excavations in Northern Chile. pp. 173-318, 46 figures, 7 tables, wrappers. $50.00

B527. BIRD (J.) and EKHOLM (G.). Pre-Columbian Gold Sculpture. 32pp, 25pp of photographs, Museum of Primitive Art, New York, 1958. $15.00

B528. BIRD (Traveller). Tell Them They Lie: The Sequoyah Myth. 144pp, plus index, illus, Los Angeles, 1971 (1st ed.), d.j. $20.00

B529. BIRKET-SMITH (K.). (Report of the Fifth Thule Expedition 1921-24, Reports of the Danish Ethnographical Expedition to Arctic America, 1921-24, Vol. VI, No. 2, Copenhagen, 1945) Ethnographical Collections from the Northwest Passage. 291pp, 189 photographs of approx. 500 objects of Netsilik and Copper Eskimo material Culture, cloth. $275.00
___Another Copy. Same. $150.00

B530. BIRKET-SMITH (K.) et al. The Eyak Indians of Copper River Delta, Alaska. 592pp, 18 figures in text, 15pp of photographs, 3pp of maps, inscribed by author, the definitive study of the ethnology of these Prince William Sound Athapaskan people, Copenhagen, 1938. $195.00
___Another Copy. Same, wrappers. $100.00

B531. BIRKET-SMITH (K.) and JENNESS (D.). The Eskimos.
xiv, 250pp, 31pp of photographs, map, cloth, New York,
1935. $58.00
___Another Copy. Same, London, 1959. $45.00
___Another Copy. Revised, enlarged edition,
New York, 1972. $50.00

B532. BIRKET-SMITH (K.). (Report of the Fifth Thule Expedition 1921-24, Reports of the Danish Ethnographical Expedition to Arctic America, 1921-24, Vol. VI, No. 3,
Copenhagen, 1930) Contributions to Chipewyan Ethnology. 113pp, 38 figures, wraps.
$125.00

B533. BIRT (Hal, Jr.). Arizona Indian Trade Tokens. 20pp,
photographs, lrge 8vo, wrappers, n.p., 1970. $15.00

B534. BISCHOFF (William N.). A Sketch of Jesuit Activities in
the Pacific Northwest. The Jesuits in Old Oregon, 1840-
1940. 205pp, plus index, maps, appendix, notes, bibliography, map endpapers, cloth, Caldwell, 1945 (1st
ed.). $17.00

B535. BISHOP (Morris). The Odyssey of Cabaza de Vaca.
298pp, plus index, illus, bibliogrpahy, New York, 1933
(1st ed.). $40.00
___Another Copy. Same. $35.00

B536. BISHOP (Nathaniel H.). A Thousand Miles' Walk Across
South America. The Pampas and the Andes. 310pp,
3 illus, Boston, 1883 (11th ed.).
$20.00

B537. BJORKLUND (Karna). The Indians of Northwestern America. Illustrated by Lorence Bjorklund, Dodd Mead, New
York, 1969, d.j. $10.00

B538. BLACK (G. A.). (Indiana Historical Society Prehistory
Research Series, Vol. 2, No. 5, Indianapolis, 1944) Andel Site, Vanderburgh County, Indiana. vi, pp 451-522,
folding map, plans, pls, wraps.
$15.00

B539. BLACK (G. A.). Angel Site. (2 Volumes). 605 double
column pp, plus index, photographs, maps, drawings,
boxed. Several years archaeological, historical and ethnological study at this Indiana site, resulting in much
detailed information. Indianapolis, 1967.
$85.00

B540. BLACKBIRD (Andrew J.) or, (Mac-Ke-Te-Pe-Nas-Sy). The
Indian Problem, from the Indians' Standpoint. 22pp, 2
illus, 5 ads, wrappers, New Harbor Springs, MI, 1900.
$25.00

B541. BLACKBURN (Thomas C.) Editor. December's Child; A
Book of Chumash Oral Narratives. 359pp, illus, glossary, bibliography. First large collection of oral literature from any Southern California tribe, and the first
collection of any kind from the Chumash. Berkeley, 1975

(1st ed.), d.j. $28.00

B542. (BLACKFEET). (Montana Heritage Series, No. 4, 1961)
Blackfeet Man--James Willard Schultz. 32pp, photographs,
color cvr illus by C. M. Russell, wraps.

$25.00

B543. (BLACKFOOT). (House of Representatives Misc. Document
No. 59, 33:1, Washington, 1854) Blackfeet Indians, Gros-
Ventre, and Others. Report by Isaac I. Stevens and J.
Mullen of Encounters with Indians. 6pp, removed.

$15.00

B544. (BLACKFOOT READER). First Reader in the English and
Blackfoot Languages, with Pictures and Words, for Use
Among the Blackfoot Tribes in the Northwest Territories.
88pp, many illus, including alphabets, cloth, Montreal,
C. O. Beauchemin, 1886. $135.00

B545. (BLACK HAWK). Black Hawk. Ma-Ka-Tai-Me-She-Kia-Kiak.
Black Hawk; an Autobiography. Edited by Donald Jack-
son. 206pp, portrait frontis, illus, bibliography, index,
Univ. of Illinois Press, 1955 (2nd printing), d.j.

$20.00

B546. (BLACK HAWK). The Great Indian Chief of the West: or,
Life and Adventures of Black Hawk. 288pp, portrait,
index, cvrs detached, stained, Cincinnati, 1858.

$35.00

B547. BLAINE (Martha Royce). The Ioway Indians. 364pp, 4to,
illus, index, maps, bibliography, Norman, 1979 (1st ed.),
d.j. $35.00
_____Another Copy. Same. $25.00

B548. BLAIR (Emma Helen). The Indian Tribes of the Upper
Mississippi Valley and Region of the Great Lakes as De-
scribed by Nicolas Perrott ... de la Potherie...., Morrell
Marston ... and Thomas Forsyth.... 372pp; 252pp (2
Volumes), plus index, photographs, other illus, map,
bibliography. Major work on the tribes of this area,
Iroquois, Hurons, Sac and Fox, etc. Cleveland, 1911
and 1912 (1st editions). $200.00
_____Another Copy. Same. $195.00

B549. BLANCHARD (Kendall). (Navaho Historical Publications,
Historical Series No. 1, Window Rock, 1971) The Ramah
Navajos: A Growing Sense of Community in Historical
perspective. 50pp, 4to, map, wraps.

$12.00

B550. BLANTON (R. E.). Monte Alban, Settlement Patterns at the
Ancient Zapotec Capitol. xxvi, 451pp, 132 figures, cloth,
New York, 1978. $30.00

B551. BLEDSOE (Anthony). Indian Wars of the Northwest. A
California Sketch. 505pp, errata, San Francisco, 1885
(1st ed.). $125.00
_____Another Copy. Oakland, 1956. $35.00

B552. BLICHFELDT (E. H.). A Mexican Journey. 270pp, 44 illus, decorated cloth, New York, 1912. $30.00

B 553. BLISH (Helen H.). A Pictographic History of the Oglala
Sioux. Drawings by Amos Bad Heart Bull. Text by Helen
R. Blish. Introduction by Mari Sandoz. 530pp, 4to,
illus, bibliography, Lincoln, 1967 (1st ed.). $50.00
All aspects of Sioux life are depicted in the 415 draw-
ings of which 32 are in color.
___Another Copy. Same. $50.00
___Another Copy. Same. Limited to 200 signed
and numbered copies, boxed. $100.00
___Another Copy. Same as above. $80.00
___Another Copy. Same as above. $95.00

B 554. BLOCK (D.). In Search of El Dorado: Spanish Entry into
Moxos, A Tropical Frontier, 1550-1767. 391pp, wrappers,
Univ. Microfilms facsimile of Doctoral thesis, some under
lining, 1981. $25.00

B 555. BLODGETT (J.) et al. Cape Dorset. 113pp, 63pp of photographs, map, Exhibition Catalogue, Winnipeg Art Gallery,
1980. $17.00

B 556. BLODGETT (Jean). The Coming and Going of the Shaman,
Eskimo Shamanism and Art. Large 4to, illus, some in
color, wraps, Winnipeg Art Gallery, 1978.
$45.00

B 557. BLODGETT (J.). Eskimo Narrative. 48pp, 62 illus, Exhibition Catalogue, Winnipeg Art Gallery, 1979.
$12.00

B 558. BLODGETT (J.). The Mulders Collection of Eskimo Sculpture. 28pp, 42 photographs, Winnipeg, 1976.
$10.00

B 559. BLODGETT (Jean). Kenojuak. 251pp, 161 prints, 33 pls,
a retrospective of the work of Canada's renowned Eskimo
artist, Toronto, 1985. $50.00

B 560. BLODGETT (J.). Tuu'Luq/Anguhadluq. 28pp, 46 b/w
and 2 color illus, wraps, Exhibition Catalogue, Winnipeg
Art Gallery, 1976. $10.00

B 561. BLOM (Frans). (Middle American Research Series, Publication No. 4, Tulane Univ., 1932) Commerce, Trade and
Monetary Units of the Maya. pp 531-556, map, wrappers.
$15.00

B 562. BLOM (Frans). La Vida de los Mayas. Illus, wraps, Mexico, 1944. $10.00

B 563. BLOM (Frans). (Middle American Research Series, Publication No. 4, Tulane Univ., 1932) The Maya Ball-Game
Pok-ta-pok (called Tlachtli by the Aztec). pp 485-530,
37 pls and figures, wraps. $20.00

B 564. BLOM (Frans). (Alma Egan Hyatt Foundation, Vol. 1, No.
2, New York, 1934) Maya Research (Mexico and Central
America). pp 61-145, 17 photographs, 27 figures, 3
maps, wraps. $45.00

B 565. BLOM (Frans). (Alma Egan Hyatt Foundation, Vol. 1, No.

1, New York, 1934) Maya Research (Mexico and Central America). 60pp, 3 photographs, 82 figures, wraps.
$40.00

B566. BLOM (Frans). (Middle American Research Series, Publication No. 4, Tulane Univ., 1932) The "Negative Batter" at Uxmal. pp 559-566, 5 pls, figures, wraps.
$15.00

B567. BLOM (Frans) and LAFARGE (Oliver). Tribes and Temples: A Record of the Expedition to Middle America, Conducted by the Tulane University of Louisiana in 1925. (2 Volumes). 536pp total the 2 volumes, 374 figures, 6 appendices on linguistics, primarily devoted to Mayan sites, New Orleans, 1926.
$200.00

B568. BLOM (Frans) et al. (Middle American Research Series, Pamphlet, Tulane Univ., 1933) A Maya Skull from the Uloa Valley, Honduras. 24pp, 17 pls, figures, wraps.
$15.00

B569. BLOMBERG (Rolf). Chavante (Indians of Brazil). 119pp, illus, some in color, New York, 1961 (1st American ed.).
$25.00

B570. BLOMBERG (Rolf). The Naked Aucas. 191pp, illus, map, New Jersey, 1957, d.j. (torn).
$30.00

B571. BLOOMFIELD (J. K.). The Oneidas. Illus, Alden Bros., New York, 1907.
$85.00

B572. BLUMENTHAL (Walter Hart). American Indians Dispossessed. Fraud in Land Cessions Forced Upon the Tribes. 200pp, bibliography, cloth, Philadelphia, 1955, d.j.
$40.00

BOAS (Franz). See also BAE Bulletin Nos. 20, 26, 27, and 59.

B573. BOAS (Franz). (American Museum of Natural History, Vol. XIV, Part VI, New York, 1901) A. F. Stone's Measurements of Natives of the Northwest Territories. 16pp, plus 5pp of photographs, wrappers.
$15.00

B574. (Boas Anniversary Volume) Anthropological Papers Written in Honor of Franz Boas. 559pp, portrait, papers include: Beauty Among the American Indians; Maya Pronoun; Kwakiutl Story, Decorative Art; Aymara; Pawnee; Peruvian Cloth; Others, 4to, rebound in linen, New York, 1906.
$150.00

B575. BOAS (Franz). Anthropology and Modern Life. 236pp, plus references, half cloth, New York, 1928 (1st ed.).
$12.00

B576. BOAS (Franz). Bella Bella Texts. 291pp, includes myths in English with Bella Bella vocabulary, New York, 1928.
$50.00

_____Another Copy. Same. $48.00
_____Another Copy. American Folklore Soc., 1932. $45.00

B577. BOAS (Franz). (American Museum of Natural History, Vol. XIV, Part V, New York, 1901) A Bronze Figurine from

British Columbia. 2pp, plus 2 illus, author's edition, wrappers. $12.00

B578. BOAS (Franz). (American Museum of Natural History, Vol. IX, Article X, New York, 1897, 1976 reprint) Decorative Art of the Indians of the North Pacific. 60pp, 81 illus, cloth. $25.00

___Another Copy. New York, 1897, author's edition extracted, cloth over wraps. $40.00

B579. BOAS (Franz). (American Museum of Natural History, Vol. XV, Part I, 1901) The Eskimo of Baffin Land and Hudson Bay. 370pp, 172 drawings of artifacts, 3pp of photographs, wrappers. $185.00

B580. BOAS (Franz). (American Museum of Natural History, Memoirs, Jesup North Pacific Expedition, New York, 1900) Facial Paintings of the Indians of Northern British Columbia. pp 13-24, plus 6 pls with multiple illus, folio (10" x 14"), cloth. $100.00

___Another Copy. AMNH, Memoirs, Vol. II, Part I, 1898. 24pp, 6pp pls containing 93 faces, wraps. $58.00

B581. BOAS (Franz). (Columbia Univ. Contributions to Anthropology, Vol. XX, New York, 1934) Geographical Names of the Kwakiutl Indians. 83pp, 22 fold-out maps, cloth. $40.00

B582. BOAS (Franz). (University Museum, Anthropological Publications, Vol. VIII, No. I, Philadelphia, 1917) Grammatical Notes on the Language of the Tlingit Indians. 179pp, wrappers. $30.00

B583. BOAS (Franz). Handbook of American Indian Languages. (2 Volumes). Part I: 1,069pp. Part II: 903pp. The Netherlands, 1969 reprint of BAE Bulletin No. 40. $90.00

B584. BOAS (Franz). (American Museum of Natural History Bulletin, Vol. XVII, Part IV, New York, 1905) The Huntington California Expedition. Anthropometry of Central California. pp 347-380, photographs, wrappers. $45.00

B585. BOAS (Franz). Keresan Texts. (in two parts). Part I: 312pp, 1925. Part II: 344pp, 1928. Cloth, New York. $75.00

B586. BOAS (Franz). Kwakiutl Ethnography. Edited by Helen Codere. xxxvii, 439pp, frontis, numerous illus and photographs, map, complete bibliography of Boa's works, index, Univ. of Chicago, 1966 (1st ed.), d.j. $42.00

Edited by Codere in a manner to complete and round out the information or fill gaps as this is the first publication of Boas' manuscript which was incomplete at the time of his death.

___Another Copy. Same. $30.00

B587. BOAS (Franz) Editor. Kwakiutl Tales. viii, 495pp, Columbia Univ., 1910 (1st ed.). $45.00

B588. BOAS (Franz). (Columbia University Contributions to Anthropology, Vol. XXVI, Part II--Texts, New York, 1943) Kwakiutl Tales. 221pp, cloth. $48.00

B589. BOAS (Franz). (American Museum of Natural History Memoirs, Vol. V, Part II, New York, 1905) Kwakiutl Texts. pp 271-402, wrappers. $95.00

B590. BOAS (Franz). (American Museum of Natural History Memoirs, Vol. V, Part III, New York, 1905) Kwakiutl Texts. pp 403-502, wrappers. $95.00

B591. BOAS (Franz). The Mind of Primitive Man. 294pp, cloth, New York, 1929 (reprinted). $12.00

B592. BOAS (Franz). Primitive Art. 376pp, 323 illus, cloth, Oslo, 1927, New York, 1955. $30.00

This classic work, published in 1927 in Oslo for the Instituttey fur Sammenligende Kultur Forskning, but with a text in English, deals with all "primitive" cultures and peoples, but the emphasis is strongly North American, particularly Northwest Coast. For better than half a century this volume has been "must" reading. The text, a model of easily understood scholarship, is accompanied by hundreds of illustrations. (EAP)
____Another Copy. Oslo, 1951. $45.00

B593. BOAS (Franz). (Columbia University Contributions to Anthropology, Vol. X, New York, 1930) Religion of the Kwakiutl Indians, Parts I & II. (2 Volumes). 574pp, cloth. $95.00
____Another Copy. Same. $65.00
____Another Copy. Same. $65.00
____Another Copy. Same. $85.00

B594. BOAS (Franz). (American Folklore Society, Vol. XI, New York, 1917, 1st ed.) Folk-Tales of Salishan and Sahaptin Tribes. 205pp, wraps. $45.00

B595. BOAS (Franz). The Social Organization and the Secret Societies of the Kwakiutl Indians. Report of the U.S. National Museum for the Year 1895. 738pp, 215 figures, 51 pls, rebound in green cloth. $90.00

B596. BOCKSTOCE (J.). (Univ. of Alaska Monograph No. 38, 1979) The Archaeology of Cape Nome, Alaska. xiii, 133pp, 9pp of photographs, 28 figures, 3 maps, wraps. $40.00

B597. BOCKSTOCE (J. R.). (Pitt Rivers Museum Monograph Series, No. 1, Oxford, 1977) Eskimos of Northwest Alaska in the Early 19th Century. 139pp, 77 figures, 11 pls, wrappers. $30.00

B598. BODARD (Lucien). Green Hell. The Massacre of the Brazilian Indians. 291pp, photographs, map, cloth, New York, 1971. $12.00

B599. BODE (Barbara). The Dance of the Conquest of Guatemala. 85pp, illus, wrappers, Tulane Univ. 1961. $20.00

B600. BODGE (George W.). Soldiers in King Philip's War, Being a Critical Account of That War, with a Concise History of the Indian Wars of New England from 1620-1677. 502pp, 3 pls, 3 maps, appendix, has additional appendix containing corrections and new material, Boston, 1906. (3rd ed.). $75.00

B601. (BODMER, KARL). People of the First Man: Life Among the Plains Indians, the First Hand Account of Prince Maximilian's Expedition Up the Missouri River, 1833-1834. 256pp, numerous illus, approx. 50 color pls, 4to, New York, 1982, d.j. $75.00

B602. BOELTER (Homer H.). Portfolio of Hopi Kachinas. 62pp, plus index, 6 annotated color pls (11" x 14"), bibliography, color pls loose in protective envelope and slipcased. Hollywood, CA, 1969 (1st ed.). $150.00

B603. BOELTER (Homer H.) and DENTZEL (C. S.). Portfolio of Hopi Kachinas. 128pp, 16 full-page color lithographs, 39 sml drawings in a bound volume; the 16 color lithographs, unbound, in a portfolio, buckram in slipcase, Los Angeles, 1969. $350.00
Each color lithograph is accompanied by a synopsis of a Hopi Cult. Brilliant lithographs, splendid lettering, papers and binding, edition limited to 1,000 numbered and signed copies. (EAP)
___Another Copy. Same. $400.00

B604. BOEMUS (J.). Costumi, le Leggi et L'Usanze di Tutte le Genti; Divisi in Tre Libri ... e Tradotti per Lucio Fauno In Questa Nostra Lingua Volgare. Et Aggiontovi di Nuovo il Quarto Libro, Nelqual si Narra i Costumi et L'Usanze Dell'Indie Occidentali Overo Mondo Nuovo, da M. Pre Gieronimo Giglio. 240pp (four parts, books in one), several woodcuts in text and on title page. Book IV (leaves 193-240) relates to the New World (America). This is believed to be the first edition in which Book IV appears. 16mo, later vellum cvr, chipped, no foxing, Venetia, per Giovanni Bonadio, 1564. $575.00

B605. BOGLAR (L.) and KOVACS (T.). Indian Art from Mexico to Peru. text, 26pp, 251 pls with 40 in color, sml 4to, most of the artifacts come from the Ethnographical Museum, Budapest, 1983. $60.00

B606. BOGORAS (W.). (Publications of the American Ethnological Society, Vol. V, 1917) Korak Texts. vii, 153pp, wraps. $40.00
___Another Copy. Same. $30.00

B607. BOHANNON (Charles). Excavations at the Pharr Mounds, Prentiss and Itawamba Counties, Mississippi, and Excavations at the Bear Creek Site.... 163pp, illus, wraps, National Park Service, Washington, 1972. $20.00
___Another Copy. Same. $12.00

B608. BOLLAERT (William). Antiquarian, Ethnological, and Other Researches in New Grenada, Ecuador, Peru and Chile. 279pp, pls, frontis, rebacked, London, Trubner & Co., 1860 (1st ed.). $65.00

Field: 146. "Cyclopedia of the records of South
American Antiquities. Vocabularies of several Indian
dialects are given. Plates, ornaments, utensils, buildings, or idols. Author brings rare combination of learning, ability and zeal." (RMW)

B609. BOLLER (Henry A.). Among the Indians. Eight Years in
the Far West, 1858-1866. Embracing Sketches of Montana
and Salt Lake. 428pp, lrge folding map, original cloth,
Philadelphia, 1868. $1,000.00
Field: 147. Graff: 341. Howes: B-579. Sabin:
6221. Streeter Sale: 3079. Boller entered the fur trade
on the Upper Missouri in 1858, in the service of the
American Fur Company. Most of the book deals with his
experiences with the Indians in Montana as a trader for
the company, and his account is one of the most vivid
and well-written narratives of the trade, and one of the
few for the period in question. (WR)
_____Another Copy. Lakeside Classic, Chicago,
1959. $25.00

B610. BOLLES (John S.). Las Monjas, A Major Pre-Mexican
Architectural Complex at Chichen Itza. 304pp, oblong
4to, illus with photographs and plans, index, Norman,
1977 (1st ed.), d.j. $30.00

B611. BOLSTER (M. H.). Crazy Snake and the Smoked Meat Re-
bellion. 221pp, 21 illus, Boston, 1976. $20.00

B611a. BOLTON (Herbert E.). Coronado, Knight of Pueblo and
Plains. 491pp, 8vo, 2 maps, appendix, bibliography
and index. New York & Albuquerque, 1949 (1st
this ed.), d.j. $30.00

B612. BOLTON (Herbert E.). The Padre on Horseback: A
Sketch of Eusebio Francisco Kino--S. J. Apostle to the
Pimas. 90pp, map endpapers, drawings by William Wilke,
marbled bds, San Francisco, 1932 (1st ed.), d.j. $75.00

B613. BOLTON (R. P.). Indian Life of Long Ago in the City of
New York. 167pp, frontis, 30 pls, edition limited to 500
numbered copies, 4to, red cloth, New York, 1934.
$125.00
_____Another Copy. New York, 1971. $35.00

B614. BONAPARTE (Prince Roland). Le Habitants de Suriname:
Notes Recueillies a l'Exposition Coloniale d'Amsterdam en
1883. viii, 226pp, 59 full-page color photographs, 7
smaller photographs, 13 full-page color drawings of objects of material culture, 1 double-page color map, 1
fold-out color map, tissue guards, folio (12 1/2" x 18"),
Chaudenat I, 765, A. Quantin, Paris, 1884. $1,500.00
One of the most important works to have been published on the anthropology and ethnology of the Surinam
of Dutch Guiana, this work contains magnificent photographs and drawings. This copy of this rare publication
has been rebound and is in fine condition.

B615. BONAVIA (D.). Mural Painting in Ancient Peru. xi, 224pp, 16pp of color photographs, 92 b/w photographs, 35 drawings, cloth, Bloomington, 1985. $80.00

A meticulously researched and accurate record of all murals thus far discovered in the Central Andes, this study of an art form that flourished for more than 2,000 years before European contact was originally published in Spanish in 1974. This English edition expands the treatment of murals discussed in the 1974 edition and incorporates new information. Many of the illustrations in this seminal work--black and white and color photographs, drawings and site plans--are published here for the first time. (EAP)

B616. BONNELL (George W.). Topographical Description of Texas to which is Added an Account of the Indian Tribes. 150pp, facsimile reprint of rare 1840 edition, cloth, Austin, 1964. $15.00

BONNERJEA (Biren). See BAE Bulletin No. 178.

B617. BOOS (Frank). (Instituto Nacional Antropologia e Historia, Mexico, 1966) Colecciones Leigh y Museo Frissell de Arte Zapoteca. 121pp, 103 pls, in folio with ties, text in Spanish and English, wraps. $40.00

B618. BOOS (F.). (Instituto Nacional de Antropologia e Historia, Mexico, 1964) Mexico I. Las Urnas Zapotecas en el Real Museo de Ontario. 154pp, in a folio, Spanish and English text, 32pp photographs, wraps. $15.00

B619. BOOS (F.). (Instituto Nacional de Antropologia e Historia, Mexico, 1968) Mexico III. Colecciones Leigh, Museo Frissell de Arte Zapoteca. 45pp, 28 pls in folio with ties. $40.00

B620. BOOS (Frank). (Instituto Nacional de Antropologia e Historia, Mexico, 1964) Urnas Zapotecas en el Real Museo de Ontario. 87pp, 33 pls in folio with ties, text in Spanish and English. $45.00

B621. BORDEAUX (William J.). Sitting Bull. Tanka-Iyotaka. 7pp, frontis, wrappers, some material in this scarce pamphlet not available elsewhere, n.p., n.d. $25.00

B622. BOSSU (Jean B.). Travels Through That Part of North America Formerly Called Louisiana. (2 Volumes). Vol. I: viii, 407pp. Vol. II: (2), 432pp. Index, modern cloth, London, T. Davies, 1771 (1st English ed.). $425.00

Field: 157. "The first volume is almost entirely filled with historical and personal sketches of the Southern Indian Tribes."

B623. BOTURINI (Lorenzo). Idea de una Nueva Historia General de la America Septentrional. Fundada Sobre Material Copioso de Figuras, Simbolos, Caracteres y Geroglificos, Cantares y Manuscritos de Autores Indios.... (38), 167, (1), (8), (1)-96pp. Old limp vellum, sml quarto, lacks the frontis, some trivial worming, some waterstaining to the last four numbers in the imprint. Madrid, Juan de Ziniga, 1746. $500.00

Sabin: 6834. Medina Bha: 3408. Griffin: 1360. The first edition of this interesting and important work, to which is appended the "Catalogo del Museo Historico Indiano ...," listing the superb collection of manuscripts, maps and books which the author assembled during his eight years' residence in Mexico. Benaduci exerted great effort toward the collection of primary materials, learning the native languages, and making friends with the natives. Unfortunately, his marvelous library was confiscated by the Viceroy of Mexico, and due to neglect and abuse, is now virtually lost but for a small residue preserved in the Bibliotheque Nationale. "No collection of Mexican native materials before or since has equalled (it)...," Griffin. (WR)

B624. BOUCHARD (J. F.). (Inst. Francais d'Etudes Andines, Memoires 34, Paris, 1984) Recherches Archeologiques Dans la Region de Tumaco (Colombie). 205pp, 38pp of photographs, 43 figures, wraps. $35.00

B625. BOULTON (Alfred). Art in Aboriginal Venezuelan Ceramics. 252pp, numerous illus, text in Spanish and English, 4to (10" x 13"), Caracas, 1978. $100.00

B626. BOUNDS (Thelma V.). The Story of the Mississippi Choctaws. 25pp, illus, written for young readers, but with accurate information, wraps, Chilocco, 1958. $10.00

B627. BOURKE (John G.). An Apache Campaign in the Sierra Madre. An Account of the Expedition in Pursuit of the Hostile Chiricahua Apaches in the Spring of 1883. 112pp, plus ads, illus, 12 pls, New York, 1886 (1st ed.). $200.00

_____Another Copy. New York, 1958, d.j. $30.00
_____Another Copy. Same, sections of d.j. laid in. $20.00
_____Another Copy. New York, 1958, lacks d.j. $10.00

B628. BOURKE (John G.). The Medicine Men of the Apache. 100pp, 4to, illus, index, bibliography, Pasadena, 1971. $25.00

_____Another Copy. Same. $22.00

B629. BOURKE (John G.). Not for General Perusal. The Urine Dance of the Zuni Indians of New Mexico.... 4pp and title, in a modern binder, New York, 1885. $400.00

Evidently the rarest of Bourke separates on the odiferous ceremonies of the Zuni. As the Eberstadts put it: "Zany Zunies wee-wee in their teepees." Eberstadt: 123:21. (WR)

_____Another Copy. 7pp, wraps, n.p., 1920. $40.00
One of 100 copies privately printed, the second edition of this title originally printed in 1885.

B630. BOURKE (John G.). On The Border With Crook. xiii, 491pp, illus, 4pp advs, original pictorial cloth, New York, 1891 (1st ed.). $200.00

Howes: B-654. Graff: 367. Jenwein: 61. Rader:
426. Published in 1891, the year after General Crook's
death, this work by one of his staff is a readable primary
source for the campaigns which subjugated the Apaches.
In Edwin Corle's words, General Crook was the only White
man who ever made the Apaches cry ... he understood
them and the best of them loved him. It is a great pity
he couldn't have guided their destinies for another twenty
years. (TE)

B631.   BOURKE (John G.). Scatalogic Rites of All Nations. 483pp,
plus index, extensive bibliography, Washington, DC,
1891 (1st ed.). $300.00
___Another Copy. New York, 1934. $50.00

B632.   BOURKE (John G.). The Snake-Dance of the Moquis of
Arizona, Being a Narrative of a Journey from Santa Fe,
New Mexico, to the Villages of the Moqui Indians of
Arizona.... 371pp, frontis, 31 pls, many of them chromo-
lithographed, cloth, New York, 1884. $300.00
Graff: 368. Howes: B-655. Bourke's first large
ethnological work, based on his visit to the Hopi pueblos
in the summer of 1881.
___Another Copy. Printed in Edinburgh, some
                        copies have New York im-
                        print. Same as above. $300.00
___Another Copy. Chicago, 1962. $40.00
___Another Copy. Tucson, 1984. $18.00

B633.   BOURKE (John G.). With General Crook in the Indian
Wars. 59pp, 2 folding maps in color, 11 illus by Remington, Palo Alto, 1968 (limited ed.). $30.00

B634.   BOURNE (Benjamin Franklin). The Captive in Patagonia:
or, Life Among the Giants. A Personal Narrative....
233pp, frontis, illus, stamped cloth, slight foxing, signature starting, Boston, 1853. $125.00
Cowan: p. 65. Eberstadt: 103:39. The author was
captured at Patagonia on a schooner voyage to California,
escaped after three months and reached the gold mines
in February, 1850. Eberstadt lists a New York edition
of the same year, with additional 10 pages. An unusual
South American Indian captivity. (WR)
___Another Copy. Same. $55.00

B635.   BOUSEMAN (C. B.). (Southern Methodist University,
Archaeology Research Program, 1974) Archaeological
Assessment Alibates National Monument. 52pp, plus pls,
maps, bibliography, lrge 8vo, wrappers. $10.00

B636.   BOUSEMAN (C. B.). (Southern Methodist University,
Archaeology Research Program, 1974) Archaeological
Assessment Carlsbad Cavern National Park. 36pp, plus
pls, maps, bibliography, lrge 8vo, wrappers. $10.00

B637.   BOUSEMAN (C. B.). (Southern Methodist University,
Archaeology Research Program, 1974) Archaeological
Assessment Lake Meredith Recreation Area. 65pp, plus
pls, maps, bibliography, lrge 8vo, wrappers. $10.00

B638. BOUSEMAN (C. B.) and ROHRT (M.). (Southern Methodist University, Archaeology Research Program, 1974) Archaeological Assessment Big Bend National Park. 81pp, plus pls, maps, bibliography, lrge 8vo, wrappers. $10.00

B639. BOVALLIUS (Carl). (Swedish Society of Anthropology and Geography, Stockholm, 1886) Nicaraguan Antiquities. 52pp, 41 lithographic pls, 4 are in color, 2 folding maps, 1/2 cloth, bds. $250.00

___Another Copy. Managua, 1970. $70.00

B640. BOWDEN (Charles). Killing the Hidden Waters. 174pp, illus, index, maps, photographs, Austin, 1977 (1st ed.), d.j. $15.00

BOWDITCH (Charles P.). See BAE Bulletin No. 28.

B641. BOWDITCH (Charles). The Numeration, Calendar Systems and Astrological Knowledge of the Mayas. 339pp, 19 pls, original cloth, Cambridge, privately printed, 1910. $175.00

B642. BOWER (R. E.). The Unreached Indian, A Treatise on Indian Life and Indian Missions. 124pp, illus, wraps, Kansas City, 1920. $20.00

BOWERS (Alfred W.). See BAE Bulletin No. 194.

B643. BOWERS (Alfred W.). Mandan Social and Ceremonial Organization. xvi, 427pp, 44 figures, cloth, Chicago, 1950. $38.00

___Another Copy. Same. $45.00

___Another Copy. Same. $30.00

___Another Copy. Same. $25.00

B644. BOWMAN (Isaiah). Desert Trails of Atacama. 362pp, illus with photographs, 8vo, cloth, expedition to the desert of Atacama and the high ranges and plateaus of the central Andes mountains, much ethnographical information on the natives, American Geographical Society, 1924. $25.00

B645. BOWNAS (Samuel). An Account of the Captivity of Elizabeth Hanson, Late of Kachecky in New-England: Who with Four of Her Children, and Servant-Maid, Was Taken Captive by the Indians, and Carried Into Canada. 28pp, rebound in cloth, London, James Phillips, 1787 (new ed.). $145.00

B646. BOYD (Louise A.). (American Geographic Society, Special Publication No. 30, New York, 1948) The Coast of Northeast Greenland, With Hydrographic Studies in the Greenland Sea. (2 Volumes). Vol. I: xi, 339pp, 193 photographs and drawings. Vol. II: 7 fold-out maps with 5 fold-out photographs loose in cloth cvrd folio, cloth. $98.00

B647. BOYD (Julian P.) Editor. Indian Treaties Printed by Benjamin Franklin, 1736-1762. lxxxviii, 340pp, map, endpaper maps, index, edition of 500 copies, folio, contains 13 treaties reproduced in facsimile, with historical and biographical notes, Philadelphia, Historical Society for Pennsylvania, 1938 (1st ed.). $250.00

BOYD (Mark F.). See BAE Bulletin No. 169.

B648. BOYD (Maurice). (Linn Pauahty and the Kiowa Historical and Research Society, Consultant) Kiowa Voices. Ceremonial Dance, Ritual and Song. Volume I. 164pp, colored reproductions of Kiowa artists, photographs, drawings, music, poems, map, bibliography, index, Fort Worth, Texas, 1981 (1st ed.), d.j. $25.00
___Another Copy. Same, lacks d.j. $25.00

B649. BOYD (Robert K.). Two Indian Battles. 18pp. limited to 500 copies, wrappers, reprint of 1928 edition, describes battles of Birch Coulee and Little Big Horn, Grand Rapids, MI, 1972. $12.00

B650. BOYD (Thomas). Simon Girty: The White Savage. (8), 252pp, New York, 1928 (1st ed.). $60.00

BOYD (William C.). See BAE Bulletin No. 143, Vol. 6.

B651. BOYLE (David). Annual Report of the Canadian Institute, 1887. 58pp, 117 illus of artifacts excavated during the year, to include pottery, clay pipes, stone pipes, gorgets, totems, axes, beads, flints, objects of bone, horn and shell, wrappers, Toronto, 1888. $35.00
___Another Copy. Same. $25.00

B652. BOYLE (David). Notes on Primitive Man in Ontario. viii, 98pp, illus of over 260 artifacts, pipes, pottery, points, blades, effigies, etc., half leather, Toronto, Warwick Bros. and Rutter, 1895 (1st ed.). $75.00

B653. BRADBURY (John). Travels in the Interior of America in the Years 1809, 1810, and 1811. 364pp, imitation morocco, Ann Arbor, 1966. $20.00

B654. BRADFIELD (Wesley). (School of American Research, Monograph No. 1, Santa Fe, 1931) Cameron Creek Village: A Site in the Mimbres Area in Grant County, New Mexico. 127pp, plus 108 pls, folding site plan, stiff printed wrappers. $85.00

B655. BRADFORD (Alexander W.). American Antiquities and Researches Into the Origin and History of the Red Race. 435pp, New York, Dayton and Saxon, 1841 (1st ed.). $80.00
___Another Copy. Same, Good copy. $50.00
___Another Copy. Same. Rebound. $125.00

B656. BRADLEY (Zorro). Site Bc 236, Chaco Canyon National Monument, New Mexico. 127pp, illus, wrappers, National Park Service, Washington, 1971. $15.00

B657. BRADOMIN (J. M.). Historia Antigua de Oaxaca. 355pp, 192 photographs and drawings, Oaxaca, 1978. $18.00

B658. BRADY (Cyrus Townsend). Northwestern Fights and Fighters. xxvi, 373pp, ads, 23 pls, 8 maps, frontis portrait, cloth, New York, 1907 (1st ed.). $35.00

B659. BRADY (Cyrus T.). South American Fights and Fighters. 342pp, illus, New York, 1910. $25.00

B660. BRAIN (J. P.). On the Tunica Trail (Louisiana Indians). 22pp, maps, illus, bibliography, decorative wrappers, Baton Rouge, 1977 (1st ed.). $10.00

B661.   BRAIN (J. P.). Tunica Treasure. 347pp, 481 photographs, 173 figures, 4pp color photographs, 62 maps, 21 tables, wraps, Cambridge, 1980. $50.00

B662.   BRAINERD (G. W.). The Maya Civilization. 93pp, illus with 25 figures, 2 maps, wraps, Los Angeles, 1963.
                                                                          $20.00

    _____Another Copy. Southwest Museum, Los
                    Angeles, 1954. $12.00
    _____Another Copy. Los Angeles, 1963. $10.00

B663.   BRAINERD (G. W.). (Univ. of California Anthropological Records, Vol. 19, 1958) The Archaeological Ceramics of Yucatan. 378pp, illus, 4to, cloth. $85.00

B664.   BRAINERD (Thomas). The Life of John Brainerd, the Brother of David Brainerd, and His Successor as Missionary to the Indians of New Jersey. xii, (9)-492pp, frontis, pls, index, Philadelphia, Presbyterian Publishing Committee, 1865 (1st ed.). $100.00

B665.   BRAND (D. G.). (Smithsonian Institute of Social Anthropology, Publication No. 11, 1951) Quiruga, A Mexican Municipio. v, 242pp of text containing 4 maps, plus 35pp of photographs, wraps. $30.00
    _____Another Copy. Same. $20.00

B666.   BRANDON (Oscar T.). Fetishes and Carvings of the Southwest. 64pp, 4to, color illus, Santa Fe, 1976 (1st ed.). $18.00
    _____Another Copy. Same. $15.00
    _____Another Copy. Same. $10.00

B667.   BRANDT (Richard B.). Hopi Ethics. A Theoretical Analysis. 386pp, plus index, notes, bibliography, Chicago, 1954 (1st ed.), d.j. $40.00
    _____Another Copy. Same. $55.00

B668.   BRANSFORD (J. F.). (Smithsonian Contributions to Knowledge, Vol. XXV, 1885) Archaeological Researches in Nicaragua. 102pp, 2pp of photographs, 134 figures, cloth, worn. $150.00
    U.S. Navy expeditions in 1876 and 1877 and the collections acquired during the expeditions are described in this rare, century old publication. 788 objects were collected (many are illustrated), examples of which--for many--had never before been seen. Also included in this 509 page volume is Prehistoric Fishing in Europe and North America by C. Rau, a 342 page paper that contains 405 figures, many of them illustrations of aboriginal hooks, sinkers and carved objects found in North America and South America and the Pacific.
    _____Another Copy. Same. $115.00
    _____Another Copy. Same. $100.00

B669.   BRANSON (Oscar). Fetishes and Carvings of the Southwest. 64pp, photographs, wrappers, Santa Fe, 1976 (1st ed.). $10.00

B670. BRASSER (Ted J.). "Bo' jou, Neejee!" Profiles of Canadian Indian Art. 204pp, 191 culture object photographs (some in color), plus reproductions of early paintings depicting Indians, bibliography, endpaper maps, stiff wrappers, Ottawa, 1976. $20.00

B671. BRASSER (T. J.). (National Museum of Man, Ethnological Division Paper No. 13, Ottawa, 1974) Riding the Frontier's Crest: Mahican Indian Culture and Culture Change. iv, 91pp, 5 full-page pls, map, wrappers. $12.00

B672. BRAYER (Herbert O.). (Univ. of New Mexico, Bulletin 334, Albuquerque, 1939) Pueblo Indian Land Grants of the "Rio Abajo," New Mexico. 135pp, map, bibliography, wrappers. $15.00
____Another Copy. Same. $25.00
____Another Copy. Same. $15.00

B673. BRAYTON (Matthew). The Indian Captive. A Narrative of the Adventures of.... 68pp, 16mo, facsimile of the 1860 edition, Tucson, 1964. $15.00

B674. BREAZALE (J. F.). The Pima and His Basket. 146pp, 132 figures, Arizona Archaeological and Historical Society, Tucson, 1923 (1st ed.). $100.00
____Another Copy. Same, signed by author. $35.00
____Another Copy. 1982 reprint. $10.00

B675. BRENNAN (Louis A.). American Dawn. A New Model of American Prehistory. 378pp, plus index, drawings, chart, bibliography, London, 1970 (1st printing). $15.00
____Another Copy. New York, 1970. $15.00
____Another Copy. New York, 1971, signed by author, d.j. $22.00

B676. BRENNAN (Louis) Editor. Archaeology of Eastern North America. Volume 2, No. 1. 98pp, illus, wraps, Bronson Museum, Attleboro, MA, 1974. $10.00

B677. BRENNAN (Louis A.). Artifacts of Prehistoric America. 218pp, plus index, photographs, drawings, over 500 American stone age artifacts catalogued, identified and pictured, Harrisburg, 1975 (1st ed.), d.j. $20.00

B678. BRETERNITZ (D. A.). (Univ. of Arizona, Anthropological Papers, No. 1, 1959) Excavations at Nantack Village, Point of Pines, Arizona. xi, 77pp, 48 figures, wraps. $24.00

B679. BRETON (Adela). (Univ. of Pennsylvania, Transactions, Vol. II, Part I, 1906) Some Notes on Xochicalco. pp 51-65, 13 figures, 8 pls, rebound in cloth. $45.00

B680. BREUMMER (F.). The Arctic. 224pp, 62 color and 71pp of b/w photographs, 2 maps, cloth, Montreal, 1974. $50.00

B681. BREUNIG (R.) and LOMATUWAY'MA (M.). (Special Edition, Plateau, Vol. 54, Flagstaff, 1983) Kachina Dolls. 32pp, 26 color and 12 b/w photographs, chart, wraps. $10.00

B682. BREW (John Otis). (Peabody Museum Papers, Vol. 21, Cambridge, 1946) Archaeology of Alkali Ridge, Southeastern Utah. 345pp, 192 figures, wraps. $45.00

B683. BREW (John Otis). (Papers of the Excavators Club, Vol. 2, No. 1, Cambridge, 1943) A Selected Bibliography of American Indian Archaeology East of the Rocky Mountains. v, 90pp, wrappers. $25.00

B684. BRIGGS (Alton). (Texas Historical Survey Committee, Archaeological Report No. 9, Austin, 1971) An Archaeological Survey of Ingram Reservoir. 73pp, illus, wrappers. $12.00
    ____Another Copy. Same. $10.00

B685. BRIGHAM (William). Guatemala: Land of the Quetzal. Illus, New York, Scribner's, 1887. $50.00

B686. BRILL (Charles). Indian and Free: A Contemporary Portrait of Life on a Chippewa Reservation. Text and photographs by author, 144pp, lrge 8vo, cloth, Minneapolis, 1975. $20.00

B687. BRIMLOW (George F.). The Bannock Indian War of 1878. 241pp, endpaper maps, cloth, Caldwell, 1938. $50.00

B688. BRINE (Lindesay). Travels Amongst American Indians, Their Ancient Earthworks and Temples, including a Journey in Guatemala, Mexico, and Yucatan, and a visit to the Ruins of Patinamit, Utatlan, Palenque and Uxmal. 429pp, frontis, 32 pls, 10 maps and plans, 6 text illus, original decorated cloth, London, 1894. $150.00
    ____Another Copy. Same. $150.00
    ____Another Copy. Same, newly rebound in cloth. $100.00

B689. BRININSTOOL (E. A.). Crazy Horse the Invincible Oglala Sioux Chief. Inside Stories by Actual Observers of a Most Treacherous Deed Against a Great Indian Leader. 87pp, frontis, 8pp of photographs, Wetzel Publishers, 1949 (1st ed.), d.j. $70.00
    ____Another Copy. Same. $75.00

B690. BRININSTOOL (E. A.). Fighting Indian Warriors. True Tales of the Wild Frontiers. 353pp, New York, n.d., d.j. $12.00

B691. BRINTON (Daniel G.). The American Race: A Linguistic Classification and Ethnographic Description of the Native Tribes of North and South America. 392pp, wear at spine ends, cloth, New York, 1891 (1st ed.). $65.00
    ____Another Copy. Same. $60.00

B692. BRINTON (Daniel G.). The Lenape and Their Legends. 262pp, figures, index, with complete text and figures (in red) of the Walum Olum, or Red Score, No. 5 of Brinton's Library of Aboriginal America, Philadelphia, D. G. Brinton, 1885. $50.00
    ____Another Copy. Same. $35.00
    ____Another Copy. Same, New York, 1969. $20.00

B693. BRINTON (Daniel G.). A Lenape-English Dictionary.

Edited with Additions. 236pp, Philadelphia, 1888.
$85.00

___Another Copy. Philadelphia, 1889. $90.00

B694. BRINTON (Daniel G.). The Myths of the New World: A Treatise on the Symbolism and Mythology of the Red Race in America. 360pp, index. New York, 1968. $17.00

B695. BRINTON (Daniel G.). Notes on the Floridian Peninsula, Its Literary History, Indian Tribes and Antiquities. viii, (13), 202pp, 12mo, printed wrappers, Philadelphia, J. Sabin, 1859. $185.00

Howes: B-779. "Contains the first attempt at a Florida bibliography; only 100 copies said to have been printed."

B696. BRINTON (Daniel G.). On the Cuspidform Petroglyphs, or So-Called Birdtrack Sculptures of Ohio. Offprint from the Proceedings of the Academy of Natural Sciences of Philadelphia, 1884. pp 275-277, wraps. $10.00

B697. BRINTON (Daniel G.) Editor. (Brinton's Library of Aboriginal American Literature, No. 8, Philadelphia, 1890) Rig Veda Americanus: Sacred Songs of the Ancient Mexicans, with a Glossary in Nahuatl. 95pp, frontis, original cloth. $125.00

___Another Copy. Same. $95.00

B698. BRISBIN (Gen. James S.). Brisbin's Stories of the Plains; or, Twelve Years Among the Wild Indians, Chiefly from the Diaries and Manuscripts of George P. Belden. Detailing the Habits, Manners, Customs, Costumes, Fights, Ceremonies, Religious Ideas and Mode of Life Generally of the Wild Indians; Together with a Biographical Sketch of "Belden," The White Chief, from His Early Childhood in New Philadelphia, Ohio, to His Tragic Death at the Hands of Treacherous Indians on the Plains. 541pp, gilt decorative cloth, slipcase, St. Louis, 1881. $85.00

Howes: B-781. Best edition, adds "Stories of the Plains."

___Another Copy. Cincinnati, 1872, spotting on cvrs. $17.00

___Another Copy. Cincinnati, 1872. $30.00

___Another Copy. Athens, 1974, d.j. $15.00

B699. BRITT (Albert). Great Indian Chiefs. A Study of Indian Leaders in the Two Hundred Year Struggle to Stop the White Advance. 274pp, bibliography, endpaper maps, New York, 1938 (1st ed.), d.j. $25.00

B700. BRITTON (Davis). The Truth About Geronimo. 253pp, frontis, illus, New Haven, 1929 (1st ed.). $75.00

B701. BRODER (Patricia Janis). Hopi Painting. The World of the Hopis. 311pp, plus index, paintings in b/w and color, photographs, New York, 1978 (1st ed.), d.j.
$25.00

Large volume with 32 full-page color plates and over 200 b/w plates. Includes biographical sketches of

today's leading Hopi artists.
    Another Copy. New York, 1979, d.j. $20.00

B702. BRODERICK (Therese). The Brand. A Tale of the Flat-head Indian Reservation. 271pp, portrait, cloth, Seattle, 1909 (1st ed.). $50.00
    Another Copy. Same. $25.00

B703. BRODY (J. J.). The Chaco Phenomenon. 28pp, 72 figures, wrappers, Maxwell Museum of Anthropology, 1983. $12.00

B704. BRODY (J. J.). Indian Painters and White Patrons. 238pp, 4to, illus, index, bibliography, Albuquerque, 1971 (1st ed.), d.j. $30.00
    Another Copy. Same, lacks d.j. $45.00

B705. BRODY (J. J.) and LE BLANC (S. A. and C. J.). Mimbres Pottery, Ancient Art of the American Southwest. 128pp, 127 b/w and 42 color photographs, cloth, New York, 1983. $45.00
    Another Copy. Same. $30.00

B706. BROOKES (Samuel) and INMON (Byron). (Mississippi Archaeological Survey Report No. 3, Jackson, 1973) Archaeological Survey of Claiborne County, Mississippi. 76pp, text figures, wrappers. $10.00

B707. BROPHY (William A.) et al. The Indian. America's Unfinished Business. 227pp, plus index, photographs, Norman, 1966 (1st ed.), d.j. $17.00
    Another Copy. Norman, 1968, d.j. $10.00
    Another Copy. Norman, 1972, d.j. $15.00

B708. BROTHERSTON (G.). (British Museum Occasional Paper No. 38, 1982) A Key to the Mesoamerican Reckoning of Time, The Chronology Recorded in Ancient Texts. v, 91pp, 16 pls, 20 figures, wrappers. $25.00

B709. (BROTHERTON INDIANS). (Report of the Secretary of Interior, Senate Executive Document 45, 33:2, Washington, DC, 1855, 1st edition) Claim of Brotherton Indians. 28pp. Removed. $12.00
    Another Copy. Same. $10.00

B710. BROSE (D. S.) et al. Ancient Art of the American Woodland Indians. 240pp, 52 color and 132 b/w photographs, 3 maps, Detroit Institute of Arts, 1985. $50.00
    The prehistoric art and artifacts of Indians who lived in the area stretching from the Atlantic to the edge of the Plains and from the Great Lakes to the Gulf of Mexico were exhibited in 1985 and 1986 at three museums. This material, very seldom published (some never published) and even less seldom exhibited, is stunningly beautiful and ranges from objects that are elegantly simple to those that are very complex. The nearly 200 photographs and lively, scholarly text in this catalogue document the great power and beauty of these pieces. (EAP)
    Another Copy. Same. $35.00

B711. BROSE (D. S.) and GREBER (N.). Hopewell Archaeology, the Chilicothe Conference. xiv, 309pp, 33 photographs, 110 figures, Kent, Ohio, 1979. $45.00

B712. BROWDER (N. C.). The Cherokee Indians and Those Who
Came After. Notes for a History of the People Who
Settled Western North Carolina. 406pp, plus index,
drawings, map, bibliography, Hayesville, NC, 1980 (2nd
printing), d.j. $20.00
___Another Copy. Hayesville, NC, 1973. $17.00
B713. BROWER (Kenneth) Editor. Navajo Wildlands "as long as
the rivers shall run": Photographs by Philip Hyde, text
by Stephen C. Jett, with Selections from Willa Cather,
Oliver LaFarge and Others. Extracts from Navajo Creation Myth and Navajo Chants. 159pp, folio, illus, folding map, San Francisco, 1967 (1st ed.), d.j. $50.00
Large (10" x 14") in size, a beautiful volume of the
Sierra Club's "Exhibit Format Series." Full color illus
supplemented with descriptive text.
B714. BROWMAN (D. L.) Editor. Early Native Americans. Prehistoric Demography, Economy and Technology. vii,
478pp (25 papers), approx. 100 photographs and drawings, cloth, The Hague, 1980. $30.00
B715. BROWN (Allen). Indian Relics and Their Values. 109pp,
many photographs and other illus, Chicago, 1942 (1st
ed.). $20.00
B716. BROWN (C. S.). Archaeology of the Mississippi. 400pp,
354 illus, cloth, Peabody Museum, 1926, 1973. $48.00
B717. BROWN (Estelle Aubrey). Stubborn Fool. A Narrative.
309pp, illus with photographs, about life on the Indian
reservations, Caldwell, 1952 (1st ed.), d.j. $15.00
___Another Copy. Same, lacks d.j. $10.00
B718. BROWN (Frank and Marie). Mission to the Headhunters.
252pp, New York, 1961 (1st ed.), d.j. $20.00
B719. BROWN (D.) et al. (Univ. of Texas at San Antonio,
Center for Archaeological Research, Survey Reports,
No. 35, 1977) Archaeological Assessment of Two Sites
in Vicinity of Floodwater Retarding Structure No. 11,
Salado Creek.... 23pp, wrappers. $10.00
B720. BROWN (Dee). Bury My Heart at Wounded Knee. An
Indian History of the American West. 487pp, illus, in-
dex, New York, 1970 (1st ed.), d.j. $25.00
B721. BROWN (Douglas Summers). The Catawba Indians. The
People of the River. 400pp, frontis, illus, bibliography,
index, cloth, Univ. of South Carolina Press, 1966 (1st
ed.), d.j. $30.00
B722. BROWN (F. M.). America's Yesterday. 319pp, 52 illus,
includes Pueblos, Basketmakers, Mayas, Aztecs, Incas,
Mound-Builders, Philadelphia, 1937. $20.00
B723. BROWN (Joseph Epes) Editor. The Sacred Pipe: Black
Elk's Account of the Seven Rites of the Oglala Sioux.
xx, 144pp, 4 illus, index, Norman, 1967 (1st ed.), d.j.
                                                $20.00
___Another Copy. Norman, 1971. $15.00
___Another Copy. Norman, 1975. $18.00

B724. BROWN (Lionel). (Publications in Salvage Archaeology,
    No. 5, Lincoln, 1967) Pony Creek Archaeology. 121pp,
    illus, wrappers. $20.00

B725. BROWN (Mark). The Flight of the Nez Perce. 480pp,
    7 maps, 4 being double page, notes, bibliography, in-
    dex, New York, 1967 (1st ed.), d.j. $35.00
    ___Another Copy. Same, lacks d.j. $30.00
    ___Another Copy. Same. $21.00

B726. BROWN (Michael F.). Tsewa's Gift: Magic and Meaning
    in an Amazon Society. Washington, 1986, d.j. $20.00

B727. BROWN (Vinson). The Pomo Indians of California and
    Their Neighbors. 64pp, illus, index, folding map,
    wrappers, Healdsburg, 1969 (1st ed.). $10.00

B728. BROWN (William C.). The Indian Side of the Story ...
    Indian Wars and Treatment Accorded the Indians in
    Washington Territory, East of the Cascades in the
    Period, 1853-1889. xiii, 469pp, plus 26 photographs on
    16 pls with description on verso, index, Spokane, for
    Author, 1961 (1st ed.). $55.00

B729. BROWNE (Gertrude Bell). Hot Suns and the Great White-
    ness. A Story Depicting the Finer Customs and Cere-
    monials of Indian Life; and Includes the Great Battle Be-
    tween the Mohegans and Narragansetts, in 1643. 95pp,
    stiff wraps, Norwich, 1927. $20.00

B730. BROWNE (J. Ross). Adventures in Apache Country. A
    Tour Through Arizona and Sonora. 535pp, illus, fac-
    simile of the 1871 first edition, New York, 1974, d.j.
        $12.00
    ___Another Copy. Same. $25.00

B731. BROWNE (J. Ross). (Senate Executive Document 46, 36:1,
    Washington, DC, 1860) Correspondence Between Indian
    Office and the Present Superintendents and Agents in
    California, and J. Ross Browne. 44pp. Removed.
        $30.00

B732. BROWNE (J. Ross). The Indians of California. Edition
    of 500 copies. Illus with 3 pls after the author, half
    cloth, bds, San Francisco, Grabhorn Press, 1944, d.j.
        $85.00

B733. BROWNE (J. Ross). (Senate Executive Document No. 40,
    35:1, Washington, DC, 1858) Report ... Late Indian
    War in Oregon and Washington Territories. 66pp. First-
    hand accounts of the massacre of the Whitmans at Wailat-
    pu. Removed. $85.00

B734. BROWNELL (Charles). The Indian Races of North and
    South America.... With Numerous and Diversified Colored
    Illustrations. 720pp, illus (40 hand-colored), worn
    leather, rebacked, New York, 1856. $40.00
    ___Another Copy. Boston, 1853. $45.00
    ___Another Copy. Hartford, 1865, 760pp,
        added chapter. $55.00
    ___Another Copy. New York, 1858. Die

Indianischen Racen von Nord
und Sud Amerika. $45.00

B735. BRUCE (Robert). Pawnee Naming Ceremonial Near Pawnee,
       Oklahoma, Armistice Day, November 11, 1932. 36
       double-column pp, photographs, wrappers, New York,
       1933. $10.00

B736. BRUCE S. (Roberto). Lacandon Texts and Drawings from
       Naha. Coleccion Cientifica Linguistica. 158pp, wrap-
       pers, Mexico, 1976. $25.00

B737. BRUCE S. (Roberto). (Instituto Nacional de Antropologia
       e Historia, Mexico, 1976) Textos y Dibujos Lancandones
       de Naja: Trilingual Edition, Lancandon-Spanish-English.
       158pp, illus, wrappers. $25.00
       ___Another Copy. Same. $20.00

B738. BRUMBLE (H. David). An Annotated Bibliography of
       American Indian and Eskimo Autobiographies. 177pp,
       index, lists 577 items with descriptive annotation for
       each, Lincoln, 1981 (1st ed.). $25.00
       ___Another Copy. Same. $15.00

B739. BRUNDAGE (Burr Cartwright). Empire of the Inca.
       396pp, illus with photographs, Norman, 1963 (1st ed.),
       d.j. $40.00
       ___Another Copy. Same. $25.00

B740. BRUNDAGE (B. C.). The Jade Steps, A Ritual Life of
       the Aztecs. xiv, 280pp, 8 illus, cloth, Salt Lake City,
       1985. $35.00
       ___Another Copy. Same. $20.00

B741. BRUNDAGE (B. C.). Lords of Cuzco: A History and
       Description of the Inca People in Their Final Days. xiii,
       458pp, notes, bibliography, Norman, 1967. $45.00
       ___Another Copy. Same, has d.j. $20.00
       ___Another Copy. Same. $20.00

B742. BRUNHOUSE (F. L.). In Search of the Maya: The First
       Archaeologists. 243pp, story of Del Rio, Dupaix, Wal-
       deck, Stephens, Bourbourg, Le Plungeon, etc., Albu-
       querque, 1973. $20.00
       ___Another Copy. 1974 reprint. $15.00

B743. BRUNHOUSE (R. L.). Frans Blom: Maya Explorer.
       291pp, illus, Albquerque, 1976 (1st ed.). $25.00

B744. BRUNHOUSE (R. L.). Sylvanus G. Morley and the World
       of the Ancient Mayas. 341pp, plus index, photographs,
       maps, bibliography, Norman, 1971 (1st ed.), d.j.
                                                   $15.00

BRYAN (Alan). See BAE Bulletin No. 179.

B745. BRYAN (Bruce). (Southwest Museum Papers No. 22, Los
       Angeles, 1970) Archaeological Explorations on San
       Nicolas Island. 160pp, 4to, illus, endpaper maps, at-
       tractive hardbound volume detailing findings of the 1926
       L. A. Museum Expedition and the Southwest Museum Ex-
       pedition of 1958-60. (1st ed.). $25.00
       ___Another Copy. Same. $20.00

B746. BRYAN (K.) (Smithsonian Misc. Collections, Vol. 122, No. 7, 1954) The Geology of Chaco Canyon, New Mexico, In Relation to the Life and Remains of the Prehistoric Peoples of Pueblo Bonito. 65pp, 3 figures, 11pp of photographs, wrappers. $18.00

B747. BRYDE (John F.). Modern Indians. 535pp, maps, wrappers, n.p., 1969. $12.00

B748. BUCK (Daniel). Indian Outbreaks. 284pp, frontis, 8 pls, Mankato, Minnesota, privately printed, 1904 (1st ed.). $70.00

Howes: B-914. Covers Spirit Lake Massacre, Chief Little Crow, Lake Shetek Massacre, New Ulm, Battle of Red Wood Ferry, narratives of Justina Krieger and Justina Boelter.
___Another Copy. Same. $35.00
___Another Copy. Minneapolis, 1965. $10.00

B749. BUECHEL (Eugene). A Grammar of Lakota, the Language of the Teton Sioux Indians. 372pp, plus index, wraps, St. Francis Mission, 1939. $25.00

B750. BULL (Norris L.) (Connecticut Archaeological Appraisal No. 1, Hartford, 1931) Monolithic Axe Found in Connecticut. 22pp, 2 pls, printed wraps. $12.00

B751. BULLARD (W. R.). (Peabody Museum Papers, Vol. XLIV, No. 2, 1962) The Cerro Colorado Site and Pithouse Architecture in the Southwestern United States Prior to A.D. 900. xii, 205pp, 28 figures, 16pp photographs, wrappers. $30.00

B752. BULLEN (P.). (Peabody Foundation for Archaeology Papers, Vol. 1, No. 3, Phillips Academy, 1949) Excavations in Northeastern Massachusetts. xii, 156pp, 19 figures, 20pp of photographs, wrappers. $35.00
___Another Copy. Same. $35.00

BULLEN (Ripley P.). See also BAE Bulletin No. 169.

B753. BULLEN (Ripley P.) Editor. Proceedings of the 2nd International Congress for the Study of Pre-Columbian Cultures in the Lesser Antilles. vii, 146pp (17 papers, text in English and French), approx 100 photographs, drawings and maps, Barbados Museum and Historical Society, St. Anns Garrison, 1968. $20.00

B754. BULLEN (R. P.) et al. (Florida Anthropological Society, Publication No. 10, 1978) The Tick Island Site, St. Johns River, Florida. 25pp, 4to, 60 illus, wrappers. $15.00

B755. BUNCH (Roland and Roger). The Highland Maya: Patterns of Life and Clothing in Indian Guatemala. 97pp, illus (some in color), Josten's Publications, Visala, 1977. $15.00

B756. BUNKER (Robert). The First Look at Strangers. 151pp, illus, photographs, account of four groups of young students that lived and worked with the Papago and Navaho which was sponsored by Russell Sage Foundation, New Brunswick, 1959 (1st ed.), d.j. $15.00

B757. BUNKER (Robert). Other Men's Skies. 256pp, illus, map,
        portraying Indian life in the southwest, Bloomington,
        1956 (1st ed.), d.j. $20.00
        ___Another Copy. Same. $12.00
B758. BUNZEL (R. L.). Introduction to Zuni Ceremonialism.
        Removed from Smithsonian Institute Bureau of American
        Ethnology Annual Report No. 47, Washington, 1932.
        pp 467-544, rebound. $17.00
B759. BUNZEL (Ruth L.). (Columbia Univ. Contributions to
        Anthropology, No. 8, New York, 1929) The Pueblo
        Potter: A Study of Creative Imagination in Primitive
        Art. xii, 134pp, 38 pls, some pls in two colors, original
        bds. $125.00
        ___Another Copy. Rebound in 1/4 leather,
                          New York, 1929. $185.00
        ___Another Copy. Rebound in later cloth with
                          original wraps bound in,
                          New York, 1929. $150.00
B760. BUNZEL (Ruth L.). Zuni Katchinas. Extract from Smith-
        sonian 47th Annual Report for the Year 1932. pp 837-
        1,086, pls 21-61, 4to, wrappers. $125.00
B761. BUNZEL (R. L.). Zuni Origin Myths. Extracted from
        Smithsonian Annual Report No. 47 for the Year 1932.
        pp 545-609, rebound. $17.00
B762. BUNZEL (R. L.). Zuni Ritual Poetry. Extracted from
        Smithsonian Annual Report No. 47 for the Year 1932.
        pp 611-835, rebound. $22.00
B763. BURDICK (Usher L.). The Last Days of Sitting Bull,
        Sioux Medicine Chief. 188pp, illus, map, Baltimore,
        1941 (1st ed.). $65.00
           A well documented account of the Ghost Dance craze
        that led to Sitting Bull's death and the Wounded Knee
        massacre. Agent McLaughlin's papers and correspondence
        pertaining to these events are recorded in the appendix.
B764. (BURBANK, E. A.). Burbank Among the Indians, As Told
        by Ernest Royce. Edited by Frank Taylor. 232pp, color
        frontis, 55pp of illus, pictorial cloth, Caldwell, 1944
        (1st ed.), d.j. $50.00
        ___Another Copy. 1946, 2nd printing. $40.00
B765. BURGER (O.). Venezuela, Ein Fuhrer Durch Das Land
        und Seine Wirtschaff. vii, 272pp, 1 fold-out map, cloth,
        Leipzig, 1922. $22.00
B766. BURGER (R. L.). (Univ. of California Publications in
        Anthropology, No. 14, 1984) The Prehistoric Occupation
        of Chavin De Huantar, Peru. xv, 403pp, 445 figures,
        4 maps, wrappers. $40.00
B767. (BURIALS). (Illinois State Museum, Reports of Investi-
        gations, No. 15, Springfield, 1969) (No Title). 82pp,
        36 full-page photographic pls of burials and artifacts,
        8vo, wrappers. $15.00
B768. BURLAND (C. A.). An Account of Page One of Codex

Fejervary Mayer. 16 unnumbered pp, stiff wraps, page I of codex reproduced in serigraph by Louis Ewing, a pre-Columbian manuscript, Santa Fe, Museum of Navajo Ceremonial Art, 1950. $40.00

___Another Copy. Same. $25.00

B769. BURLAND (C. A.). Art and Life in Ancient Mexico. 112pp, 47 illus of artifacts from the British Museum and private collections, Oxford, 1948. $45.00

B770. BURLAND (C.) and FORMAN (W.). The Aztecs, Gods and Fate in Ancient Mexico. 128pp, 122 color photographs, cloth, London, 1975, 1985. (See Item #772.) $30.00

Published in 1975 under the title "Feathered Serpent and Smoking Mirror," this reissue includes all the great Werner Forman photographs that made this volume so popular. The highly readable text reviews the history of the Aztec Empire from 2,000 BC to the death of Montezuma at the hands of the conquistadors.

B771. BURLAND (C.). Eskimo Art. 96pp, 100 illus, 4to, bibliography, index, London, 1973, d.j. $20.00

___Another Copy. Same, lacks d.j. $30.00

___Another Copy. Same, lacks d.j. $22.00

B772. BURLAND (C.) and FORMAN (W.). Feathered Serpent and Smoking Mirror, Gods and Fate in Ancient Mexico. 128pp, 122 color photographs, cloth, London, 1975. $25.00

___Another Copy. Same. $12.00

B773. BURLAND (C. A.). The Gods of Mexico. 219pp, illus, London, 1967 (1st English ed.), d.j. $40.00

___Another Copy. Same. $20.00

B774. BURLAND (C. A.). Montezuma. Lord of the Aztecs. 265pp, plus index, photographs, many in color, bibliography, New York, 1975 (1st American ed.), d.j. $17.00

B775. BURLAND (C. A.). North American Indian Mythology. 153pp, 24 color pls, over 100 illus total, lrge 8vo, New York, 1965. $10.00

___Another Copy. London, 1970. $20.00

B776. BURLAND (C. A.). The People of the Ancient Americas. 157pp including 3pp index, photographs, some in color, drawings, maps, London, 1970 (1st ed.), d.j. $12.00

___Another Copy. Same. $12.00

___Another Copy. Same. $10.00

B777. BURLAND (C. A.). Peru Under the Incas. 144pp, illus, New York, 1967. $25.00

B778. BURNFORD (Sheila). Without Reserve. 242pp, drawings by Susan Ross, account of the Cree and Ojibwa Indians of Ontario Province, Boston, 1969 (1st ed.), d.j. $12.00

B779. BURNS (Robert I.). The Jesuits and the Indian Wars of the Northwest. xvi, 511pp, color frontis, 36pp of photographs, 9 maps, 3 are folding, bibliography, index, New Haven, 1966 (1st ed.), d.j. $40.00

___Another Copy. Same, lacks d.j. $30.00

B780. BURNETT (E. K.). (Contributions from Museum of the American Indian, Vol. XIII, New York 1944) Inlaid Stone and Bone Artifacts from Southern California. 60pp, 71 pls, 4to, illus, bibliography, wraps.　$35.00
___Another Copy. Same.　$25.00
___Another Copy. Same.　$20.00

B781. BURNETT (E. K.). (Heye Foundation: Contributions from the Museum of the American Indian, Vol. 14, New York, 1945) The Spiro Mound Collection in the Museum. Also: Historical Sketch of the Spiro Mound Forrest E. Clements. 68pp, 94 pls, wrappers.　$45.00

B782. BURNETTE (Robert). The Tortured Americans. 176pp, illus with photographs, account of the Indian in Modern America, Englewood Cliffs, 1971 (1st ed.).　$20.00

B783. BURT (Jesse) and FERGUSON (Robert B.). Indians of the Southeast: Then and Now. 304pp, frontis, illus with drawings and photographs, bibliography, index, pictorial cloth, Abington Press, 1973, d.j.　$20.00
___Another Copy. Same.　$12.00
___Another Copy. Same, lacks d.j.　$10.00

B784. BURTON (Frederick R.) American Primitive Music, with Special Attention to the Songs of the Ojibways. 281pp, appendix of 28 Ojibway songs with English words, frontis, New York, 1909.　$75.00
___Another Copy. Same.　$85.00
___Another Copy. Same.　$85.00

B785. BURTON (Jimalee). Indian Heritage, Indian Pride: Stories that Touched My Life. xvi, 176pp, illus with b/w and color pls, lrge 8vo, Cherokee Indian artist recounts tales and legends learned in childhood, Norman, 1974 (1st ed.), d.j.　$30.00
___Another Copy. Same, lacks d.j.　$20.00

B786. BURWASH (Major L. T.). Canada's Western Arctic. Report on Investigations in 1925-26, 1928-29, and 1930. 116pp, 8vo, illus with photographs, maps, including 1 folding, printed wrappers, Ottawa, F. A. Acland, 1931.　$25.00
　　　　Account of investigations from the MacKenzie Delta to King William Island and Hudson Bay, on the Eskimos, natural resources, fur trade, and on the area in which the Franklin Expedition was lost.

B787. BUSCHMANN (J. Carl E.). Die Verwandtschafts-Verhaltniffe Der Athapaskischen Sprachen. Zweite Abtheilung Des Apache. (1), (195), 252pp, 4to, bds, Berlin, Dummler, 1863 (1st ed. thus).　$150.00
　　　　Very scarce study linking the Apache and Athabaskan languages. Pilling, Athapaskan, p. 17. Field: 217.

BUSHNELL (David I., Jr.). See also BAE Bulletin Nos. 48, 69, 71, 77, and 83.

B788. BUSHNELL (David I., Jr.). (Smithsonian Misc. Collections, Vol. 81, No. 4, Washington, 1928) Drawing by Jacques

Lemoyne de Morgues of Saturioua, A Timucua Chief in Florida, 1564. 10pp, illus, wraps. $10.00

B789. BUSHNELL (David I., Jr.). (Smithsonian Misc. Collections, Vol. 99, No. 15, Washington, 1940) Evidence of Early Indian Occupancy Near the Peaks of Otter, Bedford County, Virginia. 14pp, photographs, drawing, map, wrappers. $10.00

B790. BUSHNELL (David I., Jr.). (Smithsonian Misc. Collections, Vol. 96, No. 4, Washington, 1937) Indian Sites Below the Falls of the Rappahannock, Virginia. 65pp, 11 figures, 21pp of photographs, wrappers. $28.00
___Another Copy. Same. $40.00

B791. BUSHNELL (David I., Jr.). (Smithsonian Misc. Collections, Vol. 94, No. 5, Washington, 1935) The Manahoc Tribes in Virginia, 1608. 56pp, 11 figures, 21pp of photographs, wrappers. $28.00
___Another Copy. Same. $18.00

B792. BUSHNELL (David I., Jr.). (Smithsonian Misc. Collections, Vol. 89, No. 12, Washington, 1934) Tribal Migrations East of the Mississippi. 9pp, 4 maps, wrappers. $10.00

B793. BUSHNELL (David I., Jr.). (Smithsonian Misc. Collections, Vol. 99, No. 1, Washington, 1940) Sketches by Paul Kane in the Indian Country, 1845-1848. 25pp, 11 illus, wrappers. $17.00

B794. BUSHNELL (G. H. S.). Ancient Arts of the Americas. 287pp, 197 b/w and 55 color photographs, wrappers, New York, 1965. $17.00

B795. BUSHNELL (G. H. S.). (Cambridge Univ. Museum of Archaeology and Ethnology, Occasional Pub. I, 1951) Archaeology of the Santa Elena Peninsula in Southwest Ecuador. xv, 155pp containing 52 figures, plus 5pp of photographs of artifacts, cloth. $35.00

B796. BUSHNELL (G. H. S.). The First Americans, the Pre-Columbian Civilizations. 144pp, extensive illus with photographs, many in color, New York, 1968 (1st ed.), d.j. $15.00
___Another Copy. Same. $10.00

B797. BUSHNELL (G. H. S.). Peru, ancient Peoples and Places. 216pp, 71 photographs, 12 line drawings, map, cloth, New York, 1958. $22.00
___Another Copy. Same. $10.00
___Another Copy. Same, New York, 1963. $15.00

B798. BUTCHER (Devereux). Exploring Our Prehistoric Indian Ruins. 64pp, illus, Washington, DC, 1952 (2nd ed.). $15.00

B799. BUTLER (James D.). Pre-Historic Wisconsin. Annual Address Given Before State Historical Society of Wisconsin, February 18, 1876. 22pp, 4 pls, stitched self wraps, Madison, 1876. $15.00

B800. BUTLER (James D.). Prehistoric Pottery from Missouri

and Arkansas in the Museum of the State Historical Society of Wisconsin. 4pp, plus photograph. Also: Prehistoric Remains in the St. Francis Valley (William J. Seever). 3pp, plus photograph, wrappers, Madison, 1894 (1st ed.). $12.00

B801. BUTLER (Mary). Three Archaeological Sites in Somerset County, Pennsylvania. 79pp, illus, map, printed wrappers, Harrisburg, Pennsylvania Hist. Commission, 1939. $18.00
___Another Copy. Same. $15.00
___Another Copy. Same. $30.00

B802. BUTLER (Robert). A Guide to Understanding Idaho Archaeology. 143pp, photographs, drawings, map, bibliography, Idaho State Museum, Pocatello, 1966. $10.00
___Another Copy. Same, 1968 (revised). $25.00

B803. BUTTERFIELD (Consul W.). An Historical Account of the Expedition Against Sandusky Under William Crawford in 1782. x, 403pp, portrait, cloth, Cincinnati, Robert Clarke Co., 1873 (1st ed.). $70.00
___Another Copy. Same. $110.00

B804. BUTTERFIELD (Consul W.). History of Brule's Discoveries and Explorations, 1610-1626. With a Biographical Notice of the Discoverer and Explorer, Who Was Killed and Eaten by Savages. 184pp, 1 errata, maps, pls, index, weak hinges, cloth, Cleveland, Helman-Taylor, 1898 (1st ed.). $85.00

B805. BUTTERFIELD (Consul W.). History of the Seneca County. 252pp, cloth, Sandusky, Campbell & Sons, 1848. $175.00
Howes: B-1064. "2,000 copies printed, 1,300 burned." Contains much on the Indians of the Ohio Country.

B806. BUTTREE (Julia M.). The Rhythm of the Redman. In Song, Dance and Decoration. xvii, 280pp, color frontis, pls, illus, musical scores, bibliography, index, decorative cloth, illus by Ernest Thompson Seton, the author's spouse, New York, 1930 (1st ed.). $45.00
___Another Copy. Same. $65.00
___Another Copy. Same, New York, 1938. $30.00

B807. BUXTON (Mary H.) et al. The Eskimo. 29pp, 4to, illus, wrappers, Museum of Fine Arts, Houston, 1969. $12.00

BYERS (Douglas S.). See also BAE Bulletin No. 180.

B808. BYERS (Douglas S.). The Prehistory of the Tehuacan Valley. (5 Volumes). Peabody Foundation, Andover, 1967-1972. Vol. 1: Environment and Substance. viii, 331pp, 187 figures, 38 tables, 1967. Vol. 2: The Non-Ceramic Artifacts. xiii, 258pp, 175 figures, 32 tables, 1967. Vol. 3: Ceramics. xi, 306pp, 157 figures, 72 tables, 1970. Vol. 4: Chronology and Irrigation. xi, 290pp, 99 figures, 15 tables, 1972. Vol. 5: Excavations and Reconnaissance. xii, 529pp, 201 figures, 1972. $250.00

B 809. BYERS (D. S.) and JOHNSON (F.). (R. S. Peabody
Foundation for Archaeology, Vol. 1, No. 1, Andover,
1940) Two Sites on Martha's Vineyard. 104pp, 7 pls,
printed wrappers. $15.00

BYINGTON (Cyrus). See BAE Bulletin No. 46.

B 810. BYNNER (Witter). Indian Earth. xvi, 77pp, cloth, contains poems based upon Southwest subjects to include
specific dances at some of the Pueblos, New York, 1929
(1st ed.). $40.00

-C-

C1. CACHOT DE GIRARD (R. C.). La Religion en el Antiguo
Peru. 147pp, 121 figures, 5pp drawings. Lima, 1959.
$30.00

C2. (CADDO). (House of Representatives Document 25, 27:2,
Washington 1841, 1st print.) Caddo Indian Treaty.
48pp, 3pp, removed. $10.00

C3. CADOZ (D. A.). Archaeological Studies of the Susque-
hannock Indians of Pennsylvania. 217pp, 141 illus, folding maps and profiles, notes, index. Harrisburg, 1936
(1st ed.). $22.00

C4. CADOZ (D. A.). (Museum of the American Indian, Notes
and Monographs, New York, 1920) Native Copper Objects of the Copper Eskimo. 22pp, 10 full-page photographs, 1pp drawings, wrappers. $30.00

C5. CAHLANDER (A.) and BAIZERMAN (S.). Double-Woven
Treasures from Old Peru. viii, 198pp, 138 b/w and 20
color photographs, 74 drawings, cloth. St. Paul, 1985.
$47.00
This new publication is a comprehensive look at the
varieties of pre-Columbian double cloth in museum and
private collections around the world. It contains more
than 200 illus and a text that describes in detail the examples studied by the authors, and discusses exactly
how each of the variety of textiles was woven. Many of
the types of double-woven textiles that are illus are
quite rare, and many have never before been published.
(EAP)

C6. CAIN (H. Thomas). Pima Indian Basketry. 40pp, 4to,
illus, some in color, wrappers. Phoenix, Heard Museum,
1962. $15.00

C7. CALASANCTIUS (Sister Marie J.). The Voice of Alaska:
A Missionary's Memories. 340pp, 8pp, folding map,
photographic pls, decorative wrappers a bit worn. Author spent 17 years among the Indians of the Yukon.
Smith: 1374. Quebec, 1935 (1st ed. in English)
$30.00

C8. CALDERON DE LA BARCA (Mme). Life in Mexico During a
     Residence of Two Years in That Country (2 Volumes).
     Vol. I: xii, 412pp. Vol. II: xi, 427pp. Engraved
     frontis, ex-library, half leather. Boston, 1843 (1st ed.).
                                                         $60.00
CALDWELL (Joseph R.). See also BAE Bulletin No. 154.
C9. CALDWELL (Joseph R.). (American Anthropological Assn.
     Memoir No. 88, 1958) Trend and Tradition in the Pre-
     history of the Eastern United States. xiv, 88pp, 14
     figures. $14.00
C10. CALDWELL (Martha B.). Annals of Shawnee Methodist Mis-
     sion and Indian Manual Labor School. 120pp, illus,
     wrappers. Informative chronology of the historic old
     mission from 1825 to 1865. Topeka, 1939 (1st ed.).
                                                         $40.00
     ___Another Copy. Same. $15.00
CALDWELL (Warren W.). See also BAE Bulletin Nos. 179 and 189.
C11. CALDWELL (Warren W.). (Publications in Salvage Archaeol-
     ogy, River Basin Survey, Lincoln, 1966) The Black
     Partizan Site. 145pp, illus, wrappers. $20.00
C12. (CALENDAR STONE, MEXICO). Vortrag Uber den Mexican-
     ischen Calendar-Stein, Gehalten von Prof. Ph. Valentini.
     32pp, folding pl, inscribed by author, wrappers. New
     York, 1878. $45.00
C13. CALIFANO (M.). Etnografia de los Mascha de la Amazonia
     Sud Occidental del Peru. 315pp, 22 full-page photo-
     graphs, 4 drawings, approx 100 illus of objects of mate-
     rial culture, 4 maps. Buenos Aires, 1982. $40.00
C14. (CALIFORNIA). (University of California Archaeological
     Research Facility, Contribution No. 30, 1976) Studies in
     California Paleopathology. 119pp, wrappers. $20.00
C15. (CALIFORNIA). (Senate Executive Document 4, Special
     Session, Washington, 1853) Report of the Secretary of
     the Interior, Communicating ... the Correspondence be-
     tween the Department of the Interior and the Indian Agents
     and Commissioners in California. 405pp, modern cloth,
     leather label, map, table. An enormous and very infor-
     mative compilation of first hand accounts of the state of
     the affairs of the California Indians at the time, including
     treaty negotiations, reservation policies, etc. $125.00
C16. (CALIFORNIA). (House of Representatives Executive Docu-
     ment 91, 43:1, Washington 1874, 1st print.) Mission In-
     dians of Southern California. 16pp, removed. Conditions
     and policies toward these Indians. $10.00
C17. (CALIFORNIA INDIANS). (Senate Report No. 1522, 48:2,
     Washington, 1855, 1st print.) Conditions of the Indians
     Upon the Round Valley Indian Reservation in California.
     197pp, 2 folding maps, index, removed. Life on the
     reservation in late 19th Century. $35.00
C18. (CALIFORNIA INDIANS). (Contributions of University of

California Archaeological Research Facility, No. 23, Berkeley, 1975) Ethnographic Interpretations: 12-13; Socio-Religious Aspects of Resource Management, and Practice of Warfare Among California Indians. 109pp, 4to, bibliography, map, wrappers. $12.00

C19. (CALIFORNIA INDIANS). Indians of California. 12 folders in a case, illus. Book Club of California, 1973. $25.00

C20. (CALIFORNIA INDIANS). (University of California Archaeological Research Facility Contribution No. 25, 1975) The Northern California Indians. 221pp, wrappers. $35.00

C21. (CALIFORNIA INDIANS). (University of California Archaeological Research Facility Contribution No. 9, Berkeley, 1970) Papers on California Ethnography. 158pp, 4to, wrappers. Articles by various authors covering census matters, rancheria names, mission records, basketry, culture, etc. $20.00
___Another Copy. Same. $15.00

C22. (CALIFORNIA INDIANS). (University of California Archaeological Research Facility Contribution No. 31, 1976) The Round Valley Indians of California by Amelia Susman: An unpublished Chapter in "Acculturation in Seven or Eight American Indian Tribes." 108pp and illus, wrappers. $35.00

C23. (CALIFORNIA INDIANS). (University of California Archaeological Research Facility Contribution No. 28, 1975) Stephen Powers, California's First Ethnologist and Letters of Stephen Powers to John Wesley Powell Concerning Tribes of California. 94pp, wrappers. $25.00

C24. (CALIFORNIA INDIANS). (University of California Archaeological Research Facility Contribution No. 22, 1974) Two Papers on the Physical Anthropology of California Indians. 57pp, 4to, wrappers. $10.00

C25. CALLEROS (Cleofas). El Paso's Missions and Indians. 55pp, illus with drawings by Jose Cisneros and photographs, map, wrappers. El Paso, 1951. $10.00
___Another Copy. Same. $10.00

C26. CALVIN (R.). Sky Determines, an Interpretation of the Southwest. 354pp, cloth. New York, 1934. $49.00
___Another Copy. Albuquerque, 1948. $35.00

C27. CAMERON (John). (Report of the Canadian Arctic Expedition, Vol. XII, Central Eskimos, Part C, Ottawa, 1923) Osteology of the Western and Central Eskimo. 67pp, illus, wrappers. $19.00

C28. CAMPBELL (E. W.) et al. (Southwest Museum Papers No. 11, Los Angeles, 1937, 1st ed.) The Archaeology of Pleistocene Lake Mohave. 118pp, maps, photographs, figures, bibliography, wrappers. $15.00

C29. CAMPBELL (Elizabeth W.). (Southwest Museum Papers No. 7, Los Angeles, 1963) An Archaeological Survey of the Twenty-Nine Palms Region. Introduction by Edwin F. Walker. 93pp, illus, map, wrappers. $12.00

C30. CAMPBELL (Marion). The Boyhood of Tecumseh. 193pp, cloth. Philadelphia, 1940.

C31. CAMPBELL (T. A.). (University of Texas, Center for Archaeological Research, Report on Archaeology and History of San Juan Bautista Mission Area, No. 3, San Antonio, 1979) Ethnohistoric Notes on Indian Groups association with three Spanish Missions. 76pp, bibliography, wrappers. $10.00

C32. CAMPBELL (T. J.). Pioneer Priests of North America, 1642-1710. (3 Volumes). Vol. 1, Among the Iroquois. xvi, 350pp. Vol. 2, Among the Hurons. xvi, 411pp. Vol. 3, Among the Algonquins. xxii, 312pp. pls, maps, indices, decorative cloth. New York, American Press, 1911, 1913, 1914. $80.00

C33. (CANADIAN ESKIMO ART). Canadian Eskimo Art. 40pp, 37 photographs. Dept. of Northern Affairs and Natural Resources, Ottawa, 1959. $12.00

C34. (CANADIAN INDIANS). Indian Self-Government in Canada: Report of the Special Committee. 203pp, illus, issue No. 40, Ottawa, 1983, wrappers. $20.00

C35. (CANADIAN INDIANS). (Canada Dept. of Mines, Bulletin No. 50, Ottawa, 1928) National Museum of Canada, Annual Report for 1926. Includes Archaeological Investigations in Bering Strait, 1926, by D. Jenness. 126pp, wrappers. $20.00

C36. (CANADIAN INDIANS). National Museum of Canada: Annual Report for 1927. Includes papers on Beothuk Indians, Kitchen Middens, Materia Medica of the Bella Coola Indians, Ottawa, 1929, wrappers. $20.00

C37. (CANADIAN INDIANS). National Museum of Canada: Annual Report for the Fiscal Year 1949-50. Included are 20 article reports, five being well-illus articles dealing with Eskimo or Northwest Coast art and archaeology. 261pp, Ottawa, 1951. $17.00
_____Another Copy. Same. $25.00

CANALS (Frau Salvadore). See BAE Bulletin No. 143.

C38. CANCIAN (Frank). Economics and Prestige in a Maya Community. The Religious Cargo System in Zincantan. 213pp plus index, photographs, charts, appendices, bibliography, glossary. Standord CA, 1965 (1st ed.), d.j. $15.00

C39. CANESTRELLI (Philip S. J.). A Kootenai Grammar. 5pp, 144pp, 1st reprinting of Jesuit Father Canestrelli's rare work. Spokane, 1959, limited ed. $40.00

C40. CANESTRELLI (Philip). Nchaumen/Lu Kaeks-Suaum L'agal/ potu Hoi La Sainte Messe. 1pp. St. Ignatius (1891?) $75.00
        A rare St. Ignatius Mission single-sheet imprint. This broadside gives the Kalispel version of 3 prayers recited after low mass. Pilling attributes this imprint to Father Canestrelli, and dates it 1891. Mr. Philipp Callagahn, S.J., in his manuscript checklist of mission imprints,

suggests that since Pope Leo XIII ordered these prayers to be said after Mass in 1884, it is more probable that the Missionaries would have printed them for Indian use in 1885. (GFH)

C41. CANFIELD (Gae Whitney). Sarah Winnemucca of the Northern Paiutes. 306pp, illus, map, bibliography, index. Covers Sarah Winnemucca's life from birth in 1844 to death in 1891. Much on her tireless work for the physical welfare and education of the Paiutes and all Indians. Norman, 1983 (1st ed.), d.j. $22.00
_____Another Copy. Same. $20.00

C42. CANNON (C. J.). Lazaro in the Pueblos. The Story of Antonio Espejo's Expedition into New Mexico. 197pp, 1 color-4 b/w drawings, cloth. Boston & New York, 1931. $37.00

C43. CAPITAN (M. Le R.). Quelques Caracteristiques de l'Architecture Maya dans la Yucatan Ancien. Extrait des Mem. de l'Academie des Inscriptions et Belles Lettres Tome XII, 2 Partie, Paris, 1912. 32pp, 13 illus, on 5 pls, 12 figures, wrappers. $45.00

C44. CAPPS (Benjamin). The Indians. 240pp, 4to, illus, bound in imitation padded leather. New York, 1974. $15.00

C45. CAPPS (Benjamin). The Warren Wagontrain Raid. 298pp, photographs, maps, notes, index. New York, 1974 (1st ed.). $25.00
_____Another Copy. 1974 reprint, 233pp, index. $15.00

CAPRON (Louis). See also BAE Bulletin No. 151.

C46. CAPRON (Louis). The Medicine Bundles of the Florida Seminole and the Green Corn Dance. 55pp, illus, wrappers. Offprint from Bureau of American Ethnography Bulletin 151, Anthropological Paper, No. 35. $10.00

C47. (CAPTIVITY). (Rister, Carl Coke). Comanche Bondage; Dr. John Charles Beale's Settlement of La Villa de Delores on Las Moras Creek in Southern Texas in the 1830s, with an Annotated Reprint of Sarah Ann Horn's Narrative of Her Captivity Among the Comanches, Her Ransom by Traders in New Mexico and Return Via the Santa Fe Trail. 212pp, illus, map, bibliography, index, deckle edges. Glendale, 1955. $50.00

C48. (CAPTIVITY). Events in Indian History. 632pp (?) (last few pages of appendix are missing), full calf, 8 engravings, (tears in pls), hinges weak. Lancaster, G. Hills, 1841. $25.00

C49. (CAPTIVITY). (Meredith, Grace E.). Girl Captives of the Cheyenne; a True Story of the Capture and Rescue of Four Pioneer Girls, 1874. 140pp, illus, 12mo, new frnt endpapers. Los Angeles, 1927. $85.00

C50. (CAPTIVITY). Han Staden: The True History of His Captivity, 1557, (Brazil). Translated and Edited by Malcolm Letts, with an Introduction and Notes. 191pp, maps, cloth. London, 1928. $15.00

C51. (CAPTIVITY). The Indian Captive; or, A Narrative of the Captivity and Sufferings of Zadock Steele, Related by Himself, to Which is Prefixed an Account of the Burning of Royalton. Frontis, 166pp, folding map, limited to 526 copies, boxed, paper labels. Springfield, 1908. $75.00
___Another Copy. Same. $55.00

C52. (CAPTIVITY). The Indian Captivity of O. M. Spencer. 188pp, frontis, 12mo. Chicago, Lakeside Press, 1917. $25.00
___Another Copy. New York, 1968. $25.00

C53. (CAPTIVITY). A Narrative of the Captivity of Mrs. Johnson, Containing an Account of Her Sufferings, During Four Years, with the Indians and French. 111pp, leather backed bds. New York, 1841. $75.00
Newberry "Narratives of Captivities," No. 123. The first edition was printed in New Hampshire, 1796. (B. Fein)

C54. (CAPTIVITY). Narrative of the Capture and Providential Escape of Misses Frances and Almira Hall, Two Respectable Young Women ... Likewise is Added the Interesting Narrative of Captivity and Sufferings of Philip Brigdon. 24pp, frontis, pictorial wrappers, rebound in 1/4 morocco and cloth, original wrappers saved in binding. New York, 1832. $600.00
Ayer: 210. Buck: 244. Howes: H-61. The uncommon original edition of this popular captivity. The Hall sisters were spirited away from a settlement on the Fox River by members of the Sac and Fox tribe; they suffered the usual indignities and witnessed the Indians' continued molestations of frontier settlements during their captivity. The sisters survived, perhaps because Brigdon "an unfortunate Kentuckian" kept them company. Howes suggests authorship by W. P. Edwards, the perpetrator of the Lewis captivity account; Howes also suggests this first edition appeared in St. Louis, though others disagree. (WR)

C55. (CAPTIVITY). A Narrative of the Horrid Massacre by the Indians, of the Wife and Children of the Christian Hermit, a Resident of Missouri with a Full Account of His Life and Sufferings, Never Before Published. 24pp, plain wrappers, stitched. St. Louis, 1840. $1,250.00
Ayer: 214. Howes: N-14. Missouri Imprints: 280. This tract describes the captivity of the author, after the massacre of his family, in Missouri in 1815. He was evidently taken northwards to Iowa, and made his escape from there, returning to northern Missouri to live as a hermit. This last sheds some doubts on the veracity of the tale, since this withdrawal from the world and turning to God after a disastrous brush with the wild is a common theme of several other Indian Captivities and ephemeral publications of the period. The work in any case is a rare western imprint and is listed by Ayer as fact. (WR)

C56. (CAPTIVITY). Plummer, Clarissa, pseud. Narrative of the
        Captivity and Extreme Sufferings of Mrs. Clarissa Plum-
        mer Who, with Mrs. Caroline Harris ... Were, in the
        Spring of 1835 ... Taken Prisoners by ... the Comanche
        Tribe of Indians, While Emigrating to Texas.... 24pp,
        original wrappers bound in, rear wrapper reinforced,
        last leaf torn, affecting about fifteen words, supplied in
        expert facsimile, half calf, marbled bds. New York,
        Perry and Cooke, 1838. $3,250.00
           Streeter: 1320. Wagner-Camp: 71. Raines: p.166.
        Rader: 2686. Howes: P-427. Graff: 3310. Ayer:
        209. Field: 1223. Jones: 1018. This is a sensational-
        ized version of the "Rachael Plummer's Narrative," pub-
        lished in Houston in 1838 and known in only one copy,
        in the Western Americana Collection at Yale. This edition
        is only slightly less rare than the Houston issue. (WR)
C57. (CAPTIVITY). The Surprising Adventures and Sufferings
        of John Rhodes, A Seaman of Workington.... 250pp,
        1/2 leather, marbled bds by Bayntun. New York, R.
        Cotton, 1798 (1st ed.). $450.00
           Sabin: 70763. Field: 1298. Ayer, Supplement 1,
        123. Field: "There is nothing in this narrative to attest
        its truth ... contains some curious details of the customs
        of the Indians of Central America." (RMW)
        _____ Another Copy. Same. Rebound in calf
                            backed marbled bds with
                            morocco label stamped in
                            gilt. $300.00
C58. CARDENAS (Juan de). (Vol. IX Coleccion de Incunables
        Americanos, Madrid, 1945) Problems y Secretos Mara-
        villosos de las Indias. Facsimile of Mexico 1591 edition.
        248pp, wrappers. $40.00
C59. CARDOS DE M. (Amalia). (Acta Anthropologia, Vol. II,
        No. 1, Mexico, 1959) El Comercio de los Mayas Antiguos.
        151pp, illus wrappers. $25.00
C60. CARLETON (James Henry). Diary of an Excursion to the
        Ruins of Abo, Quarra and Gran Quivira in New Mexico
        in 1853. Under the Command of Major James Henry Carle-
        ton. 61pp, map, 16mo, limited to 750 copies. Complete
        reprint of report originally appearing in the 9th Annual
        Report of Smithsonian Institution. Santa Fe, 1965, d.j.
                                                      $20.00
C61   CARLSON (Roy L.). (University of Colorado Anthropology
        Series, No. 10, 1965) Eighteenth Century Navajo Fort-
        resses of the Gobernador District. viii, 116pp, pls,
        maps, figures, bibliography, wrappers. $15.00
C62. CARLSON (Roy) (Editor). Indian Art Traditions of the
        Northwest Coast. 214pp, 4to, illus, wrappers. Simon
        Fraser University, Burnaby, 1976. $30.00
C63. CARMACK (R. M.) and MONDLOCH (J. L.). El Titulo de
        Totonicapan. 283pp, illus, 4to, wrappers. UNAM,
        Mexico, 1983. $35.00

C64. CARMACK (R. M.). The Quiche Mayas of Utatlan. 435pp, illus. Norman, 1981 (1st ed.). $30.00

C65. CARMICHAEL (A.). Indian Legends of Vancouver Island. 97pp, 16 woodcuts and etchings by J. Semeyn, cloth. Toronto, 1922. $50.00

C66. CARMICHAEL (E.) et al. Hidden Peoples of the Amazon. 96pp, 57 b/w and 8 color photographs, 20 drawings, 2 maps. British Museum, 1985. $13.00

C67. CARMICHAEL (Elizabeth). Turquoise Mosaics from Mexico. 40pp, illus, some in color, wrappers. British Museum, 1970. $12.00

C68. CARPENTE (E.) et al. Eskimo. 68pp, 13 photographs, 26 b/w drawings of persons, places, 11 b/w drawings of artifacts, 4 color drawings, 2 maps, cloth, folio ($11\frac{1}{4}$" x $12\frac{1}{4}$"). Toronto, 1959. $40.00

C69. CARPENTER (E.). Eskimo Realities. 217pp, illus, photographs of artifacts. New York, 1973. $40.00
___Another Copy. Same. $25.00

C70. CARPENTER (Frank). Adventures in Geyser Land. 341pp, illus, bibliography. Yellowstone, Yellow Wolfe, Nez Perce War, eye-witness account of Chief Joseph's retreat, originally published in 1878. Caldwell, 1935. $60.00
___Another Copy. $25.00

C71. CARR (Bob). A Night Ride in Arizona. 10pp, 8pp, photographs, limited ed., signed by author, wrappers. On the Paiute Indians. Verdi, NV, 1968 (1st ed.). $10.00

C72. CARR (Lucien). The Food of Certain American Indians and their Methods of Preparing It. 38pp, wrappers. Separate printing from the Proceedings of the American Antiquarian Society. Worcester, 1895. $15.00

C73. CARR (R. F.) and HAZARD (J. E.). Tikal Reports. (Number 11). iv, 26pp of text, plus 10 lrg unbound fold-out maps in folio. University Museum, Philadelphia, 1961. $30.00

C74. CARRASCO (Pedro). (America Indigenas, Vol. 11, No. 2, 1951) Las Culturas Indigenas de Oaxaca, Mexico. pp100-114, with summary in English, wrappers. $10.00

C75. CARRASCO (Pedro). Los Otomies. 355pp, illus, limited to 500 copies, wrappers. Mexico, 1950. $45.00

C76. CARRASCO (Pedro). (Middle American Research, Tulane University, 1952) Tarascan Folk Religion: An Analysis of Economic, Social and Religious Interactions. 63pp, wrappers. $15.00

C77. CARRE (L.). Les Arts Anciens de l'Amerique. xxiv, 120pp of text and 26 full-page photographs. Musee des Arts Decoratifs, Palais du Louvre, Pavillion de Marsan, Paris, 1928. $55.00

C78. CARRIGHAR (Sally). Moonlight at Midday. 392pp plus index, photographs. New York, 1958 (1st ed.), d.j. $10.00

C79. CARRIKER (Robert C.). The Kalispel People. 104pp,

photographs (some in color), map, brief reading list, signed by a tribal chieftain, wrapper. From the Indian Tribal Series. Phoenix, 1973 (1st ed.). $15.00

C80. CARRINGTON (Henry B.). The Indian Question. An Address. 32pp, 2 fold-out maps, photographs, reprint of 1884 ed. New York, 1973. $10.00

C81. CARRINGTON (Mrs. Henry B.). As-Sa-Ra-Ka Home of the Crows; Being the Experience of an Officer's Wife on the Plains.... 284pp, folding map (repaired), illus, re-backed, some cvr wear. Philadelphia, 1868 (1st ed.). $200.00

_____Another Copy. Same. $175.00

_____Another Copy. Philadelphia, 1878 (4th ed., revised and enlarged).... With an Outline of Indian Operations and Conferences from 1865 to 1878. 378pp, 5pp of advs, 15 pls, 2 folding maps, inscribed and signed by Col. Carrington. $90.00

C82. CARROLL (John M.) (Editor). The Eleanor H. Hinman Interviews on the Life and Death of Crazy Horse. 48pp. 1pp, drawings by Larry Bjorklund, signed by Hinman, Carroll and illustrator, limited to 100 copies. New Brunswick, NJ, 1976 (1st ed.). $60.00

_____Another Copy. Same. $45.00

C83. CARROLL (John M.). The Papers of the Order of Indian Wars. 287pp, illus. Ft. Collins, 1975 (1st ed.), d.j. $30.00

C84. CARROLL (John M.). Sitting Bull Fraud. 11pp, photographs on wrappers, limited to 100 copies, signed by Carroll. Interesting reproduction of a rare pamphlet with Carroll's explanation that purports to show Sitting Bull's knowledge of Latin, French, Greek, German, English, etc. A curious fraud of the 1870s. Bryan, TX, 1978 (1st ed.). $10.00

C85. CARTER (Anthony). (Indian Heritage Series, No. 2, Vancouver, 1968, 1st ed.) This is Haida. 139pp, lrg 8vo, photographs, d.j. $15.00

C86. CARTER (G. F.). (Viking Fund Publications in Anthropology, No. 5, 1945) Plant Geography and Culture History in the American Southwest. 140pp, 27 figures. $19.00

CARTER (John G.). See BAE Bulletin No. 119.

C87. CARTWRIGHT (George). A Journal of Transactions and Events, During a Residence of Nearly Sixteen Years on the Coast of Labrador; Containing Many Interesting Particulars, Both of the Country and Its Inhabitants, Not Hitherto Known (3 Volumes). 287pp, 505pp, 248pp, 15pp, frontis of author in Arctic garb, 2 lrg folding maps, calf with marbled bds. Newark, 1792. $3,250.00

Lande: 106. TPL: 586. Sabin: 11150. The author, formerly a British army officer, made six expeditions to Newfoundland and Labrador between 1770 and 1786. The journals describe his explorations, hunting and trapping along the coast. The volumes contain extensive descriptions of Indians, Eskimos and the fauna he encountered. (WR)

C88. CARVAJAL (Gaspar De). The Discovery of the Amazon, According to the Account of Friar Gaspar de Carvajal (1541-1543), and Other Documents. Published with an Introduction by Jose T. Medina. Translated by Bertram T. Lee. 467pp, map, facs, cloth. New York, 1934. $20.00

    The manuscript was discovered and published by Medina in 1894. This is the first English translation. (CLR)

C89. CARVER (Norman Jr.). Silent Cities of Mexico and the Maya. 216pp, 170 photographs, site plans. Kalamazoo, 1986. $30.00

C90. CASAGRANDE (L. B.) and BOURNS (P.). Side Trips, The Photography of Sumner W. Matteson 1898-1908. 249pp, 173 photographs, wrappers. Milwaukee, 1983. $40.00

CASANOVA (Eduardo). See BAE Bulletin No. 143.

C91. CASANOWICZ (Immanuel M.). (U.S. National Museum Bulletin No. 148, Washington, 1929, 1st ed.) Collections of Objects of Religious Ceremonial in the United States National Museum. viii, 207pp, photographic pls, index, wrappers. $25.00

C92. CASAS (Bartolome de las). Il Supplice Schiavo Indiano.... 118pp, 2pp, sml quarto, half calf, stain running at gutter of leaves, title-leaf cracking at gutter. Venice, Marco Ginammi, 1636. $200.00

    Alden: 636/14. Sabin: 11236. Medina BHA 1085n. JCB (3)II:434. The first Italian edition of Las Casas' Sixth Tract, in which the case for the restoration of freedom to the Indians is discussed based on judicial and other authorities. The text appears in parallel column with the original Spanish text. (WR)

C93. CASE (Rev. and Mrs. Harold W.). 100 Years at Ft. Berthold. The History of Fort Berthold Indian Mission 1876-1976. 575pp, photographs, map, signed by Mrs. Case. The mission, missionaries and various Indians of the Mandan, Hidatsa and Ree tribes that resided at this reservation. Ft. Berthold, 1977 (1st ed.), d.j. $15.00

C94. CASEBIER (Dennis G.). Camp Beale's Springs and the Hualpai Indians. 233pp plus index, photographs, drawings, maps, notes, endpaper maps, signed by author. Detailed account of this Arizona army outpost 1871-1874, with much on relations and warfare with the Indians in Northwestern Arizona. Norco, CA, 1980 (1st ed.). $25.00

    _____Another Copy. Same. $20.00

C95. CASH (Joseph H.). The Sioux People. 106pp, photographs (some in color), maps, wrappers, signed by tribal chieftain. Part of the Indian Tribal Series. Phoenix, 1971 (1st ed.). $17.00

C96. CASO (A.). The Aztecs, People of the Sun. xvii, 125pp, 16pp photographs, 41 color drawings by M. Covarrubias, cloth. Norman, 1958. $45.00
___Another Copy. Norman, 1978. $18.00

C97. CASO (A.). Bibliografia de las Artes Populares de Mexico. Memorias del Instituto Nacional Indigenista, Vol. I, No. 2. pp83-132, several pls, one in color, 4to, wrappers. Mexico, 1950. $40.00

C98. CASO (A.). Interpretacion del Codice Gomez de Orozco. 20pp, fold-out color photograph in rear pocket, 8 figures, decorated bds and cloth. Mexico City, 1954. $20.00

C99. CASO (A.) et al. (Instituto Nacional de Antropologia e Historia, Mexico, 1967) La Ceramica de Monte Alban. 471pp, 401 illus, 32 color pls, bibliography, appendix, lrg 4to, many artifacts displayed, cloth. $100.00
___Another Copy. Same. $95.00

C100. CASO (A.). Thirteen Masterpieces of Mexican Archaeology. Translated by E. Mackie, J. R. Acosta. 131pp, text in English and Spanish, 13 illus (several in color), sml 4to, wrappers. Mexico City, 1938. $50.00
___Another Copy. Same. $50.00
___Another Copy. Same. $45.00
___Another Copy. Same. $17.00

C101. CASO (A.) and BERNAL (I.). (Instituto Nacional de Antropologia e Historia, Memorias II) Urnas de Oaxaca. 389pp, 527 illus, mostly photographs. Mexico City, 1952. $135.00

C102. CASSELLS (E. S.). The Archaeology of Colorado. vi, 325pp, 148 figures. Boulder, 1983. $24.00

C103. CASTETTER (E. F.) and OPLER (M. E.). The Ethnobiology of the Chiricahua and Mescalero Apache. 63pp, wrappers. University of New Mexico, Albuquerque, 1936. $35.00

C104. CASTETTER (E. F.) and UNDERHILL (R. M.). (University of New Mexico Bulletin 275, Albuquerque, 1935) Ethnobiology of the Papago Indian. 84pp. $17.00

C105. CASTETTER (Edwards) and BELL (Willis). Yuman Indian Agriculture, Primitive Subsistence on the Lower Colorado and Gila Rivers. Folding map. University of New Mexico, 1951. $35.00

C106. CASTILE (G. P.) (Editor). The Indians of Puget Sound, The Notebooks of Myron Eells. xix, 470pp, 296 photographs, 2 maps, cloth. Seattle, 1985. $48.00
     Nearly a century after it was written, here for the first time, is the historic monograph of missionary Myron Eells. The writing began in 1875, and the work was revised for the next twenty years. In a classic ethnographic approach, Eells includes chapters on all elements of Puget Sound Indian life, with particular emphasis on material culture. There are many fascinating 19th Century photographs, in addition to the many photographs of artifacts

collected by Eells--most of which have not been previously published. (EAP)

C107. CASTILE (G. P.). North American Indians. An Introduction to the Chichimeca. 302pp plus index, photographs, drawings, notes. A general study, including pre-Columbian period, contact and conflict with western cultures, the reservation system, modern policies. New York, 1979 (1st ed.), d.j. $20.00
   ___Another Copy. Same. $15.00
   ___Another Copy. Same. $10.00

C108. CASTILLO (Bernal Diaz Del). Historie Verdique de la Conquete de la Nouvelle-Espagne. Translated by D. Jourdaney. xxxii, 952pp, 4 color maps, leather and marbled bds, gold stamping. Paris, G. Masson, n.d. (1877 or 1878) (2d ed.). $75.00

C109. CASTILLO (H.) et al. Chaquicocha: Community in Progress. 91pp, photographs, wrappers. Study in Andes. Cornell University, 1964. $10.00

C110. CASTILLO (H.) et al. (Cornell Peru Project, Report No. 4, Cornell, 1964) Mito: The Orphan of its Illustrious Children. 102pp, illus, wrappers. $20.00
   ___Another Copy. Same. $10.00

C111. CASTLETON (Kenneth). Petroglyphs and Pictographs of Utah (2 Volumes). Wrappers, illus (some in color). Utah Museum of Natural History, Salt Lake City, 1978.
    $50.00

C112. CASTRO (Fernando). La Ciudad de Queretaro. Forword in English. 39 drawings, 4to, limited ed, #482/2,000, signed presentation copy. Mexico, 1975. $40.00

C113. CASTRO (Fernando). Presencia Azteca en La Ciudad de Mexico. iv, 36 pls (drawings) with descriptions in English and Spanish, Presentacion de Miguel Leon Portilla, limited ed, #2062/2,550, 4to, boxed. Mexico, 1977.
    $60.00

CASTRO POZO (Hildebrando). See also BAE Bulletin No. 143.

C114. CASWELL (Mrs. Harriet). Our Life Among the Iroquois Indians. 321pp, frontis, illus, decorated cloth, spine spotted, Boston, Chicago, 1892. $75.00
   ___Another Copy. Congregational Sunday School Pub. Society, Boston, 1892. $50.00

C115. CATALDO (J. M.). Jesus-Christ-Nim Kinne Uetas-Pa Kut Ka-Kala Time-Nin I-Ues Pilep-Eza-Pa Taz-Pa Pamtai-Pa Numipu-Timt-Ki (The Life of Jesus Christ from the Four Gospels in the Nez Perce Language). xix, 386pp, stiff wrappers. Portland, Schwab Printing, 1915. $85.00

C116. Catalog to Manuscripts at the National Anthropological Archives, Department of Anthropology, National Museum of Natural History, Smithsonian Institution (4 Volumes). 2,855pp (14¾" x 10½"), 22,800 cards, cloth. Boston, 1975. $595.00

This unique series of manuscripts represents, to a
great extent, documents collected by the Bureau of
American Ethnology between 1879 and 1965, and produced
by their scholars, or collected by the Smithsonian, or
obtained by gifts from anthropologists, soldiers, missionaries, and private collectors. Approximately 40,000 individual items are described under about 5,000 main entries. The catalog consists of three sections: an alphabetical file that relates to Indians of North America,
North of Mexico, a geographical file concerning peoples
of Mexico and Central America, and a numerical file that
indicates the subject under which the other two section's
cards have been filed. (EAP)

C117. CATHERWOOD (F.). Views of Ancient Monuments in Central America, Chiapas and Yucatan by F. Catherwood,
Arch. In a 21" x 16½" linen portfolio, there are 25 full-
page color lithographs and a 24pp text. Barre Pub.,
1965. $875.00

This special limited edition of 500 copies is a facsimile
of Catherwood's rare London, 1884, edition considered
by many to have been the most beautiful work on the
Maya. It was printed from one of the few hand-colored
sets done of that magnificent work. Included in the
linen envelope portfolio are the 25 hand-colored plates
printed on 100% rag content Brentwood vellum, an outline map showing the cities and monuments visited by
Catherwood and John L. Stephens from 1839 to 1842 and
by Catherwood in 1844, and a facsimile of Catherwood's
24 page text. (EAP)

CATLIN (George)

George Catlin was born in Wilkes-Barre, Pennsylvania,
May 26, 1796. He was trained as a lawyer and practiced
briefly in Lucerne, PA. A self-taught artist, he was
elected to Pennsylvania Academy of Fine Arts in 1824,
members of which at that time included Charles Willson
Peale, Rembrandt Peale and Thomas Sully. He was apparently inspired to his lifelong activity by a visit of an
Indian delegation to Washington, D.C.

In the spring of 1830 he travelled with General William
Clark to Prairie du Chien and Fort Crawford and in the
fall to Kansa Indian villages on the Kansas River. In
1831 he travelled up the Missouri and Platte Rivers with
Indian agent John Dougherty. In 1832 he travelled
aboard the first steamboat to ascend the Missouri to Fort
Union at the mouth of the Yellowstone River as a guest
of the American Fur Co. In 1834 he accompanied Col.
Henry Dodge and the Dragoons into the country of the
Comanche and Wichita Indians in present day Oklahoma.
In 1835 he ascended the Mississippi River as far as the
Falls of St. Anthony. In 1836 he visited the Upper Mis-
sissippi Valley via the Great Lakes.

These excursions formed the basis for most of his
work. Catlin began exhibiting his paintings and collection of artifacts beginning in 1833. His Indian Gallery
opened in New York City at Clinton Hall in 1837 with
great success. He took his exhibit to England in 1839
where it was exhibited for nearly five years. He travelled to France, exhibiting from 1845-1848. He returned
to England in this year, but the exhibition ran heavily
into debt. The majority of Catlin's collection passed into
the hands of an American, Joseph Harrison, as security
for his paying off Catlin's debt. The collection was unearthed in 1879 by Thomas Donaldson and was donated
to the U.S. Government by Harrison's widow. (RMW)

C118. CATLIN (George). Catalogue Descriptive and Instructive
of Catlin's Indian Cartoons. 99pp, printed wrappers,
appendix B contains a "Brief Synopsis of the Author's
Roamings...." New York, Baker and Bodwin, 1871.
$125.00

C119. CATLIN (George). Catalogue Raisonne de la Galerie Indi-
enne de Mr. Catlin Renfermant des Portraits, des Paysages, des Costumes, etc.... 47pp, modern bds.
Paris, Imprimerie de Wittersheim, 1845. $135.00

C120. CATLIN (George). A Descriptive Catalogue of Catlin's
Indian Gallery; Containing Portraits, Landscapes, Costumes, etc., ... North American Indians. Exhibited for
Nearly Three Years, With Great Success, in the Egyptian
Hall, Piccadilly, London. 48pp, 8vo, self wrappers.
London, C. & J. Allard, n.d. (c.1842). $300.00
     Catlin sought to sell his collection "by far the most
extensive and the finest ... of tribal costumes and other
articles ever assembled" to the U.S. Government as a
nucleus for a great National Museum. Unable to do so,
he took it abroad, possibly with the hope of selling it
there. This catalogue is from the period of its first exhibition at London's Egyptian Hall. (RMW)
     ____Another Copy. Published by author, at His Indian
Collection, No. 6, Waterloo Place, 1848.... Also Opinions
of the Press in England, France and the United States.
92pp, 8vo, self-wrappers, sewn. $125.00

C121. (CATLIN). Episodes from Life Among the Indians and Last
Rambles. Edited and with an Introduction by Marvin
Ross. 354pp, illus with 163 scenes and portraits.
Norman, 1979. $40.00

C122. CATLIN (George). Last Rambles Amongst the Indians of
the Rocky Mountains and the Andes. 2pp, (v)-x, 1pp,
361pp, pls, illus, 1/2 leather, marbled bds. New York,
Appleton, 1867 (1st American ed.). $95.00
     American edition with the English sheets. Sequel to
"Life Amongst the Indians." Both contain new bibliographical information. (RMW)

C123. CATLIN (George). Letters and Notes on the Manners,

Customs and Condition of the North American Indians (2 Volumes). Vol. 1: viii, 264pp. Vol. 2: viii, 266pp, 3 maps (1 folding), 309 pls, errata slip, rebound in 3/4 morocco. Howes: C-241. Sabin: 11536. London, Author, 1841 (1st ed., 1st issue). $750.00

___Another Copy. Same. Original cloth with paper labels, lacks errata leaf. $750.00

___Another Copy. London, 1857 (9th ed.) Illustrations of the Manners, Customs and Condition of the North American Indians: With Letters and Notes Written During Eight Years of Travel and Adventure Among the Wildest and Most Remarkable Tribes Now Existing (2 Volumes). Vol. I: viii, 264pp, 114 engravings, map, also fold-out map. Vol. II: viii, 266pp, 246 engravings, map, green morocco cvrs, morocco decorated gilt spines, marbled endpapers. Howes: C-251. Sabin: 11537. $275.00

___Another Copy. London, 1866 (10th ed.) Rebound. 264pp, 266pp, 360 engravings. $200.00

___Another Copy. London, 1880. 298pp, 303pp, 400 illus on 180 pls, 8vo, 3 maps, black and gilt publishers cloth. Plates are uncolored. $200.00

___Another Copy. Philadelphia, Leary, Stuart & Co., 1913. (2 Volumes). Vol. 1: ix, 1pp, 298pp. Vol. 2: xii, 303pp, 3 colored maps, one is folding, 320 color pls, gilt decorated cloth. $300.00

___Another Copy. Verlag Continent, Berlin, 1924. Die Indianer und Die Wahrend Eines Achtjathrigen Aufenthalts Unter Den Wildesten Ihrer Stamme Erlebten. Abentheuer und Schicksale. 255pp, 24 color pls, cloth. $85.00

___Another Copy. Edinburgh, J. Grant, 1926. (2 Volumes). Vol. 1: 298pp. Vol. 2: 303pp, 322 color pls, 2 color maps, decorated red linen cvrs. $395.00

___Another Copy. Same. $300.00

___Another Copy. Same. Spines and fore-edges smoke darkened. $190.00

___Another Copy. New York, 1975, edited and with an introduction by Michael M. Mooney, 366pp, 160 illus and pls, 8 pls are in color, 4to, d.j. $25.00

C124. CATLIN (George). Life Amongst the Indians. A Book for Youth. ix, 366pp, 16 adv pp, pls, decorative cloth, fraying, loose. Howes: C-242. "Episodes in the author's life not found elsewhere." London, Sampson, Low, 1861 (1st ed.). $80.00

___Another Copy. New York, 1867, xii, 339pp, 14 pls, original green decorated cloth, head and foot of spine frayed. $75.00

___Another Copy. London, 1874, 352pp, 14pls, decorated cloth, gilt edges, cvrs lightly worn, one page tear. $65.00

C125. CATLIN (George). North American Indian Portfolio. Folio,

31 lithographed pls by Day & Hague, original leather-backed marbled bds, frnt cvr detached, backstrip loose. London, n.d. (c.1844). $12,000.00
Howes: C-243. Field: 258. The first edition of this work was issued with 25 plates of Catlin's most popular paintings carefully drawn and lithographed. Within the year the number was increased to 31 plates, with some of the set colored. Howes: "As graphic delineations of Indian hunting and dancing scenes, these plates rank next to those of Bodmer." Field: "These beautiful views of scenes in Indian life are probably the most truthful ever presented to the public." (RMW)
____Another Copy. Chicago, Swallow Press, 1970. North American Indian Portfolio. Introduction by Harold McCracken. xx, 25 pls, from drawings of the author made during 8 years travel amongst 48 of the wildest and most remote tribes of savages in North America. Limited to 1000 copies, folio (23" x 18"), reproduction of the 1844 ed. $300.00

C126.   (CATLIN, George). Notice sur les Indiens Ioways, et Sur le Nuage Blanc, Venus des Plaines du Haut-Missouri, Pres des Montagnes Rocheuses ... Sous la Conduite de G. H. C. Melody.... 24pp of text 8 leaves of woodcut illus after Catlin, with 9 illus, printed and pictorial wrappers. Paris, 1845. $550.00
The party of Iowa Indians arrived in England in mid-1844, in tow of their sponsor, G. H. C. Melody. Here they met George Catlin, who was exhibiting his paintings at Egyptian Hall in Piccadilly. He contracted with them to perform there, and then, with Melody took them on an English tour. This was such a success that a French tour was undertaken in April, 1845. The Iowans made a great hit, appearing before Louis Philippe and getting rave reviews in the press. This rare pamphlet, describing the dances, the reception with the King, and the Indians themselves, with woodcut illustrations after Catlin, must have appeared very shortly after the Tuileries performance Sabin: 47467. (WR)

C127.   CATLIN (George). O-Kee-Pa: A Religious Ceremony: And Other Customs of the Mandans. 8pp, 52pp. With: "Folium Reservatum." n.p., n.d. (Separately and Privately Printed by the Author, 1867), 4pp, tall octavo, original cloth gilt and blindstamped, with 13 full-page colored pls depicting the Mandan Torture Ceremony. It is the only presentation copy we know of or can discover to exist. It is inscribed "To Monsr. W. Neuhaus from the author George Catlin, 1868." London, 1867. $5,000.00
George Catlin (1796-1872), who passed some fourteen years among the various North American Indian tribes and left the most authentic anthropological record of an already vanishing people, wrote O-Kee-pa in response to

an article appearing in an 1866 issue of Truebner's monthly catalogue. This attributed the authorship of an indescribably lascivious pamphlet on the secret customs of the Mandans to Catlin (see Sabin: 11528). O-Kee-pa is as much a defense of Catlin as the Mandans, a tribe who were mostly to be found on the west side of the Missouri River, most of whom were destroyed by a smallpox epidemic in 1837. Catlin states in his Preface that of all the numerous customs which he had recorded, nothing was so peculiar and surprising as the O-Kee-pa ceremony of the Mandans. Laid in is the extremely rare original "Folium Reservatum" in which Catlin provides the complete details of the ceremony of the Buffalo dance, the sexual nature of which was considered too shocking for the general public and thus separately printed for "scientific men." The curious rite of O-Kee-pa is shown in "horrible fidelity" in the 13 color plates. Catlin: pp101-108, 25 A & B. Howes: C-244. Field: 262. Sabin: 11543. Wagner-Camp: 84. (WR)

_____Another Copy. Philadelphia, J. B. Lippincott, 1867 (1st American ed.). vii, 52pp, 13 color lithographs (Photo-lith Simonau & Toovey), lrg 8vo, ex-library, original gilt stamped cloth, English sheets with Philadelphia imprint. $1,750.00

From the introductory letter by Prince Maximilian of Neuwied: "Your letter came safely to hand and revived the quite forgotten recollections of my stay amongst the Indian tribes of the Missouri, now thirty-three years past.

"The Mandan tribe, which we both have known so well, and with whom I passed a whole winter, was one of the first to be destroyed by a terrible disease, when all ... died; and it is doubtful if a single man of them remained to record the history, customs and religious ideas of his people.

"Not having been like yourself, an eye-witness of those remarkable starvations and tortures of the O-KEE-PA, but having arrived later, and spent the whole of the winter with the Mandans, I received from all the distinguished chiefs ... the most detailed and complete description of the O-KEE-PA festival, when the young men suffered a great deal; and can attest your relation of it to be a correct one, after all that I heard and observed myself." (RMW)

_____Another Copy. Yale University, 1967, Centennial Ed., d.j. Edited and with introduction by John Ewers. 103pp plus index, 13 color illus, bibliography. $45.00

_____Another Copy. Same. Folium reservatum included. $30.00

C128. CATON (John Dean). The Last of the Illinois and a Sketch of the Pottawatomies. 55pp, later wrappers. Also includes Caton's "Origin of the Prairies." Chicago, Fergus, 1876. $35.00

____Another Copy. Same. $40.00

____Another Copy. Same. $40.00

C129. CAUGHEY (John W.). McGillivray of the Creeks. xviii, 385pp, bibliography, index, review copy in blue wrappers. University of Oklahoma, Norman, 1938 (1st print.) $85.00

____Another Copy. Same. d.j. $45.00

____Another Copy. Norman, 1959 (2nd print.) cloth, d.j. $15.00

____Another Copy. Same. $12.00

C130. CAULKINS (Frances M.). (New London Historical Society Occasional Publication, Vol. I, Norwich, 1903) Some Records of Groton. Edited by Emily S. Gilman. 96pp, limited to 300 copies, account of Mason's expedition against the Pequots in 1637 and Benedict Arnold's expedition in 1781, illus, maps, cloth. $10.00

C131. CAVANAUGH (Beverly). Music of the Netsilik Eskimo: A Study of Stability and Change. 198/372pp, plus sml record (33 rpm), 10 pls, 4to, wrappers. National Museum of Canada, Ottawa, 1982. $45.00

CAVE (A. J. E.). See also BAE Bulletin No. 123.

C132. CAVERLY (R. B.). Heroism of Hannah Dustin, Together with the Indian Wars of New England. 408pp, 9 pls, original bds. Boston, 1874 (1st ed.). $45.00

____Another Copy. Same. $35.00

C133. (CAYUSE). (House of Representatives Executive Document 45, 33:1, Washington, 1845, 1st print.) Expenses of the Cayuse War. 8pp, removed. Monies spent for troops, with some account of events of the war. $20.00

C134. (CENSUS). Indian Population in the United States and Alaska, 1910. 285pp, maps, one large folding color map. Washington, 1915. $20.00

C135. (CENSUS). (House of Representatives Report 53, 29:2, Washington, 1847, 1st print.) Statistics, Etc., of the Indian Tribes. 23pp, removed. Early census with comments on conditions of Indians on reservation lands. $17.00

C136. (CENSUS). Peace Establishment. Number of Indians in Oregon, California and New Mexico, etc...... 12pp, removed from House of Representatives Document 76. Lists the number of Indians believed to be in the new territories, the number of military posts needed and the number of troops. Washington, 1848. $50.00

C137. (CENSUS). (House of Representatives Executive Document 158, 41:2, Washington, 1970, 1st print.) Number of Indians in Various Tribes. 5pp, removed. Census, giving reported numbers for 1840s to 1869. $15.00

C138. CERAM (C. W.). The First American: The Story of

North American Archaeology. 357pp, illus. New York, 1971, (1st ed.). $20.00
___Another Copy. Same. $15.00
___Another Copy. Same. $10.00

C139. CERNY (C.). Navaho Pictorial Weaving. 32pp, 22 illus, wrappers. Museum of New Mexico, 1975. $10.00

C140. CERVANTES (Enrique A.). Loza Blanca y Azulejo de Puebla. Tomo Primero. xi, 305pp, pls, figures, index, small 4to, wrappers, includes approx 100 tipped in pls of fine examples of pottery from the 16th through the 20th Century. Vol. 1 only. Mexico, 1939 (1st ed.) limited. $125.00

C141. CERVANTES (M. A.). Treasures of Ancient Mexico, From the National Anthropological Museum. 96pp, 204 color photographs, cloth. New York, 1978. $12.00

C142. CERWIN (Herbert). Bernal Diaz, Historian of the Conquest. 228pp plus index, photographs, drawings, appendix, bibliography. Norman, 1963 (1st ed.). d.j. $20.00
First bibliography of Diaz to be published in English, he served on the Coroba and Grijalva expeditions to Yucatan and was with Cortes. (TNL)

C143. CHAFE (W. L.). (Smithsonian Contributions to Anthropology, Vol. 4, 1967) Seneca Morphology and Dictionary. v, 125pp, cloth. $27.00
___Another Copy. Same. $20.00

C144. CHALMERS (Harvey). The Last Stand of the Nez Perce. 288pp, index. New York, 1962, d.j. $25.00

CHAMBERLAIN (Alexander F.). See BAE Bulletin No. 59.

C145. CHAMPE (F. W.). The Matachines Dance of the Upper Rio Grande. 113pp, 23 color and 8 b/w photographs, 93 figures, one 33 1/3 record of "Matachines music of San Ildefonso Pueblo," cloth. Lincoln, 1983. $30.00

C146. CHANNEN (E. R.) and CLARKE (N. D.). (Ottawa National Museum, Anthropological Papers No. 8, Ottawa, 1965) The Copeland Site: A Precontact Huron Site in Simcoe County, Ontario. 27pp, illus, wrappers. $10.00

C147. CHANNING (A.) and FROST (F. T.). The American Egypt. A Record of Travel in Yucatan. frontis, illus, includes travels to Chichen Itza, Labna, Sayil, Uxmal, Palenque, Cancun, Copan, Kabah. London, 1909 (1st ed.). $125.00

C148. CHAPIN (Howard M.). Sachems of the Narragansetts. 117pp, 8 pls, genealogical charts, cloth. Rhode Island Historical Society, 1931. $20.00

C149. CHAPLIN (Ralph). Only the Drums Remembered. 27pp, portrait, wrappers. Chief Leschi and White settlers. n.p., 1960 (1st ed.). $10.00

C150. CHAPMAN (A.). Mats Totemiques, Amerique du Nord, Cote Nord-ouest. 24pp, 9 photographs, wrappers. Musee de l'Homme, 1965. $10.00

C151.   CHAPMAN (Carl H.). The Archaeology of Missouri, II.
        334 double-column pp plus index, drawings, photographs,
        maps, bibliography. Early, middle and late woodland
        period plus early and middle Mississippi periods. Colum-
        bia, 1980 (1st ed.), d.j. $25.00
C152.   CHAPMAN (K. M.). (School of American Research, 1970,
        1977) The Pottery of San Ildefonso Pueblo. xvi,
        260pp, 174 color pp of designs, 5 figures, cloth. Ex-
        cellent text details all aspects of San Ildefonso Pottery,
        including its origins, forms, decoration, firing and
        styles. $48.00
        ____Another Copy. same, d.j. $35.00
C153.   CHAPMAN (Kenneth M.). (Memoirs of the Laboratory of
        Anthropology, Vol. 1, Santa Fe, 1938, 1st ed.) The
        Pottery of Santo Domingo Pueblo: A Detailed Study of
        its Decoration. xiv, 192pp, 34 text figures, 79 color
        pls, map, inscribed and signed by author, stiff printed
        wrappers. Laid in are 9 personal letters and cards
        signed by Dr. Chapman as "Chap" and 6 newspaper
        clippings concerning his career and death. $200.00
            Saunders: 1497. Swadesh: 570 "The definitive
        work on Santo Domingo pottery." Dr. Chapman was 92
        when he passed away in 1968.
        ____Another Copy. Santa Fe, 1938. $125.00
        ____Another Copy. Santa Fe, 1953, 192pp, 4to, wrap-
        pers, includes 79 half-tone full-page pls and many fig-
        ures and photographs in the text, limited to 1,000 copies.
                                                           $35.00
        ____Another Copy. Same. $27.00
        ____Another Copy. Albuquerque, 1977, 208pp, 79pp of
        color motifs and designs, 33 figures, cloth. $45.00
        ____Another Copy. Same. $30.00
C154.   CHAPMAN (K. M.). Pueblo Indian Pottery. Volume 1.
        a 22pp text in English and French, 21 loose color litho-
        graphs in a 12" x 14" folio with ties. Nice, Alexander
        C. Szwedzicki, 1938. $495.00
            This extremely scarce publication with its eagerly
        sought lithographs is only partially complete. Of the
        50 lithographs, 21 are present in this folio. All the
        lithographs are in VG condition. This edition was limited
        to 750 copies. The text is signed by Szwedzicki.
C155.   CHAPMAN (K. M.). (Laboratory of Anthropology General
        Series, Bulletin 4, Santa Fe, 1938 1st ed.) Pueblo Indian
        Pottery of the Post-Spanish Period. 14pp, illus, stiff
        printed wrappers. Saunders: 1500. $20.00
        ____Another Copy. Santa Fe, 1950 (3rd ed.) 15pp,
        15 photographs. $17.00
C156.   CHAPMAN (William M.). Remember the Wind. A Prairie
        Memoir. 240pp, drawings by Douglas Gorsline, endpaper
        maps. Life on the Sioux Standing Rock Reservation.
        Philadelphia, 1965 (1st ed.). $12.00

C157. Chapters in the Prehistory of Eastern Arizona, III. (Fieldiana: Anthropology, Vol. 65, 1975) 186pp, 40 photographs, 3 figures, 11 tables. $24.00

C158. CHARLEVOIX (Pierre Francis-Xavier de). Journal of a Voyage to North America ... Containing the Geographic Description and Natural History of That Country, Particularly Canada. Together with an Account of the Customs, Characters, Religion, Manners and Traditions of the Original Inhabitants (2 Volumes). 8pp, 382pp; 8pp, 380pp, 4pp, 22pp, 3/4 gilt morocco, folding map, bound complete with half titles, ads in second volume. London, Printed for R. and J. Dodsley, 1761. $1,200.00

Howes: C-308, "b". Graff: 651. Sabin: 12139. Clark: 1-60. Field: 283. Charlevoix was sent to Canada by the Jesuits at the age of 23. After four years of missionary work, he returned to France, whereupon he accepted the commission for this trip from the regent of France. During the years 1720-22, he traveled in the Great Lakes region, and down the Mississippi. Although his trip was publicly admitted to be for the purpose of inspecting interior posts and settlements, he was actually under orders to seek out information relating to the existence of a passage to the Pacific via Continental North America. (WR)

C159. CHARNAY (Desire). The Ancient Cities of the New World, Being Voyages and Explorations in Mexico and Central America, From 1857-1882. xlvi, 514pp, 2pp ads, 208 engravings of which 24 are full page pls, 3 maps, one is folding (18" x 12½"), decorated cloth, t.e.g. New York, 1887. $175.00

___Another Copy. Same. 2" cut on spine. $135.00
___Another Copy. Same. Blue cloth, gilt lettering. $125.00
___Another Copy. Same. $80.00

C160. CHARNAY (Desire). Revue d'Ethnographhie (In Two Parts). Part I: La Civilisation Tolteque. 25pp, 7 illus. Part II: Les Tolteques au Tabasco et dans le Yucatan. 36pp, 11 illus. Paris, 1885. $100.00

C161. CHASE (Francis). Gathered Sketches from the Early History of New Hampshire and Vermont; Containing Vivid and Interesting Accounts ... of the Adventures of Our Forefathers. 215pp, illus, cloth. Indian captivities of Gerish, Rogers, Goodwin, M'Coy, Howe, Steele, etc. Ayer: 46. Claremont, NH, 1856 (1st ed.). $45.00
___Another Copy. Same. $35.00
___Another Copy. Somersworth, NH, 1970, d.j. $15.00

C162. CHASE (K.). (Plateau, Vol. 54, No. 1, 1982) Navajo Painting. 32pp, 22 color and 8 b/w photographs. $10.00

C163. CHATEAUBRIAND (Francois A. R.). Voyages en Amerique, (Moeurs des Sauvages). i, 399pp, portrait, pl, 1/4 gilt

tooled leather, marbled bds. Paris, Bethune et Plon, 1839.
$90.00

Howes: C-325. "The distinguished author, fascinated by Indian character, roamed in 1791 throughout our interior frontiers, from western New York to the Floridas." This copy contains an unusual view of Niagara from the rocks just below the falls. (RMW)

C164. CHENEY (Roberta C.). (Interpretation by Kills Two). The Big Missouri Winter Count. 63pp, illus by Ralph Shane, map, bibliography, wrappers. Sioux Indian accounting for the years 1796-1926. Happy Camp, CA, 1979 (1st ed. thus).
$10.00

C165. CHENEY (T. A.). Ancient Monuments in Western New York. From 13th Annual Report of the Regents, New York State Cabinet of Natural History. pp 37-52, plus 12 maps, 14 figures of artifacts, a folding map showing location of ancient monuments, wrappers.
$75.00

C166. (CHEROKEE). Cherokee Hymn Book, Compiled from Several Authors and Revised. 96pp, title page in English and Cherokee, 12mo, original leather backed bds. Philadelphia, American Baptist Publication Society, 1866.
$225.00

C167. (CHEROKEE). Cherokee Testament (Title in Cherokee) 408pp, loose leaf "Cherokee Alphabet," cloth. New York, American Bible Society, 1860.
$150.00

C168. (CHEROKEE). Constitution and Laws of the Cherokee Nation. Printed in the Cherokee Language Using Alphabet invented by Sequoya in 1821. 340pp, 1/2 calf, marbled bds, lacks backstrip. The Cherokee Press, 1892.
$225.00

C169. (CHEROKEE). The Gospel of John the Apostle in Cherokee and English. 83pp, wrappers. n.p. 1948. $15.00

C170. (CHEROKEE). Review of an Article in the North American for January 1830, on the Present Relations of the Indians. n.p., n.d. (Boston, 1830)
$55.00

Sabin: 70202. Field: 1296. The article reviewed was by Lewis Cass. "Many intelligent men ... have expressed great indignation that ... the interests of the unoffending Cherokees should be sacrificed to promote the selfish ends of an individual, who has thus prostituted his talents in fabricating a plausible and sophisticated defence of manifest injustice and oppression." (RMW)

C171. (CHEROKEE). Report ... Civilization of the Several Indian Tribes. 23pp, folding table, removed. Cherokee laws and a list of Indian country schools. Washington, 1822, (1st print.).
$20.00

C172. (CHEROKEE). (House of Representatives Document 136, 18:1, Washington, 1824, 1st print.) Proposals Made by Certain Cherokee Indians, for the Cession of their Lands to the United States. 16pp, removed. Trade of Indian land for land on reservation.
$12.00

C173. (CHEROKEE). (House of Representatives Document 106, 20:1, Washington, 1828, 1st print.) Negotiation for Cherokee Lands. 40pp, removed. $15.00

C174. (CHEROKEE). (House of Representatives Document 89, 21:1, Washington, 1830, 1st print.) Intrusions on Cherokee Lands. 49pp, removed. Complaints of settlers and other Indians being on Cherokee lands. $15.00

C175. (CHEROKEE). (House of Representatives Document 6, 20: 2, Washington, 1828, 1st print.) Cherokee Council To Col. H. Montgomery. 13pp, removed. Appeals to agent Montgomery for fairness by the government. $15.00

C176. (CHEROKEE). (House of Representatives Report No. 227, Feb. 24, 1830) Report from Committee on Indian Affairs: Removal of Indians. 32pp, 1/4 leather, marbled bds, cvrs starting. Argument in favor of Cherokee dispersion to Indian Territory west of the Mississippi ... the best prospect for perpetuating their race. $50.00

C177. (CHEROKEE). Memorial of a Delegation From the Cherokee Indians. 8pp, removed, stapled, foxed. Washington, 1831. $250.00
After years of bitter feuding over land between the state of Georgia and the Cherokees, the state had begun appropriating Cherokee lands. This document constitutes an appeal by the Indians to the government to stop the state in this action and to increase the holdings of the Cherokees. The Courts, although sympathetic to the plight of the Indians, found that because they were not citizens of the U.S., or a foreign nation (as contended by the Indians themselves), they could not appear as a party to a suit in the Supreme Court. (WR)

C178. (CHEROKEE). Removal of the Cherokees ... Letter from the Secretary of War.... 26pp, removed, stitched. Gives orders for the forcible removal, if necessary, of the Cherokees from Georgia to Indian Territory. Washington, 1838. $35.00

C179. (CHEROKEE). (House of Representatives Document 386, 23:1, Washington, 1834, 1st print.) Memorial of John Ross and Others, Delegates from the Cherokee Indians, Complaining of Injuries Done Them, and Praying For Redress. 31pp, removed. $20.00

C180. (CHEROKEE). (House of Representatives Document 91, 23:2, Washington, 1835, 1st print.) Cherokee--Indians. Memorial of a Council Held at Running Waters. 19pp, removed. Constitution of the Cherokee Nation and land title requests. $10.00

C181. (CHEROKEE). (House of Representatives Document 286, 24:1, Washington, 1836, 1st print.) Memorial and Protest of the Cherokee Nation. 167pp, removed. Indian protest to the New Echota treaty of 1835. $20.00
___Another Copy. Same. $100.00

C182. (CHEROKEE). (House of Representatives Document 403,

24:1, Washington, 1836, 1st print.) Enrolements, Emigration and Improvements of the Cherokees Residing East of the Mississippi. 376pp, removed. $30.00

C183. (CHEROKEE). (House of Representatives Document 99, 25:2, Washington, 1938, 1st print.) Memorial of A Delegation of the Cherokee Nation Remonstrating Against The ... Treaty of December, 1835. 49pp, removed. Pleas for better treatment by the government, and the answer that the government will not open negotiations and wants the Indians to be started West irregardless of the weather. $30.00

C184. (CHEROKEE). (House of Representatives Document 316, 25:2, Washington, 1838, 1st print.) Memorial of the Cherokee Delegation. 7pp, removed. Protesting White outrages toward the Cherokee. $10.00

C185. (CHEROKEE). (House of Representatives Document 453, 25:2, Washington, 1838, 1st print.) Removal of the Cherokees. 26pp, removed. Military correspondence relating to the problems of relocating the Indians to the West. $12.00

C186. (CHEROKEE). (House of Representatives Document 222, 26:1, Washington, 1840, 1st print.) Cherokee--Indians. 23pp, removed. Land negotiations. $10.00

C187. (CHEROKEE). (Senate Document No. 347, 26:1, Washington, 1840, 1st print.) Report from the Secretary of War ... Present State of the Difficulties Which have Existed ... Between the Government and the Cherokee People. 62pp, removed. $20.00

C188. (CHEROKEE). (House of Representatives Document 110, 27:3, Washington, 1843, 1st print.) Cherokee Treaty. 8pp, removed. Treaty of 1835. $10.00

C189. (CHEROKEE). (Senate Document 140, 28:2, Washington 1845, 1st print.) Report of the Secretary of War ... Examination Into the Causes and Extent of the Discontent and Difficulties Among the Cherokee Indians. 143pp, removed. $20.00

C190. (CHEROKEE). (House of Representatives Document 92, 29:1, Washington, 1846, 1st print.) Information Relative to Outrages Lately Committed in the Cherokee Nation. 69pp, removed. $25.00

C191. (CHEROKEE). (House of Representatives Document 185, 29:1, Washington, 1846, 1st print.) Cherokee Disturbances. 233pp, folding map of Cherokee Lands in North Carolina, removed. Detailed account of Indian troubles, land frauds. $45.00
___Another Copy. Same. $125.00

C192. (CHEROKEE). (Senate Document 301, 29:1, Washington, 1846, 1st print.) Documents in Relation to Difficulties Existing in the Cherokee Nation of Indians. 9pp, removed. Detailing murders, burning, etc. $10.00

C193. (CHEROKEE). (Senate Document 408, 29:1, Washington,

1846, 1st print.) Cherokee Indians Residing in North Carolina. 24pp, removed. Claims for monies due Indians from early treaties. $10.00

C194. (CHEROKEE). (House of Representatives Executive Document, 30:1, Washington, 1848) Cherokee Indians. Message of the President ... Transmitting a Communication from the Secretary of War, and a Report from the Commissioner of Indian Affairs, in Relation to the Cherokee Indians. 32pp, removed. The results of the settlement required by the treaty of August, 1846, including a list of the appropriations entailed by the enacting of the treaty. $75.00

C195. (CHEROKEE). (House of Representatives Miscellaneous Document 8, 30:1, Washington, 1848, 1st print.) Cherokee Indians. 71pp, removed. Pleas for annuities and fairness. $15.00

C196. (CHEROKEE). (Senate Executive Document 28, 30:2, Washington, 1849, 1st print.) Claims Against the Cherokees, Under the Treaty of August 6, 1846. 189pp, removed. Troubles caused by Cherokees dissatisfied with treaty provisions, including attacks on Lewis & Clark and other explorers, claim of lands outside allotted territory, etc. $20.00

C197. (CHEROKEE). (House of Representatives Report 632, 31:1, Washington, 1848, 1st print.) Cherokee Indians in North Carolina. Disturbances and treaties. $12.00

C198. (CHEROKEE). (Senate Document, Special Session, Washington, 1849) Memorial of Will P. Ross, W. S. Coodey and John Drew, in behalf of the Old Settlers, or Western Cherokee, Complaining that they have been Deprived of Certain Rights Accruing Under Treaty Stipulations, etc. 5pp, removed. Claiming that the government is continuing in its tradition of not abiding by treaties with the Cherokees, the one here in question the treaty of 1846. $40.00

C199. (CHEROKEE). (House of Representatives Miscellaneous Document 150, 41:2, Washington, 1870, 1st print.) Cherokee Neutral Lands. 20pp, removed. Argument that payments for lands east of the Mississippi should be withdrawn since the Indians were given lands in the "outlet." $10.00

C200. (CHEROKEE). (House of Representatives Executive Document 54, 47:2, Washington, 1883, 1st print.) Cherokee Lands in Indian Territory. 39pp, removed. Description and valuation of land. $10.00

C201. (CHEROKEE). (Senate Executive Document 86, 48:1, Washington, 1884, 1st print.) Amount Appropriated March 3, 1883, for Cherokee Nation, and Legislation to Protect the Rights of Adopted Citizens of Said Nation. 25pp, removed. Names of adopted citizens and text of treaty. $10.00

C202. (CHEROKEE). (Senate Executive Document 82, 49:1, Washington, 1886, 1st print.) Legislation in Behalf of Certain Cherokee Indians. 11pp, removed. Providing funds for Oklahoma lands for the Cherokee. $10.00

C203. (CHEROKEE). (House of Representatives Report 3768, 51:2, Washington, 1891, 1st print.) Cherokee Outlet. 27pp, removed. 6.5 million acres set aside for Indians. $10.00

C204. (CHEROKEE). (Senate Executive Document 56, 52:1, Washington, 1892, 1st print.) An Agreement with the Cherokee Indians For the Cession of Certain Lands. 39pp, removed. Cherokee Outlet lands, Oklahoma. $10.00

C205. (CHEROKEE). (Senate Executive Document 63, 52:1, Washington, 1892, 1st print.) Title By Which the Cherokee Nation Hold the Cherokee Outlet. 28pp, removed. Attempts to reclaim this Indian territory. $10.00

C206. (CHEROKEE). (Senate Miscellaneous Document 43, 52:2, Washington, 1893, 1st print.) Opening up of the Cherokee Outlet for Settlement. 5pp, removed. Arguments for opening the Cherokee Strip. $10.00

C207. (CHEROKEE). (Senate Executive Document 20, 53:2, Washington, 1894, 1st print.) Claim of John T. Heard for Services Rendered the Western Cherokee Indians. 11pp, removed. Heard, attorney for Western Cherokees, seeks damages against the U.S. Government. $10.00

C208. (CHEROKEE). Moneys Due The Cherokee Nation. 32pp, folding color map of treaty lands in Alabama, the Carolinas, Georgia and Tennessee, removed. Government Printing Office, Washington, 1900. $15.00

C209. (CHEROKEE). (Senate Document 215, 56:1, Washington, 1900, 1st print.) Memorial of Eastern or Emigrant Cherokees. 99pp, removed. Request for funds due under treaties and, contrary to Government opinion, expenses for "removal" to the West. $15.00

C210. (CHEROKEE). (Senate Document 213, 56:2, Washington, 1901, 1st print.) Agreements With Cherokee and Muscogee or Creek Indians. 53pp, removed. Infringement on Cherokee land, oil and mineral rights. $15.00

C211. (CHEROKEE). (Senate Document 227, 59:2, Washington, 1907, 1st print.) Eastern Cherokees. 47pp, removed. Payments for lands and contracts. $10.00

C212. CHESTNUT (V. K.). Plants Used by the Indians of Mendocino County, California. 128pp, illus, maps, index, wrappers. Separate printing of material originally published in Vol. VII of Contributions from U.S. National Herbarium. Ft. Bragg, 1974. $10.00

C213– CHEVALIER (Francois) La Formation des Grands Domaines
C214. au Mexique: Terre et Societe aux XVI-XVII Siecles. 480pp, 15 pls, folding map, wrappers. Institut d'Ethnologie, Paris, 1952. $50.00

C215. (CHEYENNE). (Senate Executive Document 16, 48:2, Washington, 1885, 1st print.) Message of President ... In Relation to the Condition of the Cheyenne and Arapaho Indians. 27pp, removed. Detailed inventory of conditions, possessions, crimes. $12.00
___Another Copy. Same. $15.00

C216. (CHEYENNE AND ARAPAHO). Sand Creek Papers-- Testimonies and Statements Reflecting Facts Concerning the Killing of Cheyenne and Arapaho Indians on November 29, 1864, by the Third Colorado Volunteers. 63pp, typescript, fabric backed wrappers. #86/about 200 copies. Black Forest, CO, 1959. $36.00

C217. (CHEYENNE AND CROW). Laws, Resolutions and Memorials of the Territory of Montana, Passed at the Fourteenth Regular Session of the Legislative Assembly, Held in Helena, the Seat of Government of Said Territory, Commencing January 12, A.D. 1885, and Ending March 12, A.D. 1885. x, 251pp. Acts include provisions for the Cheyenne and Crow Indians, etc. Helena, 1885 (1st ed.). $30.00

C218. (CHICKASAW). (House of Representatives Document 8, 29:1, Washington, 1845, 1st print.) Chickasaw Fund. 97pp, removed. Investigation into investment of Chickasaw funds by the Indian Agent and others for possible fraud. $12.00

C219. (CHICKASAW). (House of Representatives Document 190, 29:1, Washington, 1846, 1st print.) Chickasaw Indians. 127pp, removed. Land claims with supporting documents. $10.00

C220. (CHICKASAW). (House of Representatives Document 195, 29:1, Washington, 1846, 1st print.) Chickasaw Indians. 21pp, removed. Further information on land claims. $10.00

C221. (CHIEF JOSEPH). Chief Joseph's Own Story. 33pp, frontis, chapter decorations, handset type, stiff wrappers. Reprinted from the North American Review of April, 1879. $10.00

C222. CHINCHILLA (C. S.). Kunst der Maya, Aus Statts und Privatbesitz der Republik Guatemala. 256pp, 80 full page b/w and 6 full page color photographs of objects, 3 b/w and color field photographs, 5 figures, map. Exhibition Catalogue, Rautenstrauch-Joset-Museum, Cologne, 1966) $35.00

C223. (CHIPPEWA). (House of Representatives Executive Document 12, 48:1, Washington, 1st print.) Lands to Chippewa Indians, Lake Superior. 8pp, 2 maps. $10.00

C224. (CHIPPEWA). (House of Representatives Executive Document 76, 48:1, Washington, 1884, 1st print.) Damages to Chippewa Indians. 37pp, removed. Loss of lands due to reservoirs. $10.00

C225. (CHIPPEWA). (Senate Executive Document 115, 49:2,

Washington, 1887, 1st print.) Chippewa Indians In Minnesota. 133pp. Treaty and rejective responses of Indians. $15.00

C226. (CHIPPEWA AND DAKOTA). Chippewa and Dakota Indians; A Subject Catalogue of Books, Pamphlets, Periodical Articles and Manuscripts in the Minnesota Historical Society. 131pp, 4to, wrappers. Completely reproduces in facsimile the card catalog of the Minnesota Historical Society's holdings on Chippewa and Dakota Indians. Lists about 2,000 items. St. Paul, 1970. $15.00
___Another Copy. Same. $12.00

C227. (CHIPPEWA LANGUAGE). Kekitchemanitomenahn Gahbemahjetnnunk Jesus Christ, Otoashke Wawweendummahgawin. 484pp, rebacked in leather, title page backed. Albany, Packard and Van Benthuysen, 1833 (1st ed.).
$350.00
___Another Copy. Same. Frnt cvr detached but present, leather. $300.00

C228. CHITTENDEN (Hiram Martin) and RICHARDSON (A. T.). Life, Letters and Travels of Father Pierre-Jean DeSmet, S.J. 1801-1873. (4 Volumes). Lrge 8vo, Vol. 1: xvi, 402pp. Vol. 2: ix, pp403-794. Vol. 3: vi, pp795-1212. Vol. 4: vi, pp1213-1624. Folding pocket map, 13 pls, other illus. New York, Harpers, 1905.
$550.00
Howes: C-392. Detailed account of Fr. DeSmet's travels among the Indians of the Far West.
___Another Copy. Same. $550.00
___Another Copy. Same. $550.00
___Another Copy. New York, 1969. Life, Letters and Travels of Father Pierre-Jean DeSmet, S.J.: Missionary Labors and Adventures Among the Wild Tribes of the North American Indians. Edited from the Original Unpublished Manuscript, Journals and Letter Books and from his Printed Works (2 Volumes). 1,624pp total both vols., index, folding map, complete facsimile reprint of the 1905 ed. $60.00

C229. (CHOCTAW). Contract of Moses Perry to Teach Among The Choctaws. One sheet manuscript, signed. Agent William Armstrong hires Perry to teach for $500 for a one-year period. Perry's retained duplicate copy. n.p., 1835. $75.00

C230. (CHOCTAW). (House of Representatives Document 39, 19:2, Washington, 1827, 1st print.) Encroachments By White Men Upon Choctaw Lands In the Territory of Arkansas. 8pp, removed. Indian refusal to sell more of their land. $10.00

C231. (CHOCTAW). (Senate Document 188, 27:2, Washington, 1842, 1st print.) Treaty of Dancing-Rabbit Creek. 13pp, removed. Claims by Indians for monies and supplies. $10.00

C232. (CHOCTAW). (Senate Document 86, 28:2, Washington, 1845, 1st print.) Contracts for Removal and Subsistence of the Choctaw Indians. 53pp, removed. $15.00

C233. (CHOCTAW). (House of Representatives Reports 193, 28:2, Washington, 1845, 1st print.) Choctaw Academy in Kentucky. 13pp, removed. Conditions and activities at school. $12.00

C234. (CHOCTAW). (House of Representatives Document 189, 29:1, Washington, 1846, 1st print.) Choctaw Treaty. 9pp, removed. Claims under 1830 treaty. $10.00

C235. (CHOCTAW). (S. Rep. Com. 374, 35:2, Washington, 1859, 1st print.) Memorial of P. P. Pitchlynn and Others, Choctaw Delegates. 18pp, removed. Unfair treatment claims against the U.S. $10.00

C236. (CHOCTAW). (House of Representatives Executive Document 82, 36:1, Washington, 1860, 1st print.) Choctaws-- Amount Due. 39pp, removed. Settlements under earlier treaties. $10.00

C237. (CHOCTAW). (Senate Miscellaneous Document 90, 41:2, Washington, 1870, 1st print.) Memorial of the Choctaw Nation of Indians. 12pp, removed. Protesting one government for all Indian Territory and the railroad through their lands. $10.00

C238. (CHOCTAW). (Senate Miscellaneous Document 106, 41:2, Washington, 1870, 1st print.) Memorial of a Committee on Behalf of the Colored People of the Choctaw and Chickasaw Tribes of Indians. 7pp, removed. Requesting equal rights with White people. $10.00

C239. (CHOCTAW). (House of Representatives Miscellaneous Documents 94, 42:3, Washington, 1873, 1st print.) Choctaw Claims. 31pp, removed. Mississippi Choctaw frauds, etc. $10.00

C240. (CHOCTAW). (Senate Miscellaneous Document 121, 43:1, Washington, 1874, 1st print.) Memorial of P. P. Pitchlynn, Delegate of Choctaw Nation of Indians. 73pp, removed. Requesting monies due Choctaws. $12.00

C241. (CHOCTAW). (House of Representatives Miscellaneous Document 294, 43:1, Washington, 1874, 1st print.) Remonstrance of the Choctaw Delegates. 11pp, removed. Concerning the rights of Black freedmen living among the Choctaw to lands and money. $10.00

C242. (CHOCTAW). (House of Representatives Executive Document 47, 43:2, Washington, 1874, 1st print.) Liabilities of Choctaw Indians to Individuals. 29pp, removed. Individuals claiming money from grant paid for lands taken over by the Government. $10.00

C243. (CHOCTAW). (House of Representatives Miscellaneous Document 40, 44:1, Washington, 1876, 1st print.) Claims of the Choctaw Nation. 95pp, removed. Review of treaties from the 1830s which still had not been settled. $15.00

C244. (CHOCTAW). (House of Representatives Report 499, 44:1, Washington, 1876, 1st print.) Choctaw Indians. 23pp, removed. Seeking to settle claims under the 1830 treaty. $10.00

C245. (CHOCTAW). (House of Representatives Executive Document 34, 45:3, Washington, 1879, 1st print.) Choctaw Claim. 49pp, removed. Claims arising under the treaty of 1855. $12.00

C246. (CHOCTAW). (Senate Executive Document 42, 52:1, Washington, 1892, 1st print.) Act to Pay the Choctaw and Chickasaw Indians for Certain Lands Now Occupied By the Cheyenne and Arapahoe Indians. $10.00

C247. (CHOCTAW). (House of Representatives Document 490, 56:2, Washington, 1901) Agreement with Choctaw and Chickasaw Nations. 16pp, removed. Treaty for town sites and other allotments. $10.00

C248. (CHOCTAW). (Senate Document 707, 60:2, Washington, 1909, 1st print.) Revenues, etc., of the Choctaw, Chickasaw, Cherokee, Creek and Seminole Tribes. 42pp, removed. Revenue accounting for 1898-1909. $10.00

C249. (CHOCTAW). (Senate Document 730, 60:2, Washington, 1909, 1st print.) Memorial of Choctaw Indians. 8pp, removed. Protesting tribal rolls being opened. $10.00

C250. (CHOCTAW). (Senate Document 553, 61:2, Washington, 1910, 1st print.) Choctaw and Chickasaw Indians. 11pp, removed. Allotments to individuals. $10.00

CHORIS (M. Louis). A Russian of German stock, was born March 22, 1795. He received his artistic training in Moscow. He made drawings of Botanical specimens for naturalist E. A. Marschall von Bieberstein in the Caucauses prior to accompanying the Kotzebue Expedition as Official Artist. Aside from this work he produced a second, Vues et Paysages des Regions Equinoxialles (Paris, 1826). He was killed by robbers on March 22, 1827, en route to Vera Cruz. Choris drew some of the prints for Voyages Pittoresque in stone himself. Others were done by Victor Adam, Franquelin, Marlet, Vorblin and Noblin. The lithographs were executed by the firm Langlume. The large map was engraved by Ambroise Tardieux, Graveur du Depot de la Marine. (RMW)

C251. CHORIS (M. Louis). Voyage Pittoresque Author du Monde, avec des Portraits de Sauvages d'Amerique, d'Asie, d'Afrique, et des Iles du Grande Ocean; des Paysages, des Vues Maritimes, et Plusieurs Objects d'Histoire Naturelle;.... pp (4), vi, 17, (3)-20, 10, 3, 24, 22, 28, 19, 6, (2), (2), 3 maps (1 folding), frontis (portrait of Romanzoff), engraved in-text music scores, 104 hand-colored lithographs pls, contemporary 1/2 gilt tooled calf and marbled bds, the margin of 3 pls and 2 text leaves have been expertly repaired, folding map has a short tear, expertly repaired, some minor foxing and stain, folio in size, published: Paris, Didot, 1822. $20,000.00

Issued in 22 parts, the work is divided into 12 sections: I: "Traversee de Cronstadt au Chili"; II: "Ile de Paques ou Vaihiou, et Ile Rumanzoff" (I and II. Coasts of Africa and South America, South Pacific, 12 pls); III: "Kamtchatka, le Golfe de Kotzebue et la Terre des Tchouktchis" (Kamtchatka Island, Kotzebue Sound, Alaska. 10 pls); IV: "Port San Francisco et ses habitants" (14 pls); V: "Iles Sandwich" (Hawaiian Islands, 19 pls); VI: "Iles Radak" (South Pacific, 19 pls); VI: "Iles Radak" (South Pacific, 19 pls); VII: "Iles Aleoutiennes" (Aleutian Islands); VIII: "Iles S. Georges et S. Paul" (in Bering Sea); IX: "Ile S. Laurent" (in Bering Sea) (VII-IX, 23 pls); X: "Iles d'Mariannes"; XI: "Iles Philippines" (X and XI, 7 pls); XII: Notice sur les Iles de Corail du Grand Ocean, par M. Adelbert de Chamisso.

Howes: C-397. Sabin: 12884. Ladda-Mocarski 84. Streeter 4: 2461. The artist Louis Choris accompanied the Russian navigator and explorer Otto von Kotzebue aboard the vessel Rurik, sent by Count Romanzoff, 1815-1818, for the purpose of exploring Oceania and searching for a Northwest Passage. In 1816 Kotzebue discovered 399 islands in the South Seas, made extensive surveys in the Bering Strait, discovering Kotzebue Sound and visited Unalaska. In 1817 he visited California and Hawaii, and discovered Romanzov Island in the Marshall Island Group.

Hill, Pacific Voyages, p. 52: "This work has great American interest because of its lithographs and its accounts of California, the Queen Charlotte Islands, the Aleutians, St. Laurence Island in the Bering Sea, and Kotzebue Sound in Alaska. The lithographs are of all aspects of native life and culture." (RMW)

C252. CHRISTIAN (Jane M.). (Southwest Studies, Vol. 11, Nos. 3 and 4, El Paso, 1964, 1965) The Navajo. A People in Transition, Part One and Part Two. 72pp, photographs, maps, wrappers. $15.00

C253. CHURCH (Col. George Earl). Aborigines of South America. 314pp, 8vo, cloth, lrg folding map at end, edited by Clement Markham, includes Caraibes, Tapuyas, Amazoma, Chiriguanos, Abipones. London, 1912 (1st ed.).

$50.00

____Another Copy. Same. $50.00

C254. CHURCH (Thomas). The Entertaining History of King Philip's War, Which Began in the Month of June, 1675. As Also of Expeditions More Lately Made Against the Common Enemy, and All Indian Rebels, in the Eastern Parts of New-England.... 199pp, frontis portraits of Benjamin Church and King Philip, both engraved by

Paul Revere, full calf. Newport, Solomon Southwick, 1772. $1,650.00

Vail: 611. Church: 1091. Evans: 12352. Sabin: 12997. The second edition, after the exceedingly rare first published in Boston, 1716. One of the most popular narratives of King Philip's War, mainly narrating the prowess and adventures of Benjamin Church, one of the most important officers in the war, by his son Thomas. Neither of the Revere engravings is based on the persons depicted; the portrait of Church is stolen from a 1768 portrait of Charles Churchill, with a powderhorn added, while the one of King Philip is based on Verelst's engravings of the Indian Kings of Canada. Despite its fraudulent character, it is the first portrait of an Indian printed in America. (WR)

C255. CHURCH (Thomas). The History of Philip's War ... 1675 and 1676. 360pp, 12mo, frontis, index, leather. Exeter, NH, J. & B. Williams, 1829 (2d ed.). $65.00
___Another Copy. Same. $50.00

C256. CHURCHHILL (Claire Warner). Slave Wives of Nehalem. 103pp, index, ethnology of North Oregon Coast Indians. Portland, 1933, d.j. $25.00

C257. CISNEROS (C. C.). Demografia y Estadistica Sobre el Indio Ecuatoriano. iii, 348pp, limited to 900 copies, inscribed by author. Quito, 1948. $35.00

C258. CISNEROS (F. G.). Maternity in Pre-Columbian Art. 147pp, illus with 95 photographs, text in Spanish and English. Salamanaca, 1970. $35.00

C259. (CLAIMS). (House of Representatives House Bill 13199, 65:3, Washington, 1918) "A Bill to refer all claims of the Cherokee, Creek and Seminole Indians, whether as individuals or otherwise, to the Court of Claims." 2pp, removed, folded. $10.00

C260. CLARK (A. McFadyen) (Editor). (National Museum of Man, Paper 27, 1975) Proceedings: Norther Athapaskan Conference, 1971 (2 Volumes). Vol. I: v, 349pp, map, fold out chart. Vol. II: pp350-803, 5 figures. $30.00

C261. CLARK (Ann). About the Pine Ridge Porcupine. 73pp, drawings, Juvenile book with text in English and Sioux, oblong 4to, wrappers. Office of Indian Affairs, Washington, 1941. $25.00

C262. CLARK (Ann). Brave Against the Enemy. 215pp, illus, text in English and Sioux, red cloth. U.S. Indian Service, 1944. $30.00

C263. CLARK (Ann). Bringer of the Mystery Dog. 84pp, Juvenile book with text in English and Sioux, oblong 4to, wrappers. Office of Indian Affairs, Washington, (c. 1941) $25.00

C264. CLARK (Ann). The Hen of Wahpeton. 97pp, illus, text in English and Sioux, wrappers. Dept. of the Interior, n.d. (c. 1945). $25.00

C265. CLARK (Ann). There Still Are Buffalo. 86pp, drawings,
       Juvenile book with text in English and Sioux, oblong
       4to, wrappers. Office of Indian Affairs, Washington,
       1942. $25.00

C266. CLARK (Ann). Singing Sioux Cowboy. 114pp, text in
       English and Sioux, wrappers. Dept. of Interior, n.d.
       (c. 1940s). $25.00

C267. CLARK (Ann N.). Father Kino: Priest to the Pimas.
       xi, 176pp, juvenile. New York, 1963 (1st ed.), d.j.
                                                        $15.00

C268. CLARK (D. W.). (National Museum of Man, Paper 18,
       Ottawa, 1974) Archaeological Collections from Norutak
       on the Kobuk-Alatna River Portage, Northwestern Alaska.
       65pp, 9pp photographs. $12.00
       ___Another Copy. Same. $12.00

C269. CLARK (D. W.). (National Museum of Man, Paper 20,
       Ottawa, 1974) Contributions to the Later Prehistory of
       Kodiak Island, Alaska. 181pp, 30pp of photographs,
       wrappers. $12.00

C270. CLARK (D. W.). (National Museum of Canada, Paper 35,
       1975) Koniag-Pacific Eskimo Bibliography. 97pp,
       wrappers. $10.00

C271. CLARK (Ella E.). Indian Legends from the Northern
       Rockies. 250pp, plus 24pp of photographs, notes,
       bibliography, index. Myths, legends, personal narra-
       tives and traditions related by Indian storytellers.
       Norman, 1966 (1st ed.), d.j. $35.00
       ___Another Copy. Same. Cloth. $15.00
       ___Another Copy. Norman, 1973 (3rd print.)
                         map, d.j. $18.00
       ___Another Copy. Same. $15.00

C272. CLARK (Galen). Indians of the Yosemite Valley and Vicin-
       ity. Their History, Customs and Traditions. xviii,
       110pp, illus, 12mo, cloth. Indian lives and habits, hints
       to visitors, Indian place names. Yosemite Valley, CA,
       1904 (1st ed.). $20.00
       ___Another Copy. Same. $35.00
       ___Another Copy. Yosemite Valley, CA, 1910,
                         112pp. $25.00

C273. CLARK (G. H.). (University of Oregon, Anthropological
       Papers No. 13, 1977) The Coast of Shelikof Strait,
       1963-1965. xiv, 247pp of photographs, 58 figures,
       22 tables, wrappers. $18.00

C274. CLARK (I. C.). Indian and Eskimo Art of Canada.
       203pp, 105 b/w and 15 color photographs, cloth. Bar-
       celona, 1976. $30.00
          Photographs of classic, historic Canadian Eskimo and
       Indian art. The photographs, all full-page, are the best
       pieces from eleven Canadian museums. Text in English,
       French, German and Spanish.
       ___Another Copy. Barcelona, 1970, xii, 120 full-page

photographic pls by D. Darbois, several pls in color,
oblong sml 4to. $25.00

C275. CLARK (Jerry E.). The Shawnee. 98pp, illus, map endpapers, bibliographical essay, pictorial cloth. University of Kentucky Press, 1977. $15.00

C276. CLARK (J. (Joshua) V. H.) Indian Camp-Fires, and
Hunting Grounds of the Red Men; or, Lights....
375pp, colored frontis and plate, modern cloth. New
York, Derby & Jackson, 1860. $35.00

C277. CLARK (J. (Joshua) V. H.). Lights and Lines of Indian
Character and Scenes of Pioneer Life. 375pp, portrait,
cloth. Syracuse, E. H. Babcock, 1854, (1st ed.).
                                                            $40.00
Field: 324 "Lighter results of his research ...
traditions, legends and the romantic shades of character
and life of the aborigines here find a place." (RMW)

C278. CLARK (J. W.) and IVEY (J. E.). (University of Texas,
Texas Archeological Survey, Research Report 32, Austin, 1974, 1st ed.) Martin Lake, Rusk and Panola Counties, Texas. 198pp, pls, maps, bibliography, lrg 8vo,
wrappers. $10.00

C279. CLARK (Laverne H.). They Sang for Horses: The Impact
of the Horse on Navaho and Apache Folklore. Illus by
De Grazia, color frontis. University of Arizona, Tucson,
1966, d.j. $85.00
___Another Copy. Same. $10.00

C280. CLARK (Leonard). Yucatan Adventure. 256pp, photographic illus. London, 1959, ex-library (1st ed.).
                                                            $30.00

C281. CLARK (W. P.). The Indian Sign Language, with Brief
Explanatory Notes of the Gestures Taught Deaf-Mutes
... and a Description of Some of the Peculiar Laws, Customs, and War Signals of Our Aborigines. 443pp, folding map, ads. cloth. Philadelphia, 1885. $150.00
___Another Copy. Same. $95.00

C282. CLARKE (Eleanor P.). (University of Arizona Social Science Bulletin 9, Tucson, 1935) Designs on the Prehistoric Pottery of Arizona. 76pp, illus, some are in
color, wrappers. $35.00

C283. CLARKE (Mary W.). Chief Bowles and the Texas Chero-
kees. 154pp, pls, maps, bibliography, index. Chief
Bowles died fighting removal in the last conflict between
Cherokees and Whites in Texas. University of Oklahoma,
1971 (1st ed.), d.j. $25.00
___Another Copy. Same. $15.00

C284. CLARKE (N. T.). (New York State Museum Bulletin 288,
1931) The Wampum Belt Collection of the New York
State Museum. pp85-121, 14 full-page photographs, in-
scribed by author. $30.00
___Another Copy. Same. Not signed, self-
                        wrappers. $15.00
___Another Copy. Same. $15.00

C285. CLAVIJERO (Francisco J.). Historia Antiqua de Mexico. Traduccion del Italiano por J. Joaquin de Mora. Prefacio por Julio le Riverend Brusone. In Two Parts. Part I: 271pp. Part II: 327pp. 19 illus, both parts bound in one volume. $75.00

C286. CLAY (Jehu C.). Annals of the Swedes on the Delaware. 232pp, 17 illus, frontis, includes Indian Missions. Chicago, 1938 (4th ed.). $30.00

C287. CLEMENTS (Lydia). The Indians of Death Valley. 23pp, illus, bibliography, decorative wrappers. Hollywood, 1962 (revised ed.). $12.00

C288. CLIFFORD (Georgia). Indian Legends of the Mississippi Valley. 113pp, illus. St. Louis, 1946 (3rd ed.). $25.00

C289. CLIFFORD (Paul). Art of Costa Rica: Pre-Columbian Painted and Sculpted Ceramics from the Sackler Collections. Essays by Doris Stone, et al. 307pp, over 250 illus with many in color (photographs), 4to, full leather. Exhibition catalogue, Washington, 1985, d.j. $150.00

C290. CLIFTON (James). The Prairie People, Continuity and Change in Potawatomi Indian Culture, 1665-1965. xx, 529pp, photographs and maps, notes, bibliography, index, an extensive study of the Potawatomi tribe, focusing specifically on the Prairie Band. University of Kansas, 1977 (1st ed.), d.j. $25.00

C291. CLINE (W.). (General Series in Anthropology No. 6, Menasha, 1938) The Sinkaietk of Southern Okanagon of Washington. 262pp, 35 figures, map. $67.00

C292. CLOWSER (Don C.). Dakota Indian Treaties, From Nomad to Reservation. 258pp, maps, bibliography, wrappers. Deadwood, 1974 (1st ed.). $15.00

C293. CLUM (Woodworth). Apache Agent. The Story of John P. Clum. 292pp, illus, index. Boston, 1936 (1st ed.). $85.00

Adams Guns: 446. Powell, SW 100 #19. Rader: 848. Clum was the first mayor of Tombstone, the founder of its famous paper, the "Epitaph," the first Indian agent of the San Carlos Apaches. He and his scouts captured Geronimo in 1877. (TNL)

___Another Copy. Same. $65.00
___Another Copy. Same. $60.00

C294. COAN (C. F.). The Adoption of the Reservation Policy in the Pacific Northwest. 38pp, wrappers. Off-print from the Oregon Historical Quarterly. Portland, 1922. $15.00

C295. COATSWORTH (E. S.). The Indians of Quetico. 58pp, color frontis, 9 pls, 12mo. Toronto, 1957. $15.00
___Another Copy. Same. $10.00

C296. COBB (William H.) et al. Monument to and History of the Mingo Indians. 32pp, plus 3pp insert numbered 17a, b & c, about a local controversy involving the Mingo

Indians and the location of their camps in West Virginia, cloth. n.p., 1921. $30.00
___Another Copy. Same. $30.00

C297. CODERE (H.). (American Ethnological Society Monograph XVIII, 1950) Fighting with Property, A Study of Kwakiutl Potlatching and Warfare, 1792-1930. viii, 136pp, 6 figures, 20 tables, fold-out map in rear pocket, cloth. $30.00

C298. (CODEX). (Fuentes Para la Historia de Mexico, 1948) Anales de Tlatelolco y Codice de Tlatelolco. Version Preparada y Anotado por Heinrich Berlin, con Una Interpretacion del Codice por Robert H. Barlow. 128pp, plus 5 pls and Codice, 1 pl folds out 36" in length. $75.00

C299. (CODEX). Codice Chimalpopoca: Anales de Cuauhtitlan. Translated from Nahuatl by Primo Feliciano Velazquez. 162pp, plus facsimiles, wrappers. Mexico, 1975 (2d ed.). $25.00

C300. (CODEX). Codice de Dresden: Manuscripto Pictorico Ritual Maya. 74 hand-colored pls (accordian folded), with deer-skin covers in a hand-made leather slipcase, limited to 50 copies, this copy un-numbered. Echaniz, Mexico, 1947. $850.00

C301. (CODEX). (Instituto Nacional de Antropologia e Historia, Serie. Investigaciones No. 5, Mexico, 1961) Codice Laud. Intro. Sececcion y Notas por Carlos Martinez Marin. 34pp, 46pls, wrappers. $35.00

C302. (CODEX). The Codex Perez and the Book of Chilam Bilam of Mani. 209pp. Norman, 1979, d.j. $25.00
___Another Copy. Same, missing d.j. $18.00

C303. (CODEX). Codex Persianus. Amended Reproduction of the Facsimile Edition Printed in Paris in 1887. Introduction by Dr. F. Anders. Introduction 41pp with German text, 22 accordian folded pp, in the original size (5" x 10"), folding box with leather spine. Graz, 1968. $250.00

C304. (CODEX). Codice Ramirez: Relacion del Origen de los Indios que Habitan Esta Nueve Espana Segun Sus Historias. Examen de la Obra con un Anexo por Manual Orozco y Berra. 16th-Century Manuscript. 294pp, wrappers. Mexico, 1944. $100.00

C305. (CODEX). Codex Tro-Cortesianus (Madrid): True and Accurate Color Facsimile Edition. Introduction by Dr. F. Anders. 112 folding pp (5" x 9"), 49pp introduction in German with summary in English, boxed. Graz, 1967. $600.00
Longest of the Mayan documents, the original preserved in Madrid, supposedly brought from Mexico by Cortes, hence the name. (B. Fein)

C306. (CODEX). Codex Vaticanus "A"--3738. Introductory note in English. 1pp, 96 color pls, both sides plated in book form (10" x 14"), leather spine, manuscript composed between 1570 and 1589 on the plateau of Mexico. Graz, Austria, 1979. $375.00

C307. (CODEX). Codice Xolotl. Edicion, Estudio y Apendice de Charles E. Dibble (2 Volumes). Vol. I: 164pp. Vol. II: 10 folding pls which are color facsimiles of codex, folio. Mexico, 1980 (2d ed.). $75.00

C308. (CODEX). Coleccion de Mendoza O Codice Mendocino Documento Mexicano del Siglo XVI.... liv, 80pp, folio, loose in folder with string ties, lacking backstrip. Facsimile of the important Codex Mendicino, the original of which is in the Bodliean Library at Oxford. Mexico, 1925. $225.00

C309. (CODEX). Facsimile of an Ancient Mexican Codex Belonging to Lord Zouche of Harynworth, England. Introduction by Zelia Nuttall. 35pp descriptive booklet, 84 color pls (accordian folded), specially made folding linen box. Peabody Museum, Cambridge, 1902. $900.00

C310. (CODEX AUBIN). Histoire de la Nation Mexicaine Depuis le Depart d'Aztlan Jusqu'a l'Arrivee des Conquerants Espagnols (et au Dela 1607).... (2)ff., ff. 1-2 then pp. 3-158; (2)ff., iii(iv blank), 63pp, sml octavo, original wrappers, cloth, clamshell case. Paris, Ernest Leroux, 1893. $750.00

First edition of this codex. Through the use of chromolithography, the publisher reproduces the 16th Century original. The pictographic codex is accompanied by Aubin's commentary. Dating from the last third of the 16th Century, the codex is the history of the Nahua nation from the time of its departure from Aztlan to the time of the Spanish conquest. Was printed in an edition of 170 copies. (WR)

C311. CODY (Rev. Edmund R.). History of the Coeur d'Alene Mission of the Sacred Heart. 48pp, illus, bibliography, wrappers. Jesuit mission among the Indians. n.p., 1930 (1st ed.). $20.00

C312. CODY (Iron Eyes). Indian Talk; Hand Signals of the American Indians. 112pp, illus with 246 photographs showing Indian hand signals. Healdsburg, 1970. $10.00

COE (Joffre L.). See BAE Bulletin No. 180.

C313. COE (Michael). America's First Civilization: Discovering the Olmec. Illus, some in color. New York, 1968, d.j. $15.00

C314. COE (Michael D.). Classic Maya Pottery at Dumbarton Oaks. 16 color pls loose in cloth folio with 30pp descriptive booklet. Washington, 1975. $25.00

C315. COE (Michael D.) and FLANNERY (Kent V.). Early Cultures and Human Ecology in South Coastal Guatemala. xi, 136pp, 50 illus, 32 pls, 4to, 15 tables. Smithsonian Press, 1967. $45.00

_____Another Copy. (Smithsonian Institution Contributions

to Anthropology, Vol. 3, 1967) Cloth. $35.00
___Another Copy. Same. Wrappers. $15.00

C316. COE (M. D.). (Peabody Museum, Papers Vol. LIII, 1961)
La Victoria, An Early Site on the Pacific Coast of Guatemala. xiv, 163pp of text containing 12 figures, 18 tables,
plus 48pp of photographs and drawings of hundreds of
ceramic and stone artifacts. $67.00

C317. COE (Michael) and DIEHL (Richard). In the Land of the
Olmec. (2 Volumes) Vol. I: The Archaeology of San
Lorenzo Tenochtitlan. 416pp, 511 illus. Vol. II: The
People of the River. 198pp, 104 illus, boxed. Austin,
1980. $100.00
___Another Copy. Same. $100.00

C318. COE (Michael D.). The Jaguar's Children--Pre-Classic
Central Mexico. 126pp, 208 illus, maps. New York,
1965, d.j. $25.00

C319. COE (Michael D.). Lords of the Underworld--Masterpieces
of Classic Maya Ceramics. 142pp, 20 folding color pls,
figures. Princeton University, 1978, d.j. $50.00
___Another Copy. Same. $60.00

C320. COE (Michael D.). The Maya. 252pp, 83 photographs,
44 drawings, 7 maps, cloth. New York, 1966. $25.00

C321. COE (Michael D.). The Maya Scribe and His World.
184pp, 278 b/w pls, 28 color pls, photographs, several
are roll-out, all by Justin Kerr, oblong folio (11" x
17"), limited to 1,000 copies, includes what some con-
sider the Fourth Maya Book of Pre-Columbian origin, the
Grolier Codex. $350.00

C322. COE (M. D.) and GROVE (D.) (organizers). (BENSON,
E. P., Editor). The Olmec and their Neighbors, Essays
in Memory of Matthew W. Stirling. xi, 346pp, 264
figures, cloth. Dumbarton Oaks, 1981. $60.00
Twenty essays in memory of Matthew W. Stirling--
ethnologist, pioneer archaeologist, discoverer of the Olmec civilization, Chief of the Bureau of American Ethnol-
ogy--grace the pages of this publication. Written with
obvious affection, these essays add even more to our
understanding of the Olmec and their arts. Among the
contributors are Coe, Phillip Drucker, Elizabeth Benson,
Peter J. Furst, Robert Heizer, David Joralemon and
Ignacio Bernal. Also included is a full bibliography of
Stirling's writings. (EAP)

C323. COE (Ralph). Sacred Circles: Two Thousand Years of
North American Indian Art. 252pp 4to, illus, some are
in color, wrappers. Nelson Art Gallery, Kansas City,
1977. $35.00

C324. COE (William R.). Piedras Negras Archaeology: Artifacts,
Caches and Burials. 176pp, 69 figures of multiple arti-
facts, inscribed by author, 4to, wrappers. University
Museum, Philadelphia, 1959. $60.00
___Another Copy. Philadelphia, 1959, x, 315pp, 69pp
of figures. $40.00

C325. COEL (Margaret). Chief Left Hand, Southern Arapaho.
338pp, illus, index, maps, bibliography. Norman, 1981,
(1st ed.), d.j. $20.00
___Another Copy. Norman, 1981, Civilization of the
American Indian Series, Vol. 159. $20.00

C326. COEHLO (V. P.). Enterramentos de Cabecas da Cultura
Nasca. vii, 401pp, wrappers. Sao Paulo, 1972. $40.00

C327. COFFEEN (Herbert) (Editor). (The Teepee Book, Vol. 1,
No. 9, Sheridan, WY, 1915) 8vo, original wrappers,
illus. Articles include "Camping with Indians" by Charles
Eastman, and "The Fight" by Badger Clark, etc.
$35.00

C328. COFFEEN (Herbert) (Editor). (The Teepee Book, Vol. 2,
No. 1, Sheridan, WY, 1916) 8vo, original wrappers,
illus. Articles include "Some Adventures of Sweet Root,"
etc. $35.00

C329. COFFEEN (Herbert) (Editor). (The Teepee Book, Vol. 2,
No. 2, Sheridan, WY, 1916) 8vo, original wrappers,
illus. Articles include Indian stories, etc. $35.00

C330. COFFEEN (Herbert) (Editor). (The Teepee Book, Vol. 2,
No. 3, Sheridan, WY, 1916) 8vo, original wrappers,
illus. Articles include fine photographs by Indian photographer Richard Throssel and Crow Indian Myths, etc.
$30.00

C331. COFFEEN (Herbert) (Editor). (The Teepee Book, Vol. 2,
No. 9, Sheridan, WY, 1916) 8vo, original wrappers,
illus. Articles include Crow War Bonnet Myth, etc.
$30.00

C332. COFFER (William E.). Spirits of the Sacred Mountains,
Creation Stories of the American Indian. 122pp, illus,
bibliography, index, New York, 1978. $18.00
Traditional creation stories of Indian tribes and the
first to bring an American Indian point of view to the
theory of the origin of human life. Unlike popular treat-
ments of Indian stories as legends and myths, this well-
researched account draws directly on oral tradition.
(GFH)

C333. COFFIN (E. F.). (Museum of the American Indian, Miscellaneous Publications No. 48, 1932) Archaeological Exploration of a Rock Shelter in Brewster County, Texas.
72pp, 25 photographs and 6 drawings of artifacts, fold-
out map. $24.00

C334. COFFIN (Morse H.). (Edited, with introduction and notes
by Alan W. Farley) The Battle of Sand Creek. 5 portrait pls, limited to 300 copies. Waco, 1965. $30.00

C335. COGOLLUDO (Lopez). Historia De Yucatan (3 Volumes).
lxviii, 452pp, 373pp, 465pp, includes introduction from
the 1867 ed. by Martin De Escarza, originally published
in 1668, wrappers. Campeche, 1954-55 (4th ed.).
$150.00

C336. COHEN (Felix S.). Felix S. Cohen's Handbook of Federal

Indian Law. 662pp, 4to, index, bibliography. Albuquerque, 1971. $75.00

C337. COHEN (F. S.). Handbook of Federal Indian Law, With
Reference Tables and Index. xxiv, 662pp, cloth. U.S.
Dept. of Interior, 1945. $40.00

C338. COHEN (M. M.). Notices of Florida and the Campaigns.
240pp, frontis, folding map, original stamped cloth.
Charlestown, SC, Burges and Honour, 1836 (1st ed.).
$325.00

Field: 339. "Personal narrative and journal of Seminole war."

C339. COHEN (Ronald). (Department of Northern Affairs, Ottawa,
1962) An Anthropological Survey of Communities in the
MacKenzie-Slave Lake Region of Canada. 119pp, wrappers, ex-library. $12.00

C340. COHODAS (Marvin). Oegikup. Washoe Fancy Basketry
1895-1935. 114pp, photographs, maps, oblong, wrappers.
Over 200 photographs of fine baskets from an exhibition
at the University of British Columbia. Vancouver,
1979 (1st ed.). $20.00

C341. (COHOE). A Cheyenne Sketchbook. 93pp plus index,
photographs, 12 color pls, commentary by E. Adamson
Hoebel and Karen Daniels Peterson. Sketches of the old
Cheyenne plains life by Cohoe, drawn while he was a
prisoner at Ft. Marion, Florida, in 1875-76. Norman,
1964 (1st ed.) d.j. $20.00

C342. COLBY (Benjamin) and L. VAN DEN BERGHE (Pierre).
Ixil Country, A Plural Society in Highland Guatemala.
illus. University of California, Berkeley, 1969, d.j.
$20.00
___Another Copy. Same. $20.00

C343. COLDEN (Cadwallader). The History of the Five Indian
Nations of Canada, Which are Dependent on the Province
of New York in America, and are the Barrier Between the
English and French in that Part of the World. xvi, (4),
90, iv, 91-90, 283pp, folding map, full calf, gilt, front
hinge weak. London, 1747. $1,000.00

Streeter Sale: 868. Vail: 435. Sabin: 14273.
Wroth, American Bookshelf, pp91-95. For decades the
only reliable colonial history of the Iroquois, and one
which colored Enlgish and American policy throughout the
18th Century. Lawrence Wroth says this "was almost the
only book in English that pretended to give anything beyond the most general information about the manners,
customs, history and organization of that confederacy of
Indians...." Wroth goes on to praise the book for several more pages. The first edition of this work was issued in New York in 1727. This second edition is vastly
expanded, the whole second part being made up of Cold-
en's "Papers Relating to the Indian Trade," issued first
in New York in 1724. According to Wroth, about 300

copies of this edition were issued before the substitution of the titlepage with a later date. (WR)

___Another Copy. London, T. Osborne, 1747 (1st English ed.) pp(xx), 204, 283, (1), full calf, neatly rebacked, lacks map. $250.00

Howes: C-560. "First history of the Iroquois Confederation." Sabin: 14273. Field: 342 (RMW)

___Another Copy. New York, 1902 (2 Volumes) 264pp, 387pp, folding map, 12mo, t.e.g., slipcase, reprint of the 1727 first history and first historical work printed in New York. $50.00

C344. COLE (Cyrenus). I Am a Man: The Indian Black Hawk. Portrait, 312pp, original red cloth, gilt. Iowa, 1938 (1st ed.). $75.00
___Another Copy. Same. $60.00
___Another Copy. Same. $25.00

C345. COLE (D.). Captured Heritage, The Scramble for Northwest Coast Artifacts. xvi, 373pp, 29 photographs, 11 drawings, 3 maps, cloth. Seattle, 1985. $27.00
___Another Copy. Same. $15.00

C346. COLE (Faye-Cooper) et al. (University of Chicago, 1951) Kincaid: A Prehistoric Illinois Metropolis. Illus, d.j. $50.00

C347. COLE (Faye-Cooper) and DEUEL (T.). Rediscovering Illinois: Archaeological Explorations in and Around Fulton County. xvi, 295pp, illus, 36 pls, maps (some folding), endpaper maps, glossary, index, inscribed by both authors. University of Chicago, 1937 (1st ed.), d.j. $45.00
___Another Copy. Same. $25.00

C348. COLE (W. H.). The Great Serpent Mound. 24pp, folding photographic panorama, maps, figures, 12mo. n.p., n.d. (c. Columbus, Ohio, Ohio State University Archeology and History Society, 1890, 1st ed.). $30.00

C349. COLEMAN (A. P.). Ice Ages: Recent and Ancient. 296pp, illus, maps, cloth. London, 1926. $12.00

C350. COLEMAN (Emma L.). New England Captives Carried to Canada between 1677 and 1760, during the French and Indian Wars (2 Volumes). pp438; 452, illus, cloth. Portland, Maine, Southworth Press, 1925. $75.00

C351. COLES (Robert). The Last and First Eskimos. 149pp, 100 duotone photographs by A. Harris. New York Graphic Society, 1970. $35.00

C352. Collection of the Massachusetts Historical Society Vol. VI, 3rd Series. 300pp, half morocco. Includes "History of the Pequot Wars" by Underhill, "History of the Pequot War" by Vincent, "Description of New England," by Gorges, "Captivity Among the Delaware Indians From 1756 to 1759" by Gibson. Boston, 1837. $25.00

COLLIER (Donald). See also BAE Bulletin No. 143.

C353. COLLIER (Donald) et al. (University of Washington

Publications in Anthropology, Vol. 9, No. 1, Seattle,
1942) Archaeology of the Upper Columbia Region.
178pp, illus, wrappers. $35.00
___Another Copy. Same. $25.00
___Another Copy. Same. $35.00
___Another Copy. Same. Ex-library. $12.00

C354. COLLIER (G. A.). Fields of the Tzotzil, the Ecological
Bases of Tradition in Highland Chiapas. xv, 255pp,
37pp of photographs, 17 figures, 12 maps, 27 tables,
cloth. Austin, 1975. $20.00

C355. COLLIER (J.). The Indians of America. xi, 325pp, 17
photographs, 2 maps, cloth. New York, 1947. $23.00

C356. COLLIER (John). Patterns and Ceremonials of the Indians
of the Southwest. 192pp, illus by Ira Moskowitz with
over 100 lithographs and drawings, cloth, #1409/1475
Copies, signed by author and artist. On Hopi, Zuni,
Navaho and Apache life styles. New York, 1949 (1st
ed.), d.j. $125.00
___Another Copy. Same. $55.00
___Another Copy. New York, 1972, American Indian
Ceremonial Dances: Navajo, Pueblo, Apache, Zuni, 192pp,
approx 200 illus revised ed. $25.00

C357. COLLIER (John, Jr.) and BUITRON (Anibal). (University
of Chicago, 1949) The Awakening Valley: The Photographic Record of a Social Miracle Among the Indians of
Ecuador. Illus, d.j. $38.00

C358. COLLINS (H. B.). Archaeology of the Bering Sea Region.
pp453-468, plus 11pp of photographs, wrappers, offprint
of Smithsonian Report for 1933. $20.00

C359. COLLINS (H. B.). (Smithsonian Miscellaneous Collections
Vol. 96, No. 1, 1937) Archaeology of St. Lawrence Is-
land, Alaska. x, 431pp, 26 figures, 84pp photographs.
                                                           $185.00
___Another Copy. Same. $45.00

C360. COLLINS (H. B.). (National Museum of Canada Bulletin
No. 118, Ottawa, 1950) Excavations of Frobisher Bay,
Baffin Island, N.W.I., a preliminary report. pp18-44,
illus, plus 11 pls, wrappers. $25.00

C361. COLLINS (H. B.) et al. The Far North--2000 Years of
American Eskimo and Indian Art. 320pp, 15 color and
350 b/w photographs, 3 maps, cloth. Washington, 1973.
                                                           $40.00
   This indispensible catalogue accompanied an exhibition
of astonishing beauty held at the National Gallery that
presented an extraordinary variety of objects--half of
them Eskimo, and the rest mostly Tlingit, with some
Athabaskan and Haida--loaned by institutions throughout
the world. Great photographs and documentations for
each object and informative essays on the cultures represented. Many of the objects, particularly from museums
in Russia, Finland and Germany, had never before been

exhibited outside of their borders. This publication is
one of only a handful of great Eskimo and Indian art
catalogues produced over the past several decades.
(EAP)

___Another Copy. Same. $45.00
___Another Copy. Same. $30.00
___Another Copy. Same. $25.00

C362. COLLINS (H. B.). (Smithsonian Miscellaneous Collections
       Vol. 100, 1940) Outline of Eskimo History. pp533-592,
       1 figure, 6pp photographs, fold-out map, essays in his-
       torical anthropology of North America. $30.00

C363. COLLINS (H. B.). (Smithsonian Miscellaneous Collections
       Vol. 81, No. 14, 1929) Prehistoric Art of the Alaskan
       Eskimo. 52pp of text, plus 24pp of photographs of 106
       bone and ivory objects, wrappers. $25.00

___Another Copy. Same. $20.00
___Another Copy. Seattle, 1969. $12.00

C364. COLLINS (H. B.). Warpath and Cattle Trail. xix, 296pp,
       illus. Ranch life among the Cheyennes and Arapahoes
       in Oklahoma Territory. New York, 1928 (1st ed.).
                                                        $40.00

C365. COLLINS (June McCormick). Valley of the Spirits. The
       Upper Skagit Indians of Western Washington. 256pp plus
       index, photographs, drawings, maps, bibliography.
       Seattle, 1974 (1st ed.), d.j. $15.00

___Another Copy. Same. $12.00

C366. COLLINS (M. B.). (University of Texas Archeological Sur-
       vey Papers, No. 16, Austin, 1969 1st ed.) Test Excava-
       tions of Amistad, 1967. 103pp, maps, pls, bibliography,
       large 8vo, wrappers. $10.00

COLOMBIA. See No. C373.

C367. COLSON (Elizabeth). The Makah Indians: A Study of an
       Indian Tribe in Modern American Society. xvi, 308pp,
       maps, bibliography, index. Author lived with these
       Neah Bay, Washington Indians. University of Minnesota,
       1953 (1st ed.), d.j. $50.00

___Another Copy. Manchester University Press,
                      1953, d.j. $75.00
___Another Copy, Manchester, England, 1953. $35.00

COLTON (Harold S.). See also BAE Bulletin No. 104.

C368. COLTON (Harold S.). Black Sand: Prehistory in Northern
       Arizona. viii, 132pp, illus, maps, bibliography, index.
       Prehistoric Southwest Indians. University of New Mexi-
       co, 1960 (1st ed.), d.j. $50.00

___Another Copy. Same. $25.00
___Another Copy. Westport, CT, 1973. $20.00

C369. COLTON (H. S.). Hopi Kachina Dolls, with a Key to
       Their Identification. 160pp, 14 color and 33 b/w photo-
       graphs, 330 line drawings, cloth. Albuquerque, 1949,
       1959 (revised ed.). $24.00

___Another Copy. Same. $25.00
___Another Copy. Same. $15.00

C370. COLTON (H. S.). (Museum of Northern Arizona Bulletin
4, Flagstaff, 1933) Pueblo II in the San Francisco Mountains, Arizona. 75pp, 24 illus, later cloth. $50.00
C371. COLTON (Harold S.). (Museum of Northern Arizona Bulletin 22, Flagstaff, 1946, 1st ed.) Archaeology of the
Region of Flagstaff, Arizona. 328pp, pls, maps, bib-
liography, index, limited issue. $50.00
C372. COLUCCIO (F.). Folklore de las Americas. 466pp, 237
photographs. Buenos Aires, 1948. $55.00
C373. (COLUMBIA). Anthropology Series, Vol. XX, No. 2, Chi-
cago, 1936. Archaeology of Santa Marta, Columbia.
Part I. Section I. 272pp, illus with 99 pls of objects
of stone, shell, bone and metal, wrappers. $85.00
C374. (COMANCHE). Three Years Among the Comanches, the
Narrative of Nelson Lee, the Texas Ranger. 179pp,
Norman, 1957, 1st thus. $25.00
C375. COMAS (J.). (Instituto Pan Americano de Geografia e
Historia, Mexico, 1953) Bibliografia Selectiva de las Cul-
turas Indigenas de America. xxviii, 292pp, 5 fold-out
maps, limited to 2,000, wrappers. $25.00
C376. (COMMISSIONERS' REPORT). Fourteenth Annual Report
of the Board of Indian Commissioners for the Year 1882.
67pp, folding map, index. Washington, 1883 (1st ed.).
$50.00
C377. COMPTON (Margaret). American Indian Fairy Tales:
Tales of Snow Bird, The Water Riger, etc. 201pp, illus
by W. C. Greenough, frontis, 10 full-page pls, tales
were obtained through the Smithsonian Institute and came
from the Journals of Schoolcraft, Catlin and Copway, pictorial inset frnt cvr. New York, 1907. $22.00
C378. COMUNALE (A. R.). Art on Stone by the American Indian
in New Jersey. 75pp, drawings of pictographs and other work on stone. New York, 1963 (1st ed.), d.j.
$25.00
C379. CONANT (A. J.). Foot-Prints of the Vanished Races in
the Mississippi Valley. 122pp, illus. St. Louis, 1879.
$50.00
C380. CONCLIN (George). The Great Indian Chief of the West:
or, Life and Adventures of Black Hawk. 288pp, index,
appendices, engravings. Philadelphia, H. M. Rulison,
1856. $65.00
C381. (CONFEDERATED TRIBES). Corporate Charter of the ...
of the Warm Springs Reservation of Oregon. 6pp,
wrappers, Washington, 1938 (1st ed.). $10.00
C382. CONN (Richard). Native American Art in the Denver Art
Museum. 351pp, illus, over 500 pls (100 in color) 4to,
bibliography. Seattle, 1979 (1st ed.), d.j. $50.00
The Native American art collection of the Denver Art
Museum was the first, and for many years the only, collection of native art based on esthetic and historic criteria.
Covers Northeast, Southeast, Subarctic, Woodlands, Plains,

Southwest, California, Northwest Coast and Arctic.
(GFH)

    ____Another Copy. Same. $45.00

    ____Another Copy. Same. $30.00

C383. CONNAWAY (John) and McGAHEY (Samuel). (Mississippi
Dept. of Archives and History Tech. Report No. 1,
Jackson, 1971) Archaeological Excavation at the Boyd
Site, Tunica County, Mississippi. 86pp, 4to, illus,
wrappers. $12.00

C384. CONSUEGRA (D.). Ornamentacion Calada en la Orfebreria
Indigena Precolombina (Musica y Tolima). 232pp, 53
photographs. Museo Del Oro, Bogota, 1968. $25.00

    ____Another Copy. Same. $35.00

C385. CONTE (C.) et al. Maya Culture and Costume, A Catalogue of the Taylor Museum's E. B. Ricketson Collection
of Guatemalan Textiles. 120pp, 49 color and 94 b/w
photographs, 5 figures, 1 map. Taylor Museum, 1984.
          $24.00

CONZEMIUS (Eduard). See also BAE Bulletin No. 106.

C386. (COOK, Charles H.). Among the Pimas, or the Mission
to the Pima and Maricopa Indians. 136pp, frontis, 4
pls, 12mo, half cloth, bds. Albany, New York, 1893.
          $60.00

    ____Another Copy. Same. $50.00

    ____Another Copy. Same. $35.00

C387. COOK (Frederick). Journals of the Military Expedition of
Major General John Sullivan Against the Six Nations of
Indians in 1779. 581pp, 5 pocket maps, other maps,
illus, errata, some light foxing. Albany, New York,
1887, 1st thus. $75.00

    ____Another Copy. Same. $55.00

C388. COOK (Sherburne F.). The Conflict Between the California
Indians and White Civilization. 522pp, index, charts.
Berkeley, 1976. $25.00

    Originally issued as "Ibero-Americana Series Nos. 21,
22, 23 and 24." Now all 4 parts reprinted in hard cover
volume. One of the most informative works ever published on relations between the California Indian and White
Man. (GFH)

    ____Another Copy. Same. $15.00

    ____Another Copy. Same. $10.00

C389. COOK (Sherburne). The Extent and Significance of Disease among the Indians of Baja California 1697-1773.
40pp, wrappers. Berkeley, 1937 (1st ed.). $10.00

C390. COOK (Sherburne). The Historical Demography and Ecology
of the Teotlalpan. 59pp, wrappers. University of California, Berkeley, 1949. $15.00

C391. COOK (Sherburne) and BORAH (Woodrow). The Indian
Population of Central Mexico 1531-1610. 109pp, wrappers.
University of California, Berkeley, 1960. $15.00

C392. COOK (S. F.). (University of California at Berkeley,

Publications in Anthropology, Vol. 12, 1976) The Indian
Population of New England in the Seventeenth Century.
91pp, wrappers.
$19.00
___Another Copy. Same. $18.00

C393. COOK (Sherburne). The Population of the California Indians, 1769-1970. 222pp, index, maps, charts. A complete and final estimate of the native California population
of 310,000 in 1769 and less than 30,000 by 1865. Berkeley, 1976 (1st ed.), d.j. $35.00
___Another Copy. Same. $30.00

C394. COOK (Sherburne) and BORAH (Woodrow). The Population
of the Mixteca Alta 1520-1960. 89pp, wrappers. University of California, Berkeley, 1968. $15.00

C395. COOK (S. F.). Population Trends Among the California
Mission Indians. 48pp, 5 figures in text, wrappers.
Berkeley, 1940 (1st ed.). $12.00

C395a. COOK (Sherburne) Santa Maria Ixcatlan: Habitant, Population Subsistence. 75pp, wrappers. University of
California, Berkeley, 1958. $15.00

C396. COOK (W. A.). The Bororo Indians of Matto Grosso Brazil.
pp48-62, 1pp photographs, offprint from Smithsonian
Miscellaneous Collections, Vol. 50, 1907. $12.00

C397. COOKE (David C.). Fighting Indians of the West. 208pp,
illus with photographs, profiles of ten major Indian
Chiefs. New York, 1960. $20.00
___Another Copy. Same. $10.00

C398. COOKE (P. S.). (Senate Executive Document 58, 34:3,
Washington, 1857, 1st print.) Report of ... The Action
at Bluewater, Nebraska Territory, with the Sioux Indians, September 3, 1955. 4pp, removed. $20.00

C399. COOLIDGE (Dane). The Last of the Seris (California Indians) frontis, 264pp, 18 photographs. The strange
story of the Seris, their myths and poetry. This isolated tribe was visited by the Norsemen. New York,
1939 (1st ed.), d.j. $25.00
___Another Copy. Same. $30.00
___Another Copy. Same. $22.00
___Another Copy. Same. $17.00

C400. COOLIDGE (Dane and Mary Roberts). The Navaho Indians.
x, 361pp, illus, endpaper map, cloth, Boston, 1930.
$39.00
___Another Copy. Same. 2 sepia photographs tipped in
on rear flyleaves. Rader: 917. Campbell: p.113.
Saunders: 904. Kluckhohn: p.71. $45.00

C401. COOLIDGE (Mary Roberts). The Rain Makers: Indians of
Arizona and New Mexico. 326pp, illus, index. Boston,
New York, 1929 (1st ed.). $35.00
___Another Copy. Boston, 1929. $20.00

C402. COON (Carleton S.). The Hunting Peoples. 400pp plus
index, drawings, maps, endpaper map, bibliography.
Covers all existing hunting cultures, in regard to

equipment, travel, methods, social organization, marriage rites, myths and healing on the Northwest Indians and Eskimo. Boston, 1971 (1st ed.), d.j. $15.00
_____Another Copy. Same. $15.00

C403.   COOPER (Jacob). Red Pioneers, Romance of Early Indian Life in the West. 251pp, frontis, pictorial cloth, decorative endpapers. McMinville, for author, 1928. $20.00

COOPER (Paul L.). See also BAE Bulletin No. 169.

C404.   COOPER (Paul L.). Archaeological Investigations in Heart Butte Reservoir Area, North Dakota. pp1-40, 12 photographic pls, folding maps, bibliography, wrappers. Offprint from Smithsonian River Basin Survey Papers, Washington 1958. $10.00

C405.   COOPER (Paul L.). (Smithsonian Miscellaneous Collections, Vol. 126, No. 2, Washington, 1955) The Archaeological and Paleontological Salvage Program in the Missouri Basin, 1950-51. 99pp, folding map, references, 12 photographic pls, wrappers. $15.00
_____Another Copy. Same. $12.00

C406.   COPWAY (George). (Kah-Ge-Ga-Gah-Bowh) Indian Life and Indian History by an Indian Author ... Particularly ... The Ojibways. 256pp, decorated cloth. Boston, A. Colby and Co., 1858. $50.00

C407.   COPWAY (George). The Life, History and Travels of Kah-Ge-Ga-Gah-Bowh, Written by Himself. 224pp, engraved frontis, later cloth. Philadelphia, 1847 (2d ed.).
                                                          $60.00

        Howes: C-770. "Contains much information on the Ojibway Indians."
_____Another Copy. New York, S. W. Benedict, 1850. $45.00

C408.   COPWAY (George). Organization of a New Indian Territory, East of the Missouri River ... by the Indian Chief Kah-Ge-Ga-Gah-Bowh. 32pp, disbound. New York, 1850. $225.00
        Howes: C-771. The half-breed Ojibway chief proposes most of the area of Iowa and some of Southern Minnesota as an Indian territory for the northern tribes of the United States, along with some remarks on Indian-White relations. (WR)

C409.   CORDAN (W.). Secret of the Forest: On the Track of the Maya and Their Temples. 223pp, 54 illus, ex-library. New York, 1964. $25.00

C410.   CORDOVA-RIOS (Manuel) and LAMB (F. Bruce). Wizard of the Upper Amazon. 203pp, maps, appendix. New York, 1971 (1st ed.), d.j. $10.00
        Rios spent 7 years as a captive of the Amahuaca Indians, thus learning of their culture, customs and knowledge of healing properties of plants.

C411.   CORDRY (D. B. & D. M.). (Southwest Museum, Papers, No. 14, Los Angeles, 1941) Costumes and Textiles of the Aztec Indians of the Cuetzlan Region, Puebla, Mexico. 60pp, 22 illus. $12.00

C412. CORDRY (Donald). Mexican Indian Costumes. Foreword by Miguel Covarrubias. 373pp, 4to, illus, index, bibliography, maps. Austin, 1968 (1st ed.), d.j. $45.00
___Another Copy. University of Texas, 1968 (2d print.) $35.00

C413. CORDRY (Donald). Mexican Masks. 280pp, 312 illus, most are in color. University of Texas Press, 1980. $40.00
___Another Copy. Same. $20.00

C414. CORKRAN (David H.). The Cherokee Frontier. Conflict and Survival, 1740-62. 286pp plus index, illus, map, bibliography. Norman, 1962 (1st ed.), d.j. $25.00

C415. CORKRAN (David H.). The Creek Frontier, 1540-1783. 343pp, frontis, 8 illus, 2 maps, bibliography, index, cloth. Norman (1st ed.), d.j. $20.00

C416. (CORNELIUS, Elias). The Little Osage Captive ... Added Some Interesting Letters, Written by Indians. 184pp, 18mo, frontis, pl, vignettes, advs, leather backed bds. York, W. Alexander & Sons, 1824 (1st English ed.). $80.00
Ayers: 55. "The Little Osage captive was rescued by missionaries from amongst the Cherokees, and given the name Lydia Carter." (RMW)

C417. CORNELY (F. L.). El Arte Decorativo Preincaico de los Indios de Coquimbo y Atacama (Diaguitas Chilenos). 47pp, 19pp (13" x 8½") of color pls, 8 figures. La Serena, 1962. $38.00

C418. CORONA NUNEZ (Jose)., Mitologia Tarasca. 112pp, 14 pls. Mexico, 1957 (1st ed.), d.j. $40.00

C419. CORSER (H. M.) (Editor). Through the Ten Thousand Islands of Alaska. 46pp, 26 photographs, wrappers. Nugget Shop, Juneau, n.d. (c.1925). $15.00

C420. CORSER (H. H.). Totem Lore of the Alaska Indians and Land of the Totem. 48pp, 28 photographs, rebound in later stiff bds. Wrangell, n.d. (c.1910) (2d ed.). $40.00
___Another Copy. Juneau, n.d. (c.1923) 102pp, many illus, wrappers. $25.00
___Another Copy. Wrangell, AK, 1940, 116pp, 2 adv, illus, decorative wrappers. $25.00
___Another Copy. Same. $20.00

C421. CORSON (C.). Maya Anthropomorphic Figurines from Jaina Island, Campeche. 176pp, 4to, 135 illus, wrappers. Ramona, Ballena Press, 1976. $45.00

C422. (CORTES). Historia de Nueva Espana Escrita por Su Esclarecido Conquistador, Hernan Cortes. Augmented with other documents and notes by Francisco Antonio Lorenzana. 400+pp, folding map, facsimile of 1770 ed., woven cloth cvrs, drawings, leather labels. $75.00

C423.   CORWIN (Hugh D.). Comanche and Kiowa Captives in
        Oklahoma and Texas. 237pp, many illus. Guthrie, OK,
        1959. $50.00

C424.   COSGROVE (C. B.). (Peabody Papers, Vol. XXIV, No.
        2, 1947) Caves of the Upper Gila and Hueco Areas in
        New Mexico and Texas. xv, 181pp, 48 figures, 1 color
        pl, 55pp photographs. $175.00
                This is from the same 1924-27 excavation that yielded
        the classic Mimbres pottery from Swarts Ruin.

C425.   COSGROVE (H. S. and C. B.). (Peabody Papers, Vol.
        XV, No. 1, 1932) The Swarts Ruin, a Typical Mimbres
        Site in Southeastern New Mexico. Report of the Mimbres
        Valley Expedition, Seasons of 1924-27. xxiii, 178pp,
        17 figures, 236pp photographs and drawings, principally
        of Mimbres pottery, 3 maps, original wrappers. $250.00

C426.   COSSIO DEL POMAR (Felipe). The Art of Ancient Peru.
        224pp, 61 pls, 23 in color, text figures. New York,
        1971, d.j. $70.00
        ___Another Copy. Same. $75.00
        ___Another Copy. Same. $60.00

C427.   COSSIO DEL POMAR (Felipe). Arte del Peru PreColumbia.
        214pp, color frontis, 65 pls with 23 in color, 4to.
        Mexico, 1949. $85.00
        ___Another Copy. Same. $75.00

C428.   COTLOW (Lewis). Amazon Head Hunters. 243pp, inscribed
        by author, map. New York, 1953 (1st ed.). $25.00

C429.   COTLOW (Lewis). The Twilight of the Primitive. 246pp,
        b/w and color photographs, maps, index. New York,
        1971 (1st ed.), d.j. $10.00

C430.   COTTER (J. L.). (National Park Service, Archaeological
        Research Series, No. 4, 1958) Archaeological Excava-
        tions at Jamestown, Virginia. x, 299pp, 92 lrg photo-
        graphs, 28 figures, 1 fold-out map. $40.00

C431.   COTTER (J. L.). (National Park Service, Series No. 1,
        1951) Archaeology of the Bynum Mounds Mississippi.
        vi, 112pp, 20pp photographs, 5 figures. $24.00

C432.   COTTERILL (R. S.). The Southern Indians: The Story
        of the Civilized Tribes Before Removal. xiii, 255pp,
        illus, bibliography, index. University of Oklahoma,
        1954 (1st ed.), d.j. $30.00
        ___Another Copy. Same. $25.00

C433.   COURLANDER (Harold). The Fourth World of the Hopis.
        230pp, decorations by Enrico Arno. Hopi legends and
        traditions. New York, 1971 (1st ed.), d.j. $20.00

C434.   COURLANDER (Harold). Hopi Voices; Recollections, Tradi-
        tions and Narratives of the Hopi Indians. Recorded,
        Transcribed and Annotated by Harold Courlander.
        255pp, glossary, bibliography. Albuquerque, 1982
        (1st ed.), d.j. $20.00
        ___Another Copy. Same. $18.00

C435.   COURLANDER (Harold) (Editor). Xava, Albert. Big

Falling Snow. A Tewa-Hopi Indian's Life and Times and the History and Traditions of His People. 179pp, photographs, map endpapers, index. New York, 1978 (1st ed.). $10.00

C436. COUTO DE MAGALHAES (Agenor). Encantors d'Oeste. 224pp, 183 photographs, many of Indians, 4to. Rio de Janeiro, 1945. $35.00

C437. COVARRUBIAS (Luis). Mexican Native Arts and Crafts. 36pp, map, watercolor drawings by author, wrappers. Mexico, n.d. $25.00

C438. COVARRUBIAS (M.). The Eagle, The Jaguar and the Serpent, Indian Art of the Americas. 373pp, 48pp b/w photographs, 110 figures 12pp color pls, cloth. New York, 1954. $97.00
___Another Copy. Same. $75.00
___Another Copy. Same. $40.00

C439. COVARRUBIAS (M.) (Editor). El Arte Indigena de Norteamerica: Exposicion Celebrada en el Museo Nacional de Antropologia. 103pp, 92 photographs, 4to, wrappers. Museo Nacional, 1945. $60.00
___Another Copy. Same. $48.00

C440. COVARRUBIAS (M.). Indian Art of Mexico and Central America. 360pp, 12 color pls, 146 figures. New York, 1957, d.j. $85.00
___Another Copy. Same. $90.00
___Another Copy. Same. $75.00

C441. COVARRUBIAS (M.). Mexico South, the Isthmus of Tehuantepec. xxviii, 436pp, viii, 91 figures, 9 color pls by author, 93 pls, folding map. New York, A. Knopf, 1946 (1st ed.). $40.00
___Another Copy. Same. $45.00

C442. COVARRUBIAS (M.). Mezcala: Ancient Mexican Sculpture. 36pp, 50 illus. New York, Emmerich Gallery, 1956. $25.00

C443. COWAN (Richard A.). The Archaeology of Barrell Springs Site, Pershing County, Nevada ... With Analysis of Faunal Remains by David H. Thomas. 48pp, illus, maps, charts, bibliography, 4to, wrappers. Obsidian industry, rhyolite industry, projectile points, scrapers, worked bone objects, etc. Berkeley, 1972 (1st ed.). $15.00

C444. COX (Ross). (STEWART, Edgar I. and Jane R., Editors). The Columbia River, or Scenes and Adventures During a Residence of Six Years ... Among Various Tribes of Indians hitherto unknown; Together With "A Journey Across the American Continent." 388pp plus index, maps, illus. Norman, 1957 (1st print.), d.j. $20.00

C445. COY (Owen). The Humboldt Bay Region, 1850-1875: A Study in the American Colonization of California. illus, folded map. California State Historical Assn., Los Angeles, 1929. $75.00

C446. COYLER (Vincent). Peace With the Apaches of New Mexico and Arizona: Report of Vincent Coyler, 1871. 58pp, wrappers. Tucson, 1964. $15.00

Reprint of Board of Indian Commissioners 1872 editions. Coyler was a member of the board and was appointed by President Grant to go to the Southwest and report on the condition of the Apaches. His reports are from Camp Grant, Camp McDowell, Pinos Altas, Ft. Craig, etc., and most show the inhuman treatment the Indians received from the white man. (GFH)

C447. COZZENS (Samuel Woodworth). The Marvellous Country, or, Three Years in Arizona and New Mexico.... 532pp, index, illus. Minneapolis, 1967, d.j. $10.00

C448. CRABTREE (Don E.). Experiments in Flintworking. Illus, bibliography, wrappers. Raw materials, tools, techniques, research, practices. Idaho State University Pocatello, 1971. $25.00

C449. CRAD (Joseph). Trailing Through Siberia. xii, 269pp, 1pp, two maps, 1 folding, cloth. Travel Book Club, London, 1939. $20.00

The title is deceptive. There is much about the author's experiences in Alaska around the turn of the century. Quite a bit of information on Eskimos of Kotzebue Sound, and Shamans.

C450. CRAIGHEAD (Jas. R. E.). Black Hawk. A Romance of the Black Hawk War. Told in Spenserian Verse. 108pp, cloth. Creston, Iowa, 1930. $12.00

C451. CRAINE (Eugene R.) and REINFORP (Reginald C.). (Editors and Translators). (Civilization of the American Indian Series Vol. 98, Norman, 1970 1st ed.) The Chronicles of Michoaian. 244pp, index, 44 pls, map, bibliography, d.j. $17.00

C452. CRAKES (Sylvester, Jr.). Five Years a Captive Among the Black-Feet Indians, or, a Thrilling Narrative of the Adventures, Perils and Sufferings, Endured by John Dixon and His Companions, Among the Savages of the Northwest Territory of North America.... 244pp, frontis, pls, original cloth, tear in one leaf with no loss, signature starting. Columbus, 1858. $850.00

The text is based, according to Crakes, upon Dixon's notes which were found at Santa Fe in the possession of a descendant of Castro Urego, for whom Dixon worked after his escape and until his death. The highly romantized style of the narrative led to past suspicions about the authenticity of the tale, but the consensus today is that the captivity is authentic, although it probably occurred later than the ascribed date of 1806. Wagner-Camp: 299. Graff: 903. Ayer Supplement: 37. Howes: C-850. Streeter Sale: 3065. (WR)

C453. CRAMPTON (C. Gregory). The Zunis of Cibola. 201pp, square 4to, illus, index, maps, bibliography. Salt Lake City, 1979, d.j. $30.00

The first examination and portrayal of the Zunis from historical documentation. An important section of this book is a 34 page exhaustive bibliography of significant works relating to the Zunis. Illustrated with full-page photographs by Hillers, Vroman, Nusbaum, Wittick and Black. (GFH)

_____Another Copy. Salt Lake City, 1979. $25.00

C454.   CRANE (Leo). Desert Drums. The Pueblo Indians of New Mexico 1540-1928. 393pp, many photographs. Rader: 952. Boston, 1925 (1st ed.). $27.00

_____Another Copy. Same. $20.00

_____Another Copy. Boston, 1928, als from author tipped in. $75.00

_____Another Copy. Same. d.j. $65.00

C455.   CRANE (Leo). Indians of the Enchanted Desert. 364pp, cloth. The author's experiences as an Indian agent among the Hopi in the teens and 20s. Boston, 1925. Rader: 953. $65.00

_____Another Copy. Same. $50.00

_____Another Copy. Same. $35.00

C456.   CRANE (Warren E.). Totem Tales. 95pp, pls. 39 various tribal legends. Juvenile. New York, 1932 (1st ed.). $25.00

C457.   CRANTZ (David). The History of Greenland: Containing a Description of the Country and its Inhabitants ... Translated from the High Dutch.... (2 Volumes). Vol. I: 60pp, 405pp. Vol. II: 497pp, 1pp. Two folding maps, four folding pls, full calf. London, printed for the Brethren's Society, 1767. $900.00

Field: 383. Sabin: 17457. Pilling: 921. First edition in English of this work, first published in Dutch in 1765, and here translated by Gambold. One of the major important works on the history of the missionary experience among the Indians of Greenland of the Moravian Bretheren. "The minute journal of the noble Moravian Bretheren gives us in their language the phases of Aboriginal life and peculiarities which daily presented themselves. No tribe of American savages has been more closely or intelligently studied. Specimens of their language are given...." Field. Another English edition of 1820 is abridged, and this edition presents the best text. (WR)

C458.   CRAPANZANO (Vincent). The Fifth World of Enoch Maloney. 242pp, 1pp. Modern Navaho. New York, 1969 (1st ed.), d.j. $10.00

C459.   CRAPANZANO (Vincent). The Fifth World of Forster Bennett: Portrait of a Navaho. 245pp. New York, 1972 (1st ed.), d.j. $10.00

C460.   CRARY (Margaret). Susette La Flesch: Voice of the Omaha Indians. 173pp, bibliography, index. New York 1973 (1st ed.). $10.00

C461. CRAWFORD (Isabel). Kiowa. 242pp, illus, history of a
       blanket Indian Mission. New York, 1915. $30.00

C462. CRAWFORD (J. M.) (Editor). Studies in Southeastern In-
       dian Languages. viii, 453pp, maps. 10 essays on
       Shawnee, Choctaw, Chickasaw, etc. University of
       Georgia, 1975 (1st ed.). $25.00
       ___Another Copy. Same. $27.00
       ___Another Copy. Same. $18.00

C463. CRAWFORD (M. H.) and WORKMAN (P. L.). Methods and
       Theories of Anthropological Genetics. 498pp, plus in-
       dex, maps, charts, bibliography. A School of American
       Research publication. Albuquerque, 1973 (1st ed.),
       d.j. $25.00

C464. CRAWFORD (Oswald). By Path and Trail. xi, 225pp,
       7 pls, travels in Arizona, New Mexico and Baja, Indians
       of Northern Mexico and lower California. Press of the
       International Catholic, 1908 (1st ed.). $45.00

C465. (CREEK INDIANS). No. I. of Documents Accompanying
       the President's Communications to Congress, the 8th
       Day of December, 1801. Letter from the Principal Agent
       for Indian Affairs, South of the Ohio. 11pp, stitched.
       Washington, 1801. $750.00
           Shaw & Shoemaker: 1476. A letter from Benjamin
       Hawkins, principal agent for Indians south of the Ohio
       River, describing the Creek Indians. He describes
       meeting with the Indians, their stockraising and agri-
       culture, their production of cotton weaving and nut
       oil, the difficulties of depredations on Whites committed
       by hunting parties, trade with the United States, and
       expenditures of the agency (including $12.50 per head
       paid the Creeks for the return of runaway slaves).
       A most important document, quite rare, as most docu-
       ments of this period other than session laws. (WR)

C466. (CREEK INDIANS). A treaty of Limits Between the United
       States of America, and the Creek Nation of Indians, 16th
       June, 1802. 8pp, disbound. Printed by Order of the
       Senate of the United States, Washington, December 29,
       1802. $1,000.00
           Sabin: 96609. Shaw & Shoemaker: 3451. An early
       and important treaty with the Creeks, negotiated for the
       United States by J. Wilkinson, B. Hawkins, and A.
       Pickens, ceding to the United States in exchange for
       payment lands in Florida. An uncommon document, not
       in Gilcrease-Hargrett, and located in only two copies by
       Shaw & Shoemaker. (WR)

C467. (CREEK INDIANS). (House Report No. 1, Washington 1822)
       Treaties With the Creek and Cherokee Indians. 10pp,
       2pp, removed. Agreement and comments on the Indian
       Reserves in Georgia. $10.00

C468. (CREEK INDIANS). (House of Representatives Document
       165, Washington, 1826) Message from the President of

the United States: Treaty with the Creek Nation of Indians: Also, A Copy of a Treaty, Superseded by the
Same, Signed at Indian Springs on the 12th of January,
1825. 15pp, wrappers. $35.00

C469. (CREEK INDIANS). (House of Representatives Document
276, 24:1, Washington, 1836, 1st print.) Creek Indian
Hostilities. 413pp, removed. Causation of the Creek
Indian War. $30.00

C470. (CREEK INDIANS). (House of Representatives Document
154, 24:2, Washington, 1837, 1st print.) Creek Indians
--Hostilities with. 61pp, removed. Detailing hostilities
with Indians, mostly in Mississippi. $15.00

C471. (CREEK INDIANS). (House of Representatives Document
78, 25:2, Washington, 1838, 1st print.) Court of In-
quiry--Operations in Florida. 832pp, pp121-206, 2 folding maps, removed. Creek and Seminole War, narratives of battles, other military operations. $15.00

C472. (CREEK INDIANS). (House of Representatives Document
274, 25:2, Washington, 1838, 1st print.) Contract--
General Jesup, Creek Chiefs.... 173pp, removed.
Attempts to remove the Creeks from their land so that
the Whites could settle thereon. $20.00

C473. (CREEK INDIANS). (House of Representatives Document
452, 25:2, Washington, 1838, 1st print.) Alleged Frauds
on Creek Indians. 102pp, removed. Defrauding of the
Indians in the transfer of their lands to the Government.
$15.00

C474. (CREEK INDIANS). (House of Representatives Executive
Document 15, 33:2, Washington, 1854, 1st print.) Creek
and Seminole Indians. 33pp, removed. Causes of the
war between and reports of incidences. $12.00

C475. (CREEK INDIANS). Accounts with Creeks, Choctaws, Etc.
Letter ... Transmitting the Accounts of the Superintendent of Indian Affairs of the Southern Superintendency.
116pp, disbound. Washington, 1863. $35.00

C476. (CREEK INDIANS). (Senate Executive Document 75, 47:1,
Washington, 1882, 1st print.) Cession of Certain Lands
in the Indian Territory Occupied by the Seminole Indians. 9pp, folding map, removed. $15.00

C477. (CREEK INDIANS). (Senate Executive Document 50, 48:2,
Washington, 1885, 1st print.) Indian Territory, Lands
Acquired by Treaty from the Creek and Seminole Indians.
71pp, 2 folding maps of the territory, removed. $35.00

C478. (CREEK INDIANS). (House of Representatives Document
252, 55:3, Washington, 1899, 1st print.) Agreement with
Creek Nation. 13pp, removed. 1899 Treaty. $10.00

C479. CREEL (Darrell) et al. (University of Texas Archaeological
Survey Report No. 62, San Antonio, 1979) Excavations
at 41Lk106, a Prehistoric Occupation Site in Live Oak
County, Texas. 44pp, photographs, maps, bibliography,
wrappers. $10.00

C480. CREMONY (John C.). Life Among the Apaches. 322pp, half calf, ex-library, minor markings. San Francisco, 1868. $225.00

Cremony served as interpreter to Bartlett on the Arizona boundary survey, and his narrative is one of the best accounts of the Apaches and neighboring tribes. Field: 387. Howes: C-879. Graff: 915. (WR)

____Another Copy. Same. Original cloth. $225.00

____Another Copy. New York, 1951. 322pp, illus. $35.00

____Another Copy. Tucson, 1954. 322pp, pictorial cloth, illus by Wm. Harrison Bryant. $35.00

____Another Copy. Alexandria, 1980, 322pp, bound in full leather, gilt lettering. $25.00

____Another Copy. New York, 1981. Time-Life Books. 322pp. $15.00

C481. CRESSMAN (L. S.). (Carnegie Institution of Washington, Publication 538, 1942) Archaeological researches in the Northern Great Basin. xvii, 158pp, 1 map, 39 tables, 102pp photographs, drawings and maps. $145.00

C482. CRESSMAN (Luther). (University of Oregon Monograph Studies in Anthropology, Bulletin No. 1, Eugene, 1936) Archaeological Survey of the Guano Valley Region in Southeastern Oregon. 48pp, wrappers. $15.00

C483. CRESSMAN (Luther). Prehistory of the Far West. Homes of Vanished Peoples. xv, 248pp, color frontis, maps, photographic illus, 33pp bibliography, index. University of Utah, Salt Lake City, 1977 (1st ed.), d.j. $20.00

C484. CROCKER (J. C.). Vital Souls, Bororo Cosmology, Natural Symbolism, and Shamanism. xiii, 380pp, 18 illus, 6 tables, cloth. Tucson, 1985. $40.00

C485. CRONAU (Rodolfo). America: Historia de So Descubrimiento Desde los Tiempos Primitivos Hasta los Mas Modernos. (3 Volumes). pp 408, 337 and 404, profusely illus, 3 color pls. Barcelona, 1892. $100.00

C486. CRONYN (G. W.). The Path of the Rainbow, An Anthology of Songs and Chants from the Indians of North America. xxxii, 347pp, black cloth, gilt decorations. New York, 1918 (2d print.). $24.00

____Another Copy. Same. $30.00

C487. CROSBY (Harry W.). The Cave Paintings of Baja California. 189pp, 4to, illus, index, maps, bibliography. La Jolla, 1984, d.j. $35.00

C488. CROSBY (Thomas). Among the An-ko-me-nums or Flathead Tribes of the Pacific Coast. 243pp, illus. Author was a missionary to the Flathead. Smith: 2134. Toronto, 1907 (1st ed.). $75.00

C489. (CROW). (Senate Executive Document 43, 51:2, Washington, 1891, 1st print.) Agreement for the Sale of the Western Part of the Crow Indian Reservation in Montana.

26pp, removed. Text of negotiations and agreements.
$15.00

C490. Crow Texts, Collected, Translated and Edited by Robert
H. Lowie. xiii, 550pp, cloth, the author's personal
copy, bearing his bookplate. Berkeley, 1960. $57.00
___Another Copy. Same. No bookplate. $47.00

C491. CROWDER (David L.). Tendoy, Chief of the Lemhis.
139pp, illus, index, map, wrappers. Caldwell, 1969
(1st ed.). $25.00

C492. CROWDER (Jack L.). Stephanie and the Coyote. 32pp,
text in English and Navaho, wrappers. U.S. Indian
Service, 1970. $10.00

C493. (CROWN RESERVATION). Letter from the Secretary of
Interior ... Regarding the Leasing of and on the Crown
Indian Reservation in Montana Territory.... 45pp, re-
moved. Describes the leasing of these lands in eastern
Montana for cattle ranching. Washington, 1885. $60.00

C494. CRUMINE (N. R.) (Editor). Ritual Symbolism and Ceremonialism in the Americas: Studies in Symbolic Anthropology (2 Volumes). pp178; 291, wrappers. University
of Colorado, 1979. $27.00

C495. CRUMRINE (Lynne S.). (University of Arizona Anthropology Papers no. 5, Tucson, 1961, 1st ed.) The Phonology of Arizona Yaqui, with Texts. 43pp, wrappers.
$10.00

C496. CRUSE (Thomas). Apache Days and After. Edited with
an Introduction by Eugene Cunningham. 329pp, frontis,
33pp photographs, gilt stamped pictorial cloth. Caldwell, Caxton Press, 1941 (1st ed.), d.j. $150.00
___Another Copy. Same. $125.00

C497. CRUXENT (J. M.) and ROUSE (I.). An Archaeological
Chronology of Venezuela (2 Volumes). Vol. I: 320pp
of text. Vol. II: 226pp of text, 201 figures, 104pp
of photographs. Washington, 1958. $95.00
___Another Copy. Washington, 1961. Spanish language
ed. Arqueologia Cronologica de Venezuela. Estudios
Monograficos, VI. $85.00

C498. CRUZ (Pacheco). Usos, Costumbres, Religion y Super-
sticiones de Los Mayas. 294pp, illus, stiff wrappers.
Merida, 1960. $45.00

C499. (CUERO, Delfina). (Baja California Travel Series No. 12,
Los Angeles, 1968) The Autobiography of Delfina Cuero,
A Diegueno Indian as Told to Florence C. Shipek.
67pp, folding map. (1st ed.). $35.00

C500. CULBERT (T. P.). (New World Archaeological Foundation.
Brigham Young University Paper No. 19, 1969) The
Ceramic History of the Central Highlands of Chiapas,
Mexico. 91pp, 38 illus. $12.00

C501. CULBERT (T. Patrick) (Editor). The Classic Maya Collapse. 543pp plus index, photographs, diagrams, drawings, maps. A major work on the collapse which occurred

in the 8th and 9th Centuries. Albuquerque, 1973 (1st
ed.), d.j. $27.00
___Another Copy. Same. $35.00

C502. (CULTURE). (University of California Archaeological Research Facility, Contribution No. 4, 1967) Colossal
heads of the Olmec Culture. 170pp, illus wrappers.
                                                  $35.00

C503. (CULTURE). New Interpretations of Aboriginal American
Culture History. viii, 135pp, figures, bibliography,
wrappers. 9 articles including Sources of Northwestern
Coast Culture; Prehistoric Culture Development in Eastern U.S., etc. Anthropological Society of Washington,
1955. $12.00

C504. CUMMINGS (Byron). Cuicuilco and the Archaic Culture
of Mexico. 56pp, illus, wrappers. University of Arizona,
1933. $15.00

C505. CUMMINGS (Byron). First Inhabitants of Arizona and the
Southwest. 251pp, numerous photographic pls, 29 color
pls, bibliography. Tucson, 1953 (1st ed.). $50.00
___Another Copy. Same. $30.00
___Another Copy. Same. $45.00

C506. CUMMINGS (Byron). Indians I Have Known. 55pp, illus,
account by noted archaeologist who made friends among
the Indians of Arizona and Southern Utah. Tucson,
1952 (1st ed.), d.j. $20.00
___Another Copy. Same. $25.00

C507. CUMMINGS (Byron). Kinishba. A Prehistoric Pueblo of
the Great Pueblo Period. 128pp, folding map inside back
pocket, colored pls, photographs, drawings, maps, rebound. Tucson, 1940 (1st ed.). $25.00
___Another Copy. Same. $40.00
___Another Copy. Same. $50.00

C508. CUMMINGS (Lewis). I Was a Head-Hunter. 338pp. Boston, 1941 (1st ed.). $25.00

C509. CUNNINGHAM (Caroline). Talking Stone. Early American
Stories Told Before the White Man's Day on this Continent by the Indians and Eskimos. 116pp, illus with
woodcuts. New York, 1939 (1st ed.), d.j. $20.00

C510. CUNNINGHAM (Frank). General Stand Watie's Confederate
Indians. xiv, 242pp, illus with photographs and
sketches, frontis portrait, decorative cloth, #80 of un-
specified number, inscribed and dated by author. San
Antonio, 1959. $75.00
    Stand Watie, a Cherokee, was the only Indian to at-
tain general officer rank in the Confederate Army, and
after official end of the Civil War, Watie and his troops
continued fighting. (SP)
___Another Copy. Same. $35.00

C511. CUNOW (H.). Geshichte und Kultur des Inkareiches.
xvi, 208pp, 4 full-page photographs, cloth. Amsterdam,
1937. $35.00

C512. (CUOA, Rev. A.). Etudes Philologiques sur Quelques
Langues Sauvages de l'Amerique. 160pp, printed wrap-
pers. Sabin: 17980. Field: 391. Montreal, Dawson
Bros., 1866 (1st ed.). $250.00

C513. CUOA (J. A.). Etudes Philologiques sur Quelques Langues
Sauvages de l'Amerique, Par N.O., Ancien Missionaire.
160pp, Dawson Bros., Montreal, 1866. and: Judgement
Errone de M. Ernest Renan sur les Langues Sauvages,
par l'Auteur des Etudes Philologiques. 114pp, Dawson
Bros., Montreal, 1869 (2d ed.). The Pair. $135.00
Both items, without original wrappers, in new loose
wrappers. Discussion of the works of Schoolcraft and
Duponceau; grammars of Algonquin and Iroquois languages
and comparisons to other languages. Sabin: 17980-81.
___Another Copy. Same. $55.00

C514. CUOQ (Rev. Father). Aiamie Tipadjimo8in Masinaigan Ka
Ojitogobanan Kaiat Ka Niina8isi Metate8ikonaie8igobanen.
339pp (2), 1/2 leather, marbled bds. Montreal, J. Lovell,
1859 (1st ed.). $400.00
Field: 389. Sabin: 46820. Pilling: BLNAI, 947.
Also includes "Ka Titc Tebeninimang Jezos, Ondaje Aking"
Montreal, J. Lovell, 1861, 1st ed., pp396. Field: 390.
Sabin: 46821. Pilling: 949. History of Old Testament
and Life of Jesus in Algonquin Language.

C515. CURTIN (Jeremiah). Myths of the Modocs. 389pp. Outstanding compilation of myths of the Indians that inhabited
the California-Oregon border area; most were told to Curtin in 1884 by one of the oldest living Modocs at that time.
complete reprint of 1912 ed. New York, 1971. $16.00

C516. CURTIN (Jeremiah). Seneca Indian Myths. 516pp, New
York, 1922 (1st ed.), d.j. $60.00

C517. CURTIN (L. S. M.). By The Prophet of the Earth. 146pp,
photographs, serigraph hand printed by Louie Ewing,
inscribed and signed by author, bds with attached d.j.
as issued, designed by Merle Armitage, drawings by
Gerri Chandler. Santa Fe, 1949, (1st ed.), d.j.
$125.00
Powell S. W. Century: 22. Marks: p.70. Powell:
"Ethnobotany of the Pima Indians in the Sal River Valley
of Arizona, based on field work by Mrs. Curtin, sponsored
by the Pueblo Grande Laboratory of the City of Phoenix.
The volume is another of the stunning Southwest series
designed by Merle Armitage. 'Prophet of the Earth' is
a Pima appellation for God." (TE)

C518. CURTIN (L. S. M.). Healing Herbs of the Upper Rio
Grande. 381pp, 4pp, 30 photographic pls, foreword by
Mary Austin, drawings by P. G. Napolitano, endpaper
maps, errata slip laid in, inscribed and signed by author,
bds, designed by Merle Armitage. Laid in is a personal
note and a Christmas card with a note from the author
which mentions the tragedy in the author's family. Santa
Fe, 1947 (1st ed.). $150.00

Swadesh: 796. Marks: p.71. Powell S. W. Century:
23: "Ethnobotany and medical folklore of the Pueblo Indians and the Spanish settlers of northern New Mexico,
again in Merle Armitage format. That Mrs. Curtin was a
protege of F. W. Hodge is all the pedigree her work re-
quires." (TE)

C519. CURTIN (L. S. M.). (Southwest Museum Leaflet No. 27,
Los Angeles, 1957) Some Plants Used by the Yuki Indians of Round Valley, Northern California. 20pp, illus,
wrappers. $10.00

C520. (CURTIS, Edward S.). Edwin S. Curtis: The Kwakiutl,
1910-1914, from the Estate of Edward S. Curtis. 20pp,
19 pls, wrappers. Fine Arts Gallery, University of California, 1976. $10.00

C521. (CURTIS, Edward S.). In a Sacred Manner We Live.
Photographs of the North American Indian by Edward S.
Curtis. 152pp, photographs, notes, references, introduction and commentary by Don D. Fowler, selection of
photography by Rachel J. Homer. New York, 1972 (1st
ed.), d.j. $20.00

C522. CURTIS (Edward S.). Indian Days of Long Ago. x,
225pp, approx 175 illus, illus with photographs by the
author and drawings by F. N. Wilson, cloth. World Book
Pub., 1915. $65.00
____Another Copy. Same. $75.00
____Another Copy. Same. $85.00

C523. CURTIS (Edward S.). Indian Life and Indian Lore. In
the Land of the Head-Hunters. 113pp, cloth and bds,
Indian tales illustrated with posed photographs (in
photogravure) of Northwest Coast Indians. New York,
1915. $100.00

C524. CURTIS (Edward S.). In the Land of the Head-Hunters.
xi, 113pp, illus with photographs, decorated bds, Yonk-
ers on Hudson, 1915 (1st ed.). $75.00
____Another Copy. World Book Pub., 1915, ex-
                   library. $35.00

C525. CURTIS (Edward S.). The North American Indian, Being
a Series of Volumes Picturing and Describing the Indians
of the United States and Alaska. Edited by Frederick
Webb Hodge, Chief of the Bureau of American Ethnology.
Foreword by Theodore Roosevelt. (40 Volumes)   20
text volumes, each with an accompanying portfolio as
follows:
I.   Apache, Jicarillas, Navaho; II: Pima, Papago, Qua-
hatika, Mohave, Yuma, Maricopa, Walapai, Havasupai,
Apache-Mohave; III: Teton Sioux, Yankonai, Assinaboin;
IV: Apsaroke, Hidatsa; V: Mandan, Arikara, Atsina;
VI: Piegan, Cheyenne, Arapaho; VII: Yakima, Klickitat,
Interior Salish, Kutenai; VIII: Nez Perce, Walla Walla,
Umatilla, Cayuse, Chinook Tribes; IX: Salishan Tribes
of the Coast, Chimakum, Quilliute, Willapa; X: Kwakiutl;

XI: Nootka, Haida; XII: Hopi; XIII: Hupa, Yurok, Karok, Wiyot, Tolowa, Tututni, Shasta, Achomawi, Klamath; XIV: Kato, Wailake, Yuki, Pomo, Wintun, Maidu, Miwok, Yokuts; XV: Southern California Shoshoneans, Dieguenos, Plateau Shoshoneans, Washo; XVI: The Tiwa, The Keres; XVII: The Tewa, The Zuni; XVIII: Chipewyan, Cree, Sarsi; XIX: Wichita, Southern Cheyenne, Oto, Comanche; XX: Nunivak, King Island, Little Diomede Island, Cape Prince of Wales, Kotzebue.

500 sets of this work were projected but only 272 were completed. This set is number 100. The text volumes are bound in gilt decorated half and full leather, and the 20 portfolios are bound in quarter leather by H. Blackwell. Text and gravures are printed on Van Gelder handmade paper. The set contains over 2,200 photogravure plates after photographs by Curtis. Norwood, Mass. The Plimpton Press, 1907-1930, (1st ed.). $95,000.00

The finest and most valuable work ever done on the American Indian and Alaskan Indian and Eskimo. The work of photographing these many Indians from most of the tribal groups still existing in North America at the turn of the Century was carried on by Curtis for over 30 years. It is, without question, the most comprehensive work on the American Indian and a landmark in the history of photography. Howes: C-965. Truthful Lens: 40. (RMW)

Curtis' monumental photographic folios are among the most cherished and valuable of all publications dealing with the North American Indian, and contain the most sought after photographs of these peoples. The New York Herald described this project as "...the most gigantic undertaking in the making of books since the King James edition of the bible." (EAP)

____Another Copy. Volume XIV only. Norwood, 1924.
$3,250.00

____Another Copy. Volume XV only. Norwood, 1926.
$4,500.00

____Another Copy. Volume XVIII only. Norwood, 1928.
$6,000.00

Each of the above three volumes are folio ($21\frac{1}{2}$" x 26"), 3/4 board and linen, with ties, containing 36 photogravures, each of which is 18" x $27\frac{1}{4}$", and a one page listing and description of each photogravure. The photogravure images are printed on Holland Van Gelder paper.

C526. CURTIS (Edward S.). Portraits from North American Indian Life. Introduction by A. Colman and T. McLuhan. xv, 81 pls, Promontory Press, New York, 1972, d.j.
$20.00

____Another Copy. Secaucus, NJ, 1985, oblong sml 4to (9" x 12"). $45.00

C527. CURTIS (Edward S.). (Gifford, Barry, Editor and

introduction) Selected Writings of Edward S. Curtis.
Excerpts from Volumes I-XX of the North American Indian. 141pp plus illus, 4 pls, portrait photograph on
frnt wrapper. Comments on Indian mythology, ceremonies, medicine men, religion, arts, warfare, etc.
Berkeley, 1976 (1st ed.). $10.00

C528. CURTIS (Natalie) (Editor). The Indian Book: An offering
by the Indians of Indian Lore, Musical, and Narrative,
to Form a Record of the Songs and Legends of Their
Race. 2nd Edition, With Additional Material. 582pp,
color frontis, illus with numerous photographs and original drawings by the Indians, decorated cloth. New
York, 1907. $85.00
____Another Copy. New York, 1935. $40.00

C529. CUSHING (F. H.) et al. (American Anthropology, Vol.
24, No. 3, 1922) Contributions to Hopi History. pp 253-
299, illus with photographs, wrappers. $30.00

C530. CUSHING (F. H.). My Adventures in Zuni. 59pp, 37
illus, cloth. Palmer Lake, 1967 reprint. $12.00

C531. CUSHING (F. H.). The Nation of the Willows. First
printing in book form of articles appearing in two 1882
issues of "Atlantic Monthly." Narrative of Cushing's
trip to the Havasupai Indians in 1882. 75pp. Flagstaff, 1965, d.j. $12.00

C532. CUSHING (F. H.). (Museum of American Indian, Notes
and Monographs, Vol. 8, New York, 1974) Zuni Bread-
stuff. 673pp, 27 pls, paperback. $25.00
____Another Copy. Same. $19.00

C533. CUSHING (F. H.). Zuni Folk Tales. xxix, 4pp, 373pp,
11 pls, introduction by Mary Austin, foreword by J. W.
Powell, cloth. New York, 1931 (2d ed.). $50.00
Howes: C-972. Campbell: p.155. Saunders: 1535.
Dobie: p.29. The author was one of the pioneer ethno-
logists and an adopted member of the Zuni tribe. Dobie:
"Cushing had rare imagination and sympathy. His re-
telling of tales are far superior to verbatim recordings."
(TE)
____Another Copy. Same. $60.00

C534. CUSICK (David). David Cusick's Sketches of Ancient History of the Six Nations, Comprising, First, a Tale of
the Foundation of the Great Island (Now North America).
35pp, pls, later limp leather, original printed wrappers
bound in. Sabin: 18142. Lockport, NY, Turner and
McCollum, 1848 (3rd ed.). $135.00

C535. CUTLER (Jervis). Topographical Description of the State
of Ohio, Indiana Territory, and Louisiana, Comprehend-
ing the Ohio and Mississippi Rivers, and Their Principal
Tributary Streams.... 219pp, leaf of errata, 5 woodcut
pls, half calf and marbled bds. Boston, 1812. $2,000.00
Wagner-Camp: 10. Field: 395. Graff: 963. Howes:
C-984. Streeter: 1775. Shaw & Shoemaker: 25204.

Despite the title, the better part of this work is devoted to describing the Trans-Mississippi West. The most interesting section is Charles Le Raye's journal describing his experiences from 1801 to 1803 as a captive of the Sioux and his travels to the Rocky Mountains. There is also an essay on Indian tribes between the Mississippi and the Rockies, a description of the Red River Country, and the descriptions of Ohio and Indiana promised in the title. The plates include one of the first views of Cincinnati and two interesting plates of Flathead Indians. (WR)

-D-

D1.   DABNEY (Owen P.).   The Lost Shackle, or Seven Years With the Indians.   True Story.   98pp, 12mo, some illus, pictorial wrappers.   Salem, 1897. $30.00
        Ayer Supp: 38.   Rader: 1017.   Smith: 2201.   Relates to the captivity of Lillian Ainsley, probably fiction.
        ___Another Copy.   Same. $25.00
        ___Another Copy.   Same. $25.00
D2.   DAIFUKU (H.).   (Peabody Papers, Vol. XXXIII, No. 1, 1961) Jeddito 264.   A Report on a Basket Maker III-Pueblo Site.   xii, 86pp, 17 figures, 10pp photographs.   (Reports of the Awatovi Expedition, Report No. 7) $35.00
D3.   (DAKOTA).   (House of Representatives Executive Document 147, 39:1, Washington, 1866, 1st print.)   Indian Affairs in Dakota.   25pp, removed, outrages and frauds against the Indians by Yankton and other Indian Agents. $17.00
D4.   (DAKOTA).   (Senate Executive Document 22, 39:2, Washington, 1867, 1st print.)   Information in Relation to the Condition of the Indians Now Located in the Vicinity of Lake Traverse and Fort Wadsworth, Dakota Territory....   12pp, removed, report after the 1862 outbreaks. $15.00
D5.   (DAKOTA).   (House of Representatives Miscellaneous Document 9, 42:3, Washington, 1872, 1st print.)   Dakota Indian War of 1862.   13pp, removed, expenses and documents relating thereto. $10.00
D6.   (DAKOTA).   (House of Representatives Executive Document 71, 48:1, Washington, 1884, 1st print.)   Right of Way Through Lake Traverse Indian Reservation.   42pp, removed, testimony in favor thereof. $12.00
D7.   (DAKOTA).   (Senate Report No. 439, 60:1, Washington, 1908, 1st print.)   Sale of Portion of Surplus Lands On Cheyenne River and Standing Rock Reservations.   24pp, removed, negotiations, conditions on reservations, helplessness of Indians. $15.00
D8.   DALE (E. E.) and LITTON (G.).   Cherokee Cavaliers, Forty Years of Cherokee History as Told in the Correspondence

of the Ridge-Waite-Boudinot Family. 342pp, 7 photographic illus, 1 fold-out genealogy table. Norman, 1939.
$34.00

D9. DALE (E. E.). The Indians of the Southwest: A Century of Development Under the United States. 299pp, 32 photographs, 5 maps, inscribed by author. Norman, 1949. $18.00
___Another Copy. Same. no inscription, 283pp, illus, 3 maps, cloth. Norman, 1949, d.j. $35.00
___Another Copy. Same. ex-library, 5 maps, 283pp. $21.00

D10. DALL (W. H.). (Smithsonian Contributions to Knowledge, No. 318, Washington, 1878) On the Remains of Later Pre-Historic Man, Obtained from Caves in the Catherina Archipelago, Alaska Territory and Especially from Caves of the Aleutian Islands. 35pp, plus 4pp index, 10 pls (Heliotype), 4to (9" x 12"), rebound in 1/2 leather.
$150.00

D11. DALL (W. H.). (United States Geographical and Geological Survey, Contributions to North American Ethnology, Vol. I, Washington, 1877) Tribes of the Extreme Northwest. and: Tribes of Western Washington and Northwestern Oregon, by George Biggs. 361pp, color illus, 4to, 2 folding maps, cloth, rebacked with original spine laid on.
$75.00

D12. DEMAS (D.). (National Museum of Canada, Bulletin No. 196, 1963) Igluligmiut Kinship and Local Groupings: A Structural Approach. vii, 216pp, 47 figures, 7 tables.
$27.00
___Another Copy. Same, errata slip, wrappers. $15.00
___Another Copy. Same. $10.00

D13. (DANCES). (Eastern Association of Indian Affairs, Bulletin 3, New York, 1924) Concerning Indian Dances. 16pp, 12 illus by Tewa and Hopi boys, pictorial self wrappers in protective folder. Contains 5 letters from anthropologists Goddard, Hodge, Parsons, Spinden and Boas on the decency, or indecency, of certain Pueblo Indian dances and ceremonies. $15.00

DANGBERG (Grace M.). See also BAE Bulletin No. 164.

D14. DANSON (Edward Bridge). (Papers of Peabody Museum, Vol. XLIV, No. 1, Cambridge, MS, 1957, 1st ed.) An Archaeological Survey of West Central New Mexico and East Central Arizona. 133pp plus 8 photographs, figures in text, charts, maps, bibliography, wrappers. $25.00
___Another Copy. Same, ex-library. $18.00

D15. DANZINGER (Edmund Jefferson, Jr.). (Civilization of the American Indian Series, Vol. 148, Norman, 1978, 1st ed.) The Chippewas of Lake Superior. 254pp plus index, photographs, maps, drawings, notes, bibliography, d.j.
$15.00

D16. DANZINGER (Edmund J.). Indians and Bureaucrats:

Administering the Reservation Policy During the Civil War.
240pp, index, bibliography, folding map. Urbana, 1974
(1st ed.), d.j. $15.00
___Another Copy. Same. $15.00

D17. DAUGHERTY (Richard D.). The Yakima People. 104pp,
b/w and color photographs, maps, wrappers. Phoenix,
1973 (1st ed.). $15.00
___Another Copy, Indian Tribal Council, Phoenix, 1972,
color frontis, photographic illus, stiff wrappers, signed
by Robert Jim, chairman of the Yakima Tribal Council.
                                                                             $12.00

D18. DAVENPORT (J. W.) and CHELF (C.). (Witte Memorial
Museum, Bulletin 5, San Antonio, (c. 1935), 1st ed.
Painted Pebbles from the Lower Pecos and Big Bend Re-
gions of Texas. 43pp, figures, wrappers. $12.00

D19. DAVIDSON (D.). (Museum of the American Indian, Notes
and Monographs, Vol. X, No. 9, 1928) Decorative Art
of the Tetes de Boule of Quebec. 45pp, 30 photographs,
14pp color illus. $17.00

D20. DAVIDSON (D. S.). (Museum of the American Indian,
Notes and Monographs, No. 46, New York, 1928, 1st ed.)
Family Hunting Territories in Northwestern North America.
34pp, folding map, Tlingit Indians of Alaska, wrappers.
                                                                             $15.00
___Another Copy. Same. $10.00

D21. DAVIES (Nigel). The Aztecs: A History. 363pp, illus.
London, 1973. $30.00
___Another Copy. Same. $17.00

D22. DAVIES (Nigel). (Civilization of the American Indian
Series, Vol. 144, Norman, 1977, 1st ed.) The Toltecs
Until the Fall of Tula. 533pp, frontis, illus, bibliography,
notes, index, references, d.j. $20.00
___Another Copy. Same. Cloth. $15.00

D23. DAVIS (Barbara A.). Edward S. Curtis: The Life and
Times of a Shadow Catcher. Portrait, 256pp, over 200
photographs, 16pp of full color illus, 4to (10" x 13").
San Francisco, 1985 (1st ed.), d.j. $45.00
___Another Copy. Same. $59.00

D24. DAVIS (Britton). The Truth About Geronimo. Life with
the Apache Scouts. 253pp, index, illus with photographs.
Yale University Press, New Haven, 1929, d.j. $100.00
The narrative of Lt. Davis is the intimate relation of
his three years experience in a military capacity with the
Apache of the Southwest. Lt. Davis was a Company Com-
mander. Thirty-five men, eight half grown boys, and
101 women and children maintained themselves 18 months
against 5,000 troops, 500 Indian auxiliaries and an unknown number of civilians. The Indian losses in killed
were six men, 2 large boys, two women and one child.
(WS)
___Another Copy. Same. $45.00

____Another Copy. Same. $45.00
____Another Copy. New Haven, 1963 (2d ed.) 237pp, photographs, foreword by Robert M. Utley, index.
$10.00

D25. DAVIS (E. C.). Ancient Americans, the Archaeological Story of Two Continents. 311pp, 28pp of photographs, cloth. New York, 1931, 1975. $15.00

D26. DAVIS (E. H.). (Museum of the American Indian, Notes and Monographs, Vol. III, No. 4, 1920) The Papago Ceremony of Vikita. 21pp, 13pp photographs, spine reinforced. $23.00

D27. DAVIS (E. L.) and BROTT (C. W.). (San Diego Museum of Man, Papers, No. 6, 1969) The Western Lithic Co-Tradition. xi, 97pp, 38 illus. $12.00

D28. DAVIS (E. Mott) and CORBIN (James E.). (State Building Commission Report No. 5, Austin, 1967) Archaeological Investigations at Washington-on-the Brazos State Park in 1966. 58pp, photographs, drawings, map, bibliography, wrappers. $10.00
____Another Copy. Same. $10.00

DAVIS (Irvine). See also BAE Bulletin No. 191.

D29. DAVIS (James T.). Trade Routes and Economic Exchange Among the Indians of California. 71pp, maps, bibliography, appendix, 4to, wrappers, informative account with an appendix that correlates the aboriginal Indian trails with modern California thoroughfares. Ramona, 1974 (1st ed.). $12.00

D30. DAVIS (Joshua). Candi Token Wayusica. 8pp, portrait on cvr, 12mo, self wrappers, Sioux language. Santee, NE, 1903. $35.00

D31. DAVIS (Ogilvie H.). Aboriginal Human Effigy Portrayal--Northeast. 88pp, 29 pls, 6 line drawings, portrays objects in stone, bone and ceramics, wrappers, n.p., 1972. $20.00

D32. DAVIS (P. W.). (British Columbia Provincial Museum, Heritage Record No. 10, 1980) Bella Coola Texts. 322pp. $17.00

D33. DAVIS (R. H.). Three Gringos in Venezuela and Central America. frontis, 66 illus. New York, 1896 (1st ed.). $25.00

D34. DAVIS (Robert). Native Arts of the Pacific Northwest From the Rasmussen Collection of the Portland Art Museum. 165pp, illus. Stanford University Press, 1949 (2d print.) d.j. $35.00
____Another Copy. Same. $55.00

D35. DAVIS (Rev. William L.). A History of St. Ignatius Mission, An Outpost of Catholic Culture on the Montana Frontier. 147pp, map, index, signed by author. Spokane, 1954 (1st ed.). $60.00

D36. DAWDY (Doris). (Contributions from Museum of American Indian, Vol. XXI, Part 2, New York, 1968, 1st ed.)

Annotated Bibliography of American Indian Painting.
Lists over 250 printed sources of material on Indian art.
$10.00

D37. DAWES (H. L.). (Senate Report No. 670, 46:2, Washington, 1880, 1st print.) Report ... On the Removal of the Northern Cheyennes From the Sioux Reservation to the Indian Territory.... 534pp, index, removed. Edges of a few leaves chipped. Testimony and reports on movement of the Indians, sickness and deaths, conditions on the reservation and new lands, etc. $85.00

D38. DAWSON (G. M.). Report on the Queen Charlotte Islands and on the Haida Indians of the Queen Charlotte Islands. 189pp of text, plus 14pp of drawings of artifacts. These are but two of the nine papers contained in this 406pp report (Geological Survey of Canada). Other areas covered are geology, marine life, explorations, etc., numerous illus, maps, charts, cloth. Montreal, 1880. $135.00

D39. DAWSON (S. J.). Report on the Exploration of the Country Between Lake Superior and the Red River Settlement, and Between the Latter Place and the Assiniboine and the Saskatchewan. 43pp, 4 folding maps, folio, rebound in cloth. Toronto, John Lovell, 1859 (1st ed.). $175.00

D40. DAWSON (Thomas F.) and SKIFF (F. J. V.). The Ute War: A History of the White River Massacre and the Privations and Hardships of the Captive White Women Among the Hostiles on the Grand River. 192pp, 3/4 brown polished calf, gilt. Denver, 1879. $1,200.00
Streeter Sale: 2194. Howes: D-161. Ayer, Supplement: 42. Graff: 1028. The primary contemporary account of the events which led up to the removal of the Ute Indians from their lands west of the 107th meridian. (WR)

____Another Copy. Boulder, 1964, 208pp. illus, advs, specially printed title page, comments and notes by Dr. Nolie Mummey, wrappers in a specially made folding cloth case, facsimile of 1879 ed. $55.00

D41. DeACOSTA (Fray Joseph). Historia Natural y Moral de las Indias, Publicado en Sevilla, Ano de 1590 (2 Volumes). pp485, 392, wrappers. Ahora Fielmente Reimpres, Madrid, 1894. $45.00

D42. DEAN (J. S.). Chronological Analysis of Tsegi Phase Sites in Northeastern Arizona. 220pp, 53 illus, 33 tables. Tucson, 1969. $20.00

D43. DeANGULO (Jaime). Coyote's Bones; Selected Poetry and Prose. Edited by Bob Callahan. 88pp, 12mo, Indian myths of early Indians in California. San Francisco, 1974. $20.00

D44. DeANGULO (Jaime). How the World Was Made and Shabegok. (2 Volumes) pp104; 112, enclosed in slipcase, illus, notes, myths and folklore of northern California Indians. Berkeley, 1976. $20.00

D45. deBENAVIDES (Alonso). Memorial Que Fr. Juan de San-
        tander ... Comisario General de Indias, Presenta a la
        Majestad ... Don Felipe Curato. 62pp, lacks wrapper,
        minor soiling on title and last page, else a fine unopened
        copy. Museu Nacional, Mexico, 1899, (2d ed., in Span-
        ish) $475.00
            First printed in Madrid in 1630, this publication is
        one of the primary sources for the history of early 17th
        Century New Mexico. It is particularly important for its
        descriptions of the various Indian groups, especially the
        Apaches, and for the litany of miracles and conversions
        brought about by the Franciscan missionaries. It was
        published as part of the Franciscan effort to have New
        Mexico elevated to a bishopric. Palau: 27145. Sabin:
        4636 and 76810. Streeter: 134. Wagner Spanish South-
        west: 33. (EAP)

D46. DEBENEDETTI (Salvador). L'Ancienne Civilisation des
        Barreales du Nord-Ouest Argentin: La Cienega et la
        Aguada d'Apres les Collections Privess et les Documents
        de Benjamin Muniz Baretto. 58pp, plus 58 pls, folio,
        some pls in color, wrappers. Paris, les Editions, G.
        Van Oest, 1931. $350.00
        ___Another Copy. Same. $350.00
        ___Another Copy. Same. $300.00

D47. DEBENEDETTI (Salvador). Las Ruinas del Pucara. 142pp,
        color frontis, folding map, 26 pls (photogravures), re-
        bound in cloth and marbled bds. Buenos Aires, 1930.
                                                                     $95.00

D48. DEBO (Angie). And the Still Waters Run: The Betrayal
        of the Five Civilized Tribes. 417pp, illus, wrappers.
        Princeton University Press, 1973. $10.00

D49. DEBO (Angie). Geronimo--The Man, His Time, His Place.
        480pp, 3 maps, illus. Norman, 1976 (1st ed.), d.j.
                                                                     $25.00
        ___Another Copy. Norman, 1977, d.j. $15.00
        ___Another Copy. Norman, 1982, lrg format
                                paperback. $12.00

D50. DEBO (Angie). A History of the Indians of the United
        States. 363pp plus index, photographs, bibliography.
        Norman, 1970 (1st print.), d.j. $17.00
        ___Another Copy. Same. Cloth. $24.00

D51. DEBO (Angie). The Rise and Fall of the Choctaw Repub-
        lic. 299pp plus index, photographs, drawings, maps,
        bibliography, purple-brown cloth of the 1st state bind-
        ing. Norman, 1934 (1st ed.). $50.00
        ___Another Copy. Norman, 1961 (2d ed.) cloth, 314pp,
        frontis, illus, bibliography, index. $20.00

D52. DEBO (Angie). The Road To Disappearance. 388pp plus
        index, photographs, maps, bibliography, presentation
        copy signed by author. A History of the Creek Indians,
        from the early 1700s to the beginning of the 20th

Century. Norman, 1941 (1st ed.). $45.00
___Another Copy. Same. $35.00

D53. DeBOOY (Theodor). (Museum of the American Indian, Notes and Monographs, Vol. 1, No. 2, New York, 1919) Santo Domingo Kitchen-Midden and Burial Mound. pp107-137, 12mo, 15 pls, wrappers. $25.00

D54. DeBORHEGYI (S. F.). (Contributions in Anthropology and History, No. 1, Milwaukee Public Museum, 1980) The Pre-Columbian Ballgames, A Pan-Mesoamerican Tradition. 30pp, 25 photographs of many artifacts, map. $12.00

D55. DEDERA (Don). Navajo Rugs. How to Find, Evaluate, Buy and Care for Them. 111pp, b/w and color illus, bibliography, index, wrappers. Flagstaff, 1979 (3rd print.) $10.00

D56. DEFENBACH (Byron). Red Heroines of the Northwest. 301pp, pls, map, Sacajawea and Jane Silcott. Caldwell, 1929 (1st ed.). $65.00
___Another Copy. Same. $50.00

D57. DeFOREST (John W.). History of the Indians of Connecticut from the Earliest Known Period to 1850. xxvi, 509pp, folding map (Connecticut in 1639), pls, index. Hartford, W. J. Hammersley, 1851 (1st ed.). $135.00
Howes: D-216: "Best account of these tribes."
___Another Copy. Same. 535pp, 8 engravings, 1 figure of 19 Indian autographs, fold-out map, later cloth, tear in the lower corner of pp199 and 200, with loss of some text. $87.00
___Another Copy. Hartford, 1851 (1st ed., 2d print.) cloth rebacked with original spine laid on. $50.00
___Another Copy. Hartford, 1852. $45.00

D58. De GEREZ (Toni). 2-Rabbit, 7-Wind: Poems from Ancient Mexico retold from Nahuatl Texts. New York, 1971, d.j. $10.00

D59. DeGOEJE (C. M.). Bidrage Tot de Ethnographe der Surinaamsche Indianen. 117pp, 11pp color and b/w drawings, 5pp of photographs, linen and bd cvrs. Leiden, E. J. Brill, 1906. $165.00

D60. DeGOMARA (Francisco Loquez). The Conquest of the West India (New Spain). 408pp. Readex Facsimile, 1966. $30.00

D61. DeGRUYTER (W. Jos.). A New Approach to Maya Hieroglyphs. 71pp, bibliography, one large folding pl. Amsterdam, 1946 (1st ed.). $30.00
___Another Copy. Same, ex-library. $22.00

D62. DeHASS (Wills). History of the Early Settlement and Indian Wars of Western Virginia.... 416pp, illus, pls (1 folding), original gilt decorated cloth. Wheeling WV, H. Hoblitzell, 1851 (1st ed.). $150.00
Title continues: "Also, Biographical Sketches of Col. Ebenezer Zane, Major Samuel M'Culloch, Lewis Wetzel,

General Andrew Lewis...." Howes: D-223. "Valuable
compilation based on reliable sources." (RMW)
___Another Copy. Wheeling & Philadelphia, 1851, frontis,
illus, 3/4 leather. $125.00

D63. DeHELLER (J.). (El Museo del Oro, Estudios, Vol. 1, No.
1, Bogota, 1971) Bibliography of Pre-Hispanic Gold Work
of Columbia. 126pp text in English and Spanish, 6 full-
page photographs, fold-out map. $45.00

D64. DeHUFF (Elizabeth Willis). Taytay's Tales: Collected and
Retold. xiii, 213pp, illus by Fred Kabotie and Otis
Polelonema, 8 color pls, pictorial cloth, collection of
Pueblo folktales by a Santa Fe author and illustrated by
2 young Hopi men. Campbell: p.156; Dobie: p.29.
Saunders: 1556. New York, 1922. $75.00

D65. DeHUMBOLDT (Alexander). Personal Narrative of Travels
to the Equinoctial Regions of the New Continent, During
the Years 1799-1804. 432pp, newly rebound. Philadelphia, M. Carey, December 23, 1815. $175.00

D66. DeHUMBOLDT (Alexander). Researches Concerning the
Institutions and Monuments of the Ancient Inhabitants of
America. (2 Volumes). Vol. 1: iv, 411pp. Vol. 2:
324pp, 19 pls (some in color), original paper covered
bds. London, Longman, Hurst, et al., 1814. $275.00
Field: 740. Valuable study of Mesoamerican Indians.

D67. DeJARNETTE (D. L.). Archaeological Salvage in the Walter F. George Basin of the Chattahoochee River in Alabama. xiii, 237pp, pls, maps, bibliography, index.
University of Alabama, 1975 (1st ed.). $15.00

D68. DeJARNETTE (D. L.) and WIMBERLY (S. B.). (University of Alabama, Geological Survey of Alabama, Museum
Papers, No. 17, 1941) Bessemer Site. xii, 122pp, figures, bibliography, index, wrappers. $20.00

D69. DeKORNE (John C.) (Editor). Navaho and Zuni for Christ.
Fifty Years of Indian Missions. 208pp, illus. Grand
Rapids, MI, 1947. $10.00

D70. De La CRUZ (Raul). Ritos y Costumbres de Nuestros
Pueblos Primitivos. 147pp, 8 illus, wrappers. Mexico,
1964. $20.00

D71. De La FUENTE (Beatriz). Arte Prehispanico Funerario,
el Occidente de Mexico. 181pp, 90 full-page b/w and
12 full-page color photographs, cloth. Mexico City,
1974. $35.00
___Another Copy. Same. $50.00

D72. De La FUENTE (Beatriz). Escultura Monumental Olmeca:
Catalogo. 353pp, illus. Mexico, 1973. $55.00

D73. De La FUENTE (J.). (Serie Cientifica 1. Mexico, 1949)
Yalaag: Una Villa Zapoteca Serrana. 382pp, 16pp
photographs, wrappers. $35.00

D74. De LaGARZA (Mercedes). La Conciencia Historica de los
Antiguos Mayas. 141pp, wrappers. Mexico, 1975.
$15.00

D75. DeLAGUNA (Frederica). (University of Washington, Publications in Anthropology, Vol. 13, Seattle, 1956) Chugach Prehistory: The Archaeology of Prince William Sound Alaska. 289pp, illus, wrappers. $45.00

D76. DeLAGUNA (Frederica) (Editor). Selected Papers from the American Anthropologist 1888-1920, with an Essay "The Beginnings of Anthropology in America" by A. Irving Hollowell. Evanston, 1960. $25.00

D77. DeLAGUNA (Frederica). (Smithsonian Contributions to Anthropology, Vol. 7, 1972) Under Mount Saint Elias: The History and Culture of the Yakutat Tlingit (3 Volumes). Part I: xxiii, 550pp, 61 figures, 26 maps. Part II: ppxxiv-xlvi, 551-913, 13 figures. Part III: ppxlvii, xlix, 914-1395, 218pp photographs and drawings.
$350.00
____Another Copy. Same. $165.00
____Another Copy. Same. $125.00
____Another Copy. Same. Parts I and II only. $195.00

D78. DeLAMEIRAS (Brigitte) and PEREYRA (A.). (Instituto Nacional Antropologia e Historia, Coleccione Cientifica 13, Mexico, 1974) Terminologia Agrohidraulica Perhispanica Nahua. 125pp, wrappers. $15.00

D79. DeLAND (Charles Edmund). Tragedy of the White Medicine. A Story of Indian Mystery, Revenge and Love. 135pp, Sioux lore and legends. New York, 1913 (1st ed.).
$25.00

D80. DeLANDA (Friar Diego). (PAGDEN, A. R., Editor and Translator). Diego de Landa's Account of the Affairs of Yucatan. The Maya. 183pp plus index, drawings, photographs, facsimiles, notes, bibliography, the only contemporary Spanish account at time of conquest, customs, beliefs, etc. DeLanda was Missionary priest in Yucatan in the 1500s. Chicago, 1975, (1st print.) d.j.
$15.00

D81. DeLANDA (Friar Diego). (Peabody Museum Papers Vol. XVIII, Cambridge, 1941) Landa's Relacion de las Cosas de Yucatan: A Translation Edited with Notes by Alfred Tozzer. 395pp, 4to, wrappers. $75.00

D82. DeLANDA (Friar Diego). Relacion de las Cosas de Yucatan. Introduccion por Andel Ma. Garibay K. xv, 252pp, illus, wrappers. Mexico, 1982. $35.00

D83. DeLANDA (Friar Diego). Yucatan Before and After the Conquest. Translated with Notes by William Gates. 162pp, includes related documents, maps, and illus. Baltimore, The Maya Society, 1937 (2d ed.). $125.00

D84. DELANEY (Robert W.). The Southern Ute People. 102pp, b/w and color photographs, maps, wrappers, part of the Indian Tribal Series. Phoenix, 1974 (1st ed.). $10.00

D85. DeLa PENA MONTENEGRO (Alonso). Intinerario Para Parochos de Indios.... 28ff, 697pp, 1pp, 43ff, sml quarto, contemporary stiff vellum with (defective) button ties, two minor contemporary ownership inscriptions, few light waterstains. En Amberes: En Casa de Juan Bautista Verdussen, 1726. $300.00

Palau: 217534. Sabin: 59623. First printed in 1668, this is a very important study by the Bishop of Quito, Ecuador, of the Andean Indians, their society, laws, customs, history and beliefs. It was composed in order to better prepare priests for the task of proselytizing the Indians. It is a most important ethnohistorical source for the study of colonial (and by inference, pre-Hispanic) era Andean Indians. This later edition, approximately the fourth, is revised and improved and has a very useful index, directing the reader to such sections as treat of "drunkenness," "adulthood," "chocolate," "tobacco," "slavery," "witchcraft" and much more. (WR)

D86. DeLARA (Manuel Tunon) Introduction. From Incas to Indios. 25pp, 77pp photographs by Werner Bischof, Robert Frank, Pierre Verger, 4to. Paris, 1956. $50.00

D87. DeLas CASAS (Bartolome). Il Supplice Schiavo Indiano.... (bound with) La Liberta Pretesa dal supplice Schiavo Indiano.... (bound with) Istoria, o Brevissima Relazione Della Distruzzione Dell'Indie Occidentali.... (3 volumes bound together) 118pp, 2pp, 155pp, 5pp, 8pp, 150pp, 2pp. Engraved title vignettes, contemporary stiff vellum, ex-library, bound complete with the publisher's advs. Venice, Marco Ginammi, 1636-40-43.

$400.00

Alden: 636/14; 640/46; 643/29. Sabin: 11236; 11245; 11244. Medina BHA: 1085n. Palua: 46956-7. JCB (3)II: 434; 281; 228. Field Sale: 1269-70. The first work is the first Italian edition of DeLas Casas' Sixth Tract, in which the case for the restoration of freedom to the Indians is discussed based on judicial and other authorities. In each work, the texts are printed parallel with the original Spanish texts. The second work is the first and only 17th-Century Italian printing of the Third Tract, in which twenty reasons why the Indians should not be bound into slavery to the Spaniards are discussed. The third work is the third Italian edition of the First Tract, in which are outlined the abuses of the Indians by the Spaniards in their most succinct form. (WR)

D88. DeLas CASAS (Bartolome). La Liberta Pretesa sul Supplice Schiavo Indiano.... 2pp, 155pp, 3pp, engraved title vignette, 3/4 19th Century crimson morocco, t.e.g., ex-library, partially untrimmed. Venice Marco Cinammi, 1640. $300.00

Alden: 640/46. Sabin: 11245. Medina GHA 1085n. The first and only 17th Century printing of DeLas Casas' Third Tract, in which twenty reasons why the Indians should not be bound into slavery to the Spaniards are discussed. (WR)

D89. DeLas CASAS (Bartolome). Los Indios de Mexico y Nueva
Aspana Antologia. Prologo, Apendices y Notas de Ed-
mundo O'Gorman. 225pp, illus, wrappers. Mexico,
1966. $20.00
D90. DeLa VEGA (Garcilaso). The Florida of the Inca: The
Fabulous De Soto Story. 655pp, first complete English
translation. Austin, 1961. $50.00
D91. DeLa VEGA (Garcilaso). Los Comentarios Reales de los
Incas. Anataciones y Concordancias con las Cronicas
de Indias por Horacio H. Urteaga. (6 Volumes). pp378,
353, 400, 330, 435, 400. wrappers. Lima, 1941-1946
(2d ed.). $90.00
D92. DeLa VEGA (Garcilaso). (Rycaut, Paul, Translated by)
The Royal Commentaries of Peru, In Two Parts. (8),
1019, (8)pp, portrait, 8 pls (of 9), index, folio, very
worn leather, cvrs loose, some stains. London, Miles
Flesher, for Jacob Tonson in Chancery Lane, 1688.
                                                            $300.00
___Another Copy. Austin, 1966, d.j. 1487pp plus in-
dex, translated by Harold V. Livemore. $30.00
___Another Copy. Same. $25.00
D93. DeLAVELLE (J. A.), et al. Culturas Precolombianas, Arte
y Tesoros del Peru. 195pp, 54pp of color photographs,
6pp of b/w of textiles, 40pp of color and 6pp b/w
photographs of ceramics, 14pp of color and 7pp b/w
photographs of ornaments and figures, cloth. Lima,
1984. $125.00
D94. (DELAWARE INDIANS). The Life of David Brainerd, Mis-
sionary to the Indians: with an Abridgement of His
Diary and Journal from President Jonathan Edwards by
John Styles. 292pp with 29pp appendix, early full leather.
Boston, 1812 (1st American Ed.). $60.00
D95. (DELAWARE INDIANS). Walam Olum, or Red Score: The
Migration Legend of the Lenni Lenape, or Delaware In-
dians, Customs and Products on the Theory of the Ethnic
Unity of the Race. Frontis, 487pp, numerous illus,
decorated cloth. New York & London, 1906. $85.00
___Another Copy. Lakeside Press for Indiana Historical
Society, 1954, translated from a manuscript by Constan-
tine S. Rafinesque, written in 1833, 379pp, with full re-
production of all the pictographs, with numerous inter-
pretations. $85.00
___Another Copy. Indianapolis, 1954. 369pp plus in-
dex, profusely illus with original texts, map endpapers.
                                                            $40.00
D96. DELGADO (A.). (New World Archaeological Foundation.
Brigham Young University Papers Nos. 17-18, 1965)
Archaeological Research at Santa Rosa, Chiapas and in
the Region of Tehuantepec. 124pp, 100 figures. $12.00
D97. DELLENBAUGH (Frederick S.). The North Americans of
Yesterday: A Comparative Study of North American

Indian Life, Customs and Products, on the Theory of the Ethnic Unity of the Race. frontis, 487pp, numerous illus, decorated cloth. New York & London, 1906.
$85.00

____Another Copy. New York, 1900, 1906
(3rd print.) $75.00

____Another Copy. New York, 1906 (2d ed.) $40.00

D98. DELORES (Juan). (University of California Publications in American Archaeology and Ethnology, Vol. 10, No. 5, Berkeley, 1913) Papago Verb Stems. 22pp, wrappers. $20.00

D99. DELORIA (V., Jr.). Indians of the Pacific Northwest: From the Coming of the White Man to the Present Day. 207pp, illus. New York, 1977 (1st ed.). $15.00

D100. DELOS REYES (Antonio). Arte in Lengua Mixteca. Octavo, treed sheep with red and green morocco labels and a bit of gilt tooling, original wrappers bound in, a reprint of the 16th Century Mexico Mixtec grammar, Mixtec being the language spoken in the regions of Tepuzculula and Yanguitlan. Vinaza: 84 (original ed.) and 689 (reprint). Sabin: 70393 (original ed.) Alencon: Typographie E. Renaut-de Broise, 1889.
$225.00

D101. DeMALLIE (Raymond J.) (Editor). The Sixth Grandfather; Black Elk's Teachings Given to John G. Neihardt. 452pp, illus, index, maps, bibliography. Lincoln, 1984 (1st ed.), d.j. $25.00

D102. DeMARCOS (Saavedra). Confessonario Breve Activo, y Passivo, en Lengua Mexicana.... 12mo, sewn as issued. Imprenta Real del Superior Gobierno, y del Nuevo Rezado, de Dona Maria de Rivera, Mexico, 1746. $1,500.00

Garcia Icazbalceta Lenguas: 176. Medina (Mexico): 3798. Sabin: 74650. Palau: 283406. Probably different from Vinaza: 321. A manual, based on the Ten Commandments, for aiding priests in hearing the confessions of their Indian parishioners. The first half suggests different phrases or confessions the natives might use to admit to breaking each of the commandments; the second provides the clergyman with a flock of questions to ask to help him get a better sense of the gravity of their transgressions. The text is printed in double-column format, with Spanish on the left and Nahuatl, the most widely used language among Mexican Indians in the 18th Century on the right. This is, according to Medina and other bibliographers, the second edition, although the first has been seen by neither Sabin nor Medina and is not recorded in Vinaza or Palau. (WR)

D103. DeMEZIERES (Athanase). Athanase De Mezieres and the Louisiana-Texas Frontier, 1768-1780. Edited and

Annotated by Herbert E. Bolton (2 Volumes). pp392; 351, folding map, illus, t.e.g., original red cloth. Cleveland, Arthur H. Clark Co., 1914. $300.00
 Howes: B-584. Jenkins Basic Texas Books 41: "The best insight into the Indians of Texas during the period." (BF)

D104. DEMING (Terese O. and Edwin W.). Cosel With Geronimo on His Last Raid: The Story of an Indian Boy. xvii, 125pp, illus, 6 color pls. True experience of an Indian boy of seven who followed his family on the warpath. Philadelphia, 1938 (1st ed.), d.j. $60.00

D105. DEMING (Terese O. and Edwin W.). Indian Child Life. 101pp, illus, 18 color pls, color cvr illus, slipcase. New York, 1927, d.j. $85.00

D106. DEMING (Terese O. and Edwin W.). The Indians In Winter Camp: A Story of Indian Life. 126pp, color illus, decorative cloth. Indian Life Series #2. Chicago, 1931 (1st ed.). $35.00
 ___Another Copy. New York, 1931. $15.00

D107. DEMING (Terese O. and Edwin W.). Indians of the Pueblos: A Story of Indian Life. 224pp, color pls, decorative cloth, Indian Life Series #4. Chicago, 1936 (1st ed.). $30.00

D108. DEMING (Terese O. and Edwin W.). Indians of the Wigwams: A Story of Indian Life. 239pp, color pls, decorative cloth, Indian Life Series #5. Chicago, 1938 (1st print.). $30.00
 ___Another Copy. Same. Ex-library. $15.00

D109. DEMING (Terese O. and Edwin W.). Little Eagle: A Story of Indian Life. 96pp, color illus, decorative cloth, Indian Life Series #1. Chicago, 1931 (1st ed.). $40.00

D110. DEMING (Terese O. and Edwin W.). Many Snows Ago. 96pp, illus, 18 color pls, oblong 8vo, decorative cloth, slipcase. New York, 1929 (1st ed.). $75.00

D111. DEMING (Terese O. and Edwin W.). Red People of the Wooded Country: A Story of Indian Life. 191pp, color pls, decorative cloth, Indian Life Series #3, rehinged. Chicago, 1932 (1st ed.). $25.00

D112. DeMOTOLINIA (Fray Toribio). History of the Indians of New Spain. Translated and annotated with a biobibliographical study of the author by Francis Steck. 358pp, ex-library. Washington, 1951. $50.00

D113. DEMPSEY (Hugh A.). Crowfoot, Chief of the Blackfeet. 226pp, illus, index, maps, bibliography. Norman, 1974, d.j. $22.00
 ___Another Copy. Norman, 1972 (1st ed.) Civilization of the American Indian, Series Vol. 122. $17.00

D114. DENEUAN (William M.) (Editor). The Native Population of the Americas in 1492. 351pp. Wisconsin, 1976. $30.00

DENIG (Edwin T.). See also BAE Bulletin No. 151.

D115. DENIG (Edwin T.). Five Indian Tribes of the Upper Missouri: Sioux, Arickaras, Assiniboines, Crees, Crow. Edited and with an Introduction by John C. Ewers. 217pp including bibliography and index, 12 pls, map. Norman, 1961 (1st ed.), d.j. $35.00

Mr. Denig was a fur trader on the upper Missouri from 1833-1858. Father DeSmet received information on the Indians from Denig and encouraged him to write. This is first complete publication of his recently discovered manuscript.

_____Another Copy. Same. $30.00
_____Another Copy. Same. $25.00

D116. DENIG (Edwin T.). (Smithsonian Institution BAE Anthropology Papers No. 13, Washington, 1953, 1st ed.) Of the Crow Nation. 74pp, 6 pls, wrappers. $10.00

D117. DeNIZA (Fray Marcos) Discovery of the Seven Cities of Cibola. 59pp, printed wrappers, translated from the account contained in Documentos Ineditos del Archivo Indias by Percy M. Baldwin and issued as the first publication of the Historical Society of New Mexico. Albuquerque, 1926. $45.00

D118. DENNIS (Wayne). The Hopi Child. 197pp, illus, bibliography, index. New York, 1940 (1st ed.). $15.00

DENSMORE (Frances). See also BAE Bulletin Nos. 45, 53, 61, 75, 80, 86, 90, 93, 102, 110, 124, 133, 136, 151, 161 and 165.

D119. DENSMORE (Frances). The American Indians and Their Music. 143pp, 4 pls, half fabricoid, bds, 1 signature repaired, 8 songs with scores. New York, 1926 (1st ed.). $55.00

D120. DENSMORE (Frances). (Southwest Museum Papers No. 10, Los Angeles, 1936) Cheyenne and Arapaho Music. 111pp, wrappers. $20.00

_____Another Copy. 1964. 110pp, 10 photographs. $12.00

D121. DENSMORE (Frances). Chippewa Music. 557pp, illus, bibliography, index. A detailed inquiry into the music, customs and oral traditions of the Chippewa (Ojibway) Indians. Originally issued as 2 separate volumes by the BAE in 1910 and 1913. This one-volume edition is a complete reprint of the 2 volumes, with informative new introduction by ethnomusicologist Thomas Venum. Minneapolis, 1973, d.j. $30.00

D122. DENSMORE (Frances). (Museum of the American Indian, Notes and Monographs, Vol. XI, No. 3, 1948) A Collection of Specimens from the Teton Sioux. pp165-204 and 24 pls, ex-library, 12mo, wrappers. $45.00

_____Another Copy. Same. $45.00

D123. DENSMORE (Frances). Music of the Maidu Indians of California. 67pp, 7 illus, cloth. Southwest Museum,

Los Angeles, 1958. $14.00
____Another Copy. Same. ex-library. $10.00
____Another Copy. Same. Museum Publication
    VII. $15.00
____Another Copy. Same. stiff printed
    wrappers. $20.00

D124. DENSMORE (Frances). (Southwest Museum Papers, No.
12, Los Angeles, 1938) Music of the Santo Domingo
Pueblo, New Mexico. 186pp, illus, includes much
ethnographic information, including a photograph of a
crystal ball used by Shamans in diagnosing illness
caused by witchcraft; original edition, wrappers.
                                         $60.00

D125. DENSMORE (Frances). Pawnee Music. xviii, 128pp,
illus, cloth. Washington, 1929 (1st ed.). $20.00

D126. DENTZEL (C.). The Art of the Indian Southwest. 32pp,
38 b/w, 4 color photographs. Exhibition catalogue
Newport Harbor Museum, Balboa, 1971. $12.00

D127. DePAREDES (Ignacio). Catecismo Mexicano.... Plate,
16ff, 170pp, 2pp. Includes one rather skillful full-
page engraving by Ortuno depicting Saint Francis
Xavier preaching to Indian children. Octavo, contemporary sheep with gilt spine and cvr borders,
rubbed, inkstains on title page, not affecting text,
complete with both Spanish and Nahuatl title pages.
Imprenta de la Biblioteca Mexicana, Mexico, 1758.
                                   $1,250.00
Medina (Mexico): 4500. Palau: 269110. Garcia
Icazbalceta Lenguas: 56. Vinaza: 341. The translation by Padre Paredes, who was one of the most important Nahuatl scholars of the period, of Ripalda's
Spanish language catechism into Nahuatl, which was
the language of the Aztecs. The headings, licenses
and indices are in Spanish, suggesting that this volume
was intended strictly for the use of Spanish missionaries. (WR)

D128. DePAREDES (Ignacio). Promptuario Manual Mexicano.
23ff, 380pp, xc, the copperplate engraving of St. Ignatius found in some copies is not here present. Sml
quarto, 19th Century half morocco, part of the pre-
liminaries misbound. Imprenta de la Biblioteca Mexicana, Mexico, 1759. $1,000.00
Vinaza: 344. Garcia Icazbalceta Lenguas: 57.
Medina (Mexico): 4568. Sabin: 58575. A renowned
work in Nahuatl and Spanish by the 18th Century's
greatest student of the Aztec language. Handsomely
produced by one of Mexico's best 18th Century presses,
the work is composed of 52 sermons and 40 moral discussions in Nahuatl meant to explain points of Catholic
theology. (WR)

D129. DePINA CHAN (B. B.). (Instituto Nacional de Antropologia e Historia) Valle de Guadalupe: Jalisco. 122pp, 23 photographs, 8 maps, one is fold-out. Mexico City, 1980. $10.00

D130. DePONCINS (G.). Eskimos. 105pp, 63 full-page photographs, map, cloth. New York, 1949. $50.00

D131. DePONCINS (G.). Kabloona. xii, 339pp, 27 b/w and 4 color drawings, 32pp photographs, cloth. New York, 1941. $24.00

D132. DEPONS (F.). Travels in South America, During the Years 1801, 1802, 1803 and 1804 ... With a View of the Manners and Customs of the Spaniards and the Native Indians (2 Volumes). Vol. 1: lii, 503pp. Vol. 2: (xii), 384pp, folding map, original calf, rebacked. London, Longman, Hurst, Rees and Orme, 1807.
$250.00

Important early documentation of Indians of South America both before and after the arrival of Whites. Includes a description of the slaughter of the Indians and the Search for El Dorado. Field: 421. (RMW)

D133. DePOURTALES (Count Albert-Alexander). (SPAULDING, George F., Editor) On the Western Tour with Washington Irving. The Journals and Letters of.... 85pp, illus, index. Norman, 1968 (1st ed.), d.j. $12.00

D134. DeRIBAS (Andres Perez). Padre Provincial of the Company of Jesus of New Spain (Mexico). My Life Among the Savage Nations of New Spain. Written in the Year A.D. 1644 and entitled "Triumphs of Our Saintly Faith Among Peoples, the Most Barbarous and Savage of the New Orb" Translated in the Condensed Form by Thomas Antonio Robertson. 304pp, lrg 8vo, illus, maps, index. Los Angeles, 1968. $35.00

D135. (DeROCHEFORT Charles) Histoire Naturelle et Morale des les Antilles de l'Amerique, Enrichie d'un Grand Nombre de Belles Figures en Taille Douce, des Places & des Raretes les Plus Considerables, Qui y Song Descrites. Avec un Vocabulaire Caraibe. Seconde Edition. (34), 583, (13)pp, engraved frontis, 3 double-page views, many in text illus, recent full leather, lrg 8vo. Roterdam, Arnout Leers, 1665. $900.00

Sabin: 72316. Field: 1313. "In this work ... have been preserved very many curious and interesting particulars of the life, habits and characters of the Carib Indians, more especially of the Apalachites. The last eighteen chapters ... are entirely devoted to the relation of these particulars, with a copious vocabulary of their language." (RMW)

D136. DeROSIER (Arthur H., Jr.). The Removal of the Choctaw Indians. 201pp plus index, illus, maps, bibliography, first of the tribal removals to the west. Knoxville, 1970 (1st ed.), d.j. $15.00

_____Another Copy. Knoxville, 1972, d.j. $10.00

D137. DeSAHAGUN (B.). The Florentine Codex. Translated
from the Aztec into English, with notes by C. E.
Dibble and J. O. Anderson. The monumental and
encyclopedic study of native life in Mexico at the time
of the Spanish conquest took Sahagun over 30 years to
complete. His manuscripts, confiscated in about 1575,
disappeared for over 200 years before their existence
became known in 1793 at the Medicea Laurenziana Library in Florence. In the late 1940s a microfilm copy
became available, and translators Anderson and Dibble
commenced a 35-year effort that culminated with the
writing of the Introductory Volume and the complete
translation of the entire manuscript--one of the most
distinguished contributions in the fields of the anthropology, ethnology and linguistics of 16th-Century
Mexico. (EAP)
___Introductory Volume: Sahagun's Prologues and In-
terpolations, General Bibliography, General Indices.
xv, 137pp, 15 b/w and 2 full-page color photographs.
Cloth. School of American Research, 1982. $55.00
___Book 1 (The Gods). 84pp, 43 illus, cloth. School
of American Research, 1970, 1978 (2d ed., revised).
                                                 $28.00
___Book 2 (The Ceremonies). 247pp, 66 illus, cloth.
School of American Research, 1981 (2d ed., revised).
                                                 $60.00
___Book 3 (The Origin of the Gods). 70pp, 19 illus,
cloth. School of American Research, 1978 (2d ed.,
revised). $28.00
___Book 4 and 5 (The Soothsayers, The Omens).
196pp, 113 illus, cloth. School of American Research,
1957, 1979. $60.00
___Book 6 (Rhetoric and Moral Philosophy). 260pp,
52 illus, cloth. School of American Research, 1969,
1976 (2d print.). $60.00
___Book 7 (The Sun, The Moon and Stars, and the
Binding of the Years). 81pp, 22 illus, cloth. School
of American Research, 1953, 1977. $28.00
___Book 8 (Kings and Lords). 89pp, 100 illus, cloth.
School of American Research, 1954, 1979. $30.00
___Book 9 (The Merchants). 97pp, 110 illus, cloth.
School of American Research, 1959, 1976. $30.00
___Book 10 (The People). 197pp, 197 illus, cloth.
School of American Research, 1961, 1974. $48.00
___Book 11 (Earthly Things). 297pp, 965 illus, cloth.
School of American Research, 1963, 1975. $70.00
___Book 12 (The Conquest of Mexico). 126pp, 161
illus, cloth. School of American Research, 1975 (2d
ed., revised. $44.00
D138. DeSAPIR (O. L.). (Smithsonian Contributions to Anthro-
pology, Vol. 8, 1968) Cultural Chronology of the

Gulf of Chiriqui, Panama. 154pp, 55 figures containing hundreds of drawings, 20pp photographs, 12 tables, cloth. $40.00

D139. DeSCHWEINITZ (Edmund). The Life and Times of David Zeisberger: The Western Pioneer and Apostle of the Indians. 747pp, index, original green cloth, gilt, early missionary account, geographical glossary of Indian towns, settlements, forts and rivers. Philadelphia, 1879 (1st ed.). $145.00

D140. DESERONTYON (John). (Museum of the American Indian, Notes and Monographs, Vol. 10, No. 8, 1928) A Mohawk Form of Ritual of Condolence, 1782. pp87-110, 12 facsimile illus, 12mo, wrappers. $20.00

D141. DeSMET (Father Pierre-Jean). Annales de la Propagation de la Foi. Tome Dix-Huitieme. 576pp, index, half-calf, marbled bds, light foxing. Lyon, 1846 (1st ed.). $110.00

D142. DeSMET (Father Pierre-Jean). Letters and Sketches with a Narrative of a Year's Residence Among the Indian Tribes of the Rocky Mountains. (iii)-(xi), (13)-252pp, frontis, 10 pls (lacks plate 7), folding pl (lithographs by P. S. Duvall), full red gilt leather, marbled endpapers by Zaehnsdorf. Philadelphia, M. Fithian, 1843 (1st ed.). $650.00
Howes: D-283. Sabin: 82262. Field: 1423. Wagner-Camp: 102:1: "Father DeSmet gave more than three decades of service to the cause of the American Indian. His voluminous, articulate writings, in the form of letters ... described his wards with accuracy and sympathy." (RMW)

D143. DeSMET (Father Pierre-Jean). Voyages aux Montagnes Rocheuses. 240pp, frontis, recently rebound, interior shows library stamps. Howes: D-288. Lille, France, 1859 (4th ed.). $45.00

D144. DeSMET (Father Pierre-Jean). Mission de l'Oregon et Voyages dans les Montagnes Rocheuses on 1845 et 1846. 408pp, frontis 12 pls, engraved title, leather backed, marbled bds, hinge cracked at engraved title, leather backed, marbled bds, hinge cracked at engraved title. Paris, Librairie de Poussielgue-Rusand, 1848. $150.00
Howes: D-286. Sabin: 82266. Field: 1425. Sabin: "The lithographed plates are identical with those in the New York edition ... from which this translation (Bourliz, M., Translator) seems to have been first made. In the latter part, however, it follows the other French edition published at Ghent." (RMW)

D145. DeSMET (Father Pierre-Jean). New Indian Sketches. 175pp, frontis pl, 1 pl in text, rebacked, 2 maps pasted to endpaper. New York, D. & J. Sadlier, 1863 (1st ed.). $250.00
Howes: D-285. Field: 1427. Includes memoir of Louise Sighouin, a Coeur d'Alene Indian.

D146. DeSMET (Father Pierre-Jean). Origin, Progress and Prospects of the Catholic Mission to the Rocky Mountains. 12pp, 2pp, limited to 300 copies, wrappers. Fairfield, WA, 1967. $10.00

D147. DeSMET (Father Pierre-Jean). Western Missions and Missionaries, A Series of Letters. First Translation of Cinquante Nouvelles Lettress. 532pp, 4pp ads, frontis, gilt pictorial cloth, new endpapers. New York, 1863. $125.00

    Smith: 9568. "Two of Father DeSmet's journeys here described are especially worth noticing. First is his visit to the Sioux in 1848, and second is description of the Grand Desert in 1851." (OTB)

    ____Another Copy. Same. Portrait added to blank endpaper, later leather, ex-library. Howes: D-289. Sabin: 82277. Field: 1426. $135.00

D148. DeSMIDT (Leon S.). Among the San Blas Indians of Panama: Giving a Description of Their Manners, Customs and Beliefs. 95pp, photographs, bibliography, decorative wrappers. "Tule" tribe. Troy, 1948 (1st ed.). $25.00

D149. DeSOLIS (Antonio). Historia de la Conquesta de Mexico, Poblacion y Progresos de la America Septentrional, Conocida por el Nombre de Nueva Espana (5 Volumes). ppxlvii, 251; 316; 304; 303; 268, 16 mo, full calf, engravings. Madrid, Cano, 1798-1799. $200.00

    Field: 1465. "This work affords the most minute narration of the slaughter of the Indians of Mexico by the Spaniards, and the prodigies of valor exhibited by iron-mailed warriors in fighting naked savages." (RMW)

D150. DeTAPIA ZENTENO (Carlos). Noticia de la Lengua Huasteca, Que en Beneficio de sus Nacionales de Orden del Ilmo. Sr. Arzobispo de Esta Santa Iglesia Metropolitana y a sus Expensas.... Sml quarto, contemporary vellum. Imprenta de la Bibliotheca Mexicana, Mexico, 1767. $1,800.00

    Vinaza: 355. Garcia Icazbalceta Lenguas: 73. Medina (Mexico): 5187. Sabin: 94355. Palau: 327486. A pristine copy of an exceedingly rare grammar, and the only grammar to exist in Huasteca, the northern dialect of the Maya that was spoken in Puebla, Veracruz and San Luis Potosi. The work also includes a Spanish-Huastec dictionary extending to 40 pages. Tapia Zenteno was not only an important Mexican linguist and professor of Mexican languages at the Royal University but was also a comisario for the Inquisition.

    Provenance: Maggs, Bibliotheca Americana V:4678; acquired by G. R. C. Conway; on his death to Vizconde Gavito.

D151. DeTRUEBA y COSIO (Don Teleforo). History of the Conquest of Peru by the Spaniards. 341pp, 12mo, spine repaired. Edinburgh, 1830. $125.00

D152. DEUEL (Leo). Conquistadors Without Swords: Archaeologists in the Americas, an Account with Original Narratives. 647pp, illus, index, maps, includes accounts
by 42 pioneer archaeologists. New York, 1967 (1st
ed.). $20.00
___Another Copy. Same. d.j. $15.00

D153. DEUSS (K.). Indian Costumes from Guatemala. 72pp,
54 color and 33 b/w photographs, 70 drawings, 3 maps.
Twickenham, 1981. $20.00

D154. DeVALDIVA (L.). (Peabody Museum Papers, Vol. III,
No. 5, 1913) Discovery of a Fragment of the Printed
Copy of the Work on the Millcayac Language. 36pp,
photographs of 4 pages of the work, wrappers. $17.00
___Another Copy. Same. $15.00

D155. DEVEL (T.). American Indian Ways of Life, An Interpretation of the Archaeology of Illinois and Adjoining
Areas. 80pp, 38 figures. Illinois State Museum, 1958,
1968. $15.00

D156. DEVEL (T.). (Illinois State Museum, Scientific Papers,
Vol. 5, 1952) Hopewellian Communities in Illinois.
271pp, 94pp, illus. $30.00

DEVEREUX (George). See also BAE Bulletin No. 175.

D157. DEVEREUX (George). (From: Journal of American Folklore, Vol. 61, No. 241, 1948) Mohave Coyote Tales.
pp 233-255, wrappers. $15.00

D158. DEVEREUX (George). Reality and Dream: Psychotherapy
of a Plains Indian. 438pp, 12pp illus, index, prefaces
by Karl Menninger and Robert H. Lowie. New York,
1951 (1st ed.), d.j. $35.00
___Another Copy. New York, 1969, 615pp, illus,
index, bibliography, d.j. $20.00
___Another Copy. Same. $12.00

D159. DEVORE (Paul T.) (Editor). The Black Moccasin. 79pp,
illus, life on the Blackfeet Indian reservation as recorded by John Tatsey, cloth, limited to 250 copies.
Spokane, 1971, d.j. $25.00

D160. DeVORSEY (Louis, Jr.). The Indian Boundary in the
Southern Colonies, 1763-1775. 267pp, illus with 29
maps, bibliography, index, cloth. University of North
Carolina, 1966, d.j. $25.00
___Another Copy. Same. $18.00

D161. DeWALD (T.). The Papago Indians and Their Basketry.
49pp, 100 b/w and 79 color photographs. Tucson,
1979. $14.00

D162. DEWDNEY (S.) and KIDD (K. E.). Indian Rock Paintings
of the Great Lakes. 135pp, 6 color and 39 b/w photographs, 116 drawings, 6 maps, cloth. Toronto, 1962.
$34.00
___Another Copy. Same. d.j. $15.00

D163. DEWDNEY (S.). The Sacred Scrolls of the Southern
Ojibway. 191pp, b/w and color photographs, oblong.
Toronto, 1975 (1st ed.). $15.00

D164. DeZARATE (Don Augustin). Histoire de la Decouverte et de la Conquete du Perou (2 Volumes) Vol. 1: xl, 360pp. Vol. 2: iv, 479pp, 14 engraved pls, one folding map. Paris, Compagnie des Libraries, 1716.
$300.00

___Field: 1706: "Early narrative of the Spanish Conquest fully confirms the terrible story of Las Casas. The prints are principally descriptive of the horrible cruelties perpetrated by the Spanish monsters on the Indians." (RMW)

D164a. D'HARCOURT (R. & M.). La Musique des Incas et Ses Survivances. Text volume: 575pp, engraved frontis, Plate volume: xxiii, 39 photogravure pls, 2 in color, over 300 artifacts shown. Paris, 1925. $285.00

D165. D'HARCOURT (R.). Primitive Art of the Americas. 199pp, 160 b/w and 4 color photographs, 2 maps, linen cvr. New York, 1950.
$65.00

___Another Copy. Same. Hinges repaired. $45.00

___Another Copy. Arts de l'Amerique (French edition), Paris, 1948.
$42.00

D166. D'HARCOURT (R.). (University of Washington, Seattle, 1962) Textiles of Ancient Peru and Their Techniques. Illus, revised American Edition.
$75.00

D167. D'HARCOURT (R.). El Arte del Indo en los Estados Unidos. 58pp, 16 full-page photographs, 1pp drawings. National Indian Institute, Washington, 1943. $29.00

D168. DIAL (Adolph L.). The Only Land I Know: A History of the Lumbee Indians. 188pp, illus, bibliography, San Francisco, Indian Historical Press, 1975 (1st ed.), d.j.
$15.00

The Lumbee Indians lived in Robeson County, North Carolina. The story of their beginnings, their struggle for recognition and their militant fight against racial prejudice is told in this book.

D169. DIAZ DEL CASTILLO (Captain Bernal). The Discovery and Conquest of Mexico, 1517-1521. Edited from the only exact copy of the original manuscript by Genaro Garcia. Translated, with introduction and notes by A. P. Maudsley. A new introduction by Harry Block. xxii, 263pp, 45 color drawings by Miguel Covarrubias, sheepskin leather binding, hubs on spine, (8 3/4" x 12 3/4") in size, gold stamping, laid and toned paper, especially watermarked with a design by Covarrubias. This edition was printed in Mexico City in 1942 for the Limited Editions Club. This is copy number 388, and is signed by the printer, the editor and the illustrator. The original edition "Historia Verdadera de la Conquista de la Nueva-Espana" was published in Madrid in 1632.
$475.00

___Another Copy. London, 1933, 596pp. $35.00

___Another Copy. New York, 1956, 478pp. $15.00

_____Another Copy. New York, 1927, The True History
of the Conquest of Mexico Written in the Year 1568,
562pp, 14 pls, cloth, reprint of the London 1800 edition;
Diaz who accompanied Cortez, offers many important details not to be found elsewhere, d.j. $75.00

D170.   DIBBLE (Charles E.).   Codex en Cruz (2 Volumes).
Vol. I: 68pp of text containing 73 figures. Vol. II:
Atlas, 50pp of facsimiles. 4to (9" x 12"), post-
conquest Mexican Codex, relating to events beginning
in 1402, Salt Lake City, 1981. $45.00

D171.   DIBBLE (Charles E.).   Codice Xolotl (2 Volumes). Vol.
I: 166pp, 3 charts. Vol. II: 12 fold-out color photographs, 20 fold-out pages of b/w photographs, folio,
cloth, in cloth cvrd slipcase. Mexico City, 1951, 1980.
                                                        $70.00

D172.   DIBBLE (D. S.) and PREWITT (E. R.). (University of
Texas, Archaeological Survey Reports, No. 3, Austin,
1967, 1st ed.) Amistad Reservoir, 1964-1965. 125pp,
illus, maps, bibliography, lrg 8vo, wrappers. $12.00

D173.   DIBBLE (D. S.) and DAY (K. C.). (University of Utah--
Anthropological Papers, No. 57, Salt Lake City, 1962)
A Preliminary Survey of the Fontenelle Reservoir,
Wyoming, and other articles. 71pp, 43pp, maps,
photographs, figures, bibliography, indices, lrg 8vo,
wrappers. $15.00

DICK (Herbert W.). See also BAE Bulletin No. 154.

D174.   DICK (H. W.). (School of American Research, Monograph
No. 27, Santa Fe, 1965) Bat Cave, 114pp, 61 illus,
wrappers, Mogollon culture exploration in New Mexico.
                                                        $35.00

D175.   DICKENSON [Dickinson] (Jonathan). God's Protecting
Providence, Man's Surest Help and Defense, in Times
of Greatest Difficulty and Most Eminent Danger, Evi-
denced in the Remarkable Deliverance of Robert Barrow,
With Divers Other Persons, from the Devouring Waves
of the Sea, Amongst Which They Suffered Shipwreck;
and also from the Cruel Devouring Jaws of the Inhuman
Canibals of Florida. (xiv), 126pp, 4pp ads, 12mo,
gilt decorated calf. London, Mary Hinde, n.d. (c.
1759) (5th ed.). $300.00
Field: 426. Howes: D-317. Fascinating Indian
captivity, and the first book of general interest published in Philadelphia. (RMW)
_____Another Copy. Yale Historical Anns., Mss. 19,
New Haven, 1943, Jonathan Dickinson's Journal; or, God's
Protecting Providence. Being the Narrative of a Journey
from Port Royal in Jamaica to Philadelphia Between August 23, 1696, and April 1, 1697. Edited by Evangeline
Andrews and Charles Andrews. 252pp, illus, cloth.
                                                        $25.00

D176.   DICKERSON (Philip). History of the Osage Nation, Its

People, Resources and Prospects (wrapper title).
144pp, lacks wrappers. (Pawhuska, 1906). $200.00
Confusion exists concerning this Oklahoma book.
Only a very few copies were initially distributed because
the author, who was also the publisher, went bankrupt
shortly after publication. We are told that a remainder
of this item was found by a Kansas City bookseller in
the 1940s, lacking wrappers, and that he had blue and
pink wrappers made. In content, this pamphlet contains
much information on the Osage in Oklahoma, and the
history of the northeastern part of the state. (WR)

D177. DICKEY (Herbert S.). My Jungle Book. 298pp, illus
with photographs, Orinoco River, includes Maquiritari,
Guaharibo Indians. Boston, 1932. $25.00

D178. DICKEY (Thomas) et al. The Kings of El Dorado: Treasures of the World. 176pp, numerous color illus, includes Colombia, Ecuador, Peru, 4to. New York,
1982. $25.00

D179. (DIEGUENO). The Autobiography of Delfina Cuero, A
Diegueno Indian, as told to Florence C. Shipek; interpreter, Rosalie Pinto Robertson. 67pp, photographic
frontis, folding map at back, limited to 600 copies.
Los Angeles, 1968 (1st ed.). $20.00

DIESELDORFF (E. P.). See BAE Bulletin No. 28.

D180. DIESELDORFF (H. Q.). X Balm Q'ue, El Pajaro Sol, El
Traje Regional de Coban. v, 38pp, 15 lrg color and
8 b/w photographs, 2 drawings. Museo Ixchel del
Traje Indigena de Guatemala, 1984. $20.00

D181. DIETERICH (M.), et al. Guatemalan Costumes. 96pp,
23pp of color and 20pp of b/w photographs, 4pp of
drawings, 3 maps. Phoenix, 1979. $30.00
A Heard Museum exhibition catalogue reflected almost
a decade of field research and collecting and it provides
a dazzling visual presentation of contemporary Guatemalan Highland costume. Great photographs and excellent data on each illustrated garment. (EAP)

D182. DIETRICH (Margaretta S.). The Navajo in No-Man's Land.
10pp, stiff printed wrappers, problems of the Navajo
living off the reservation, separate reprint from the New
Mexico Quarterly, Vol. XX, No. 4. Albuquerque, 1950.
    $10.00

D183. DIGBY (A.). Maya Jades. 48pp, 16pp of photographs, 4
figures. London, 1964. $10.00

D184. DILLEHAY (T. D.). (University of Texas, Archeological
Survey Research Reports, No. 51, Austin, n.d., 1st
ed.) Prehistoric Subsistence Exploitation in the Lower
Trinity River Delta, Texas. 193pp, pls, maps, bibliog-
raphy, lrg 8vo, wrappers. $10.00
____Another Copy. Same. $10.00

D185. DILLON (B. D.). Salinas de los Nueve Cerros Guatemala,
Preliminary Archaeological Investigations. 94pp, 29pp
of drawings and photographs. Socorro, 1977. $15.00

D186. DIN (Gilbert C.) and NASATIR (Abraham P.). The Imperial Osage-Spanish-Indian Diplomacy in the Mississippi Valley. 417pp plus index, illus, maps, bibliography, the Osages to 1808. Norman, 1983 (1st ed.), d.j.
$30.00
___Another Copy. Same. $22.00

D187. DINGUS (R.). The Photographic Artifacts of Timothy O'Sullivan. 158pp, 64 nineteenth century photographs, cloth. Albuquerque, 1982. $45.00

D188. DIOMEDI (Father A.). Sketches of Modern Indian Life. 79pp, plain paper wrappers, original and only edition of a rare and little known work. Only a few copies were printed for private use ... Soliday II: 333. Ex-library, n.p., n.d. (Written in 1879, published c. 1894 in Woodstock, MD?) $325.00
Father Diomedi went to the Rocky Mountains in the 60s ... relates to Indians of Montana, Idaho and Washington. Father Diomedi founded Lewiston, Idaho, and St. Ignatius missions. (OTB)

D189. DIPESO (C.). (Amerind Foundation, No. 5, Dragoon, 1951) The Babocomari Village Site on the Babocomari River, Southeastern Arizona. xii, 248pp, 49 figures.
$40.00

D190. DIPESO (C.). Casas Grandes. A Fallen Trading Center of the Gran Chichimeca. Vols. 4-8 (5 Volumes). pp474; 925; 551; 532; 415 plus indices, illus, maps. Covers dating, architecture, ceramics and shell, stone and metal, bones, burials and commerce. The detailed source materials and data upon which Vols. 1-3 were based. Dragoon and Flagstaff, 1974 (1st ed.). $185.00
___Another Copy. Same. All 8 volumes. $250.00
___Another Copy. Same. Volumes 1-3 only. $75.00

D191. DIPESO (C.). (Amerind Foundation No. 6, Dragoon, 1953) The Sobaipuri Indians of the Upper San Pedro Valley, Southeastern Arizona. xii, 285pp, 92 photographs, 32 figures. $47.00
___Another Copy. Same. $65.00
___Another Copy. Same. $30.00

D192. (DISBURSEMENTS). (Senate Executive Document 20, 35:1, Washington, 1858, 1st print.) Indian Disbursements. 330pp, removed. Indian allotments. $25.00

D193. DISSELHOFF (H. D.). Alltag Im Alten Peru. 155pp, 13pp of color and 93pp of b/w photographs, 8pp of drawings of artifacts, principally from European museums and private collections, map, cloth. Munich, 1960. $45.00

D194. DISSELHOFF (H.) and LINNE (S.). The Art of Ancient America. 274pp, 148 b/w and 110 color photographs, cloth. New York, 1960. $25.00
___Another Copy. New York, 1961, 274pp, 60 color pls. $25.00

D195. DISSELHOFF (H.). Daily Life in Ancient Peru. 156pp,

175 illus, some in color, 4to. New York, 1967, d.j.
$45.00

D196. DISTRONG (W.), et al. (University of California Publications in American Archaeology Vol. 29, No. 1, 1930) Archaeology of the Dalles-Deschutes Region. vii, 154pp, 22 figures, map, 22pp of photographs, map, spine repaired. $57.00

D197. DIXON (Joseph K.). The Vanishing Race: The Last Great Indian Council; A Record in Picture and Story of the Last Great Indian Council Participated in by Eminent Indian Chiefs from nearly every Indian Reservation in the United States, Together with the Story of their Lives as told by Themselves ... and the Indians' Story of the Custer Fight. xviii, 222pp, plus 80 photogravures, Indians, costumes, families, decorated cloth, photographs by Joseph K. Dixon although they were copyrighted by Rodman Wanamaker. New York, Doubleday Page, 1913 (1st ed.). $100.00
____Another Copy. Same. $125.00
____Another Copy. Garden City, 1914 (2d revised ed.), xvii, 231pp, 80 photogravure pls, index. $85.00
____Another Copy. New York, n.d. reprint of 1913 ed., d.j. $14.00

D198. DIXON (Margaret Denny). Pocahontas, The Princess of the Old Dominion; A Historical Novel of the First Virginia Colony. 132pp, cloth. Richmond, 1953, d.j.
$10.00

DIXON (Roland B.). See also BAE Bulletin No. 40, Part 1.

D199. DIXON (R. B.). (American Museum of Natural History Bulletin, Vol. XVIII, Part III, 1905) The Northern Maidu. pp119-346, 67 illus, repairs to spine, rear wrapper missing. $135.00
This was the first major publication on the Maidu of Northeastern California, and provided a full ethnographic examination of this people, with particular emphasis on their religion and material culture, especially basketry and feather work. (EAP)

D200. DOBYNS (Henry F.). The Apache People (Coyotero). 106pp, b/w and color photographs, maps, signed by tribal chieftain, part of the Indian Tribal Series, wrappers. Phoenix, 1971 (1st ed.). $15.00

D201. DOBYNS (H. F.) and EULER (R.). (Prescott College, Studies in Anthropology, No. 1, Arizona, 1967) The Ghost Dance of 1889 Among the Pai Indians of Northwestern Arizona. 67pp, 4 photographs, map. $30.00

D202. DOBYNS (H. F.) and EULER (R. C.). The Havasuapi People. 71pp, 1pp, b/w and color photographs, map, signed by tribal chieftain, part of the Indian Tribal Series, wrappers. Phoenix, 1971 (1st ed.). $15.00

D203. DOBYNS (H. F.). The Mescalero Apache People. 106pp b/w and color photographs, maps, signed by tribal

chieftain, part of Indian Tribal Series, hard cvr.
Phoenix, 1973 (1st ed.). $20.00
___Another Copy. Same. $17.00

D204. DOBYNS (H. F.) and EULER (R. C.). The Navaho People. 100pp, b/w and color photographs, maps, signed by tribal chieftain, part of the Indian Tribal Series, wrappers. Phoenix, 1972 (1st ed.). $15.00
___Another Copy. Albuquerque, 1986, The Navajo Indians. 121pp, 24 illus, maps, wrappers. $10.00

D205. DOBYNS (H. F.). The Papago People. 106pp, b/w and color photographs, maps, signed by tribal chieftain, part of the Indian Tribal Series, wrappers. Phoenix, 1972 (1st ed.). $15.00

D206. DOCKSTADER (Frederick J.) (Compiler). The American Indian in Graduate Studies: A Bibliography of Theses and Dissertations. Parts 1 and 2. 399pp, 426pp, each indexed. Ex-library, covers 1890-1973. Heye Foundation, New York, 1957 and 1974 (1st eds.). $40.00

D207. DOCKSTADER (Frederick J.). Great North American Indians; Profiles in Life and Leadership. 386pp, photographs, paintings, other illus, 4to, index, life histories of 300 Indian leaders from all regions and tribes active between 1600 and 1977, includes all the famous chiefs plus many lesser-known and more recent individuals. New York, 1977 (1st ed.), d.j. $34.00

D208. DOCKSTADER (F. J.). Indian Art in America. The Arts and Crafts of the North American Indian. 224pp, 180 b/w and 69 color illus, cloth. New York, 1961. $65.00
___Another Copy. New York, 1961 (4th print.) Indian Art in North America, Arts and Crafts. Title change and addition to bibliography. $49.00

D209. DOCKSTADER (Frederick). Indian Art in Middle America. 221pp, 248 illus, many are tipped in color pls. New York, Graphic Society, 1964 (1st ed.). $60.00
___Another Copy. Same. $65.00
___Another Copy. London, 1964. $60.00

D210. DOCKSTADER (F. J.). Indian Art in South America, Pre-Columbian and Contemporary Arts and Crafts. 222pp, 201 b/w and 49 lrg color photographs, cloth. New York, 1967. $125.00
___Another Copy. South American Indian Art, London, 1967. $125.00

D211. DOCKSTADER (Frederick J.). Indian Art of the Americas. 304pp, photographs by Carmelo Guadagno, some in color, maps, bibliography, wide range of artifacts illus. Museum of American Indian, Heye Foundation, New York, 1973 (1st ed.). $20.00
___Another Copy. Same. $16.00

D212. DOCKSTADER (F. J.). Indianer Nordamerikas. 290pp, 93 b/w, 8 color full-page photographs. Rautenstrauch-Joest-Museum, Cologne, 1969. $18.00

D213. DOCKSTADER (Frederick J.). (Cranbrook Institute of
Science, Bulletin 35, Bloomfield Hills, MI, 1954, 1st
ed.) The Kachina and the White Man. 179pp plus index, photographs, color illus, b/w drawings of kachinas
by author, glossary, bibliography, maps. $35.00
___Another Copy. Same. d.j. $30.00
___Another Copy. Same. Presentation copy, signed
in full. $50.00
___Another Copy. Albuquerque, 1985. 202pp, illus.
                                                  $20.00
D214. DOCKSTADER (F. J.). Masterworks From the Museum of
the American Indian. 64pp, 209 photographs. Exhibition catalogue, Metropolitan Museum of Art, New York,
1973. $18.00
D215. DOCKSTADER (F.). Weaving Arts of the North American
Indian. 224pp, 100 b/w and 62 color photographs,
cloth. New York & London, 1978. $35.00
D216. DODDRIDGE (Joseph). Logan, The Last of the Race of
Shikellemus, Chief of the Cayuga Nation. 76pp, lrg
8vo. Cincinnati, Robert Clarke, 1868. (reprinted from
the Virginia Edition of 1823). Bound with: Jacob,
John J. "A Biographical Sketch of the Life of the Late
Captain Michael Cresap." 158pp. Cincinnati, Uhlhorn,
1866. With the Appendix: Lieutenant Boyer. "A Jour-
nal of Wayne's Campaign ... Against the Northwestern
Indians." 23pp. Cincinnati, Uhlhorn, 1866. The three
titles bound together is an edition limited to 300 copies.
                                                  $125.00
___Another Copy. Parsons, WV, 1971. Logan, the Last
of the Race of Skikellemus, Chief of the Cayuga Nation.
A Dramatic Piece to which is Added the Dialogue of the
Backwoodsman and the Dandy. First Recited at the
Buffaloe Seminary, July 1st, 1821. Reprinted from the
Virginia edition of 1823, with an appendix relating to
the Murder of Logan's Family for William Dodge. 76pp,
cloth. $22.00
D217. DODDRIDGE (Joseph). Notes on the Settlement and Indian
Wars of the Western Parts of Virginia and Pennsylvania
From 1763-1783, Inclusive. Together with a View of the
State of Society, and Manners of the First Settlers of the
Western Country. 331pp, index, decorated cloth. Al-
bany, New York, 1876. $85.00
    Howes: D-390. Ayer: 75, 76. Field: 437. First
edition of this important work was published in 1824,
the second, with new material, is this edition. (TA)
D218. DODGE (J. R.). Red Men of the Ohio Valley: An Abor-
iginal History. x, 13-435pp, ads, frontis, illus, original cloth. Springfield, OH, Ruralist Publishers, 1860
(2d print.). $95.00
Field: 439. "Concentrates on early white contacts with
Indians of Kentucky, Ohio, Indiana and Illinois." (RMW)

D219. DODGE (Richard I.). The Plains of the Great West and
       Their Inhabitants, Being a Description of the Plains,
       Game, Indians, etc., of the Great North American
       Desert. lv, 448pp, plus 19 pls, folding map, table of
       Indians living in the United States. Putnam, 1877
       (1st ed.). $125.00
D220. DODGE (Col. Richard Irving). Our Wild Indians: 33
       years' Personal Experience Among the Red Men of the
       Great West. Frontis, 653pp, 6 chromolithographed pls
       of Indian artifacts, illus, rebound. Hartford, 1882.
                                                            $50.00
       ___Another Copy. Hartford, 1883, 653pp, frontis, 6
       color pls, numerous engravings on steel and wood, gilt
       decorated brown cloth. $60.00
       ___Another Copy. New York, 1959. 657pp, 6 pls of
       multple artifacts. $35.00
D221. DOERING (H.). Old Peruvian Art. 93pp, 12 full-page
       color and 64 full-page b/w photographs, (9½" x 13") in
       size. London, 1936. $90.00
D222. DOLFIN (John). Bringing the Gospel in Hogan and Pueb-
       lo. 376pp, photographs, bibliography, much on the
       customs and life of the Zuni and Navajos by the author,
       who was a missionary among them from 1896. Grand
       Rapids, 1921 (1st ed.). $45.00
D223. DOMENECH (Abbe Em). Seven Years' Residence in the
       Great Deserts of North America (2 Volumes). Vol. 1:
       xxiv, 445pp. Vol. 2: xxii, 465pp, 59 colored and half-
       tone pls, folding hand-colored map of Indian Tribes of
       North America, cloth. London, Longman Green & Co.,
       1860 (1st ed.). $350.00
       Field: 444. Howes: D-410. Fine plates of Indian
       artifacts, utensils, weapons and of the Western lands.
       (RMW)
       ___Another Copy. Same. $300.00
D224. DONALDSON (T.). (Smithsonian Institution, Annual Re-
       port of the Board of Regents, Washington, 1886) The
       George Catlin Indian Gallery in the United States Na-
       tional Museum, With Memoir and Statistics ... To July,
       1885. Part II. vii, 939pp, 142pp drawings, 2 fold-out
       maps, cloth cvr, spine repaired. $165.00
       ___Another Copy. Same. modern calf. $225.00
D225- DONALDSON (Thomas C.) (Editor). Reports on Indians
D226. Taxed and Not Taxed.... (6), 683pp, maps, some fold-
       ing, 19 pls in full color, one is folding, pls, large thick
       quarto, rebound in cloth. Washington, 1894. $750.00
       Howes: D-148. One of the most important and ex-
       haustive treatments of the American Indian in the nine-
       teenth century. As American Indians had not been
       treated in detail in previous censuses, it was decided
       under the administration of Superintendent Robert Porter
       to prepare this mammoth undertaking which pays

scrupulous, detailed attention to the present state of the American Indian of the time. Included are discussions of Indian populations by state, status reports on life on the reservations, disbursement of populations on and off reservations, progress in schooling and employment, etc. The highly prized lithographed color pls of Indian life by noted artists are the best such works undertaken in a government publication, and are of exceptional quality. A large map shown "Indian Reservations of the United States...," another linguistic stocks, and another the Indian territory. Numerous single page maps show reservations. (WR)

D227. DONNAN (Christopher B.) and MACKEY (C. J.). Ancient Burial Patterns of the Moche Valley, Peru. 408pp, numerous illus. Texas, 1978. $45.00

D228. DONNAN (C. B.) and McCLELLAND (E.). The Burial Theme in Moche Iconography. 46pp, 44 photographs. Washington, 1979. $12.00

D229. DONNAN (C. B.) (Editor). Early Ceremonial Architecture in the Andes. A Conference at Dumbarton Oaks, Oct. 8-10, 1982. 289pp (12 papers), 112 figures, cloth. Washington, 1985. $40.00

D230. DONNAN (Christopher). Moche Art of Peru: Pre-Columbian Symbolic Communication. illus, some in color, 4to, wrappers. Museum of Cultural History, Los Angeles, 1978. $40.00
____Another Copy. Same. 205pp. $38.00

D231. DONNAN (C. B.) and COCK (G. A.) (Editors). The Pacatnumu Papers, Volume I. 188pp (12 papers), text in English and Spanish, 6 color photographs of textiles, 26 drawings, 28 maps and plans, fold-out map in rear pocket, wrappers. Museum of Cultural History, 1986. $30.00

D232. DORMAN (Rushton M.). The Origin of Primitive Superstitions. 398pp, index, 5 pls, of which 4 are in color, other text illus, cloth. Philadelphia, Lippincott, 1881 (1st ed.). $50.00

D233. DORN (Ed) and LUCAS (Leroy). The Shoshoneans: The People of the Basin-Plateau. Illus, stamp of magazine on endpaper, review slip laid in, because of the photo subject material, this book was recalled and pulped by the publishers. New York, 1966, d.j. $75.00

D234. DORRIS (Michael). Native Americans, 500 Years After. Photographs by Joseph C. Farber. 333pp, 4to, illus with hundreds of photographs showing the condition of the American Indian in the 1970s, index, map. New York, 1975 (1st ed.), d.j. $35.00

D235. DORSEY (G. A.). (Field Columbian Museum, Publication 75, Anthropology Series, Vol. IV, 1903) The Arapaho Sun Dance; The Ceremony of the Offerings Lodge. xii, 228pp text, plus 137pp of color and b/w photographs and drawings. $185.00

This seminal study by the great anthropologist vastly overshadowed anything previously written on this ceremony, and has remained, in the more than eighty years since its publication, one of the principal works on the Sun Dance. A massive work, the splendid text is accompanied by 137pp of photographs of the ceremony and the dancers. (EAP)

    Another Copy. Same. $125.00
    Another Copy. Same. $100.00
    Another Copy. Same. $45.00
    Another Copy. Millwood, 1973. $138.00

D236. DORSEY (G. A.). (Field Museum Anthropological Series, Vol. II, No. 5, 1901) Archaeological Investigations on the Island of La Plata, Ecuador. pp247-280 (some uncut) of text containing 10 figures and 2 fold-out maps, plus 62pp of photographs of objects. $59.00

One of the first investigations to be made of this island, the 1892 expedition led by the author was remarkably productive. The unearthed treasure cache made its way to the Field Museum, where it was later exhibited. Many of the finer objects are illustrated in the photographs; the text provides details on the objects unearthed, with particular emphasis on stylistic differences. (EAP)

D237. DORSEY (G. A.). (Field Museum of Natural History, Publication 23, Anthropology Series, Vol. II, No. 2, 1898) A Bibliography of the Anthropology of Peru. pp55-206. $85.00

D238. DORSEY (G. A.). (Field Columbian Museum, Anthropology Series, Vol. 9, Chicago, 1905) The Cheyenne (2 Volumes). Vol. I: Ceremonial Organization. 55pp, 17 pls with several in color. Vol. II: The Sun Dance. 186pp, 50 pls with several in color, wrappers. $225.00

As part of Dorsey's studies of Plains Indian ceremonies and social structures, the fieldwork and research for this volume were completed at a time when it was still possible to view the Sun Dance and to receive firsthand information from members of the tribe who had participated in all aspects of tribal ceremonies in the mid to late 19th century; the text, as with all Dorsey tomes, is scholarly and accurate, yet easily read. The illustrations include many photographs and drawings of the ceremonies, dancers, war bonnets, painted shirts, and other objects of material culture. The reprint is out of print, and the original 1905 editions have been out of print for over half a century. (EAP)

    Another Copy. Same. Vol. I only. $75.00
    Another Copy. Same. Vol. I only. $65.00
    Another Copy. Same. Vol. I only. $70.00
    Another Copy. Same. Vol. II only. $165.00
    Another Copy. Same. Vol. II only. $85.00

____Another Copy. Glorieta, 1971, 213pp, 24 color and 44 b/w full-page pls, plus 108 photographs and drawings, cloth. (2 Volumes). $40.00

____Another Copy. Fairfield, Washington, 1975, 55pp, 12 pls, limited to 300 copies, Vol. I only. $28.00

____Another Copy. Same. Vol. I only. $25.00

D239. DORSEY (George A.). (From: American Anthropologist, Vol. 5, 1903) How the Pawnee Captured the Cheyenne Medicine Arrows. pp644-658, in a binder. $10.00

____Another Copy. Same. $10.00

D240. DORSEY (G. A.). Indians of the Southwest. 223pp, 184 photographs, 34 drawings, 1 fold-out map. Chicago, 1903. $57.00

D241. DORSEY (G. A.) and MURIE (James R.). (Field Museum of Natural History, Publication 479, Vol. 27, No. 2, Chicago, 1940) Notes on Skidi Pawnee Society. pp67-119, bibliography, index, one text illus, wrappers. $25.00

D242. DORSEY (G. A.). (Field Museum Publication 102, Anthropological Series, Vol. VII, No. 2, 1905) The Ponca Sun Dance. 26pp text, plus 35 full-page photographs and color drawings. $24.00

____Another Copy. Same. 21pp, wrappers. $75.00

D243. DORSEY (G. A.). The Stanley-McCormick Hopi Expeditions. pp219-222. Offprint from "Science," N.S. 13: 319, (February, 1901) Brief review of explorations in these Hopi studies. $15.00

D244. DORSEY (George). Traditions of the Caddo. 136pp. Carnegie Institute, Washington, 1905. $45.00

D245. DORSEY (G. A.). (Field Columbian Museum, Publication 88, Anthropology Series, Vol. VII, No. 1, 1904) Traditions of the Osage. 60pp. $28.00

____Another Copy. Ex-library. $18.00

D246. DORSEY (George A.). Traditions of the Skidi Pawnee. xi, 366, 6pp, photographic pls, bibliography, index. Boston & New York for the American Folk-Lore Society, 1904 (1st ed.). $65.00

DORSEY (James Owen). See also BAE Bulletin Nos. 11 and 47.

D247. DORSEY (James O.). (Contributions to North American Ethnology, Vol. VI, 1890.) The Cegiha Language. xviii, 794pp, myths, stories, letters of the Omaha and Ponca tribes, rebound in brown cloth. $125.00

____Another Copy. Same. $90.00

____Another Copy. Same. $50.00

____Another Copy. Same. $40.00

D248. DORSEY (J. Owen). On the Comparative Phonology of Four Siouan Languages. Offprint for Smithsonian Report of 1883. 11pp, wrappers. $18.00

D249. DORWIN (John T.). (Indiana Historical Society Prehistoric Research Series, Vol. 4, No. 3, 1966) Fluted Points and Late-Pleistocene Geochronology in Indiana. pp141-188, illus, maps, bibliography, wrappers. $10.00

D250. DOUGHTY (Paul) and NEGRON (Luis). (Cornell Peru
Project, Report No. 6, Cornell, 1964) Pararin: A
Break with the Past. 74pp, wrappers. $18.00

D251. DOUGLAS (F. H.) et al. Indian Art of the United States.
200pp, 200 b/w and 16 color photographs, cloth. Exhibition Catalogue, Museum of Modern Art, New York,
1941. $58.00
___Another Copy. Same. $50.00
___Another Copy. New York, 1969 $25.00
___Another Copy. Same. $20.00

D252. DOWNEY (Fairfax) and JACOBSEN (Jacques Noel, Jr.).
The Red/Bluecoats. The Indian Scouts of the U.S.
Army. 201pp plus index, photographs, drawings, bib-
liography. Ft. Collins, CO, 1973 (1st ed.). $12.00

D253. DOWNES (Randolph C.). Council Fires on the Upper
Ohio: A Narrative of Indian Affairs in the Upper Ohio
Valley Until 1795. 367pp, map, index. University of
Pittsburgh Press, 1940 (1st ed.), d.j. $35.00
___Another Copy. Same. $25.00

D254. DOWNS (James F.). (University of California Publications
in Anthropology, Vol. 1, Berkeley, 1964) Animal Husbandry in Navajo Society and Culture. 104pp, maps,
charts, bibliography, wrappers. $15.00
___Another Copy. Same. $10.00

D255. DOZIER (Edward). (University of California Publications
in American Archaeology and Ethnology, Vol. 44, No.
3, Berkeley, 1954) The Hopi-Tewa of Arizona. pp359-
376, 4 figures, 4 maps, wrappers. $40.00

D256. DRAGOO (Don W.). (Carnegie Museum Anthropology
Series, No. 1, Pittsburgh, 1959, 1st ed.) Archaic
Hunters of the Upper Ohio Valley. pp139-246, illus,
bibliography, wrappers. $20.00

D257. DRAGOO (Don W.). Mounds for the Dead: An Analysis
of the Adena Culture. 315pp, illus, bibliography, index, cloth. Carnegie Museum, Pittsburgh, 1963, (1st
ed.). $65.00

D258. DRAKE (Benjamin). The Life and Adventures of Black
Hawk: With Sketches of Keokuk, the Sac and Fox Indians, and the Late Black Hawk War. 288pp including
index, frontis, 7 full-page woodcut pls, 1/2 leather,
cloth cvrd bds. Cincinnati, 1847 (7th ed.). $40.00

D259. DRAKE (Benjamin). Life of Tecumseh and of His Brother,
The Prophet; with a Historical Sketch of the Shawanoe
Indians. 235pp, cloth. Cincinnati, 1852. $45.00
___Another Copy. Cincinnati, 1858. $40.00

D260. DRAKE (Samuel G.). Biography and History of the Indians
of North America; Comprising a General Account of
Them, and Details in the Lives of All the Most Distin-
guished Chiefs. 518, (30)pp, 8 pls, 8vo, full calf.
Boston, Perkins, 1834. $75.00
___Another Copy. Boston, 1857. Biography and

History of the Indians of North America, from Its First
Discovery. 720pp, index added this ed. $60.00
___Another Copy. Boston, 1861. 720pp, frontis, 11
pls. $50.00
___Another Copy. New York, Hurst & Co., n.d. (c.
1880) (15th ed.) The Aboriginal Races of North Amer-
ica; Comprising Biographical Sketches of Eminent Indi-
viduals, and.... 787pp, decorated cloth. $25.00
___Another Copy. Same. $20.00
D 261. DRAKE (Samuel G.). Early History of New England; Be-
        ing a Relation of Hostile Passages Between the Indians
        and European Voyagers and First Settlers, to the Close
        of the War with the Pequots, In the Year 1637.... 309pp,
        large 8vo, rebound in half leather. Boston, Drake,
        1864. $125.00
        Field: 459. Reprinting of a rare work by Increase
        Mather, "A Relation of the Troubles Which Have
        Hap'ned in New England, by reason of the Indians
        There from the Year 1614 to the Year 1675." (RMW)
D 262. DRAKE (Samuel G.). Indian Captivities; or, Life In The
        Wigwam. Being True Narratives of Captives Who Have
        Been Carried Away by the Indians, From the Frontier
        Settlements of the United States, From the Earliest
        Period to the Present Time. 360pp, woodcut illus, half
        leather. Auburn, NY, 1850. $25.00
        ___Another Copy. Same. $40.00
        ___Another Copy. Boston, 1844, title starts "Tragedies
        of the Wilderness..., 4 full-page engravings. $85.00
D 263. DRAKE (Samuel G.). The Old Indian Chronicle: Being
        a Collection of Exceedingly Rare Tracts, Written and
        Published in the Time of King Philip's War. Introduc-
        tion and Notes by S. G. Drake. xii, 333pp, newly
        rebound, sml 4to, folding map. Boston, 1867. $125.00
D 264. DRAKE (Samuel G.). A Particular History of the Five
        Years French and Indian War in New England and Parts
        Adjacent, From March 15, 1744, to the Treaty with the
        Eastern Indians, October 16, 1749, Sometimes Called
        Governor Shirley's War. 312pp, sml 4to, frontis, text
        illus. Albany, Joel Munsell, 1870. $75.00
D 265. DRAPER (William R.). Stories About Indian Maidens, Un-
        usual Sex and Marriage Customs Among the Osage In-
        dians. 32pp, stapled wrappers. Girard, KS, 1946
        (1st ed.). $12.00
D 266. DREW (L.). Haida, Their Art and Culture. 111pp, 85
        b/w and 26 color photographs, 20 drawings, 1 map of
        Haida villages, cloth. Surrey, 1982. $18.00
        ___Another Copy. Same. Soft cover. $10.00
D 267. DRIMMER (Frederick) (Editor). Scalps and Tomahawks:
        Narratives of Indian Captivity. 378pp, accounts of 15
        survivors during 1750-1870. New York, 1961 (1st
        ed.), d.j. $15.00

D268. DRINNON (Richard). White Savage. The Case of John
      Dunn Hunter. 282pp, memoirs of John Dunn Hunter's
      captivity with the Indians, bibliography, index. New
      York, 1972 (reprint of London ed., 1824), d.j. $15.00
      _____Another Copy. Same. $12.00
      _____Another Copy. Same. $15.00
D269. DRISCOLL (B.). Baffin Island. 128pp, 133 photographs,
      1 map. Winnipeg, 1983. $10.00
D270. DRIVER (H. E.). (Transactions of the American Philo-
      sophical Society, New Series, Vol. 47, Part 2, 1957)
      Comparative Studies of North American Indians. pp165-
      456, 18 drawings, 13 diagrams, 20 tables, 163 maps.
                                                        $40.00
      _____Another Copy. Philadelphia, 1960. $37.00
D271. DRIVER (H. E.). (University of California Anthropologi-
      cal Records, Vol. 1, No. 2, 1937) Culture Element
      Distributions: VI. Southern Sierra Nevada. 104pp,
      1 map. $30.00
D272. DRIVER (H. E.). (University of California Publications
      in American Archaeology and Ethnology, Vol. 36, No.
      3, Berkeley, 1936) Wappo Ethnography. 46pp, 1
      figure, 2 maps. $29.00
D273. DRIVER (Harold and Wilhelmine). Ethnography and Accul-
      turation of the Chichimeca-Jonaz of Northeast Mexico.
      265pp, 32 figures, wrappers. International Journal,
      American Linguistics, 1963. $35.00
DRUCKER (Philip). See also BAE Bulletin Nos. 133, 140, 141,
      144, 153, 157, 168, and 170.
D274. DRUCKER (P.). (University of California Publications in
      American Archaeology and Ethnology, No. 35, No. 7,
      Berkeley, 1939) Contributions to Alsea Ethnography.
      22pp. $18.00
D275. DRUCKER (P.). (University of California Anthropological
      Records, Vol. 9, No. 3, Berkeley, 1950) Culture Ele-
      ment Distributions: XXVI. Northwest Coast. 142pp,
      78 drawings. $57.00
D276. DRUCKER (Philip). Indians of the Northwest Coast.
      208pp, 104 Illus. New York, 1955 (1st ed.), d.j.
                                                        $40.00
      _____Another Copy. Same. $47.00
      _____Another Copy. 1963, wrappers. $12.00
D277. DRUCKER (P.). (University of California Anthropological
      Records, Vol. 2, No. 6, Berkeley, 1940) Kwakiutl
      Dancing Societies. 34pp, 2 figures, map. $30.00
      _____Another Copy. Same. $30.00
D278. DRUCKER (Philip). (Smithsonian Miscellaneous Collections,
      Vol. 107, No. 8, Washington, 1947) Some Implications
      of the Ceramic Complex of La Venta. 9pp, plus 6 pls,
      wrappers. $20.00
D279. DRUCKER (Philip). To Make My Name Good: A Re-
      examination of the Southern Kwakiutl Potlatch. 157pp,

index, bibliography. Berkeley, 1967 (1st ed.), d.j.
$25.00

New interpretation of an often misunderstood ceremonial feast which the Kwakiutl of British Columbia
used to validate hereditary status, distribute wealth,
pay debts.

D280. DRUMMOND (D. E.). (University of Oregon, Anthropological Papers No. 21, 1981) The Naknek Region, 1960-1975.
xii, 277pp, 17pp of photographs, 80 figures, wrappers.
$22.00

D281. DRURY (Clifford M.). Chief Lawyer of the Nez Perce Indians. 304pp, color frontis, illus, map, signed. Glendale, 1979. $25.00
____Another Copy. Same. Not signed. $25.00

D282. DRURY (Clifford M.). (Northwest Historical Series, Vol.
IV, Glendale, 1958, 1st ed.) The Diaries and Letters
of Henry H. Spalding and Asa Bowen Smith relating to
the Nez Perce Mission 1838-1842. 368pp plus index,
photographs, maps, colored frontis. $50.00
____Another Copy. Same. signed by author. $50.00

D283. DRURY (Clifford M.). Elkanah and Mary Walker. Pioneers Among the Spokanes. 283pp, frontis, 28pp illus,
notes, bibliography, index, pictorial gilt cloth, endpaper maps, limited to 500 signed copies. Caldwell,
1940 (1st ed.), d.j. $100.00

Mary Walker's diaries of life at Tshimakain mission
provide one of the most detailed accounts of frontier
life.

D284. DRURY (Clifford). Henry Harmon Spalding. Pioneer of
Old Oregon. 438pp, frontis, 28pp illus, bibliography,
index, endpaper maps, was early NW missionary to the
Indians. Caldwell, 1936 (1st ed.), d.j. $75.00

D285. DRURY (Clifford M.). Nine Years with the Spokane Indians: The Diary, 1838-1848, of Elkanah Walker.
547pp, illus, map, index. Glendale, 1976 (1st ed.).
$30.00
____Another Copy. Same. $26.00

D286. DUBOIS (C.). (General Series in Anthropology, No. 7,
Menasha, 1938) The Feather Cult of the Middle Colum-
bia. 45pp. $37.00
____Another Copy. Same. stiff wrappers. $25.00

D287. DUBOIS (C. G.). (University of California Publications
in American Archaeology and Ethnology, Vol. 8, No. 3,
1908) The Religion of the Luiseno Indians Southern
California. 118pp, 4pp photographs, 3 figures. $45.00

D288. DUBOIS (C.). (University of California Publications in
American Archaeology and Ethnology, Vol. 36, No. 1,
1935) Wintu Ethnography. 148pp, 3pp photographs,
11 figures, 1 map. $49.00

D289. DUBY (G.). Chiapas Indigena. 148pp, 138 lrg photographs, cloth. Mexico City, 1961. $40.00

D290. DUCHAUSSOIS (R. P.). Aux Glaces Polaires--Indiens et
Esquimaux. 440pp, photographic pls, folded map,
wrappers. Paris, Nouvelle Oeuvre des Missions, 1928.
$45.00

D291. DUCHAUSSOIS (P.). Mid Snow and Ice. The Apostles of
the North-west. 328pp, photographs, folding colored
map, Catholic missionaries to the Indians and Eskimos,
late 1800s on. London, 1923 (1st ed.), d.j. $60.00
____Another Copy. Same. $50.00

D292. DUERDEN (J. E.). (Journal, Institute of Jamaica, Vol.
2, No. 4, 1897) Aboriginal Indian Remains in Jamaica.
50pp, 7 pls illus artifacts, wrappers. $60.00

D293. DUFF (Wilson). Anthropology in British Columbia, No.
5. 151pp, illus, wrappers. British Columbia Museum,
Victoria, 1956. $35.00
____Another Copy. Same. $10.00
____Another Copy. Same. $10.00

D294. DUFF (Wilson) et al. Arts of the Raven: Masterworks
by the Northwest Coast Indian. 80pp, pls, decorative
wrappers, pieces from private and public sources. Exhibition catalogue, Vancouver Art Gallery, 1967 (1st
ed.). $20.00

D295. DUFF (Wilson). (Anthropology in British Columbia, Memoirs No. 4, Victoria, 1959) Histories, Territories and
Laws of the Kitwancool. 45pp, illus, wrappers. $12.00

D296. DUFF (Wilson). Images: Stone: B.C., Thirty Centuries
of Northwest Coast Indian Sculpture. 191pp, photographs, map, square 4to, catalogue of an exhibition of
British Columbia Indian sculpture, includes photographs
of 136 items with excellent descriptive text. Seattle,
1975 (1st ed.), d.j. $40.00

D297. DUFF (W.) et al. Masterpieces of Indian and Eskimo Art
from Canada. 276pp, 147 b/w and 6 color photographs.
Paris, 1969. $45.00
In a dazzling 1969 exhibition at the Musee de l'Homme
185 seldom seen masterpieces of Canadian Indian and
Eskimo art were displayed. 126 of these great objects
were Eskimo and Northwest Coast; the remaining 59 were
from the Plains and Eastern regions of Canada. The
photographs are large; the data for each object is very
complete. Text in both English and French, out of
print. (EAP)

D298. DUFF (W.). (Provincial Museum Memoir, Victoria, 1952,
1st ed.) The Upper Stalo Indians of the Fraser Valley,
British Columbia. 146pp, illus, bibliography. $30.00
____Another Copy. Same. Wrappers. $15.00

D299. DUFFER (K.). (University of British Columbia Museum
of Anthropology, Museum Note No. 10, 1983) A Guide
To Buying Contemporary Northwest Coast Indian Art.
28pp, 35 photographs, 14 drawings, 1 map. $10.00

D300. DUFFIELD (L. F.) and JELKS (E.). (University of Texas,

Dept. of Anthropology, Archaeology Series, No. 4, 1961) The Pearson Site. 83pp, bibliography, pls of pottery, trade beads, etc., 8vo, wrappers. $12.00

D301. DUFFIELD (Lathel). The Strawn Creek Site: A Mixed Archaic and Neo-American Site at Navarro Mills Reservoir, Navarro County, Texas. 69pp, illus, wrappers. Austin, Texas Archaeological Salvage Project, 1963.
$18.00

D302. DUGUID (Julian). Tiger-Man. 298pp, Jaguar hunting in Paraguay, illus (photographs). London, 1932. $20.00

D303. DUMOND (D. E.). The Eskimos and Aleuts. 180pp, 119 photographs and drawings, cloth. London, 1977.
$32.00
The prehistory and history of the Eskaleut peoples are closely examined--with the emphasis very much on their artistic and material cultures--in this volume. The artistic and technological achievements of the Eskimos and their cousins, the Aleuts, are traced via abundant, good illustrations and a fine text. (EAP)

D304. DUNCAN (K. C.). Bead Embroidery of the Northern Athapaskans. xiii, 560pp, 116pp photographs and drawings, 7 maps, facsimile, printed on microfilm xerography on acid-free paper, of the author's 1982 doctoral dissertation. Reproduction of photographs extremely poor. Cloth. Ann Arbor, 1985. $100.00
Embroidery, primarily on costume, has been the prominent Athapaskan art form through time. This study fills an important gap in the knowledge of the art of this Subarctic people who, in the late 18th Century incorporated beads into their established design tradition. Exacting and thorough this systematic analysis of the style characteristics of Northern Athapaskan bead embroidery closely examines each of the major regions and their styles. Photographs of bead embroidery in 34 U.S. and 13 Canadian Museum collections and 3 private collections. (EAP)

D305. DUNCAN (Kate). Some Warmer Tone: Alaska Athapascan Bead Embroidery. 64pp, 4to, illus, some in color, wrappers. University of Alaska, Fairbanks, 1984.
$20.00

D306. DUNN (Caroline). (Indiana Historical Society Prehistory Research Series, Vol. 1, No. 2, Indianapolis, 1937) Jacob Piatt Dunn: His Miami Language Studies and Indian Manuscript Collection. 35pp, bibliography of Dunn's works and list of his material in the Indiana State Library, wrappers. $10.00

D307. DUNN (John). History of the Oregon Territory and British North-American Fur Trade, with an Account of Habits and Customs of the Principal Native Tribes.... viii, 359pp, folding map (44x33cm). London, Edw. and Hughes, 1844 (1st ed.). $750.00

D308. DUNN (John). A Reference Grammar for the Coast Tsimshian Language. 91pp, 4to, wrappers. National Museum of Canada, Ottawa, 1979. $15.00

D309. DUNN (J. P.). Massacres of the Mountains; A History
of the Indian wars of the Far West, 1815-1875. 670pp,
illus, map, bibliography, index, causes and results of
Indian Uprisings in the West, including Whitman massacre, Oatman tragedy, Custer massacre, etc. New York,
1958. $32.00

D310. DUNN (Lt. Col. William R.). "I Stand By Sand Creek."
158pp, illus, maps, index, stiff wrappers, a defense
of Col. John M. Chivington and the Third Colorado
Cavalry. Fort Collins, 1985. $10.00

D311. (DUPAIX NARRATIVES). Magnificent Account with 166
Lithographed Plates. Dupaix, Capt. Antiquites Mexi-
caines: Relation des Trois Explorations en 1805-07,
pour la Recherche des Antiquites du Pails, Notamment
celles de Mitla et de Palenque, with 166pls lithographed
by Thierry Frers, a large proportion finely hand-
colored. (2 volumes). Tall folio (13 3/4" x 12½"),
later red morocco. Paris, 1834. $15,000.00
        One of the great source-books for Mexican antiquities,
with splendid color plates. The Dupaix narratives, undertaken by order of the King of Spain, are printed in
both Spanish and French; it will be remembered that the
same explorations furnished most of the material for the
great Lord Kingsborough publication. Excellent copy
throughout, the plates being separately bound, with
lithographed title, except for Warden's account of North
American antiquities, which has 10 plates (printed on 6
sheets) bound in the text volume. (ABS)

D312. DuPONCEAU (M. and P.). Memoire Sur le System Grammatical des Langues de Quelques Nations Indiennes de
l'Amerique du Nord. xvi, 646pp, 8vo, quarter leather,
front cvr detached. Paris, 1838 (1st ed.). $85.00
        Field: 469. "One of the first attempts subsequent
to that of Mr. Gallatin, to systematize the aboriginal
languages, and determine the laws of their construction."
(RMW)

D313. DUQUE GOMEZ (Luis). Exploraciones Arqueologicas en
San Agustin. 510pp, illus, folded charts, wrappers.
Bogota, 1964. $50.00

D314. DURAN (Fray Diego). The Aztecs: The History of the
Indies of New Spain. First translation into English.
381pp, frontis, illus, many illus from codices of the
16th Century, 4to. New York, 1964 (1st ed.).
                                                 $50.00

____Another Copy. Same. $40.00

D315. DURAN (Fray Diego). Book of the Gods and Rites and the
Ancient Calendar. xxiv, 502pp, 8 color and 55 b/w photographs, map, cloth. Norman, 1971, 1975. $35.00

D316. DURATSCHEK (Sister Mary). Crusading Along Sioux Trails. A History of the Catholic Missions of South Dakota. xiii, 235pp, keyed map, numerous photographs, index, bibliography. St. Meinrad The Grial, 1947, (1st ed.), d.j. $30.00

D317. DURKEE (Caroline Cain) (as told to) Willie Whitewater. The Story of W. R. Hennell's Life and Adventures Among the Indians.... 309pp, photographs, large folding map of old Pony Express route, Indian agent of the Kickapoo, Iowas, Pottawatomies, Chickasaw, Sak and Fox in Kansas from 1899. Kansas City, 1950, (1st ed.), d.j. $20.00

D318. DUSTIN (C. Burton). Peyotism and New Mexico. 51pp, illus, autographed by author, stiff pictorial wrappers, a description of the use of peyote in religious cere-monies at Taos Pueblo and on the Navajo Reservation with the incorporation of Peyotism into the Native American Church. Farmington, 1960 (1st ed.). $50.00

D319. DUTTON (Bertha P.). Friendly People: The Zuni In-dians. 28pp, illus, maps, reading list, wrappers. Santa Fe, 1963. $12.00
____Another Copy. Santa Fe, 1968. $10.00

D320. DUTTON (Bertha). A History of Plumbate Ware. Re-printed from El Palacio, Vol. 49, Nos. 10, 11 and 12, 1942. 50pp, 12 photographs of Plumbate Vessels, 12mo, wrappers. $25.00
____Another Copy. Same. $25.00
____Another Copy. American School of Research, Santa Fe, 1943, 49pp, 12 photographs. $15.00

D321. DUTTON (Bertha). Indians of the American Southwest. xxix, 298pp, 16pp photographs, 4 maps, bibliography, index. Prentice Hall, 1975 (1st ed.), d.j. $20.00

D322. DUTTON (B. P.). (University of New Mexico Bulletin, Monograph Series Vol. 1, No. 6, 1938) Leyit Kin, A Small House Ruin. Chaco Canyon, New Mexico. 101pp, 5 figures, 2 graphs, 30 tables, 21pp photographs, spine reinforced. $34.00
____Another Copy. Same. $30.00

D323. DUTTON (B. P.). New Mexico Indians, Pocket Handbook. 96pp, 22 photographs, inscribed by author. New Mexi-co Assn. on Indian Affairs, 1948. $19.00

D324. DUTTON (Bertha). The Rancheria, Ute and Southern Paiute Peoples: Indians of the American Southwest. 124pp, 4to, illus, wrappers. Englewood Cliffs, 1976 (1st ed.). $10.00
____Another Copy. Same. $10.00

D325. DUTTON (Bertha P.). Sun Father's Way: The Kiva Murals of Kuaua. 237pp, 115 text figures, 22 pls, sml 4to, Albuquerque, 1963 (1st ed.) d.j. $60.00
____Another Copy. Same. $30.00

D326. DWIGHT (Sereno E.). Memoirs of the Rev. David

Brainerd ... Taken from His Own Diary. By Rev.
Jonathan Edwards.... 507pp, full calf, hinges weak.
New Haven, S. Converse, 1822. $145.00
___ Another Copy. Same. $135.00

D327. DWYER (Jane Powell) (Editor). The Cashinahua of Eastern Peru. 238pp, 4to, illus, wrappers. Haffenreffer
Museum of Anthropology, Brown University, 1975.
$25.00

D328. DYCK (Paul). Brule: The Sioux People of the Rosebud.
xii, 365pp, approx. 175 c. 1890s photographs by John
Anderson, who spent over 40 years at Rosebud, large
8vo, inscribed, slipcase, half-title rehinged with tape.
Flagstaff, 1971 (1st ed.). $60.00
___ Another Copy. Same. d.j. $45.00

D329. DYK (Walter). Son of Old Man Hat. A Navaho Autobiography. 378pp, 8vo. Howes: D-625. New York, 1938
(1st ed.). $65.00
___ Another Copy. Same, cloth, d.j. $65.00
___ Another Copy. Same. Saunders: 1075. Wallace
XIV 91. $20.00
___ Another Copy. Viking Fund Publications in Anthropology No. 8, 1947. A Navaho Autobiography. 218pp,
map, 16 full-page photographs. $37.00

D330. DYOTT (G. M.). Man Hunting in the Jungle. 323pp,
illus, frontis, search for three lost explorers. New
York, 1930. $20.00

-E-

E1. EAGLE (D. Chief). Winter Count. iv, 230pp, endpaper
maps, about clash of White Man and Indian on Sioux
Hunting grounds, Colorado Springs, 1967 (1st ed.),
d.j. $12.00

E2. EARLE (Edwin). Hopi Kachinas. Text by E. A. Kennard.
xlpp, 28 color pls, original decorated cloth, 4to, (9" x
12"), New York, J. J. Augustin, 1938 (1st ed.).
$200.00
___ Another Copy. Same. $200.00
___ Another Copy. Same. $225.00

E3. EASBY (E. K.). Ancient Art of Latin America from the
Collection of Jay C. Leff. 144pp, 144 photographs,
4 maps and charts, New York, 1966. $15.00
___ Another Copy. Same. $12.00

E4. EASBY (E. K.) and SCOTT (J. F.). (Exhibition Catalogue,
Metropolitan Museum of Art, New York, 1970) Before
Cortes, Sculpture of Middle America. 322pp, 352 sepia-
tone and 27 color photographs, wrappers. $125.00
___ Another Copy. Same. $100.00

____Another Copy. Same. $95.00
____Another Copy. Same. $85.00
____Another Copy. Same. $85.00

E5.   EASBY (E. K.). Pre-Columbian Jade from Costa Rica.
104pp, 36 color and 33 b/w photographs by L. Boltin,
New York, 1968. $40.00
____Another Copy. Same. $25.00

E6.   EASTBURN (Rev. Joseph). Memoirs of ... Stated Preacher
in the Mariner's Church, Philadelphia. Edited by Ashbel
Green. 208pp, portrait. Also contains: "A Faithful
Narrative of the Many Dangers and Sufferings, As Well
As Wonderful Deliverances of Robert Eastburn, During
His Late Captivity Among the Indians." pp 183-208.
Third edition of this scarce Indian Captivity, originally
published in 1758, whole volume published in Philadel-
phia, G. W. Mentz, 1828. $60.00

E7.   (EASTBURN, Robert). The Dangers and Sufferings of Robert
Eastburn, and His Deliverance from Indian Captivity.
76pp, limited to edition of 250 copies, cloth. Cleveland,
1904 (1st ed. thus). $20.00

E8.   EASTMAN (Charles A.). From the Deep Woods to Civilization. 206pp, photographs, index, autobiography of the
nephew of Sitting Bull, Boston, 1916 (1st ed.), d.j.
                                                   $30.00
____Another Copy. Same, lacks d.j. $15.00

E9.   EASTMAN (Charles A.). Indian Boyhood. 289pp, illus by
E. L. Blumenschein, cloth with pictorial overlay, New
York, 1905 (1st ed., 4th impression). $22.00
____Another Copy. Same, New York, 1911. $20.00

E10.   EASTMAN (Charles A.). Indian Heroes and Great Chief-
tains. 241pp, illus, Boston, 1921. $30.00
____Another Copy. Same, Boston, 1923. $12.00
____Another Copy. same, Boston, 1923. $15.00

E11.   EASTMAN (Charles A.). Red Hunters and the Animal People. 247pp, tinted frontis, decorated cloth, New York,
104 (1st ed.). $20.00
____Another Copy. Same, New York, 1905. $35.00

E12.   EASTMAN (Charles A.). The Soul of the Indian: An Interpretation. 170pp, Boston, 1911. $30.00
____Another Copy. Same. $18.00

E13.   EASTMAN (Charles and Elaine). Wigwam Evenings: Sioux
Folk Tales Retold. 253pp, frontis and 17 full-page pls
by Edwin Willard Deming, Boston, 1909 (1st ed.).
                                                   $25.00
____Another Copy. Same, tipped in signature of
                   Charles Eastman. $35.00
____Another Copy. Same. $22.00

E14.   EASTMAN (Edwin). Seven and Nine Years Among the
Comanches and Apaches, An Autobiography. 310pp,
cloth, a bogus Indian captivity, put out by a patent
medicine company, but highly amusing, New Jersey,
1879. $50.00

_____Another Copy. Same, New Jersey, 1873,
1st ed. $45.00
_____Another Copy. Same, Toyahvale, 1964. $20.00

E15. EASTMAN (Elaine G.) Pratt; the Red Man's Moses. 285pp, story of Richard Henry Pratt, founder of the Carlisle Indian School, Norman, 1935, d.j. $45.00
_____Another Copy. Same, lacks d.j. $35.00

E16. (EASTMAN, Elaine). Sister to the Sioux. The Memoirs of Elaine Goodale Eastman, 1885-91. Edited by Kay Graber. xiii, 175pp. 8 photographs, map, cloth, Lincoln, Univ. of Nebraska, 1978 (1st ed.), d.j. $20.00

E17. EASTMAN (Mary H.). The American Aboriginal Portfolio. 84pp, 26 engraved pls, 4to, decorated cloth, engraved title page, Philadelphia, Lippincott, 1853 (1st ed.). $750.00
    Handsome volume, with fine pls by Mrs. Eastman's husband, Seth Eastman. Each plate is accompanied by a short explanatory essay.

E18. EASTMAN (Mary H.). The American Annual: Illustrative of the Early History of North America. 126pp, 21 engraved pls, original gilt decorated cloth, Philadelphia, c.1854. $750.00
    Howes: E-18. Illustrated by her husband, Seth Eastman, the pls mainly reflect Indian life in the Southwest Pueblos and in the Minnesota area.

E19. EASTMAN (Mary H.). Chicora and Other Regions of the Conquerors and the Conquered. 126pp, with 21 full-page engraved pls of Plains and Southwest Indians, decorated cloth, lrge 8vo, Philadlephia, Lippincott, Grambo & Co., 1854 (1st ed.). $425.00
    Note: This is the first edition, the reprint in Item 18 above shows title change.

E20. EASTMAN (Mary H.). Dahcotah; or, Life and Legends of the Sioux Around Fort Snelling. 268pp, illus, 4 lithographs by Seth Eastman, quarter leather, New York, John Wiley, 1849 (1st ed.). $125.00
    Field: 478. Mary Eastman spent the years 1841 through 1848 at Fort Snelling where her husband was stationed. During this period, the Eastmans entertained many Indians in their home and undertook a dual recording of the Dakota. Seth ... portrayed them on canvas, Mary ... elicited their stories and legends for a written record. This extended acquaintance gave her a realistic yet sympathetic perspective ... unusual for her day. Perceiving that the day of the Dakota is far spent, she decided to gather their stories and legends for publication. The resulting work is believed to have inspired Longfellow to write "Hiawatha" a few years later. (RMW)
_____Another Copy. Same, Minneapolis, 1962. $20.00
_____Another Copy. Same. $12.00

E21. EATON (T. H.) and SMITH (G.). Birds of the Navaho

Country. vii, 75pp, 18pp of drawings, map, National
Youth Administration, Berkeley, 1973. $30.00

E22. EATON (T. H.). Geology of the Navajo Country. 20pp,
4 hand-drawn fold-out charts, map, Berkeley, 1937.
$30.00
___Another Copy. Same. $17.00

E23. ECCLESTON (Robert). The Mariposa Indian war, 1850-51.
Diaries of Robert Eccleston. Edited by C. G. Crampton.
160pp, frontis, folding map, bibliography, index, Salt
Lake City, 1957 (1st ed.). $45.00

E24. ECHEVARRIA y VEYTIA (M. F.). Los Calendarios Mexicanos. 167 unbound photographic leaves in board and
linen folio (10 1/4" x 13 1/2") with ties; each photograph
is of a stone, jade, or ceramic object; this appears to
be the plate volume of a two-volume set, folio is scuffed
and soiled, published in Mexico about 1905-1915. $135.00

E25. ECKERT (Allan W.). Blue Jacket, War Chief of the Shawnees. 177pp, frontis, map, cloth, Boston, 1969 (1st ed.),
d.j. $20.00
___Another Copy. Same, Boston, 1969, 2nd
printing. $15.00

E26. (ECUADOR). Manuscript Document Discussing the Indians
of Ecuador. 12pp, folio, disbound, n.p., 1781. $375.00
Describes a visit to the Indians of the Pueblo of
Cuenca in the Assuay Province in 1781. Written in legible Spanish hand. A typed transcript accompanies the
document.

E27. EDDY (Frank W.). (Museum of New Mexico, Papers in
Anthropology, Publication No. 4, Santa Fe, 1961) Excavations at Los Pinos Phase Sites in the Navajo Reservoir District. 106pp, 76 figures, 4 tables, stiff pictorial
wrappers, limited to 500 copies. $20.00

E28. EDDY (F. W.). (Museum of New Mexico, Papers in Anthropology, Publication No. 15, Santa Fe, 1966) Prehistory
in the Navajo Reservoir District, Northwestern New
Mexico. Parts I & II. 631pp, 62 figures, 27 tables,
wrappers. $30.00
___Another Copy. Same, Part I only. $10.00

E29. EDMONDS (H. M. W.). (Anthropology Papers, Univ. of
Alaska, Vol. 13, No. 2, 1966) The Eskimo of St. Michael
and Vicinity. 143pp, 32 photographs, plus numerous
figures, wrappers. $25.00
___Another Copy. Same. $18.00

E30. EDMONSON (M. S.). (Middle American Research. Tulane
Univ., Publication 35, 1971) The Book of Counsel: The
Popol Vuh of the Quiche Maya of Guatemala. 273pp, the
Quiche text with a new English translation, wrappers.
$75.00
___Another Copy. Same. $62.00

E31. EDMONSON (M. S.). (Middle American Research. Tulane
Univ., Publication 30, 1965) Quiche-English Dictionary.

      168pp, wrappers. $45.00

      _____Another Copy. Same. $40.00

E32. EDMONSON (M. S.). Status Terminology and the Social Structure of the North American Indians. 87pp, American Ethnological Society, Seattle, 1958. $30.00

      _____Another Copy. Same. $17.00

      _____Another Copy. Same. $12.00

E33. EDMUNDS (David R.). The Potawatomis; Keepers of the Fire. 366pp, illus, Norman, 1980 (2nd ed.,), d.j. $20.00

E34. (EDUCATION). (Senate Document No. 179, 58:3, Washington, DC, 1905) Care and Education of Indians in Sectarian and Denominational Schools. 63pp. Removed. $15.00

E35. (EDUCATION). Catalogue of the Industrial School at Carlisle, Pennsylvania. 116pp, oblong 8vo, cloth and decorated bds, full-page photographs of students at work, brief history of school, Carlisle, 1902. $65.00

E36. (EDUCATION). Civilization of the Indian Tribes. 23pp, folding table of expenditures on schools, etc. Removed. Washington, DC, 1822. $12.00

      _____Another Copy. Same. $10.00

E37. (EDUCATION). Correspondence on the Subject of Teaching the Vernacular in Indian Schools, 1887-88. 27pp, printed wrappers, U.S. Indian Office, Washington, DC, 1888. $75.00

E38. (EDUCATION). Indian Education: A National Tragedy-- A National Challenge. 220pp, wrappers, Senate Report No. 91-501, Washington. DC, 1969. $20.00

E39. (EDUCATION). Indian Industrial School, Carlisle, Pennsylvania. (4), 64pp, pls, oblong 16mo, printed pictorial wrappers, Carlisle, n.d., c.1896. $50.00

E40. (EDUCATION). (Senate Executive Document 106, 49:1, Washington, DC, 1886) Purchase of a Tract of Land for an Indian Training School. 4pp, folding map. Removed. $10.00

E41. EDWARDS (Jonathan). An Account of the Life of the Late Reverend Mr. David Brainerd, Minister of the Gospel, Missionary to the Indians. First English Edition, including his "Journal While Among the Indians." xii, 504pp, original calf, Edinburgh, J. Gray and G. Alston for W. Gray, 1765. $125.00

      Field: 486. Howes: E-56. Rev. Brainerd was one of the earliest of American missionaries to work among the Indians.

      _____Another Copy. Same, 360pp, illus, 12mo, cloth, New York, n.d., c.1845. $20.00

E42. (EDWARDS, William P.). Narrative of the Capture and Providential Escape of Misses Frances and Almira Hall ... Likewise is Added the Interesting Narrative of the Captivity and Sufferings of Philip Brigdon, A Kentuckian,

Who Fell Into the Hands of the Merciless Savages ...
Communicated by Persons of Respectability Living in the
Neighborhood of the Captives. (2), (5)-24pp, frontis,
half leather, marbled bds, with the original illus wraps
bound in, n.p. 1832 (1st ed.). $450.00
>Howes: H-61. Field: 635. Ayer: 210. Subtitle:
"Two respectable young women (sisters) of the ages 16
and 18, who were taken prisoners by the Savages, at a
frontier settlement near Indian Creek, in May last, when
fifteen of the inhabitants fell victims to the bloody Tomahawk and Scalping Knife; among whom were the parents
of the unfortunate females."

E43. (EEL RIVER INDIANS). (House of Representatives Executive
Document No. 279, 20:1, Washington, DC, 1828) Treaty
with Eel River Indians. 7pp. Removed. $35.00

E44. EELLS (Rev. M.). Ten years of Missionary Work Among
the Indians at Skokomish, Washington Territory, 1874-
1884. 271pp, illus, cloth, Boston, 1886 (1st ed.).
$30.00

E45. EELLS (Myron). The Twana, Chemakum, and Klallam Indians of Washington Territory. From Smithsonian Annual
Report for the Year 1887. pp605-681, wraps, Washington,
1889. $10.00

E46. EGAN (Ferol). Sand in a Whirlwind. The Paiute War of
1860. 310pp, photographs, notes bibliography, map
endpapers, index, Garden City, NY, 1972 (1st ed.),
d.j. $15.00

E47. EGGAN (F.) Editor. Social Anthropology of North American
Indian Tribes. xvii, 456pp (8 papers), cloth, Chicago,
1937. $40.00
___Another Copy. Same. $25.00
___Another Copy. Same. $15.00

E48. EGGAN (F.). Social Organization of the Western Pueblos.
xvii, 373pp, 26 figures, map, 10 tables, cloth, Chicago,
1950 (1st ed.), d.j. $45.00
___Another Copy. Same, lacks d.j. $40.00
___Another Copy. Same. $40.00
___Another Copy. Same, 1969, 5th printing. $10.00

E49. EGGLESTON (Edward) and SEELYE (Lillie). Montezuma
and the Conquest of Mexico. 385pp, illus, original pictorial cloth, New York, Dodd Mead, 1880 (1st ed.).
$45.00

E50. EGGLESTON (Edward) and SEELYE (Lillie). Tecumseh and
the Shawnee Prophet. 332pp, map, frontis, appendix,
cloth, New York, 1878. $25.00
___Another Copy. Same. $30.00
___Another Copy. Same. $18.00

E51. EGGLESTON (George Cary). Red Eagle and the Wars with
the Creek Indians of Alabama. Famous American Indians.
346pp, frontis, illus, cloth, New York, 1878. $25.00
___Another Copy. Same. $20.00

E52. EICKEMEYER (Carl) and WESTCOTT (Lilian). Among the
Pueblo Indians. 195pp, 40pp of photographs, decorated
cloth, New York, 1895 (1st ed.). $65.00
___Another Copy. Same. $45.00

E53. EIDE (Arthur H.). Drums of Diomede: The Transforma-
tion of the Alaska Eskimo. House-Warven, Hollywood,
1952, d.j. $75.00
___Another Copy. Same. $60.00

E54. EKHOLM (Gordon F.). Ancient Mexico and Central America. 128pp, photographs in b/w and color by Lee Bolton,
bibliography, pictorial wraps, New York, 1970 (1st ed.).
$10.00

E55. EKHOLM (Gordon F.). (American Museum of Natural History, Anthropology Papers, New York, 1944) Excavations at Tampico and Panuco in the Huasteca, Mexico.
pp 321-512, 56 pls, over 200 Huastec artifacts, wraps.
$60.00
___Another Copy. Same. $50.00

E56. EKHOLM (Gordon F.). Stone Sculpture from Mexico. 30
full-page and half-page photographs, 1 drawing, Museum of Primitive Art, 1959. $15.00

E57. EKHOLM (S. M.). (New World Archaeological Foundation.
Brigham Young Univ. Paper No. 25, 1969) Mound 30a
and the Early Preclassic Ceramic Sequence of Izapa,
Chiapas, Mexico. 102pp, 78 figures, wrappers. $12.00

E58. ELIOT (John). Indian Primer; or, The Way of Training
Up of Our Indian Youth in the Good Knowledge of God.
lvi, 150pp, reprinted from the original edition of 1669,
modern wraps, Edinburgh, 1877. $35.00

E59. ELIOT (S. A.). Report Upon the Conditions and Needs of
the Indians of the Northwest Coast. 28pp, ex-lib,
wraps, Washington, 1915. $25.00

E60. ELLENBECKER (John G.). The Indian Raid on the Upper
Little Blue in Southern Nebraska During the Sixties.
23pp, pictorial wrappers, n.p., n.d. $40.00
___Another Copy. Same. $25.00

E61. ELLIOT (E.). The Savage, My Kinsman. 159pp, over 75
photographs, many of the Aucas Indians, New York,
1961 (1st ed.). $25.00

E62. ELLIS (F. H.). (Garland American Indian Ethnohistory
Series, 1974) Pueblo Indians I. 386pp, cloth. $37.00

E63. ELLIS (George W.) and MORRIS (John E.). King Philip's
War, Based on the Archives and Records of Massachu-
setts, Plymouth, Rhode Island and Connecticut and Con-
temporary Letters and Accounts. 326pp, illus, map, cloth,
New York, 1906. $40.00
___Another Copy. Same. $35.00

E64. ELLIS (H. Holmes). Flint-Working Techniques of the Amer-
ican Indians. 63pp, illus, 4to, bibliography, wraps,
Columbus, Ohio, 1965 (2nd printing). $17.00
___Another Copy. Same. $12.00

E65. ELLIS (Richard N.). General Pope and U.S. Indian Policy.
287pp, illus, index, bibliography, Albuquerque, 1970
(1st ed.), d.j. $20.00
___Another Copy. Same, lacks d.j. $18.00
___Another Copy. Same. $15.00
E66. ELMENDORF (Mary L.). Nine Mayan Women: A Village
Faces Change. 159pp, illus, wrappers, New York,
1976. $10.00
E67. ELMENDORF (W. W.). (Washington State Univ., Research
Studies, Monographic Supplement No. 2, 1960) The
Structure of Twana Culture, and Other Articles. (16),
576pp, maps, figures, bibliography, index, wrappers.
$25.00
___Another Copy. Same, ex-lib. $30.00
E68. ELMORE (Francis). (Univ. of New Mexico, Monograph
Series, Vol. 1, No. 7, Albuquerque, 1944) Ethnobotany
of the Navajo. 136pp, wrappers. $35.00
___Another Copy. Same. $28.00
___Another Copy. Same. $30.00
E69. EMBREE (Edwin R.). Indians of the Americas. Historical
pageant. 260pp, woodcut illus, cloth, Boston, 1939.
$10.00
E70. EMERSON (Dorothy). Among the Mescalero Apaches. The
Story of Father Albert Braun, O.F.M. xiii, 224pp, frontis
portrait, photo illus, map, bibliography, index, Tucson,
Univ. of Arizona, 1973 (1st ed.), d.j. $20.00
___Another Copy. Same. $18.00
E71. EMERSON (Ellen Russell). Indian Myths or Legends,
Traditions, and Symbols of the Aborigines of America
Compared with Those of Other Countries Including
Hindostan, Egypt, Persia, Assyria and China. xviii,
677pp, illus, folding map, t.e.g., pictorial cloth, inner
hinges cracked, Boston, 1884 (1st ed.). $50.00
EMERSON (N. B.). See BAE Bulletin No. 38.
E72. EMERSON (William C.). The Seminoles: Dwellers of the
Everglades, the Land, History and Culture of Florida
Indians. 72pp, illus with 32 photographs, bibliography,
New York, 1954, d.j. $15.00
___Another Copy. Same. $10.00
E73. EMMART (Emily). (Smithsonian Misc. Collections, Vol. 94,
No. 2, Washington, DC, 1935) Concerning the Badianus
Manuscript, An Aztec Herbal "Codex Barberini, Latin
241" (Vatican Library). 14pp plus illus, one illus is in
color, wrappers. $15.00
___Another Copy. Same. $12.00
E74. EMMERICH (Andre). Gold und Silberschmuck Aus Dem
Pre-Columbischen America. 24 illus, wrappers, Basel,
1964. $15.00
E75. EMMERICH (Andre). Masterpieces of Pre-Columbian Art,
from the Collection of Mr. and Mrs. Peter G. Wray.
54pp, 24pp of color photographs, map, Emmerich Gallery,

New York, 1984. $22.00
____Another Copy. Same. $25.00

E76. EMMERICH (Andre). Sweat of the Sun and Tears of the
Moon: Gold and Silver in Pre-Columbian Art. 216pp,
222 figures (several in color), Seattle, 1965 (1st ed.).
$65.00
____Another Copy. Same. $50.00
____Another Copy. Same, New York, 1984. $58.00

E77. EMMITT (Robert). The Last War Trail. The Utes and the
Settlement of Colorado. 328pp, plus index, drawings
by Bettina Steinke, bibliography, Norman, 1954 (1st
ed.), d.j. $25.00
____Another Copy. Same. $32.00
____Another Copy. Same. $21.00
____Another Copy. Same, Norman, 1972, d.j. $15.00

E78. EMMONS (Della Gould). Leschi of the Nisquallies. 416pp,
endpaper maps, Minneapolis, T. S. Denison, 1965 (1st
ed.), d.j. $35.00

E79. EMMONS (Della Gould). Sacajawea of the Shoshones.
316pp, bibliography, endpaper maps, pictorial cloth,
Portland, 1943 (1st ed.). $30.00
____Another Copy. Same, has d.j. $15.00

E80. EMMONS (G. T.). (American Museum of Natural History,
Memoirs, Vol. III, Part IV, 1907) The Chilkat Blanket.
pp 329-401, 57 figures, 2pp b/w photographs, 2 pp color
drawings, 4pp of descriptions of illus, bound in later
cloth over original wraps. $150.00
____Another Copy. Same, in wrappers. $175.00

E81. EMMONS (G. T.). (Museum of the American Indian, Notes
and Monographs, No. 35, 1923) Jade in British Columbia
and Its Use by the Natives. 53pp, 25 pls with 24 in
color, 12mo, wrappers. $125.00
____Another Copy. Same. $75.00

E82. EMMONS (G. T.). (Univ. of Pennsylvania Museum, Anthropology Publications, Vol. 4, No. 1, 1979) The Tahltan
Indians. 120pp, wrappers. $20.00

E83. EMMONS (G. T.). (Museum of the American Indian, Notes
and Monographs, New York, 1921) Slate Mirrors of the
Tsimshian. 21pp, 5 pls, wrappers. $20.00

E84. EMMONS (G. T.). (American Museum of Natural History,
Anthropological Papers, Vol. XIX, Part I, New York,
1916) Whale House of the Chilkat. 33pp plus pls (4 in
color), wrappers. $60.00

E85. ENCISO (Jorge). Design Motifs of Ancient Mexico. 153pp
plus ads, designs are printed in four colors but only
one color per page, New York, 1953. $20.00

E86. ENGEL (F.). (Transactions of the American Philosophical
Society, New Series, Vol. 53, Part 3, 1963) A Pre-
ceramic Settlement on the Central Coast of Peru: Asia,
Unit 1. 139pp, 279 figures, inscribed by author, wraps.
$70.00
____Another Copy. Same, not inscribed. $60.00

E87. ENGEL (F.). (Hunter College, Dept. of Anthropology Papers, 1983) Prehistoric Andean Ecology, Man, Settlement and Environment in the Andes. Stone Typology. 185pp, 122pp of photographs and drawings of sites and objects, with particular emphasis on pre-Columbian fish hooks and other fishing devices used in the cold Pacific waters of South America, wraps. $40.00
___Another Copy. Same. $25.00

E88. ENGLISH (J. S.). Indian Legends of the White Mountains. 92pp, 16mo, illus, cloth, Boston, 1915. $12.00
___Another Copy. Same. $20.00

E89. ENOCHS (J. B.). Little Man's Family. (Primer and Reader). 30pp; 78pp. Illustrated by Gerald Nailer, printed in the English and Navajo language, stiff pictorial wrappers, Bureau of Indian Affairs, Indian School Print Shop, Phoenix, 1953; 1955 (3rd ed.). $30.00

E90. ERDOES (Richard). The Pueblo Indians. 128pp, photographs, 4to, index, New York, 1967 (1st ed.), d.j.
$12.00

E91. ERDOES (Richard). The Rain Dance People. 276pp, plus index, photographs, drawings, bibliography, New York, 1976 (1st ed.), d.j. $15.00
___Another Copy. Same. $12.00

E92. ERDOES (Richard). The Sound of Flutes and Other Indian Legends, as Told by Lame Deer, Jenny Leading Cloud, Leonard Crow Dog, and Others. 131pp, color illus, New York, 1976. $35.00

E93. ERDOES (Richard). The Sun Dance People: The Plains Indians, Their Past and Present. Illus (photographs by author), New York, 1972 (1st ed.), d.j. $35.00

E94. E. REY (E. Tabio y). Prehistoria de Cuba. 280pp, illus, wrappers, Havana, 1966. $35.00

E95. ERNST (Alice H.). The Wolf Ritual of the Northwest Coast. ix, 107pp, illus, pls, map, wrappers, photographs of dancers, masks, etc., Univ. of Oregon, 1952 (1st ed.). $35.00
___Another Copy. Same, ex-lib. $15.00

E96. EROS (Dennis). The American Indian Artifact Catalogue and Price Guide, Vol. 1, No. 1. 96pp, illus with photographs, wrappers, Watsonville, 1974. $10.00

E97. EROSA PENICHE (J.). Guide Books to the Ruins of Uxmal. 50pp, 17 illus, map, wrappers, Merida, 1948. $15.00

E98. (ESKIMO). Aux Glaces Polaires, Indiens et Esquimaux. 488pp, 33 photographs, Paris, 1922. $40.00

E99. (ESKIMO). (Senate Executive Document No. 14, 51:2, Washington, DC, 1890) Condition of the Natives in Alaska. 5pp. Removed. $12.00

E100. (ESKIMO). (Univ. of Alaska, Anthropology Papers, Vol. 10, No. 2, 1963) Early Man in the Western American Arctic, A Symposium. 136pp, 10 papers total, illus, wrappers. $18.00

E101. (ESKIMO). Eskimo Cook Book. 36pp, illus, 12mo, wrappers, recipes prepared by students of Shishmaref Day School, Shishmaref, Alaska, n.d., c.1950. $18.00

E102. (ESKIMO). Eskimo Songs and Stories, Collected by Knud Rasmussen on the Fifth Thule Expedition. Selected and Translated by Edward Field. 102pp, color illus by Kiakshuk and Pudlo, New York, 1975. $25.00

E103. (ESKIMO). Eskimo Songs, Songs of the Copper Eskimo. Report of the Canadian Arctic Expedition, 1913-18, Vol. XIV, Ottawa, 1925. $22.00

E104. (ESKIMO). (Univ. of Alaska, Anthropological Papers, Vol. 16, No. 2, 1974) Includes Eskimo warfare in Northwest Alaska. Also: Ethnohistory of Disease and Medical Care Among the Aleut. 69pp, 33 illus, wraps. $12.00

    Another Copy. Same. $18.00

E105. (ESKIMO). (Arts Canada, Special Issue, December, 1971, January, 1972, Nos. 162-163) The Eskimo World. 144pp, illus with hundreds of color and b/w photographs of Eskimo artifacts, wrappers. $30.00

E106. (ESKIMO). We Don't Live in Snow Houses Now: Reflections of Arctic Bay. 191pp, illus, wrappers, includes recently carved objects, interviews with modern Eskimos, Ottawa, 1976. $20.00

E107. (ESKIMO ART). Arctic Quebec. 48pp, 34 prints illus with text, original wrappers, Quebec, 1974. $10.00

E108. (ESKIMO ART). Baker Lake. 48pp plus price list, 44 prints with photographs of the artists, original wrappers, Edmonton Art Gallery, 1970. $12.00

E109. (ESKIMO ART). Baker Lake. 52pp, 47 prints in color and b/w, prices, original wrappers, Edmonton Art Gallery, 1971. $12.00

E110. (ESKIMO ART). Baker Lake. 52pp plus price list, shows 41 prints, original wrappers, Edmonton Art Gallery, 1972. $12.00

E111. (ESKIMO ART). Canadian Eskimo Art. 40pp, many illus, rear photograph is of famous sculpture "Birds in a Tree" by a Frobisher Bay Artist who had never seen a tree, Ottawa, 1959. $10.00

E112. (ESKIMO ART). Canadian Eskimo Art. 40pp, 43 illus, wrappers, Minister of Northern Affairs, 1960. $10.00

E113. (ESKIMO ART). Cape Dorset. 83pp with 81 graphics illus in b/w and color, photographs of artists included, Cape Dorset, 1976. $10.00

E114. (ESKIMO ART). The Coming and Going of the Shaman: Eskimo Shamanism and Art. 246pp, 169 illus, 4to wraps, Winnipeg Art Gallery, 1978. $45.00

    Another Copy. Same. $38.00

E115. (ESKIMO ART). Holman Eskimo Prints. 32pp, illus, Holman Galleries, 1970. $12.00

E116. (ESKIMO ART). Inuit Artist of Sugluk. 72pp, illus,

bibliography, art, sculpture, historical and biographical
information, P. Q., 1976. $10.00

E117. (ESKIMO ART). Karoo Ashevak. 76pp, 46 photographs,
Winnipeg Art Gallery, 1977. $10.00

E118. (ESKIMO ART). Masterpieces of Indian and Eskimo Art
from Canada. 300pp, over 100 illus, several full-page
color pls, lrge 8vo, wrappers, Paris, 1969. $60.00

E119. (ESKIMO ART). Sculpture/Inuit. 493pp, 405 photographic
illus in b/w and color, index, lrge 8vo, Inuit sculptures,
with explanatory text and historical introduction, Toronto, 1971. $30.00

E120. (ESKIMO ART). Sculpture of the Inuit: Masterworks
of the Canadian Arctic. 63pp, essays in French and
English, 405 pls with 12 in color, wraps, Toronto,
1971. $75.00
___Another Copy. Same, ex-lib. $50.00

E121. (ESKIMO ART). Survival: Life and Art of the Alaskan
Eskimo. 96pp, 50 illus, several in color, sml 4to,
wrappers, Newark Museum, 1977. $25.00
___Another Copy. Same, some stain in margins. $12.00

E122. (ESKIMO ART). Tivi Etook. 44pp, many illus, wraps,
George River, 1975. $10.00

E123. (ESKIMO ART). The Zazelenchuk Collection of Eskimo
Art. 88pp, 8 color and 122 lrge b/w photographs of
objects in one of the finest collections of Canadian
Eskimo art, wrappers, Winnipeg Art Gallery, 1978.
$12.00
___Another Copy. Same. $15.00

E124. (ESKIMO ARTIFACTS). Canadian Eskimo Artifacts.
32pp, illus, Ottawa, 1970. $10.00

E125. (ESSAYS). (Smithsonian Misc. Collections, Vol. 100,
Washington, DC, 1940) Essays in Historical Anthropology of North America. 600pp (16 essays), cloth, published in Honor of John R. Swanton. $95.00

E126. ESTRADA (Emilio). Arte Aborigen del Ecuador: Sellos
o Pintaderas. 62pp, 166 illus, wrappers, Mexico,
1959. $25.00

E127. ESTRADA (Emilio). Los Huancavilcas: Ultimas Civilizaciones Pre-historicas de la Costa del Guayas. Publication del Museo Victor Emilio Estrada No. 3. 82pp, 50
figures, 8 charts, wrappers, Guayaquil, 1957. $30.00

E128. ESTRADA (Emilio). Prehistoria de Manabi. Publication
del Museo Victor Emilio Estrada No. 4. 176pp, 132 illus,
14 charts, wrappers, Guayaquil, Ecuador, 1957. $45.00
___Another Copy. Same. $25.00

E129. ESTRADA (Emilio). Ultimas Civilizaciones Prehistoricas
de la Cuenca del Rio Guayas. Publication de Museo
Victor Emilio Estrada. 87pp, 72 illus, 5 folding charts,
wraps, Guayaquil, Ecuador, 1957. $40.00
___Another Copy. Same. $25.00

E130. (ETHNOLOGY). (Univ. of California Archaeological

Research Facility, Contribution No. 23, 1975) Ethnographic Interpretations 12-13. 109pp, wrappers.

$20.00

___Another Copy. Same. $15.00

E131. (ETHNOLOGY). Transactions of the American Ethnological
Society. Volume I. xiv, 491pp, 4 advs pls (some folding), modern cloth, New York, Bartlett & Welford, 1845
(1st ed.). $110.00

Includes Gallatin, A. "Notes on the Semi-Civilized
Nations of Mexico." Schoolcraft, H. R. "Observations
of Grave Creek Mound." Troost, G. "Ancient Remains
in Tennessee." Field: 1564.

E132. (ETHNOLOGY). Transactions of the American Ethnological
Society. Volumes 1 and 2. Vol. 1: xvi, 491pp. Vol.
2: clxxxviii, 298, 151pp, folding maps, plans, pls, half
leather with marbled bds, original wrappers bound in,
New York, 1845; 1848 (1st editions). $400.00

Contains important articles on American ethnology,
including E. G. Squier, "Observations on the Aboriginal
Monuments of the Mississippi Valley"; Hale's work on
North American Indian languages; Albert Gallatin, "Hale's
Indians of North-west America...," "Notes on the Semi-
Civilized Nations of Mexico, Yucatan, and Central Amer-
ica"; "Ancient Remains in Tennessee"; "Grave Creek
Mound in Western Virginia" by Henry Schoolcraft. The
Gallatin "Hale's Indians...," contains a version of the
great Wheat map 417 "Map of the Indian Tribes of North
America About 1600 A.D...." lithographed by Endicott
of New York. (RMW)

E133. ETZENHOUSER (Rudolf). Engravings of Prehistoric Specimens from Michigan, U.S.A. 39pp, photographs, wrappers, Detroit, 1910. $10.00

E134. EULER (Robert C.) and DOBYNS (Henry F.). The Hopi
People. 106, (1)pp, illus with b/w and color photographs, maps, signed by tribal chieftain, wrappers, part
of Indian Tribal Series, Phoenix, 1971 (1st ed.).

$15.00

E135. EULER (Robert C.). The Paiute People. 105pp, b/w and
color photographs, maps, signed by tribal chieftain,
wrappers, one of Indian Tribal Series, Phoenix, 1972
(1st ed.). $15.00

E136. EVANS (Allen Roy). Meat. A Tale of the Reindeer Trek,
1929-1935. 288pp, 8vo, photographic pls, cloth, London, Hurst & Blackett, n.d., c.1936. $20.00

Story of the six year effort to drive a herd of reindeer from western Alaska to Canada to supply Canadian
Eskimos.

E137. EVANS (Bessie and May G.). American Indian Dance Steps.
xviii, 104pp of text containing 8pp of drawings, plus
8pp of original color paintings by "... Poyage, San Ildefonso Indian," cloth, New York, 1931 (1st ed.). $150.00

___Another Copy. Same. $25.00

EVANS (Clifford). See also BAE Bulletin Nos. 160, 167, and 177.

E138. EVANS (Clifford) and MEGGERS (B. J.). (Smithsonian Contributions to Anthropology, Vol. 6, Washington, 1968) Archaeological Investigations on the Rio Napo, Eastern Ecuador. 127pp, 94 pls, 80 figures, 2 fold-out maps, cloth. $35.00

    ___Another Copy. Same. $35.00

    ___Another Copy. Same. $20.00

E139. EVANS (G. L.) and CAMPBELL (T. N.). (Texas Memorial Museum Notes, No. 11, 1970, 2nd ed.) Indian Baskets of the Paul T. Seashore Collection. 65pp, 55 b/w and 5 color photographs, 2 drawings, wrappers. $10.00

    ___Another Copy. Same, Austin, 1952, 1st ed. $20.00

E140. EVANS (H.) et al. Mimbres Indian Treasure in the Land of Baca. Excavating An Ancient Pueblo Ruin. xi, 333pp, 241 b/w and 6 color photographs, 107 drawings, 4 maps, cloth, Kansas City, 1985. $50.00

This study of Mimbres pottery exploration is constructed around the Evans collection of Mimbres pottery, excavated by Evans on land he leased, called the Baca ruins. The bulk of the text--very interestingly written--recounts the Evans' experiences in excavating the site. The collection consists of 153 bowls, and each is full described. All items in the collection appear in photographs taken in 1973.

E141. EVARTS (Jeremiah). Essays on the Present Crisis in the Condition of the American Indians. 112pp, lacks cvr, Boston, Perkins and Marvin, 1829 (1st ed.). $90.00

First published in the National Intelligencer under the signature of William Penn (pseudonym for Jeremiah Evarts). Gives arguments concerning Indian (Cherokee) rights to their lands, including the collision between the Government and individual states, in this instance, Georgia.

EWERS (John C.). See also BAE Bulletin Nos. 151, 159, 164, and 186.

E142. EWERS (John C.). Blackfeet Crafts. 66pp, illus, wrappers, Lawrence, Haskell, 1945. $18.00

E143. EWERS (John C.). The Blackfeet: Raiders of the Northwestern Plains. xviii, 348pp, 24 maps and illus, Norman, 1958 (1st ed.), d.j. $25.00

    ___Another Copy. Same, Norman, 1961. $37.00

    ___Another Copy. Same, Norman, 1958, d.j. $30.00

    ___Another Copy. Same. $30.00

E144. EWERS (John C.). Charles Bird King, Painter of Indian Visitors to the Nation's Capitol. Reprint from Smithsonian Annual report, 1953. pp 463-473, pls, bibliography, wrappers, Washington, DC, 1954. $15.00

E145. EWERS (John C.). (Smithsonian Misc. Collections, Vol. 134, No. 7, Washington, DC, 1957) Early White Influence Upon Plains Indian Painting: George Catlin and

Carl Bodmer Among the Mandan, 1832-1834. 11pp, 12
pls, wrappers. $15.00
___Another Copy. Same. $18.00

E146. EWERS (John C.). The Emergence of the Plains Indian
as the Symbol of the North American Indian. Offprint,
Smithsonian Annual Report for 1964. pp531-544, 18pp
of photographs, wrappers. $12.00

E147. EWERS (John C.). (Smithsonian Misc. Collections, Vol.
110, No. 7, Washington, DC, 1948) Gustavus Sohon's
Portraits of the Flathead and Pend D'Oreille Indians,
1854. 68pp, 22 pls, wrappers. $45.00
___Another Copy. Same. $17.00
___Another Copy. Same. $15.00

E148. EWERS (John C.). Hair Pipes in Plains Indian Adornment.
pp 29-85, plus 25pp of photographs, 6 maps, Washington,
DC, 1957, Ohsweken, 1985 (reprint). $10.00
___Another Copy. Same. $10.00

E149. EWERS (John C.). The Horse in Blackfoot Culture, With
Comparative Material from Other Western Tribes. (Reprint of BAE Bulletin 159). 358pp, plus index, 17 pls
of photographs and drawings, bibliography, cloth,
Washington, 1969. $17.00

E150. EWERS (John C.). Indian Art in Pipestone: George Catlin's Portfolio in the British Museum. 80pp, oblong 4to,
illus, bibliography, Washington, DC, 1979 (1st ed.).
$25.00
Well-illustrated work that reflects Catlin's serious
and long sustained interest in Indian tobacco pipes of
stone and clay. Illustrations include 6 color pls.
___Another Copy. Same. $20.00

E151. EWERS (John C.). Indian Life on the Upper Missouri.
214pp, plus index, photographs, map, bibliography,
Norman, 1968 (1st ed.), d.j. $25.00
___Another Copy. Same. $20.00

E152. EWERS (John C.). Murals in the Round, Painted Tipis
of the Kiowa and Kiowa-Apache Indians. 56pp, 30 b/w
and 19 color photographs, Washington, DC, 1978.
$15.00
___Another Copy. Same. $18.00

E153. EWERS (J. C.). Plains Indian Painting. xiv, 70pp, 39pp
of photographs, 5pp of drawings, decorated cloth, Stanford, 1939. $150.00

E154. EWERS (J. C.). The Role of the Indian in National Expansion. (2 Parts). Part I: The Background of Aboriginal America. Part II: Removing the Indian Barrier.
190pp (offset, probably a very limited printing), 9 maps,
U.S. Dept. of Interior, National Park Service, 1928.
$45.00

E155. EWERS (J. C.). Teton Dakota, Ethnology and History.
108pp, 17 full-page b/w and color illus, Berkeley, 1938
(revised ed.). $28.00
___Another Copy. Same. $18.00

E156.   EWING (Douglas C.). Pleasing the Spirits: A Catalogue
        of a Collection of American Indian Art. 401pp, illus,
        pls, map, bibliography, index, lrge 8vo, approx 480
        objects illus for study and comparison, New York, 1982
        (1st ed.), d.j. $125.00
        ____Another Copy. Same. $45.00
E157.   E-YEH-SHURE (Blue Corn). I Am a Pueblo Indian Girl.
        27 unnumbered pp, pictorial title label laid on, illus,
        introduction by Oliver LaFarge, edition of 500 num-
        bered and signed copies, cloth, New York, 1939 (1st
        ed.). $75.00
            A narrative of the life of an Isleta Pueblo girl. Each
        of her eleven subjects is illustrated by an outstanding
        Indian artist--Navajo, Apache, Pueblo--with a picture
        especially painted for this book.
E158.   EZELL (P. H.). (American Anthropological Association,
        Memoirs, No. 90, Menasha, 1961) Hispanic Accultura-
        tion of the Gila River Pimas. x, 171pp, 4 photographs,
        4 tables, map, plus 3 fold-out maps, wrappers. $25.00
        ____Another Copy. Same. $10.00
        ____Another Copy. Same. $12.00

                            -F-

F1.   FABREGA (Horacio, Jr.) and SILVER (Daniel B.). Illness
        and Shamanistic Curing in Zinacatan. An Ethnomedical
        Analysis. 280pp, plus index, charts, map, bibliography,
        Stanford, CA, 1973 (1st ed.), d.j. $20.00
F2.   FAGG (W.) Editor. Eskimo Art in the British Museum.
        30pp b/w photographs, 2pp color photographs, map,
        wraps, London, n.d. $22.00
F3.   FAHEY (John). The Flathead Indians. 361pp, plus index,
        illus, map, bibliography, Norman, 1974 (1st ed.), d.j.
                                                            $25.00
F4.   FAHEY (John). The Kalispel Indians. 234pp, 52 photo-
        graphs, Norman, 1986. $20.00
FAIRBANKS (Charles H.). See also BAE Bulletin No. 180.
F5.   FAIRBANKS (Charles H.). (National Park Service, Archaeo-
        logical Research Series, No. 3, 1956) Archaeology of
        the Funeral Mound, Ocmulgee National Monument, Geor-
        gia. vi, 95pp, 28pp of photographs, 6 figures, wraps.
                                                            $22.00
F6.   FAIRBANKS (Charles H.) and GOFF (J. H.). (Garland
        American Indian Ethnohistory Series, 1974) Cherokee
        and Creek Indians. 639pp, cloth. $40.00
        ____Another Copy. Same. $25.00
F7.   FAJARDO (J. Garcia). Fonetica del Espanol de Valladolid,
        Yucatan. 105pp, wrappers, Mexico, 1984. $15.00

F8.   FALCK (R. and E.). Tetes de Harpons Eskimo. 56pp, 12pp
      of drawings of 138 harpoon heads, Museum National d'His-
      toire Naturelle, Paris, 1963. $12.00

F9.   FALK (Randolph). Lelooska. (Kwakiutl Family of Wood
      Carvers.) 144pp, 4to, illus with approx. 200 photographs,
      wrappers, Millbrae, 1976. $25.00
      ___Another Copy. Same, Millbrae, 1979. $22.00

F10. FALKNER (Thomas). A Description of Patagonia and the
      Adjoining Parts of South America. Introduction and
      Notes by A. Neumann. 168pp, folding map, 4to, full
      size facsimile of 1774 edition, limited to 1,000 copies,
      Chicago, 1935. $65.00

F11. FALLON (Carol). The Art of the Indian Basket in North
      America. 56 partially double-column pp, photographs,
      map, bibliography, wrappers, Lawrence, Kansas Museum
      of Art, 1975 (1st ed.). $10.00

F12. FANCOURT (Charles St. John). The History of Yucatan
      from its Discovery to the Close of the Seventeenth Cen-
      tury. xvi, 340pp, folding map of Yucatan, 1/4 leather,
      marbled bds, London, J. Murray, 1854 (1st ed.).
                                                          $150.00

      Focuses primarily on the Indians of the peninsula,
      their culture, languages, conditions and association with
      the Spanish invaders.

F13. FARABEE (W. C.). (Peabody Museum Papers, Vol. X,
      Cambridge, 1922) Indian Tribes of Eastern Peru. xiv,
      193pp, 28pp of photographs, 20 figures, fold-out map,
      wrappers. $65.00

F14. FARABEE (W. C.) and SHOTRIDGE (L.). (Museum Journal,
      Univ. Museum, Philadelphia, March, 1922) Recent Dis-
      coveries of Ancient Wampum Belts and Land Otter-Man.
      pp 46-59, 4 photographs, wrappers. $15.00

F15. FARB (Peter). Man's Rise to Civilization: As Shown by
      the Indians of North America from Primeval Times to the
      Coming of the Industrial State. 332pp, illus, index,
      bibliography, New York, 1968 (1st ed.), d.j. $12.00
      ___Another Copy. Same. $10.00

F16. FARNSWORTH (Dewey and E. W.). The Americas Before
      Columbus. 176pp, lrge 4to, photographic illus, bibliogra-
      phy, About and shows Mexican and Central American
      Antiquities, El Paso, 1947 (1st ed.). $35.00
      ___Another Copy. Same, Salt Lake City, 1956,
                        3rd ed., d.j. $45.00

F17. FARON (L. C.). Mapuche Social Structure. xvi, 247pp,
      7 figures, Chicago, 1961. $20.00
      ___Another Copy. Same. $15.00

F18. FARR (William E.). The Reservation Blackfeet, 1882-1945.
      A Photographic History of Cultural Survival. 205pp, plus
      index, photographs, maps, bibliography, Seattle, 1984,
      d.j. $25.00

F19. FARRAND (Livingston). (American Museum of Natural

History, Memoirs, Jesup North Pacific Expedition, New York, 1900) Basketry Designs of the Salish Indians. pp 391-399, 15 illus in text, plus 3 pls which have 40 photographs of baskets, folio (10" x 14"), newly rebound in linen. $125.00

___Another Copy. Same, original wrappers. $75.00

___Another Copy. Same. $45.00

F20. FARRAND (Livingston). (American Museum of Natural History, Memoirs, Jesup North Pacific Expedition, New York, 1900) Traditions of the Chilcotin Indians. 54pp, folio (10" x 14"), 32 myths, including 6 Raven stories, newly rebound in linen. $75.00

___Another Copy. Same, original wrappers. $55.00

F21. FARRAND (Livingston). (American Museum of Natural History, Memoirs, Jesup North Pacific Expedition, New York, 1902) Traditions of the Quinault Indians. pp 77-132, original wrappers. $55.00

___Another Copy. Same. $50.00

F22. FARRINGTON (O. C.). (Field Museum Publication No. 18, Geological Series, Vol. 1, No. 2, Chicago, 1897) Observations on Popocatepetl and Ixtaccihuatl. pp 71-120, containing 2 figures, and 11pp of photographs, fold-out map, wrappers. $50.00

___Another Copy. Same. $65.00

F23. FAST (J. E.) and CAYWOOD (L. R.). (Southwestern Monuments, Special Report No. 2, n.d., c.1940) Life Figures on Hohokam Pottery. 4pp, 5 leaves of drawings and figures, wrappers. $12.00

___Another Copy. Same. $15.00

F24. FAWCETT (D. M.) and CALLANDER (L. A.). Native American Painting, Selections from the Museum of the American Indian. 96pp, 44 color and 27 b/w photographs, New York, 1982. $35.00

Seventy-one previously unexhibited paintings and drawings from the Museum of the American Indian were exhibited in 1982. The exhibition--which contained a representative sample of the Museum's collection of 1,500 paintings and drawings--ranged from ledger drawings done in the mid-19th century to work done as recently as 1982. The seventy-one paintings are reproduced very handsomely--particularly those in color--in this catalogue of the exhibition, which includes a cultural and alphabetical listing of the entire 1,500 paintings and drawings in the collection. (EAP)

F25. FAWCETT (Col. P. H.). Lost Trails, Lost Cities. Edited by Brian Fawcett. xvi, 332pp, illus, pls, maps, index, recounting 7 expeditions into the Amazon Basin, Col. Fawcett made an 8th expedition and vanished, New York, 1953 (1st American ed.), d.j. $20.00

___Another Copy. Same. $20.00

F26. FEATHERSTONHAUGH (G. W.). A Canoe Voyage Up the

Minnay Sotor. (2 Volumes). Vol. I: xiv, 416pp. Vol. II: viii, 351pp. 2 maps, 2 pls, cloth, hinges weak, London, Richard Bentley, 1847 (1st ed.). $250.00

    Howes: F-67. Field: 530. Scarce narrative of Indian life and customs.

    ____Another Copy. Same. $200.00

    ____Another Copy. Same, Minnesota Historical Society, 2 vols., 1970. $30.00

F27. FEDER (Norman). American Indian Art. 446pp, color frontis, 59 tipped in color pls, 242 illus, oblong 4to, Abrams, New York, 1969 (1st ed.). $95.00

    ____Another Copy. Same, New York, 1982, d.j. $40.00

F28. FEDER (N.). American Indian Art Before 1850. 32pp, 43 photographs, wrappers, Denver, 1965. $18.00

F29. FEDER (N.) and MALIN (E.). Indian Art of the Northwest Coast. 96pp, 44 lrge photographs, 3 drawings, Denver Art Museum Quarterly, 1962, 1968. $17.00

F30. FEDER (N.). North American Indian Painting. 24pp, photographs, lrge 8vo, wrappers, Greenwich, CT, 1967 (1st ed.). $12.00

F31. FEDER (N.). Two Hundred Years of North American Indian Art. 128pp, 150 b/w and 8 color photographs, Whitney Museum, 1971. $28.00

    ____Another Copy. Same. $15.00

F32. FEE (Chester). Chief Joseph: The Biography of A Great Indian. xiii, 346pp, frontis map, 10 pls including 3 maps, notes, bibliography, index, W. Erikson, 1936 (1st ed.), d.j. $90.00

    ____Another Copy. Same, lacks d.j. $75.00

    ____Another Copy. Same, lacks d.j. $75.00

F33. FEEST (C. F.). Indianer Nordamerikas. Heute & Gestern. 36pp, 30 b/w and 9 color photographs, 1 drawing, 2 maps, Exhibition catalogue, Museum fur Volkerkunde, Vienna, 1986. $12.00

F34. FEHRENBACH (T. R.). Comanches. The Destruction of A People. 557pp, plus index, drawings, b/w and color photographs, maps, bibliography, New York, 1974 (1st ed.), d.j. $40.00

    ____Another Copy. Same. $45.00

    ____Another Copy. Same, New York, 1983, lacks d.j. $20.00

F35. FEJOS (Paul). (Viking Fund Publications in Anthropology, No. 1, New York, 1943, 1st ed.) Ethnography of the Yagua. 144pp, figures, map, 55 pls, glossary, index, bibliography, stiff wrappers. $20.00

    ____Another Copy. Same. $25.00

    ____Another Copy. Same, ex-lib, cloth. $18.00

FENNER (Clarence N.). See BAE Bulletin No. 52.

F36. FENNER (P. R.). Indians, Indians, Indians: Stories of Tepees and Tomahawks, Wampum Belts and War Bonnets, Peace Pipes and Papooses. 288pp, illus, New York, 1950 (1st ed.), d.j. $10.00

F37. FENSTERMAKER (Gerald B.). Seneca Indians. Home Life and Culture. 120pp, photographs, drawings, York, PA, 1944. $12.00

FENTON (William N.). See also BAE Bulletins Nos. 128, 149, 156, 164, and 180.

F38. FENTON (William N.). American Indian and White Relations to 1830. 122pp, plus index, bibliography, Chapel Hill, NC, 1957 (1st ed.). $17.00
___Another Copy. Same, New York, 1957. $10.00

F39. FENTON (William N.). Iroquois Suicide: A Study in the Stability of a Culture Pattern. Offprint, Smithsonian Anthropological Papers, Washington, 1941. pp 79-137, 3 photographic pls, bibliography, printed wrappers. $10.00

F40. FENTON (William N.). Masked Medicine Societies of the Iroquois. Extracted from Smithsonian Annual Report for year 1940. pp 397-430, 25 pls, wrappers. $25.00
___Another Copy. Same, cloth. $12.00

F41. FENTON (William N.). (Smithsonian Misc. Collections Vol. 111, No. 15, Washington, DC, 1950) The Roll Call of Iroquois Chiefs, A Study of Menomonie from the Six Nations Reserve. 73pp, 3 figures, 12pp of photographs, wrappers. $33.00
___Another Copy. Same. $15.00
___Another Copy. Same, Ontario, 1983. $15.00

F42. FENTON (William N.). Songs from the Iroquois Longhouse.... 34pp, illus, wrappers, Smithsonian, Washington, 1942. $15.00
___Another Copy. Same. $10.00

F43. FERGUSON (Alice L.). Moyaone and the Piscataway Indians. 44pp, pls, maps, wrappers, about Maryland Indians, Washington, DC, 1937 (1st ed.). $15.00

F44. FERGUSON (H. L.). (Museum of the American Indian, Notes and Monographs, Vol. XI, No. 1, 1935) Archaeological Exploration of Fishers Island, New York. 44pp, 13pp of photographs, wrappers. $10.00

F45. FERGUSON (T. J.) and HART (E. R.). A Zuni Atlas. xiii, 154pp, 41 photographs, 6 figures, 44 maps, cloth, Norman, 1985. $38.00

F46. FERGUSSON (Erna). Dancing Gods. Indian Ceremonials of New Mexico and Arizona. 276pp, plus drawings by noted Southwestern artists, 16 photographic pls, New York, 1931. $30.00
___Another Copy. Same. $75.00
___Another Copy. Same, Albuquerque, 1957. $50.00
___Another Copy. Same, 1966, xvi, 206pp. $22.00

F47. FERGUSSON (Erna). (The New Mexico Quarterly, Vol. IV, No. 3, Albuquerque, 1934) Indians of Mexico and New Mexico. Entire issue in original wrappers. $15.00

F48. FERNANDEZ (Diego). Primera Parte de la Historia del Peru. pp 361, 446, two parts in one volume, cloth and vellum,

Madrid, 1913. $90.00

___Another Copy. Same. $120.00

F49. FERNANDEZ PIEDRAHITA (Lucas). Historia General de las
Conquistas del Nuevo Reyno de Granada. 10 preliminary
leaves, 62pp, one title-leaf, pp 63-599, pp 600-606, index,
3 engraved titles, depicting 31 portraits of famous Indians
and the Spanish conquerors, as well as four battle scenes,
sml folio, old vellum, Antwerp, 1688. $3,950.00

JCB: p.189. Palau: 89568. Sabin: 62704. Maggs
V: 4417. Medina Bha: 1816. Only this first part was
ever published of this exhaustive work, usually considered
the standard early history of what is now Colombia. It
covers the period to 1562, and begins with an account
of the natives and their customs, laws and kingdoms previous to the Conquest. The author, Bishop Fernandez
Piedrahita, was born in Bogota in 1624. He had literary
ambitions from his youth, and developed a considerable
reputation as a preacher and political figure in New
Granada. In 1661 he was called to Spain to defend himself against charges made there, which he did so success-
fully that he was made a Bishop. During his six years
in Spain, from 1663 to 1669, he wrote this work, having
at his disposal the manuscripts of Gonzalo Ximenez de
Quesada, the conqueror of New Granada. He then returned to Colombia where he worked among the Indians in
poverty until his death in 1688, the same year his work
was published. Although the imprint states Antwerp as
the place of publicaiton, the JCB catalogue suggests it
may have been printed in Seville. (WR)

F50. FERNDON (E. N.). (School of American Research, Monograph 16, 1953) Tonala Mexico. An Archaeological Survey. xvi, 126pp of text containing 1 map and 52 photographs, 15pp of figures, 6 fold-out plans, wraps.
$40.00

___Another Copy. Same, rebound in library
cloth, ex-lib with markings. $30.00

F51. FERNOW (Berthold). The Ohio Valley in Colonial Days.
299pp, index, lrge 8vo, original stiff wraps, Albany,
J. Munsell, 1890 (1st ed.). $95.00

Howes: F-92. Covers Indians of the Ohio Valley
and the Indian wars.

F52. FERRIS (Ida M.). The Sauks and Foxes in Franklin and
Osage Counties, Kansas. 63pp, illus, wrappers, separate
printing of material from Kansas Historical Collections,
Vol. XI, n.p., n.d., c.1911. $20.00

F53. FERRIS (Robert G.) Editor. Soldier and Brave. Indian
and Military Affairs in the Trans-Mississippi West....
260pp, plus index, photographs, drawings, maps, New
York, 1963 (1st ed.), d.j. $20.00

___Another Copy. Same, New York, 1971, en-
larged ed. 407pp, bibliog-
raphy added. $12.00

F54. FEUCHTWANGER (Franz). The Art of Ancient Mexico. 109 photographs by Irmgard Groth-Kimball, 4to, includes private collection of Miguel Covarrubias, London, 1954 (1st ed.), d.j. $75.00

FEWKES (Jesse Walter). See also BAE Bulletin Nos. 41, 50, 51 and 70.

F55. FEWKES (Jesse Walter). Ancestor Worship of the Hopi Indians. From Smithsonian Annual Report for 1921, Washington, 1922. pp 485-506, 7 pls, wraps. $15.00

F56. FEWKES (Jesse Walter). Antiquities of the Upper Verde River and Walnut Creek Valley, Arizona. From 28th Annual Smithsonian Report, Washington, 1913. pp 181-220, pls nos. 79-102, wraps. $25.00
____Another Copy. Same. $18.00

F57. FEWKES (Jesse Walter). (Smithsonian Misc. Collections, Vol. 68, No. 1, Washington, 1917) Archaeological Investigations in New Mexico, Colorado, and Utah. 38pp, illus, wrappers. $15.00

F58. FEWKES (Jesse Walter). Certain Antiquities of Eastern Mexico (Ruins of Cempoalan). From Smithsonian 25th Annual Report, Washington, 1907. pp 227-296, 26 figures, 35 pls, wraps. $50.00

F59. FEWKES (Jesse Walter). (Smithsonian Misc. Collections, Vol. 74, No. 2, Washington, 1923) Designs on Prehistoric Pottery from the Mimbres Valley, New Mexico. 47pp, 21pp of drawings of 140 pots, wrappers. $40.00
____Another Copy. Same. $30.00
____Another Copy. Same, ex-lib. $17.00

F60. FEWKES (Jesse Walter). (Museum of the American Indian, Contributions, Vol. II, No. 2, 1915) Engraved Celts from the Antille. 12 drawings of 9 celts, wraps. $18.00

F61. FEWKES (Jesse Walter). (American Anthropologist, Vol. 11, 1898) The Feather Symbol in Ancient Hopi Designs. 14pp, 10 figures, Philadelphia, wrappers. $14.00

F62. FEWKES (Jesse Walter). Hopi Katchinas Drawn by Native Artists. 190pp, illus in color, reprint by the Rio Grande Press of the 21st Smithsonian Annual Report, Glorieta, 1982. $25.00
____Another Copy. Same. $20.00

F63. FEWKES (Jesse Walter). (Hemenway Southwestern Archaeological Expedition, Journal of American Ethnology and Archaeology. Volume I, Boston, 1891) Included articles are: A Few Summer Ceremonials at Zuni Pueblo. 62pp, 10 illus, 1 color plate ... Zuni Melodies. 30pp.... Reconnoissance of Ruins and Zuni Reservation. 140pp, folding map, wrappers. $125.00
____Another Copy. Same, paper over bds. $100.00

F64. FEWKES (Jesse Walter). (Hemenway Southwestern Archaeological Expedition, Journal of American Ethnology and Archaeology. Volume II, Boston, 1891) Included articles are: A Few Summer Ceremonials at the Tusayan Pueblos.

160pp, illus ... Natal Ceremonials: Hopi. 16pp ... A Ruin in Casa Grande, Arizona. 16pp, wrappers.

$125.00

F65. FEWKES (Jesse Walters). (Smithsonian Institution Annual Report to July, 1885) Contains: The Tusayan Ritual; A Study of the Influence of Environment on Aboriginal Cults. The Cliff Villages of the Red Rock Country. The Tusayan Ruins of Sikyatki and Awatobi, Arizona. xlii, 837pp, 35pp of illus, cloth. $68.00
___Another Copy. Same, ex-lib. $40.00
___Another Copy. Same, rebound in later cloth. $50.00

F66. FEWKES (Jesse Walter). Sun Worship of the Hopi Indians. From Smithsonian Report for 1918. pp 493-526, plus 11pp of pls, wrappers. $40.00
___Another Copy. Same. $20.00

F67. FEWKES (Jesse Walter). Tusayan Snake Ceremonies. From Smithsonian Report No. 16, Washington, 1897. pp 267-311, pls, rebound in cloth. $22.00

F68. FEWKES (Jesse Walter). Two Summers' Work in Pueblo Ruins. From Smithsonian 22nd Annual Report, 1904, Part I. 195pp, 122 figures, 70 pls with several in color, 4to, rebound in red leather and cloth. $45.00
___Another Copy. Same, cloth. $45.00

F69. FEWKES (Jesse Walter) and GENIN (A.). Fire Worship of the Hopi Indians. Also: Notes on the Dances, Music, and Songs of the Ancient and Modern Mexicans. From Smithsonian Institute Annual Report, June 30, 1920. pp 589-611 and pp 657-759, 13pp illus, 10pp photographs, cloth. $38.00

F70. FEWKES (Jesse Walter) and MEYER (H.). Preliminary Account of an Expedition to the Pueblo Ruins Near Winslow, Arizona in 1896. Also: Bows and Arrows in Central Brazil. From Smithsonian Institute Annual Report to July, 1896. li, 727pp total whole volume, extracts ... pp 517-541, 28pp illus. pp 549-591, 5pp illus, leather with marbled bds. $75.00
___Another Copy. Same, cloth. $55.00
___Another Copy. Same, ex-lib. $30.00

F71. FEY (Harold E.) and MCNICKLE (D'Arcy). Indians and Other Americans. Two Ways of Life Meet. 214pp, map, notes, index, New York, 1959 (1st ed.). $10.00

F72. FIELDER (Mildred). Sioux Indian Leaders. 160pp, early photographs, 4to, bibliography, index, Seattle, 1975 (1st ed.), d.j. $27.00
___Another Copy. Same, New York, 1981, d.j. $15.00
___Another Copy. Same, lacks d.j. $10.00

F73. FIELDS (V. M.). The Hover Collection of Karok Baskets. 112pp, 128 photographs, 6 drawings, 1 map, Clarke Memorial Museum, 1985. $30.00
The Hover Collection, perhaps the largest and most

important collection of Karok basketry, was acquired in the early 1980s by the Clarke Memorial Museum in Eureka, California. This catalogue documents a major material culture collection of this northwest California Indian people--about which there has been little written in literature. In addition to photographs, there is a good essay on Karok ceremonies, ethnography and material culture. (EAP)

____Another Copy. Same. $18.00

F74. FIERO (D. C.) et al. (MNA Research Paper II, Flagstaff, 1980) The Navajo Project, Archaeological Investigations Page to Phoenix 500KV Southern Transmisison Line. 299pp, 87 illus, 20 tables, wraps. $17.00

F75. FINLAYSON (Duncan). Traits of American Indian Life and Character by a Fur Trader. 107pp, 6 pls, limited to 500 copies, first reprint of 1853 edition which recent research indicates that Peter Ogden was the author, San Francisco, Grabhorn Press, 1933. $125.00

F76. FINLEY (James B.). Autobiography of Rev. James B. Finley; or, Pioneer Life in the West. 455pp, frontis, 7 pls, original cloth, Cincinnati, Methodist Book Concern, 1853 (1st ed.). $125.00
Howes: F-143. Field: 539. A classic narrative of the Old Northwest, with many reminiscences of Indians and events in Kentucky, Ohio, and the Mississippi Valley.
____Another Copy. Same, rebound in later cloth. $80.00

F77. FINLEY (James B.). History of the Wyandott Mission, at Upper Sandusky, Ohio. 432pp, full calf, Cincinnati, J. F. Wright & L. Swormsteldt, 1840 (1st ed.). $150.00
Howes: F-144. Field: 538. The author was a missionary who worked for several years among the Wyandotts, beginning in 1819. His account of his labors, Indian customs and village life are among the best early narratives of these Ohio Valley Indians.

F78. FINLEY (Rev. James B.). Life Among the Indians. 548pp, plus 4pp ads, portrait and 4 pls, decorated cloth. Cincinnati, 1857 (1st ed.). $90.00
____Another Copy. Same, 548pp, cloth, hinges weak, Cincinnati, n.d., c.1880s $75.00
____Another Copy. Same. $10.00

F79. FINLEY (James B.). Selected Chapters from the History of the Wyandott Mission at Upper Sandusky, Ohio. Printed Under the Direction of the Methodist Episcopal Church. 147pp, selected chapters from 1840 edition, cloth, Cincinnati, 1916. $15.00

F80. FINNERTY (W. Patrick). (Pacific Coast Archaeological Society, Occasional Paper No. 1, Ramona, 1981, reprint) Community Structure and Trade at Isthmus Cave: A Salvage Excavation on Catalina Island. 30pp, 4to, illus, 30 item bibliography, wrappers. $15.00
____Another Copy. Same. $10.00

F81. FINNIE (Richard). Lure of the North. 222pp, plus index,
photographs, endpaper maps, much on the Eskimo,
Philadelphia, 1940 (1st ed.), d.j. $25.00

FISHER (Edna). See BAE Bulletin No. 133.

FISHER (Margaret W.). See BAE Bulletin No. 125.

F82. FISHER (Reginald G.). (Univ. of New Mexico Archaeology
Series Bulletin, Vol. 1, No. 1, Albuquerque, 1930) The
Archaeological Survey of the Pueblo Plateau. 22pp, plus
lrge folding map, 2 maps in text, 1 folding map, wraps.
$15.00

_____Another Copy. Same. $18.00
_____Another Copy. Same. $10.00

F83. FISKE (Elizabeth French). I Lived Among the Apaches:
An Appreciation of the Virtues and Emotions of the Indian American. 165pp, Pasadena, 1947 (1st ed.), d.j.
$45.00

First-hand account of the Apaches. Author traveled
with her husband while he worked for the Bureau of Indian Affairs as field-representative at San Carlos, Parker,
Whiteriver, Old Fort McDowell, etc.

_____Another Copy. Same. $35.00

F84. FISKE (Frank). The Taming of the Sioux. 186pp, photographs, Bismark, ND, 1917 (1st ed.). $100.00

Luther High Spot, 98. The 1862-63 Sioux War, the
Little Big Horn, the Messiah craze, the death of Sitting
Bull, Wounded Knee; Paints Brown (A Sioux who was in
the Custer fight) relates his account of the affair.

F85. FITTING (James E.). The Archaeology of Michigan. A
Guide to the Prehistory of the Great Lakes Region.
274pp, 123 illus, 4to, cloth, Garden City, NY, 1970.
$35.00

_____Another Copy. Same. $25.00

F86. FITTING (James E.). (Univ. of Michigan Anthropology
Papers, No. 24, Ann Arbor, 1965) Late Woodland Cultures of Southeastern Michigan. 165pp, 48 illus, wraps.
$18.00

_____Another Copy. Same. $15.00

F87. FITZHUGH (W. W.) Editor. Cultures in Contacts. The
European Impact on Native Cultural Institutions in Eastern North America, A.D. 1000-1800. vi, 320pp, 39
figures, Anthropological Society, Washington, 1985.
$45.00

F88. FITZHUGH (W. W.). (Smithsonian Contributions to Anthropology, No. 16, Washington, 1972) Environmental Archaeology and Cultural Systems in Hamilton Inlet, Labrador,
A Survey of the Central Labrador Coast from 3000BC to
the Present. xix, 299pp, 87 photographs, 80 figures,
cloth. $40.00

_____Another Copy. Same, wrappers. $20.00
_____Another Copy. Same. $10.00

F89. FITZPATRICK (W. S.). Treaties and Laws of the Osage

Nation as Passed to November 26, 1890. (25), 103pp, printed wrappers, facsimile reprint of Cedar Vale, Kansas, 1895 printing, Santa Anna, 1967. $12.00

F90. (FIVE NATIONS). The Four Kings of Canada. Being a Succinct Account of the Four Indian Princes Lately Arriv'd from North America. 47pp, 12mo, London, 1710 (reprinted London, Garrett & CO., 1891). $65.00
   Field: 553. "Tale of the Four Chiefs from the Five Nations brought to England in the early 1700's to cement the alliance between the Iroquois and the British in their war with the French."

F91. FLADMARK (K. F.). British Columbia Prehistory. x, 150pp, 8 full-page color photographs, 29pp of b/w photographs, 6pp of b/w drawings, 3 maps, wrappers, National Museum of Man, 1986. $22.00
   ____Another Copy. Same. $30.00

F92. FLAGG (Edmund) and DESMET (Pierre Jean). Travels in the Far West, 1836-1841. (2 Volumes). Edited by Reuben Gold Thwaites. Vol. I: FLAGG (E.) The Far West: or, A Tour Beyond the Mountains. 370pp. Vol. II: DESMET (Pierre J.) Letters and Sketches,.... 411pp. Both volumes illus with facsimiles, drawings, folding map, newly rebound, Cleveland, 1906 (1st ed.). $50.00

F93. FLANNERY (K. V.) and BLANTON (R. E.). (Univ. of Michigan, Museum of Anthropology, No. 15, 1982) Monte Alban's Hinterland, Part I: The Prehistoric Settlement Patterns of the Central and Southern Part of the Valley of Oaxaca, Mexico. xv, 506pp, 77 figures, 83pp of site maps, 77pp of grid squares, wrappers. $30.00
   ____Another Copy. Same. $40.00

FLANNERY (Regina). See BAE Bulletin No. 133.

F94. (FLATHEAD). (Senate Executive Document 221, 51:1, Washington, 1890, 1st printing) Draught of a Bill for the Sale, etc., of Lands of the Flathead Indians of Montana. 35pp, folding map. Removed. $15.00

F95. FLEMING (Henry Craig). (Museum of the American Indian, Contributions, Vol. VIII, No. 2, New York, 1924) Medical Observations on the Zuni Indians. 10pp, plus 8pp of pls, wrappers. $10.00
   ____Another Copy. Same. $15.00

F96. FLEMING (Rev. John). A Short Sermon: Also Hymns, in the Muskogee or Creek Language. 35pp, 18mo, self wraps, Boston, Crocker & Brewster, 1835. $100.00
   The pamphlet consists of the alphabet, pp 3-4; the sermon and hymns in Muskokee, pp 5-11, pp 13-35.

F97. FLETCHER (Alice C.). Historical Sketch of the Omaha Tribe of Indians in Nebraska. 12pp, 11 pls, folding map of reservation, wrappers, Washington, 1885. $125.00

F98. FLETCHER (Alice C.). Indian Story and Song from North America. 126pp, Boston, 1900. $75.00

F99. FLETCHER (Alice C.). (Peabody Museum Archaeological and Ethnological Papers, Vol. I, No. V, Cambridge, 1893)

A Study of Omaha Indian Music. 152pp, original wrappers. $35.00

___Another Copy. Same, rebound in cloth. $40.00

F100. FLETCHER (J. G.). John Smith, Also Pocahontas. 303pp, frontis, 5 illus, cloth, New York, 1928. $20.00

___Another Copy. Same. $15.00

F101. (FLINT). Flint Implements; an Account of Stone Age Techniques and Cultures. 108pp, illus, bibliography, index, wrappers, Trustees, British Museum, London, 1968. $10.00

___Another Copy. Same. $15.00

___Another Copy. Same. $22.00

F102. FLINT (Timothy). Indian Wars of the West: Containing Biographical Sketches of Those Pioneers Who Headed the Western Settlers in Repelling the Attacks of the Savages. 240pp, sml 8vo, rebound in cloth, Cincinnati, E. H. Flint, 1833 (1st ed.). $200.00

Howes: F-201. Field: 545. Contains much first-hand information on the customs, monuments, and antiquities of the Western Indians.

___Another Copy. Same, 1/2 leather, marbled bds, 1833 (1st ed.). $250.00

___Another Copy. Same, full calf, 1833 (1st ed.). $175.00

F103. (FLORIDA). (Smithsonian Misc. Collections, Vol. 95, No. 16, Washington, DC, 1936) A 17th Century Letter of Gabriel Diaz Vara Calderon, Bishop of Cuba, Describing the Indians and Indian Missions of Florida. 17pp, 12 pls, wrappers. $25.00

___Another Copy. Same. $30.00

___Another Copy. Same. $18.00

F104. FLORNEY (B.). Jivaro (Amazon). 224pp, illus, London, 1953. $20.00

___Another Copy. Same. $15.00

F105. FLYNN (A. J.). The American Indian as a Product of Environment, with Special Reference to the Pueblos. 275pp, 8 photographs, cloth, Boston, 1907 (1st ed.). $45.00

___Another Copy. Same. $20.00

___Another Copy. Same. $33.00

FOGELSON (Raymond D.). See BAE Bulletin No. 180.

F106. FOLAN (William J.) et al. Coba: A Classic Maya Metropolis. 253pp, illus, with Coba archaeological mapping project containing 22 folding maps, boxed, New York, 1983. $50.00

___Another Copy. Same, box missing. $30.00

F107. FOLAN (William J.). (Middle American Research. Tulane Univ., Publication 26, No. 9, 1969) The Open Chapel of Dzibilchaltun, Yucatan. 19pp, 11 figures, wrappers. $10.00

F108. FOLAN (W. J.) and DEWHIRST (J.) Editors. The Yuquot

Project, Volume 3. Glassware, Glass Beads, Clay Tobacco Pipes, Ceramics, Mexican Sherds, All from or Excavated at Yuquot, British Columbia. 186pp, 33 lrge
photographs, 31 figures, wrappers, Ottawa, 1981.
$20.00

F109. (FOLKLORE). Honne, The Spirit of the Chehalis. The
Indian Interpretation of the Origin of the People and
Animals. As Narrated by George Saunders. 204pp,
(3)pp, frontis, illus, cloth, n.p., 1925. $20.00
___Another Copy. Same. $30.00

F110. FONTANA (Bernard L.). Of Earth and Little Rain; the
Papago Indians. With Photographs by John P. Schaefer.
162pp, oblong 8vo, illus, some in color, index, bibliography, map, Flagstaff, 1981 (1st ed.). $30.00

F111. FONTANA (B. L.) et al. Papago Indian Pottery. 176pp,
129 illus, Seattle, 1962. $38.00
___Another Copy. Same, has d.j. $28.00
___Another Copy. Same. $15.00

F112. FORBES (Jack D.). Apache, Navaho, and Spaniard.
xxvi, 304pp, 8 full-page pls, 4 maps, index, bibliography, Norman, 1960 (1st ed.), d.j. $30.00
___Another Copy. Same. $30.00
___Another Copy. Same. $25.00

F113. FORBES (Jack D.). Native Americans of California and
Nevada. 202pp, illus, maps, index, Healdsburg, 1969
(1st ed.). $17.00
___Another Copy. Same. $10.00
___Another Copy. Same. $12.00

F114. FORBES (Jack D.). Warriors of the Colorado: The
Yumas of the Quechan Nation and Their Neighbors.
378pp, illus, index, bibliography, Norman, 1965 (1st
ed.), d.j. $30.00
Full history of the Yumas from earliest Spanish exploration through 1850s. Much on Yuma influence of
history of Southern California, Arizona and Sonora.
___Another Copy. Same. $35.00
___Another Copy. Same. $20.00

F115. FORBIS (Richard G.). (Univ. of Calgary, Dept. of
Archaeology, Occasional Papers No. 4, Calgary, 1977)
Cluny. An Ancient Fortified Village in Alberta. 81pp,
tables, photographs, drawings, maps, references, ap-
pendix, wrappers. $10.00
___Another Copy. Same. $15.00

F116. FORBIS (Richard G.). (National Museum of Canada, Bulletin No. 180, Contributions to Anthropology, Part I,
1960) The Old Woman's Buffalo Jump. 123pp, illus
with 19 figures, 5 pls, wrappers. $15.00

F117. FORCE (M. F.). Some Early Notices of the Indians of
Ohio. 40pp, original wrappers, Cincinnati, Robert
Clarke, 1879 (1st ed.). $85.00
Paper delivered before the Historical and Philosophical

Society of Ohio regarding early reports from travelers
and explorers on encounters with Indians in Ohio.

F118.　FORD (Clellan S.). Smoke from Their Fires; The Life of
a Kwakiutl Chief. (11), 248pp, portrait, map, New
Haven, 1941 (1st ed.). $60.00

F119.　FORD (J. A.). Louisiana Geological Survey, Anthropological Study, Dept. of Conservation, Study No. 2, 1936)
Analysis of Indian Village Site Collections from Louisiana
and Mississippi. xi, 285pp, illus, bibliography, index,
wrappers. $35.00
___Another Copy. Same, ex-lib, cloth. $22.00

F120.　FORD (J. A.). (Louisiana Geological Survey, Anthropologi-
cal Study, Dept. of Conservation, Study No. 1, 1935)
Ceramic Decoration Sequence at an Old Indian Village
Site Near Sicily Island, Louisiana. 41pp, pls, maps,
index, wrappers. $20.00
___Another Copy. Same. $25.00

F121.　FORD (J. A.). (Smithsonian Contributions to Anthropology, Vol. 11, Washington, 1969) A Comparison of
Formative Cultures in the Americas. xvi, 211pp, 32
figures, 22 fold-out charts, cloth. $35.00

F122.　FORD (J. A.) and WILLEY (G.). (Louisiana Dept. of Con-
servation, Anthropology Study No. 3, 1940) Crooks
Site, a Marksville Period Burial Mound in La Salle Par-
ish, Louisiana. xi, 148pp, 59 figures, wraps. $30.00
___Another Copy. Same. $25.00
___Another Copy. Same. $18.00

F123.　FORD (J. A.). (American Museum of Natural History,
Anthropological Papers, Vol. 47, Part 1, 1959) Eskimo
Prehistory in the Vicinity of Point Barrow, Alaska.
272pp of text containing 118 figures, plus 13pp of photo-
graphs, wrappers. $90.00
___Another Copy. Same. $45.00
___Another Copy. Same. $68.00

F124.　FORD (J. A.). (American Museum of Natural History,
Anthropological Papers, Vol. 44, Part I, 1951) Green-
house: A Troyville-Coles Creek Period Site in Avayelles
Parish, Louisiana. 132pp, 49 figures, 23pp of photo-
graphs, wrappers. $40.00
___Another Copy. Same. $30.00
___Another Copy. Same. $25.00

F125.　FORD (J. A.). (American Museum of Natural History,
Anthropological Papers, Vol. 50, Part 1, 1963) Hopewell
Culture Burial Mounds Near Helena, Arkansas. 56pp,
figures, 10 pls, bibliography, wrappers. $20.00

F126.　FORD (J. A.). (American Museum of Natural History,
Anthropological Papers, Vol. 44, Part 3, 1952) Measurements of Some Prehistoric Design Developments in the
Southeastern United States. pp 313-384, 23 figures,
wrappers. $22.00

F127.　FORD (J. A.). (American Museum of Natural History,

Anthropological Papers, Vol. 48, Part 2, 1961) Menard
Site: The Quapaw Village of Osotouy on the Arkansas
River. pp 133-191, 20 figures, 10pp of photographs,
wrappers. $35.00
___Another Copy. Same. $17.00
___Another Copy. Same. $15.00

F128. FORD (J. A.) and WEBB (C. H.). (American Museum of
Natural History, Anthropological Papers, Vol. 46, Part
1, 1956) Poverty Point, a Late Archaic Site in Louisiana. 142pp, 6pp of photographs, 45 figures, wrappers.
$27.00
___Another Copy. Same. $15.00

F129. FORD (J. A.) and WILLEY (G.). (American Museum of
Natural History, Anthropological Papers, Vol. 43, Part
1, 1949) Surface Survey of the Viru Valley, Peru.
89pp of text, 3 figures, 6 fold-out maps and graphs,
plus 7pp of photographs, wrappers. $45.00
___Another Copy. Same. $30.00

F130. FORD (J. A.) et al. (Memoirs of the Society for American
Archaeology, American Antiquity, Vol. 2, Menasha and
Salt Lake City, 1945) Tchefuncte Culture, Early Occu-
pation of Lower Mississippi Valley. xii, 113pp, pls,
figures, illus, bibliography, wrappers. $18.00
___Another Copy. Same. $22.00

F131. FORDE (C. D.). (Univ. of California Publications in
American Archaeology and Ethnology, Vol. 28, No. 4,
Berkeley, 1931) Ethnography of the Yuma Indians.
204pp, 9pp of photographs, 17 figures, 2 fold-out maps,
wraps. $60.00
___Another Copy. Same. $45.00

F132. FORDE (C. D.). Habitat, Economy and Society: A Geographical Introduction to Ethnology. 500pp. frontis,
108 illus and maps, New York, 1949 (7th ed.), d.j.
$35.00

F133. FOREMAN (Grant). Advancing the Frontier, 1830-1860.
363pp, illus, index, folding maps, bibliography, Norman,
1968, d.j. $20.00

F134. FOREMAN (Grant). The Five Civilized Tribes. 431pp,
plus index, illus, folding map, Norman, 1934 (1st ed.).
$75.00
___Another Copy. Same, Norman, 1966. 2nd
ed. $20.00

F135. FOREMAN (Grant) Editor. Indian Justice. A Cherokee
Murder Trial at Tahlequah in 1840. As Reported by
John Howard Payne. 105pp, plus index, illus, map,
Oklahoma City, 1934 (1st ed.), d.j. $45.00
___Another Copy. Same, lacks d.j. $40.00

F136. FOREMAN (Grant). Indian Removal. Emigration of the
Five Civilized Tribes of Indians. 415pp, 5 folding maps,
plate illus, Norman, (1st printing of new ed.), d.j.
$32.00

       ____Another Copy. Same, Norman, 1956, d.j. $20.00
       ____Another Copy. Same, Norman, 1956, d.j. $10.00

F137. FOREMAN (Grant). Indians and Pioneers: The Story of the American Southwest Before 1830. 300pp, index, bibliography, 8 full-page pls, map, Norman, 1936, d.j.
                                             $30.00

F138. FOREMAN (Grant). The Last Trek of the Indians. 358pp, plus index, 1 photograph, 8 folding maps, bibliography, from the treaty with the Delaware in 1778 to the removal to Oklahoma. Chicago, 1946 (1st ed.), d.j. $45.00
       ____Another Copy. Same, lacks d.j. $30.00
       ____Another Copy. Same, lacks d.j., 2nd ed. $14.00

F139. FOREMAN (Grant). Sequoyah. 90pp, index, illus, cloth, Norman, 1938 (1st ed.), d.j. $60.00
       ____Another Copy. Same, lacks d.j. $45.00
       ____Another Copy. Same, Norman, 1959, d.j. $20.00
       ____Another Copy. Same, Norman, 1959, d.j. $10.00

F140. FOREMAN (Grant). A Traveler in Indian Territory. The Journal of Ethan Allen Hitchcock, Late Major General in the United States Army. 262pp, plus index, illus, folding map, Cedar Rapids, 1930 (1st ed.). $50.00

F141. FORREST (Earle R.) and HILL (E. B.). Lone War Trail of the Apache Kid. 143pp, photographs, illus, color plate, bibliography, index, Pasadena, 1947 (1st ed.).
                                             $45.00
       ____Another Copy. Same, deluxe ed., #169 of
                        250 copies. $50.00

F142. FORREST (Earle R.). Missions and Pueblos of the Old Southwest. 386pp, 32 photographic illus, blue cloth, Cleveland, Arthur H. Clark, 1929. $90.00
       ____Another Copy. Same, some spotting. $65.00

F143. FORREST (Earl R.). The Snake Dance of the Hopi Indians. 172pp, photographs, endpaper maps, bibliography, index, Los Angeles, 1961, d.j. $25.00
       ____Another Copy. Same. $22.00
       ____Another Copy. Same, lacks d.j. $15.00
       ____Another Copy. Same, lacks d.j. $12.00

F144. FORREST (Earle R.). With Camera in Old Navaholand. 274pp, 125 photographs, index, Norman, 1970 (1st ed.), d.j. $17.00
       ____Another Copy. Same. $22.00

F145. FORRESTER (Robert E.). The Ham Creek Site ... (Archaeology). 46pp, photographs, drawings, bibliography, spiral bound, Ft. Worth, 1964. $10.00

FORSTEMANN (E.). See BAE Bulletin No. 28.

F146. FORSTEMANN (E.). (Peabody Museum Papers, Vol. IV, No. II, Cambridge, 1906) Commentary on the Maya Manuscript in the Royal Public Library of Dresden. 238pp, 2pp of pls, wrappers. $74.00
       ____Another Copy. Same, ex-lib. $60.00

F147. FORTUNE (R. F.). (Columbia Univ. Contributions to

Anthropology, Vol. CIV, 1932) Omaha Secret Societies. 200pp, cloth. $50.00

F148. FOSTER (George M.). (Smithsonian Institute of Social Anthropology, Publication No. 6, 1948) Empire's Children, The People of Tzintzuntzan. v, 297pp, 36 figures, 16pp of photographs, 2 maps, wrappers. $40.00
____Another Copy. Same. $35.00
____Another Copy. Same. $25.00

F149. FOSTER (George M.). A Primitive Mexican Society. 115pp, illus, 8 b/w photographs, American Ethnological Society, Seattle, London, 1966. $35.00
____Another Copy. Same, Seattle, 1942, cloth. $25.00

F150. FOSTER (George M.). (Univ. of California Anthropological Records, Vol. 5, No. 3, Berkeley, 1944) A Summary of Yuki Culture. iv, 92pp, 15 figures, 2 maps, wraps. $37.00
____Another Copy. Same. $15.00
____Another Copy. Same. $25.00
____Another Copy. Same. $25.00

F151. FOSTER (John W.). Pre-Historic Races of the United States of America. 415pp, 72 figures, index, cloth, much on the Mound Builders, Chicago, 1874 (3rd ed.). $12.00
____Another Copy. Same, Chicago, 1878, 4th ed. $10.00
____Another Copy. Same, Chicago, 1881, 5th ed. $15.00
____Another Copy. Same, Chicago, 1887, 6th ed. $45.00

F152. FOSTER (Michael K.). (National Museum of Canada, Canadian Ethnology Service, Paper No. 20, Ottawa, 1974) From the Earth to Beyond the Sky: An Ethnographic Approach to Four Longhouse Iroquois Speech Events. 448pp, wrappers. $28.00
____Another Copy. Same, cloth. $38.00
____Another Copy. Same, cloth, ex-lib. $25.00

F153. FOSTER (M. and G.). (Smithsonian Institute of Social Anthropology, Publication No. 8, 1948) Sierra Popoluca Speech. 45pp, lrge 8vo, wrappers. $10.00

F154. FOSTER (Robert). The North American Indian Doctor, or Nature's Method of Curing and Preventing Disease According to the Indians ... Also, a Materia Medica of Indian Remedies.... 154, (2)pp, index, 12mo, linen backed bds, lacks free frnt endpapers, Canton, Ohio, for author by Smith and Bevin, 1838 (1st ed.). $275.00

F155. FOUCHET (M. P.). Terres Indiennes. Over 50 photographs, 2 color pls (Codices), 4to, wrappers, Lausanne, 1955. $25.00

F156. FOULKS (Edward). (American Anthropological Assoc., Anthropological Studies, No. 10, Washington, DC, 1972) The Arctic Hysterias of the North Alaskan Eskimo. 162pp, illus, wrappers. $17.00

FOWKE (Gerard). See also BAE Bulletins Nos. 23, 37, 44, and
76.

F157. FOWKE (Gerard). Archaeological History of Ohio: The
Mound Builders and Later Indians. xvi, 760pp, fold-
out frontis, 303 figures, photographs, and drawings,
brown cloth, from the Press of Fred J. Heer, Columbus, Ohio, 1901 (1st ed.). $55.00
___Another Copy. Same, Columbus, 1902. $65.00
___Another Copy. Same, Columbus, 1902. $45.00

F158. FOWKE (Gerard). Prehistoric Objects Classified and Described. 32pp, 14 pls of artifacts, wraps, Missouri Historical Society, St. Louis, 1913 (1st ed.). $15.00

F159. FOWLER (Don D. and Catherine S.) Editors. (Smithson-
ian Contributions to Anthropology, Vol. 14, 1971)
Anthropology of the Numa: John Wesley Powell's
Manuscripts on the Numic Peoples of Western North
America, 1868-1880. 300 double column pp, plus index,
photographs, maps, wrappers. $30.00
___Another Copy. Same. $25.00

F160. FOWLER (Don D.) Editor. In A Sacred Manner We Live:
Photographs of the North American Indians by Edward
S. Curtis. Introduction and Commentary by Don D.
Fowler. 152pp, 4to, illus, New York, 1972, d.j.
$20.00
120 representative photographs from Curtis's monumen-
tal "The North American Indian."

F161. FOWLER (M. L.). (Illinois State Museum Scientific Papers,
Vol. VIII, No. 1, 1957) Ferry Site, Hardin County,
Illinois. 36pp, 2 1/2 pp photographs, 14 figures, wrap-
pers. $13.00
___Another Copy. Same. $10.00

F162. FOWLER (M. L.). (Illinois State Museum, Reports of Investigations, No. 4, Springfield, 1956) Modoc Rock
Shelter. 58pp, lrge 8vo, illus, wrappers. $10.00

F163. FOWLER (M. L.). (Illinois State Museum Scientific Papers,
Vol. VII, No. 1, 1957) Rutherford Mound, Hardin
County, Illinois. 44pp, 14pp of photographs, 5 figures,
wrappers. $15.00

F164. FOX (A. A.) and HESTER (T. R.). (Univ. of Texas
Archaeological Survey Report No. 22, San Antonio,
1976) Archaeological Test Excavations at Mission San
Francisco de la Espada. 28pp, photographs, plans,
bibliography, wrappers. $10.00

F165. FOX (A. A.) and HESTER (T. R.). (Univ. of Texas
Archaeological Survey Report No. 18, San Antonio,
1976) An Archaeological Survey of Coleto Creek, Victoria and Golind Counties, Texas. 84pp, photographs,
maps, bibliography, wrappers. $10.00

F166. FOX (D. E.). (Texas Historical Commission, Office of
State Archaeologist, Special report No. 3, Austin, 1970)
Archaeological Salvage Mission San Jose.... 53pp, plus
maps and pls, bibliography, wrappers. $12.00

F167. FOX (D. E.). (Univ. of Texas Archaeological Survey Report No. 72, San Antonio, 1979) An Intensive Survey of Sixteen Prehistoric Archaeological Sites in Starr County, Texas. 49pp, photographs, drawings, maps, bibliography, wrappers. $10.00

F168. FOX (Daniel E.). (Univ. of Texas, Center for Archaeological Research, Special Report No. 8, San Antonio, 1979) The Lithic Artifacts of Indians at the Spanish Colonial Missions, San Antonio, Texas. 47pp, drawings, bibliography, wrappers. $12.00

F169. FOX (Daniel E.) et al. (Texas Historical Commission Archaeological Survey Report No. 12, Austin, 1974) Archaeological Resources of the Proposed Cuero Reservoir. 311pp, photographs, drawings, maps, charts, bibliography, wrappers. $10.00

F170. FOX (John W.). Quiche Conquest. 322pp, 43 figures, 11 maps, includes a thorough analysis of Pre-Columbian Sites, Albuquerque, 1978. $30.00

FRACHTENBERG (Leo J.). See BAE Bulletins Nos. 40, Part II, and 67.

F171. FRANCIS (Convers). Life of John Eliot, the Apostle to the Indians. 357pp, full calf, Boston, 1836 (1st ed.). $12.00

F172. FRANCK (H.). Trailing Cortez Through Mexico. 373pp, 76 photographic illus, New York, 1935. $25.00

F173. FRANCK (H.). Working North from Patagonia. 650pp, 176 illus, map, New York, 1921 (1st ed.). $35.00

F174. FRANK (L.) and HARLOW (F.). Historic Pottery of the Pueblo Indians, 1600-1880. xvi, 160pp, 166 b/w and 32 lrge color photographs, 1 map, cloth, Boston, 1975. $45.00
   This volume, the first comprehensive account of Pueblo pottery of the historic period--from about 1600 to 1880, contains large, very handsome photographs of 198 historic period pots from major museum and private collections. In addition to an important text, there is a full description for each of the illustrated pots.
   ____Another Copy. Same, Boston, 1974, 1st ed. $35.00
   ____Another Copy. Same, Boston, 1978. $30.00

F175. FRANK (Larry) and HOLBROOK (Millard J., II). Indian Silver Jewelry of the Southwest, 1868-1930. 209 mostly double-column pp, many illus, photographs, some in color, Boston. 1978 (1st ed.), d.j. $30.00
   ____Another Copy. Same. $25.00
   ____Another Copy. Same. $50.00

F176. FRAU (Salvador C.). Las Civilizaciones Prehispanicas de America. 565pp, 142 figures, 78 pls, bibliography, wrappers, Buenos Aires, 1959. $35.00

F177. FRAZIER (Kendrick). People of Chaco: A Canyon and Its Culture. 224pp, illus, New York, 1986 (1st ed.). $20.00

_____Another Copy. Same. $28.00

F178.   FREDERICKSON (N. Jaye) and GIBB (Sandra). The
        Covenant Chain, Indian Ceremonial and Trade Silver.
        166pp, plus index, photographs, drawings, some in
        color, maps, bibliography, Ottawa, 1980 (1st ed.),
        d.j. $30.00
_____Another Copy. Same. $25.00

FREED (J. Arthur). See BAE Bulletin No. 192.

F179.   FREEMAN (John F.). A Guide to Manuscripts Relating to
        the American Indian in the Library of the American
        Philosophical Society. x, 491pp, bibliography, index,
        total of 3,995 entries, American Philosophical Society,
        Philadelphia, 1966, d.j. $35.00

F180.   FREILE (Juan Rodriguez). The Conquest of New Granada
        (Colombia). 228pp, translation of a 16th century work,
        boxed, Folio Society, London, 1961. $30.00

FREIRE-MARRECO (Barbara). See BAE Bulletin No. 55.

FRENGUELLI (Joaquin). See BAE Bulletin No. 143.

F181.   FREUCHEN (Dagmar) Editor. Peter Freuchen's Book of the
        Eskimo. 441pp, pls, endpaper maps, Cleveland, 1961
        (1st ed.), d.j. $12.00
_____Another Copy. Same. $18.00
_____Another Copy. Same, lacks d.j. $12.00

F182.   FREY (M.). The Apaches of the Rio Grande; A Story of
        Indian Life. Translated by Brita Mack. Introduction
        by Ray Allen Billington. 85pp, illus, wrappers, Los
        Angeles, 1978. $15.00
        Only English translation of a piece of fiction that was
        originally published in German in the 1880s. Includes
        the illustrations from the unique copy of the original
        edition at the University of Texas. (GFH)

F183.   FRIEDE (Juan) and KEEN (Benjamin) Editors. Bartolome
        de las Casas in History. 632pp, illus, 3 maps, Dekalb,
        1971. $40.00

F184.   FRIEDERICI (George). Indianer und Anglo-Amerikaner.
        Ein Geschichtlicher Uberlick. ("History of the Indians
        of North America."--Rader: 1488). 147pp, modern
        wraps, Braunscheig, Germany, 1900. $25.00

F185.   FRIEDLANDER (E.) and PINYAN (P. J.). (Univ. of New
        Mexico, Center Anthropological Studies, Ethnology Re-
        port Series, No. 1, Albuquerque, 1980) Indian Use of
        the Santa Fe National Forest: A Determination from
        Ethnographic Sources. vi, 51pp, 12 figures, wraps.
                                                            $12.00

F186.   FRIEDMAN (M.). Annual Report United States Indian
        School. Carlisle, Pennsylvania ... for the Year Ending
        June 30, 1910. 20pp, plus pls, pictorial wrappers,
        string tied, Carlisle, Carlisle Indian Press, 1910.
                                                            $35.00

F187.   FRIKEL (P.). Os Tiriyo Seu Sistema Adaptativo. 323pp,
        66pp of illus, summary in English, Hanover, 1973.
                                                            $85.00

Principally of objects of material culture of the Tiriyo
Indians, a Carib tribe who reside in Northeast Brazil,
on the Brazilian side of the Tumucumaque mountain
range.
____Another Copy. Same, rebound in cloth,
ex-lib. $60.00

F188. FRISBIE (Charlotte). Kinaalda. A Study of the Pueblo
Girl's Puberty Ceremony. xiii, 437pp, photographic
illus, bibliography, index, Middleton, Wesleyan Univ.,
1967 (1st ed.), d.j. $35.00
The Kinaalda and its myth, the ceremony, the music,
most of the text is devoted to the music, some 75 songs
with Navajo text and translation and melodies.
____Another Copy. Same. $30.00

F189. FRISBIE (Charlotte) Editor. Navajo Blessingway Singer;
The Autobiography of Frank Mitchell, 1881 to 1967.
446pp, illus, index, Tucson, 1978 (1st ed.), d.j.
$30.00
____Another Copy. Same, lacks d.j. $30.00

F190. FRISBIE (Charlotte). Southwestern Indian Ritual Drama.
xii, 372pp, illus, references, index, 12 essays on rituals
of Indians in Arizona and New Mexico, including songs
of Zuni Katchinas, Hopi Ogres, etc., Univ. of New
Mexico, 1980 (1st ed.), d.j. $35.00
____Another Copy. Same. $40.00

F191. FRISON (George C.). Folsom Tools and Technology at
the Hanson Site, Wyoming. 135pp, illus, map, index,
well illus scholarly account of artifacts discovered at
Hanson Site in Big Horn County, Albuquerque, 1980
(1st ed.). $30.00
____Another Copy. Same. $20.00
____Another Copy. Same. $17.00

F192. FRONVAL (G.) and DUBOIS (D.). Indian Signals and
Sign Language. 81pp, more than 350 color illus, mainly
photographs, cloth, New York, 1985. $13.00
____Another Copy. Same. $17.00

F193. FROST (John). The Book of the Indians of North America:
Illustrating Their Manners, Customs, and Present State.
283pp, illus, engraved title, cloth, worn and taped.
New York, D. Appleton, 1845. $15.00
____Another Copy. Same. $25.00

F194. FROST (John). Indian Battles, Captivities, and Adventures. 408pp, illus, rebound in cloth, New York,
Derby & Jackson, 1859. $35.00

F195. FROST (John). Thrilling Adventures Among the Indians:
As Well As Incidents in the Recent Indian Hostilities
in Mexico and Texas. 448pp, engraved illus, hand-
colored frontis of Sioux Warrior, blind stamped leather,
Philadelphia, J. W. Bradley, 1850. $60.00

F196. FUHRMANN (Ernst). Kulturen der Erde: Peru II.
24pp, 100 pls, 4to, contains 100 full-page pls from

Pre-Columbian Peruvian collections of Hamburg, Frankfort, Vienna Museums, Germany, 1922.   460.00

F197. FUHRMANN (Ernst). (Material zur Kultur und Kunstgeschichte Aller Volker. Band I. Hagen, 1922) Reich der Inka. Texteil: Sprache und Kultur im Altesten Peru. Bildteil: Keramik, Weberei und Monumentalbau. 146pp, 96 full-page photographs, cloth. $95.00
    ___Another Copy. Same, illus hard bd cvr. $85.00

F198. FUHRMANN (Ernst). Tlinkit U. Haida. 104pp, 61 full-page photographs of art objects, Kulturen der Erde, Hagen jw. und Darmstadt, 1923. $95.00

F199. FUHRMANN (Ernst). Tlinkit U. Haida. Indianerstamme der Westkuste von Nordamerika. Kultische Kunst und Mythen des Kulturkreises. 46pp (1)pp, photographic pls, wrappers, Hagen, Germany, 1922 (1st ed.). $75.00

F200. FULTON (A. R.). The Red Men of Iowa; Being a History of the Various Aboriginal Tribes Whose Homes Were in Iowa; Sketches of Chiefs, Traditions, Indian Hostilities, Incidents and Reminiscences; With a General Account of the Indians and Indian Wars of the Northwest; Also an Appendix Relating to the Pontiac War. 559pp, 26 pls, index, cloth, Des Moines, 1882 (1st ed.). $150.00
    ___Another Copy. Same. $90.00

F201. FULTON (W. S.). (Museum of the American Indian, Contributions, Vol. XII, Nos. 1, 2, 3, New York, 1934, 1934, 1938) Archaeological Notes on Texas Canyon, Arizona. No. 1: 23pp, map, 20pp of photographs, 1934. No. 2: 23pp, map, 14pp of photographs, 1934. No. 3: 22pp, 2 figures, 23pp of photographs, 2pp drawings, 1938. Wrappers. $80.00
    ___Another Copy. Same, Parts 1, 2, 3. $60.00
    ___Another Copy. Part 1 only. $25.00
    ___Another Copy. Part 2 only. $25.00
    ___Another Copy. Part 3 only. $24.00
    ___Another Copy. Part 3 only. $30.00

F202. FULTON (W. S.). An Archaeological Site Near Gleeson, Arizona. 66pp, plus 27 pls, 4to, illus, folding map, wrappers, Dragoon, Arizona, 1940. $20.00

F203. FULTON (W. S.). A Ceremonial Cave in the Winchester Mountains, Arizona. 61pp, 13pp of photographs, cloth, Dragoon, Arizona, 1941. $50.00
    ___Another Copy. Same, wrappers. $22.00

F204. FUNDABURK (Emma Lila) Editor. Southeastern Indians: Life Portraits, A Catalogue of Pictures, 1564-1860. 135pp, illus from the 16th to the 19th century, Luverne, Alabama, 1958, d.j. $60.00

F205. FUNDABURK (Emma) and FOREMAN (Mary D.). Sun Circles and Human Hands: The Southeastern Indians Art and Industry. 227pp, plus index, photographs, drawings, maps, bibliography, for the author, Luverne, Alabama,

1957, d.j. $28.00
___Another Copy. Same. $20.00
F206. FURST (J. L.). (Institute for Mesoamerican Studies,
       No. 4, Albany, 1978) Codex Vindobonensis Mexicanus
       I: A Commentary. 396pp, 103 figures, 50 tables,
       wrappers. $40.00
       ___Another Copy. Same. $28.00
F207. FURST (Jill). Pre-Columbian Art of Mexico. 128pp, folio,
       illus, map, bibliography, New York, 1980 (1st ed.),
       d.j. $35.00
           Large 12" by 15" volume. Presents in full-color with
       four fold-out pls, and 93 others, architectural sites and
       objects of both ceremonial and mundane use.
F208. FURST (Peter) Editor. Flesh of the Gods: The Ritual
       Use of Hallucinogens. 304pp, studies by Wasson, Le-
       Barre, Reichel-Dolmatoff, others, New York, 1972.
                                                        $35.00
F209. FURST (Peter). Selections from the Pre-Columbian Collec-
       tion of Constance McCormick Fearing. 32pp, 40 photo-
       graphs, mostly full-page, Santa Barbara Museum, 1967.
                                                        $10.00

                            -G-

G1.   GABEL (Norman E.). A Comparative Study of the Papago.
       96pp, 28 photographs, wrappers. University of New
       Mexico Press, Albuquerque, 1949. $20.00
       ___Another Copy. Same. $20.00
G2.   GABRIEL (Ralph Henry). Elias Boudinot, Cherokee and
       His America. 190pp, cloth, presentation inscription by
       author. Norman, 1941. $75.00
       ___Another Copy. Same. No inscription. $35.00
       ___Another Copy. Same. d.j. $25.00
G3.   GADDIS (Vincent H.). American Indian Myths and Myster-
       ies. 220pp, index, bibliography. Radnor, 1977 (1st
       ed.). $10.00
G4.   GAILLAND (Rev. Maurice). Potewatemi Nemewinin Ipi
       Menenigamowinin. 119pp, frontis, stamped calf, expertly
       rebacked. Pilling Algonquian, p. 198. St. Louis, 1866.
                                                        $200.00
G5.   GALARZA (J.). Lienzos de Chiepetlan. 505pp, 14pp of
       b/w and 2pp of color photographs, 87pp of figures,
       cloth, inscribed by author. Mexico City, 1972. $55.00
G6.   GALL (John F.) and WEBB (David K.) (Editors). The
       Massacre of the Wigton Family with an account of the
       trial of Samuel Mohawk, the Murderer. 8pp, wrappers.
       Chillicothe, OH, 1934. $10.00
G7.   GALLAGHER (P.). (Yale University Publications in

Anthropology, No. 76, 1979) La Pitia: An Archaeological
Series in Northwestern Venezuela. xiv, 249pp, 8pp of
photographs, 61 figures, 6 tables. $40.00
___Another Copy. Same. $30.00

G8. GALINDO (Enrique V.). Nankijukima Religion, Usos y
Costumbres de los Salvajes del Oriente del Ecuador.
349pp, half calf and bds. Ambato, 1895, Indians of
Ecuador, based on the experiences of the author in
1893-1894. Ambato, 1895. $275.00

G9. GALLATIN (Albert). (Transactions and Collections of the
American Antiquarian Society, Vol. II, Cambridge, 1836)
Synopsis of the Indian Tribes of North America, East
of the Rockies. xxx (2), 574pp, errata, folding hand-
colored map, rebound in green linen and bds. $225.00
Besides the title above, this volume also includes Col.
Juan Galindo's "Description of the Ruins of Copan," one
of the earliest reports on the site. The "Synopsis" is
one of two important works on Indian languages produced
by Gallatin. It includes extensive grammars and vocabularies for over seventy tribes and his classification of them
into families. It is one of the fundamental 19th century
studies of Indian languages. The folding hand-colored
map is best of the western country up to this time.
Howes: G-30. Pilling: 1391. (CY)

G10. GALLENCAMP (Charles). Maya: The Riddle and Rediscov-
ery of a Lost Civilization. 240pp, illus, cloth. New
York, 1959, d.j. $15.00
___Another Copy. New York, 1976 (revised, expanded,
2d ed.) 220pp, illus. $16.00
___Another Copy. New York, 1985 (3rd revised ed.).
$23.00

G11. GALLENCAMP (C.) and JOHNSON (R. E.) (Editors). Maya
Treasures of an Ancient Civilization. 240pp, 82 color
and 156 b/w photographs, 2 maps, cloth. New York,
1985. $48.00
The largest and most comprehensive collection of Mayan
art ever exhibited in North America visited six U.S. and
Canadian museums in 1985-87. In this catalogue of the
collection, 275 wondrous objects--jade, wood, shell,
ceramics, gold, semi-precious stones, ornaments and im-
plements--are illustrated in large, very fine photographs.
Six essays review the culture of the ancient Maya and
Maya iconography, ceramics, sculpture and architecture.
(EAP)

G12. GALLO (Miguel Mujica). Gold in Peru. Meisterwerke der
Goldschmiedekunst aus der Pra-Pnkazeit, dem Inkareich
und der Ubergansra. Mit einer Einfuhrung von Raul
Porras Barrenechea. 300pp, 146 mounted color pls, 4to,
cloth, boxed. Berlin, 1939. $150.00
___Another Copy. Recklinghausen, 1959. The Gold of
Peru: Masterpieces of the Goldsmiths Work of Pre-Incan

and Incan Time and the Colonial Period. 296pp, 144
tipped in color pls.
$135.00
____Another Copy. Recklinghausen, 1967. (German
title). 294pp, 134 full-page color photographs of 326
objects, cloth, text in German.
$97.00
GALVAO (Eduardo). See also BAE Bulletin No. 143.
G13. GALVIN (John) (Editor). Through the Country of the
Comanche Indians in the Fall of the Year 1845. The
Journal of a U.S. Army Expedition Led by Lieutenant
James W. Abert of the Topographical Engineers. 77pp,
index, bibliography, color pls, folio, folding map, lim-
ited to 5,000 copies. John Howell, 1970.
$65.00
G14. GAMBOA (F.). Das Portrait Mexikos. 58pp, 31 full-page
photographs. Vienna, 1968.
$10.00
GANN (Mary). See also BAE Bulletin No. 123.
GANN (Thomas). See also BAE Bulletin Nos. 64 and 123.
G15. GANN (Thomas). Ancient Cities and Modern Tribes. 256pp,
frontis, illus with numerous photographs and figures.
New York, 1926.
$50.00
____Another Copy. London, 1926.
$40.00
____Another Copy. New York, 1929. 48 photo-
graphs.
$50.00
G16. GANN (Thomas and Mary). Archaeological Investigations
in the Corozal District of British Honduras. pp1-66,
figures, 10 photographic pls, bibliography, printed wrap-
pers, offprint Smithsonian Anthropological Papers, Wash-
ington, 1939.
$10.00
G17. GANN (Thomas). Glories of the Maya. 279pp, illus with
photographs. London, 1939.
$50.00
____Another Copy. New York, 1939.
$40.00
G18. GANN (T.) and THOMPSON (J. E.). The History of the
Maya, from the Earliest Times to the Present Day. x,
264pp, 26 pp of photographs and drawings, cloth. New
York, 1931. (1st ed.).
$35.00
____Another Copy. Same.
$35.00
G19. GANN (Thomas). In an Unknown Land. (Belize). 263pp,
illus with photographs, also includes various sites in
Yucatan, original cloth. New York, Scribner's, 1924.
$40.00
____Another Copy. Same.
$25.00
G20. GANN (Thomas). Maya Cities: A Record of Explorations
and Adventure in Middle America. 256pp, 55 illus (most
are photographs), includes Tuluum, Tzibanche, Uaxac-
tun, Tikal, sml tear title page. London, 1927 (1st ed.).
$45.00
____Another New York, 1928.
$50.00
G21. GARCES (Francisco). A Record of Travels in Arizona and
California, 1775-1776. Edited by John Galvin. x, 117pp,
color frontis, 8 pls (2 folding maps), glossary, index,
references, limited to 1250 copies by Lawton Kennedy.
San Francisco, John Howell, 1965.
$75.00

G22. GARCIA (Gregorio). Origen de los Indios del Nuevo
        Mundo E. Indias Occidentales.... (16)ff, 336pp, (40)ff,
        folio. Imprenta de Francisco Martinez Abad, Madrid,
        1729. $850.00
            Sabin: 26567. Maggs Bibliotheca Americana: I:634.
        Medina BHA: IV:2713. The corrected and expanded
        second edition of this famous treatise. Sabin writes that
        it is a "work of vast erudition. All that has ever been
        imagined as to the origin of the Americans, and the man-
        ner in which this New World was peopled, is gathered
        here." The evidence of possible Jewish origins is given
        extended discussion. The book is based on Garcia's
        own experience in the New World, unpublished manu-
        scripts in his possession and indigenous oral and written
        sources. All of the fifth section is composed of "native
        Indian accounts of their origin, and is divided into sec-
        tions which treat separately of the various distinct tribes
        of Mexico and Peru" (Maggs). (WR)
G23. GARCIA-BARCENA (J.). (Coleccion Cientifica, Prehistoria,
        No. 110, INAH, Mexico City, 1982) El Preceramico de
        Aguacatengo, Chiapas, Mexico. 87pp, 21 figures, wrap-
        pers. $10.00
G24. GARCIA GRANDOS (Rafael). Estudio Comparativo de los
        Signos Cronograficos en los Codices Prehispanicos de
        Mexico. (Sobretiro de las Actas de la Primera Sesion,
        Congreso Internacional de Americanistas) pp419-469,
        wrappers. INAH, Mexico, 1939. $30.00
G25. GARCIA ROSELL (Cesar). Diccionario Arqueologico del
        Peru. 406pp, plus illus, wrappers. Soc. Geog. de Lima,
        Lima, 1964. $25.00
GARCIA VALDEZ (Pedro). See BAE Bulletin No. 143.
G26. GARDENER (Lion). Relation of the Pequot Warres, Written
        in 1660 by Lieutenant Lion Gardener. Now First Printed
        From the Original Manuscript. xxxii, 33pp, stiff wrap-
        pers, hand-made paper, limited to 102 copies. Acorn
        Club Publication 4, Hartford, 1901. $50.00
        ____Another Copy. Same. $40.00
G27. GARDNER (Erle Stanley). The Hidden Heart of Baja.
        25pp, photographs, Indian cave paintings. New York,
        1962 (1st ed.) d.j. $10.00
G28. GARFIELD (Viola). Historical Aspects of Tlingit Clans
        in Angoon, Alaska. 15pp, wrappers, reprint from Amer-
        ican Anthropology, Vol. 49, No. 3, 1947. $10.00
G29. GARFIELD (V. E.). Meet the Totem. 54pp, 13 lrg draw-
        ings, wrappers. Sitka, 1951. $10.00
G30. GARFIELD (V. E.). Tsimshian Clan and Society. pp169-
        339, pls, 2 folding maps, glossary, bibliography, wrap-
        pers. University of Washington, 1939 (1st ed.). $35.00
G31. GARFIELD (V. E.) and WINGERT (P. S.). (American
        Ethnological Society Publication No. 18, New York, 1951,
        1st ed.) The Tsimshian: Their Arts and Music. 290pp,
        18 illus, plus 8 pls. $60.00

G32. GARFIELD (Viola E.) and FORREST (Linn A.). The Wolf
and the Raven: Totem Poles at Southeastern Alaska.
151pp, 67 photographs of totem poles. University of
Washington, Seattle, 1948 (1st ed.), d.j. $35.00
___Another Copy. Same. $40.00
___Another Copy. Same. $25.00
___Another Copy. 1961, wrappers. $10.00
G33. GARIBAY K. (Angel M.). La Literature de los Aztecas.
138pp, wrappers. Mexico City, 1964. $15.00
G34. GARLAND (Hamlin). The Book of the American Indian.
6pp, 274pp, 37 pls (4 color), large 8vo, illus by Fred-
eric Remington, owner's inscription. New York & Lon-
don, 1923 (1st ed.), d.j. $250.00
___Another Copy. Same. $135.00
___Another Copy. New York, 1923, later
print. $65.00
___Another Copy. Same. $50.00
G35. GARNER (Van H.). The Broken Ring; The Destruction of
the California Indians. 226pp, illus, index, bibliography,
maps. Tucson, 1982 (1st ed.), d.j. $25.00
___Another Copy. Same. $15.00
G36. GARROW (Patrick H.). The Mattamuskeet Documents: A
Study in Social History. 79pp, charts, maps, wrappers.
Raleigh, NC, 1979 (3rd print.). $10.00
G37. GARST (Shannon). Crazy Horse. Great Warrior of the
Sioux. 260pp, illus, bibliography. Boston, 1950.
                                                    $10.00
G38. GATES (W. E.). (Peabody Museum Papers, Vol. VI, No.
1, 1910) Commentary Upon the Maya-Tzental Perez
Codes, With a Concluding Note Upon the Linguistic
Problem of the Maya Glyphs. 64pp, 2 full-page color
codices, numerous sml drawings in text. $50.00
___Another Copy. Same. $35.00
___Another Copy. Same. $30.00
G39. GATES (William) (Editor). The De La Cruz-Badiano Aztec
Herbal of 1552. Translation and Commentary by Wm.
Gates. xxxii, 144pp, 150 illus, English translation of
text of Codex Barb. Lat. 241. Maya Society, Baltimore,
1939. $95.00
G40. GATES (William). Outline Dictionary of Maya Glyphs with
a Concordance and Analysis of Their Relationships.
Color frontis, wrappers, extracts from Maya Society,
Publication No. 1, John Hopkins Press, Baltimore, 1931.
                                                    $30.00
GATSCHET (Albert S.). See also BAE Bulletin No. 108.
G41. GATSCHET (A. S.). (Peabody Museum Papers, Vol. 1,
No. 2, 1891) The Karankawa Indians, The Coast People
of Texas. 101pp, wrappers. $45.00
___Another Copy. Same. Wrappers missing. $40.00
G42. GATSCHET (A. S.). (Contributions to North American
Ethnology, Vol. II, Washington, 1890. 1891) The

Klamath Indians of Southwestern Oregon (2 Volumes). Vol. I: cvi, 711pp. Vol. II: 711pp. Monumental work that contains a Klamath-English and English-Klamath dictionary, a detailed study of their grammar, a presentation of Klamath texts and an Ethnographical sketch.
$185.00

_____Another Copy. Same. Vol. I only, newly rebound.
$45.00

G43.   GATSCHET (A. S.). (Contributions to North American Ethnology, Vol. II, Part II, 1890) The Klamath Indians of Southwestern Oregon, Dictionary of the Klamath Language. 705pp, original cloth.
$135.00

G44.   GAY (Carlo). Text by. Guerrero: Stone Sculpture From the State of Guerrero. 20pp, 19 photographs. Exhibition catalogue, Finch College Museum of Art, wrappers. New York, 1965.
$50.00

G45.   GAY (Carlo). Mezcala Stone Sculpture: The Human Figure. 39pp, illus with 60 photographs, frontis, wrappers. Museum of Primitive Art, New York, 1967.
$25.00

_____Another Copy. Same.
$17.00

G46.   GAY (Carlo). Xochipala; The Beginnings of Olmec Art. 63pp, square 4to, illus. Princeton, 1974.
$22.00

_____Another Copy. Same.
$20.00

_____Another Copy. Same.
$15.00

G47.   GAY (E. Jane). With the Nez Perces; Alice Fletcher in the Field 1889-92. 188pp, illus, index, map. Lincoln, 1981 (1st ed.), d.j.
$22.00

_____Another Copy. Same.
$20.00

G48.   GAYTON (A. H.) and KROBER (A. L.). (University of California Publications in American Archaeology and Ethnology, Vol. 24, No. 1, 1927) The Uhle Pottery Collections from Nazca. 46pp, 21 pls, 8vo, wrappers.
$30.00

G49.   GAYTON (A. H.). (University of California Anthropological Records, Vol. 10, No. 1, Berkeley, 1948) Yokuts and Western Mono Ethnography. I: Tulare Lake, Southern Valley and Central Foothill Yokuts. 141pp, 1 full-page photographs of Yokut baskets, 14 figures, 1 map.
$57.00

G50.   GAYTON (A. H.). (University of California Anthropological Records, Vol. 10, No. 2, Berkeley, 1948) Yokuts and Western Mono Ethnography. II: Northern Foothill Yokuts and Western Mono. 166pp, 1pp photograph of baskets, 5 figures, 5 maps.
$57.00

GEARING (Fred O.). See also BAE Bulletin No. 180.

G51.   GEARING (Fred). The Face of the Fox: A Book About American Indians, White Men, The Cultural Traditions that Separate Them, and What Can Be Done About Their Estrangement. Chicago, Aldine, 1970, d.j.
$18.00

G52.   GEARING (Fred). (American Anthropological Assn., Memoirs No. 93, Menasha, 1962) Priests and Warriors:

Social Structures for Cherokee Politics in the Eighteenth
Century. 124pp, wrappers. $17.00
___Another Copy. Same. $13.00
___Another Copy. Same. $10.00

G53. GEBHART-SAYER (A.). The Cosmos Encoiled: Indian
Art of the Peruvian Amazon. 32pp, 6pp b/w and 4pp
color photographs, 5pp drawings, 1 map. New York,
1984. $13.00

G54. GEHM (Katherine). Sarah Winnemucca. Most Extraordinary
Woman of the Paiute Nation. 196pp, reading list, photographs, map endpapers, biography of this remarkable
Paiute woman who fought for just treatment of the people
from the government and helped to lessen the problems
of the Bannock War. Phoenix, 1975 (1st ed.), d.j.
$17.00

G55. GEIOGAMAH (Nanay). New Native American Drama. 24pp,
133pp, introduction by Jeffrey Huntsman, photographs.
Three plays, the first collection of plays by an Indian
playwright. Norman, 1980 (1st ed.). $10.00

G56. GEIST (O. W.) and RAINEY (F. G.). (University of
Alaska, Miscellaneous Publications, Vol. II, 1936)
Archaeological excavations at Kukulik, St. Lawrence Is-
land. 410pp, 78 photographs, 45 drawings, 8 maps.
$135.00
___Another Copy. Same. $85.00
___Another Copy. Same. $75.00
___Another Copy. Same. $65.00

GENTRY (Howard Scott). See also BAE Bulletin No. 186.

G57. GENTRY (Howard S.). The Warihio Indians: Of Sonora-
Chihuahua. An Ethnographic Survey. pp63-144, 11
photographs pls, bibliography, printed wrappers, offprint Smithsonian Anthropological Papers, Washington,
1963. $10.00

G58. (GEORGIA). (House of Representatives Document 98, 21:1,
Washington, 1830, 1st print.) Report and Remonstrance
of the Legislature of Georgia, In Relation to the Indian
Tribes Within that State. 13pp, removed. $17.00

G59. (GEORGIA). (House of Representatives Document 200,
27:2, Washington, 1842, 1st print.) Depredations by
Indians and United States Troops in Georgia. 74pp, removed, murders of settlers, burnings by Indians.
$25.00

G60. GERALD (R. E.) et al. (Garland American Indian Ethnohistory Series, 1974) Apache Indians III. 358pp, cloth.
$32.00

G61. GESSNER (Robert). Massacre. A Survey of Today's
American Indian. x, 418pp, 6 pls, much on Sioux, In-
dian Bureau abuses, etc. New York, 1931 (1st ed.).
$25.00
___Another Copy. Same. $12.00

G62. GHEERBRANT (A.). The Incas. xlviii, 432pp, 4 color

and 12 b/w photographs, 23pp drawings, cloth. New
York, 1961. $35.00

G63. (GHOST DANCE). Ghost Dancer in the West: The Sioux
at Pine Ridge and Wounded Knee in 1891. 12pp, 4to,
illus, first separate printing of two articles from the
Illustrated American for 1891, wrappers. Ramona, 1976.
$10.00

G64. GIAGO (Tim). (Nawica Kjici) Notes from Indian Country.
Vol. I. 395pp plus index, bibliography, writings by an
Oglala Sioux for his weekly news column in the Rapid
City Journal, expressing the Indian viewpoint and trying
to correct false views of the Indian. Pierre, 1984 (?)
(1st ed.), d.j. $20.00

G65. GIBBS (George A.). A Dictionary of the Chinook Jargon,
or, Trade Language of Oregon. xiv, 44pp, 18x28.5cm,
wrappers, Chinook was the jargon used by several Northwest tribes and fur traders to facilitate trade. No. 12
of Shea's American Linguistics, New York, Cramoisy, 1863
(1st ed.). $150.00
___Another Copy. Same. $100.00

G66. GIBBS (George). George Gibbs' Journal of Redick McKee's
Expedition Through Northwestern California in 1851.
Edited and Annotations by Robert F. Heizer. 88pp, 4to,
wrappers. Berkeley, 1972. $12.00
Reprints California material from Schoolcraft's "Histori-
cal and Statistical Information Respecting the History,
Condition and Prospects of Indian Tribes of the United
States." (GFH)

G67. GIBBS (George). (Smithsonian Miscellaneous Collections,
No. 160, Washington, 1963) Instructions for Research
Relative to the Ethnology and Philology of America. ii,
33pp, stitched self wrappers. $15.00

G68. GIBBS (George). Notes on the Tinneh or Chepwyan Indians of British and Russian America. Extracted from
Smithsonian Annual Report for 1866. pp304-327, 10 illus,
wrappers. Washington, 1867. $25.00
___Another Copy. Same. $17.00

G69. GIBBS (George). (Contributions to North American Ethnology, Vol. I, Part II, Washington, 1877) Tribes of Western Washington and Northwest Oregon. ix, pp157-361,
cloth, pocket map, edge wr, innerhinges repaired.
$75.00
___Another Copy. Same. Ex-library. $125.00

G70. GIBSON (Arrell M.). The Chickasaws. 297pp plus index,
photographs, maps, bibliography, first full history of
the Chickasaws. Norman, 1971 (1st ed.), d.j. $35.00
___Another Copy. Same. $25.00

G71. GIBSON (A. M.). The Kickapoos: Lords of the Middle
Border. 391pp, bibliography, index, 16 illus, map.
Norman, 1963 (1st ed.), d.j. $30.00
___Another Copy. Same. $25.00

G72. GIDDINGS (J. L.). Ancient Men of the Arctic. 448pp, 152 illus, cloth. New York, 1967. $35.00
___Another Copy. Seattle, 1985, wrappers. $20.00
G73. GIDDINGS (J. L.). Archaeology of Cape Denbigh. 503pp, 73pp photographs, 16 tables, cloth. Providence, 1964. $60.00
The 1948-52 excavations in Alaska fully revealed the three major cultural phases of the Western Arctic. This intensive study fully documents those excavations, what they found and what the finds meant. More than 1,200 artifacts--many carved and made from bone, wood, ivory, stone, bark, slate and grass--are illustrated. (EAP)
G74. GIDDINGS (J. L.). (University of Pennsylvania Museum, Philadelphia, 1952) The Arctic Woodland Culture of the Kobuk River. 143pp, 46 illus, wrappers, covers faded. $25.00
G75. GIDDINGS (J. L.). (University Museum Bulletin Vol. 20, No. 2, 1956) Forest Eskimos, an Ethnographic Sketch of Kobuk River People in the 1880s. 58pp, 15 illus. $12.00
G76. GIDDINGS (J. L.). (Studies of Northern People, No. 1, Alaska, 1961) Kobuk River People. 166pp, illus, wrappers. $20.00
___Another Copy. Same. Ex-library. $12.00
G77. GIDDINGS (Ruth Warner). Yaqui Myths and Legends. 180pp, illus. University of Arizona, Tucson, 1959, d.j. $10.00
___Another Copy. Same. $20.00
___Another Copy. Same. $15.00
___Another Copy. Same. 73pp, wrappers. $15.00
G78. GIDLEY (M.). Kopet: A Documentary Narrative of Chief Joseph's Last Years. 108pp, 4to, illus, map, index. Seattle, 1981 (1st ed.), d.j. $25.00
Combines narrative and documentary material, including previously unpublished items by Joseph himself, with a generous selection of full-page illustrations, many of them photographs never before published.
___Another Copy. Same. $15.00
G79. GIFFEN (Fannie Reed). Oo-Mah-Ha Ta-Wa-Tha (Omaha City). 94pp, cloth, describes the settlement of Omaha and the Omaha tribe of Indians in the 1860's and 1870's and the mission to them where the author grew up. n.p., 1898. $60.00
G80. GIFFEN (Naomi). The Roles of Men and Women in Eskimo Culture. 113pp, bibliography, wrappers. University of Chicago, 1930 (1st ed.). $20.00
G81. GIFFORD (Douglas) and HOGGARTH (Pauline). Carnival and Coca Leaf, Some Traditions of the Quechua Aylla. St. Martins Press, New York, 1976, d.j. $20.00
GIFFORD (E. W.). See also BAE Bulletin No. 97.
G82. GIFFORD (Edward W.). California Indian Nights Entertainments. 323pp, 9 pls, folding map, index, maroon cloth.

Glendale, Arthur H. Clarke, 1930 (1st ed.). $120.00
    Another Copy. Same. $45.00

G83. GIFFORD (Edward Winslow). (University of California
Publications in American Archaeology and Ethnology,
Vol. 22, No. 2, Berkeley, 1926) Californian Anthropometry. pp217-390, pls (photographs of the people), 3
maps, wrappers. $10.00

G84. GIFFORD (Edward Winslow). (University of California
Publications in American Archaeology and Ethnology, Vol.
18, Berkeley, 1922) Californian Kinship Terminologies.
pp1-285, 29 maps, wrappers. $12.00

G85. GIFFORD (E. W.). (University of California Anthropology
Records, Vol. 9, No. 1, Berkeley, 1947) Californian
Shell Artifacts. 132pp, illus with drawings, wrappers.
$25.00
    Another Copy. Same. $25.00
    Another Copy. Same. $39.00

G86. GIFFORD (E. W.). (University of California Anthropological Records, Vol. 14, No. 4, 1955) Central Miwok Ceremonies. 62pp, 1 photograph. $24.00

G87. GIFFORD (E. W.). (University of California Anthropological Records, Vol. 4, No. 1, 1940) Culture Element Distributions: XII Apache Pueblo. 213pp, some underlining, 31 drawings, 4 diagrams, 2 maps. $45.00

G88. GIFFORD (E. W.). (University of California Publications
in American Archaeology and Ethnology, Vol. 11, No. 5,
1916) Dichotomous Social Organization in South Central
California. 6pp. $15.00

GILBERT (William Harlen, Jr.). See also BAE Bulletin No. 133.

G89. GILL (John) (Compiler). Gill's Dictionary of the Chinook
Jargon. 84pp, decorative wrappers, 12mo, includes the
Lord's Prayer and others. Portland, 1909 (15th ed.).
$15.00

G90. GILL (Richard G.). White Water and Black Magic. 369pp,
illus, travels in the upper Amazon and the use of curare
as a medicine, cloth. New York, 1940, d.j. $20.00

G91. GILLES (Albert S., Jr.). Comanche Days. 126pp, memoirs
of an Indian trader in Faxton, Oklahoma, cloth. Dallas,
1974, d.j. $20.00
    Another Copy. Same. $15.00
    Another Copy. Same. $15.00

GILLIN (John). See also BAE Bulletin Nos. 128 and 143.

G92. GILLIN (John). (Peabody Museum Papers Vol. XIV, No.
2, Cambridge, 1936) The Barama River Caribs of British
Guiana. 274pp, illus, wrappers. $35.00

G93. GILLIN (J.). (Smithsonian Institution, Institute of Social
Anthropology, No. 3, 1945) Moche, A Peruvian Coastal
Community. vii, 166pp of text containing 8 figures, map
and 26pp photographs. $45.00
    Another Copy. Same. $15.00

G94. GILLIN (John). The Quichua-speaking Indians of the

Province of Imbabura (Ecuador). pp167-228, 9 photographic pls, bibliography, printed wrappers, offprint
Smithsonian Anthropological Papers, Washington, 1941.
$10.00

G95.   GILLMAN (C.). (Minnesota Historical Society, St. Paul,
1982) Where Two Worlds Meet: The Great Lakes Fur
Trade. 143pp, 212 b/w photographs, maps, 24 color
photographs. $30.00
From 1600 to 1850 Europeans traded their manufactured
goods for Indian furs. The European goods were then
used to make or modify Indian artifacts. The result,
as we see in this stunning exhibition catalogue, was a
wonderful tradition of functional, decorative artifacts by
Great Lakes Indian tribes. Four essays in the catalogue
are accompanied by excellent photographs of artifacts--
pipes, tomahawks, clothing, tools, birch-boxes, glass
beads, etc. (EAP)

G96.   GILLMOR (Frances). Flute of the Smoking Mirror. A Portrait of Nezahualcoyotl, Poet King of the Aztecs. 183pp,
illus, map endpapers. University of New Mexico Press,
1949 (1st ed.), d.j. $22.00
____Another Copy. Same. $30.00

G97.   GILLMOR (F.) and WETHERILL (L. W.). Traders to the
Navahos, the Story of the Wetherills of Kayenta. 265pp,
9pp photographs, cloth. Boston & New York, 1934.
$60.00
____Another Copy. Same. d.j. $35.00
____Another Copy. Boston, 1934, d.j. $15.00

G98.   GILMORE (Kathleen). Cultural Variation on the Texas
Coast: Analysis of an Aboriginal Shell Midden, Wallis-
ville Reservoir, Texas. 108pp, 4to, illus, wrappers.
University of Texas Archaeological Survey, Austin,
1974. $20.00
____Another Copy. Same. $10.00

G99.   GILMORE (M. R.). (University of Texas, Anthropology
Papers Series, Bulletin Vol. 1, No. 5, 1937) An Interesting Vegetal Artifact From the Pecos.... 39pp, illus,
bibliography, 8vo, wrappers, also with other articles.
$10.00

G100.   GILMORE (Melvin R.). Notes on Gynecology and Obstetrics
of the Arikara Tribe of Indians. 12pp, wrappers, offprint of an article from Michigan Academy of Sciences,
Vol. 1, Ramona, 1980. $10.00

GILMORE (Raymond M.). See BAE Bulletin No. 143.

G101.   GILPIN (Laura). The Enduring Navaho. 277pp, 219 b/w
and 22 color photographs, cloth. Austin, 1968, 1980
(5th print.). $50.00
Quite probably the foremost photographer of the
Navaho, Laura Gilpin took most of the photographs between 1950 and 1965 that appear in this volume. Though
there are many photographs of ceremonies and artifacts,

this is really a volume of photographs of the people, the
land on which they have lived and the traditional ceremonies that bind them together. Fine essays accompany
the wonderful photographs in this volume that has, in
the years since it was first published, become a classic.
(EAP)

    Another Copy. Austin, 1968, 256pp, b/w and color
illus, bibliography. $40.00

    Another Copy. Austin, 1969. $50.00

G102.   GILPIN (Laura). The Pueblos: A Camera Chronicle.
124pp, 75 photographs, 2 maps, cloth. New York,
1941. $135.00

G103.   (GIORDA, J. and BANDINI, J.). Lu Tel Kaimintis Kolinzuten Kuitlt Smiimii. Some Narratives from the Holy
Bible, in Kalispel. Compiled by the Missionaries of the
Society of Jesus. 140, 14pp, half morocco, original
wrappers bound in. St. Ignatius, Montana, 1879.
                                                $275.00

    Schoenberg, Jesuit Mission Presses: 6. McMurtie:
113. Pilling: 1557. The second edition of this collection, the first having appeared in 1876. Van Gorp suggests that only 225 copies of each edition were printed.
Pilling only notes this edition. (WR)

G104.   GIORDA (J.) et al. Szmimie-S Jesus Christ. A Catechism
of the Christian Doctrine in the Flat-Head or Kalispel
Language Composed by the Missionaries of the Society
of Jesus. Part 1. 17pp, wrappers, prayers and
Catechism. Jesuit Mission Press, Montana, 1880, (1st
ed.). $95.00

    Another Copy. Same. $75.00

G105.   GIRARD (R.). El Popul-Vuh, Fuente Historia. El Popol-
Vuh como Fundamento de la Historia Maya-Quiche. 461pp,
104 illus, numbered copy. Guatemala City, 1952.
                                                $55.00

G106.   GIRARD (Rafael). Indios Selvaticos de la Amazonia Peruana Mexico. 356pp, illus. Mexico, 1958. $45.00

G107.   GIRARD (Rafael). Los Mayas Eternos. 487pp, 250 photographs, text 94pp with illus. Mexico, 1962. $60.00

G108.   GLADWIN (Harold Sterling). (Gila Pueblo, Medallion Papers No. XXXIII, Globe, 1945, 1st ed.) The Chaco
Branch Excavations at White Mound and in the Red Mesa
Valley. ix, 159pp, 47 pls, 27 figures, stiff printed
wrappers, inscribed and signed by author. $50.00

G109.   GLADWIN (Harold S.). (Southwest Museum Papers, No. 2,
Los Angeles, 1970) Excavations at Casa Grande, Arizona,
February 12-May 1, 1927. 30pp, illus, bibliography,
wrappers, reprint of the 1928 1st ed. $10.00

G110.   GLADWIN (H. S.) et al. (Gila Pueblo, Medallion Papers
No. XXV, XXVI, 1937) Excavations at Snaketown (2
Volumes). Vol. I: "Material Culture." xviii, 305pp,
115 figures, 215pp photographs. Vol. II: "Comparisons

and Theories." xiv, 167pp, 25pp photographs, 8pp
charts, 7pp maps. $250.00

G111. GLADWIN (Harold S.). (Medallion Papers No. XXXVIII,
Globe, AZ, 1948 1st ed.) Excavations at Snaketown,
Vol. IV. Review and Conclusions. 267pp, photographs,
drawings, maps, bibliography, wrappers. $40.00

G112. GLADWIN (Harold S.). A History of the Ancient Southwest. xx, 383pp, illus, maps, decorative cloth, from
A.D. 400 to A.D. 1400. Wallace II: 41. Portland,
1957 (1st ed.), d.j. $30.00

G113. GLADWIN (H. S.). (Medallion Papers No. XXXVI, Globe,
1946, privately printed for Gila Pueblo) Tree Ring
Analysis. Problems of Dating II. The Tusayan Ruin.
21pp, 14 figures, wrappers. $30.00
___Another Copy. Same. $12.00

G114. GLADWIN (Harold S.). (Medallion Paper No. XXXVII,
Globe, AZ, n.d. (c.1946) 1st ed.). Tree-Ring Analysis. Tree-Rings and Droughts. 36pp, 1 pl, bibliography,
wrappers. $12.00

G115. GLADWIN (W. & H. S.). A Method for Designation of
Cultures and Their Variations. 30pp, 11 fold-out charts,
Gila Pueblo, 1934. $28.00

G116. GLANDER (W. P.) et al. (Southern Methodist University
Archaeology Research Program, 1973, 1st ed.) Archaeology Resources Milehigh. 32pp, pls, maps, bibliography,
wrappers. $10.00

G117. GLASER (Lynn). Indians or Jews? An Introduction to a
Reprint of Manasseh Ben Israel's The Hope of Israel
(1652). 160pp, illus, map, attempts to show that the
American Indians are the descendants of the lost tribes.
Gilroy, 1973 (1st ed.). $20.00
___Another Copy. Same. Ex-library, rebound. $12.00

G118. GLASSLEY (Ray H.). Pacific Northwest Indian Wars.
266pp, photographs, bibliography, wars of 1848-1879.
Portland, 1953 (1st ed.), d.j. $40.00
___Another Copy. Same. $25.00
___Another Copy. Same. $20.00
___Another Copy, 1972, 258pp, endpaper maps. $12.00

G119. GLEASON (Duncan). Sketches and Paintings from Mexico.
With Commentaries by Dorothy Gleason. 42pp, portrait,
color frontis, 20 full-page b/w and color illus, inscribed
by Dorothy Gleason, hand bound by Robert Cowan,
limited to 500 copies. Los Angeles, 1963, (1st ed.).
$27.00

G120. GLOB (P. V.). Eskimo Settlements in Northeast Greenland. (Danish Expedition to greenland 1926-39). 40pp,
9 maps. Meddelesser om Greenland, bd. 144, Nr. 6,
Copenhagen, 1946. $28.00

G121. GLUBOK (S.). The Art of the Plains Indians. 55pp, 58
photographs, cloth cover, juvenile. New York, 1975.
$15.00

G122.   GLUBOK (S.). The Art of the Southeastern Indians.
        50pp, 59 photographs, cloth, juvenile. New York,
        1978. $18.00
G123.   GLUBOK (S.). The Art of the Southwest Indians. 50pp,
        58 photographs, cloth, juvenile. New York, 1971.
                                                           $17.00
G124.   GLUBOK (S.). The Art of the Woodland Indians. 50pp,
        69 photographs, cloth, juvenile. New York, 1976.
                                                           $15.00
GODDARD (Pliny Earl). See also BAE Bulletin No. 40, Pt. 1.
G125.   GODDARD (Pliny Earl). (University of California, Publi-
        cations in American Archaeology and Ethnology, Vol.
        24, No. 5, 1929) The Bear River Dialect of Athapascan.
        32pp, wrappers. $22.00
G126.   GODDARD (P. E.). (American Museum of Natural History,
        Anthropological Papers, Vol. X, Part IV, New York,
        1916) The Beaver Indians. 90pp, wrappers. $35.00
        ___Another Copy. Same. $30.00
        ___Another Copy. Same. $15.00
G127.   GODDARD (P. E.). (American Museum of Natural History,
        Anthropological Papers, Vol. X, Parts V and VI, 1917)
        Beaver Texts and Beaver Dialect. pp295-546 (some un-
        cut), 191 figures. $99.00
        ___Another Copy. Same. $27.00
G128.   GODDARD (P. E.). (University of California Publications
        in American Archaeology and Ethnology, Vol. 10, No.
        7, 1914) Chilula Texts. 90pp, wrappers. $35.00
G129.   GODDARD (P. E.). (American Museum of Natural History,
        Anthropological Papers, Vol. XI, Part V, 1914) Dancing
        Societies of the Sarsi Indians. 10pp, wrappers. $20.00
G130.   GODDARD (P. E.). (University of California Publications
        in American Archaeology and Ethnology, Vol. 11, No.
        1, 1912) Elements of the Kato Language. 176pp, illus,
        wrappers. $45.00
G131.   GODDARD (P. E.). (University of California Publications
        in American Archaeology and Ethnology, Vol. 17, No.
        4, 1924) Habitat of the Pitch Indians, a Wailaki Divi-
        sion. 8pp, wrappers. $18.00
G132.   GODDARD (P. E.). (University of California Publications
        in American Archaeology and Ethnology, Vol. 1, No. 2,
        1904) Hupa Texts. 286pp, wrappers. $60.00
        ___Another Copy. Same. $35.00
G133.   GODDARD (P. E.). (American Museum of Natural History,
        Handbook Series No. 10, 1924) Indians of the North-
        west Coast. 175pp, 145 drawings, 37 photographs,
        cloth. $57.00
        ___Another Copy. New York, 1934. $25.00
        ___Another Copy. 1945. $45.00
G134.   GODDARD (P. E.). (American Museum of Natural History,
        Handbook Series No. 2, 1913) Indians of the South-
        west. 191pp, 71 illus, mostly photographs, cloth,
        slipcase. $57.00

      ____Another Copy. Same. $35.00
      ____Another Copy. 1927. $35.00
      ____Another Copy. 1931. $30.00
      ____Another Copy. Same. $25.00
      ____Another Copy. New York, 1975. $12.00

G135. GODDARD (P. E.). (University of California Publications in American Archaeology and Ethnology, Vol. 5, No. 3, 1909) Kato Texts. 173pp, illus, wrappers. $35.00

G136. GODDARD (P. E.). (University of California Publications in American Archaeology and Ethnology, Vol. 1, No. 1, 1903) Life and Culture of the Hupa. 140pp, 30pp photographs, 10 figures, 1 map. $125.00
      ____Another Copy. Same. $100.00

G137. GODDARD (P. E.). (University of California Publications in American Archaeology and Ethnology, Vol. 3, 1905) The Morphology of the Hupa Language. 344pp, wrappers. $45.00
      ____Another Copy. Same. $75.00
      ____Another Copy. Same. Ex-library. $35.00

G138. GODDARD (P. E.). (American Museum of Natural History, Anthropological Papers, Vol. XXIV, Parts I & II, 1918) Myths and Tales from the San Carlos Apache. 139pp, cloth. $49.00
      ____Another Copy. Same. Part I only. $35.00

G139. GODDARD (P. E.). (American Museum of Natural History, Anthropological Papers, Vol. XXIV, Part II, 1919) Myths and Tales from the White Mountain Apache. 52pp, wrappers. $25.00

G140. GODDARD (P. E.). (American Museum of Natural History, Anthropological Papers Vol. XXXIV, Part I, 1933) Navajo Texts. 179pp, wrappers. $45.00

G141. GODDARD (P. E.). (University of California Publications in American Archaeology and Ethnology, Vol. 10, No. 6, 1914) Notes on the Chilula Indians of Northwestern California. 23pp, illus, wrappers. $32.00

G142. GODDARD (P. E.). (University of California Publications in American Archaeology and Ethnology, Vol. 5, No. 1, 1907) The Phonology of the Hupa Language. Part I, The Individual Sounds. 19pp, illus wrappers. $17.00

G143. GODDARD (P. E.). (University of California Publications in American Archaeology and Ethnology, Vol. 23, No. 6, 1928) Pitch Accent in Hupa. 5pp, wrappers. $10.00

G144. GODDARD (P. E.). (American Museum of Natural History, Guide Leaflet Series No. 73, 1928) Pottery of the Southwestern Indians. 32pp, 35 photographs, 2 drawings. $30.00
      ____Another Copy. 1931. $24.00
      ____Another Copy. Ramona, 1971. $10.00

G145. GODDARD (P. E.). (American Museum of Natural History, Anthropological Papers, Vol. XXIV, Part III, 1919) San Carlos Apache Texts. 220pp, wrappers. $37.00

G146. GODDARD (P. E.). (University of California Publications in American Archaeology and Ethnology, Vol. 11, No. 3, 1915) Sarsi Texts. 88pp, wrappers. $45.00

G147. GODDARD (P. E.). (American Museum of Natural History, Anthropological Papers, Vol. X, Parts I and II, 1912) Texts and Analysis of Cold Lake Dialect, Chipewyan. 170pp, wrappers. $37.00

G148. GODDARD (P. E.). (American Museum of Natural History, Anthropological Papers, Vol. XXIV, Part IV, 1920) White Mountain Apache Texts. 156pp, wrappers. $37.00

G149. GODFREY (Carlos E.). The Lenape Indians. Their Origin and Migrations to the Delaware. An Address Before the Trenton Historical Society, Nov. 20, 1919. 16pp, printed wrappers. Trenton, 1919. $12.00

G150. GOETZ (Delia) and MORLEY (Sylvanus G.). Popol Vuh, the Sacred Book of the Ancient Quiche Maya. 256pp, index, map facsimiles, bibliography, English version from the Spanish translation by Adrian Recinos. Norman, 1953 (1st print.), d.j. $20.00
_____ Another Copy. 1961 (5th print.), d.j. $10.00

G151. GOETZ (H.). The Inuit Print. 268pp, 155 b/w and 12 color illus, all half or full-page, Ottawa, 1977. $25.00
_____ Another Copy. cloth. $45.00

G152. GOETZMANN (Wm. H.) and SLOAN (Kay). Looking Far North. The Harriman Expedition to Alaska 1899. 236pp plus index, photographs, bibliography, notes. New York, 1982 (1st ed.), d.j. $25.00

GOGGIN (John M.). See also BAE Bulletin No. 180.

G153. GOGGIN (J. M.) et al. (Yale University Publications in Anthropology, Nos. 41, 42, 1949) Excavations on Upper Matecumbe Key, Florida. also: Excavations in Southeast Florida. 109pp, 8pp of photographs, 8 figures, 4 tables; 154pp, 16pp photographs, 8 figures. The pair. $45.00

G154. GOGGIN (J. M.). (Yale University Publications in Anthropology, No. 47, 1952) Space and Time Perspective in Northern St. Johns Archaeology, Florida. 147pp, 9 figures, 12pp photographs. $35.00

G155. GOLD (Douglas). A Schoolmaster with the Blackfeet Indians. 287pp, author taught school on the Blackfoot Reservation from 1914 to 1934 and kept a record of events in the Indian country and of his experiences with the Blackfeet. Caldwell, 1963 (1st ed.), d.j. $25.00
_____ Another Copy. Same. $20.00

GOLDEN (Bernard). See also BAE Bulletin No. 189.

G156. GOLDEN (Gertrude). Red Moon Called Me: Memoirs of an Indian Service Schoolteacher. (Oregon). 211pp. San Antonio, 1954 (1st ed.), d.j. $15.00

G157. GOLDENWEISER (Alexander). Early Civilization: An Introduction to Anthropology. 428pp, includes Eskimo, Tlingit, Haida, Iroquois, chapters on Religion and Magic, newly rebound. New York, 1922 (1st ed.). $60.00

GOLDFRANK (Esther S.). See also BAE Bulletin No. 181.
G158. GOLDFRANK (Esther). (Smithsonian Contributions to
Anthropology, Vol. 5, 1967) The Artist of "Isleta
Paintings" in Pueblo Society. 227pp, cloth. $20.00
___Another Copy. Same. $15.00
___Another Copy. Same. wrappers. $10.00
G159. GOLDFRANK (E. S.). (American Ethnology Society,
Monograph 8, New York, 1945, 1st ed.) Changing Con-
figurations in the Social Organization of a Blackfoot
Tribe During the Reserve Period (The Blood of Alberta,
Canada). 73pp, illus, bibliography. also: Monograph
9: "Observations on Northern Blackfoot Kinship" by
L. M. Hanks, Jr., and Jane Richardson (31pp). $15.00
G160. GOLDFRANK (E.S.). (American Anthropological Assn.
Memoirs, No. 33, 1927) The Social and Ceremonial Or-
ganization of Cochiti. 129pp, 7 fold-out charts. $37.00
___Another Copy. Same. $35.00
___Another Copy. Same. $25.00
GOLDMAN (Irving). See also BAE Bulletin No. 143.
G161. GOLDMAN (Irving). The Mouth of Heaven: An Introduc-
tion to Kwakiutl Religious Thought. xvi, 265pp, illus,
map endpapers, bibliography, index. New York, 1975
(1st ed.) d.j. $15.00
G162. GOLDSCHMIDT (Walter) (Editor). (American Anthropologi-
cal Assn. Memoirs, No. 89, 1959) The Anthropology of
Franz Boas. 165pp, wrappers. $20.00
G163. GOLDSCHMIDT (W.). (University of California Publications
in American Archaeology and Ethnology, Vol. 42, No.
4, 1951) Monlaki Ethnography. 148pp, 3 figures, 1
map. $37.00
G164. GOMEZ (Zapata). Mascaras Mayas: Veinte Dubujos de
Piezas Arcaicas. iv, 20pls, wrappers, Con un Commen-
tario de Antonio Mediz Bolio. Mexico, 1934. $30.00
G165. GONCALVES DE LIMA (Oswaldo). El Maguey y El Pulque
en los Codices Mexicanos. Edition of 5,000 copies, 72
figures in text, bibliography. Mexico City, 1978, d.j.
                                                     $35.00
G166. GONZALEZ DE HOLGUIN (Diego). Vocabulario de la Lengua General de Todo el Peru Llamada Lengua Qquichua,
O del Inca. Corregido y Renovada Conforme A la Pro-
piedad Cortesana del Cuzco ... Libro Segundo del
Vocabulario de la Lengua Qquichua General del Peru,
Que Comienca por el Romance. 4; 375; 332 leaves.
Repairs to the outer margins of the first two leaves,
not affecting text. Some shaving of headlines. The last
two leaves containing the Privilegios of the press, are
not present in this copy. These were evidently an
afterthought, since the colophon on the last leaf de-
clares this work finished, August 8, 1608. Modern dark
green morocco, fillet borders, slipcased. (Ciudad de los
Reyes, Francisco del Canto, 1608). $7,500.00

Medina (Lima): 42. An exceedingly rare early Lima imprint. This compilation, the first comprehensive Quicha-Spanish and Spanish-Quicha dictionary, has the added distinction, at over 700 leaves, of being the largest work printed in South America to that time. With the grammar, printed the year before, Gonzalez de Holguin produced a lasting monument in Indian languages. (WR)

G167. GONZALEZ R. (Luis). Etnologia y Mison en la Primeria Alta 1715-1740. 357pp, wrappers. Mexico, 1977.
$20.00

G168. GONZALEZ RUL (Francisco). (Instituto Nacional Antropologia e Historia) La Litica en Tlatelolco. 35pp, plus 8 pls, wrappers. Mexico City, 1979. $15.00

G169. GOODALL (Edward A.). Sketches of American Indian Tribes, 1841-1843. Introduction and Notes by M. N. Menezes. 63 color pls, 6 monochrome pls, map, bibliography. London, 1977 (1st ed.). $30.00
___Another Copy. Same. $15.00
___Another Copy. Same. $15.00

G170. GOODCHILD (P.). Survival Skills of the North American Indians. 234pp, 200 figures (approx), cloth. Chicago, 1984. $30.00

G171. GOODFELLOW (John C.). The Totem Poles of Stanley Park. 44pp, pls, wrappers. Vancouver, BC, n.d. (c.1928) (1st ed.). $20.00

G172. GOODMAN (F. S.). The Embroidery of Mexico and Guatemala. 81pp, 34 color and 63 b/w photographs, 27 drawings, cloth. New York, 1976. $30.00

G173. GOODMAN (James B.). The Navajo Atlas; Environments, Resources, People, and History of the Dine Bikeyah. 109pp, 4to, illus, contains 48 maps, several charts and explanatory text in 6 sections. Norman 1982 (1st ed.), d.j. $25.00
___Another Copy. Same. $20.00

G174. GOODMAN (J. T.). The Archaic Maya Inscriptions. Appendix from: Biologia Centrali-Mericana (Archaeology). 149pp, illus, numerous glyphs, tables, folio (10" x 13"), original blue wrappers, 1897. $150.00

G175. GOODRICH (S. G.). Lives of Celebrated Indians. 315pp, frontis, illus, cloth, Boston, 1855. $25.00
___Another Copy. Same. part of cabinet library. $20.00
___Another Copy. Boston, 1868. $40.00

G176. GOODWIN (G.). The Social Organization of the Western Apache. xx, 701pp, 10pp photographs, 4 figures, 7 maps, cloth. Chicago, 1942. $57.00
___Another Copy. Same. $85.00
___Another Copy. Same. $70.00
___Another Copy. Same. $42.00

G177. GOODWIN (William B.). The Ruins of Great Ireland In

New England. 424pp, pls, figures, maps, bibliography, examination of ancient stone works. Boston, 1946, (1st ed.). $45.00

G178. GOOSSEN (Irvy W.). Navajo Made Easier. A Course in Conversational Navajo. 271pp. Flagstaff, 1979 (3rd print, revised). $10.00

G179. GORDON (G. B.) and MASON (J. A.). Examples of Maya Pottery in the Museum and Other Collections. (In Two Parts). Part I: 25 pls with 22 in color. Part II: 25 pls with 21 in color. Plate list with each part. University Museum, Philadelphia, 1925-1928 (Lacks part three which was published in 1943), plates are 18" x 15" in size in wrappers in original worn portfolio with ties, color types were printed in London. $575.00

Important and now rare early pictorial surveys of Maya vase painting. Folio plates of hand-drawn and watercolor reproductions of Maya polychrome and molded vases from important institutional collections. Plates are printed on heavy laid paper. (CY)

G180. GORDON (George Byron). In the Alaskan Wilderness. 246pp, maps (2 folding), illus, t.e.g. Smith: 3680. Wickersham: 2043. Philadelphia, 1917 (1st ed.). $50.00

G181. GORDON (Suzanne). Black Mesa: The Angel of Death. 105pp, illus, problems of present-day Hopi Life. New York, 1973. $20.00

G182. GOTTFREDSON (Peter) (Editor, Compiler). History of the Indian Depredations in Utah. 352pp, illus, signed by author, a 20pp supplement by author and a full-page TLS of author to E. A. Brininstool tipped in, covers from 1847 to the 1860s. Salt Lake City, 1919 (1st ed.). $125.00

G183. GOWANLOCK (Theresa) and DELANEY (T.). Two Months in the Camp of Big Bear, the Life and Adventures of.... 136pp, numerous illus in text, cloth. Parkdale, 1885. $425.00

The two women were captured at the time of the Frog Lake massacre in North Saskatchewan in 1885; they were sole survivors. They were rescued after two harrowing months. Although in two parts, there is but one pagination. One of the last Indian captivities, chronologically. Graff: 605. Ayer, Supplement: 60. Peel: 602. (WR)

G184. GRABURN (Nelson). (Department of Northern Affairs, Ottawa, 1964). Taqagmiut Eskimo Kinship Terminology. 222pp, stapled wrappers, tape repair to spine, slight ink marks in table of contents. $15.00

G185. GRAHAM (I.). (Middle American Research, Tulane University Publication 33, 1967) Archaeological Explorations in El Peten, Guatemala. 107pp, 81 figures. $40.00

G186. GRAHAM (Isabella H.). Lion Gardiner, A Tale of the

Pequot War. 122pp, frontis, 16mo, cloth, privately
printed, n.p., 1918. $10.00

G187. GRAHAM (J. A.) (Editor). Ancient Mesoamerica, Selected
Readings. xiv, 366pp, 128 figures. Palo Alto, 1981
(2d ed.). $20.00

G188. GRANADOS y GALVEZ (J. J.). Tardes Americanas: Gob-
ierno Gentil y Catolico: Breve y Particular Noticia de
Toda la Historia Indiana: Sucesos, Casos Notables, y
Cosas Ignoradas, Desde la Entrada de la Gran Nacion
Tulteca a Esta Tierra de Anahuac, Hasta los Presentes
Tiempos. Trabajadas por un Indio, y un Espanol. 36
leaves, 540pp, 3 engraved plates. Spanish calf, gilt,
slight wear to hinges, else very good. Palau: 108426.
JCB III: 2467. Mexico, 1778. $2,000.00
According to Palau, this work is very rare, and al-
most all of the known examples are imperfect. This
copy is complete, with some slight wear to the title-page.
The work is particularly valuable as it includes material
on now lost Testerian and Tarascan manuscripts. There
is also much on the pre-Conquest history of the Toltecs
and tribes in Sonora and the area of Gran Chichimeca.
This copy belonged to the noted ethnologist Frederick
Starr, with his bookplate. (WR)

G189. GRANBERG (Wilbur). People of the Maguey: The Otomi
Indians of Mexico. Illus. New York, 1970, d.j.
$10.00

GRANGE (Roger T., Jr.). See also BAE Bulletin No. 169.

G190. GRANGE (Roger T.). (Nebraska Historical Society Publications in Anthropology, No. 3, 1968, 1st ed.). Pawnee
and Lower Loup Pottery. 235pp, 36 full-page pls, 4to,
original wrappers. $20.00

G191. GRANT (Mrs. Anne). Memoirs of an American Lady:
With Sketches of Manners and Scenery in America, as
They Existed Previous to the Revolution. 344pp, 12mo,
includes an account of the Five Nations, Mohawk mode
of life. New York, D. & C. Bruce, 1809. $150.00

G192. GRANT (B. C.). Taos Indians. 127pp, 27 illus, signed
by author, wrappers. Taos, 1925 (1st ed.) Rader:
1646. $125.00
_____Another Copy. Same, without inscription. $85.00
_____Another Copy. Same. $65.00
_____Another Copy. Same. $50.00
_____Another Copy. Same. $45.00
_____Another Copy. Same. $40.00
_____Another Copy. Glorieta, 1976, cloth. $20.00

G193. GRANT (Campbell). Rock Art of the American Indian.
178pp, 16 pls in color and 150 b/w photographic pls.
New York, 1967. $35.00
_____Another Copy. Same. d.j. $22.00
_____Another Copy. Promontory Press Reprint. $25.00

G194. GRANT (Campbell). (Baja California Travel Series, No.

33, Los Angeles, 1974) Rock Art of Baja California: With Notes on the Pictographs of Baja California by Leon Diguet (1895). 146pp, illus, index, folding map, illus include 9 full color pls. (1st ed.). $35.00

G195. GRANT (C.) et al. (Maturango Museum Publication No. 4, China Lake, 1968) Rock Drawings of the Coso Range, Inyo County, California. xii, 145pp, 106 photographs, 155 drawings, 7 maps, wrappers. $20.00

G196. GRANT (C.) and HEIZER (R. F.). The Rock Paintings of the Chumash, A Study of a California Indian Culture. 199pp, 31 color photographs, 114 b/w photographs and drawings, 6 maps, cloth. Berkeley, 1965. $50.00

G197. GRAVES (William W.). The First Protestant Osage Missions 1820-1837. 272pp, bibliography, index. Oswego, 1949 (1st ed.). $30.00
___Another Copy. Same. $17.00

G198. GRAVES (W. W.). Life and Letters of Rev. Father John Schoenmakers, S.J., Apostle to the Osages. 144pp, index, photographs, Catholic mission in Kansas in the 1840s. Rader: 1655. Adams Guns: 861. Parsons, KS, 1928 (1st ed.). $15.00

G199. GRAVIER (R. P. Jacques). Relation on Journal de Voyage du ... en 1700 depuis le page des Illinois jasqu'a l'embouchereda Mississippi. 68pp, bound in cloth, ex-library but no external marks, limited to 100 copies, signed by publisher John G. Shea, one of the earliest accounts of Kaskaskia. Howes: G-328. New York, 1859 (1st ed.). $75.00

G200. GRAYBILL (Florence Curtis). Edward Sheriff Curtis: Visions of a Vanishing Race. 303pp, lrg 4to, illus, lrg 13" x 10" volume containing over 175 photographs, many of them reproduced for the first time and made directly from Curtis's own glass-plate negatives and original prints. $30.00

G201. GRAYMONT (Barbara). The Iroquois in the American Revolution. 359pp, map frontis, illus, cloth. Syracuse University Press, 1972 (1st ed.), d.j. $25.00

G202. GREEN (Charles R.). Sac and Fox Indians in Kansas. Mokohoko's Stubbornness. Some History of the Band of Indians Who Stayed Behind their Tribe 16 Years as given by Pioneers. 20 unnumbered pp, 1 photograph, wrappers. Rader: 1667. Olathe, KS, 1914 (1st ed.). $10.00

G203. GREEN (D. F.) and LOWE (G. W.). (New World Archaeological Foundation, Brigham Young University Paper No. 20, 1967) Altamira and Padre Piedra, Early Preclassic Sites in Chiapas, Mexico. 133pp, 97 figures. $12.00

G204. GREEN (Samuel A., MD.). Groton During the Indian Wars. 214pp, cloth. Groton, Mass, 1883. $12.00

G205. GREENE (A. C.). The Last Captive. The Lives of Herman Lehmann, Who was Taken By the Indians As A Boy

From His Home in Texas, 161pp, illus from photographs, bibliography, printed on tan paper, special bound and boxed, signed by author, limited to 250 copies. Austin, 1972 (1st ed.). $100.00

____ Another Copy. Encino Press, 1st trade ed. $25.00

____ Another Copy. Same. $15.00

G206. GREENE (Alma). Tales of the Mohawks. 186pp, drawings by R. G. Miller, myths, legends and stories told by clan mother of the Mohawks. Canada, 1975, (1st ed.), d.j. $12.00

G207. GREENGO (R. E.). (Memoirs, Society for American Archaeology, Vol. 30, No. 2, 1964) Issaquena: An Archaeological Phase in the Yazoo Basin of the Lower Mississippi Valley. viii, 130pp, 44 illus, 85 tables. $17.00

____ Another Copy. Same. $10.00

G208. GREENMAN (E.). (University of Michigan Museum, Anthropology Contribution No. 11, 1951) Old Birch Island Cemetery and the Early historic Trade Route, Georgian Bay, Ontario. viii, 69pp, 7 figures, 26pp photographs. $23.00

G209. GREENMAN (E.). (University of Michigan Museum of Anthropology, Occasional Contributions No. 6, 1937) The Younge Site: an Archaeological record from Michigan. xii, 172pp, 9 figures, 10 maps, 33pp photographs. $34.00

G210. GREGG (Elinor D.). The Indians and the Nurse. 173pp. Norman, 1965 (1st ed.), d.j. $15.00

G211. GREGORIE (Anne King). Notes on the Sewee Indians and Indian Remains, Christ Church Parish, Charleston County, South Carolina. 23pp, illus, wrappers. Charleston Museum, 1925. $20.00

G212. GREGORY (Jack) and STRICKLAND (Rennard). Sam Houston with the Cherokees 1829-1833. 182pp plus index, photographs, drawings, maps. Austin and London, 1967 (1st ed.), d.j. $17.00

G213. GREY (Herman). Tales from the Mohaves. Foreword by Alice Marriott. 96pp. Norman, 1980 (1st ed.). $12.00

G214. GREY OWL. The Men of the Last Frontier. 253pp, photographs, drawings, the life of the Ojibway. London, 1935 (5th ed.). $10.00

G215. GRIDLEY (M. E.). Indian Legends of American Scenes. 127pp, 13 full-page color illus, cloth. Chicago, 1939. $27.00

G216. GRIDLEY (Marion). Indians of Today. 232pp, illus. Chicago, 1960 (1st ed.). $20.00

G217. GRIEDER (Terrence). The Art and Archaeology of Pashash. 268pp, 203 illus, richest pre-Columbian burial ever scientifically excavated (approx 500 A.D.). University of Texas, 1978. $45.00

____ Another Copy. Same. d.j. $25.00

____ Another Copy. Same. $22.00

G218. GRIEWE (W. P.). Primitives Sudamerika. 251pp, 5 full-page photographs, 22 drawings, map, cloth. Cincinnati, 1893. $95.00

GRIFFIN (James B.). See also BAE Bulletin No. 133.

G219. GRIFFIN (J. B.). (Indiana Historical Society Prehistory Research Series, Vol. 2:3, Indianapolis, 1941) Additional Hopewell Material from Illinois. pp165-223, illus, pls, wrappers. $20.00

G220. GRIFFIN (J. B.). Archaeology of the Eastern United States. 392pp, plus 195 figures and maps, 4to. Chicago, 1952 (1st ed.). $85.00
____Another Copy. Same. $78.00
____Another Copy. Same. $50.00
____Another Copy. Chicago, 1972. $75.00

G221. GRIFFIN (J. B.) et al. (University of Michigan, Museum of Anthropology Memoirs No. 2, 1970) The Burial Complexes of the Knight and Norton Mounds in Illinois and Michigan. 198pp of text containing 41 figures, plus 177pp of photographs. $47.00

G222. GRIFFIN (J. B.). The Fort Ancient Aspect, its Cultural and Chronological Position in Mississippi Valley Archaeology. xv, 392pp, 18pp figures, 10 maps, additional 314pp with 157pp of photographs of artifacts from Fort Ancient Site, cloth. Ann Arbor, 1943. $77.00
____Another Copy. Same. $65.00

G223. GRIFFIN (J. B.) (Editor). (University of Michigan Museum of Anthropology Papers No. 17, 1961) Lake Superior Copper and the Indians: Miscellaneous Studies of Great Lakes Prehistory. ix, 189pp, 21 figures, 5 maps, 33pp of illus, bds. $22.00
____Another Copy. Same. wrappers. $20.00

G224. GRIFFIN (John W.). The Florida Indian and His Neighbors. Papers delivered at Rollins College, 1949. 168pp, wrappers. Winter Park, 1949. $35.00

G225. GRIFFIN (J. W.). (National Park Service, Publications in Archaeology No. 13, 1974) Investigations in Russell Cave, Russell Cave National Monument, Alabama. xiv, 127pp, 61 figures. $18.00

G226. GRIFFIN (J. W.). (Florida Anthropological Society Publications No. 2, 1950) The Safety Harbor Site, Pinellas County, Florida. 42pp, 3pp photographs. $12.00

G227. GRIFFIS (Joseph K.). Tahan. Out of Savagery into Civilization. An Autobiography. 263pp, photographs. New York, 1915 (1st ed.). $40.00

G228. GRIFFITH (A. Kinney). The First Hundred Years of Nino Cochise. (As Told to Author.) 364pp, illus with photographs. New York, 1971 (1st ed.). $35.00

G229. GRIFFITH (A. Kinney). Mickey Free, Manhunter. 239pp, illus, frontis portrait, cloth, story of Mickey Free, an Indian Scout in the Arizona Territory during the 1870s and 1880s, who died in 1913. Caldwell, ID, 1969 (1st ed.), d.j. $25.00

G230. GRIFFITH (J. S.). Legacy of Conquest, The Arts of
Northwest Mexico. 32pp, 13 full-page photographs,
exhibition catalogue of Taylor Museum, Colorado
Springs, 1967. $10.00

G231. GRIFFITH (W. J.). (Middle American Research Institution,
Vol. II, No. 3, 1954) The Hasinai Indians of East
Texas, as Seen By Europeans, 1687-1772. pp 43-167,
2 maps. $28.00

G232. GRIM (John A.). The Shaman: Patterns of Siberian and
Ojibway Healing. 258pp, illus. Norman, 1983. $20.00

G233. GRIMM (William C.). Indian Harvests. 127pp, illus by
Ronald Himler, food plants from Nature. New York,
1973 (1st ed.). $12.00

G234. GRINDE (Donald A.). The Iroquois and the Founding of
the American Nation. 175pp. California, 1977, d.j.
                                                  $15.00

G235. GRINNELL (George Bird). Blackfoot Lodge Tales. 310pp,
index, Blackfoot tribal history, customs, organization
and stories. London, 1893 (1st English ed.). $75.00
____Another Copy. New York, 1908, cloth. $25.00
____Another Copy. New York, 1920. $35.00

G236. GRINNELL (G. B.). The Cheyenne Indians, Their History
and Ways of Life (2 Volumes). pp 358; 450, illus with
photographs by Elizabeth C. Grinnell and Mrs. J. E.
Tuell, map, inscribed by author in both volumes, TLS
from author laid in. Yale University Press, 1923 (1st
ed.). $150.00
____Another Copy. Same, no inscription. $225.00
____Another Copy. New Haven, 1924 (2d print.)
358pp, 430pp. $150.00
____Another Copy. New York, 1962, xix, 359pp, vi,
430pp, 25pp photographs. $135.00

G237. GRINNELL (G. B.). The Fighting Cheyennes. 431pp,
11 maps, inscribed by author, typed note from author
laid in. New York, 1915 (1st ed.). $100.00
____Another Copy. Norman, 1956, 435pp plus index.
                                                  $17.00
____Another Copy. Norman, 1963 (3rd print.), 453pp,
15 illus. $35.00
____Another Copy. Same. $15.00
____Another Copy. University of Oklahoma, 1966,
454pp, illus, maps, d.j. $20.00

G238. GRINNELL (G. B.). The North American Indians of Today. 185pp, illus with photographs by F. A. Rinehart,
a total of 55 full-page portraits, original decorated cloth,
4to. London, 1900, (1st ed.). $250.00
____Another Copy. Same. $150.00
____Another Copy. Chicago, 1900. $100.00

G239. GRINNELL (G. B.). (From the Writings of) Pawnee,
Blackfoot and Cheyenne. 301pp, history and folklore
of the Plains Indians. New York, 1961 (1st ed.), d.j.
                                                  $20.00

___Another Copy. Same. $17.00

G240. GRINNELL (G. B.). Pawnee Hero Stories and Folk-Tales,
with Notes on the Origin, Customs, and Character of
the Pawnee People. xxi, 417pp, illus with drawings,
original cloth. New York, 1889. $75.00
___Another Copy. Same. small hole in cloth at edge
of spine. $55.00
___Another Copy. Same. $60.00
___Another Copy. New York, 1893, 446pp. $85.00
___Another Copy. New York, 1912, 446pp, frontis,
cloth. $50.00

G241. GRINNELL (G. B.). (American Anthropological Society
Vol. 7, 1905) Some Cheyenne Plant Medicines. pp37-
43, in a binder. $10.00

G242. GRINNELL (G. B.). The Story of the Indians. 268pp
plus index, photographs. Rader: 1699. Larned: 646.
New York, 1895 (1st ed.). $45.00
___Another Copy. New York, 1917, 230pp. $35.00

G243. GRINNELL (G. B.). Two Great Scouts and Their Pawnee
Battalion: Frank J. and Luther H. North; pioneers of
the great West, 1862-1865, and their defense of Union
Pacific. 298pp, folding map, index. Cleveland, 1928.
$105.00

G244. GRINNELL (G. B.). When Buffalo Ran. 114pp, frontis,
photographic illus, decorative cloth-covered bds. New
Haven, 1920 (1st print.). $95.00
___Another Copy. Same. $40.00
___Another Copy. New Haven, 1932 (4th print.)
$17.00

G245. GROSVENOR (Abbie J.). Winged Moccasins: A Tale of
The Adventurous Mound-Builders. x, 291pp, illus,
juvenile. New York, 1933 (1st ed.). $12.00

G246. GROTH-KIMBALL (I.) and FEUCHTWANGER (F.). The
Art of Ancient Mexico. illus, some in color. New York,
1954 (2d print.), d.j. $45.00

G247. GROVE (David). (Studies in Pre-Columbian Art and
Archaeology, No. 6, Washington, 1970) The Olmec
Paintings of Oxtotitlan Cave, Guerrero, Mexico. 36pp,
color frontis, illus, wrappers. $15.00

G248. GROVE (D. C.). Chalcatzingo, Excavations on the Olmec
Frontier. 184pp, 15 color and 82 b/w photographs,
44 figures, cloth. New York, 1984. $40.00
The artifacts found at Chalcatzingo, particularly the
monumental rock carvings--similar in many ways to the
art of the Olmec, had made this site's relationship to the
Olmec centers a mystery until the Chalcatzingo excavations in the 1970s. This fascinating volume delineates
the results of the excavations and demonstrates the intimate relationship of Olmec and Chalcatzingo artists.
Some of the photographs were taken at the site; a number of the illustrated objects have not been published
before. (EAP)

G249. GROVES (G. I.). Famous American Indians. 272pp, index. Chicago, 1943. $25.00

G250. GRUBB (W. Barbrooke). A Church in the Wilds. 287pp,
23 illus, 2 maps, decorated cloth. New York, 1914
(1st ed.). $45.00

G251. GRUMET (Robert S.). Native American Place Names in
New York City. 79pp, evaluation of ethnohistoric docu-
mentary evidence for Indian occupation of New York
City, wrappers. New York, 1981. $15.00

G252. GUAMAN POMA DE ALAYA (F.). Nueva Coronica y Buen
Gobierno (Codex Peruvien Illustre). 1,178 illus pages
and 28pp introduction, cloth. Travaux et Memoirs de
l'Institute D'Ethnologie, XXIII, Paris, 1936, 1972
(reprint). $85.00

G253. (GUATEMALA). Excavations at Seibal, Dept. of Peten.
Includes I: Major Architecture and Caches by A. L.
Smith; and II: Analysis of Fine Paste Ceramics by
Sabloff, et al. 343pp, illus, wrappers. Peabody Mu-
seum, 1982. $45.00

G254. GUBSER (Nicholas J.). The Nunamint Eskimos. Hunters
of Caribou. 363pp plus index, maps, bibliography.
New Haven, 1965 (1st ed.). $25.00

G255. GUEMPLE (Lee) (Editor). (Supplement, Proceedings of
the American Ethnological Society, 1971) Alliance in
Eskimo Society. 131pp, 4to, wrappers. $20.00
_____Another Copy. Same. $15.00

GUERNSEY (Samuel J.). See also BAE Bulletin No. 65.

G256. GUERNSEY (S. J.). (Peabody Museum Papers Vol. 12,
No. 1, 1931) Explorations in Northeastern Arizona.
121pp, 66pp photographs, 31 drawings. $50.00

G257. GUERNSEY (S. J.). (Peabody Museum Papers Vol. 12,
No. 2, 1931) Notes on the Archaeology of the Kaibito
and Rainbow Plateaus in Arizona. 27pp, 5pp photographs, 1 site map. $25.00

G258. GUILLEMIN (Jeanne). Urban Renegades. The Cultural
Strategy of American Indian. 329pp plus index, a review of the history of the Mimmac and their adaption
to present urban life. New York, 1975, d.j. $15.00

G259. GUITERAS-HOLMES (C.). Perils of the Soul: The World
Views of Tzotzil Indians. 371pp. Glencoe, 1961.
                                                       $25.00
_____Another Copy. Same. $25.00

GULICK (John). See BAE Bulletin No. 180.

GULLBERG (Jonas E.). See BAE Bulletin No. 170.

G260. GUMERMAN (G. J.). A View from Black Mesa, The Changing Face of Archaeology. xiii, 184pp, 44 figures, cloth.
Tucson, 1984. $30.00

G261. GUNN (John M.). Schat-Chen: History, Traditions and
Narratives of the Queres Indians of Laguna and Acoma.
223pp, drawings by Queres Indians, pls, decorative
cloth, native tales and myths. Although part of this

material was published in 1904, this is the first with
added material and in this form. Albuquerque, 1917,
(1st thus.). $125.00
G262. GUNN (S. W. A.). Haida Totems in Wood and Argillite.
24pp, illus, wrapper. Vancouver, Smith, 1967. $10.00
G263. GUNNERSON (D. A.). The Jicarilla Apaches: A Study in
Survival. 326pp, Illinois, 1974. $15.00
GUNNERSON (James H.). See also BAE Bulletin No. 173.
G264. GUNNERSON (J. H.). (Peabody Museum Papers Vol. 59,
No. 2, 1969) The Fremont Culture, A Study of Culture
Dynamics on the Northern Anasazi Frontier. xv, 221pp,
19 figures, 32 photographs. $42.00
G265. GUNTHER (Erna). Art in the Life of the Northwest Coast
Indians. 284pp, 74 b/w and 10 color photographs.
Portland, 1966. $20.00
____Another Copy. Same. $15.00
____Another Copy. Same. $12.00
G266. GUNTHER (E.). (University of Washington Publications
in Anthropology, Vol. 10, No. 1, 1945) Ethnobotany
of Western Washington. 61pp, map, ways in which more
than 150 plants served as food and medicine and for
clothing and other objects. $15.00
____Another Copy. Seattle, 1973. 71pp, illus, bibliog-
raphy, map, 4to, index. $17.00
____Another Copy. Same. no map. $10.00
G267. GUNTHER (E.). (University of Washington Publications
in Anthropology, Vol. 2, No. 5, Seattle, 1928) A
Further Analysis of the First Salmon Ceremony. 44pp,
1 figure, 1 fold-out table. $30.00
G268. GUNTHER (E.). Indian Life on the Northwest Coast of
North America. 291pp, 63 illus of artifacts, cloth.
Chicago & London, 1972. $30.00
____Another Copy. Chicago, 1972. $15.00
G269. GUNTHER (E.). (University of Washington Publications
in Anthropology, Vol. 4, No. 1, 1930) The Indians of
Puget Sound. 83pp, 3 figures, 2pp photographs.
                                                $38.00
G270. GUNTHER (E.). (University of Washington Publications
in Anthropology, Vol. 1, No. 5, 1927) Klallam Ethnog-
raphy. 138pp, 1 figure. $48.00
____Another Copy. Same. $37.00
G271. GUNTHER (E.). (University of Washington Publications
in Anthropology, Vol. 1, No. 4, 1925) Klallam Folk
Tales. 57pp, wrappers. $35.00
____Another Copy. Same. $24.00
G272. GUNTHER (E.). Northwest Coast Indian Art. 101pp, over
75 illus, wrappers, exhibition catalogue. Seattle World's
Fair, 1962. $35.00
____Another Copy. Same. $28.00
____Another Copy. Same. $15.00
G273. GUNTHER (E.). The Permanent Collection, Volume One.

"Northwest and Eskimo Art." 64pp, 150 photographs, 1 map. Bellingham, 1975. $10.00

G274. GUTHE (A. K.). (Rochester Museum of Arts and Sciences, Research Records No. 11, 1958) The Late Prehistoric Occupation in Southwestern New York: An Interpretive Analysis. v, 100pp, 32pp photographs, 2 figures. $12.00

G275. GUTHE (C. E.). Peabody Museum Papers, Vol. VI, No. II, 1921. A Possible Solution of the Number Series on Pages 51 to 58 of the Dresden Codex. 31pp, fold-out illus of Dresden Codex pages 51-58. $25.00

G276. GUTHE (Carle E.). Pueblo Pottery Making: A Study at the Village of San Ildefonso. viii, 89pp plus 35 pls, 11 figures, cloth, portrait frontis (Maria Martinez). Rader: 1714. Campbell, p. 135. Swadesh: 573. Saunders: 1650. New Haven, 1925 (1st ed.). $250.00

G277. GUTIERREZ SOLANA (Nelly) and HAMILTON (Susan). Las Esculturas en Terracota de el Zapotal, Veracruz. 251pp, illus, wrappers. Mexico, 1977. $35.00

G278. GUZMAN (V.) and MERDADER (Y.). Bibliografia de Codices, Mapas y Lienzos del Mexico Prehispanico y Colonial. (2 Volumes) 470pp, 2 fold-out charts. Mexico City, 1979. $22.00

-H-

HAAG (William G.). See also BAE Bulletin No. 129.

HAAS (Mary R.). See also BAE Bulletin No. 180.

H1. HABEL (S.). (Smithsonian Contributions to Knowledge, No. 269, Washington, 1878) The Sculptures of Santa Lucia Cosumalwhuapa in Guatemala, With an Account of Travels in Central America and on the West Coast of South America. 90pp, 8 pls (albertypes), one pl repaired, rebound in 1/2 leather, marbled endpapers, edges. $150.00

H2. HABER (Grace Stevenson). With Pipe and Tomahawk. The Story of Logan, the Mingo Chief. 126pp, photograph, illus, bibliography. New York, 1958 (1st ed.). $10.00

H3. HABERLAND (H.) Onnervogel und Raubwal, Indianisch Kunst der Nortwestkuste Nordamerikas, (Thunderbird and Killer Whale, Indian Art of the Northwest Coast of North America). 292pp, 280 b/w and 16 color photographs. Hamburg, 1979. $40.00

What probably was the most important exhibition of Northwest Coast art ever to be mounted on the European continent was held in 1979 in Hamburg. Many objects, previously unpublished, were drawn from museums throughout Europe, U.S. and Canada. This exceptional catalogue contains not only great photographs of classic pieces, but has photographs of contemporary Northwest Coast objects done in a traditional manner by modern day master carvers-craftsmen. Text in German. (EAP)

H4. HABERLAND (W.). The Art of North America. 256pp, 95 b/w and 60 color illus, cloth. Baden-Baden, 1964, 1968. $25.00

H5. HABERLAND (W.). Das Gaben Sie Uns, Indianer Und Eskimo Ais Erfinder Und Entdecker. (They Gave Them To Us, Indians and Eskimos as Inventors and Discoverers). 62pp, 8pp of photographs, 23 figures. Exhibition catalogue, Hamburg Museum fur Volkerkunde, 1975. $10.00

H6. HABERLY (Lloyd). Pursuit of the Horizon: A Life of George Catlin. xiii, 239pp, pls. First Catlin biography. New York, 1948 (1st ed.) tear, some wear to d.j.
$20.00
____Another Copy. Same. $15.00

H7. HACK (J. T.). (Peabody Papers, Vol. XXXV, No. 1, 1942) The Changing Physical Environment of the Hopi Indians of Arizona. xxii, 85pp, 54 figures, 12pp photographs. $35.00
____Another Copy. Same. Wrappers. $35.00

H8. HACK (J. T.). (Peabody Museum Papers, Vol. 35, No. 2, 1942) Prehistoric Coal Mining in the Jeddito Valley, Arizona. 24pp, 5 pls, 4to, wrappers. $30.00
____Another Copy. Same. $17.00
____Another Copy. Same. $16.00

H9. HACKETT (Charles W.). Coronado Cuarto Centennial Publications, Vols. VIII and IX, Albuquerque, 1942, (1st ed.). Revolt of the Pueblo Indians of New Mexico and Otermin's Attempted Reconquest 1680-1682 (2 Volumes). ccx, 262pp; xx, 430pp, translations of original documents by Charmion Clair Shelby. $150.00
____Another Copy. Albuquerque, 1970. Map, limited to 1000 copies, cloth, slight wear to top edge of d.j.
$100.00
____Another Copy. Same. $100.00
____Another Copy. Same. d.j. $75.00

H10. HAEBERLIN (H. K.). (American Anthropological Assn., Memoirs, Vol. III, No. 1, 1916) The Idea of Fertilization in the Culture of the Pueblo Indians. 55pp, wrappers.
$35.00

H11. HAEBERLIN (H.) and GUNTHER (E.). (University of Washington Publications in Anthropology, Vol. IV, No. 1, Seattle, 1930, 1952) The Indians of Puget Sound. 88pp, 2pp of photographs, 3 figures, wrappers. $20.00
____Another Copy. 1971 (8th print.) $12.00

H12. HAFEN (LeRoy R.). The Indians of Colorado. 52pp, illus with photographs, line drawings and facsimiles, wrappers. Denver, 1952. $10.00

H13. HAGAN (William T.). Indian Police and Judges. Experiments in Acculturation and Control. 183pp plus index and photographs, bibliography. Adams Guns: 889. New Haven, 1966 (1st ed.) d.j. $12.00

H14. HAGAN (William T.). The Sac and Fox Indians. 276pp plus index, illus, two maps, bibliography, review copy. A comprehensive study with emphasis on the period from 1804 to present. One of two bindings, with top edge stained orange. Norman, 1958 (1st ed.) d.j. $17.00
___Another Copy. Same. Top edge stained yellow, d.j. $17.00
___Another Copy. Norman, 1980, d.j. $20.00

H15. HAGEMANN (Elizabeth Compton). Navaho Trading Days. 388pp, index, illus with 318 photographs taken by the author in the 1920's and 30's. University of New Mexico, 1966, d.j. $30.00

H16. HAIG-THOMAS (David). Tracks in the Snow. x, 303pp, photographic pls, 8vo, maps, cloth. Oxford University Press, New York, 1939, d.j. $25.00

H17. HAIL (B. A.). Hau, Kola! The Plains Indian Collection of the Haffenreffer Museum of Anthropology. 256pp, 355 photographs and drawings, including 16pp of color photographs. Providence, 1980. $40.00
About half of the Museum's Plains holdings (mostly late 19th-early 20th Century) are illustrated and described in this catalogue of one of the most important Plains Indian collection extant. Fine illustrations, good essays on Plains art and excellent, elaborate descriptions of each object. (EAP)

H18. HAILE (Father B.). (Bolingen Series LIII) Beautyway-- A Navajo Ceremonial. Myth Recorded and Translated by the Author with Variant Myth Recorded by Maud Oakes. Sandpaintings Recorded by L. Armer, F. Newcomb and M. Oakes, edited with Commentaries by L. C. Wyman. xii, 218pp, 7 text figures, 3 charts and maps, 16 silk-screened pls, 83pp pamphlet in rear pocket, original 1/2 cloth. New York, 1957. $125.00
___Another Copy. Same. $75.00

H19. HAILE (Father Berard) et al. Emergence Myth According to the Hanelthnayhe of Upward-Reaching Rite. 13 serigraph color pls by Louie Ewing, small stain on frnt endpaper. Museum of Navajo Ceremonial Art, Santa Fe, 1949, d.j. $100.00

H20. HAILE (Fr. B.). An Ethnologic Dictionary of the Navaho Language. 109 illus, cloth. St. Michaels, 1910, 1968. $59.00

H21. HAILE (Fr. B.). Head and Face Masks in Navajo Ceremonialism. 136pp, 3pp photographs of masks, 14pp of

colored lithographs of masks, 4 figures, cloth, #140 of
500 copies. Laid in are four Christmas cards signed by
the author, the official formal announcement of his diamond jubilee, a newsletter about his stroke and hospital-
ization in Santa Fe, a newspaper report of the celebration
of his jubilee at the hospital. St. Michaels Press, 1947
(1st ed.). $275.00
___Another Copy. Same. #473 of 500 copies. $100.00
___Another Copy. Same. $125.00
___Another Copy. Same. d.j. $100.00
H22. HAILE (Fr. B.). Learning Navaho.
    Vol. 1: 184pp, Boston, 1959. $35.00
    Vol. 3: 166pp, St. Michaels, 1947. $45.00
    Vol. 4: 296pp, St. Michaels, 1948. $45.00
    ___Another Copy. All four volumes. Vols. 1 and 2 are
    bound together as are Vols. 3 and 4. Cloth covers. St.
    Michaels, 1971. $95.00
H23. HAILE (Berard). Legend of the Ghostway Ritual In the
    Male Branch of Shootingway (Part One). Suckingway, Its
    Legend and Practice (Part Two). xviiii, 372pp, two
    folding color pls, inscribed and signed by the author,
    printed in both Navaho and English, stiff printed wrap-
    pers. Laid in is the last Christmas card signed by the
    author, a newsletter from the Church about his death and
    a newsletter signed by a nephew about his last days....
    St. Michaels, 1950 (1st ed.). $110.00
H24. HAILE (Fr. B.). (American Tribal Religions, Vol. 2, Flag-
    staff, 1978, 1st ed.) Love-magic and Butterfly People.
    172pp, wrappers, printed in both Navaho and English.
                                                $14.00
H25. HAILE (Fr. B.). A Manual of Navaho Grammar. xi, 324pp.
    One of the most important publications on Navaho Linguis-
    tics. St. Michaels, 1926. $95.00
H26. HAILE (Fr. B.). The Navaho Fire Dance or Corral Dance:
    A Brief Account of its Practice and Meaning. 4pp, 57pp,
    illus by Jean Margerite, Paul Scales and Bruno Butz, stiff
    pictorial wrappers. Some wrinkling on four pp. St.
    Michaels, 1946 (1st ed.). $35.00
    ___Another Copy. Same. Wrappers. $35.00
    ___Another Copy. Same. $30.00
H27. HAILE (Fr. B.). Navaho Sacrificial Figurines. 100pp,
    illus, inscribed and signed by author, stiff printed wrap-
    pers. Printed in both Navaho and English. Chicago,
    1947. $75.00
    ___Another Copy. Same. $47.00
H28. HAILE (Fr. B.). The Navaho War Dance: A Brief Narra-
    tive of its Meaning and Practice. 50pp, 9 illus. St.
    Michaels, 1946. $30.00
    ___Another Copy. Same. Stiff pictorial wrappers.
                                                $30.00
    ___Another Copy. Same. $20.00

H29.   HAILE (Fr. B.). (Yale University Publications in Anthro-
       pology, No. 17, New Haven, 1938, 1st ed.) Origin
       Legend of the Navaho Enemy Way: Text and Transla-
       tion. 320pp, 2 pls, text figures, printed wrappers, in-
       scribed by author. Laid in is a thank you note signed
       by the author. $185.00
            Saunders: 976. Kluckhohn: p.34. "The most ex-
       tensive Navaho text, scrupulously recorded with a wealth
       of linguistic commentary."
H30.   HAILE (Fr. B.). Origin Legend of the Navaho Flintway:
       Text and Translation. xi, 319pp, inscribed and signed
       by the author, stiff printed wrappers. Saunders: 4893.
       Chicago, 1943 (1st ed.). $150.00
H31.   HAILE (Fr. B.). Prayer Stick Cutting In A Five Night
       Navaho Ceremonial of the Male Branch of Shootingway.
       xvi, 229pp, 4 drawings, 7 photographs, 9 fold-out color
       pls, another 14pp text. Chicago, 1947. $70.00
            ___Another Copy. Same. Inscribed and signed by au-
       thor, with tipped in color photograph of author, signed
       Christmas card and Jubilee card and a newspaper article
       about author's death, stiff printed wrappers. $125.00
H32.   HAILE (Fr. B.). Starlore Among the Navaho. 43pp ex-
       cluding pls, 13 pls in color (3 folding), inscribed by
       author, printed in both Navaho and English with star
       charts, stiff printed wrappers, Santa Fe, Museum of
       Ceremonial Art, 1947 (1st ed.). $110.00
H33.   HAILE (Fr. B.). (LUCKERT, Karl W., Editor). (American
       Tribal Religions, Vol. 7, Lincoln, 1981, 1st ed.) Upward
       Moving and Emergence Way. 238pp, drawings, wrappers.
       The Gishin Biye Version. English text only. $12.00
H34.   HAILE (Fr. B.). (LUCKERT, Karl W., Editor). (American
       Tribal Religions, Vol. 5, Flagstaff, 1979. 1st ed.)
       Waterway. A Navajo Ceremonial Myth told by Black Mus-
       tache Circle. 152pp, photographs of sandpaintings,
       printed in both English and Navaho, wrappers. A
       gradually vanishing ceremony now usually confined to the
       cutting of prayer sticks. $13.00
H35.   HAILE (Fr. B.). (LUCKERT, Karl W., Editor). (American
       Tribal Religions, Vol. 6, Lincoln, 1981, 1st ed.) Women
       Versus Men. A Conflict of Navajo Emergence. 118pp,
       wrappers, printed in Navaho and English. $10.00
H36.   HAINES (Elijah M.). The American Indian (Uh-Nish-In-Na-
       Ba). The Whole Subject Complete in One Volume. 821pp,
       many illus, maps, glossary of Indian names, lrge 8vo.
       Chicago, Mas-Sin-Na-Gan Co., 1888 (1st ed.). $90.00
            ___Another Copy. Same. Decorated cloth. $80.00
            ___Another Copy. Same. Full leather, t.e.g. $100.00
            ___Another Copy. Same. 3/4 leather, rebacked in cloth
       with part of leather backstrip laid down. $50.00
H37.   HAINES (Francis). The Buffalo. The True Story of Ameri-
       can Bison and Their Hunters from Prehistoric Time to

the Present. 242pp, index, illus. New York, 1970 (1st
ed.), d.j. $20.00

H38. HAINES (Francis). The Nez Perces, Tribesmen of the
Columbia Plateau. xvii, 326pp, 16 pls, 3 maps, bibliog-
raphy, index, essay, pictorial cloth. Norman, 1955
(1st ed.), d.j. $45.00
___Another Copy. Same. Sunned d.j. $50.00
___Another Copy. Same. $50.00
___Another Copy. Same. Ex-library. $25.00
___Another Copy. Norman, 1972. 365pp, frontis, illus,
bibliographical essay, index, cloth, d.j. $25.00

H39. HAINES (Francis). Red Eagles of the Northwest. The
Story of Chief Joseph and his people. 258pp plus index,
frontis, map endpapers. Smith: 3964. Portland, OR,
1939 (1st ed.) in original fragile d.j. a bit chipped.
                                                            $65.00

H40. HAINES (Francis). Where did the Plains Indians Get Their
Horses? Printed wrappers. Offprint. Inscribed to historian Herbert O. Brayer. n.p., 1938. $20.00

H41. HAIRY SHIRT (Leroy). Lakota Woonspe Wowapi. 202pp,
illus, presents the non-Lakota speaking student with a
systematic introduction to speaking, reading and writing
in Lakota language. Aberdeen, SD, 1973. $35.00

H42. (HAISLA INDIANS). (University of California Anthropology
Records, Vol. 2, No. 5, Berkeley, 1940) The Social Organization of the Haisla of British Columbia. pp169-220,
wrappers. $20.00

HALBERT, Henry S. See also BAE Bulletin No. 46.

HALE, Edward E. See also BAE Bulletin No. 25.

H43. HALE (J. P.). History and Mystery of the Kanawah Valley.
18pp, pl, original wrappers. The discovery of an early
wooden carving. West Virginia Historical and Antiquarian
Society, 1897. $10.00

H44. HALE (J. P.). Some Local Archaeology. 14pp, sketch,
wrappers. Small sticker on frnt wrap. Opening of mound
and examination of ancient stone works at 20-Mile Creek.
West Virginia Historical and Antiquarian Society, 1898.
                                                            $12.00

H45. HALKETT (John). Historical Notes Respecting the Indians
of North America. 408pp, errata, deluxe leather, rebacked. London, Archibald, Constable, 1825 (1st ed.).
                                                           $375.00
        Field: 633. Halkett, son-in-law of Lord Selkirk,
founder of the Red River Settlement, traveled in Canada
in 1822 and made extensive notes on the Indians and attempts to civilize them.

H46. HALL (Charles Francis). Arctic Researches and Life Among
the Esquimaux, Being the Narrative of an Expedition in
Search of Sir John Franklin, in the Years 1860, 1861 and
1862. xxviii, 595pp, folding map, 100 illus, original

cloth. New York, Harper & Bros., 1865 (1st ed.).

$100.00

_____Another Copy. New York, 1866. $75.00

H47. HALL (Edwin S., Jr.) et al. Northwest Coast Indian Graphics, an Introduction to Silk Screen Prints. 144pp, 94 b/w and 16 color drawings, cloth. Seattle, 1981.

$45.00

_____Another Copy. Same. d.j. $25.00

H48. HALL (E. T., Jr.). (Museum of Northern Arizona, Bulletin 20, Flagstaff, 1942) Archaeological Survey of Walhalla Glades. 32pp, photographs, graphs, maps, bibliography, wrappers. $10.00

H49. HALL (Edward Twitchell, Jr.). (Columbia Studies in Archaeology and Ethnology, Vol. 2, Part 1, New York, 1944) Early Stockaded Settlements in the Governador, New Mexico. A Marginal Anasazi Development from Basket Maker III to Pueblo I Times. 94pp, 37 figures, wrappers.

$40.00

_____Another Copy. Same. $35.00

H50. HALL (Robert L.). The Archaeology of Carcajou Point. With an Interpretation of the Development of Oneota Culture in Wisconsin. Vol. 1. 191pp plus index, references. Madison, 1962 (1st ed.), d.j. $12.00

_____Another Copy. Vol. 2, 148pp, drawings, photographs, tables, maps, stiff wrappers, spiral binding. $10.00

H51. HALL (W. S.). The Red Indian. Currier & Ives Prints No. 2. 5 double-column pp plus tissue guards with titles and 8 full-color reproductions of Currier & Ives Indian scenes which are tipped in. Some chipping of paper over bds spine. London, 1931 (1st ed.). $15.00

_____Another Copy. London & New York, 1931. $35.00

H52. HALLE (Louis J.). River of Ruins. (Down the Usumacinta, the Peten Area of Mexico and Guatemala). 334pp, 20 photographs, inscribed. New York, 1941 (1st ed.), d.j. $40.00

_____Another Copy. Same. $10.00

H53. HAMILTON (Charles) (Editor). Cry of the Thunderbird. 274pp plus index, drawings, map, bibliography. Indians relating Indian experiences. New York, 1950 (1st print.) chips to d.j. $15.00

H54. HAMILTON (Henry W.). (Missouri Archaeologist, Vol. 14, Columbia, 1952) The Spiro Mound. 276pp, 152 full-page pls. Pipes, textiles, pottery, points, etc., at the great Mound-Builder site. $30.00

H55. HAMMER (O.) and D'ANDREA (J.) (Editors). Treasures of Mexico from the Mexican National Museums. 206pp, 194 b/w and 30 color photographs. cloth. Los Angeles, 1978. $16.00

H56. HAMMOND (N.). Corozo Project, British Museum. 92pp of text and 90pp of photographs, drawings, maps, charts. Interim Report for Center of Latin American Studies, University of Cambridge, 1973. $22.00

H57. HAMMOND (N.) and WILLEY (G. R.). Maya Archaeology
      and Ethnohistory. viii, 292pp (14 papers), 69 figures,
      cloth. Austin, 1979. $40.00
      ___Another Copy. Same. $30.00
      ___Another Copy. Same. $30.00
H58. HAMMOND (N.). Meso-American Archaeology: New Ap-
      proaches. 474pp, illus. Austin, 1974. $25.00
H59. HAMY (E. T.). Descripcion, Historia y Exposicion de
      Codice Borbonico por Francisco del Paso y Troncoso Con
      un Comentario Explicativo. (Facsimile of the Codex pub-
      lished in Paris in 1899) (2 Volumes) Vol. I: Text.
      429pp. Vol. II: 38 color plates (Accordian folded),
      folio (16" x 16"), decorated cloth, leather spines, Aztec
      Codex: Original in Bourbon Palace, Paris, hence the name.
      Mexico, 1980. $250.00
H60. (Handbook of Middle American Indians.) Supplement:
      Vol. I. (Archaeology). Edited by J. A. Sabloff. 463pp,
      illus, 14 different studies. Austin, 1981. $55.00
H61. HANDY (Edward). Zuni Tales. Reprinted from Journal of
      American Folklore, Vol. 31, No. 122, 1918. pp 451-471,
      wrappers. $10.00
H62. HANKE (Lewis). Aristotle and the American Indians. A
      Study in Race Prejudice in the Modern World. 160pp,
      plus index, appendices, illus. How the early Spanish
      treatment of the Indians evolved. Bartolome de las Casas
      against the views of Juan Gines de Sepulveda, who sup-
      ported the Aristotelean view that some men are born to
      slavery. Chicago, 1959 (1st ed.), d.j. $15.00
H63. HANNA (Warren L.). The Life and Times of James Willard
      Schultz (Apikino). 382pp, illus with photographs, por-
      trait. Norman, 1986, d.j. $25.00
      ___Another Copy. Same. $20.00
H64. HANNUM (Alberta). Paint The Wind. 206pp, 8 color pls,
      bds, illus by Beatien Yazz. A Story of a Navaho with
      color reproductions of paintings by a Navaho artist.
      Wallace: XIV 124. New York, 1958 (1st ed.), d.j.
                                                    $25.00
      ___Another Copy. Same. $10.00
H65. HANS (Fred M.). The Great Sioux Nation. 586pp, illus,
      index. Minneapolis, 1964, limited reprint ed., light wear
      to d.j. $20.00
H66. HANSON (James Austin). Metal Weapons, Tools and Orna-
      ments of the Teton Dakota Indians. 118pp, illus, index.
      Lincoln, 1975 (1st ed.). $30.00
      ___Another Copy. Same. d.j. $16.00
      ___Another Copy. Same. $15.00
H67. HAPGOOD (C. H.). Mystery in Acambaro, An Account of
      the Ceramic Collection of the Late Waldemar Julsrud, in
      Acambaro, GTO, Mexico. 43pp, 56 lrge photographs.
      Winchester, 1973. $18.00
H68. HARDIE (J. A.). (House of Representatives Executive

Document No. 286, 43:1, Washington, 1874, 1st print.)
Dakota Indian War Claims of 1862. 143pp, removed.
History of wars, listing of soldiers. $30.00

H69. HARDIN (Margaret Ann). Gifts of Mother Earth; Ceramics
in the Zuni Tradition. 51pp, b/w and color photographs,
bibliography, wrappers. Phoenix, 1983 (1st ed.).
$12.00

H70. HARDING (A. D.) and BOLLING (P.). Bibliography of
Articles and Papers on North American Indian Art.
363pp, bound in later wrappers. Indian Arts and Crafts
Board, Washington, n.d. $40.00
___Another Copy. Washington, n.d. (c.1940) $15.00
___Another Copy. New York, 1969, cloth. $30.00
___Another Copy. Same. $30.00
___Another Copy. Same. $20.00
___Another Copy. Same. $25.00
___Another Copy. Same. $25.00

H71. HARDOY (Jorge E.). Pre-Columbian Cities. xxxvi,
602pp, maps, plans, views, 4to. New York, 1973.
$25.00
___Another Copy. Same. (1st American ed.) $25.00
___Another Copy. Same. d.j. $40.00
___Another Copy. Same. $40.00

H72. HARDY (Arnulfo). Palenque: Pasado y Presente (Chiapas). 96pp, 16 photographs, wrappers. $10.00

H73. HARDY (M. E.). Little Ta-Wish: Indian Legends from
Geyserland. Frontis, 154pp, illus with photographs and
drawings. New York, 1914 (1st ed.). $20.00

H74. HARE (Lloyd C. M.). Thomas Mayhew Patriarch to the
Indians (1593-1682).... 225pp plus index, illus, maps.
One of the early colonizers of Martha's Vineyard and
Nantucket, missionary to the Indians. New York, 1932
(1st ed.), d.j. $17.00

H75. HARGRAVE (Lyndon Lane). Report on Archaeological
Reconnaissance in the Rainbow Plateau Area of Northern
Arizona and Southern Utah. 56pp, 4to, illus, maps,
bibliography, wrappers. Berkeley, 1935. $15.00

H76. HARGRETT (Lester). The Gilcrease-Hargrett Catalogue
of Imprints. 400pp, illus, index. Norman, 1972 (1st
ed.). $30.00
Lists hundreds of printed items in the Gilcrease Institute Library with brief descriptions of each item.
Most of the items listed deal with the Five Civilized Tribes.

H77. HARMON (Daniel W.). A Journal of Voyages and Travels
in the Interior of North America. 432pp, half-title, portrait, map, no errata slip, rebound in leather. Andover,
Flagg and Gould, 1820 (1st ed.). $275.00
Howes: H-205. Streeter: 3692. Field: 656. Important, very scarce, early account of Indians, with an
extensive vocabulary of the Cree language.
___Another Copy. New York, Barnes, 1903. xxiii,
382pp, frontis, folding map. $40.00

H78. HARMON (George Dewey). Sixty Years of Indian Affairs. Political, Economic and Diplomatic. 1789-1850. 414pp plus index, bibliography. Chapel Hill, 1941 (1st ed.). $20.00

H79. HARNER (Michael). The Jivaro: People of the Sacred Falls. 233pp, 24 pls. New York, 1972 (1st ed.), d.j. $25.00

H80. HARNER (M. J.) and ELSASSER (A. B.). Art of the Northwest Coast. 112pp, 87 photographs, map. Lowie Museum, Berkeley, 1965, wrappers. $15.00

H81. HARNEY (Wm. S.). (Senate Executive Document 130, 34:1, Washington, 1856, 1st print.) Council With The Sioux Indians at Fort Pierre with Nine Tribes of Sioux Indians. 39pp, removed. $50.00
Meetings with Sioux leaders after the Sioux massacre of Lt. J. L. Grattan and his 29 men in 1854, and the Army response in raids on the Sioux carried out in 1855. Gen. Harney calls for renegade Indians to be brought to Army justice.

H82. HARP (Elmer, Jr.). (Arctic Institute of North America Technical Paper No. 8, Montreal, 1961) The Archaeology of the Lower and Middle Thelon, Northwest Territories. 74pp, pls, maps, bibliography, wrappers, inscribed. $10.00

H83. HARPER (J. Russell). Paul Kane's Frontier. xviii, 350pp, b/w and color illus, color frontis, gilt cloth, includes "Wanderings of an Artist among the Indians of North America" by Paul Kane. Fort Worth, 1971 (1st ed.) d.j. $75.00
In the 1840s Kane traveled from the Great Lakes to the Pacific coast. This work elevates Kane to a major North American artist.

HARRINGTON (John P.). See also BAE Bulletin Nos. 55, 56, 84, 94, 107, 157 and 164.

H84. HARRINGTON (John P.). Exploration of the Burton Mound at Santa Barbara, California. pp23-168 containing 2 figures, plus 27pp of photographs, cloth. Removed from Smithsonian Institute Bureau of American Ethnology Annual report No. 44, Washington, 1928. $45.00

H85. HARRINGTON (John P.). An Introductory Paper on the Tewa Language, Dialect of Taos, New Mexico. 48pp, wrappers, offprint from American Anthropologist. n.p., 1910. $12.00
_____Another Copy. Same. $15.00
_____Another Copy. Same. $10.00

H86. HARRINGTON (John P.). Karuk Indian Myths. 34pp, wrappers. Complete reprint of BAE Bulletin 107. Gives myths in both original Karuk language and English translation. Ramona, 1972. $10.00

H87. HARRINGTON (John P.). A New Original Version of Boscana's Historical Account of the San Juan Capistrano

Indians of Southern California. 62pp, 2 pls, map on frnt cvr. Ann Arbor, 1966, reprint. $10.00

H88. HARRINGTON (M. R.). (Southwest Museum Leaflet No. 26, Los Angeles, 1955) Ancient Life Among the Southern California Indians. 38pp, illus, wrappers. $10.00

H89. HARRINGTON (M. R.). (Museum of the American Indian, Notes and Monographs, New York, 1921) Cuba Before Columbus (2 Volumes). 246pp, 260pp, frontis, 107 pls. $200.00

___Another Copy. Same. $200.00

H90. HARRINGTON (M. R.). (Museum Journal, Vol. III, No. 1, Philadelphia, 1912) The Devil Dance of the Apache. Also: The Northwest Coast Collection. pp6-15, 5 photographs. $12.00

H91. HARRINGTON (M. R.). Dickon Among the Indians. Illustrated by Clarence Ellsworth. 368pp, bibliography. Philadelphia, 1938. $35.00
About Delaware Indians as they lived in New Jersey and Pennsylvania before the coming of the Whites.

H92. HARRINGTON (M. R.). (Southwest Museum Papers, No. 8, Los Angeles, 1963) Gypsum Cave, Nevada. 197pp, illus, maps, wrappers. Well-illustrated work on the archaeological findings in a cave near Las Vegas. $12.00

H93. HARRINGTON (M. R.). (Southwest Museum Leaflet No. 15, Los Angeles, 1942) Indians of the Plains. 47pp, illus, pictorial wrappers. Detailed descriptions of costumes, living conditions and culture. $10.00

H94. HARRINGTON (M. R.). (American Museum of Natural History, Anthropological Papers, Vol. I, Part VI, 1908) Iroquois Silverwork. pp351-369 (containing 2 figures), 6pp photographs, frnt and rear wrappers missing, spine reinforced, else Very Good. $30.00

H95. HARRINGTON (M. R.). (Museum of the American Indian, Notes and Monographs, Vol. XII, 1971) The Ozark Bluff Dwellers. 233pp, 126 illus. $17.00

H96. HARRINGTON (M. R.). (Southwest Museum Papers No. 17, Los Angeles, 1957, 1st ed.) A Pinto Site at Little Lake, California. vi, 91pp, illus, 54 figures, cloth and bds, some wear and soil. $15.00

H97. HARRINGTON (M. R.). (Museum of the American Indian, Notes and Monographs, New York, 1921) Religion and Ceremonies of the Lenape. 249pp, color frontis, 12mo, 9pls. $75.00

H98. HARRINGTON (M. R.). (University Museum Anthropological Publications, Vol. IV, No. 2, Philadelphia, 1914) Sacred Bundles of the Sac and Fox Indians, Illustrated by Specimens in the George G. Heye Collection. 220pp, 20pp of photographs, 15pp of drawings. $30.00
This publication on sacred bundles collected by the expedition under George G. Heye examines these objects that were so highly venerated by the Sac and Fox of

Oklahoma. The sacred bundles, which contained charms, amulets and fetishes are classified according to type, and each bundle in the collection is described in detail. (EAP)

H99. HARRINGTON (M. R.). (Museum Journal, Vol. 1, No. 3, Philadelphia, 1910) Some Customs of the Delaware Indians. pp52-60, 6 lrge photographs, wrappers. $12.00

H100. HARRINGTON (M. R.). (Southwest Museum Papers No. 18, Los Angeles, 1961) Tule Springs, Nevada, With Other Evidences of Pleistocene Man in North America. 146pp, illus, bibliography, wrappers. $10.00

H101. HARRIS (B. W.). (House of Representatives Report 63, 43:1, Washington, 1874, 1st print.) Nez Perce Indian Reservation in Idaho. 10pp, removed. Purchase of 640 acres for a reservation, with reprinted early documents and letters about the Nez Perce, dating from 1847. $15.00

H102. HARRIS (Thaddeus M.). A Discourse Delivered Before the Society for Propagating the Gospel Among the Indians and Others in North America, 6th November, 1832. With Report of the Select Committee. 50pp, removed. Cambridge, Mass., 1823. $20.00
Includes an account of the arrival of the first group of Stockbridge Indians at Green Bay, Wisconsin, where a large tract of land had been purchased for resettlement.

H103. HARRISON (J. B.). The Latest Studies on Indian Reservations. 233pp, printed wrappers. Philadelphia, 1887. $125.00
Notes on reservation in Dakota, Washington, Montana, Nebraska, Idaho and Oregon, followed by impressions of Indian education and missionaries. Harrison was acting as a representative of the Indian Rights Assn.
____Another Copy. Same. Original wrappers, rear cvr detached. $90.00

H104. HARROD (Howard L.). Mission Among the Blackfeet. 218pp, illus, index, bibliography, map. Norman, 1971 (1st ed.), d.j. $20.00
____Another Copy. Same. $20.00

H105. HARROD (Howard L.). Renewing the World, Plains Indian Religion and Morality. xiv, 213pp, 7 drawings, map, cloth. Tucson, 1987. $40.00

H106. HARSTON (J. Emmor). Comanche Land. 206pp, illus. History of the vast area from Arkansas River to Rio Grande and from eastern Texas to Arizona. San Antonio, 1963 (1st ed.). $17.00
____Another Copy. Same. D.j. $15.00
____Another Copy. Same. $15.00
____Another Copy. Same. $12.00
____Another Copy. San Antonio, 1963 (2d print.) $10.00

H107. HART (Jeff). Montana--Native Plants and Early People. 75pp, illus, bibliography, oblong 4to, wrappers. Legends about the uses of 60 plants native to Montana. Helena, 1976 (1st ed.). $10.00

H108. HARTJE (K.) et al. Signale Indianischer Kunstler. 131pp, 30pp photographs, 71 b/w photographs, 1 drawing. Berlin, 1984. $37.00

HARTLE (Donald D.). See also BAE Bulletin No. 185.

H109. HARTLEY (William). Osceola, The Unconquered Indian. 293pp, early photographs and paintings, other illus, bibliography, map, index. Biography of the great Seminole leader and history of the 2nd Seminole War of 1835-42. New York, 1973, d.j. $17.00

H110. HARTMAN (C. V.). Archaeological Researches in Costa Rica. Illustrations by J. Cerderquist (Photoengraver). 195pp of text containing 479 photographs and drawings, plus an additional 348pp containing 87 full-page pls, both b/w and color. Consisting of photographs of hundreds of stone figures and ceramic vessels, bowls and containers, buckram cvrs. Royal Ethnographical Museum, 1901. $775.00

H111. HARTMAN (C. V.). (Carnegie Museum Memoirs, Vol. 3, No. 1, Pittsburgh, 1907) Archaeological Researches on the Pacific Coast of Costa Rica. 95pp, 44 pls displaying over 400 artifacts, 22 examples in color of jade, folio, wrappers. $400.00

H112. HARTMAN (H.). George Catlin und Balduin Mollhausen, Zwei Interpreten des Indianer und des Alten Westens. 156pp, 33pp of Catlin drawings, 1pp drawings of artifacts in the Mollhausen collection, 2 maps, cloth. Berlin, 1963. $40.00

H113. HARTMAN (H.). Kachina, Figuren der Hopi-Indianer. 286pp, 106 b/w and 52 color drawings and photographs. Exhibition catalogue, Museum fur Volkerkunde, Berlin, 1978.

H114. HARTWIG (G.). The Polar World: A Popular Description of Man and Nature in the Arctic and Antarctic Regions of the Globe. xviii, 550pp, 8 color pls, 3 folded maps, many woodcuts in text, original decorated cloth. Longmans, green, London, 1869, 1874 (2nd ed.). $50.00

H115. HARVEY (Byron). (Museum of the American Indian, Contributions, Vol. XXIV, New York, 1970) Ritual in Pueblo Art: Hopi Life in Hopi Painting. 180pp, 4to, illus, reproduces 185 examples of Pueblo art with paragraph of explanatory text for each, 5 color pls, bibliography, wrappers. $25.00
　　　Another Copy. Same. $20.00

H116. HARVEY (Fred). The Great Southwest, Along the Santa Fe. 64pp, 30 full-page color drawings and photographs, decorated cvr. Kansas City, 1923 (7th ed.). $69.00

H117. HARVEY (Henry). History of the Shawnee Indians from
the Years 1681 to 1854, Inclusive. 316pp, sml 8vo,
cloth. Cincinnati, Ephraim Morgan & Sons, 1855.
$100.00

Howes: H-275. Field: 663. Contains an extensive
history of the tribe, with an account of the loss of its
traditional lands in Ohio, from eye-witness accounts of
the author.
____Another Copy. New York, 1971, portrait frontis.
$20.00
____Another Copy. Millwood, 1977. $15.00

H118. HASKELL (Thomas Nelson). The Indian Question.
Y-oung K--onkaput, the King of the Utes; a Legend of
Twin Lakes and Occasional Poems. 257pp, 145pp, 92pp,
illus, gilt decorated cloth. Denver, 1889 (1st ed.).
$75.00

H119. HASSRICK (Royal B.). The Sioux, Life and Customs of
a Warrior Society. 337pp, illus, index, bibliography,
maps. Norman, 1977, d.j. $20.00

H120. HATHAWAY (Benjamin). The League of the Iroquois, and
Other Legends. From the Indian Muse. Portrait, 12mo,
decorative cloth. Chicago, 1882. $35.00

H121. HATT (G.). (American Anthropology Association, Memoirs,
Vol. III, No. 3, 1916) Moccasins and Their Relations
to Arctic Footwear. 102pp, 89 figures, spine reinforced. $60.00

H122. HAURY (E. W.). (Peabody Papers, Vol. XXIV, No. 1,
1945) The Excavation of Los Muertos and Neighboring
Ruins in the Salt River Valley, Southern Arizona. xv,
223pp, 133 figures, 29pp photographs. $77.00

H123. HAURY (E. W.) and CUBILLOS (J. C.). (University of
Arizona, Social Science Bulletin No. 22, 1953) Investigaciones Arqueologicas en la Sabana de Bogota, Colombia. 104pp, 7pp photographs, 32 figures. $15.00

H124. HAURY (E. W.). Mogollon Culture in the Forestdale
Valley, East-Central Arizona. xix, 454pp, 21 photographs, 150 drawings, 11 tables, cloth. Tucson, 1985.
$44.00

Three separate reports on the inhabitants of the
Forestdale Valley are contained in this volume. Two of
the reports--on Bear Ruin and on the Bluff Site--were
originally published in 1940 and 1947, respectively, and
have long been out of print. The third, on Tia Kii
Pueblo, completes the trilogy. The appearance of the
three reports in one volume offers for the first time the
complete cultural history of the Valley. The information
contained in the reports was instrumental in the Mogollon
being classified as a separate culture, rather than as a
close relative of their neighbors, the Anasazi. (EAP)

H125. HAURY (E. W.). (Medallion Papers No. XX, Gila Pueblo,
1936) The Mogollon Culture of Southwestern New Mexico.
ix, 146pp, 32pp photographs and drawings. $60.00

H126. HAURY (E. W.). (Medallion Papers No. XIX, Gila Pueblo,
       1936) Some Southwestern Pottery Types, Series IV.
       v, 49pp, 4pp photographs, 4 figures, 5 fold-out charts.
                                                           $40.00
H127. HAURY (E. W.). The Stratigraphy and Archaeology of
       Ventana Cave Arizona. xxvii, 599pp, pls, folding maps
       and tables, bibliography, index. Some wear and stains.
       University of New Mexico, 1950 (1st ed.). $20.00
H128. HAUSMAN (Gerald). Sitting On The Blue-eyed Bear.
       Navajo Myths and Legends. 130pp, drawings by Sidney
       Hausman, bibliography. Westport, CT, 1975 (1st ed.)
       d.j. $15.00
H129. HAVEN (Samuel F.). (Smithsonian Contributions to Knowl-
       edge, Vol. 8, Washington, 1856) Archaeology of the
       United States, Vestiges of Antiquity. 168pp, includes
       physiological researches, American Indian languages,
       rebound in cloth, 4to. $75.00
H130. HAVILAND (W. A.). (Middle American Research. Tulane
       University, Publication 26, No. 5, 1968) Ancient Low-
       land Maya Social Organization. 25pp. $10.00
H131. HAVILAND (W. A.). (Middle American Research. Tulane
       University, Publication 26, No. 3, 1966) Maya Settle-
       ment Patterns: A Critical Review. 26pp. $10.00
H131a. HAVINS (Thomas Robert). Beyond the Cimarron: Major
       Earl Van Dorn in Comanche Land. 113pp, bibliography,
       drawings. Brownwood, The Brown Press, TX, 1969
       (1st ed.) d.j. $25.00
H132. HAWKINS (Col. Benjamin). (Collections of the Georgia
       Historical Society, Vol. 3, Part 1, Savannah, 1848)
       A Sketch of the Creek Country, In the Years 1798
       and 1799. 88pp, 8vo, original wrappers. $185.00
            Field: 668. Howes: H-318. Hawkins was a govern-
       mental official working with the Indians for over 30 years.
       This work is derived from his extensive notes and ob-
       servations. This title was issued as an "extra" 25 years
       before the actual volume 3 of the Georgia Historical Col-
       lections was published. (RMW)
       ____Another Copy. New York, 1971. Facsimile reprint.
                                                           $10.00
H133. HAWLEY (Florence M.). Field Manual of Prehistoric
       Southwestern Pottery Types. 126pp, printed wrappers.
       Albuquerque, University of New Mexico, 1936. $30.00
H134. HAWLEY (Florence M.). (University of New Mexico, Bul-
       letin, Monograph No. 2, 1934) The Significance of the
       Dated Prehistory of Chetro Ketl, Chaco Canon, New
       Mexico. x, 80pp, 18pp of pls, later cloth over original
       wrappers. $40.00
H135. HAWLEY (Florence M.). Some Factors in the Indian Prob-
       lem in New Mexico. 48pp, illus, wrappers. Albuquer-
       que, 1948. $15.00
H136. HAWTHORN (A.). Art of the Kwakiutl Indians, and Other

Northwest Coast Tribes. xxx, 410pp, 537 b/w photographs, 3 maps, 32pp of color photographs, cloth, inscribed by author. Seattle, 1967. $135.00

H137. HAWTHORN (Audrey). Kwakiutl Art. 268pp plus index, figures, photographs, appendices, glossary, many full color photographic pls, maps. Enlarged and revised. Seattle, 1979 (1st thus), d.j. $45.00

H138. HAWTHORN (Audrey). People of the Potlatch. 48pp, 109 photographs, oblong 8vo. Vancouver, B.C., 1954.
                                                        $15.00
____Another Copy. Vancouver Art Gallery, 1965.
                                                        $20.00

H139. HAWTHORN (H. B.) et al. The Indians of British Columbia. A Study of Contemporary Social Adjustment. ix, 499pp, index. University of California Press and U.B.C., 1958, (1st ed.), d.j. $40.00
____Another Copy. Same. $45.00
____Another Copy. 1960 (2d print.) $30.00

H140. HAYDEN (Ralston). The Senate and Treaties 1789-1817. The Development of the Treaty-making Functions of the United States Senate during their Formative Period. 226pp, bibliography, index. New York, 1920 (1st ed.) d.j. $25.00
____Another Copy. Same. $20.00

H141. (HAYDEN SURVEY). Bulletin of the U.S. Geological and Geographic Survey of the Territories. Vol. II, Nos. 1-4. xii, 392pp, pls, maps, index, ex-library, 1/2 leather, marbled bds and endpapers, worn. Partial contents: "A Notice of Ancient Ruins of Southwestern Colorado..." by W. H. Holmes, pp3-24, 14 pls; "A Notice of the Ancient Ruins in Arizona and Utah Lying About the Rio San Juan" by W. H. Jackson, pp25-46, 9 pls (including large folding map of ruins). Government Printing Office, Washington, 1876. $65.00

H142. (HAYDEN SURVEY). Bulletin of the U.S. Geological and Geographic Survey of the Territories. Vol. III, Nos. 1-4. ix, 856pp, pls, map, index, ex-library, rebound in cloth, original wrappers bound in. Partial contents: "Researches in Kjokkenmoddings and Graves of Former Population of the Coast of Oregon" by Paul Schumacher, pp27-35, 8 pls; "The Twana Indians of the Skokomish Reservation in Washington Territory" by M. Eells, pp57-120, 3 pls. Government Printing Office, Washington, 1877. $45.00

H143. HAYES (Jess G.). Apache Vengeance: True Story of Apache Kid. 185pp, illus by Horace T. Pierce, pictorial cloth. Albuquerque, 1954 (1st ed.) d.j. $30.00
Wallace: X52. Adams Six-Guns: 954: "One of the best and most thorough books written about Apache Kid, the notorious Indian Outlaw." (TE)
____Another Copy. Same. $30.00

H144. HAYNE (Coe). Redman on the Big Horn. 123pp, story of "Swift Eagle" based on Crow legends. Ft. Custer Crow Agency, Philadelphia, 1930 (3rd print.). $30.00

H145. HAYS (Arthur H.) Notawkah: Friend of the Miamis. 430pp, map endpapers. John Corrington, the Miami and Shawnee Indians in Wabash County, Indiana, 1761-2. Caldwell, 1936, d.j. $45.00

H146. HAYS (H. R.). Children of the Raven: The Seven Indian Nations of the Northwest Coast. 314pp, illus, map, index. Explores the society, environment and history of the Tlingit, Tsimshian, Haida, Kwakiutl, Bella Coola, Nootka and Coast Salish. New York, 1975, (1st ed.), d.j. $25.00

H147. HAZEN (Reuben W.). History of the Pawnee Indians. 80pp, frontis. Fremont, NE, 1893 (1st ed.). $65.00

H148. HEBARD (Grace Raymond). Sacajawea, A Guide and Interpreter of the Lewis and Clark Expedition, with an account of the travels of Toussaint Charbonneau, and of Jean Baptiste, the expedition Papoose. 340pp, illus, folding map, bibliography, index. Details one of the most romantic and heroic stories of the westward expansion. Contains much on Sacajawea's later life at Fort Bridger. Glendale, 1967. $45.00

H149. HECKEWELDER (John). An Account of the History, Manners, and Customs of the Indian Nations, Who Once Inhabited Pennsylvania and Neighbouring States. lii, iv, 3pp, 464pp, errata, rebound in half leather, in transactions of the American Philosophical Society. Philadelphia, A. Small, 1819. $125.00

Field: 679. Howes: H-390. Concentrates on the customs and languages of the Indians, especially the Delaware and Shawnese tongues. The Vocabulary is quite complete and correct. (RMW)

____Another Copy. Philadelphia, 1876, new and revised edition with an introduction and notes by Rev. Wm. Reichel, portrait, 465pp, original cloth. $125.00

____Another Copy. Same. $80.00

____Another Copy. Same. Cvr fade, lacks part of paper spine label, ex-library. $80.00

____Another Copy. New York, 1971, facsimile reprint. d.j. $10.00

H150. HECKEWELDER (John). A Narrative of the Mission of the United Brethren Among the Delaware and Mohegan Indians, from its Commencement, in the Year 1740, to the Close of the Year 1808. xii, 17pp, 429pp, 1 errata, portrait, full leather, cvrs detached. Philadelphia, M'Carty and Davis, 1820 (1st ed.). $175.00

Sabin: 31205. Field: 678. Howes: H-392. "Standard authority on the Moravian missions in Pennsylvania, Ohio, etc." (RMW)

____Another Copy. Same. Tear to last page. $150.00

H151. HEDGES (F. A. Mitchell). Land of Wonder and Fear.
265pp, illus, map. New York, 1931 (1st ed.). $35.00
H152. HEDRICK (Basil C.) et al. The Mesoamerican Southwest.
Readings of Archaeology, Ethnohistory and Ethnology.
178pp, notes, index. Carbondale, 1974 (1st ed.) d.j.
$15.00
___Another Copy. Same. $10.00
___Another Copy. Same. Ex-library. $10.00
H153. HEDRICK (Basil C.) et al. (Editors). The North Mexican
Frontier: Readings in Archaeology, Ethnohistory and
Ethnography. 255pp. Southern Illinois University,
1971, d.j. $15.00
___Another Copy. Same. $10.00
H154. HEGEMANN (Elizabeth Compton). Navaho Trading Days.
388pp, bibliography, 4to, a remarkable narrative with
318 photographs from the 1920s and 1930s recording life
among the Hopi, Navaho. University of New Mexico
Press, Albuquerque, 1963 (1st ed.), d.j. $45.00
___Another Copy. Same. Cloth. $25.00
H155. HEIDENREICH (C. Adrian) (Editor). Ledger Art of the
Crow and Gross Ventre Indians: 1879-1897. 32pp,
many photographs and color and b/w illus from the
ledgers, errata, color decorative wrappers, limited to
about 300 copies. Includes an excellent essay on the
background and interpretation of the art. Yellowstone
Art Center, Billings, 1985. $20.00
H156. HEIDERSTADT (Dorothy). Indian Friends and Foes. A
Baker's Dozen. Portraits from Pocahontas to Geronimo.
126pp plus index, drawings by David Humphreys Miller,
bibliography, portrait endpapers. Also Pontiac, Brant,
Tecumseh, Sacajawea, Black Hawk, Sequoya, Osceola,
Crazy Horse, Sitting Bull and Cochise. New York,
1958 (1st ed.), d.j. $17.00
H157. HEIDERSTADT (Dorothy). More Indian Friends and Foes.
138pp plus index, drawings by David Humphreys Miller,
bibliography. Sketches of the Lives of King Philip,
Little Turtle, John Ross, Popé, Little Crow, Roman
Nose, Red Cloud, Capt. Jack, Washakie, Joseph, etc.
New York, 1963 (1st ed.), d.j. $15.00
___Another Copy. Same. $10.00
H158. HEIGHAN (C. W.) and RIDDELL (F. A.). The Maru Cult
of the Pomo Indians, a California Ghost Dance Survival.
144pp, 18 photographs, 16 figures, 1 map, cloth. Los
Angeles, 1972. $20.00
HEIZER (Robert F.). See also BAE Bulletin Nos. 133, 143 and
151.
H159. HEIZER (Robert F.) and MASSEY (William C.). (Smithson-
ian Institution BAE Anthropology Papers No. 39, Wash-
ington, 1953, 1st ed.) Aboriginal Navigation Off the
Coasts of Upper and Baja California. pp285-311, photographs, drawings, bibliography, wrappers. $10.00

H160.　HEIZER (Robert F.).　Aconite Poison Whaling in Asia and
America.　An Aleutian Transfer.　pp 415-468, 7 photo-
graphic pls, bibliography, printed wrappers.　Offprint
Smithsonian Anthropological Papers, Washington, 1943.
$10.00

H161.　HEIZER (Robert F.).　(Contributions of University of
California Archaeological Research Facility, No. 10,
Berkeley, 1970)　Archaeology and the Prehistoric Great
Basin Lacustrine Subsistence Regime as Seen from Love-
lock Cave, Nevada.　202pp, 4to, illus, bibliography,
maps, wrappers.　　　　　　　　　　　　　　$20.00

H162.　HEIZER (Robert F.).　The Archaeology of Bambert Cave,
Amador County, California.　87pp, drawings, photographs, maps, bibliography, 4to, wrappers.　Scholarly
account with drawings of artifacts plus photographs in
pocket.　Berkeley, 1973 (1st ed.).　　　　　　$15.00
____Another Copy.　Same.　　　　　　　　　　$12.00

H163.　HEIZER (Robert F.) and ELSASSER (Albert).　(University
of California Archaeology Reports, No. 59, Berkeley,
1963)　The Archaeology of Bowers Cave, Los Angeles
County, California.　83pp, illus, wrappers.　Bound
with Reprints of Early Notes on Santa Barbara Archaeology, 83pp, wrappers.　　　　　　　　　　　　$15.00

H164.　HEIZER (Robert F.) and COOK (S. F.).　(University of
California Anthropological Records 12:2, Berkeley, 1949)
The Archaeology of Central California: A Comparative
Analysis of Human Bone From Nine Sites.　29pp, stiff
wrappers.　　　　　　　　　　　　　　　　　$17.00
____Another Copy.　Same.　　　　　　　　　　$10.00

H165.　HEIZER (Robert F.) and KRIEGER (Alex).　(University of
California Publications in American Archaeology and
Ethnology, Vol. 47, No. 1, Berkeley, 1956)　The
Archaeology of Humboldt Cave, Churchill County, Nev-
ada.　190pp, wrappers, illus.　　　　　　　　$75.00

H166.　HEIZER (Robert F.) et al.　(University of California
Anthropological Records, Vol. 20, No. 4, Berkeley,
1961)　The Archaeology of Two Sites at Eastgate,
Churchill County, Nevada.　36pp, 9pp drawings and
photographs, 2 maps.　　　　　　　　　　　　$18.00

H167.　HEIZER (Robert F.).　(University of California Anthropo-
logical Records, Vol. 17, No. 1, Berkeley, 1956)
Archaeology of the Uyak Site Kodiak Island, Alaska.
205pp, 85pp photographs, 68 figures, 29 tables.　$60.00
____Another Copy.　Same.　　　　　　　　　　$45.00
____Another Copy.　Same.　　　　　　　　　　$45.00

H168.　HEIZER (Robert F.) (Editor).　(Contributions of University
of California Archaeological Research Facility, No. 6,
Berkeley, 1970)　A Bibliography of California Archaeology.　78pp, 4to, lists hundreds of printed items under
29 subject headings, wrappers.　　　　　　　　$15.00
____Another Copy.　Same.　　　　　　　　　　$12.00

H169.   HEIZER (Robert F.).   California Indian History: A Clas-
        sified and Annotated Guide to Source Materials.   90pp,
        map, 4to, index, wrappers.   Lists 685 works on Califor-
        nia Indians.   Ramona, 1975 (1st ed.). $15.00
        ___Another Copy.   Same. $10.00
H170.   HEIZER (R. F.) and WHIPPLE (M. A.).   The California
        Indians, a Source Book.   492pp, 15 illus, 12 maps,
        cloth.   Berkeley, 1951, d.j. $12.00
        ___Another Copy.   1965, d.j. $20.00
        ___Another Copy.   1970. $27.00
        ___Another Copy.   1971, d.j. $25.00
H171.   HEIZER (Robert F.).   The California Indians vs. The
        United States of America; Evidence Offered in Support
        of Occupancy, Possession and Use of Land in California
        by the Ancestors of Enrolled Indians of California.
        130pp, 4to, wrappers.   Offprint of House of Representa-
        tives Document 4497.   Socorro, 1978 (1st ed. thus).
                                                            $15.00
H172.   HEIZER (Robert F.).   Catalogue of the C. Hart Merriam
        Collection of Data Concerning California Tribes and Other
        American Indians.   80pp, 4to, wrappers.   Berkeley,
        1969. $15.00
H173.   HEIZER (Robert F.).   (University of California Reports
        of Archaeological Survey, No. 10, Berkeley, n.d.)
        A Cave Burial From Kern County, California.   Bound
        With the Archaeology of Site Ker-74 by F. A. Riddell.
        35pp, wrappers, text figures. $17.00
H174.   HEIZER (Robert F.).   Check List and Index to Reports of
        the University of California Archaeology Survey Nos.
        32(1955) to 74(1968); Check List of Contribution...,
        No. 1(1965) to No. 30(1976); and other Information...,
        1948-1972.   94pp.   Berkeley, 1976. $16.00
H175.   HEIZER (Robert F.) (Editor).   A Collection of Ethnographi-
        cal Articles on the California Indians.   103pp, 4to,
        map, wrappers, 21 articles originally published between
        1851 and 1920.   Ramona, 1976 (1st ed.). $15.00
H176.   HEIZER (Robert F.) (Editor).   The Destruction of Califor-
        nia Indians; A Collection of Documents from the Period
        1847-1865, in Which are Described Some of the Things
        That Happened to Some of the Native People of California.
        321pp, illus.   Santa Barbara, 1974 (1st ed.), d.j.
                                                            $20.00
        ___Another Copy.   Same. $17.00
        ___Another Copy.   Same. $10.00
H177.   HEIZER (Robert F.).   The Eighteen Unratified Treaties of
        1851-1852 Between the California Indians and the United
        States Government.   101pp, 4to, maps, wrappers.
        Berkeley, 1972 (1st ed.). $20.00
            Full text of all 18 treaties and names of all signa-
        tories.   Taken together they give an excellent picture
        of the ludicrous and dishonest treaties foisted on the

Indians by the government. The treaties divided prac-
tically the entire state among various "tribes"; they were
never ratified by the Senate and the whole affair was
marked "Secret" and not revealed until a half century
later. (GFH)

H178. HEIZER (Robert F.) and COOK (S. F.). (University of
California Archaeology Reports, No. 17, Berkeley, 1952)
The Fossilization of Bone: Organic Components and
Water. 24pp, wrappers. $15.00

H179. HEIZER (Robert F.). (University of California Publications
in American Archaeology and Ethnology, Vol. 42, No.
3, Berkeley, 1947) Francis Drake and the California
Indians, 1579. pp251-302, pls 18-21, 1 figure in text,
2 illus, cloth. D.j. $18.00
    Heizer's analysis and conclusion that Drake, the first
Englishman to see and describe the Indians of upper
California, landed in territory occupied by the coast
Miwok speaking Indians at Drake's Bay.
____Another Copy. Same. $27.00
____Another Copy. Same. $15.00
____Another Copy. Same. $12.00

H180. HEIZER (Robert F.) (Editor). George Gibb's Journal of
Redick McKee's Expedition Through Northwestern Califor-
nia in 1851. 88pp, 4to, wrappers. Department of
Anthropology, Berkeley, 1974. $20.00

H181. HEIZER (Robert F.). Great Basin Projectile Points:
Forms and Chronology. 43pp, illus, maps, bibliography
4to, wrappers. Socorro, 1978 (1st ed.). $11.00

H182. HEIZER (Robert F.) and KROEBER (Theodora) (Editors).
Ishi, the Last Yahi. A Documentary History. 242
double-column pp, photographs, maps, music, oblong.
Berkeley, 1979 (1st ed.), d.j. $17.00
    Some 40 documents dealing with Ishi or his tribe of
Northern California Indians. Much on Ishi after he left
the wild life in 1911 to eventually serve as a source for
much of our knowledge of this tribe and way of life.
(TNL)

H183. HEIZER (Robert F.). Languages, Territories and Names
of California Indian Tribes. Folded maps in pocket.
University of California, Berkeley, 1966. $55.00
____Another Copy. Same. D.j. $33.00

H184. HEIZER (Robert F.). (University of California, Reports
No. 75, Berkeley, 1972) List and Index to Reports of
the University of California Archaeological Surveys,
Nos. 32 to 74. 80pp, wrappers. $12.00

H185. HEIZER (Robert F.) (Editor). Narrative of the Adventures
and Sufferings of John R. Jewitt While Held a Captive
of the Nootka Indians of Vancouver Island 1803 to 1805.
111pp, 4to, illus, wrappers. Ramona, 1975. $18.00

H186. HEIZER (Robert F.). (University of California Anthropological Records, Vol. 15, No. 1, 1952) The Mission Indian

Vocabularies of Alphonse Pinart. 84pp, stiff wrappers.
$25.00
H187. HEIZER (Robert F.). (University of California Anthropological Record, Vol. 15, No. 2, 1955) The Mission Indian Vocabularies of H. W. Henshaw. 117pp, stiff
wrappers. $30.00
H188. HEIZER (Robert F.) and BAUMHOFF (M. A.). Prehistoric
Rock Art of Nevada and California. 412pp, 4to, illus,
wrappers. University of California, Berkeley, 1962.
$35.00
____Another Copy. Berkeley, 1984. xvii, 412pp,
24pp photographs, 200 figures. $28.00
H189. HEIZER (Robert F.) (Editor). Reprints of Various Papers
on California Archaeology, Ethnology and Indian History.
139pp, 4to, wrappers. 27 articles. Berkeley, 1973
(1st ed.). $30.00
____Another Copy. Same. $15.00
H190. HEIZER (Robert F.) (Editor). Seven Early Accounts of
the Pomo Indians and Their Culture. 63pp, illus, map,
4to, wrappers. University of California Archaeological
Research Facility, Berkeley, 1975) $25.00
____Another Copy. Same. $15.00
____Another Copy. Same. $10.00
H191. HEIZER (Robert F.) (Editor). Some Last Century Ac-
counts of the Indians of Southern California. 92pp,
4to, wrappers. 17 articles. Ramona, 1976 (1st ed.).
$11.00
H192. HELFRITZ (Hans). Mexican Cities of the Gods: An
Archaeological Guide. 180pp, 111 illus, includes 15
pre-Columbian sites. New York, 1970. $20.00
H193. HELLMUTH (N. H.). (University of Northern Colorado,
Museum of Anthropology, Katunob, No. 4, 1970) Pre-
liminary Bibliography of the Chol, Lacandon, Yucatec,
Itza, Mopan and Quejache of the Southern Maya Low-
lands, 1524-1969. xviii, 114pp. $20.00
H194. HELLMUTH (Nicholas). (Corpus of Maya Art, Vol. II,
FLAAR, California, 1985) Maya Cylindrical Tripods and
Related Early Classic Art: Iconography and Form.
244pp, 5 photographs, 4to, wrappers. A catalogue of
described objects, located world-wide. $60.00
H195. HELM (June). The Indians of the Subarctic. A Critical
Bibliography. 92pp, wrappers. Bloomington, IN, 1976
(1st ed.). $10.00
H196. HELPS (Sir Arthur). The Life of Pizarro, With Some Account of His Associates in the Conquest of Peru. 320pp,
full leather, decorated spine, 5 raised bands. London,
1869 (2d ed.). $90.00
H197. HELPS (Sir Arthur). The Spanish Conquest in America
and Its Relation to the History of Slavery and to the
Government of Colonies. (4 Volumes). 369pp, 365pp,
400pp, 374pp, several folding maps, a new edition with

an introduction, maps and notes by M. Oppenheim.
London, 1902-1904. $125.00

H198. HEMMING (John). The Conquest of the Incas. 624pp
plus index, photographs, drawings, maps, notes. New
York, 1970 (1st American ed.), wear to d.j. $15.00

H199. HEMMING (John). Machu Picchu. 172pp, approximately
135 color and b/w photographs, 80 drawings, cloth.
New York, 1981. $22.00

H200. HEMMING (John). Red Gold: The Conquest of the
Brazilian Indians. 677pp, 31 illus. Mass., 1978, d.j.
$30.00

____Another Copy. Cambridge, MA, 1978 (1st ed.),
d.j. $17.00

HENCKEL (Carlos). See BAE Bulletin No. 143.

HENDERSON (J.). See also BAE Bulletin Nos. 54 and 56.

H201. HENDERSON (J. S.). (Yale University Publications in
Anthropology, No. 77, 1979) Atopula, Guerrero and
Olmec Horizons in Mesoamerica. xi, 256pp, 93 figures,
5 tables. $30.00

H202. HENDRON (J. W.). Frijoles; a Hidden Valley in the New
World. Edited by Dorothy Thomas. Drawings by Joce-
lyn Taylor. xii, 92pp, map endpapers, and other maps,
diagrams in pocket on back endpaper, illus, bibliography,
glossary, index. Earliest occupation of the Rio Grande
Valley by prehistoric Indians. Santa Fe, 1946 (1st
ed.). $50.00

____Another Copy. Same. $10.00

HENDRY (Jean). See also BAE Bulletin No. 191.

H203. HENDRY (Jean). (Smithsonian Institution Anthropology
Papers No. 74, Washington, 1964, 1st ed.) Iroquois
Masks and Maskmaking at Onondaga. pp349-410, photo-
graphs, wrappers. $10.00

H204. HENRY (J. & Z.). (American Orthopsychiatric Assn.,
Research Monograph, No. 4, New York, 1944) Doll Play
of Pilaga Indian Children. xii, 132pp, cloth. $35.00

H205. HENRY (Thomas R.). Wilderness Messiah. The Story of
Hiawatha and the Iroquois. 276pp plus index, bibliography. New York, 1955 (1st ed.). $10.00

HENSHAW (H. W.). See also BAE Bulletin No. 2.

HERNANDEZ DeALVA (Gregorio). See also BAE Bulletin No. 143.

H206. HERNDON (W. L.) and GIBBON (L.). Explorations of the
Valley of the Amazon, Made Under the Direction of the
Navy Department (3 Volumes). Vol. I: iv, 414pp, 16
pls. Vol. II: x, 339pp, 36 pls. Map Vol. III: 3
fold-out maps for Herndon's report. Cloth. Washington,
1853-1854. $265.00

One of the earlier and scientifically more important
expeditions to the Amazon, the 1850-51 expedition was
considered a seminal journey, and devoted considerable
time to the ethnology and remarkable antiquities of the
indigenous population. Sabin: 31524: "Contains minute,

accurate and very interesting accounts of the Aborigines of the Andes, and the Amazon and its tributaries."
___Another Copy. Same. $250.00
___Another Copy. Same. $175.00
___Another Copy. Vols. I and II only, cvrs worn, scattered foxing. $225.00
___Another Copy. Vols. I and II only, cvrs worn and soiled, inner hinges repaired, scattered foxing. $175.00

H207. HERRERA (Antonio De). Historia General de los Hechos de los Castelanos, en las Islas y Tierra-Firme del Mar Oceano. (10 Volumes). Decorated title pages, illus, 13 folding maps, wrappers. Asuncion de Paraguay: Editorial Guarania, 1944. $350.00

H208. HERSKOVITS (Melville J.). Franz Boas: The Science of Man in the Making. 131pp. New York, 1953. $15.00

H209. HERTZ (Rudolf). Congregational Woope. 24pp, 12mo, wrappers. Sioux Indian Language. Santee, NE, 1926. $35.00

H210. HERTZBERG (Hazel W.). The Search for an American Indian Identity. 362pp, index. New York, 1971, d.j. $15.00

HERZOG (Ernesto). See also BAE Bulletin No. 143.

H211. HESS (Thom.). Dictionary of Puget Salish. 770pp, map, bibliography. The most comprehensive dictionary yet attempted for any Salishan language. Seattle, 1976, (1st ed.). $35.00
___Another Copy. Same. $25.00

H212. HESS (William). The Epistle of Paul the Apostle to the Corinthians, Translated into the Mohawk Language. 55pp, stiff wrappers. New York, Howe and Bates, 1836. $125.00

H213. HESTER (James J.). Museum of New Mexico Papers in Anthropology, No. 6, Santa Fe, 1962, (1st ed.). Early Navajo Migrations and Acculturation in the Southwest. 138pp, photographs, maps, tables, drawings, plans, bibliography, wrappers. $15.00

H214. HESTER (James J.) and NELSON (S. M.) (Editors). (Simon Fraser University Department of Archaeology, Publication No. 5, 1978) Studies in Bella Bella Prehistory. v, 141pp, 80 figures, wrappers. $22.00

H215. HESTER (Thomas R.). (Texas State Building Commission, Report No. 15, Austin, 1969) Archaeological Investigations in Kleberg and Kennedy Counties, Texas. 78pp, photographs, drawing, map, bibliography, wrappers. $10.00

H216. HESTER (Thomas R.). (University of Texas Archaeological Survey Report No. 42, San Antonio, 1977) Archaeological Research at the Hinojosa Site ... Jim Wells County, ... Texas. 45pp, pls, maps, bibliography, wrappers. $10.00

H217. HESTER (Thomas R.). (University of Texas at San

Antonio, Center for Archaeological Research, Survey
Report No. 3, 1974, 1st ed.) Archaeological Survey
Areas Proposed for Modification In Salado Creek Water-
shed, Bexar.... 34pp. $10.00

H218-219. HESTER (Thomas R.) et al. (University of Texas at San
Antonio, Center for Archaeological Research, Survey
Report No. 6, 1975, 1st ed.) Archaeological Survey
Comal River Watershed, Comal County, Texas. 28pp.
$10.00

H220. HESTER (Thomas R.) (Editor). (University of Texas,
Center for Archaeological Research, Regional Studies,
No. 1, San Antonio, 1975) Archaeology and History
Resources in the San Antonio-Guadalupe River Basins:
a Preliminary Statement. 70pp, maps, bibliography.
$10.00

H221. HESTER (Thomas R.). Great Basin Atlatl Studies. 81pp,
illus, maps, bibliography, 4to, wrappers. Good descriptive and distributional information on early atlatls (spear-
throwers) found in various parts of Nevada. Ramona,
1974 (1st ed.). $10.00

H222. HESTER (Thomas R.) et al. (University of Texas, Center
for Archaeological Research, Regional Studies, No. 2,
San Antonio, 1975) An Initial Archaeological and Historical Assessment of Three Proposed Dam Sites in Gonzales
and Kendal Counties, Texas. 32pp, photographs, drawing, maps, bibliography, spiral bound. $10.00

H223. HESTER (Thomas R.) and HAMMOND (Norman) (Editors).
(University of Texas Center for Archaeological Research,
Special Report No. 4, San Antonio, 1976) Maya Lithic
Studies: Papers from the 1976 Beliz Field Symposium.
190pp, drawings, maps, bibliography, wrappers.
$10.00

H224. HESTER (Thomas R.). Review and Discussion of Great
Basin Projectile Point. Form and Chronology. 39pp,
illus, map, bibliography, 4to, wrappers. Berkeley,
1973 (1st ed.). $10.00

H225. HESTER (Thomas R.) and HILL (T. C.). (University of
Texas Center for Archaeological Research, Special Report
No. 1, San Antonio, 1975) Some Aspects of Late Prehistoric and Protohistoric Archaeology in South Texas.
35pp, drawing, maps, bibliography. $10.00

H226. HESTER (Thomas R.). (University of Texas at San Antonio, Center for Archaeological Research, Special Report, No. 2, 1976, 1st ed.) Texas Archaic: Symposium.
97pp, maps, illus, bibliography, large 8vo, wrappers.
$15.00

H227. HEUSSER (Albert H.). Homes and Haunts of the Indians.
105pp plus index, drawings, photographs. Archaeology
in New Jersey and New York. Paterson, NJ, 1923
(1st ed.). $12.00

HEWETT (E. L.). See also BAE Bulletin Nos. 32 and 54.

H228. HEWETT (E. L.). Ancient Andean Life. 356pp, 37 photographs, fold-out map, cloth cvr. Indianapolis, 1939.
$55.00
___Another Copy. Same. $40.00

H229. HEWETT (E. L.). Ancient Life In The American Southwest
With An Introduction On The General History Of The
American Race. xvii, 392pp plus 32 pls, illus, map end-
paper, cloth. Indianapolis, 1930 (1st ed.) wear and soil
to d.j. $50.00
Murphey: 137. Campbell: p.238. Excellent treatise
on Indians of the Southwest, including Pueblo, Hopi
and much on Chaco Canyon.
___Another Copy. Same. $35.00
___Another Copy. Same. $25.00
___Another Copy. New York, 1943 (2d ed.), d.j.
$15.00

H230. HEWETT (E. L.). Ancient Life in Mexico and Central
America. 364pp, frontis, illus with photographs. Indianapolis, 1936 (1st ed.). $50.00

H231. HEWETT (E. L.). (Archaeological Institute of America,
Art and Archaeology Magazine, Vol. IV, No. 6, Washington, December, 1916) Entire issue in original wrappers. Numerous articles concerning American archaeology. Murphey: 75-76. $20.00

H232. HEWETT (E. L.). (Archaeological Institute of America,
Art and Archaeology Magazine, Vol. IX, No. 1, Washington, January, 1920) Entire issue in original wrappers. Numerous articles concerning American archaeology. Murphey: 94-95. $20.00

H233. HEWETT (E. L.). (Archaeological Institute of America,
Art and Archaeology Magazine, Vol. X, Nos. 1-2,
Washington, July-August, 1920) Entire issue in original
wrappers. Numerous articles concerning American
archaeology. Murphey: 96-97. $15.00

H234. HEWETT (E. L.). (Archaeological Institute of America,
Art and Archaeology Magazine, Vol. XI, Nos. 1-2,
Washington, January-February, 1921) Entire issue in
original wrappers. Numerous articles concerning American archaeology. Murphey: 100-101. $25.00

H235. HEWETT (E. L.). (Archaeological Society, Art and
Archaeology Magazine, Vol. XVI, Nos. 1-2, Washington
1923) Entire issue in original wrappers. Numerous
articles concerning American archaeology. Murphey:
108-109. $20.00

H236. HEWETT (E. L.). The Chaco Canyon and Its Monuments.
234pp, illus, cloth. University of New Mexico and School
of American Research, Albuquerque, 1936. $65.00
Saunders: 457. Murphey: 161. Campbell: p.238.
One of the best archaeological histories of Chaco Canyon, monument of a civilization that died before Columbus arrived which comes alive as presented in this
detailed study. (TE)

      ___Another Copy. Same. $45.00
      ___Another Copy. Albuquerque, 1960. $50.00

H237. HEWETT (E. L.). (Papers of the School of American Archaeology, No. 10, Santa Fe, 1909) The Excavations at El Rito de los Frijoses in 1909. 23pp, 13 figures. Murphey: 59. Saunders: 459. $18.00
      ___Another Copy. Same. $15.00
      ___Another Copy. Same. $12.00

H238. HEWETT (E. L.) and MAUZY (Wayne). Landmarks of New Mexico. Illus. University of New Mexico, Albuquerque, 1953 (3rd ed.), d.j. $25.00

H239. HEWETT (E. L.). (Papers of the School of American Archaeology, No. 3, Santa Fe, 1909) The Pajaritan Culture. 10pp. $17.00

H240. HEWETT (E. L.). Pajarito Plateau and Its People. Illus, folded chart. University of New Mexico, 1953 (2d ed.), d.j. $75.00

H241. HEWETT (E. L.) and DUTTON (Bertha P.). The Pueblo Indian World: Studies on the Natural History of the Rio Grande Valley in Relation to Pueblo Indian Culture. 176pp, illus, folded maps, cloth. Albuquerque, 1945 (1st ed.) d.j. $40.00
      Murphey: 220. Campbell: p. 116. Excellent treatise by knowledgeable writers which also includes appendices of The Southwest Indian Languages and The Sounds and Structures of the Aztecan Languages by J. P. Harrington.
      ___Another Copy. Same. $27.00

H242. HEWETT (E. L.). Two Seasons Work in Guatemala. 17pp, illus, wrappers. Offprint from Bulletin of Archaeological Institute of America, June, 1911. $20.00
      ___Another Copy. Same. $20.00

HEWITT (J. N. B.). See BAE Bulletin No. 123.

H243. HEYE (George G.). (Museum of the American Indian, Notes and Monographs, Vol. 7, No. 1, 1919) Certain Aboriginal Pottery from Southern California. 46pp, 19 pls, 12mo, wrappers. $35.00

H244. HEYE (George G.). (Heye Foundation: Contributions From the Museum of the American Indian, Vol. 5, No. 3, New York, 1919) Certain Mounds in Haywood County, North Carolina. 31pp, 43pp, 5 pls, wrappers. $15.00

H245. HEYE (George G.). (Museum of American Indian, Contributions, Vol. II, No. 1, 1915) Exploration of a Munsee Cemetery Near Montague, New Jersey. 78pp, 22 figures, 33pp photographs, fold-out map, wrappers soiled, else fine. $57.00

H246. HEYE (George G.). (Museum of the American Indian, Notes and Monographs, Vol. V, No. 2, 1921) A Mahican Wooden Cup. 8pp, 1 photograph. $12.00

H247. HEYERDAHL (Thor). American Indians in the Pacific.
821pp, 90 pls, 11 maps, references, index, cloth, lrge
8vo. Chicago, Rand McNally, 1953 (1st American ed.).
$60.00
___Another Copy. Same. d.j. $45.00
___Another Copy. London, Allen & Unwin, 1952.
American Indians in the Pacific: The Theory Behind
the Kon-Tiki Expedition. illus. d.j. $95.00

H248. HIBBEN (Frank C.). Digging Up America. 239pp, including index, illus with photographs. New York, Hill
& Wang, 1960. $12.00

H249. HIBBEN (Frank). (Smithsonian Miscellaneous Collections
Vol. 99, No. 23, Washington, 1941) Evidences of Early
Occupation in Sandia Cave, New Mexico, and Other Sites
in the Sandia-Manzano Region. 64pp, illus, folded
maps, wrappers. $18.00

H250. HIBBEN (Frank C.). Kiva Art of the Anasazi at Pottery
Mound. 145pp, illus with 108 illus in color, oblong 4to.
Las Vegas, 1975 (1st ed.), d.j. $35.00

H251. HIBBEN (Frank C.). The Lost Americans. 196pp. Theory on the earliest Americans in easy to understand
style. Folsom, Sandia man, Uyma, etc. New York,
1946, (1st print.) d.j. $15.00

H252. HIBBEN (Frank C.). Treasure in the Dust: Exploring
Ancient America. 311pp. New York, Philadelphia,
1951, (1st ed.). $20.00
___Another Copy. Philadelphia, 1951. Signed by
author. $15.00

H253. HICKERSON (H.). (American Anthropological Assn. Memoir 92, 1962) The Southwestern Chippewa, an Ethnohistorical Study. vi, 110pp, 3 maps. $14.00
___Another Copy. Same. $10.00

H254. HIGGINSON (Thomas Wentworth). (Harpers Monthly Magazine, New York, August, 1882) The First Americans.
Entire issue in original printed wrappers. Concerning
the Pueblo. Saunders: 479. $12.00

H255. HIGHLEY (Lynn) et al. (University of Texas Archaeological Survey Report No. 27, San Antonio, 1977) An
Archaeological and Historical Assessment of the Tule
Lake Tract, Nueces County, Texas. 23pp, drawing,
map, bibliography, wrapper. $10.00

H256. HIGHWATER (Jamake). Anpao. An American Indian
Odyssey. 256pp, illus. Philadelphia, 1977 (3rd print.).
$10.00

H257. HIGHWATER (Jamake). Fodor's Indian America. 431pp,
illus, index. A good guidebook to America's Indians
written by an Indian from the Indian point of view,
with much on the cultural aspects of the Indians. New
York, 1975, (1st ed.), d.j. $22.00
___Another Copy. Same. $15.00

H258. HIGHWATER (Jamake). Ritual of the Wind: North

American Ceremonies, Music and Dances. 192pp, illus, with several rare photographs, sml 4to. New York, 1977 (1st ed.) d.j. $35.00
___Another Copy. Same. $25.00
___Another Copy. Same. $20.00
___Another Copy. Same. $25.00

H259. HIGHWATER (Jamake). Song from the Earth: American Indian Painting. 224pp, 130 b/w and 32 color illus, cloth. Boston, 1976. $40.00
___Another Copy. Same. Wrappers. $23.00

H260. HIGHWATER (Jamake). The Sweet Grass Lives On, Fifty Contemporary North American Indian Artists. 192pp, 150 b/w and 64 color photographs, cloth. New York, 1980. $60.00
This vivid visual anthology, a gallery of the achievements of 50 contemporary North American Indian artists, is a lavishly illustrated volume that presents the works of many of the finest Indian painters and sculptors. The work of each artist is illustrated and is accompanied · by a biographical sketch. (EAP)

H261. HILDRETH (Samuel). Contributions to the Early History of the North-West, Including the Moravian Missions in Ohio. 240pp, mainly a history of Northeast Ohio and the Moravian Indian Missions. Cincinnati, 1864 (2d ed.). $60.00
___Another Copy. Same. Modern cloth. $50.00

HILGER (Sister M. Inez). See also BAE Bulletin Nos. 146 and 148.

H262. HILGER (Sister M. Inez). (Smithsonian Miscellaneous Collections, Vol. 133, Washington, 1957) Araucanian Child Life and Its Cultural Background. 422pp plus index, illus, maps. Comprehensive study of this tribe which inhabits Chile and Argentina. $17.00

H263. HILGER (Sister M. Inez). The First Sioux Nun. Sister Marie-Josephine Nebraska, S.G.M., 1859-1894. 157pp, drawings by Sister Mary Michael Kaliher, map, glossary, note from author laid in, author's signed presentation on title page. Milwaukee, 1963, (1st ed.), d.j. $15.00

H264. HILL (B. and R.). Indian Petroglyphs of the Pacific Northwest. 314pp, more than 900 photographs and drawings, cloth. Seattle, 1975. $30.00
___Another Copy. Same. d.j. $25.00

H265. HILL (Jim Dan). (Overland Monthly and Out West Magazine, Vol. LXXXII, No. 12, San Francisco, 1924) The Seven Cities of Cibola. Entire issue in original wrappers. $10.00

H266. HILL (J. L.). The Passing of the Indian and Buffalo. 47pp, illus, wrappers. Historical sketch of the extermination of the American Bison. Also some material on Western Indian Wars. Long Beach, CA n.d., (c.1917) (1st ed.). $25.00
___Another Copy. Same. $20.00

H267. HILL (Leonard U.). John Johnston and the Indians in the Land of the Three Miamis. With Recollections of Sixty Years by John Johnston. 198pp, cloth. Reprint of 1915 edition. Howes: J-137. Piqua, OH, 1957. $25.00

H268. HILL (Ruth Beebe). Hanta Yo. 834pp, cloth. Information about two families of the Teton Sioux from the late 1700's to 1830's taken from tanned hide record. Garden City, 1979 (1st ed.), d.j. $15.00
   ___Another Copy. Same. $10.00
   ___Another Copy. Same. $12.00

H269. HILL (W. W.). (Yale University Publications in Anthropology, No. 18, 1938) The Agricultural and Hunting Methods of the Navaho Indians. 193pp, 4pp photographs, 12 figures. $50.00
   ___Another Copy. Same. $47.00

H270. HILL (W. W.). An Ethnography of Santa Clara Pueblo, New Mexico. 576pp, 34 photographs, 44 drawings, cloth. Albuquerque, 1982. $50.00
   A product of field research spanning nearly eighty years, this publication presents an incomparable picture of the traditions and customs of a small community of Tewa-speaking Indians. J. A. Jeancon's unpublished field notes, made between 1904 and 1930, and Hill's unfinished manuscript--edited, annotated and completed by Lange--have created a vivid picture of a fascinating and complex pueblo, with strong emphasis on ceremonial organization and material culture. The definitive work on Santa Clara Pueblo. (EAP)

H271. HILL (W. W.). (General Series in Anthropology, No. 9, Menasha, 1943) Navaho Humor. 28pp. $27.00

H272. HILL (W. W.). (University of New Mexico Bulletin Anthropology Series, Vol. 2, No. 3, Albuquerque, 1937) Navajo Pottery Manufacture. 23pp, illus with 4 pls, wrappers. $20.00

H273. HILL-TOUT (C.). The Native Races of the British Empire. British North American I. The Far West. The Home of the Salish and Dene. xiv, 263pp of text, plus 32 full-page photographs, map, gilt decorated cloth. London, 1907. $95.00

H274. HIND (Henry Youle). British North America. Reports of Progress, Together with a Preliminary and General Report, on the Assiniboine and Saskatchewan Exploring Expedition.... 219pp, 4to, green cloth, 6 folding maps, 2 pls, several illus. London, Stationery Office, 1860. $225.00

H275. HINES (Gustavus). A Voyage Round the World: With a History of the Oregon Mission: And Notes of Several Years Residence on the Plains, Bordering on the Pacific Ocean: Comprising an Account of Interesting Adventures Among the Indians. 6pp, 9-437pp, original cloth. Howes: H-505. Buffalo, G. H. Derby, 1850 (1st ed.). $75.00

H276. HINES (J.). The Red Indians of the Plains. Thirty Years' Missionary Experience in the Saskatchewan. 322pp, photographs, drawings, maps. London, 1915 (1st ed.). $80.00

H277. HINMAN (Marjory B.). Onaquaga: Hub of the Border Wars. 113pp, Onaquaga was an Iroquoian Village; also a large amount of material on Joseph Brant. n.p., 1975. $15.00
_____Another Copy. Same. $10.00

H278. HINSDALE (Wilbert B.). Archaeological Atlas of Michigan. 38pp, plus 20 large detailed maps of portions of the state, each showing mounds, villages, burying grounds, enclosures, ancient copper excavations, earthworks, etc., folio (19" x 24"). Ann Arbor, University of Michigan, 1931 (1st ed.). $150.00

H279. HINTON (T. B.). (University of Arizona, Anthropological Papers, No. 4, 1959) A Survey of Indian Assimilation in Eastern Sonora. 32pp, 13 photographs, 3 maps.
                                                         $15.00

H280. HIRST (Stephen). Havsuw 'Baaja: People of the Blue Green Water. 251pp plus index, photographs by Lois Hirst, maps, notes, bibliography. Tribal council sanctioned history of the Havasupai. Supai, AZ, 1985 (1st ed.), d.j. $18.00

H281. HIRST (Stephen). Life In A Narrow Place. The Havasupai of the Grand Canyon. 293pp plus index, photographs by T. & L. Eiler, bibliography, notes. New York, 1976 (1st ed.), d.j. $15.00

H282. HOAD (Louise). Kickapoo Indian Trails. 129pp, color frontis, 21 full-page illus by Cecil Smith, endpaper maps. Caldwell, Caxton Press, 1944 (1st ed.). $20.00

H283. HOADLEY (Mabel). Chi-Keeta and the Puk-Wudj Is. 146pp, color frontis, 11 full-page pls by Robert Holcomb, Juvenile novel of Indian legend. Caldwell, Caxton Press, 1950 (1st ed.). $15.00

H284. HOBLER (P. M.) (Editor). (Simon Fraser University Department of Archaeology, Publication No. 10, 1982) Papers on Central Coast Archaeology. viii, 140pp, 73 figures, 15 tables. wrappers. $22.00

H285. HOBSON (Richard). (Papers of the Peabody Museum, Harvard, Vol. XLII, No. 3, Reports of the Rimrock Project Values Series, No. 5, Cambridge, MA 1954) Navaho Acquisitive Values. 37pp, tables, references, list of museum publications. $20.00
_____Another Copy. Same. $17.00
_____Another Copy. Same. $15.00

HODGE (Frederick Webb). See also BAE Bulletin Nos. 24, 30, 36 and 154.

H286. HODGE (F. W.). (Museum of the American Indian, Notes and Monographs, Vol. III, No. 2, 1920) The Age of the Zuni Pueblo of Kechipauan. 16pp, 5 full-page

photographs, map, lacking frnt wrapper, spine rein-
forced. $17.00

H287. HODGE (F. W.) (Editor). Handbook of American Indians
North of Mexico (2   Volumes)   972pp and 1221pp, photo-
graphs, drawings, bibliography. Howes: H-556.
Dustin: 134. Washington, 1907 (1st eds.). $125.00
___Another Copy. Washington, 1912, ex-library.
                                                                                        $100.00
___Another Copy. New York, 1969. $85.00

H288. HODGE (F. W.). Handbook of Indians of Canada. 632pp,
folding maps. Reprint of the Ottawa 1913 ed. New
York, 1969. $30.00

H289. HODGE (F. W.). (Heye Foundation, Indian Notes and
Monographs, Vol. III, No. 3, 1920) Hawikuh Bonework.
149pp, illus, wrappers. $45.00

H290. HODGE (F. W.). History of Hawikuh New Mexico, One of
the So-called Cities of Cibola. xviii, 155pp of text containing figures, 26 full-page photographs, issued jointly
by the F. W. Hodge Anniv. Pub. Fund and Museum of
the American Indians. Printed by the Ward Ritchie
Press, Southwest Museum, 1937. $125.00
___Another Copy. Same. $125.00
___Another Copy. Same. $35.00

H291. HODGE (F. W.). Pueblo Snake Ceremonies. pp133-149,
wrappers. Offprint, American Anthropologist, Vol. 9,
No. 4, 1896). $10.00

H292. HODGE (F. W.). Pueblo Snake Ceremonials. 4pp, wrappers. Separate printing of material from the American
Anthropologist. n.p., 1896. $10.00

H293. HODGE (F. W.). Turquois Work of Hawikuh, New Mexico.
30pp, 2 color pls, 4to, wrappers. Museum of the American Indian, New York, 1921. $50.00

H294. HODGE (Gene Meany). Four Winds: Poems from Indian
Rituals. 34 unnumbered pp, illus by author, signed by
author on title page. Santa Fe, 1972 (1st ed.). $20.00

H295. HODGE (Gene Meany). Four Winds: Poems from Indian
Indian Kachina Dolls with Related Folktales. Forward
by Dr. Frederick W. Hodge, 129pp. Flagstaff, 1967.
                                                                                         $50.00
___Another Copy. Same. d.j. Facsimile of the 1936
edition. $45.00
___Another Copy. Same. $20.00

H296. HODGE (William H.). (University of Arizona Anthropology
Papers, No. 11, Tucson, 1969) The Albuquerque Navajos. 76pp, 4to, maps, bibliography, wrappers. $12.00

H297. HODGE (William). A Bibliography of Contemporary North
American Indians. 310pp. New York, 1976. $25.00
___Another Copy. Same. $20.00

H298. HODGSON (Adam). Letters from North America, Written
During a Tour in the United States and Canada (2 Volumes). Vol. 1: xvi, 405pp, errata. Vol. 2: iv, 459pp,

errata, frontis, folding map, illus, half leather, marbled bds, rebacked. London, Hurst, Robinson & Co., 1824.

$400.00

Howes: H-560. "Best Edition." Field: 705. "Mr. Hodgson's account of his visit to the Creek and Choctaw Indians ... contain interesting particulars relating to the aborigines and their antiquities." (RMW)

H299. HOEBEL (E. A.). (American Anthropological Assn. Memoirs, No. 54, 1940) The political Organization and Law-Ways of the Comanche Indians. 149pp. $28.00

HOFFMAN (Bernard G.). See also BAE Bulletin No. 191.

H300. HOFFMAN (Charles F.). Wild Scenes in the Forest and Prairie (2 Volumes). Vol. 1: viii, 292pp. Vol. 2: iv, 284pp. Half leather. London, Bentley, 1840.

$150.00

Howes: H-567. Field: 707. "The Indian legends and stories narrated ... are still truthful to the phases of aboriginal life which the author had witnessed." (RMW)

H301. HOFFMAN (Charles F.). A Winter in the West (2 Volumes). Vol. 1: 282pp. Vol. 2: 286pp. Original cloth, edge wear. New York, Harper Bros., 1835 (2d ed.).

$225.00

Howes: H-568. Field: 706. Field cites the voluminous notes and interesting details about Indians and gives these volumes "a high rank in aboriginal literature." (RMW)

H302. HOFFMAN (G.) and WADE (E. L.). Indianische Kunst Im 20 Jahrhundert. Malerei, Keramik and Cachinafiguren Indianische Kulturen in den USA. 373pp, 326 b/w and 101 color photographs, 4 maps, cloth. Munich, 1985.

$64.00

Published to accompany a major show of 20th-Century American Indian paintings that travelled to West German and Swiss museums in 1984 and 1985. The exhibition included 172 drawings and paintings from the late 19th Century to the present and a group of Pueblo pottery and kachinas (historic and contemporary). Ten essays (in the German text) describe the historical antecedents of the collection, which each object (drawn from 25 European and U.S. public and private collections) is fully described and illustrated in large, very fine photographs. (EAP)

H303. HOFFMAN (J. J.). (Publications in Salvage Archaeology, River Basin Survey No. 11, Lincoln, 1968) The La Roches Site. 123pp, illus, wrappers. $20.00

H304. HOFFMAN (Walter James). The Graphic Art of the Eskimos. pp739-968 from the 1895 Report of the U.S. National Museum, 82pls, drawings, map, bound separately in cloth. Washington, 1897. $45.00

____Another Copy. Same. Rebound in green linen.

$90.00

___Another Copy. New York, 1975. Cloth. $75.00

H305. HOFFMAN (W. J.). The Menomini Indians. lxi, 328pp, 38 full-page pls, 55 figures, cloth. Extracted from BAE Annual Report 14, 1896 and bound by itself. $85.00

H306. HOFFMAN (W. J.). "The Mide 'wiwin or 'Great Medicine Society' of the Ojibwa." pp143-300, illus, b/w and color pls. From the Smithsonian Institution BAE Annual Report No. 7, Washington, 1891. $20.00

H307. HOFMANN (Charles) (Editor). (Museum of the American Indian Contributions, Vol. XXIII, New York, 1968) Frances Densmore and American Indian Music; A Memorial Volume. 127pp, illus, wrappers. $12.00

H308. HOIG (Stan). The Battle of the Washita: The Sheridan-Custer Indian Campaign of 1867-69. 268pp, photographs, bibliography, index. Garden City, 1976 (1st ed.), d.j. $15.00

H309. HOIG (Stan). Peace Chiefs of the Cheyennes. xiv, 206pp, photographs, map, bibliography, index. University of Oklahoma, 1980 (1st ed.), d.j. $20.00
___Another Copy. Same. $15.00
___Another Copy. Same. $13.00
___Another Copy. Same. $10.00

H310. HOIJER (Harry). Tonkawa. An Indian Language of Texas. 148pp, wrappers. From Handbook of American Indian Language, Vol. III. New York, 1933. $17.00

H311. HOIJER (Harry) et al. (University of California Publications in Linguistics, No. 29, Berkeley, 1963 (1st ed.) Studies in the Athapaskan Languages. 154pp, 4to, wrappers. $20.00

H312. (HOKKAIDO). (University of Wisconsin, Arctic Anthropology, Vol. IV, No. 1, 1967) 261pp, maps, pls, bibliography, wrappers, large 8vo. Numerous articles including "Annotated Bibliography of the Archaeology of Hokkaido," "Preceramic Period of Hokkaido," and others. $18.00

H313. HOLDER (Preston). The Hoe and the Horse on the Plains. A Study of Cultural Development Among North American Indians. xii, 176pp, plus 8 pls, bibliography, index, University of Nebraska, Lincoln, 1970 (1st ed.), d.j. $15.00

H314. HOLE (Frank) (Editor). (Rice University Department of Anthropology, Technical Report No. 2, Houston, 1974) Archaeological Investigations along Armand Bayou, Harris County, Texas. 96pp, photographs, drawings, maps, bibliography $10.00

HOLLAND (C. G.). See also BAE Bulletin Nos. 160 and 173.

H315. HOLLAND (C. G.). (Smithsonian Institution Contributions to Anthropology, No. 12, Washington, 1970) An Archaeological Survey of Southwest Virginia. 194pp, 28 pls, 4to, some damage to end of spine. $45.00
___Another Copy. Same. $35.00

    ____Another Copy. Same. $30.00

    ____Another Copy. Same. $18.00

H316. HOLLAND (C. G.). Preceramic and Ceramic Cultural Patterns in Northwest Virginia. pp1-139, figures, folding charts, bibliography, printed wrappers. Offprint Smithsonian Anthropological Papers, Washington, 1960. $15.00

    ____Another Copy. Same. $10.00

H317. HOLLING (H. C.). The Book of Indians. 125pp, over 300 drawings, 6 full-page color pls, Juvenile, cloth. New York, 1935. $28.00

    ____Another Copy. Same. D.j. $15.00

H318. HOLLISTER (G. H.). Mount Hope; or, Philip, King of the Wampanoags: A Historical Romance. 280pp, cloth, foxed. New York, 1851. $35.00

H319. HOLLISTER (U. S.). The Navajo and His Blanket. 144pp of text containing 22 b/w photographs, plus 10 leaves of color pls, cloth cvr, photographic insert. Denver, 1903. $395.00

    Howes H-603. One of the first extensive works on Navajo weaving. Hollister was a famous collector of Navajo blankets and here writes about the Navajos and his great collection.

    ____Another Copy. Same. $250.00

    ____Another Copy. Same. $175.00

    ____Another Copy. Glorieta, 1972. $25.00

    ____Another Copy. Same. $20.00

H320. HOLLMANN (Clyde) and MITCHUM (John). Black Hawk's War. 124pp plus index, photographs, lithographs, port frontis. Philadelphia, 1973 (1st ed.), d.j. $10.00

H321. HOLLOWAY (W. L.). Wild Life on the Plains and Horrors of Indian Warfare by a Corps of Competent Authors and Artists Being a Complete History of Indian Life, Warfare and Adventure in American West With Full Description of the Messiah Craze, Ghost Dance, Life of Sitting Bull. 592pp, many illus, 3/4 leather. St. Louis, 1891 (1st ed.). $55.00

H322. HOLM (Bill). Box of Daylight: Northwest Coast Indian Art. 148pp, 245 b/w and 18 color photographs, 10 drawings, 2 maps, cloth. Seattle, 1983. $50.00

    More than 200 Northwest Coast objects--rarely seen and few previously published--drawn from private collections in the Northwest were exhibited at the Seattle Art Museum. These private collections--in the "home" of Northwest Coast art--contain more than their share of great objects, all of which are illustrated in this Catalogue of the exhibition. The text contains very complete data and interpretation for each object. (EAP)

    ____Another Copy. Same. Soft Cvr. $30.00

H323. HOLM (Bill) and QUIMBY (George). Edward S. Curtis in the Land of the War Canoes: A Pioneer Cinematographer in the Pacific Northwest. 132pp, oblong 4to, illus, index, bibliography. $45.00

Authors restored and edited a motion picture shot by Curtis in 1914 that portrayed the Kwakiutl Indians and their culture. This book is a history of the motion picture and its restoration. Illustrated with 57 full-page stills from the movie. (GFH)

____Another Copy. Same. Ex-library. $30.00
____Another Copy. Same. D.j. $25.00

H324. HOLM (Bill) and REID (W.). Form and Freedom, A Dialogue on Northwest Coast Indian Art. 265pp, 138 b/w and 50 color photographs. Houston, 1975. $30.00
____Another Copy. Same. $15.00
____Another Copy. Same. $15.00

H325. HOLM (Bill). Northwest Coast Indian Art: An Analysis of Form. 115pp, illus with over 75 figures. Seattle, 1965. $20.00
____Another Copy. Seattle, 1967, d.j. $15.00
____Another Copy. Seattle, 1971. $10.00
____Another Copy. Seattle, 1976. $10.00

H326. HOLM (Stan). Crooked Beak of Heaven. 96pp, photographs, map, bibliography, wrappers. Well illustrated presentation of masks and other ceremonial art of the Northwest Coast. Seattle, 1972 (1st print.). $15.00

HOLMBERG (A. R.). See also BAE Bulletin No. 143.

H327. HOLMBERT (A. R.). (Smithsonian Institution, Institute of Social Anthropology, Publication No. 10, 1950) Nomads of the Long Bow, The Siriono of Eastern Bolivia. iv, 104pp, 7pp photographs, map. $30.00
____Another Copy. Same. $25.00
____Another Copy. Same. $20.00
____Another Copy. University of Chicago, 1966, iii, 111pp, 7pp photographs. $10.00

H328. HOLMBERG (H. J.). Holmberg's Ethnographic Sketches. x, 133pp, fold-out map in rear pocket. Edited by N. W. Falk, translated by F. Jaensen. Originally published 1855-63. Fairbanks, 1985. $30.00

H329. HOLMER (N. M.) and WASSEN (S. H.). (Etnologiska Studier. Etnografiska Museet, Goteborg No. 21, 1953) The Complete Mu-Igala in Picture Writing, A Native Record of a Cuna Indian Medicine Song. 159pp, 33pp in b/w and 1pp in color of picture writing, inscribed by S. H. Wassen. $25.00

H330. HOLMER (N. M.) and WASSEN (S. H.). (Etnologiska Studier. Etnografiska Museet, Goteborg No. 27, 1963) Dos Cantos Shamanisticos de los Indios Cunas. 150pp. $15.00

H331. HOLMER (N. M.) and WASSEN (S. H.). (Etnologiska Studier. Etnografiska Museet, Goteborg No. 20, 1952) Inatoipippiler, or the Adventure of Three Cuna Boys and New Cuna Myths. 105pp, 1 color pl. $15.00

H332. HOLMER (N. M.) and WASSEN (S. H.). (Etnologiska
       Studier. Etnografiska Museet, Goteborg No. 23, 1958)
       Nia-Ikala, Canto Para Curar la Locura. 137pp, 6 illus.
                                                    $15.00

H333. HOLMES (Abiel). A Discourse, Delivered Before the Soci-
       ety for Propagating the Gospel Among the Indians and
       Others in North America. 68pp, original self wrappers,
       historical notes treat aboriginal affairs, give estimated
       population of Eastern Tribes. Boston, 1808. $75.00

H334. HOLMES (John). Historical Sketches of the Missions of
       the United Brethren for Propagating the Gospel Among
       the Heathen, From Their Commencement to the Present
       Time. 8pp, 472pp, diced calf, joints worn. Dublin,
       Printed by R. Napper, 1818. $250.00
          Sabin: 32606. Field: 712 (2d ed. only). The au-
       thor was Minister of the Brethren's Congregation in
       Dublin, and here records a history of their missions
       among the Delaware and Iroquois, as well as in Green-
       land, Labrador, the West Indies and South America.
       (WR)
       ___Another Copy. Same. Ex-library. $165.00
HOLMES (William H.). See also BAE Bulletin Nos. 3, 7, 21, 23,
       52 and 60.

H335. HOLMES (W. H.). Aboriginal Pottery of the Eastern United
       States. 201pp of text, 79 figures, 127pp photographs,
       drawings, cloth, gilt spine. Extracted from the 10th
       Annual Report of the Bureau of American Ethnology,
       1903. $130.00

H336. HOLMES (W. H.). (Field Museum, Anthropology Series,
       Vol. 1, No. 1, Publications 8 and 16, Chicago, 1895-97)
       Archaeological studies Among the Ancient Cities of Mexi-
       co, Parts 1 and 2. Part 1: Monuments of the Yucatan.
       Part 2: Monuments of Chiapas, Oaxaca and the Valley
       of Mexico. Original gilt-stamped linen. $125.00
          Holmes' 1897 study of the monuments and figures of
       Chiapas, Oaxaca and the Valley of Mexico was one of the
       earliest serious archaeological studies of the area, and
       remains one of the most respected. (EAP)
       ___Another Copy. Part 2 only. 196pp, 31 full-page
       and double-page drawings, 80 figures. $49.00

H337. HOLMES (W. H.). Flint Implements and Fossil Remains
       from a Sulphur Spring at Afton, Indian Territory.
       pp233-252, 26 pls, wrappers. From U.S. National Mu-
       seum Report for 1901, Washington, 1903. $20.00

H338. HOLMES (W. H.). Pottery of the Ancient Pueblos. 102pp,
       146 illus. Extracted from 4th Annual Report of Bureau
       of American Ethnology, Washington, 1886, Seattle 1971
       reprint. $14.00

H339. HOLMES (W. H.). Stone Implements of the Potomac-
       Chesapeake Tidewater Province. 152pp, 4to, 103 pls,
       29 figures. Extracted from the Bureau of American
       Ethnology 15th Annual Report, Washington, 1897. $50.00

H340. HOLTVED (Erik). (Meddelelser om Gronland, Bd. 182,
Nr. 2, Kobenhavn, 1967) Contribution to Polar Eskimo
Ethnography. 180pp, figures, wrappers, presentation
copy. $58.00

H341. HOLTZ (G.). Indian Skin Paintings from the American
Southwest. xiv, 248pp, 18 full-page photographs, 3
drawings, 3 maps, cloth. Norman, 1970. $19.00

HOLZINGER (C. H.). See also BAE Bulletin No. 180.

H342. HONIGMANN (John J.). (Yale University Publications in
Anthropology, No. 40, 1949) Culture and Ethos of
Kaska Society. 365pp of text containing 7 figures, plus
12pp of photographs, wrappers. $70.00
___Another Copy. Same. $60.00
___Another Copy. Same. $25.00

H343. HONIGMANN (John and Irma). Eskimo Townsmen. 278pp,
illus, wrappers, wear to slipcover. University of Ottawa, 1965. $35.00

H344. HONIGMANN (John). (Publications in Anthropology, No.
33 and 34, Yale University, 1946) Ethnography and
Acculturation of the Fort Nelson Slave. Bound with
Mason Notes on the Indians of the Great Slave Lake
Area. 169pp and 42pp, illus, wrappers. $35.00

H345. HONIGMANN (John J.). (Yale University Publications in
Anthropology, No. 51, 1954) The Kaska Indians: An
Ethnographic Reconstruction. 163pp, 6 figures. $40.00
___Another Copy. Same. $40.00
___Another Copy. Same. $17.00
___Another Copy. New Haven, 1964. $30.00

H346. HONIGMANN (John J.). (National Museum of Canada, Bulletin No. 178, 1962) Social Networks in Great Whale
River. vi, 110pp, 9pp photographs, 2 maps. $28.00

H347. HONORE (Pierre). In Quest of the White God: The Mysterious Heritage of South American Civilization. Translated from the German. Illus. London, 1963, d.j.
$25.00

H348. HOOPER (Lucile). (University of California Publications
in American Archaeology and Ethnology, Vol. 16, No.
6, Berkeley, 1920) The Cahuilla Indians. pp315-380,
wrappers. $25.00
___Another Copy. Same. $20.00

H349. HOOTON (Earnest A.). (Peabody Museum Papers, Vol.
VIII, No. 1, Cambridge, 1920) Indian Village Site and
Cemetery Near Madisonville, Ohio. 135pp, illus, folded
map, wrappers. $20.00
___Another Copy. Same. With C. C. Willoughby,
146pp, 30pp illus. $24.00

H350. HOOVER (Herbert T.). The Chitimacha People. 100pp,
drawings, b/w and color photographs, maps, wrappers.
Indian Tribal Series. Phoenix 1975 (1st ed.). $12.50

H351. (HOPEWELL). (Illinois State Museum Scientific Papers,

Vol. 12, 1970, 2d print.) Hopewellian Studies. 156pp,
illus, bibliography. $10.00

H352. (HOPI). The Year of the Hopi. Paintings and Photographs by Joseph Mora, 1904-06. 87pp, photographs,
paintings, bibliography, pictorial wrappers. $10.00

H353. HOPKINS (D. M.) and GIDDINGS (J. L. Jr.). (Smithsonian Miscellaneous Publications, Vol. 121:11, Washington, 1953) Geological Background of the Iyatayet
Archaeological Site, Cape Denbigh, Alaska. 33pp,
illus, wrappers. $15.00

H354. HOPKINS (Sarah Winnemucca). Life Among the Paiutes.
268pp, cloth. Boston, 1883. $150.00
A remarkable book, written by an Indian woman about
her life and especially the course of White-Indian con-
tact in the Great Basin. The fate of her tribe before
and during the reservation period are told in detail.
The manuscript was edited for publication by Mrs. Horace
Mann. Graff: 1950. Rader: 1927. (WR)
____Another Copy. Same. Life Among the Paiutes;
Their Wrongs and Claims. $150.00
____Another Copy. Same. $75.00

H355. HOPPER (J. H.) (Editor). Indians of Brazil in the Twen-
tieth Century. xxx, 256pp (5 papers), 52 b/w drawings, 5pp colored pls of feathered objects, 26 photographs, 14 maps, cloth. Institute for Cross-Cultural
Research, Washington, 1967. $45.00

H356. HORAN (James D.). The McKenney-Hall Portrait Gallery
of American Indians. 373pp, 4to, illus. New York
1972 (1st ed.). $45.00
Large 9" x 12" volume includes the 128 color portraits of some of the most famous Indians in American
history as painted over 150 years ago by a group of
the country's most perceptive artists and originally issued in a 3-volume portfolio in 1836. The author has
written individual biographies of each of the Indians
based on firsthand source material and also a full length
biography of Col. McKenney. (GFH)
____Another Copy. Same. $35.00
____Another Copy. Same. Limited to 249 copies, signed
by author, boxed, 1/2 leather. $125.00

H357. HORAN (J. D.). North American Indian Portraits. 120
Full Color Plates from the McKenney-Hall Portrait Gallery
of American Indians. 128pp, 120 full-page color pls.
New York, 1975. $12.00

H358. HORCASITOS (Fernando). The Aztecs Then and Now.
168pp, 54 photographs, 22 drawings, 5 maps. Mexico
City, 1979. $12.00

H359. HORCASITOS (Fernando) (Translator and editor). Life
and Death in Milpa Alta: A Nahuatl Chronicle of Diaz
and Zapata. xx, 187pp, foreword by Miguel Leon-
Portilla, drawings by Alberto Beltran, map, from the

Nahuatl recollecitons of Dona Luz Jimenez, cloth. Norman, 1972 (1st ed.) d.j. $15.00

    This work is a collection of Nahuatl texts on the epoch of Porfirio Diaz (1876-1910) and the revolution (1910-19) that overthrew his regime. It is here published in Nahuatl, or Aztec, and English. It is the first documentation from the Indian point of view of the revolution and the region over which Carranza and Zapata fought for control of Mexico's destiny. (TE)

____Another Copy. Same. $20.00

____Another Copy. Same. Civilization of the American Indian Series, Vol. 117. $15.00

H360. HORKHEIMER (H.). (Instituto Arqueologico de la Universidad Nacional de Trujillo, 1944) Vistas Arqueologicas del Noroeste del Peru. 83pp, 84 illus, fold-out map, decorated cloth, inscribed by author. $28.00

____Another Copy. Same. $25.00

H361. HORSE CAPTURE (G. P.) and BALL (G.) (Editors). Fifth Annual Plains Indian Seminar in Honor of Dr. John C. Ewers. 146pp, 75 photographs, 5pp drawings, 1 map. Cody. 1980. $38.00

    In honor of the life work of one of the major figures in Plains Indian ethnology, this seminar was dedicated. The papers presented reflected both the affection and respect in which the honoree was held, and they concentrated on topics identified with him. Among the eight well-illustrated papers in this out of print volume are those dealing with Plains Indian ceremonial shirts, Crow ledger art, Crow beadwork and the art and culture of the Northern Plains from 1875 to 1881. (EAP)

H362. HORSE CAPTURE (G. P.). Indian Feathers. Yesterday's Tradition, Today's Care, Tomorrow's Prize. 39pp, 23 photographs, 2 drawings, history and conservation of Indian artifacts with eagle feathers. Cody, 1982.
$28.00

H363. HORSE CAPTURE (G. P.) (Editor). Native American Ribbonwork: A Rainbow Tradition. Fourth Annual Plains Indian Seminar. 56pp, 25 photographs, 21 figures, 1 map. Cody, 1980. $30.00

H364. HORSMAN (Reginald). Matthew Elliott, British Indian Agent. xiii, 256pp, notes, bibliography, index, map. A furtrader in the Ohio Valley in the years immediately preceding the Revolutionary War. Detroit, Wayne University, 1964 (1st ed.), d.j. $20.00

HORTON (Donald). See also BAE Bulletin No. 143.

H365. HOSMAN (Elene). Ambiente de Altiplano: Fotos de Peru y Bolivia, Tipos y Costumbres Populares--la Nota Colonial --el Acento Incaico y PreIncaico. 22pp, 147 illus photographs by author, 4to. Buenos Aires, n.d. $35.00

H366. (HOSTILITIES). A Further Brief and True Narration of the Great Swamp Fight in the Narragansett Country,

December 19, 1675. 6pp, 12pp, limited to 300 copies.
Facsimile reproduciton of the 1676 ed. of which there
are only 2 known copies, details the great fight in which
some 500 Narragansett Indians (excluding count of women
and children) were slain, with 30 colonists slain. Providence, RI, 1912. $35.00

H367. (HOSTILITIES). Penhallow's Indian Wars. A Facsimile
Reprint of the First Edition ... Boston ... 1726. With
Notes of Earlier Editors and Additions from the Original
Manuscript. 134pp plus 42pp of notes, 2pp bibliography
and index, notes, index and introduction by Edward
Wheelock. Best early summary of New England's early
Indian wars. Howes: P-201. Field: 1203. Boston,
1924. $10.00

H368. (HOSTILITIES). (House of Representatives Document 434,
25:2, Washington, 1838) Indians Hostile on Western
Frontier. 10pp, removed. Problems with Indians killing
settlers' stock and raiding farms in winter. $18.00

H369. (HOSTILITIES). (House of Representatives Executive
Document 1, 31:2, Washington, 1850) Correspondence
On The Subject of Indian Hostilities in Texas, New
Mexico and California. 113pp, removed, in protective
wrappers. $65.00
___Another Copy. Same. $60.00

H370. (HOSTILITIES). (Senate Executive Document 22, 33:2,
Washington, 1855, 1st print.) Indian Hostilities. 7pp,
removed. Reports from Fort Laramie and Fort Pierce.
                                                         $15.00

H371. (HOSTILITIES). (House of Representatives Executive
Document 93, 34:1, Washington, 1856, 1st ed.) Indian
Hostilities in Oregon and Washington. 144pp, removed.
                                                         $45.00

H372. (HOSTILITIES). (House of Representatives Executive
Document 118, 34:1, Washington, 1856, 1st ed.) Indian
Hostilities in Oregon and Washington Territories. 58pp,
removed. $35.00

H373. (HOSTILITIES). (House of Representatives Executive
Document 11, 36:1, Washington, 1860, 1st ed.) Claims
growing out of Indian Hostilities in Oregon and Washington in 1855 and 1856. 132pp, removed. $45.00

H374. (HOSTILITIES). (House of Representatives Executive
Document 69, 36:1, Washington, 1860) Indian Hostilities
in New Mexico, 64pp, removed, wrappers. Reports on
continued difficulties with the Navaho in late 1859 and
early 1860 with details on skirmishes and the difficulty
of campaigns against them. Powell Serial Set, 1051.
                                                         $45.00

H375. (HOSTILITIES). (Senate Executive Document 13, 40:1,
Washington, 1867, 1st print.) Indian Hostilities on the
Frontier. 127pp, removed. Reports on the Fort Phil.
Kearney massacre, from Fort Dodge, Dakota Territory,
etc. $40.00

H376. (HOSTILITIES). (House of Representatives Executive
Document 44, 41:2, Washington, 1869) Suppressing Indian Hostilities in Utah. 8pp, removed. The hostilities
of 1865-67. $10.00

HOSTOS (Adolfo de). See also BAE Bulletin No. 143.

H377. HOTZ (Gottfried). Indian Skin Paintings from American
Southwest. Two Representations of Border Conflicts
Between Mexico and the Missouri in Early 18th Century,
xiv, 248pp, 18pp of photographs, 3 maps, paper cvrd
bds. Norman, 1970 (1st ed.) d.j. $25.00
___Another Copy. Same. $22.00
___Another Copy. Same. $12.00

H378. HOUER (H.). (Viking Fund Publications in Anthropology,
No. 6, 1946) Linguistic Structures of Native America.
423pp. $30.00

H379. HOUGH (Franklin B.) (Editor). Diary of the Siege of
Detroit in the War with Pontiac. xxiii, 304pp, index,
4to, half leather, limited to 136 copies. Albany, J.
Munsell, 1860 (1st ed.). $300.00
Howes: H-675. Sabin: 33138. Field: 719. Also
contains: "Narrative of the Principal Events of the
Siege by Major R. Rogers; A Plan for Conducting Indian
Affairs by Col. Bradstreet." Howes: "The diarist was
Lt. Jehu Day. Here first printed from his ms." (RMW)

H380. HOUGH (Franklin B.). (Third Annual Report of the Regents of the University, Albany, 1850) Notice of Several Ancient Remains of Art, in Jefferson and St. Lawrence Counties, New York State. Revised Ed. pp101-
105, plus 5 pls, which are drawings of ancient burial
places, wrappers. $35.00

H381. HOUGH (Franklin B.) (Editor). Proceedings of the Commissioners of Indian Affairs, Appointed by Law for the
Extinguishment of Indian Titles in the State of New York
(2 Volumes). Vol. 1: 255pp. Vol. 2: 257-501pp.
3 folding maps, index, half leather, marbled bds. Albany, J. Munsell, 1861. $225.00
Field: 723. Record of the taking of lands from the
Six Nations in New York, with maps of the Indian lands.
___Another Copy. 1861, the 2 volumes bound together,
same collation. $200.00

HOUGH (Walter). See also BAE Bulletin No. 35.

H382. HOUGH (Walter). (Report of the U.S. National Museum,
1901) Archaeological Field Work in Northeastern Arizona.
The Museum-Gates Expedition of 1901. pp279-358, plus
101 pls of multiple artifacts, including 30 color pls illus
ancient pottery, excavations include Forestdale, Linden,
Scorse Ranch, Canyon Butte Wash, Stone Ax Ruin,
Jettyto Valley Ruins, newly rebound in blue linen.
$125.00

H383. HOUGH (Walter). (U.S. National Museum, Vol. 42, Washington, 1912) Censers and Incense of Mexico and Central
America. pp109-137, 14 pls (29 illus). $35.00

H384. HOUGH (Walter). (Proceedings of U.S. National Museum, Vol. 81, Part 7, Washington, 1932) Decorative Designs on Elden Pueblo Pottery, Flagstaff, Arizona. 21pp, illus with 10 full-page photographs, map, wrappers.
$12.00

H385. HOUGH (Walter). Exploration of Ruins in the White Mountain Apache Indian Reservation, Arizona. 21pp of text plus 10pp photographs. Offprint of Proceedings of the U.S. National Museum, Vol. 78, Washington, 1930.
$24.00

H386. HOUGH (Walter). (Smithsonian: U.S. National Museum Bulletin 139, Washington, 1926) Fire as an Agent in Human Culture. 270pp, 40 photographs, wrappers.
$25.00

H387. HOUGH (Walter). "Fire-making Apparatus in the U.S. National Museum." pp531-587 from the 1888 Report of the National Museum, drawings, bound in later cloth. Washington, 1888. $15.00

H388. HOUGH (Walter). (Proceedings of the U.S. National Museum, Vol. 54, Washington, 1919) The Hopi Indian Collection in the United States National Museum. pp235-296 containing 48 figures, plus 26 leaves of photographs and 9 leaves of drawings of Hopi artifacts. Frnt and rear wrappers missing, else very good. $39.00

H389. HOUGH (Walter). (Smithsonian Institution Annual Report, Washington, 1896) The Lamp of the Eskimo. pp1027-1057, 4 figures, 24pp of drawings, 24pp descriptions, offprint of Annual Report, original wrappers, spine reinforced. $40.00

H390. HOUGH (Walter). The Moki Snake Dance. 68pp, 64 half-tone illus from special photographs, decorative wrappers. Passenger Dept., Santa Fe Route, n.p. (Chicago), 1899. $30.00

H391. HOUGLAND (Willard). Santos. A Primitive American Art Collection of Jan Kleijkamp and Ellis Monroe. 44pp, map, photographs, bibliography, wrappers. New York, 1946 (1st ed.). $25.00

H392. HOULIHAN (P. T.) and SELSER (C.). (Intro) One Thousand Years of Southwestern Indian Ceramic Art. 28pp, 12pp color photographs and 5 full-page b/w photographs. Exhibition Catalogue, ACA American Indian Arts, New York, 1981. $10.00

H393. HOUSTON (James A.). Canadian Eskimo Art. 40pp, 4to, illus, wrappers. Ottawa, 1964. $10.00

H394. HOWARD (Donald M.). Primitives in Paradise; The Monterey Peninsula Indians. 72pp, illus, map, wrappers. Monterey, 1975 (1st ed.). $10.00

H395. HOWARD (Edgar B.). (Museum Journal, Vol. 24, Nos. 2-3, Philadelphia, 1935) Evidence of Early Man in North America. 175pp, 25 pls, folding plan, small 4to, wrappers. Folsom and Yuma artifacts. $25.00

H396. HOWARD (G. D.). (Yale University Publications in Anthropology, No. 37, 1947) Prehistoric Ceramic Styles of
Lowland South America, Their Distribution and History.
95pp of text containing 15 figures, 3 tables and 15pp of
photographs. $45.00

H397. HOWARD (Helen A.) and McGRATH (Dan L.). War Chief
Joseph. 368pp, appendices, index, notes, references,
bibliography, color frontis, 14 full-page pls, color map.
Caldwell, 1958 (4th print), d.j. $25.00
___Another Copy. Caldwell, 1941 (1st ed.), 362pp,
pls, colored frontis of Joseph, maps, bibliography,
geneology, index. $50.00
___Another Copy. Caldwell, 1952 (3rd ed.). $25.00

HOWARD (James H.). See also BAE Bulletin Nos. 173, 189 and
195.

H398. HOWARD (James H.). (University of Nebraska Studies in
the Anthropology of North American Indians, Lincoln,
1984) The Canadian Sioux. 207pp, index, map, bibliography, cloth. $20.00
___Another Copy. Same. $18.00

H399. HOWARD (James H.). Oklahoma Seminoles, Medicine,
Magic and Religion. 279pp, illus, index, bibliography.
Norman, 1984 (1st ed.), d.j. $25.00
___Another Copy. Same. $23.00
___Another Copy. Civilization of the American Indian
Series, Vol. 166, Norman, 1984, 266pp plus index,
photographs, drawings, notes, bibliography. $20.00

H400. HOWARD (James H.) (Editor and Translator). The War-
rior Who Killed Custer. The Personal Narrative of
Chief Joseph White Bull. 82pp, b/w and color illus,
bibliography, from White Bull's 1931 account. Luther
High Spot, 106. Lincoln, 1968 (1st print.) d.j. $20.00
___Another Copy. Lincoln, 1969 (2d print.) no d.j.
                                                           $10.00

H401. HOWARD (Joseph H.). Drums in the Americas. 316pp
plus index, photographs, maps, drawings, glossary,
bibliography, notes. Much on American Indian drums.
New York, 1967 (1st print.). $20.00

H402. HOWARD (O. O.). Famous Indian Chiefs I Have Known.
364pp, illus (several by George Varian). Cochise, Capt.
Jack, Joseph, Red Cloud, Sitting Bull and others.
Howe: H-709. Rader: 1954. New York, 1908 (1st
print.). $45.00
___Another Copy. Same. $95.00

H403. HOWARD (O. O.). My Life and Experiences Among our
Hostile Indians. A Record of Personal Observations,
Adventures and Campaigns Among the Indians of the
Great West.... 570pp, frontis, 46 pls with 10 in color,
cloth rebacked in morocco. Hartford, 1907. $125.00
___Another Copy. Same. $150.00
___Another Copy. Hartford n.d. (c.1907). $100.00

H404. HOWARD (O. O.). Nez Perce Joseph, an Account of His
Ancestors, His Lands, His Confederates, His Enemies,
His Murders, His War, His Pursuit and Capture. xii,
274pp, 2 frontis portraits, 2 maps, one is folding.
Boston, Lee and Shepard, 1881 (1st ed.). $350.00
___Another Copy. Same. $350.00
___Another Copy. Same. $200.00

H405. HOWE (Carrol B.). Ancient Tribes of the Klamath Country. 248pp plus index, photographs, sources, map endpapers. Good illus of artifacts. Portland, OR, 1968
(1st ed.). $25.00
___Another Copy. Same. $15.00
___Another Copy. Same. $15.00
___Another Copy. Portland, 1969, d.j. $15.00

H406. HOWLEY (James P.). The Beothuks or Red Indians: The
Aboriginal Inhabitants of Newfoundland. 348pp, frontis,
17 pls of implements and ornaments, 14 drawings, 9
illus, 4to. The results of 40 years of research, including interviews with persons who had actual contact with
some of the aborigines. Cambridge, London, 1915 (1st
ed.). $250.00
___Another Copy. Toronto, 1974, facsimile in smaller
format of 1915 ed. $40.00

H407. HOXIE (Frederick E.) A Final Promise: The Campaign
to Assimilate the Indians, 1880-1920. 350pp, illus, bibliography. Lincoln, 1984 (1st ed.). $25.00

H408. HOYLE (R. L.). Peru. 243pp, 76 b/w and 91 color
photographs (many full page), 4 maps, cloth. Geneva,
1966. $50.00
    The seven epochs of ancient Peruvian cultural de-
velopment are examined in this volume (part of the
"Archaeologia Mundi" series) that deals with every medium of Peruvian art. The bulk of the illustrations are
of objects from the Herrera Museum, Lima, and most have
never before been published. (EAP)
___Another Copy. Cleveland, 1966, d.j. $20.00

H409. HOYT (E.). Antiquarian Researches: Comprising a History of the Indian Wars in the Country Bordering Connecticut River and Parts Adjacent, and Other Interesting Events ... With Notices of Indian Depredations.
312 pp, engraved title, folding view of Hoyt's house in
Deerfield, rebound, untrimmed. Greenfield, MA, Ansel
Phelps, 1824 (1st ed.). $150.00
___Another Copy. Same. Later half linen. $85.00

HRDLICKA (Ales). See also BAE Bulletin Nos. 33, 34, 38, 42,
52, 62, 66, 143 and 182.

H410. HRDLICKA (Ales). Alaska Diary, 1926-1931. 414pp, portrait, 232 figures (most are photographs). Lancaster,
1943. $50.00

H411. HRDLICKA (Ales). The Anthropology of Kodiak Island.
xix, 486pp, bibliography, index, illus with photographs.
Philadelphia, Wistar Institute, 1944. $100.00

H412. HRDLICKA (Ales). Catalog of Human Crania in the U.S. National Museum Collections. Eskimo in General. 260pp, wrappers. Offprint from Proceedings U.S. National Museum, Vol. 91, Washington, 1942. $10.00

H413. HRDLICKA (Ales). The "Chichimecs" and Their Ancient Culture with Notes on the Tepecanos and the Ruins of La Quemada Mexico. 55pp, illus, wrappers. Offprint from American Anthropologist, Vol. 5, No. 3. $20.00
___Another Copy. Same. $18.00

H414. HRDLICKA (Ales). (American Museum of Natural History, Anthropological Papers, Vol. V, Part II, 1910) Contribution to the Anthropology of Central and Smith Sound Eskimo. pp177-280, plus 15pp of photographs, wrappers. $55.00
___Another Copy. Same. $25.00

H415. HRDLICKA (Ales). (Smithsonian Miscellaneous Collections, Vol. 101:4, Washington, 1941) Diseases of and Artifacts on Skulls and Bones from Kodiak Island. 14pp, 11 pls, 8vo, wrappers. $15.00

H416. HRDLICKA (Ales). An Eskimo Brain. 48pp, illus, wrappers. New York, Knickerbocker Press, 1901. $25.00
___Another Copy. Same. $25.00

H417. HRDLICKA (Ales). The Most Ancient Skeletal Remains of Man. pp491-552, 41 pls, wrappers. Reprinted from Smithsonian Annual Report, Washington, 1914. $20.00
___Another Copy. Same. $10.00

H418. HRDLICKA (Ales). Notes on the Indians of Sonora Mexico. 40pp, illus, wrappers. Offprint from American Anthropologist, Vol. 6, No. 1. $20.00
___Another Copy. Same. $18.00

H419. HRDLICKA (Ales). A Painted Skeleton from Northern Mexico with Notes on Bone Painting Among the American Aborigines. 24pp, figures, wrappers. Offprint from the American Anthropologist, Vol. 3, 1910. $13.00
___Another Copy. Same. $10.00

H420. HRDLICKA (Ales). The Painting of Human Bones Among the American Aborigines. 10pp, color illus, wrappers. Reprint from Smithsonian for 1904, Government Printing Office, Washington. $15.00

H421. HRDLICKA (Ales). (Smithsonian Institution, Miscellaneous Collections, Vol. 99, No. 3, Washington, 1946) Ritual Ablation of Front Teeth in Siberia and America. 32pp, illus, wrappers. $30.00
___Another Copy. Same. $10.00

H422. HRDLICKA (Ales). (Smithsonian Miscellaneous Collections, Vol. 56, No. 16, Washington, 1911) Some Results of Recent Anthropological Exploration in Peru. 16pp, illus, 1 in color, wrappers. $10.00

H423. HSU (D. P.) et al. (Texas Historical Commission Survey Reports, No. 3, Austin, n.d., 1st ed.) Appraisal of Archaeological Resources Big Cyprus (Franklin

County) Reservoir. 53pp, illus, maps, bibliography, lrg 8vo, wrappers. $10.00

H424. HSU (D. P.) and RALPH (R. W.). (Texas Historical Commission Survey Reports, No. 1, Austin, 1968, 1st ed.) Appraisal of Archaeological Resources of Cibolo Reservoir, Wilson County, texas. 58pp plus 8 pls, illus, maps, bibliography, lrg 8vo, wrappers. $10.00

H425. HSU (D. P.). (Texas Historical Commission Survey Reports, No. 2, Austin, 1968, 1st ed.) Appraisal Archaeological Resources Timber Creek and Bois d'Arc Reservoirs Fannin County, Texas. 29pp plus 4 pls, illus, maps, bibliography, lrg 8vo, wrappers. $10.00

H426. HSU (D. P.). (Texas Historical Commission Survey Reports, No. 4, Austin, 1969, 1st ed.) Appraisal of Archaeology Resources Titus County Reservoir, Titus, Camp and Franklin Counties, Texas. 38pp, illus, maps, bibliography, lrg 8vo, wrappers. $10.00

H427. HSU (D. P.). (Texas Historical Commission Survey Reports, No. 5, Austin, 1969, 1st ed.) Arthur Patperson Site, a Mid-Nineteenth Century Site, San Jacinto County, Texas. 51pp, illus, maps, bibliography, lrg 8vo, wrappers. $10.00

H428. HUBBARD (J. Niles). An Account of Sa-Go-Ye-Wat-Ha; or, Redjacket and His People, 1750-1830. xvi, 9-356pp, index, frontis, illus, cloth. Albany, Joel Munsell, 1886. $60.00

H429. HUBBARD (Jeremiah). Forty Years Among the Indians. 200pp, pls, 12mo. Quaker missionary to various tribes in Kansas, Missouri and Oklahoma. Light cvr soil and wear. Miami, OK, 1913 (1st ed.). $200.00

H430. HUBBARD (William). A Narrative of the Indian Wars in New England, from the First Planting Thereof in the Year 1607, to the Year 1677. 8pp, 288pp, full calf. Boston, 1775. $300.00
     Howes: H-756. Field: 731. Important authority on these Indian Wars.
     ___Another Copy. Norwich, CT, 1802, 16mo, modern quarter morocco, raised bands. $60.00
     ___Another Copy. Stockbridge, MA, 1803, 12mo, calf. $50.00
     ___Another Copy. Brattleborough, Wm. Fessenden, 1814, 359pp, original leather. $125.00
     ___Another Copy. Roxbury, MA, 1865, xxxiv, 292pp, 303pp, lrg 4to, folding map, revised ed. with notes by Samuel G. Drake, number 10 of 50 large paper copies in a total edition of 350, this is considered the "best" modern edition, half maroon morocco. $175.00

H431. HUCKEL (J. F.) (Editor). American Indians. First Families of the Southwest. 30 color illus, rugs, blankets, pottery, general life styles of the Indians, wrappers. Kansas City, 1928 (4th ed.). $25.00
     ___Another Copy. Same. $15.00

H432. HUDDLESTON (Lee Eldridge). (Latin American Monographs
No. 11, Institute of Latin American Studies, Austin,
1967) Origins of the American Indians, European Concepts, 1492-1729. ix, 179pp, wrappers. $25.00
___Another Copy. Austin, 1972 (3rd print.) d.j.
$10.00

H433. HUDSON (A. E.). (Yale University Publications in Anthropology, No. 20, 1938, 1964) Kazak Social Structure,
109pp, map. $35.00

H434. HUDSON (Charles). The Southeastern Indians. 557pp
plus index, drawings, photographs, map, notes, bibliography. Full coverage from Prehistory to removal.
University of Tennessee, 1980 (3rd print.) d.j. $15.00

H435. HUDSON (Dee T.). (San Diego Museum Papers No. 13,
1977) Chumash Wooden Bowls, Trays and Boxes. 37pp,
6 illus, wrappers. $12.00
___Another Copy. Same. $10.00

H436. HUDSON (Dee T.). (Ethnic Technology Notes, No. 13,
San Diego, 1974) Chumash Archery Equipment. 34pp,
2pp photographs, 1pp drawings, 1 figure, 1 map.
$10.00

H437. HUDSON (Travis) and UNDERHAY (Ernest). (Anthropological Papers, No. 1, Socorro, 1978) Crystals in the
Sky: An Intellectual Odyssey Involving Chumash Astronomy, Cosmology and Rock Art. 164pp, wrappers.
$25.00

H438. HUDSON (Travis) et al. (Editors). (Santa Barbara Bicentennial Historical Series, Vol. 4, Santa Barbara, 1977,
1st ed.) The Eye and The Flute. Chumash Tradition
History and Ritual, as told by Fernando Librado Kit-
sepawat. 133pp plus index, frontis painting in color,
illus by Campbell Grant, glossary, bibliography, map
endpapers, limited to 500 copies. $35.00

H439. HUDSON (T.) and BLACKBURN (T. C.). The Material
Culture of the Chumash Interaction Sphere. Vol. 1:
Food Procurement and Transportation. 392pp, 245
illus, cloth. Palo Alto, 1982. $50.00
After the massive acquisition of Chumash artifacts
by the great museums in the late 19th Century, most of
the artifacts were virtually forgotten for many years.
This volume contains 245 photographs and drawings of
objects used in hunting, fishing, gathering and trans-
portation--from nets, trays, harpoons and burden
baskets to cradleboards and the famous Chumash plank
canoes. (EAP)
___Another Copy. Same. Soft cover. $30.00

H440. HUDSON (T.) and BLACKBURN (T. C.). The Material
Culture of the Chumash Interaction Sphere. Vol. II:
Food Preparation and Shelter. 453pp, 427 figures, 3
tables. Palo Alto, 1983. $60.00
This is the second volume in a series that illus

virtually every material object used by the Chumash and
their neighbors, the Kitanemuk and Gabrielino. Vol. II
contains photographs and drawings of items associated
with storage, processing, cooking, serving, housing,
firemaking and furnishing--everything from bottles,
baskets and bowls to blankets, beds and buildings.
Most of the objects have not been previously described
or illus--nor has much of the ethnographic data been
previously published--and are from over forty museum
and private collections around the world. (EAP)

H441. HUDSON (T.) and BLACKBURN (T. C.). The Material
Culture of the Chumash Interaction Sphere. Vol. III:
Clothing, Ornamentation and Grooming. 375pp, 187
photographs and drawings, 1 map, cloth. Menlo Park,
1985. $60.00
    Vol. III in this series, dealing with the rich diversity
of items associated with nonsecular body adornment,
represents a significant addition to the literature, containing as it does a wealth of new data and illus on
Chumash costumes, dances and adornments. The illus
objects--drawn from collections in the U.S., Spain,
France, the U.S.S.R., and England--are for the most
part unpublished and are catalogued in meticulous detail
in a text that disproves earlier historical accounts of
Chumash clothing and ornamentation. (EAP)
____Another Copy. Same. Soft Cover. $40.00

H442. HUGHES (Charles C.). Eskimo Boyhood. An Autobiography in Psychosocial Perspective. 429pp, drawings, references, map endpapers. A young Eskimo relates his
life during the 1930s and 1940s. Lexington, KY, 1974.
                                                  $12.00

H443. HUGHES (Herbert). The Indian Miguels, Chiefs and Scholars. 71pp, illus, well illus work on the Indians in and
around Fort Yuma on the California side of the Colorado
River, wrappers. n.p., 1980. $12.00

H444. HUGHES (J. T. and P. S.). (Texas Historical Commission
Survey Reports, No. 24, Austin, 1978, 1st ed.)
Archaeology Mackenzie Reservoir. 204pp, illus, maps,
bibliography, lrg 8vo, wrappers. $17.00
____Another Copy. Same. $12.00

H445. HUGHES (Thomas). Indian Chiefs of Southern Minnesota;
Containing Sketches of the Prominent Chieftains of the
Dakota and Winnebago Tribes from 1825 to 1865. 196pp,
illus, index. Source work in the study of the Sioux,
particularly the Wabash Dynasty, the Red Wing Dynasty
and the Shakpay Dynasty. Minneapolis, 1969, (2nd ed.),
d.j. $17.00

H446. HULBERT (A. B.) and SCHWATZE (W. N.) (Editors).
(Ohio Archaeological and Historical Quarterly, Vol. XIX,
Nos. 1 & 2, 1910) David Zeisberger's History of North
American Indians. 189pp. $47.00
____Another Copy. Same. $30.00

H447. HULSIZER (A.). Religion and Culture in the Curriculum of the Navaho and the Dakota. xxv, 344pp, 11 tables, cloth. Federalsburg, 1940. $30.00

H448. HUME (Ivor N.). Historical Archaeology. xiii, 355pp, v, illus, bibliography, index. A handbook for amateur or student archaeologist. New York, 1969 (1st ed.), d.j. $15.00

H449. HUMFREVILLE (J. Lee). Twenty Years Among Our Hostile Indians. xiii, 479pp, illus with photographs. New York, 1899. $85.00

H450. HUMPHREY (Herman). Indian Rights and Our Duties. 24pp, 12mo, removed. Albany, Indian Rights Assn., 1831. $50.00
    Field: 741. Strong plea for better treatment of Indians by White conquerors.

H451. HUMPHREY (R. L.) and STAFFORD (D.) (Editors). Pre-Llano Cultures of the Americas: Paradoxes and Possibilities. ix, 150pp (6 papers) 73 figures. Anthropological Society of Washington, 1979. $18.00

H452. HUMPHREY (Seth K.). The Indian Dispossessed. 298pp, Boston, 1906 (revised ed.). $30.00

H453. HUMPHREYS (David). An Historical Account of the Incorporated Society for the Propagation of the Gospel in Foreign Parts. xxxii, 356pp, 2 folding maps, one of the Carolinas and one of New England, 8vo, rebound in half leather, marbled bds. London, Joseph Downing, 1730 (1st ed.). $750.00
    Howes: H-795. Account of early contacts with the Iroquois, Mohawks and other tribes, translation of the Bible into Indian languages, missions to North and South Carolina. (RMW)

H454. HUNDLEY (Will M.). Squawtown. My Boyhood Among the Last Miami Indians. 209pp, drawings by R. W. Hall with color frontis, ex-library but no spine or exterior marking. Caldwell, 1939 (1st ed.). $10.00
    As a young boy in 1875, the author lived on the Mississinewa Reservation with those Miami Indians under Francis Godfrey that had not been forced to remove to Indian Territory. (TNL)

H455. HUNGRY WOLF (A. & B.). The Blackfoot Craftworker's Book. 79pp, 202 photographs, 20 drawings. Invermere, 1977. $27.00

H456. HUNGRY WOLF (Beverly). The Ways of My Grandmothers. 249pp plus index, drawings, photos. A young woman of the Blood tribe tells of tribal history, legends, myths and the material culture of her tribe. New York, 1980 (1st ed.), d.j. $15.00

H457. HUNT (D. C.) et al. Karl Bodmer's America. xi, 376pp, 257 color and 102 b/w full-page pls. Cloth. Omaha, 1984. $99.00
    The most admired of the many painters of the early

American West, Karl Bodmer, accompanied his patron,
Prince Maximilian of Wied, during a year-long expedition
into the upper Missouri wilderness in 1833 and 1834.
The result was the best visual record we have of that
landscape and those people and their artifacts. The
sketches and portraits that constitute such an historically
significant record of that expedition were organized by
the Joslyn Art Museum into a very important exhibition.
This oversize (12" x 12") catalogue of the expedition--
reproducing for the first time this major corpus of Bodmer's original work--discusses and superbly illustrates
this collection and reviews the artist's life work. (EAP)

H458.   HUNT (Eva). (American Antiquities, Vol. 43, No. 4,
         1978). The Provenience and Contents of the Porfirio
         Diaz and Fernando Leal Codices. pp673-689, wrappers.
         $10.00

H459.   HUNT (Jack). Land Tenure and Economic Development of
         the Warm Springs Indian Reservation. 16pp, 4to, illus,
         maps, wrappers. Los Angeles, 1970. $10.00

H460.   HUNT (W. Ben) and BURSHEARS (J. F.). American In-
         dian Beadwork. 63pp, pls, some in color, 4to, printed
         wrappers, text illus. Milwaukee, 1951. $15.00

H461.   HUNT (W. Ben). Indiancraft. 124pp, profusely illus,
         cloth, index. Milwaukee, 1953 (4th print.). $15.00

H462.   HUNT (W. B.). Indian Crafts and Lore. 112pp, approx
         800 color drawings, decorated cloth. New York, 1951.
         $29.00

H463.   HUNTER (John D.). Manners and Customs of Several In-
         dian Tribes Located West of the Mississippi. 402pp,
         8vo, rebound in cloth. Philadelphia, Author, 1823
         (1st ed.). $200.00
             Howes: H-813. Sabin: 33920. Field: 743. Includes
         Hunter's account of a journey across the mountains to
         the Pacific Ocean and the Indian Materia Medica. (RMW)
         ___Another Copy. London, Longman, Hurst, Reese,
         Orme and Brown, 1823 (1st ed.). Old half leather
         splitting along front joint, 10pp, 448pp. $100.00
         ___Another Copy. London, Longman, Hurst, et al.,
         1823, New Ed. (same year as 1st English and American
         eds.). "Memoirs of a Captivity Among the Indians of
         North America, from Childhood to the Age of Nineteen:
         With Anecdotes Descriptive of Their Manners and Cus-
         toms." Same Collation. $150.00
         ___Another Copy. London, 1824. "Memoir of a Captiv-
         ity Among the Indians, From Childhood to the Age of
         Nineteen: With Anecdotes Descriptive of Their Manners
         and Customs. To Which is Added, Some Account to the
         Soil, Climate, and Begatable Productions of the Territory
         Westward of the Mississippi." xii, 468pp, portrait, half
         calf. Enlarged 3rd ed. Added to this ed. is "Reflections

on the different states and conditions of society; with
the outlines of a plan to ameliorate the circumstances of
the Indians of North America," pp449-468. $100.00
___Another Copy. Minneapolis, 1957. 402pp, limited
facsimile reprint of the Philadelphia, 1823 ed. $25.00
___Another Copy. New York, 1973. With Richard
Drinnon as Editor. 252pp, portrait frontis, notes, map
endpaper, based on 1824 ed., d.j. $10.00

H464.   HUNTER (Martin). Canadian Wilds. 277pp. Tells about
the Hudson's Bay Company, Northern Indians and their
modes of hunting and trapping, etc. Worn, good.
Columbus, OH, 1907. $20.00

H465.   HUNTER (Milton R.). Utah Indian Stories. xi, 282pp,
8pp photographs. Salt Lake City, 1946. (1st ed.)
$25.00

H466.   HURALT (J.). La Vie Materielle des Noirs Refugies Boni
et des Indiens Wayana du Haut-Maroni. 142pp, 16pp
drawings and photographs, 16 tables, 13 figures.
Paris, 1965. $25.00

H467.   HURALT (J.). Les Indiens Wayana de la Guane Francaise.
164pp, 16pp photographs and drawings. Paris, 1968.
$35.00

H468.   HURLEY (Vic). Arrows Against Steel: The History of
the Bow. 227pp, index. New York, 1975 (1st ed.)
d.j. $17.00

H469.   HURST (D.) et al. (American Museum of Natural History,
Anthropological Papers, Vol. 55, Part 2, 1978) The
Anthropology of St. Catherines Island. I: Natural and
Cultural History. pp157-248, 39 photographs, drawings,
maps. $24.00

H470.   HURST (E. A.). Ad-em-nel-la, An Indian Love Story in
Verse, and Other Poems. 145pp, 1 photograph, cloth,
presentation copy inscribed by author. Kansas City,
1915. $24.00

H471.   HUSTED (Wilfred). (Publications in Salvage Archaeology,
River Basin Surveys, No. 12, Lincoln, 1969) Bighorn
Canyon Archaeology. 138pp, illus, wrappers. $20.00

H472.   HUTCHENS (Alma). Indian Herbalogy of North America:
A Study of Anglo-American, Russian and Oriental Lit-
erature on Indian Medical Botanics of North America with
Illustrations. 382pp, bibliography. Ontario, 1974, (5th
ed.). $45.00
___Another Copy. Same. $35.00

H473.   HUTTON (S. K.). By Eskimo Dog-Sled and Kayak. A
Description of a Missionary's Experiences and Adventures
in Labrador. xii, 17pp, 219pp, 8vo, pls, map, original
cloth. London, 1930. $20.00

H474.   HUXLEY (Francis). Affable Savages: An Anthropologist
Among the Urubu Indians of Brazil. 285pp, map, kinship chart, 13 photographs. New York, 1957, d.j.
$20.00

H475. HUXLEY (M.). Farewell to Eden. Photographs by C.
Capa. 244pp, 48pp of color and 96pp of b/w photographs of the Amahuaca Indians of the Peruvian Montana, 3 maps, cloth. New York, 1964. $45.00

H476. HUYGHE (Rene) (Editor). Larousse Encyclopedia of Prehistoric and Ancient Art. 400pp, b/w and color photographs, maps, index. Pre-Columbia Central and South
American art. New York, 1967, reprint. $12.00

H477. HYATT (Robert D.) et al. (Southern Methodist University
Contributions to Anthropology, No. 12, Dallas, 1974)
Archaeological Research at Cooper Lake, 1970-1972.
93pp, photographs, maps, bibliography, wrappers.
$10.00

H478. HYATT (Robert D.) and DOEHNER (K.). (Southern
Methodist University Contributions to Anthropology, No.
15, Dallas, 1975) Archaeological Research at Cooper
Lake, Northeast Texas, 1973. 84pp, photographs, drawings, bibliography, wrappers. $10.00

H479. HYDE (Dayton). The Last Free Man: The True Story
Behind the Massacre of Shoshone Mike and His Band of
Indians in 1911. 264pp, illus. New York, 1973 (1st
ed.). $20.00
___Another Copy. Same. d.j. $15.00

H480. HYDE (George E.). Indians of the High Plains: From
the Prehistoric Period to the Coming of Europeans.
xiii, 231pp, pls, maps, bibliography, index. University
of Oklahoma, 1959 (1st ed.), d.j. $30.00
___Another Copy. Same. $27.00
___Another Copy. Norman, 1976. $18.00

H481. HYDE (George E.). Indians of the Woodlands: From Pre-
historic Times to 1725. With typed note from author
about a bad review in the Pennsylvania Historical Review.
Norman, 1962, d.j. $85.00
___Another Copy. Same. Signed, 295pp. $20.00
___Another Copy. Norman, 1969, 292pp. $40.00

H482. HYDE (George E.). Pawnee Indians. 304pp, frontis,
illus, 3 maps (2 folding). Denver, 1951 (1st ed.),
d.j. $45.00
___Another Copy. Same. $30.00
___Another Copy. Norman, 1974, d.j. $20.00

H483. HYDE (George E.). Red Cloud's Folk. 331pp, inscribed,
with typed note by author concerning effigy mounds
with simple sketches. Norman, 1957 (2d. print.).
$75.00
___Another Copy. Norman, 1957 (2d. print. of 2d re-
vised ed.). $12.00

H484. HYDE (George E.). A Sioux Chronicle. 320pp plus index, illus, maps. Continuation of Red Cloud's Folk,
this is concerned with the years 1878-1890. Covers the
trying reservation years culminating in the disastrous
Ghost Dance craze. Norman, 1956 (1st ed.), d.j.
$25.00

___Another Copy. Same. $40.00
___Another Copy. Same. $25.00
___Another Copy. Norman, 1980, d.j. 331pp. $20.00

H485. HYDE (George E.). Spotted Tail's Folk: A History of the Brule Sioux. 329pp, illus, index, maps, bibliography. Norman, 1961 (1st ed.), d.j. $30.00
___Another Copy. Same. $30.00
___Another Copy. Norman, 1974, 361pp, revised with some changes and added illus. $18.00
___Another Copy. Same. $20.00

H486. HYER (Joseph K.) and STARRING (William). Dahcotah Dictionary of the Sioux Language. 36pp, wrappers. Facsimile reprint of 1866 1st ed., limited to 300 copies. New Haven, 1968. $25.00

Produced by young Army lieutenants at Ft. Laramie, Dakota in 1866, only six copies of original are known.

-I-

I1. IBANEZ (J. S. C.) and GORDILLO (O. R.). Tres Estudios en Arqueologia de Veracruz. 83pp, 3pp of photographs, 15pp of maps and plans, limited to 500 copies, wrappers. Mexico City, 1985. $20.00

I2. (IDAHO). (Senate Miscellaneous Document 32, 43:1, Washington, 1874, 1st print) Proposed Indian Reservations in Idaho and Washington. 11pp, removed, sites and rules for allowing Indians to reside there. $12.00

I3. IDELL (Albert) (Translator and Editor). The Bernal Diaz Chronicles: The True History of the Conquest of Mexico. 414pp, maps, cloth. Garden City, 1956 (1st ed.), d.j. $25.00

I4. IKTOMI (Lila Sica). America Needs Indians. 425pp, several illus and pls, pictorial cloth, very satiric commentary on White-Indian relations and an appeal for better treatment of Indians. Denver, Bradford (1st ed.), 1937, d.j. $45.00
___Another Copy. Same, folding diagram in rear pocket, mainly uncut and unopened. $25.00

I5. ILIFF (Flora Gregg). People of the Blue Water: My Adventures Among the Walapai and Havasupai Indians. 271pp, 24 illus, report on the isolated Indian tribes of the Colorado River canyons, by a woman who lived and worked among the American Indians for many years. New York, 1954 (1st ed.). $20.00
___Another Copy. Same. d.j. $17.00
___Another Copy. Same. $10.00

I6. (ILLINOIS). (Illinois Archaeology Survey, Bulletin 1, 1973, 5th print) Illinois Archaeology. 62pp, illus,

8vo, wrappers, authoritative summary of prehistory and
early history. $10.00

I7. (ILLINOIS). (Illinois Archaeology Survey, Bulletin 8, 1971)
Mississippian Site Archaeology in Illinois, I: Site Reports from the St. Louis and Chicago Areas. 250pp,
over 100 illus, maps, 8vo, wrappers. $12.00

I8. IM THURN (E. F.). Among the Indians of Guiana. 445pp,
color frontis, 8 pls with 2 in color, 43 figures, folding
map. London, 1883. $100.00

IMBELLONI (Jose). See BAE Bulletin No. 143.

I9. (INCA). (American Ethnological Society, Monograph IV,
1941) An Analysis of Inca Militarism. vii, 85pp, cloth.
$25.00

I10. (INDIAN AFFAIRS). Binney, Charles C. In the Supreme
Court of the United States. October Term, 1899. The
United States Appellant vs. the Choctaw Nation and the
Chickasaw Nation. Brief for the United States. (4),
281pp, 12 folding maps, front wrapper present, rear
lacking. Washington, 1899. $300.00

The brief of the United States in a complex lawsuit
involving the rights of the Choctaw and Chickasaw to
lands they either leased or sold to the Government in the
Indian territory, as well as questions of whether the
tribes were properly reimbursed for lands ceded in the
Southeast. As part of the evidence this brief reproduces
twelve maps from the seventeenth century up to Pike as
the basis for earlier treaty stipulations. (WR)

I11. (INDIAN AFFAIRS). A Brief Account of the Proceedings
of the Committee, Appointed in the year 1795 by the
Yearly Meeting of Friends of Pennsylvania, New Jersey,
&c, for Promoting the Improvement and Gradual Civilization of the Indian Natives. 45pp, original wrappers.
Philadelphia, Kimber, Conrad & Co., 1805. $75.00

Field: 183. "Early commentary on the treatment of
the Indians, and a plea for the improvement of their conditions." (RMW)

I12. (INDIAN AFFAIRS). Condition of the Indian Tribes. Report of the Joint Special Committee Appointed Under
Joint Resolution of March 3, 1965, with Appendix.
532pp, index, original cloth. Washington, 1867.
$125.00

I13. (INDIAN AFFAIRS). Report of the Commissioner of Indian
Affairs, 1877. Fold-out map titled, Indian Reservations
in the U.S. and Number of Indians Belonging thereto,
1877 (color coded), Commissioner's report, 77 agents
reports, 237pp of tables, 33pp pamphlet titled "Are the
Indians Dying Out?", 34pp index. Washington, Government Printing Office, 1877. $85.00
____ Another Copy. Same. $65.00

I14. (INDIAN AFFAIRS). Report of the Commissioner of Indian
Affairs, 1878. 438pp, fold-out map (color coded),

additional map, Sioux Reservation. Washington, Government Printing Office, 1878. $95.00

115. (INDIAN AFFAIRS). Report of the Commissioner of Indian Affairs, 1879. Fold-out map of Indian Reservations west of the 83rd Meridian and the number of Indians belonging thereon. Additional 16 maps showing Indian Reserves and territory. 392pp, including index. Washington, 1879. $125.00

116. (INDIAN AFFAIRS). Report of the Commissioner of Indian Affairs, 1881. 476pp including index, cloth, fold-out map 15½" x 22" in 3 color highlights, lists all ratified treaties and agreements with the Indians. Washington, Government Printing Office, 1881. $100.00
Contains removal of the Mescalero Apaches, Indian disturbances in New Mexico and Arizona, Indian Police, reservations, liquor, Little Chief's band of Cheyennes.

117. (INDIAN AFFAIRS). Report of the Commissioners of Indian Affairs, 1882. 525pp, folding map, ex-library. Washington, Government Printing Office, 1882. $60.00

118. (INDIAN AFFAIRS). Report of the Commissioner of Indian Affairs, 1883. 466pp, fold-out map 19 3/4" x 31½" highlighted in 5 colors, cloth. Washington, Government Printing Office, 1883. $95.00
Contains: education, Commission to the Sioux of Dakota (10,167,360 acres ceded to the U.S.), the Turtle Mountain country in Dakota (another 9,000,000 gone), Creek difficulties, deplorable condition of Indians in Montana.

119. (INDIAN AFFAIRS). Report of the Commissioner of Indian Affairs, 1885. 140pp, with folding map in color showing the locations of Indian Reservations in 1885. Washington, 1886. $50.00

120. (INDIAN AFFAIRS). Report of the Commissioner of Indian Affairs, Accompanying the Annual Report of the Secretary of Interior, for the Year 1861. 221pp, original cloth, includes reports from the various Indian agents, particularly interesting this year due to the influence, the commissioner assets, of the Confederate States in fomenting restlessness among the tribes. Washington, 1861. $125.00

121. (INDIAN AFFAIRS). Report of the Commissioner of Indian Affairs, 1867. 397pp, old calf and bds, made by superintendency districts. Washington, 1868. $75.00

122. (INDIAN AFFAIRS). Report of Indian Affairs to the Secretary of the Interior for the Fiscal Year Ended June 30, 1913. 296pp, 71 tables, lrge fold-out map of Indian Reservations in the U.S., cloth. Washington, 1914. $19.00

123. (INDIAN AFFAIRS). The Southwest Indian Report; A Report of the U.S. Commission on Civil Rights, 171pp, 4to, wrappers. Washington, 1973. $15.00

124. (INDIAN AFFAIRS). Report of the Committee on Indian Affairs: Petition of Alexander J. Robison, Asking

Compensation for Medical Services Rendered to the Emigrating Creek Indians West of the Mississippi River. 1pp, disbound in binder. House of Representatives Report No. 172, Washington, 1834. $35.00

125. (INDIAN AFFAIRS). (House of Representatives Document No. 181, Washington, 1835) Letter from the Secretary of War Transmitting a List of the Names of Persons Employed in 1834. 4pp, disbound in binder, list of agents, interpreters, blacksmiths, etc., plus salary of each.
                                                                 $35.00

126. (INDIAN AFFAIRS). (Senate Executive Document 4, Washington, 1853) Report of the Secretary of the Interior Communicating ... the Correspondence Between the Department of the Interior and the Indian Agents and Commissioners in California. 405pp, map, table, modern cloth.
                                                                $125.00
An enormous and very informative compilation of first hand accounts of the state of affairs of the California Indians at the time, including treaty negotiations, reservation politics, etc.

127. (INDIAN AFFAIRS). (Senate Executive Document, 32:2, Washington, 1853) Letter from the Secretary of the Interior, Communicating the Report of Edward F. Beals, Superintendent of Indian Affairs in California, Respecting the Condition of Indian Affairs in that State. 18pp, removed. $50.00
Reports from various local agents regarding the conditions of the Indians in their respective jurisdictions, concluding with a list of recommendations by Beale, including financial support and abolition of Indian agencies.

128. (INDIAN AFFAIRS). (House of Representatives Executive Document 76, 4:2 (sic.--could be 34:2), Washington, 1859, 1st ed.) Indian Affairs on the Pacific. 256pp, removed. $35.00
Covers Indian affairs and what was known of the various tribes in California, and in the territories of Washington and Oregon. Some of the material covers the area of Arizona. Information on the Nez Perce and the hostilities in the northwest.

129. (INDIAN AFFAIRS). Accounts with Creeks, Choctaws, etc. Letter ... Transmitting the Accounts of the Superintendent of Indian Affairs of the Southern Superintendency. 116pp, removed, describes payments to these tribes in southern Kansas during the Civil War. Washington, 1863. $35.00

130. (INDIAN AFFAIRS). (Senate Executive Document 58, 52:1, Washington, 1892, 1st print.) Affairs of the Indians at the Pine Ridge and Rosebud Reservations in South Dakota. 185pp plus large folding colored map of Montana Territory dated, 1887, removed, also covers North Cheyenne Reservation. $35.00

131. (INDIAN DEPARTMENT). Message from the President of the

United States, Transmitting a Statement of Expenditures and Receipts in the Indian Department. 10pp, wrappers, printed by Gales and Seaton, Washington, 1821. $35.00

132. (INDIAN PEACE MEDALS). (National Portrait Gallery, Washington, 1985) Peace and Friendship: Indian Peace Medals in the United States. 32pp, illus, 4to, wrappers, catalog of these rare medals from public and the very few private collections, including the history of the medals. $10.00

133. (INDIAN RIGHTS ASSOCIATION). Third Annual Report. 40pp, wrappers. Philadelphia, 1886. $20.00

134. (INDIAN RIGHTS ASSOCIATION). Tenth Annual Report. 76pp, includes a visit to South Dakota, Colorado and Oklahoma by P. Garrett. 21pp, Phila., 1893. $30.00

135. (INDIANS). The American Heritage Book of Indians. 424pp, 100 or more color and b/w photographs, cloth. New York, 1961. $30.00
____Another Copy. 1982. $30.00

136. (INDIANS). The Indian. The Northwest. 1600-1900. The Red Man. The War Man. The White Man. 114pp, photographs, paintings, drawings, b/w and color maps. Dustin: 150. Smith: 1662. Chicago, 1901 (1st ed.). $20.00

137. (INDIANS). (Pacific R.R. Report of Explorations and Surveys, to Ascertain the Most Practicable and Economical Route for a Railroad From the Mississippi River to the Pacific Ocean, Washington.) Vol. 3: Indians. 4to, includes Choctaw, Yuma, Pima, Cherokee, Pueblo, Navaho, Acoma, Pai-ute, tinted pls, cvrs wrn and off, some lvs loose, 1855-1860. $60.00
____Another Copy. Same. cvrs off, text loose, lacks pls. $15.00

138. (INDIANS). (National Geographic Society, Washington, 1955, 1st ed.) Indians of the Americas. A Color-illustrated Record. 424 double-column pp plus index, photographs, drawings (many in color), some by W. Langton Kihn, others by H. M. Herget, d.j. $15.00

139. (INDIAN WARS). Barbarities of the Enemy Exposed.... 192pp, 12mo, ex-library, disbound, trimmed, ink spots in text. Worcester, I. Sturtevant, 1814. $40.00
Sabin: 3296. Field: 76: "Testimony criminating the British Military Officers in the horrible massacres perpetrated by the Indians after the surrender of the Americans as prisoners of war on several occasions." (RMW)

140. (INDIAN WARS). Indian Narratives: Containing a Correct and Interesting History of the Indian Wars, from the Landing of Our Pilgrim Fathers, 1620, to General Wayne's Victory, 1794. 276pp, 8vo, original decorated cloth. Claremont, NH, Tracy, 1854. $85.00
____Another Copy. Same. Ex-library. $50.00

141. INGENTHORN (Elmo). Indians of the Ozark Plateau.

173pp, illus, map, index, wrappers. Point Lookout, MO,
1970 (1st ed.). $10.00

142. INGSTAD (Helge). The Land of Feast and Famine. xiii,
332pp, 8vo, photographic illus, folded map, original cloth.
New York, 1933. $35.00
Narrative of the author's travels 1930-31 in the region
of Great Slave Lake and upper Thelon River, his hunting
activities, life among the "Caribou-eater" Indians of the
Barren Grounds.

143. INNIS (Ben). Bloody Knife. Custer's Favorite Scout.
202pp, illus, bibliography, index, Bloody Knife served
with Custer in the 1873 Yellowstone Expedition, the 1874
Black Hills Expedition and lost his life during the Little
Big Horn Campaign. Ft. Collins, 1973, (1st ed.), d.j.
$20.00

144. (INTER-TRIBAL CONFERENCE). Proceedings of the Nevada
Inter-Tribal Indian Conference May 1 & 2, 1964. 92pp,
4to, wrappers, edited and published by the Center for
Western North American Studies, University of Nevada,
on Indian problems in Nevada. Reno, 1964 (1st ed.).
$55.00

145. INVERARITY (R. B.). Art of the Northwest Coast In-
dians. 243pp, 279 photographs, cloth, Berkeley, 1950.
$67.00
___Another Copy. Same, wear to d.j. $45.00
___Another Copy. Same, strip of d.j. backstrip miss-
ing. $35.00
___Another Copy. Same. $30.00

146. INVERARITY (R. B.). (Washington State Museum, Series
No. 1, 1946) Northwest Coast Indian Art. 30pp, 26
photographs, 1 drawing, map, spiral binding, exhibition
catalogue. $17.00

147. (IROQUOIS). Art et Artisanate des Indiens Iroquois.
31pp, 15 photographs, exhibition catalogue, Rennes Museum, 1964. $10.00

148. IRVINE (Keith) (Editor). Encyclopedia of Indians of the
Americas (North and South America). 458pp, color
frontis, numerous illus, 4to (9"x11"), (Volume I only),
includes articles by Dockstader, Deloria, Brew, Grindley,
Spencer, others, a full chronology, 25,000 B.C. to A.D.
1974. $60.00

149. IRVING (John Treat Jr.). Indian Sketches Taken During
an Expedition to the Pawnee Tribes (1833). Edited and
Annotated by John Francis McDermott. 275pp, index,
bibliography, cloth. Norman, 1955 (reprint of Howes:
I-79), d.j. $30.00
___Another Copy. Same. $30.00
___Another Copy. Same. $20.00

150. IRWIN (Charles) (Editor). The Shoshoni Indians of Inyo
County California, The Kerr Manuscript. 92pp, illus,
wrappers. Socorro, 1980. $20.00

151. IRWIN (H. J. and C. C.). (Denver Museum of Natural History, proceedings No. 8, Denver, 1959, 1st ed.) Excavations at the Lodaiska Site in the Denver, Colorado, Area. viii, 156pp, pls, figures, maps, bibliography, wrappers, many illus of flints. $25.00
___Another Copy. Same. $15.00

152. ISHIDA (E.) (Expedition Director). Andes. The Report of the University of Tokyo Scientific Expedition to the Andes. (3 Volumes). Vol. I: Andes. Reports of Expeditions in 1958 and 1960. 528pp, approx 750 photographs, drawings, rubbings and maps, Tokyo, 1960. Vol. II: Andes 2, Excavations at Kotosh, Peru, 1960. (S. Izumi and T. Sono) 214pp of text containing several hundred drawings and maps, 3 color pls, plus 181pp of photographs and drawings. Tokyo, 1963. Vol. III: Excavation at Pechiche and Garbanzal, Tumbes Valley, Peru. (S. Izumi and K. Terada.) v, 109pp, 11 figures, plus 42pp of photographs and drawings. Tokyo, 1966. All volumes bound in fine linen.
$495.00
An expedition of immense scientific importance, the University of Tokyo Scientific Expeditions to the Andes uncovered a plethora of new material and resulted in the publication of these three volumes. Each volume is 12"x8½" in size, beautifully illustrated, and printed on splendid paper. Approximately 1/3 of the text of Vol. I is in English; the balance is in Japanese. The texts for Vols. II and III are entirely English.

153. ISHIDA (E.) (Editor). (Fine Arts of the World, Vol. 24, Tokyo, 1962) Precolumbian Americas. 251pp (text in Japanese), 140pp of color and b/w photographs, cloth, inscribed by author. $45.00

154. (ISSUE OF ARMS). (House of Representatives Miscellaneous Document, 39:2, Washington, 1967) Issue of Arms to Indians. Letter from the Secretary of War, Addressed to the Chairman of the Committee of Military Affairs, Relative to the Issue of a Large Number of Arms to the Kiowas and Other Indians. 4pp, removed, fear of hostilities breaking out due to the sale of arms and ammunition to Indians by agents and traders, notable for the account of the Indians' perspective in the matter. $30.00

155. IVANOFF (Pierre). En el Pais de los Mayas. 253pp, illus with 28 photographs. Barcelona, 1970. $15.00

156. IVANOFF (Pierre). Mayan Enigma: The Search for a Lost Civilization. 202pp, illus. New York, 1971. $25.00

157. IVES (Joseph C.). Report on the Colorado River of the West. (Five Parts in One). 131pp, 3 maps, 25 pls; 14pp, 154pp, 6 pls; 30pp; 6pp; xxxii; 2 maps are folding, 8 color pls of Indians, newly rebound in linen, new endpapers. Washington, Government Printing Office, 1861. $300.00

IVES (Ronald L.). See BAE Bulletin No. 123.

158. IVEY (J. E.) et al. (University of Texas Archaeological
Survey Report No. 32, San Antonio, 1977) An Initial
Archaeological Assessment of Areas Proposed for Modification at Ft. McIntosh, Webb County, Texas. 20pp,
maps, bibliography, wrappers. $10.00

159. IWANSKA (Alicja). Purgatory and Utopia. A Mazahua Indian Village of Mexico. 214pp, photographs, glossary,
an anthropological study of tribe of Central Mexico.
Cambridge, MA, 1971 (1st ed.), d.j. $15.00

160. IZCU (Elena). El Arte Peruano en la Escuela. (L'Art
Peruvien a l'Ecole--Peruvian Art in School.) Part I:
4 color pls, 30 b/w worksheets. 4to, text loose in pictorial stiff printed wrappers as issued, 18pp and pls,
18pp and pls. Paris, 1925-26. $75.00
Ornate schoolbooks to teach Peruvian children Inca
designs, the worksheets on thin boards, text in Spanish,
French and English.

161. IZQUIERDO (Anna Luisa). La Educacion Maya en los Tiempos
Prehispanicos. 93pp, wrappers. UNAM, Mexico, 1983.
$15.00
___Another Copy. Same. $12.00

162. IZUMI (S.) et al. (University of Tokyo Museum, Bulletin
No. 3, 1972) Excavations at Shillacoto, Huanuco, Peru.
vii, 82pp of text containing 15 figures, plus 46 pp of
photographs and 14pp of drawings, wrappers. $35.00

-J-

J1. JABLOW (J.). (Monographs of the American Ethnological
Society, No. XIX, 1951) The Cheyenne in Plains Indian
Trade Relations 1795-1840. ix, 100pp, 2 maps, cloth.
$27.00

J2. JACOBS (Melville). (University of Washington, Publications
in Anthropology, Vol. 8, No. 2, 1940) Coos Myth Texts.
pp129-259. $30.00
___Another Copy. Same. wrappers. $17.00

J3. JACOBS (M.). (University of Washington, Publications in
Anthropology, Vol. 8, No. 1, 1939) Coos Narrative and
Ethnologic Texts. pp1-126, index, wrappers. $18.00

J4. JACOBS (M.). The Fate of Indian Oral Literatures in Oregon. pp90-99, wrappers. Reprint from Northwest Review, Vol. 5, No. 3, 1962. $10.00

J5. JACOBS (M.) et al. (University of Washington Publications
in Anthropology, Vol. II, 1945) Kalapuya Texts. 394pp,
index, wrappers. $25.00

J6. JACOBS (M.). (Columbia University Contributions to
Anthropology, Vol. 19, Parts I and II, New York, 1934)

Northwest Sahaptin Texts. pp291, 238, wrappers.
$60.00

___Another Copy. New York, 1937, cloth, 2 volumes,
529pp. $75.00

___Another Copy. New York, 1934, Part I only. 291pp.
$15.00

___Another Copy. Columbia University Press, 1937,
Part II only. $20.00

J7. JACOBS (M.). The People Are Coming Soon: Analysis of
Clackamas Chinook Myths and Tales. xii, 359pp, wrappers, 56 analyses. University of Washington Press, 1960
(1st ed.). $18.00

J8. JACOBS (M.). (American Folklore, Vol. 65, No. 256, 1952)
Psychological Inferences From a Chinook Myth. pp121-
138. $10.00

J9. JACOBS (M.). (University of Washington Publications in
Anthropology, Vol. 4, No. 2, Seattle, 1931) A Sketch of
Northern Sahaptin Grammar. pp85-292, wrappers.
$15.00

J10. JACOBS (M. M.). Kachina Ceremonies and Kachina Dolls.
72pp, 11 half-page color photographs of 52 kachinas, 13
drawings. Pittsburgh, 1980. $18.00

J11. JACOBS (Wilbur R.). Diplomacy and Indian Gifts. Anglo-
French Rivalry Along the Ohio and Northwest Frontiers,
1748-1763. 208pp, frontis, illus, endpaper maps, bibliography, index, cloth. Stanford University Press, London,
1950 (1st ed.), d.j. $25.00

___Another Copy. Stanford, 1950. $30.00

J12. JACOBS (W. R.). Dispossessing the American Indian.
Indians and Whites on the Colonial Frontier. 229pp plus
index, photographs, maps, appendices, footnotes, notes
on sources. New York, 1972, d.j. $10.00

J13. JACOBSEN (Johan A.). Alaskan Voyage: 1881-1883, An
Expedition to the Northwest Coast of America. Translated
by Erna Gunther from the German Text of Adrian Woldt.
266pp, 60 illus showing some Eskimo and Indian artifacts.
Chicago, 1977. $25.00

___Another Copy. Same. $17.00

J14. JACKS (Jerry D.) and HAMMACK (Nancy G.). Indian
Jewelry of the Prehistoric Southwest. 44pp, color photographs, map, wrappers. Tucson, 1975 (1st ed.). $10.00

J15. JACKSON (A. T.). (University of Texas, Publications Vol.
3, No. 2, Austin, 1938) The Fall Creek Sites, and other
articles. 153pp, maps, plates, figures, bibliography,
site and artifact photographs, lrg 8vo, wrappers. $35.00

___Another Copy. Same. $18.00

J16. JACKSON (A. T.). (University of Texas Anthropology Papers, Vol. 11, Study No. 27, 1938) Picture Writing of
Texas Indians. 515pp, 607 photographs and drawings of
several thousand pictographs, petroglyphs and designs,
49 maps. $165.00

___Another Copy. Same. 490pp, bibliography, index,
slipcase, wrappers. $125.00
___Another Copy. Same. color frontis. $125.00

J17. JACKSON (Helen Hunt). A Century of Dishonor, a Sketch
of the United States Government's Dealings with Some of
the Indian Tribes. x, 514pp, 4pp ads. Boston, Robert
Bros., 1891. $20.00

J18. JACKSON (Sheldon). Reports on Education in Alaska:
with Illustrations and Maps. 53pp, photogravures of
groups of Eskimos, 3/4 leather. Senate Executive Document, Washington, 1886. $125.00

J19. JACKSON (Sheldon). Report on the Introduction of Domestic Reindeer into Alaska. Jackson was a leader of the
movement to bring reindeer into Alaska to help natives
become self-sufficient again. These reports are full of
information about and photographs of native life, villages,
whaling, Revenue Service ships, Indian totems, bands,
schools, etc.
___2nd Report, n.p., 1893. 39pp plus folding map,
photographs, index, 8vo, removed. $45.00
___3rd Report, n.p., 1894. 187pp plus 2 folding maps,
photographs, index, 8vo, removed. $40.00
___4th Report, n.p., 1894. 100pp plus folding map,
photographs, index, 8vo, removed. $40.00
___6th Report, n.p., 1896. 144pp plus photographs, in-
dex, 8vo, removed. $35.00
___8th Report, n.p., 1898. 149pp plus 2 folding maps,
photographs, index, 8vo, removed. $35.00
___13th Report, n.p., 1904. 192pp plus large folding
map, photographs, index, 8vo, removed. $35.00

J20. JACKSON (William Henry). Descriptive Catalogue of Photographs of North American Indians. 124pp, wrappers.
Washington, 1877. $250.00
List of photographs taken on the Hayden Survey that
have Indians in them, with Jackson's annotations.
___Another Copy. Government Printing Office, Report
1978. $10.00

J21. JAEGER (E.). Council Fires. 253pp, 117 pls, drawings,
overview of council fires, including dances, masks, etc.
New York, 1949. $20.00

J22. JAHODA (Gloria). The Trail of Tears: The Story of the
American Indian Removals, 1813-1855. 356pp, illus
(16 pls of Indian Chiefs). New York, 1975 (1st ed.),
d.j. $40.00
___Another Copy. Same. $20.00

J23. JAMES (Ahlee). Tewa Firelight Tales. 248pp, illus by Awa
Tsireh and others, decorative cloth. New York, 1927
(1st ed.). $65.00
Campbell: p.159. Saunders: 1727. These tales were
gathered by the author during three years residence at
San Ildefonso Pueblo. This charming work contains ten

color plates executed by Indian artists. (TE)
    Another Copy. Same. $25.00
J24. JAMES (C. D., III). (Museum of Northern Arizona, Research Paper 1, 1976) Historic Navajo Studies in Northeastern Arizona. 142pp, 51 figures, 11 tables. $16.00
J25. JAMES (Edwin). A Narrative of the Captivity and Adventures of John Tanner ... During Thirty Years Residence
Among the Indians in the Interior of North America.
426pp, engraved portrait, half leather, marbled bds.
New York, G. and C. and H. Carvill, 1830 (1st ed.).
        $650.00
    Howes: J-42. Ayer: 290. Field: 772. James re-
corded the captivity and life of John Tanner among the
Chippeway, Ojibway and Ottawa Indians from interviews
with Tanner. "His relation of his life among the Northern
Indians, is probably the most minute if not authentic detail
of their habits, modes of living and social customs ever
printed." Also contains much information on Indian lan-
guages, alphabets and dialects. (RMW)
    Another Copy. Same. bds rebacked in cloth.
        $500.00
    Another Copy. London, 1830, tall 8vo, 3/4 leather
and label. $850.00
    Another Copy. Minneapolis, 1956, d.j. $15.00
    Another Copy. New York, Garland Series of American
Indian Ethnohistory, 1975. $35.00
J26. JAMES (George Wharton) (Editor). (The Basket Fraternity,
Vol. II, No. 4, Pasadena, 1904, 1st ed.) The Basket:
The Journal of the Basket Fraternity or Lovers of Indian
Baskets and Other Good Things. 64pp, illus, stiff pic-
torial wrappers, the last issue published of this periodical
edited by James. $25.00
J27. JAMES (G. W.). Indian Basketry. 238pp, 300 illus of
baskets, decorated cloth. Pasadena, 1901 (1st ed.).
        $85.00
    Another Copy. Same. $85.00
    Another Copy. New York, 1902 (2d ed., revised
and enlarged). $45.00
    Another Copy. New York, 1903 (3rd ed.) with How
To section of 136pp. $75.00
    Another Copy. New York, 1970 (reprint of 1903).
        $40.00
    Another Copy. Glorieta, 1975. $30.00
    Another Copy. Glorieta, 1982. $20.00
J28. JAMES (G. W.). Indian Blankets and Their Makers. xvi,
213pp, 232 b/w photographs and drawings, 32 full-page
color photographs, decorated buckram cvr, in original
cardboard shipping box with lithograph of Navajo textile
on box cvr. McClurg & Co. 1914. $450.00
    Another Copy. Same. $395.00
    Another Copy. pp103-213, frontis, index, 114 b/w

photographs and drawings, 16 full-page color photographs, these pages of this volume principally deal with 1885-1910 weaving. Bound in later cloth, gilt lettering on spine read "Indian Blankets." "James, Part II." $135.00

___Another Copy. Chicago, 1920, in original box, 213pp, 64 illus and 32 color pls. $150.00

___Another Copy. New York, 1937, xvi, 213pp, 222 b/w photographs and drawings, 32pp full-page color photographs. $195.00

___Another Copy. Same. Scuffed cvr. $175.00

___Another Copy. Same. 4" split along spine. $165.00

___Another Copy. Same. ex-library, numbers on spine, cloth. $90.00

___Another Copy. Same, newly rebound. $110.00

___Another Copy. Glorieta, 1970. $25.00

___Another Copy. Glorieta, 1974. $25.00

J29. JAMES (G. W.). The Indians of the Painted Desert Region: Hopis, Navahoes, Wallapais, Havasupais. xxi, 268pp plus 40 pls, illus, 3pp advs, pictorial cloth. Rader: 2051. Saunders: 2236. Boston, 1903 (1st ed.). $100.00

___Another Copy. Same. $45.00

___Another Copy. Boston, 1907, presentation copy, inscribed by author. $95.00

___Another Copy. Same. no inscription. $79.00

J30. JAMES (G. W.). New Mexico, the Land of the Delight Makers.... 462pp plus index, folding full-color map, illus (8 in color), bibliography. Rader: 2053. Dykes High Spot: 107. Boston, 1920, 1st impression. $40.00

J31. JAMES (G. W.). What the White Race May Learn from the Indian. 269pp, illus with photographs, original red cloth. Chicago, Lakeside Press, 1908 (1st ed.). $85.00

___Another Copy. Same. $40.00

J32. JAMES (Harry). Red Man, White Man. 286pp, endpaper maps, designed and illus by Don Perceval, a novel woven into Hopi culture. San Antonio, Naylor, 1958, (1st ed.), d.j. $15.00

J33. JAMES (James A.). English Institutions and the American Indian. 59pp, wrappers. Baltimore, Johns Hopkins, 1894. $12.00

J34. JAMES (John). My Experiences with Indians. 147pp, cloth. Austin, 1925. $125.00

     Rader: 2060. The author taught school to the Choc- taws from 1884 to 1888, and discusses their life and his peculiar situation. Other scenes of life in North Texas during the period. (WR)

___Another Copy. Same. $125.00

___Another Copy. Same. $27.00

J35. JAMES (W. C.). A. A. Chesterfield. Ungava Portraits, 1902-04. 48pp, 18pp of photographs, map, text in Eng- lish and French, wrappers. Exhibition catalogue, Ether- ington Art Center, Kingston, 1982. $10.00

JARRELL (Myrtys). See also BAE Bulletin No. 115.
J36. JARVIS (Samuel F.). (Collections of the New York Histori-
cal Society for 1821, Vol. 3, New York, 1821) A Discourse
on the Religion of the Indian Tribes of North America.
pp183-268, original cloth. $90.00
Includes study in Indian languages, with an interesting
comparison of Delaware and Hebrew. The author believed
that the Indians were members of the lost tribes of Israel.
(BF)
JEANCON (J. A.). See also BAE Bulletin No. 81.
J37. JEANCON (J. A.). (Smithsonian Miscellaneous Collections,
Vol. 81:12, Washington, 1929) Archaeological Investigations In The Taos Valley, New Mexico, During 1920.
29pp, 15 pls, 8vo, wrappers. $20.00
____Another Copy. Same. $18.00
J38. JEFFERSON (Thomas). Notes on the State of Virginia; With
an Appendix Relative to the Murder of Logan's Family.
363pp, 1 folding table of Indian tribes and populations
between 1607 and 1669, 12mo, rebound in quarter leather.
Trenton, Wilson and Blackwell, July 12, 1803 (1st ed. with
the Appendix noted on the title page). $200.00
JELKS (Edward B.). See also BAE Bulletin No. 179.
J39. JELKS (Edward). Excavations at Texarkana Reservoir,
Sulphur River, Texas. 78pp and 17 illus, wrappers, offprint from BAE Bulletin 179, River Basin Survey Paper
No. 21. Washington, 1961. $10.00
J40. JELKS (E.) and TUNNELL (C.). (University of Texas,
Department of Anthropology, Archaeology Series, No. 2,
1959) The Harroun Site. 63pp plus 15 pls and maps,
bibliography, 8vo, wrappers. $15.00
J41. JELKS (E.). (University of Texas, Department of Anthropology, Archaeology Series, No. 5, 1962) The Kyle Site.
114pp, 35 photographs, 8vo, wrappers. $12.00
J42. JELM (J.). (National Museum of Canada, Bulletin 176,
1961) The Lynx Point People: The Dynamics of a North-
ern Athapaskan Band. v, 193pp, 8 figures, 6 tables.
                                                    $33.00
J43. JENKS (A. E.). (American Anthropological Association,
Memoirs, No. 56, Menasha, 1941, 1st ed.) Ethnography
of the Kutenai. 201pp, map, pls, bibliography, wrappers.
                                                    $15.00
J44. JENKS (A. E.). (American Anthropological Association,
Memoirs, No. 49, 1937) Minnesota Browns Valley Man and
Associated Burial Artifacts. 49pp, 8pp photographs, 5
figures. $19.00
____Another Copy. Same. $10.00
J45. JENNESS (A. D.). (National Museum of Man, Canadian
Ethnology Service, Paper No. 93, 1984) Coast Salish
Gambling Games. xi, 143pp, 34pp photographs, drawings
and maps. $12.00
____Another Copy. Same. $10.00

J46.   JENNESS (Aylette). Dwellers of the Tundra: Life in an
         Alaskan Eskimo Village. 114pp, photographs by Jonathan
         Jenness. Toronto, 1970. $20.00
JENNESS (Diamond). See also BAE Bulletin No. 133.
J47.   JENNESS (Diamond). The Carrier Indians of the Bulkley
         River. Their Social and Religious Life. pp469-586. 11
         photographic pls, bibliography, printed wrappers, offprint
         Smithsonian Anthropological Papers, Washington, 1943.
                                                                    $10.00

J48.   JENNESS (D.). (Report of the Canadian Arctic Expedition,
         1913-1918, Ottawa, 1924) Eskimo Folk-Lore: Eskimo
         String Figures. 192pp, 229 figures, wrappers. $35.00
         ____Another Copy. Same. $25.00
J49.   JENNESS (D.). (Report of the Canadian Arctic Expedition,
         1913-1918, Ottawa, 1924) Eskimo Folk-Lore: Myths and
         Traditions from Northern Alaska, the Mackenzie Delta and
         Coronation Gulf. 90pp, wrappers. $35.00
J50.   JENNESS (D.). (National Museum of Canada Bulletin No.
         85, Ottawa, 1937, 1st ed.) The Indian Background of
         Canadian History. 46pp, maps, wrappers, population
         movements, origins, etc. $20.00
J51.   JENNESS (D.). (Ottawa National Museum, Bulletin No. 65,
         Anthropology Series No. 15, 1932) Indians of Canada.
         x, 446pp, color frontis, photographic illus, bibliography,
         index, lrg folding map in rear pocket. $80.00
         ____Another Copy. Ottawa, 1958 (4th ed.) 425pp, b/w
         and color illus, maps, cloth. $25.00
         ____Another Copy. Ottawa, 1963, cloth. $25.00
         ____Another Copy. Ottawa, 1967, (6th ed.). $55.00
         ____Another Copy. n.d. $50.00
J52.   JENNESS (D.). (National Museum of Canada, Bulletin No.
         78, Ottawa, 1938) The Ojibwa Indians of Parry Island,
         Their Social and Religious Life. vi, 115pp, bds, inner
         hinge repaired. $47.00
         ____Another Copy. 1935, (1st ed.), inscribed. $25.00
J53.   JENNESS (D.). (Report of the Canadian Arctic Expedition,
         1913-1918, Vol. XII, Southern Party, 1913-1916, Ottawa,
         1922) The Life of the Copper Eskimo. 277pp, 51 photo-
         graphs, 18 drawings and 2 maps in text, plus 9pp of
         photographs and 1 fold-out map in rear pocket, wrappers.
                                                                    $90.00
J54.   JENNESS (D.). The People of the Twilight. xii, 6, 247pp,
         photographic pls, map, original cloth. New York, Mac-
         Millan, 1928 (1st ed.), d.j. $65.00
         Jenness' narrative of his life with Coronation Gulf
         Eskimos during Stefansson's Canadian Arctic Expedition,
         1914-17. Arctic Bibliography: 8048. (HL)
         ____Another Copy. Same. newly rebound. $45.00
         ____Another Copy. Same. $30.00
J55.   JENNESS (D.). (Ottawa National Museum, Anthropology
         Series No. 20, 1937) The Sekani Indians of British

Columbia. 82pp, illus, wrappers. $35.00
   ___Another Copy. Same. $30.00
   ___Another Copy. Same. $25.00
J56.   JENNINGS (Francis). The Invasion of America: Indians, Colonialism, and the Cant of Conquest. xvii, 369pp, illus, maps, bibliography, index, "Settlement" of America from the Indian point of view. University of North Carolina Press, 1976 (2d print.). $15.00
JENNINGS (Jesse D.). See also BAE Bulletin Nos. 131 and 164.
J57.   JENNINGS (J. D.). (University of Utah--Anthropological Papers, No. 81, Salt Lake City, 1966) Glen Canyon: A summary. vii, 84pp, figures (some lrg folding), bibliography, lrg 8vo, wrappers. $12.00
J58.   JENNINGS (J. D.). Prehistory of North America. 376 double-column pp plus index, drawings, charts, maps, New York, 1968 (1st ed.). $10.00
J59.   JENNINGS (J. D.). (University of Utah, Anthropological Papers, No. 98, 1978) Prehistory of Utah and the Eastern Great Basin. xii, 263pp, 241 figures. $30.00
J60.   JERNIGAN (E. Wesley). Jewelry of the Prehistoric Southwest. 260pp, 4to, illus include 100 drawings plus photographs and some full color pls, covers three cultures--Hohokam, Mogollon and Anasazi--index, map. Santa Fe, 1978 (1st ed.), d.j. $35.00
   ___Another Copy. Same. $30.00
   ___Another Copy. Same. $24.00
J61.   JESKE (J. A.). (Milwaukee Public Museum Bulletin Vol. III, No. 2, Milwaukee, 1927) The Grand River Mound Group and Camp Site. 67pp, 17 figures, 13pp photographs, wrappers. $30.00
J62.   JESUP (Gen. T. S.). (House of Representatives Document 80, 27:3, Washington, 1843, 1st print.) Report ... In Relation to a Claim of the Creek Indians. 52pp, removed, reports and orders dealing with the Indian war in Alabama. $15.00
J63.   JEWITT (John R.). Narrative of the Adventures and Sufferings of John R. Jewitt, Only Survivor of the Crew of the Ship Boston, During a Captivity of Nearly 3 Years Among the Savages of Nootka Sound. 204pp, frontis pl. Middletown, Seth Richards, 1815. $175.00
      Field: 777. Howes: A-189. Expanded from the author's journals by Richard Alsop. This narrative relates a frightening confrontation between the visiting sailors and the Nootka Sound natives. It also gives many particulars of the life and customs of the Indians. A Nootka vocabulary is included. (RMW)
   ___Another Copy. New York, Andrus, Gauntlett Co., 1851, 166pp, illus, full calf. $120.00
   ___Another Copy. London, 1896, 256pp, illus, index, cloth. $35.00
   ___Another Copy. Fairfield, WA, 1967, 186pp, drawings,

photographs, facsimiles, errata slip, limited to 1522
copies. $12.00

J64.   JIJON Y CAAMANO (J.). Maranga. Contribucion Al Cono-
cimiento de los Aborigines del Valle del Rimac, Peru.
vii, 511pp of text containing 219 figures, plus 104pp of
pls and 18 fold-out maps and plans, wrappers. Quito,
1949. $90.00

J65.   JILEK (W. G.). Indian Healing, Shamanic Ceremonialism in
the Pacific Northwest Today. 182pp, 30 b/w and 9 color
photographs, 2 drawings. Surrey, 1982. $15.00

J66.   JOCHELSON (Waldemar). Archaeological Investigations In
the Aleutian Islands. ix, 145pp, pls, figures, folding
map, glossary, bibliography, index, lrg 8vo, wrappers,
ex-library. Carnegie Institute, Washington, 1925, (1st
ed.). $50.00
       Russian sponsored expedition of 1909-10. The manu-
scripts, drawings, maps, plates, etc., were saved from
destruction by the Revolutionary mob in 1917 and rewrit-
ten with additional material. (RMW)

J67.   JOCHELSON (W.). (American Museum of Natural History,
Anthropological Papers, Vol. XXXIII, Part II, 1933) The
Yakut. 225pp, 107 illus containing over 200 photographs
and drawings, wrappers. $90.00

J68.   JOHN (Elizabeth A. H.). Storms Brewed in Other Men's
Worlds; The Confrontation of Indians, Spanish and French
in the Southwest, 1540-1795. 805pp, index, bibliography,
cloth. Texas A & M University Press, 1975 (1st ed.),
d.j. $30.00
       ____Another Copy. Same. $30.00
       ____Another Copy. Same. lacks d.j. $20.00

J69.   JOHNASEN (Dorothy O.) (Editor). Robert Newell's Memoranda: Travles in the Teritory of Missourie; Travle to
the Kayuse War; together with a Report on the Indians
South of the Columbia River. 159pp, folding map, uncut,
opened, limited to 1000 copies. Portland, 1959 (1st ed.).
                                                           $35.00

J70.   JOHNSON (Anna C.) Pseudo. Minnie Myrtle. The Iroquois;
or, The Bright Side of Indian Character. (3), 317pp,
18 advs, frontis, pls, decorated cloth. New York, Appleton, 1855 (1st ed.). $150.00
       Howes: J-125. Sabin: 36183. Field: 791. "Compila-
tion ... relating to the Six Nations, legendary, historical
and biographical. The author lived among the Senecas
for several months ... and was adopted into the tribe...."
(RMW)

J71.   JOHNSON (Bobby H.). The Coushata People. 104pp, b/w
and color photographs, maps, signed by tribal chieftain,
wrappers, part of the Indian Tribal Series. Phoenix,
1976 (1st ed.). $10.00

J72.   JOHNSON (Broderick H.) (Editor). Denetsosie. 51pp,
photographs, drawings by Andy Tsinajinnie, wrappers,

the biography of a Navaho council/medicine man. Rough
Rock, AZ, 1969. $10.00

J73.   JOHNSON (E. B.) (Editor). Animal Stories the Indians
Told. 155pp, illus. New York, 1927 (1st ed.). $25.00

J74.   JOHNSON (E. L.) and BERNICK (K.). Hands of Our Ancestors, The Revival of Salish Weaving at Musqueam.
32pp, 45 photographs, 2 drawings, map, wrappers. UBC
Museum of Anthropology, Vancouver, 1986. $10.00

J75.   JOHNSON (E. Pauline). (Tekahionwake) Flint and Feathers:
The Complete Poems of E. Pauline Johnson. 166pp, frontis,
decorated cloth, Indian poetess born on Six Nations' Reserve. Toronto, 1928. $20.00

J76.   JOHNSON (E. P.). (Tekahionwake) Legends of Vancouver.
138pp, illus. Vancouver, 1913 (6th ed.). $10.00

JOHNSON (Frederick). See also BAE Bulletin No. 143.

J77.   JOHNSON (F.) (Editor). (Peabody Foundation for Archaeology, Papers, Vol. 4, No. 1, Phillips Academy, 1949) The
Boylston Street Fishweir II. A Study of Geology, Paleo-
botany and Biology of a Site on Stuart Street. viii,
133pp, 14pp photographs, 15 figures. $19.00

J78.   JOHNSON (F.) and RAUP (H. M.). (Peabody Foundation
for Archaeology, Papers, vol. 1, No. 2, Phillips Academy,
1947) Grassy Island. Archaeological Investigations on an
Indian Site, Taunton River, Massachusetts. viii, 68pp,
3pp photographs, 9 figures. $20.00

J79.   JOHNSON (F.) et al. (Peabody Foundation Archaeology Papers, Vol. 6, Andover, 1964) Investigations in Southwest
Yukon. Numbers 1 and 2. 488pp, 94 figures, fold-out
map. $67.00
_____Another Copy. Same, wrappers. $25.00

J80.   JOHNSON (F.) et al. (Peabody Foundation for Archaeology
Papers, Vol. 3, Phillips Academy, 1946) Man in Northeastern North America. viii, 345pp (12 papers), 21 figures,
1 photograph. $32.00

J81.   JOHNSON (F.). (Memoirs, Society for American Archaeology
American Antiquities, Vol. XVII, No. 1, Part 2, n.d.)
Radiocarbon Dating. 65pp, wrappers. $20.00

J82.   JOHNSON (F. Roy). Tuscaroras, Mythology-Medicine-
Culture   (2 Volumes). Vol. I: 265pp, 26 illus, cloth.
Vol. II: 284pp, 33 illus, cloth. Murfreesboro, 1967,
1968. $35.00

J83.   JOHNSON (J. B.). (University of New Mexico Publications
in Anthropology, No. 6, 1950) The Opata: An Inland
Tribe of Sonora. 55pp, 3pp photographs of dance masks.
                                                    $35.00
_____Another Copy. Same. $15.00

J84.   JOHNSON (Kenneth M.). (Famous California Trials, No.
6, Los Angeles, 1966, 1st ed.) K-344, or Indians of
California vs. The United States. 97pp, illus, limited to
500 copies, an important survey of the legal problems of
Indian ownership of land from the earliest times to the

present, especially relating to the case known as K-344
of the 1920s, in which the whole history of Indian land
ownership was examined. $55.00

J85. JOHNSON (L.) et al. (Texas Memorial Museum Bulletin No.
5, Austin, 1962) Salvage Archaeology Canyon Reservoir....
126pp, illus, pls, bibliography, wrappers. $15.00

J86. JOHNSON (L., Jr.). (Texas Memorial Museum, Bulletin 12,
Austin, 1967) Towards Statis. Overview of Archaic Cultures, Central and South Texas. 110pp, pls, bibliography, wrappers. $10.00

J87. JOHNSON (Olga W.). Flathead and Kootenay. The Rivers,
the Tribes and the Regions Traders. 392pp, frontis,
28pp of photographs, folding map, bibliography, index.
A. H. Clark, 1969 (1st ed.). $50.00

J88. JOHNSON (Ronald). The Art of the Shaman. 32pp, illus,
wrappers. University of Iowa, Museum of Art, 1973.
                                                       $15.00

J89. JOHNSON (W. Fletcher). Life of Sitting Bull and History
of the Indian War of 1890-91. A Graphic Account ...
story of the Sioux Nation.... 587pp, illus, map. Rader:
2101. Dustin: 155. n.p., 1891. $12.00
____Another Copy. Same. 606pp, wear to top of back-
strip. $12.00
____Another Copy. Same. Salesman's prospectus. $25.00

J90. JOHNSTON (Bernice E.). California's Gabrielino Indians.
198pp, illus, gilt decorated buckram. Southwest Museum,
Los Angeles, 1962. $25.00
____Another copy, F. W. Hodge Anniversary Publication,
Vol. VIII, Los Angeles, 1962. index. $20.00

J91. JOHNSTON (B. E.). Two Ways in the Desert; A Study of
Modern Navajo-Anglo Relations. 334pp, illus, the John-
stons were prime movers in an historic effort to save living space for the Navajos, and this work covers their efforts 1896 through World War II. Pasadena, 1972 (1st ed.),
d.j. $25.00

J92. JOHNSTON (Charles M.) (Editor). The Valley of the Six
Nations: A Collection of Documents on the Indian Lands
of the Grand River. xcvi, 344pp, illus, 2 folding maps,
color frontis. Toronto, Champlain Society, 1964. $35.00
____Another Copy. 1971, d.j. $20.00
____Another Copy. Same. $15.00

JOHNSTON (Denis Foster). See also BAE Bulletin No. 197.

J93. JONAITIS (A.). Northwest Coast Indian Art from California
Collections. 16pp, 25 photographs. Davis, 1980. $10.00

J94. JONES (Charles C.). Antiquities of the Southern Indians,
Particularly of the Georgia Tribes. 532pp, 30pls, 3 woodcuts, original green cloth, light water staining on margin
of some pages. Howes: J194. New York, 1873 (1st ed.).
                                                       $275.00
____Another Copy. Same. $225.00

J95. JONES (Charles C., Jr.). Historical Sketch of Tomo-Chi-Chi,

Mico of the Yamacraws. 133pp, wrappers, presentation
copy signed and dated by the author, biography of this
intelligent, generous Indian Chief. Howes: J-198.
Field: 796. New York, Albany, Joel Munsell, 1868
(1st ed.). $25.00

J96.   JONES (Daniel W.). Forty Years Among the Indians.
378pp. Salt Lake City, 1960, d.j. $20.00
____Another Copy. Same, 1000 copies printed. $22.00
____Another Copy. Salt Lake City, n.d., reprint of
1960 edition. $10.00

J97.   JONES (David). A Journal of Two Visits Made to Some
Nations of Indians on the West Side of the River Ohio,
1772-1773. With Biographical Note by H. G. Jones. 8vo,
120pp, wrappers, limited to 250 copies. New York,
Joseph Sabin, 1865. $125.00
A Missionary's account of the Delaware and Shawnee
tribes in 1772. Thomas Hutchins and George Rogers
Clark were his traveling companions. This account was
originally published in 1774.

J98.   JONES (Douglas C.). The Treaty of Medicine Lodge. The
Story of the Great Treaty Council as Told by Eyewit-
nesses. 230pp, plus index, photographs, some drawings,
bibliography, author's signed presentation copy with a
small sketch of an Indian head by author. Norman,
1966 (1st ed.), d.j. $25.00
____Another Copy. Same. $25.00
____Another Copy. Same. Lacks d.j. $20.00
____Another Copy. Same. Frayed d.j. $17.00

J99.   JONES (George). The History of Ancient America, Anterior
to the Time of Columbus. xx, 462pp, engraved title, index, half leather, marbled bds, endpapers. London,
Longman, Brown, Green and Longmans, 1843 (2d ed.).
                                                             $90.00
Field: 801. Howes: J-214. W. H. Blumenthal: "Book-
men's Bedlam," pp202-03. Perhaps the queerest character in the annals of the American stage was George Jones,
who forsook England about 1828 and came to be known
as Count Johannes.... His stage career began about
1833 and his favorite role was Hamlet ... until he became
too mad to portray even the Mad Prince. He was admitted
to the Bar of New York about 1862 as a sort of joke, and
he always appeared in a velvet coat with many decorations.
The Second edition, has same date and collation as the
first edition. Attempts to prove America was discovered
nearly 2,000 years before Columbus and that Indians trace
back to the Tyrians. (CLR) (RMW)
____Another Copy. Same. ....Columbus; Providing the
Identity of the Aborigines with the Tyrians and Israelites;
and the Introduction of Christianity into the Western
Hemisphere by the Apostle St. Thomas, engraved extra
title. $50.00

J100.   JONES (Grant D.). Anthropology and History in Yucatan.
        292pp, 24pp bibliography, contains essays by leading
        scholars on the Maya. Austin, 1977. $35.00
        ____Another Copy. Same, ex-library. $22.00
J101.   JONES (J.). The Art of Precolumbian Gold, The Jan
        Mitchell Collection. 248pp, 80 full-page color and 78
        b/w photographs, 19 drawings, 5 maps, cloth. Boston,
        1985. $49.00
            The Mitchell collection of pre-Columbian gold, one of
        the most important collections, private or museum, ex-
        tant, was exhibited in 1985 at the Metropolitan Museum of
        Art. This book, published in conjunction with the exhi-
        bition, contains six essays by authorities in the field and
        a full catalogue of the exhibition. The photographs are
        especially fine, an extensive description of each illustrated
        object. (EAP)
J102.   JONES (J.). (Smithsonian Contributions to Knowledge 259,
        Washington, 1879) Explorations of the Aboriginal Remains
        of Tennessee. x, 170pp, 85 illus. $165.00
            More than a century ago this major paper introduced
        to many scholars the burial customs of the Mound Build-
        ers of Tennessee and the rich, sophisticated artifacts un-
        covered during the excavations of the burial sites in 1868
        and 1869. Out of print for almost 90 years, this study
        concentrates on the sites at Big Harpeth River, Old Town
        and Maury County, and illustrates some wonderful arti-
        facts excavated at these sites, including beads, belts, in-
        tact ceramic vessels, stone pipes, stone idols and ceramic
        figures. (EAP)
JONES (J. A.). See also BAE Bulletin No. 157.
J103.   JONES (James A.). Tales of an Indian Camp. (3 Volumes).
        Vol. 1: xxxiii, 312pp. Vol 2: iv, 336pp. Vol. 3:
        iv, 341pp. Later 1/2 calf, marbled bds. London, H.
        Colburn and R. Bentley, 1829 (1st ed.). $200.00
            Howes: J-219. Sabin: 36521. Field: 799. "The
        copious and numerous notes scattered through the vol-
        umes upon Indian history and customs, have also an
        authenticity which entitles them to respect." (RMW)
J104.   JONES (James Athern). Traditions of the North American
        Indians. (3 Volumes) Vol. I: (30), 213pp. Vol. II:
        (6), 336pp. Vol. III: (4), 341pp, 6 pls, later calf.
        London, 1829. $300.00
            Howes: J-219. The second edition, but issued under
        a different title (the first being "Tales of an Indian Camp")
        and with the author named, but published in the same
        year, by the same publisher, and probably only differing
        from the first in title page and the introduction in Vol.
        I. Full of exotic tales, mainly from eastern Indian tribes,
        with explanations which might or might not hold up today.
        (WR)
J105.   JONES (Joan Megan). The Art and Style of Western

Indian Basketry. 56pp, b/w and color photographs, wrappers. Surrey, BC, n.d., (1st ed.). $10.00

J106. JONES (J. M.). (Thomas Burke Museum, Research Report No. 1, Seattle, 1968) Northwest Coast Basketry and Culture Change. 60pp, 67 illus. $18.00

J107. JONES (Joseph). (Smithsonian Contributions to Knowledge No. 259, Washington, 1876) Explorations of the Aboriginal Remains of Tennessee. 171pp, 4to, 84 figures, newly rebound in linen. $125.00

J108. JONES (Julie) (Editor). Photographs by Justin Kerr. The Art of Pre-Columbian Gold: The Jan Mitchell Collection. 85pp, 80 color pls with full descriptions, 4to. London, 1985. $40.00

J109. JONES (Julie). El Dorado: The Gold of Ancient Columbia. 150pp, illus, some in color, wrappers. Museo del Oro, Bogota, 1974. $20.00

J110. JONES (Livingston F.). A Study of the Tlingits of Alaska. 261pp, 16 pls, 6 advs, map, index, the author lived among the Tlingits on the Northwest Coast for twenty years and reports on their language, customs, art, etc. New York, 1914 (1st ed.). $55.00

J111. JONES (Louis Thomas). Highlights of Puebloland. 107pp, illus. San Antonio, 1968 (1st ed.). $17.00
＿＿Another Copy. Same. $12.00

J112. JONES (L. T.). Aboriginal American Oratory; The Tradition of Eloquence Among Indians of the United States. 136pp, illus. Los Angeles, 1965 (1st ed.). $12.00
＿＿Another Copy. Same. $10.00

J113. JONES (Oakah L.). Pueblo Warriors and Spanish Conquest. 225pp, illus index, maps. Norman, 1966 (1st ed.). $25.00
Procedures, organization and significance of the native Pueblo warriors that the Spanish used to augment their own troops to hold the Southwest 1692-1794.
＿＿Another Copy. Same. d.j. $22.00
＿＿Another Copy. Same. $20.00

J114. JONES (Peter). History of the Ojibway Indians. viii, 278pp, 24pp ads, 16 pls, original cloth, rebacked. London, A. W. Bennett, 1861. $85.00
Howes: J-238. Field: 797. Origin of the Indians, religion and ceremonies, material culture, languages, medicines and diseases, etc.

J115. JONES (P. M.). (University of California Anthropological Records, Vol. 17, No. 2, 1956) Archaeological Investigations on Santa Rosa Island in 1901. 84pp, 44pp photographs, 1 map. $30.00

J116. JONES (Suzi) (Editor). Pacific Basket Makers: A Living Tradition. 80pp, photographs, map, bibliography, exhibition catalogue. University of Alaska, 1983 (1st ed.). $10.00

J117. JONES (T. J.) et al. The Navajo Indian Problem, An

Inquiry Sponsored by the Phelps-Stokes Fund. xvi,
127pp, map. New York, 1939. $24.00

J118.   JONES (Tom) (Copyrighter). The Last of the Buffalo
comprising a history of the buffalo herd of the Flathead
Reservation and an account of the great round up. 6
unnumbered pp of text, 23pp of photographs, oblong,
wrappers, in original mailing envelope. Cincinnati, 1909.
$25.00

J119.   JONES (W.). (American Ethnological Society Publications,
Vol. 1, Leyden, 1907) Fox Texts. 383pp, cloth, inscribed by A. L. Kroeber. $59.00

JONES (Walter B.). See also BAE Bulletin No. 129.

JONES (William). See also BAE Bulletin Nos. 40, Part I, and 125.

J120.   JONES (William). (Supplement, American Anthropology,
Vol. 6, No. 3, New York, 1904) Some Principles of Algonquian Word Formation. pp369-411, wrappers. $15.00

J121.   JONES (W. K.). (Smithsonian Institution Contributions to
Anthropology, Vol. 2, No, 5, 1969) Notes on the History
and Material Culture of the Tonkawa Indians. v, pp65-
81, 13pp photographs, 3pp of maps. $24.00

J122.   JORALEMON (Peter). A Study of Olmec Iconography.
95pp, 266 illus, 4to, wrappers. Washington, 1971.
$25.00

____Another Copy. (Studies in Pre-Columbian Art and
Archaeology, No. 7, Washington, 1970). $12.00

J123.   JORDAN (W. F.). Glimpses of Indian America. 203pp
plus index, photographs, map front endpaper. New York,
1923 (1st ed.). $10.00

J124.   JORDON (Jan). Give Me the Wind. 253pp and 2pp, biographical novel of the life of John Ross, Cherokee Chief.
Englewood Cliffs, NJ, 1973 (1st ed.), d.j. $10.00

J125.   JOSEPH (A.) et al. The Desert People, A Study of the
Papago Indians of Southern Arizona. xvii, 288pp, 20pp
photographs, 5 maps, cloth. Chicago, 1949. $35.00
____Another Copy. Same. $30.00

J126.   JOSEPHY (A. M.) (Editor). The American Heritage Book
of Indians. 424pp, profusely illus, 4to. New York,
1961. $25.00

J127.   JOSEPHY (A. M.). The Artist Was A Young Man. The
life story of Peter Rindisbacher. 92pp plus index, drawings (some in color), notes, bibliography. Ft. Worth,
1970 (1st ed.), d.j. $15.00

J128.   JOSEPHY (A. M.). Chief Joseph's People and Their War.
22pp, illus, wrappers. Yellowstone Library and Museum,
1964. $10.00

J129.   JOSEPHY (A. M.). The Indian Heritage of America.
384pp, illus, maps, ex-library. New York, 1968 (1st
ed.), d.j. $14.00
____Another Copy. New York, 1968 (3rd print.), d.j.
$10.00

____Another Copy. New York, 1970, d.j. $15.00

J130. JOSEPHY (A. M.). The Nez Perce Indians and the Opening of the Northwest. 705pp, illus, index, maps. New
Haven, 1965 (1st ed.), d.j. $60.00
Author traces the history of the Nez Perce from the
time of Lewis and Clark through Chief Joseph's fighting
retreat over the Lolo trail in 1877. First edition is scarce
and in demand as later printings were abridged. (GFH)
___Another Copy. Same. $40.00
___Another Copy. Same. $40.00

J131. JOSEPHY (A. M.). The Patriot Chiefs; A Chronicle of
American Indian Leadership. 364pp, 9 portraits, map at
beginning of each chapter by Daniel Brownstein, index,
bibliography, cloth. New York, 1965 (4th print.), d.j.
$25.00
___Another Copy. Same. edge-frayed d.j. $14.00
___Another Copy. New York, 1962 (2d print.). $10.00

J132. JOSEPHY (A. M.). Red Power. The American Indians'
Fight for Freedom. 259pp. New York, 1971 (1st ed.),
d.j. $12.00
___Another Copy. Same, lacks d.j. $10.00

J133. JOSSELYN (John). New-England Rarities Discovered: In
Birds, Beasts, Fishes, Serpents and Plants of that Country. Together With the Physical Chyrugical Remedies
Wherewith the Natives Constantly Use to Cure Their Dis-
tempers, Wounds and Sores. Also a Perfect Description
of the Indian Squa, In all Her Bravery.... iv, 114pp,
leaf of ads, leaf displaying the publisher's woodcut
dragon, several woodcuts in text, 2 leaves, pp45-48 and
one folding woodcut supplied in facsimile, 16mo, modern
calf. London, G. Widdowes, 1672 (1st ed.). $1,900.00
Howes: J-255. Field: 779. The first work on the
natural history of New England. The Description of Indian herbal medicines takes up a goodly portion of this
work. (RMW)

J134. JOYCE (Thomas A.). Central American and West Indian
Archaeology, Being an Introduction to the Archaeology of
the States of Nicaragua, Costa Rica, Panama and the
West Indies. xvi, 270pp, 28 full-page b/w and 1 full-
page color photograph, 64 figures, 2 maps, cloth. New
York, 1916. $96.00
___Another Copy. Same. ex-library. $65.00
___Another Copy. New York, 1973, all b/w photographs.
$60.00

J135. JOYCE (T. A.). Maya and Mexican Art in "The Studio."
191pp, approx 75 illus of artifacts and sites, color frontis
of Zouche Codex, edge wr, slight tear on spine. London,
1927. $45.00
___Another Copy. Same. $50.00

J136. JOYCE (T. A.). Mexican Archaeology: An Introduction to
the Archaeology of the Mexican and Mayan Civilizations
of Pre-Spanish America. xvi, 87 figures, 25 pls, 1 pl

in color, 3 maps and charts, several are folding, original
cloth. London, Medici Society, 1920. $75.00
    Another Copy. New York, 1969, 384pp. $25.00
    Another Copy. Same. $15.00

J137. JOYCE (T. A.) et al. Report of the British Museum Expedition to British Honduras 1927-1930. (4 parts). Offprint from the Journal of the Royal Anthropological Institute, Vol. LVII, 1927; Vol. LVIII, 1928; Vol. LIX,
1929 and Vol. LX, 1930. 82pp, 40 pls, numerous figures
and charts, excellent plates illustrating objects excavated
during the Expedition, wrappers. $60.00
    Another Copy. Vol. LVIII, 1928 only, pp323-350,
2 maps, 1 plan, 12pp photographs. $30.00

J138. JOYCE (T. A.). A Short Guide to the American Antiquities in the British Museum. 53pp, 12 pls, 48 illus,
lacks cvrs. London, 1912. $35.00

J139. JOYCE (T. A.). South American Archaeology, An Introduction to the Archaeology of the South American Continent with Special Reference to the Early History of
Peru. 307pp, 37 figures containing drawings of about
100 objects, 36pp of photographs of several hundred objects, 1pp of color photographs, cloth. New York, 1912.
$75.00

J140. JUDD (Mary) (Compiler). Wigwam Stories Told By North
American Indians. ix, 278pp, illus, glossary, some
photographs by George W. James. Boston, 1909. $12.00

JUDD (Neil M.). See also BAE Bulletin No. 82.

J141. JUDD (Neil M.). (Smithsonian Miscellaneous Collections,
Vol. 70, No. 2, Washington, 1919) Archaeological Investigations at Paragonah Utah. 22pp, illus, wrappers.
$15.00

J142. JUDD (Neil M.). (Smithsonian Miscellaneous Collections,
Vol. 147, No. 1, Washington, 1964, published with grant
from the Nat. Geographic Soc.) The Architecture of
Pueblo Bonito. 349pp, illus, wrappers. $75.00

J143. JUDD (Neil M.). The Bureau of American Ethnology, a
Partial History. xi, 139pp, 8pp of photographs, index,
includes bibliography of BAE Annual Reports, Bulletins,
Contributions to North American Ethnology, Introductions
and Miscellaneous Publications. Norman, 1967 (1st ed.),
d.j. $25.00
    Another Copy. Same. $10.00

J144. JUDD (Neil M.). (From: U.S. National Museum Proceedings, Vol. 77, Part 5, Washington, 1930) The Excavation
and Repair of Betatakin (Navaho National Monument,
Arizona). pp1-77, pls 1-46, wrappers. $35.00
    Another Copy. Same. $15.00

J145. JUDD (Neil M.). (Smithsonian Miscellaneous Collections,
124, published with grant from Nat. Geographic Soc.,
Washington, 1954) The Material Culture of Pueblo Bonito.
397pp, 101 illus, wrappers. $75.00

J146. JUDD (Neil M.). (Smithsonian Miscellaneous Collections, Vol. 138, No. 1, Washington, 1959) Pueblo del Arroyo, Chaco Canyon, New Mexico. 222pp, illus, wrappers. $45.00

J147. JUDD (Neil M.). Two Chaco Canyon Pit Houses. From Smithsonian Annual Report for 1922, pp399-413, 7 pls, printed wrappers. Washington, 1924. $20.00

J148. JUDGE (W. James). Paleoindian Occupation of the Central Rio Grande Valley in New Mexico. x, 361pp, figures, tables, bibliography, index, wrappers. University of New Mexico, 1977 (2d print.). $10.00

J149. JUDSON (Katherine B.). Myths and Legends of California and the Old Southwest. 193pp, profusely illus with Zuni Sandpaintings, Yuma Indians, etc., decorated cloth. Chicago, A. C. McClurg, 1912 (1st ed.). $35.00

J150. JUDSON (K. B.). Myths and Legends of the Pacific Northwest: Especially of Washington and Oregon. 145pp, photographic pls, folding map, decorative cloth with photograph. Chicago, 1910, (1st ed.). $40.00

JUDSON (Sheldon). See also BAE Bulletin No. 154.

J151. JUDSON (Sheldon). (Smithsonian Miscellaneous Collections, Vol. 121, No. 1, Washington, 1953) Geology of the San Jon Site, Eastern New Mexico. 70pp, illus wrappers. $18.00

J152. JUNEK (Oscar W.). Isolated Communities: A Study of a Labrador Fishing Village. Foreword by Clark Wissler, illus, New York, American Book Co., 1937. $35.00

-K-

K1. KABOTIE (Fred). Designs from the Ancient Mimbrenos, with a Hopi Interpretation. 94pp, folio, illus, signed, leather backed buckram, slipcased, limited to 100 copies. Kabotie is a major figure in 20th Century Indian Art, working in both Anglo and Hopi worlds. $250.00

K2. (KACHINAS). Dancing Kachinas, A Hopi Artist's Documentary. 38pp, 48 color paintings by Cliff Bahnimptewa. Heard Museum, 1971. $15.00

K3. (KACHINAS). Kachina: Horst Antes Collection. 176pp, 412 Kachinas illus (many in color), text in German, 4to, stiff wrappers. West Germany, 1981-82. $125.00

K4. (KACHINAS). Kachinas. 32pp, 35 photographs of 68 kachinas. Los Angeles, 1967. $10.00

K5. (KACHINAS). Kachinas-Paone. 94pp, 15pp of color and 103 full and half-page b/w photographs. Exhibition catalogue, Contemporary Arts Museum, Houston. Austin, 1976. $19.00

K6. KAEMLEIN (W. R.). An Inventory of Southwestern American

Indian Specimens in European Museums. 240pp. Arizona
State Museum, Tucson, 1967. $30.00

K7. KAHLENBERG (Mary Hunt) and BERLANT (Anthony). The
Navajo Blanket. 112pp, large 4to, b/w and color illus.
Los Angeles Museum of Art, 1972. $25.00
___Another Copy. Same. $15.00
___Another Copy, Los Angeles, 1972 paper edition, 3rd
print. $12.00

K8. KALM (Peter). Norra Americansa Farge-Orter.... 8pp,
disbound. Abo. 1763. $550.00
Larson: 396. A dissertation by Kalm upon Indian
uses of plants for dyeing in America. Kalm describes
methods of making dyes from plants, tattooing, body
painting and clothing dyes. (WR)

K9. KAMENSKII (A.). Tlingit Indians of Alaska. xvii, 166pp,
9 full-page photographs, wrappers. Odessa, 1906, Fairbanks, 1985. $30.00

K10. KAMER (Helene). Arts Pre-Colombiens. 36pp, 36 illus,
(7"x11") in size, wrappers. Exhibition catalogue, Paris,
1971. $20.00

K11. KAMER (Helene). Mexique Pre-Colombien. 40pp, 40 illus
(7"x11") in size, wrappers. Exhibition catalogue, Paris,
1976. $20.00

K12. KAMPEN (M. E.). The Sculptures of El Tajin, Veracruz,
Mexico. 195pp, illus. Gainesville, 1972. $35.00

K13. KAN (M.) et al. Sculpture of Ancient West Mexico. xxxii,
206pp, 4to, wrappers. Exhibition catalogue, The Proctor
Stafford Collection, Los Angeles, 1970. $65.00
___Another Copy. Same. 116pp, 206 illus. $60.00
___Another Copy. Same. $35.00

K14. KANE (Elisha Kent). Arctic Explorations: The Second
Grinnell Expedition in Search of Sir John Franklin, 1853,
54, 55 (2 Volumes). pp464, 467, folding maps, engravings, illus, original cloth. Philadelphia, Childs and Peterson, 1856 (1st ed.). $90.00
Field: 812. Sabin: 37001. Arctic Biblio: 8373.
Much of this work is taken with a detailed description of
the Eskimo people, their customs, living quarters, costumes,
dances, language, etc.
___Another Copy. London, Trubner & Co. $115.00

K15. KANE (Paul). Wanderings of an Artist Among the Indians
of North America from Canada to Vancouver's Island and
Canada Through the Hudson's Bay Company's Territory
and Back Again. xvii, 455pp, folding map, 8 color pls,
13 woodcuts, morocco, gilt, hinges weak. London, 1859.
$1,500.00
Howes: K-7. Graff: 2262. Wagner-Camp: 332:1,
Peel: 212. Abbey: 663. Field: 811. Streeter: 3727.
Kane travelled west with Sir George Simpson in 1846
and travelled extensively around the Oregon territory in
1847, finally returning to Canada in the following year.

An accomplished artist, his work is now recognized as some of the most significant illustrations of North American aboriginal life of this period. (WR)

____Another Copy. Toronto, Radisson Society, 1925, liv, 329pp, 2 portrait pls, d.j. $50.00

____Another Copy. Rutland, 1968, 329pp. $35.00

K16. KAPPLER (Charles J.) (Editor and Compiler). Kappler's Indian Affairs: Laws and Treaties (7 Volumes) Vol. I: leather, covers detached, 1904 (2d revised ed.). Vols. II-VII, cloth, reprints. All Indian Laws and Treaties through 1971, indexed. $450.00

____Volumes I-V. 1065pp, 1074pp, 756pp, 1194pp and 829pp plus indices, rebound, Washington 1903, 1904, 1913, 1929 and 1941. $400.00

____Volumes I and II, 1st ed. Calf cvrs, one loosening, one detached, laws and treaties to 1902. $150.00

____Vol. I. Washington, 1975. $65.00

____Vol. II. 1904 2d revised ed, calf cvrs loosening, treaties to 1904. $45.00

____Vol. V. Reprint, laws 1927-38. $45.00

KARSTEN (Rafael). See also BAE Bulletin No. 79.

K17. KARSTEN (Rafael). The Civilization of the South American Indians: With Special reference to Magic and Religion. Kegan Paul, London, 1926. $35.00

K18. KARSTEN (R.). Indian Tribes of the Argentine and Bolivian Chaco, Ethnological Studies. x, 236pp, 23 photographs, 2 drawings, fold-out map, Societas Scientiarum Fennica, Helsingfors, 1932. $45.00

____Another Copy. Same. $15.00

K19. KARSTEN (Rafael). (Commentationes Humanarum. Litterarum Tomux XVI, No. 1, Copenhagen, 1950) A Totalitarian State of the Past; The Civilization of the Inca Empire in Ancient Peru. 288pp, illus, wrappers. $45.00

____Another Copy. Same. $40.00

K20. KASHEVAROFF (A. P.). Descriptive Booklet on the Alaska Historical Museum. 52pp, 27 lrg photographs illus hundreds of Northwest Coast and Eskimo artifacts. Alaska Historical Assn, Juneau, n.d. $40.00

K21. KATZ (F.). The Ancient American Civilizations. xvi, 386pp of text, plus 48pp of photographs of artifacts and archaeological sites, 3 maps, cloth. London, 1972. $30.00

K22. KATZ (Jane B.) (Editor and Compiler). We Rode the Wind. 110pp, drawings, sources. Recollections of 19th Century tribal life, material from Eastman, Stands in Timber, Two Leggings, Standing Bear, Wm. Warren's Ojibway history, Jim Whitewolf, Black Elk. Minneapolis, 1975, (1st ed.), d.j. $10.00

K23. KATZ (S. R. and P. R.). (Texas Historical Commission State Archaeologist Survey Report, No. 16, Austin, 1976, (1st ed.) Archaeological Investigation of Lower Tule Canyon, Briscoe County, Texas. 147pp, illus, maps, bibliography, lrg 8vo, wrappers. $12.00

K24. KATZENBERG (Dena). And Eagles Sweep Across the Sky:
Indian Textiles of the North American West; Navaho
Blankets and Rugs; Baskets of the West. 151pp, 111
illus with 8 color pls. Baltimore Museum of Art, 1977.
$25.00

___Another Copy. Same. $15.00

K25. KAUFMAN (A.) and SELSER (C.). The Navajo Weaving
Tradition, 1650 to the Present. 150pp, 181 color and 36
b/w photographs, 1 drawing, 2 maps. New York, 1985.
$35.00

More and better photographs of Navajo weaving than
any previous publication. A good study of the history of
Navajo weaving, the text provides a fine overview of this
art form, with particular emphasis on the classic period
and on contemporary Navajo weaving. The color photographs are remarkably rich and each of them illustrates
textiles (most are previously unpublished) and is completely described. (EAP)

K26. KAUT (C. R.). (University of New Mexico Publications
in Anthropology, No. 9, 1957) The Western Apache Clan
System: Its Origin and Development. vi, 99pp, 13 illus.
$24.00

___Another Copy. Same. inscribed by author. $22.00
___Another Copy. Same. wrappers. $20.00

K27. KEATING (William H.). Narrative of an Expedition to the
Source of St. Peter's River, Lake Winnepeek, Lake of the
Woods, etc., etc. Performed in the Year 1823 (2 Volumes). Vol. I: xiv, 9-439pp, folding map. Vol. II:
vi, 5-459pp, 15 pls, including music scores, rebound in
cloth, Philadelphia, Carey and Lea, 1824 (1st ed.).
$275.00

Howes: K-20. Field: 949. Pilling: 2066. Sabin:
37137. The scientist W. Keating served as geologist and
Historiographer for the Long Expedition, sent to explore
the headwaters of the Mississippi River. The artist Samuel
Seymour contributed views of Lake Travers, Winnepeek
River, Lake of the Woods, Lake Superior, along with Indian portraits and village scenes. An important western
artist, although little is known about his life, Seymour is
generally regarded as the first white artist in the trans-
Mississippi West. Field: "The work is almost a cyclopedia
of material relating to the Indians of the explored territory. Nothing escaped the attention of the gentlemen ...
of the Sioux and Chippewa tribes ... the most valuable
studies we have of these people." (RMW)

___Another Copy. London, 1825, Vol. I: (16), 458pp.
Vol. II: (6), 248pp, 156pp, map 8 pls, 3 tables, original
bds, t.e.g. $250.00

K28. KEEL (B. C.). The Conservation and Preservation of
Archaeological and Ethnological Specimens. 65pp, wrappers.
Southern Indian Studies, Vol. 15, 1963. $20.00

___Another Copy. Same. $18.00

K29. KEELER (Clyde E.). Land of the Moon Children: The Primitive San Blas Culture in Flux. 207pp, illus. Athens, GA, 1956 (1st ed.), d.j. $25.00

K30. KEEN (Benjamin). The Aztec Image in Western Thought. xii, 668pp, 57 illus, 2 maps. Rutgers University, 1957. $25.00
___Another Copy. New Brunswick, NJ, 1971, d.j. $30.00
___Another Copy. Same. $50.00

K31. KEESING (F. M.). (American Philosophical Society, Memoirs, Vol. X, 1939) The Menomini Indians of Wisconsin, a Study of Three Centuries of Cultural Contact and Change. xi, 261pp, 8pp illus, 5 diagrams. $29.00

KEHOE (Thomas F.). See also BAE Bulletin No. 173.

K32. KEITH (Marshall). An Indian Odyssey. The Story of Chief Washakie, the Upright Aborigine. 218pp, frontis, Caldwell, Caxton Press, 1935 (1st ed.), d.j. $25.00

K33. KEITHAHN (Edward). Alaskan Igloo Tales. 138pp, illus by George Ahgupuk, oblong wrappers. Seattle, Seal Publishers, 1958. $15.00

K34. KEITHAHN (E. L.). Monuments in Cedar, the Authentic Story of the Totem Pole. 160pp, 189 b/w and 8 color photographs, cloth. Seattle, 1963. $40.00
___Another Copy. New York, Bonanza reprint, 1963, d.j. $12.00
___Another Copy. Same. $10.00

K35. KEITHAHN (E. L.). Native Alaskan Art in the State Historical Museum, Juneau, Alaska. 76pp, 62pp photographs, Juneau, 1959. $30.00

K36. KELEMEN (Pal). Medieval American Art (2 Volumes). 414pp, 306 pls with descriptions, pre-Columbian arts of the Americas, 4to. New York, 1946. $100.00
___Another Copy. New York, 1956, one volume edition, 414pp, 308 pls, 4to. $65.00

K37. KELER (C. E.). Cuna Indian Art. 192pp, illus, several in color pls. New York, 1968. $30.00

K38. KELKER (Nancy L.). America Before Columbus: Pre-Columbian Art in the Collection of the San Antonio Museum Association. 132pp, illus, 8 color pls and 57 photographs, decorated embossed cvr. Exhibition catalogue, San Antonio Museum Assn, 1985, d.j. $30.00

K39. KELLAR (James). (Indiana Historical Society, Prehistory Research, Vol. III, No. 3, 1955) The Atlatl in North America. 70pp, illus, wrappers. $25.00

K40. KELLER (J. E.). (Texas Highway Department Publications in Archaeology, Vol. 2, 1973, 1st ed.) The Black Dog Village Site. 67pp, maps, pls, bibliography, lrg 8vo, wrappers. $10.00

KELLEY (A. R.). See BAE Bulletin No. 119.

K41. KELLEY (William Fitch). Pine Ridge 1890: An Eye Witness Account of the Events Surrounding the Fighting at Wounded

Knee. 267pp, illus, photographs, lrg folding map, bibliography. San Francisco, 1971 (1st ed thus). $20.00

K42.   KELLY (Fanny). Narrative of My Captivity Among the Sioux
Indians. With a Brief Account of General Sully's Indian
Expedition in 1865. 12 pls, shaken, cloth. Hartford,
1871. $40.00
Mrs. Kelly was held captive for 5 months. She was
an astute observer, and gives much insight into Indian
life during the changing times and how the Indians
viewed the encroaching march of white settlers.
_____Another Copy. Hartford, Mutual Publishing Co.,
1872, 285pp, 8vo, 12 full-page pls, blue cloth. $25.00
_____Another Copy. Chicago, 1891. $20.00

K43.   KELLY (Isabel). The Archaeology of the Autlan-
Tuxcacuesco Area of Jalisco. Parts 1 and 2. 98pp and
292pp, illus, wrappers. University of California, Berkeley, 1945, 1949. $75.00
_____Another Copy. Part 1 only. $25.00

K44.   KELLY (I. T.). (University of California Publications in
American Archaeology and Ethnology, Vol. 24, No. 7, 1930)
The Carvers Art of the Indians of Northwestern California.
35pp, 17pp photographs, 7 figures. $30.00
_____Another Copy, Ramona, 1971, reprint, 34pp, 4to,
illus, wrappers. $10.00

K45.   KELLY (I. T.). (University of California Publications in
American Archaeology and Ethnology, Vol. 31, No. 3,
1932) Ethnology of the Surprise Valley Paiute. 175pp,
16pp photographs, 10 figures, 1 map. $59.00

K46.   KELLY (I.). (Viking Fund Publications in Anthropology,
No. 7, 1947) Excavations at Apatzingan, Michoaca. 227pp
of text containing 100 figures, 27 tables, plus 24pp of
photographs. $40.00

K47.   KELLY (I. T.) and VAN VALKENBURGH (R. V.). Paiute
Indians II: Southern Paiute Ethnography. also: Cheme-
huevi Notes. 225pp, 29pp, 7pp photographs, 19 figures,
2 maps. Reprint on University of Utah Anthropological
Papers No. 69, 1964. New York, 1976. $30.00

K48.   KELLY (I. T.). (University of California Publications in
American Archaeology and Ethnology, Vol. 24, No. 6,
1930) Peruvian Cumbrous Bowls. 17pp, fold-out with
drawings of 138 bowls. $15.00

K49.   KELLY (I. T.). (University of California Anthropology
Records, Vol. 2, No. 4, Berkeley, 1939)   Southern Paiute
Shamanism. pp151-167, 4to, wrappers. $20.00

K50.   KELLY (I. T.) and PALERM (A.). (Smithsonian Institution
Institute of Social Anthropology, Publication 13, 1952)
The Tajin Totonac. Part 1. History, Subsistence, Shelter
and Technology. xiv, 364pp of text containing 69 figures,
21 tables, 33pp photographs. $45.00
_____Another Copy. Same. $40.00
_____Another Copy. Same. $15.00

K51. KELLY (I. T.). (University of California Publications in
American Archaeology and Ethnology, Vol. 24, No. 9, 1930)
Yuki Basketry. 40pp, 16pp photographs, 5 figures.
$47.00
___Another Copy. Same. bound in later cloth. $35.00
K52. KELLY (Jane Holden). Yaqui Women; Contemporary Life
Histories. 265pp, map, four life histories relating per-
sonal accounts of the Yaqui wars, deportation from Sonora
into virtual slavery, life as soldaderas with the Mexican
Revolutionary army, emigration to Arizona to escape per-
secution and life in the modern Yaqui communities. Lin-
coln, 1978 (1st ed.), d.j. $25.00
K53. KELLY (Joanne M.). Cuna. 440pp, frontis, cloth. New
York & London, 1966, d.j. $15.00
K54. KELLY (Lawrence C.). The Navajo Indians and Federal
Indian Policy 1900-1935. 210pp plus index, maps, bibliog-
raphy. Tucson, 1968 (1st ed.), d.j. $15.00
___Another Copy. Same. $17.00
___Another Copy. 1970 (2d print.), d.j. $12.00
K55. KELLY (Lawrence C.). Navajo Roundup: Selected Cor-
respondence of Kit Carson's Expedition Against the Nava-
jo, 1863-1865. 192pp, illus, index, folding map in pocket.
Boulder, CO, 1970 (1st ed.), d.j. $20.00
___Another Copy. Same. $17.00
K56. KELLY (Roger E.) et al. Navaho Figurines Called Dolls.
75pp, photographs, drawings by Harry Walters, map,
bibliography, wrappers, one of the few works to deal
with this subject and the most comprehensive. Santa Fe,
1972 (1st ed.). $12.00
K57. KELLY (T. C.) and HESTER (T. R.). (University of
Texas Center for Archaeological Research, Survey Re-
ports No. 10, San Antonio, 1975) Additonal Archaeological
Survey in Dry Comal Watershed, Comal County, Texas.
29pp. $10.00
K58. KELLY (T. C.) and HESTER (T. R.). (University of
Texas Archaeological Survey Report No. 15, San Antonio,
1975) Archaeological Investigations at Four Sites in Comal
County, Texas. 22pp, photographs, map, bibliography,
wrappers. $10.00
K59. KELLY (T. C.) and HESTER (T. R.). (University of
Texas Archaeological Survey Report No. 17, San Antonio,
1976) Archaeological Investigations at Sites in the Upper
Cibolo Creek Watershed, Central Texas. 33pp, photo-
graphs, drawings, map, bibliography, wrappers. $10.00
K60. KELLY (T. C.) and HESTER (T. R.). (University of
Texas Center for Archaeological Research, Survey Report
No. 20 1976) Archaeological Investigations Sites Near
Matalia, Texas. 19pp, drawings, map, bibliography,
wrappers. $10.00
K61. KELLY (T. C.) and HIGHLEY (L.). (University of Texas
Archaeological Survey Report 65, San Antonio, 1979)

The Jackpump Project. An Archaeological Survey of Portions of Karnes and Gonzales Counties, Texas. 39pp,
photographs, maps, bibliography, wrappers. $10.00

K62. KELLY (William H.). (University of Arizona, First Annual
Report of Bureau of Ethnic Research, Tucson, 1953) In-
dians of the Southwest: A Survey of Indian Tribes and
Indian Administration in Arizona. 129pp, wrappers.
                                                    $18.00

K63. KELLY (W. H.). The Papago Indians of Arizona: A Population and Economic Study. 129pp, wrappers. University
of Arizona, Tucson, 1963. $18.00

K64. KELM (H.). Handwerk Der Shefferville-Naskapi (Kanada).
Ausstellung Des Stammes Der Naskapi Im Museum Fur
Volkerkunde Der Stadt Frankfurt Am Main. 28pp, 16pp
photographs, map, wrappers. Frankfurt, 1979. $10.00

K65. KELSEY (C. E.). Census of Non-Reservation California
Indians 1905-1906. 118pp, 4to, wrappers, actual count of
the number of surviving native Californians (including names
and number of children) in each of the 36 counties in which
Kelsey made investigations. Berkeley, 1971 (1st ed.).
                                                    $25.00
_____Another Copy. Same. $15.00

K66. KELTON (Dwight H.). Indian Names of Places Near the
Great Lakes. (Volume 1. All published). 55pp, 10pp
ads, original cloth. Detroit, author, 1888. $30.00
Focuses on the considerable Indian history found in
the sources of names like Chicago, Detroit, Huron, Mani-
tou, Pontiac, Wabash, etc.

K67. KENDALL (A.). The Art and Archaeology of Pre-Columbian
Middle America: An Annotated Bibliography of Works in
English. 324pp, cloth. Boston, 1977. $60.00

K68. KENDALL (A.). The Art of Pre-Columbian Mexico, An
Annotated Bibliography of Works in English. 115pp, 654
entries. Austin, 1973. $12.00

K69. KENDALL (Edward A.). Travels Through the Northern
Parts of the United States, in the Years 1807 and 1808.
(3 Volumes). Vol. 1: xii, 330pp. Vol. 2: viii, 309pp.
Vol. 3: viii, 312pp, rebound in cloth, 8vo. New York,
I. Riley, 1809 (1st ed.). $150.00

K70. KENNARD (E. A.) et al. Field Mouse Goes to War.
(Tusan Homichi Tuwvota). 76pp, text in English and
Hopi, illus, 13 full-page drawings. Bureau of Indian
Affairs, 1943. $24.00

K71. KENNARD (E. A.). Hopi Kachinas. 106pp, 4to, (50pp
text plus 28 full-page color plates by artist Edwin Earle)
with paragraph of descriptive text for each picture. New
York, 1971. $25.00

K72. KENNEDY (Mary Jeanette). Tales of a Trader's Wife (Life
on the Navajo Indian Reservation) 1913-1938. 61pp,
photographs, author's signed presentation. Albuquerque,
1965 (1st ed.). $17.00

K73. KENNEDY (Michael) (Editor). The Assiniboines, from the
      Accounts of the Old Ones. Told to First Boy (James
      Larpenteur Long). lxxv, 209pp, 8pp illus from paint-
      ings by Bodmer, Catlin, Kane, bibliography, index,
      reprint of the very scarce "Land of Nakoda." Norman
      1961 (1st ed. thus), d.j. $25.00
      ___Another Copy. Same. $30.00
      ___Another Copy. Same. $20.00
K74. KENNER (Charles L.). A History of New Mexican-Plains
      Indian Relations. 250pp, illus, index, bibliography, map.
      Norman, 1969 (1st ed.), d.j. $25.00
      ___Another Copy. Same. $15.00
K75. KENT (Kate Peck). (SW Mon. Assoc. Tech. Series, Vol.
      3, Part 2, Globe, AZ, 1954 (1st ed.) Montezuma Castle
      Archaeology. Part 2: Textiles. 102pp, photographs,
      drawings, bibliography, wrappers. $12.00
K76. KENT (K. P.). Navajo Weaving, Three Centuries of
      Change. x, 139pp, 24pp of color photographs and 65
      b/w photographs, 17 drawings, 1 map, cloth. Santa Fe,
      1985. $40.00
      The history of Navajo weaving from 1650 to the present
      is traced by one of the foremost authorities on ethnic tex-
      tiles. Reflecting the latest research and information--
      some of it amassed (though previously unpublished) by
      Joe Ben Wheat--and based partly on the School of Ameri-
      can Research collection of more than 400 Navajo textiles,
      the beauty and creativity of this tradition are graphically
      shown. All the textiles in the School's collection are listed
      in the appendix, with detailed descriptions given for each
      textile illustrated in this book.
      ___Another Copy. Same. Soft cvr. $200.00
K77. KENT (K. P.). Pueblo Indian Textiles. A Living Tradi-
      tion. 111pp plus index, photographs (some in color), draw-
      ings, wrappers, covers the evolution of tools, materials
      and the textiles themselves. Santa Fe, 1983 (1st ed.).
                      $15.00
K78. KENTON (E.) (Editor). Black Gown and Redskins: Ad-
      ventures and Travels of the Early Jesuit Missionaries in
      North America. 527pp, map, ex-library. New York,
      1956. $25.00
K79. KENTON (Edna) (Editor). The Indians of North America:
      from "The Jesuit Relations and Allied Documents ... 1610-
      1791".... (2 Volumes). 597pp, 579pp, illus, maps,
      notes. New York, 1927 (1st thus.). $30.00
K80. KEPHART (Horace). Captives Among the Indians. First
      Hand Narratives of Indian Wars, Customs.... 240pp,
      (Adventure Series #3), cloth. New York, 1915. $20.00
K81. KERMODE (F.). Guide to the Anthropological Collection in
      the Provincial Museum. viii, 69pp, 26pp photographs.
      British Columbia Provincial Museum, Victoria, 1909.
                      $50.00

K82. KERR (J.). 50 Figures from a Site in Veracruz. 91pp,
44 full-page photographs. Exhibition catalogue, Merrin
Gallery, New York, 1970. $12.00

K83. KESSELL (John L.). Mission of Sorrows. Jesuit Guevavi
and the Pimas, 1691-1767. 215pp plus index, photographs,
bibliography, map endpapers. Tucson, 1970 (1st ed.),
d.j. $15.00

K84. KETCHUM (William). An Authentic and Comprehensive History of Buffalo, With Some Account of its Early Inhabitants,
Both Savage and Civilized, Comprising Historic Notices of
the Six Nations, or Iroquois Indians.... (2 Volumes).
Vol. 1: xvi, 432pp. Vol. 2: viii, 443pp, index, 2 maps,
original cloth. Buffalo, NY, Rockwell, Baker and Hill,
1864. $60.00
    Howes: K-110. Field: 824. Contains narratives of
early explorers, French and Indian Wars, War of the Six
Nations against the Colonies, much on Indian tribes and
contacts with whites.

K85. KEUR (Dorothy L.). (Supplement to American Antiquity,
Vol. 7, No. 2, Menasha, WI, 1941) Big Bend Mesa: An
Archaeological Study of Navaho Acculturation, 1745-1812.
Frontis, 90pp, 7 photographs and figures, wrappers.
                                                   $25.00
____Another Copy. Same. $20.00

K86. (KEYES, Hervey). The Forest King; or, The Wild Hunter
of the Adaca. 63pp, 12mo, original pictorial wrappers,
Mohawk Indians. New York, 1878. $15.00

K87. (KICKAPOO). Life and Scenes Among the Kickapoo Indians, Their Manners, Habits and Customs.... Texas
Charlie's Adventures ... Discovery of the Wondrous Kickapoo Medicine Men ... Their Remedies and the Marvelous
Curses Effected by Them. 174pp, illus, self-wrappers,
8vo, resewn, facts, lore, anecdotes, medical information
and "useful" statistics. Medical guide/almanac Kickapoo
Remedy promo. New Haven, n.d. (c.1890). $35.00

K88. (KICKAPOO). Kickapoo Indians. Letter ... Relative to the
Kickapoo Indians Now in Mexico. 6pp, removed, Indians
were raiding over the border into Texas. Washington,
1868. $20.00

K89. (KICKAPOO). (Senate Document 215, 60:1, Washington,
1908) Affairs of the Mexican Kickapoo Indians (Vol. 1
only). 900pp, folding pls, index, theft of Indian lands
and goods, murder, liquor sales, etc., in Texas, Oklahoma and Arizona. $30.00

K90. KICKINGBIRD (Kirke) and DUCHENEAUX (Karen). One
Hundred Million Acres. 232pp plus index, foreword by
Vine Deloria, Jr., long-standing disputes and problems
regarding Indian land/land claims. New York, 1973 (1st
print.). $10.00

KIDDER (Alfred, II). See also BAE Bulletin Nos. 65 and 143.

K91. KIDDER (Alfred, II). (Peabody Museum Papers, Vol. 26,

No. 1, Cambridge, 1944) Archaeology of Northwestern
Venezuela. 178pp, 18 pls, wrappers. $60.00

K92. KIDDER (A.). The Artifacts of Pecos. xvi, 314pp, many
      photographs, bibliography, lrg 8vo, one of the scarcest,
      and certainly one of the best illustrated, of the reports
      on the Peabody Foundation investigations, 1915-1925 at
      this New Mexico site. Yale University Press, New Haven,
      1932 (1st ed.). $150.00
      ___Another Copy. Same. $150.00
      ___Another Copy. Same. $60.00

K93. KIDDER (A. V.). (Carnegie Institute Publication No.
      576, Washington, 1947) The Artifacts of Uaxactun,
      Guatemala. 76pp, plus 21 pls of over 100 artifacts, 4to,
      wrappers. $125.00
      ___Another Copy. Same. $95.00
      ___Another Copy. Same. $33.00

K94. KIDDER (A. V.) and JENNINGS (J. D.). (Carnegie Insti-
      tution Publication No. 561, 1946) Excavations at Kaminal-
      juyu, Guatemala. ix, 284pp of text containing 102 figures,
      plus 18pp of plans, 162pp of photographs and explanatory
      text, 14pp b/w drawings, text, 8pp color drawings and
      text. $250.00

K95. KIDDER (A. V.). An Introduction to the Study of South-
      western Archaeology, With a Preliminary Account of the
      Excavation at Pecos. vii, 158pp, 25 figures, 50pp photo-
      graphs and drawings, cloth. Phillips Academy and Yale
      University Press, New Haven, 1924. $95.00
      One of the landmark publications in southwestern
      archaeology, this study was the first regional synthesis,
      and remains one of the seminal volumes on Pueblo archaeol-
      ogy. During Kidder's work at Pecos--documented on these
      pages--he pioneered both the use of stratigraphy and the
      application of ethnological data to the interpretation of
      archaeological remains. The bulk of the illustrations are
      of ceramic bowls and vessels. (EAP)
      ___Another Copy. Same. Cloth. $95.00
      ___Another Copy. 1924 (2d print.). $75.00
      ___Another Copy. Same. $60.00
      ___Another Copy. New Haven, 1962, ix, 377pp, 50pp
      of photographs and drawings, 31 figures, soft cvr. $24.00
      ___Another Copy. New Haven, 1968, d.j. $25.00

K96. KIDDER (A. V.). (Peabody Foundation for Archaeology
      Papers, Vol. 5, Phillips Academy, 1958) Pecos, New
      Mexico: Archaeological Notes. xx, 360pp, 72pp photo-
      graphs and drawings. $45.00
      ___Another Copy. Same. $90.00
      ___Another Copy. Same. in later cloth. $45.00
      ___Another Copy. Same. wrappers. $40.00

K97. KIDDER (Frederic). The Expeditions of Captain John
      Lovewell, and His Encounters With the Indians; Including
      a Particular Account of the Pequauket Battle, With a History

of that Tribe; and a Reprint of Rev. Thomas Symme's Sermon. 138pp, i, map, sml 4to, half morocco, one of 200 sml quarto copies in an edition of 235. Boston, 1865. $50.00

KILPATRICK (Anna Gritts and Jack Frederick). See also BAE Bulletin No. 196.

K98. KILPATRICK (Jack F. and Anna G). Friends of Thunder. Folktales of the Oklahoma Cherokees. 197pp, few illus, notes. Dallas, 1964 (1st ed.), d.j. $15.00

K99. KILPATRICK (Jack F.). The Wahnenauhi Manuscript: Historical Sketches of the Cherokees. pp175-213, 4 pls, bibliography, printed wrappers, offprint Smithsonian Anthropological Papers, Washington, 1966. $10.00

K100. KILPATRICK (Jack F. and Anna G.). (Smithsonian Contributions to Anthropology, Vol. 2, No. 3, Washington, 1967, 1st ed.) Muskogean Cham Songs Among the Oklahoma Cherokees. 12pp, music, references, sml folio, wrappers. $10.00

K101. KILPATRICK (Jack F. and Anna G.) (Editors). New Chota Letters. 130pp, bibliography, material appearing in the first Indian language periodical printed in America (Cherokee). Dallas, 1968 (1st ed.), d.j. $15.00

K102. KILPATRICK (Jack F. and Anna G.). (Smithsonian Contributions to Anthropology, Vol. 2, No. 6, Washington, 1970, 1st ed.) Notebook of a Cherokee Shaman. 43pp, list of references cited, wrappers. $10.00

K103. KILPATRICK (J. F. and A. G.). Run Toward the Nightland: Magic of the Oklahoma Cherokees. 197pp, Dallas, 1967 (1st ed.), d.j. $20.00

K104. KILPATRICK (Jack F. and Anna G.) (Editors and translators), (Civilization of the American Indian Series, Vol. 81, Norman, 1965, 1st ed.) The Shadow of Sequoyah. Social Documents of the Cherokees, 1862-1964. 111pp plus index, illus, bibliography, d.j. $15.00

K105. KIMBALL (Irmgard Groth). Mayan Terracottas. xiii, 44pp, profusely illus, 4to. New York, 1961. $60.00

K106. KIMBALL (Yeffe) and ANDERSON (Jean). The Art of American Indian Cooking. 215pp, illus, index. Garden City, 1965. $10.00

K107. KIMM (S. C.). The Iroquois. A History of the Six Nations of New York. 122pp, frontis, original wrappers bound in later limp leather. Middleburgh, NY, 1900. $15.00

K108. KING (A. R.). (Middle American Research, Tulane University, Publication 18, No. 4, 1955) Archaeological Remains from the Cintalapa Region, Chiapas, Mexico. 31pp, 20 figures. $10.00

K109. KING (Blanche Busey). Under Your Feet: The Story of the American Mound Builders. xii, 169pp, 37 pls not included in pagination, inscription by author, cloth. New York, 1939 (1st ed.). $40.00

K110. KING (General Charles). A Daughter of the Sioux. A
Tale of the Indian Frontier. 306pp, frontis, with illus
by Remington and Deming, cloth with pictorial overlay.
New York, 1903 (1st ed.). $15.00

K111. KING (Charles Bird). The Redwood Library Collection
North American Indian Portraits by Charles Bird King.
47pp b/w and color illus, wrappers, 21 remarkable Indian
portraits, unpriced copy of the sale whose prices ranged
from $7500 to $30,000. New York, 1970. $10.00

K112. KING (Dale S.). (Museum of Northern Arizona, Bulletin
23, 1949) Nalakihu: Excavations at a Pueblo III Site on
Wupatki National Monument, Arizona. 183pp, illus,
wrappers, folded charts. $25.00
____Another Copy. Same. $18.00

K113. KING (J. C. H.). Artificial Curiosities from the Northwest
Coast of America. Native American Artifacts in the Brit-
ish Museum Collected on the Third Voyage of Capt. James
Cook. 119pp, 134 pls with 25 in color, 4to. British
Museum, 1981. $90.00

K114. KING (J. C. H.). Portrait Masks From the Northwest
Coast of America. 95pp plus index, drawings, b/w and
color photographs, wrappers. New York, 1979 (1st
American ed.). $15.00
____Another Copy. London, Thames and Hudson, 1979,
96pp, 52 b/w and 48 color photographs. $18.00
____Another Copy. Same. $13.00

K115. KING (J. C. H.). Smoking Pipes of the North American
Indian. 63pp, 44 photographs, map, bibliography, dis-
cusses 100 pipes from the British Museum, wrappers.
London, 1977 (1st ed.). $18.00
____Another Copy. Same. $17.00
____Another Copy. Same. $10.00

K116. KING (Jeff). Where the Two Came to their Father: A
Navaho War Ceremonial. 86pp of text, 18 pochoir pls
18"x24" in size in cloth portfolio, text and paintings
recorded by Maud Oakes, commentary by Joseph Campbell,
explanation of pls is in text, portfolio soiled and edge
worn, library bookplate inside frnt cvr, small red mark-
ers in lower left margin of each pl. New York, Pantheon,
1943 (Bollingen Series, I). $1,200.00
____Another Copy. Same. $1,150.00
____Another Copy. Same. repair to spine and cvr, li-
brary stamps on text, back of pls and linen cvr.
$975.00

K117. KING (J. L.). Ancient Mexico, An Overview. 133pp, 44
photographs and drawings, cloth. Albuquerque, 1985.
$18.00

K118. KING (Patrick). Pueblo Indian Religious Architecture.
30 photographs, wrappers. Utah, 1975. $10.00

K119. KING (Titus). Narrative of Titus King of Northhampton,
Massachusetts. A Prisoner of the Indians of Canada,

1755-1758. 21pp, printed wrappers. Connecticut Historical Society, Hartford, 1938. $12.00
    Matthews: American Diaries: pp63. First printing
of the manuscript.

K120. KINGSBOROUGH (Lord R. K.). Antiguedades de Mexico,
Basada en la Recopilacion de Lord Kingsborough. Vol.
III (Antiquities of Mexico, Comprising Facsimiles of Ancient Mexican Paintings and Hieroglyphics). 451pp, 143
full and half-page color codices, cloth cvr with leather
insert. Mexico City, 1964. $59.00
    Special facsimile reprint of Kingsborough's monumental
nine volumes, London 1831-1848. Volume III was originally
published in 1831. Volume II is of the Codice Vaticanos-
Rios. This codex is post-Columbian, and bears the number 3738 in the Vatican Library, under the title of
"Codice Latino." The color reproduction is fine in the
color plates and was taken directly from the original in
the Vatican Library. (EAP)

K121. KINGSTON (W. H. G.). Adventures Among the Indians.
242, (16)pp, ads, cloth. Chicago, 1888. $15.00

K122. KINIETZ (W. V.). (Cranbrook Institute of Science, Bulletin 25, 1947) Chippewa Village, the Story of Katikite-
gon. ix, 259pp, 53 photographs, cloth. $44.00
    ___Another Copy. Same. $25.00

K123. KINIETZ (W. V.). (Museum of Anthropology, University
of Michigan, Occasional Contribution No. 10, 1940) The
Indians of the Western Great Lakes, 1615-1766. xiv,
427pp. $57.00
    ___Another Copy. Ann Arbor, 1965, 410pp plus index,
map, bibliography, cloth. $12.00
    ___Another Copy. Same. $10.00

K124. KINNEY (J. P.). A Continent Lost--A Civilization Won.
Indian Land Tenure in America. 356pp plus index, illus,
bibliography, errata page. Baltimore, 1937 (1st ed.),
d.j. $20.00

K125. KINSEY (W. Fred, III). Lower Susquehanna Valley Prehistoric Indians. 125 double-column pp, photographs
(many in color), drawings, maps, limited to 900 copies.
Ephrata, PA, 1977 (1st ed.). $17.00

K126. KINZIE (Mrs. John H.). Wau-Bun: Early Days in the
Northwest. Introduction and Notes by L. Kellogg. xxi,
390pp, 9 pls, original cloth. Menasha, 1948. $10.00

K127. (KIOWA INDIANS). Kiowa Indian Art: Watercolor Painting
in Color by the Indians of Oklahoma. Introductory essay
by Jamake Highwater. Portfolio with 30 plates (6 in color
by offset lithography), loose as issued, 15"x11" in size,
facsimile of 1929 edition, published by C. Zwedzicki at
Nice, France, limited to 750 copies, this copy marked as
complimentary copy. Santa Fe, Bell Editions, 1979.
                                              $175.00

K128. (KIOWA INDIANS). (Senate Document 170, 56:1, Washington,

1900, 1st print.) Kiowa, Commanche and Apache Indians --Ratification of Agreement. 86pp, 30pp, 31pp, removed, Indians given farm lands unsuitable for agriculture.
$20.00

K129. KIP (Lawrence). Army Life on the Pacific; A Journal of the Expedition Against the Northern Indians, The Tribes of The Coeur D'Alenes, Spokans and Pelouzes, In the Summer of 1858. vi, 144pp, original cloth, 12mo. Redfield, NY, 1859 (1st ed.). $275.00

K130. KIP (Lawrence). The Indian Council at Walla Walla, May and June 1855: A Journal. 28pp, stapled self wrappers. Eugene, 1897. $25.00

K131. (KIP, William Ingraham). Few Days at Nashotah. 31pp, self-wrappers, library stamp, author describes his visit to the Nashotah mission in Minnesota. Howes: K-177. Albany, 1849. $75.00
_____Another Copy. Same. $45.00

K132. KIRCHHOFF (H.). Peru, Ayer y Hoy, Past and Present. 135pp, 146 photographs, color map, cloth. Buenos Aires, 1951 (numbered copy). $35.00
_____Another Copy. Same. $35.00

KIRCHHOFF (Paul). See BAE Bulletin No. 143.

K133. KIRK (Ruth). Exploring Washington Archaeology. 112pp, 4to, illus, index, maps. Seattle, 1978 (1st ed.), d.j.
$20.00
Highlights the 1977 discovery on the Olympic Peninsula of a mastodon that was hunted and butchered by man 12,000 years ago. Other Archaeological excavations that are discussed and illustrated are the Marnes Man and Lind Coulee sites in eastern Washington, the Hoko River project and the Ozette excavations.
_____Another Copy. Same. $15.00
_____Another Copy. Same. $13.00

K134. KIRK (R. F.). Introduction to Zuni Fetishism. 65pp, 11 photographs. American School of Research, Santa Fe, 1948. $30.00

K135. KIRK (Ruth F.). Southwestern Indian Jewelry. 24pp, illus, wrappers. Santa Fe, 1945 (1st ed.). $10.00

K136. KIRKBY (Anne). (Museum of Anthropology, Memoirs No. 5, Ann Arbor, 1973) The Use of Land and Water Resources in the Past and Present Valley of Oaxaca, Mexico. 174pp, illus, wrappers. $25.00

K137. KIRKLAND (Forrest). (Text by Newcomb, W. W., Jr.) Rock Art of Texas Indians. xiv, 239pp, 160 illus (32 in color), bibliography, index, 4to, reproduces Kirkland's watercolors of petroglyphs and pictographs. University of Texas Press, 1967 (1st ed.), d.j. $35.00

K138. KISSELL (M. L.). (American Museum of Natural History Anthropology Papers, Vol. XVII, Part IV, 1916) Basketry of the Papago and Pima. pp115-264, 81 photographs and drawings, rebound in later cloth. $80.00
_____Another Copy. Same. $35.00

KIVETT (Marvin F.). See BAE Bulletin No. 154.

K139.   KLAH (Hasteen). (Museum of Navajo Ceremonial Art,
        Navajo Religion Series, Vol. 1, Santa Fe, 1942, 1st ed.)
        Navajo Creation Myth: The Story of the Emergence.
        237pp, portrait, 15 color pls of sand paintings, recorded
        by Mary C. Wheelright, limited to 1000 copies, case bind-
        ing by Hazel Dreis, cloth. $250.00
             Saunders: 1353. Swadesh, 748. Mary Wheelright,
        founder of the Museum of Navajo Ceremonial Art, met
        Hasteen Klah, a well-known Navajo Medicine Man, through
        Mr. and Mrs. A. J. Newcomb at their trading post.
        Through Klah's help and by encouraging other members
        of the Navajo Nation, much of what we now know about
        their religion came through him. (TE)

K140.   (KLAMATH INDIANS). (Senate Executive Document 140,
        50:2, Washington, 1889, 1st print.) Report Relative to
        the Survey and Sale of the Klamath Indian Reservation.
        23pp, removed. $10.00

K141.   (KLAMATH INDIANS). (Senate Executive Document 62,
        53:3, Washington, 1895, 1st print.) Survey of the
        Klamath Indian Reservation in Oregon. 21pp, 6 folding
        maps, removed. $20.00

K142.   (KLAMATH INDIANS). (Senate Document 131, 54:1,
        Washington, 1896, 1st print.) Memorial on Behalf of
        The Klamath and Modoc Tribes ... in the State of Ore-
        gon. 29pp, removed, erroneous land surveys. $10.00

K143.   (KLAMATH INDIANS). (Senate Document 93, 54:2,
        Washington, 1897, 1st print.) Klamath Indian Boundary
        Commission. 19pp, removed, large folding colored map
        of the Klamath Reservation in Oregon. $15.00

K144.   KLEIN (Bernard) and ICOLARI (Daniel) (Editors). Refer-
        ence Encyclopedia of the American Indian. 536pp, cloth,
        lists all government agencies, associations, tribal councils,
        schools, arts and crafts, ships, government publications,
        alphabetical and subject bibliographies, etc. New York,
        1967, d.j. $25.00

K145.   KLEIN (C.) (Editor). Art of Pre-Columbian America.
        40pp, 20 photographs. Exhibition catalogue, Meadow
        Brook Art Gallery, Rochester, 1976. $10.00

K146.   KLEIN (O.). La Ceramica Mochica. 156pp, 59pp of photo-
        graphs, 31pp of drawings, map, inscribed by author.
        Universidad Tecnica Federico, Santa Maria, Valparaiso,
        1967. $25.00

K147.   KLEIVAN (I.) and SONNEL (B.). (Iconography of Reli-
        gions, Section VIII, Fasc. 2, Leiden, 1985) Eskimos,
        Greenland and Canada. ix, 43pp text, 48pp photographs.
                                                            $47.00
             The religion of the original inhabitants of the Canadian
        Arctic and Greenland is discussed in the text. Rites of
        passage, hunting rituals, the role of the Shaman and
        other rituals are discussed. Most of the illustrations of

the rituals and the ritual artifacts are from the National Museum, Copenhagen.

K148. KLEMEN (P.). Medieval American Art. (2 Volumes). Vol. I: (Text) 413pp. Vol. II: (Illustrations) 378pp, 306 pls containing approx 1300 photographs of pre-Columbian architecture, sculpture, pottery, weaving, metal-work, jade and other semiprecious stones, murals and miscellaneous applied arts, cloth. New York, 1943. $195.00

K149. KLIMEK (S.). (University of California Publications in American Archaeology and Ethnology, Vol. 37, No. 1, 1935) The Structure of California Indian Culture. 70pp, 6 diagrams, 6 maps. $30.00

KLUCKHOHN (Clyde). See also BAE Bulletin No. 196.

K150. KLUCKHOHN (Clyde) and SPENCER (K.). A Bibliography of the Navaho Indians. xiv, 92pp, cloth. New York, 1940. $99.00

___Another Copy. Same. $35.00
___Another Copy. Same. $30.00

K151. KLUCKHOHN (C.). (American Anthropological Assn, Memoirs No. 53, 1940) An Introduction to Navaho Chant Practice, with an Account of the Behavior Observed in Four Chants. 214pp, 10pp photographs, rebound in cloth. $50.00

___Another Copy. Same. original cloth. $47.00

K152. KLUCKHOHN (C.) and LEIGHTON (D.). The Navaho. xx, 258pp, 8pp photographs, 12 figures, cloth. Cambridge, 1946. $47.00

___Another Copy. Same. without inscription, rebound in library cloth cvrs. $37.00
___Another Copy. Cambridge, 1947 (2d print.), 252pp, index, illus, bibliography, map endpapers. $12.00
___Another Copy. 1948, slight stain on page edges. $31.00
___Another Copy. 1951. $35.00
___Another Copy. 1974. $27.00

K153. KLUCKHOHN (C.). (Peabody Museum Papers Vol. XXII, No. 2, 1944) Navaho Witchcraft. x, 149pp, inscribed by author. $57.00

___Another Copy. Same, wrappers. $45.00
___Another Copy. Boston, 1962, cloth. $30.00

K154. KLUCKHOHN (C.) and REITER (P.). (University of New Mexico Bulletin 345, 1939) Preliminary Report on the 1937 Excavations, BC 50-51, Chaco Canyon, New Mexico. 190pp, 16 figures, 9 maps, 9 tables, 14pp photographs. $37.00

___Another Copy. Same. $20.00

K155. KLUCKHOHN (C.). To the Foot of the Rainbow: A Tale of 25 Hundred Miles of Wandering on Horseback Through the Southwest's Enchanted Land. Illus, slight cvr wr, New York, Century Co., 1927. $25.00

K156. KNACK (Martha). (Anthropological Papers, No. 19,

Socorro, 1980) Life is With People: Household Organization of the Contemporary Southern Paiute Indians. 106pp, wrappers. $15.00

K157. KNEALE (Albert). Indian Agent. 429pp, frontis, 30pp of photographs, 8 text maps, author spent thirty years as an agent among the western tribes. Caldwell, Caxton Press, 1950 (1st ed.), d.j. $35.00

___Another Copy. Same. $27.00

___Another Copy. Same. no d.j. $22.00

K158. KNOBLOCK (Byron W.). Banner-Stones of the North American Indian. 596pp, index, bibliography, 270 full-page pls, limited to 50 deluxe copies, half leather with raised bands, gilt decorated spine, slipcased, signed by author. LaGrange, IL, author, 1939 (1st ed.). $400.00

An exhaustive study of the types, methods of manufacture, use and distribution of these pre-historic carved stone works. Also includes articles by Warren K. Moorehead, Fay-Cooper Cole, Henry C. Shetrone, George A. West and William S. Webb.

___Another Copy. Same. cloth. $350.00

___Another Copy. Same. d.j. $175.00

___Another Copy. Same. Popular edition. $95.00

K159. KNOROZOV (Y. V.). (Peabody Russian Translation Series, Vol. IV, 1967) Selected Chapters from the Writing of the Maya Indians. v, 152pp, 461 sml drawings of graphemes. $30.00

K160. KNUDTSON (Peter N.). The Wintun Indians of California and Their Neighbors. 95pp, photographs, drawings, folded map in pocket, bibliography, index. Happy Camp, 1977 (1st ed.). $15.00

___Another Copy. Same. $12.00

K161. KOCH (Ronald P.). Dress Clothing of the Plains Indians. 219pp, illus, bibliography, index, account covering feathers, color and painted designs, quillwork, trade beads, hair and headgear, skins and shirt, leggings, etc. Norman, 1977 (1st ed.), d.j. $34.00

___Another Copy. Same. $30.00

___Another Copy. Same. $25.00

K162. KOCH-GRUNBERG (T.). Zwei Jahre Bei De Indianer In Nordwest-Brasiliens. xii, 416pp, 12 full-page sepia photographs and 56 drawings of dancers, masks and artifacts uncovered during the 1903-1905 expedition, fold-out map. Stuttgart, 1923. $185.00

K163. KOSOK (Paul). Life, Land and Water in Ancient Peru. 264pp, numerous illus which include pre-Columbian artifacts, 4to. New York, 1965. $75.00

K164. KOWTA (Makoto). (University of California Publications in Anthropology, Vol. 6, 1969) The Sayles Complex: A Late Milling Stone Assemblage from Cajon Pass and the Ecological Implications of its Scraper Planes. 101pp, illus, wrappers. $20.00

K165. KRAMER (F. W.). (Etnologiska Studier, Etnografiska
Museet, Goteborg, No. 30, 1970) Literature Among the
Cuna Indians. 166pp. $15.00

K166. KRAUSE (A.) and GUNTHER (E.). The Tlingit Indians.
Results of Trip to the Northwest Coast of America and
the Bering Straits. viii, 310pp, 32 figures, 4pp draw-
ings, hard cvr. American Ethno. Society, Seattle, 1956.
$57.00
___Another Copy. Same. $45.00
___Another Copy. Same. $40.00
___Another Copy. Same. $25.00

K167. KIRCKBERG (W.) and KUTSCHER (G.). Altmexikanische
Kulturen, Mit Einem Anhang uber die Kunst Altmexikos.
644pp, 193 photographs, 309 drawings, 2 maps, cloth.
Berlin, 1966. $35.00
___Another Copy. Same. $30.00

K168. KRICKEBERG (Von Walter). Inka, Maya und Azteken:
Versunkener Kulturen Lebendige Volker. Kurt P. Kar-
feld (Photographer). xxv, 48 color pls, 4to, Munich,
n.d., d.j. $30.00

K169. KRICKEBERG (W.) et al. Pre-Columbian American Religions. 365pp, 13 illus, New York, 1969 (1st American
ed.), d.j. $45.00
___Another Copy. London, 1968, d.j. $45.00
___Another Copy. Same. $35.00

K170. KRIEGER (Alex D.). (University of Texas, Publications
No. 4640, Austin, 1946) Culture Complexes and Chronology in Northern Texas With Extension of Puebloan Datings
to the Mississippi Valley. 366pp, folding map, figures
(some folding), pls, bibliography, index, lrg 8vo, wrappers. $150.00

K171. KRIEGER (H. W.). (U.S. National Museum Bulletin 156,
Washington, 1931) Aboriginal Indian Pottery of the
Dominican Republic. 165pp of text, 56pp of photographs.
$35.00
___Another Copy. Same. $30.00

K172. KRIEGER (H. W.). The Aborigines of the Ancient Island
of Hispaniola. pp 473-506, 27 pls, removed from Smithsonian Annual Report for 1929. Arawaks, Washington,
1930. $25.00
___Another Copy. Same. $20.00

K173. KRIEGER (H.). American Indian Costumes in the U.S.
National Museum, Washington, D.C. pp623-661, 36 pls,
wrappers, offprint from Smithsonian Report for 1928.
$30.00

K174. KRIEGER (H. W.) et al. (Smithsonian Annual Report for
the Year ending June 30, 1927) Indian Villages of Southeast Alaska. also: The Interpretation of Aboriginal
Mounds by Means of Creek Indian Customs. also:
Friedrich Kurz, Artist-Explorer. xii, 580pp, of which
these three papers are pp467-494, 16 pp photographs of

totem poles, house posts, villages; pp495-506, 6 figures, 7pp photographs; pp507-527, 6 figures, 8pp illus of Hidatsa, Crow, Cree, Mandan and other Plains people, cloth. $47.00

___Another Copy. Same. Indian Villages of Southeast Alaska only. pp467-494, 16 pls, wrappers. $15.00

KROEBER (Alfred L.). See also BAE Bulletin Nos. 78 and 143.

K175. KROEBER (Alfred L.) and WISSLER (C.). (American Museum of Natural History, Bulletin Vol. XVIII, Parts I, II, III and IV, 1902, 1904 and 1907) The Arapaho. Vol. I: General Description, Decorative Art and Symbolism. Vol. II: Ceremonial Organization. Vol. III: Decorative Art of the Sioux Indians. Vol. IV: Religion. 466pp of text containing 180 figures, plus 99 pp of pls, later morocco and marbled hard bd cvrs, also bound at the end of this volume is "Primitive Art, a Guide Leaflet to Collections in the American Museum of Natural History," 1904, 39pp, approx 50 photographs and drawings.
$275.00

___Another Copy. Same. Vol. I only. pp1-150, 46 figures, 31pp of b/w and color pls, frnt wrapper chipped and repaired, rear wrapper missing, some pp uncut.
$59.00

___Another Copy. Same. Vol. IV only. pp279-454, 76 figures, 31pp photographs, drawings, repairs to spine.
$69.00

___Another Copy. Lincoln, 1983, facsimile reprint, Vols. I, II and IV only. $10.00

K176. KROEBER (A. L.). (University of California Publications in American Archaeology and Ethnology, Vol. 12, No. 3, 1916) Arapaho Dialects. 67pp, wrappers. $35.00

K177. KROEBER (A. L.). (Field Museum, Anthropology Memoirs, Vol. II, No. 1 and 2, Chicago, 1926) Archaeological Explorations in Peru, Parts I and II. Part I: Ancient Pottery from Truhillo. Part II: The Northern Coast. 43pp, illus, wrappers; 115pp, illus, wrappers. $55.00

___Another Copy. Same. $50.00

K178. KROEBER (A. L.). (Field Museum, Anthropology Memoirs Vol. II, No. 4, 1937) Archaeological Explorations in Peru: Canete Valley. pp221-273, plus 22pp of illus.
$70.00

___Another Copy. Same. $40.00

K179. KROEBER (A. L.). The Archaeology of California. 42pp, from the Putnam Anniversary Volume, Cedar Rapids, 1909. $24.00

K180. KROEBER (A. L.). (University of California Publications in American Archaeology and Ethnology, Vol. 17, No. 7, 1925) Archaic Culture Horizons in the Valley of Mexico. 35pp, illus, wrappers. $35.00

___Another Copy. Same. $20.00

K181. KROEBER (A. L.). (University of California Publications

in American Archaeology and Ethnology, Vol. 23, No. 4,
1927) Arrow Release Distributions. 13pp, map, wrappers.
$10.00

K182. KROEBER (A. L.). (University of California Publications
in American Archaeology and Ethnology, Vol. 2, No. 4,
1905) Basket Designs of the Indians of Northwestern
California. pp105-164, drawings, 6 photographic pls,
wrappers. $30.00

K183. KROEBER (A. L.). (American Museum of Natural History,
Anthropological Papers, Guide Leaflet No. 55, 1922)
Basketry Designs of the Mission Indians. 34pp, photo-
graphs of 18 baskets, 84 drawings of designs. $35.00
____Another Copy. Same. $50.00
____Another Copy. 1932 (3rd print.). $25.00

K184. KROEBER (A. L.). (University of California Publications
in American Archaeology and Ethnology, Vol. 17, No. 2,
1920) California Culture Provinces. 18pp, wrappers.
$15.00
____Another Copy. Same. $10.00

K185. KROEBER (A. L.). (University of California Publications
in American Archaeology and Ethnology, Vol. 12, No. 9,
1917) California Kinship Systems. 57pp, wrappers.
$40.00

K186. KROEBER (A. L.). (University of California Publications
in American Archaeology and Ethnology, Vol. 12, No. 2,
1916) California Place Names of Indian Origin. 38pp,
wrappers. $35.00

K187. KROEBER (A. L.). (University of California Publications
in American Archaeology and Ethnology, Vol. 9, No. 2,
1910) The Chumash and Costanoan Languages. 34pp,
wrappers. $20.00

K188. KROEBER (A. L.). Cultural and Natural Areas of Native
North America. 242pp, 28 maps (some folding), index,
presentation copy. University of California, 1939 (1st
ed.). $115.00
____Another Copy. Berkeley, 1947 (2d ed.), d.j.
$27.00
____Another Copy. Berkeley, 1964 (4th print.). $47.00

K189. KROEBER (A. L.) and GIFFORD (E. W.). (University of
California Publications in American Archaeology and
Ethnology, Vol. 37, No. 4, 1937) Culture Element Dis-
tributions IV: Pomo. 137pp, maps, wrappers. $30.00

K190. KROEBER (A. L.). (University of California Anthropological Papers, Vol. 5, No. 1, 1939) Culture Element Distribution XI: Tribes Surveyed. 5pp, folded map.
$10.00

K191. KROEBER (A. L.). (University of California, Anthropological Records, Vol. 6, No. 1, 1941) Culture Element
Distributions XV: Salt, Dogs, Tobacco. 20pp, stiff
wrappers. $10.00
____Another Copy. Same. $10.00

K192.   KROEBER (A. L.). Decorative Symbolism of the Arapaho.
        pp308-336, drawings, in later paper over bds, ex-library.
        Separate printing from the American Anthropology Vol.
        3, 1901, and Kroeber's doctorial thesis. New York,
        1961. $20.00
K193.   KROEBER (A. L.). (University of California Publications
        in American Archaeology and Ethnology, Vol. 13, No. 8,
        1922) Elements of Culture in Native California. 70pp,
        4 maps. $27.00
K194.   KROEBER (A. L.). (American Museum of Natural History
        Bulletin, Vol. XII, 1899) The Eskimo of Smith Sound.
        pp265-327, 54 figures, 4pp pls, spine reinforced. $95.00
K195.   KROEBER (A. L.). (University of California Publications
        in American Archaeology and Ethnology, Vol. 47, No. 2,
        1957) Ethnographic Interpretations, 1-6. 48pp. $17.00
K196.   KROEBER (A. L.). (University of California Publications
        in American Archaeology and Ethnology, Vol. 47, No. 3,
        1959) Ethnographic Interpretations, 7-11. 75pp. $20.00
K197.   KROEBER (A. L.). (University of California Publications
        in American Archaeology and Ethnology, Vol. 8, No. 2,
        1908) Ethnography of the Cahuilla Indians. 70pp, 30pp
        photographs of baskets, pestles, pottery and other ob-
        jects of material culture. $59.00
        ___Another Copy. Same. wrappers $25.00
        ___Another Copy. Same. wrappers. $20.00
K198.   KROEBER (A. L.). Handbook of the Indians of California.
        all maps nicely reprinted. California Book Co., Berkeley,
        1953 (reprint). $100.00
        ___Another Copy. Same. xviii, 995pp, 83pp illus,
        including 10 maps (2 lrg maps in rear pocket, bibliogra-
        phy, index, reprint of 1925 ed. $60.00
K199.   KROEBER (A. L.). (University of California Publications
        in American Archaeology and Ethnology, Vol. 4, No. 4,
        1907) Indian Myths of South Central California. 82pp,
        wrappers. $45.00
        ___Another Copy. Same. 94pp. $35.00
K200.   KROEBER (A. L.) and GIFFORD (E. W.). Karok Myths.
        Edited by Grace Buzaljko, foreword by Theodora Kroeber,
        folkloristic commentary by Alan Dundes, linguistic index
        by Wm. Bright. 380pp, illus, index, map. Berkeley,
        1980 (1st ed.), d.j. $25.00
K201.   KROEBER (A. L.) and WATERMAN (T. T.). (University
        of California Publications in American Archaeology and
        Ethnology, Vol. 35, No. 6, 1938) The Kepel Fish Dam.
        31pp, wrappers. $15.00
K202.   Kroeber Anthropology Papers, No. 1. iii, 86pp. (6 pa-
        pers), 1 photograph, 2 maps. Berkeley, 1950. $18.00
K203.   KROEBER (A. L.). (University of California Publications
        in American Archaeology and Ethnology, Vol. 9, No. 3,
        1911) The Languages of the Coast of California, North of
        San Francisco. 162pp, wrappers. $45.00
        ___Another Copy. Same. $10.00

K204. KROEBER (A. L.). (University of California Publications in American Archaeology and Ethnology, Vol. 2, No. 2, 1904) The Languages of the Coast of California, South of San Francisco. 52pp, wrappers. $40.00

K205. KROEBER (A. L.). (University of California Publications in American Archaeology and Ethnology, Vol. 8, No. 1, 1908) A Mission Record of the California Indians from a Manuscript in the Bancroft Library. 27pp, wrappers. $30.00

K206. KROEBER (A. L.). (University of California Anthropological Records, Vol. 11, No. 2, 1951) A Mohave Historical Epic. 105pp, folded maps, stiff wrappers. $25.00
    ___Another Copy. n.d. $20.00
    ___Another Copy. 1948. $20.00

K207. KROEBER (A. L.). (University of California Anthropology Papers, Vol. 27, 1972) More Mohave Myths. 160pp, 9 pls, wrappers. $35.00
    ___Another Copy. Same. $20.00

K208. KROEBER (A. L.) and HARNER (M. J.). (University of California Anthropological Records Vol. 16, No. 1, 1955) Mohave Pottery. 36pp, 8pp photographs, 2 figures. $30.00
    ___Another Copy. Same. 20pp, plus 8 pls, wrappers. $25.00
    ___Another Copy. Same. $18.00

K209. KROEBER (A. L.) and KROEBER (C. B.). (University of California Publications in Anthropology, Vol. 10, 1973) A Mohave War Reminiscence 1854-1880. 97pp, illus, map in pocket. $25.00
    ___Another Copy. Same. $20.00

K210. KROEBER (A. L.). (University of California Publications in American Archaeology and Ethnology, Vol. 23, No. 9, 1928) Native Culture of the Southwest. 24pp. $23.00

K211. KROEBER (A. L.). (University of California Publications in American Archaeology and Ethnology, Vol. 8, No. 5, 1909) Notes on the Shoshonean Dialects of Southern California. 34pp, wrappers. $25.00
    ___Another Copy. Same. $15.00

K212. KROEBER (A. L.) et al. (Contributions of University of California Archaeological Research Facility, No. 9, 1970) Papers on California Ethnography. 158pp, 4to, wrappers. $15.00

K213. KROEBER (A. L.). (University of California Publications in American Archaeology and Ethnology, Vol. 40, No. 8, 1953) Paracas Cavernas and Chavin. 36pp, 7pp photographs of ceramic vessels. $35.00
    ___Another Copy. Same. $30.00

K214. KROEBER (A. L.). (University of California Publications in American Archaeology and Ethnology, Vol. 29, No. 4, 1932) The Patwin and Their Neighbors. 170pp, maps, wrappers, stain to top edges. $45.00

K215.   KROEBER (A. L.). (Viking Fund Publications in Anthro-
        pology, No. 4, 1944) Peruvian Archaeology in 1942.
        151pp, 48 illus of hundreds of objects. $35.00
K216.   KROEBER (A. L.). (University of California Publications
        in American Archaeology and Ethnology, Vol. 10, No. 1,
        1911) Phonetic Constituents of the Native Languages of
        California. 12pp, wrappers. $12.00
        ___Another Copy. Same. $10.00
K217.   KROEBER (A. L.). (University of California Publications
        in American Archaeology and Ethnology, Vol. 10, No. 3,
        1911) Phonetic Elements of the Mohave Language. 51pp,
        illus, wrappers. $45.00
K218.   KROEBER (A. L.). (Fieldiana Anthropology, Vol. 44,
        No. 1, Chicago, 1954) Proto-Lima, A Middle Culture of
        Peru. 157pp, 95 illus, 8 tables. $25.00
        ___Another Copy. Same. $20.00
K219.   KROEBER (A. L.). (University of California Publications
        in American Archaeology and Ethnology, Vol. 4, No. 6,
        1902) The Religions of the Indians of California. 37pp,
        wrappers. $42.00
K220.   KROEBER (A. L.). (Southwest Museum Papers, No. 6,
        Los Angeles, 1964) The Seri. 60pp, wrappers. $15.00
        ___Another Copy. Same. $10.00
K221.   KROEBER (A. L.). (University of California Publications
        in American Archaeology and Ethnology, Vol. 11, No. 4,
        1915) Serian, Tequistlatecan, and Hokan. 11pp, wrap-
        pers. $15.00
K222.   KROEBER (A. L.). (University of California Anthropology
        Records, Vol. 11, No. 1, 1948) Seven Mohave Myths.
        68pp, wrappers. $20.00
        ___Another Copy. Same. $18.00
        ___Another Copy. Same. $15.00
K223.   KROEBER (A. L.). (University of California Publications
        in American Archaeology and Ethnology, Vol. 4, No. 3,
        1907) Shoshonean Dialects of California. 100pp, wrap-
        pers. $20.00
K224.   KROEBER (A. L.) and WATERMAN (T. T.). Source Book
        in Anthropology. 571pp, illus, includes Boas, Lowie,
        Goddard, Wissler, etc. New York, 1931 (1st thus.).
                                                             $25.00
K225.   KROEBER (A. L.). (University of California Publications
        in American Archaeology and Ethnology, Vol. 43, No. 4,
        1956) Toward A Definition of the Nazca Style. 106pp,
        15pp photographs of ceramic vessels, 12 figures. $65.00
        ___Another Copy. Same. $45.00
K226.   KROEBER (A. L.). (University of California Archaeologi-
        cal Survey Reports, No. 56, 1962) Two Papers on the
        Aboriginal Ethnography of California. 58pp, wrappers.
                                                             $20.00
K227.   KROEBER (A. L.) and STRONG (W. D.). (University of
        California Publications in American Archaeology and

Ethnology, Vol. 21, Nos. 1 and 2, 1924) The Uhle Collections from Quincha. Also: Explorations at Chincha, by M. Uhle. 94pp of text containing 28 figures, 22pp of photographs, 2 maps. $75.00

K228. KROEBER (A. L.). (University of California Publications in American Archaeology and Ethnology, Vol. 21, No. 5, 1925) The Uhle Collections from Moche and The Uhle Collections from Supe. 72pp containing 5 figures, and 20pp photographs. $55.00

K229. KROEBER (A. L.). (University of California Publications in American Archaeology and Ethnology, Vol. 21, No. 7, 1926) The Uhle Pottery Collections from Chancay. 39pp, illus, wrappers. $50.00

K230. KROEBER (A. L.). (University of California Publications in American Archaeology and Ethnology, Vol. 21, No. 3, 1924) The Uhle Pottery Collection from Ica. 39pp of text containing 17 figures, 15pp of photographs. $55.00
_____Another Copy. Same. $50.00

K231. KROEBER (A. L.) and GAYTON (A. H.). (University of California Publications in American Archaeology and Ethnology, Vol. 24, No. 1, 1927) The Uhle Pottery Collections from Nazca. 46pp, illus, wrappers. $50.00

K232. KROEBER (A. L.). (Ibero-Americana: 8, Berkeley, 1934) Uto-Aztecan Languages of Mexico. 26pp, map, wrappers. $15.00

K233. KROEBER (A. L.). (University of California Publications in American Archaeology and Ethnology, Vol. 24, No. 4, 1929) The Valley Nisenan. 37pp, wrappers. $22.00

K234. KROEBER (A. L.) (Editor). (American Anthropology Assn, Memoirs No. 42, 1935) Walapai Ethnography. 293pp, illus, wrappers. $50.00
_____Another Copy. Same. $45.00
_____Another Copy. Same. $32.00
_____Another Copy. Same. $25.00

K235. KROEBER (A. L.). (University of California Publications in American Archaeology and Ethnology, Vol. 4, No. 5, 1907) The Washo Language of East Central California and Nevada. 63pp, wrappers. $37.00
_____Another Copy. Same. $27.00

K236. KROEBER (A. L.) and GIFFORD (E. W.). (University of California Anthropological Records, Vol. 13, No. 1, 1949) World Renewal, a Cult System of Native Northwest California. 155pp, illus, stiff wrappers. $67.00

K237. KROEBER (A. L.). (University of California Publications in American Archaeology and Ethnology, Vol. 2, No. 5, 1907) The Yokuts Language of Southern Central California. 210pp, wrappers. $40.00

K238. KROEBER (A. L.). (University of California Publications in American Archaeology and Ethnology, Vol. 16, No. 8, 1920) Yuman Tribes of the Lower Colorado. 11pp. $18.00
_____Another Copy. Same. wrappers. $15.00

K239. KROEBER (A. L.). Yurok Myths. 484pp plus index,
bibliography, review copy, originally collected as early
as 1901-07, Kroeber's crowning achievement in the field
of Indian mythology. Berkeley, 1976 (1st ed.), d.j.
$25.00

____Another Copy. Same. $25.00

____Another Copy. Same. $30.00

K240. KROEBER (A. L.). (University of California American
Museum of Natural History Papers Vol. XVIII, Part II,
1917) Zuni Kin and Clan. 165pp, folded charts, wrap-
pes. $45.00

K241. KROEBER (Theodora). Alfred Kroeber, A Personal Con-
figuration. xi, 292pp, 27 photographs, cloth. Berkeley,
1970. $28.00

K242. KROEBER (T.) and HEIZER (R. F.). Almost Ancestors;
The First Californians. 167pp, 117 photographs, 4to.
San Francisco, 1968 (1st ed.), d.j. $30.00

____Another Copy. Same. $10.00

K243. KROEBER (T.). Ishi in Two Worlds: A Biography of
the Last Wild Indian in North America. 255pp, illus with
photographs, bibliography. Berkeley, 1961. $15.00

____Another Copy. Same. $10.00

KROLL (W. J.). See BAE Bulletin No. 166.

K244. KRUTT (M.). Les Figurines en Terre du Mexique Occidental. 162pp, 166 photographs. University of Brux-
elles, 1975. $18.00

KUBLER (George). See also BAE Bulletin No. 143.

K245. KUBLER (George). The Art and Architecture of Ancient
America: The Mexican, Maya and Andean Peoples.
420pp, 192 illus. Maryland, 1975 (2d ed.), d.j. $60.00

____Another Copy. Baltimore, 1962, 609pp, 168pp of
photographs, 119 figures, 4 maps, 3 charts, cloth.
$60.00

K246. KUBLER (G.). (Smithsonian Institute, Institute of Social
Anthropology, Publication 14, 1952) The Indian Caste
of Peru, 1795-1940. vi, 68pp of text containing 1 figure,
20 maps, 9 tables, 2pp photographs. $15.00

____Another Copy. Same. $15.00

____Another Copy. Same. $10.00

K247. KUBLER (G.). (Connecticut Academy of Arts and Sciences Memoirs, Vol. 18, New Haven, 1969) Studies in
Classic Maya Iconography. 111pp, 99 figures, 4to.
$35.00

K248. KUPPERMAN (K. O.). Settling with the Indians: The
Meeting of English and Indian Cultures in America.
224pp. Toronto, 1980. $20.00

KURATH (Gertrude Prokosch). See also BAE Bulletin Nos. 156,
180 and 187.

K249. KURATH (G. P.). (National Museum of Canada Bulletin
220, Ottawa, 1968) Dance and Song Rituals of Six Nations Reserve, Ontario. xiv, 205pp, 26pp photographs.
93 figures. $13.00

K250. KURATH (G. P.) and MARTI (S.). (Viking Fund Publica-
tions in Anthropology, No. 38, New York, 1964, 1st ed.).
Dances of Anahuac: The Choreography and Music of
Precortsian Dances. xix, 251pp, maps, illus, pls, bib-
liography, index, stiff wrappers. $25.00
K251. KURJACK (E. B.). (Middle American Research Institute
Publication No. 38, New Orleans, 1974) Prehistoric Low-
land Maya Community and Social Organization (Dzibilchal-
tun). 105pp, 28 figures, wrappers. $35.00
KURZ (Rudolph Friederich). See also BAE Bulletin No. 115.
KUTSCHE (Paul). See also BAE Bulletin No. 180.
K252. KUTSCHER (G.). Ancient Art of the Peruvian Coast.
32pp of text in English and Spanish, plus 80pp of
photographs with captions in English and German.
Berlin, 1955. $45.00
K253. KUTSCHER (Von Gerdt). Chimu: Eine Altindische
Hochkultur. (Peru) 11pp, 80 pls, 4to. Berlin, 1950.
$75.00
K254. KVASNICKA (Robert) and VIOLA (Herman, Jr.) (Editors).
The Commissioners of Indian Affairs, 1824-1977. 381pp
plus index, foreword by Philleo Nash. Lincoln, 1979
(1st ed.), d.j. $20.00

-L-

LA BARRE (Weston). See BAE Bulletin No. 143.
L1. LA BARRE (Weston). (American Anthropologist, Vol. 50,
No. 1, Part 2, Memoir No. 68, 1948) The Aymara In-
dians of the Lake Titicaca Plateau, Bolivia. 249pp, plus
13pp of photographs, wrappers. $20.00
L2. LA BARRE (Weston). The Ghost Dance: Origins of Re-
ligion. 677pp, New York, 1970. $40.00
L3. LA BARRE (Weston). (Yale Univ. Publications in Anthro-
pology, No. 19, 1938) The Peyote Cult. 192pp, 2pp of
photographs, 7 figures, wrappers. $35.00
_____Another Copy. Hamden, 1964, new enlarged edition.
$15.00
L4. LABBE (A. J.). Colombia Before Columbus. The People,
Culture and Ceramic Art of Pre-Hispanic Colombia.
207pp, 4to, 171 illus, 61 color pls, stiff wrappers, New
York, 1986. $20.00
LADD (John). See BAE Bulletin No. 193.
L5. LAFARGE (Oliver). All the Young Men. 272pp, cloth,
volume of short stories about the Navajos, Boston, 1935
(1st ed.). $35.00
L6. LAFARGE (Oliver). As Long as the Grass Shall Grow.
140pp, illus with photographs, a look at the Indian in
American Society in 1940, New York, 1940 (1st ed.), d.j.
$15.00

L7.   LAFARGE (Oliver). The Door in the Wall. viii, 303pp,
      cloth, collection of stories that probe the mystery of an
      anthropologist's life, Boston, 1965 (1st ed.), d.j. $15.00
L8.   LAFARGE (Oliver). The Enemy Gods. 325pp, a work of
      fiction based on Navajo ritual and about the Navajo, cloth,
      Boston, 1937 (1st ed.). $39.00
      ___Another Copy. Same, signed by author, d.j. $25.00
L9.   LAFARGE (Oliver). Laughing Boy. 302pp, signed by au-
      thor, cloth, Boston, 1929. $30.00
         Dobie, p.181: "Laughing Boy grew out of the author's
      ethnological knowledge of the Navajo Indians."
L10. LAFARGE (Oliver). A Pictorial History of the American In-
      dian. 272pp, illus, contains 350 illus with some in color,
      cloth, New York, 1956 (1st ed.), d.j. $30.00
      ___Another Copy. Same. $30.00
      ___Another Copy. Same, New York, 1957. $10.00
      ___Another Copy. Same, New York, 1974. $15.00
L11. LAFARGE (Oliver). Santa Eulalia. The Religion of a
      Cuchumatan Indian Town. 211pp, illus with photographs,
      endpaper maps, bibliography, index, cloth, Univ. of Chi-
      cago Press, 1947, d.j. $22.00
      ___Another Copy. Same. $50.00
      ___Another Copy. Same. $35.00
L12. LAFARGE (Oliver) and BYERS (Douglas). (Middle Ameri-
      can Research Institute, Publication No. 3, Tulane Univ.,
      1931) The Year Bearer's People (Ethnology of Jacaltenan-
      go, Guatemala). 379pp, color frontis, illus, lrge 4to,
      wrappers. $65.00
L13. LAFITAU (Per. Joseph Francois). Moeurs des Sauvages
      Ameriquains, Compare'es au Moeurs des Premiers Temps.
      (2 Volumes). Vol. I: (22), 610pp. Vol. II: (12),
      490pp(41), 42 pls, 2 maps, index, errata, contemporary
      full tooled leather, 4to, Paris, 1724 (1st ed.). $900.00
         Howes: L-22. Sabin: 38596. Field: 850. Howes:
      "Comprehensive and meticulous information on the Iroquois
      and other Northern tribes acquired by a long residence
      among them." Field: "The work is a grand cyclopedia
      of Indian history and customs at that date. The numerous
      engravings, although most of them remind us of De Bry,
      are finely executed illustrations of aboriginal life and
      peculiarities."
LA FLESCHE (Francis). See also BAE Bulletins Nos. 101 and 109.
L14. LA FLESCHE (Francis). A Dictionary of the Osage Lan-
      guage. Edited by W. David Baird. 406pp, cloth,
      Phoenix, 1975, d.j. $35.00
L15. LA FLESCHE (Francis). Omaha Bow and Arrow Makers.
      From, Smithsonian Annual Report for 1926, Washington,
      1927. pp 487-494, 4 pls, wrappers. $10.00
L16. LAHOTAN (Baron). New Voyages to North America. Con-
      taining an Account of the Several Nations of that Vast
      Continent ... to Which is Added, a Dictionary of the

Algonkine Language, Which is Generally Spoke in North-
America. (2 Volumes). Vol. I: (xxiv), 280pp, errata,
frontis, map and 8 (of 9) other maps and pls, (Map of
New France in facsimile). Vol. II: (ii), 302pp, adv. leaf,
(xiii) index, 10 pls. Conforms to the collation in Howes:
L-25. Field: 852. Original calf, one volume rebacked,
London, H. Bonwicke, et al., 1703 (1st ed. in English).
$350.00
A narrative of considerable value for its account of
the author's travels in the Great Lakes regions. Especially
interesting plates, including several on beaver hunting,
Indian villages, costumes, implements, etc. (RMW)

L17. LAIDLAW (S. J.). (Idaho State Univ. Museum Occasional
Papers, No. 3, 1960) Federal Indian Land Policy and
the Fort Hall Indians. iii, 61pp, bibliography, wrappers.
$10.00

L18. LAIRD (Irma). The Modoc Country. 147pp, frontis, 13pp
illus, bibliography, index, folding map tipped in at rear,
designed and printed by Lawton Kennedy, Alturas, for
author, 1971 (1st ed.). $25.00

L19. LAIRD (W. David). Hopi Bibliography; Comprehensive and
Annotated. 733pp, index, wraps, Tucson, 1977 (1st
ed.). $20.00
Lists 2,935 printed items on the Hopi with both subject
and title index. Informative annotations on each title.

L20. LAMB (F. W.). Indian Baskets of North America. 155pp,
215 b/w and 10 color photographs, 33 drawings, 8 maps,
cloth, Riverside, 1972 (1st ed.), d.j. $30.00
The basket weaving areas of North America--Northwest
Coast, Northern and Southern California, Great Basin,
Southwest, Southeast, Northeast and Eskimo, are examined
in this volume. Many photographs of baskets in a number
of western museums and private collections.
____Another Copy. Same. $25.00

L21. LAMB (Kaye W.) Editor. Sixteen Years in the Indian Country. The Journal of Daniel William Harmon, 1800-1816.
277pp, illus, map, Toronto, 1957. $35.00

L22. LAMBERT (M. F.) and AMBLER (J. R.). (School of American Research, Monograph No. 25, Santa Fe, 1961) Survey
and Excavations of Caves in Hidalgo County, New Mexico.
107pp, 57 illus, wrappers. $12.00
____Another Copy. Same. $10.00

L23. LANCASTER (J.) et al. Archaeological Excavations in Mesa
Verde National Park, Colorado, 1950. viii, 118pp, 72 pls,
9 tables, National Park Service, 1954. $30.00
____Another Copy. Same. $23.00

L24. LANCASTER (Richard). Piegan. A Look from Within at
the Life, Times and Legacy of an American Indian Tribe.
359pp, illus by Nancy McLaughlin, cloth, Garden City,
New York, 1966 (1st ed.), d.j. $20.00
____Another Copy. Same. $15.00

L25. LANDA (Diego de). (Peabody Museum Papers, Vol. 18,
      Cambridge, 1941) Landa's Relacion de las Cosas de
      Yucatan. Edited with notes by A. M. Tozzer. 394pp,
      illus, cloth, inscribed by Tozzer. $150.00

L26. LANDA ABREGO (Maria Elena). (Instituto Nacional Antro-
      pologia e Historia, Mexico, 1962) Contribucion al Estudio
      de la Formacion Cultural del Valle Poblano-Tlaxcalteca.
      213pp, 25 illus, folding map, wrappers. $25.00

L27. LANDERS (Leif C. W.). (Southwest Museum Papers No.
      19, Los Angeles, 1965) The Chumash Indians of Southern
      California. 158pp, 4to, illus, bibliography, wrappers.
                                                            $15.00
      ___Another Copy. Same. $18.00

L28. LANDERHOLM (Carl) Editor. Notices and Voyages of the
      Famed Quebec Mission to the Pacific Northwest; Being the
      Correspondence, Notices, etc., of Fathers Blanchet and
      Demers.... While on Their Arduous Mission to the En-
      gages of the Hudson's Bay Company and the Pagan Natives
      1838 to 1847.... 243pp, illus, folding map, pictorial cloth,
      limited to 1,000 copies, index, Portland, 1956 (1st ed.).
                                                            $40.00
      ___Another Copy. Same. $35.00

L29. LANDES (Ruth). The Mystic Lake Sioux, Sociology of the
      Mdewakantonwan Santee. x, 224pp, bibliography, index,
      Madison, Univ. of Wisconsin, 1968 (1st ed.), d.j. $25.00
      The "Mystic Lake Sioux" were the easternmost band of
      Sioux, living on the Mississippi in the area from present
      day Winona to the Falls of St. Anthony and up the Minne-
      sota River as far as Shakopee.
      ___Another Copy. Same. $20.00
      ___Another Copy. Same. $20.00

L30. LANDES (Ruth). Ojibwa Religion and the Midewiwin.
      250pp, illus, index, bibliography, Madison, 1968 (1st
      ed.) d.j. $20.00

L31. LANDGRAF (J. L.). (Peabody Museum Papers, Vol. LXII,
      No. 1, 1954) Land Use in the Ramah Area of New Mexico,
      An Anthropological Approach to Areal Study. vii, 97pp,
      17 figures, fold-out map, wrappers. $25.00
      ___Another Copy. Same. $25.00
      ___Another Copy. Same. $23.00
      ___Another Copy. Same.   ~ $22.00

L32. LANDIS (D. H.). A Brief Description of Indian Life and
      Indian Trade of the Susquehannock Indians. 48pp,
      double-column print, frontis, 21 full-page pls of artifacts
      and drawings by John Wyth, limited edition of 150 copies
      of which 100 were offered for sale, signed by author,
      wrappers, Lancaster, 1929. $45.00
      ___Another Copy. Same, unsigned. $35.00

L33. LANDSMAN (Anne C.). Needlework Designs from the
      American Indians. Traditional Patterns of the South-
      eastern Tribes. 36pp, plus 1pp of text, illus of 122

designs, index, 8pp of color photographs, New York, 1977 (1st ed.), d.j. $15.00

L34. (LAND TITLES). Message from the President ... to Confirm the Title to Certain Land in the Indian Territory to the Cheyenne and Arapahoes.... 82pp, two folding maps, disbound, Washington, DC, 1883. $85.00

Reviews treaties with the tribes and describes lands. The maps show proposed reservation lands along the Canadian River in western Oklahoma. (WR)

LANDY (David). See BAE Bulletin No. 180.

L35. LANG (John D.) and TAYLOR (Samuel). Report of a Visit to Some of the Tribes of Indians, Located West of the Mississippi River. 34pp, original wraps, New York, Mahlon Day & Co., 1843 (1st printing). $150.00

Howes: L-72. Field: 855. Visit by two Quakers to the Winnebagoes, Shawnees, Kickapoos, Delawares, Choctaws, Cherokees, Kansas, Osage, and other groups.

L36. LANGE (Algot). The Amazon Jungle, Adventures in Remote Parts of the Upper Amazon River, Including a Sojourn Among Cannibal Indians. xx, 405pp, 86 photographs, 1 color pl, linen and morocco gilt cvr, ridged spine, linen endpapers, New York, 1912. $65.00

___Another Copy. Same, decorated cloth. $50.00

___Another Copy. Same, decorated cloth. $45.00

L37. LANGE (Algot). The Lower Amazon. 468pp, frontis, 109 illus, with over 75 photographs, 6 maps, decorated cloth, t.e.g., New York, 1914 (1st ed.). $30.00

L38. LANGE (C. H.). Cochiti, A New Mexico Pueblo, Past and Present. xxiv, 618pp of text containing 35 figures, primarily multiple drawings of objects of material culture, including 11pp of drawings of "Ka'tsina masks" and 2 maps (one is fold-out in rear pocket), plus 28pp of photographs, mostly of dances and ceremonies, cloth, Austin, 1959. $60.00

L39. LANGE (C. H.) and RILEY (C. L.) Editors. The Southwestern Journals of Adolph F. Bandelier, 1880-1882. 462pp, illus, Albuquerque, 1966 (1st ed.). $75.00

___Another Copy. Same. $40.00

L40. LANGE (C. H.) and RILEY (C. L.) Editors. The Southwestern Journals of Adolph F. Bandelier, 1883-1884. 471pp, plus 2 maps and index, photographs, drawings, bibliography, endpaper maps, Albuquerque, 1970 (1st ed.), d.j. $45.00

L41. LANGE (C. H.) and RILEY (C. L.) Editors. The Southwestern Journals of Adolph F. Bandelier, 1885-1888. 558pp, 44pp bibliography, Albuquerque, 1975 (1st ed.). $75.00

L42. LANGE (F.) et al. Yellow Jacket, A Four Corners Anasazi Ceremonial Center. 52pp, 30 photographs of artifacts, 11 maps and plans, Boulder, 1986. $10.00

L43. (LANGUAGES). Dictionary of the Chinook Jargon, or Indian Trade Language of the North Pacific Coast. (3),

33pp, decorated wrappers, Victoria, British Columbia, 1877. $225.00

L44. (LANGUAGES). Dineh Bizad Navajo, His Language: A Handbook for Beginners in the Study of the Navajo Language. 128pp, cloth, New York, n.d., c.1945. $25.00

A handbook originally published in 1932 by Missions of the Presbyterian Church. Contains classified word lists and a English-Navajo list.

L45. (LANGUAGES). An Ethnologic Dictionary of the Navaho Language. 536pp, illus, printed wrappers, The Franciscan Fathers, St. Michaels, 1910 (1st ed.). $125.00

Relatively early work combining language and archaeology which used native informants both for language and illustrations.

L46. (LANGUAGES). (Univ. of California Publications in Linguistics, Vol. 10, Berkeley, 1951) Papers from the Symposium on American Indian Linguistics. 68pp, wraps. $20.00

L47. (LANGUAGES). A Vocabulary of the Navaho Language. (2 Volumes). pp 228; 212, edition limited to 325 copies, both volumes bound together in cloth over the original wraps, The Franciscan Fathers, St. Michaels, 1912.
$175.00

L48. (LANGUAGE IMPRINT). Ajokertutsit Pijarialiksuit. Apertsutit Kigutsillo. Attortaujut Illagene Evangeliumiune. (Eskimo). 13pp, original wrappers. Evangelical Free Church Catechism. Naineme Nenertaumajut. 1907.
$75.00

L49. (LANGUAGE IMPRINT). (Belcourt, Georges Antoine) Anamihe-Masinahigan. Jesus ot Ijittwawin. (6), 209pp, 16mo, cloth, Kebekong (i.e., Quebec) otenang, Cote et Cie, 1859. $150.00

Peel: 205. S. & T.: 5838. Text in Saulteaux Dialect. Second edition, originally published in 1839. Consists of Primer Lessons, Numerals, Prayers, Catechism, Prayers for Mass, and Hymns. Pilling: Algonquian Languages, p.39.

L50. (LANGUAGE IMPRINT). Catholic Prayers and Hymns in the Tinneh Language (bound with:) Tinneh Indian Catechism of Christian Doctrine. (2), 39, (1), (2), 22pp, bound with floral cloth over stiff wrappers, Holy Cross Mission, Kosoreffski, Alaska, Indian Boys' Press, 1897. $325.00

Two important and early Alaskan Indian Language imprints; according to Streeter, "...these two books are the only ones listed in the Imprints catalogue at the New York Public Library as printed at Holy Cross, on the west side of the Yukon ... and are the earliest listed under any of the towns of the Seward Peninsula." It is not ascertainable which of the two imprints was printed first. (WR)
____Another Copy. Same. $50.00

L51. (LANGUAGE IMPRINT). Chahta Holisso. Ai Isht Ia Ummona. (Choctaw). 72pp, disbound, Boston, printed for the

American Board of Commissioners for Foreign Missions,
1835. $325.00
    Gilcrease: p.110. Pilling: p.96. Spelling and gram-
mar with woodcuts. According to Gilcrease, this was au-
thored by Alfred Wright and Cyrus Byington. Identified
on the title page as the third edition, revised although he
does not locate earlier printings. (WR)
L52. (LANGUAGE IMPRINT). Chahta Na-Holhtina: or, Choctaw
Arithmetic. 72pp, disbound, Boston, printed for the
American Board of Commissioners for Foreign Missions,
1835. $325.00
    Gilcrease: p.109. Pilling: p.98. Gilcrease attributes
authorship to Alfred Wright. The entire text is in Choctaw. (WR)
L53. (LANGUAGE IMPRINT). (Lacombe, Albert) Four Lines in
Syllabic Characters, (Livre de Prieres, Etc., en Saulteaux). 382pp, woodcut seal of Oblates, 14 full-page
religious woodcuts, some signed Jules Marion, 16mo, cloth,
Montreal Beauchemin & Valois, 1880. $125.00
L54. (LANGUAGE IMPRINT). Iapi Oaye. Volume II, No. 3.
4pp, folio, Dakota Mission, Greenwood, Dakota Territories,
1873. $65.00
    Complete 4 page March, 1873 issue of "The Word Car-
rier," a newspaper issued by Rev. J. P. Williamson at the
Dakota Mission, Greenwood, Dakota Territory. The paper
is over half in the Dakota language with the last page in
English.
L55. (LANGUAGE IMPRINT). (La Brosse, Jean Baptiste de)
Nehiro-Iriniui Aiamihe Massinahigan, Shatshegutsh, Mitine-
kapitsh, Iskuamiskutsh, Netshekatsh, Misht', Assinitsh,
Shekutimitsh, Ekuanatsh, Ashuabmushuanitsh, Piakua-
gamitsh ... Uabistiguiatsh ... Broun gaie Girmor, 1767.
96pp, A-B, E, G-K, M-P, R signatures in fours, full
calf, bds slightly warped. $7,500.00
    Tremaine, Canadian Imprints: 105. TPL Catalogue:
411. Pilling: Algonquian 281. Lande: 1895. A most
interesting early work of prayers and catechisms in Mon-
tagnai Indian tongue. This manual is one of the first
works of any length printed in Quebec, the second site
of printing in Canada. The first printing there was in
1764, and the printers, Brown & Gilmore, were the first
printers to operate there. This work was prepared for
the use of the Montagnais Indians, an Algonquian tribe,
at missions in the Saguenay country, by Father Jean Baptiste La Brosse, a Jesuit father who worked among the
Montagnais from 1756 to 1782. (WR)
L56. (LANGUAGE IMPRINT). Neh Nase Tsi Shok8atak8en Ne
Sonk8aianer Iesus-Keristos. (The Holy Gospels Translated from the Authorized English Version into the Iroquois Indian Dialect.) 324pp, 16mo, original cloth, ex-
lib, Montreal, J. Lovell & Son, for British and Foreign
Gospel Society, 1880 (1st ed.). $175.00

L57.   (LANGUAGE IMPRINT).   Presbyterian Tawoope Qa Wicasta
       Wakan Tawowcon.   Translations into Sioux from the
       Presbyterian Government and Discipline, including Forms
       for Special Occasions by John Eastman, George Firecloud,
       A. F. Johnson, J. P. Williamson.   96pp, 12mo, Santee,
       Nebraska, 1915. $65.00
       ____Another Copy.   Same. $95.00
       ____Another Copy.   Disbound, damp stain in margins.
                                                              $35.00
L58.   (LANGUAGE IMPRINT).   (Prevost, Jules L.)   Culic Whutana
       Kunacu Yit.   Tadluonu Khuva Whykainiwhulit.   Kowhulud
       By Khudidash.   Dowhudoduwon Cithlotalton Yulh.   36pp,
       sewn into stiff cloth printed wrappers, (Tanana, Alaska,
       1907). $150.00
            Tourville: 3685.   Wickersham: 1140.   An interesting
       hymnal, based on translations made by McDonald, Canham
       and the compiler.   It was evidently useful, because Tour-
       ville notes a second edition issued eight years later; Tour-
       ville and Wickersham also call for only 32pp in this edition,
       while this copy has a full 36pp.
L59.   (LANGUAGE IMPRINT).   Smiimii Lu Tel Kaimintis Kolinzuten.
       (Kalispel).   Narratives from the Holy Scriptures in Kalis-
       pel.   140, 14pp, grey printed wrappers, St. Ignatius
       Print, Montana, 1879. $200.00
            Only one work was produced on the St. Ignatius Press
       before this item, and that was a pamphlet in Latin for the
       Jesuit order.   The present work was the first book and
       the first Indian language production.   Prepared by Father
       Giorda, it contains narratives from the Old and New Testa-
       ments.   Wrappers for the first edition of 1876 were used
       on this 1879 work.   Schoenberg 6.   (WR)
L60.   (LANGUAGE IMPRINT).   Suptraction Ubvalo Illangerterinek.
       Tafel XIII.   Instruction card in arithmetic for Eskimos
       of Labrador.   n.d., c.1860. $60.00
L61.   (LANGUAGE IMPRINT).   Testamentetak Tamedsa: Nalegapta
       Piulijipta Jesusib Kristusib Apostelingitalo Pinniarningit
       Okausingillo.   (Eskimo).   (3), (279)-637pp, modern full
       leather, London, W. M'Dowall, 1840 (1st ed.). $260.00
            Pilling, Eskimo p.88-89.   Labrador Eskimo New Testa-
       ment excluding four gospels.
L62.   (LANGUAGE IMPRINT).   Tan Teladakadidjik Apostalewidjik.
       (Acts of the Apostle in Micmac Language).   140pp, 16mo,
       full leather, British and Foreign Bible Society, Bath,
       1863. $135.00
            Pilling, Bibliography: 3809.   In phonetic characters.
       Probably translated by Rev. S. T. Rand.
L63.   (LANGUAGE IMPRINT).   Wowapi Wakan Kin.   (The New
       Testament in the Dakota Language).   Translated from the
       original Greek by Stephen R. Riggs.   408pp, full leather,
       New York, American Bible Society, 1895. $125.00
L64.   LANNING (E. P.).   (Univ. of California Publications in

American Archaeology and Ethnology, Vol. 46, No. 2, 1963) A Ceramic Sequence for the Piura and Chira Coast, North Peru. 150pp, 33pp of photographs, 23 figures, wrappers. $55.00

L65. LANTIS (M.). Eskimo Childhood and Interpersonal Relationships, Nunivak Biographies and Genealogies. xv, 215pp, 7 figures, 10 charts, map, bds, American Ethnological Society, 1960. $25.00
___Another Copy. Same. $20.00

L66. LANTIS (M.). (Univ. of Kentucky Studies in Anthropology, No. 7, Lexington, 1970 [1st ed.], d.j.) Ethnohistory in Southwestern Alaska and Southern Yukon. 301pp, plus index, illus, maps, bibliography. $17.00

L67. LAPHAM (I. A.). (Smithsonian Contributions to Knowledge, Vol. VII, 1855) The Antiquities of Wisconsin, as Surveyed and Described by I. A. Lapham, Civil Engineer, Etc., on Behalf of the American Antiquarian Society. xii, 95pp, 61 wood engravings, 65pp of maps and plans, cloth. $135.00

L68. LAPINER (A. C.). Art of Ancient Peru. 36pp, 56 photographs, map, Arts of the Four Quarters, New York, 1968. $10.00

L69. LAPINER (A. C.). Pre-Columbian Art of South America. 460pp, 910 illus, 225 in color, 4to, New York, Abrams, 1976, d.j. $275.00

L70. LA POINTE (James). Legends of the Lakota. 160pp, Indian Historian Press, San Francisco, 1976. $15.00

LARCO HOYLE (Rafael). See also BAE Bulletin No. 143.

L71. LARCO HOYLE (Rafael). Cronologia Arqueologica del Norte Peru. 87pp, 25 full-page pls of ceramic artifacts, plus 25 smaller photographs, 2 maps, wraps, Buenos Aires, 1948. $45.00

L72. LARCO HOYLE (Rafael). La Ceramica de Vicus (Peru). 46pp, 44 figures, wrappers, Lima, 1965. $25.00

L73. LARIMER (Sarah L.). The Capture and Escape; or, Life Among the Sioux. 252pp, 5pls, cloth, Claxton, Remsen & Haffelfinger, Philadelphia, 1870 (1st ed.). $45.00
A rather worn copy with a couple of plates pulled but present, and sewing a bit loose, considerable edge wear. A scarce narrative; the author was captured by the Sioux en route to the gold fields of Idaho, but later eluded her captors.

L74. LARMOUR (W. T.). Inunnit. The Art of the Canadian Eskimo. 104 double-column pp, photographs, drawings, wrappers, n.p. (Ottawa), 1974. $15.00

L75. LARNED (I. A.). The Antiquities of Wisconsin. Removed from Smithsonian Contributions to Knowledge, Washington, 1855. xii, 95pp, 55 pls, maps, other illus, 4to, plain wrappers, early work on the Moundbuilders. $75.00

L76. LARSON (Charles R.). American Indian Fiction. 204pp, plus index, notes, appendix, bibliography, Albuquerque, 1978 (1st ed.), d.j. $10.00

L77. LARSON (H.) and RAINEY (F.). (American Museum of Natural History, Anthropology Papers, Vol. 42, 1948) Ipiutak and the Arctic Whale Hunting Culture. 376pp, 59 figures, 100pp of photographs (artifacts), wrappers. $135.00

    ___Another Copy. Same, rebound in cloth. $90.00
    ___Another Copy. Same, original wrappers. $90.00

L78. LARRALDE (S. L.) and CHANDLER (S. M.). (Bureau of Land Management: Utah. Cultural Resource Series, No. 11, Salt Lake City, 1981) Archaeological Inventory ... Seep Ridge Cultural Study Tract.... 237pp, illus, maps, bibliography, lrg 8vo, wrappers. $15.00

L79. LAS CASAS (Fr. Bartolome De). Los Indios de Mexico y Nueva Espana Antologia. Antologis Edicion. 225pp, illus, wrappers, Mexico, 1966. $20.00

L80. LATHROP (Donald W.). Ancient Ecuador Culture, Clay and Creativity, 3,000 to 300 B.C. 110pp, 604 illus, 4to, wrappers, Field Museum, Chicago, 1975. $25.00

L81. LATORRE (Felipe A. and Dolores L.). The Mexican Kickapoo Indians. 388pp, plus index, photographs, notes, bibliography, Austin, 1976 (2nd printing), d.j. $15.00

L82. LATROBE (Charles J.). The Rambler in Mexico. 309pp, folding map, cloth, London, 1836 (1st English ed.). $90.00

L83. LATTA (Frank F.). Handbook of Yokuts Indians. 765pp, 4to, illus, index, endpaper maps, revised and enlarged 2nd ed. of basic work on these San Joaquin Valley Indians, Santa Cruz, 1977. $30.00
    ___Another Copy. Same. $25.00

L84. LAUBIN (Reginald and Gladys). American Indian Archery. 174pp, plus index, b/w and color photographs, drawings, bibliography, Norman, 1980 (1st ed.), d.j. $85.00

L85. LAUBIN (Reginald). Indian Dances of North America: Their Importance to Indian Life. 538pp, 4to, illus, index, 25 full-page color pls, Norman, 1979, d.j. $35.00
    ___Another Copy. Same. $30.00

L86. LAUBIN (Reginald). The Indian Tipi, Its History, Construction and Use. xviii, 208pp, color frontis, 9pp photographs, 45 sketches, Norman, 1957 (1st ed.). $30.00
    ___Another Copy. Same. $25.00

L87. LAUGHLIN (R. M.). (Smithsonian Contributions to Anthropology, Vol. 19, 1975) The Great Tzotzil Dictionary of San Lorenzo Zinacantan. 609pp, 2 photographs, 3 figures, 5 fold-out maps, wrappers. $35.00
    ___Another Copy. Same. $20.00
    ___Another Copy. Same. $45.00
    ___Another Copy. Same. $30.00

L88. LAUGHLIN (R. M.). (Smithsonian Contributions to Anthropology, Vol. 23, 1977) Of Cabbages and Kings, Tales from Zinacantan. x, 427pp, 12 figures, 8 maps, wrappers. $25.00

___Another Copy. Same. $35.00

L89. LAUGHLIN (R. M.). (Smithsonian Contributions to Anthropology, Vol. 22, 1976) Of Wonders Wild and New. xii, 178pp, 11 photographs, 3 maps, wrappers. $20.00

___Another Copy. Same. $25.00

___Another Copy. Same. $10.00

L90. LAURENT (J.). New Familiar Abenakis and English Dialogues. The First Vocabulary Ever Published in the Abenakis Language, Comprising: The Abenakis Alphabet, the Key to the Pronunciation and Many Grammatical Explanations, to Which is Added the Etymology of Indian Names of Certain Localities, Rivers, Lakes, etc. 230pp, decorative cloth, Indian Village of St. Francis, Province of Quebec, 1884. $70.00

___Another Copy. Same. $175.00

L91. LAVACHERY (H. A.). Les Arts Anciens d'Amerique au Musee Archeologique de Madrid. 129pp, 51 pls, red cloth with original wrappers bound in, edition is limited to 300 copies, Anvers (Eds. De Sikkel), 1929. $95.00

___Another Copy. Same. $125.00

L92. LAVEILLE (E.). The Life of Father DeSmet, S.J., 1801-1873. Translated by Marian Lindsay. 590pp, 1pp, plus index, frontis drawing, bibliography, folding map in back pocket, New York, 1915 (1st American ed.). $35.00

___Another Copy. Same, Chicago, 1981 reprint. $20.00

L93. LAWRENCE (D. H.). Mornings In Mexico. 189pp, cloth, much about the American Southwest, with a long section on the Hopi Snake Dance, New York, 1934, d.j. $25.00

L94. (LAWS). Constitution and Laws of the Muskogee Nation. 243pp, cloth, Muskogee Indian Territory, 1893. $325.00

Compiled and Codified by Arthur P. McKellop. The compiler, a Creek was born in the Indian Territory in 1858. He later attended Wooster University in Ohio. He served his nation later in many important posts, not the least being his compilation and codification of the Creek laws. Foreman locates only four copies. Eberstadt: 113:364. Foreman, pp. 44-45. Hargrett: 182. (WR)

L95. LEACH (Douglas Edward). Flintlock and Tomahawk. New England in King Philips' War. 304pp, illus, New York, 1958 (1st ed.). $35.00

___Another Copy. Same, d.j. $15.00

L96. LEACOCK (E. B.) and LURIE (N. O.) Editors. North American Indians in Historical Perspective. 498pp, studies by Fenton, Hickerson, Weltfish, Opler, others, New York, 1971 (1st ed.). $25.00

___Another Copy. Same. $15.00

L97. LE BEAU (Claude). Geschichte Des Herrn C. Le Beau, Advocat Im Parlament. Oder Merckwurdige und Neue Reise Zu Denen Wilden Des Nordlichen Theils Von America.... 319, (368)pp, 7 pls, folding map, half vellum, marbled bds, Erfurt, 1752. $650.00

Sabin: 39582. Lande: 512. TPL: 168. Gagnon:
1992. First German edition, after the first edition in
French of 1738.

L98.   LECKIE (William H.). Military Conquest of the Southern
Plains. 269pp, 4 maps, plate illus, Norman, 1963,
(1st ed.), d.j. $28.00
___Another Copy. Same. $25.00
___Another Copy. Same, lacks d.j. $18.00

L99.   LEDESM (Raul). Maquijat. Santiago Del Estero (El Leg-
endario Pueblo Indigena). 191pp, illus wrappers, Argentina, 1961. $50.00

L100. LEE (L. P.). History of the Spirit Lake Massacre! 8th
March, 1857 and of Miss Abigail Gardiner's Three Months'
Captivity Among the Indians. 48pp, printed wrappers,
New Britain, CT, 1857. $175.00
Howes: L-210. Ayer: 181. Miss Lee was captured
in northern Iowa by the Sioux. Harrowing tale told in
Gruesome detail. (WR)
___Another Copy. Iowa City, 1951. $10.00

L101. LEE (Melicent). Indians of the Oaks. 245pp, illus, wrappers, a novel but ethnographically accurate (Southern
Dieguenos), Ramona, 1978. $14.00

L102. LEE (Nelson). (Garland Library of Narratives of North
American Indian Captivities, Vol. 75, New York, 1977)
Three Years Among the Comanches. 224pp, cloth.
                            $45.00

L103. LEE (T. A.) and NAVARRETE (C.). (New World Archaeological Foundation. Brigham Young Univ. Paper No. 40,
1978) Mesoamerican Communications Routes and Cultural
Contacts. 265pp, 20 symposium papers by various authors, 36 figures, 19 tables, wrappers. $35.00
___Another Copy. Same. $20.00

L104. LEFREE (Betty). (Univ. of New Mexico, School of American
Research, Monograph No. 29, 1975) Santa Clara Pottery
Today. 114pp, illus, some in color, wrappers. $12.00
___Another Copy. Same. $15.00

L105. LEFTWICH (Regal H.). Chiricahua Anniversary. 51pp,
photographs, wrappers, Almagordo, New Mexico, 1963
(1st ed.). $10.00

LEHMANN (Henri). See also BAE Bulletin No. 143.

L106. LEHMANN (Henri). Archeologie du Sud-Quest Colombien.
Offprint of Journal de la Societe des Americanistes,
Nouvelle Serie, XLII, 1953, pp 199-270, 26 photographs
and drawings in text plus 10pp photographs, fold-out
map, Musee de l'Homme, Paris, 1953. $30.00

L107. LEHMANN (Henri). L'Art PreColumbian. Collecion "Carre-
four Des Arts." 76pp, 94 illus (8 pls in color), artifacts
from museums world-wide, Paris, 1960. $30.00

L108. LEHMANN (Henri). Mixco Viejo. 53pp, illus, 14 photographs, 2 plans, ceremonial center of Maya (Pokoman
Group), wrappers, Guatemala, n.d. $15.00

L109. LEHMANN (Henri). Pre-Columbian Ceramics. 160pp, 52
b/w and 17 color photographs, 60 drawings, cloth, Paris,
1959, New York, 1962. $30.00
___Another Copy. Les Ceramiques Precolombienes.
Paris, 1959. $25.00

L110. LEHMANN (Walter). (Orbis Pictus Band 8. Berlin, n.d.)
Altmexikanische Kunstgeschichte. 27pp, 48 pls, overview
of Pre-Columbian artifacts, wrappers. $35.00

L111. LEHMANN (Walter) and DOERING (H.). The Art of Old
Peru. 208pp, consisting of 68pp of text containing 63
figures and 12pp of color photographs and 128pp of b/w
photographs, cloth, Berlin, 1924, New York, 1974.
                                                         $70.00
Classic in its field, this full historical survey of the
art of Peru and neighboring regions contains an abundance
of large illustrations of ceramics, metal work, and textiles.
The illustrations are arranged in a chronological sequence,
more than half of them, both tapestry and pottery, were
taken from an extraordinary private collection in
Schlachtensee, all of which were previously unpublished.
(EAP)
___Another Copy. E. Weyhe, New York, 1924. $175.00
___Another Copy. Same. $200.00

LEHMER (Donald J.). See also BAE Bulletin No. 158.

L112. LEHMER (Donald J.) and JONES (David). (River Basin
Survey, Publications in Salvage Archaeology, No. 7,
Lincoln, 1968) Arikara Archaeology: The Bad River
Phase. 170pp, illus, wrappers. $20.00

L113. LEHMER (D. J.). (National Park Service, Anthropological
Papers, No. 1, 1971) Introduction to Middle Missouri
Archaeology. x, 206pp, 114 figures, cloth. $17.00

L114. LEHMER (D. J.). (Univ. of Arizona Bulletin Vol. XIX,
No. 2, 1948) The Jornada Branch of the Mogollon. 99pp,
36 photographs, 24 figures, wrappers. $20.00

L115. LEICHT (Herbert). Pre-Inca Art and Culture. 253pp,
48 pls of multiple artifacts, New York, 1960. $45.00

L116. LEIGH (R. W.). (Univ. of California Publications in American Archaeology and Ethnology, Vol. 23, No. 10,
Berkeley, 1928) Dental Pathology of Aboriginal California.
53pp, illus, folded charts, wrappers. $25.00
___Another Copy. Same. $10.00

L117. LEIGHTON (Alexander and Dorthea). (Peabody Museum
Papers, Vol. 40, No. 1, Cambridge, 1949) Gregorio,
the Hand-Trembler. 177pp, wrappers. $35.00

L118. LEIGHTON (Alexander and Dorthea). The Navaho Door.
An Introduction to Navaho Life. xviii, 149pp of text,
plus 36pp of photographs, cloth, Cambridge, 1944.
                                                         $25.00
___Another Copy. Same. $40.00
___Another Copy. Same. $30.00
___Another Copy. Same. $25.00

L119. LEIGHTON (D.) and KLUCKHOHN (C.). Children of the
People. The Navaho Individual and His Development.
xvi, 277pp, 19 photographs, 5 figures, 20 tables, 3 maps,
Cambridge, 1948. $40.00

L120. LEKSON (S. H.). (National Park Service, Publications in
Anthropology 18B, Albuquerque, 1986 reprint) Great
Pueblo Architecture of Chaco Canyon, New Mexico.
xviii, 299pp, 131pp of photographs and drawings, wrappers. $27.00

L121. LELAND (C. G.). The Algonquin Legends of New England; or, Myths and Folklore of the Micmac, Passamaquoddy, and Penobscot Tribes. 379pp, illus, brown
cloth, gilt lettering, Boston, New York, 1884 (1st ed.).
                                                    $45.00

L122. LEMOS (P. J.). Indian Decorative Designs. 60pp, 28
full-page pls, 18 drawings, rebound in later cloth, School
Arts Magazine, Worcester, 1926. $18.00

L123. LENZ (Mary Jane). The Stuff of Dreams: Native American
Dolls. 96pp, 81 illus, 4to, wrappers, New York, 1986.
                                                    $16.00

L124. LEON (F. de P.). Los Esmaltes de Urupan. 176pp, 52
full-page hand-colored drawings of enamels, Mexico City,
1939. $150.00
        This beautiful volume, written by Professor Francisco
de P. Leon in 1922 and published in 1939, is still considered to be the finest volume published on the lovely
enamels of Uruapan. The 52 hand-colored drawings are
dazzling in their quality and richness. (EAP)

L125. LEON (Dr. Nicolas). Lyobaaor Mistlan. Historical-
Descriptive Guide. 53pp, 54 photographs, several folding maps, plans, text in Spanish and English, decorated
cloth, extensive coverage of the Mitla ruins, Mexico,
1901. $125.00

L126. LEON-PORTILLA (Miguel). Aztec Thought and Culture:
A Study of the Ancient Nahuatl Mind. 237pp, illus,
Norman, 1982, d.j. $20.00

L127. LEON-PORTILLA (M.). Pre-Columbian Literatures of
Mexico. 191pp, Norman, 1969 (1st ed.), d.j. $35.00
        ____Another Copy. Same. $15.00
        ____Another Copy. Same. $22.00

L128. LEON-PORTILLA (Miguel). Religion de los Nicaraos:
Analisis y Comparacion de Tradiciones Culturales Nahuas.
116pp, 4 pls, wrappers, Mexico, 1972. $25.00

L129. LEON-PORTILLA (Miguel). Time and Reality in the Thought
of the Maya. 171pp, plus index, drawings, bibliography,
references, Boston, 1973 (1st English printing), d.j.
                                                    $15.00

LEOPOLD (A. Starker). See BAE Bulletin No. 170.

L130. LE PAGE DU PRATZ (A. S.). Histoire de la Louisiane,
Contenant la Decouverte de Ce Vaste Pays, Sa Description Geographique, Unvoyage Dans les Terres; l'Histoire

Naturelle; Les Moeurs, Costumes and Religion des Natur-
els Avec Leurs Origines.... (3 Volumes). Vol. 1: xvi,
358pp (no errata). Vol. 2: 441pp. Vol. 3: 454pp,
folding map of Louisiana territory, folding plan of New
Orleans, 40 pls, 12mo, leather, Paris, De Bure, Dela-
guette, Lambert, 1758 (1st ed.). $400.00
    Howes: L-266. Field: 911. Focuses on French
claims to the southern part of the territory and on the
Indian tribes in the area, including the war with the
Chickasaw, Indian languages, customs, and ceremonies.
(RMW)

L131. LE PLONGEON (Alice). Here and There in the Yucatan.
Miscellanies. 146pp, cloth, New York, 1886. $150.00
    Memories of travels in search of Mayan ruins with her
husband Augustus.

L132. LE PLONGEON (Augustus). Queen Moo and the Egyptian
Sphinx. 277pp, 73 pls, cloth, New York, 1900 (2nd
ed.). $225.00
    Puts forth the eccentric explorer-archaeologist's the-
ory of Egyptian-Maya links.
    ____Another Copy. Same. $175.00

L133. LERY (Jean). Historia Navigationis in Brasiliam Quae et
America Dicitur. 29 unnumbered leaves, 340pp, 8 unnumbered leaves of index, 7 full-page woodcuts, in
pagination, and one folding plate, full green morocco,
gilt, Geneva, 1594. $3,000.00
    Borba De Moraes: p.471. European Americana:
594/32. Sabin: 40154. JCB: (3) 1:333. The second
Latin edition of Lery's classic account, and the fifth
overall, preceded by French editions of 1578, 1580, and
1585 and the first Latin edition of 1586. All the early
editions are rare. Lery, a Protestant pastor, came to
Brazil in 1556 and stayed for about a year. Much of this
time he lived with the Indians, and as great an authority
as Levi-Strauss credits him with the most accurate observations on the Tupi Indians made in the sixteenth
century, and calls his work one of the classics of anthropological observation. The illustrations show domestic
and war scenes of the Indians. (WR)

L134. LESLIE (C. M.). Now We Are Civilized: Study of the
World View of the Zapotec Indians of Mitla, Oaxaca.
108pp, 12 photographs, Detroit, 1960 (1st ed.), d.j.
                                                    $25.00
    ____Another Copy. Same. $15.00
    ____Another Copy. Same. $10.00

L135- LESSER (A.). (Columbia Univ. Contributions to Anthro-
136.   pology, Vol. XVI, 1933) The Pawnee Ghost Dance Hand
Game. 339pp, 3pp photographs, 13 figures, cloth.
                                                    $70.00
    ____Another Copy. Madison, 1978. $27.00
    ____Another Copy. Same. $10.00
    ____Another Copy. New York, 1933. $40.00

L137.   LESUEUR (Jacques). (Museum of the American Indian Con-
         tributions, Vol. XII, No. 5, New York, 1952) History of
         the Calumet and of the Dance. 22pp, color frontis,
         wrappers. $15.00
L138.   LETTERMAN (Edward). From Whole Log to No Log. His-
         tory of the Indians Where the Mississippi and the Minne-
         sota Rivers Meet. 268pp, plus index, photographs, maps,
         appendix, bibliography, Minneapolis, 1969 (1st ed.),
         d.j. $12.00
    ___Another Copy. Same. $10.00
L139.   (SOUTH AMERICAN LETTERS). Cartas de Indias. Edicion
         Facsimile. (2 Volumes). pp 459; 418, reprint of 1877
         Madrid edition with important 16th century documents to
         include Guatemala and Chiapas. limited edition of 500
         copies, wraps, Guadalajar, Mexico, 1970. $125.00
L140.   LEUPP (Francis). The Indian and His Problem. cracked
         frnt hinge, New York, 1910. $20.00
L141.   LEUPP (Francis). In Red Man's Land. Study of the
         American Indian. 161pp, frontis, illus, bibliography,
         wrappers, New York, Chicago, 1914. $15.00
L142.   LEVANTO (Leonardo). Cathecismo de la Doctrina Christi-
         ana, en la Lengua Zaapotec. (4)ff., 32pp, sml quarto,
         contemporary limp vellum. Puebla: por la Viuda de
         Miguel de Orteaga, y por su Origin la en la Oficina Pala-
         foxian, 1776. $950.00
         Vinaz: 362.   Garcia Icazbalcet Lenguas: 125. Medina
         (Puebla): 956. Palau: 137035. Sabin: 40732. Zapotec
         is one of the indigenous languages of Oaxaca, Mexico,
         and was spoken by the builders of Monte Alban and
         Mitla. This work contains prayers, the Ten Command-
         ments, the Seven Deadly Sins in that language and, ad-
         ditionally, bilingual catechism. Virtually every concerned
         bibliographer has noted that the introductory matter is
         dated 1732 and has theorized the existence of an Oaxaca
         edition of that date. They all, however, have overlooked
         the fact that three licenses ("del gobierno," "del ordi-
         nario," and "de la religion") were required for publication
         in colonial South America. The religious license was not
         granted until 1752, thus ruling out an edition of 1732.
         The existence of a lost 1752 edition (printed in Puebla),
         is, however distinctly possible, especially given the word-
         ing of the imprint. (WR)
L143.   LEVI (M. Carolissa). Chippewa Indians of Yesterday and
         Today. 367pp, plus index, drawings by Peter Whitebird,
         New York, 1956 (1st ed.), d.j. $35.00
LEVI-STRAUSS (Claude). See also BAE Bulletin No. 143.
L144.   LEVI-STRAUSS (Claude). La Vie Familiale et Sociale des
         Indiens Nambikwar (Brazil). Extrait du Journal de la
         Societe des Americanistes, Nouvelle Serie, Tomo 37,
         Paris, 1948. 132pp, 7 pls, wrappers. $25.00
L145.   LEVI-STRAUSS (Claude). The Way of the Masks. 259pp,

58 b/w and 4 color photographs, 2 drawings, 3 maps,
cloth, Seattle, 1982. $27.00

L146. LEWIS (Anna). Chief Pushmataha. American Patriot.
The Story of the Choctaws' Struggle for Survival.
200pp, plus index, 2 illus, bibliography, New York, 1959
(1st ed.), d.j. $12.00
___Another Copy. Same. $15.00

L147. LEWIS (Rev. Arthur). The Life and Work of the Rev.
E. J. Peck Among the Eskimos. xvi, 350pp, pls, map,
original cloth, London, 1908 (3rd ed.). $35.00
Missionary work, 1876-1902, in Canadian Arctic.

L148. LEWIS (C.). Indian Families of the Northwest Coast.
xi, 224pp, cloth, Chicago, 1970. $30.00
___Another Copy. Same. $15.00
___Another Copy. Same. $20.00

L149. LEWIS (Henry Morgan). The Indian Journals, 1859-1862.
236pp, 16 full color pls (full-page), Ann Arbor, 1959
(1st ed.), d.j. $36.00
___Another Copy. Same. $45.00
___Another Copy. Same, lacks d.j. $30.00
Note: Listed elsewhere under Editor: WHITE (Leslie A.).

L150. LEWIS (James Otto). The Aboriginal Port-Folio. Lithographed by Lehman and Duval, No. 8 (7) Bank Alley.
Folio (49x30cm), 9 Numbers, Nos. 1-9, 72 color pls.
Advertising leaves inserted at beginning of Nos. 1, 2,
3. Original blue printed wraps, sewn, tissue guards.
Advertisement "From The Numerous Notices" on the rear
wraps of Nos. 5 and 6, occasional, minor, skillful repairs
to wraps. The first part has inscribed on frnt wrap:
"To Dr. Worrall from the Publisher J. O. Lewis," in
clamshell box. Philadelphia, 1835-6. $30,000.00
    The Aboriginal Port-Folio represents the first attempt
at a collection of portraits of the North American Indian,
preceding McKenney and Hall's History of the Indian
Tribes of North America, and the works of George Catlin.
It is the earliest effort of several of the pioneers of
American lithography and color printing and it is considered the rarest of art publications about the western
Indians.
    About the Port-Folio Henry R. Schoolcraft wrote:
"Altogether it is to be regarded as a valuable contribution.... He has painted the Indian lineaments on the
spot, and is entitled to patronage--not as supplying all
that is desirable, or practicable, perhaps, but as a first
and original effort. We should all cherish such a work."
    This Aboriginal Port-Folio represents the first business
venture by both George Lehman and Peter S. Duval.
Their association during the years 1835 and 1836 produced
this work as well as lithographs for McKenney and Hall's
great History of the Indian Tribes of North America.
George Lehman was born in Lancaster County, Pa. An

"extremely competent artist," he "painted, engraved, aqua-tinted and handcolored a number of views of Pennsylvania towns that are well kncwn." The lithographer Peter S. Duval ("one of the most important of them all"-- Peters) was brought from France in 1831 by the firm of Childs and Inman, who also employed George Lehman. Cephas G. Childs, regarded as one of the outstanding American lithographers, and Henry Inman, painter and engraver (who incidentally contributed portraits to McKenney and Hall's work), produced lithographs which were regarded as among the best of the era. While in the employ of Childs and Inman, 1831-35, Duval began to gather around him a group of first rate lithographers who were to work with him in later years. He is regarded as a pioneer of color printing and produced the first specimen of lithotint "Grandma's Pet." Peter S. Duval and his group occupy one of the most important places in American lithography. Among the later productions of Duval's company are James Simpson's "Journal of a Military Reconnaissance." Herndon and Gibbon's "Exploration of the Valley of the Amazon." and many other government publications; De Smet's "Letters and Sketches"... etc. (RMW)

____Another Copy. The American Indian Portfolio: An Eyewitness History, 1823-1828. 96pp, 16 full-page color pls, edition limited to 200 copies, Kent, Ohio, 1980.
$150.00
____Another Copy. Same. $150.00

L151. LEWIS (William S.) and PHILLIPS (Paul C.) Editors. The Journal of John Work. 190pp, plus index, illus, colored map, bibliography, trader to the Flatheads and Blackfeet, Cleveland, 1923 (1st ed.). $100.00
____Another Copy. Same. $125.00
____Another Copy. Same. $75.00

L152. LEWIS (Oscar). (American Ethnological Society Monograph VI, 1942) The Effects of White Contact Upon Blackfoot Culture. 73pp, cloth. $24.00
____Another Copy. Same, wrappers. $12.00
____Another Copy. Same, Seattle, 1973. $10.00
____Another Copy. Same, Seattle, 1973. $12.00

L153. LEWIS (Oscar). Anthropological Essays. 523pp, maps, index, 24 essays on Blackfeet, New York, 1970 (1st ed.).
$30.00
____Another Copy. Same, d.j. $15.00

L154. LEWIS (Richard). I Breathe A New Song: Poems of the Eskimo. 128pp, numerous illus by Oonark, Ny, 1971 (1st ed.). $30.00
____Another Copy. Same. $25.00

L155. LEWIS (T. M.) and KNEBERG (M.). Hiwassee Island: An Archaeological Account of Four Tennessee Indian Peoples. x, 188pp, maps, figures, tables, 118 pls, some in color,

bibliography, index, wrappers, Univ. of Kentucky, 1946
(1st ed.). $45.00
___Another Copy. Same. $35.00
___Another Copy. 1979, 4th printing, d.j. $20.00
___Another Copy. Same. $25.00

L156. LEWIS (Thomas M. N.) and KNEBERG (Madeleine). Tribes
That Slumber. Indians of the Tennessee Region. 196pp,
frontis, illus by Madeleine Kneberg, end paper maps,
1/2 cloth, bds, Univ. of Tennessee Press, 1960, d.j.
                                                        $25.00
___Another Copy. Same. $30.00
___Another Copy. Same. $25.00

L157. LIBBY (O. G.). The Arikara Narrative of the Campaign
Against the Hostile Dakotas June, 1876. 276pp, 7 folding
maps, 18 pls, index, Bismarck, 1920. $135.00
___Another Copy. Same. $75.00
___Another Copy. Same, New York, 1973. $20.00

L158. LIEBERKUHN (Samuel). The History of Our Lord and
Saviour Jesus Christ. Translated Into the Delaware Indian Language by the Rev. David Zeisberger. viii,
222pp, later cloth, American Ethnological Society, New
York, Daniel Fanshaw, 1821. $150.00

L159. LIEBLER (H. Baxter). Boil My Heart for Me (Navaho).
194pp, photographs, New York, 1969 (1st ed.), d.j.
                                                        $10.00

L160. LIGHT (D. W.). (Glenbow-Albert Institute Occasional
Paper No. 6, Alberta, 1972) Tattooing Practices of the
Cree Indians. 23pp, illus with figures and photographs,
wrappers. $12.00

L161. LILLY (Eli). Prehistoric Antiquities of Indiana. xvi,
293pp, index, bibliography, 53 full-page photographic
pls, illus endpapers, 4to, printed at Lakeside Press,
Indianapolis, Indiana Historical Society, 1937 (1st ed.).
                                                        $150.00
___Another Copy. Same, signed by author. $165.00

L162. LINARES (O.) and RANERE (A.) Editors. (Peabody Museum Monographs, No. 5, Cambridge, 1980) Adaptive
Radiations in Prehistoric Panama. 530pp, illus, wraps.
                                                        $20.00

L163. LINCOLN (Charles H.). Narratives of the Indian Wars,
1675-1699. 300pp, plus index, 2 maps (one folding),
facsimile, New York, 1913. $20.00
___Another Copy. Same. $15.00

L164. LINCOLN (Louise) Editor. Southwest Indian Silver from
the Doneghy Collection. 189 double-column pp, many
photographs, map, bibliography, wrappers, Minneapolis,
1982 (1st ed.). $16.00
___Another Copy. Same, cloth. $30.00
___Another Copy. Same, wrappers. $18.00
___Another Copy. Same. $12.00

L165. LINDERMAN (Frank B.). American: The Life Story of a

Great Indian, Plenty-coups, Chief of the Crows. xi,
313pp, illus by H. M. Stoops, cloth, New York, 1930
(1st ed.). $30.00
____Another Copy. Same. $25.00
____Another Copy. Same. $35.00
____Another Copy. London, 1930. $25.00
____Another Copy. London, n.d. $35.00
____Another Copy. Same. Plenty-Coups: Chief of the
Crows. New York, 1972. $15.00
Originally published in 1930 under title "American":
This is a complete reprint.

L166. LINDERMAN (Frank B.). Blackfeet Indians. 66pp, 50pp
of color drawings (10 1/4 by 12 inches) by W. Reiss,
decorated bds, St. Paul, Great Northern Rail-Way, 1935.
    $60.00
____Another Copy. Same. $125.00

L167. LINDERMAN (Frank B.). Indian Why Stories, Sparks from
War Eagle's Lodge-Fire. xiii, 236pp, color frontis, color
title page illus, color cvr plate, 7 color text pls, 11 illus
by C. M. Russell, New York, Scribner's, 1915 (1st ed.).
    $100.00
Dykes High Spots of Western Illustrators, No. 41:
Has 12 b/w line engravings in addition to the color pls.
Has 22 first appearance illus. Dykes: "The fine color
pls are some of Russell's best, showing his understanding
of the Indians and their legends."
____Another Copy. Same. $100.00
____Another Copy. Same. $60.00

L168. LINDERMAN (Frank B.). Old Man Coyote (Crow). 254pp,
illus by Herbert Morton Stoops, New York, 1932. $15.00

L169. LINDERMAN (Frank B.). Out of the North. This portfolio contains full-color pls of 24 Blackfoot Indians, by
Winold Reiss, Great Northern Railway, 1947. $125.00

L170. LINDERMAN (Frank B.). Pretty-Shield: Medicine Woman
of the Crows. 256pp, illus, cloth, New York, 1972,
d.j. $15.00
Originally published as "Red Mother" in 1932, this is
a complete reprint. Account of Crow Indian life prior to
the reservation period. Consists primarily of Linderman's
conversations with the elderly Crow woman, Pretty-Shield.
____Another Copy. Red Mother. 256pp, illus by Herbert
M. Stoops, New York, 1932. $40.00

L171. LINDQUIST (G. E. E.). The Indian in American Life.
180pp, index, folding map, wrappers, New York, 1944
(3rd printing). $10.00

L172. LINDSAY (A. J.). (Museum of Northern Arizona Bulletin
No. 45, Flagstaff, 1968) Survey and Excavations North
and East of Navaho Mountain, Utah, 1959-1962. 412pp,
256 figures containing photographs and drawings, wrappers. $25.00

L173. LINDUFF (Katheryn M.). Ancient Art of the Middle

Americas. 124pp, 149 photographs, selections from J. C.
Leff Collection, wrappers, Huntington Galleries, 1974.
$20.00

L174. LINES (M. de) and LINES (J. A.). Costa Rica, Monumentos Historicos Arqueologisos. 221pp of text, plus
35pp of photographs, fold-out map, San Jose, C. R.,
1974. $30.00

L175. LINK (Margaret S.). The Pollen Path. A Collection of
Navaho Myths Retold by Margaret Schevill Link. xiv,
205pp, 1 color pl, 22 drawings, cloth, Stanford, 1956.
$58.00
___Another Copy. Same. $35.00
___Another Copy. Same. $45.00
___Another Copy. Same. $32.00

L176. LINNE (S.). Archaeological Researches at Teotihuacan,
Mexico. 236pp, over 300 figures, maps, appendices,
Ethnographical Museum of Sweden, printed in English by
Oxford University Press, wrappers, 1934. $175.00

L177. LINNE (S.). Darien in the Past: The Archaeology of
Eastern Panama and Northwestern Colombia. 318pp, 62
figures, 14 maps, 42pp bibliography, figures are of
multiple artifacts, wrappers, Goteborg, 1929. $90.00

L178. LINNE (S.). El Valle y la Ciudad de Mexico en 1550:
Relacion Historica Fundad Sobre un Mapa Geografico, que
se Conserva en la Biblioteca de la Universidad de Upp-
sala. xv, 220pp, 55 text illus, 12 folding pls, 24" x 36"
color facsimile map in rear pocket, bound in cloth, Stockholm, 1948. $225.00
Extraordinarily accurate description of the city and
the Valley of Mexico, with great detail. Done c.1555 by
Indian Colegio de Santa Cruz in Tlatelolco. (CY)

L179. LINNE (S.). (Ethnographical Museum of Sweden, New
Series, Publication No. 7, 1942) Mexican Highland Cultures, Archaeological Researches at Teotihuacan, Cal-
pulalpan and Chalchicomula in 1934-1935. 223pp, 333 figures, map, fold-out plan, wrappers. $145.00
___Another Copy. Same. $135.00
___Another Copy. Same, rebound in cloth. $95.00

L180. LINNE (S.). Treasures of Mexican Art, Two Thousand
Years of Art and Art Handicraft. 131pp, 95 b/w photographs, mostly full-page, 4 full-page color photographs,
map, wrappers, National Museum, Stockholm, 1956.
$35.00

L181. LINTON (Ralph). Acculturation in Seven American Indian
Tribes. xiii, 526pp, cloth, New York, 1940. $30.00
___Another Copy. Same. $22.00
___Another Copy. Same. $35.00

L182. LINTON (Ralph). (Field Museum Leaflet No. 8, Chicago,
1923) Annual Ceremony of the Pawnee Medicine Men.
20pp, 2 full-page photographs, wrappers. $14.00

L183. LINTON (Ralph). (Field Museum of Natural History,

Chicago, 1923) Purification of the Sacred Bundles: Ceremony of the Pawnee. 11pp, frontis pl, the account of this ceremony has been compiled from the unpublished notes of Dr. G. A. Dorsey, wrappers. $12.00

L184. LINTON (Ralph). (Field Museum of Natural History, Leaflet No. 5, Chicago, 1922) The Thunder Ceremony of the Pawnee. 19pp, 4pp full-page photographs, wrappers.
$28.00

LIPKIND (William). See BAE Bulletin No. 143.

L185. LIPPS (Oscar H.). The Navajos. 136pp, plus 17 pls, limp cloth, color frontis, Cedar Rapids, 1909 (1st ed.).
$45.00

L186. LIPTON (B.). Survival: Life and Art of the Alaskan Eskimo. 96pp, 44 b/w and 14 color photographs, Newark, 1977. $12.00

L187. LISMER (M.). Seneca Splint Basketry. 40pp, 15 lrge photographs, 11 figures, 2 maps, wrappers, Washington, DC, 1941, Ontario, 1982. $10.00

L188. LISTER (Florence and Robert). Earl Morris and Southwestern Archaeology. illus, Univ. of New Mexico, 1968, d.j. $27.00

L189. LISTER (R. H. and F. C.). Aztec Ruins on the Animas, Excavated, Preserved, and Interpreted. viii, 120pp, 65pp of photographs, 7pp of drawings, map, Albuquerque, 1987. $20.00

L190. LISTER (R. H. and F. C.). Chaco Canyon, Archaeology and Archaeologists. xiv, 284pp, 80 half and full-page photographs and drawings, cloth, Albuquerque, 1981.
$48.00
        Tucked away in the craggy desert of northwestern New Mexico, Chaco Canyon is one of North America's richest archaeological areas. This extensive study fully documents the discovery, history and research done at each of the spectacular major ruins, and provides a particularly valuable list of all pertinent information on each of Chaco Canyon's investigated sites. (EAP)
___Another Copy. Same, soft cvr. $20.00

L191. LISTER (R. H. and F. C.). (Univ. of Colorado, Anthropological Series No. 9, Boulder, 1964) Contributions to Mesa Verde Archaeology; I site 499, Mesa Verde National Park, Colorado. 91pp, 29 photographs, 12 figures, rebound in cloth. $25.00

L192. LISTER (Robert). (Univ. of New Mexico, Publications in Anthropology, No. 5, 1949) Excavations at Cojumatlan Michoacan, Mexico. 106pp, illus, wrappers. $30.00
___Another Copy. Same. $18.00

L193. LISTER (R. H. and F. C.). Those Who Came Before, Southwestern Archaeology in the National Park System. 184pp, 63 b/w and 15 color photographs, 3 charts, 4 maps, cloth, Tucson, 1983. $45.00
___Another Copy. Same. $25.00

L194. LITTLEFIELD (Daniel F.) and PARINS (J. W.). American
       Indian and Alaskan Native Newspapers and Periodicals,
       1826-1924. 482pp, Connecticut, 1984. $45.00
L195. LITTLEFIELD (Daniel F.). The Cherokee Freedmen from
       Emancipation to American Citizenship. 265pp, plus index,
       photographs, maps, bibliography, Westport, CT, 1978
       (1st ed.). $15.00
L196. LITTLEFIELD (Daniel F.). The Chickasaw Freedmen. A
       People Without a Country. 236pp, plus index, photo-
       graphs, maps, bibliography, Westport, CT, 1980 (1st
       ed.). $15.00
       ___Another Copy. Same. $12.00
L197. LLEWELLYN (K. N.) and HOEBEL (E. Adamson). The
       Cheyenne Way: Conflict and Case Law in Primitive
       Jurisprudence. xiv, 360pp, pictorial cloth, Norman,
       1941 (1st ed.). $45.00
       ___Another Copy. Same, 1953, d.j. $30.00
       ___Another Copy. Same, 1961. $25.00
       ___Another Copy. Same, 1978, d.j. $20.00
L198. LLOYD (J. William). Aw-Aw-Tam, Indian Nights. The
       Myths and Legends of the Pimas. 241pp, 1 photographic
       pl, printed on brown pulp paper, n.p., published by
       the author, paper bds, 1911. $40.00
L199. LOBB (Allan). Indian Baskets of the Northwest Coast.
       118pp, plus index, b/w and color photographs, drawings
       by Barbara Paxson, Portland, 1978 (1st ed.), d.j.
                                                          $20.00
L200. LOCHER (G. W.). The Serpent in Kwakiutl Religion: A
       Study in Primitive Culture. viii, 118pp, pls, bibliogra-
       phy, wrappers, Leyden, 1932 (1st ed.). $35.00
L201. LOCKE (L. L.). The Ancient Quipu, or Peruvian Knot
       Record. 84pp of text containing 17 figures, map, plus
       59pp of photographs, decorated gilt cloth, American Mu-
       seum of Natural History, 1923. $40.00
       ___Another Copy. Same. $28.00
L202. LOCKE (L. L.). (Museum of the American Indian, Contri-
       butions, Vol. VII, No. 5, New York, 1927) Peruvian
       Quipu. 12pp, plus one 7pp fold-out diagram, 1 photo-
       graph, wrappers. $12.00
L203. LOCKE (L. L.). (American Museum of Natural History
       Anthropological Papers, Vol. XXX, Part II, 1928) Sup-
       plementary Notes on the Quipus in the American Museum
       of Natural History. pp 39-73, 1pp of drawings, wrappers.
                                                          $22.00
       ___Another Copy. Same. $17.00
       ___Another Copy. Same. $20.00
L204. LOCKE (Raymond F.) Editor. The American Indian.
       253pp, plus index, photographs, drawings, map, Indian
       history by various authors, New York, 1970 (1st print-
       ing), d.j. $15.00
L205. LOCKETT (H.). Along the Beale Trail, Photographic

Account of Wasted Range Land. 56pp, 25 full-page photographs, U.S. Office of Indian Affairs, 1939. $15.00

L206. LOCKETT (H.) and HARGRAVE (Lyndon L.) et al. (Museum of Northern Arizona Bulletin No. 26, Flagstaff, 1953) Woodchuck Cave. Basketmaker II Site in Isegi Canyon, Arizona. 32pp, plus index, photographs, map, bibliography, wrappers. $12.00

L207. LOCKWOOD (Frank C.). The Apache Indians. (18), 348pp, photographs, 2 folding maps, index, MacMillan, New York, 1938 (1st printing). $60.00
___Another Copy. Same. $75.00
___Another Copy. Same, some fading to backstrip.
                $75.00
___Another Copy. Same. $85.00

L208. LOCKWOOD (Frank C.). The Life of Edward E. Ayer. 300pp, illus, index, Chicago, 1929 (1st ed.), d.j.
                $50.00

L209. LOEB (E. M.). (Univ. of California Publications in American Archaeology and Ethnology, Vol. 33, No. 2, Berkeley, 1933) The Eastern Kuksu Cult. 108pp, 1 figure, map, fold-out table, wrappers. $57.00
___Another Copy. Same. $40.00

L210. LOEB (E. M.). (Univ. of California Publications in American Archaeology and Ethnology, Vol. 33, No. 1, 1932) The Western Kuksu Cult. 137pp, wrappers. $50.00

L211. LOMMEL (A.). Altamerikanische Kunst Mexico-Peru. 240pp, 89 b/w and 20 color photographs, Museum fur Volkerkunde, Munich, 1961. $25.00

L212. LONG (James Larpenteur). The Assiniboines. From the Accounts of the Old Ones as Told to First Boy. Edited by Michael S. Kennedy. 197pp, plus index, maps, illus, bibliography, Norman, 1961 (1st ed. thus), d.j. $20.00

L213. LONGACRE (William A.) Editor. Reconstructing Prehistoric Pueblo Societies. 247pp, index, maps, bibliography, Albuquerque, 1970 (1st ed.), d.j. $20.00
___Another Copy. Same. $15.00

L214. LONGFELLOW (Henry W.). The Song of Hiawatha. xviii, 242pp, 22 photogravure pls, 379 text illus from designs by Frederic Remington, modern quarter morocco, raised bands, t.e.g., Boston, Riverside Press, 1892 (1st ed., 2nd printing). $100.00

L215. LONG LANCE (Chief Buffalo Child). Long Lance. xv, 278pp, frontis, pictorial cloth, New York, 1928. $35.00
Dobie, p.34. Dobie: "Long Lance was Blackfoot only by adoption, but his imagination incorporated him into tribal life more powerfully than blood could have. He is said to have been a North Carolina mixture of Negro and Croatan Indian; he was a magnificent specimen of manhood with swart Indian complexion. He fought in the Canadian Army during World War I, and thus became acquainted with the Blackfeet. No matter what the facts of his life,

he wrote a vivid and moving autobiography of a Blackfoot Indian in whom the spirit of the tribe and the natural life of the Plains during buffalo days were incorporated. In 1932 in the California home of Anita Baldwin, daughter of the spectacular "Lucky" Baldwin, he absented himself from this harsh world by a pistol shot." (TE)

     ____Another Copy. Same. $20.00
     ____Another Copy. Same. $18.00
     ____Another Copy. Same. $20.00

L216. LONGSTREET (Stephen). War Cries on Horseback. The Story of the Indian Wars of the Great Plains. 335pp, (1), photographs, map, endpaper map, Garden City, NY, 1970 (1st ed.), d.j. $15.00

L217. LONGYEAR (J. M.). Peabody Museum, Memoirs, Vol. IX, No. 2, 1944) Archaeological Investigations in El Salvador. xi, 120pp, 14pp of photographs, wrappers. $125.00
     ____Another Copy. Same. $100.00

L218. LONGYEAR (J. M.). (Carnegie Institute Publication No. 597, 1952) Copan Ceramics. Study of Southeastern Maya Pottery. xiii, 114pp of text containing 3 maps, 14 tables, plus 118pp of photographs and drawings of artifacts and another 82pp of explanatory text, wrappers. $125.00

L219. LONNEAUX (Martin J., S.J.). Mass Book and Hymnal in Innuit: Missarchutit Kalikat. 129pp, cloth, small printing, scarce, Chaneliak, Alaska, 1950 (1st ed.). $35.00

L220. LOOK (Al). Ute's Last Stand at White River and Mill Creek, Western Colorado in 1879. 105pp, photographs, drawings, reproductions of author's paintings in color, Denver, 1972 (1st ed.), d.j. $25.00

L221. LOOMIS (Augustus W.). Scenes in the Indian Country. 283pp, 2 pls, 16mo, later leather backed cloth, Philadelphia, Presbyterian Board, 1859 (1st ed.). $110.00
     Howes: L-461. Sabin: 77463. Field: 1358. Account of a year among the Creek Indians along the Arkansas River.
     ____Another Copy. Same, 3 pls. $95.00
     ____Another Copy. Same, rebound in later cloth. $80.00

L222. LOPEZ GOMARA (Francisco). La Terza Parte delle Historie dell' Indie, nella Quale Particolarmente Si Tratta dello Scoprimento della Provincia di Iucatan Detta Nuova Spagna & delle Cose Degne di Memoria, Fatte da Spagnuoli nella Conquista della Grande & Meravigliosa Citta di Messico & delle Altre Provincie ad Essa Sottoposte. Venetia, G. Ziletti, 1566. Thk 16mo, old vellum, title leaf backed, first line of title removed, some preliminary leaves lacking, text is complete. $450.00
     Sabin: 13052. Very early, and rare history of the Indians of Central America, and their conquest. Gomara was a respected historian, and this history contains good information on Indian Tribal groups, customs, and cities.

L223. LORANG (Sister May Corde). Footloose Scientist in Mayan
America. Illus. Scribner's, New York, 1966, d.j.
$20.00

L224. LORING (J. M. L.). Pictographs and Petroglyphs of the
Oregon Country. (2 Volumes). Part I: Columbia River
and Northern Oregon. 325pp, 6 photographs, 255 draw-
ings. Part II: Southern Oregon. xi, 355pp, 12 photo-
graphs, 466 drawings. Institute of Archaeology, Los
Angeles, 1982, 1983. $68.00
____Another Copy. Same. $50.00
____Another Copy. Same. $75.00

L225. LORRAIN (D.). (Texas Historical Commission, Report No.
12, Austin, 1968) Archaeological Excavations in Northwestern Crockett County, Texas. 71pp, illus, pls, maps,
bibliography, lrge 8vo, wrappers. $10.00

L226. LORRAIN (D.). (Southern Methodist University Contributions to Anthropology, No. 4, Dallas, 1969) Archaeological Excavations in the Fish Creek Reservoir. 160,
(2)pp, photographs, maps, limited to 100 copies, wrappers. $10.00
____Another Copy. Same. $12.00
____Another Copy. Same. $15.00

L227. LOSKIEL (George H.). Geschichte Der Mission Der Evan-
gelischen Bruder Unter Den Indianern in Nordamerika.
(16), 784, (1)pp, original bds, Barby, 1789. $500.00
Howes: L-474. Sabin: 42109. Thomson: 732. Field:
952. The first edition, first state of this important work
(with six-line errata). A very important and official account of missionary work among the Indians of the frontier:
Ohio, Pennsylvania, New York, from 1735 to 1787, including details on the Gnadenhutten and Salem massacres,
the activities of the Moravians and their missions, and
what is reputed to be the first mention in a book of the
discovery of oil in Pennsylvania. The first edition is to
be preferred to the translations in that significant material pertaining to tribes which had become friendly in the
intervening years was deleted in the translations and later
editions. (WR)
____Another Copy. Barby, 1789 (1st ed., 2nd issue).
$250.00
____Another Copy. London, 1794 (1st ed. in English).
$375.00
____Another Copy. Same as above. $275.00
____Another Copy. Same. $350.00

L228. LOTHROP (D. W.). The Upper Amazon. 256pp, 75 photographs and 42 drawings of several hundred pots, sherds,
and designs, cloth, London, 1970, 1979. $25.00

L229. LOTHROP (Gloria Ricci). Recollections of the Flathead
Mission by Fr. Gregory Mengarini, S.J. Frontis map,
4 illus, Glendale, 1977 (1st ed.), d.j. $20.00

LOTHROP (Samuel K.). See also BAE Bulletin No. 143.

L230. LOTHROP (Samuel K.). (Peabody Museum, Memoirs, Vol.
IX, No. 3, 1950) Archaeology of Southern Veraguas,
Panama. 127pp, 150 photographs and drawings of over
500 objects, wrappers. $120.00
___Another Copy. Same. $95.00

L231. LOTHROP (S. K.). (Peabody Museum Papers, Vol. LI,
Cambridge, 1963) Archaeology of the Diquis Delta, Costa
Rica. x, 142pp of text containing 82 figures, 8 tables,
plus 51pp of photographs of gold, stone and ceramic objects and figures, wrappers. $65.00

L232. LOTHROP (S. K.). Azteken-Maya-Inkas, Kunst und Kultur
in Mittel-und Sudamerik. 247pp, 85 color and 62 b/w
photographs, all lrge, many full-page, 43 figures, map,
cloth, Skira, Geneva, 1964, 1980. $70.00

L233. LOTHROP (S. K.). (Peabody Museum Papers, Vol. L, No.
1, Cambridge, 1957) A Chancay-Style Grave at Zapalla,
Peru. An Analysis of its Textiles, Pottery and Other
Furnishings. 90pp, 17pp of photographs, 10 figures,
wrappers. $40.00

L234. LOTHROP (S. K.). (Peabody Museum Memoirs, Vol. VII,
Cambridge, 1937) Cocle, An Archaeological Study of Central Panama. Historical Background, Excavations at the
Sitio Conte. Artifacts and Ornaments. xvii, 327pp, 271
figures, 3 color pls, 29 tables, wrappers. $225.00

L235. LOTHROP (S. K.). (Peabody Museum Memoirs, Vol. VIII,
Cambridge, 1942) Cocle, An Archaeological Study of
Central Panama. Pottery of the Sitio Conte and Other
Archaeological Sites. xiii, 292pp, 491 figures, 3 color
pls, 6 tables, wrappers. $225.00

L236. LOTHROP (S. K.). Essays in Pre-Columbian Art and
Archaeology. 507pp, illus, Harvard Univ., 1961. $85.00

L237. LOTHROP (S. K.). (American Antiquities, Vol. 6, No. 3,
1941) Gold Ornaments of Chavin Style from Chongoyape,
Peru. pp 250-262, illus of 25 different artifacts, wrappers. $20.00

L238. LOTHROP (S. K.). (Museum of the American Indian, Contributions No. 10, 1928) The Indians of Tierra Del Fuego.
244pp of text containing 105 photographs and drawings,
plus extra 19 pp of more photographs, wraps. $97.00

L239. LOTHROP (S. K.) and MAHLER (J.). (Peabody Museum
Papers, Vol. L, No. 2, Cambridge, 1957) Late Nazca
Burials in Chavin, Peru. 102pp, 19pp of photographs,
2pp diagrams, 14 figures, wrappers. $40.00
___Another Copy. Same. $35.00

L240. LOTHROP (S. K.) and VAILLANT (G. C.) et al. The
Maya and Their Neighbors. xxi, 606pp (34 papers) of
text containing 41 figures, plus 20pp of photographs,
cloth, New York, 1940. $60.00

L241. LOTHROP (S. K.), FOSHAG (W. F.) and MAHLER (J.).
Pre-Columbian Art, Robert Woods Bliss Collection. 287pp,
113pp of color and 53pp of b/w photographs, 5 drawings,

      2 maps, cloth, London, 1957. $375.00

      ___Another Copy. New York, 1958. $250.00

      ___Another Copy. Same. $250.00

L242. LOTHROP (S. K.). Treasures of Ancient America: The Arts of the Pre-Columbian Civilizations from Mexico to Peru. Lrge 4to, color illus, xiv, 229pp, 85 color and 60 b/w photographs, map, cloth, Skira, Geneva, 1964, d.j. $175.00

      ___Another Copy. Same. $95.00

      ___Another Copy. Same, lacks d.j. $75.00

      ___Another Copy. Same, lacks d.j. $60.00

L243. LOTHROP (S. K.). Zacualpa: A Study of Ancient Quiche Artifacts. 103pp, 107 illus, 7 pls with 3 in color, Carnegie Institute, Washington, DC, 1936. $125.00

      ___Another Copy. Same. $90.00

L244. LOTT (Milton). Dance Back the Buffalo. 406pp, endpaper maps, novelized history of Ghost Dance Religion, Boston, 1959 (1st ed.), d.j. $15.00

L245. LOUD (L. L.). (Univ. of California Publications in American Archaeology and Ethnology, Vol. 13, No. 3, 1919) Ethnogeography and Archaeology of the Wiyot Territory. 216pp, 15 figures, 10 tables, 18pp of photographs, 3pp of maps, signed by author, wraps. $90.00

L246. LOUD (L. L.). (Univ. of California Publications in American Archaeology and Ethnology, Vol. 17, No. 6, 1924) The Stege Mounds at Richmond, California. 18pp, 1 figure, 2pp photographs of sinkers, pestles, and charmstones, wrappers. $24.00

L247. LOUDON (Archibald). A Selection of Some of the Most Interesting Narratives, of Outrages, Committed by the Indians in Their Wars, with the White People. x, 302pp; 357pp (2 Volumes in One), originally published at Carlisle, 1808, New York 1971 (reprint). $20.00

      ___Another Copy. Same, d.j. $25.00

      ___Another Copy. Same. $17.00

      ___Another Copy. Same. $12.00

LOUNSBURY (Floyd G.). See also BAE Bulletin No. 180.

L248. LOUNSBURY (Floyd G.). (Yale Univ. Publications in Anthropology, No. 48, 1953) Oneida Verb Morphology. 111pp, wrappers. $18.00

L249. LOUNSBURY (Floyd G.). A Semantic Analysis of the Pawnee Kinship Usage. Reprinted from "Language," Vol. 32, No. 1, 1956. pp 158-194, in binder. $15.00

L250. LOVE (William Deloss). Sampson Occum and the Christian Indians of New England. 379pp, illus, cloth, Boston, 1899. $35.00

      ___Another Copy. Same. $25.00

L251. LOWE (G. W.) and AGRINIER (P.). (New World Archaeological Foundation. Brigham Young Univ. Papers 8-11, 1961) Excavations at Chiapas De Corzo, Chiapas, Mexico. 202pp, 108 figures, 55pp of photographs, wraps. $25.00

      ___Another Copy. Paper No. 8 only. $10.00

L252. LOWE (G. W.) et al. (New World Archaeological Foundation. Brigham Young Univ. Paper No. 31, 1980) Izapa: An Introduction to the Ruins and Monuments. xix, 349pp, 183 figures, 8 tables, wrappers. $30.00
___Another Copy. Same. $20.00

L253. LOWE (G. W.). (New World Archaeological Foundation. Brigham Young Univ. Paper No. 12, 1962) Mound 5 and Minor Excavations, Chiapa De Corzo, Chiapas, Mexico. 144pp, 46 figures, 34 pls, wraps. $12.00

LOWIE (Robert H.). See also BAE Bulletin No. 143.

L254. LOWIE (Robert H.). (American Museum of Natural History Anthropological Papers, Vol. IV, Part I, 1909) The Assiniboine. 270pp, 17 drawings of artifacts, 3pp of photographs, later bds over original wrappers. $90.00

L255. LOWIE (Robert H.). The Complete Bibliography of Robert H. Lowie. 44pp, wrappers, Berkeley, 1966. $15.00

L256. LOWIE (Robert H.). The Crow Indians. xxii, 350pp, illus, bibliography, index, New York, 1935 (1st ed.). $85.00
___Another Copy. Same. $85.00
___Another Copy. Same, chipped d.j. $65.00
___Another Copy. Lincoln, 1983, no photographs, wrappers. $10.00

L257. LOWIE (Robert H.). (Univ. of California Publications in American Archaeology and Ethnology, Vol. 29, No. 2, 1930) A Crow Text, with Grammatical Notes. pp 155-175, wrappers. $22.00
___Another Copy. Same. $20.00

L258. LOWIE (Robert H.). (Univ. of California Publications in American Archaeology and Ethnology, Vol. 39, No. 1, 1941) The Crow Language: Grammatical Sketch and Analyzed Text. 142pp, wrappers. $50.00
___Another Copy. Same. $35.00
___Another Copy. Same. $35.00

L259. LOWIE (Robert H.). Crow Word Lists. Crow-English and English-Crow Vocabularies. x, 411pp, cloth, Berkeley, 1960. $50.00
___Another Copy. Same. $40.00

L260. LOWIE (Robert H.). (American Museum of Natural History, Anthropological Papers, Vol. XI, Part X, 1915) Dances and Societies of the Plains Indians. pp 803-835, 5 photographs, wrappers. $30.00
___Another Copy. Same. $20.00

L261. LOWIE (Robert H.). (Univ. of California Publications in American Archaeology and Ethnology, Vol. 36, No. 5, Berkeley, 1939) Ethnographic Notes on the Washo. 52pp, 2 figures, wrappers. $35.00
___Another Copy. Same. $25.00

L262. LOWIE (Robert H.). (Indiana Historical Society, Vol. 1, No. 6, 1939) Hidatsa Texts. pp 173-239, wrappers. $15.00

L263. LOWIE (Robert H.). (American Museum of Natural History, Anthropological Papers, Vol. XXX, Part VII, 1929) Hopi Kinship. 27pp, wrappers. $20.00

L264. LOWIE (Robert H.). (American Museum of Natural History, Anthropological Handbook No. 1, 1954) Indians of the Plains. xiii, 222pp, 105 illus, cloth. $40.00
____Another Copy. Same. $15.00
____Another Copy. Same, New York, 1943 (1st ed.). $12.00

L265. LOWIE (Robert H.). (American Museum of Natural History, Anthropological Papers, Vol. XXI, Part III, 1922) The Material Culture of the Crow Indians, pp 201-270, 19 figures, wrappers. $100.00
____Another Copy. Same. $25.00

L266. LOWIE (Robert H.). (American Museum of Natural History, Anthropology Papers, Vol. XXV, Part I, New York, 1918) Myths and Traditions of the Crow Indians. 308pp, wraps. $45.00
____Another Copy. Same. $25.00

L267. LOWIE (Robert H.). (American Museum of Natural History, Anthropological Papers, Vol. II, Part II, New York, 1909) The Northern Shoshone. pp 165-306, figures, pls, bibliography, wrappers. $75.00
____Another Copy. Same. $20.00

L268. LOWIE (Robert H.). (American Museum of Natural History, Anthropological Papers, Vol. IV, Part II, New York, 1910) Notes Concerning New Collections. pp 271-337, 42 figures, 5pp of photographs, wrappers. $48.00

L269. LOWIE (Robert H.). (American Museum of Natural History, Anthropological Papers, Vol. XXX, Part VI, New York, 1929) Notes on Hopi Clans. 57pp, wraps. $25.00

L270. LOWIE (Robert H.). (American Museum of Natural History, Anthropological Papers, Vol. XX, Part III, New York, 1924) Notes on Shoshonean Ethnography. 128pp, 36pp of photographs and drawings, wrappers. $50.00
____Another Copy. Same. $35.00

L271. LOWIE (Robert H.). (American Museum of Natural History, Anthropological Papers, Vol. XXV, Part II, New York, 1922) The Religion of the Crow Indians. 136pp, 7 figures, wrappers. $45.00
____Another Copy. Same. $40.00
____Another Copy. Same. $25.00
____Another Copy. Same. $20.00
____Another Copy. Same, New York, 1976, cloth. $33.00

L272. LOWIE (Robert H.). Robert H. Lowie, Ethnologist: A Personal Record. 198pp, 12pp of photographs, bibliography, Berkeley, 1959 (1st ed.), d.j. $25.00
Lowie's own story with much on his lifelong study of the Crow Indians of Montana and of his seven visits to their reservation beginning in 1907. Also material on the Indians of Alberta and the American Southwest. (GFH)

    ___Another Copy. Same. $25.00
    ___Another Copy. Same. $20.00

L273. (LOWIE, ROBERT H.) Robert H. Lowie. Biography. Edited by R. E. Murphy. viii, 179pp, cloth, New York, 1972. $17.00
    ___Another Copy. Same, d.j. $22.00

L274. LOWIE (Robert H.). (American Museum of Natural History, Anthropological Papers, Vol. IX, Part II, New York, 1912) Social Life of the Crow Indians. 69pp, wrappers. $25.00

L275. LOWIE (Robert H.). (American Museum of Natural History, Anthropological Papers, Vol. XI, Part III, New York, 1913) Societies of the Crow, Hidatsa, and Mandan Indians. pp 145-358, 7 figures, wrappers. $60.00
    ___Another Copy. Same, rear wrap missing. $45.00

L276. LOWIE (Robert H.). (American Museum of Natural History, Anthropological Papers, Vol. XI, Part XI, New York, 1916) Societies of the Kiowa. pp 837-851, wraps. $17.00

L277. LOWIE (Robert H.). (Univ. of California Publications in American Archaeology and Ethnology, Vol. 40, No. 1, Berkeley, 1942) Studies in Plains Indian Folklore. 28pp, wrappers. $20.00
    ___Another Copy. Same. $18.00
    ___Another Copy. Same. $22.00

L278. LOWIE (Robert H.). (American Museum of Natural History, Anthropological Papers, Vol. XVI, Part I, New York, 1915) The Sun Dance of the Crow Indians. 50pp, 11 figures, wrappers. $55.00
    ___Another Copy. Same, frnt and rear wraps missing. $40.00

L279. LOWIE (Robert H.). (American Museum of Natural History, Anthropological Papers, Vol. XVI, Part V, New York, 1919) The Sun Dance of the Shoshoni, Ute, and Hidatsa. pp 387-431, 4 figures, wrappers. $40.00
    ___Another Copy. Same. $30.00
    ___Another Copy. Same. $15.00

L280. LOWIE (Robert H.). (American Museum of Natural History, Anthropological Papers, Vol. XXX, Part II, New York, 1919) The Tobacco Society of the Crow Indians. 93pp, illus, wrappers. $35.00

L281. LUCKERT (Karl W.). Coyoteway; A Navajo Holyway Healing Ceremonial. With Johnny C. Cooke, Navajo Interpreter and Additional Texts by Mary C. Wheelright, Maud Oakes and Others. 260pp, illus, bibliography and index, the first complete recording of this full nine-night Navajo ceremonial which had been thought to be extinct, Tucson, 1979. $35.00
    ___Another Copy. Same. $43.00
    ___Another Copy. Same, soft cvr. $24.00

L282. LUCKERT (Karl W.). (American Tribal Religions, Vol. 3,

Flagstaff, 1978, 1st ed.) Navajo Bringing-Home Ceremony. The Claus Chee Sonny Version of Deerway Ajilee. 208pp, illus with photographs, map, bibliography, wrappers. $15.00

L283. LUCKERT (Karl W.). (American Tribal Religions, Vol. 1, Flagstaff, 1977, 1st ed.) Navajo Mountain and Rainbow Bridge Religion. 157pp, illus with photographs, bibliography, wrappers. $10.00

L284. LUDEWIG (Hermann E.). The Literature of American Aboriginal Languages. With Additions and Corrections by Prof. William W. Turner. Edited by Nicolas Trubner. 258pp, index, New York, 1971. $25.00
Complete reprint of the London 1848 edition. Field: "It contains notices of treaties on the languages and dialect spoken by 1,030 tribes, or by Aboriginal peoples, known under as many names; and as a monument of industry is scarcely excelled." Field: 959 (Indian Bibliography)
___Another Copy. Same. $17.00

L285. LUGO (Bernardo de). Gramatica en la Lengua General del Nuevo Reyno. Llamada Mosca. 22, 158 leaves, 5 leaves lacking (title, last leaf of introduction, leaves 84, 85 and 158 of text), 12mo, calf and bds, Madrid, 1619. $650.00
Sabin: 42667. Medina: 683. Alden: 619/75. JCB: (3)II: 135. Bernardo de Lugo's grammar of the Chibcha language of the Indians of Colombia.

L286. LUIS (Cocco). El Imperio Yanomamo de las Amazonas Venezolanas. Offprint of America Indigena, Vol. 34, No. 1, 1974. pp 39-62, wrappers. $10.00

L287. LUMBRERAS (Luis G.). Peoples and Culture of Ancient Peru. 248pp, 232 illus, Smithsonian Press, Washington, DC, 1977. $25.00

L288. LUMHOLTZ (C.). (American Museum of Natural History Memoirs, Vol. III, Part III, 1904) Decorative Art of the Huichol Indians. pp 279-327, 170 figures, 1 plate, inscribed by author, wrappers. $85.00

L289. LUMHOLTZ (C.). El Arte Simbolico y Decorativo de Los Huicholes. 402pp, 461 figures in text, wraps, Mexico, 1986. $25.00

L290. LUMHOLTZ (C.). Los Indios del Noroeste, 1890-1898. 86pp, over 50 photographs, oblong 8vo, wrappers, Instituto Nacional Indigenista, Mexico, 1982. $35.00

L291. LUMHOLTZ (C.). New Trails in Mexico: An Account of One Year's Exploration in North-Western Sonora, Mexico and South-Western Arizona, 1909-1910. 411pp, numerous illus, photographs of Papago Indians, artifacts, 2 color pls, 2 maps in rear pocket, appendix with Papago, Pima, Cocopa Indians, vocabularies of, t.e.g., Scribner's, New York, 1912 (1st ed.). $100.00
___Another Copy. Same. $95.00
___Another Copy. Same, rebound, ex-lib. $75.00

L292. LUMHOLTZ (C.). Unknown Mexico. A Record of 5 Years Exploration Among the Tribes of the Western Sierra Madre; in the Tierra Caliente of Tepic and Jaliscoc; and Among the Terascos of Michoacan. (2 Volumes). Vol. I: 530pp, over 200 illus, 6 color pls, 1 folding map in color. Vol. II: 496pp, over 200 illus, 9 color pls, 1 color folding map, 1 double-page map. Decorative cloth, photographic portrait on frnt of each volume, slipcased, Scribner, New York, 1902 (1st ed.). $250.00

L293. LUMHOLTZ (C.). (American Museum of Natural History Memoirs, Vol. III, part I, New York, 1900) Symbolism of the Huichol Indians. 228pp of text containing 291 drawings of Huichol artifacts, 3pp color illus, 1pp b/w illus, 1pp photographs, 2 maps, folio, full leather. $275.00
___Another Copy. Same, original wrappers. $225.00

L294. LUMMIS (Charles F.). Bullying the Moqui. Edited with an Introduction by Robert Easton. 132pp, illus, index, map, account of attempts to forcibly civilize the Hopi Indians, Prescott, 1968, d.j. $20.00
___Another Copy. Same. $20.00

L295. LUMMIS (Charles F.). The Land of Poco Tiempo. xii, 310pp, 38 illus including some of the earliest photographs ever recorded of Penitente ceremonies, special edition, generally most desirable with gilt decorated cloth, fine paper, New York, 1893, 1921, 1925. $85.00
___Another Copy. Same. $35.00

L296. LUMMIS (Charles F.). Mesa, Canon and Pueblo. xvi, 517pp, 67pp of color photographs, decorated cloth, New York, 1938. $60.00
___Another Copy. Same, 1925, 1st ed., frnt hinge loose. $12.00

L297. LUMMIS (Charles F.). Pueblo Indian Folk-Stories. x, 257pp, illus, decorated cloth, New York, 1910. $25.00
Originally published under the title of "The Man Who Married the Moon," this edition enlarged with the addition of new material.

L298. LUMMIS (Charles F.). Some Strange Corners of Our Country. The Wonderland of the Southwest. xi, 270pp, many illus, decorated cloth, New York, 1892 (1st ed.). $85.00
___Another Copy. Same. $60.00
___Another Copy. Same. $60.00

L299. LUMPKIN (Wilson). The Removal of the Cherokee Indians from Georgia. Two volumes in one. pp 369; 328. Limited edition of 500 copies, New York, 1907. $150.00
Author served two terms as Governor of Georgia and later as U.S. Commissioner to the Cherokees. The period covered in the text is primarily 1827 through 1841. Lumpkin introduced the Indian Removal Resolution in Congress, but did have some sympathy for the Indians plight.
___Another Copy. Same, New York, 1971. $25.00

L300. LUNA PARRA de GARCIA SAINZ (G.) and ROMANDIA de
CANTU (G.). En el Mundo de la Mascara. 132pp, 108
color photographs, many full page, cloth, Mexico City,
1978. $47.00
A study of Mexican masks, arranged by type and
usage of mask, this volume is filled with exceptional color
photographs of masks and dances, perhaps none of which
have been previously published. The text (in Spanish)
discusses the history of each of the various mask types
and describes in detail the dances in which they are
worn. (EAP)

L301. LUOMALA (K.). Navaho Life of Yesterday and Today.
vii, 115pp, 7 pls, National Park Service, Berkeley, 1938.
                                                                       $40.00

L302. LURIE (Nancy) (Editor). Mountain Wolf Woman: Sister of
Crashing Thunder: The Autobiography of a Winnebago
Indian. xx, 141pp, photographic pls, map, Ann Arbor,
1961 (1st ed.). $15.00

L303. LURIE (N.). North American Indian Lives. xii, 72pp,
22 lrge photographs, 2 maps, wrappers, Milwaukee Public
Museum, 1985. $12.00

L304. LUTZ (M. M.). (Ottawa National Museum of Man, Paper
No. 41, Ottawa, 1978) The Effects of Acculturation on
Eskimo Music of Cumberland Peninsula. 168pp, maps,
phonograph record in back pocket, 4to, wrappers.
                                                                       $35.00

L305. LUVERA (Paul). How to Carve Totem Poles. 157pp, illus,
some in color, wrappers, Seattle, 1977. $15.00

L306. LYFORD (C. A.). Iroquois Crafts. 97pp, 69 photographs,
19 drawings of Iroquois designs, Lawrence, 1945. $28.00
____Another Copy. Same. $18.00
____Another Copy. Same, Ontario, 1982. $10.00

L307. LYFORD (C. A.). Ojibwa Crafts. 216pp, 145 illus, inscribed by author, Lawrence, 1943. $35.00
____Another Copy. Same, no inscription. $25.00

L308. LYFORD (C. A.). Quill and Beadwork of the Western
Sioux. 116pp, 81 illus, special cloth, Lawrence, 1940.
                                                                       $35.00
____Another Copy. Same, wrappers. $28.00
____Another Copy. Same, cloth. $30.00
____Another Copy. Same, 1954, wrappers. $18.00
____Another Copy. Same, 1954, wrappers. $25.00

L309. LYMAN (C. M.). The Vanishing Race and Other Illusions:
Photographs of Indians by Edward S. Curtis. (2 Volumes). 158pp; 128 photographs, cloth, Washington, DC,
1982. $35.00
These two very interesting--and very different studies
of the work of Edward S. Curtis present opposite views
of the life and work of the brilliant photographic artist.
The first volume, purportedly the most comprehensive
biography of Curtis to date, reviews his early work, his

documentation of the Harriman Expedition and the task of publishing the 20 volume set of "The North American Indian." 150 pages of his "luminous visions of life in another age" contain many previously unpublished photographs, including work from his days in Hollywood as a still photographer for Cecil B. DeMille. A laudatory, important study of the romantic controversial artist.

In the second volume, Christopher Lyman examines Curtis's motivations and methods for creating his stunning images. Using more than 120 of the photographs to set the man and his work in historical context, Lyman analyzes Curtis's attitudes and shows how they affected his work, and he suggests that Curtis was able to manipulate both his subjects and his medium to create a composite image that appealed to cultural stereotypes of "Indianness." The result is a controversial work, highly critical on racial and ethnic grounds--though applauding and acknowledging Curtis's magnificent photography. (EAP)

L310. LYNN (Warren M.) et al. (Texas Historical Commission Archaeological Survey Report No. 20, Austin, 1977) Cultural Resource Survey of Choke Canyon Reservoir. Live Oak and McMullen Counties, Texas. 273pp, photographs, maps, bibliography, wrappers. $10.00

L311. LYNOTT (Mark J.). (Southern Methodist University Contributions to Anthropology, No. 16, Dallas, 1975) Archaeological Excavations at Lake Lavon, 1974. 136pp, ads, wrappers. $10.00

-M-

M1. McALLESTER (D. P.). (Peabody Papers, Vol. 41, No. 3, 1954) Enemy Way Music, A Study of Social and Esthetic Values as Seen in Navaho Music. 106pp, 47pp songs. $47.00

M2. McALLESTER (David). Peyote Music. 104pp, music, wrappers, New York, 1949. $25.00

M3. McALLISTER (J. G.). (Texas Memorial Museum Bulletin 17, 1970) Daveko, Kiowa-Apache Medicine Man. 61pp, 17pp photographs. $14.00

M4. McBETH (Kate C.). The Nez Perces Since Lewis and Clark. 272pp, photographs. Rader: 2271. Smith: 6186. New York, 1908 (1st ed.). $50.00

M5. McBRIDE (Elizabeth Nelson). Along Indian Trails. 93pp, illus, wrappers. n.p., 1939. $15.00

M6. McBRIDE (G. M.). (American Geographical Society Research Series No. 5, New York, 1921) The Agrarian Communities of Highland Bolivia. 27pp, 5 figures. $20.00

M7. McBRYDE (F. W.). (Smithsonian Institution, Institute of

Social Anthropology, No. 4, 1945) Cultural and Historical Geography of Southwest Guatemala. xv, 184pp of text containing 2 figures, 47pp photographs, 25 maps, some are fold-out. $60.00

M8. McCALL (Capt. Hugh). The History of Georgia, Containing Brief Sketches of the Most Remarkable Events up to the Present Day (2 Volumes). Vol. 1: viii, 376pp. Vol. 2: viii, 424pp. Full calf, joints weak, ex-library. Savannah, Seymour and Williams, 1811, 1816 (1st ed.). $400.00

First history of Georgia. Sabin erroneously calls for a map. Streeter: "A fundamental Georgia history and the chief source on the border wars with the Creeks and Cherokees; one of the rarest of state histories." (RMW)

M9. McCALLUM (James Dow) (Editor). (Dartmouth College MS Series, No. 1, Hanover, NH, 1932, 1st ed.) The Letters of Eleazar Wheelock's Indians. 316pp plus index, illus. These curious letters reflect the various reactions of Indians exposed to the learning, religion and customs of the Calvinistic New Englanders in the mid-1700s. $10.00

M10. McCARTHY (T. L.) et al. A Bibliography of Navaho and Native American Teaching Materials. viii, 103pp. Rough Rock, 1983 (revised ed.). $15.00

M11. McCLARKAN (Burney B.) et al. (Texas Archaeological Salvage Project, No. 8, Austin, 1966) Excavations in Toledo Bend Reservoir, 1964-65. 85pp, photographs, map, bibliography, wrappers. $10.00

M12. McCLINTOCK (Walter). (Southwest Museum Leaflet No. 2, Los Angeles, n.d.) The Blackfoot Beaver Bundle. 20pp, illus, wrappers. $10.00

M13. McCLINTOCK (Walter). (Southwest Museum Leaflet No. 8, Los Angeles, n.d.) Blackfoot Warrior Societies. 30pp, 16mo, illus, wrappers. $10.00

M14. McCLINTOCK (Walter). Old Indian Trails. 336pp, illus with color and b/w photographs, index, decorated cloth. Boston, 1923 (1st ed.). $125.00

In 1896, in the company of Gifford Pinchot, the author as photographer was part of an expedition to the forest area of Northwestern Montana, part of which later became Glacier National Park. After the expedition, he stayed on and was adopted into Chief Mad Wolf's Blackfoot tribe. This book relates 15 years close association and is based on his records of everything he saw and heard: their customs and legends and religious beliefs. (WS)

___Another Copy. Same. $80.00
___Another Copy. Same. $65.00

M15. McCLINTOCK (Walter). The Old North Trail of Life, Legends and Religion of the Blackfeet Indians. 532pp, plus index, photographs, colored frontis. Howes: M-45. Smith: 6228. London, 1910 (1st ed.). $85.00

M16. McCLINTOCK (Walter). (Southwest Museum Leaflet No. 6, Los Angeles, 1936) Painted Tipis and Picture-Writing of the Blackfoot Indians. 26pp, 18 photographic pls, illus, wrappers. $12.00

___Another Copy. Same. $10.00

M17. McCLURKAN (B. B.) et al. (University of Texas, Archaeological Survey Papers, No. 8, Austin, 1966, 1st ed.) Excavations at Toledo Bend Reservoir, 1964-1965. 85pp, maps, pls, bibliography, lrg 8vo, wrappers. $10.00

M18. McCLURKAN (B. B.). (University of Texas, Archaeological Survey Papers, No. 12, Austin, 1968, 1st ed.) Livingston Reservoir, 1965-6 ... Late Archaic and Neo-American Occupations. 115pp, maps, pls, bibliography, lrg 8vo, wrappers. $12.00

___Another Copy. Same. $10.00

M19. McCOMBE (Leonard) et al. Navaho Means People. 159pp, illus, cloth. Photographs of life among the Navaho Indians in the late 1940s with descriptive text. Wallace XIV, 108. Cambridge, 1951 (1st ed.), d.j. $30.00

M20. McCONKEY (Harriet). Dakota War Whoop. 395pp, frontis, 5 illus, 12mo. Chicago, Lakeside Press, 1965. $30.00

___Another Copy. Same. Cvrs slightly spotted. $20.00

M21. McCORMICK (O. F., III). (Southern Methodist University Archaeology Research Program, 1973, 1st ed.) Archaeological Excavations Lake Monticello. 123pp plus pls, maps, bibliography, 8vo, wrappers. $10.00

M22. McCORMICK (O. F., III). (Southern Methodist University Contributions in Anthropology, 1973, 1st ed.) Archaeology Resources Lake Monticello Area, Titus County, Texas. 115pp, maps, pls, bibliography, large 8vo, wrappers.
$10.00

M23. McCOSKER (S. S.). (Ethnologiska Studier. Etnografiska Museet, Goteborg. No. 33, 1974) The Lullabies of the San Blas Cuna Indians of Panama. 190pp, 18 figures, 10 tables. $15.00

M24. McCOWN (T. D.). (University of California Publication, in American Archaeology and Ethnology, Vol. 39, No. 4, 1945) Pre-Incaic Huamachuco, Survey and Excavations in the Region of Huamachuco and Cajabamba. x, 399pp, 16pp photographs, 22 figures, 8 fold-out maps. $65.00

M25. McCOY (Isaac). History of Baptist Indian Missions: Embracing Remarks on the Former and Present Condition of the Aboriginal Tribes; Their Settlement within the Indian Territory, and Their Future Prospects. 611pp, original cloth, lacks free blank endpapers. Washington, 1840.
$600.00

Wagner-Camp: 81. Howes: M-68. Pilling: 2365. Sabin: 4312. Streeter: 1804. Field: 982. Graff: 2589. The title of this work is somewhat misleading, since it is primarily an account of McCoy's career among the Indians from 1817 on, much of it concerning the explorations and opening of the Indian Territory. Field calls this "the work of a highly intelligent man, who recorded with

the judgment of an historian, while he labored with the
zeal of an ecclesiastic; and the result of his early philosophical observations has been to give us a valuable record
of the characteristic traits of the Indian tribes he lived
among." After 1830 McCoy lived in the Indian Territory
and Kansas working among the Indians, and this is a primary source for this period. (WR)

    ____Another Copy. Same. Rebound in cloth. $300.00

M26.   McCOY (Isaac). Remarks on the Practicability of Indian
Reform, Embracing Their Colonization. 47pp, half morocco.
Boston, 1827. $350.00

    Howes: M-70. Field: 985. Graff: 2591. Howes:
"One of the earliest suggestions for a reservation on which
to colonize and educate western Indians." (WR)

M27.   McCRACKEN (Harold). George Catlin and the Old Frontier.
131 illus plus 36 color pls. New York, Dial, 1959 (1st
ed.), d.j. $60.00

    ____Another Copy. Same. 216pp, cloth. $50.00

    ____Another Copy. Same. $20.00

M28.   McCREIGHT (M. I.). Chief Flying Hawk's Tales. The
True Story of Custer's Last Fight, as told by Chief Fly-
ing Hawk to M. I. McCreight. 56pp plus photographs.
Duston: 55. New York, 1936 (1st ed.). $35.00

M29.   McCREIGHT (M. I.). Firewater and Forked Tongues; A
Sioux Chief Interprets U.S. History. 104pp, pls (2 by
C. M. Russell including one first appearance, frontispiece
in color), appendix, index, inscribed by author, deluxe
edition limited to 250 copies. Early Sioux history as told
by Chief Flying Hawk who survived the Custer battle.
Pasadena, 1947, d.j. $50.00

    ____Another Copy. Same. 180pp, illus, the Sioux Cal-
endar. $22.00

    ____Another Copy. Same. $20.00

M30.   (McCULLOH, James H., Jr.). Researches on America; Being an Attempt to Settle Some Points Relative to the Aborigines of America, etc., "By an officer of the United States
Army." 8pp, 131pp, original bds rebacked in cloth.
Baltimore, 1816 (1st ed.). $50.00

    ____Another Copy. Baltimore, 1829 (3rd ed.) Researches,
Philosophical and Antiquarian, Concerning the Aboriginal
History of America. 535pp, folding map, original bds,
hinges cracked, scattered foxing of text. $400.00

    Field: 987. Howes: M-79. Sabin: 43134. American
Imprints: 39357. The third edition, greatly enlarged,
with slightly altered title, and the best textual edition.
Field describes this edition as "the most complete and
valuable essay upon the subject of which it treats," for
which the first and second editions were "Mere Sketch(es)."
McCulloh devotes chapters to Indian languages, physiog-
nomy, social structure, the Indians of Guatemala, Florida,
Peru and Mexico, Indian artifacts and so forth. (WR)

    ____Another Copy. Same. $175.00

M31. MacCURDY (George Grant). (Connecticut Academy of Arts and Sciences, Memoirs, Vol. III, New Haven, 1911) A Study of Chiriquian Antiquities. 249pp, 380 illus, and 49 pls of multiple artifacts, with many in color, cloth, some water staining, primarily to pls margins only. $175.00
   Based on collections belonging to Yale University. Supplemented by private collections, notably those of George G. Heye and Minor C. Keith.
   ___Another Copy. New York, 1976. $60.00
   ___Another Copy. Same. Ex-library. $45.00
M32. McCURDY (James G.) and NEWELL (Gordon). Indian Days at Neah Bay. 123pp, photographs. Autobiography of handicapped pioneer boy while living with Makah Indians. Seattle, 1961 (1st ed., limited), d.j. $50.00
   ___Another Copy. Same. $45.00
M33. McDANIEL (James) et al. Reply of the Delegates of the Cherokee Nation to the Demands of the Commissioner of Indian Affairs, May, 1866. 14pp, printed wrappers a bit chipped and detached. Refusal of the Cherokees to assent to certain demands made by the government preliminary to the negotiation of a treaty with them, including grants of lands to railroads, changes in the land holdings of the nation set out in the Treaty of 1835, etc. Eberstadt: 133:809. Washington, 1866. $250.00
McDERMOTT (John Francis). See also BAE Bulletin No. 147.
M34. McDERMOTT (John F.). Seth Eastman, Pictorial Historian of the Indians. 270pp, b/w and color illus. Norman, 1961 (1st ed.), d.j. $32.00
   ___Another Copy. Same. $30.00
M35. McDERMOTT (John F.) (Editor). Tixier's Travels on the Osage Prairies. Translated from the French by A. J. Salvan. 309pp, frontis, 8 illus, 2 folding maps. Norman, 1940 (1st ed.), d.j. $75.00
   Originally published in French as "Voyage aux Prairies, Louisiane et Missouri 1839-1840." Tixier traveled with the Osages on a buffalo hunt.
   ___Another Copy. Same. $45.00
   ___Another Copy. Same. $30.00
   ___Another Copy. Norman, 1968 (2d print.). $15.00
M36. MacDONALD (G. F.). Ninstints, Haida World Heritage Site. 66pp, 55 b/w and 11 color photographs, 9 drawings, 2 maps, wrappers. Vancouver, 1983. $12.00
M37. MacDONALD (G. F.). (National Historic Parks and Sites, Canada, 1984) The Totem Poles and Monuments of Git-wangak Village. 160pp, 176 photographs, wrappers. $18.00
M38. McDONALD (Lucile). Swan Among the Indians: Life of James G. Swan, 1818-1900: Based Upon Swan's Hitherto Unpublished Diaries and Journals. 233pp, illus, index, endpaper maps. Portland, 1972 (1st ed.), d.j. $25.00
   In-depth biography of James Swan, who did the first

and finest scientific research among the coastal Indians of
Washington Territory. He was the first teacher at the
Makah Indian Reservation at Neah Bay, wrote the first
major literary work from the new territory and was its
first artist.

M39. McGEE (Robert). (National Museum, Publications in Archaeology, No. 2, Ottawa, 1972) Copper Eskimo Prehistory.
136pp, illus, wrappers. $18.00

McGEE (W. J.). See also BAE Bulletin Nos. 17 and 18.

M40. McGEE (W. J.). Seri Indians of Bahia Kino and Sonora,
Mexico. 406pp, facsimile reprint of BAE Annual Report,
72 new photographs with 32 in color, decorated simulated
leather. Rio Grande Press, 1971. $50.00

M41. McGEE (W. J.). The Sioux Indians. A Socio-Ethnological
History. 119pp, illus, wrappers. New York, 1973.
$10.00

M42. McGEE (W. J.) et al. The Sioux Indians. Three articles
reprinted from the 10th and 15th Smithsonian Annual Reports. 138pp, 4to, wrappers. New York, 1973. $12.00

McGEEIN (Donald F.). See BAE Bulletin No. 192.

M43. McGIMSEY (C. R., III) and DAVIS (H. A.). (Arkansas
Archaeological Survey, Publications in Archaeology, 1969)
Indians of Arkansas. also: What is Archaeology. 70pp,
10 photographs, 1 drawing, 2 maps. $17.00

M44. McGIMSEY (C. R., III). Public Archaeology. 265pp, State-
supported programs. New York, 1972 (1st ed.), d.j.
$10.00

M45. McGINNIS (Dale) and SHARROCK (Floyd W.). The Crow
People. 106pp, photographs (some in color), maps, signed
by tribal chieftain, wrappers. Part of the Indian Tribal
Series. Phoenix, 1972 (1st ed.). $15.00

M46. McGLOIN (John Bernard). Eloquent Indian: The Life of
James Bouchard, California Jesuit. 380pp, illus, index,
bibliography. Stanford, 1949 (1st ed.), d.j. $35.00
Bouchard was the first Indian ordained a Catholic
priest in the United States. The book covers his life in
Kansas, Nevada and Oregon, in addition to well over 100
pages on his activities in Northern California from 1861-
1889.

M47. McGOVERN (W. M.). Jungle Paths and Inca Ruins. xi,
526pp, 31pp of photographs, 2 maps, cloth. New York,
1927. $35.00

M48. McGRAW (A. J.). (University of Texas Archaeological Survey Report No. 76, San Antonio, 1979) A Preliminary
Archaeological Survey for the Conquista Project in Gonzales, Atascosa and Live Oak Counties, Texas. 31pp,
photographs, drawings, maps, bibliography, wrappers.
$10.00

M49. McGRAW (A. J.) and VALDEZ (F., Jr.). (University of
Texas at San Antonio, Center for Archaeological Research
Survey Reports No. 43, 1977) Preliminary Assessments in

Archaeology Resources, Tobins Oakwell Farm, San Antonio, Texas. 20pp. $10.00

M50. McGREEVY (S.) et al. Shared Horizons: Navajo Textiles. 60pp, 16 full-page color photographs. Santa Fe, 1981. $16.00

M51. McGREEVY (S. B.) and WHITEFORD (A. H.). Translating Tradition: Basketry Arts of the San Juan Paiute. 64pp, 141 b/w and 9 color photographs, 1 map, 1 chart. Santa Fe, 1985. $15.00

M52. MacGREGOR (Gordon). Warriors Without Weapons: A Study of the Society and Personality Development of the Pine Ridge Sioux. 228pp, illus, index, map, bibliography. Chicago, 1951. $20.00

M53. McGREGOR (J. C.). Southwestern Archaeology. x, 403pp, 162 figures, cloth. New York, 1941. $37.00

M54. McGREGOR (James H.). The Wounded Knee Massacre From the Viewpoint of the Sioux. 140pp, illus, printed wrappers. Author was former Superintendent of U.S. Indian Service. Minneapolis, 1950, reprint. $20.00

M55. McGUIRE (Joseph D.). Classification and Development of Primitive Implements. pp227-36, chipped wrappers. Offprint from American Anthropologist, July 1896. $15.00

M56. McGUIRE (J. D.). (U.S. National Museum Report for 1897) Pipes and Smoking Customs of the American Ab- origines. pp351-645, 239 illus, 4 maps, newly rebound. $90.00
_____Another Copy. Same. $85.00

M57. McINTIRE (William G.). Prehistoric Indian Settlements of the Changing Mississippi River Delta. x, 113pp, pls, maps (several folding), bibliography, wrappers. Louisi- ana State University, Baton Rouge, 1958 (1st ed.). $17.00

M58. McINTOSH (John). The Origin of the North American In- dians; With a Faithful Description of their Manners and Customs, Religions, Languages, Dress and Ornaments. 345pp, illus, some are in color, original decorated leather. New Edition, Improved and Enlarged. New York, Nafis and Cornish, 1843. $50.00
_____Another Copy. New York, 1850. $60.00
_____Another Copy. New York, 1853. $65.00
_____Another Copy. New York, 1855. $85.00
_____Another Copy. Same. $60.00

M59. McKEE (Barbara) and JOYCE (Edwin & Harold). Havasupai Baskets and Their Makers: 1930-1940. 142pp, photo- graphs, drawings, bibliography. McKee was a naturalist at the Grand Canyon during these years. Flagstaff, 1975 (1st ed.), d.j. $25.00
_____Another Copy. Same. $25.00
_____Another Copy. Same. $17.00

M60. McKENNEY (Thomas L.). Documents and Proceedings Re- lating to the Formation and Progress of a Board in the

City of New York, for the Emigration, Preservation and
Improvement of the Aborigines of America, July 22, 1829.
48pp, original printed wrappers. New York, Vanderpool
and Cole, 1829 (1st ed.). $65.00
    Contains letters and addresses by Thomas L. McKenney,
Andrew Jackson and others interested in getting the Indians moved West of the Mississippi River.

M61. McKENNEY (Thomas L.) and HALL (James). History of the
Indian Tribes of North America, With Biographical Sketches
and Anecdotes of the Principal Chiefs (3 Volumes). pp
333; xvii, 9-920; iv, 17-392, royal 8vo, 120 hand-colored
pls, gilt decorated leather, Philadelphia, D. Rice and
A. N. Hart, 1855. $3,200.00
    Howes: M-129. Field: 922. The most colorful, orig-
inal and authentic portraits of Indians done before mid-
century. The portraits are by Charles Bird King, many
based on original paintings by J. O. Lewis, others done
on site in Washington, D.C. All the original paintings
on which these plates were based were destroyed in a fire
at the Smithsonian in 1865. Each portrait is accompanied
by text with biographical information on the individual and
his or her tribe. The lithographs in this edition were
executed by the firm of J. T. Bowen. (EAP)
    ___Another Copy. Edinburgh, John Grant, 1933. Vol.
I: lxii, 442pp. Vol. II: 458pp. Vol. III: xvi, 355pp.
123 full-page pls in color, 2 photogravure portraits, 2
color maps, blue gilt cloth covers, edited by F. W. Hodge.
$475.00
    ___Another Copy. Same. Ex-library. $400.00
    ___Another Copy. Same. $275.00
    ___Another Copy. Totowa, NJ, 1972. Reprint of 1933
ed. pp442, 458, 355, 2 folding maps, 122 color pls, d.j.
$150.00

M62. McKENNEY (Thomas L.). Memoirs, Official and Personal;
With Sketches of Travels Among the Northern and Southern Indians; Embracing a War Excursion, and Descriptions
of Scenes Along the Western Borders. (2 Volumes).
ppviii, 17-340; vi, 9-136, 13 pls, frontis portrait, facsimiles, some foxing, rebound in half-leather, contains the
hand-colored frontis to Vol. 2, of Pocahontas, which is
frequently missing, most lithographs by the firm of P. S.
Duvall. New York, Paine and Burgess, 1846. $200.00
    ___Another Copy. Same. All pls missing. $50.00

M63. McKENNEY (Thomas L.). Sketches of a Tour to the Lakes,
of the Character and Customs of the Chippeway Indians,
and of the Incidents Connected with the Treaty of Fon Du
Lac. also: A Vocabulary of the Lagic, or Chippeway
Language. 494pp, plus 27 lithographed or engraved pls,
original linen backed bds, cloth slipcase. Baltimore, 1827.
$450.00
    Howes: M-132. Sabin: 43407. Classic work by the

noted Indian Commissioner, describing his travels among the Chippewa in 1826.

___Another Copy. Minneapolis, 1959, d.j. $20.00

___Another Copy. Barre, Mass., Imprint Society, 1972. 414pp, i, 29 pls, some colored, quarter morocco, boxed, limited edition. Reprint of 1827 ed. $40.00

___Another Copy. Same. $35.00

M64. McKENZIE (Parker). (Monograph of School of American Research, No. 12, Santa Fe, 1948) Popular Account of the Kiowa Indian Language. 21pp, 4to, wrappers, limited to 500 copies. $10.00

M65. McKEOWN (Martha P.). Linda's Indian Home. 79pp, text on even page, photograph on opposing page, pictorial endpapers, 21x21.5cm, juvenile picture story of Indians at Celilo Falls on Columbia River, photographic illus are by Archie McKeown. Portland, 1956 (1st ed.), d.j.

    $15.00

M66. McKERN (W. C.). (Milwaukee Public Museum Bulletin, Vol. III, No. 4, 1930) The Kletzien and Nitschke Mound Groups. 56pp, 24pp photographs, cloth. $40.00

M67. McKERN (W. C.). (Milwaukee Public Museum Bulletin Vol. III, No. 3, 1928) The Neale and McClaughry Mound Groups. 204pp, 31 figures, 23pp photographs, 3 maps, wrappers. $35.00

___Another Copy. Same. $20.00

M68. McKIMMIN (Dugald). The Maya. 37 pls or sketches, part colored, 4to, full calf, 34 leaves of thin boards on cloth hinges reproducing in facsimile the author's manuscript. Aberdeen, Scotland, n.d. (c.1963). $75.00

Apparently a subscription work, published in a very limited edition. Author's Prospectus: "Copan was one of the great cities of the Mayan civilization, whose story is told in a reconstruction by Dugald McKimmin based on the facts established by archaeologists and the author's personal interpretation of the monuments. The volume is illustrated in tone, line and colour by the author, with additional drawings by Elizabeth McKimmin. The illustrations are of three types (1) direct drawings of the monuments and relics; (2) reconstructions based on a study of Mayan paintings; and (3) purely personal drawings and paintings of the jungle and jungle life; the Mayan background." (CLR)

M69. McLAUGHLIN (James). My Friend the Indian. 404pp plus index, illus, frnt blank endpaper missing, else nice. About the Sioux. Howes: M-147. Dustin: 179. Luther High Spot: 87. Boston, 1910 (1st ed. but not 1st print.). $30.00

___Another Copy. Seattle, 1970. The Superior Edition of My Friend the Indian. Paintings by Daniel S. Buisson and the Three Missing Chapters, with a Preface and Epilogue by Rev. Louis F. Pfaller, OSB. xv, 126pp, illus

photographs, 4to, padded cloth, boxed. Reprint of 1910
ed. $25.00
___Another Copy. Same. $15.00
___Another Copy. Seattle, 1970, limited ed., xv, 126pp,
illus, lrg 8vo, index, puffy vinyl, slipcase. $15.00

M70. McLAUGHLIN (Mrs. Marie L.). Myths and Legends of the
Sioux. 200pp, stories related by older Sioux Indians to
author, whose husband was Indian Agent. Bismarck, 1916.
$85.00
___Another Copy. Same. $59.00

M71. McLEAN (John P.). (Western Reserve Historical Society
Tract 90, Cleveland, 1901) Archaeological Collection of
the Western Reserve Historical Society. pp190-272, 25
pls, printed wrappers. $15.00

M72. McLEAN (John). Notes of a Twenty-Five Years' Service in
the Hudson's Bay Territory (2 Volumes). pp308; 328,
8vo, original cloth. London, R. Bentley, 1849. $225.00
Sabin: 43514. Field: 996. Narrative of travel among
the Indians of Canada, with extensive observations on their
customs, dress, hunting methods, costumes and languages.
(RMW)

M73. MacLEAN (J. P.). The Mound Builders; Being an Account
of a Remarkable People that Once Inhabited the Valleys of
the Ohio and Mississippi, Together with an Investigation
into the Archaeology of Butler County, Ohio. 233pp,
64 illus, 1 fold-out map, cloth (worn), spine and hinge
repaired. Cincinnati, 1879. $95.00
___Another Copy. Same. $85.00

M74. MacLEAN Y ESTENOS (Roberto). Presencia del Indio en
America. 275pp, wrappers. Mexico, 1958. $20.00

M75. McLENDON (S.). (University of California Archaeological
Research Facility, Contributions, No. 37, Berkeley, 1977)
Ethnographic and Historical Sketch of the Eastern Pomo
and Their Neighbors, The Southeastern Pomo. 64pp, 20
full-page photographs from archival sources, 1 map,
wrappers. $18.00

McLEOD (B. H.). See also BAE Bulletin No. 166.

M76. MacLEOD (W. C.). The American Indian Frontier. xxiii,
598pp, 13 maps, cloth. New York, 1928. $30.00

M77. McLOUGHLIN (Anthony). Palenque and the Maya Gems of
Puuc. 63pp, illus. New York, 1976. $15.00

M78. McLUHAN (T. C.). Touch the Earth; A Self Portrait of
Indian Existence. Illus with photographs, notes, statements and writings by North American Indians recounting
the nature and fate of the Indian way of life. New York,
1971 (1st ed.). $20.00
___Another Copy. Same. 185pp, d.j. $10.00

M79. McMILLAN (Donald B.). Etah and Beyond, or Life Within
Twelve Degrees of the Pole. xix, 287pp, photographs,
maps, index. Aboard the Bowdoin, along Labrador Coast,
to Etah on the Northwest coast of Greenland, much on
Eskimos. Boston, 1927, (1st ed.). $25.00

M80. McMILLAN (Donald B.). Four Years in the White North. xx, 426pp, photographic pls, maps, index. Considerable information on Etah Eskimos and their Arctic environment. New York and London, 1918 (1st ed.). $75.00
___Another Copy. Boston & New York, 1925, New, Revised Ed. xxii, 428pp, photographs, maps, map endpapers, index. $15.00

M81. McNAIR (P. L.) and HOOVER (A. L.). (British Columbia Provincial Museum, Special Publication No. 7, 1984) The Magic Leaves, a History of Argillite Carving. 211pp, 252 color photographs, 1 drawing, 1 map, cloth. $44.00
___Another Copy. Same. Soft cvr. $33.00
Primarily a catalogue of the argillite carving collection of the British Columbia Provincial Museum, this publication examines this collection--perhaps the most representative collection extant--and identifies sixteen types of argillite carvings that fit into a recognized chronological sequence. A detailed history of argillite carving is presented, as is a classification of each piece in the collection and the identity of the carver. Excellent photographs of every carving in the collection. (EAP)

M82. MacNEISH (R. S.). (Transactions of the American Philosophical Society, New Series, Vol. 44, Part 5, 1954) An Early Archaeological Site Near Panuco, Vera Cruz. pp539-641, 36 figures, inscribed by author. $45.00

M83. MacNEISH (R. S.). (National Museum of Canada, Contributions to Anthropology, Bulletin No. 162, Ottawa, 1957) The Callison Site in the Light of Archaeological Survey of SW Yukon. 52pp of 131pp, photographs, map, bound in later cloth. $12.00

M84. MacNEISH (R. S.) et al. The Central Peruvian Prehistoric Interaction Sphere. xii, 97pp, 8 figures, 3 tables. Andover, 1975. $15.00

M85. MacNEISH (R. S.). First Annual Report of the Tehuacan Archaeological-Botanical Project. 32pp, 15 figures. Peabody Foundation for Archaeology, Andover, 1961. $12.00

M86. MacNEISH (R. S.). (National Museum of Canada, Bulletin 157, Ottawa, 1958) An Introduction to the Archaeology of Southeast Manitoba. v, 184pp, 20pp photographs, 24 figures, 8 tables. $14.00

M87. MacNEISH (R. S.). (National Museum of Canada, Bulletin 124, Ottawa, 1952) Iroquois Pottery Types, A Technique for the Study of Iroquois Prehistory. 165pp, 32pp of photographs, 23 figures. $29.00

M88. MacNEISH (R. S.). (Transactions of the American Philosophical Society, New Series, Vol. 48, Part 6, 1958) Preliminary Archaeological Investigations in the Sierra de Tamaulivas, Mexico. 210pp, 48 figures, many full-page. $60.00

M89. MacNEISH (R. S.). Second Annual Report of the Tehuacan Archaeological-Botanical Project. 42pp, 16 figures, Peabody Foundation for Archaeology, Andover, 1962. $12.00

M90. McNELEY (James Kale). Holy Wind in Navajo Philosophy.
109pp plus index, appendix of Navajo texts, references.
A major study in the field of ethno-psychology and which
contradicts some previous concepts regarding Navajo belief.
Tucson, 1981 (1st ed.), d.j. $25.00

M91. McNICHOLS (Charles). Crazy Weather. 195pp. New York,
1944, d.j. $10.00
    Powell: 77: "...packed with the lore and legends of
the once fierce Mojaves who thought nothing of whipping
their Apache neighbors...."

M92. McNICKLE (D'Arcy). Indian Man: A Life of Oliver LaFarge.
xiii, 242pp, index. University of Indiana Press, 1971
(1st ed.), d.j. $12.00

M93. McNICKLE (D'Arcy). They Came Here First. The Epic of
the American Indian. 318pp plus index, illus, source notes.
Philadelphia, 1949 (1st ed.), d.j. $15.00
    ___Another Copy. New York, 1975, 307pp. $10.00

M94. McNICOL (Donald M.). The Amerindians from Acuera to
Sitting Bull, from Donnacona to Big Bear. 341pp, bibliography, index, cloth. New York, 1937 (1st ed.),
d.j. $20.00
    ___Another Copy. Same. $15.00

M95. McNITT (Frank). The Indian Traders. xiv, 393pp, color
photograph, 24pp b/w photographs, cloth. $50.00
    ___Another Copy. Same. $35.00
    ___Another Copy. Norman, 1963 (2nd print.). $44.00
    ___Another Copy. Norman, 1972 (3rd print.). $20.00

M96. McNITT (Frank). Navajo Wars. 477pp, military campaigns,
slave raids, reprisals. University of New Mexico, 1972
(1st ed.). $35.00
    ___Another Copy. Same. $30.00

M97. McNITT (Frank). Richard Wetherill: Anasazi. 362pp,
maps and drawings by author, photographs, decorative
cloth. Albuquerque, 1957 (1st ed.). $30.00
    Adams Herd: 1418. Best biography of Wetherill, who
discovered the ruins at Mesa Verde and explored Pueblo
Bonito at Chaco Canyon. He was also an Indian trader
in the Four Corners area. (TE)
    ___Another Copy. Albuquerque, 1966, d.j. 370pp,
photographs. $25.00

M98. McREYNOLDS (Edwin C.). The Seminoles. 375pp plus
index, illus, bibliography, maps. First really extensive
history of this tribe. Norman, 1957 (1st print.), d.j.
                                                         $20.00
    ___Another Copy. Same. $15.00
    ___Another Copy. Norman, 1967, d.j. $20.00

M99. McTAGGART (Fred). Wolf That I Am: In Search of the
Red Earth People. 195pp, encounters with present day
Mesquakie Indians (Iowa River). Boston, 1976, (1st
ed.), d.j. $15.00
    ___Another Copy. Same. $12.00

M100. McVEY (E. E.). The Crow Scout Who Killed Custer.
32pp, illus, wrappers. Conjecture that his guide, Mitch
Bouyer, led Custer into a trap. Billings, 1952, (1st
ed.). $15.00

M101. McWHORTER (Lucullus V.). The Crime against the Yakima. 56pp, photographs. Concerning the wrongs done
to the Yakimas. Smith: 6474. No. Yakima, WA, 1913
(1st ed.). $50.00
____Another Copy. Same. $45.00

M102. McWHORTER (L. V.). Hear Me, My Chiefs! Nez Perce
History and Legend. xxiv, 640pp, photographs, maps,
map endpapers, bibliography, index. Tribal wars, coming of the whites, etc. Caldwell, 1952 (1st ed.), d.j.
                                                                 $175.00
____Another Copy. Caldwell, 1983, d.j. $25.00

M103. McWHORTER (Lucullus V.). Tragedy of the Wahk-shum.
Prelude to The Yakima Indian War, 1855-56. 44pp,
errata slip, map, photographs, wrappers, limited to 750
copies, signed by author, prospectus laid in. Includes
eyewitness account of the killing of Indian Agent Andrew
J. Bolon. Smith: 6476. Yakima, 1937. $75.00
____Another Copy. Fairfield, WA, 1968. Tragedy of the
Wahk-Shum: The Death of Andrew J. Bolon, Indian Agent
to the Yakima Nation. 44pp, frontis, 10 full-page pls,
map, limited to 476 copies, green cloth. $25.00

M104. McWHORTER (Lucullus). Yellow Wolf: His Own Story.
324pp, frontis, 24pp photographs, endpaper maps, bibliography, index. Caldwell, 1940 (1st ed.). $175.00
____Another Copy. Caldwell, 1948 (2d print.). 328pp,
frontis, 32pp photographs, d.j. $125.00
____Another Copy. Same. $85.00
____Another Copy. Same. $65.00
____Another Copy. Caldwell, 1983. 328pp, illus, index,
bibliography, d.j. $20.00

M105. MADEIRA (Percy C.). (Museum Journal, Vol. 22, No. 2,
Philadelphia, 1931) An Aerial Expedition to Central Amer-
ica. 153pp, 33 pls, includes Coba, Tuluum, Uxmal,
Chichen-Itza, Yachilan, Yaxha, wrappers. $30.00

MADISON (Lee G.). See BAE Bulletin No. 189.

M106. MADSEN (Brigham D.). The Bannock of Idaho. 382pp,
illus, color frontis, map endpapers, bibliography, index.
Branch of North Paiutes and the history of their struggle
to preserve their tribal entity. Caldwell, 1958 (1st ed.),
d.j. $70.00
____Another Copy. Same. $50.00
____Another Copy. Same. $35.00
____Another Copy. Same. $30.00

M107. MADSEN (Brigham D.). The Northern Shoshoni. 259pp,
4to, illus, index, maps, bibliography. Caldwell, 1980
(1st ed.), d.j. $30.00
____Another Copy. Same. $25.00
____Another Copy. Same. $25.00

M108. MAGOFFIN (R. V. D.) and DAVIS (Emily C.). The Romance of Archaeology. 339pp plus index, illus. New York, 1929. $10.00

M109. MAHON (John K.). History of the Second Seminole War 1835-42. 371pp plus index, photographs, map, lrg folding map inside back cvr, notes, bibliography. Gainesville, FL, 1980 (1st print.), d.j. $20.00

M110. MAHOOD (R. I.) (Editor). Photographer of the Southwest, Adam Clark Vroman, 1856-1916. 127pp, 91 full-page photographs, 12 smaller photographs, cloth. Ward Richie Press, 1961. $125.00

M111. MAILS (Thomas E.). Dog Soldiers, Bear Men and Buffalo Women: A Study of Societies and Cults of the Plains Indians. Color frontis, 384pp, illus by author, 4to. New Jersey, 1973, d.j. $75.00
____Another Copy. New York, 1973. $40.00

M112. MAILS (Thomas E.). Fools Crow. Assisted by Dallas Chief Eagle. Illustrated by the author. 286pp, illus, notes, bibliography, index, appendix, a unique account of the ancient tribal traditions, cherished and preserved despite the efforts of the white society to extinguish them. Garden City, 1979 (1st ed.). $22.00
____Another Copy. Same. $12.00

M113. MAILS (Thomas E.). The Mystic Warriors of the Plains. 618pp, 4to, illus, index, bibliography, maps. New York, 1972, d.j. $50.00
    Large thick volume, illustrated with 1,000 detailed drawings and 32 full-page color plates. Describes the life styles of the plains Indians at the height of their culture, when they were still relatively untouched by the White man's influence. Day-by-day activities, social customs, Governments, training of the young, role of the warrior, etc. Large section devoted to their religion, their supernatural beliefs, practice of medicine and ceremonial practices.
____Another Copy. Same. $30.00

M114. MAILS (Thomas E.). The People Called Apache. 447pp, illus, index, bibliography, maps, illus with 16 full-color reproductions of author's paintings, 4to, 300 photographs and drawings. Englewood Cliffs, 1974 (1st ed.), d.j. $85.00
____Another Copy. Same. Cloth. $50.00
____Another Copy. Same. 1st trade ed. $45.00
____Another Copy. Same. New York, 1974, 1981. $28.00

M115. MAILS (T. E.). Plains Indians, Dog Soldiers, Bear Men and Buffalo Soldiers. 384pp, approx. 250 photographs and drawings, cloth. New York, 1973. $30.00

M116. MAILS (T. E.). The Pueblo Children of the Earth Mother (2 Volumes) Vol. I: The Heritage, Culture, Crafts and Traditions of the Anasazi Ancestors of the Pueblo Indians.

xxi, 522pp, 19 color pls, over 500 individual drawings.
Vol. II: The Culture, Crafts and Ceremonials of the
Pueblo Indians of Yesterday and Today. x, 534pp, 25
color pls, over 500 individual drawings, small folio,
cloth. New York, 1983. $165.00

M117. MAILS (T. E.). Sundancing at Rosebud and Pine Ridge.
395pp, photographs, drawings by author (some in color).
Detailed work with material from Eagle Feather and some
earlier anthropologists. Sioux Falls, SD, 1978 (1st ed.)
d.j. $35.00
___Another Copy. Same. $30.00

M118. MAKEMSON (Maud W.). The Book of the Jaguar Priest.
A Translation of the Book of Chilam Balam of Tizimin,
with Commentary. 238pp, bibliography, index. Vassar
College, New York, 1951, d.j. $25.00
___Another Copy. Same. $15.00

M119. MALAURIE (Jean). The Last Kings of Thule: A Year
Among the Polar Eskimos of Greenland. 295pp, illus.
London, 1956. $20.00

M120. MALER (Teobert). (Peabody Museum Memoirs, Vol. 4,
No. 2, Cambridge, 1908) Explorations in the Department
of Peten, Guatemala and Adjacent Regions, Topoxte,
Naranjo, Yaxha, Benque Viejo. pp55-127, 30 pls which
are photogravures of stellae, 4to, wrappers. $125.00

M121. MALER (Teobert). (Peabody Museum Memoirs, Vol. II,
No. 1, 1901, New York, 1970 reprint) Researches in the
Central Portion of the Usumatsintla Valley, 1898-1900.
75pp, 33 pls, folding map. $40.00

M122. MALER (Teobert). (Peabody Museum Memoirs, Vol. II,
No. 2, 1901, New York 1970 reprint) Researches in the
Central Portion of the Usumatsintla Valley, 1898-1900.
216pp, 96 pls. $65.00

M123. MALIN (Edward). A World of Faces: Masks of the Northwest Coast Indians. b/w and color illus, presentation
copy. Portland, 1978. (1st ed.). $35.00
___Another Copy. Same. $15.00

M124. MALLERY (Garrick). (Smithsonian Bureau of American
Ethnology, Introductions, Washington, 1880) Introduction
to the Study of Sign Language Among the North American
Indians as Illustrating the Gesture Speech of Mankind.
iv, 72pp, 33 unnumbered figures, bound in blue cloth.
                                                     $75.00

M125. MALLET (Thierry). Glimpses of the Barren Lands.
142pp, illus with drawings, cloth and paper over bds.
Northern Indians and Eskimos and Chipewa Indians.
New York, 1930 (1st ed.). $10.00

M126. MALLOUF (R. F.) and BASKIN (B. J.). (Texas Historical
Commission Survey Reports, No. 19, Austin, 1976, 1st
ed.) Archaeological Investigation Tehuacana Creek Watershed Hill and McLennan Counties, Texas. 58pp, illus,
maps, bibliography, lrg 8vo, wrappers. $12.00

M127. MALLOUF (R. J.) and TUNNELL (C.). (Texas Historical
Commission Survey Reports, No. 22, Austin, 1977, 1st
ed.) Archaeological Reconnaissance Lower Canyons of
the Rio Grande. 71pp, illus, maps, bibliography, lrg
8vo, wrappers. $12.00

M128. MALLOUF (R. J.) et al. (Texas Historical Survey Committee Archaeological Report 11, Austin, 1973) An Assessment of the Cultural Resources of Palmetto Beal Reservoir, Jackson County, Texas. 218pp, photographs,
drawings, maps, bibliography, wrappers.' $10.00

M129. MALLOUF (R. J.). (Texas Historical Commission Survey
Reports No. 18, Austin, 1976, 1st ed.) Investigations of
Proposed Big Pine Lake, 1974-5, Lamar and Red River
Counties, Texas. 557pp, illus, maps, bibliography, lrg
8vo, wrappers. $20.00

M130. MALLOUF (R. J.). (Texas Historical Commission Survey
Reports No. 33, Austin, 1981, 1st ed.) Plow Damage,
Chert Artifacts. 62pp, illus, plates, maps, bibliography,
lrg 8vo, wrappers. $10.00

M131. MALLOUF (R.) and ZAVALETA (A.). (Texas Historical
Commission Special Reports, No. 25, Austin, 1979, 1st
ed.) Unland Site. 32pp, plus maps and pls, bibliography,
lrg 8vo, wrappers. $10.00

M132. MALONE (Henry Thompson). Cherokees of the Old South.
A People in Transition. 8 illus, 2 maps, index, bibliography, notes, cloth. University of Georgia Press, Athens,
1956, d.j. $20.00

M133. MALOTKI (Ekkehart) and LOMATUWAY'MA (Michael).
(American Tribal Religions, Vol. 9, Lincoln, 1984, 1st
ed.) Hopi Coyote Tales. Istutuwutsi. 343pp, drawings
by Anne-Marie Malotki, alternating pages of Hopi and
English text, wrappers. $13.00

MALOUF (Carling). See also BAE Bulletin No. 185.

M134. MANDELBAUM (David). (American Museum of Natural History, Anthropological Papers, Vol. XXXVII, Part II, New
York, 1940) The Plains Cree. 150pp, wrappers. $25.00

M135. MANFRED (Frederick). The Manly-Hearted Woman. 185pp,
novel of Yankton Dakota Indian Legend and Spiritual
belief. New York, 1975 (1st ed.), d.j. $12.00

M136. MANGELSDORF (P. C.) and REEVES (R.). (Texas Agricultural Experiment Station Bulletin 574, 1939) The
Origin of Indian Corn and its Relatives. 315pp, 95 illus,
pp273-302 deal with corn and its relation to the culture
and civilization of the Americas, wrappers. $25.00
_____Another Copy. Same. $17.00

M137. MANRING (B. F.). The Conquest of the Coeur D'Alenes,
Spokanes and Palouses. The Expeditions of Colonels
E. J. Steptoe and George Wright Against the Northern
Indians in 1858. 280pp, photographic illus, biographical
sketches, pictorial cvr. Spokane, 1912. $85.00
_____Another Copy. Same. $75.00

M138. MANYPENNY (George W.). Our Indian Wards. 26pp,
436pp, quarto, cloth, hinges started. Cincinnati,
1880. $125.00
Manypenny was the Commissioner of Indian Affairs and
Chairman of the Sioux Commission, and although the early
chapters of this work are devoted to congress with the
Indians in the Northeast, the majority of the work is a
history of Indian relations in the West, the Camp Grant
massacre, Harney's campaign, the operations of Dun and
Dowling, Custer, Sherman, Sheridan and the Comanche
removal to Wichita agency, etc. Howes: M-268.

M139. MARANDA (Lynn). (National Museum of Canada, Mercury
Series, Ethnology No. 93, n.p., 1984, 1st ed.) Coast
Salish Gambling Games. xi, 143pp, photographs, figures,
bibliography, lrg 8vo, wrappers. Detailed study of history and customs of games, game structure and attending
spirit power affiliations. $15.00

M140. MARCANO (G.). (Instituto Nacional de Antropologia e
Historia, Caracas, 1971) Etnografia Precolombiana de
Venezuela. 366pp, 82 figures, 6 maps. $30.00

M141. MARCANO (S. G.). Ethnographie Precolombienne du
Venezuela, Valles d'Aragua et de Caracas. 91pp of text
and 19pp of illus containing 57 drawings, fold-out map,
frnt wrapper chipped, rear wrapper missing, spine repaired. Paris, A. Hennuyer, 1889. $55.00

M142. MARCOY (Paul). A Journey Across South America from
the Pacific Ocean to the Atlantic Ocean (2 Volumes).
Vol. I: Travels in; Ilay, Arequipa, Lampa, Cuzco,
Echarati, Chulutuqui, Tunkini, Paruitcha, Tumbuyu.
Vol. II: Travels in; Sarayacu, Tierra Blanca, Nauta,
Tabatinga, Santa Maria de Belen. Extensive travels
along the Amazon and in Peru, recording scenes with
native tribes. 600 wood engravings, 12 color maps,
original edition published in Paris, 1869, London edition
of 1875 had 525 engravings, the original Paris edition
had 626 engravings, this edition contains more engravings
than the 1875 edition calls for. Folio, occasional foxing,
rebound in 3/4 leather with five raised bands. London,
1874. $450.00
____Another Copy. New York, Scribner, 1875. Vol. I:
524pp. Vol. II: 496pp, illus with 525 wood engravings
drawn by E. Riou and 10 maps from drawings by the
author, 4to (9" x 12"), edge wr, inner hinges started.
                                                       $250.00
____Another Copy. Same. original green gilt stamped
cloth, a.e.g. $135.00

M143. MARCUS (Joyce). Emblem and State in the Classic Maya
Lowlands. 302pp, illus, 4to. Washington, 1976. $20.00

M144. MARCY (Randolph B.). Explorations of the Red River of
Louisiana in the Year 1852. 16pp, 320pp, 65 pls, 12 of
which are tinted, 2 lrg maps in separate folder, original

black cloth. House of Representatives Document 65, Washington, Nicholson, 1854. $350.00

Howes: M-276. Field: 1006. Report contains authentic information regarding the peculiar customs of the Indians of the Southern Plains, their mode of warfare, the construction of their dwellings and villages. (WS)

___Another Copy. Washington, Tucker, 1854, (1st ed., 2d issue). $250.00

M145. MARCY (Col. R. B.). Thirty Years of Army Life on the Border Comprising Descriptions of the Indian Nomads.... 442pp, pls, light cover wear. New York, 1866 (1st ed.). $190.00

M146. MARDOCK (Robert Winston). The Reformers and the American Indian. 245pp, index, bibliography. Columbia, 1971 (1st ed.). $15.00

M147. MARGARET (Helene). Father DeSmet. 356pp. Milwaukee, 1940 (1st ed.). $45.00

M148. MARISCAL (F. E.). (Contribution de Mexico al XXIII Congreso Americanistas, Mexico City, 1928) Estudio Arquitectonico de las Ruinas Mayas Yucatan y Canpeche. 109pp, 73 photographs, 16pp of site plans of Mayan ruins, bds, decorated endpapers, folio (16" x 12").

M149. MARKHAM (Clements R.). A History of Peru. 556pp, frontis, illus, 5 maps, one of the maps is folding and in color, 3/4 leather with marbled bds. Chicago, 1892, (1st ed.). $85.00

___Another Copy. Same. $65.00

M150. MARKHAM (Clements R.). Travels in Peru and India While Superintending the Collection of Chincona Plants and Seeds in South America. xviii, 572pp, folding map, other maps and pls, half leather, marbled bds. London, 1862 (1st ed.). $150.00

Sabin: 44616. "The wonderful story of Tupac Amaru, the last of the Incas, his insurrection, defeat and horrible execution is here related at length." (RMW)

M151. MARMONTEL (Jean Francois). Les Incas: or, the Destruction of the Empire of Peru (2 Volumes). Vol. 1: x, xxvi, 263pp. Vol. 2: iv, 296pp. 12mo, original calf, one cvr detached. London, J. Nourse, P. Elmsly, E. Lyde, 1777 (1st ed. in English). $75.00

Sabin: 44653. detailed account, including the death of the Inca royal family, with conversations recorded.

___Another Copy. London, 1808. Les Incas, ou la Destruction l'Empire du Perou. 416pp, rebound. $60.00

___Another Copy. Paris, Ledentu, 1817 (2 Volumes), Vol. 1: xxxiv, 288pp. Vol. 2: 322pp, 12mo, calf, 1 backstrip loose. $65.00

MARQUEZ MIRANDA (Fernando). See BAE Bulletin No. 143.

M152. MARQUEZ (Pietro). Due Antichi Monumenti di Architectura Messicana. iv, 47pp, engraved title, 4 folding engraved pls, fine painting on hand made paper, 1/2 leather and

marbled bds, new endpapers, some staining in upper margins. Rome, Salmoni, 1804. $550.00
 Early treatise on the Temple De Tajin (Totonac culture in Vera Cruz), and the Xochicalco Pyramid in Morelos.

M153. MARQUINA (I.). (Instituto Nacional de Antropologia e Historia, Memorias I, Mexico City, 1951) Arquitectura Prehispanica. 988pp, 476 photographs, 291 drawings, 33 figures, inscribed by author, cloth. $225.00
 ___Another Copy. Mexico City, 1964 (2d ed.) 1,055pp, 291 pls (10 in color), 476 photographs, appendix, 27 pls, 4to. $200.00
 ___Another Copy. Same. $150.00

M154. MARQUINA (I.). (Contribucion de Mexico al XXIII Congreso de Americanistas, Mexico City, 1928) Estudio Arquitectonico Comparativo de los Monumentos Arqueologicos de Mexico. 82pp of text containing 51 figures, plus 109 leaves of color and b/w illus of artifacts and structures and 10 fold-out color and b/w leaves, folio (16" x 12") half leather. $195.00
 ___Another Copy. Same. $250.00

M155. MARQUIS (Arnold). A Guide to America's Indians: Ceremonials, Reservations and Museums. 267pp, 4to, illus, maps, bibliography, index. Norman, 1974, (1st ed.), d.j. $30.00
 ___Another Copy. Norman, 1975, d.j. $20.00

M156. MARQUIS (Thomas B.). Memories of a White Crow Indian. 356pp, illus. New York, 1928 (1st ed.). $90.00
 ___Another Copy. Same. $65.00

M157. MARQUIS (Thomas B.). (Custer Battle Museum, Series of Custer Pamphlets, Harding, MO, 1934) Rain-In-The-Face and Curly, the Crow. 8pp, map, wrappers. Debunks popular speculation about these Indians. $20.00

M158. MARQUIS (Thomas B.). (Custer Battle Museum, Series of Custer Pamphlets, Harding, MO, 1933) She Watched Custer's Last Battle. 8pp, wrappers. The observations of Kate Bighead. $20.00

M159. MARQUIS (Thomas B.). (Custer Battle Museum, Series of Custer Pamphlets, Harding, MO, 1934) Sitting Bull and Gall, the Warrior. 8pp, wrappers. $10.00

M160. MARQUIS (Thomas B.). (Custer Battle Museum, Series of Custer Pamphlets, Harding, MO, 1933) Sketch Story of the Custer Battle: A Clashing of Red and Blue. 8pp, wrappers. $20.00

M161. MARQUIS (Thomas B.). (Custer Battle Museum, Series of Custer Pamphlets, Harding, MO, 1935) Two Days After the Custer Battle, the Scene There as Viewed by William H. White, a Soldier with Gibbon in 1876. 8pp, wrappers. $20.00

M162. MARQUIS (Thomas B.). A Warrior Who Fought Custer. 384pp, maps. Midwest Co., Minnesota, 1931 (1st ed., 1st state). $100.00

M163. MARQUIS (Thomas B.). (Custer Battle Museum, Series of
Custer Pamphlets, Harding, MO, 1933) Which Indian
Killed Custer? Custer Soldiers Not Buried. 10pp,
wrappers. $20.00

M164. MARRIOTT (Alice) and RACHLIN (C. K.). American Indian Mythology. 211pp, illus, cloth. New York, 1968,
d.j. $12.00
___Another Copy. Same. $10.00

M165. MARRIOTT (Alice). The Black Stone Knife. 180pp, 3pp,
illustrated by Harvey Weiss, author's signed presentation.
Kiowa history and legend. New York, 1957, (1st ed.),
d.j. $15.00

M166. MARRIOTT (Alice) and RACHLIN (C. K.). Dance Around
the Sun. The Life of Mary Little Bear Inkanish:
Cheyenne. 229pp plus index, photographs. New York,
1977, (1st ed.), d.j. $12.00
___Another Copy. Same. $10.00

M167. MARRIOTT (Alice). Greener Fields: Experiences Among
The American Indians. 274pp, inscribed and signed by
author, cloth. New York, 1953, (1st ed.). $20.00
___Another Copy. Same. $12.00

M168. MARRIOTT (Alice). Indians on Horseback. 133pp plus
index, drawings by Margaret Lefranc, map, bibliography,
Plains Indians before the reservation period. New York,
1948, (1st ed.), d.j. $35.00

M169. MARRIOTT (Alice). Maria: The Potter of San Ildefonso.
315pp, 25 illus, cloth. Norman, 1948. $30.00
___Another Copy. Same. $21.00
___Another Copy. Norman, 1954, inscribed by Maria.
$40.00
___Another Copy. Norman, 1970, 294pp, bibliography,
d.j. $15.00

M170. MARRIOTT (Alice) and RACHLIN (C. K.). Peyote. 104pp
plus index, drawings, laid in is letter from the publisher
submitting this book for Western Writers of America 1971
award, the origin and growth of the Peyote religion among
the American Indian. New York, 1971 (1st ed.), d.j.
$20.00

M171. MARRIOTT (Alice). The Ten Grandmothers. xiv, 306pp,
cloth. Norman, 1945 (1st ed.). $25.00
Dobie: p.35. Major SW: p.95. Campbell: p.180:
"Kiowa Indian history presented in terms of the recollec-
tions of a kiowa man and woman. Dramatic and very hu-
man. Admirably written and strictly from the Indian
point of view." (TE)
___Another Copy. Same. $25.00
___Another Copy. Same. $20.00
___Another Copy. 8th print. $10.00

M172. MARRIOTT (Alice). These Are The People: Some Notes
On The Southwestern Indians. 67pp plus 10 pls, limited
to 1000 copies, signed by the author, designed by Merle

Armitage, stiff wrappers. Santa Fe, 1949 (1st ed.),
d.j. $50.00
   Kobler: p.43. Marks: p.75. Powell SW Century:
66. Powell: "There is no better introduction and guide
to the subject than this glowing little volume, beautifully
conceived and written, and designed by Merle Armitage."
(TE)

M173. MARSH (Charles S.). The Utes of Colorado. People of
the Shining Mountain. 186pp plus index, photographs,
drawings, maps, bibliography, Ute history, legends,
material culture. Boulder, 1982 (1st ed.), d.j. $20.00

M174. MARSH (Winifred Petchey). People of the Willow. The
Padimuit Tribe of the Caribou Eskimo. 63pp, b/w and
color illus, map, oblong. Toronto, 1976 (1st ed.), d.j.
                                                                  $15.00

M175. MARSHALL (Mr. Chief Justice John). Opinion of the
Supreme Court of the United States, at January Term,
1832 ... In the Case of Samuel A. Worcester ... Versus
the State of Georgia. 39pp, 8vo, rebound in cloth.
Washington, 1832. $150.00
   Howes: M-318. Field: 1017. Very important docu-
ment, reviewing the history of American Indian treaties.
(RMW)

M176. MARSHALL (Robert). Arctic Village. 399pp, illus. New
York, 1933. $20.00

M177. MARTIN (Fran.). Raven-Who-Sets-Things-Right; Indian
Tales of the Northwest Coast. 90pp, illus. New York,
1975, (1st ed. thus). $10.00

M178. MARTIN (George C.). (Southwest Texas Archaeological
Society, White Memorial Museum, Big Bend Blanket Maker
Papers, Bulletin, 3, San Antonio, 1933) Archaeological
Exploration of Shumla Caves. 92pp plus index, photo-
graphs, drawings, wrappers. $10.00

M179. MARTIN (Paul S.). (Field Museum of Natural History
Anthropology Memoirs, Vol. 5, Millwood, 1977, reprint
ed.) Anasazi Painted Pottery in Field Museum of Natural
History. 284pp, 4to, contains 125 full-page pls of Anasazi pottery, index, map. $30.00

M180. MARTIN (P. S.). (Fieldiana Anthropology Vol. 53, 1955)
Chapters in the Prehistory of Eastern Arizona, I. 244pp,
78 photographs, 21 tables. $24.00

M181. MARTIN (P. S.). (Fieldiana Anthropology Vol. 55, 1964)
Chapters in the Prehistory of Eastern Arizona, II.
261pp, 79 illus, 18 tables. $24.00

M182. MARTIN (P. S.). (Fieldiana Anthropology Vol. 57, 1967)
Chapters in the Prehistory of Eastern Arizona, III.
178pp, 107 figures. $24.00

M183. MARTIN (P. S.). (Fieldiana Anthropology Vol. 38, No.
1, Chicago, 1949) Cochise and Mogollon Sites, Pinelawn
Valley, Western New Mexico. 232pp, 78 figures. $40.00

M184. MARTIN (P. S.). (Fieldiana Anthropology Vol. 51, No.

1, 1960) Excavations in the Upper Colorado Drainage, Eastern Arizona. 129pp, 61 photographs, tools, stones, awls, knives, sherds and pots. $19.00

M185. MARTIN (P. S.) et al. (Fieldiana Anthropology Vol. 46, Chicago, 1956) Higgins Flat Pueblo, Western New Mexico. 218pp, 85 photographs. $30.00

During 1953 the Field Museum Expedition excavated a portion of a large pueblo on Higgins Flat. Fourteen rooms were excavated and two of the plazas were trenched. Uncovered were hordes of artifacts--several hundred of which are pictured--including stone and clay animal effigies, bracelets, textile fragments, cut and carved shell ornaments, knives, axes, and some lovely intact bowls, a number of which are relatively scarce in this area. This out of print report of the excavation of this pueblo, occupied during the Tularosa Phase and probably abandoned about 1250 A.D., contains full details of the excavation and photographs of several hundred of the excavated artifacts. (EAP)

M186. MARTIN (Paul S.) et al. Indians Before Columbus. Frontis, 582pp, 122 illus. Chicago, 1948. $40.00

____Another Copy. Chicago, 1950. 582pp, 117 illus, includes North American Indians plus three chapters on the Eskimo. $35.00

____Another Copy. Chicago, 1967 (9th print.) Indians before Columbus. Twenty Thousand Years of North American History Revealed by Archaeology. 543pp plus index, extensive bibliography, illus map endpapers. $12.00

M187. MARTIN (P. S.) et al. (Fieldiana Anthropology Vol. 49, No. 1, Chicago, 1957) Late Mogollon Communities, Four Sites of the Tularosa Phase, Western New Mexico. 144pp, 56 photographs. $28.00

M188. MARTIN (P. S.). (Chicago Field Museum of Natural History. Vol. XXIII, Nos. 1, 2 and 3, 1936, 1938 and 1939) (3 Volumes). Lowry Ruin in Southwestern Colorado, and Archaeological Work in the Ackmen-Lowry Area, and Modified Basket Maker Sites, Ackmen-Lowry Area. 646pp, 250pp photographs of many hundreds of objects, numerous tables, charts, maps and drawings. $135.00

____Another Copy. Vol. 2 only. pp219-304, 4 figures, 5 maps, 67pp photographs. $47.00

____Another Copy. Vol. 3 only. pp305-499, 82 figures, 19 maps, 1 color pl. $47.00

M189. MARTIN (P. S.) et al. (Fieldiana Anthropology Vol. 52, Chicago, 1961) Mineral Creek Site and Hooper Ranch Pueblo, Eastern Arizona. 181pp, 95 photographs. $34.00

M190. MARTIN (P. S.) et al. (Fieldiana Anthropology Vol. 40, Chicago, 1952) Mogollon Cultural Continuity and Change. The Stratigraphic Analysis of Tularosa and Cordova Caves. 528pp, 179 photographs. $50.00

A major breakthrough in the study of Mogollon culture
--as well as Anasazi and Hohokam--was achieved in 1950
and 1951 by the excavation of Mogollon artifacts and
perishable material from the Tularosa and Cordova Caves
and testing them by stratigraphic sequence. This heavily
detailed report of these archaeological excavations (and
the excavations done by the same team from 1939-1950)
and the major contributions made to the study of these
cultures is meticulously delineated in this voluminous
study. Out of print for quite some time, this remains
one of the historically more important volumes on Southwest archaeology. (EAP)
_____Another Copy. Same. $55.00

M191. MARTIN (P. S.). (Colorado Magazine, Vol. VII, No. 1,
Denver, 1930) The 1929 Archaeological Expedition of the
State Historical Society.... 44pp, 9 pls, 3 figures,
wrappers. Pueblo Excavations. $18.00

M192. MARTIN (P. S.) et al. (Fieldiana Anthropology Vol. 38,
No. 3, 1950) Sites of the Reserve Phase, Pine Lawn
Valley, Western New Mexico. pp403-577, 77 figures and
full-page photographs. $38.00

M193. MARTIN (P. S.) et al. (Field Museum Anthropology Series,
Vol. 32, Nos. 1, 2 and 3, Chicago 1940, 1943 and 1947)
The Su Site, Excavations at a Mogollon Village, Western
New Mexico. Part 1: 97pp, 42pp photographs and drawings; Part 2: pp98-271, 49 photographs and drawings,
12 maps; Part 3: pp272-382, 42 photographs and drawings, 12 maps. $100.00
_____Another Copy. New York, 1968 reprint, all three
volumes bound into one. $70.00
_____Another Copy. Part 2 only, Chicago, 1943, pp101-
271, pls, maps, bibliography, index, wrappers. $45.00
_____Another Copy. Part 3 only, Chicago, 1947, pp282-
382, including index, photographs, drawings, maps,
bibliography, wrappers. $25.00

M194. MARTIN (P. S.) et al. (Fieldiana Anthropology Vol. 51,
No. 2, Chicago, 1960) Table Rock Pueblo Arizona.
170pp, 101 illus. $23.00

M195. MARTIN (P. S.) et al. (Fieldiana Anthropology Vol. 38,
No. 2, Chicago, 1950) Turkeyfoot Ridge Site, A Mogollon Village, Pine Lawn Valley, Western New Mexico.
pp235-396, 65 figures. $34.00

M196. MARTINEAU (LaVan) (DenDOOVEN, Gueneth Reed, Editor).
The Rocks Begin to Speak. 200pp plus index, photographs, drawings, bibliography, detailed attempt to explain Indian pictographs. Las Vegas, NV, 1976 (2d print.).
                                                      $10.00

M197. MARTINEZ (H. P.). Yucatan. An Annotated Bibliography
of Documents and Manuscripts on the Archaeology and
History of Yucatan in Archives and Libraries of Mexico,
North America and Europe. 133pp, text in Spanish,
cloth. Campaeche, 1943, Salisbury, 1980. $40.00

M198. MARWITT (J. P.). (University of Utah, Anthropology Papers, No. 95, 1970) Median Village and Fremont Culture Regional Variation. 193pp, 90 illus, 4to, wrappers.
$20.00

M199. MASAYESVA (V.) and YOUNGER (E.). Hopi Photographers/Hopi Images. 111pp, 6 full-page color photographs, 53pp b/w, 37 smaller b/w photographs, cloth. Tucson, 1983.
$38.00

M200. (MASCOUTENS). (Milwaukee Public Museum Bulletins, Vol. IV, Nos. 1, 2 and 3, 1924, 1926 and 1927) The Mascoutens of Prairie Potawatomi. Part 1: Social Life and Ceremonies, 262pp, 2 figures, 8pp photographs. Part 2: Notes on the Material Culture. 63pp, 12pp photographs. Part 3: Mythology and Folklore. 85pp, cloth.
$150.00
___Another Copy. Same. Each of the three parts is in its original wrapper, spine reinforced.
$120.00

M201. MASON (B. S.). The Book of Indian--Crafts and Costumes. 118pp, approx 85 photographs, 200 drawings, cloth. New York, 1946.
$19.00

M202. MASON (B. S.). Dances and Stories of the American Indian. 269pp, illus with photographs and drawings, cloth. New York, 1944, (1st ed.).
$25.00
___Another Copy. New York, 1944 (4th print.) d.j.
$25.00
___Another Copy. New York, 1944.
$17.00

M203. MASON (B. S.). Drums, Tom-toms and Rattles. Primitive Percussion Instruments for Modern Use. 206pp plus index, drawings. New York, 1938, (1st ed.), d.j.
$25.00
___Another Copy. Same.
$20.00

M204. MASON (Gregory). Silver Cities of Yucatan. Preface by Herbert Spinden. Illus, map. New York, Putnams, 1927.
$35.00

MASON (J. Alden). See also BAE Bulletin No. 143.

M205. MASON (J. Alden). (Field Museum Anthropological Series, Vol. XX, Nos. 1, 2 and 3, 1931, 1936 and 1939) Archaeology of Santa Marta, Columbia, the Tairona Culture. (3 Volumes). Part I: Report on Field Work. Part II: Objects of Shell, Bone and Metal. Part II, Section 2: Objects of Pottery. 418pp of text (some uncut), plus 272 pages of photographs and drawings, 2 fold-out maps.
$195.00
The definitive work on the Tairona culture, this three-volume set was published in the 1930s and has been out of print for several decades. The many thousands of objects that were excavated during the 1922-23 Marshall Field Archaeological Expedition to Columbia provide a remarkably complete picture of Tairona culture, and are the largest corpus of Tairona material unearthed. Several thousand of the objects are illustrated and discussed in each of the three volumes. (EAP)

M206. MASON (J. A.). (American Museum of Natural History, Anthropological Papers, Vol. 39, No. 3, 1945) Costa Rican Stonework, the Minor C. Keith Collection, pp193-317, 44 figures, 61pp of photographs. $85.00

M207. MASON (J. A.). (University of California Publication, in American Archaeology and Ethnology, Vol. 10, No. 4, Berkeley, 1912) The Ethnology of the Salinan Indians. 145pp, 17pp photographs. $69.00

M208. MASON (J. A.). (Museum Journal, University Museum, June, 1928) A Remarkable Stone Lamp from Alaska. pp170-194, 5 lrg photographs of the lamp, wrappers. $18.00

M209. MASON (J. A.). (Field Museum Anthropology Leaflet No. 16, 1924) Use of Tobacco in Mexico and South America. 15pp of text, plus 6pp of photographs of pipes, gourds, tubes, etc. $15.00

M210. MASON (John). A Brief History of the Pequot War. Written by Major John Mason, a Principal Actor Therein. xxii, 20pp, (Sabin's Reprint No. 7) half leather. New York, 1869. $25.00

M211. MASON (John A.). (Eastern New Mexico University Contributions in Anthropology, Vol. 4, No. 1, 1972) The Ceremonialism of the Tepecan. 44pp, illus, wrappers. $15.00

M212. MASON (Louis E.). Life and Times of Major John Mason of Connecticut, 1600-1672. 350pp, illus, cloth. New York, 1935, d.j. $15.00

M213. MASON (Otis T.). Aboriginal American Basketry. pp171-548, 248pls, several in color, extracted from Smithsonian Annual Report, 1902, U.S. National Museum, 1904. $175.00
___Another Copy. Same. $150.00
___Another Copy. Glorieta, 1970, pp171-528, containing 212 figures plus 248 b/w and color photographs, cloth. $79.00
___Another Copy. Same. $45.00
___Another Copy. Glorieta, 1972. $75.00

M214. MASON (Otis T.). (Smithsonian Institution, Annual Report for the Year Ending June 30, 1900) Aboriginal American Harpoons: A Study in Ethnic Distribution and Invention. pp189-304, 91 figures, 19pp drawings. Also included in this xvi, 737pp volume is "Anthropological Studies in California" by W. H. Holmes, and "A Collection of Hopi Pigments" by W. Hough. Cloth. $175.00
___Another Copy. Same. $60.00
___Another Copy. Seattle, 1974. 112pp, 111 illus of hundreds of harpoons and harpoon parts, wrappers. $18.00

M215. MASON (Otis T.). (U.S. National Museum Report for Year 1902, Washington, 1904) Aboriginal American Pottery. 548pp, 248 pls, several in color, original cloth. $150.00

M216. MASON (Otis T.). Aboriginal Skin Dressing; A Study
        Based on Material in the U.S. National Museum. pp553-
        589, plus 32 pls, new wrappers, from National Museum
        Report for 1889. $45.00

M217. MASON (Otis T.). An Account of Recent Progress in
        Anthropology (for the Years 1879 and 1880). 2pp, 49pp,
        printed wrappers, from Smithsonian Report for Year
        1880, No. 432, Washington, 1881. $20.00

M218. MASON (Otis T.). An Account of the Progress in Anth-
        ropology in the Year 1881. 27pp, bibliography, wrappers,
        ex-library, includes 17pp bibliography of the year's
        publications, Smithsonian Institution, Washington, 1883.
                                                            $10.00

M219. MASON (Otis T.). An Account of Recent Progress in
        Anthropology in the Year 1884. 2pp, 41pp, printed
        wrappers, from Smithsonian Report for Year 1884, Wash-
        ington, 1885. $15.00

M220. MASON (Otis T.). "Basket-work of the North American
        Aborigines." pp291-300 plus 64 pls, extracted from 1884
        Report of the U.S. National Museum, bound separately
        in cloth. Washington, 1885. $45.00

M221. MASON (Otis T.). (American Anthropology, January,
        1889) The Beginnings of the Carrying Industry. pp21-
        46, 8 figures, wrappers. $10.00

M222. MASON (Otis T.). Cradles of the American Aborigine.
        pp161-202 with 45 figures, bound separately in new
        cloth, extracted from the 1887 Report of the U.S. Na-
        tional Museum. Washington, 1887. $12.00
        ___Another Copy. Seattle, 1974 facsimile, 61pp, 45
        illus. $13.00

M223. MASON (Otis T.). (Government Printing Office, Part P,
        Bulletin of United States National Museum, No. 39,
        Washington, 1902) Directions for Collectors of American
        Basketry. 31pp, 44 figures, chipped wrappers, ex-
        library, includes list of basket-making tribes. $25.00

M224. MASON (Otis T.). Indian Basketry: Studies in a Textile
        Art Without Machinery (2 Volumes). pp254, 273, 248
        pls, 212 text figures, decorated cloth, enhanced version
        of U.S. National Museum Report, with tipped in color pls
        and fine paper. New York, Doubleday, 1904. $350.00
        ___Another Copy. London, 1905, 2 volumes, 518pp plus
        index, 248 pls in b/w and color, other illus, bibliography.
        The English edition is better from printing and binding
        standpoint. $250.00

M225. MASON (Otis T.). The Man's Knife Among the North
        American Indians: A Study in the Collections of the U.S.
        National Museum. pp725-748, from National Museum Re-
        port for 1897, 20 illus in folder. $20.00

M226. MASON (Otis T.). Pointed Bark Canoes of the Kutenai
        and Amur. 15pp of text containing 6 figures, plus 5pp
        of photographs and drawings, wrappers. Smithsonian,
        Washington, 1901. $22.00

M227. MASON (Otis T.). A Primitive Frame for Weaving Narrow
Fabrics. pp487-510 plus 10 pls, rebound in later cloth,
from the Smithsonian Institution Report of U.S. National
Museum for 1899. Washington, 1899. $12.00

M228. MASON (Otis T.). (Smithsonian Institution Annual Report
for the Year Ending June 30, 1894) Primitive Travel and
Transportation. and: A Study of Primitive Methods of
Drilling, by J. D. McGuire. xxvi, 1,030pp, extracts are
pp237-595, 260 illus, 25 full-page pls; and pp 623-757,
200 illus, cloth cvr. $67.00
___Another Copy. Primitive Travel and Transportation
only. $15.00

M229. MASON (Otis T.). The Ray Collection from Hupa Reservation. pp205-244 plus 3pp of drawings, 25 other pls
of drawings in text but not in pagination, bound separately in new cloth, from Part 1 of the 1886 Smithsonian
Annual Report, Washington, 1886. $12.00

M230. MASON (Otis T.). The Technic of Aboriginal American
Basketry. pp109-128, 32 figures, from American Anthropologist, Vol. 3, No. 1, 1901. $17.00

M231. MASON (Otis T.). Throwing Sticks in the National Mu-
seum. pp279-289, plus 17pp of pls and 17pp of descrip-
tions, wrappers, from Smithsonian Institute Annual Re-
port for the Year 1884, Part I. $22.00
___Another Copy. Same. $10.00
___Another Copy. Seattle, 1975 reprint. $10.00
___Another Copy. Also: Basket Work of the North
American Aborigines and A Study of Eskimo Bows in the
U.S. National Museum. 458pp, approx 75pp of pls, cloth.
Smithsonian Institution Annual Report for the Year 1884.
$90.00

M232. MASON (Otis T.). The Ulu, or, Woman's Knife of the
Eskimo. pp411-416, plus 20pp of pls and 20pp of descriptions, wrappers, offprint from Smithsonian Institution Annual Report for 1890, Part II. $20.00

M233. MASONS (R. J.). Great Lakes Archaeology. 449pp, 135
illus of over 500 artifacts, cloth. New York, 1981.
$60.00

M233a. (MASSACHUSETTS). Collections of the Massachusetts Historical Society for the Year 1792. iv, 288pp, original
calf, valuable collection of documents relating to the Indians and the settlement of New England. Field: 1020.
Boston, Munroe and Francis, 1806. $85.00

MASSEY (William C.). See also BAE Bulletin No. 151.

M234. MASSEY (William C.). (University of California Anthropology
Records, vol. 16, No. 8, Berkeley, 1961) A Burial Cave
in Baja California: The Palmer Collection, 1887. 25pp,
4to, illus, maps, bibliography, wrappers. $12.00
___Another Copy. Same. $10.00

M235. MASSON (Marcelle). A Bag of Bones: Legends of the
Wintu Indians of Northern California. 130pp, illus, map.
Healdsburg, 1966 (1st ed.). $17.00

M236. MATHENY (R. T.). (New World Archaeological Foundation. Brigham Young University Paper No. 27, 1970) The Ceramics of Aguacatal, Campeche, Mexico, 155pp, 53 figures. $12.00

M237. MATHER (Increase). Early History of New England; Being a Relation of the Hostile Passages Between the Indians and the European Voyagers and First Settlers: And a Full Narrative of Hostilities, to the Close of the War With the Pequots, 1637: Also a Detailed Account of the Origin of the War With King Philip. 309pp, 4to, cloth, spine relined. Albany, J. Munsell, 1864. $60.00

M238. MATHER (Samuel). An Attempt to Shew That America Must be Known to the Ancients. 35pp, 8vo, rebound in half leather. Boston, J. Kneeland, T. Leverett, H. Knox, 1773 (1st ed.). $225.00

M239. MATHEWS (John Joseph). The Osages, Children of the Middle Waters. 823pp, 4 maps, pronunciation key, bibliography, index. Norman, 1961 (1st ed.), d.j. $50.00
___Another Copy. Same. $45.00
___Another Copy. Norman, 1973, 826pp, index, maps, bibliography, d.j. $35.00

M240. MATHEWS (John Joseph). Talking to the Moon. 244pp, illus (some by author). Chicago 1945 (2d print.), d.j. $12.00
Dobie: "A wise and spiritual interpretation of the black-jack country of eastern Oklahoma, close to the Osages, in which John Joseph Mathews lives...." (GFH)
___Another Copy. Norman, 1981. $17.00

M241. MATHEWS (John Joseph). Wah'Kon-Tah, the Osage and the White Man's Road. 360pp, 11 illus, cloth. Norman, 1932 (1st ed.). $40.00
___Another Copy. Same. $15.00
___Another Copy. Norman, 1968 (2d Print.). $10.00

M242. MATHIASSEN (Therkel). (Museum of the American Indian, Notes and Monographs, Vol. 6, No. 1, 1929) Some Specimens from the Bering Sea Culture. pp33-55, 12mo, 12 illus, wrappers. $25.00

M243. MATSCHAT (Cecil H.). Seven Grass Huts: An Engineer's Wife in Central and South America. 281pp, 4 illus. New York, 1939. $15.00

MATTES (Merrill J.). See BAE Bulletin No. 176.

M244. MATTHEWS (Washington). The Mountain Chant: A Navajo Ceremony. 87pp, 3 double page color sand paintings, 6 full-page illus, 10 drawings (outprint of Smithsonian Institution BAE Annual Report Five, 1887) $48.00
___Another Copy. Glorieta, 1970, pp379-564, 10 illus, 9 pls with 4 pls in color, 4to. $35.00

M245. MATTHEWS (Washington). Navaho Legends, Collected and Translated by Washington Matthews. viii, 299pp, 7 full-page photographs, 42 figures (mostly photographs and drawings of artifacts), 1 map, cloth. Reprint of Memoirs

of the American Folk-Lore Society, Boston, 1897. Millwood, 1976. $59.00

M246. MATTHEWS (Washington) and GODDARD (P. E.). (University of California Publications in American Archaeology
and Ethnology, Vol. 5, No. 2, 1907) Navaho Myths,
Prayers and Songs, with Texts and Translations. 43pp.
$45.00

M247 MATTHEWS (Washington). Navajo Silversmiths. pp167-178,
3 pls, rebound. Removed from Smithsonian Institute
Bureau of American Ethnology Annual Report No. 2,
Washington, 1884. $17.00

M248. MATTHEWS (Washington). (American Museum of Natural
History Memoirs, Vol. VI, 1902. Publications of the
Hyde Southwestern Expedition) The Night Chant, A
Navaho Ceremony. xvi, 332pp of text, 19 figures, 5pp
color pls, 3pp photographs, later black linen cloth,
folio (11" x 14"). $450.00

Washington Matthews, one of the first scholars to
witness and receive instructions in Navaho ceremonies
and myths and the attendant songs and prayers produced
his seminal work in 1902 in his superb monograph on the
Night Chant. This ceremony, performed only in the late
autumn or winter, was observed by Matthews on numerous
occasions. This work, by far the most detailed examination of this or any other Navaho ceremony at that time,
remains one of the bulwark studies of Navaho religion
and ceremony. (EAP)

___Another Copy. Same. $395.00

M249. MATTHIESSEN (Peter). Indian Country. 338pp, endpaper maps. New York, 1984. $18.00

___Another Copy. Same. $15.00

MATTOS (Anibal). See BAE Bulletin No. 143.

M250. MAUD (R.). A Guide to British Columbia Indian Myth
and Legend, a Short History of Myth-collecting and A
Survey of Published Texts. 218pp, 18 full-page photographs. Vancouver, 1982. $17.00

M251. MAUDSLAY (A. P.). Biologia Centrali-Americana or, Contributions to the Knowledge of the Fauna and Flora of
Mexico and Central America. Edited by E. D. Godman
and O. Salvin. (4 Plate Volumes). Folio (13" x 20"),
Archaeology: Vol. I: iv, 119 pls, 22 in color. Vol. II:
iv, 98 pls, 6 in color. Vol. III: iv, 82 pls, 17 in color.
Vol. IV: iv, 93 pls, 15 in color. Cloth with new leather
spines. Text volume and appendix supplied in facsimile.
Includes Copan, Quirigua, Chichen-Itza, and Palenque,
fine heliogravures, plus drawings (chromolithograph and
pochoir). London, for the Editors, 1895-1902 (1st ed.).
$3,800.00

Griffin: 1188. "Remains a monument in MesoAmerican
archaeology, and most of its photographs are unsurpassed
to this day." (BF)

___Another Copy. Norman, 1983, Biologia Centrali-
Americana or, Contributions to the Knowledge of the
Fauna and Flora of Mexico. Introductions by Francis
Robicsek, Appendix by J. T. Goodman. (4 Volumes).
pp288, 182, 226 and 272, illus classic work includes Pre-
Columbian stellae, 4to (8" x 11"). $250.00

M252. MAXWELL (G. S.). Navajo Rugs, Past, Present and Future. 72pp, 24 color and 20 b/w photographs. Palm
Desert, 1963, 1973. $12.00

M253. MAXWELL (M. B.). (National Museum of Canada Bulletin
No. 170, 1960) An Archaeological Analysis of Grant
Land, Ellesmere Island, Northwest Territories. iv,
109pp, 17pp of photographs, 10 figures, 2 maps. $40.00

M254. MAXWELL (M. S.). (Archaeological Survey of Canada,
Paper No. 6, 1973) Archaeology of the Lake Harbor District, Baffin Island. 363pp, 72 line drawings, 36 charts,
wrappers. $17.00

M255. MAY (Robin). Indians. 63pp, 4to, illus with early photographs and prints. New York, 1983 (1st ed.), d.j.
                                                        $12.00
___Another Copy. Same. $10.00

M256. (MAYA). (Carnegie Institute Supplemental Publication,
No. 46, Washington, 1955) Ancient Maya Paintings of
Bonampak, Mexico. 36pp of text, plus 3 paintings of
murals by Antonio Tejada (fold-out), 4to, wrappers.
                                                        $25.00

M257. (MAYA). Historia Antigua de Zinacantan. 49pp, illus,
text in Yucatec and Spanish. Mexico, 1983. $15.00
___Another Copy. Same. $12.00

M258. (MAYA). Jaina Figurines: A Study of Maya Iconography.
71pp, illus with 25 figures, wrappers. Princeton, 1975.
                                                        $45.00

M259. (MAYA). Los Mayas, The Manuel Barbancho Ponce Mayan
Art Collection. 64pp, 106 b/w and 55 color photographs.
Exhibition Catalogue, Dalhousie University Art Gallery,
1978. $15.00

M260. (MAYA). Maya Art and Civilization, Revised and Enlarged
with added Illustrations by H. S. Spinden. 432pp, 65
pls, 86 figures. Falcon Wing Press, Colorado, 1957.
                                                        $65.00

M261. (MAYA). Maya: Keramik und Skulptor aus Mexiko. Die
Manuel Barbachano. Frankfurt, Ponce-Kollection, Dec.
1974 to Jan. 1975. Numerous photographs, wrappers.
                                                        $15.00

M262. (MAYA). Volume in Maya and Spanish Comprising Two
Different Texts. Text I: 81 leaves (131pp of text),
A portion of "Recetarios" by Juan Pio Perez which includes remedies for various ailments. Text II: Cuaderno
de Teabo. Dated 1803, 80pp, text in Maya, contains
remedies, list of plants, loose in wrappers, text slightly
wormed but entirely legible. $3,500.00

M263. (MAYA). Maya: Treasures of an Ancient Civilization.
240pp, illus wrappers, exhibition catalogue. New York,
1985. $25.00
___Another Copy. Same. $20.00
M264. (MAYA). Ritual of the Bacabs. 193pp, 4 pls, first Eng-
lish translation of a Colonial Mayan Manuscript. Norman,
1965, d.j. $35.00
___Another Copy. Same, no d.j., ex-library. $20.00
M265. (MAYA). Tulum: Guia Oficial. 68pp, illus, map, 12mo,
wrappers. Mexico, 1979. $10.00
M266. MAYBURY-LEWIS (David). The Savage and the Innocent.
(Tribes of Brazil). 270pp, 42 illus. London, 1965.
                                                         $15.00
M267. MAYER (Brantz). Mexico, As It Was and As It Is.
389pp, profusely illus with wood engravings, decorated
cloth, rebacked with original spine laid on, foxed. New
York, 1844. $90.00
M268. MAYER (Brantz). Tah-Gah-Jute or Logan and Captain
Michael Cresap; A Discourse. 86pp, original wrappers,
errata leaf. J. Murphy & Co., for Maryland Historical
Society, Baltimore, 1851 (1st ed.). $85.00
Howes: M-451. Field: 1039. Defense of Cresap
against the charge, repeated by Thomas Jefferson, of
killing the family of the famous Indian Chief Logan.
(RMW)
M269. MAYER (K. H.). Classic Maya Relief Columns. 32pp,
16 pls, wrappers, 4to. Ramona, 1981. $20.00
M270. MAYER (K. H.). Maya Monuments: Sculptures of Unknown Provenance in Europe. 44pp, 55 pls, wrappers,
4to. Ramona, 1978. $12.00
M271. MAYER (K. H.). Maya Monuments: Sculptures of Unknown Provenance in the United States. 86pp, 84 pls,
4to, wrappers. Ramona, 1980. $20.00
M272. MAYER (Peter J.). Miwok Balanophagy: Implications for
the Cultural Development of Some California Acorn-Eaters.
39pp, bibliography, 4to, wrappers. Investigates the
subsistence behavior of the Miwok who inhabited the
Sierra Nevada, focusing primarily on the acorn as a food
resource and on the possible dependence of them on this
source of nourishment. Berkeley, 1976 (1st ed.).
                                                         $10.00
M273. MAYER-OAKES (William J.). (Annals of Carnegie Museum,
Anthropological Series, No. 2, Pittsburgh, 1955) Pre-
history of the Upper Ohio Valley: An Introductory
Archaeological Study. 296pp, 120 pls, 30 figures, 30
maps, cloth, d.j. $35.00
___Another Copy. Same. Ex-library. $25.00
M274. MAYHALL (Mildred R.). The Kiowas. 301pp, illus.
Norman, 1962 (1st ed.). $35.00
___Another Copy. Same. $25.00
___Another Copy. Same. $25.00

_____Another Copy. Norman, 1971 (2d ed.) 364pp, illus, map, d.j. $16.00

M275. MAYS (B.). Ancient Cities of the Southwest. A Pictorial Guide to the Major Prehistoric Ruins of Arizona, New Mexico, Utah and Colorado. 131pp, 46 photos, 16 drawings, 10 maps. San Francisco, 1982. $13.00

M276. MAYS (B.). Indian Villages of the Southwest. A Practical Guide to the Pueblo Indian Villages of New Mexico and Arizona. 105pp, 63 photographs, 2 maps. San Francisco, 1985. $14.00

M277. MAZIERE (Francis). Expedition Tumuc-Humac (Guianas). 249pp, illus. New York, 1955. $20.00

M278. MAZIERE (Francis). Indiens d'Amazonie. 78pp, 90 photographs, with several in color by Dominique Darbois. Paris, n.d., d.j. $40.00

M279. MAZZANOVICH (Anton). (Edited and arranged by BRININSTOOL, E. A.) Trailing Geronimo. 322pp, illus. Author was a private soldier and scout under Carr, Crook and others. Los Angeles, 1926 (1st ed.). $60.00

M280. (MAZZUCHELLI, Samuel). Memoirs, Historical and Edifying, of a Missionary Apostolic.... 375pp, frontis, maps (one large folding) 3/4 leather, some wear to ends of spine, rear hinge cracked. First English translation of his experiences in missionary work to the Indians in Michigan, Wisconsin, Iowa and Illinois. Howes: M-457. Chicago, 1915 (1st ed.). $45.00

M281. MEACHAM (A. B.). Wi-Ne-Ma (The Woman-Chief) and Her People. 168pp, frontis portrait, other illus, original cloth. Hartford, American Publishing Co., 1876 (1st ed.). $125.00
Modoc Indian chief, with accounts of Captain Jack, Scar-Face Charley, and the Oregon Indian Wars.

M282. MEAD (C. W.). (American Museum of Natural History, Handbook Series No. 11, 1924) Old Civilizations of Inca Land. 117pp, frontis, illus, 1 fold-out map, index, pictorial cloth. $25.00
_____Another Copy, 1932 (2d ed.) 141pp, 55 illus, fold-out map, cloth. $30.00

M283. MEAD (C. W.). (American Museum of Natural History, Guide Leaflet No. 46, New York, 1922, 3rd enlarged ed.) Peruvian Art, As Shown on Textiles and Pottery. 24pp, 1pp photographs, 7 pp containing 102 drawings. $20.00
_____Another Copy. 1929 edition. $12.00

M284. MEAD (G. R.). (Colorado State College, Occasional Publications in Anthropology, Archaeology Series No. 5, 1968) Rock Art North of the Mexican-American Border. An Annotated Bibliography. 64pp, wrappers. $10.00

M285. MEAD (M.). The Changing Culture of an Indian Tribe. 313pp, cloth, inscribed by Oliver LaFarge. Columbia University Contributions to Anthropology, New York, 1932. $47.00
_____Another Copy. Same. $25.00

M286. MEADE (Joaquin). La Huasteca: Epoca Antigua. 378pp,
       207 pls, wrappers. Publicaciones Historicas, Mexico,
       1942. $60.00
M287. MEANS (Florence Crannell). Sagebrush Surgeon. 166pp.
       The story of Clarence Salsbury, long-time medical mis-
       sionary to the Navajos. New York, 1956 (1st print.),
       d.j. $10.00
M288. MEANS (Philip A.). Ancient Civilizations of the Andes.
       596pp, color frontis, 223 illus, light shelf wr. New York
       & London, 1931 (1st ed.). $50.00
       ___Another Copy. Same. $32.00
M289. MEANS (Philip A.). Ancient Civilizations of the Andes.
       xviii, 586pp, pls, figures, bibliography, index. Author
       served as Director of National Museum of Archaeology in
       Lima. Companion volume to "Fall of the Inca...." New
       York, 1931 (1st ed.). $35.00
       ___Another Copy. Same. $50.00
       ___Another Copy. Same. $30.00
       ___Another Copy. New York, 1936. $25.00
M290. MEANS (Philip A.). Fall of the Inca Empire and the
       Spanish Rule in Peru. 1530-1780. xii, 351pp, pls,
       maps, bibliography, glossary, index. Companion volume
       to "Ancient Civilizations...." New York, 1932 (1st ed.).
                                                          $35.00
       ___Another Copy. Same. $25.00
M291. MEANS (Philip). Peruvian Textiles: Examples of the pre-
       Incaic Period. 27pp, plus 24 pls, 4to (9" x 12"), Metro-
       politan Museum of Art, New York, 1930, d.j. $90.00
       ___Another Copy. Same. $85.00
M292. MEANS (P. A.). (Smithsonian Miscellaneous Collections,
       Vol. 66, No. 14, Washington, 1917) Preliminary Survey
       of the Remains of the Chippewa Settlements on La Pointe
       Island, Wisconsin. 15pp, 2 maps, wrappers. $20.00
M293. MEANS (Philip A.). A Study of Peruvian Textiles. 85pp
       plus 70pp of photographic pls, drawings, bibliography,
       examples as found in the Boston Museum of Fine Arts.
       Boston, 1932 (1st ed.). $45.00
M294. MEANS (Philip A.). (Transactions, CT Academy of Arts
       and Sciences, Vol. 21, 1917) A Survey of Ancient
       Peruvian Art. pp 315-442, 17 pls of multiple artifacts,
       wrappers. $45.00
M295. MEDEM (F.). El Cocodrilo. Estudio Inicial Sobre las
       Representaciones Zoomorfas Precolumbinas en el Arte
       Indigena de Colombia. 96pp, 37 half-page photographs
       of artifacts, 2 maps, wrappers. Bogota, 1953. $25.00
M296. MEDINA (Elsie E.). El Alma de Campeche en la Leyenda
       Maya. 82pp, wrappers. Mexico, 1947. $10.00
M297. MEDINA (Jose Toribio). The Discovery of the Amazon:
       According to the Account of Friar Gaspar de Gaspar de
       Carvajal and Other Documents. 465pp, light shelf wr.
       American Geographical Society, 1934. $50.00
       ___Another Copy. Same, rebound, ex-library. $30.00

M298. MEDINA (J. T.). Los Aborijenas de Chile. xvi, 427pp, 40 leaves containing 232 lrg drawings, 1/4 morocco, marbled bds. Santiago, 1882. $375.00

MEGGERS (Betty J.). See also Bulletin Nos. 143, 167 and 177.

M299. MEGGERS (Betty) and EVANS (Clifford) (Editors). (Smithsonian Institution, Miscellaneous Collections, Vol. 146, No. 1, Washington, 1963) Aboriginal Culture Development in Latin America: An Interpretative Review. 146pp, folded charts, stiff wrappers. $38.00
___Another Copy. Same. 148pp. $35.00
___Another Copy. Same. $12.00

M300. MEGGERS (B. J.) et al. (Smithsonian Contributions to Anthropology, Vol. 1, 1965) Early Formative Period of Coastal Ecuador: The Valdivia and Machalilla Phases. xvii, 234pp of text containing 115 figures, plus 196pp of photographs. $60.00
___Another Copy. Same. $45.00

M301. MEGGERS (Betty). Ecuador. (Ancient Peoples and Places Series). Illus. New York, 1966, d.j. $25.00

M302. MEIGHAN (Clement W.). (Baja California Travel Series, No. 13, Los Angeles, 1969 1st ed.) Indian Art and History: The Testimony of Prehistoric Rock Paintings in Baja California. 79pp, illus, printed by Grant Dahlstorm at Castle Press in an edition of 850 copies. $40.00

M303. MEIGHAN (Clement W.). (Southwest Museum Papers, No. 23, Los Angeles, 1972) The Maru Cult of the Pomo Indians. 134pp, 4to, illus, bibliography. $20.00
___Another Copy. Same. $25.00

M304. MEIGHAN (Clement W.) (Editor). Seven Rock Art Sites in Baja California. 236pp, illus, bibliography, 4to, wrappers. Las Pintas Petroglyphs, Rock Art of Velicata, Rock Art of Tinaja de Refufio, Los Pozos Rock Art Site, Bahia Coyote Rock Art, etc., by various contributors. Socorro, 1978 (1st ed.). $17.00

M305. MELATI (J. C.). Indios Do Brasil. 208pp of text, containing 13 figures and 5pp of maps, plus 26pp of photographs, wrappers. Brasilia, 1972 (2d ed.). $25.00

M306. MELDGAARD (J.). Eskimo Sculpture. 94pp, 77 photographs, bds. Copenhagen, 1959. $40.00
___Another Copy. London, 1960, cloth. $50.00
___Another Copy. New York, 1960, 48pp, 75 photographs. $30.00

M307. MENDEZ (Eugenio Fernandez). Art and Mythology of the Taino Indians of the Greater West Indies. 95pp, 32 pls, 4to, limited to 2,000 copies. San Juan, 1972. $40.00

M308. MENDIETA (Geronimo De Fray). Historia Eclesiastica Indiana (4 Volumes). pp185, 214, 227 and 255, wrappers, important Franciscan 16th Century source on Ethnohistory. Griffin: 1410. Mexico, 1945. $135.00

M309. MENDIETY (Rosa Ma.) and DEL AMO R. XALAPA (Silvia). Plantas Medicinales del Estado de Yucatan. 428pp, illus,

2 color pls, sml 4to (8" x 11"), wrappers. Mexico, 1981.
$45.00

M310. MENENDEZ (Carlos A.) and HOLM (Olaf). Excavaciones
Arqueologicas en San Pablo: Informe Preliminar. 14pp,
28 pls, map, wrappers. Guayaquil, 1960. $25.00

M311. MENGARINI (Fr. Gregory). Recollections of the Flathead
Mission: Containing Brief Observations both Ancient and
Contemporary Concerning this Particular Nation. Edited
with biographical introduction by Gloria Ricci Lothrop.
256pp, illus, index, bibliography, map. Glendale, 1977
(1st ed.). $25.00
___Another Copy. Same. $20.00
___Another Copy. Same. $15.00

M312. (MENOMINEE INDIANS). (House of Representatives Executive Document 47, 36:1, Washington, 1860, 1st print.)
Charges Against A. D. Bonesteel, U.S. Agent For the
Menominee Indians. 9pp, removed. Fraud and abuse
charges. $10.00

M313. (MENOMINEE INDIANS). (House of Representatives Document 490, 59:2, Washington, 1907, 1st print.) Sale of
Certain Timber on Menominee Indian Reservation, Wisconsin. 23pp, 3 maps, removed. $10.00

M314. MENZEL (D.) and ROWE (J. H.). (University of California
Publications in American Archaeology and Ethnology, Vol.
50, 1964) The Paracas Pottery of Ica. Study in Style
and Time. xiv, 399pp, 15pp photographs, 64 figures.
$90.00

M315. MERA (H. P.). Alfred I. Barton Collection of Southwestern Textiles. 99pp, 165 photographs, 3 full page color
drawings. San Vicente Foundation, Santa Fe, 1949 (2nd
print.). $97.00

M316. MERA (H. P.). (Laboratory of Anthropology, Bulletin
19, Santa Fe, 1945) Indian Silverwork of the Southwest:
Band Bracelets: Embossed. 15 unnumbered pp, illus,
stiff wrappers. $10.00

M317. MERA (H. P.). (Laboratory of Anthropology, General
Series, Bulletin No. 18, Santa Fe, 1945) Indian Silver
Work of the Southwest Illustrated: Band Bracelets:
Filed and Stamped. 16pp, 12 pls, wrappers. $25.00
___Another Copy. Same. $20.00
___Another Copy. Same. $15.00

M318. MERA (H. P.). (Laboratory of Anthropology, Bulletin 17,
Santa Fe, 1944) Indian Silverwork of the Southwest:
Bridles. 15 unnumbered pp, illus, stiff wrappers.
$20.00
___Another Copy. Same. $10.00

M319. MERA (H. P.). Indian Silverwork of the Southwest, Illustrated. Volume One. 128pp, 195 photographs. Globe,
1959. $16.00
___Another Copy. Same. wrappers. $12.00
___Another Copy. Same. $10.00

M320. MERA (H. P.). (University of New Mexico, Laboratory of
Anthropology, Bulletin 3, Santa Fe, 1938) Navajo
Blankets of the "Classic" Period. 16pp, 7pp of photo-
graphs, wrappers. $30.00
___Another Copy. Same. $29.00
___Another Copy. Same. $15.00

M321. MERA (H. P.). (Laboratory of Anthropology, Bulletin 10,
Santa Fe, 1940) Navajo Rugs of the Crystal and Two
Gray Hills Type. 15pp, 6 photographs. $29.00

M322. MERA (H. P.). Navajo Textile Arts. 102pp, 96 photographs, pictorial bds, limited to 1,250 copies, book designed by Merle Armitage, inscribed by author. Laboratory of Anthropology, Santa Fe, 1947. $135.00
___Another Copy. Santa Fe, n.d. (c. 1947) $75.00
___Another Copy. Santa Fe, 1948. $40.00
___Another Copy. Santa Barbara, 1975, reprint of
1947 ed., 122pp, illus, with added index. $12.00

M323. MERA (H. P.). (Laboratory of Anthropology Bulletin 14,
Santa Fe, 1943) Navajo Twilled Weaving. 16pp, 6
photographs. $24.00

M324. MERA (H. P.). (Laboratory of Anthropology Bulletin 14,
Santa Fe, 1944) Navajo Woven Dresses. 16pp, 5pp
photographs. $29.00

M325. MERA (H. P.). Negative Painting on Southwest Pottery.
6pp, 1 pl, printed wrappers. Reprinted from Southwestern Journal of Anthropology, Vol. 1, No. 1, 1945.
                                                     $10.00

M326. MERA (H. P.). (University of New Mexico, Laboratory
of Anthropology, Santa Fe, 1938) Pictorial Blankets.
12pp, 8 photographs, wrappers. $30.00

M327. MERA (H. P.). (Laboratory of Anthropology, Memoirs
Vol. IV, Santa Fe, 1943) Pueblo Indian Embroidery.
73pp, 24pp b/w photographs and drawings, 2pp color
photographs, wrappers, designed by Merle Armitage.
                                                     $95.00
___Another Copy. Same. $60.00
___Another Copy. Same. $45.00

M328. MERA (H. P.). (Laboratory of Anthropology, Memoirs
Vol. II, Santa Fe, 1937, 1st ed.) The "Rain Bird,"
A Study in Pueblo Design. 113pp, 48 pls, 176 draw-
ings by Tom Lea stiff printed wrappers. $350.00
    Saunders: 1830. Hinshaw-Lovelace: 20. Dykes,
Lea 200. This volume presents the variations of the Rain
Bird motif as it appears on Pueblo pottery with 176 draw-
ings all by Tom Lea in two colors and monochrome. An
important ethnological study as well as an important Lea
item, since this is the first book completely illustrated by
Lea. (TE)
___Another Copy. Same. $375.00
___Another Copy. Same. $195.00
___Another Copy. Same. $45.00

M329. MERA (H. P.). (American Anthropological Assn., Memoirs
No. 51, 1938) Reconnaisance and Excavation in South-
western New Mexico. 94pp, 24pp photographs. $24.00
M330. MERA (H. P.). (Laboratory of Anthropology Bulletin 11,
Santa Fe, 1940) The Serrate Designs of Navajo Blanketry.
16pp, 4 photographs, 1 figure. $27.00
M331. MERA (H. P.). (Laboratory of Anthropology Bulletin 5,
Santa Fe, 1938) The "Slave Blanket." 15 unnumbered
pp, illus, stiff wrappers. $15.00
M332. MERA (H. P.). (Laboratory of Anthropology Bulletin 2,
Santa Fe, 1938) The So-Called "Chief Blanket." 16pp,
7 photographs. $30.00
___Another Copy. Same. $15.00
___Another Copy. 1938 (2d print.). $25.00
M333. MERA (H. P.). (Laboratory of Anthropology Memoirs,
Vol. III, Santa Fe, 1939) Style Trends of Pueblo Pot-
tery, in the Rio Grande and Little Colorado Cultural Area:
From the Sixteenth to the Nineteenth Century. 164pp,
67 full-page b/w and color pls, fold-out map. $90.00
___Another Copy. Same. Ex-library. $65.00
M334. MERA (H. P.). (Laboratory of Anthropology, Bulletin 9,
Santa Fe, 1939) Wedge-Weave Blankets. 16pp, 5 photo-
graphs, 6 figures. $27.00
M335. MERA (H. P.). (Laboratory of Anthropology, Bulletin 12,
Santa Fe, 1940) The Zoning Treatment in Navajo Blanket
Design. 16pp, 6 photographs. $27.00
M336. MERCER (H. C.). The Antiquity of Man in the Delaware
Valley. 83pp, 30 figures, wrappers. Reprinted from
Publication of the University of Pennsylvania, Vol. 6.
Boston, 1897. $20.00
M337. MERIAM (Lewis) (Technical Director). The Problem of
Indian Administration. Report of a Survey Made at the
Request of ... Hubert Work, Secretary of the Interior,
and Submitted to Him, February 21, 1928. 847pp plus
index, fading to backstrip, few pencil notes on frnt
endpapers. Baltimore, MD, 1928 (1st ed.). $12.00
M338. MERIDA (Carlos). Estampas del Popul-Vuh: 10 Color
Lithographs. Includes introductory booklet in English
and Spanish, folio (12" x 16"), pls loose as issued, limited to 100 copies, once signed by artist, cloth spine,
orange bds, some edge wr. Graphic Art Publications,
Mexico, 1943. $850.00
An outstanding work by a major Mexican artist ...
"I did not wish to make illustrations nor create an alle-
gory, but to penetrate and render very free poetic ver-
sions of Mythological wonders." (BF)
M339. MERIDA (C.). Mexican Costume. A 16pp text plus 25
unbound color pls in a board and linen folio (13¼" x
16½") in size, limited to 1000 copies. Pocahontas Press,
Chicago, 1941. $135.00
M340. MERRIAM (A. P.). (Viking Fund Publication in Anthropology,

No. 44, Chicago, 1967) Ethnomusicology of the Flathead
Indians. 403pp, 4to, stiff wrappers. $35.00
___Another Copy. New York, 1967. 403pp, illus, stiff
wrappers. $30.00
___Another Copy. Same. $15.00

M341. MERRIAM (C. Hart). Boundary Descriptions of California
Indian Stocks and Tribes. 35pp, 4to, describes the
boundaries of 25 California tribes, wrappers. Berkeley,
1974 (1st ed.). $18.00

M342. MERRIAM (C. Hart). (Smithsonian Miscellaneous Collections, Vol. 78, No. 3, Washington, 1926, 1st ed.) The
Classification and Distribution of the Pit River Indian
Tribes of California. 52pp plus 27 photographic pls,
folding color map, mainly uncut and unopened, wrappers.
$25.00

M343. MERRIAM (C. Hart). Studies of California Indians.
233pp, 48 photographic pls, illus, bibliography, maps,
4to, index, ethnographic accounts, notes on material
culture, comparative records, etc. Berkeley, 1962,
d.j. $55.00

M344. MERRILL (Robert H.). (Cranbrook Institute Bulletin 24,
Michigan, 1945) The Calendar Stick of Tshi-Zun. Hau-
Kau. 6pp, color frontis, 3 illus, wrappers. $15.00

M345. MERWIN (R. E.) and VAILLANT (G. C.). (Peabody Museum Memoirs, Vol. III, No. 2, 1932) The Ruins of
Holmul, Guatemala. xiv, 107pp of text containing 36
figures, plus 36pp of photographs, 1 color pl. $150.00

METCALF (George). See BAE Bulletin No. 185.

M346. METHVIN (J. J.). Andele, or, the Mexican-Kiowa Captive.
A Story of Real Life Among the Indians. 184pp, pls,
original cloth. Louisville, 1899. $150.00
Ayer: 85. Graff: 2764. Howes: M-562. Little
Andele was taken by the Apache, rescued and adopted
by the Kiowa, and immortalized by the Reverend Methvin
in this authentic, yet patronizing little book. It is up
to the reader to ascertain which was the worst fate.
(WR)
___Another Copy. Same. $125.00
___Another Copy. Louisville, Pentecostal Herald Press,
1899 (2d ed.) all leaves prior to title page missing, frnt
hinge cracked, binding worn. $40.00

METRAUX (Alfred). See also BAE Bulletin No. 143.

M347. METRAUX (A.). (Universidad Nacional de la Plata Museo,
1930, Revista, Tomo XXXII.) Contribution a l'Etude
l'Archeologie du Cours Superieur, et Mayen de l'Amazone.
pp145-185 containing 35 photographs and drawings, another
5pp photographs, fold-out map, spine repaired. $35.00

M348. METRAUX (Alfred). The History of the Incas. 205pp,
photographs, map, bibliographic essay. New York, 1969,
(1st American ed.), d.j. $10.00

M349. METRAUX (A.). Revista del Instituto de Etnologia, de la

Universidad Nacional de Tucuman. (Tomo III) 2 papers on Bolivian Indian secret societies and material culture and 2 other papers, 32pp of photographs, 3pp of color and b/w drawings of Chiriguano decorative designs.
$45.00

M350. METRAUX (A.) and PLOETZ (H.). Revista del Instituto de Etnologia, de la Universidad Nacional de Tucuman. (Tomo I). pp107-293, Entrega 2a, 1930. $30.00

M351. (MEXICAN ART). Arte de Jalisco. "De los Prehispanicos a Nuestro Dias." 100pp, 90 illus (2 in color) wrappers. Museo Nacional de Arte Moderno, Mexico, 1963. $35.00

M352. (MEXICAN ART). Masterworks of Mexican Art. 296pp, 151 lrg photographs. Los Angeles County Museum of Art, 1963. $15.00

M353. (MEXICO). El Norte de Mexico y el Sur de Estados Unido. Tercera Reunion de Mesa Redondo Sobre Problemas Antropologicos de Mexico y Centro America. xv, 362pp, figures, tables, 3 text maps, 32 fold-out maps. Mexico City, Castillo de Chapultepec, 1943. $55.00

M354. (MEXICO). (Instituto Nacional de Antropologia e Historia, Vol. 5 & 6, Mexico City, 1952) Tlatoani. 92pp, 112 photographs and drawings. $18.00

M355. MEYER (Hermann). (Report of Smithsonian Institution, Washington, 1896) "Bows and Arrows in Central Brazil." pp549-591, 4 pls of drawings, folding color map, bound in later cloth. $12.00

M356. MEYER (Roy W.). History of the Santee Sioux: United States Indian Policy on Trial. 434pp, illus, index, maps, bibliography. Lincoln, 1967 (1st ed.), d.j. $30.00
____Another Copy. Same. $25.00
____Another Copy. Same. $20.00

M357. MEYER (Roy W.). The Village Indians of the Upper Missouri: The Mandans, Hidatsas and Arikaras. 354pp, illus, index. Lincoln, 1977 (1st ed.), d.j. $20.00

M358. MEYERS (A.). Die Inka In Ekuador, Untersuchungen Ahand Ihrer Materiellen Hinterlassenschaft. 186pp containing 37 figures, 14 tables, plus 56pp addenda containing 12pp of drawings, 5pp of photographs, 2 maps. Bonn, BAS 6, 1976. $35.00

M359. MEYERS (Albert Cook) (Editor and introduction). William Penn's Own Account of the Lenni Lenape or Delaware Indians. 91pp plus index, photographs, foreword by John E. Pomfret. Somerset, NJ, 1970 (revised ed.).
$10.00

M360. MEZA (Otilia). Leyendas Aztecas. 133pp, illus, 8 color pls, wrappers. Museo Nacional de Mexico, 1934. $35.00

M361. MICHELS (Joseph W.). The Kaminaljuyu Chiefdom. 283pp, 81 illus, 4to, Penn State University Press, 1979. $30.00

MICHELSON (Truman). See also BAE Bulletin Nos. 72, 85, 87, 89, 95, 105, 114, 119 and 123.

M362. MICHELSON (Truman). Linguistic Classification of Cree

and Montognais-Naskapi Dialects. pp66-95, map, printed
wrapper, offprint Smithsonian Anthropological Papers,
Washington, 1939. $10.00

M363. MICHELSON (Truman). Preliminary Report on the Linguistic Classification of Algonquian Tribes. pp221-308, folding table, folding colored map, index, tall 8vo, decorative cloth, inscribed to Dr. Alfred L. Kroeber from Edwin
Emerson. Extract from 28th BAE Annual Report. Gov-
erment Printing Office, Washington, 1913. $20.00

M364. (MICHIGAN). Information in Relation to the Superintendency of Indian Affairs, in the Territory of Michigan.
132pp, removed, expenses for support and removal.
Washington, 1822 (1st print.). $25.00

M365. MIJANGOS (Juan de). Espeio Divino en Lengua Mexicana....
(8)ff., 562pp, (1)ff. Quarto, 19th Century half morocco
with gilt spine, title page mounted, lrge title page device,
lrge ornamented woodcut initials and four woodcut engravings, lacks final two leaves (tables). En Mexico. En la
Emprenta de Diego Lopez Daualos, 1607. $4,000.00
      Medina (Mexico): 238. Puttick & Simpson: 1138.
Palau: 168872. Garcia Icazbalceta Lenguas: 45. Vinaza:
119. A very early Augustinian work in Nahuatl, the language of the Aztecs. According to Medina, who calls
this a "buena impresion," the book is printed using Elze-
vier characters and is thus "the largest book printed in
Nahuatl," a claim we think may be inaccurate. According
to several sources, the book is excessively rare. It does
not appear in Brunet, Rich or LeClerc. (WR)

M366. MIJANGOS (Juan de). Primera Parte del Sermonario Dom-
inical, y Sanctoral, en Lengua Mexicana.... (9)ff.,
564pp, (46)ff. Bears both an engraved portrait of St.
Augustine on the titlepage and a far less sophisticated
cut of the Saint preaching to a native Indian at his feet
on the verso. Quarto, contemporary limp vellum, lacking
ties, piece of title page torn away and replaced, parts of
three words supplied in manuscript. En Mexico. En la
Imprenta del Licenciado Iuan de Alcacar, 1624.
$4,250.00
      Medina (Mexico): 370. Palau: 169164. Garcia Icaz-
balceta Lenguas: 46. Puttick & Simpson: 1137. Vinaza:
158. A rare volume of sermons for the church year in
Nahuatl, the indigenous language of Mexico spoken by
the majority of Indians. The author, a native of Oaxaca
and an Augustinian, dedicated himself to the needs of the
native Indians. (WR)

M367. MILANICH (J. T.) and FAIRBANKS (C. H.). Florida
Archaeology. 306pp, 44 illus, hard bd cvr. New York,
1980. $37.00

M368. MILANICH (J. T.) and STURTEVANT (Wm. C.). Francisco
Pareja's 1613 Confessionario: A Documentary Source for
Timucuan Ethnography. 121pp, frontis. Tallahassee,
1972. $35.00

M369. MILBRATH (S.). (Studies in Pre-Columbian Art and
Archaeology, No. 23, Washington, 1979) A Study of Ol-
mec Sculptural Chronology. 75pp, 78 photographs and
drawings. $18.00
M370. MILES (Charles). Indian and Eskimo Artifacts of North
America. 244pp, 4to, illus, index, bibliography. New
York, 1963, d.j. $15.00
M371. MILES (Nelson A.). (Senate Executive Document 117,
49:2, Washington, 1887) Letter from the Secretary of
War transmitting ... correspondence with General Miles
relative to the surrender of Geronimo. 77pp, recently
rebound in 1/4 leather and silk cloth. $150.00
____Another Copy. Same. $65.00
M372. MILLAR (George). Orellana Discovers the Amazon.
303pp, drawings, map (one folding), bibliography.
Based on facts, but author uses fictional devices. Part
of Pizarro's force braving the Amazon in 1541. London,
1954 (1st ed.). $10.00
M373. (MILLE LAC RESERVATION). (House of Representatives
Executive Document 148, 48:1, Washington, 1884, 1st
print.) Mille Lac Indian Reservation in Minnesota.
18pp, removed. $10.00
M374. MILLER (Alfred J.). Braves and Buffalo, Plains Indian
Life in 1837. Water-Colours of Alfred J. Miller with Descriptive Notes by the Artist. Introduced by Michael
Bell. 176pp, 79 full-page color pls, oblong 4to. Toronto,
1973 (1st ed.), d.j. $30.00
Done by Miller when he accompanied Wm. Drummond
Stewart on his 1837 trip through Wyoming and the
Rockies; each plate is accompanied by page of descriptive
text by Miller. Many of the pictures are on the Wyoming
part of the journey and include what is perhaps the only
visual record extant of old wooden Ft. Laramie. (GFH)
____Another Copy. Same. $20.00
MILLER (Carl F.). See BAE Bulletin Nos. 164, 176, 182, 185 and
189.
M375. MILLER (David H.). Custer's Fall: The Indian Side of
the Story. xiii, 271pp, illus, map endpapers. The
results of interviews with 71 Indian participants. New
York, 1957 (1st ed.). $20.00
____Another Copy. New York, 1957 (2d print), d.j.
                                                              $15.00
M376. MILLER (David H.). Ghost Dance. 318pp, index, well-
researched history of the Messiah Craze of the Sioux in
1890. New York, 1959 (1st ed.), d.j. $25.00
____Another Copy. Same. $17.00
M377. MILLER (J.) and EASTMAN (C. M.) (Editors). The
Tsimshian and Their Neighbors of the North Pacific Coast.
xxii, 343pp, 24 photographs, 19 figures, 14 tables, 3
maps, cloth. Seattle, 1984. $24.00
M378. MILLER (Joaquin). Paquita, The Indian Heroine. A True

Story. 445pp, illus, ads, full leather, worn, couple of
signatures loose. Hartford, 1881. $25.00

M379.   MILLER (Joaquin). Unwritten History: Life Amongst the
Modocs. 445pp, illus, ads, half leather, marbled bds and
endpapers. Pleas for better treatment for the California
Indians, with extracts from Reports of the Commissioner
of Indian Affairs relating to the Modocs. Hartford, CT,
1874 (1st American ed.). $70.00
____Another Copy. Same. $45.00

M380.   MILLER (Joseph). Monument Valley and the Navajo Country: Arizona ... Utah. 96pp, illus, cloth. Powell
Gathering II 1216. New York, 1951 (1st ed.). $20.00

M381.   MILLER (Leo). In the Wilds of South America: Six Years
of Exploration in Columbia, Venezuela, British Guiana,
Peru, Bolivia, Argentina, Paraguay and Brazil. 242pp,
over 70 photographs, color frontis, newly rebound.
New York, Scribner's, 1918. $60.00
____Another Copy. Same. $35.00
____Another Copy. Same. hinges split, ex-library.
                                                           $35.00
____Another Copy. Same. $25.00

M382.   MILLER (M.). Indian Arts and Crafts. 118pp, 37 illus,
cloth. New York, 1972. $15.00

M383.   MILLER (Nathan). The Child in Primitive Society. 302pp
plus index, bibliography, general study including references to many American Indian tribal customs. New York,
1928, d.j. $27.00

M384.   MILLER (Polly and Leon). Lost Heritage of Alaska: The
Adventure and Art of the Alaskan Coast Indian. 289pp,
approx 200 illus. New York, 1967 (1st ed.). $55.00
____Another Copy. Same. $35.00
____Another Copy. Same. $28.00
____Another Copy. Same. $25.00

M385.   MILLIGAN (Edward). Dakota Twilight. The Standing
Rock Sioux, 1874-1890. 184pp plus index, photographs,
appendix, bibliography, notes, maps. Indian viewpoint
of Little Big Horn. Hicksville, NY, 1976 (1st ed.),
d.j. $15.00
____Another Copy. Same. $15.00
____Another Copy. Same. $12.00

M386.   MILLIGAN (Edward A.). High Noon on the Greasy Grass.
The Story of the Little Big Horn by Indians Who Were
There (cover title). 35 unnumbered pp, photograph
frontis, limited to 500 copies, signed by author, wrappers,
contains Kills Eagle's account and the account of Two
Bulls. Bottineaux, ND, 1972 (1st ed.). $15.00

M387.   MILLIGAN (Edward A.). A Sun Dance of the Sioux (cover
title). 27 unnumbered pp, photographs, wrappers.
Bottineaux, ND, 1969. $10.00

M388.   MILLIKEN (W.). Art of the Americas. Picture Book, No.
2. 58pp, 5pp of color, 44pp b/w photographs, 2 maps.
Cleveland Museum of Art, 1946. $20.00

M389. MILLON (R.). The Teotihuacan Map. Vol. I, Part One:
Text. xvi, 154pp, 61pp of photographs, 8pp of maps and
charts. Vol. I, Part Two: Maps. xiii, 147 individual
map sheets, each with acetate overlay, 3 fold-out maps
in snap button external pocket, cloth. Austin, 1973.
$89.00
___Another Copy. Same. $60.00
MILLS (John E.). See BAE Bulletin No. 176.
M390. MILLS (William C.). Archaeological Atlas of Ohio. xi,
photographs, 88 maps, folio, hinges loose, some cvr fading. A classic in Ohio archaeology. Maps, county by
county, showing distribution of prehistoric remains,
archaeological description of each county, Indian trails
and over 5,000 prehistoric earthworks.
Archaeological and Historical Society, Columbus, OH,
1914 (1st ed.). $175.00
M391. MILLS (William C.). Certain Mounds and Village Sites in
Ohio. Volume 2 only. xv, 288pp, index, lrg 8vo, cloth,
many color and b/w photographs and maps, covers Seip
Mound, Tremper Mound, Westenhaver Mound, and
archaeological remains of Jackson County. Columbus,
F. J. Heer, 1917. $150.00
M392. MILLS (William C.). Certain Mounds and Village Sites in
Ohio. Volume 3 only. xv, 412pp, index, lrg 8vo, cloth,
many photographic illus, maps, plans, covers Feurt
Mounds, Ulrich Mounds, Flint Ridge and the Mound City
Group. Columbus, F. J. Heer, 1922. $150.00
M393. MILLS (William C.). Certain Mounds and Village Sites in
Ohio. Volume 4 only. 305pp, lrg 8vo, cloth, many
photographic illus, maps, plans, covers Campbell Island
and Hine Mound Sites, the Wright Group of Earthworks,
the Hopewell Group. Columbus, F. J. Heer, 1923.
$135.00
M394. MILTON (John R.) (Editor). The American Indian Speaks.
194pp, 24 pls (12 in color), stiff pictorial wrappers,
collection of poetry, fiction, art, music and commentary
by contemporary Indians. Vermillion, 1969. $20.00
M395. MILTON (R.) and DREWITT (B.). (Transactions of the
American Philosophical Society, New Series, Vol. 55, Part
6, 1965) The Pyramid of the Sun at Teotihuacan: 1959
Investigations. 94pp, 125 figures. $45.00
M396. MINARDI (V.). Arte Maya Del Guatemala. 114pp, 100
photographs, 19 drawings. Instituto Italo-Latino Ameri-
cano, Rome, 1969. $25.00
M397. MINDELEFF (Cosmos). The Cliff Ruins of Canyon de
Chelly, Arizona. pp73-138, drawings, photographic pls,
folding map, newly separately bound, light marginal
waterstain on 2pp. From Smithsonian Institution BAE
Annual Report No. 16, Washington, 1897. $20.00
M398. MINDELEFF (Victor). A Study of Pueblo Architecture,
Tusayan and Cibola. pp3-228, drawings, 31 pls of

photographs, maps, drawings, newly separately bound.
From Smithsonian Institution BAE Annual Report No. 8,
Washington, 1893. $25.00

M399. MINELLI (L. L.). Arte e Rituali Nell'antico Peru. 111pp,
29pp of photographs, map. Exhibition Catalogue, Museo
Civico Archeologico Ethnologico, Modena, 1980. $18.00

M400. MINER (H. Craig). The Corporation and the Indian:
Tribal Sovereignty and Industrial Civilization in Indian
Territory, 1865-1907. 236pp, index, bibliography.
Columbia, 1976 (1st ed.), d.j. $15.00
_____Another Copy. Same. $10.00

M401. MINER (William Penn). History of Wyoming, in a Series
of Letters. 488 (2), 104pp, 2 folding maps, 2 pls, disbound. History of the Wyoming Valley of Pennsylvania,
scene of many Indian battles and tragic massacres.
Howes: M-648. Field: 1068. Philadelphia, J. Crissy,
1845 (1st ed.). $45.00

M402. MINGE (Ward Alan). Acoma, Pueblo in the Sky. 180pp,
illus, map endpapers, bibliography, 4to, index. Good
account of Acoma which traces the social, economic and
political history of its inhabitants over 400 years. Albuquerque, 1976 (1st ed.), d.j. $25.00
_____Another Copy. Same. $17.00

MISHKIN (Bernard). See also BAE Bulletin No. 143.

M403. MISHKIN (B.). (Monograph of the American Ethnological
Society, No. 3, New York, 1940) Rank and Warfare
Among the Plains Indians. 65pp, cloth. $27.00
_____Another Copy. Seattle, 1975. $10.00

M404. (MISSIONARIES). (Santa Barbara Bicentennial Historical
Series, Vol. 1, Santa Barbara, 1976, 1st ed.) As the
Padres Saw Them. California Indian Life and Customs
as Reported by the Franciscan Missionaries, 1813-1815.
170pp, photographs, drawings, notes, introduction notes
and translation by Maynard Geiger, anthropological commentary notes and appendices by Clement W. Meighan,
limited to 500 copies. $35.00

M405. (MISSIONARIES). Some Account of the Conduct of the
Religious Society of Friends Towards the Indian
Tribes.... 247pp, rebound in cloth, lacks map, ex-
library. London, E. Marsh, 1844 (1st ed.). $40.00

M406. (MISSIONS). Indian Tribes and Missions: A Handbook
of General History of the American Indians. Early Missionary efforts and missions of the Episcopal Church.
Pages non-consecutively numbered, approx 200pp, numerous photographic illus, cvr soiled, lacks frnt endpaper.
Hartford, 1926. $50.00

M407. (MISSIONS). Philip Everhard; or, a History of the Baptist Indian Missions in North America. 108pp, 1/2 leather, hinges started. Boston, 1831. $50.00

M408. MITCHELL (Annie R.). Jim Savage and Tulareno Indians.
118pp, illus, map, index. Savage, a California mountain

man, became ruler over hundreds of Tulareno Indians.
He openly exploited them in his trading posts and in
his mining activities. He led the famed Maripose Battalion against them in the Indian War of 1851-52, and,
on one of his forays, discovered Yosemite. Los Angeles,
1957 (1st ed.), d.j. $45.00

M409. MITCHELL (Emerson Blackhorse). Miracle Hill: The
Story of a Navaho Boy. 230pp, index. Norman, 1967
(1st ed.), d.j. $25.00
___Another Copy. Same. $15.00

M410. MITCHELL (J. Leslie). The Conquest of the Maya.
folded map. London, Jarrold, 1934. $40.00

M411. MITCHELL (Joseph). The Missionary Pioneer, or a Brief
Memoir of the Life, Labours and Death of John Stewart
(Man of Colour), Founder, Under God of the Mission
Among the Wyandotts at Upper Sandusky, Ohio. 96pp,
original paper cvrd bds, new leather backstrip and end-
papers, 1/4 leather slipcase. New York, Joseph Mitchell,
printed by J. C. Totten, 1827 (1st ed.). $375.00
    Howes: M-680. Graff: 2837. Sabin: 49704.
Thompson: 839. Stewart was an extraordinary man,
a Negro born in Virginia about 1790, who believed he was
called to preach to the Indians of the Old Northwest.
He traveled through the wilderness from Marietta to the
Upper Sandusky, where he established a mission after
gaining the trust of the natives. He remained among the
Wyandotts for seven years. (RMW)

M412. MITCHELL (Marie). The Navajo Peace Treaty of 1868.
145pp, illus, index, bibliography, map. New York,
1973 (1st ed.), d.j. $15.00
___Another Copy. Same. $12.00
___Another Copy. Same. $10.00

M413. MITCHELL (Rev. S. H.). The Indian Chief, Journeycake.
108pp, sml 8vo, photographic frontis, 5 photographic pls,
much information on the Delaware tribe at the time of
the tribe's removal to Kansas, and final removal to Indian
Territory. Philadelphia, American Baptist Publication
Society, 1895 (1st ed.). $35.00
___Another Copy. Same. $15.00

M414. MITCHENER (C. H.). Ohio Annals. Historic Events in
the Tuscarawas and Muskingum Valley, and in Other
Portions of the State of Ohio. Adventures of Post,
Heckewelder and Zeisberger. Legends and Traditions
of the Kophs, Mound Builders, Red and White Men. viii,
358pp, blind stamped cloth. Dayton, OH, T. W. Odell,
1876 (1st ed.). $65.00
___Another Copy. Same. Ex-library. $60.00
___Another Copy. Same. $55.00

M415. MOCHON (Marion J.). Masks of the Northwest Coast;
The Samuel R. Barrett Collection. 102pp, lrg 8vo, frontis
in color, illus, wrappers. Milwaukee Public Museum,
1966. $22.00

_____Another Copy. Milwaukee, 1968 (2d print.). $10.00

M416. MOCTEZUMA (Eduardo Matos). Una Visita al Templo Mayor. 77pp, 44 illus, wrappers. Mexico City, 1981. $20.00

M417. (MODOC). (House of Representatives Executive Document 201, 42:3, Washington, 1873, 1st print.) Modoc Indians. 12pp, removed, narratives of Indian attacks on settlers. $20.00

M418. (MODOC). (House of Representatives Executive Document 122, 43:1, Washington, 1874, 1st print.) Modoc War. Message from the President ... copies of Correspondence and Papers relative to the war with the Modoc Indians in Southern Oregon and Northern California during the years 1872 and 1873. 330pp, bound in later cloth. In addition, contains the proceedings of the military commission which tried and condemned the Modoc leaders. The major document on the Modoc War. $75.00

M419. (MODOC). (House of Representatives Executive Document 45: 43:2, Washington, 1874, 1st print.) Modoc War Claims. 119pp, removed. Accounts and brief history of the war. $35.00

M420. MOFFETT (Thomas C.). The American Indian on the New Trail; the Red Man of the United States and the Christian Gospel. 316pp, illus, folding map, index, appendix. New York, 1914 (1st ed.). $25.00

_____Another Copy. Same, wrappers. $15.00

_____Another Copy. Same. $14.00

M421. (MOHAWK SAINT). Katherine Tekakwitha: The Lily of the Mohawks. Cause for Beatification and Canonization; Being the Original Documents First Published at the Vatican Polyglot Press, Now Done in English. Portrait, 468pp, decorated endpapers, full leather. 17th Century Mohawk, nominated as the first Catholic Saint in the United States. New York, 1940 (1st ed.). $125.00

M422. MOHR (Walter H.). Federal Indian Relations, 1744-1788. 247pp, map, cloth. University of Pennsylvania Press, 1933. $20.00

M423. MOISES (Rosalio). The Tall Candle: The Personal Chronicle of a Yaqui Indian. 251pp, maps, index, firsthand account of the Yaqui and Sonoran history through the final Yaqui uprising of 1926. Lincoln, 1971 (1st ed.), d.j. $27.00

_____Another Copy. Same. $15.00

M424. MOISES HERRERA et al. Estado Actual de los Principales Edificios Arqueologicos de Mexico. 263pp, illus, lrg 4to, wrappers. Mexico, 1928. $85.00

M425. MONCKTON (Elizabeth). White Canoe and Other Legends of the Ojibwats. Prepared from Legends Heard from the Indians Themselves by the Author. 8 original pyrographic drawings on birch by the author, decorated cloth. New York, 1904 (1st ed.). $45.00

M426. MONNEY (James). The Sacred Formulas of the Cherokees. pp 301-397, 4 pls, newly separately bound, from Smithsonian Institution BAE Annual Report No. 7, Washington, 1892. $20.00

M427. (MONTANA). (House of Representatives Executive Document 312, 42:2, Washington, 1872, 1st print.) Montana Indian War Claims of 1867. 10pp, removed. $10.00

M428. (MONTANA). (House of Representatives Executive Document 164, 42:3, Washington, 1872, 1st print.) Montana Indian War Claims of 1867. 32pp, removed, damage claims and supply lists. $17.00

M429. (MONTANA). (Senate Document 117, 54:1, Washington, 1896, 1st print.) Agreement Made ... With the Indians of The Fort Belknap Reservation in Montana.... 32pp, removed, copy of the agreement and transcript of the negotiations carried on by George B. Grinnell and others. $20.00

M430. (MONTANA). (Senate Document 118, 54:1, Washington, 1896, 1st print.) Agreement Made ... With the Indians of The Fort Belknap Reservation In Montana.... 36pp, removed, text of treaty negotiations over mineral lands (copper, gold and silver) owned by the Indians. Final price: $1,500,000. $20.00

M431. MONTELL (G.) and ROYEM (C.). (Oslo Etnografiske Museums, Skrifter Bind 5, Hefte 1, 1926) An Archaeological Collection from the Rio Loa Valley, Atacama. 46pp, 54 illus. $35.00

M432. MONTELL (Gosta). Dress and Ornaments in Ancient Peru. Archaeological and Historical Studies. 263pp, illus, wrappers. London, Oxford House, n.d., (c.1929). $55.00
____Another Copy. Goteborg, 1929, iv, 272pp, 96 illus, wrappers. $45.00

M433. MONTGOMERY (John L.). (University of Texas, Center for Archaeological Research, Special Report No. 6, San Antonio, 1978) The Mariposa Site: A Late Prehistoric Site on the Rio Grande Plain of Texas. 155pp, photographs, drawings, maps, bibliography, wrappers. $10.00

M434. MONTHAN (Guy and Doris). Art and Indian Individualists. The Art of Seventeen Contemporary Southwestern Artists and Craftsmen. 191pp plus index, photographs, many in color, bibliography, foreword by Lloyd Kiva New, covers Tona Da, R. C. Gorman, Allan Houser, Charles Loloma, Grace Medicine Flower, Preston Monongye, Fritz Scholder and others. Flagstaff, 1975 (1st ed.) d.j. $35.00

M435. MONTI (Franco). Precolumbian Terracottas. 158pp, 71 color pls, cloth. London & New York, 1969, d.j. $15.00
____Another Copy. Same. $12.00
____Another Copy. Same. $10.00

M436. MONTURE (Ethel Brant). Canadian Portraits. Brant.

Crowfoot. Oronhyatekha. Famous Indians. 158pp, index, drawings. Toronto, 1960 (1st ed.). $10.00

M437. MOODY (Ralph). Geronimo. Wolf of the Warpath. 186pp, illus by Eggenhofer. New York, 1958. $14.00

M438. MOOK (Maurice A.). (University of Pennsylvania, Journal, Washington Academy of Science, Vol. XXXIV, No. 6 and 7, 1944) Algonkian Ethnohistory of the Carolina Sound. pp178-228, map, wrappers. Early Algonkian Tribes and towns. $12.00

M439. MOON (Grace). The Magic Trail. Illustrated by Carl Moon. 244pp, endpaper maps, cloth. New York, 1929, (1st ed.). $25.00

M440. MOON (Sheila). A Magic Dwells: A Poetic and Psychological Study of the Navaho Emergence Myth. 206pp, cloth, Middletown, 1970 (1st ed.). $20.00
____Another Copy. Same. d.j. $15.00
____Another Copy. Wesleyan University Press, 1970, d.j. $18.00

MOONEY (James). See also BAE Bulletin Nos. 22 and 99.

M441. MOONEY (J.). Calendar History of the Kiowa Indians. 332pp, 211 illus, extracted from BAE 17th Annual Report, 1898, Washington, 1979 reprint. $14.00

M442. MOONEY (J.). Siouan Tribes of the East. 101pp, 101 illus, cloth, reprint of BAE Bulletin 22. New York, 1970. $15.00

M443. MOORE (C. B.). (Journal of the Academy of Natural Sciences of Philadelphia, Vol. XIV, 1912) Some Aboriginal Sites on Red River. 164pp, 138 b/w photographs and drawings, 7 full-page (14" x 8") color photographs, morocco and gilt cvr, hubs on spine, marbled endpapers, presentation copy, inscribed by author. $185.00

M444. MOORE (Earl). Silent Arrows. Indian Lore and Artifact Hunting. 197pp, extensive photographic illus, 4 are in color, references, index. Klamath Falls, 1977. $15.00

M445. MOORE (Jacob B.). Annals of the Town of Concord, in the County of Merrimack, and State of New Hampshire, from its First Settlement in the Year 1726 ... to Which is Added a Memoir of the Penacook Indians. 112pp, 8vo, original wrappers bound in, cloth. Concord, Author, 1824 (1st ed. thus). $55.00

M446. MOORE (J. H.). The Political Condition of the Indians and the Resources of the Indian Territory. 62pp, wrappers, loose disbound. St. Louis, 1874. $650.00

M447. MOORE (Martin). Memoirs of the Life and Character of Rev. John Eliot, Apostle of the North American Indians. 174pp, 24mo, full leather, some stain, foxing. Boston, T. Bedlington, 1822 (1st ed.). $135.00
Sabin: 50421. Field: 1087. "The compiler of this little work, being stationed on the ground where Eliot planted his first Indian Church and organized his first Indian town, has naturally felt a deep interest in his character." (p. iii)

M448. MOORE (William V.). (pseudon. for John Frost) Indian
Wars of the United States.... 328pp, 16pp, advs,
illus, pls, color frontis, rebacked. Philadelphia, W. A.
Leary & Co., 1850. $55.00
    Sabin: 26039. Field: 1088. Sabin: "This is the
first work of this prolific author, if such a term can be
applied to a notorious pilferer."
___Another Copy. Philadelphia, 1853, cloth, rebound.
$55.00
___Another Copy. Philadelphia, 1860 (1850). $65.00
M449. MOOREHEAD (Warren K.). The American Indian in the
United States. Period 1850-1914. 440pp, index, 2
folding maps, many photographs, including several
photogravures taken on the Wanamaker Expedition by
Joseph K. Dixon, cloth. Andover, Mass, Andover Press,
1914 (1st ed.). $110.00
___Another Copy. Same. $250.00
___Another Copy. Same. $250.00
___Another Copy. Same, ex-library. $90.00
M450. MOOREHEAD (Warren K.). Archaeology of the Arkansas
River. Supplemental papers included are J. B. Tho-
burn, the Prehistoric Cultures of Oklahoma; Charles
Peabody, the Exploration of Jacobs Cavern. 204pp, 76
figures, 11 pls. New Haven, 1931. $90.00
___Another Copy. Same. $69.00
M451. MOOREHEAD (Warren). Archaeology of Maine: Being a
Narrative of Explorations in that State, 1912-1920, To-
gether With Work at Lake Champlain, 1917. Illus.
Andover Press, Andover, 1922. $100.00
M452. MOOREHEAD (Warren K.). (Dept. of Archaeology, Phil-
lips Academy, Bulletin V, Andover, 1912) Certain
Peculiar Earthworks Near Andover, Massachusetts. 55pp,
21 photographs, 6 folding maps, wrappers. $25.00
M453. MOOREHEAD (Warren K.). Etowah Papers: Exploration
of the Etowah Site in Georgia. 178pp, 104 illus, 4to,
New Haven, 1932. $90.00
___Another Copy. Same. Ex-library. $50.00
M454. MOOREHEAD (Warren K.). Fort Ancient: The Great Pre-
historic Earthwork of Warren County, Ohio ... With an
Account of its Mounds and Graves. xii, 129pp, 37 pls,
folding map, green cloth, Cincinnati, Robert Clark,
1890 (2d ed.). $85.00
___Another Copy. Same. $97.00
___Another Copy. Phillips Academy Dept. of Anthro-
pology Bulletin No. IV, Andover Press, 1908, 166pp,
illus, wrappers. $25.00
M455. MOOREHEAD (Warren K.). (Field Museum of Natural History, Publication 211, Anthropological Series Vol. VI,
No. 5, 1922) The Hopewell Mound Group of Ohio.
101pp of text, 68 figures, drawings of hundreds of objects, 48pp pls containing photographs and drawings of
over 150 objects, 1 fold-out map. $78.00

Moorehead's study remains one of the most sought-after publications on the culture of the Hopewell people. This long out of print volume discusses Hopewell culture, the late 19th-Century excavations under the author's direction, and the objects unearthed. Most of the hundreds of objects illustrated were presented to the Field Museum at the end of the 19th Century. (EAP)

    ____Another Copy. Same. $125.00

    ____Another Copy. Same. $60.00

M456. MOOREHEAD (Warren K.). (Ohio State Archaeological and Historical Society Quarterly, Vol. 7, Columbus, 1899) Indian Tribes of Ohio Historically Considered. pp1-109, original cloth. $15.00

M457. MOOREHEAD (Warren K.). The Merrimack Archaeological Survey. 79pp, 44 maps and illus of artifacts and sites. Peabody Museum, Salem, Mass, 1931 (1st ed.), wrappers. $45.00

M458. MOOREHEAD (Warren K.). Primitive Man in Ohio. xvi, 246pp, index, 54 illus, cloth, examination of Flint Ridge, Port Ancient, Chillicothe, Hopewell and many other prehistoric sites in Ohio. New York, 1892 (1st ed.). $110.00

M459. MOOREHEAD (Warren K.). A Report of The Susquehanna River Expedition. 143pp, 37 pls, index, bibliography, original wrappers. Andover, Andover Press, 1938 (1st ed.). $40.00

    ____Another Copy. Same. $30.00

    ____Another Copy. Same. $20.00

M460. MOOREHEAD (Warren K.). The Stone Age in North America. An Archaeological Encyclopedia.... (2 Volumes). Vol. 1: xiv, 457pp. Vol. 2: viii, 417pp. Lrg 8vo, original green cloth, over 700 color and b/w photographs of artifacts, illus, index, bibliography. Boston, Houghton Mifflin, 1910 (1st ed.). $225.00

M461. MOOREHEAD (Warren K.). Stone Ornaments Used by the Indians in the U.S. and Canada, Being a Description of Certain Charm Stones, Gorgets, Tubes, Bird Stones, Etc. 448pp, 262 illus, spine ends frayed, rear hinge started, ex-library, numbers on spine, rear pocket removed. Andover, 1917. $125.00

M462. MOOREHEAD (Warren K.). Tonda: A Story of the Sioux. 309pp, appendix by Major Marcus A. Reno, photographs by D. F. Barry, R. A. Rinehart, others, includes Custer battle, decorated cloth. Cincinnati, Robert Clark, 1904 (1st ed.). $55.00

M463. MOORE-WILSON (Minnie). The Seminoles of Florida. 126pp, photographs, 22pp Seminole vocabulary. Philadelphia, 1896 (1st ed.). $35.00

    ____Another Copy. New York, Moffat Yard, 1910. $15.00

M464. MOORHEAD (Max L.). The Apache Frontier: Jacobo

Ugarte and Spanish-Indian Relations in Northern New
Spain, 1769-1791. 309pp, illus, 12pp photographs, 8
maps, sources, index. Norman, 1968 (1st ed.). $30.00
___Another Copy. Same. d.j. $30.00
___Another Copy. Same. d.j. $20.00
___Another Copy. Norman, 1976, d.j. $20.00

M465. MOORHOUSE (Major Lee). Souvenir Album of Noted Indian Photographs. 25pp of photographs interleaved with
22pp of descriptive text, tied wrappers, 28.5 x 23.5 cm.
Pendleton East Oregonia, 1906 (2d ed.). $50.00
    Major Moorhouse was Superintendent of Umatilla Indian
Agency near Pendleton. It was here that he began his
hobby of photographing Indian tribal life. Smith:
6996.
___Another Copy. Same. $50.00

M466. MORGAN (C.) and O'CALLAGHAN (E. B.) (Editors).
The Documentary History of the State of New York.
(Volume 1 only) 786pp, 13 maps and plans, newly re-
bound, 26 papers, many relating to the Indian tribes
(Iroquois, Mohawk, Onondagoes). Albany, 1849. $60.00

MORGAN (Lewis H.). See also BAE Bulletin No. 128.

M467. MORGAN (Lewis H.). Ancient Society. Or Researches in
the Lines of Human Progress from Savagery through Bar-
barism to Civilization. 564pp, index. Howes: M-803/
Chicago, n.d. $20.00

M468. MORGAN (L. H.). (Contributions to North American
Ethnology, Vol. IV, Washington, 1881) Houses and
House-Life of the American Aborigines. xiv, 281pp, fron-
tis, 56 photographs (including 28 pls) and drawings,
cloth. $125.00
___Another Copy. Same. $50.00
___Another Copy. Same. Ex-library. $40.00

M469. MORGAN (L. H.) (WHITE, Leslie A., Editor). The Indian
Journals, 1859-62. 229pp, index, 16 color pls, over 100
other illus, maps, notes, oblong 4to. Ann Arbor, MI,
1959 (1st ed.) d.j. $45.00
___Another Copy. Same. $40.00
___Another Copy. Same. $30.00

M470. MORGAN (Lewis). League of the Ho-de-no-sau-nee, or
Iroquois. 477pp, pls, other illus, some folding, folding
map. New York, Rochester, 1851 (1st ed.). $200.00
    Howes: M-804. Field: 1091. Larned: 668. Howes
shows 1851 edition is first, another 1901 edition which is
limited to 300 copies, 1901 edition is 2 volumes. (WS)
___Another Copy. New York, 1901, ...With Additional
Material Edited and Annotated by Herbert M. Lloyd (2
Volumes). 338pp, 332pp, maps, pls, some in color.
$100.00
___Another Copy. New York, 1904 (2 volumes in 1),
670pp, two lrg (18½" x 21½") colored maps, 2 color pls,
92 other illus, lrg 8vo. $75.00

_____Another Copy. New York, 1922 (2 Volumes in 1) 338pp, 332pp, pls, maps (folded). $97.00

_____Another Copy. Same. $60.00

M471. MORGAN (Lewis H.). (Third Annual Report of the Regents on the Condition of the State Cabinet of Natural History, Albany, 1850, revised ed.) Report to the Regents of the University, Upon the Articles Furnished to the Indian Collection. pp65-97, 27 illus of Indian Artifacts, 17 hand-colored pls of Iroquois Indian artifacts, mostly beadwork, usual off-setting on these pls.
    $175.00

_____Another Copy. Albany, 1850, New York Senate Report 75, 18 colored by hand pls, text figures, new wrappers added, largely costumes. $35.00

M472. MORGAN (Lewis H.). (In: Archaeological Institute of America, First Annual Report, 1879-1880, Cambridge, 1880) A Study of the Houses of the American Aborigines; with suggestions for the Exploration of the Ruins in New Mexico, Arizona and Central America. pp29-80, 13 pls, text figures, complete report, cloth, rebacked, ex-library, 163pp. $25.00

M473. MORGAN (Lewis H.). (Smithsonian Contributions to Knowledge, Vol. 17, Washington, 1871) Systems of Consanguinity and Affinity of the Human Family. 590pp, re-bound, ex-library, includes Eskimo, Cree, Cherokee, Iroquois, Ojibwas, Pueblo Indians, with tables of 80 different Indian languages. $250.00

M474. MORIARTY (James Robert). Chinigchinix; An Indigenous California Indian Religion. 59pp, maps. Los Angeles, 1969 (1st ed.). $10.00

M475. MORLAN (R. E.). (National Museum of Canada, Mecury Series, No. 11, 1973) The Later Prehistory of the Middle Porcupine Drainage, Northern Yukon Territory. xxvi, 583pp, 24pp of photographs, 46 figures, 81 tables, 2 maps, wrappers. $25.00

M476. MORLAN (R. E.). (National Museum of Man, Mecury Series, No. 7, 1973) A Technological Approach to Lithic Artifacts from Yukon Territory. 44pp, 15pp of photographs, 5pp of drawings, wrappers. $10.00

MORLEY (Sylvanus G.). See also BAE Bulletin No. 57.

M477. MORLEY (S. G.). The Ancient Maya. 520pp, 95 pls, 57 figures. Stanford University Press, 1946 (1st ed.).
    $45.00

_____Another Copy. Same. $25.00

_____Another Copy. Stanford, 1947 (2d ed.) signed by author. $40.00

_____Another Copy. Stanford University Press, Oxford University Press, California, London, 1947 (2d ed.).
    $25.00

M478. MORLEY (S. G.). The Book of the People: Popol Vuh. The National Book of the Ancient Quiche Maya. Linen

cvr, slipcase, edition limited to 1,500 copies. Limited
Editions Club, Los Angeles, 1954. $185.00
    This English version was made by Sylvanius Morley
from the translation into Spanish by Adrian Recinos, with
a Pronouncing Dictionary compiled by Lucille Weil. Illustrations by Everett Jackson.

M479. MORLEY (Sylvanius G.). The Excavation of the Cannonball
Ruins in Southwestern Colorado. 14pp, illus, folding
map, wrappers. n.p., 1908. $12.00
____Another Copy. Same. $10.00

M480. MORLEY (S. G.). (American Journal of Archaeology, Vol.
15, No. 2, 1911) The Historical Value of the Books
of Chilan Balam. pp195-214, in a binder. $15.00
____Another Copy. Same. wrappers $10.00

M481. MORLEY (S. G.). The Inscriptions at Copan. 643pp, 33
pls, 91 text figures, 12pp bibliography, 4to, major work
on the Maya of Copan, Honduras. Carnegie Institute,
Washington, 1920. $475.00

M482. MORLEY (S. G.). (Middle American Research, Tulane
University, Publication 26, No. 8, 1969) The Stela Plat-
form at Uxmal, Yucatan, Mexico. 30pp, 23 figures.
                                                  $12.00

M483. (MORONGO INDIANS). Engineering an Economic Feasibility
Investigation from Rehabilitation and Betterment of the
Morongo Irrigation Project, Morongo Indian Reservation,
California. 65pp, 4to, maps, 2 lrg folding maps in rear
pocket, report prepared by VTN Consolidated for the
Morongo Bank of Mission Indians under the auspices of
the Bureau of Indian Affairs. Irvine, 1976. $50.00

M484. MORRIS (A. A.). Digging in the Southwest. 301pp,
51 photographs, cloth. New York, 1933. $38.00

M485. MORRIS (A. A.). Digging in Yucatan. 279pp, frontis,
illus with 40 photographs, interesting account of an
excavation by artist who assisted her husband, Earl H.
Morris. New York, 1931 (1st ed.). $35.00
____Another Copy. New York, Junior Literary Guild,
1931, 291pp, 38 illus, cloth. $30.00

M486. MORRIS (E. H.). (Carnegie Institution of Washington,
Publication 533, 1941) Anasazi Basketry, Basketmaker
II through Pueblo II. 138pp, 21pp photographs, 7pp
designs, 11pp drawings, fold-out map, cloth. $165.00

M487. MORRIS (E. H.) and SHEPARD (A. O.). (Carnegie Institution Publication 519, Washington, 1939) Archaeological
Studies in the La Plata District, Southwestern Colorado
and Northwestern New Mexico, and: Technology of La
Plata Pottery. xxiv, 298pp, 67 figures, 321 photographic pls. $275.00

M488. MORRIS (E. H.) and BURGH (R. F.). (Carnegie Institution Publication 604, Washington, 1954) Basket Maker II
Sites Near Durango, Colorado. x, 135pp, drawings,
maps, 88pp photographs. $125.00

M489. MORRIS (E. H.). (American Museum of Natural History, Anthropological Papers, Vol. XXVIII, Part II, 1927) The Beginning of Pottery Making in the San Juan Area; Unfired Prototypes and the Wares of the Earliest Ceramic Period. 73pp, illus, wrappers. $27.00

M490. MORRIS (E. H.). (American Museum of Natural History, Anthropological Papers, Vol. XXVI, Parts III, IV, 1924) Burials in the Aztec Ruin, The Aztec Ruin Annex. 114pp, illus, folded maps, wrappers. $27.00

M491. MORRIS (E. H.). (American Museum of Natural History, Anthropological Papers, Vol. XXVI, Part II, 1921) The House of the Great Kiva at the Aztec Ruin. 37pp, illus, wrappers, folded maps, cvrs loose. $15.00

M492. MORRIS (E. H.). (American Museum of Natural History, Anthropological Papers, Vol. XXVI, Part V, 1928) Notes on Excavations in the Aztec Ruin. 161pp, illus, wrappers. $27.00

M493. MORRIS (E. H.). (Carnegie Institute Publication 406, Washington, 1931) The Temple of the Warriors at Chichen Itza, Yucatan (2 Volumes). With illustrations by Jean Charlot and Ann Axtell Morris. 4to, original cloth, boxed, somewhat shaken. Vol. I: Text. xiv, 485pp, color frontis (Turquoise Mosaic). Vol. II: Illustrations. 170 full-page pls with 80 in color, 323 figures. Plates 1-27: Temple of the Warriors and edifices related thereto, folding map, 1 lithographed water color by Charlot. Plates 28-129: includes drawings, bas reliefs reproducing original colors as found by Jean Charlot. Drawings by A. A. Morris in full color plus 2 folding plates of N. W. Collonade Dais in full color. Plates 130-170: Murals by A. A. Morris includes folding pls of Sea Coast Village and Temple of Chac Mool, lithographed in full color. $950.00
One of the most detailed excavation reports ever produced, describing the work of four seasons, 1924-1928. Illustrated with before and after photographs. Morris was aided by noted archaeologists including Ruppert, Thompson, Morley, etc. Work was enhanced by the Mexican Muralist Charlot's watercolors. (BF)

M494. MORRIS (W. F.). Luchetik, The Woven Word from Highland Chiapas. 38pp, 35pp of drawings, 1 full-page photograph, map. San Cristobal de las Casas, 1983. $12.00

MORRISON (J. P. E.). See BAE Bulletin No. 129.

M495. MORRISON (T. F.). The Osage treaty of 1865: An Address. 8pp, 4to, wrappers, gives historical background of this treaty as well as text of the treaty itself. St. Paul, 1925 (1st ed.). $15.00

M496. MORROW (Mabel). Indian Rawhide: An American Folk Art. 243pp, 4to, illus with 140 drawings, 40 are in color, index, bibliography. Norman, 1975 (1st ed.), d.j. $45.00

_____Another Copy. Same. $30.00

M497. MORSE (Jedidiah). A Report to the Secretary of War on
        Indian Affairs, Comprising a Narrative of a Tour Per-
        formed in the Summer of 1820, Under a Commission From
        the President, for the Purpose of Ascertaining the Actual
        State of the Indian Tribes in Our Country. ivc, 400pp,
        handcolored folding map, portrait, modern quarter moroc-
        co, raised bands, first edition, first issue without errata
        slip. New Haven, 1822. $200.00
            Includes extracts from the journals of other travelers
        such as Captain John R. Hall down the Arkansas;
        Wagner-Camp: 25. "This is certainly the most complete
        and exhaustive report of the condition, numbers, names,
        territory and general affairs of the Indians ever
        made...." Field: No. 1098 (CLR)
            Howes: M-843. Sabin: 50945.
        _____Another Copy. Same. $335.00

M498. MORSS (N.). (Peabody Museum Papers, vol. XII, No. 2,
        Cambridge, 1931) Notes on the Archaeology of the Kai-
        bito and Rainbow Plateaus in Arizona. 18pp, 5pp of
        photographs, 2 maps. $19.00

M499. MORTON (Freidrich). Xelahuh (Adventures in the Maya
        Lowlands). Translated from the German edition of 1950.
        Illus. London, n.d. $13.00

M500. MORTON (Samuel G.). Crania Americana; or, A Compara-
        tive View of the Skulls of Various Nations of North and
        South America.... (4), v, 296pp, frontis, folio, 78 pls,
        colored map, in text illus, errata, original cloth. Phila-
        delphia, J. Dobson, 1839. $500.00
            Sabin: 51022. Field: 1100. Neither reference men-
        tions the frontispiece portrait of Ongapatonga (Big Elk),
        Chief of the Omawhaws. Lithography by John Collin,
        Philadelphia. (RMW)

M501. MORTON (Sarah W. A.). Ouabi: or the Virtues of Na-
        ture. An Indian Tale. In Four Cantos. 52pp, frontis,
        later leather backed bds, left edge frontis trimmed
        through rule, presentation copy from George Ticknor.
        Boston, I. Tomas, E. T. Andrews, 1790 (1st ed.).
                                                       $175.00

M502. MORTON (Thomas). New English Canaan or New Canaan.
        Containing an Abstract of New England, Composed in
        Three Books. The Firste Booke Setting Forth the
        Originall of the Natives ... the Country ... The Third
        Booke Setting Forth, What People are Planted There, What
        Remarkable Accidents Have Happened Since the First
        Planting of It, Together with Their Tenents and Practice
        of Their Church. 96 leaves, full red crushed morocco,
        gilt. Amsterdam, Frederick Stam, 1637. $12,500.00
            Church: 437. JCB (3)2:265. Streeter Sale: 616.
        Sabin: 51028. One of the classic accounts of the early
        settlements of New England, looked to increasingly by

modern historians and anthropologists for its unbiased
and detailed accounts of Indian life in early New England,
internecine struggles among the colonists, and descriptions of flora and fauna. Morton first came to New England in 1622 and lived there until his expulsion by the
Plymouth colonists a decade later. He was particularly
sympathetic to the way of life of the Indians, and provides extensive descriptions of customs, hunting and
planting, artifacts and lifestyles in the first section of
the work. The second provides a remarkable account
of the landscape and ecology of New England. The final
section of Morton's account is the most famous historically,
since it gives an account of his long and often amusing
feud with the Plymouth Colony and a description of his
separate settlement at Merr-mount, where his close association with the Indians of the area and his open defi-
ance of the laws of the Plymouth settlers provided one
of the more colorful episodes in early New England.
(WR)

M503. MOSCOWITZ (I.) and COLLIER (J.). American Indian
Ceremonial Dances: Navajo, Pueblo, Apache, Zuni.
192pp, 147 drawings, cloth, revised edition of Patterns
and Ceremonials of the Indians of the Southwest. New
York, 1972. $18.00

M504. MOTT (Mrs. D. W.). Legends and Lore of the Long Ago.
232pp, illus, frontis, cloth. Los Angeles, 1929, d.j.
                                                   $20.00

M505. (MOUNDBUILDERS). Eighth Annual Report of the Peabody Museum. Description of an Excavation and a Collection of Articles of Pottery and Stone. 30pp, illus,
wrappers. Cambridge, 1875. $35.00

M506. MOZINO (Jose Mariano). Noticias de Nutka: An Account
of Nootka Sound in 1792. Translated and Edited by Iris
Wilson. University of Washington, Seattle, 1970, d.j.
                                                   $22.00

M507. MUELLE (J. C.). (University of California Publications in
American Archaeology and Ethnology, Vol. 39, No. 3,
1943) Concerning the Middle Chimu Style. 14pp of text
containing 1 figure, 2pp of photographs. $20.00

M508. MULLAN (John). (Senate Executive Document 32, 35:2,
Washington, 1859) Topographical Memoir and Map of
Colonel Wright's Late Campaign Against the Indians of
Oregon and Washington Territories. 82pp, folding map
of Col. Steptoe's Battlefield, May, 1858, removed. One
of Mullan's lesser-known works, written while he was
working on the Fort Benton to WallaWalla wagon road,
for which he is justly famous. Col. Steptoe was well
known for shepherding emigrant trains overland to the
West in the 1850s. $125.00

M509. MULLER (G. F.) and URNESS (C.). Bering's Voyages:
The Reports from Russia. vii, 221pp, 2 illus, 23 maps,

wrappers. St. Petersburg, 1758, Fairbanks, 1986.
$30.00

M510. MULLOY (W.). (University of Wyoming Publications, Vol. XVIII, No. 1, Laramie, 1954) Archaeological Investigations in the Shoshone Basin of Wyoming. 70pp, maps, pls, wrappers, reprint. $10.00

M511. MULLOY (W.) and STEEGE (S. C.). (University of Wyoming Publications, Vol. XXXIII, No. 3, Laramie, 1967) Continued Archaeological Investigations Along N. Platte River in E. Wyoming. pp169-233, maps, pls, wrappers. $10.00

M512. MULLOY (W.). (Wyoming Archaeologist, Vol. 7, No. 1, 1964) McKean Site in Northwest Wyoming, and other Articles. 41pp, maps, illus, lrg 8vo, wrappers. $10.00

M513. MUMEY (Nolie). The Singing Arrow. A Navaho Indian Story of Love and Truth. 89pp, 4to, photographic illus, limited to 1,000 signed copies, based on legendary characters of the Navaho Indians. The Golden Bell Press, Denver, 1958, d.j. $50.00
____Another Copy. Same. Unopened. $25.00
____Another Copy. Same. Uncut and unopened.
$15.00

MUNIZ (Manuel Antonio). See BAE Bulletin No. 143.

M514. MUNK (J. A.). Southwest Sketches. 311pp, 133 illus, Indians of Arizona, Rader, 2458. New York, 1920 (1st ed.). $45.00

M515. MURDOCK (George Peter). Ethnographic Bibliography of North America. 393pp, entries listed by individual tribes making this the most useful edition. New Haven, 1960 (3rd ed.). $50.00
____Another Copy. 454pp, map, 4to, Vol. I: General North America. New Haven, 1975 (4th ed.). $35.00

M516. MURDOCK (John). "A Study of Eskimo Bows in the U.S. National Museum." pp307-316 plus 11 pls of drawings, map, from the Report of U.S. National Museum for 1884, bound in later cloth, Washington, 1884. $15.00
____Another Copy. Same. Wrappers. $10.00

M517. MURIE (James R.). (American Museum of Natural History, Anthropological Papers, Vol. XI, Part VI, 1914) Pawnee Indian Societies. 99pp, wrappers. $30.00

M518. MURILLO (Gerardo) (Dr. Atl). Iglesias de Mexico. Volume V: Altares. 94pp, text and watercolor by Dr. Atl (Gerardo Murillo), 37 photographs by Kahlo, folio. Mexico, 1925. $125.00

M519. MURPHEY (Edith VanAllen). Indian Uses of Native Plants. 81pp, illus, index, map, wrappers, informative work on ethnobotany of Indians of Nevada, Southern California, Utah and Arizona. Ft. Bragg, n.d. (c.1959). $15.00
____Another Copy. Same. $10.00

M520. MURPHY (James E.). Let My People Know: American Indian Journalism, 1828-1978. 230pp, index, bibliography. Norman, 1981 (1st ed.), d.j. $18.00

M521. MURPHY (Robert F.). (University of California Anthropological Records No. 16, Berkeley, 1960, 1st ed.)
Shoshone-Bannock Subsistence and Society. 50pp, map,
bibliography, 4to, wrappers, history, social and political organization and ecology of the Shoshone and Bannock
of Wyoming and Idaho. $40.00

M522. MURPHY (R. F.) and QUAIN (B.). (American Ethnological
Society, Monograph XXIV, 1955) The Trumai Indians of
Central Brazil. xii, 108pp, 4pp of photographs, map,
cloth. $30.00
____Another Copy. Same. $20.00

MURRA (John). See BAE Bulletin No. 143.

M523. MURRAY (Charles A.). Travels in North America During
the Years 1834, 1835 and 1836. Including a Summer
Residence with Pawnee Tribe in Remote Prairies of Missouri (2 Volumes). Vol. 1: xvi, 473pp. Vol. 2: xi,
372pp, 2 frontis, half morocco, marbled bds. London,
Bentley, 1839 (1st ed.). $325.00
    Howes: M-193: "Best account of the Pawnees while
yet uncontaminated by whites." (OTB)
____Another Copy. Same. $350.00
____Another Copy, Harper & Bros., 1839 (1st American
ed.) (2 Volumes) Vol. 1: 324pp. Vol. 2: vii, 13pp,
247pp, original cloth, rebacked. $300.00

M524. MURRAY (Hugh). An Historical and Descriptive Account
of British North America (3 Volumes). pp352; 356; 388.
Maps, (2 folding), pls, index, 12mo, full leather, one
map torn at attachment. Edinburgh, Oliver & Boyd,
1839 (2d ed.). $150.00
____Another Copy. Harper & Bros., 1840 (1st American
ed.) (2 volumes) pp312;290. index, gilt lettered cloth.
                                                        $65.00

M525. MURRAY (Keith A.). The Modocs and Their War. 330pp,
illus, index, bibliography, map, an account of the Modoc
War which gives the history of the war in detail and also
explains the concepts and religious beliefs behind some
of the Modoc's most surprising moves, first available
edition, as first edition destroyed by fire. Norman,
1959 (2d print.). $20.00
____Another Copy. Norman, 1976. $25.00

M526. MURRAY (William H.). Pocahontas and Pushmataha. xv,
106pp, illus, bibliography. Oklahoma City, 1931 (2d
ed.). $10.00

M527. (MUSEUM OF AMERICAN INDIAN). Indian Notes Vol. II,
No. 2, April, 1925. Contains "Arikara Basketry" by
M. R. Gilmore; "The Crow Skull Medicine Bundle," by
W. Wildschut; "An Unusual Pomo Basket," by W. C.
Orchard. 55pp, photographs. $22.00

M528. (MUSEUM OF AMERICAN INDIAN). Indian Notes Vol. III,
No. 3, 1926. Contains: "Stone Sculptures from the
Finca Arevalo," by S. K. Lothrop; "The Stone Collars of

Porto Rico," by M. H. Saville. 73pp, photographs and
figures, wrappers. $30.00

M529. (MUSEUM OF AMERICAN INDIAN). Indian Notes Vol. III,
No. 4, October, 1926. Contains: "Indian Use of the
Silver Gorget" by A. Woodward; "The Arikara Consola-
tion Ceremony" by M. R. Gilmore; "Crow War Bundle of
Two Leggings" by W. Wildschut. 98pp, photographs.
$25.00

M530. (MUSEUM OF AMERICAN INDIAN). Indian Notes Vol. IV,
No. 2, April, 1927. Contains: "The Potters of Gauta-
jiagua, Salvador" by S. K. Lothrop; "Nose Ornaments
of Gold" by W. C. Orchard; "Objects from the Canadian
Northwest" by D. A. Cadzow; "Some Tolowa Specimens"
by A. Woodward. 82pp, numerous photographs. $35.00
___Another Copy. Same. $25.00

M531. (MUSEUM OF AMERICAN INDIAN). Indian Notes Vol. IV,
No. 3, July, 1927. Contains: "A Nicoyan Polychrome
Vase" by S. K. Lothrop; "Some Gold Ornaments from
South America" by M. H. Saville. 117pp, photographs
and figures, wrappers. $25.00

M532. (MUSEUM OF AMERICAN INDIAN). Indian Notes Vol. V,
No. 3, July, 1928. Contains: "A Pipe of Unique Form
from Pecos, New Mexico" by A. V. Kidder; "Mohegan
Beadwork on Birch Bark" by F. G. Speck. 84pp, photographs, figures. $25.00

M533. (MUSEUM OF AMERICAN INDIAN). Indian Notes Vol. V,
No. 4, October, 1928. Contains: "Shell Carvings from
Colombia" by M. H. Saville; "Santiago Atilan, Guatemala"
by S. K. Lathrop. 112pp, photographs and figures,
wrappers. $25.00

M534. (MUSEUM OF AMERICAN INDIAN). Indian Notes Vol. VI,
No. 1, January, 1929. Contains: "Some Specimens from
the Bering Sea Culture" by T. Mathiassen; "The Dakota
Ceremony of Hunka" by M. R. Gilmore. 96pp, photographs. $35.00

M535. (MUSEUM OF AMERICAN INDIAN). Indian Notes Vol. VI,
No. 2, April, 1929. Contains: "Boundaries and Hunt-
ing Groups of the River Desert Algonquin" by F. G.
Speck; "The Peace Tomahawk Algonkian Wampum" by J.
Keppler; "A Montagnais Prayer-Book and a Mowak
Primer" by R. Gaines. 95pp, photographs, figures.
$27.00

M536. (MUSEUM OF AMERICAN INDIAN). Indian Notes Vol. VII,
No. 1, January 1930. Contains: "Notes on the Gay
Head Indians of Massachusetts" by G. Tantaquidgeon;
"The Senaca New-Year Ceremony and Other Customs"
by H. M. Converse. 128pp, photographs, figures.
$30.00

M537. (MUSEUM OF AMERICAN INDIAN). Indian Notes Vol. VII,
No. 2, April, 1930. Contains: "The Paraphernalia of
the Duwamish Spirit-Canoe Ceremony" by T. T.

Waterman; "A Massachusetts Pot and an Eskimo Lamp" by W. C. Orchard. 147pp, photographs, figures.
$30.00

M538. (MUSEUM OF AMERICAN INDIAN). Indian Notes Vol. VII, No. 3, July, 1930. Contains: "Coiled Gambling Baskets of the Pawnee and Other Plains Tribes" by G. Weltfish; "Wampum Collection" by G. G. Heye. 131pp, photographs and figures.
$35.00

M539. (MUSEUM OF AMERICAN INDIAN). Indian Notes Vol. VII, No. 4, October, 1930. Contains: "Ornamental Designs in Southwestern Pottery" by T. T. Waterman; "Newly Discovered Straw Basketry of the Wampanuag Indians of Massachusetts" by G. Tantaguidgeon; "Mistassini Notes" by F. G. Speck. 172pp, 74 photographs.
$39.00

M540. (MUSIC). Authentic Music of the American Indian. (set of three 12-inch stereo records) Contains the music of over 20 western tribes including Sioux, Apache, Hopi, Navaho, Crow, Pawnee, Tewa, Pima, etc., actually performed by native American Indians; war dances, honor songs, social and folk songs, ceremonial songs and chants, in box. Los Angeles, n.d.
$20.00

M541. MYERS (Fred). (Smithsonian Institution, Washington, 1986) Pintupi Country, Pintupi Self: Sentiment, Place and Politics Among the Western Desert Aborigines, d.j.
$18.00

M542. MYRTLE (Minnie) (Anna C. Johnson). The Iroquois; or, the Bright Side of Indian Character. 317pp, illus, foxing, newly rebound. Howes: J-125. New York, 1855 (1st ed.).
$15.00

-N-

N1. NABOKOV (Peter). Two Leggings; The Making of a Crow Warrior. Based on a Field Manuscript by William Wildschut. xxv, 226pp, 16pp illus, maps, bibliography, notes, index, appendix. New York, 1967 (1st ed.). $30.00
_____Another Copy. Same. $20.00
_____Another Copy. Same. Foreword by John Ewers, crayon mark on d.j. $10.00

N2. NADAL (Mora V.). Compendio de Historia del Arte Pre-Columbiano de Mexico y Yucatan. 271pp, 75 drawings, 12mo, ex-library. Buenos Aires, 1940. $30.00

N3. NADEAU (Remi). Fort Laramie and the Sioux Indians. 324pp plus index, photographs, maps, other illus, notes, bibliography, map endpapers. Englewood Cliffs, NJ, 1967 (1st ed.), d.j. $20.00

N4. NADER (Laura). (University of California Publications in American Archaeology and Ethnology, Vol. 48, No. 3,

1964) Talea and Juquila: A Comparison of Zapotec Social Organization. 101pp, text figures, wrappers.
$30.00

___Another Copy. Same. $10.00

N5. NADILLAC (Marquis de). Pre-historic America. Edited by W. H. Dall. First Edition in English. 566pp, 219 engravings, original gilt stamped cloth. New York, 1884.
$45.00

N6. NAMMACK (Georgiana). Fraud, Politics and Dispossession of the Indians. The Iroquois Land Frontier in the Colonial Period. 128pp, 11 illus, some are maps, bibliography, index. Norman, 1969 (1st ed.), d.j. $15.00

___Another Copy. Same. $10.00

N7. NAPOLI (Ignacio M.). (Baja California Travel Series No. 19, Los Angeles, 1970) The Cora Indians of Baja California; The Relacion of Father Ignacio Maria Napoli, S.J., Sept. 20, 1721. Translated and Edited by James R. Moriatry III. 76pp, illus, folding map, limited to 500 copies. $30.00

___Another Copy. Same. $25.00

N8. (NARRAGANSET INDIANS). The Narraganset Chief; or, the Adventures of a Wanderer. Written by Himself. 195pp, pages stained and foxed, full leather with cvrs detached. New York, J. K. Porter, 1832. $85.00
Howes: N-11. Sabin: 51771. Purports to be the story of an Indian raised and educated in the East.
(BF)

N9. NASH (Manning). (University of Texas, Vol. 6 in a series, Austin, 1967) Handbook of Middle American Indians: Social Anthropology. 597pp, illus, index, bibliography, 4to. $40.00

N10. NASH (M.). (American Anthropological Assn, Memoir 87, Menasha, 1958) Machine Age Maya: The Industrialization of a Guatemalan Community. 118pp, folded charts, wrappers. $15.00

N11. NASH (R. C.). (Museum of the American Indian, Notes and Monographs, No. 52, New York, 1939) Calendrical Interpretations of a Golden Breastplate from Peru. 16pp, 1 illus, wrappers. $10.00

N12. (NAVAHO INDIANS). The Art of the Navaho, from the Alfred I. Barton Collection. 24pp, exhibition catalogue from Lowe Art Museum, 1975. $10.00

N13. (NAVAHO INDIANS). Navaho Customs. A Booklet of the History, Beliefs and Knowledge of Navaho Indians. vi, 105pp, illus, pictorial wrappers, twenty articles from earlier publications (1932-1952) of the Museum of Northern Arizona Society of Science and Art. Flagstaff, 1954.
$10.00

N14. (NAVAHO INDIANS). Our Friends the Navahos. 32pp, illus, map, stiff pictorial wrappers, printed professionally for the Members of the Young People's Fellowship, Church

of the Holy Faith, contains eight plates by Laura Gilpin.
Santa Fe, 1957. $25.00

N15. (NAVAHO INDIANS). Navahoana, A List of Publications on
the Navaho Indian. 16pp. St. Michaels Press (c.1949).
$13.00

N16. (NAVAHO INDIANS). (Senate Document 216, 56:2, Washington, 1901) Navaho Indian Reservation, Arizona and
New Mexico: Mineral Claims. 97pp, folding color map
of the reservation lands, removed. $20.00

N17. (NAVAHO INDIANS). The Navajo. vi, 24pp, 16 b/w
photographs of the trading post, the reservation and
rugs; 15 color and 1 b/w half-page photographs of Navajo
rugs offered for sale at the trading post, along with a
full description and price for each rug, complete reprint
of a catalogue published by M. B. Moore, Indian Trader,
of the Crystal Trading Post, New Mexico, in 1911. Albuquerque, 1986. $17.00

N18. (NAVAHO INDIANS). The Navajo: A Long Range Program
for Navajo Rehabilitation. Report of J. A. Krug, Secretary of the Interior. 51pp, 4to, wrappers. $15.00

N19. (NAVAHO INDIANS). A Ten Year Program for the Navajo,
Prepared at the Request of the Hon. Julius A. Krug,
Secretary of the Interior, December, 1947. 80pp, 1 fold-
out map. $17.00

N20. (NAVAHO INDIANS). Treaty Between the United States of
America and the Navajo Tribe of Indians, with a Record
of the Discussions that Led to its Signing. Introduction
by Martin A. Link. 26pp, wrappers, the negotiations of
May, 1868 at Ft. Sumner, New Mexico, plus a complete
printing of the treaty. Flagstaff, 1968. $12.00
____Another Copy. Same. $10.00

N21. (NAVAHO INDIANS). (Senate Executive Document 68, 52,
Washington, 1893) Condition of the Navajo Indian Country. 50pp, from Secretary of the Interior to President
Benjamin Harrison dealing with a full inspection of the
Navajo country. Text contains a number of figures,
17 very large fold-out maps, 3/4 red morocco, 1/4 kid
cvr, hubs on spine, worn. $90.00

N22. NAVARRETE (C.). (New World Archaeological Foundation,
Brigham Young University Paper No. 7, 1960) Archaeological Explorations in the Region of the Frailesca, Chiapas, Mexico. 43pp, 49 figures. $15.00

N23. NAVARRETE (C.). (New World Archaeological Foundation,
Brigham Young University, Paper No. 4, 1959) A Brief
Reconnaissance in the Region of Tonala, Chiapas, Mexico.
10pp, 8 figures. $10.00

N24. NAVARRETE (C.). (New World Archaeological Foundation,
Brigham Young University, Paper No. 21, 1966) The
Chipanec, History and Culture. 111pp, 102 figures.
$12.00

N25. NAVARRETE (C.). (New World Archaeological Foundation,

Brigham Young University, Paper No. 3, 1959) Exploration at San Agustin, Chiapas, Mexico. 16pp, 10 figures.
$10.00

N26. NAVARRETE (Carlos) et al. Observaciones Arqueologicas
en Coba, Quintana Roo. 90pp, illus, folded charts, maps,
wrappers. Mexico, 1979. $25.00

N27. NAVARRETE (Carlos) and MUNOZ (L. L.). Reconocimiento
Arqueologica del Sitio "Dos Pilas." Petexbatun, Guatemala. 68pp, 39 illus, includes several photographs of
carved stellae, wrappers. Guatemala, 1963. $25.00

N28. NEIHARDT (John G.). Black Elk Speaks. Being the Life
Story of a Holy Man of the Ogalala Sioux as told to....
280pp, illus by Standing Bear (some in color). Dustin:
211. Luther High Spot: 89. New York, 1932 (1st ed.).
$45.00

N29. NEIHARDT (J. G.). Indian Tales and Others. 306pp,
New York, 1926 (1st ed.). $25.00

N30. NEIHARDT (John G.). Patterns and Coincidences. A
Sequel to All is But A Beginning. 122pp. Columbia,
MO, 1973 (1st ed.), d.j. $10.00

N31. NEIHARDT (J. G.). The Song of the Indian Wars. 231pp.
New York, MacMillan, 1925 (1st ed.). $40.00

N32. NEIHARDT (J. G.). When the Tree Flowered. An Authentic Tale of the Old Sioux World. 248pp. New York, 1951
(1st print.), d.j. $15.00

N33. NEITZEL (R. S.). (American Museum of Natural History,
Anthropological Papers, Vol. 51, Part 1, 1965) Archaeol-
ogy of the Fatherland Site: The Grand Village of the
Natchez. 108pp, 21 figures, 16pp of photographs.
$39.00
____Another Copy. Same. $25.00
____Another Copy. Same. $20.00

N34. NELSON (Bruce). Land of the Dacotahs. 343pp plus index, photographs, bibliography. Minneapolis, 1946
(1st ed.). $20.00
____Another Copy. 1947 (2d print.). $10.00

N35. NELSON (F. W.). (New World Archaeological Foundation,
Brigham Young University, Paper No. 33, 1973) Archaeological Investigations at Dzibilnocac, Campeche, Mexico.
142pp, 107 figures. $14.00

N36. NELSON (John Louw). Rhythm for Rain. xi, 273pp, illus,
pls, cloth, life of and with Hopi Indians. Boston, 1937,
(1st ed.), d.j. $60.00
____Another Copy. Same. $40.00
____Another Copy. Same. $40.00
____Another Copy. Same. slight wear to d.j. $25.00
____Another Copy. Same. $25.00

N37. NELSON (J. R.). Lady Unafraid. 278pp, signed by author, story of Rebecca Jewel Francis, who spent the
year 1862 as a Missionary and teacher among the Ojibway
Indians, wear at spine ends, part of frnt cvr faded.
Caldwell, Idaho, 1951. $35.00

N38. NELSON (Kjerstie). Marriage and Divorce Practices in Native California. 47pp, bibliography, 4to, wrappers,
criteria in choosing a spouse, pre-marital sex, love magic,
bride purchase, courting, divorce, child custody, etc.
Berkeley, 1975. $12.00

N39. NELSON (N. C.). (University of California Publications in
American Archaeology and Ethnology, Vol. 7, No. 5,
Berkeley, 1910) The Ellis Landing Shellmound. pp357-
426, 15 pls of multiple artifacts, wrappers. $35.00

N40. NELSON (N. C.). (American Museum of Natural History,
Anthropological Papers, Vol. XXII, Part I, 1917) Contributions to the Archaeology of Mammoth Cave and Vicinity, Kentucky. 73pp, illus, text figures, wrappers, cvr
missing. $20.00

N41. NELSON (R. K.). Hunters of the Northern Ice. xxiv,
429pp, 16pp photographs, cloth. Chicago, 1969. $34.00

N42. NELSON (R.). Hunters of the Northern Forest, Designs
for Survival Among the Alaskan Kutchin. 339pp, 29
illus, cloth. Chicago, 1973. $25.00
____Another Copy. Same. $18.00

N43. NEQUATEWA (E.). (Museum of Northern Arizona, Bulletin
No. 8, Flagstaff, 1936) Truth of a Hopi and Other Clan
Stories of Shung-Opovi. 114pp, 1 photograph, limited to
600 copies, cloth. $45.00
____Another Copy. Flagstaff, 1947, limited to 1500
copies, edited by Mary-Russell Colton, d.j., 136pp,
pictorial cloth. $20.00

N44. NESBITT (Paul H.). The Ancient Mimbrenos: Based on
Investigations at the Mattocks Ruin, Mimbres Valley, New
Mexico. 105pp, 43 pls of multiple artifacts, cloth with
original wrappers bound in, sml 4to. The Logan Museum,
Beloit, 1931 (1st ed.). $65.00

N45. NESBITT (P. H.). (From: American Antiquities, Vol. 2,
No. 4, 1937) A Stone Carving in Bas-Relief from the
Upper Gila Area. pp264-266, 1 pl, in binder. $10.00

N46. NEUENSWANDER (H. L.) and ARNOLD (D. E.). Cognitive
Studies of Southern Mesoamerica. xxxi, 283pp, 8 maps,
approx 40 charts. Dallas, 1977, 1981. $25.00

NEUMAN (Robert W.). See also BAE Bulletin Nos. 185 and 189.

N47. NEUMAN (R. W.) and SIMMONS (L. A.). (Louisiana Geological Survey No. 4, Anthropological Study, State of Louisiana, Dept. of Conservation, 1940) A Bibliography Relative to Indians of the State of Louisiana. 72pp. $20.00

N48. (NEVADA). (Southwest Museum Papers No. 4, Los Ange-
les, 1930, 1st ed.) Contains: Introduction, by M. R.
Harrington (26pp); Mesa House, by Irwin Hayden (66pp);
An Unusual Burial in Mesa House Ruin, by Louis Schell-
back (12pp) and Paiute Cave, by M. R. Harrington (20pp).
                                                            $40.00
____Another Copy. Los Angeles, 1970. $11.00

N49. (NEVADA). (Senate Report 221, 56:1, Washington, 1900,

1st print.)   Reimbursement for Moneys Expended, etc.,
in Repelling and Suppressing Indian Invasions and Hostilities in Nevada.   11pp, removed, narrative of the Indian
Wars with accounts of claims. $15.00

N50. NEVE y MOLINA (Luis de).   Regalas de Orthographia,
Diccionario, y Arte del Idioma Othomi, Breve Instruccion
para los Principiantes.... 24pp, 106pp, frontis portrait
in crude facsimile, sml quarto, contemporary limp vellum,
upper corner of first two leaves torn, affecting some text
on verso of second, some minor worming, good copy with
uncommon engraved errata leaf.   Imprenta de la Bibliotheca Mexicana, Mexico, 1767. $600.00
        Medina (Mexico) 5174. Pilling: 2738. Sabin: 52413.
The author was a native Otomi, born in the environs of
Mexico City. He entered the Seminary there where he
served as professor of the Otomi language. This is a
general manual for the language, which has been called
one of the most interesting of the native languages of
Mexico, spoken by the Indians of the northwest part of
the Anahuac Valley and parts of the provinces of Michoacan. (WR)

N51. NEWCOMB (Charles). Throw His Saddle Out. 246pp, novel
relating experiences on Navaho reservation. Flagstaff,
1970. $16.00

N52. NEWCOMB (Franc Johnson). Hosteen Klah, Navaho Medicine Man and Sand Painter. 221pp plus index, illus,
bibliography, traces of water stain at lower corners.
Norman, 1964, (1st ed.). $15.00
____Another Copy. Same. d.j. $30.00
____Another Copy. Norman, 1971, 227pp, illus, maps,
bibliography, index, d.j. $20.00

N53. NEWCOMB (F. J.). Navaho Folk Tales. xix, 203pp, 27
b/w drawings, 1 color pl, cloth. Museum of Navaho
Ceremonial Art, 1967. $35.00

N54. NEWCOMB (F. J.). Navaho Neighbors. 236pp, illus, index. Norman, 1966 (1st ed.), d.j. $25.00
____Another Copy. Same. $20.00

N55. NEWCOMB (F. J.). Navajo Omens and Taboos. 79pp plus
12 photographs, foreword by Chee Dodge, 1 two-page
color sand painting, limited to 1000 copies, cloth with
printed title labels, promotional brochure and order blank
laid in. Santa Fe, 1940 (1st ed.). $150.00
        Saunders: 1176. Kluckhohn, p.55. The author lived
among the Navajo for twenty-seven years accumulating the
material for this book from direct observation. (TE)

N56. NEWCOMB (Hervey). The Wyandot Chief; or, the History
of Barnet, a Converted Indian; and His Two Sons; with
Some Account of the Wea Mission. frontis, 92pp, early
cloth. Boston, 1835. $125.00

N57. NEWCOMB (William). North American Indians: An Anthropological Perspective. Goodyear, 1974, paper ed. $15.00

N58. NEWCOMB (W. W., Jr.). The Indians of Texas from Prehistoric to Modern Times. xviii, 404pp, illus, pls, 4
maps, bibliography, index. University of Texas, Austin,
1961 (1st ed.). $35.00

N59. NEWCOMB (W. W., Jr.). The People Called Wichita.
104pp, b/w and color photographs, drawings, maps,
signed by tribal chieftian, wrappers, part of the Indian
Tribal Series. Phoenix, 1976 (1st ed.). $10.00

N60. NEWCOMB (W. W.) and KIRLAND (Forrest). The Rock Art
of Texas Indians. Illus, 239pp, maps, bibliography, 4to,
index. University of Texas, Austin, 1967, (1st ed.),
d.j. $70.00
___Another Copy. Same. $25.00

N61. NEWCOMB (W.). (Texas Memorial Museum, Museum Notes,
No. 8, Austin, 1958) Skeleton of Yellowhouse Canyon.
12pp, wrappers. $10.00

N62. NEWELL (H. P.) and KRIEGER (A. D.). (Society of American Archaeology, Memoir, No. 5, 1949) The George C.
Davis Site, Cherokee County, Texas. xv, 255pp, 60
figures, 20pp tables. $40.00
___Another Copy. Same. $25.00

N63. NEWELL (Robert). Memoranda: Travels in the Territory
of Missourie; Travel to the Kayuse War, Together with a
Report on the Indians South of the Columbia River. 159pp,
frontis, 2 maps, designed and printed by Lawton Kennedy, edited by Dorothy O. Johnasen, limited to 1000 copies,
cloth. Portland, OR, 1959, (1st ed.). $65.00

NEWMAN (Marshall T.). See also BAE Bulletin Nos. 129, 143,
154, 164 and 166.

N64. NEWMAN (M. T.) and WILLEY (G. R.). (Peabody Museum,
Papers, Vol. XXVII, No. 4, 1947) Indian Skeletal Material from the Central Coast of Peru. 71pp of text containing 26 tables and maps, plus 7pp of photographs.
$25.00

N65. NEWMAN (Sandra Corrie). Indian Basket Weaving. How
to Weave Pomo, Yurok, Pima and Navaho Baskets. 91pp,
many b/w and color photographs, bibliography, wrappers.
Flagstaff, 1974 (1st ed.). $12.00

N66. NEWMAN (S.). (Viking Fund Publications in Anthropology,
No. 2, 1944) Yokuts Language of California. 247pp.
$25.00

N67. NEWMAN (S.). (University of New Mexico Publications in
Anthropology, No. 14, 1965) Zuni Grammar. 77pp.
$19.00

N68. (NEW MEXICO). (Eastern New Mexico University, Contributions in Anthropology, Vol. 1, No. 2, 1968) Excavations at En Medio Shelter, New Mexico. iv, 44pp, maps,
illus, bibliography, wrappers. $10.00

N69. (NEW SPAIN). Descripcion de la Nueva Espana en el Siglo
SVII, por El Padre Fray Antonio Vazquez de Espinosa, y
Otros Documentos del Siglo SVII. 254pp of text, plus 9

leaves of engravings, calf, marbled endpapers. Mexico
City, 1844. $70.00

N70. (NEW TESTAMENT). El Evangelio de Jesu Christo Segun
San Lucas en Ayamara y Espanol. Traducido ... al Aymara por Don Vicente Pazoskanki.... 2ff, 130pp, 12mo,
19th century brown morocco embossed in blind, a.e.g.,
ex-library with perforation stamp on titlepage, accession
date rubber-stamped in gutter of another page, and shelf
number in white on spine. Londres: Impreso por J.
Moyes, 1829. $300.00

Darlow & Moule: 1519. The first printing of any portion of the Bible in Aymara, the native language of Bolivia
and the secondary language of the Inca empire. (WR)

N71. (NEWS). News from New-England, Being a True and Last
Account of the Bloody Wars Carried on Betwixt the In-
fidels, Natives, and the English Christians, and Converted Indians of New England, by a Factor of New-
England to a Merchant in London, 1676. 20pp, 4pp advs,
cloth. Boston, reprinted for Samuel G. Drake, April,
1850. $35.00

___Another Copy. 4to, printed wrappers, 20pp, one of
75 lrge paper copies. $35.00

N72. NEWSOM (J. A.). The Life and Practice of the Wild and
Modern Indian. frontis, vi, 219pp, author came to Okla-
homa in 1879 at the age of six. He lived among the
Cheyenne and Seminole Indians for 20 years. Oklahoma
City, Harlow Publishers, 1923 (1st ed.). $45.00

N73. NEWSON (T. M.). Thrilling Scenes Among the Indians.
With a Graphic Description of Custer's last fight with
Sitting Bull. 241pp, drawings. Howes: N-127. Dustin:
477. Chicago, 1884 (1st ed.). $100.00

N74. NEWTON (Norman). Thomas Gage in Spanish America.
214pp, illus, 17th century English traveler in Mexico
and Central America. New York, 1969. $20.00

N75. (NEZ PERCE). (House of Representatives Executive Document 307, 42:2, Washington, 1872, 1st print) Nez Perce
Indian Reservation in the Territory of Idaho. 4pp, removed. $10.00

N76. (NEZ PERCE). (Senate Executive Document 82, 50:2,
Washington, 1889, 1st print.) Letter from Secretary of
War ... Information Relative to Services of Volunteers in
the Nez Perce War. 27pp, removed, names of the volunteers along with events of the war. $25.00

N77. (NEZ PERCE). (Senate Executive Document 31, 53:2,
Washington, 1894, 1st print.) Agreement with the Nez
Perce Tribe of Indians in Idaho. 68pp, removed, text of
the agreement, and testimony on it, to transfer over
32,000 acres of Nez Perce land to the United States.
$30.00

N78. NIBLACK (A. P.). (National Museum Report for 1888,
Washington, 1890.) The Coast Indians of Southern

Alaska and Northern British Columbia. pp225-386, 70
pls (multiple artifacts), 2 folding charts, (whole volume),
some cvr wr. $125.00
___Another Copy. Same. bound in cloth covered bds.
                                                               $65.00
N79. NICHOLS (David A.). Lincoln and the Indians: Civil War
      Policy and Politics. 223pp, bibliography, index. Colum-
      bia, 1978 (1st ed.), d.j. $17.00
      ___Another Copy. Same. $15.00
      ___Another Copy. Same. $12.00
NICHOLS (Frances S.). See BAE Bulletin No. 152.
N80. NICHOLS (J. B.). Little Man's Family, Dine Yahzi
      Ba'Atchini. Bureau of Indian Affairs, 2 Volumes, The
      first publications in Navajo of anything except for the
      Bible and related material. Primer: 30pp, 28 drawings;
      1940, 1950. Reader: 78pp, 35 drawings, 1950 (revised).
                                                               $25.00
N81. NICHOLS (Phebe Jewell). Tales from an Indian Lodge;
      Memominee Indian Reservation, Wisconsin. 47pp, wrap-
      pers. n.p., n.d. $15.00
N82. NICHOLSON (H. B.) and KEBES (E. Q.). Art of Aztec
      Mexico, Treasures of Tenochtitlan. 188pp, 111 b/w and
      30 color photographs, 37 drawings, 1 map. National
      Gallery of Art, Washington, 1983. $40.00
          A wonderful exhibition of Aztec art, the first truly
      representative survey of the art of the Aztec people held
      outside Mexico, drawn from museums around the world, but
      particularly from Mexico's National Museum of Anthropology
      and the Templo Mayor, was held at the National Gallery of
      Art. The discovery of the ritual heart of the Aztec Em-
      pire--at the Templo Mayor and the sacred precinct of
      Tenochtitlan--has brought to light much new information
      that is discussed in the text of this out of print catalogue
      of the exhibition. Wonderful photographs--especially those
      in color--of the objects, some of which have never before
      been in view away from the excavation sites. (EAP)
N83. NICHOLSON (H. B.) et al. Pre-Columbian Art from the
      Land Collection. 276pp, 180 b/w and 16 color photo-
      graphs. San Francisco, 1979. $35.00
          One of the most important private collections of pre-
      Columbian art in the U.S. is the subject of this excep-
      tional, extensive catalogue. The Land's Mesoamerican
      collection has just received many plaudits, and this hand-
      some volume, with its fine text and first-rate photographs,
      rubbings and drawings, illustrates the wealth and depth
      of the collection. (EAP)
      ___Another Copy. Same. $25.00
N84. NICHOLSON (Irene). Firefly in the Night: A Study of
      Ancient Mexican Poetry and Symbolism. London, Faber,
      1959, d.j. $25.00
N85. NICHOLSON (Irene). Mexican and Central American

Mythology, 141pp, illus, sml 4to. London, 1967, (1st
ed.). $25.00
___Another Copy. over 100 illustrations of pre-
Columbian artifacts, reprint. $20.00
NICKERSON (Norton H.). See BAE Bulletin No. 158.
N86. NIELSEN (George R.). The Kickapoo People. 104pp, b/w
and color photographs, maps, signed by tribal chief,
wrappers, part of the Indian Tribal Series. Phoenix,
1975 (1st ed.). $10.00
N87. NIETHAMMER (Carolyn). American Indian Food and Lore.
178pp plus indices, drawings, notes, bibliography.
150 recipes with medical uses also given. New York,
1974 (1st ed.), d.j. $15.00
NIMUENDAJU (Curt). See also BAE Bulletin No. 143.
N88. NIMUENDAJU (Curt) and LOWIE (R. H.). (Catholic University of America, Anthropology Series, No. 8, 1939).
The Apinaye. vi, 189pp, 30 photographs. $30.00
N89. NIMUENDAJU (C.). (Fjarde Foldjen, Band 31, No. 2,
Goteborg, 1926) Die Palikur-Indianer und Ihre Nach-
barn. 144pp, 44 photographs of artifacts, fold-out map.
$35.00
N90. NIMUENDAJU (Curt). (University of California Publications
in American Archaeology and Ethnology. Vol. 41, 1946)
The Eastern Timbira. 358pp, 3 maps, 42 pls of multiple
artifacts, translated and edited by Robert Lowie, wrap-
pers. $60.00
___Another Copy. Same. $80.00
N91. NIMUENDAJU (Curt). (University of California Publications
in American Archaeology and Ethnology, Vol. 45, 1952)
The Tukuna. 167pp and illus, edited by Robert Lowie
and Translated by W. D. Hoehthal, wrappers. $80.00
N92. NOEMI (Maria) and RAMIREZ (Q.). (Instituto Nacional
Antropologia e Historia, Serie Investigaciones, No. 22,
Mexico, 1972) Los Matlatzincas Epoca Prehispanica y
Epoca Colonial Hasta, 1650. 142pp, wrappers. $20.00
___Another Copy. Same. $21.00
N93. NOGUERA (Eduardo). La Ceramica Arqueologica de
MesoAmerica. 412pp, over 150 illus. Mexico, 1965.
$100.00
N94. NOMLAND (Gladys Ayer). (University of California Publi-
cations in American Archaeology and Ethnology, Vol.
36, No. 2, 1935) Sinkyone Notes. pp149-178, one
photograph, map, wrappers. $12.00
___Another Copy. Same. $10.00
N95. NOON (J. A.). (Viking Fund Publications in Anthropology,
No. 12, 1949) Law and Government of the Grand River
Iroquois. 186pp. $25.00
N96. NORDENSKIOLD (Erland). (Ethnographical Museum,
Ethnographical Studies No. 10, Goteborg, 1938) An
Historical and Ethnological Survey of the Cuna Indians.
Arranged by Henry Wassen. 686pp, plus color illus,
wrappers. $185.00

___Another Copy. Same. $125.00

N97.   NORDENSKIOLD (G.).   Cliff Dwellers of the Mesa Verde,
       Southwestern Colorado, Their Pottery and Implements.
       383pp, 64 color photographs, 97 sml b/w photographs
       and drawings, 34pp of lrge b/w photographs, 11pp of
       lrge drawings, cloth. Stockholm, 1893, Glorieta, 1979.
                                                  $40.00
       ___Another Copy. Same. $25.00

N98.   NORDENSKIOLD (G.).   Ruiner af Klippboningar I Mesa
       Verde's Canons. (4), 193, (1), (4)pp, plus map and
       plates not reckoned in pagination, numerous textual
       illus, folio, original half calf with gilt, and gilt decor-
       ated cloth, t.e.g., edge wr. Stockholm, P.A., Nor-
       stedt, 1893. $500.00
           An extraordinarily interesting and visually beautiful
       work on the cliff-dwellers of Mesa Verde and environs,
       distinguished by twelve outstanding photogravure plates
       (on 9 sheets; one double-spread) of the cliff dwellings,
       evidently by the author, including views of Mountain
       Sheep Canyon, the Cliff Palace, the Balcony House, etc.
       These views are supplemented by several full-page
       tinted maps, numerous other plates and textual illustra-
       tions after photographs of artifacts, other ruins, etc.

N99.   NORDENSKJOLD (O.).   Antarctica, Two Years Amongst the
       Ice of the South Pole. 626pp, 228 illus, 2 fold-out
       maps. Hamden, 1977. $40.00

N100. NORDENSKJOLD (O.).   Sud-Amerika, ein Zukenftsland der
       Menscheit. Natur/Mensch/Wirtschaft. xii, 245pp, 75
       photographs, 2 figures, 8 maps, cloth. Stuttgart,
       1928. $40.00

N101. NORDQUIST (D. L. and G. E.).   Twana Twined Basketry.
       viii, 94pp, 83 illus, wrappers. Ramona, 1983. $30.00
       ___Another Copy. Same. $25.00

N102. NORIEGA (Raul).   Registry of Eclipses of the Sun on Two
       Monuments of Ancient Mexico. 18pp, illus, wrappers.
       Mexico, 1956. $20.00

N103. NORMAN (Benjamin M.).   Rambles in Yucatan.... 304pp,
       12 adv. pp, many illus, pls (lithographs by Endicott),
       maps, 1/2 leather, marbled bds. J. and H. G. Lang-
       ley, 1843 (1st ed.). $150.00
           Field: 1138. Sabin: 55494. Sabin: "Including a
       valuable ethnological disquisition, and a vocabulary of
       the Maya tongue, with a sketch of the grammar." (RMW)
       ___Another Copy. New York, 1843 (3rd ed.). $60.00

N104. NORMAN (V. G.).   (New World Archaeological Foundation,
       Brigham Young University Paper No. 30, 1973, 1976)
       Izapa Sculpture. (2 Volumes). Vol. I: 68pp, 64
       photographs, 1973. Vol. II: 260pp, 261 figures and
       photographs, 26 tables, 1976. $75.00

N105. NORTH (Luther).   Man of the Plains. Recollections of
       Luther North, 1856-1882. Edited by Donald Danker.

Foreword by George Bird Grinnell. xx, 350pp, 9 maps, appendices, chronology, index. Lincoln, University of Nebraska, 1961 (1st ed.). $25.00

North led Pawnee Scouts during Plains Indian Wars of the 60s and 70s. North completed his recollections in 1925 and except for extracts in Grinnell's "Two Great Scouts," it has until now remained unpublished. (OTB)

N106. NORTHROP (D. Henry). Indian Horrors; or, Massacres by the Red Man. 600pp, illus. n.p., n.d. (c.1890). $30.00

N107. (NORTHWEST COAST). Art of the Shaman. 32pp, 36 illus, (some in color), wrappers. University of Iowa Museum of Art, 1973. $10.00

N108. (NORTHWEST COAST). An Art Perspective of the Pacific Northwest, from the Collection of Dr. and Mrs. F. R. Stenzel. 32pp, 89 photographs of paintings by Western artists. Exhibition catalogue, Montana Historical Society, 1963. $13.00

N109. (NORTHWEST COAST). Arts of a Vanished Era. 63pp, 80 illus, wrappers. Bellingham, Washington, 1968. $15.00

N110. (NORTHWEST COAST). (Seattle Anthropology Society and the University of Washington Student Davidson Anthropology Society, Vol. 1, No. 1, 1955; Vol. 3, No. 2, 1957) Davidson Journal of Anthropology. Lrge 8vo, pls, figures, bibliographies, wrappers, six issues, all published, Northwest Coast and Plateau Indians. $60.00

N111. (NORTHWEST COAST). Der Lachs in der Vorstellung der Indianer des Westlichen Nord-Amerika. pp23-71, Jahrbuch des Museums fur Volkerkunde zu Leipzig, Berlin, 1965, wrappers. $35.00

N112. (NORTHWEST COAST). Northwest Coast Indian Art, The Collection of Ulfert Wilke. 20pp, 19 lrge photographs. Exhibition catalogue, Cedar Rapids Art Center, 1970. $12.00

N113. (NORTHWEST COAST). (Museum of the American Indian, Leaflet No. 5, 1926) A Rare Salish Blanket. 15pp, 1 color photograph, 8 drawings. $15.00

N114. (NORTHWEST COAST). Stones, Bones and Skin: Ritual and Shamanic Art. 180pp, profusely illus, 4to, also includes Pre-Columbian Cultures, Indians of North America, cloth. Toronto, 1977. $45.00

N115. NOURSE (J. E.) (Editor). Narrative of the Second Arctic Expedition Made by Charles F. Hall ... and Residence Among the Eskimos During the Years 1864-1869. (50), 644pp, many illus, photographs and pls, folding colored pocket map of the North Polar Regions, index, rebound in cloth, lrge 8vo. Government Printing Office, Washington, 1879. $90.00

_____Another Copy. Same, rebound, no map. $65.00

N116. NOWOTNY (Karl A.). Mexikanische Kostbarkeiten aus

Kunstkammern der Renaissance. 80pp, 26 pls, with 3 in color of Pre-Columbian Featherwork, wrappers. Vienna, 1960. $40.00

N117. NOYES (Al). In the Land of Chinook or the Story of Blaine County. 147pp plus index, photographs, other illus, photograph of C. M. Russell and reproduction of one of his letters. Howes: N-218. Herd: 1690. Adams Guns: 1625. n.p. 1917 (1st ed.). $85.00

N118. NULIGAK (Translated and Edited by Maurice Metayer). I, Nuligak. 208pp, drawings by Ekootak, map endpapers, autobiography of a member of the Kitigariukment tribe of Canadian Eskimo, born in 1895. Toronto, 1966 (1st ed.), d.j. $10.00

N119. NUNEZ A. (Lautaro). Desarrollo Cultural Prehispanico del Norte de Chile. 48pp, 7pls, wrappers. Chile, 1965. $15.00

N120. NUNEZ A. (Lautaro). Prospeccion Arquelogica en el Norte de Chile. 35pp, 6 pls, wrappers. Chile, 1965.
$15.00

N121. NUNGAK (Zebedee) and ARIMA (E.). (Ottawa National Museum, Bulletin No. 235, Ottawa, 1969) Eskimo Stories. Unikkaatuat. 137pp, 4to, illus, wrappers.
$18.00

N122. NUNLEY (Parker) and HESTER (Thomas). (University of Texas Archaeological Survey Report No. 7, San Antonio, 1975) An Assortment of Archaeological Resources in Portions of Starr County, Texas. 100pp, photographs, drawings, maps, bibliography, spiral bound. $10.00

N123. NUNO (Ruben Bonifaz). The Art in the Great Temple: Mexico-Tenochtitlan. 188pp, 91 color pls, 4to. Instituto Nacional de Antropologia e Historia, Mexico, 1981.
$75.00
____Another Copy. Same. $65.00

N124. NURGE (Ethel) (Editor). The Modern Sioux, Social Systems and Reservation Culture. 352pp, index, bibliography. Lincoln, 1977. $25.00
____Another Copy. Same. $20.00
____Another Copy. Same. $20.00

N125. NUSBAUM (Aileen). Zuni Indian Tales. 167pp, six double-page color drawings, illus by Margaret Finnan, decorative cloth, originally published under the title of The Seven Cities of Cibola, a collection of Zuni Folk Tales retold for children, some of which were gathered while the author's husband was on the Hodge expedition excavating Hawikuh. New York, 1926. $35.00

N126. NUSSBAUM (D.). Deric With the Indians. x, 204pp, 24pp of photographs. New York, 1927 (1st ed., 2d impression). $24.00

N127. NUTTALL (Z.). (Peabody Museum, Papers, Vol. 1, No. 3, 1891) The Atlatl or Spear Thrower of the Ancient Mexicans. 40pp, 3pp drawings, 7 figures, wrappers missing. $55.00

N128. NUTTALL (Z.) (Translator). (Peabody Museum Papers, Vol. 11, No. 2, Cambridge, 1926) Official Reports Sent to His Majesty, Philip II, in 1580. 39pp, 2 pls, wrappers. $20.00

N129. NUTTALL (Z.). (Peabody Museum Papers, Vol. I, No. VII, 1904) A Penitental Rite of the Ancient Mexicans. 36pp, 5pp of photographs, 8 figures. $65.00

N130. NYBROTEN (Norman) (Editor). (University of Idaho Bureau of Business and Economic Research, Report No. 9, Moscow, ID, 1964, 1st ed.) Economy and Conditions of the Fort Hall Indian Reservation. 194pp plus index, photographs, maps, wrappers. $10.00

N131. NYE (Wilber S.). Bad Medicine and Good: Tales of the Kiowas. 291pp, illus by Nick Eggenhofer, index. Norman (1st ed.). $25.00
_____Another Copy. Norman, 1969, d.j. $20.00

N132. NYE (W. S.). Plains Indian Raiders. The Final Phases of Warfare from the Arkansas to the Red River. 407pp plus index, bibliography, photographs, military subduing of the Kiowas, Kiowa-Apaches, Arapaho, Cheyenne and Comanche, includes a collection of photographs by W. S. Soule done 1867-1875 of southern Plains Indians, together with explanations. Norman, 1969 (1st ed.), d.j. $30.00
_____Another Copy. Same. $26.00

N133. NYSTEL (Ole T.). Lost and Found; or, Three Months with the Wild Indians. A Brief Sketch of the Life of Ole T. Nystel, Embracing His Experiences While in Captivity to the Comanches, and Subsequent Liberation from Them, Reflections and Religious Experience. 26pp, plus inserted testimonial leaf, original printed wrappers. Dallas, Wilmans Bros., 1888. $750.00
Not in Eberstadt, Decker or Ayer. Graff: 3057. Howes: N-233. Ole Nystel was captured by the Comanches in Bosque Country, in the spring of 1867 at the age of fourteen. For the first few weeks of his period of captivity, he was subjected to numerous indignities and abuses, but was finally accepted by the Tribe due to his having displayed courage during a thunderstorm. After several attempts at escape, the Indians felt it best to be shed of him, and traded him for $250 in goods at a post on the Arkansas River. Nystel made his way back home to Texas, indignant that Indians would be traded with in Kansas, only to return and maraud in Texas. The remainder of the narrative deals with the author's account of Indian customs, and the large part providence played in his experience. (WR)

-O-

O1. OAKES (Maud). The Two Crosses of Todos Santos: Sur-
vivers of Mayan Religious Ritual. 274pp, 20 pls, sml 4to.
New York, 1951 (1st ed.). $45.00
O2. OBER (F. A.). Travels in Mexico and Life Among the
Mexicans. 190 illus, yellow decorated cloth, some shelf
wear, overall a very good copy, includes: Yucatan, Cen-
tral and Southern Mexico. Boston, 1884. $75.00
___Another Copy. Boston, 1885. xxii, 672pp, spine
frayed, light stain to covers and margin. $45.00
___Another Copy. Same. $165.00
___Another Copy. Same. inner hinges reinforced with
tape. $35.00
O3. OBEREM (U.). Estudios sobre la Arqueologia del Ecuador.
142pp of text, plus 37pp of figures. BAS 3, Bonn, 1975.
                                                      $30.00
O4. OBERG (K.). (Smithsonian Institution, Institute of Social
Anthropology, Publication No. 15, 1953) Indian Tribes
of Northern Matto Grasso, Brazil. 144pp, 10pp of photo-
graphs, 14 charts, 3 maps. $35.00
___Another Copy. Same. wrappers. $30.00
___Another Copy. Same. $15.00
O5. OBERG (K.). (Smithsonian Institution, Institute of Social
Anthropology, Publication No. 9, 1949) The Terena and
the Caduveo of Southern Matto Grasso, Brazil. 72pp of
text containing 4 maps, 2 charts, 24pp of photographs.
                                                      $20.00
___Another Copy. Same. wrappers. $15.00
O6. OBLIGADO (P.). Tradiciones de Buenos Aires. 441pp,
rebound in cloth with original wrappers bound in, 4to,
(7"x11"). Buenos Aires, 1888. $75.00
O7. O'CALLAGHAN (E. B.). The Documentary History of the
State of New York. (Volume I Only). 786pp, 13 maps,
plans (one lacking), newly rebound, includes: Iroquois,
Onondaga, Mohawk, account of the expedition against the
Onondagoes in 1696. Albany, 1849. $75.00
O8. OCAMPO (E.). Apolo y Mascara, la Estetica Occidental
Frente a las Practicas Artisticas de Otras Culturas.
206pp, wrappers. Barcelona, 1985. $15.00
O9. OCCOM (Samson). A Sermon, Preached at the Execution of
Moses Paul, an Indian, Who was Executed ... for the Mur-
der of Mr. Moses Cook, of Waterbury.... 24pp, sml 8vo,
original wrappers. Boston, John Boyles, 1773. $100.00
Field: 1148. Sabin: 56635. Occom, the author, was
the first Indian pupil of the Celebrated Eleazer Wheelock,
at his school in Lebanon, 1742.... He established a
school among the Montauk Indians on Long Island in
1755. (RMW)
O10. OCHOA (Lorenzo) (Editor). Estudios Preliminares Sobre los
Mayas de las Tierras Bajas Noroccidentales. 127pp, plus

illus, folded charts, wrappers. Mexico, 1978. $25.00

O11. O'CONNELL (James F.). The Prehistory of Surprise Valley.
57pp, illus, bibliography, 4to, wrappers. Ramona,
1975, (1st ed.). $15.00

     Surprise Valley runs for 60 miles along the western
edge of the Great Basin in extreme northeastern California
and adjacent areas of northwestern Nevada. A scholarly
account of archaeological investigations of the area and
reconstruction of prehistoric subsistence and settlement
patterns.

    ___Another Copy. Same. $10.00

O12. O'CROULEY (P. A. V.). A Description of the Kingdom of
New Spain by Sr Don Pedro Alonso O'Crouley. 1774.
Edited and translated by Sean Galvin. 146pp plus index,
b/w and color illus, maps, appendices, bibliography, designed by Lawton and Alfred Kennedy, Mexico, New Mexico, California, Texas. San Francisco, 1972 (1st thus.).
   $25.00

O13. O'DELL (Scott). Sing Down the Moon. 138pp, Boston,
1970 (1st ed.). $15.00

O14. ODENS (Peter). The Indians and I: Visits with the
Dieguenos, Quechans, Fort Mohaves, Zunis, Hopis,
Navajos and Paiutes. 80pp, illus, wrappers. El Centro,
1971 (1st ed.). $10.00

O15. OEHLER (C. M.). The Great Sioux Uprising. 272pp, illus,
notes, index, Sioux massacres of the 1860s. New York,
1959, (1st ed.). $25.00

    ___Another Copy. Same. d.j. $15.00

O16. OEHLER (Gottlieb F.) and SMITH (D. Z.). Description of
a Journey and Visit to the Pawnee Indians ... 1851 ...
a Description of the Manners and Customs of the Pawnee
Indians. 32pp, rebound in 3/4 leather with repaired frnt
wrapper bound in. New York, 1914 (1st ed. in separate
format). $25.00

    ___Another Copy. Same. $25.00

    ___Another Copy. Same. $20.00

    ___Another Copy. Fairfield, WA, 1974, facsimile reprint,
limited to 300 copies. $10.00

O17. OEHM (V. P.). Investigaciones Sobre Mineria y Metalurgia
en el Peru Prehispanico, una Vision Critica Actualizada.
134pp, 4 figures, 9 maps. BAS 12, Bonn, 1984. $30.00

O18. OETTERING (Bruno). Morphological and Metrical Variation
in Skulls from San Miguel Island, California. I: The
Sutura Nasofrontalis. 85pp, wrappers. New York,
1920. $10.00

O19. OETTERING (B.). (Heye Foundation, Indian Notes and
Monographs, No. 39, New York, 1925) Skeletal Remains
from Santa Barbara. I: Craniology. 168pp, illus,
wrappers. $18.00

    ___Another Copy. Same. errata slip. $10.00

O20. OETTERING (B.). (Southwest Museum Paper No. 5, Los
Angeles, 1930, 1st ed.) The Skeleton from Mesa House.

A Physical Investigation. 48pp, illus, bibliography, index, wrappers, detailed description of a skeleton discovered in 1926 in Overton, Clark County, Nevada.
$12.00

O21. OFFICER (James E.). Indians in School: A Study of the
Development of Educational Facilities for Arizona Indians.
148pp, illus, 4to, wrappers. University of Arizona, Tuc-
son, 1958. $20.00

O22. OGDEN (John C.). An Excursion into Bethlehem and Nazareth, in Pennsylvania, in the Year 1799; with a Succinct
History of the Moravians. (1 leaf), 167, (1 errata)pp,
12mo, later 1/2 leather, cloth. Philadelphia, C. Cist,
1800 (1st ed.). $175.00
     Howes: O-37. Field: 1152. Sabin: 56815. Includes
a short narration of the massacre of Christian Indians at
Salem and Gnaddenhutten. (RMW)

O23. (Ogden, Peter Skene). Traits of American-Indian Life and
Character. By a Fur Trader. (16), 220, plus 16 adv
pp, half leather, bds. London 1853. $1,750.00
     Field: 1562. Wagner-Camp: 232. Graff: 3076.
Howes: F-139. Sketches of life in Oregon mainly concerned with Indians, but with notes on the fur trade.
At one time this work was attributed to Duncan Findlayson,
but it is now generally agreed that the noted English fur
trader Peter Skene Ogden was the author. Ogden was a
trader and trapper for the Hudson's Bay Co., and this
book recounts his experiences in Oregon and the Northwest from 1820s on, including an account of Jedediah
Smith in Oregon in 1828. (WR) (GFH)
     ____Another Copy. San Francisco, Grabhorn Press, 1933,
107pp, 4to, illus. $125.00
     ____Another Copy. Same. $125.00
     ____Another Copy. Same. cloth, limited to 500 copies.
$75.00
     ____Another Copy. Fairfield, WA, n.d. (c. 1986),
157pp, gilt simulated leather, limited to 398 numbered
copies. $30.00

O24. OGLE (Ralph Hedrick). Federal Control of the Western
Apaches 1848-1886. 259pp, map, bibliography, index,
how the government asserted its authority over the
Apaches of southeastern Arizona and southwestern New
Mexico from the acquisition of the territory to the sur-
render of Geronimo. Albuquerque, 1970, d.j. $15.00

O25. OGLESBY (Catharine). Modern Primitive Arts of Mexico,
Guatemala, and the Southwest. 226pp, 12 photographs,
includes Tribal arts of the Pueblo and Navaho. New
York, 1939 (1st ed.). $40.00

O26. OGLETHORPE (Gen. James). (Collections of the Georgia
Historical Society, Vol. 2, Savannah, 1842, 1st print)
A New Voyage to Georgia ... A Curious Account of the
Indians. 8vo, contains other articles. $75.00

O27. (OHIO). (Ohio Archaeological and Historical Publications, Vol. 1, 1887) Contents include: Aboriginal History of Butler County; Ancient Earthwork near Oxford; Archaeology in Ohio, Blennerhassett; Mounds and Earthworks of Ohio; The Serpent Mound, etc. 8vo, green cloth.
$25.00

O28. (OHIO). (Ohio Archaeological and Historical Publications, Vol. 2, 1888) Contents include: Aboriginal Implements; Opening of a Mound, by W. K. Moorehead, etc. 8vo, green cloth. $20.00

O29. (OHIO). (Ohio Archaeological and Historical Publications, Vol. 3, 1891) Contents include: Fort Ancient; Indian Massacre of Moravians, etc. 8vo, green cloth. $15.00

O30. (OHIO). (Ohio Archaeological and Historical Publications, Vol. 4, 1895) Contents include: Fort Ancient, with map, by W. K. Moorehead, etc. 8vo, green cloth. $15.00

O31. (OHIO). (Ohio Archaeological and Historical Publications, Vol. 5, 1897) Contents include: Archaeological Field Work (by W. K. Moorehead, etc.) 8vo, green cloth.
$15.00

O32. (OHIO). (Ohio Archaeological and Historical Publications, Vol. 7, 1899) Contents include: Indian Tribes of Ohio; Report of Field Work (both by W. K. Moorehead, etc.) 8vo, green cloth. $25.00

O33. (OHIO). (Ohio Archaeological and Historical Publications, Vol. 8, 1900) Contents include: Indian Trial of Ohio; Archaeological Field Work; Narrative of Captivity of Abel Janney, etc. 8vo, green cloth. $15.00

O34. (OHIO). (Ohio Archaeological and Historical Publications, Vol. 11, 1903) Contents include: Ohio Mound Builders; Shaker Mission to Shawnee Indians, etc. 8vo, green cloth. $15.00

O35. (OHIO). (Ohio Archaeological and Historical Publications, Vol. 12, 1903) Contents include: Ancient Works at Marietta; Hopewell Copper Object, etc. 8vo, green cloth. $15.00

O36. (OHIO). (Ohio Archaeological and Historical Publications, Vol. 14, 1905) Contents include: Mound Builders; Miamisburg Indian Mound, etc. 8vo, green cloth. $15.00

O37. (OJIBWAYS). (Collections of the Minnesota Historical Society, Vol. V, St. Paul, 1885) History of the Ojibway Nation. 535pp, frontis. $75.00

O38. O'KANE (Walter Collins). The Hopis: Portraits of a Desert People. 267pp, color photographs, cloth. Norman, 1958 (3rd print.), d.j. $15.00

O39. O'KANE (W. C.). Sun in the Sky. The Hopi Indians of the Arizona Mesa Lands. xvii, 261pp, 53pp of photographs, 18 drawings of designs and decorations. Norman, 1950. $40.00
_____Another Copy. Same. $30.00
_____Another Copy. Same. d.j. $15.00

___Another Copy. Norman, 1950 (2d print), d.j.
$10.00

O40. (OKLAHOMA). Official Souvenir Number and Program of the Convention-Exposition of the Society of Oklahoma Indians. 64pp, photographs, wrappers, from the second annual convention. Ponca City, OK, 1925. $35.00

OLBRECHTS (Frans M.). See BAE Bulletin No. 99.

O41. O'LEARY (T. J.). Ethnographic Bibliography of South America. xxiv, 387pp, 13 maps. New Haven, 1963.
$40.00

O42. OLSEN (Evelyn Guard). Indian Blood. 253pp, map frontis, cloth. Parsons, WV, 1967, d.j. $15.00

O43. OLSEN (S. J.). (Peabody Papers, Vol. LVI, No. 2, 1968) Fish, Amphibian and Reptile Remains from Archaeological Sites. Part I. Southeastern and Southwestern United States. xvii, 137pp, 78pp of photographs and drawings.
$22.00

O44. OLSEN (S. J.). (Peabody Papers Vol. LVI, No. 1, 1964) Mammal Remains from Archaeological Sites. Part I. Southeastern and Southwestern United States. xii, 162pp, 116pp illus. $25.00

O45. OLSON (James). Red Cloud and the Sioux Problem. xiii, 375pp, 25pp of photographs, bibliography, index, endpaper maps. Lincoln, University of Nebraska, 1965 (1st ed.), d.j. $30.00
___Another Copy. Same. lacks d.j. $20.00

O46. OLSON (R. L.). (University of California Anthropological Records, Vol. 14, No. 5, Berkeley, 1955) Notes on the Bella Bella Kwakiutl. 34pp. $23.00

O47. OLSON (R. L.). (University of California Anthropological Records, Vol. 14, No. 3, Berkeley, 1954) Social Life of the Owlekeno Kwakiutl. 56pp, 4 figures, map. $24.00

O48. OLSON (R. L.). (University of California Anthropological Records, Vol. 2, No. 5, 1940) The Social Organization of the Haisla of British Columbia. 36pp. $22.00

O49. OLSON (Ronald D.). (University of Washington Publications in Anthropology, Vol. 2, No. 1, Seattle, 1927) Adze, Canoe, and House Types of the Northwest Coast. 38pp, 4 pls, wrappers. $20.00
___Another Copy. Same. $19.00

O50. OLSON (Ronald). (University of Washington Publications in Anthropology, Vol. 6, No. 1, 1936) The Quinault Indians. 190pp, wrappers. $45.00
___Another Copy. Same. presentation copy signed by author. $38.00

O51. O'MEARA (Walter). Daughters of the Country; The Women of the Fur Traders and Mountain Men. 368pp, illus, bibliography, index. Good account of a neglected aspect of western history--the racial and sexual confrontation of the Indian women and the white men on the frontier. Author traces this relationship from earliest times showing the Indian woman as victim of mass rape, as slave concubine, trading post and rendezvous prostitute and hospitality gift to a passing trader. New York, 1968 (1st ed.), d.j. $25.00

O52.   O'MEARA (W.). The Last Portage. 289pp, illus, index. Biography of John Tanner who was kidnapped by the Shawnee in 1789 and later traded to the Ojibway. Tanner adopted Ojibway way of life and became a member of the tribe living with them for 30 years before returning to white civilization. Boston, 1962 (1st ed.), d.j. $25.00

O'NEALE (Lila M.). See also BAE Bulletin No. 143.

O53.   O'NEALE (Lila M.). (Field Museum, Anthropology Memoirs, Vol. II, No. 3, 1937) Archaeological Explorations in Peru: Textiles of the Early Nazca Period. pp119-220, plus 2 full-page photographs and 34pp of drawings.
     $125.00

O54.   O'NEALE (L. M.). (University of California Anthropological Records, Vol. 9, No. 2, 1949) Chincha Plain-Weave Cloths. 18pp of text containing 8 figures, map, and 9pp of photographs. $30.00
_____Another Copy. Same. $25.00

O55.   O'NEALE (L. M.). Mochica (Early Chimu) and Other Peruvian Twill Fabrics. pp269-294, 6pp of photographs, 7 figures, offprint, Southwestern Journal of Anthropology, 1946. $15.00

O56.   O'NEALE (L. M.). Tejidos de los Altiplanos de Guatemala. (2 Volumes). pp462, 325, 130 illus, wrappers. Guatemala, 1980. $75.00
_____Another Copy. Same. ex-library. $65.00

O57.   O'NEALE (L. M.). (Carnegie Institution Publication No. 567, 1945) Textiles of Highland Guatemala. x, 319pp of text, plus 73pp of figures, another 73pp of text explaining figures, and 57pp of photographs with text page for each. $275.00
_____Another Copy. Same. 4to, cloth. $50.00

O58.   O'NEALE (L. M.) and CLARK (B. J.). (University of California Publications in American Archaeology and Ethnology, Vol. 40, No. 4, 1948) Textile Periods in Ancient Peru III: The Gauze Weaves. 68pp containing 10 figures, 12 diagrams and 20pp of photographs. $75.00
_____Another Copy. Same, wrappers. $18.00

O59.   O'NEALE (L. M.). (Carnegie Institute Publication 574, 1948) Textiles of Pre-Columbian Chihuaha. Foreword by A. V. Kidder, 86pp, 17pp of photographs, 17 figures.
     $65.00
_____Another Copy. Same. $65.00
_____Another Copy. Same. $40.00

O60.   O'NEALE (L. M.). (University of California Publications in American Archaeology and Ethnology, Vol. 32, No. 1, Berkeley, 1932) Yurok-Karok Basket Weavers. 184pp plus 58 photographic pls, drawings in text, wrappers.
     $37.00

O61. OPLER (Morris E.). Among the Western Apache. Edited
by Grenville Goodwin, 103pp, index. Arizona, 1973.
$12.00

O62. OPLER (M. E.). An Apache Life-way. 482pp plus index,
photographs, bibliography, the economic, social and religious institutions of the Chiricahua Indians. Chicago,
1941 (1st ed.). $50.00

O63. OPLER (M. E.). The Character and Derivation of the
Jicarilla Holiness Rites. 98pp, 1 full-page color draw-
ing. University of New Mexico, 1943. $35.00
____Another Copy. Same. color frontis, wrappers.
$25.00
____Another Copy. Same. $25.00

O64. OPLER (M. E.). (Publication of the Hodge Anniversary
Fund, Vol. V, Los Angeles, 1964) Childhood and Youth
in Jicarilla Apache Society. 170pp, illus, map, bibliography, wrappers. $15.00
____Another Copy. Same. $12.00

O65. OPLER (M. E.). (American Anthropological Assn, Memoir
52, Menasha, 1938, 1st ed.) Dirty Boy: A Jicarilla Tale
of Raid and War. 80pp, stiff printed wrappers. $60.00
Saunders: 770. An Apache tale of the spurned and
ill-treated youth who puts his detractors to shame by
performing incredible feats of speed and bravery. It is
a description of Jicarilla Apache concepts of raid, war,
relationship and status that presents a picture of many
important aspects of the culture. (TE)
____Another Copy. Same. $24.00
____Another Copy. Same. $20.00
____Another Copy. Same. $12.00

O66. OPLER (M. E.) (Editor). Grenville Goodwin Among the
Western Apache. 103pp, index, bibliography. Univer-
sity of Tucson, 1973 (1st ed.), d.j. $22.00
____Another Copy. Same. $15.00
____Another Copy. Same. $12.00

O67. OPLER (M. E.). (Memoirs of American Folklore Society,
Vol. XXXVI, New York, 1940) Myths and Legends of
the Lipan Apache Indians. 296pp, index, bibliography.
$35.00

O68. OPLER (M. E.). (American Folk-Lore Society Memoirs,
Vol. XXXVII, 1942) Myths and Tales of the Chiricahua
Apache Indians. xiv, 114pp, cloth. $34.00

O69. (ORATORS). Speeches Delivered by Several Indian Chiefs.
Also, an Extract of a Letter from an Indian Chief. 23pp,
stiff wrappers. New York, S. Wood, 1812, (1st ed.).
$50.00

O70. ORCHARD (Wm. C.). (Contributions from Museum of
American Indian, Heye foundation, Vol. XI, New York,
1975, 2d ed.) Beads and Beadwork of the American
Indian.... 168pp, 41 pls (some in color), photographs,
drawings, wrappers. $10.00

O71. ORCHARD (Wm. C.). Indian Porcupine-quill and Beadwork.
      13pp, wrappers, written for the Exposition of Indian
      Tribal Arts. New York, 1931 (1st ed.). $10.00
O72. ORCHARD (Wm. C.). (Leaflet of Museum of the American
      Indian, No. 5, New York, 1926) A Rare Salish Blanket.
      15pp, lrge 4to, stiff wrappers, includes details of actual
      technique of weaving as well as description and full-color
      illus of a classic example, 9"x13" in size. $15.00
      ___Another Copy. Same. $35.00
O73. ORCHARD (Wm. C.). (Contributions from the Museum of
      American Indian, Heye Foundation, Vol. IV, No. 1, New
      York, 1971, 2d ed) The Technique of Porcupine Quill
      Decoration Among the North American Indians. 85pp,
      30 photographic pls (some in color), 6 figures, wrappers.
                                                         $10.00
O74. ORCHARD (W. J.). The Stone Age on the Prairies.
      160pp, illus, decorated cloth. Toronto, 1942. $35.00
O75. ORCUTT (Samuel). The Indians of the Housatonuc and
      Naugatuck Valleys. (Connecticut). 220pp, illus, cloth.
      Hartford, 1882. $40.00
      ___Another Copy. Same. $35.00
      ___Another Copy. Hartford 1882, reprinted 1972.
                                                         $30.00
O76. (OREGON). (Senate Executive Document 47, 30:1, Wash-
      ington, 1848) Indian Difficulties in Oregon. 8pp, re-
      moved, early announcement of the Oregon Indian War and
      some narrative of attacks and events. $40.00
O77. (OREGON). (Senate Executive Document 46, 37:2, Wash-
      ington, 1862, 1st print.) Indian War Claims in Oregon
      and Washington Territory. 12pp, removed, claims of
      soldiers and persons holding war bonds. $10.00
O78. (OREGON). (Government Printing Office, Washington,
      1874) Official Copies of Correspondence Relative to the
      War with Modoc Indians in 1872-1873. 330pp, removed,
      1st print, massive, important source document with eye-
      witness accounts of the Oregon Indian Wars. $60.00
O79. (OREGON). (Senate Executive Document 121, 47:1, Wash-
      ington, 1882, 1st print) Malheur Indian Reservation in
      ... Oregon. 4pp, plus large folding map showing Indian
      lands in 1879, removed. $35.00
O80. (OREGON). (Senate Executive Document 25, 53:1, Wash-
      ington, 1893, 1st print.) Treaties with Certain Indians
      in Oregon. 58pp, folded map colored in outline, removed,
      contains copies of treaties in force. $35.00
O81. (OREGON AND WASHINGTON). (Senate Executive Document
      34, 33:1, Washington, 1854) Communications from Secre-
      tary of Interior ... Treaties with the Indians in Oregon
      and Washington Territories, 16pp, removed, letters from
      Isaac Stevens detailing a great council of Indians at Fort
      Benton to ease Indian-White tensions, Expedition to the
      Nez Perce and other tribes, trading with fur companies,
      etc. $35.00

O82. (OREGON AND WASHINGTON). Report of the Secretary of War ... all the Letters of the Governor of Washington Territory, Addressed to Him During the Present Year; and Copies of all the Correspondence Relative to the Indian Disturbances in the Territories of Washington and Oregon. 68pp, sewn, describes events in the Rogue River War. Washington, 1856. $75.00

O83. (OREGON AND WASHINGTON). (House of Representatives Executive Document 118, 34:1, Washington, 1856) Indian Hostilities in Oregon and Washington Territories. 58pp, removed, details of battles with Indians, supplies used, etc. $30.00

O84. (OREGON AND WASHINGTON). (House of Representatives Executive Document 45, 35:1, Washington, 1858, 1st print.) Expenses of the Indian Wars in Washington and Oregon Territories. 16pp, removed, review of activities and pay for soldiers. $15.00

O85. (OREGON AND WASHINGTON). (House of Representatives Executive Document 11, 36:1, Washington, 1860, 1st print.) Claims Growing Out of Indian Hostilities in Oregon and Washington in 1855 and 1856. 132pp, removed, reports of operations during the War, and expenses for materials, troops, lodging, etc. $30.00

O86. (OREGON AND WASHINGTON). (House of Representatives Executive Document 46, 36:2, Washington, 1861, 1st print.) Depredations and Massacre by the Snake River Indians. 16pp, removed, narratives of several massacres and attacks on emigrants. $35.00

O87. (OREGON AND WASHINGTON). (Senate Executive Document 24, 42:3, Washington, 1873, 1st print.) Indian Hostilities in the Year 1856. 68pp, removed, reports of the War, with expenses incurred. $30.00

O88. ORR (Charles) (Editor). History of the Pequot War. xxii, 149pp, map, contemporary accounts of Mason, Underhill, Vincent and Gardener, reprinted from Collections of the Mass. Historical Society, cloth. Cleveland, 1897. $25.00

O89. ORTIZ (A.). Hopi Kachina Dolls. 24pp, 14 full-page photographs. Exhibition catalogue, Moore College Art Gallery, Philadelphia, 1975. $12.00

O90. ORTIZ (A.). The Tewa World. Space, Time, Being and Becoming in a Pueblo Society. xviii, 197pp, 11 figures, cloth. Chicago, 1969. $30.00
      ____Another Copy. Same. d.j. $12.00
      ____Another Copy. Same. $10.00

O91. ORTON (J. R.). Camp Fires of the Red Men, or, A Hundred Years Ago. 401pp, illus by Walcott, embossed cloth. New York, 1855 (1st ed.). $25.00

O92. (OSAGE INDIANS). (House of Representatives Report, No. 15, 1851) 12pp, outlines irregularities of Indian agent, removed. $20.00

O93. (OSAGE INDIANS). (Senate Executive Document 6, 44:1,

Washington, 1875, 1st print.) Report of the Commissioners
Appointed to Investigate the Affairs of the Osage Indian
Agency. 108pp, removed, testimony and eye-witness
accounts of frauds against Indians, agency conditions.
$20.00

O94. (OSAGE INDIANS). (House of Representatives Executive
Document 73, 47:1, Washington, 1882, 1st print.)
Claim of Charles Ewing Against the Osage Indian Nation.
Letter from the Secretary of the Treasury ... Transmitting the Papers in the Claim of.... 52pp, removed, it
appears that Ewing was contracted by the Osage tribe as
their attorney, problems arose when the Osages sold a
tract of land and refused to pay Ewing a fee for the
transaction. $45.00
_____Another Copy. Same. $17.00

O95. (OSAGE INDIANS). (House of Representatives Document
643, 57:1, Washington, 1902, 1st print.) Adjustment of
Osage Traders' Claims. 103pp, removed, adjustment of
amounts owed traders by Indians after federal audits.
$10.00

O96. (OSAGE INDIANS). (Senate Document 63, 65:1, Washington, 1917, 1st print.) Osage Indian Leases in Oklahoma. 31pp, removed, oil and mining leases. $15.00

O97. OSBORN (Chase S. and Stellanova). "Hiawatha" with its
Original Indian Legends. 255pp including 1p index of
legends, photographs, Chippewa bibliography, introduction by Frank Murphy. Lancaster, PA, 1944 (1st ed.).
$15.00

OSBORNE (Carolyn). See also BAE Bulletin No. 192.

O98. OSBORNE (C. M.). (University of California, Anthropological
Records, Vol. 13, No. 2, 1950) Shaped Breechcloths
from Peru. 36pp, 4pp photographs, 16 figures. $15.00

OSBORNE (Douglas). See also BAE Bulletin Nos. 166 and 179.

O99. OSBORNE (D.) and KATZ (B. S.) (Editors). (Memoirs of
the Society for American Archaeology, American Antiquity,
Vol. 19, Menasha and Salt Lake City, 1965, 1st ed.)
Contributions of the Wetherill Mesa Archaeological Project.
xviii, 230pp, illus, figures, bibliography, wrappers.
$17.00

O100. OSBORNE (Harold). Indians of the Andes: Aymaras and
Quechuas. 266pp, illus with 30 photographs. Cambridge,
1952 (1st ed.). $40.00
_____Another Copy. Same. $35.00
_____Another Copy. Same. $20.00
_____Another Copy. New York, 1973, reprint, cloth,
279pp, 30 photographs, 2 maps. $15.00

O101. OSBORNE (Lilly De Jongh). Indian Crafts of Guatemala
and El Salvador. 278pp, 81 pls. Norman, 1965 (1st
ed.). $35.00

O102. OSGOOD (C.) and HOWARD (G. D.). (Yale University
Publications in Anthropology, Nos. 27, 28 and 29, 1943)

An Archaeological Survey of Venezuela; Excavations at Ronquin, Venezuela; Excavations at Tocoron, Venezuela. 313pp of text containing 54 figures, and 38pp of photographs. $80.00

O103. OSGOOD (C.) and ROUSE (I.). (Yale University Publications in Anthropology, Nos. 25 and 26, 1942) The Ciboney Culture of Cayo Redondo, Cuba; Archaeology of the Maniabon Hills, Cuba. 186pp of text containing 15 figures and 14pp of photographs, 7 tables. $65.00

O104. OSGOOD (C.). (Yale University Publications in Anthropology, No. 14, New Haven, 1936.) Contributions to the Ethnography of the Kutchin. 189pp text, 30 figures, 10pp of photographs. $57.00

Considered to be the most complete study on the ethnography of the eight Kutchin tribes of the Yukon Territory, Osgood's monographs of this Athapaskan speaking group very heavily emphasizes their material culture. Few Kutchin artifacts are exhibited in museums and even fewer found in galleries or auctions. Meticulously detailed, includes illustrations of artifacts never before published. (EAP)

___Another Copy. New Haven, 1979 reprint. $30.00

O105. OSGOOD (C.). (Yale University Publications in Anthropology, No. 7, New Haven, 1936) The Distribution of the Northern Athapascan Indians. 23pp, map, wrappers. $15.00

O106. OSGOOD (C.). (Yale University Studies in Anthropology, No. 16, New Haven, 1936, 1970 reprint) The Ethnography of the Tanaina. 229pp of text, 32 figures, 14pp of photographs. $30.00

The Tanaina nation, an Athapaskan Speaking people of the south coast of Alaska in and around Cook Inlet, had been the subject of no major study prior to the 1936 publication of this monograph. This and de Laguan's "The Archaeology of Cook Inlet, Alaska" remain the two major studies of the ethnography of this people. The focus is on material and social culture; the illustrated artifacts are principally from collections in Russian, Danish, German and U.S. Museums and most appear in no other publication. (EAP)

O107. OSGOOD (C.). (Yale University Publications in Anthropology, No. 74, 1971) The Han Indians, A Compilation of Ethnographic and Historical Data on the Alaska-Yukon Boundary Area. 173pp, 17 figures, 3pp of photographs. $40.00

___Another Copy. Same. $35.00
___Another Copy. Same. $19.00

O108. OSGOOD (C.). Ingalik Material Culture. 512pp, 144 illus. New Haven, 1940. $68.00

Masks, baskets, boxes, fish skin and fur bags, bowls, pots, clubs, knives, scrapers and scores of other objects made and used by the Ingalik Indians are closely examined in this monumental study of the material culture of this Northern Athapaskan people. The research was done in the 1930s and was published as study No. 22 in the Yale University Publications in Anthropology. (EAP)

O109. OSGOOD (C.). (Yale University Publications in Anthropology, No. 56, 1959) Ingalik Mental Culture. 195pp, 10 figures. $40.00

O110. OSGOOD (C.). (Yale University Publications in Anthropology, No. 53, 1958) Ingalik Social Culture. 289pp, 20pp figures (masks). $70.00

O111. OSKISON (John M.). Tecumseh and His Times. The Story of a Great Indian. 244pp, frontis, endpaper maps, index, cloth. New York, 1938 (1st ed.), d.j. $50.00
___Another Copy. Same. $35.00

O112. OSTERMANN (H.) (Editor). (Reports of the Danish Ethnographical Expedition to Arctic America, 1921-24, Vol. X, No. 3, Copenhagen, 1952) The Alaskan Eskimos, As Described in the Posthumous Notes of Dr. Knud Rasmussen. 292pp, 20 photographs, map, wrappers. $125.00

O113. OSTERMANN (H.) (Editor). (Reports of the Danish Ethnographical Expedition to Arctic America, 1921-24, Vol. X, No. 2, Copenhagen, 1942) The Mackenzie Eskimos, After Knud Rasmussen's Posthumous Notes. 166pp, approx 12 photographs, 4 drawings, wrappers. $95.00

O114. OSWALD (Felix L.). Summerland Sketches, or, Rambles in the Backwoods of Mexico and Central America ... with Numerous Illustrations.... 425pp, frontis, illus, pictorial cloth, gilt, t.e.g., edgeworn, internally a bit soiled and loose, overall quite good. Philadelphia, 1880. $150.00
The travels of the author after leaving his post as director of a poor military hospital in Vera Cruz, from Sonora to Colima, the lake region of Falisco to Yucatan, Guatemala and the Sierra Negra. Much description of the wildlife and fauna encountered, as well as various Indian tribes, with 76 illustrations. (WR)

OSWALT (Wendell H.). See also BAE Bulletin No. 199.

O115. OSWALT (W. H.). Eskimos and Explorers. 361pp, 70 illus, 2 maps, cloth. Novato, 1979. $23.00

O116. OSWALT (W. H.). This Land Was Theirs: A Study of the North American Indian. 617pp, illus, index, endpaper maps, bibliography. New York, 1973. $20.00

O117. OSWALT (W. H.). A Western Eskimo Ethnobotany. pp16-36. Offprint from Anthropological Papers of the University of Alaska, Vol. 6, No. 1, December, 1957. $10.00

O118. OTIS (D. S.). The Dawes Act and the Allotment of Indian
    Lands. Edited with Introduction by Francis Paul Prucha.
    206pp, index. Norman, 1973, d.j. $20.00
    ___Another Copy. Same. lacks d.j. $15.00
O119. OTIS (Raymond). Indian Art of the Southwest: An Ex-
    position of Methods and Practices. 27 unnumbered pp,
    illus, printed wrappers. Saunders: 2320. Weigle:
    p.30 n13. Santa Fe, 1935. $25.00
O120. OTERO (Gustavo Adolfo). La Piedra Magica: Vida y
    Costumbres de los Indios Callahvayas de Bolivia.
    292pp, photographs, wrappers. Mexico, 1951. $35.00
    ___Another Copy. Same. rebound in cloth. $25.00
O121. OTS CAPDEQUI (J. M.). El Estado Espanol en las Indias.
    181pp, wrappers. Mexico, 1965 (4th ed.). $15.00
O122. (OTTAWA INDIANS). Ottawa Indians of Kansas. Letter
    from the Secretary of the Interior.... 9pp, removed,
    the 1862 treaty. Washington, 1863. $25.00
O123. OURADA (Patricia K.). The Menominee Indians. A His-
    tory. 267pp plus index, photographs, drawings, notes,
    bibliography, maps. Foreword by Donald J. Merthrong,
    first history of the Menominees. Norman, 1979 (1st
    ed.), d.j. $15.00
    ___Another Copy. Norman, 1980, 274pp, 33 illus, d.j.
    $35.00
O124. OVER (W. H.). (University of South Dakota, Circular
    No. 1, Vermillion, 1934) Archaeology in South Dakota.
    9pp, drawings, wrappers. $10.00
O125. OWEN (Mary A.). Folk-Lore of the Musquakie Indians of
    North America, and Catalogue of Musquakie Beadwork
    and Other Objects in the Collection of the Folk-Lore
    Society. 147pp, plus 8 pls of multiple artifacts, includ-
    ing 2 color pls of designs, original cloth. David Nutt,
    Publisher, London, 1904. $125.00
    ___Another Copy. Same. $87.00
O126. OWEN (Roger C.). (University of Arizona, Anthropological
    Papers, No. 3, Tucson, 1959) Marobavi: A Study of
    an Assimilated Group in North Sonora. 53pp, illus,
    wrappers. $15.00
    ___Another Copy. Same. $10.00
O127. OWEN (R. C.) et al. The North American Indians: A
    Sourcebook. Includes a bibliography of 200 films on
    American Indians. New York, 1967. $35.00
O128. OWENS (Thomas C.). The Yokaia: A History of the
    Ukiah Valley Indians, 1579-1978. 47pp, 4to, illus, map,
    wrappers. Fort Bragg, 1980, (1st ed.). $12.00
    ___Another Copy. Same. $10.00

P1.   PACKARD (Gar.). Suns and Serpents; The Symbolism of
      Indian Rock Art. 64pp, 74 photographs, 20 drawings,
      index, wrappers, meanings of over 70 symbols found on
      rock carvings made by ancient Puebloid Indians of
      Arizona and New Mexico. Santa Fe, 1974 (1st ed.).
                                                         $10.00
P2.   PADDEN (R. C.). The Hummingbird and the Hawk: Con-
      quest and Sovereignty in the Valley of Mexico, 1503-1541.
      319pp. Ohio, 1967 (1st ed.), d.j. $15.00
P3.   PAEZ (Don Ramon). Wild Scenes in South America; or,
      Life in the Llanos of Venezuela. 502pp, tinted frontis,
      34 illus, frnt cvr faded, water stains along margins,
      original cloth with edge wr. New York, Scribner's,
      1862 (2d ed.). $60.00
P4.   PAIGE (Harry W.). Songs of the Teton Sioux. xv, 201pp,
      illus, bibliography, index, includes later songs of the
      Ghost Dance and Peyote cult. Los Angeles, Westernlore,
      1970 (1st ed.), d.j. $25.00
      ____Another Copy. Same. $15.00
      ____Another Copy. Same. $12.00
P5.   PAINTER (C. C.). Cheyennes and Arapahoes Revisited and
      a Statement of Their Agreement and Contract with Attor-
      neys. 62pp, original printed wrappers. Philadelphia,
      1893. $125.00
           A report by an agent of the Indian Rights Association
      on the state of the Indian reservations and the degree
      to which the treaty of 1867, and other treaties, had not
      been fulfilled.
P6.   PAINTER (C. C.). A Visit to the Mission Indians of South-
      ern California, and Other Western Tribes. 29pp, wrap-
      pers. Philadelphia, 1886. $125.00
           Acting as agent of the Indian Rights Association,
      Painter visited with various tribes, including the Apaches,
      Papagoes, Pimas and Paiutes in Nevada, Idaho and Oregon
      as well as California, and notes here his observations of
      their respective conditions and relations with the Whites.
P7.   PAINTER (M. T.). With Good Heart, Yaqui Beliefs and
      Ceremonies in Pascua Village. xxxvi, 533pp, 29pp
      photographs, cloth. Tucson, 1986. $50.00
P8.   PAINTER (Muriel Thayer). The Yaqui Easter Ceremony at
      Pascua. 40pp, map, wrappers. Tucson, 1950 (1st ed.).
                                                         $10.00
P9.   PALACIOS (E. J.). Arqueologia de Mexico: Culturas Arcaica
      y Tolteca. 80pp, 49 figures, wrappers. Mexico, 1947.
                                                         $40.00
P10. PALACIOS (E. J.). (Contribucion de Mexico al XXIII Con-
      greso de Americanistas, Mexico City, 1928) En los
      Confines de la Selva la Candona. Exploraciones en el

Estado de Chiapas, Mayo-Agosto 1926. 215pp, 116 photographs, 11 figures, 5 color pls, fold-out color pl, bds, sml folio (9"x13"), spine repaired. $125.00
___Another Copy. Same. $85.00

P11. (PALENQUE ROUND TABLE SERIES) In 1973 a group of key Maya scholars convened the first Palenque Round Table; subsequent meetings were held in 1974, 1978 and 1980. The conference, now recognized as the preeminent forum for Maya specialists, attracted scholars of the highest caliber from around the world. These volumes have become essential tools for all serious students of the Maya and have attracted the foremost Maya scholars as contributors. (EAP)
___Volume II (M. G. Robertson, Editor) First Palenque Round Table, 1973: Part 2. 143pp, 87 b/w photographs, 56 drawings, 3 tables, 4 charts, wrappers. $25.00
___Volume IV (M. G. Robertson and D. C. Jeffers, Editors) Third Palenque Round Table, 1978: Part 1. 232pp, 76 b/w photographs, 132 drawings, 2 maps, 6 tables, 2 charts, wrappers. $45.00
___Volume V (M. G. Robertson, Editor) Third Palenque Round Table, 1978: Part 2. 242pp, 130 b/w and 4 color photographs, 101 drawings, map, 2 tables, cloth. $50.00

P12. PALLADINO (L. B.). Indian and White in the Northwest. xxvi, 411pp, many photographs, folding map, bibliography, blue cloth, early missions among the Blackfeet, Piegan, Cheyenne and Crow. Howes: P-40. Baltimore, 1894 (1st ed.). $250.00
___Another Copy. Same. 3/4 leather. $125.00
___Another Copy. Lancaster, PA, 1922 (2d print.) xx, 512pp, photographs, index, decorative leatherette. $85.00
___Another Copy. Same. $95.00
___Another Copy. Same. green cloth, gilt lettering. $65.00

P13. PALMATARY (H. C.). The River of the Amazons. Its Discovery and Early Exploration, 1500-1743. 140pp, map, inscribed by author, cloth. New York, 1965. $15.00

P14. PALMER (R. A.). (Smithsonian Institution, Smithsonian Scientific Series, Vol. 4, 1929, 1949) The North American Indians, an Account of the American Indians North of Mexico, Compiled from Original Sources. 319pp, 11 figures, 85 full-page color and b/w pls. Rader: 2580. $28.00
___Another Copy. New York, 1934. $10.00
___Another Copy. New York, 1975. $20.00

P15. PALMER (William R.). Pahute Indian Legends. 134pp, illustrations. Salt Lake City, 1946 (1st ed.), d.j. $20.00
___Another Copy. Same. $17.00

P16. PALOU (Fray Francisco). Life and Apostolic Labors of the Venerable Father Junipero Serra.... 338pp, illus with 2 pls, folding map, original cloth. Pasadena, 1913.
$60.00

P17. PANCOAST (Chalmers Lowell). (American Museum Journal, Volume XVIII, No. 4, New York, April, 1918) Last Dance of the Picuris. Illustrated article appearing in Journal, entire issue in original pictorial wrappers, ceremony of one of the New Mexico Pueblos with photographs by the author. Saunders: 1855. $25.00

P18. PANCOAST (Henry S.). Impressions of the Sioux Tribes in 1882. With Some First Principles of the Indian Question. 28pp, printed wrappers. Philadelphia, 1883.
$125.00
The author was a Philadelphia do-gooder out visiting the Indians; he provides, however, a good account of the Dakotas and the reservations. (WR)

P19. PANNELL (Walter). Redmen's Horizons. 53pp, wrappers, about the Pueblos. Los Angeles, 1945. $10.00

P20. PARDUCCIZ (R. & I.). Un Sitio Arqueologico Al Norte de la Cuidad: Fase Buayaquil. 84pp, 18pp of photographs, 12 figures, 3 site maps. Casa de la Cultura Ecuatorian, Guayaquil, 1970. $20.00

PARK (Willard Z.). See also BAE Bulletin No. 143.

P21. PARK (W.). (Northwestern University Studies, Social Sciences, No. 2, Evanston, 1939, 1st ed.) Shamanism in Western North America, A Study in Cultural Relationships. viii, 166pp, cloth. $47.00
___Another Copy. Same. $35.00

P22. PARKER (Aaron F.). Forgotten Tragedies of Indian Warfare in Idaho. 10pp, self-wrappers, the Sheepeater campaigns of 1878-89--the last Indian wars in Idaho Country. Grangerville, ID, 1925 (1st ed.). $20.00

P23. PARKER (A. C.). (New York State Museum, Archaeology Bulletin No. 235 and 236, 1922) The Anthropological History of New York. 470pp, pp471-743, index, many illus and maps, 8vo, original wrappers. $70.00
___Another Copy. Same. $35.00
___Another Copy. Same. Part I only. $35.00
___Another Copy. Same. Part II only. $35.00

P24. PARKER (A. C.). (New York State Museum Archaeology Bulletin, No. 184, Albany, 1916) The Constitution of the Five Nations. 158pp, 8 pls, map, index, wrappers.
$35.00
___Another Copy. (c. 1965) reprint. $10.00

P25. PARKER (A. C.). (New York State Museum Bulletin 117, Archaeology 14, 1907) Excavations in an Erie Indian Village and Burial Site at Ripley, Chautauqua County, New York. 96pp, 27 figures, 38pp photographs and drawings. $50.00
___Another Copy. Same. $50.00

P26. PARKER (A. C.). The Indian How Book. 335pp, illus,
      Indian lore. New York, 1927 (1st ed.). $12.00
      ___Another Copy. Garden City, 1937. $15.00
P27. PARKER (Arthur C.). The Life of General Ely S. Parker.
      xiv, 346pp, pls, index, last Grand Sachem of the Iro-
      quois and General Grant's Military Secretary. Buffalo
      Historical Society, 1919 (1st ed.). $65.00
P28. PARKER (Arthur C.). Red Jacket: Last of the Seneca.
      228pp. New York, 1952 (1st ed.). $35.00
P29. PARKER (Arthur C.). Seneca Myths and Folk Tales.
      465pp, illus. Buffalo Historical Society, 1923. $60.00
P30. PARKER (Arthur C.). Skynny Wyndy and Other Indian
      Tales. 262pp, drawings by Will Crawford (some in
      color). Dykes: 50. Crawford: 44. New York, 1926
      (1st ed.). $20.00
P31. PARKER (Donald Dean) (Editor). The Recollections of
      Philander Prescott. Frontiersman of the Old Northwest
      1819-1862. 263pp plus index, bibliography. Prescott
      was Supervisor of Indian farming for the Sioux 1849-
      1856. Lincoln, NE, 1966 (1st ed.), d.j. $12.00
P32. PARKER (Mack). The Amazing Red Man. 66pp, details
      the contributions the Indian has made to White civiliza-
      tion in the fields of Medicine, Art, Humor, Education,
      Philosophy, etc. San Antonio, 1972, d.j. $10.00
P33. PARKER (Samuel). Journal of an Exploring Tour Beyond
      the Rocky Mountains ... in the Years 1835-37 ... Cus-
      toms of the Natives.... 371pp, folding map, index, fac-
      simile of 1838 1st ed. Howes: P-89. Rader: 2600.
      Minneapolis, 1967, d.j. $10.00
P34. PARKER (Thomas). The Cherokee Indians. With Special
      Reference to Their Relations with the United States Gov-
      ernment. 116pp, cloth, ex-library, 1907. $30.00
      ___Another Copy. Same. $25.00
P35. PARKHILL (Forbes). The Last of the Indian Wars. 121pp
      plus index, photographic frontis, map, bibliography, the
      1915 war between Utes and cowboys in the Four Corners
      area. New York, 1962, d.j. $12.00
      ___Another Copy. Same. $12.00
P36. PARKMAN (Francis). (Preface) Historical Account of
      Bouquet's Expedition Against the Ohio Indians, in 1764.
      xxiii, 162pp, folding maps, pls, index, cloth. R.
      Clarke, 1868 (1st ed.). $95.00
         Field: 1182. Includes translation of Dumas' "Bio-
      graphical Sketch of General Bouquet."
P37. PARKMAN (Francis, Jr.). History of the Conspiracy of
      Pontiac and the War of the North American Tribes Against
      the English Colonies After the Conquest of Canada.
      xxiv, 630pp, 4 maps, Marietta public library slips pasted
      in and pocket pasted at rear. Boston, Charles Little
      and James Brown, 1851. $185.00
      ___Another Copy. Boston, 1863 (3rd ed. with addi-
      tions), 632pp, 3 maps, cloth. $25.00

P38. PARKS (D. R.). (Garland Studies in American Indian Linguistics, New York, 1976) A Grammar of Pawnee.
361pp. $40.00

PARSONS (Elsie Clews). See also BAE Bulletin No. 181.

P39. PARSONS (Elsie C.). American Indian Life, 419pp, cloth
and bds, collection of essays by well-known anthropolo-
gists. New York, 1922. $50.00
___Another Copy. New York, 1925, with C. G. La-
Farge, linen. $59.00
___Another Copy. Lincoln, 1967. $45.00
___Another Copy. New York, 1983. $12.00

P40. PARSONS (E. C.). Further Notes on Isleta. pp149-169,
wrappers, offprint American Anthropologist, Vol. 23,
No. 2, 1921. $20.00

P41. PARSONS (E. C.). (American Anthropological Assoc,
Memoirs, No. 39, 1933) Hopi and Zuni Ceremonialism.
108pp, wrappers. $30.00
___Another Copy. 1976 reprint. $18.00

P42. PARSONS (E. C.). Isleta, New Mexico. pp193-406, pls,
drawings, bibliography, rebound, removed from Smithsonian Institute BAE Annual Report No. 47, Washington,
1932. $27.00

P43. PARSONS (E. C.). (American Folk-Lore Society, Memoirs
vol. XXII, 1929) Kiowa Tales. xxii, 151pp, 3 fold-out
charts, cloth. $40.00

P44. PARSONS (E. C.). (American Anthropological Assoc, Memoirs No. 57, 1941) Notes of the Caddo. 76pp, 7 illus,
fold-out chart, map. $25.00
___Another Copy. Same. wrappers. $10.00

P45. PARSONS (E. C.). Pueblo Indian Folk-Tales, Probably of
Spanish Provenance. pp216-263, stapled wrappers,
extracted from Journal American Folklore, Vol. 31, No.
120, 1918. $20.00

P46. PARSONS (E. C.). Pueblo Indian Religion (2 Volumes).
xiii, 1,275pp, illus, 26 pls (some in color), folding
tables, maps, cloth. Chicago, 1939 (1st ed.). $250.00
Saunders: 1877. Swadesh: 58: "excellent, comprehensive and comparative." This thorough work also analyzes the relations of Pueblos with other tribes in the
Southwest and in Mexico with comparative tables for
ceremonial organization, spirits and ceremonies. (TE)
___Another Copy. Same. $175.00
___Another Copy. Same. $125.00

P47. PARSONS (E. C.). (Department of Archaeology, Phillips
Academy, Southwestern Expedition Paper No. 3, New
Haven, 1925, 1st ed.) The Pueblo of Jemez. xiv, 144pp,
18 text figures, 18 pls, 7 folding genealogical charts in
rear pocket (not called for in contents), cloth. $150.00
Saunders: 1878. The field-work for this study was
done in 1921-22 by the author. This publication was
produced as part of the series by Alfred V. Kidder about

Pecos, since Jemez is connected in many ways with Pecos, both linguistic and historic. (TE)

P48. PARSONS (E. C.). The Social Organization of the Tewa of New Mexico. 309pp, folded charts, wrappers. New York, 1929. $89.00
  ___Another Copy. Same. $50.00
  ___Another Copy. New York, 1964. $39.00

P49. PARSONS (E. C.). Taos Pueblo. 121pp, 13pp photographs, fold-out map. Menasha, 1938. $57.00
  ___Another Copy. New York, 1970, 136pp, 33 photographs, cloth. $30.00

P50. PARSONS (E. C.). (American Folk-Lore Society, Memoirs Vol. XXXIV, New York, 1940) Taos Tales. vii, 185pp, cloth. $40.00
  ___Another Copy. Same. $45.00

P51. PARSONS (E. C.). (University of California Publications in American Archaeology and Ethnology, Vol. 17, No. 3, 1922) Winter and Summer Dance Series in Zuni in 1918. 45pp, wrappers. $35.00

P52. PARSONS (J. R.). (Memoirs, Museum of Anthropology, University of Michigan, No. 3, 1971) Prehistoric Settlement Patterns in the Texcoco Region, Mexico. 390pp, 57 pls, wrappers. $35.00

P53. PARSONS (L.). (Milwaukee Public Museum, Anthropology Paper, No. 12) Bilbao Buatemala, An Archaeological Study of the Pacific Coast Cotzumalhuapa Region. (2 Volumes). Vol. I: 198pp, 23pp of photographs, 77 figures, 3 fold-out charts, 1967. Vol. II: 274pp, 66 photographs, 16 figures, 8 tables, 1969, wrappers.
   $65.00

P54. PARSONS (L.). Pre-Columbian America: The Art and Archaeology of South, Central and Middle America. 193pp, 201 photographs. Milwaukee, 1974. $16.00

P55. PARSONS (Marl L.). (Texas State Building Commission, Report No. 7, Austin, 1967) Anthropological Investigations in Crosby and Dickens Counties, Texas. 108pp, photographs, drawings, maps, bibliography, wrappers.
   $10.00

P56. PARSONS (Usher, M.D.). Indian Names of Places in Rhode Island; Collected for the Rhode Island Historical Society. 32pp, printed wrappers. Providence, 1861. $25.00

P57. PARRY (Albert). Tattoo; Secrets of a Strange Art as Practiced Among the Natives of the United States. 184pp, illus, bibliography, index. New York, 1933.
   $35.00

P58. PARRY (Ellwood). The Image of the Indian and the Black Man in American Art, 1590-1900. 182pp plus index, illus, notes, bibliography. New York, 1974 (1st print.), d.j.
   $15.00

P59. PARRY (William E.). Journal of a Second Voyage for the Discovery of a North-West Passage from the Atlantic

to the Pacific; Performed in the Years 1821-22-23, in His
Majesty's Ships Fury and Hecla. (8), xxx, (1), 571, (1
errata)pp, 31 pls, 4 folding maps, 4 folding profiles,
modern 1/4 gilt-stamped leather, marbled bds. London,
J. Murray, 1824 (1st ed.). $500.00
    Sabin: 58864. Arctic: 13142. Hill: p.226: "This
work deals with the characteristics of the Eskimos and is
a treatise on aboriginal life as well as a narrative of
scientific discoveries." (RMW)

P60. PASZTORY (Esther). Aztec Art. 335pp, 394 illus, 75 color
pls, 4to. New York, 1983. $60.00

P61. PASZTORY (E.). Aztec Stone Sculpture. 46pp, 29 photographs. New York, 1976. $10.00

P62. PATTERSON (E. Palmer, II). The Canadian Indian: A
History since 1500. 203pp plus index, photographs,
drawings, maps, footnotes, bibliography. Don Mills,
Ontario, Canada, 1972 (1st ed.), d.j. $12.00

P63. PATTERSON (J. B.) (Editor). Life of Ma-Ka-Tai-Me-She-
Kai-Kiak or Black Hawk ... Dictated by Himself. 155pp,
portrait, 12mo, bds, rebacked. Boston, 1834. $90.00
____Another Copy. Same, lower margin of 7 lvs clipped.
$40.00

P64. PATTERSON (J. T.). (University of Texas Bulletin Vol.
1, No. 2, 1937) Boat-Shaped Artifacts of the Gulf Southwest States. 131pp, 176 photographs. $40.00
____Another Copy. Same. $20.00

P65. PATTERSON (J. T.). (University of Texas, Anthropology
Papers Series, Bulletin Vol. 1, No. 4, 1936) The
Corner-Tang Flint Artifacts of Texas. 54pp, illus,
signed by L. Speir, 8vo, wrappers. $17.00
____Another Copy. Same. $15.00

P66. PATTERSON (J. T.). (University of Texas, Anthropology
Papers Series, Bulletin Vol. 1, No. 5, 1937) Supplemental Notes on the Corner-Tang Artifacts, with other articles. 39pp, illus, bibliography, 8vo, wrappers. $10.00

P67. PATTERSON (Nancy L.). Canadian Native Art: Arts and
Crafts of Canadian Indians and Eskimos. 180pp, illus
with 55 figures and 15 color pls. New York, 1973.
$35.00
____Another Copy. Ontario, 1973. $10.00

P68. PATTERSON (T. C.). (University of California Publications
in Anthropology, Vol. 13, Berkeley, 1966) Pattern and
Process in the Early Intermediate Period Pottery of the
Central Coast of Peru. x, 180pp, 8pp photographs,
22pp figures, wrappers. $25.00

P69. PAUL (A.). (Goteborgs Ethnografisk Museum, 1979)
Paracas Textiles, Selected from the Museum's Collections.
56pp of text containing 19 drawings, plus 19pp of b/w
and 8pp of color photographs. $30.00

P70. PAUL (Frances). Spruce Root Basketry of the Alaska
Tlingit. 80pp, 36 photographs, 64 drawings, wrappers.

Washington, 1944. $18.00
____Another Copy. Lawrence, 1944. $10.00
____Another Copy. Lawrence, Haskell, n.d. $15.00
____Another Copy. Sitka, 1982, 96pp. $12.00

P71. PAUL (J. R.) et al. Designs of the Mimbrenos, An Exhibition of Zoomorphic Decorations on Indian Pottery From Mimbres River Valley, New Mexico. 20pp, 11 photographs, 2 drawings, 1 map. New Haven, 1956. $13.00

P72. (PAWNEE INDIANS). Description of a Journey and Visit to the Pawnee Indians by Brn. Gottlieb F. Oehler and David Z. Smith, April 22-May 18, 1851, and a Description of the Manners and Customs of the Pawnee Indians by Dr. D. Z. Smith. 32pp, self-wrappers, reprinted from the Moravian Church Miscellany of 1851-52. New York, 1914. $60.00

P73. (PAWNEE INDIANS). (Senate Executive Document 16, 52:2, Washington, 1893) In the Senate ... Message from the President ... an agreement of the Pawnee Indians for the cession of certain lands in the Territory of Oklahoma. 14pp, removed, in later protective wrapper. $15.00

P74. PAYER (Julius). New Lands Within the Arctic Circle: Narrative of the Discoveries of the Austrian Ship "Tegetthoff" in the Years 1872-1874. 399pp, color frontis, numerous full-page and text wood engravings, gilt pictorial cloth, some shelf wr, neat ex-library. New York, 1877. $90.00

P75. PAYNE (Doris Palmer). Captain Jack. Modoc Renegade. 259pp, illus, history of the Modoc Wars in California 1873-1874. Portland, 1958, d.j. $20.00
____Another Copy. Same. $15.00
____Another Copy. Same. $12.00

P76. PAYNE (Edward W.). Photographs of Interesting and Outstanding Specimens of Indian Relics from the Edward W. Payne Stone Age Collection. 156pp, oblong 8vo, Springfield, Williamson, 1937 (1st ed.). $85.00
    Most of these full-page plates illustrating single items and groups of artifacts from the extensive Payne collection, considered the largest collection of prehistoric and pre-Columbian artifacts ever assembled by an individual. Attempts were made to sell it as a whole, but no individual or institution had the facilities to store it. (RMW)

P77. PAYNE (John H.). Indian Justice; A Cherokee Murder Trial at Tahlequah in 1840. Edited by Grant Foreman. 132pp, illus, map, index. Oklahoma City, 1934. $45.00

P78. PAYTIAMO (James). Flaming Arrow's People by an Acoma Indian. 158pp, color illus by author, personal experiences and interpretation of Acoma life by an Acoma Indian. New York, 1932 (1st ed.). $125.00

P79. PEABODY (C.). (Peabody Museum Papers, Vol. III, No. 2, 1904) Exploration of Mounds, Coahoma County, Mississippi. 42pp, 15pp photographs, 2pp drawings, cloth over original wrappers. $50.00

P 80. PEABODY (Charles) and MOOREHEAD (W. K.). (Phillips Academy, Dept. of Archaeology Bulletin II, Andover, 1906) The So-Called "Gorgets." 100pp, 19 pls, wrappers. $20.00

P 81. PEABODY (George A.). South American Journals, 1858-1859. Edited by J. C. Phillips. xvi, 209pp, lrg 8vo, limited to 581 copies, marbled bds. Printed at the Southworth-Anthoesen Press, Peabody Museum, Salem, 1937. $75.00

P 82. PEALE (Albert Charles). (United States Geological Survey No. 110, Washington, 1893) The Paleozoic Section in the Vicinity of Three Forks, Montana, with Petrographic Notes by George Perkins Merrill. 56pp, illustrated pls, double-pp color map, printed wrappers. $15.00

P 83. PEALE (Arthur L.). Memorials and Pilgrimages in the Mohegan Country. 50pp, 2 maps, illus, cloth. Norwich, CT, 1930. $10.00

P 84. PEALE (Arthur L.). Uncas and the Mohegan-Pequot. 183pp, illus, cloth, inscribed. Boston, 1939, d.j. $15.00

P 85. PEARCE (A. S.). (Carnegie Institute Publication No. 491, 1938) Fauna of the Caves of Yucatan. 304pp, 8pp of photographs, 319 figures. $150.00

P 86. PEARCE (J. E.) and JACKSON (A. T.). (University of Texas, Anthropology Papers Series, Bulletin Vol. 1, No. 3, 1933) A Prehistoric Rock Shelter in Val Verde County, Texas. 143pp, bibliography, maps, figures, photographs of artifacts, sites, flints, textiles, etc., 8vo, wrappers. $15.00

P 87. PEARCE (J. E.). (University of Texas Bulletin No. 3537, Anthropological Papers Vol. 1, No. 1, Austin, 1935) Tales That Dead Men Tell. 133pp, photographs, index, bibliography, wrappers. $25.00
___Another Copy. Same. $15.00
___Another Copy. Same. $10.00

P 88. PEARCE (Roy H.). The Savages of America. A Study of the Indian and the Idea of Civilization. 244pp plus index, frontis, covers from 1609 to 1851 on the attempt to civilize the Indian and the end result. Baltimore, 1953 (1st ed.), d.j. $15.00
___Another Copy. Same. $10.00

P 89. PECK (George). Wyoming; Its History, Stirring Incidents, and Romantic Adventures (Pennsylvania). 432pp, illus, cloth. New York, 1868. (3rd ed.). $50.00
Ayer: 233. Field: 1191. "Composed so largely of original material, the author has given even that portion which is merely compiled an additional value." (CLR)

P 90. PECKHAM (Howard H.) (Editor). Captured by Indians. True Tales of Pioneer Survivors. 238pp, text illus, cloth backed bds. Rutgers University Press, 1954, d.j. $25.00

P91. PEIRCE (Ebenezer W.). Indian History, Biography and
       Genealogy: Pertaining to the Good Sachem Massacoit of
       the Wampanoag Tribe and His Descendants. 261pp, illus,
       appendix, cloth. North Arlington, Mass, 1878. $35.00

P92. PEIRSON (D.). (Smithsonian Institution, Institute of Social
       Anthropology, Publication No. 12, 1951) Cruz das
       Almas, A Brazilian Village. x, 226pp of text with 13
       figures, 2 maps and 20pp photographs. $25.00

P93. PEISSEL (M.). The Lost World of Quintana Roo (Yuca-
       tan). 306pp, illus, maps, cloth. New York, 1963,
       d.j. $15.00
       ____Another Copy. Same. $12.00

P94. PEITHMANN (I. M.). Echoes of the Red Man. 134pp,
       photographs of Hopewell and other artifacts. New York,
       1955 (1st ed.). $15.00

P95. PEITHMANN (Irvin). Red Men of Fire: A History of the
       Cherokee Indians. Illus. Springfield, 1964, d.j.
                                                     $12.00

P96. PELTIER (Jerome). Warbonnets and Epaulets. 385pp,
       photographs, notes and sources, the Steptoe-Wright
       Campaigns of 1858 in Washington Territory. Montreal,
       1971 (1st ed.). $15.00

P97. PENAFIEL (Dr. Antonio). Coleccion de Documentos Para
       la Historia Mexicana Publicadas. 13pp of prologue in
       Spanish. 133pp of text in Nahuatl language, 4to, con-
       tains: Cantares en Idioma Mexicano. Inpresos Segun
       el Manuscrito Original Que Existe en la Biblioteca.
       Mexico, 1899. $250.00

P98. PENAFIEL (Antonio). Nombres Geograficos de Mexico:
       Catalogo Alfabetico de los Nombres de Lugar Perteneci-
       entes al Idioma "Nahuatl." Estudio Jeroglifico del
       Codice Mendocino. Two separate volumes, one being
       an atlas. 260pp, illus, Mexico, 1885. Atlas volume:
       39 pls containing 462 glyphs in original colors, 4to
       (8"x12"), Mexico, 1884. Both volumes bound in 1/4
       leather, neat ex-library. $400.00

P99. PENDERGAST (David) (Editor). Palenque: The Walker-
       Caddy expedition to the Ancient Maya City, 1839-1840.
       213pp, 36 pls, cloth. Norman, 1967, d.j. $18.00
       ____Another Copy. Same. $15.00
       ____Another Copy. Same. $12.00

P100. PENHALLOW (Samuel). The History of the Wars of New
       England with the Eastern Indians.... 138pp, 36pp,
       cloth, ex-library, reprint of the rare Boston, 1726 ed.,
       includes appendix with Gardner's account of the Pequot
       Wars. Cincinnati, W. Dodge, 1859. $125.00
          Howes: P-201. Sabin: 59655. Howes: the "best
       early summary of New England's Indian Troubles."
       ____Another Copy. Same. $100.00
       ____Another Copy. Same. $35.00
       ____Another Copy. Concord, NH, 1824, Penhallow's

Indian Wars (in "Collections of the New Hampshire Historical Society, 1924, Volume I") pp13-135, complete volume with 336pp total, cloth backed bds. $85.00
___Another Copy. Boston, 1924. Facsimile of 1726 ed. 51pp. $40.00

P101. PENNINGTON (C. W.). The Pima Bajo of Central Sonora, Mexico. (2 Volumes). Vol. I: The Material Culture. xvii, 410pp, 39pp of photographs and drawings, 1 map, cloth. Salt Lake City, 1980. $47.00
Vol. II: Vocabulario en la Lengua Nevome. xxix, 129pp, cloth. Salt Lake City, 1979. $27.00
  This work focuses on the culturally more advanced Pima Bajo, about whom few studies have been done. Archival material over the past 300 years was extensively analyzed, and the author spent several summers doing fieldwork. The result is the most comprehensive study done on this people. Volume I is concerned with their material culture, while Volume II discusses the language and presents the vocabulary in an edited version of a 17th century manuscript. (EAP)

P102. PENNINGTON (C. W.). The Tepehaun of Chihuahua, Their Material Culture. 413pp, 63 photographs, 2 maps in text, 1 map in rear pocket. Salt Lake City, 1969.
          $24.00

P103. PEPPER (G. H.). (American Anthropological Assn. Memoirs, Vol. II, Part 4, 1908) An Hidatsa Shrine and the Beliefs Respecting It. 54pp, 4pp photographs, 3 figures.
          $40.00

P104. PEPPER (G. H.). Hyde Expedition. Ceremonial Deposits Found in an Ancient Pueblo Estufa in Northern New Mexico, U.S. A. 8pp, 6 photographs, inscribed by author, wrappers and pages chipped and clipped at corners. New York, 1899. $30.00

P105. PEPPER (G. H.). (Museum of the American Indian, Notes and Monographs, Vol. X, No. 7, 1921) A Wooden Image from Kentucky. 25pp, 3 illus. $10.00

P106. PERCEVAL (Don). From Ice Mountain; Indian Settlement of the Americas. With an Introduction by Frank Waters. 74pp, color illus, the theory of population migration across the Bering Strait as recounted by a talented artist and narrator. Flagstaff, 1979 (1st ed.). $15.00

P107. PERCEVAL (Don). A Navaho Sketch Book. 98pp, illus in color and b/w, small 4to, descriptive text by Clay Lockett. Flagstaff, 1962 (1st ed.), d.j. $50.00
___Another Copy. Flagstaff, 1974. $25.00

P108. PERDUE (Theda). Slavery and the Evolution of Cherokee Society 1540-1866. 198pp, maps, notes, bibliography, index. Knoxville TN, 1981 (2d print.) d.j. $10.00

P109. PERERA (V.) and BRUCE (R. D.). The Last Lords of Palenque: The Lacandon Mayas of the Mexican Rain Forest. 333pp, 19pp photographs, map. Berkeley, 1982. $12.00

P110. PEREZ (Manual). Farol Indiano, y Gvia de Curas de Indios. Summa de los Cinco Sacramentos.... (bound with)
Arte de el Idioma Mexicano.... by Manual Perez. 46pp,
192pp, 4pp, 80pp, 4pp, small quarto, contemporary limp
vellum, leather ties, frnt hinge separated, AAS duplicate,
Francisco de Ribera Calderon, Mexico, 1713. $2,000.00
    Sabin: 60913, 60911. Pilling: 2954, 2955. Medina:
2370, 2371. Stevens Historical Nuggets: 2133, 2134.
Father Perez was professor of the Mexican language at
the Royal University for 22 years, and left a body of
work on the language of fundamental importance. The
first work is an abridgement of the sacraments for use
by missionaries to the Indians; the second a study of
the Mexican idiom, including pronunciation and general
grammatical constructions, etc. All authorities agree as
to the rarity and importance of both works. (WR)

P111. PEREZ DE BARRADAS (Jose). Arqueologia Agustiniana
Excaviones Arqueologicas Realizadas de Marzo a Diciem-
bre de 1937. 169pp, plus 189 full-page pls, 4to, wrappers. Imprenta Nacional, Bogota, 1943. $125.00
    ___Another Copy. Same. $100.00

P112. PEREZ DE BARRADAS (J.). Eighty Masterpieces from
the Gold Museum. 186pp, 76 full-page b/w photographs,
4 full-page color photographs. Banco de la Republica,
Bogota, 1954. $25.00

P113. PEREZ DE BARRADAS (Jose). Orfebreria Prehispanica de
Colombia: Estilo Calima (2 Volumes). Vol. I: Text.
367pp, 200 figures, 20 full-page photographs, Vol. II:
Plate Volume. 300 pp photographs, 20pp text, folio.
Museo de Oro Bogota, 1954. $300.00
    ___Another Copy. Same. $225.00
    ___Another Copy. Same. $175.00

P114. PEREZ DE BARRADAS (Jose). Orfebreria Prehispanica de
Colombia: Estilos Tolima y Muisca (2 Volumes). Vol.
I: Text. 385pp, 147 drawings and photographs, 10
full-page color photographs, map. Vol. II: Laminas.
21pp text, plus 287pp photographs. Museo de Oro, Madrid, 1958. $300.00
    ___Another Copy. Same. $150.00
    ___Another Copy. Same. Plate volume only. $150.00

P115. PEREZ DE BARRADAS (Jose). Orfebreria Prehispanica de
Colombia: Estilos Quimbaya y Otros (2 Volumes). Vol.
I: Texto. xxiii, 355pp, 109 photographs and drawings,
12 full-page color photographs. Vol. II: Laminas.
22pp text plus 298pp of photographs. $150.00

P116. PEREZ DE RIBAS (Andres). My Life Among the Savage
Nations of New Spain. 256pp, 4to, illus, index, map,
first English printing of work originally printed in Spain
in 1645. Consists of three sections. One of the best
accounts extant of 17th-century Mexico. Los Angeles,
1968 (1st ed., thus), d.j. $25.00

___Another Copy. Same. $45.00

___Another Copy. Same. $25.00

P117. PERKINS (David) and TANIS (Norman). Native Americans of North America. 558pp, index, limited to 500 copies, bibliography based on collections in the Library of California State University, Northridge, listing over 3400 entries listed by subject matter. Northridge, CA, 1975 (1st ed.). $12.00

P118. PERKINS (James H.). (J. M. Peck, 2nd ed.) Annals of the West. 808pp, later cloth. St. Louis, J. R. Albach, 1850 (2d ed., revised and enlarged). $55.00
    Howes: 231. Sabin: 60955. Field: 1199: "It is a great collection of details of frontier warfare; but contains little material that is new ... yet it is much esteemed as a history of Western Settlement." (RMW)

P119. PERROT (Nicolas). Memoire sur les Moeurs, Coutumes et Religion des Sauvages de l'Amerique Septentrionale. 241pp, illus. Montreal, 1973. $30.00

P120. PERRY (William J.). The Children of the Sun. A Study in the Early History of Civilization. 551pp, 16 maps. New York, n.d., (c.1923). $15.00

P121. PERSINGER (Joseph). The Life of Jacob Persinger Who Was Taken by the Shawnee Indians When an Infant; with a Short Account of the Indian troubles in Missouri; and a Sketch of the Adventures of the Author. 24pp, wrappers, Sturgeon, MO, 1861. Reprint, n.d. $10.00

P122. (PERU). Antiquidades Peruanas by Rivero and Tschudi (2 Volumes). Vol. I: Text. 328pp, color frontis, text engravings (9"x12") in size. Vol. II: Atlas. Lithographic frontis, 58 color pls (22"x24") in size, rebound in cloth. Vienna, 1851. $3,000.00

P123. (PERU). (Davenport Academy of Sciences, Proceedings Vol. 13, 1914.) Includes: The Nazca Pottery of Ancient Peru by Max Uhle. 16pp, 3 illus; also: The Davenport Collection of Nazca and Other Peruvian Pottery by Edward Putnam, pp17-45, 27 pls, 2 pls are in color, contains 250 examples of Pre-Columbian Pottery, wrappers. $50.00

P124. (PERU). Die Eroberung von Peru: Kultur und Untergang der Inkas. Original text by William Prescott. 478pp, 4to, 74 fine illus primarily of Peruvian pre-Columbian artifacts, map. Vienna, 1937. $60.00

P125. (PERU). Gold Aus Peru. Aus Dem Goldmuseum: Lima. 100pp, 50 illus, includes several examples of pottery, wrappers, exhibition catalogue. Hindesheim, West Germany, 1977. $20.00

P126. (PERU). Indianer Gestern und Heute. 78pp, illus, includes early drawings, photographs of sites, artifacts, current Indians, wrappers. Basel Museum Catalogue, 1971-72. $15.00

P127. (PERU). Indios Selvaticos de la Amazonia Peruana.

356pp, 207 photographs, 100 figures, wrappers. Mexico, 1958. $35.00

P128. (PERUVIAN ART). (Exhibition Catalogue, XXVI Congreso International de los Americanistas, Sevilla, 1935, Madrid, 1935) Arte Peruano. Colleccion Juan Larrea. 22pp text, 4 figures, 100pp photographs. $95.00

P129. (PERUVIAN ART). Gold of the Andes, Treasures of Peru. 60pp, 5pp of color, 20pp of b/w photographs, chart, map, exhibition catalogue. Brooklyn and de Young Memorial Museum, 1963. $12.00

P130. (PERUVIAN ART). Les Tresors du Perou. 104pp, 59pp of photographs, 2 drawings, map, table. Exhibition catalogue, Petit Palais, Paris, 1958. $12.00

P131. (PERUVIAN ART). Peruvian Paintings by Unknown Artists, 800 B.C. to 1700 A.D. 36pp, 20pp of b/w and color photographs. Exhibition catalogue, Center for Inter-American Relations, 1973. $15.00

PETERSEN (Karen Daniels). See also BAE Bulletin No. 186.

P132. PETERSEN (Karen Daniels). Howling Wolf, A Cheyenne Warrior's Graphic Interpretation of his People. 64pp, 12 full-page color pls, 8 b/w and 3 color photographs, 3 b/w, 2 color drawings, cloth. Palo Alto, 1968.
$29.00
____Another Copy. Same. $35.00
____Another Copy. Same. $27.00
____Another Copy. Same. $15.00

P133. PETERSEN (Karen Daniels). Plains Indian Art from Ft. Marion. 340pp, oblong 4to, illus, index, bibliography. Norman, 1971 (1st ed.), d.j. $35.00
From 72 frightened homesick Plains Indians imprisoned at Ft. Marion in the 1870s came this series of drawings depicting their former life on the plains. An analysis and interpretation of the drawings accompany the fine reproductions of the drawings themselves. Also biographies of the Indian artists.

P134. PETERSON (Harold L.). (Contributions from the Museum of American Indian, Vol. XIX, New York, 1971, 1st revised ed.) American Indian Tomahawks. 142pp, 97 photographic pls, frontis, drawings, bibliography, appendix. $17.00

P135. PETERSON (S.). Lucy M. Lewis, American Indian Potter. 218pp, 54pp of color and 43pp of b/w photographs, 12pp of sepia-tone archival photographs of Acoma Pueblo and dancers, 1 map, cloth, Tokyo, 1984. $70.00
The first detailed study of the work of famed Acoma potter, Lucy M. Lewis, this publication presents her pots and discusses the Acoma pottery process--and Lucy's acclaimed innovations. More than 100pp of photographs illustrate her pots, selected historical Acoma pots and a glimpse of Acoma Pueblo and its life.

P136. PETITOT (Emile). Traditions Indiennes du Canada

Nord-Ouest (1862-1882). Textes Originaux and Traduction Litterale. 446pp, rebound, original torn wrappers present. Allecon, 1888. $175.00

P137. PETITOT (E.). Traditions Indiennes du Canada Nord-Ouest: Traditions, Legendes, Contes, Chansons, Proverbes, Devinettes, Superstitions, Tome XXIII. 546pp, cloth. Paris, 1886. $100.00
___Another Copy. Paris, 1967, cloth. $30.00

P138. (PETROGLYPHS). (University of California Archaeological Research Facility Contribution No. 20, 1974) Four Great Basin Petroglyph Studies. 130pp, illus, wrappers. $25.00

PETRULLO (Vincenzo). See also BAE Bulletin No. 123.

P139. PETRULLO (Vincenzo). The Diabolic Root. A Study of Peyotism, the New Indian Religion, among the Delawares. 185pp, illus, bibliography, library perforations on title, newly rebound. Philadelphia, 1934 (1st ed.). $30.00

P140. PETRULLO (V. M.). (University Museum, Museum Journal Vol. XXIII, No. 2, Philadelphia, 1932) Primitive Peoples of Matto Grosso Brazil. 174pp, illus, folded map, wrappers. $45.00

P141. PETRULLO (V.). The Yaruros of the Capanaparo River, Venezuela. pp163-288, 15 photographic pls, bibliography, printed wrappers, offprint Smithsonian Anthropological Papers, Washington, 1939. $10.00

P142. PETSCHE (Jerome E.). (Smithsonian Institution Publications in Salvage Archaeology, No. 10, Lincoln, 1968) Bibliography of Salvage Archaeology in the United States. 162pp, 4to, printed wrappers. $15.00

P143. PETTER (Rudolphe). Zixtxuisto, or, Cheyenne Reading Book. 36pp, 19.5cm, printed wrappers, first printing of the Cheyenne language, only two known copies. Gilcrease-Hagrett: p.94. Quakerston, Stauffer, 1895 (1st ed.). $750.00

P144. PETTIT (Benjamin Marie) (Edited by Irving McKee). (Indiana Historical Society, 1941) The Trail of Death Letters of ... (Potawatomi removal). 141pp, wrappers. $15.00

P145. PETTITT (George). (University of California at Berkeley, Anthropological Records Vol. 14, No. 1, 1949) The Quileute of La Push, 1775-1945. Illus, bound presentation copy, spotted cvrs. $62.00

P146. PHELPS (Martha B.). Francis Slocum, the Lost Sister of Wyoming (Pennsylvania). 167pp, 6 color and 2 b/w pls, Indian captivity of Francis Slocum. New York, 1905 (1st ed.). $25.00

P146. PHILLIPS (George Harwood). Chiefs and Challengers; Indian Resistance and Cooperation in Southern California. 225pp, illus, index. Berkeley, 1975 (1st ed.), d.j. $25.00
___Another Copy. Same. $22.00

        ___Another Copy. Same. $22.00
        ___Another Copy. Same. $20.00

P147. PHILLIPS (P.) et al. (Peabody Museum Papers, Vol. XXV, 1951) Archaeological Survey in the Lower Mississippi Alluvial Valley, 1940-1947. xii, 530pp, 39pp photographs, 73 figures, 17 tables. $50.00

P148. PHILLIPS (P.). (Peabody Museum Papers, Vol. 60, 1970) Archaeological Survey in the Lower Yazoo Basin, Mississippi, 1949-1955 (2 Volumes). 1,000pp, 637 illus of several thousand objects. $59.00

P149. PHILLIPS (P.) and BROWN (J.). Pre-Columbian Shell Engravings From The Craig Mound at Spiro, Oklahoma. This six-volume series--the most lavish ever published by the Peabody Museum--examined the ceremonial artifacts and engravings on gorgets and cups that constitute the largest corpus of figural and decorative art that has ever come out of a single site in the United States and that is unequalled in North America as a single source of pre-historic and decorative art. These magnificent examples of Southeastern Indian Art are reproduced in full-page two color plates (in the cloth bound editions only; the plates in the soft cover editions are black and white) that contain actual size reproductions of the rubbings of the engravings on the cups and gorgets from this great site. Volume VI, in addition to dealing with the final phase of the Craig style, contains a summary of the study, the complete bibliography for the six volumes, and an extensive index. The cloth bound volumes, printed on permanent, acid-free paper, are part of a limited edition of 500 copies. (EAP)

        ___Volumes 1-3. 640pp, 129 pls, 271 figures. Soft cvr. 1978. $55.00

        ___Volume IV. The Craig School: Phase A. 149pp (14"x18"), 69-full-page pls and 69 drawings, cloth. Cambridge, 1979. $98.00

        ___Volume V. The Craig School: Phase B. 210pp (14"x18"), 71 pls and 71 drawings, cloth. Cambridge, 1980. $98.00

        ___Volume VI. The Craig School: Phase C. 220pp (14"x18"), 61 pls and 61 drawings, cloth. Cambridge, 1983. $98.00

        ___Volumes IV-VI. The Craig School: Phases A-C. 580pp (9"x11½"), 201 pls and 201 drawings. Soft cvr. Cambridge, 1983. $55.00

P150. PHILLIPS (R. B.). Patterns of Power, The Jasper Grant Collection and Great Lakes Indian Art of the Early Nineteenth Century. 151pp, 26 color and 74 b/w photographs. Kleinburg, 1984. $30.00

        Organized around a collection of Great Lakes Indian art presented to the National Museum of Ireland in 1902 by the descendants of Jasper Grant, a British Army officer who collected the artifacts between 1802 and 1809, this exhibition visited three Canadian museums in 1984 and 1985. The Grant collection, showing virtually no European influence, contained a number of unique pieces, and was exhibited with several other important collections to form this important assemblage, the theme of which was symbolism in Great Lakes Indian design. Every piece in the exhibition is illustrated in excellent photographs; the text is English and French. (EAP)

P151. PICKERING (John). An Essay on a Uniform Orthography for the Indian Languages of North America. 42pp, sml 4to, modern leather backed bds, first separate ed., reprinted from American Academy of Arts and Sciences "Memoirs" Vol. 4. Cambridge University Press, 1820.
$100.00

P152. PIDGEON (William). Traditions of De-Coo-Dah. An Antiquarian Researches ... Mound Builders ... Elk Nation ... Evidences of an Ancient Population.... 334pp, pls (1 folding), 1/4 leather and cloth, cvrs detached. New York, Thayer, Bridgman and Fanning, 1853 (1st ed.). $85.00
Howes: P-351. Sabin: 62698. Field: 1214: "Record of personal examination of a great number of ancient mounds ... and of the traditions regarding them, obtained from an aged Sioux chief. Hypothesis ... rendered almost useless by their blending with baseless hypothesis and unreliable traditions. The numerous plates afford very clear illustrations of many remains of Indian structures." (RMW)
___Another Copy. New York, 1858. $65.00

P153. (PIEGAN INDIANS). (House of Representatives Executive Document 269, 41:2, Washington, 1870, 1st print.) Piegan Indians. Letter from the Secretary of War ... in Relation to the Late Expedition Against the Piegan Indians in the Territory of Montana. 74pp, bound in later 1/4 leather. $125.00

P154. PIERCE (William Henry). From Potlatch to Pulpit; Being the Autobiography of the Rev. William Henry Pierce, Native Missionary to the Indian Tribes of the Northwest Coast of British Columbia. Edited by Rev. J. P. Hicks. 176pp. Vancouver, 1933 (1st ed.), d.j. $40.00

P155. PIERSON (Abraham). Some Helps for the Indians: A Catechism in the Language of the Quiripi Indians of New Haven Colony. xi, 67pp, printed wrappers, reprinted from original edition of 1658. Hartford, 1873. $35.00
___Another Copy. New wrappers, one of 100 copies, reprinted from the Collections of the Conn. Historical Society, Vol. 3. $25.00

P156. PIERSON (Donald). (Smithsonian Institute of Social Anthropology, Publication No. 12, 1951) Cruz Das Almas:

A Brazilian Village. 226pp, pls, figures, maps, glossary, bibliography, index, lrg 8vo, wrappers. $15.00

P157.   PIKE (D. G.). Anasazi, Ancient People of the Rock. 189pp, 110 color and 17 b/w photographs, cloth. New York, 1974. $30.00

P158.   PIKE (R. E.) and MADSEN (D. B.). (Bureau of Land Management: Utah. Cultural Resource Series No. 9, Salt Lake City, 1981, 1st ed.) Excavation of Two Anasazi Sites in Southern Utah. 237pp, 110pp, illus, photographs, maps, bibliography, lrg 8vo, wrappers. $15.00

P159.   PIKE (Zebulon). An Account of Expeditions to the Sources of the Mississippi and Through the Western Parts of Louisiana, to the Sources of the Arkansaw, Kansas, La Platte and Pierre Juan Rivers; Performed by order of the Government of the United States during the Years 1805, 1806 and 1807, and a Tour Through the Interior Parts of New Spain.... 484pp, folding map, bound in dark red imitation morocco, complete reprint of original 1810 edition. Ann Arbor, 1966. $15.00

P160.   PILGRIM (Mariette). Oogaruk, the Aleut. 223pp, color frontis, 21pp illus, illus endpapers. Caldwell, Caxton Press, 1947 (1st ed.), d.j. $20.00

P161.   PILKINGTON (W.) (Editor). The Journals of Samuel Kirkland, 18th Century Missionary to the Iroquois, Government Agent, Father of Hamilton College. 459pp, portrait. Clinton, New York, 1980. $35.00

PILLING (James C.). See also BAE Bulletin Nos. 1, 5, 6, 9, 13, 14, 15, 16 and 19.

P162.   PILLING (James C.). Proof Sheets of a Bibliography of the Languages of the North American Indians. 1135pp, 29 pls, 4,308 main entries and approx 3,000 supplemental entries. Facsimile reprint of the BAE Miscellaneous Publications No. 2, 1885, of which there were only 100 copies printed. Brooklyn, 1970, limited to 750 copies. $95.00

P163.   PINA CHAN (R.) and NAVARRETE (C.). (New World Archaeological Foundation, Brigham Young University Paper No. 22, 1967) Archaeological Research in the Lower Grijalva River Region, Tobasco and Chiapas. 52pp, 100 figures. $10.00

P164.   PINA CHAN (Roman). (Instituto Nacional de Antropologia e Historia) Chiapas. Atlas Arqueologico de la Republica Mexicana, 2. 98pp, 29 pls, 3 lrg folding maps, wrappers. Mexico, 1967. $30.00

P165.   PINA CHAN (R.) and COVARRUBIAS (L.). El Pueblo del Jaguar (Los Olmecas Arqueologicos). 68pp of text containing 62 figures, plus 1 full-page color photograph and 19pp of b/w photographs of Olmec masks, figures, objects and reliefs, cloth. Museo Nacional de Antropologia, Mexico City, 1964. $50.00

P166. PINA CHAN (R.). Exploraciones Arqueologicas en Tingam-
bato, Michoacan. 103pp, 69 photographs, 34pp of drawings, wrappers. Instituto Nacional Antropologia e Historia, Mexico City, 1982. $15.00

P167. PINA CHAN (Roman). (Instituto Nacional de Antropologia
e Historia, Serie Investigaciones No. 24, Mexico, 1970)
Informe Preliminar de la Reciente Exploracion del Cenote
Sagrado de Chichen Itza. 59pp, 38 photographs, sml
4to (9"x11"), wrappers. $25.00

P168. PINA CHAN (R.). (Instituto Nacional de Antropologia e
Historia, Memorias VI, Mexico City, 1960) Mesoamerica.
178pp, 70 photographs, 53 drawings, 13 maps. $35.00

P169. PINA CHAN (Roman). (Instituto Nacional de Antropologia
e Historia, Mexico City, 1960) Museum of the Huaxtec
Civilization. 49pp, 16 illus, wrappers. $10.00

P170. PINA CHAN (R.). Teotenango: Segundo Informe de Ex-
ploracions Arqueologicas. 75pp of text plus 60pp of
photographs, 11pp drawings. Mexico City, 1973.
$18.00

P171. PINA CHAN (R.). (Instituto Nacional de Antropologia e
Historia, Mexico City, 1958) Tlatilco 1. 126pp, 22
photographs, 49 figures, 4 maps. $18.00

P172. PINA CHAN (R.). (Instituto Nacional de Antropologia e
Historia, Mexico City, 1958) Tlatilco 2, Traves de su
Ceramica. 54pp, 48 photographs, 12 drawings. $12.00

P173. PINA CHAN (R.). Una Vision del Mexico Prehispanico.
339pp of text, plus 63pp of photographs, 4 fold-out
maps, cloth. Mexico City, 1967. $40.00

P174. PINART (Alphonse Louis). Explorer, Linguist and
Ethnologist: A Descriptive Bibliography of the Published Works of, with Notes on His Life by Ross Par-
menter. Introduction by Carl S. Dentzel. 68pp, illus.
Los Angeles, 1966. $20.00

P175. PINART (Alphonse Louis) Voyages a la Cote Nord-Ouest
de l'Amerique Executes Durant les Annees 1870-72.
folio, 51(1)pp, 5 engraved pls, original printed wrapper.
Paris, L. Leroux, 1875. $95.00
Pinart, on a journey financed by the Imperial Academy
of Sciences of St. Petersburg, traveled to the Aleutians
and Alaskan Peninsula, and here gives his observations,
historical, ethnographical, etc ... Wickersham: 2654.
Titled Volume I, but all published. (H.L.)

P176. PINCKARD (George). Notes on the West Indies; Written
During the Expedition Under the Command of the Late
General Sir Ralph Abercromby: Including Observations
on the Island of Barbados, and the Settlements Captured
by the British Troops, upon the Coast of Guiana; Likewise Remarks Relating to the Creoles and Slaves of the
Western Colonies, and the Indians of South America....
(3 Volumes). 24pp, 448pp; 20pp, 472pp; 20pp, 456pp.
Lrg octavo, contemporary full polished calf, morocco

labels, complete with the half-titles in the first two volumes (none required in the third). The author was a
medical officer with the expedition and recorded his
narratives in epistolary form, including minute observations on the manners and customs of the Indians. Sabin:
62893. Rich, B.A.N: 1806:16. Handler: p.62. London, 1806. $600.00

P177. PITSEOLAK (Peter) and EBER (Dorothy). People From
Our Side: An Inuit Record of Seekooseelak--The Land
of the People of Cape Dorset, Baffin Island. 159pp,
many photographs, 4to, wrappers, Inuit life in old and
modern times. Indiana University Press, 1975. $10.00

P178. PITSEOLAK (Peter). Peter Pitseolak's Escape from Death
with Drawings by the Author. Introduction and Edited
by Dorothy Eber. 46pp, color illus, wrappers. Toronto, 1977. $15.00

P179. PLACE (Marion T.). Comanches and Other Indians of
Texas. 131pp, photographs and other illus, maps.
New York, 1970 (1st ed.). $10.00

P180. PLACE (Marion T.). Retreat to the Bear Paw. The
Story of the Nez Perce. 190pp, illus, endpaper maps.
New York, 1969 (1st ed.), d.j. $12.00
___Another Copy. Same, ex-library. $10.00

P181. (PLAINS INDIANS). Indianer der Prarien und Plains.
104pp, color pl, 32 paintings, plus 90 other illus, includes trips of Paul Wilhelm von Wurttemburg (1822-
24) and Maximilian zu Wied (1832-34), wrappers. Exhibition catalogue, Stuttgart, 1976. $25.00

P182. Ploughed Under: The Story of an Indian Chief, Told by
Himself. 268pp, ads, decorative cvr. New York,
Fords, Howard and Hulbert, 1881 (1st ed.). $35.00

P183. PLUMMER (Rachel). Rachel Plummer's Narrative of Twenty-
One Months Servitude as a Prisoner Among the Comanche
Indians. 29pp, cloth and bds, one of 400 copies re-
printed from the only known copy of the first edition.
Austin, 1977. $40.00

P184. POE (C.). Angel to the Papagos. 159pp, illus with photographs of Papagos, account of Goldie Richmond who
came to the Papagos reservation in 1927 and has never
left. San Antonio, 1964. $15.00

P185. POINDEXTER (Miles). The Ayar-Incas. (2 Volumes).
pp274, 359, illus. New York, 1930. $75.00
___Another Copy. Same. $100.00

P186. POINT (Nicholas). Wilderness Kingdom: Indian Life in
the Rocky Mountains, 1840-1847, the Journals and Paintings of Nicolas Point, S.J. Translated and Introduced
by Joseph Donnelly, S.J. With an Appreciation by John
C. Ewers. 274pp, 4to, illus, bibliography. New York,
1967 (1st ed.), d.j. $50.00
Large 9" by 12" volume containing the illustrated
diary of missionary Father Point who, between 1840 and

1847 lived among the Flathead, Coeur d'Alenes and Blackfeet in what now are the states of Idaho and Montana.
Reproduced here are 285 of Father Point's paintings with
232 in full-color which depict customs, family life, religion, hunting, war ceremonies, dances and costumes of
the Indians. (GFH)
    ___Another Copy. Same. $75.00
    ___Another Copy. Same. $20.00

P187. PO-LIN-GAY-SI (Mrs. Elizabeth White). the Sun Girl: A
True Story about Dawamana, The Little Hopi Indian
Maiden of Old Oraibi in Arizona--and How She Learned
to Dance the Butterfly Dance at Moencopi--As Told by
her Lifelong Friend Po-Lin-Gay-Si (Mrs. Elizabeth
White). 47pp, designed by Ben Kennedy and Wilder
Bentley, illustrated by Hopi artist Komoki, inscribed and
signed by author, snapshot of author laid in, decorated
cloth, juvenile. Berkeley, 1941 (1st ed.). $55.00

POLLARD (J. G.). See BAE Bulletin No. 17.

P188. POLLOCK (H. E. D.) et al. (Carnegie Institute, Publication 619, Washington, 1962) Mayapan Yucatan Mexico.
Illus, lrg 4to, folded charts. $63.00

P189. POLLOCK (H. E. D.). The Puuc: An Architectural Survey of the Hill Country of Yucatan and Northern Campeche, Mexico. 600pp, 933 figures, 4to, wrappers.
Peabody Museum, Cambridge, 1980. $75.00

P190. POMA (Huaman). Letter to a King. A Peruvian Chief's
Account of Life under the Incas and under Spanish
Rule. 243pp plus index, drawings in facsimile, trans-
lated, edited and introduction by Christopher Dilke, first
English translation of a major source of Incan life and
history. New York, 1978 (1st American ed.), d.j.
                                     $15.00

P191. POMA de AYALA (Felipe Guaman). Nueve Coronica y
Buen Gobierno (Codex Peruvien Illustre). xxviii, Codex
is 1100 pp, original green cloth. Paris, Institut d'Ethnologie, 1936. $150.00

P192. (POMO INDIANS). (University of California Archaeological
Research Facility Contribution No. 37, 1977) Ethnographic and Historical Sketch of the Eastern Pomo and
Their Neighbors, the Southeast Pomo. 64pp and illus,
wrappers. $22.00

P193. POND (Gideon H.). (Minnesota Historical Society, Collections, Vol. II, Part III, 1867) Dakota Superstitions.
pp32-62, complete issue, printed wrappers, contains
Dakota songs, with translations, Pond was missionary
among the Dakota Sioux from 1834-1852. $20.00

P194. PORTER (Muriel Noe). Excavations at Chupicuaro, Guana-
juato, Mexico. 67pp, plus illus, 4to, wrappers. American Philosophical Society, 1956. $45.00

P195. PORTER (M. N.). (Viking Fund Publications in Anthropology, No. 19, New York, 1953) Tlatilco and the

Pre-Classic Cultures of the New World. 104pp, 14 pls, wrappers. $45.00

P196. PORTILLA (M. L.) and HIGUERA (S. M.). Catalogo de los Codices Indigenas del Mexico Antiguo. 53pp, Supplemento del Boletin Bibliografico de la Secretaria de Hacienda No. 111, Mexico, 1957. $15.00

P197. PORTILLO (Jose L.). Quetzalcoatl: In Myth, Archaeology and Art. 246pp, numerous pls, many in color, 4to, boxed. New York, 1982. $85.00
___Another Copy. Same, missing box and d.j. $45.00

P198. (PORTRAITS). The T. B. Walker Collection of Indian Portraits. 163pp (27pp of historical commentary), 125 reproductions of paintings by Henry H. Cross of which 22 are in color, wrappers. Madison, WI, 1948. $20.00

P199. POSNANSKY (I. Arthur). Tihuanacu: The Cradle of American Man (2 Volumes). Volumes I and II bound together as one volume, illus, some in color, many folded charts. Augustin, NY, 1945. $350.00

P200. (POTTAWATOMIE INDIANS). (House of Representatives Executive Document 61, 40:3, Washington, 1869, 1st print.) Pottawatomie Claims. Letter from the Secretary of the Interior, Submitting a Report of Commissioners Under Pottawatomie Treaty of August 7, 1868, to Examine the Claims of said Tribe. 31pp, 2pp, removed, an examination of Pottawatomie treaties from 1795 to 1846, including very detailed schedules of annuities payments made and due for education, blacksmiths, tobacco, iron, etc. $40.00
___Another Copy. Same. $17.00

P201. (POTTERY). Designs of the Mimbrenos, an Exhibition of Zoomorphic Decorations on Indian Pottery from Mimbres River Valley, New Mexico. 20pp, 11 photographs, 3 drawings, map. Yale University Art Gallery, 1956. (See entry P71.) $19.00

P202. (POTTERY). Families in Pueblo Pottery. 112pp, portraits, photographs of pottery (some in color), stiff decorative wrappers, excellent artist reference which includes family trees, portraits and examples of work, shows the major families known for pottery. Maxwell Museum of Anthropology and the University of New Mexico, Albuquerque, 1974. $15.00

P203. (POTTERY). Indian Pottery of the Southwest Post Spanish Period. 52 unnumbered pp, 21 pls, stiff pictorial wrappers. Tulsa, 1958. $12.00
___Another Copy. 1963 revised ed., 64pp. $10.00

P204. (POTTERY). (Medallion Papers, No. XXI, Gila Pueblo, 1936) Some Southwestern Pottery Types, Series V. vi, 66pp, 12pp photographs, 14 figures, 3 fold-out charts, map. $57.00

P205. POUND (Arthur) and DAY (Richard E.). Johnson of the Mohawks. A Biography of Sir William Johnson. 556pp, illus, maps, cloth. New York, 1930. $30.00

P206. POUND (Arthur). Lake Ontario. 363pp, photographs, bibliography, map endpapers, index. Indianapolis, 1945, (1st ed.). $10.00

P207. POUND (Merritt B.). Benjamin Hawkins, Indian Agent. 270pp, index, bibliography. Athens, 1951 (1st ed.), d.j. $15.00

P208. POURADE (Richard F.) (Editor). Ancient Hunters of the Far West. 207pp, 4to, illus, index, bibliography, maps. San Diego, 1966 (1st ed.), d.j. $30.00
Illustrated work on Southern California's early inhabitants by various experts including Malcom Rogers, H. M. Wormington and the author, etc.
___Another Copy. Same. $19.00

POURCHET (Maria Julia). See BAE Bulletin No. 143.

P209. POWELL (Donald M.). Arizona Gathering II, 1950-1969: An Annotated Bibliography. vii, 207pp, 2,060 items listed with much on publications about the Navajo. University of Arizona Press, 1973 (1st ed.), d.j. $20.00

P210. POWELL (J.) and JENSEN (V.). Quileute, An Introduction to the Indians of La Push. 78pp, 85 photographs, 1 drawing, 2 maps. Seattle, 1976. $10.00

P211. POWELL (J. P.). Ancient Art of the Americas. 68pp, 38 photographs, map. Exhibition catalogue, Brooklyn Museum, 1959. $22.00

P212. POWELL (J. W.). Indian Linguistic Families of America North of Mexico. pp1-142, newly rebound, from Smithsonian Institution BAE 7th Annual Report, Washington, 1892. $15.00

P213. POWELL (J. W.). Introduction to the Study of Indian Languages, with Words, Phrases and Sentences to be Collected. xi, 228pp, 10 blank lves, 4 kinship charts in pocket, original cloth, 4to. Washington, 1880. $150.00

P214. POWELL (J. W.). Outlines of the Philosophy of the North American Indians. 19pp, original printed wrappers, a paper read before the American Geographical Society concerned with Indian theology, myth and custom. Not in Howes, Eberstadt, Decker, Sabin, etc. New York, 1877. $75.00

P215. POWELL (Peter J.). People of the Sacred Mountain. A History of the Northern Cheyenne Chiefs and Warrior Societies, 1830-1870, with an epilogue 1969-1974 (2 Volumes). 1416 pp plus index, 77 full-color reproductions of Indian ledger art, photographs, maps, notes, bibliography, boxed. San Francisco, 1979 (1st ed.). $150.00
___Another Copy. San Francisco, 1981. $125.00

P216. POWELL (Peter J.). Sweet Medicine: The Continuing Role of the Sacred Arrows, The Sun Dance, and the Sacred Buffalo Hat in Northern Cheyenne History (2

Volumes). 935pp total, illus, index, map, bibliography, boxed. Norman, 1969 (1st ed.). $90.00

 Contains the most comprehensive record ever made of the unique ceremonies of the Cheyenne. Volume I recounts tribal history against the background of the 2 great spiritual tragedies in Cheyenne life with much new material on their battles; Volume II records the contemporary Sacred Arrow and Sun Dance ceremonies in their entirety.

 ____Another Copy. Same. $75.00
 ____Another Copy. Same. $75.00
 ____Another Copy. Norman, 1979, 935pp, 2 volumes, boxed. $50.00

P217. POWERS (Bob). Indian Country of the Tubatulabal. 103pp, 4to, illus, index, bibliography. Tucson, 1981, (1st ed.), d.j. $25.00

P218. POWERS (Stephen). California Indian Characteristics also: Centennial Mission to the Indians of Western Nevada and California. vi, v, 57pp, illus, pls, color frontis, portrait, wrappers, No. 23 in Friends of Bancroft Library Keepsakes, these two titles originally appeared in the April, 1875, Overland Monthly and the 1876 Annual Report of the Smithsonian Institution. Berkeley, 1975 (1st ed.). $20.00
 ____Another Copy. Same. $10.00

P219. POWERS (Stephen). (Smithsonian Contributions to North American Ethnology, Vol. III, Washington, 1877) Tribes of California. 634pp, illus, 4to, cloth. $125.00
 ____Another Copy. Same, rebound in quarter leather.
                                                         $120.00
 ____Another Copy. Berkeley, 1976, complete new edition, 480pp, illus, index. $45.00
 ____Another Copy. Same. $40.00
 ____Another Copy. Same. $30.00

P220. POWERS (William K.). Oglala Religion. 233pp, illus, bibliography, index, how the Oglala Sioux have preserved their social and cultural identity despite formidable attempts by the U.S. Government to eliminate tribal societies, full accounts of rituals, dances, ceremonies, etc. Lincoln, 1977 (1st ed.), d.j. $22.00
 ____Another Copy. Same. $19.00

P221. POWERS (William K.). Yuwipi. Vision and Experience In Oglala Ritual. 106pp plus index, maps, bibliography. Lincoln, 1982 (1st ed.), d.j. $14.00

P222. PRADEAU (Alberto F.). Numismatic History of Mexico: From the Pre-Columbian Epoch to 1823. 146pp, 24 pls, wrappers, 4to, includes plate of 5 tajederas ("Hoe Money") and gold eagle of the Aztecs. Los Angeles, 1938. $85.00

P223. PRATSON (Fredrick John). Land of the Four Directions. 131pp, illus oblong 4to, documentary on the

Passamaquoddy, Maliseet and Micmac tribes of Maine
and New Brunswick, with much on their problems and
struggles in modern civilization. Old Greenwich, 1970
(1st ed.), d.j. $16.00

P224.   PRATT (Frances) and GAY (Carlo). Ceramic Figures of
Ancient Mexico. 288pp, 106 pls with 22 in color, 5
maps, folio. Graz, Austria, 1979. $125.00

P225.   PREBLE (Donna). Yamino-Kwiti; Boy Runner of Siba.
Foreword by A. L. Krober. 230pp, end maps, histori-
cal novel of Gabrielino Indians. Caldwell, Caxton
Printers, 1940 (1st ed.). $25.00

P226.   (PRE-COLUMBIAN ART). Aboriginal Cultures of the Western Hemisphere. 32pp, 30 photographs, 20 of pre-
Columbian objects, 10 of Indian objects. San Francisco,
1940. $12.00

P227.   (PRE-COLUMBIAN ART). (Carnegie Institution Supplementary Publication No. 46, 1955) Ancient Maya Paintings of Bonampak, Mexico. In a transparent folio, 36pp
text with 1 map, 1 figure and 3 loose fold-out color
paintings of murals. $25.00

P228.   (PRE-COLUMBIAN ART). Arensberg Collection. Classified
and Annotated by George Kubler. 197 illus, many are
full-page, includes all areas of Mexico plus Central
America. Philadelphia Museum of Art, 1954. $45.00
____Another Copy. Same. ex-library. $30.00

P229.   (PRE-COLUMBIAN ART). Art Ancien du Mexique et du
Perou. 32pp, 14 b/w and 2 color full-page photo-
graphs. Exhibition catalogue, Musee de Beaux-Arts,
Lyon, 1972. $12.00

P230.   (PRE-COLUMBIAN ART). The Art of Ancient Mexico.
Text and notes by Franz Feuchtwanger. 29pp, 109
photographs by Irmgard Croth-Kimball, newly rebound.
New York, 1955. $85.00

P231.   (PRE-COLUMBIAN ART). Art de l'Amerique Precolombienne. 52pp, 20 b/w and 10 color photographs--all full
page, 2 maps. Infrequently seen examples (a number of
them of stunning beauty) from the Musee Barbier Muller's collection of pre-Columbian art are illustrated, text
in French. Geneva, 1981. $18.00
____Another Copy. Geneva, n.d., 50pp, 21 b/w and
9 color photographs. $15.00

P232.   (PRE-COLUMBIAN ART). Arte Prehispanico de Mexico.
xi, 263 illus, stiff wrappers, Mexico, 1946. $30.00
____Another Copy. Same. $30.00
____Another Copy. Same. $30.00
____Another Copy. Same. Instituto Nacional de Antro-
pologia e Historia, Pre-Spanish Art of Mexico. 120pp,
263 illus. $30.00

P233.   (PRE-COLUMBIAN ART). Art Mexicain, du Precolombien
a Nors Jours, Tome I. 154pp, 72 lrg photographs.
Exhibition Catalogue, Musee National d'Art Moderne,
1952. $25.00

P234. (PRE-COLUMBIAN ART). Between Continents/Between Seas:
Precolumbian Art of Costa Rica. 240pp, 100 color and
233 b/w photographs, soft cover. New York, 1982.
$34.00
Published to coincide with the exhibition of the most
important collection of Costa Rican art ever to visit the
U.S. This truly stunning volume contains important
essays by twelve leading archaeologists, art historians
and ethnographers and over 300 photographs of spectacular creations in stone, jade, gold and ceramic. (EAP)
___Another Copy. Same. Cloth cvr. $48.00

P235. (PRE-COLUMBIAN ART). Catalogo de la Coleccion Vela de
Prehistoria Americana. 37pp, 87 pls of lithic objects
and artifacts from Bolivia, wrappers. Valencia, 1964.
$45.00

P236. (PRE-COLUMBIAN ART). Chefs-D'ouvre de l'Amerique
Pre Colombienne. 77pp, 16 pls of pre-Columbian Art
from Mexico, Antilles, Columbia and Peru, wrappers.
Au Musee de l'homme, Paris, 1947. $20.00
___Another Copy. Same. new wrappers. $12.00

P237. (PRE-COLUMBIAN ART). (Instituto Nacional de Antropologia e Historia, Mexico, 1966) Colima por Miguel
Messmacher. 141pp, 84 photographs por Alfonso Munoz,
sml 4to, wrappers. $40.00

P238. (PRE-COLUMBIAN ART). Ethnographie Ancienne de
l'Equateur. Arc de Meridien Equatorial en Amerique
du Sud, Sous le Controle Scientifique de l'Academie des
Sciences, 1899-1906. xli, 224pp, 56pp of color and b/w
photographs of ceramic vessels and figures, cvrs
chipped, spine repaired. Tome 6, Paris, 1922. $75.00

P239. (PRE-COLUMBIAN ART). Flor y Canto del Arte Prehispanico de Mexico. Introduction by Angel Garibay K.,
411 pls, most are in color, with index of illus in English, folio (11"x14"). Mexico, 1964 (1st ed.). $150.00

P240. (PRE-COLUMBIAN ART). Glanz und Untergang Des Alten
Mexiko: Die Azteken und Ihre Vorlaufer (2 Volumes).
pp225, 349, profusely illus, several in color, wrappers,
a fine collection from museums world-wide, including
Turin, Brussels, Berlin, Hamburg, Bremen, Vienna,
Mainz, 1987. $75.00

P241. (PRE-COLUMBIAN ART). Handbook of the Robert Woods
Bliss Collection of Pre-Columbian Art. 78pp, 100 illus,
with supplement, wrappers. Washington, 1963. $40.00

P242. (PRE-COLUMBIAN ART). Houses for the Hereafter: Fun-
erary Temples from Guerrero, Mexico. Introduction by
Julie Jones. 32pp, 29 photographs, bibliography,
wrappers. New York, 1987. $12.00

P243. (PRE-COLUMBIAN ART). Indian Art of the Americas.
48pp, 24 photographs, pre-Columbian, North American
Indian and Eskimo. Exhibition catalogue, Dallas Museum
of Fine Arts, 1963. $12.00

P244. (PRE-COLUMBIAN ART). Indigenous Art of the Americas:
Collection of Robert Woods Bliss. 159pp, color frontis,
over 100 illus, 4to. Smithsonian, 1947. $40.00

P245. (PRE-COLUMBIAN ART). Kunst Aus Alt Mexico. 31pp, 15
illus, wrappers. Berlin, 1961. $10.00

P246. (PRE-COLUMBIAN ART). Man-Eaters and Pretty Ladies.
107pp, over 120 illus, with some in color, covers early
art in Central Mexico from the Gulf to the Pacific, 1500
B.C. to 500 A.D., Montreal Museum of Fine Arts, 1972
(2d print.). $45.00

P247. (PRE-COLUMBIAN ART). Masterpieces from the Gold Museum. 80 illus, descriptions in English, water stains at
lower edges, wrappers. Bogota, 1954. $20.00

P248. (PRE-COLUMBIAN ART). Masterpieces of Primitive Art.
263pp, color frontis, numerous color photographs, 4to.
New York, 1978, d.j. $40.00

P249. (PRE-COLUMBIAN ART). Musestrario de Arte Peruano
PreColombino. I: Cermica. 40pp, plus 72 pls showing
over 100 artifacts. Museo Nacional, Lima, 1938. $45.00

P250. (PRE-COLUMBIAN ART). Olmec: An Early Art Style of
Precolumbian Mexico. 188pp, 39 photographs and drawings, map endpaper, cloth. Tucson, 1971 (1st ed.).
$20.00

P251. (PRE-COLUMBIAN ART). Peruvian pre-Columbian Art.
illus, 35 photographs, 4to, wrappers. Exhibition catalogue, Lowe Art Museum, Miami, 1976. $15.00

P252. (PRE-COLUMBIAN ART). Pre-Columbian Art. 38pp, 11
full-page photographs, map. Exhibition catalogue, Los
Angeles County Museum, 1940. $15.00

P253. (PRE-COLUMBIAN ART). Pre-Columbian Art. 52pp, over
100 artifacts shown from Mexico and Central America.
Exhibition catalogue, Stendahl Galleries, 1963-1965.
$15.00

P254. (PRE-COLUMBIAN ART). Pre-Columbian Art of Mexico and
Guatemala. 32pp, 42 b/w and 2 color photographs.
Exhibition catalogue, Merrin Gallery, New York, 1970.
$12.00

P255. (PRE-COLUMBIAN ART). Pre-Columbian Gold Sculpture.
28pp, illus, 4to, wrappers. Exhibition catalogue, Museum of Primitive Art, New York, 1958. $25.00

P256. (PRE-COLUMBIAN ART). Pre-Columbian Sculpture in
Wood, Shell and Bone from Peru A.D. 500-1530. 24pp,
45 illus. Emmerich Gallery, 1966. $15.00

P257. (PRE-COLUMBIAN ART). Twenty Centuries of Mexican
Art. 197pp, text in English and Spanish, 155 b/w and
20 color photographs. Exhibition catalogue, Museum of
Modern Art, New York, 1940. $27.00

P258. (PRE-COLUMBIAN ART). The Weisman Collection of Pre-
Columbian Medical Sculpture. 15pp, photographs of 41
objects, inscribed by author. Exhibition catalogue,
National Library of Medicine, Bethesda, 1966. $14.00

P259. (PRE-COLUMBIAN ART). Works of Art from Pre-Columbian
       Mexico and Guatemala. 32pp, 25 lrg photographs.
       Exhibition catalogue, Merrin Gallery, New York, 1971.
                                                          $10.00
P260. (PREHISTORIC AGRICULTURE). (University of New
       Mexico Bulletin Vol. 1, No. 5, Albuquerque, 1936)
       Symposium on Prehistoric Agriculture. 72pp. wrap-
       pers. $15.00
       ___Another Copy. Same. $10.00
P261. (PREHISTORIC RELICS). Prehistoric Relics, An Illus-
       trated Catalogue Describing Some Eight Hundred and
       Fifty Different Specimens. 165pp, 146 photographs and
       drawings of over 850 artifacts; pipes, pottery, knives,
       etc., original leather. Andover Press, Andover, 1905.
                                                          $75.00
P262. (PREHISTORY). (Geological Society of America Bulletin
       51, New York, 1940). Early Man in America. Index
       to Localities and Selected Bibliography. pp373-432, pl,
       figure, wrappers. $10.00
P263. (PREHISTORY). (Geological Society of America Bulletin
       58, New York, 1947) Early Man in America. Index to
       Localities and Selected Bibliography, 1940-1945. pp955-
       978, wrappers. $12.00
P264. (PRE-INCA ARTIFACTS). (Selected Specimens of Anti-
       quities in the Archaeological Seminary, The University
       of Tokyo, No. 14, 1954.) Pre-Inca Remains. sml tied
       folio with 12pp text in English and Japanese, 25 unbound
       leaves, each leaf containing photographs of clay vessels.
                                                          $40.00
P265. (PRE-INCA ARTIFACTS). (Selected Specimens of Anti-
       quities in the Archaeological Seminary, The University
       of Tokyo, No. 15, 1956.) Pre-Inca Remains. sml tied
       folio with 16pp of text in English and Japanese, 25 un-
       bound leaves, each leaf containing photographs of metal
       and textile artifacts. $40.00
P266. PRESCOTT (W.). Die Eroberung Von Peru. 536pp, 23pp
       of drawings, map, cloth. Vienna, 1927. $35.00
P267. PRESCOTT (W. H.). History of the Conquest of Peru,
       1524-1550. Introduction by S. E. Morrison. xxxvi,
       252pp, 30 color drawings by E. G. Jackson, sheepskin
       leather binding, hubs on spine (8 3/4"x12 3/4") in size,
       gold stamping, specially made paper, printed for the
       members of the Limited Editions Club at Imprenta Nuevo
       Mundo, Mexico City, 1957. This edition limited to 1500
       copies of which this is No. 583, and is signed by printer
       and illustrator. $350.00
       ___Another Copy. Same. #1078/1500, full leather,
       signed, boxed, taped and worn. $150.00
       ___Another Copy. Philadelphia, 1847, 1874 (revised
       ed.) 2 Volumes, Edited by J. F. Kirk. Vol. I: xvi,
       510pp. Vol. II: xx, 530pp, cloth, decorated gilt
       spines. $55.00

P268. PRESTON (Nolan E.). Two Burials from the McCann Site
and a Synposis of Lithic.... 20pp, photographs, map,
bibliography. Ft. Worth, 1971. $10.00
P269. PREUSS (K. Th.). Arte Monumental Prehistorico, Excavaciones en al Alto Magdalena y San Agostino Comparacion Arqueologica con las Manifestaciones Artisticas de
las demas Civilizaciones Americanas (2 Volumes). Vol.
I: Texto, 215pp. Vol. II: Planchas y Dibujos. 30pp
of text, plus 87 leaves of photographs and 20 leaves of
drawings--all with tissue guards. Bogota, 1931.
$145.00
The excavations of two major Columbian sites and
the magnificent stone monumental figures uncovered are
fully discussed (in Spanish text) and illustrated in this
long out of print two volume study. Vol. I details the
excavations, discusses the figures and examines the
material culture, art, religion and gods. Vol. II is
filled with illustrations of these beautiful, overwhelming
figures.
___Another Copy. Same. $150.00
P270. PREUSS (K. Th.). Bericht Uber Meine Archaologischen
und Ethnologischen Forschungsreisen in Kolumbien.
pp89-128, 14 illus (stone idols, Indians), in a binder.
Zeitschrift fur Ethnologie, Berlin, 1920-21. $25.00
P271. PREUSS (K. Th.) and MENGIN (E.). Die Mexikanische
Bilderhanschrift Historia Tolteca-Chichimeca. 130pp
of text containing 148 drawings, plus 25pp of pls, cloth.
Berlin, 1937, New York, 1968. $40.00
P272. PREWITT (E. R.). (University of Texas Archaeological
Survey, Research Report, No. 49, Austin, 1974, 1st
print.) Archaeological Investigations at the Loeve-Fox
Site, Williamson County, Texas. 147pp, plates, maps,
bibliography, lrg 8vo, wrappers. $10.00
___Another Copy. Same. $10.00
P273. PREWITT (E. R.). (Texas Historical Commission Report
No. 18, Austin, 1970, 1st ed.) Piedra del Diablo Site
Val Verde County, Texas. with: Notes ... Smithsonian
Institution.... 31pp, 52pp, illus, pls, maps, bibliogra-
phy, lrg 8vo, wrappers. $10.00
P274. (PRICE GUIDE). American Indian Artifact Price Guide
Vol. 2, No. 1, Watsonville, 1975. 120pp, 475 photo-
graphs and prices of 500 objects. $12.00
___Another Copy. Same. $11.00
P275. PRIEST (Josiah). American Antiquities.... 400pp,
folding map, pl, in text figures, later 1/2 leather,
marbled bds. Albany, 1833, Hoffman and White (2d
ed.). $60.00
Howes: P-592. Sabin: 65484. Field: 1245. First
edition also published in 1833.
___Another Copy. Albany, 1833 (3rd edition revised).
$75.00

    ____Another Copy. Same. $75.00
    ____Another Copy. Albany, 1834 (4th ed.). $40.00
    ____Another Copy. Same. $35.00
    ____Another Copy. Albany, 1835 (5th ed.). $50.00

P276. PRIESTLEY (Herbert Ingram) (Editor). (University of California Publications of the Academy of Pacific Coast History, Vol. 3, No. 2, Berkeley, 1913) The Colorado River Campaign, 1781-1782. Diary of Pedro Fages. 101pp, diary of Pedro Fages who fought the Yuma Indians in 1781-1782, wrappers. $60.00

P277. PRINCE (L. Bradford). Historical Sketches of New Mexico From the Earliest Records to the American Occupation. 320pp, 2pp, signed and dated by W. H. Pope of Santa Fe, embossed decorative cloth. Kansas City, 1883 (2d ed.). $150.00
    Howes: P0611. Graff: 3363. Rader: 2738. Saunders: 2610. Judge William Hayes Pope came to Santa Fe in 1894 and became associate editor of the New Mexican. In 1895 he resumed his profession and was appointed attorney for the Court of Private Land Claims. Later he was attorney for the Pueblo Indians, then appointed Associate Justice of the Supreme Court. (TE)

P278. PRITCHETTE (Mr.). (House of Representatives Executive Document 4, 36:2, Washington, 1860) Case of A. D. Bonesteel, Agent for the Menomonee Indians. 137pp, removed, details of Bonesteel stealing from the Indians. $20.00

P279. PROCTOR (E. D.). The Song of the Ancient People. 86pp, 11 full-page aquatints by Julian Scott, bound in full decorated suede. Boston 1893. $250.00
    Done by Hemenway Southwestern Archaeological Expedition and contains eleven aquatints of Zuni and Moqui subjects. Text printed on hand-made paper, limited edition.
    ____Another Copy. Boston, 1903. $175.00

P280. PROCTOR (Mary A.). Indians of the Winnipesauke and Pemigewasset Valleys. 67pp, photographic illus, wrappers. New Hampshire, 1930. $45.00

P281. PROSKOURIAKOFF (Tatiana). (Carnegie Institute Publication No. 558, Washington, 1946) An Album of Maya Architecture. 146pp, 36 collotype pls, numerous text figures, oblong folio, original cloth, limited to 1100 copies. $200.00
    ____Another Copy. Same. leather and bds. $135.00
    ____Another Copy. Maya Foundation, Yucatan, Mexico, facsimile ed. $135.00
    ____Another Copy. Merida, 1958, #5/1100. $150.00
    ____Another Copy. Same. #516/1100. $150.00
    ____Another Copy. Norman, 1963, xxi, 142pp, 87 illus, cloth, 8vo. $60.00

P282. PROUDFIT (S. V.). A Collection of Stone Implements from

the District of Columbia. 8pp, 4 pls, wrappers. Washington, 1890. $10.00

P283. PROULX (D. A.). (University of Massachusetts. Dept.
of Anthropology Research Report No. 2, 1968) An
Archaeological Survey of the Nepena Valley, Peru.
189pp, 21pp of photographs, 21pp of figures, 11pp plans,
map, 2 tables, wrappers. $25.00
___Another Copy. Same. Stapled mimeo. $25.00

P284. PROULX (D. A.). (University of Massachusetts. Anthropological Research Report No. 13, 1973) Archaeological
Investigations in the Nepena Valley, Peru. x, 231pp
of text containing 46 figures plus 30pp of photographs.
                                                        $15.00

P285. PROULX (Donald). (University of California Publications
in Anthropology, Vol. 5, 1968) Local Differences and
Time Differences in Nasca Pottery. 148pp, plus 31 pls,
wrappers. $35.00

P286. PRUCHA (Francis Paul). American Indian Policy in Crisis:
Christian Reformers and the Indian, 1865-1900. 456pp,
illus, index, maps. Norman, 1976 (1st ed.). $25.00
___Another Copy. Same. d.j. $17.00
___Another Copy. Same. $15.00

P287. PRUCHA (Francis P.). American Indian Policy in the
Formative Years, 1790-1834. 303pp, Cambridge, 1962
(1st ed.), d.j. $25.00

P288. PRUCHA (Francis P.). A Bibliographical Guide to the
History of Indian-White Relations in the United States.
464pp, index, wrappers. Lincoln, 1982. $10.00

P289. PRUCHA (Francis P.). The Great Father, the United States
Government and American Indians (2 Volumes).
1,302pp total, illus, index, maps, boxed, the first comprehensive history of relations between the government
and the Indians, from the Revolutionary War to 1980.
Lincoln, 1984 (1st ed.). $60.00

P290. PRUCHA (Francis P.). Indian Peace Medals in American
History. 175 pp plus index, photographs, notes, sources,
bibliography. Madison, 1971 (1st ed.), d.j. $35.00
___Another Copy. Same. $18.00
___Another Copy. Same. $15.00
___Another Copy. Same. $15.00

P291. PRUDDEN (T. Mitchell). On the Great American Plateau:
Wanderings Among the Canyons and Buttes, in the Land
of the Cliff-Dweller, and the Indians of Today. 243pp,
illus, 16mo, cloth. New York, 1906. $25.00

P292. PRUFER (Olaf H.). (Cleveland Museum of Natural History,
No. 10, Cleveland, OH, 1964) Survey of Ohio Fluted
Points. 24pp, self wrappers, map, photographs, draw-
ings, evidence of early Paleo-Indian presence in Ohio.
                                                        $10.00

P293. PURDY (C.). Pomo Indian Baskets and Their Makers.
Indians and Indian Baskets of Lake and Mendocino

Counties, California. 44pp, 38 photographs. Mendocino, n.d. $12.00
___Another Copy. Ukiah, n.d. 44pp, 33 photo-
graphs. $10.00

P294. PURDY (W. M.). (University of Utah--Anthropological
Papers, No. 37, Salt Lake City, 1959) An Outline of the
History of the Flaming Gorge Area. viii, 45pp, maps,
photographs, bibliography, lrg 8vo, wrappers. $10.00

P295. PUTNAM (C. E.). Elephant Pipes and Inscribed Tablets
in the Museum of the Academy of Natural Sciences,
Davenport, Iowa. 95pp, 3 figures. Davenport, 1885.
                                                    $40.00

P296. PUTNAM (C. E.). Elephant Pipes in the Museum of the
Academy of Natural Sciences. A Vindication for the
Authenticity of the Elephant Pipes ... From the Accusa-
tion of the Bureau of Ethnology of the Smithsonian Institution. 40pp, 1 illus. Davenport, 1885. $40.00

P297. PUTNAM (F. W.) et al. Palaeolithic Man in Eastern and
Central America. pp 421-449, 29pp, maps, wrappers,
bound in later boards, separate printing from the
Boston Society of Natural History, Vol. XXIII. Cambridge, MA, 1888. $10.00

-Q-

Q1.   (QUAPAW). Quapaw Indians--Present Conditions. 15pp.
Removed. Washington, DC, 1827. $20.00
Reports from agents on removal of Quapaw Indians.

Q2.   QUIMBY (G. I.). (Chicago Natural History Museum,
Anthropology Leaflet No. 35, Chicago, 1944) Aleutian
Islanders, Eskimos of the North Pacific. 56pp, 8pp of
photographs, 9 figures, wrappers. $24.00
___Another Copy. Same, ex-lib. $15.00

Q3.   QUIMBY (G. I.). (Field Museum, Fieldiana Anthropology,
Vol. 47, No. 2, Chicago, 1957) The Bayou Goula Site,
Iberville Parish, Louisiana. pp 91-170, 15 photographic
figures, 2 drawings, map, wrappers. $20.00
___Another Copy. Same. $15.00

Q4.   QUIMBY (G. I.). (Field Museum, Fieldiana Anthropology,
Vol. 56, No. 1, Chicago, 1966) The Dumaw Creek Site,
A Seventeenth Century Prehistoric Indian Village and
Cemetery in Oceana County, Michigan. 91pp, 31 photo-
graphic pls of artifacts, 3 drawings, wrappers. $12.00

Q5.   QUIMBY (G. I.). Indian Culture and European Trade
Goods. 217pp, 33 illus, cloth, Madison, 1966. $38.00
___Another Copy. Same. $17.00

Q6.   QUIMBY (G. I.). Indian Life in the Upper Great Lakes,
11,000 B.C. to A.D. 1800. xv, 182pp, 62 lrge

photographs, 13 figures, 2 maps, cloth, Chicago, 1960.
$28.00
Q7.   QUIMBY (G. I.). (Field Museum, Anthropology Series, Vol.
XXIV, No. 2, Chicago, 1951) The Medora Site, West
Baton Rouge Parish, Louisiana. pp 79-135, 21 figures,
wrappers. $20.00
Q8.   QOYAWAYMA (Polingysi) (Elizabeth Q. White). No Turning
Back. (As told to Vada F. Carlson). 180pp, illus,
author's signature, presentation copy, Albuquerque,
1964 (1st ed.), d.j. $20.00
      A true account of a Hopi Indian girl's struggle to
bridge the gap between the world of her people and the
world of the White man.

-R-

R1.   RADIN (Paul). (Univ. of California Publications in American Archaeology and Ethnology, Vol. 16, No. 7, Berkeley,
1920) The Autobiography of a Winnebago Indian. 92pp,
wrappers. $27.00
R2.   RADIN (Paul). Crashing Thunder: The Autobiography of
an American Indian. 202pp, decorated cloth, New York,
1926 (1st ed.). $60.00
____Another Copy. Same. $20.00
R3.   RADIN (Paul). (Indiana Univ. Publications in Anthropology
and Linguistics, Memoir No. 2, 1945) The Culture of the
Winnebago, as described by Themselves. 119pp, wraps.
$32.00
____Another Copy. Same. $10.00
R4.   RADIN (Paul). The Esoteric Rituals of the North American
Indians. 66pp, wrappers, reprint from Eranos-Jahrbuch
XIX, Zurich, 1951. $10.00
R5.   RADIN (Paul). The Evolution of an American Prose Epic:
A Study in Comparative Literature. 148pp, wrappers,
Basel, 1954. $15.00
R6.   RADIN (Paul). The Genetic Relationship of the North Ameri-
can Indian Languages. 13pp, wrappers. $17.00
R7.   RADIN (Paul). (Univ. of California Publications in American
Archaeology and Ethnology, Vol. 27, Berkeley, 1929)
A Grammar of the Wappo Language. vi, 194pp, wrappers.
$20.00
____Another Copy. Same. $32.00
____Another Copy. Same. $15.00
____Another Copy. Same. $20.00
R8.   RADIN (Paul). An Historical Legend of the Zapotecs.
29pp, wrappers, Berkeley, 1935 (1st ed.). $10.00
R9.   RADIN (Paul). Indians of South America. Illus, Double-
day, New York, 1942, 1946. $20.00

R10. RADIN (Paul). (Dept. of Mines, Anthropology Series No. 6, Ottawa, 1915) Literary Aspects of North American Mythology. 51pp, wrappers. $25.00

R11. RADIN (Paul). Monotheism Among Primitive People. 30pp, wrappers, reprint of a 1924 monograph, Baltimore, 1954.
                                                                $10.00

R12. RADIN (Paul). (Bollingen Foundation, Special Publication No. 2, and Indiana Univ. Publications in Anthropology Memoir No. 3, Baltimore, 1950) The Origin Myth of the Medicine Rite: Three Versions. The Historical Origins of the Middle Rite. 78pp, wrappers. $20.00
____Another Copy. Same. $20.00
____Another Copy. Same. $10.00
____Another Copy. Same. $30.00

R13. RADIN (Paul). The Ritual and Significance of the Winne-bago Medicine Dance. Offprint from Journal of American Folk-lore. pp149-208, wrappers, New York, 1911.
                                                                $35.00

R14. RADIN (Paul). (Bollingen Series V, New York, 1945) The Road of Life and Death, a Ritual Drama of the American Indians. xiv, 435pp, cloth. $50.00
____Another Copy. Same. $15.00

R15. RADIN (Paul). The Sacral Kingship (Cover). The Sacral Chief Among the American Indians (caption title). pp83-97, wrappers, separate printing from Studies in History of Religions, Leiden, 1959. $10.00

R16. RADIN (Paul). The Story of the American Indian. 391pp, 6 full-page color photographs, 42 b/w photographs, 17 drawings, cloth, New York, 1927, 1937. $25.00
____Another Copy. Same. $18.00
____Another Copy. Same, 1927. $15.00

R17. RADIN (Paul). (Dept. of Mines, Anthropology Series, No. 5, Ottawa, 1915) The Social Organization of the Winne-bago Indians, an Interpretation. 40pp, wrappers.
                                                                $25.00

R18. RADIN (Paul). Some Aspects of Puberty Fasting Among the Ojibwa. 10pp, wrappers, reprint from Ottawa Museum Bulletin No. 2, Ottawa, 1914. $10.00

R19. RADIN (Paul). (Univ. of California Publications in American Archaeology and Ethnology, Vol. 17, No. 1, Berkeley, 1921) The Sources and Authenticity of the History of the Ancient Mexicans. 150pp, wrappers. $35.00

R20. RADIN (Paul). The Trickster: A Study of American Indian Mythology. 221pp, penetrating study of Trickster Myth of the Indians with commentary by C. G. Jung. Includes Winnebago, Assiniboine and Tlingit Indians, New York, 1956, d.j. $15.00
____Another Copy. Same. $12.00
____Another Copy. Same, London, 1956. $12.00

R21. RADIN (Paul). (International Journal of American Linguis-tics, Memoir No. 1, Baltimore, 1948, 1st ed.) Winnebago

Hero Cycles. A Study in Aboriginal Literature. 168pp, notes, wrappers. $10.00

R22. RADIN (Paul). (Southwest Anthropology Society Papers, Vol. 1, No. 1, Santa Fe, 1915) The Winnebago Myth of the Twins: A Comparative Study. 53pp, wrappers. $30.00

R23. (RAILROADS). (Senate Executive Documents 40 and 41, 50:1, Washington, 1888, 1st printing) Railroads Through Indian Lands. 4pp; 8pp. Removed. $12.00

R24. RAINEY (F. G.). (American Museum of Natural History Anthropology Papers, Vol. XXXVI, Part IV, New York, 1939) Archaeology in Central Alaska. pp 351-405, 12 figures, wrappers. $34.00
____Another Copy. Same. $35.00
____Another Copy. Same. $28.00

R25. RAINEY (F. G.). The Vanishing Art of the Arctic. pp 3-13, 19 photographs of Old Bering Sea carved ivory objects and 19th century wooden masks, 4 drawings, 2 maps, wrappers, Philadelphia, 1959. $12.00

R26. RALEY (G. H.). A Monograph of the Totem-Poles in Stanley Park, Vancouver, B.C. 24pp, photographs, wrappers, Vancouver, 1945. $15.00

R27. RANDOLPH (J. Ralph). British Travellers Among the Southern Indians, 1660-1763. xv, 183pp, 48pp illus, 7 maps, bibliography, index, a study of Indians of the Southern colonies through the journals and memoirs of the early travellers, Norman, 1973 (1st ed.), d.j. $25.00
____Another Copy. Same. $15.00
____Another Copy. Same, lacks d.j. $10.00

RANDS (Robert L.). See also BAE Bulletin Nos. 151 and 157.

R28. RANDS (Robert L.). The water Lily in Maya Art. pp 77-153, bibliography, printed wrappers, offprint Smithsonian Anthropological Papers, Washington, 1953. $10.00

R29. RANKING (John). Historical Researches on the Conquest of Peru, Mexico, Bogota, Natchez and Talomeco, in the 13th Century, by the Mongols, Accompanied with Elephants. 479pp, 2 folding maps, 3 engraved pls of Incas of Peru, engraved portrait of Montezuma, London, 1827 (1st ed.). $500.00
    Despite the author's contention that the Mongols, together with their elephants landed in Peru, this work is a vivid description of Mexican and South American scenes, including a history of the Incas and early Mexico. (BF)

R30. RANNEY (Edward). Stonework of the Maya. 119pp, illus, wrappers, Univ. of New Mexico, 1974 (2nd printing). $15.00

R31. RAPOPORT (R. N.). (Peabody Museum Papers, Vol. 41, No. 2, Cambridge, 1954) Changing Navaho Religious Values. A Study of Christian Missions to the Rimrock Navahos. 166pp, 1 figure, 33 tables, wraps. $24.00
____Another Copy. Same. $18.00

R32. RASMUSSEN (K.). (Reports of the Danish Ethnographical
Expedition to Arctic America, 1921-24, Vol. VII, Nos.
2 and 3, Copenhagen, 1930) Intellectual Culture of the
Caribou Eskimos and Igulik and Caribou Eskimo Texts.
274pp of text, 12 maps, 23 pls, 1 fold-out map, wraps.
$195.00

R33. RASMUSSEN (K.). (Reports of the Danish Ethnographical
Expedition to Arctic America, 1921-24, Vol. IX, Copenhagen, 1931) Intellectual Culture of the Copper Eskimos. 350pp of text containing 57 figures, pls, 32pp of
photographs, 2 maps, wrappers. $225.00

R34. RAU (Charles). (Smithsonian Contributions to Knowledge,
No. 287, Washington, 1876) The Archaeological Collection of the U.S. National Museum. 104pp, 340 illus,
drawings with descriptions, primarily North American
artifacts, some examples from Mexico, 4to, rebound in
linen. $90.00
___Another Copy. Same, ex-lib. $60.00
___Another Copy. Same. $35.00

R35. RAU (Charles). Articles on Anthropological Subjects Contributed to the Annual Reports of the Smithsonian Institute from 1863 to 1877. 164pp, wrappers. $25.00
___Another Copy. Same, cloth, ex-lib. $18.00

R36. RAU (Charles). (Smithsonian Contributions to Knowledge,
No. 509, Washington, 1884) Prehistoric Fishing in Europe
and North America. 342pp, 405 illus of artifacts, 4to,
original cloth. $90.00

R37. RAUFER (Sister Marie). Black Robes and Indians on the
Last Frontier. A Story of Heroism. xiv, 489pp, 32pp of
photographs, bibliography, index, Milwaukee, 1966 (1st
ed.), d.j. $25.00
___Another Copy. Same. $20.00
___Another Copy. Same, signed, lacks d.j. $20.00

R38. RAVENHILL (Alice). (British Columbia Provincial Museum
Occasional Papers no. 5, Victoria, 1945) A Corner Stone
of Canadian Culture. An Outline of the Arts and Crafts
of the Indian Tribes of British Columbia. 103pp, plus
20 illus, wrappers. $25.00

R39. (Ravoux, Rev. Augustin). Katolik Wocekiye Wawapi Kin.
(Caption Title). 84pp, 16mo, cloth, n.p., n.d., c.
1876. $125.00
Pilling: Siouan Languages, p.58. Contains summary
of Christian doctrine, prayers, bible history, catechism
and Roman Catholic hymns (verse only) in the Isanti
dialect of the Dakota language. Embossed stamp of the
Diocese of Dakota on the frnt free-endpaper. (CLR)

R40. RAVOUX (Monsignor Augustin). Reminiscences, Memoirs,
and Lectures. 223pp, 3 illus, maroon cloth, inner hinge
started, edge wr, St. Paul, 1890. $175.00
Howes: R-75. Monsignor Ravoux came to Minnesota

in 1840; as missionary to the Sioux from 1840 to 1876. His operations covered the vast region between Dubuque and Fort Pierre. About personal experiences with Chippeway and Sioux Indians.

R41. RAY (Arthur J.). "Give Us Good Measure"; An Economic Analysis of Relations Between the Indians and the Hudson's Bay Company Before 1763. 298pp, maps, index, bibliography, Toronto, 1978 (1st ed.). $22.00
    ___Another Copy. Same. $30.00

R42. RAY (Arthur J.). Indians in the Fur Trade: Their Role as Trappers, Hunters and Middlemen in the Lands Southwest of Hudson Bay, 1660-1870. 242pp, plus index, maps, tables, graphs, bibliography, Toronto, 1974 (1st ed.), d.j. $25.00
    ___Another Copy. Same. $15.00
    ___Another Copy. Same, lacks d.j. $18.00

R43. RAY (Dorothy Jean). Aleut and Eskimo Art. Tradition and Innovation in South Alaska. 237pp, plus index, photographs, drawings, map, bibliography, Seattle, 1981 (1st ed.), d.j. $35.00
    ___Another Copy. Same, lacks d.j. $28.00

R44. RAY (D. J.). Artists of the Tundra and the Sea. 192pp, 107 photographs, 200 line drawings, Seattle, 1961, 1980. $16.00

R45. RAY (D. J.). Contemporary Indian Artists: Montana, Wyoming, Idaho. 80pp, illus, most are in color, wraps, Dept. of Interior, Washington, 1972. $12.00

R46. RAY (D. J.). Eskimo Art: Tradition and Innovation in North Alaska. 298pp, profusely illus, Seattle, 1977. $35.00
    ___Another Copy. Same, d.j. $32.00

R47. RAY (D. J.). The Eskimos of Bering Strait, 1650-1898. xvi, 305pp, 16pp of photographs, 5 maps, bibliography, index, Seattle, Univ. of Washington, 1975 (1st ed.), d.j. $25.00
    ___Another Copy. Same. $16.00

R48. RAY (D. J.). (Dept. of Interior, Native American Arts No. 2, Washington, 1969) Graphic Arts of the Alaskan Eskimo. 86pp, illus, wraps. $18.00
    ___Another Copy. Same. $10.00

R49. RAY (Verne F.). The Contrary Behavior Pattern in American Indian Ceremonialism. Reprint from Southwest Journal of Anthropology, Vol. 1, No. 1, 1945. pp 75-114, bibliography, wrappers. $10.00

R50. RAY (V. F.). (Southwest Museum, F. W. Hodge Anniversary Publication Fund Volume III, 1939) Cultural Relations in the Plateau of Northwestern America. ix, 154pp, 20 maps, 2 tables, wrappers. $38.00
    ___Another Copy. Same. $40.00
    ___Another Copy. Same. $30.00

R51. RAY (V. F.). (Univ. of Washington, Publications in

Anthropology, Vol. 7, No. 2, 1938) Lower Chinook
Ethnographic Notes. pp 29-166, 5pp of photographs,
19 figures, 7 tables, wrappers. $48.00

R52. RAY (V. F.). Primitive Pragmatists, the Modoc Indians
of Northern California. 237pp, 19 illus, American Ethnological Society, Seattle, 1963. $30.00
___Another Copy. Same, 1963 (1st ed.), d.j. $20.00
___Another Copy. Same, 1973. $12.00

R53. RAYMOND (J. Scott) et al. (Dept. of Archaeology, Univ.
of Calgary, Occasional Papers, No. 2, Calgary, 1975)
Cumancaya: Peruvian Ceramic Tradition. 143pp,
photograph, many drawings, map, wrappers. $15.00
___Another Copy. Same. $12.00

R54. RAWLS (James J.). The Indians of California; the Changing image. 293pp, illus, index, bibliography, Norman,
1984 (1st ed.), d.j. $20.00
___Another Copy. Same, lacks d.j. $12.00

R55. REA (B. D.). (Wyoming Archaeologist, Vol. 7, No. 1,
1964) Maps for Archaeologists, and Other Articles.
41pp, maps, illus, lrge 8vo, wrappers. $10.00

R56. READ (William A.). (Louisiana State Univ., Studies No.
11, Baton Rouge, 1934) Florida Place-Names of Indian
Origin and Seminole Personal Names. 80pp, plus index,
bibliography, wrappers. $10.00

R57. READ (W. A.). (Louisiana State Univ., Bulletin Vol. XIX,
No. 2, Baton Rouge, 1927) Louisiana Place-Names of
Indian Origin. 72pp, folded frontis, wraps. $25.00

R58. REAGAN (A. B.). (American Museum of Natural History
Anthropological Papers, Vol. 31, Part 5, 1930) Notes
on the Indians of the Fort Apache Region. pp 282-344,
wrappers. $25.00
___Another Copy. Same. $25.00
___Another Copy. Same. $15.00

R59. REAGAN (A. B.). Some Notes of the Grand Medicine Society of the Bois Fort Ojibwa. Offprint from American-
Illustrated, Vol. 27, No. 4, 1933. pp 502-519, 3 illus,
wrappers. $15.00

R60. REAMON (G. Elmore). The Trail of the Iroquois. How the
Iroquois Nation Saved Canada for the British Empire.
129pp, plus index, photographs, drawings, references,
New York, 1967 (1st American ed.), d.j. $12.00

R61. REBOK (Horace M.). The Last of the Mus-Qua-Kies and
the Indian Congress 1898. 70pp, photographs, stiff
wrappers, Dayton, Ohio, 1900 (1st ed.). $37.00

R62. (RED CLOUD AGENCY). Report of the Special Commission
Appointed to Investigate the Affairs of the Red Cloud
Indian Agency, July 1875; Together with the Testimony
and Accompanying Documents. 852pp, index, 1/2 leather,
marbled bds, endpapers, Washington, GPO, 1875. $65.00
Report of the alleged abuses at the Red Cloud Agency
in the Black Hills of Wyoming and the Dakotas.

R63. REDFIELD (R. and M. P.). (Carnegie Institute Contributions to American Anthropology and History, No. 32,
1940) Disease and Its Treatment in Dzitas, Yucatan.
pp 49-81, wrappers. $20.00
R64. REDFIELD (R.). The Folk Culture of Yucatan. xxiii,
416pp, 6 photographs, 10 figures, map, cloth, Chicago,
1941. $20.00
R65. REDFIELD (R.) and VILLA (A.). (Carnegie Institute
Contributions to American Anthropology and History, No.
28, 1939) Notes on the Ethnography of Tzeltal Communi-
ties of Chiapas. pp 105-119, wrappers. $20.00
R66. REDNICK (D.). The Fort Belknap Assiniboine of Montana.
A Study in Culture Change. 125pp, wrappers, New
Haven, 1938. $38.00
____Another Copy. Same. $40.00
____Another Copy. Same. $22.00
R67. REED (Erik K.). For the Dean: Essays in Anthropology
in Honor of Byron Cummings on His 89th Birthday.
307pp, illus, 22 authoritative articles on Southwestern
Anthropology by various experts, Santa Fe, 1950.
                                                       $25.00
R68. REED (Verner Z.). The Southern Ute Indians of Early
Colorado. Reprint of article from California Illustrated
Magazine for 1893. 20pp, illus, wrappers, Golden,
1980. $10.00
R69. REEL (E.). Report of the Superintendent of Indian
Schools, 1899. 54pp, wrappers, Washington, GPO,
1899. $37.00
R70. REH (Emma) and MCNICKLE (D'Arcy). Peyote and the
Indian. Official print from Scientific Monthly, No. 57,
September, 1943. pp 220-229, illus, wrappers. $10.00
R71. REICHARD (Gladys A.) and BITTANY (A. D.). Agentive
and Causative Elements in Navajo. 22pp, wrappers,
some fine points in Navajo grammar, New York, J. J.
Augustin, 1940. $25.00
____Another Copy. Same. $10.00
R72. REICHARD (Gladys A.). (Memoirs of the American Folk-
lore Society, Vol. 41, Philadelphia, 1947) An Analysis
of the Coeur d'Alene Indian Myths. x, 218pp, original
cloth. $45.00
R73. REICHARD (Gladys A.). Dezba, Woman of the Desert.
161pp, 47pp of photographs, cloth, New York, 1939.
                                                       $85.00
____Another Copy. Same. $35.00
____Another Copy. Same, rebound in linen. $95.00
R74. REICHARD (Gladys A.). (Publications of the American
Ethnological Society, Vol. XXI, New York, n.d., c.1951)
Navaho Grammar. 393, (1)pp, cloth. $45.00
____Another Copy. J. Augustin, New York, n.d.,
c.1952. $40.00
____Another Copy. Same. $32.00

R75. REICHARD (Gladys A.). (Bollingen Series, XVIII, New
York, 1950) Navaho Religion, A Study of Symbolism.
(2 Volumes). 805pp, 29 drawings, 23 charts, cloth in
slipcase. $125.00
___Another Copy. Same. $95.00
___Another Copy. Same. $35.00
___Another Copy. Same, 1953, in one volume. $30.00
___Another Copy. Same. $25.00
R76. REICHARD (Gladys A.). Navaho Shepherd and Weaver.
xviii, 222pp, 15pp photographs, 35 figures, woven linen
cvr, J. J. Augustin, New York, 1936. $185.00
___Another Copy. Same. $150.00
___Another Copy. Same. $75.00
___Another Copy. Same, Rio Grande Press, 1968.
                                                             $10.00
___Another Copy. Same, Glorieta, 1981. $18.00
R77. REICHARD (Gladys A.). Prayer: The Compulsive Word.
x, 97pp, 14pp analysis (in 25 figures) of Navajo prayers,
Monographs of the American Ethnological Society, cloth,
New York, 1944. $40.00
___Another Copy. Same, Seattle, 1966. $12.00
R78. REICHARD (Gladys A.). (Columbia Univ. Contributions to
Anthropology, Vol. VII, 1928) Social Life of the Navaho
Indians. vii, 239pp, 25 figures, 3pp of photographs of
ceremonies, numerous tables and charts, cloth. $97.00
___Another Copy. Same. $125.00
___Another Copy. Same. $65.00
R79. REICHARD (Gladys A.). Spider Woman, A Story of Navajo
Weavers and Chanters. 287pp, 15pp of photographs,
one double-page color photograph of sand painting,
New York, 1934. $185.00
___Another Copy. Same, light cvr spots, signed by
author. $195.00
___Another Copy. Same, Glorieta, 1981. $25.00
R80. REICHARD (Gladys A.). The Story of the Navajo Hail
Chant. 155pp, 4to (8" x 11"), Columbia Univ., New
York, 1944, wrappers. $60.00
___Another Copy. Same. $48.00
R81. REICHARD (Gladys A.). (Univ. of California Publications
in American Archaeology and Ethnology, Vol. 22, No. 1,
Berkeley, 1925) Wiyot Grammar and Texts. (California).
pp 1-215, photographs, wrappers. $20.00
___Another Copy. Same. $18.00
R82. REICHEL-DOLMATOFF (G.). Beyond the Milky Way: Hal-
lucinatory Imagery of the Tukano Indians. 159pp, illus,
ex-lib., California, 1978. $20.00
R83. REICHEL-DOLMATOFF (G.). Colombia. 231pp, 65pp of
photographs and drawings, 3 maps, 1 table, cloth, New
York, 1965. $30.00
R84. REICHEL-DOLMATOFF (G.). Datos Historico-Culturales
Sobre las Tribus de la Antigua Gobernacion de Santa
Marta. 131pp, 1 photograph map, Bogota, 1951. $15.00

R85. REICHEL-DOLMATOFF (G.). Excavaciones Arqueologicas en Puerto Hormiga. 60pp, wrappers, Bogota, 1965.
$20.00

R86. REICHEL-DOLMATOFF (G.). (Univ. of Chicago, 1971) Amazonian Cosmos: The Sexual and Religious Symbolism of the Tukano Indians, Illus, d.j. $23.00

R87. REICHEL-DOLMATOFF (G.). The Shaman and the Jaguar: A Study of Narcotic Drugs Among the Indians of Colombia. Illus, Temple Univ. Press, 1975. $22.00

R88. REID (Aileen A.) et al. Totonac: From Clause to Discourse. 185pp, appendices, folding chart, wrappers, treatise on Indian language of Puebla, northern Mexico, Norman, 1968 (1st ed.). $10.00

R89. REID (B.) and BRINGHURST (R.). The Raven Steals the Light. 91pp, 10 full-page drawings by Bill Reid, cloth, Vancouver, 1984. $35.00
___Another Copy. Same. $28.00

R90. REID (Hugo). The Indians of Los Angeles County. iii, 70pp, cloth, limited to 200 copies, Los Angeles 1926 (1st ed.). $30.00
(Another Copy) (Southwest Museum Papers, No. 21, Los Angeles, 1968) The Indians of Los Angeles County: Hugo Reid's Letters of 1852. Edited by Robert F. Heizer. 142pp, illus, bibliography, about the Gabrielino Indians in the mid-19th century, wrappers. $25.00
___Another Copy. Same. $20.00

R91. REID (John Phillip). A Law of Blood: The Primitive Law of the Cherokee Nation. 340pp, index, endpaper maps, New York, 1970 (1st ed.), d.j. $18.00

R92. REINA (Ruben E.). Los Itzaes de San Jose, Guatemala y Socotz, Belize, Abandonan las Primicias. From Guatemala Indigena, Vol. 1, No. 2, 1961. pp 57-64, wrappers.
$10.00

R93. REINBURG (P.). Bebidas Toxicas de los Indios del Noroeste del Amazonas: El Ayaluasca-El Yate-El Huanto. 62pp, wrappers, Lima, 1965. $15.00

R94. REITER (Paul). (Univ. of New Mexico, School of American Research, Monograph Nos. 4 and 6, Albuquerque, 1938) The Jemez Pueblo of Unshagi, New Mexico, with Notes on the Earler Excavations at "Amoxiumqua" and "Guisewa." (in two parts). Part I: 92pp, 9 figures, 23pp of photographs, fold-out map. Part II: pp 97-211, 14 figures. wrappers. $50.00
___Another Copy. Same. $50.00

R95. RELANDER (Click). Drummers and Dreamers. Smowhala the Prophet and His Nephew Puck Hyah Toot, Last Prophet of the Nearly Extinct River People, the Wanapums. 345pp, frontis, 48pp of photographs, appendix, index, bibliography, endpaper maps, Caldwell, Caxton Press, 1956 (1st ed.), d.j. $275.00
Scarce study of Smowhala, the Dreamer, religious

   leader of the Wanapums, an eastern Washington tribe.
   ___Another Copy. Same. $100.00

R96. RELANDER (Click). Strangers on the Land. 100pp, illus,
   wrappers, Yakima Indian Nation, Yakima, WA, 1962
   (1st ed.). $15.00

R97. RELANDER (Click). Treaty Centennial 1855-1955, The
   Yakimas. 63pp, illus, map, wrappers, contains treaty
   text and history of tribe, Yakima, 1955 (1st ed.).
                 $20.00
   ___Another Copy. Same. $15.00

R98. REMINGTON (Frederic). On the Apache Indian Reservations. Also: Artists Wanderings Among the Cheyennes.
   Articles reprinted from Century Magazine for 1899.
   36pp with 33 illus by author, cloth, Palmer Lake, 1974.
                 $12.00

R99. REMY (Jules). A Journey to Great-Salt Lake City....
   (2 Volumes). Vol. 1: cxxxi, 508pp. Vol. 2: vii,
   605pp, folding map pls, index, modern half leather,
   W. Jeffs, London, 1861 (1st ed. in English). $325.00
    Howes: R-210. Sabin: 69594. Field: 1279.
   Field: "Much of the space ... is devoted to descriptions
   of the Shoshoni Indians."

R100. (REMOVAL). (American Historical Association, Annual
   Report, Vol. I, Washington, DC, 1908) History of
   Events Resulting in Indian Consolidation West of the
   Mississippi. (Complete volume), pp 233-450, cloth.
                 $25.00

R101. (REMOVAL). Speeches on the Passage of the Bill for the
   Removal of the Indians, Delivered in the Congress of
   the United States, April and May, 1830. viii, 304pp,
   original paper cvrd bds, Boston, Perkins and Marvin,
   1830 (1st ed.). $90.00
    Contains a history of the forced march of the Indians
   to the West, with pleas by several, notably Davy Crockett, to preserve the rights of the Indians to their own
   lands. A most remarkable series of speeches on this
   knotty problem, the resolution of which led to the death
   of many Indians and the displacement of all of them.
   Field: 1468.
   ___Another Copy. Same, rebound in cloth. $85.00

R102. (REMOVAL). A Statement of the Indian Relations; With a
   Reply ... on the Removal of the Indians. 21pp, one
   contemporary plate supplied, later wraps, New York,
   Clayton and Van Norden, 1830 (1st ed.). $50.00

R103. RENAUD (E. B.). (Univ. of Denver, Dept. of Anthropology, 1932) Archaeological Survey of Eastern Wyoming.
   91pp, 14pp of drawings of Wyoming photographs, 1 color
   drawing, 5pp of photographs, 6pp of drawings, 1 map,
   wrappers. $40.00
   ___Another Copy. Same. $25.00

R104. RENNER (C. A.). (Wyoming Archaeologist, Vol. 16, No.

2, 1973) A Survey of Ceramic Sites in Southeastern Wyoming. 126pp, illus, lrge 8vo, maps, bibliography, wrappers. $12.00

R105. REPLOGLE (Charles). Among the Indians of Alaska. xi, 182pp, frontis, 7 pls, pictorial gilt decorated cloth, London, Headley Bros., 1904 (1st ed.). $100.00
The author was a Society of Friends in America Missionary among the Indians on Douglas Island, Alaska.
___Another Copy. Same. $85.00

R106. REPLOGLE (Emma A. M.). Indian Eve and Her Descendants. An Indian Story of Bedford County, Pennsylvania. 128pp, photographs, ex-lib., rebound, about Indian captivities occurring toward the end of the Revolution, Huntingdon, Pennsylvania, 1911 (1st ed.).
$15.00

R107. (RESERVATIONS). Federal and State Indian Reservations, an EDA Handbook. 418pp, 4to, wraps, Washington, DC, 1971. $25.00

R108. REYNIERS (F.). Ceramiques Americaines, Inventaire des Collections Publiques Francaises. 175pp, 333 photographs, 25pp of drawings, Musee National de Ceramique, Severes, 1966. $30.00
___Another Copy. Same. $22.00
___Another Copy. Same. $35.00

R109. REYNOLDS (C. R.) (Editor). American Indian Portraits from the Wanamaker Expedition of 1913. 124pp, photographs, 4to, 120 portraits that were found in a drawer at the American Museum of Natural History and have never been published, photographer is unknown, Brattleboro, VT, 1971 (1st ed.), d.j. $50.00
___Another Copy. Same. $17.00

R110. RIBEIRO (B. G.). Bases Para Classifacao Dos Adornos Plumarios Dos Indios Do Brasil. Offprint, Arquivos Do Museu Nacional Vol. XLIII, Rio Janeiro, 1957. 119pp, 55 drawings in text, 11 full-page drawings, 2 full-page photographs, stiff wraps. $45.00

R111. RICCI (Clemente). Las Pictografias de la Grutas Cordobesas y Su Interpretacion Astronomico Religiosa. 50pp, folded illus, 4to, wrappers, Buenos Aires, 1930. $75.00

R112. RICE (A. H.). The Rio Branco, Uraricuera and Parima. Surveyed by the Expedition to the Brazilian Guayana from August 1924 to June 1925. 59pp of text, plus 26pp of photographs, fold-out map, London, 1928. $22.00

R113. RICH (Edwin Gile). Hans the Eskimo. His Story of Arctic Adventure with Kane, Hayes, and Hall. viii, 288pp, illus by Rockwell Kent, cloth, Boston, 1934. $35.00
Story of Hans Hendrik, the Eskimo, 1834-1889, Greenland hunter for several American Arctic expeditions.
___Another Copy. Same. $30.00

R114. RICHARDS (C. E.). The Oneida People. 104pp, drawings, photographs, maps, one of the Indian Tribal

Series, signed by Tribal Chieftain, Phoenix, 1974 (1st ed.). $12.00

R115. RICHARDS (Eva Alvey). Arctic Mood. 282pp, illus, map endpapers, author taught Indians and Eskimos at Wainwright, Alaska 1924-26, Caldwell, 1949 (1st ed.). $10.00

___Another Copy. Same. $15.00

R116. RICHARDSON (Boyce). Strangers Devour the Land. A Chronicle of the Assault upon the Last Coherent Hunting Culture in North America, the Cree Indians of Northern Quebec.... 342pp, plus index, photographs, maps, map endpapers, New York, 1976 (1st ed.), d.j. $17.00

R117. RICHARDSON (J.). (American Ethnological Society, Monograph No. 1, 1940) Law and Status Among the Kiowa Indians. vii, 136pp, cloth. $33.00

R118. RICHARDSON (Sir John). Arctic Searching Expedition: A Journal of a Boat-Voyage.... (2 Volumes). Vol. I: viii, 413pp, 32 adv. pp, Vol. II: vii, 426pp, handcolored folding map, pls, cloth, hinges brittle, edge wr, Longman, Brown, Green, and Longmans, London, 1851 (1st ed.). $1,000.00

Sabin: 71025. Field: 1300. Field: "Exceedingly interesting work ... thronged with details of personal experiences in Indian life...." Wagner-Camp: 203:1: "Of interest to our work is ... account of the journey from Hudson's Bay by way of the Athabasca River and Great Slave Lake to the Arctic Ocean." Excellent color pls of Indians, mostly Kutchins and Crees.

R119. RICKARD (Chief Clinton) and GRAYMONT (Barbara). Fighting Tuscarora. The Autobiography of.... 178pp, plus index, photographs, maps, first autobiography of a Tuscarora Indian. Chief Rickard was a leader of the Indian rights movement and founder of the Indian Defense League of America, Syracuse, 1973 (1st ed.), d.j. $15.00

R120. RICKARDS (C. G.). The Ruins of Mexico. (Volume I). 153pp, illus with 459 photographs, 3 to each page, covers Paleque, Uxmal, Chichen Itza, Labna, Chacmultun, Itzamal, Acanceh, Litla, Xaaga, Zaachila, Tepeaca, rebound with original cloth laid on, folio, London, 1910. $250.00

R121. RICKETSON (E. B.). (Carnegie Institute Publication No. 477, 1937) Uaxactun, Guatemala, Group E-1926-1931. (2 Parts). Part I: The Excavations. Part II: The Artifacts. xi, 314pp of text containing 194 figures, plus 87pp of b/w photographs and 1 page color pls, fold-out map in rear pocket, wrappers. $225.00

R122. RICKETTS (Orval). Songs of the Navajo Country. 56pp, frontis, limited edition of 500 copies, stiff pictorial wrappers, Albuquerque, 1940 (1st ed.). $30.00

___Another Copy. Same. $42.00

RIDDELL (Francis A.). See BAE Bulletin No. 192.

R123. RIDDLE (Jeff C.). The Indian History of the Modoc
War. 295pp, illus with photographs, n.p., 1914.
$80.00
___Another Copy. Same. $60.00

R124. RIEBETH (Carolyn Reynolds). J. H. Sharp Among the
Crow Indians, 1902-1910: Personal Memories of His Life
and Friendships on the Crow Reservation in Montana
by.... 154pp, plus folding map and 12 color pls, other
maps, color and b/w illus, bibliography, notes, index,
royal 8vo, limited to 500 copies, El Segundo, 1985 (1st
ed.), d.j. $65.00

R125. (RIEL, LOUIS). The Story of ... the Rebel Chief.
176pp, drawing, cloth, Toronto, 1885 (1st ed.). $45.00

RIESENBERG (Saul H.). See BAE Bulletin No. 172.

R126. RIESTER (J.). Die Pauserna-Guarasug'wa. Monographie
Eines Tupi-Guarani-Volkes in Ostbolivien. xviii, 562pp,
120 drawings of objects of material culture, 7 maps,
approx 85pp of photographs, Collectanea Instituti
Anthropos, St. Augustin, 1972. $45.00

R127. RIGGS (Stephen R.). (Smithsonian Contributions to North
American Ethnology, Vol. VII, Washington, 1890) A
Dakota-English Dictionary. x, 665pp, original cloth.
$125.00
___Another Copy. Same. $100.00

R128. RIGGS (Stephen R.). (Smithsonian Contributions to North
American Ethnology, Vol. 9, Washington, 1893) Dakota
Grammar, Texts, and Ethnography. 238pp, 4to, cloth.
$90.00
___Another Copy. Same. $45.00
___Another Copy. Same, Minneapolis, 1973. $25.00

R129. RIGGS (Stephen R.). (Smithsonian Contributions to Knowledge, Vol. IV, Washington, 1852) Grammar and Dictionary of the Dakota Language, Collected by the Members of the Dakota Mission. xx, 338pp, cloth. $95.00
___Another Copy. Same, cloth spotted. $35.00

R130. RIGGS (Stephen R.). Mary and I. Forty Years with the
Sioux. xx, 388pp, frontis, 1 plate, Chicago, Holmes,
1880 (1st ed.). $60.00
___Another Copy. Same. $40.00
___Another Copy. Same. $50.00

R131. RIGGS (Stephen R.). Wowapi Mitawa. Tamokoce Kaga.
My Own Book. Prepared from Rev. T. H. Gallaudet's
"Mothers Primer," and "Child's Picture Defining and
Reading Book," in the Dakota Language. Profusely
illus with woodcut illustrations. 64pp, 16mo, new
wrappers, Boston, printed for the American Board of
Commissioners for Foreign Missions by Crocker and
Brewster, 1842. $500.00

R132. RIGHETTI (O. L.). Dos Conferencias, Sobre el Imperio
de las Llanuras Santiaguenas, Arqueologia Argentina.

56pp, 61 b/w and color photographs of several hundred objects, Buenos Aires, 1942. $35.00

R133. (RIGHT OF WAY). (House of Representatives Executive Document No. 31, 48:2, Washington, DC, 1884). Report from the Commissioner of Indian Affairs granting the right of way to the Jamestown and Northern Railway Co. through the Devil's Lake Indian Reservation. 10pp. Removed. $10.00

R134. (RIGHTS). (House of Representatives Misc. Document No. 49, 41:3, Washington, DC, 1871) Indian Confederacy. 6pp. Removed. $10.00
   Papers relative to the Confederacy of Indian Tribes. Plea for rights and protection for the Indian Territory.

R135. RIGHTS (Douglas). The American Indian in North Carolina. 298pp, frontis, illus, fold-out map, index, cloth, Winston-Salem, 1957, d.j. $25.00
   ___Another Copy. Same, Durham, 1947, signed.
                                                              $50.00

R136. RILEY (C. R.) et al. Coastal Salish and Western Washington Indians II. 694pp, maps, cloth, Garland American Indian Ethnohistory Series, 1974. $40.00

R137. RILEY (Glenda). Women and Indians on the Frontier, 1825-1915. 336pp, illus, index, notes, bibliography, Albuquerque, 1984 (1st ed.), d.j. $35.00
   ___Another Copy. Same. $25.00
   ___Another Copy. Same, lacks d.j. $15.00

R138. RINEHART (F. A.). Rinehart's Indians. 46 half-tone photographs of Indians, 4 color pls, decorated cloth, Omaha, 1899 (1st ed.). $225.00
   Photographs of Blackfoot, Apache, Sioux and other Indians were taken at the Indian Congress of the Trans-Mississippi and International Exposition held at Omaha in 1898.
   ___Another Copy. Paper cover edition, with 46 half-tone photographs, 2 pls. $175.00

R139. RINEHART (Mary Roberts). The Out Trail. 246pp, illus, cloth, lacks frnt flyleaf, general wear, travel experiences which include the Hopi Snake Dance, Zuni Pueblo and Navaho weavers, New York, 1923. $12.00
   ___Another Copy. Same, nr fine. $30.00
   ___Another Copy. Same, VG. $18.00

R140. RINK (Dr. Henry). Tales and Traditions of the Eskimo. With A Sketch of Their Habits, Religion, Languages and Other Peculiarities. Translated from the Danish by the Author. With Numerous Illustrations, drawn and engraved by Eskimo. xxii, 472pp (errata), 12mo, cloth, Edinburgh, London, 1875. $350.00
   Wickersham: 2672. Haycox, p.183. Arctic Bibliography: 14629. First edition in English. Author is the highest authority on the Greenland Eskimo, and his books are excellent reading.

R141. RISTER (Carl C.). Border Captives: The Traffic in Pris-
oners by Southern Plains Indians, 1835-1875. 220pp,
8 photographs, 2 maps, Norman, 1940 (1st ed.), d.j.
$40.00
___Another Copy. Same. $25.00
R142. RITCHIE (William). The Archaeology of Martha's Vineyard:
A Framework for the Prehistory of Southern New England. 253pp, 55 photographic pls, New York, 1969
(1st ed.). $40.00
RITCHIE (William A.). See also BAE Bulletin No. 180.
R143. RITCHIE (William A.). (Indiana Historical Society, Prehis-
tory Research Series, Vol. III, No. 2, 1949) The Bell-
Philhower Site, Sussex County, New Jersey. pp 149-
272, 21pp of photographs, 1pp of drawings, map,
wrappers. $30.00
R144. RITCHIE (William A.). (Research Records, Rochester Mu-
seum of Arts and Sciences, No. 4, Rochester, 1938)
Certain Recently Explored New York Mounds and Their
Probable Relation to Hopewell Culture. 42pp, figures,
pls, bibliography, wrappers. $20.00
___Another Copy. Same. $13.00
R145. RITCHIE (William A.). (New York State Museum Circular
No. 29, 1952) The Chance Horizon, An Early Stage of
Mohawk, Iroquois Cultural Development. 53pp, 9pp of
photographs, 4 figures, wrappers. $17.00
___Another Copy. Same. $10.00
R146. RITCHIE (William A.). (New York State Archaeological
Association, Researches and Transactions, Vol. XIII, No.
1, 1954) Dutch Hollow, An Early Historic Period Seneca
Site in Livingston County, New York. 98pp, 30 photo-
graphs, most are full-page, wrappers. $30.00
___Another Copy. Same. $13.00
R147. RITCHIE (William A.). (New York State Archaeological
Association, Researches and Transactions, Vol. X, No.
1, 1945) An Early Site in Cayuga County, New York.
viii, 158pp, 57pp of photographs, 1 figure, fold-out map
in pocket, wrappers. $22.00
___Another Copy. Same. $13.00
R148. RITCHIE (W. A.). (New York State Museum and Science
Service Bulletin No. 379, Albany, 1960) The Eastern
Dispersal of the Adena. 80pp, photographs, folding
chart in rear pocket, wrappers. $10.00
R149. RITCHIE (W. A.). (New York State Museum and Science
Service, Bulletin No. 372, Albany, 1959) The Stony
Brook Site and Its Relation to Archaic and Transitional
Cultures on Long Island. 169pp, 53pp of photographs,
7 figures, 2 maps, wrappers. $20.00
___Another Copy. Same. $12.00
R150. RITZENTHALER (Robert). (Milwaukee Public Museum,
Publications in Primitive Art, No. 3, Milwaukee, 1969)
Iroquois False-Face Masks. 71 double-column pp, b/w

and color photographs, bibliography, wrappers. $25.00
___Another Copy. Same. $18.00

R151. RITZENTHALER (Robert) et al. (Milwaukee Public Museum, Publications in Primitive Art, No. 2, Milwaukee, 1966) Masks of the Northwest Coast: The Samuel A. Barrett Collection. 102pp, illus, wrappers. $25.00
___Another Copy. Same, Milwaukee, 1968. $15.00

R152. RITZENTHALER (R.). (Milwaukee Public Museum Primitive Art Series No. 1, Milwaukee, 1961) The Miller Collection of Sioux Indian Drawings. 8pp of text, 36 loose folio color pls in folder, wrappers. $50.00

R153. RITZENTHALER (Robert). (Milwaukee Public Museum Handbook Series No. 4, 1953, 1979) Prehistoric Indians of Wisconsin. 46pp, 112 photographs, wrappers.
$10.00

R154. RITZENTHALER (Robert). (Milwaukee Public Museum Bulletin, Vol. 19, No. 3, 1953, 1962) The Potawatomi Indians of Wisconsin. 75pp, 21 photographs, wrappers.
$10.00

R155. RITZENTHALER (Robert) and QUIMBY (G. I.). (Fieldiana Anthropology, Vol. 36, No. 11, Chicago, 1962) The Red Ocher Culture of the Upper Great Lakes and Adjacent Areas. 33pp, 12 photographs of artifacts, wraps.
$12.00

R156. RIVERO (M. E.) and VON TSCHUDI (J. J.). Peruvian Antiquities. 306pp, illus, frontis, cloth with leather spine label, New York, 1853. $150.00

R157. RIVET (P.). El Museo del Oro. 64pp of text containing 1 color plate, color map, fold-out color map, plus 100 leaves of color photographs, Banco de la Republica, Bogota, 1948. $70.00
___Another Copy. Same. $50.00

R158. RIVET (P.). Maya Cities. 234pp, 136 photographs, 10 full-page color pls, 12pp of figures, cloth, London, 1960. $50.00
___Another Copy. Same. $45.00
___Another Copy. Same, Paris, 1954. $70.00

R159. ROBBINS (Maurice). An Archaic Village in Middleboro, Massachusetts. 85pp, 26pp, illus, maps, plans, bibliography, Massachusetts Archaeology Society, Attleboro, 1969. $15.00

ROBBINS (Wilfred W.). See BAE Bulletins Nos. 54 and 55.

R160. ROBELO (Cecilio). Toponimia: Maya-Hispano Nahoa. 38pp, 6pp of notes, facsimile of 1902 edition, a dictionary in Maya, Spanish and Nahuatl, wraps. Merida, 1973. $10.00

ROBERTS (Frank H. H. Jr.). See also BAE Bulletins Nos. 92, 96, 100, 111, 121, 126, 169, 176, 179, 182, 185, and 189.

R161. ROBERTS (Frank H. H.). (Smithsonian Misc. Collections, Vol. 94, No. 4, Washington, 1935) A Folsom Complex ... in Northern Colorado. 35pp, plus 16 pls, 8vo,

wrappers. $15.00
___Another Copy. Same. $10.00

R162. ROBERTS (Frank H. H.). (Smithsonian Misc. Collections,
Vol. 95, No. 10, Washington, 1936) Additional Information on the Folsom Complex ... in Northern Colorado.
38pp, 12 pls, 8vo, wrappers. $12.00
___Another Copy. Same. $10.00

R163. ROBERTS (Frank H. H.). (Smithsonian Misc. Collections,
Vol. 103, No. 4, Washington, 1942) Archaeological and
Geological Investigations in the San Jon District, East
New Mexico. 30pp, 9 pls, 8vo, wrappers. $12.00
___Another Copy. Same. $10.00

R164. ROBERTS (Frank H. H.). Archaeology in the Southwest.
Offprint from American Antiquities, Vol. 1, 1937. pp-
3-34, in binder. $12.00
___Another Copy. Same, self wraps. $10.00

R165. ROBERTS (Frank H. H.). (Smithsonian Misc. Collections,
Vol. 81, No. 7, Washington, 1929) Recent Archaeological
Developments in the Vicinity of El Paso, Texas. 14pp,
plus illus, wrappers. $10.00

R166. ROBERTS (Helen H.). (American Museum of Natural His-
tory, Anthropological Papers, Vol. XXXI, Part II,
New York, 1929) The Basketry of the San Carlos Apache.
pp 121-218, 27 figures containing photographs and draw-
ings of several hundred baskets and designs, later cloth.
$70.00
___Another Copy. Same. $60.00
___Another Copy. Same, wrappers. $38.00
___Another Copy. Same, later cloth. $25.00
___Another Copy. Same, Glorieta, 1972. $37.00

R167. ROBERTS (Helen H.). (Yale Univ. Publications in Anthropology, No. 12, 1936) Musical Areas in Aboriginal
North America. 41pp, figures, bibliography, wrappers.
$18.00

R168. ROBERTS (Helen H.) and JENNESS (D.). (Report on the
Canadian Arctic Expedition, 1913-18, Vol. XIV, Ottawa,
1925) Songs of the Copper Eskimos. 505pp, frontis,
musical scores, wrappers. $55.00

R169. ROBERTS (Helen H.) and SWADESH (Morris). (American
Philosophical Society, Transactions, Vol. 45, Part 3,
Philadelphia, 1955) Songs of the Nootka Indians of
West Vancouver Island. 128pp, lrge 4to, wraps.
$50.00

R170. ROBERTS (J. M.). (Peabody Museum Papers, Vol. 40,
No. 3, Cambridge, 1951) Three Navaho Households:
A Comparative Study in Small Group Culture. 118pp,
14pp of photographs, wrappers. $28.00
___Another Copy. Same. $15.00

R171. ROBERTS (W.). Stokes Carson, Twentieth-Century Trading on the Navajo Reservation. 225pp, 16pp of photographs, map, wrappers, Albuquerque, 1987. $15.00

R172.   ROBERTSON (Frank C.). On the Trail of Chief Joseph.
        230pp, written for young readers, New York, 1927
        (1st ed.). $12.00
R173.   ROBERTSON (M. G.) (Editor). Primera Vesa Redonda de
        Palenque, Part I. A Conference on the Art, Iconogra-
        phy, and Dynastic History of Palenque. 173pp, 6pp
        photographs, 133 figures, Robert Louis Stevenson
        School, Pre-Columbian Art Research, Pebble Beach,
        1974. $75.00
        ____Another Copy. Same, rebound in 1/4 leather.
                                                          $80.00
        ____Another Copy. Same, cloth. $55.00
        The following three studies will be part of a five
        volume set that will be the only complete color photo-
        graphic record of Palenque as it was before recent dam-
        age by volcanic ash and acid rain, and will be the most
        comprehensive photographic record of Palencon sculp-
        ture, painting and architecture. Volume I is a detailed
        presentation of the Maya Temple of the Instructions dis-
        covered in 1952, and the most important structure at Pal-
        enque. A work of inestimable importance, this volume
        was said, by Michael Coe, to be "...probably the best
        study we have for any Mayan site...." Volume II treats
        the Palace Houses, thought to have formed the ceremonial
        center of Palenque in the middle to late Early Classic
        period. The architecture and dates of the different
        structures, their stucco, frescoes, sculpture, glyphs
        and motifs are scrupulously studied and presented in
        hundreds of illustrations. Volume III records the period
        of late Palace Buildings, when Palenque produced some
        of the finest sculpture ever created in the Maya world.
R174.   ROBERTSON (M. G.). The Sculpture of Palenque. Vol-
        ume I: The Temple of the Instructions. xxix, 380pp,
        265pp of illus, containing 133 b/w and 96 color photo-
        graphs, 106 drawings, 9 fold-out drawings, 5 text illus,
        2 maps, 1 fold-out map in rear pocket, cloth, Princeton,
        1983. $195.00
R175.   ROBERTSON (M. G.). The Sculpture of Palenque. Vol-
        ume II: The Early Buildings of the Palace and Wall
        Paintings. xiii, 337pp, 253pp of color and b/w photo-
        graphs, drawings, and plans, cloth, Princeton, 1985.
                                                         $225.00
R176.   ROBERTSON (M. G.). The Sculpture of Palenque. Vol-
        ume III. xvii, 496pp, 334pp of color and b/w photo-
        graphs, drawings and plans, cloth, Princeton, 1985.
                                                         $225.00
R177.   ROBICSEK (Francis). Copan: Home of the Mayan Gods.
        Illus, most are in color, 4to, Heye Foundation, New
        York, 1972, d.j. $95.00
R178.   ROBICSEK (Francis). A Study in Maya Art and History:
        The Mat Symbol. 358pp, 307 b/w and 88 color illus,
        New York, 1978. $20.00

R179. ROBINSON (Alfred). Life in California: A Historical Account of the Origin, Customs, and Conditions of Indians of Alta-California. 219pp, illus are full color reproductions of early California lithographs, 4to, Oakland, 1947. $50.00

Zamorano Eighty #65. The fine limited California Centennial edition of this classic. Includes Robinson's translation of Boscana's "Chinigchinich" on the Indians of San Juan Capistrano Mission.
___Another Copy. Same. $35.00

R180. ROBINSON (Bert). The Basket Weavers of Arizona. 161pp, plus index, illus, some in color, Albuquerque, 1954 (1st ed.), d.j. $50.00

R181. ROBINSON (Doane). A History of the Dakota or Sioux Indians, from Earliest Traditions and First Contact with White Men to Final Settlement ... on Reservations. 523pp, frontis, illus, endpaper maps, index, Ross and Haines, Minneapolis, 1956 (reprint of 1904 ed.), d.j. $25.00
___Another Copy. Same. $35.00
___Another Copy. Same. $25.00
___Another Copy. Same. Minneapolis, 1974, d.j. $20.00

R182. ROBINSON (Dorothy F.). Navajo Indians Today. 80pp, photographs, endpaper maps, San Antonio, 1966 (1st ed.), d.j. $12.00
___Another Copy. Same. $10.00

R183. ROBINSON (Will). Under Turquoise Skies: Outstanding Features of the Story of America's Southwest from the Days of the Ancient Cliff-Dwellers to Modern Times. xvi, 538pp, illus, New York, 1928. $75.00
___Another Copy. Same. $45.00

R184. ROCKWELL (Wilson). The Utes, A Forgotten People. 302pp, plus index, illus, bibliography, Denver, 1956 (1st ed.), d.j. $35.00

R185. RODAS (Flavio) and RODAS (Ovidio) et al. Chichicastenango, the Kiche Indians: Their History and Culture, Sacred Symbols of Their Dress and Textiles. 155pp, 40 illus, 2 are in color, poor pulp paper, wrappers, Union Tipografka, Guatemala, 1940. $35.00

R186. RODDIS (Louis H.). The Indian Wars of Minnesota. 307pp, plus index, photographs, other illus, endpaper maps, mainly on 1862-63 troubles, but also covers briefly the 1872 Blueberry war and 1898 Leech Lake Chippewa fight, Cedar Rapids, 1956 (1st ed.), d.j. $50.00
___Another Copy. Same. $50.00

R187. RODEE (Marian E.). Old Navajo Rugs; Their Development from 1900 to 1940. 113pp, illus, bibliography, index, Albuquerque, 1982, d.j. $27.00
___Another Copy. Same. $25.00

R188. RODMAN (Selden). Artists in Tune with Their World.
       222pp, illus, 32 are in color, 4to, Indian Arts of the
       Northwest Coast, Central Canada, Mexico, South and
       Central America, New York, 1982. $35.00
R189. RODNICK (David). The Fort Belknap Assiniboine of
       Montana. A Study in Culture Change. 125pp, stiff
       wraps, New Haven, 1938 (1st ed.). $45.00
R190. RODRIGUEZ VALLEJO (Jose). Ixcatl, El Algodon Mexi-
       cano. 93pp, wrappers, Mexico, 1976. $15.00
R191. ROE (Frank G.). The Indian and the Horse. xvi, 434pp,
       pls, folding map, bibliography, index, Norman, 1955
       (1st ed.), d.j. $45.00
       ___Another Copy. Same. $30.00
       ___Another Copy. Same, lacks d.j. $25.00
R192. ROEDIGER (Victoria M.). Ceremonial Costumes of the
       Pueblo Indians. 251pp, 40 full-page colored pls, 25
       figures, map, bibliography, Berkeley, 1941 (1st ed.),
       d.j. $150.00
       ___Another Copy. Same, Berkeley, 1961. $18.00
R193. ROESSEL (R. A.). Sheep in Navaho Culture. iv, 109pp.
       35pp of appendices, 3 maps, St. Louis, 1951. $40.00
R194. ROGERS (Mrs. Charlotte). Knowledge of Today was In-
       dians' Know-How Yesterday. 18pp, illus, stiff pictorial
       wrappers, n.p. 1965. $10.00
R195. ROGERS (David Banks). Prehistoric Man on the Santa
       Barbara Coast: A Synopsis of the Results of Four Years
       of Intensive Investigation, Conducted by the Author for
       the Museum of Natural History of Santa Barbara, Cali-
       fornia, Among the Now Rapidly Vanishing Remains of
       Villages that in Former Times Occupied the Santa Bar-
       bara Valley. 452pp, illus, index, folding map, Santa
       Barbara, 1929. $50.00
       ___Another Copy. Same. $57.00
R196. ROGERS (Edward). (Royal Ontario Museum Guide No. 6,
       Ontario, 1972) Indians of the Pacific Coast. 18pp, illus,
       wrappers. $10.00
R197. ROGERS (E. S.). (National Museum of Canada Bulletin
       No. 195, 1963) The Hunting Group-Hunting Territory
       Complex Among the Mistassini Indians. 95pp, 3 maps,
       7 tables, 1 chart, wrappers. $17.00
R198. ROGERS (E. S.). (National Museum of Canada Bulletin
       No. 218, Ottawa, 1967) The Material Culture of the
       Mistassini. 150pp, 18pp of photographs, 51 figures,
       cloth. $23.00
       ___Another Copy. Same, wrappers. $15.00
R199. ROGERS (John). Red World and White: Memories of a
       Chippewa Boyhood (Chief Snow Cloud). 153pp, Norman,
       1974, d.j. $12.00
       First printing of this new edition of a work originally
       issued privately in 1957 under title "A Chippewa Speaks."
       ___Another Copy. Same. $15.00
       ___Another Copy. Same. $18.00

R200. ROGERS (Robert). A Concise Account of North America
... To Which Is Subjoined an Account of the Several
Nations and Tibes (sic) Residing.... 264pp, full
leather, gilt ruled, a.e.g., Dublin, J. Milliken, 1769.
$575.00
Howes: R-418. Sabin: 72724. Field: 1316. Howes:
"Based largely on personal knowledge, this was the first
geographical account of the American interior after Eng-
land wrested it from France, and aside from those by
Pittman and Hutchins, the most accurate of the period."

R201. ROGIN (Michael). Fathers and Children. Andrew Jackson
and the Subjugation of the American Indian. xvii, 373,
xii pp, 8pp of photographs, notes, index, Knopf, New
York, 1975 (1st ed.), d.j. $25.00
Fawn Brodie calls this "most brilliant psychoanalytic
study of an American President yet published." Explores Jackson's hostility toward Indians and responsi-
bility for their destruction.
____Another Copy. Same. $17.00

R202. ROHN (Arthur H.). Cultural Change and Continuity on
Chapin Mesa. 306pp, plus indices, photographs, plans,
maps, bibliography, a major contribution to Mesa Verde
Archaeology, Lawrence, KS, 1977 (1st ed.), d.j.
$20.00

R203. ROHN (Arthur H.). (National Park Service, Archaeology
Research Series, No. 7D, Washington, 1971) Mug House:
Mesa Verde National Park, Colorado. 280pp, lrge 4to,
560 illus, wrappers. $45.00
____Another Copy. Same. $30.00

R204. ROHNER (Ronald P.) (Editor and Compiler). Letters and
Diaries of Franz Boas, Written on the Northwest Coast
from 1886 to 1931. 322pp, plus indices, photographs,
maps, bibliography, Chicago, 1969 (1st ed.), d.j.
$15.00
____Another Copy. Same. $25.00

R205. ROLINGSON (M. A.) and SCHWARTZ (D. W.). Later
Paleo-Indian and Early Archaic Manifestations in Western
Kentucky. 168pp, illus, photographs, maps, bibliogra-
phy, index, Univ. of Kentucky, 1966 (1st ed.), d.j.
$35.00

R206. ROLLINS-GRIFFIN (Ramona). Chaco Canyon Ruins; Ancient Spirits Were Our Neighbors. 95pp, illus with
drawings and photographs, Flagstaff, 1971 (1st ed.).
$12.00
____Another Copy. Same, with d.j. $15.00

R207. ROMERO (J.). Anales Instituto Nacional de Antropologia
e Historia, Indices de la Sexta Epoca, 1939-1966. 54pp,
Mexico City, 1968. $10.00

R208. ROMERO (John Bruno). The Botanical Lore of the California Indians. New York, Vantage Press, 1954, d.j.
$15.00

R209. RONAN (Peter). Historical Sketch of the Flathead Nation.
       85pp, illus, index, complete reprint of the scarce 1890
       edition, Minneapolis, 1965, d.j. $10.00
       ___Another Copy. Same. $15.00
       ___Another Copy. Same. $10.00
R210. RONDA (James P.). Lewis and Clark Among the Indians.
       310pp, illus, index, bibliography, maps, Lincoln, 1984
       (1st ed.), d.j. $25.00
R211. RONDTHALER (Edward). The Life of John Heckewelder.
       Edited by B. H. Coates. 149pp, 2 adv., portrait,
       12mo, Philadelphia, Townsend Ward, 1847. $70.00
R212. ROOSEVELT (Anna C.) and SMITH (J. G. E.) (Editors).
       The Ancestors: Native Artisans of the Americas. 197pp,
       illus, 12 color pls and figures, Museum of the American
       Indian, wrappers, New York, 1979. $35.00
       ___Another Copy. Same. $17.00
       ___Another Copy. Same. $22.00
ROOT (William C.). See BAE Bulletin No. 143.
R213. ROSE (Dan). The Ancient Mines of Ajo. 67pp, illus,
       history of the mines of Ajo in Pima County from the
       earliest Papago Indian times, Ajo, 1936 (1st ed.).
                                                           $70.00
R214. ROSEN (Kenneth) (Editor). The Man to Send Rain Clouds.
       Contemporary Stories by American Indians. 178pp,
       photographs, New York, 1974 (1st ed.). $15.00
R215. ROSENBLAT (Angel). La Poblacion Indigena de America,
       Desde 1492 Hasta la Actualidad. 293pp, illus, 4to,
       wrappers, Buenos Aires, 1945. $60.00
       ___Another Copy. Same. $40.00
R216. ROSMAN (Abraham) and RUBEL (Paula). Feasting with
       Mine Enemy: Rank and Exchange Among the Northwest
       Coast Societies. Columbia Univ. Press, 1971, d.j.
                                                           $18.00
R217. ROSNEK (Carl) and STACEY (Joseph). Skystone and
       Silver: The Collectors Book of Southwest Indian Jewelry.
       Illus, some in color, Prentice Hall, 1976, d.j. $50.00
R218. ROSS (Bernard R.) et al. Notes on the Tinneh or
       Chepewyan Indians of British and Russian America.
       Removed from Smithsonian Museum Annual Report for the
       year 1866. pp 303-327, wraps. $15.00
R219. ROSS (K.). Codex Mendoza, Aztec Manuscript. 123pp,
       cloth, Fribourg, 1978. $30.00
R220. ROSS (Marvin C.) (Editor). George Catlin. Episodes
       from "Life Among the Indians" and "Last Rambles."
       344pp, plus index, 152 scenes and portraits by Catlin,
       color frontis, bibliography, Norman, 1959 (1st ed.),
       d.j. $35.00
R221. ROSS (Richard). (Texas Archaeological Salvage Project,
       No. 7, Austin, 1965) The Archaeology of Eagle Cave.
       163pp, photographs, drawings, bibliography, wrappers.
                                                           $10.00

R222. ROSS (R. F.) and SORROW (W. M.). (Univ. of Texas,
Texas Archaeological Survey Papers, No. 9 and 10,
Austin, 1966) Upper Rockwall and Glen Hill Sites,
Fourney Reservoir (Ross), and Pecan Springs Site
(Sorrow). 68pp, maps, pls, bibliography, lrge 8vo,
wraps. $12.00

ROTH (Walter E.). See also BAE Bulletin No. 91.

R223. ROTH (W. E.). An Inquiry into the Animism and Folklore
of the Guiana Indians. pp 107-386, photographs,
index, cloth, separate printing from Smithsonian Annual
Report No. 30, Washington, 1915. $27.00

R224. ROTHERY (Agnes). Images of Earth: Guatemala. 206pp,
illus with photographs, New York, 1934 (1st ed.).
                                                         $30.00

R225. ROUFTS (Timothy G.). The Anishinabe of the Chippewa
Tribe. 104pp, photographs, b/w and color drawings,
signed by Tribal Chieftain, wrappers, Phoenix, 1975
(1st ed.). $10.00

R226. ROUHIER (A.). Le Peyotl. La Plante Qui Fait les Yeux
Emrveilles. xii, 371pp, 46 illus, Paris, 1926. $45.00

ROUSE (Irving). See also BAE Bulletin No. 143.

R227. ROUSE (Irving) and FERGUSON (V. M.). (Yale Univ.
Publications in Anthropology, No. 44, 1951) A Survey
of Indian River Archaeology, Florida and Chronology at
South Indian Field, Florida. 292pp, 15 figures, 5 tables,
8pp of photographs; second part: 60pp, 16 figures,
7 tables, 4pp of photographs, wrappers. $60.00
____Another Copy. Same. $42.00

R228. ROUSE (Irving) and CRUKENT (J. M.). Venezuelan
Archaeology. xiii, 179pp of text containing 34 figures,
plus 55pp of photographs, cloth, New Haven, 1963.
                                                         $35.00
____Another Copy. Same. $45.00
____Another Copy. Same. $35.00

R229. ROWE (A.) et al (Editors). The Junius B. Bird Pre-
Columbian Textile Conference. 278pp, 247 illus, cloth,
Washington, DC, 1979. $60.00
This volume is the outgrowth of a conference held in
the spring of 1973, and contains fifteen of the papers
that were presented by a distinguished group of Pre-
Columbian textile scholars. The papers presented new
research in the field and covered most of the major
types of surviving pre-Columbian textiles. Very good
photographs in this volume that provides the most detailed and comprehensive account of this subject area
to date. (EAP)
____Another Copy. Same. $35.00

R230. ROWE (C. W.). (Milwaukee Public Museum, Publications
in Anthropology, No. 3, 1956, New York, 1970 reprint)
The Effigy Mound Culture of Wisconsin. 103pp, 36 illus,
cloth. $28.00
____Another Copy. Same, Milwaukee, 1956. $40.00

ROWE (John Howland). See also BAE Bulletin No. 143.

R231. ROWE (John Howland). (Univ. of California Publications in American Archaeology and Ethnology, Vol. 46, No. 1, Berkeley, 1954) Max Uhle, 1856-1944. A Memoir of the Father of Peruvian Archaeology. 134pp, 14pp of photographs, wrappers. $50.00
____Another Copy. Same. $37.00

R232. ROWE (John Howland) and MENZEL (D.) (Editors). Peruvian Archaeology: Selected Readings. 320pp, illus, 23 studies by Rowe, Bird, Sawyer, Lothrop, Mienzel, Gayton, and others, Palo Alto, 1967. $15.00

R233. ROYS (L.) and SHOOK (E. M.). (Memoirs of the Society for American Archaeology, American Antiquity, Vol. 20, Menasha and SLC, 1966) Preliminary Report on the Ruins of Ake, Yucatan. x, 54pp, illus, figures, bibliography, wrappers. $15.00
____Another Copy. Same. $12.00

R234. ROYS (Ralph L.). The Book of Chilam Balam of Chumayel. 229pp, 2 pls, illus, 4to, post-conquest book of the prophet from Yucatan, recalling pre-conquest culture. Norman, 1967. $35.00
____Another Copy. Same. $20.00

R235. ROYS (Ralph L.). (Carnegie Institute Publication No. 548, 1943) The Indian Background of Colonial Yucatan. vii, 244pp, 12pp of photographs, 2 fold-out maps, 4 maps in text, wrappers. $125.00
____Another Copy. Same, Norman, 1972. $45.00

R236. ROYS (Ralph L.). Ritual of the Bacabs. 193pp, illus, the first English translation of a Mayan colonial manuscript dealing with incantations, Norman, 1965 (1st ed.), d.j. $35.00
____Another Copy. Same, lacks d.j. $15.00

R237. RUBIN DE BORBOLLA (D. F.). (Exhibition Catalogue, Museo de Ciencias y Arte, Mexico City, 1964) Escultara Precolombina de Guerrero. 139pp, text in Spanish and English, 209 b/w photographs and drawings, 7 color photographs, 2 maps, wrappers. $40.00

R238. RUBIN DE BORBOLLA (D. F.). Mexico: Monumentos Historicos y Arqueologicos. 279pp, 232 photographs, fold-out map, Instituto Panamerican de Geografia e Historia, Mexico City, 1953. $45.00

R239. RUBIO MANE (J. Ignacio). Archivo de la Historia de Yucatan, Campeche y Tabasco. (3 Volumes). Vol. I: Documentos, 1539-1562, appendices, 1789-1795, 262pp. Vol. II: Documentos, 1542-1562, 459pp. Vol. III: Documentos, 1559-1560, 331pp. Wrappers. $90.00

R240. RUBIO ORBE (Gonzalo). Ruminahui, ATI II (Biografia). 223pp, wrappers, Quito, 1944. $25.00
____Another Copy. Same. $35.00
____Another Copy. Same. $28.00

R241. RUBY (R. H.) and BROWN (J.). The Cayuse Indians.

Imperial Tribesmen of Old Oregon. xix, 340pp, 24pp
of photographs, 8 maps, bibliography, index, Norman,
1972 (1st ed.), d.j. $35.00
___Another Copy. Same. $30.00
___Another Copy. Same, lacks d.j. $30.00

R242. RUBY (R. H.). The Chinook Indians: Traders of the
Lower Columbia River. 349pp, illus, index, bibliography, maps, Norman, 1976 (1st ed.), d.j. $25.00

R243. RUBY (R. H.) and BROWN (J. A.). Half-Sun on the
Columbia: A Biography of Chief Moses. 377pp, illus,
map, bibliography, index, Norman, 1966 (2nd printing).
                                                        $20.00

R244. RUBY (R. H.). Indians of the Pacific Northwest. A
History. 294pp, 4to, illus, index, maps, bibliography,
Norman, 1982, d.j. $35.00
Comprehensive history of the Indians of Oregon,
Washington, Idaho and Western Montana from 1750 to
1900. Large volume bound in dark green imitation
leather.
___Another Copy. Same, Norman, 1981, 1st ed.
                                                        $35.00

R245. RUBY (R. H.) and BROWN (J.). Myron Eells and the
Puget Sound Indians. 122pp, illus, Seattle, 1976 (1st
ed.). $35.00
___Another Copy. Same. $22.00
___Another Copy. Same. $28.00
___Another Copy. Same, 1978. $20.00

R246. RUBY (R. H.). The Oglala Sioux: Warriors in Transition. 115pp, New York, 1955 (1st ed.), d.j. $30.00
___Another Copy. Same. $20.00

R247. RUBY (R. H.) and BROWN (J. A.). The Spokane Indians;
Children of the Sun. 346pp, photographs, bibliography,
maps, index, Norman (1st ed.), d.j. $35.00
___Another Copy. Same. $20.00

R248. RUFFNER (E. H.). Report of a Reconnaissance in the
Ute Country Made in the Year 1873. 101pp, lrge folding
map, printed wrappers, Washington, DC, 1874. $75.00
Issued as 43rd Congress, 1st session, House Executive Document, 193, with new titlepage. One of the important, detailed government explorations of the Colorado region. The map was drawn by Prout.
___Another Copy. (House of Representatives Executive
Document 193, 43:1, Washington, 1874) (Same Title).
101pp. Removed. Calls for a map, not published.
See Hasse, p.69. $55.00

R249. RUIZ (Jose Francisco). Report on the Indian Tribes of
Texas in 1828. 44pp, lrge 4to, imitation leather,
bibliography, New Haven, 1972 (1st ed. thus). $35.00
Tall 9" by 14" volume bound in dark red imitation
morocco. Contains a facsimile reproduction of Ruiz's
manuscript report plus a full English translation and an

introduction by John C. Ewers.
___Another Copy. Same. $32.00
___Another Copy. Same. $25.00

R250. RUNNING (J.). Honor Dance: Native American Photographs. xx, 155pp, 90 color and 70 b/w photographs
of the Big Mountain Navajo, Hopi, Rio Grande Pueblos
and other tribes, cloth, Reno, 1985. $70.00

R251. RUPP (Israel Daniel). Early History of Western Pennsylvania, and of the West, and of Western Expeditions and
Campaigns from 1754 to 1833. iv, 352, 406, iv, vi pp,
2 folding maps, rebound in cloth, Pittsburgh, A. P.
Ingram, 1850. $125.00
    Howes: R-505. Field: 473. Important gathering of
information and accounts of the early expeditions against
the Indians of western Pennsylvania, siege of frontier
forts, massacre in border settlements, etc. Also contains the journals of General Washington, St. Clair,
Weiser, and letters of General Braddock. (RMW)

R252. RUPP (Israel Daniel). History of Lancaster County. To
Which is Prefixed A Brief Sketch of the Early History
of Pennsylvania. 524pp, 5 pls, 1 table, full leather,
Lancaster, G. Hill, 1844 (1st ed.). $125.00
    Howes: R-509. Sabin: 74160. Field: 1331. Field:
"History of the Moravians ... massacre of Conestoga Indians ... Border Wars ... treated ... with great minute-
ness."

R253. RUPPERT (Karl) and DENISON (John Jr.). (Carnegie Institute, Publication 543, Washington, DC, 1943)
Archaeological Re-Connaissance in Campeche, Quintana
Roo, and Peten. 150pp, 126 figures, 60 pls, 15 folded
maps, lrge 4to, wrappers. $45.00

R254. RUPPERT (K.) et al. (Carnegie Institute, Publication
602, Washington, DC, 1955) Bonopak, Chiapas, Mexico.
xii, 71pp of text containing 12pp of figures, 13pp of
b/w and color photographs, 3pp of color drawings,
wraps. $100.00
___Another Copy. Same. $150.00

R255. RUPPERT (K.). (Carnegie Institute, Publication 454,
Washington, DC, 1935) The Caracol at Chichen, Itza,
Yucatan, Mexico. xii, 294pp, 338 photographs and
drawings, 13 folded maps, wrappers. $295.00

R256. RUPPERT (K.). (Carnegie Institute, Publication 595,
Washington, DC, 1952) Chichen Itza: Architectural
Notes and Plans. 169pp, 150 illus, folding map in rear
pocket, 4to, wrappers. $175.00

R257. RUPPERT (K.). (Pre-Print: Carnegie Institute, Publication
546, Washington, DC, 1943) The Mercado, Chichen Itza,
Yucatan. pp 223-260, 35 illus, wraps. $45.00

R258. RUSH (Philip S.). The Merchandise of the American Indian.
20pp, photographs, separate printing from Dun's International Review, wrappers, n.p., n.d., c.1915. $12.00
___Another Copy. Same. $10.00

R259.   RUSHBY (Henry H.).   Jungle Memories.   388pp, 16 pls,
        about exploration of the Amazon Valley in search of
        medicinal plants (quinine), the Andes (coca), New York,
        London, 1933 (1st ed.), d.j. $65.00
R260.   RUTSCH (E. S.).   Smoking Technology of the Aborigines
        of the Iroquois Area of New York State.   252pp, 191 il-
        lus, Fairleigh, Dickinson Univ. Press, 1973, d.j.
                                                        $25.00
        ___Another Copy. Same. $20.00
        ___Another Copy. Same. $22.00
R261.   RUTTENBER (E. M.).   Footprints of the Red Men: In-
        dian Geographical Names.   Their Location and Probable
        Meaning.   241pp, cloth, New York State Historical Assn.,
        1906. $60.00
        Located on the Hudson and Delaware Rivers and Val-
        ley of the Mohawk.
        ___Another Copy. Same. $45.00
R262.   RUTTENBER (E. M.).   History of the Indian Tribes of
        Hudson's River; Their Origin, Manners and Customs....
        415pp, 5 portraits, illus, index, decorated cloth, rear
        hinge started, edge wr, not all copies issued, included
        the 5 portraits, Albany, J. Munsell, 1872 (1st ed.).
                                                        $185.00
        ___Another Copy. Same, Port Washington, 1971.
                                                        $40.00
R263.   RUXTON (George F.).   Adventures in Mexico and the
        Rocky Mountains.   viii, 332, 16 adv.pp, 12mo, original
        cloth, rebacked, London, J. Murray, 1847 (1st ed.).
                                                        $150.00
        Howes: R-553. Sabin: 74501. Field: 1335. "His
        relations of the awful ravages of the Apaches and
        Comanche ... painfully vivid. He passes for weeks
        through ruined villages, whose inhabitants have per-
        ished in merciless slaughter."
        ___Another Copy. New York, Harper & Bros., 1848,
        1st American ed., 312pp, 12mo, cloth. $95.00
R264.   RUXTON (Lt. George Augustus Frederick).   "The Migra-
        tion of the Ancient Mexicans and Their Analogy to the
        Existing Indian Tribes of Northern Mexico." pp 90-104.
        Removed. $35.00
        Mainly devoted to the Pueblo Indians of New Mexico,
        suggesting the possibility of their relation to the Aztecs
        who migrated south to Mexico at some date. No source
        given, but stated as read before the Society(?), 17th
        May, 1848.
R265.   RYAN (Marah Ellis).   The Flute of the Gods.   338pp, plus
        24 full-page pls after photographs by Edward S. Curtis,
        pictorial cloth, New York, 1909. $150.00
        The first state of the first edition, with the full
        complement of plates. A novel, though heavily steeped
        in and annotated with reference to historical material,

and of importance due to the Curtis photographs.
___Another Copy. Same. $80.00
___Another Copy. Same. $60.00
___Another Copy. Same, New York, 2nd issue, 3
Curtis pls. $35.00

R266. RYAN (Marah Ellis). Indian Love Letters. 122pp, illus
text, pictorial bds, illus endpapers, Chicago, 1907.
$12.00

R267. RYAN (T.). Dorset 75--Cape Dorset Annual Graphics
Collection. 74pp, 40 b/w and 35 color illus, cloth,
Toronto, 1975. $16.00

R268. RYAN (T.). Dorset 76--Cape Dorset Annual Graphics
Collection. 84pp, 40 b/w and 48 color illus, cloth,
Toronto, 1976. $20.00

R269. RYAN (T.). Dorset 77--Cape Dorset Annual Graphics
Collection. 80pp, 39 b/w and 80 color illus, cloth,
Toronto, 1977. $20.00

R270. RYAN (T.). Dorset 78--Cape Dorset Annual Graphics
Collection. 80pp, 66 b/w and 36 color illus, cloth,
Toronto, 1978. $20.00

R271. RYDEN (Stig). Andean Excavations. (2 Volumes). Vol.
I: The Tiahuanaco Era East of Lake Titicaca. 198pp,
147 figures. Vol. II: Tupuraya and Cayhuasi: Two
Tiahuanaco Sites. 122pp, 71 figures, maps. Ethno-
graphic Museum of Sweden, Stockholm, 1957-59. $90.00
___Another Copy. Same. $77.00
___Another Copy. Same. $55.00
___Another Copy. Same, Volume II only. $10.00

R272. RYDEN (Stig). Archaeological Researches in the Department of La Candelaria. 327pp, 150 figures, signed by
author, wrappers, Goteborg, 1936. $75.00

R273. RYDEN (Stig). The Erland Nordenskiold Archaeological
Collection from the Mixque Valley, Bolivia. 142pp, 48
figures, wrappers, contains illus of hundreds of objects, Ethnologiska Studier, Goteborg, 1956. $18.00

R274. RYDEN (Stig). (Revista De Museo Paulista, Nova Serie,
Vol. IV, Sao Paulo, 1950) A Study of South American
Indian Hunting Traps. pp 247-352, 41 figures, wrap-
pers. $25.00

R275. RYDJORD (John). Indian Place Names: Their Origin,
Evolution and Meaning, Collected in Kansas from the
Siouan, Algonquian, Shoshoean, Caddoan, Iroquoian and
Other Tongues. 380pp, illus, index, bibliography, maps,
Norman, 1982, d.j. $25.00
___Another Copy. Same, lacks d.j. $18.00
___Another Copy. Same, 1968, 1st ed., d.j. glued
to cloth cvrs. $10.00

-S-

S1. SABLOFF (J. A.) and WILLEY (G. R.). (South West Journal of Anthropology, Vol. 23, No. 4, 1967) The Collapse of Maya Civilization in the Southern Lowlands. pp311-336, wrappers. $10.00
S2. SABLOFF (J. A.) and ANDREWS (E. W.). Late Lowland Maya Civilization, Classic to Postclassic. 526pp, 35 figures, cloth. Albuquerque, 1986. $35.00
S3. (SAC AND FOX). (House of Representatives Report 88, 37:2, Washington, 1862, 1st print.) Sac and Fox Indians. 7pp. Removed. Request payment for property damaged in Kansas during the "Bleeding Kansas" period, 1854-1860. $10.00
S4. SAENA (M.). Sobre el Indio Peruano y su Incorporacion al Medio Nacional. xvi, 310pp, 101 photographs, 6 figures, Mexico City, 1933. $35.00
S5. SAIGNES (M. A.). Estudios de Etnologia Antigua de Venezuela. xx, 203pp, 1 photograph, 1 drawing, 2 figures, 4 fold-out maps and charts. Caracas, 1954. $25.00
S6. SALAS (Alberto M.). Cronica Florida del Mestizaje de las Indias. Buenos Aires, 1960, d.j. $45.00
S7. SALISBURY (O. M.). The Customs and Legends of the Tlingit Indians of Alaska. 275pp, illus. New York, 1962, d.j. $15.00
___Another Copy. Same. $15.00
___Another Copy. Same. $12.00
S8. SALISBURY (Stephen, Jr.). (From: Proceedings, American Antiquarian Society, 1876-77, Worcester, 1877). The Mayas: The Sources of Their History. 49pp, with Dr. Le Plongeon in Yucatan, His Account of Discoveries. pp54-103, 3 heliotypes, 12 photographs. $125.00
S9. SOLOMAN (Julian). The Book of Indian Craft and Indian Lore. 418pp, cloth. Collection of Material on weapons, tools, etc. New York, 1928. $35.00
___Another Copy. New York, London, 1928. $25.00
___Another Copy. New York, 1928. $10.00
S10. SALPOINTE (Rev. J. B.). Soldiers of The Cross. Notes on the Ecclesiastical History of New-Mexico, Arizona and Colorado. xiv, 299pp, 2pp, illus, index. Ex-library. Some wear and fading. Banning, CA, 1898, (1st ed.). $250.00
Eberstadt 120:179: "Printed on the local mission press by resident Indian boys. Due to the circumstances of its issuance, but a few copies were printed. The work, an important contribution to the history of the West, is the result of years of research in the ancient archives and personal association with the natives." (RMW)
S11. SANBORN (J. W.). Legends, Customs and Social Life of

the Seneca Indians of Western New York. 76pp, cloth. Gowanda, 1878. $89.00

S12. (SAND CREEK MASSACRE). (Senate Executive Document 26, 39:2, Washington, 1867, 1st print.). Sand Creek Massacre, November, 1864--Evidence Taken at Denver and Fort Lyon, Colorado Territory, by a Military Commission. 228pp. Removed. $50.00

Howes: S-80. Seventy-six days of testimony from Army officers, with Indian statements reported by officers, regarding this tragedy. The eye-witnesses are fresh and the accounts lively.

S13. SANDERS (Daniel C.). A History of the Indian Wars ... Particularly in New England. 319pp, 12mo, full leather, contents browned. Montpelier, VT, Wright and Sibley, 1812 (1st ed.). $450.00

Field: 1351. "The mystery which surrounded the authorship, history and origin of this very rare volume has been slowly dispelled by successive fragments of information. So few copies have survived the holocaust to which it was devoted that its very existence was unknown to the most zealous collectors of Indians and Vermont history." Howes: "The sensitive author, chagrined over some scornful critique of his book, sought to suppress the 1812 edition."

S14. SANDERSON (William E.). Horses Are For Warriors. 183pp, illus. Historical fiction about Nez Perce Indians. Juvenile. Caldwell, 1954, (1st ed.), d.j. $20.00

S15. SANDO (Joe S.). The Pueblo Indians. 247pp, photographs, maps, bibliography. A useful book by a Pueblo Indian. San Francisco, 1982, (2d ed.) d.j. $12.00

S16. SANDOZ (Mari). Cheyenne Autumn. xviii, 282pp, illus, folding map, decorative endpapers, cloth. The outbreak of the Northern Cheyenne under Dull Knife and Little Wolf in 1878. New York, 1953, (1st ed.). $45.00
____Another Copy. Same. Signed. d.j. $40.00

S17. SANDOZ (Mari). Crazy Horse. The Strange Man of the Oglalas. 428pp, folding map. New York, 1942, (1st ed.) d.j. $55.00
____Another Copy. New York, 1975, d.j. $15.00

S18. SANDOZ (Mari). A New Introduction ... to the Cheyenne Indians, Their History and Ways of Life by George Bird Grinnell. Portrait, wrappers, edition of 300 numbered and signed copies. New York, 1962. $50.00

S19. SANDOZ (Mari). These Were the Sioux. 118pp, illus. Customs, beliefs, philosophy and wisdom of the Sioux. New York, 1961, (1st ed.), d.j. $25.00
____Another Copy. Same. Repair to d.j. $20.00

S20. SANDSTROM (A. R. and P. E.). Traditional Papermaking and Paper Cult Figures of Mexico. xxv, 327pp, 14 color photographs, 200 drawings, 9 maps and diagrams, cloth. Norman, 1986. $35.00

S21. SANDWEISS (M. A.). Laura Gilpin, An Enduring Grace. 339pp, 126 magnificent full-page photographs taken by one of the great photographers of the Southwest, 45 smaller photographs, small folio size (9½ x 12½), Amon Carter Museum, 1986, 1st print. limited. $97.00

S22. SANFORD (Paul). Sioux Arrows and Bullets. 171pp, bibliography. The Minnesota Sioux outbreak of 1862-63, with information supplied through letters of author's great grandfather, a participant. San Antonio, 1969, (1st ed.) d.j. $15.00

S23. SANFORD (T. E.). The Story of Architecture in Mexico, including the Work of the Ancient Indian Civilizations. 363pp, 64 pls with multiple photographs. New York, 1947 (1st ed.). $40.00

S24. SANGINES (C. P.). (Academia Nacional de Ciencias de Bolivia, Publication No. 19, La Paz, 1969) Tunupa Ekako, Estudio Arquiologico Acerca de las Efigies Precolumbinas de Dorso Adunco. 381pp, 149 photographs, wrappers.
                   $40.00
_____Another Copy. Same. $35.00

S25. SANTEE (Ross). Apache Land. 216pp, illus. New York, 1947 (1st ed.). $45.00
The best of all modern writers about Southern Arizona. Santee gathers here rich lore of Apache Warriors and their bloody land and illustrates the book with his b/w drawings which perfectly complement the text.
_____Another Copy. Same. $46.00
_____Another Copy. Same. Wear to d.j. $45.00

S26. SAPIR (E.). (Smithsonian Contributions to Anthropology, Vol. 8, Washington, 1968) Cultural Chronology of the Gulf of Chiriqui, Panama. 119pp, 20 pls, 4to, wrappers.
                   $15.00

S27. SAPIR (E.). (University Museum, Anthropological Publications, Vol. 11, No. 2, Philadelphia, 1914) Notes on Chasta Costa Phonology and Morphology. 76pp, wrappers.
                   $12.00

S28. SAPIR (E.). (University of California Publications in American Archaeology and Ethnology, Vol. 13, No. 1, Berkeley, 1917) The Position of Yana in the Hokan Stock. pp1-34, bibliography, some chipping to edge of wrappers. $10.00

S29. SAPIR (E.). (Canada Dept. of Mines, Museum Bulletin No. 19, Ottawa, 1915) A Sketch of the Social Organization of the Nass River Indians. 30pp, 1 photograph. $24.00
_____Another Copy. Same. ex-library, soil to wrappers.
                   $15.00

S30. SAPIR (E.). (Canada Dept. of Mines, Memoir 90, No. 13, Anthropology Series, 1916) Time Perspective in Aboriginal America Culture, A Study in Method. vii, 87pp.
                   $24.00

S31. SAPIR (E.). (Publications in American Ethnology and

Sociology, Vol. II, Leyden, 1909, 1st ed.) Wishram
Texts. xv, 314pp, 4pp, wrappers, unopened. With:
"Wasco Tales and Myths," collected by J. Curtin.
"Wishram" was the minority dialect of Wi'cxam Indians on
Yakima Reservation, also spoken by Wascos of Warm Springs
Reservation, Oregon. $75.00
___Another Copy. Same. Inscribed by A. L. Kroeber.
                                                       $60.00

S32. SAPPER (K.). In Den Volkangegeiten Mittleamerikas und
Westindiens. vi, 334pp, 76 photographs, 2 fold-out maps,
cloth. Stuttgart, 1905. $45.00

S33. SASS (Herbert Ravenel). Hear Me, My Chiefs! 251pp,
plus index, maps, map endpapers. The Cherokee chiefs,
Sioux, Roman Nose, Beecher's Island, Chief Joseph, etc.
New York, 1940 (1st ed.), wear to d.j. $15.00

S34. SATTERTHWAITE (L.). Piedras Negras Archaeology:
Architecture. Part V. Sweathouses. 91pp, 69 figures,
Philadelphia, 1952. $20.00

S35. SAUER (Nellie Jane). American Indian Words in the Literature of the West and Southwest. 91pp, bibliography.
Thesis presented to the faculty of the Department of English, Texas Technological College, laid in are 7 original
watercolor drawings of Indian Designs by the author.
1939. $275.00

S36. SAUM (Lewis O.). The Fur Trader and the Indian.
311pp plus index, bibliography, notes, frontis. Seattle,
1965 (1st ed.), d.j. $30.00
Fully well-documented history of the relationship between the fur trader and the Indian during the entire
history of the Rocky Mountain fur trade.
___Another Copy. Seattle, 1973. $18.00
___Another Copy. Seattle, 1973. $15.00

S37. SAUNDERS (Charles Francis). Finding the Worth While in
the Southwest. 226pp, illus, index. Covers Acoma,
Hopis, Pueblos, Navaho, Zuni, etc. New York, 1928
(3rd print.) revised. $10.00

S38. SAUNDERS (Charles Francis). The Indians of the Ter-
raced Houses. 293pp, cloth. Travels among the Hopi
and Zuni at the turn of the century. New York, 1912.
                                                       $65.00
___Another Copy. Same. Some wear to extremities,
weak back hinge. $20.00
___Another Copy. Glorieta, 1973. $23.00
___Another Copy. Glorieta, 1973. $18.00

S39. SAUNDERS (L.). A Guide to Materials Bearing on Cultural
Relations in New Mexico. xvi, 528pp, cloth. School of
Inter-American Affairs, Albuquerque, 1944. $50.00

S40. SAUTER (John) and JOHNSON (Bruce). Tillamook Indians
of the Oregon Coast. 196pp, illus, index, map. Portland, 1974 (1st ed.). $15.00
Full account of the Tillamook Indians from prehistoric

to recent times. Illustrated with 150 photographs.
___Another Copy. Same. Nice. $10.00

S41. SAVAGE (William W., Jr.) (Editor). Indian Life; Trans-
forming an American Myth. 286pp, illus. Norman, 1977
(1st ed.). $15.00
___Another Copy. Same. d.j. Review copy. $10.00

S42. SAVALA (Refugio). Autobiography of a Yaqui Poet. 222pp
plus index, photographs, bibliography, wrappers. Tucson, 1980 (1st ed.). $15.00
___Another Copy. Same. $10.00

S43. SAVILLE (Marshall H.). (Contributions to South American
Archaeology, The George G. Heye Expedition) The
Antiquities of Manabi Ecuador. (2 volumes). Vol. I.
A Preliminary Report. 135pp of text containing 9 figures,
41 leaves of photographs, 19 leaves of drawings illus
stone and ceramic antiquities and designs, tissue guards
between each leaf. New York, 1907. Vol. II: Final
Report. 284pp of text containing 17 figures, 79 leaves
of photographs, 35 leaves of drawings of all types of
antiquities, designs and of the site, fold-out map, green
linen cvrs, sml folio (9½" x 13"). 1910. $575.00
___Another Copy. Vol. I only. Lrge 4to. $300.00

S44. SAVILLE (M. H.). (Museum of the American Indian, Notes
and Monographs, Vol. 6, No. 2, New York, 1929) The
Aztecan God Xipe Totec. pp151-174, 11 illus, 12mo,
wrappers, ex-library, cvrs worn. $25.00

S45. SAVILLE (M. H.). (Museum of the American Indian, Notes
and Monographs, Vol. 6, No. 5, New York, 1928) Bibliographic Notes on Palenque, Chiapas. pp119-180, 11
figures, 12mo, wrappers. $20.00

S46. SAVILLE (M. H.). (Museum of the American Indian, Notes
and Monographs, New York, 1921) Bladed Warclubs from
British Guiana. 20pp, 3 full-page photographs, 6 drawings, wrappers. $15.00

S47. SAVILLE (M. H.). (Museum of the American Indian, Indian
Notes and Monographs, Vol. 9, No. 1, New York, 1920)
The Earliest Notices Concerning the Conquest of Mexico
by Cortes in 1519. 54pp, 12mo, wrappers. $25.00

S48. SAVILLE (M. H.). (American Anthropological Society,
1899) Explorations of Zapotecan Tombs in Southern
Mexico. pp350-362, 3 pls, in a binder. $15.00

S49. SAVILLE (M. H.). A Sculptured Vase from Guatemala.
Frontis in color, 4pp, long folding pl, 4to, stiff wrappers. New York, 1919. $15.00

S50. SAWYER (Alan R.). Ancient Peruvian Ceramics. The
Nathan Cummings Collection. 141pp plus index, b/w and
color photographs, drawings, bibliography. Exhibition
Catalogue, Metropolitan Museum of Art, New York, 1966,
(1st ed.), d.j. $45.00
___Another Copy. Same, no d.j. $35.00
___Another Copy. Same. $15.00

S51. SAWYER (A. R.). Animal Sculpture in Pre-Columbian Art.
    48pp, 46pp photographs. Exhibition Catalogue, Art In-
    stitute of Chicago, 1957. $15.00
S52. SAWYER (A. R.). Mastercraftsmen of Ancient Peru.
    108pp, 71 b/w and 22 color photographs, map, chart.
    Exhibition Catalogue, Guggenheim Museum, New York,
    1968. $20.00
S53. SAWYER (A. R.). The Nathan Cummings Collection of An-
    cient Peruvian Art. 49pp, 69 photographs, 11 drawings,
    map. Art Institute of Chicago, 1954. $25.00
    ___Another Copy. Same. Wrappers. $18.00
    ___Another Copy. Same. 4to. $17.00
S54. SAWYER (Jesse) (Editor). (University of California Pub-
    lications in Linguistics, Vol. 65, Berkeley, 1973) Studies
    in American Indian Languages. 317pp, 4to.
        Ten scholarly articles by various experts, covering
    Noptinte Yukuts, Taracan, Athapaskan morphology, in-
    animate imitatives in Pomo, etc. $62.00
    ___Another Copy. Same. $35.00
    ___Another Copy. Same. Wrappers. $18.00
S55. SAYER (C.). Costumes of Mexico. 240pp, 32pp of color
    photographs, 97 b/w photographs, 89 drawings. London
    and Austin, 1985. Soft Cover. $25.00
        Though not the definitive work on the subject, this
    publication is probably the best one volume study--in
    English--on Mexican dress. A survey of native Mexican
    ᴄostume from prehistoric to modern times, this handsome,
    heavily illustrated volume traces 2,000 years of Mexican
    costume history, with emphasis on its technical and decor-
    ative aspects and the fusion of native and European
    traditions. (EAP)
    ___Another Copy. Same. Cloth. $40.00
S56. SAYLES (E. B.). (Medallion Papers, No. XXII) An
    Archaeological Survey of Chihuahua, Mexico. ix, 119pp,
    31pp of photographs, 2 figures, fold-out chart, map.
    Privately printed for the Medallion, Gila Pueblo, Globe,
    1936. $50.00
S57. SAYLES (E. B.) and ANTEVS (Ernest). The Cochise
    Culture. 81pp, illus, 4to, wrappers. Medallion Papers,
    Arizona, 1941. $50.00
S58. SCACHERI (Mabel and Mario). Indians Today. 182pp,
    illus with photographs. New York, 1936 (1st ed.), d.j.
                                                         $25.00
S59. SCAIFE (H. L.). History and Condition of the Catawba
    Indians of South Carolina. 16pp, self-wrappers. Some
    wear and soiling. Government Printing Office, Washington,
    1930, 1st print. $10.00
S60. SCHAAFSMA (Polly). Early Navaho Rock Paintings and
    Carvings. 32pp, illus, stiff pictorial wrappers. Museum
    of Navaho Ceremonial Art, Santa Fe, 1966. $12.00
S61. SCHAAFSMA (Polly). Indian Rock Art of the Southwest.

379pp, 32 color pls, 250 photographs. Albuquerque, 1980. $50.00

S62. SCHAAFSMA (Polly). (Museum of New Mexico, Papers in Anthropology No. 7, 1963, 1971) Rock Art in the Navajo Reservoir District. 74pp, 54 figures, 4 full-page color pls, wrappers. $12.00

S63. SCHAAFSMA (P.). The Rock Art of Utah, from the Donald Scott Collection. 169pp, 134 illus. Cambridge, 1971. $18.00

S64. SCHAEFER (Jack). Adolphe Francis Bandelier. 23pp. Brief accurate biographical sketch of the famed Southwest archaeologist. Wrappers. Santa Fe, 1966. $10.00

S65. SCHAEFER-SIMMERN (H.). Eskimo-Plastik Aus Kanada. 64pp, 28 full-page photographs. Kassell, 1958. $18.00

S66. SCHELE (Linda). Notebook for the Maya Hieroglyphic Writing Workshop. 124pp, illus, wrappers. Austin, 1981. $30.00

___Another Copy. Same. Ex-library. $22.00

S67. SCHELL (James P.). In the Ojibway Country: A Story of Early Missions on the Minnesota Frontier. xvi, 188pp, plus 15 pls and maps, cloth, rebound. C. H. Lee, Walhalla, ND, 1911 (1st ed.). $275.00

___Another Copy. Same. Unbound signatures. $50.00

S68. SCHELLHAUS (Paul). (Peabody Museum Papers, Vol. 4, No. 1, Cambridge, 1904) Representation of Deities of the Maya Manuscripts. 47pp, 65 figures, 1 pl, wrappers. $30.00

S69. SCHENCK (W. E.) and DAWSON (E. J.). (University of California Publications in American Archaeology and Ethnology, Vol. 25, No. 4, Berkeley, 1929) Archaeology of the Northern San Joaquin Valley. 181pp, 28pp photographs of many objects of material culture, including textile fragments, awls, tubes, whistles, bird effigies, beads, pendants, pipes, mortars and pestles. $65.00

S70. SCHERER (Joanna C.). Indians: The Great Photographs That Reveal North American Indian Life, 1847-1929. 189pp, photographs, 4to. From the great Smithsonian and Bureau of American Ethnology collections. New York, 1973, d.j. $20.00

___Another Copy. Same. $17.00

___Another Copy. New York, 1982, d.j. $15.00

S71. SCHIFFER (Michael) and HOUSE (John). (Arkansas Archaeological Survey, Research Series No. 8, 1975) The Cache River Archaeological Project: An Experiment in Contract Archaeology. 339pp, wrappers. $18.00

___Another Copy. Same. $17.00

S72. SCHLAGER (Ann P.). An Illustrated Guide to Pueblo Pottery, 1900-1975. 16pp, drawings, wrappers. Lawrence, 1980, (1st ed.). $10.00

S73. SCHLEDERMANN (P.). Eskimo and Viking Finds in the Arctic. pp574-601, 14pp of color photographs, 4pp

drawings, map, in binder, National Geographic, May,
1981. $10.00

S74. SCHLEDERMANN (P.). (National Museum of Man, Archaeological Survey of Canada, No. 38, 1974) Thule Eskimo
Pre-history of Cumberland Sound, Baffin Island, Canada.
297pp, 50pp of photographs illus 573 objects, 48 figures,
wrappers. $20.00

S75. SCHMITT (K. and I. O.). Wichita Kinship, Past and Present. 72pp, 16 figures, wrappers. Norman, n.d. (c.
1950-55). $25.00

S76. SCHMITT (Martin F.) and BROWN (Dee). Fighting Indians
of the West. 382pp, illus, end maps, bibliography, royal
8vo. Contemporary pictorial of western Indian tribes
who chose to fight rather than go to reservations. Dustin:
511. Luther High Spot: 181. New York, 1948 (1st ed.),
d.j. $45.00
____Another Copy. Same, variant binding (tan cloth),
worn and repaired d.j. $37.00
____Another Copy. Same. $35.00
____Another Copy. Same. $15.00

S77. SCHNEIDER (D. M.) et al. (University of Nebraska, Laboratory of Anthropology, Note Book No. 3, 1956) Zuni
Kin Terms and Zuni Daily Life. 137pp, 5 figures,
wrappers. $35.00

S78. SCHOENBERG (Wilfred). Jesuit Mission Presses in the
Pacific Northwest. A History and Bibliography of Imprints 1876-1899. 76pp, frontis, 9 pls, notes, copyright
page states edition of 804 copies, but is in actuality
edition of 54 copies, specially bound, containing 11 mission press fragments in a folding case inside rear cvr.
Portland, Champoeg Press, 1957, (1st ed.). $450.00
____Another Copy. Same. Facsimiles, insertions in rear
pocket. $300.00
____Another Copy. Same. Facsimiles. $40.00

S79. SCHOLDER (F.). Indian Kitsch: The Use and Misuse of
Indian Images. 64pp, 30 b/w and 20 color photographs.
Phoenix, 1979. $15.00

S80. SCHOLES (France) and ROYS (Ralph). (Carnegie Institute,
Publication 560, Washington, 1948) The Maya Chontal
Indians of Acalan-Tixchel: A Contribution to the History
and Ethnography of the Yucatan Peninsula. x, 564pp,
4 fold-out maps. $160.00
____Another Copy. Same. $75.00
____Another Copy. Norman, 1968, d.j. $35.00
____Another Copy. Norman, 1968, d.j. $17.00

S81. SCHOOLCRAFT (Henry R.). Algic Researches ... Inquiries
Respecting the Mental Characteristics of the North American Indians. Indian Tales and Legends. (2 Volumes).
Vol. 1: 248pp. Vol. 2: 5pp, 244pp (8 advs), 12mo,
cloth. New York, Harper & Bros., 1839 (1st ed.).
                                                        $175.00

S 82. SCHOOLCRAFT (Henry R.). (Proceedings, New York Historical Society, 1846) Incentives to the Study of the Ancient Period of American History: An Address. 38pp,
discusses origins of American Indians, wrappers. $45.00
_____Another Copy. New York, The Society, 1847.
$65.00

S 83. SCHOOLCRAFT (Henry R.). Information Respecting the
History, Condition and Prospects of the Indian Tribes
of the United States (5 volumes). Vol. 1: xxiii, 13-
568pp. Vol. 2: xxiv, 17-608pp. Vol. 3: 635pp. Vol.
4: xxvi, 19-668pp. Vol. 5: 712pp. Engraved titles,
figures, pls, maps. Later 1/2 leather, marbled bds.
Philadelphia, Lippincott, Grambo & Co., 1853-1856.
Howes: S-183. Sabin: 77855. Field: 1379.
This edition was printed in a smaller format without
the Volume 6 of the other editions. $900.00
_____Another Copy. Volume 6 only. 28pp, pp25-756,
portrait, 57 pls, some pls duplicating pls in previous 5
volumes, 4to, original cloth. Philadelphia, 1856. $350.00
_____Another Copy. Volume 3 only. New York, 1969,
Paladin Press reprint of 1853 edition. $45.00

S 84. SCHOOLCRAFT (Henry R.). The Myth of Hiawatha....
xxiv, 13pp, 343pp, 12mo, cloth. Philadelphia, J. B.
Lippincott & Co., 1856 (1st ed.). $100.00

S 85. SCHOOLCRAFT (Henry R.). Narrative Journal of Travels
Through the Northwestern Regions of the United States,
Extending from Detroit Through the Great Chain of
American Lakes, to the Sources of the Mississippi.
xiv, 1pp, 17pp, 419pp, 4pp, engraved title, folding map,
pls, index, later 1/2 calf. Albany, E. & E. Hosford,
1821 (1st ed.). $350.00
Howes: S-186. Sabin: 77862. Field: 1363.
Wagner-Camp 21a: "Expedition led by Lewis Cass ...
one of the many that he made as governor of Michigan for
the purpose of visiting and negotiating with various Indian tribes of the Old Northwest ... also proposed to
determine the source of the Mississippi River." Field:
"Interwoven with ... large number of incidents of Indian
history, personal experiences among the tribes ...
sketches of their principal characteristics." (RMW)
_____Another Copy. Same. Rear cvr loose, map and 1
pl hand-colored. $350.00
_____Another Copy. Same. Calf, worn, map mounted,
lacks one geological plate. $150.00
_____Another Copy. 419pp, illus, index, map, facsimile
reprint of the 1821 edition, bound in dark blue imitation
morocco. Ann Arbor, 1966. $30.00

S 86. SCHOOLCRAFT (Henry R.). Notes on the Iroquois; or,
Contributions to American History, Antiquities, and General Ethnology. xiii, 498pp (12 advs)pp, 2 color lithographs by Sarony & Major, New York, pictorial gilt cloth.
E. H. Pease & Co., 1847. $175.00

Howes: S-191. Field: 1370. "Much more pretentious but less valuable than his official report on the same subject. Intended as a popular reproduction...." (RMW)

S87. SCHOOLCRAFT (Henry R.). (From Proceedings, New York Historical Society Appendix for 1846, New York, 1847) Notices of Some Antique Earthen Vessels Found in the Low Tumuli of Florida and in the Caves and Burial Places of the Group of Indian Tribes, North of These Latitudes. pp124-136, 2 pls. $40.00

S88. SCHOOLCRAFT (Henry R.). Oneota, or the Red Race of America. Number one of eight parts. 64pp, removed, lacks wrapper, signature slightly trimmed. New York, 1844. $15.00
Title changed to "The Indian In His Wigwam" as of 1848.
___Another Copy. 416pp, lacks the two pls listed in Howes U.S.iana, 1962 (S 188), contemporary marbled bds. Graham, NY, 1848. $90.00
___Another Copy. 414pp, frontis, illus decorated cloth, rebacked, some stain, foxing, New York, Dewitt and Davenport, 1848. $60.00
___Another Copy. Buffalo, Derby and Hewson, 1848. $60.00

S89. SCHOOLCRAFT (Henry R.). Personal Memoirs of a Residence of Thirty Years with the Indian Tribes on the American Frontiers. xlviii, 17pp, 703pp, portrait, original cloth, rebacked in leather. Philadelphia, Lippincott, Grambo & Co., 1851. $200.00
Note: This copy contains the portrait of Schoolcraft not found in most copies. Howes: S-190. Sabin: 77870. Field: 1377. Wagner-Camp 203b: "Following his exploration of the Missouri in 1817 and 1818, Schoolcraft spent most of his remaining years in the Old Northwest. He joined several expeditions seeking to establish the source of the Mississippi River, and his interest in that area caused him to be appointed Indian agent for the tribes on Lake Superior ... Schoolcraft ... pioneered early anthropological and ethnological studies of the American Indian." (RMW)
___Another Copy. Ex-library, modern cloth, hinges cracked. $100.00
___Another Copy. Same. $140.00

S90. SCHOOLCRAFT (Henry R.). Report of Mr. Schoolcraft, to the Secretary of State, Transmitting the Census Returns in Relation to the Indians. (Senate Doc. No. 24). (iii)-vi, 285pp, 1pp, illus, self wrappers, sewn. Albany, 1846 (1st ed.). $150.00
Howes: S-191. Sabin: 77874. Field: 1371. Field: "This is the most valuable of Mr. Schoolcraft's works, having been executed after personal examination in an official capacity of all the tribes inhabiting New York.

There is an almost entire absence of the speculative and sentimental cogitations which so greatly marred his other works." (RMW)

S 91. SCHOOLCRAFT (Henry R.) (MASON, Philip P., Editor). Schoolcraft's Expedition to Itasca Lake. 373pp plus index, bibliography, map endpapers. This expedition discovered the real source of the Mississippi. Considerable on Indians. Howes: S-187. East Lansing, MI, 1958 (1st ed.) d.j. $15.00

S 92. SCHOOLCRAFT (Henry R.) (WILLIAMS, Mentor L., Editor). Schoolcraft's Indian Legends. 322pp, bibliography. Taken from Algic Researches, Hiawatha, Oneota, Red Race in America and Statistical Information. East Lansing, MI, 1962 (2d print.), d.j. $10.00

S 93. SCHOOLCRAFT (Henry R.). Travels in the Central Portions of the Mississippi Valley.... iv, 459pp, frontis, 2 pls, folding map, full leather, 2-inch piece of corner of map lacking, separated at some folds, lacks 1 map. New York, Collins and Hannay, 1825. $50.00
    Howes: S-193. Sabin: 77880. Field: 1364. Field: "Interesting incidents of Indian life and character, extracts from manuscript journals of the fur trader, and traditions of the aborigines ... analysis and vocabulary of the Chippewa language." (RMW)

S 94. (SCHOOLCRAFT, Henry R.). Western Scenes and Reminiscences: Together with Thrilling Legends and Traditions of the Red Men of the Forest. v, 5-495pp, colored frontis, 3 other pls, rebound, cloth. Auburn, Derby and Miller, 1853. $90.00
    Howes: S-188. Several Indian captivities and Indian songs included.

S 95. SCHOOLCRAFT (Henry R.). (House of Representatives Doc. 152, 22:1, Washington, 1832, 1st print.) Expedition Into the Indian Country. 20pp, removed. Early report by Schoolcraft of his 1831 tour in Huron Territory around Lake Superior among the Chippewas. $25.00

S 96. SCHOOLCRAFT (Henry R.). (House of Representatives War Dept. Doc. 323, 23:1, Washington, 1834, 1st print.) Schoolcraft and Allen--Expedition to North-West Indians. 68pp, folding map, removed, wrappers. $200.00
    Howes: A-148. Sabin: 77847. Wagner-Camp 47a: "Lt. Allen commanded the military escort accompanying Henry Schoolcraft on his expedition. Documents consist of Lt. Allen's report and journal.... One of the principal objects was to vaccinate the Chippewa Indians."

S 97. SCHOOLCRAFT (Henry R.). (Senate Executive Doc. 13, 33:2, Washington, 1854, 1st print.) Report ... on the State of Indian Statistics. 11pp, removed. Problems of gathering information from Indians. $15.00

S 98. SCHOOLING (Sir William). The Hudson Bay Company, 1670-1920. The Governor and Company of Adventurers

of England Trading into Hudson's Bay During Two Hundred Fifty Years. xvi, 120pp of text containing numerous drawings, plus 42pp of photographs. London, 1920.
$135.00

S 99.   SCHRABISCH (Max). Aboriginal Rock Shelters and Other Archaeological Notes of Wyoming Valley and Vicinity. 186pp, illus, maps, index. Wilkes Barre, E. B. Yordy, 1926. $20.00

S100.   SCHRABISCH (Max). Archaeology of the Delaware River Valley. 181pp, illus, tears on two pages. Concentrates on rock shelters; includes assessment of pottery. Harrisburg, PA, 1930. $35.00
___Another Copy. Light cover spotting. $20.00

S101.   SCHROEDER (Albert H.). The Changing Ways of Southwestern Indians: A Historic Perspective.... xxii, 289pp, illus, notes, index. History and social life of Southwest Indians. Glorieta, 1973. $15.00
___Another Copy. Same. $10.00

S102.   SCHROEDER (Albert H.). A Colony on the Move; Gaspar Castano de Sosa's Journal 1590-1591. 196pp, illus, maps, bibliography, index. Santa Fe, 1965, (1st ed.), d.j. $20.00
The first time a complete English translation of Gaspar Castano de Sosa's journal of his expedition from northern Mexico into New Mexico in 1590-91 has been made. The annotated commentary details the route of travel, identifies the Indians and Pueblos visited, and provides pertinent information on many points of historical and archaeological interest. Santa Fe, 1965, (1st ed.), d.j. $20.00

S103.   SCHROEDER (Albert H.). A Study of the Apache Indians. Parts I, II and III. 583pp, maps, separate bibliography. Part I: Apaches and their neighbors; Part II: The Jicarilla Apaches; Part III: The Mescalero Apaches. New York, 1974 (1st ed.). $37.00
___Another Copy. Same. $17.00

S104.   SCHUETZ (M. K.). (Texas Historical Commission, Office of State Archaeologist, Report No. 19, Austin, 1970, 1st ed.) Excavation of a Section of the Acequia Madre in Bexar County, Texas and ... at Mission San Jose.... 17pp, 31pp, illus, photographs, maps, wrappers.
$12.00
___Another Copy. Same. $10.00

S105.   SCHUETZ (M. K.). (Texas State Building Commission, Reports No. 10 and 11, Austin, 1968 and 1969, 1st ed.) The History and Archaeology of Mission San Juan Capistrano, San Antonio, Texas (2 volumes). Vol. I: 263pp, photographs, plans, drawings, maps, wrappers. Vol. II: 124pp, 9pp, photographs, drawings, bibliography, wrappers. $15.00
___Another Copy. Vol. II only. $15.00

S106. SCHULTE (Paul). The Flying Priest Over the Arctic: A Story of Everlasting Ice and Everlasting Love. xiii, 268pp, photo illus, cloth. New York (c. 1940). $15.00
Account of the author's mission work in Canadian Eastern arctic, along the western coast of Hudson Bay and on northern Baffin Island.

S107. SCHULTZ (George A.). (Civilization of the American Indian Series, Vol. 121. Norman, 1972, 1st ed.) An Indian Canaan. Isaac McCoy and the Vision of an Indian State. 223pp plus index, illus, bibliography. $15.00
___Another Copy. Same. $22.00

S108. SCHULTZ (Harold). Hombu. Urwaldleben der Brasilianischen Indianer. 35 double-column pp of text plus 125 b/w and color photographs. The daily lives of several primitive Brazilian Indian tribes. Stuttgart, 1962, (1st ed.). $25.00

S109. SCHULTZ (James Willard). Apauk; Caller of Buffalo. 226pp. Boston, New York, 1916 (1st ed.). $55.00
___Another Copy. Boston, 1916. $15.00

S110. SCHULTZ (James Willard). (Ap-I-Kun-I) On the Warpath. 245pp, frontis, illus, cloth. Boston, 1924. $22.00
___Another Copy. Boston, 1914, 274pp. $55.00

S111. SCHULTZ (James Willard) (BETTS, Wilbur W., Editor). Bear Chief's War Shirt. 146pp, drawings by Glen Eagle Speaker. Betts completed this story from Schultz's half-finished manuscript. Missoula, 1984, (1st ed.) d.j. $15.00

S112. SCHULTZ (James Willard). Black feet and Buffalo. Memories of Life Among the Indians. 384pp, cloth. Norman, 1962, d.j. $40.00
Last book of author. Inter-tribal conflict, differences between Government and Blackfeet, religious beliefs, observances.
___Another Copy. Same. $30.00
___Another Copy. 400pp. $27.00
___Another Copy. Same. $25.00

S113. (SCHULTZ, James Willard). Blackfeet Man, James Willard Schultz: Stories of the Famous Montana Indian Story Writer and an Original Map and Guide to the Beautiful Region He Loved. 32pp, 4to, illus, wrappers. Helena, 1961, (1st ed.). $10.00

S114. SCHULTZ (James Willard). Friends of My Life As An Indian. 299pp, photographs, light wear. Boston, 1923 (1st ed.). $65.00

S115. SCHULTZ (James Willard). My Life As An Indian: The Story Of A Red Woman And A White Man In The Lodges Of The Blackfeet. 426pp, several full-page photographs, (some by Grinnell), decorative cloth. Some wear to cover. Author's finest book. Howes: S-205. Smith: 9093. New York, 1907 (1st ed.). $200.00
___Another Copy. Same. $65.00

        ___Another Copy. Boston, 1907. $35.00
        ___Another Copy. Boston, 1907. $25.00

S116. SCHULTZ (James Willard). The Quest of the Fish-Dog Skin. 218pp. Boston, 1913 (1st ed.). $65.00

S117. SCHULTZ (James Willard). Rising Wolf. 253pp. Boston, 1919 (1st ed.). $65.00

S118. SCHULTZ (James Willard). Signposts of Adventure. 224pp, Glacier National Park as the Indians know it. Map. Boston, 1926. $55.00

S119. SCHULTZ (James Willard). Sinopah. The Indian Boy. 154pp. Boston, 1913 (1st ed.). $55.00

S120. SCHULTZ (James Willard). Skull Head the Terrible. 207pp. Boston, 1929 (1st ed.). $55.00

S121. SCHULTZ (James Willard) and DONALDSON (Jessie L.). The Sun God's Children. 254pp, 1pp, color frontis, illus with portraits of Blackfeet Indians by Winold Reiss, illus endpapers. Boston, New York, 1930 (1st ed.). $35.00

S122. SCHULTZ (James Willard). Why Gone Those Times? Blackfoot Tales. 271pp, illus. Norman, 1978, d.j. $20.00
        Brings together 17 superbly written stories for the first time in book form. Illustrated with paintings and bronzes by Russell. (GFH)

S123. SCHULTZ (James Willard). William Jackson, Indian Scout, His True Story Told By His Friend. 206pp, illustrated by Frank E. Schoonover. Bookplate removed from front endpapers, slight discoloration from tape to front and back, top edge of spine worn. Norman, 1962, (1st ed.). $67.00

S124. SCHULTZ (James Willard). With the Indians In The Rockies. ix, 228pp, pls, cover illus paste down. Light cover soil. Illustrations by G. Varian. The 19th Century adventures of trapper Thomas "The Fox" Fox. Boston, 1912 (1st ed.). $65.00

S125. SCHULZ (P. E.). Indians of Lassen Volcanic National Park and Vicinity. 176pp, 98 drawings of objects of material culture, 58 drawings of basketry and textile designs. Mineral, 1954. $12.00

S126. SCHULZ (Valerie-Vera). Haida: Bella Coola-Indianische Totempfahle in Nordwest Amerika. Color frontis, 25 photographs. Kassel, 1962. $20.00

S127. SCHULTZ-LORENTZEN. Dictionary of the West Greenland Eskimo Language. Reprint from Meddeleser om Gronland. 303pp, large 8vo, wrappers. Copenhagen, 1927. $85.00

S128. SCHULZE-THULIN (A.). Im Zeichen des Jaguars, Indianische Fruhkulturen in Alt-Peru. 90pp, 74 photographs, 11 drawings. Linden Museum, Stuttgart, 1974. $10.00

S129. SCHUSKY (Ernest L.). The Forgotten Sioux. 261pp plus index, photographs, map, notes, bibliography.

Ethnohistory of the Lower Brule Reservation. Chicago,
1975, (1st ed.), d.j. $15.00
S130. SCHWARTA (D. W.) et al. The Bright Angel Site.
114pp, 41 illus. Archaeology of the Grand Canyon,
School of American Research, Santa Fe, 1979. $10.00
S131. SCHWATKA (Frederick). In the Land of Cave and Cliff
Dwellers. 385pp, illus. Boston, 1899. $22.00
S132. SCHWATKA (Frederick). (Senate Executive Doc. 2, 48:2,
Washington, 1885) Report of a Military Reconnaissance
in Alaska, made in 1883. 121pp, 20 folding maps,
illus. Much on the Indians in this area. $70.00
S133. SCIDMORE (E. R.). Alaska, The Sitkan Archipelago.
340pp, 23 photographs and drawings. $47.00
S134. SCOTT (J. F.). The Art of the Taino from the Dominican
Republic. Artifacts on loan from the Museo del Hombre
Dominicano. 48pp, 2 color and 42 b/w photographs, 2
drawings, map. Gainesville, 1985. $12.00
S135. SCRIVER (Bob). No More Buffalo. Foreword by Dr.
Harold McCracken and Dr. John Ewers and others.
53 Sculptures Reproduced in Full Color, endpaper fac-
simile of Blackfeet Signers of Agreement of 1887-1888
... Establishing Reservation Boundary. xvii, 120pp,
4to, map, appendix, bibliography. Kansas City, 1982.
$55.00
S136. SCRIVNER (Fulsom). Mohave People. 144pp, pictorial
cloth. San Antonio, Naylor, 1970 (1st ed.) d.j. $15.00
S137. SCULLY (Vincent). Pueblo/Mountain, Village, Dance.
390pp, photographs, maps, notes. New York, 1975
(1st ed.), d.j. $30.00
S138. SCULLY (Virginia). A Treasury of American Indian
Herbs: Their Lore and Their Use for Food, Drugs and
Medicine. Text figures. New York, Crown, 1970 (3rd
print.). $25.00
S139. SCURLOCK (Dan) et al. (Texas Historical Commission
Archaeological Survey Report 17, Austin, 1976) An
Archaeological and Historical Survey of the Proposed
Mission Parkway, San Antonio, Texas. 351pp, photo-
graphs, maps, bibliography, wrappers. $10.00
S140. SCURLOCK (D.) et al. (Texas Historical Commission Of-
fice of State Archaeologist Special Reports, No. 11,
Austin, 1974, 1st ed.) Assess. Arch. Resources Padre
Is. National Seashore, Texas. 127pp plus maps and
pls, bibliography, large 8vo, wrappers. $15.00
S141. SEAMAN (N. G.). Indian Relics of the Pacific Northwest.
157pp, extensively illus with photographs of artifacts,
index, cloth. Portland, 1946 (1st ed.), d.j. $15.00
___Another Copy. Portland, 1956 (2nd print.), 153pp.
$10.00
___Another Copy. Portland, 1967, d.j. 255pp. $25.00
S142. SEAVER (James E.). Deh-He-Wa-Mis: or, A Narrative of
the Life of Mary Jemison: Otherwise Called the White

Woman.... 192pp, 16mo, later full calf. New York,
W. Seaver & Son, 1842. $175.00
    Howes: S-263. Sabin: 78680. Ewers: 253. Howes:
"One of the most authentic and interesting of captivity
narratives, told by one who spent a long life among the
Senecas and was the first white woman to descend the
Ohio."

S143. SECOY (F. M.). (American Ethnological Society, Mono-
graph XXI, New York, 1953) Changing Military Patterns
Of The Great Plains. (17th Century Through Early 19th
Century). viii, 112pp, 4 maps. $24.00
    Another Copy. Same. $25.00

S144. SEDGWICK (Mrs. William T.). Acoma, the Sky City. A
Study in Pueblo-Indian History and Civilization. 305pp
plus index, bibliography, map endpapers, illus. History, social organization, folktales, myths, religious beliefs, rituals, pottery, etc. Cambridge, 1926 (1st ed.).
$30.00
    Another Copy. 318pp. Cambridge, 1927 (2d Print.).
$60.00
    Another Copy. Cambridge, 1927. $35.00
    Another Copy. Cambridge, 1927. $25.00
    Another Copy. Chicago, 1963. $20.00

S145. SEGER (John H.) (VESTAL, Stan, Editor). Early Days
Among The Cheyenne and Arapaho Indians. 155pp,
illus. Memoirs of the author who founded the town of
Colony, OK, and the Model Indian Industrial School.
University of Oklahoma, 1934 (1st ed.), chips to d.j.
$55.00
    Another Copy. Cloth. 2d edition with "Traditions
of the Cheyenne Indians" added. Norman, 1934.
$35.00
    Another Copy. 146pp. Norman, 1956, d.j. $25.00
    Another Copy. Norman, 1956, d.j. $15.00

S146. SEILER (Baldinger A.). El Dorado: Goldschatze aus
Kolombein. 52pp, 26 large b/w and 4 full-page color
photographs, 3 drawings, 8 maps, 2 charts. Basel
1974. $10.00

S147. SEILER (Baldinger A.). Maschenstoffe in Sud-und Mittel
Amerika. 248pp, 24 tables, 6 maps, wrappers. Basel,
1971. $40.00

S148. SEITZ (Don C.). From Kaw Teepee to Capitol. The Life
Story of Charles Curtis, Indian, Who Has Risen to High
Estate. 223pp, frontis, illus. New York, 1928 (1st
ed.). $10.00
    Curtis, a U.S. Vice-president, was brought up as an
Indian with the Kansa tribe; his experiences during the
Indian war of 1868, etc.

S149. SEITZ (Don C.). Letters from Francis Parkman to E. G.
Squier. With Bibliographical Notes and a Bibliography
of E. G. Squier. 58pp, limited to 200 copies. Cedar

Rapids, The Torch Press, 1911 (1st ed.). $100.00
   __Another Copy. Same. $75.00

S150. SEJOURNE (Laurette). (Instituto Nacional de Antropologia e Historia) Arqueologia del Valle de Mexico. I: Culhuacan. 214pp, 135 illus. sml 4to. Mexico City, 1970, wrappers. $25.00

S151. SEJOURNE (Laurette). Arqueologia de Teotihuacan, la Ceramica. 262pp of text containing 22 color and b/w figures, many are full page, plus 64pp of photographs, cloth. Mexico City, 1966. $85.00
   __Another Copy. Mexico City, 1984. $50.00

S152. SEJOURNE (Laurette). Burning Water. Thought and Religion in Ancient Mexico. 192pp, 22 photographic illus, 82 figures, cloth. New York, n.d. (c.1956).
   $25.00
   __Another Copy. Same. $15.00

S153. SEJOURNE (Laurette). El Pensamiento Nahuatl Cifrado por los Calendarios. 407pp, 335 illus. Mexico, 1981.
   $60.00

S154. SEJOURNE (Laurette). El Universo de Quetzalcoatl. 205pp, 59 pls, many in color, several tipped in, 171 figures, illus primarily of Pre-Columbian artifacts, 1st edition with Spanish text. Mexico, 1962. $45.00

S155. SELER (Eduard). Codex Fejervary-Mayer. An Old Mexican Picture Manuscript, in the Liverpool Free Public Museum, Published at the Expense of His Excellency, the Duke of Loubat. English Edition by A. H. Keane. 210pp, 218 illus, plus 20 pls, facsimile edition, outlined in red, with glyphs and gods identified, folio (11" x 14"), newly rebound. Berlin, London, 1901-1902. $600.00

S156. SELER (Eduard). Comentarios Al Codice Borgia. Primera Edition en Espanol. 3 volumes, with reproductions of the codex. Mexico, 1980, reprint. $375.00

S157. SELER (Eduard). Die Holzgeschnitzte Pauke Von Malinalco und das Zeichen Atl-Tlachinolli. 53pp, 71 figures, cvr soiled. Vienna, 1904. $35.00

S158. SELER (Eduard). The Mexican Chronology With Special Reference to the Zapotec Calendar. From: BAE Bulletin No. 28, pp13-55, folding map, in folder. Washington, 1904. $15.00

S159. SELER (Eduard). Observations and Studies in the Ruins of Palenque. Translated by Gisela Morgner. 92pp, 19 pls, 146 illus, 4to. Robert Louis Stevenson School, 1976. $65.00
   __Another Copy. 173pp, 81pp illus, cloth. Pebble Beach, 1977. $13.00

S160. SEMENOV (S. A.) (Translated by THOMPSON, M.). Prehistoric Technology: An Experimental Study of the Oldest Tools and Artifacts From Traces of Manufacture and Wear. xii, 211pp, photographs, figures, index. 1st English translation. The result of 20 years' research on

prehistoric tools. London, 1964, some wear to d.j.
$35.00

S161.   (SEMINOLE). Message From the President ... Information
        In Relation To the War With The Seminoles.... 29pp,
        removed. Narratives of events of the war. Washington,
        1818 (1st print.). $25.00

S162.   (SEMINOLE). Message From the President ... In Relation
        To The Manner The Troops ... Now Operating Against
        The Seminole Tribe of Indians, Have Been Subsisted.
        8pp, removed. Payment and supplies for army troops.
        Washington, 1818 (1st print.). $20.00

S163.   (SEMINOLE). Seminole Campaign--Horses Lost. 24pp,
        removed, folding chart. Claims of Tennessee Volunteers
        for lost guns, horses and other equipment during the
        war. Washington, 1822 (1st print.). $15.00

S164.   (SEMINOLE). (House of Representatives Document 267,
        24:1, Washington, 1836, 1st print.) Causes of Hostil-
        ities of Seminole Indians. 22pp, removed. Treaties of
        1832 and 1833, how they were broken, the first battles.
                                                              $12.00

S165.   (SEMINOLE). (House of Representatives Document 271,
        24:1, Washington, 1836, 1st print.) Seminole Hostilities.
        272pp, removed. Important, lengthy accounting of the
        causes of the Seminole War and attempts by the Army
        to win it. Includes battles, participants, settlements.
                                                              $40.00

S166.   (SEMINOLE AND CHEROKEE). (House of Representatives
        Document 285, 25:2, Washington, 1838, 1st print.)
        Seminole and Cherokee Indians. 24pp, removed. John
        Ross negotiating for Indians. $20.00

S167.   (SEMINOLE). (House of Representatives Document 327,
        25:2, Washington, 1838, 1st print.) Seminole Indians--
        Prisoners of War. 14pp, removed. Reports of Capture
        of Indians, with names of Chiefs and others captured.
                                                              $20.00

S168.   (SEMINOLE WAR). Narrative of a Voyage to the Spanish
        Main in the Ship "Two Friends"; the Occupation of
        Amelia Island, by McGregor and Co.--Sketches of the
        Province of East Florida; and Anecdotes Illustrative of
        the Habits and Manners of the Seminole Indians....
        328pp, later half morocco and bds, bound without half
        title, errata leaf present. London, 1819. $1,250.00
            Howes: N-12. Streeter Sale: 1201. Sabin: 51782.
        Field: 1119. "Almost the whole of the volume is de-
        voted to the Seminole Indians; the barbarous character
        of the war of the Americans with them; and anecdotes
        respecting the Seminoles."--Field.

S169.   (SEMINOLE WAR). (Senate Document No. 42, Washington,
        1839) Bill to Provide for the Armed Occupation and
        Settlement of That Part of Florida Which is Now Over-
        run and Infested by Marauding Bands of Hostile Indians
        (Seminole). 3pp, removed. $25.00

S170. (SEMINOLE WAR). (Senate Document 278, 26:1, Washington, 1840, 1st ed.) Message of the President of the
U.S. ... the correspondence between the War Dept. and
Gov. Call, concerning the war in Florida. 245pp, bound
in later 1/4 leather. Major source document on this war,
covering the period 1836-1838. $75.00

S171. SENDEY (J.). The Nootkan Indian: A Pictorial. viii,
72pp, 91 photographs, most are full and half-page,
2 maps, wrappers. Alberni Valley Museum, 1977.
$17.00

S172. (SENECA INDIANS). The Case of the Seneca Indians in
the State of New York. Printed for the Information of
the Society of Friends. 256pp, index, modern plain
wrappers. Philadelphia, Merrihew and Thompson, 1840
(1st ed.). $85.00
    Field: 252: "The Senecas having, at the suggestion
of the Society of Friends, consented to sell their lands,
a controversy arose regarding the transaction which became on the part of their opponents quite acrimonious.
To justify themselves, the committee of the Society
printed this pamphlet." (RMW)

S173. SERRANO (A.). El Arte Decorativo de los Diaguitas.
137pp, 42 pls, wrappers. Cordoba, 1943. $35.00

S174. SERRANO (A.). Lineas Fundamentales de la Arqueologia
Saltena. 52pp, 19 figures, wrappers. Salta, 1963.
$20.00

S175. SERRANO (A.). Los Pueblos y Culturas Indigenas del
Litora. 125pp, 48 photographs, 2 maps. Santa Fe
(Argentina), 1955. $40.00

S176. SETEN (J. M.). Indian Costume Book. xv, 212pp, 48pp
of drawings and photographs of costumes and other objects of material culture, bound 3/4 wood and buckram,
all copies hand bound by Seton Village Press, limited to
500 copies. Santa Fe, 1938. $375.00

S177. SETON (Julia). The Pulse of the Pueblo: Personal
Glimpses of Indian Life. 249pp, frontis, decorated bds.
Slight wear at ends, else very good. Character studies
among many of the Western tribes in addition to the
Pueblo's drawn from the experiences of the author and
her husband, Ernest Thompson Seton. Santa Fe, 1939
(1st ed.). $30.00

S178. SETZLER (F. M.). (Smithsonian Misc. Collections, Vol.
100, 1940) Archaeological Perspectives in the Northern
Mississippi Valley. pp253-290, 4 maps, wrappers.
$18.00

S179. SEXTON (Bernard). Grey Wolf Stories: Indian Mystery
Tales of Coyote Animals and Men. x, 192pp, pictorial
cloth. Slight soiling. A collection of Indian tales from
several tribes, but the majority are Blackfoot. Reprint
of 1921 ed. New York, 1923. $30.00

S180. SEYMOUR (Flora Warren). Indian Agents of the Old

Frontier. 392pp plus index, photographs. Covers
agents Kit Carson, Tatum of the Kiowas, Jeffords of the
Apaches, John Clum, Arny, Meacham, Pratt, McLaugh-
lin. Smith: 9354. New York, 1941 (1st ed.). $27.00
___Another Copy. Same, d.j. $25.00
___Another Copy. New York, 1975. $30.00

S181.   SEYMOUR (Flora Warren). The Story of the Red Man.
421pp, 31 illus, 12 maps, endpaper maps. New York,
1929. $25.00
___Another Copy. New York, 1934 (2d ed.). $10.00
___Another Copy. Freeport, 1970. $12.00

S182.   SEYMOUR (Flora Warren). We Called Them Indians.
280pp, frontis, illus, index, cloth. London, New York,
1940. $20.00

S183.   SHAFER (Harry J.). (Texas Archaeological Salvage Project, No. 17, Austin, 1969) Archaeological Investigations
in the Robert Lee Reservoir Basin, West Central Texas.
101pp, pls, drawings, maps, bibliography, wrappers.
                                               $12.00
___Another Copy. Same. $10.00

S184.   SHAFER (Harry J.). (Texas Archaeological Salvage Project, No. 13, Austin, 1968) Archaeological Investigations
in the San Jacinto River Basin, Montgomery County,
Texas. 82pp, photographs, drawings, maps, bibliography, wrappers. $12.00
___Another Copy. Same. $10.00

S185.   SHAFER (Harry J.). (University of Texas, Texas Archaeological Survey Reports, No. 4, Austin, 1967, 1st ed.)
Robert Lee Reservoir, Coke County, Texas. 77pp,
maps, pls, bibliography, large 8vo, wrappers. $10.00

S186.   SHAFER (Harry J.). (University of Texas, Texas Archaeological Survey Reports, No. 7, Austin, 1971, 1st ed.)
Sanderson Canyon Watershed, Texas. 72pp, maps, pls,
bibliography, large 8vo, wrappers. $10.00

S187.   SHAFER (Harry J.) and HESTER (T. R.). (Texas Historical Survey Committee Archaeological Report 20, Austin,
1971) A Study of the Function and Technology of Certain Bifacial Tools from Southern Texas. 11pp, photographs, map, wrappers. $12.00
___Another Copy. Same. $10.00

S188.   SHAPIRO (H. L.). The Alaskan Eskimo. A Study of the
Relationship Between the Eskimo and the Chipewayan
Indians of Central Canada. pp347-383, 5pp of photo-
graphs, wrappers. American Museum of Natural History,
New York, 1931. $28.00
___Another Copy. Same. $25.00

S189.   SHARER (Robert). The Prehistory of Chalchuapa, El Salvador. (3 Volumes). Vol. I: contains Surface Surveys, excavations, Monuments and Special Deposits.
94pp, 14 figures. Vol. II: contains Artifacts and
Figurines. 211pp, numerous illus. Vol. III: contains

Pottery and Conclusions. 226pp. 4to, wrappers. University of Pennsylvania, 1978. $50.00

S190. SHARP (Mrs. Abbie Gardner). History of the Spirit Lake Massacre and Captivity of Miss Abbie Gardner. 312pp, illus, cloth. Des Moines, Iowa, 1885. $75.00

S191. SHARROCK (F. W.) and KEANE (E. G.). (University of Utah, Anthropological Papers, No. 57, Salt Lake City, 1962) Carnegie Museum Collection From Southeast Utah, and other articles. 71pp, 43pp, maps, photographs, figures, bibliography, indices, large 8vo, wrappers. $15.00

S192. SHAW (Anna Moore). Pima Indian Legends. 111pp, drawings, wrappers. Tucson, 1972 (3rd print.). $10.00

S193. SHAW (Anna Moore). A Pima Past. 262pp, photographs, wrappers. Tucson, 1974 (1st ed.). $10.00

S194. SHAW (George). The Chinook Jargon and How to Use It. A Complete and Exhaustive Lexicon of the Oldest Trade Language of the American Continent. xvi, 65pp, 3pp ads, wrappers, 15x21.5cm, photo pl on front cvr. Seattle, Rainier Printing, 1909. $45.00

S195. (SHAWNEE). (Senate Document No. 413, Washington, 1840) Claim for payment of certain debts due from Shawnee Indians. 7pp, removed. $15.00

S196. (SHAWNEE). (Senate Executive Document No. 40, 41:2, Washington, 1879, 1st print.) Shawnee Indians--Black Bob's Band. 210pp, removed. Treaty assignment of lands in Kansas, settlers claiming sections, and Indian removal. $25.00

S197. (SHAWNEE). (Senate Executive Document No 111, 49:2, Washington, 1887, 1st print.) Shawnee Indians--Lands. 254pp, removed. Plat and section maps, detailed examination of sale of land allotted to Shawnee Indians in Kansas. $25.00

S198. SHEA (John G.). Discovery and Exploration of the Mississippi Valley. lxxvii, 2pp, 268pp, portrait, folding map, cloth backed bds, limited to 500 copies. Albany, J. McDonough, 1903 (2d ed.). $60.00
Howes: S-357. Field: 1391. "Beside the valuable relations, which afford us the first accounts of the Indian tribes which inhabited the vast tract of territory, from the St. Lawrence to the Mississippi, Mr. Shea has added notes, biographical sketches and bibliographical accounts of works upon aboriginal history, which are scarcely to be overestimated." (RMW)

S199. SHEA (John G.) (Editor). Early Voyages Up and Down the Mississippi.... 191pp, index, 4to, 1/2 leather, marbled bds, original wrappers bound in, limited to 100 copies. Albany, J. Munsel, 1861 (1st ed.). $125.00
Howes: S-358. Sabin: 80023. Field: 1395: "Relations of travels and voyages ... accessible here for

the first time ... almost wholly composed of accounts of the Indian tribes they encountered ... filled with the most interesting details."

_____Another Copy. Albany, J. Munsel, 1902, limited to 500 copies, cloth. $75.00

_____Another Copy. Same, ex-library, limited to 500 copies. $65.00

S200. SHEA (John G.). History of the Catholic Missions Among the Indian Tribes of the United States, 1529-1854. 514pp, 10 adv pp, portraits, engraved title, "Facsimiles," modern cloth. New York, E. Dunigan, 1855, (1st ed.). $150.00

S201. SHEEHAN (B. W.). Seeds of Extinction: Jeffersonian Philanthropy And the American Indian. 301pp, bibliography, index. Some underlining and notes. Chapel Hill, 1973 (1st ed.), d.j. $10.00

S202. SHEEHAN (Carol). Pipes That Won't Smoke; Coal That Won't Burn. Haida Sculpture in Argillite. 214pp, b/w and color photographs, drawings, map, bibliography, small folio, stiff wrappers. Calgary, 1981 (1st ed.). $20.00

S203. SHEETS (P. D.) (Editor). Archaeology and Volcanism on Central America: The Zapotitan Valley of El Salvador. 307pp, illus, 4to. Austin, 1983. $35.00

S204. SHELTON (William). Totem Legends: Indian Totem Legends of the Northwest Coast Country by One of the Indians. 17pp, 4to, illus with photographs, pictorial wrappers. Printed by the Printing Department of the Chilocco Indian School, Tulalip Indian Reservation, Washington, n.d. (c.1900). $30.00

  Indian legends of Skay-Whah-Mish, Puyallup and Wenatchee tribes of the coast of Washington state.

S205. SHEPARD (A. O.). (Carnegie Institution Publication 609, Washington, 1956) Ceramics for the Archaeologist. xii, 414pp, 59 figures. $57.00

S206. SHEPARD (A. O.). Notes from a Ceramic Laboratory. 100pp, 8 figures. Carnegie Institution, Washington, 1977. $20.00

  Publication covers Maya blue, Oaxaca ceramics and Yucatan imitation jade ornaments.

S207. SHEPARDSON (Mary). The Navajo Mountain Community: Social Organization and Kinship Terminology. 278pp, index, map. Berkeley, 1970 (1st ed.). $30.00

_____Another Copy. Same. $30.00

_____Another Copy. Same. $24.00

_____Another Copy. Same. $20.00

S208. SHEPARDSON (Mary). (American Anthropological Assn. Memoir 96, New York, 1963) Navajo Ways in Government, A Study In Political Process. xi, 132pp. $15.00

_____Another Copy. Same. $12.00

_____Another Copy. Same. $10.00

S209. SHEPHERD (Henry A.). The Antiquities of the State of
Ohio. vi, 139pp, 4to, maps, pls of Ohio mounds,
pipes and other artifacts, etc. Robert Clarke Co.,
Cincinnati, 1890. $45.00
___Another Copy. Same. Cloth. $60.00
S210. SHERER (Lorraine M.). The Clan System of the Fort
Mojave Indians. 85pp, illús, map, limited to 300 copies.
Los Angeles, 1965. $35.00
Study of the Indians of San Bernardino County,
Calif.
___Another Copy. Same. $32.00
S211. SHERIDAN (Clair). Redskin Interlude. Illus, color
frontis. Mostly concerning Blood Reservation. London,
1938, d.j. $35.00
S212. SHERIDAN (P. H.). Record of Engagements with Hostile
Indians within the Military Division of the Missouri, from
1868 to 1882.... 112pp, original printed wrappers.
Washington, 1882. $200.00
Howes: S-395. Graff: 3753. Rader: 3180. A
valuable and detailed record of all the Indian outbreaks
from 1868 through the Chiricahua Apache outbreak near
Stein's Pass, Arizona, in 1882. The Custer skirmish
occupies several pages. One of the standard works on
the bloodiest years of western warfare. (WR)
___Another Copy. Headquarters, Military Division of
Missouri, Chicago, 1882. 120pp, cloth, leather label.
$275.00
___Another Copy. Washington, 1882, wrappers, tape
strengthening head and tail. $150.00
___Another Copy. Bellevue, NE, 1969, 112pp. $15.00
S213. SHERIDAN (Thomas) and NAYLOR (Thomas) (Editors).
Raramuri: A Tarahumara Colonial Chronicle 1607-1791.
144pp, wrappers. Northland Press, Flagstaff, 1979.
$18.00
S214. SHERWIN (Reider T.). The Viking and the Red Man.
145pp. New York, 1953. $10.00
S215. SHETRONE (Henry Clyde). The Mound-Builders. 508pp,
299 figures, original decorated cloth, ex-library with
bookplates, lettering on spine. New York, 1930 (1st
ed.). $75.00
___Another Copy. New York, 1936, d.j. $150.00
___Another Copy. New York, 1936 (3rd print.).
$75.00
S216. SHIELDS (Col. G. O.). The Blanket Indian of the North-
West. 322pp, 32 pls (some colored), index. Some cvr
spotting, light wear, limited to 500. Autographed,
subscriber's edition. New York, 1921 (1st ed.).
$150.00
___Another Copy. Same. $125.00
S217. SHIELDS (W. F.). (University of Utah, Anthropological
Papers No. 89, Salt Lake City, 1967) Collected

Miscellaneous Papers, including 1966 Excavations: Uinta Basin, etc. viii, 70pp, illus, bibliography, large 8vo, wrappers. $10.00

S218. SHIMONY (A. A.). (Yale University Publications in Anthropology, No. 65, 1961) Conservatism Among The Iroquois at the Six Nations Reserve. 302pp, 19 figures. $34.00

S219. SHINE (Michael A.). (Nebraska Academy of Sciences Publications, Vol. IX, No. 1, Lincoln, 1914) The Nebraska Aborigines As They Appeared in the Eighteenth Century. 23pp, illus, maps, wrappers. $15.00

S220. SHINKLE (James D.). Fort Sumner and the Bosque Redondo Indian Reservation. 85pp, photographs, signed by author. Roswell, NM, 1965. $15.00
____Another Copy. No inscription. $10.00

S221. SHIPP (Barnard). The Indian and Antiquities of America. xi, 451pp, frontis, 22pls, errata page following title, 18x26cm. Philadelphia, Sherman & Co., 1897 (1st ed.). $45.00

S222. SHOOK (E. M.) et al. Tikal Reports. (Numbers 1-4). v, 150pp, 26 figures. University Museum, Philadelphia, 1958. $50.00

S223. SHORRIS (E.). The Death of the Great Spirit: A Eulogy for the American Indian. 253pp. New York, 1971. $15.00
____Another Copy. Same. $10.00

S224. SHORTRIDGE (L.). Emblems of Tlingit Culture. pp350-377, 7 full-page photographs, Museum Journal, December, 1928. $20.00

S225. SHUTLER (Richard and Mary). (Nevada State Museum Anthropology Papers, No. 7, Carson City, 1962.) Archaeological Survey in Southern Nevada. 40pp, plus 35 illus, folded charts, 4to, wrappers. $18.00
____Another Copy. Same. $17.00

S226. SIBLEY (Henry). Iron Face. The Adventures of Jack Frazer, Frontier Warrior, Scout and Hunter. 206pp, frontis photograph, limited to 500 copies, prospectus laid in. Chicago, 1950 (1st ed.). (TNL) $100.00
Frazer was half Sioux. This work is an excellent look at Sioux life and thought. Much on the 1862 Sioux War. Originally in a newspaper, this is the first book publication, although written nearly 100 years previously.

S227. SIDES (Dorothy Smith). Decorative Art of the Southwestern Indians. 50 pls as issued (loose), 41 hand-colored pls, with descriptive booklet, foreword by F. W. Hodge, boxed (torn at edges), ex-library, numbers on cvr, none on pls, full description also given on back of pl, with interpretation of symbols, pls are in excellent condition. Santa Ana, CA, Fine Arts Press, 1936. $350.00
____Another Copy. 28pp plus 50 design pls, newly

rebound in cloth. New York, 1961. $15.00
___Another Copy. Same. $10.00

S228. SIEBERT (Erna) and FORMAN (Werner). North American
Indian Art (Northwest Coast). 204pp, 107 photographs
of masks, amulets, wood carvings and ceremonial dress,
4to. 1967, d.j. $75.00

S229. SIEGRIST (Roland) (Editor). Prehistoric Petroglyphs and
Pictographs in Utah. 71pp, 28 full-page b/w and color
photos, oblong 4to, wrappers. Salt Lake City, 1972
(1st ed.). $10.00

S230. (SIGOURNEY, Lydia H.). Traits of the Aborigines of
America. 284pp, (1 errata), (1 adv), modern cloth,
marbled bds, 12mo. Cambridge University Press,
Hilliard and Metcalf, Printers, 1822 (1st ed.). $175.00

S231. SIIGER (Halfdan). (National Museum, Ethnographic Series,
Vol. XI, Part I, Copenhagen, 1967) The Lepchas:
Culture and Religion of a Himalayan People, Part I.
251pp, illus, large 4to, wrappers. $45.00

S232. SILBERMAN (A.) and HIGHWATER (J.). 100 Years of
Native American Painting. 122pp, 67 b/w and 17 color
photographs. Oklahoma City, 1978. $22.00

S233. (SILETZ AGENCY). (Senate Miscellaneous Document 65,
43:1, Washington, 1874, 1st print.) Report ... In
Relation to the Condition of the Indians of the Siletz
Agency in Oregon. 7pp, removed. Review of events
relating to the settlement of Siletz lands and poor conditions of the Indians. $15.00

S234. SILVA (Arthur M.) and CHIN (William C.). California Indian Basketry. An Artistic Overview. 84pp, photographs, maps, wrappers. Detailed reference for the
California tribes. Cypress, CA, 1978. $15.00

S235. SILVERBERG (Robert). Men Against Time: Salvage
Archaeology in the United States. 202pp, illus, cloth.
New York, 1967, d.j. $10.00

S236. SILVERBERG (Robert). The Mound Builders. 276pp,
53 photographs. Greenwich, 1970, Athens, 1986.
$12.00

S237. SILVERBERG (Robert). Mound Builders of Ancient America: The Archaeology of a Myth. 369pp, 59 figures,
4to. Greenwich, 1968 (1st ed.) d.j. $40.00
___Another Copy. Same. Cloth. $30.00
___Another Copy. Same. $20.00

S238. SIMMONS (L. W.). Sun Chief, The Autobiography of a
Hopi Indian. x, 460pp, 5 illus, cloth. New Haven,
1942. $34.00
___Another Copy. New Haven, 1971, d.j. $15.00

S239. SIMMONS (Marc). Border Comanches. Seven Spanish
Colonial Documents, 1785-1819. 41pp, 12.5x22.5cm,
limited to 400 copies printed on a hand press. Santa
Fe, 1967 (1st ed.) d.j. $45.00
A remarkable series of Spanish letters and reports on

the early Comanches found in old Mexican archives and
here published for the first time in English.
___Another Copy. Same. $25.00

S240. SIMMONS (Marc). Witchcraft in the Southwest; Spanish
and Indian Supernaturalism on the Rio Grande. 184pp,
illus, bibliography. Flagstaff, 1974, (1st ed.) d.j.
$17.00

Accounts of Devil's Sabbats, were-animals, sexual
rituals, mysterious illnesses and incredible cures, Pueblo Witchcraft, Zuni Plague of Witches, Navajo and
Apache Witchcraft, herbalism and Black Magic.

S241. SIMMONS (Wm. Scranton). Cautantowwit's House. An
Indian Burial Ground on the Island of Conanicut in
Narragansett Bay. 178pp, illus, cloth. Brown Univer-
sity Press, 1970, d.j. $15.00
___Another Copy. Same. $10.00

S242. SIMMS (S. C.). (Field Columbian Museum Publication 85,
Anthropology Series, Vol. II, No. 6, Chicago, 1903)
Traditions of the Crows. pp281-324. $35.00
___Another Copy. Same. $30.00
___Another Copy. Same. Uncut, unopened, wrappers.
$10.00

S243. SIMONSEN (B. O.). (National Museum of Canada, Archaeological Survey, No. 13, 1973) Archaeological Investigations in the Hecate Strait-Milbanke Sound Area of British Columbia. 117pp, 15pp of photographs, wrappers,
2 maps. $15.00

S244. SIMPSON (Lesley Byrd). Exploitation of Land in Central
Mexico in the 16th Century. 92pp, wrappers. University of California, Berkeley, 1952. $20.00

S245. SIMPSON (Lesley Byrd) (Editor). The San Saba Papers;
A Documentary Account of the Founding and Destruction
of San Saba Mission. Translated by Paul Nathan.
157pp, folding map. San Francisco, 1959 (1st ed.).
$50.00

Book designed and printed by Lawton Kennedy. Eye-
witness accounts of the famous San Saba Massacre of
1758. Taken from the depositions of survivors. The
massacre is historically significant as it caused the
Spaniards to abandon their attempt to bring the Apaches
and Comanches into their colonial system.

S246. SIMPSON (Lesley B.). Studies in the Administration of
the Indians in New Spain I. The Laws of Durgos of
1512. II. The Civil Congregation. 128pp, pls, folding map, printed wrappers. Berkeley, 1934. $30.00
___Another Copy. Same. $25.00

S247. SIMPSON (Lesley B.). Studies in the Administration of
the Indians in New Spain. III. The Repartimento System. 160pp, printed wrappers. Berkeley, 1938. $25.00
___Another Copy. Same. Facsimiles. $10.00

S248. SIMS (Agnes C.). San Cristobal Petroglyphs. Descriptive

booklet with 10pp, 17 pls loose as issued in folder, 4to
(9" x 12"), wrappers. Santa Fe, Southwest Editions,
1950. $60.00

S249. SINGER (M.) and COHN (B. S.) (Editors). (Viking Fund
Publications in Anthropology No. 47, New York, 1948
1st ed.) Structure and Change in Indian Society.
xvi, 507pp, figures, maps, illus, bibliography, indices,
stiff wrappers. 20 articles. $10.00

S250. (SIOUX). (House of Representatives Executive Document
130, 34:1, Washington, 1856) Council with the Sioux
Indians at Fort Pierre ... Minutes of a Council ... by
General Harney, etc. 39pp, removed. Includes speeches
of Indian chiefs and revealing as to past and future problems with the Sioux. $45.00

S251. (SIOUX). (House of Representatives Report 42, 38:1,
Washington, 1864, 1st print.) Claims for Depredations
by Sioux Indians. 13pp, removed. Account of the New
Ulm, Wisconsin, massacre and other battles. $15.00

S252. (SIOUX). (House of Representatives Executive Document
58, 38:1, Washington, 1864, 1st print.) Sioux Indians
--Claims For Depredations By. 23pp, removed. Reports
by Stephen Riggs and others on killings and troubles
with settlers. $18.00

S253. (SIOUX). (House of Representatives Executive Document
126, 39:1, Washington, 1866, 1st print.) Sioux Indians
--Lands. 10pp, folding hand-colored map. $20.00

S254. (SIOUX). (Senate Executive Document 11, 40:3, Washington, 1869) Letter of the Secretary of War ... Report of
Brevet Major General Harney upon the Sioux Indians
on the Upper Missouri. 6pp, removed. Harney's efforts
to make the reservation system work with the hostile
Sioux. $10.00

S255. (SIOUX). (Senate Executive Document 28, 40:3, Washing-
ton, 1869) Letter of the Secretary of the Interior ...
an Estimate of Appropriations for the Sisseton and
Wahpeton Sioux Indians at Lake Traverse and Devil's
Lake, Dakota Territory. 6pp, removed. $12.00
___Another Copy. Same. $10.00

S256. (SIOUX). (Senate Executive Document 31, 40:3, Washington, 1869) Letter of the Secretary of the Interior ...
an Estimate of Appropriations to Supply Deficiencies in
the Appropriations for the Sioux of Dakota, Arickarees,
Gros Ventres and Mandans, Crows and Yanktons. 4pp,
removed. $10.00

S257. (SIOUX). (Senate Executive Document 9, 44th Congress,
Washington, 1876) Report of the Sioux Commission.
90pp. $35.00

S258. (SIOUX). (Senate Executive Document 30, 44:1, Washington, 1876) Red Cloud Agency, Nebraska--Information
in Relation to the Deficiency of Supplies. 12pp, removed.
Warns, just weeks before the Custer massacre, of the
unhappy state of 13,000 Sioux Indians. $25.00

S259.   (SIOUX).   (House of Representatives Executive Document
          42, 44:1, Washington, 1876, 1st print.) Sisseton and
          Wahpeton Sioux Indians. 30pp, removed. Allotments
          of land to Sioux on Lake Traverse Reservation in Dakota.
                                                                 $20.00
S260.   (SIOUX).   (House of Representatives Document 184, Wash-
          ington, 1876, 1st print.) Military Expediton Against the
          Sioux Indians. 63pp, removed. Well-known but seldom-
          seen announcement regarding the Custer Massacre.
                                                                 $225.00
S261.   (SIOUX).   (Senate Executive Document 33, 45:2, Washing-
          ton, 1878) Message from the President ... information
          in relation to the cost of the late war with the Sioux
          Indians. 3pp, removed. $10.00
S262.   (SIOUX).   (House of Representatives Executive Document
          68, 47:2, Washington, 1883, 1st print.) Sioux Indian
          Treaties. 14pp, removed. Treaty text with names of
          signers. $10.00
S263.   (SIOUX).   (Senate Executive Document, 48:1, Washington,
          1884) Letter from the Secretary of the Interior ... Re-
          port of Commissioner of Indian Affairs Submitting Copies
          of Sioux Agreements to Cession of Land to the United
          States, with Correspondence Connected Therewith.
          69pp, 2pp, 1 map, removed. A good example of Gov-
          ernment-Indian political goings-on during the period,
          with correspondence from 1882 to 1884. A colored map
          is tipped in depicting locations of various reservations
          in the Dakota Territory circa 1883. $60.00
S264.   (SIOUX).   (House of Representatives Executive Document
          11, 48:1, Washington, 1883, 1st print.) Right of Way
          to Dakota Central Railway Through Sioux Reservation,
          Dakota. 11pp, removed. Agreement with list of Indians
          signing, including Red Cloud, Spotted Tail, Little Big
          Man, Red Shirt, Gall.
S265.   (SIOUX).   (Senate Executive Document 70, 48:1, Washing-
          ton, 1884, 1st print.) Sioux Agreements to Cession of
          Land To the U.S. 69pp, folding map, removed.
                                                                 $20.00
S266.   (SIOUX).   (Senate Executive Document 51, 51:1, Washing-
          ton, 1890, 1st print.) Reports Relative to the Proposed
          Division of the Great Sioux Reservation. 308pp, re-
          moved. Testimony and narratives of a great Indian peo-
          ple entirely dependent on the Government for food and
          land. $35.00
S267.   (SIOUX).   (Senate Executive Document 27, 53:2, Washing-
          ton, 1894, 1st print.) Letter from Indian Commissioner
          Concerning Treaties with Yankton and Dakota Sioux In-
          dians. 101pp, removed. Treaty of December, 1891.
                                                                 $35.00
S268.   (SIOUX).   (Senate Executive Document 59, 43:2, Washing-
          ton, 1894, 1st print.) Sioux Mixed Blood Question.

160pp, folding map, removed. Testimony attempting to clarify which Indians have rights to lands, etc. $35.00

S269. (SIOUX). (Senate Report 9, 55:1, Washington, 1897, 1st print.) Sisseton and Wahpeton Bands of Sioux Indians. 27pp, removed. Review of land treaties and text of new agreements taking more Indian land. $20.00

S270. (SIOUX PAINTINGS). Sioux Indian Drawings. 36 color pls loose as issued, folio (12" x 16"), Milwaukee Museum Primitive Art Series, No. 1, n.d. $65.00

S271. (SIOUX WAR). A Thrilling Narrative of the Minnesota Massacre and the Sioux War of 1862-3. 273pp, pls, photographs, illus, later cloth. Chicago, A. P. Connolly, 1896 (1st ed.). $90.00

S272. SIPE (C. Hale). The Indian Chiefs of Pennsylvania. 560pp, index, sources, chronology. Butler, PA, c. 1927 (1st ed.). $75.00

Contains an overview of the Indians and biographies of several influential personalities, including Cornstalk, Logan, Cornplanter, Shikellamy, Queen Allaquippa.

S272a. SIPE (C. Hale). The Indian Wars of Pennsylvania. 793pp, pls, folding map in rear pocket, bibliography, index, errata slip dated 11/16/30 tipped in, rear hinge cracked, cloth. Harrisburg, 1929 (1st ed.). $75.00

An account of the Indian events in Pennsylvania, the French and Indian War, Pontiac's War, Lord Dunsmore's War, the Revolutionary War and the Indian Uprising of 1789 to 1795.

____Another Copy. Same. Signed presentation of author. $75.00

S273. SITGREAVES (Lorenzo). (Senate Executive Document 59, 32:2, Washington, 1853, 1st ed.) Report of an Expedition Down the Zuni and Colorado Rivers. 198pp, pls, index, 1/2 calf, marbled bds, lacks large folding map volume. $100.00

Howes: S-521. Sabin: 81472. Field: 1414. Artist Richard Kern accompanied the expedition, contributing illustrations of the Mojave, Zuni and other tribes and their country. Lithographs by Ackerman, New York. (RMW)

S274. SIVIRICHI (A.). Derecho Indigena Peru Ano. 549pp. Lima, 1946. $35.00

S275. SKINNER (A.). (Museum of the American Indian, Notes and Monographs Vol. II, No. 4, 1920) An Antique Tobacco-pouch of the Iroquois. 12pp, 2 photographs. $12.00

S276. SKINNER (A.). (American Museum of Natural History, Anthropological Papers Vol. XIII, Part II, 1915) Associations and Ceremonies of the Menomini Indians. pp167-215, 2 figures. $28.00

S277. SKINNER (A.). (Milwaukee Public Museum Bulletin, Vol. 5, No. 4, 1926) Ethnology of the Ioway Indians. 173pp, illus, wrappers. $60.00

S278.   SKINNER (A.). (American Museum of Natural History,
        Guide Leaflet Series, No. 41, New York, 1915) The
        Indians of Manhattan Island and Vicinity. 54pp, 26
        illus, wrappers. $35.00
        ____Another Copy. Science Guide, 1947, 63pp. $25.00
        ____Another Copy. Same. $20.00
S279.   SKINNER (A.). (Museum of the American Indian, Notes
        and Monographs Vol. II, No. 5, 1920) An Iroquois
        Antler Figurine. 10pp, 1 photograph. $12.00
S280.   SKINNER (A.). (Museum of the American Indian, Miscel-
        laneous Publications No. 20, 1921) Material Culture of
        the Menomini. 478pp, 79 figures, 107pp photographs,
        cloth. $195.00
        ____Another Copy. Same. $85.00
        ____Another Copy. Cvrs soiled, ex-library. $65.00
S281.   SKINNER (A.). (Museum of the American Indian, Notes
        and Monographs No. 18, New York, 1921) Notes on
        Iroquois Archaeology. 216pp, 37pls, many are photo-
        graphs, 52 figures, 12mo, cvrs soiled. $60.00
S282.   SKINNER (A.). (Milwaukee Public Museum Bulletin Vol.
        II, No. 3, 1925) Notes on Mahikan Ethnology. 19pp,
        5pp photographs, wrappers. $25.00
S283.   SKINNER (A.). (American Museum of Natural History,
        Vol. XVI, Pt. IV, New York, 1919, 1st ed.) Notes on
        the Sun Dance of the Sisseton Dakota. The Sun Dance
        of the Plains Cree. pp271-385, wrappers. With: Notes
        on the Sun Dance of the Sarsi, Notes on the Sun Dance
        of the Cree in Alberta, by Pliny Earl Goddard, and The
        Sun Dance of the Canadian Dakota, by W. D. Wallis.
                                                            $20.00
S284.   SKINNER (A.). (Milwaukee Public Museum, Bulletin Vol.
        5, No. 1, 1923) Observations on the Ethnology of the
        Sauk Indians. 58pp, 1 full-page photograph, wrappers.
                                                            $45.00
        ____Another Copy. Hard Cover reprint, 1970, Vol. 5,
        Nos. 1, 2 and 3, 180pp. $25.00
        ____Another Copy. Same. $15.00
S285.   SKINNER (A.). (American Anthropologist Vol. XII, No.
        2, 1911) War Customs of the Menomini Indians. 16pp,
        2 photographs, inscribed by author. $15.00
S286.   SKINNER (S. A.) et al. (Editors). (Southern Methodist
        University, Contributions in Anthropology, 1969, 1st
        ed.) Archaeological Investigations Sam Kaufman Site,
        Red River County, Texas. 136pp, maps, pls, bibliog-
        raphy, large 8vo, wrappers. $10.00
S287.   SKINNER (S. A.) and GALLAGHER (J.). (Southern Metho-
        dist University, Contributions in Anthropology, 1974,
        1st ed.) Evaluation of Archaeological Resources Lake
        Whitney, Texas. 94pp, maps, pls, bibliography, large
        8vo, wrappers. $10.00
S288.   SKINNER (S. A.). (Texas Historical Survey Committee

Archaeological Report 21, Austin, 1971) Historical
Archaeology of the Neches, Saline, Smith Counties,
Texas. 45pp, illus, photos, drawing, map, bibliography,
wrappers. $15.00
___Another Copy. Same. $10.00

S289. SLIGHT (Benjamin). Indian Researches: or, Facts Concerning the North American Indians. 179pp, original
cloth. Montreal, for Author, J. E. L. Miller, Printer,
1844. $150.00
Field: 1421. "Expression of the personal experience
of a candid and thoughtful man, on the structure of the
Indian language." (RMW)

S290. SLOAN (J.) and SPINDEN (H. J.) et al. Introduction to
American Indian Art, to Accompany the First Exhibition
of American Art Selected Entirely With Consideration of
Esthetic Value. (2 parts). Part I: 59pp, 22 b/w and
9 color half and full-page photographs. Part II: 166pp,
67 b/w half and full page photographs, 1 color photo pl,
28 figures, cloth on Part I, Part II in original wrappers.
New York, 1931. $185.00
___Another Copy. Same. Part I only, original wrappers.
$70.00

S291. SLOBODIN (R.). (National Museum of Canada Bulletin 179,
1962) Band Organization of the Peel River Kutchin. iv,
97pp, 4pp photographs, 3 figures, 2 maps. $30.00
___Another Copy. Same. Cloth. $15.00

S292. SLOTKIN (J. S.) (Editor). (Viking Fund Publications in
Anthropology, No. 40, 1965, 1st ed.) Readings in Early
Anthropology. xvii, 530pp, notes, index, stiff wrap-
pers. $12.00

S293. SMAILUS (Ortwin). El Maya-Chontal de Acalan: Analisis
Linguistico de un Documento de los Anos 1610-1612.
234pp, wrappers. Mexico, 1975. $20.00

S294. SMILEY (Terah L.) et al. (University of Arizona Lab of
Tree-ring Research, Bulletin 6, Tucson, 1953) A
Foundation for dating of Some Late Archaeological Sites
in the Rio Grande Area, New Mexico. 66pp, photo-
graphs, bibliography, wrappers. $20.00
___Another Copy. Same. $10.00
___Another Copy. (University of Arizona Bulletin Vol.
XXIV, No. 3, 1955) 66pp, 4 photographs, 4 figures, 1
loose fold-out map. $20.00

S295. SMILEY (Terah L.). (University of Arizona Bulletin Vol.
XXIII, No. 3, 1952) Four Late Prehistoric Kivas at
Point of Pines, Arizona. 72pp, 12pp photographs, 9
figures. $25.00

S296. SMILEY (Terah L.). (University of Arizona Bulletin Vol.
XXII, No. 4, 1951) A Summary of Tree-Ring Dates from
Some Southwestern Archaeological Sites. 32pp, 1 figure,
1 loose fold-out map. $17.00
___Another Copy. (University of Arizona, Lab of

Tree-ring Research, Bulletin 5, Tucson, 1951) 32pp, folding map, bibliography, wrappers. $10.00

S297. SMITH (A. L.) and KIDDER (A. V.). (Carnegie Institution Publication No. 594, 1951) Excavations at Nebaj Guatemala. vi, 185pp, 42pp photographs, 2pp drawings, 34 figures, 8pp of plans. $145.00

S298. SMITH (Anne M.). (Papers in Anthropology No. 17, Santa Fe, 1974, 1st ed.) Ethnography of the Northern Utes. 318pp, illus, map, bibliography, 4to, wrappers. Ute origins, shelters, food quest, clothing, adornment, life cycle, Shamanism and curing, peyote, games, etc.
$20.00

S299. SMITH (Buckingham). Rudo Ensayo. Tentativa de Ana Previncional Descripcion Geografica de la Province de Sonora.... 208pp, bound in later 1/4 leather and bds, limited to 160 copies. St. Augustine, FL, (printed in Albany, NY) 1863, 1st ed. $300.00
Howes: S-578. Compiled by unknown author (Juan Nenivig) in 1762 with considerable useful material on Apaches and other Indians of Arizona and New Mexico. (TNL)

S300. SMITH (Clinton L.) and SMITH (Jeff D.). The Boy Captives. Being the True Story of the Experiences and Hardships of ... Among the Comanche and Apache Indians. 219pp, frontis, wrappers. Bandera, TX, 1927.
$125.00
One of J. Marvin Hunter's classic productions. The Smith boys were captured by the Comanches in 1869 and held until 1874.

S301. SMITH (C. S.). (American Museum of Natural History, Anthropology Papers, Vol. 43, Part 2, 1950) The Archaeology of Coastal New York. 116pp, 8pp photographs, 3 figures. $37.00

S302. SMITH (C. S.) and GRANGER (R. T., Jr.). The Spain Site.... pp79-128, 12 photo plates, 1 fold-out map, other maps, bibliography, printed wrappers. Offprint Smithsonian Basin River Survey Papers, Washington, 1958. $10.00

S303. SMITH (Daniel) and MEIGS (R. J.). Copy of Instructions Under Which the Articles of a Treaty with the Cherokee Indians Were Formed. 17pp, removed. Foxed. Treaties were negotiated in 1804 and 1805 at Tellico, GA. Washington, 1824, 1st print. $25.00

S304. SMITH (Decost). Indian Experiences. 387pp, illus, Caxton, 1943 (1st ed.) d.j. $85.00

S305. SMITH (Decost). Martyrs of the Oblong and Little Nine. Frontis, 310pp, illus, limited to 1000 copies. The Caxton Printers, Caldwell, 1948 (1st ed.), d.j. $50.00
____Another Copy. Same. $30.00
____Another Copy. Same. $10.00

S306. SMITH (Dwight L.) (Editor). Indians of the United States and Canada. A Bibliography. 453pp including index, list of periodicals cited, list of abstractors, map endpapers, introduction by John Ewers. Santa Barbara, 1974, (1st ed.). $20.00

Subject categories and an abstract of each article appearing in periodicals from 1954 through 1972.

S307. SMITH (E. H.). Ma-Ka-Tai-Me-She-Kai-Kiak; or, Black Hawk, and Scenes in the West. 299pp, engraved title and frontis, original cloth. New York, Edward Kearny, 1848 (1st ed.). $55.00

Field: 1001. "Epic poem of the Black Hawk war, Illinois and Great Lakes Indians, Massacre of Chicago, etc." (RMW)

____Another Copy. New York, 1849. $40.00

S308. SMITH (Edmond R.). The Araucanians; or, Notes of a Tour Among the Indian Tribes of Southern Chile. 335pp, illus, rebound in cloth. New York, Harper Bros., 1855 (1st ed.). $65.00

Field: 1449. These aboriginal warriors fought the Spanish fiercely for three hundred years to save their lands, and this is almost the only authentic study of them. (RMW)

S309. SMITH (G. Hubert). (River Basin Survey, Publications in Salvage Archaeology No. 9, Lincoln, 1968) Big Bend Historic Sites. 111pp, illus, wrappers. $20.00

S310. SMITH (Harlan) and FOWKE (Gerald). (American Museum of Natural History, Memoirs, Jesup North Pacific Expedition, New York, 1901) Cairns of British Columbia and Washington. pp55-75, plus 5 pls, folio (10" x 14"), newly rebound in linen. $100.00

____Another Copy. Same. $75.00

____Another Copy. Same. Ex-library. $65.00

S311. SMITH (Herbert H.). Brazil, the Amazons and the Coast. 644pp, 4pp ads, numerous illus from sketches by J. Wells Champney and others, folding map, decorated cloth. New York, 1879. $90.00

S312. SMITH (H. G.). (Florida Anthropological Society Publication No. 4, 1956) The European and the Indian, European-Indian Contacts in Georgia and Florida. iv, 150pp, 1 photograph, chart, 6 maps. $13.00

S313. SMITH (H. G.). (Florida Anthropological Society Publications No. 1, Gainesville, 1949, New York, 1970) Two Archaeological Sites in Brevard County, Florida. 32pp, 4pp of photographs, 2 figures, wrappers. $12.00

S314. SMITH (H. I.). (Canada Dept. of Mines, Bulletin 37, Anthr. Series, No. 8, 1923) An Album of Prehistoric Canadian Art. iii, 195pp, 84pp drawings. $47.00

S315. SMITH (H. I.). (Canada Dept. of Mines, Geological Survey) The Archaeological Collection from the Southern Interior of British Columbia. 72pp, 16pp photographs, 3 figures, cloth over original wrappers. Ottawa, 1913. $47.00

    ____Another Copy. Same. Original wrappers. $37.00

S316. SMITH (H. I.). (American Museum of Natural History, Memoirs, Vol. II, Part III, 1899) Archaeology of Lytton, British Columbia. pp129-161, 117 figures, 1pp photographs, 1pp illus descriptions, chipped wrappers, reinforced spine. $87.00

S317. SMITH (H. I.). (American Museum of Natural History, Memoirs, Vol. II, Part VI, 1900) Archaeology of the Thompson River Region, British Columbia. pp401-442, viii, 50 figures, 3pp photographs, chipped wrappers, reinforced spine. $97.00

    ____Another Copy. pp254-401, 3 pls, 48 figures, wrappers. $30.00

    ____Another Copy. Cloth, 8vo, New York, 1975. $33.00

S318. SMITH (H. I.). (American Museum of Natural History, Memoirs, Vol. IV, Part II, 1901) Cairns of British Columbia and Washington. pp54-75, 7 figures, 2 maps, 5pp photographs, 5pp illus descriptions, chipped wrappers, reinforced spine. $77.00

S319. SMITH (H. I.). (American Museum of Natural History, Anthropological Papers Vol. VI, Part II, 1910) The Prehistoric Ethnology of a Kentucky Site. pp173-241, 1 figure, 64pp photographs, tissue guards, some pages uncut, frnt wrapper missing, reinforced spine, otherwise VG. $67.00

S320. SMITH (H. I.). (American Museum of Natural History, Memoirs, Vol. IV, Part IV, 1903) Shell Heaps of the Lower Fraser River, British Columbia. pp133-191, 60 figures, 2pp photographs. $97.00

S321. SMITH (H. I.). (American Museum of Natural History, Anthropological Papers, Vol. VI, Part I, 1910) The Archaeology of the Yakima Valley. 171pp, 129 figures, 16pp photographs, rear wrapper missing, spine reinforced, otherwise VG. $89.00

S322. SMITH (H. I.). Noteworthy Archaeological Specimens from Lower Columbia Valley. pp297-307, 2pp photographs, offprint, American Anthropologist, Vol. 8, No. 2, 1906. $12.00

S323. SMITH (H. P., Jr.) and McDONALD (K.). (University of Texas at San Antonio, Center for Archaeological Research, Survey Reports, No. 12, 1975, 1st ed.) Archaeological Survey Freidrich Park, Bexar County, Texas. 10pp. $10.00

S324. SMITH (Huron). (Milwaukee Public Museum Bulletin Vol. 7, No. 1, 1933) Ethnobotany of the Forest Potawatomi Indians. 230pp and illus, wrappers, frnt cvr torn in half, contents VG. $20.00

S325. SMITH (James). An Account of the Remarkable Occurrences in the Life and Travels of Col. James Smith. xii, 190pp, index, ex-library. Cincinnati, Robert Clarke, 1870. $125.00

Field: 1440. One of the most exciting and informative books on frontier life in Ohio, Kentucky and Pennsylvania. Includes Smith's captivity by the Indians from 1755 to 1759. (RMW)

S326. SMITH (J. G. E.). Arctic Art: Eskimo Ivory. 128pp, 16 color photographs, 216 b/w photographs, 4 drawings. New York, 1980. $40.00

Two hundred superb ivory carvings from the collection of the Museum of the American Indian were exhibited in the fall of 1980. Every piece in the collection-- magnificent ivory objects from all periods of Eskimo carving--is illustrated in this catalogue. (EAP)

S327. SMITH (M.). The Technique of American Indian Beadwork. iii, 102pp, 4pp color photographs and 157 b/w photographs, 25 drawings. Ogden, 1983. $15.00

S328. SMITH (Marian). (Contributions to Anthropology, Vol. XXXII, Columbia University Press, 1940) The Puyallup-Nisqually. 336pp, illus, bibliography, index.

Scholarly account of the Coast Salish Indians of the Puget Sound region. $55.00

___Another Copy. Same. $40.00

S329. SMITH (Mary Elizabeth). Picture Writing from Ancient Southern Mexico: Mixtec Place Signs and Maps. 348pp, illus, index, map. Norman, 1973 (1st ed.), d.j.
$60.00

This large 9" x 12" richly illustrated book presents a comprehensive study of the surviving Mixtec manuscripts of the pre-Hispanic and early colonial periods, including an analysis of the methods used to recount history and the relationship of the pictorial signs to the Mixtec language. (GFH)

___Another Copy. Same. $40.00

___Another Copy. Same. $35.00

S330. SMITH (M. W.) et al. (Society of American Archaeology, Memoirs Nos. 6 & 7, 1950) Archaeology of the Columbia-Fraser Region. Also: Cattle Point. viii, 46p; xii, 94pp, 4 figures and 25 figures. $25.00

S331. SMITH (Nancy). (Museum of New Mexico Research Records No. 1, Santa Fe, 1966, 1st ed.) New Mexico Indians: Economic, Educational and Social Problems. 165pp, bibliography, wrappers. $10.00

S332. SMITH (Philip H.). Legends of the Shawangunk (Shon-Gum) and Its Environs.... 212pp, review copy. Considerable material on the Indians of this New York State Catskills Mts. area. Syracuse, 1965 (1st ed.), d.j.
$12.00

S333. SMITH (R. E.). (Middle American Research. Tulane University, Publication 20, 1955) Ceramic Sequence at Uaxactun, Guatemala. 388pp, 86pp of pls, 2 volumes.
$65.00

S334. SMITH (R. E.). (Peabody Museum Papers, Vol. 75, 1987)

A Ceramic Sequence from the Pyramid of the Sun, Teot-
hihuacanm Mexico. xviii, 375pp, 63 figures containing
photographs and drawings of hundreds of artifacts,
42 tables, 3 charts, wrappers. $70.00

S335. SMITH (R. E.). (Peabody Museum Papers, Vol. 66, 1971)
The Pottery of Mayapan (2 volumes). Vol. I: 276pp.
Vol. II: 179pp. 75 pls, sml 4to, wrappers. $40.00

S336. SMITH (Rex Alan). Moon of Popping Trees. 287pp plus
index, map, bibliography. New York, 1975 (1st ed.),
d.j. $15.00
Probably the most fair view of the Ghost Dance Craze,
the death of Sitting Bull and the battle of Wounded Knee.

S337. SMITH (Thomas Buckingham). A Grammatical Sketch of the
Heve Language: Translated from an Unpublished Span-
ish Manuscript. 26pp, loose in original wrapper, 4to.
Shea's Library of American Linguistics, New York,
Cramoisy Press, 1861. $95.00
Edition of 110 copies, this being one of 10 on large
paper. Pilling: 3641. Sabin: 84381. According to
Mr. Smith's introductory notes, the Heve, a dialect of
the Pima language, was spoken in the middle of the 18th
Century by the Eudeve, a people living chiefly in the
province of the Sonora. (CY)

S338. SMITH (V. G.). Izapa Relief Carving: Form, Content,
Rules for Design, and Role in Mesoamerican Art History
and Archaeology. vii, 103pp, 53 drawings, 1 map.
Dumbarton Oaks, 1984. $27.00

S339. SMITH (Watson) et al. (Contribution of Museum of the
American Indian, Vol. XX, New York, 1966) The Excavation of Hawikuh by Frederick Webb Hodge: Report
of the Hendricks-Hodge Expedition 1917-1923. xvi, 336pp
plus 26 figures and 34 pls, stiff printed wrappers.
Laid in is a Christmas card with a personal note signed
by Ross Montgomery, a printed compliments card of
Frederick J. Dockstader, Director of the Heye Foundation, and a letter typed from the director of the Peabody Museum. $60.00
____Another Copy. Same. $25.00
____Another Copy. Same. $25.00
____Another Copy. Same. $20.00

S340. SMITH (Watson). (Peabody Museum, Papers, Vol. 37,
Cambridge, 1952) Kiva Mural Decorations at Awatovi
and Kawaik-A, With a Survey of Other Wall Paintings
in the Pueblo Southwest. 500pp, 9 full-page and double-
page color serigraph pls, 53pp of collotype reproductions
of several hundred segments of Kiva mural paintings,
28 b/w drawings (mostly full-page) of hundreds of design elements. $77.00
A survey not only of the Kiva mural decoration at
Awatovi and Kawaik-A, but other wall paintings in the
Pueblo southwest. The quality of the prehistoric mural

art encountered and its subsequent analysis (and illustrations) in this report make this volume one of the most
important published on Kiva art. (EAP)
    ___Another Copy. Same. $75.00

S341. SMITH (Watson). (Peabody Museum Papers, No. 38, 1971)
Painted Ceramics of the Western Mound at Awatovi.
630pp, 300 photographs, drawings of over 2,000 ceramics,
designs, decorations, colors, maps and charts, wrappers.
    $60.00
    ___Another Copy. Same. $45.00

S342. SMITH (Watson) and ROBERTS (John M.). (Papers of
Peabody Museum of American Archaeology and Ethnology,
Vol. 43, No. 1, 1954) Zuni Law, a Field of Values.
ix, 175pp. $34.00
    ___Another Copy. Same. $20.00

S343. SMITH (White Mountain). Indian Tribes of the Southwest.
v, 146pp, 9 drawings, inscribed by author, cloth.
Stanford, 1933. $39.00

S344. SMITH (William). Relation Historique de l'Expedition, Con-
tre les Indiens de l'Ohio in 1764. Commandee Par le
Chevalier Henry Bouquet.... xvi, 147pp, 11pp; xvi,
128pp, 4 folding maps and plans, 2 engraved pls, includes the biography of Col. Bouquet by Mons. Dumas,
later half leather. Amsterdam, Marc-Michel Rey, 1769
(1st French ed.). $700.00
    Field: 1443. Bound with second title: "Remarques
Sur les Erreurs de l'Histoire Philosophique et Politique
de Mr. Guillaume Thomas Raynal." Brussels, 1783.
    ___Another Copy. Green Cloth. Cincinnati, Robert
Clark, 1868. $80.00

S345. SMITH (W. R. L.). The Story of the Cherokees. 229pp,
illus. Rader: 2946. Cleveland, TN, 1928 (1st ed.).
    $35.00
    ___Another Copy. Same. $25.00

S346. (SMITHSONIAN). U.S. National Museum Report for 1895,
Part II. (Includes) ... BOAS (Franz) The Secret Or-
ganization and the Secret Societies of the Kwakiutl In-
dians. pp313-738, 215 illus ... HOFFMAN (W. J.)
The Graphic Art of the Eskimos. pp739-968, 82 pls.
Volume is a.e.g., 1/2 leather. Washington, 1897.
    $150.00

S347. SMOLE (W. J.). The Yanoama Indians, A Cultural Geography. 286pp, 31 photographs, 11 figures, 13 maps,
16 tables, cloth. Austin, 1976. $25.00
    ___Another Copy. Same, d.j. $14.00
    ___Another Copy. Same. $12.00

S348. SMYLY (John and Carolyn). The Totem Poles of the Ske-
dans. 119pp, 4to, illus, wrappers. University of
Washington, Seattle, 1973. $25.00
    ___Another Copy. Seattle,1975, d.j. $15.00
    ___Another Copy. Cloth. Seattle, 1976. $27.00

S349. SNARKIS (Michael J.). Le Ceramica Precolombina en Costa
Rica. 136pp, 160 color illus, text in English and Spanish, wrappers, ex-library. San Jose, 1982. $20.00

S350. SNELLING (William Joseph). Tales of the Northwest.
254pp, introduction by John T. Flanagan. Early Upper
Missouri River Indian Life. Reprint of 1830 edition.
Howes: S-738. Minnesota, 1971, d.j. $10.00

S351. SNEVE (Virginia Driving Hawk). (HUNT, H. Jane, Editor).
They Led a Nation. 44pp plus index, portraits drawn
by Loren Zephier, bibliography, tall, wrappers. Sioux
Falls, SD, 1975 (1st ed.). $10.00
    20 great Sioux leaders pictured with biographies, in-
cluding Little Crow, Inkpaduta, Gall, Red Cloud, Crazy
Horse, Sitting Bull, Hump, Spotted Tail and American
Horse.

S352. SNODGRASS (M. P.). Economic Development of American
Indians and Eskimos, 1930-1967: A Bibliography, Bureau
of Indian Affairs. 263pp, 4to, wrappers. Washington,
1968. $25.00

S353. SNOW (Charles). (University of Alabama, Geological Survey of Alabama, Museum Papers, No. 15, 1941) Anthropological Studies at Moundsville. 59pp, pls, wrappers.
Includes "Possible Evidence of Scalping." $20.00

S354. SNOW (D.) and FORMAN (W.). Archaeology of North
America. 272pp, 169 b/w and 23 color photographs,
cloth. New York, 1976. $40.00

S355. (SOCIETY OF FRIENDS). Friends in Pennsylvania in 1791
and 1792. 4pp, 14pp, 2pp, later wrappers. London,
printed by James Phillips..., 1792. $400.00
    Sabin: 60624. Prints the appeal of Chief Corn Plant-
er of the Senecas, the Friends' response, as well as the
Friends' communications with the Cherokees, Creeks,
Chickasaws, and Choctaws. Corn Planter's address is
of special interest in that it relates his wish that two
Seneca boys, along with the son of his translator, be
taken by the Friends and educated. (WR)

S356. (SOCIETY OF FRIENDS). Some Account of the Conduct of
the Religious Society of Friends Towards the Indian
Tribes in the Settlement of the Colonies of East and West
Jersey and Pennsylvania: With a Brief Narrative of
Their Labors.... 247pp, frontis map in color, plus
folding map, original cloth. London, Edward Marsh,
1844. $275.00

S357. SOLA (Miguel). Historia del Arte Hispano-Americano:
Arquitectura, Escultura, Pintura y Artes Menores en
la America Espanola Durante los Siglos XVI, XVII y
XVIII. 431pp, 51 pls, 167 text illus. Barcelona, 1935.
      $25.00

S358. SOLA (Miguel). Historia del Arte PreColombiano. 244pp,
plus 32 pls, 105 figures, color fold-out pl, includes
MesoAmerica, Andes, Argentina. Barcelona, 1936.
      $35.00

_____Another Copy. Same. $30.00

S359. SOLANA (Nelly G.) and SHAVELZON (D.). Corpus Bibliographico de la Cultura Olmeca. 137pp, limited to 2,000 copies, original wrappers. Mexico, 1980. $15.00

S360. SOLLAS (W. J.). Ancient Hunters and Their Modern Representatives. 689pp, illus, 368 illus, cloth. New York, 1924 (3rd ed. revised). $22.00

S361. SOLORZANO (M. M.). Relacion de las Ceremonias y Poblacion y Gobernacion de los Indios de la Provincia de Mechuacan. 301pp of text, plus 43 leaves of illus on fine paper, cloth, marbled bds. Morelia, 1902. $175.00

S362. SOMMER (Charles H.). "Quannah Parker" Last Chief of the Comanches. A Brief Sketch. 48pp, photographs, map. Quanah, 1945 (1st ed.). $28.00

S363. SONNE (Conway B.). World of Wakara. 235pp, illus, index, bibliography, endpaper maps. San Antonio, 1962 (1st ed.). $12.00
_____Another Copy. Same. d.j. $12.00
_____Another Copy. Same. d.j. $10.00

S364. SONNICHSEN (C. L.). The Mescalero Apaches. 303pp, illus. Norman, 1958 (1st ed.), d.j. $45.00
_____Another Copy. Same. Fine w/o d.j. $28.00
_____Another Copy. Same. Frayed d.j. $30.00

S365. (SONORA INDIANS). Missionary in Sonora: The Travel Reports of Joseph Och, S.J., 1755-1767. Translated and Annotated by Theodore E. Treutlein. 196pp, illus with 2 maps. San Francisco, 1965. $25.00
Father Och arrived at the Sonora missions and worked with the Indians for eight years. His keen eyes and memory recorded many facts of life among the Indians.

S366. SORKIN (Alan L.). American Indians and Federal Aid. 223pp plus index, bibliography. Washington, 1971, (1st ed.) d.j. $10.00

S367. SORROW (William M.). (Texas Archaeological Salvage Project, No. 18, Austin, 1969) Archaeological Investigations at the John Ischy Site, Williamson County, Texas. 62pp, photographs, drawings, maps, bibliography, wrappers. $15.00
_____Another Copy. Same. $10.00

S368. SORROW (William M.). (Texas Archaeological Salvage Project, No. 11, Austin, 1967) Excavations at Stillhouse Hollow Reservoir. 148pp, photographs, drawings, maps, bibliography, wrappers. $12.00
_____Another Copy. Same. $10.00

S369. SOUSTELLE (J.). Arts of Ancient Mexico. 311pp, 17 color and 189 b/w photographs, 39 figures, cloth. New York, 1967. $45.00

S370. SOUSTELLE (J.). El Arte del Mexico Antiguo. 175pp text containing 39 figures, plus 189pp of b/w photographs and 17pp color photographs, cloth. Barcelona, 1969. $49.00

A Text (in Spanish) by a famed authority on the pre-Columbian art of Mexico and almost 200 pages of very good photographs make this large (9½" x 11¼") almost 20 year old volume one of the better and more handsome publications on the art of this area. The major sections are: Olmec, Teotihaucan, Maya, Zapotec, Gulf Coast and Xochicalco, Toltec, Toltec-Maya in the Yucatan; Postclassic art of Cholula, Tlaxcala and Oaxaco; Aztec. (EAP)

S371.   SOUSTELLE (J.). The Four Suns, Recollections and Reflections of an Ethnologist in Mexico. xii, 256pp of text containing 22 drawings of artifacts, map, plus 16pp of photographs, cloth. New York, 1970. $25.00
A fine mixture of reminiscence, detailed anthropology, history and philosophical reflection by one of Europe's leading Pre-Columbian scholars. Author studies the ancient Mayans and Aztecs as well as the present-day Lacandones and Otomi of Mexico. (GFH)
___Another Copy. New York, 1971, d.j. $14.00
___Another Copy. New York, 1971, d.j. $15.00
___Another Copy. New York, 1971, d.j. $12.00

S372.   SOUSTELLE (J.). Mexico. 285pp, 108 b/w and 76 color photographs of pre-Columbian art objects and archaeological sites. Archaeologi Mundi, Geneva, 1967. $50.00
___Another Copy. Cleveland, 1967 (1st American ed.) d.j. $12.00

S373.   SOUSTELLE (J.). The Olmecs. The Oldest Civilization in Mexico. 210pp plus index, drawings, photographs, bibliography. Interesting summary of what is known of this civilization. Garden City, 1984 (1st American ed.), d.j. $18.00

S374.   (SOUTH DAKOTA). (South Dakota State Historical Society Historical Collections, Vol. III, 1906, 1st ed.) 592pp, plates, index, ex-library, 6 articles, including "The Aborigines of South Dakota in 2 Parts." $65.00

S375.   (SOUTH DAKOTA). (South Dakota State Historical Society Historical Collections, Vol. IV, 1908, 1st ed.) 748pp, ex-library. 11 articles including "Aborigines of South Dakota, Part 2." $65.00

S376.   (SOUTH DAKOTA). (South Dakota State Historical Society Historical Collections, Vol. XV, 1930, 1st ed.) 730pp, illus, index. Articles include "The Sioux Wars (Part 1)." $85.00

S377.   (SOUTH DAKOTA). (South Dakota State Historical Society Historical Collections, Vol. XVII, 1934, 1st ed.) 654pp, index. 6 articles including "The Sioux Wars (Part 2)."
                                                  $85.00

S378.   (SOUTH DAKOTA). (Senate Executive Document 58, 52:1, Washington, 1892, 1st print.) Affairs of the Indians at the Pine Ridge and Rosebud Reservations in South Dakota. 185pp, large folding colored map, removed.
                                                  $35.00

S379. (SOUTH DAKOTA). (Senate Executive Document 32, 53:2, Washington, 1894, 1st print.) Schedule of Names of Settlers on the Crow Creek and Winnebago Reservation ... And the Amount of Damages Sustained by Them. 117pp, removed. $25.00

S380. (SOUTH DAKOTA). (Senate Document 28, 57:1, Washington, 1901, 1st print.) Agreement With Indians of Lower Brule Reservation. 16pp, plus folding map of reservation, removed. Treaty text and names of signers. $15.00

S381. (SOUTH DAKOTA). (Senate Document 31, 57:1, Washington, 1901, 1st print.) Agreement with Indians of Rosebud Agency. 43pp, removed. Treaty and signers. $15.00

S382. (SOUTHWESTERN INDIAN ART). (Peabody Papers, Vol. XLIX, No. 1, Cambridge, 1954) Clay Figurines of the American Southwest. 115pp, 51 photographs and 10pp of drawings of hundreds of figurines. Millwood, 1978 reprint. $35.00
   A scholarly, well-written, very interesting study based on eleven figurines found in northeastern Utah. The figurines are compared to others from the Southwest (from both northern and southern traditions and others from the Northern Pueblos) and figurines from outside the Southwest (California, western Texas, the Plains, Mexico). (EAP)

S383. (SOUTHWESTERN INDIANS). Indians of the Southwest: A Survey of Indian Tribes and Indian Administration in Arizona. First Annual Report of the Bureau of Ethnic Research, Dept. of Anthropology, University of Arizona. 129pp, wrappers. Tucson, 1953. $20.00

S384. (SOUTHWEST POTTERY). Vessel and Image: Prehistoric Southwest Indian Pottery. 32pp, 44 illus, wrappers. University of Colorado, Boulder, 1977. $10.00

S385. SPARKMAN (P. S.). (University of California Publications in American Archaeology and Ethnology, Vol. 8, No. 4, Berkeley, 1908) The Culture of the Luiseno Indians. 49pp, 1 pl. $29.00

S386. SPARKS (Col. Ray G.). "Tall Bull's Captives." 29pp, wrappers. Kansas City, MO, 1962. $10.00

S387. SPAULDING (A. C.). (University of Michigan, Museum of Anthropology, Anthropology Papers No. 18, 1962) Archaeological Investigations on Agattu, Aleutian Islands. 79pp, 27pp of photographs, 4pp drawings. $17.00

S388. SPAULDING (George). On the Western Tour With Washington Irving. The Journal and Letters of Count De Pourtales. Introduction and notes by Spaulding. xiv, 96pp, 16pp of illus, double-page map, bibliography, index. Norman, 1968 (1st ed.) d.j. $25.00

S389. SPECK (Frank G.). Catawba Texts. 109pp, cloth.

Columbia University Contributions to Anthropology, New York, 1934. $27.00

S390. SPECK (Frank G.). (Museum of the American Indian, Notes and Monographs Vol. 1, No. 5, 1928) Chapters on the Ethnology of the Powhatan Tribes of Virginia. pp227-455, folding map, 134 figures, 12mo, wrappers. $75.00

____Another Copy. Same. Rebound in cloth, ex-library. $50.00

S391. SPECK (Frank G.). Cherokee Dance and Drama. 106pp, illus, wrappers. University of California, Berkeley, 1951. $15.00

S392. SPECK (Frank G.). (Milwaukee Public Museum Bulletin Vol. II, No. 2, Milwaukee, 1920) Decorative Art and Basketry of the Cherokee. 16pp, 9pp of photographs and drawings of baskets, pottery designs, wrappers. $30.00

____Another Copy. Same. $25.00

S393. SPECK (Frank G.). (Canada Dept. of Mines, Anthropology Series No. 10, 1915) Decorative Art of Indian Tribes of Connecticut. 72pp, illus, wrappers. $30.00

S394. SPECK (Frank G.). (Canada Dept. of Mines, Geological Survey, Memoir 75, Ottawa, 1915) Decorative Art of Indian Tribes of Connecticut. 73pp, 9pp of photographs of baskets, 4pp of photographs of objects of material culture, cloth. $75.00

____Another Copy. Same. Stiff printed wrappers. $50.00

S395. SPECK (Frank G.). (Canada Dept. of Mines, Anthropology Series No. 1, 1914) The Double-Curve Motive in Northeastern Algonkian Art. 17pp, 25 figures, 18 pls, wrappers. Fine. $37.00

____Another Copy. Same. $35.00

S396. SPECK (Frank G.). (University Museum, Anthropological Publications, Vol. 1, No. 1, Philadelphia, 1909) Ethnology of the Yuchi Indians. b/w and color illus, rebound. $85.00

____Another Copy. 170pp, 78 photographs, 50 drawings, wrappers. Atlantic Highlands, 1979 reprint. $25.00

S397. SPECK (Frank G.). (New England Gourd Society, Boston, 1941) Gourds of the Southeastern Indians. Illustrations. $25.00

S398. SPECK (Frank G.) and HEYE (G. C.). (Museum of the American Indian, Notes and Monographs, 1921) Hunting Charms of the Montagnais and the Mistassini. 19pp, 5 pls, 12mo, wrappers. $25.00

____Another Copy. Same. Spine reinforced. $20.00

S399. SPECK (Frank G.). (Cranbrook Institute of Science, Bulletin 23, 2d ed., 1945, 1955) The Iroquois, A Study in Cultural Evolution. 95pp, 61 photographs. $15.00

____Another Copy. 1971 print. $12.00

S 400. SPECK (Frank G.). Naskapi; The Savage Hunters of the
         Labrador Peninsula. 250pp, illus, glossary, index, map.
         Norman, 1935 (1st ed.). $35.00
         ___Another Copy. Same. $30.00

S 401. SPECK (Frank G.) and ORCHARD (W. C.). (Museum of
         the American Indian, Leaflet No. 4, New York, 1925)
         The Penn Wampum Belts. 20pp, 4 pls with 2 in color,
         stiff wrappers, 4to. $35.00

S 402. SPECK (Frank G.). Penobscot Man: The Life History of
         a Forest Tribe in Maine. 325pp, 81 illus, map, cloth.
         University of Pennsylvania Press, 1940, d.j. $35.00

S 403. SPECK (Frank G.). Rappahannock Taking Devices: Traps,
         Hunting and Fishing. 28pp, 12 photographs, 16 draw-
         ings, map. University Museum, 1946. $10.00

S 404. SPECK (Frank G.). (From: Museum of the American In-
         dian, Notes and Monographs, Vol. 4, No. 3, July, 1927)
         River Desert Indians of Quebec. pp240-252, 8 illus,
         wrappers. $25.00

S 405. SPECK (Frank G.). (Heye Foundation, Indian Notes and
         Monographs, No. 44, 1928) Territorial Subdivisions and
         Boundaries of the Wampanoag, Massachusett and Nauset
         Indians. 152pp, 78 illus, 16mo, folding map, printed
         wrappers. $20.00

S 406. SPECK (Frank G.). The Tutelo Spirit Adoption Ceremony.
         Reclothing the Living in the Name of the Dead. xix,
         125pp, 5 photographs, 11 plans, blue gilt cloth. Penn-
         sylvania Historical Commission, Harrisburg, PA, 1942.
                                                          $57.00
         ___Another Copy. With: Transcriptions and Analysis
         of Tutelo Music by George Herzog. $15.00

S 407. SPECK (Frank G.). (University Museum, Museum Journal,
         Vol. 11, No. 1, Philadelphia, 1911) A Visit to the
         Penobscot Indians and Some Huron Treaty Belts and a
         Trip to Chichen Itza. 13pp, 2 drawings, wrappers.
                                                          $12.00

S 408. SPENCE (Lewis). The Gods of Mexico. xvi, 388pp, pls,
         illus, bibliography, index. Cvr wear, spine tears.
         New York, 1923. $15.00

S 409. SPENCE (Lewis). The Magic and Mysteries of Mexico; or,
         The Arcane Secrets and Occult Lore of the Ancient
         Mexicans and Mayas. 288pp, illus, pls, index. London,
         n.d. (1st ed.), edge wear to d.j. $15.00

S 410. SPENCE (Lewis). Myths and Legends of the North Ameri-
         can Indians. xii, 393pp, 32 full-page color pls, 4 full-
         page b/w photographs, 1 map, chipped decorated suede
         cvr. London, 1916. $47.00
         ___Another Copy. London, 1922 (4th print.), cloth.
                                                          $20.00
         ___Another Copy. New York, 1986. $25.00

S 411. SPENCER (Katherine). (Memoirs of American Folklore
         Society, Vol. 48, Philadelphia, 1957, 1st ed.) Mythology

and Values: An Analysis of Navaho Chantway Myths.
240pp, wrappers. $25.00
____Another Copy.   Same. $15.00
____Another Copy.   Philadelphia, 1971. $11.00
____Another Copy.   Same. $10.00

S412.   SPENCER (Katherine).   (University of New Mexico, Pub-
        lications in Anthropology, No. 3, Albuquerque, 1947)
        Reflection of Social Life in the Navaho Origin Myth.
        140pp, wrappers. $35.00
        ____Another Copy.   Same. $28.00

S413.   SPENCER (Oliver M.).   Indian Captivity: A True Narra-
        tive of the Capture of Rev. O. M. Spencer by the In-
        dians, in the Neighborhood of Cincinnati.   160pp, 12mo,
        illus, original half leather, marbled bds.   New York,
        Lane & Scott, 1849. $50.00
        ____Another Copy.   New York, Sundy School Union,
        n.d. (c.1850). $35.00
        ____Another Copy.   172pp plus index.   New York,
        1968, d.j. $18.00

S414.   SPICER (Edward H.).   Cycles of Conquest: The Impact
        of Spain, Mexico, and the United States on the Indians
        of the Southwest, 1533-1960.   609pp, drawings by Hazel
        Fontana, bibliography, index, cloth.   University of
        Arizona, Tucson, 1962 (1st ed.). $40.00
        ____Another Copy.   599pp, Tucson, 1967 (2d ed.).
                                                     $28.00

S415.   SPICER (Edward H.).   Pascua: A Yaqui Village in Arizona.
        Illus, folded charts.   University of Chicago, 1940,
        frayed d.j. $50.00

S416.   SPICER (Edward H.).   (American Anthropological Associa-
        tion, Memoir 77, Menasha, 1954)   Potam: A Yaqui Vil-
        lage in Sonora.   220pp, illus. $25.00
        ____Another Copy.   Same. $25.00
        ____Another Copy.   Same.   Good-Very Good. $12.00

S417.   SPICER (Edward H.).   (University of Arizona, Bulletin
        Vol. VII, No. 1, 1936)   Two Pueblo Ruins in West Cen-
        tral Arizona.   115pp, 57 photographs, 25 figures.
                                                     $20.00
        ____Another Copy.   Same.   Rebound in cloth. $30.00

S418.   SPICER (Edward H.).   The Yaquis; A Cultural History.
        394pp, maps, illus, notes, references, index, double-
        column print, wrappers.   Tucson, 1980. $15.00

S419.   SPIER (Leslie).   (University of New Mexico Publications in
        Anthropology, No. 2, Albuquerque, 1946, 1st ed.)
        Comparative Vocabularies and Parallel Texts in Two
        Yuman Languages of Arizona.   150pp, wrappers.
                                                     $10.00

S420.   SPIER (Leslie).   (University of Washington Publications in
        Anthropology, Vol. 2, No. 2, Seattle, 1927)   The Ghost
        Dance of 1870 Among the Klamath of Oregon.   16pp,
        1 map. $22.00

S 421. SPIER (Leslie). (American Museum of Natural History,
Anthropological Papers Vol. XXIX, Part III, 1928)
Havasupai Ethnography. 110pp, illus, folded maps in
pocket, wrappers, cvrs loose. Good. $25.00

S 422. SPIER (Leslie). (University of California, Publications in
American Archaeology and Ethnology, Vol. 30, 1930)
Klamath Ethnography. 338pp, text figures, wrappers.
Fine. $125.00

S 423. SPIER (Leslie). (American Museum of Natural History,
Anthropology Papers, Vol. 18, Part 2, 1917) An Outline for a Chronology of Zuni Ruins. pp207-331, 18
illus, folding map, wrappers. $45.00

S 424. SPIER (Leslie). The Prophet Dance of the Northwest and
Its Derivatives: The Source of the Ghost Dance. 74pp,
1 diagram, map. Menasha, 1944. $24.00

S 425. SPIER (Leslie). The Sun Dance of the Plains Indians.
Its Development and Diffusion. pp451-527, map. From
The American Museum of Natural History Anthropology
Papers. New York, 1921 (1st ed.). $12.00

S 426. SPIER (Leslie). (American Museum of Natural History,
Anthropological Papers, Vol. XXII, Part IV, 1918) The
Trenton Argillite Culture. 59pp, folded map, wrappers,
cvrs missing. Good. $10.00

S 427. SPIER (Leslie). (University of Washington, Publications in
Anthropology, Vol. 3, No. 3, 1930) Wishram Ethnography. 150pp, 13pp photographs, 9 figures. $67.00

S 428. SPIER (Leslie). Yuman Tribes of the Gila River. xviii,
433pp, 15pp photographs, 15 figures, cloth. University
of Chicago, 1933. $60.00
___Another Copy. Same. $35.00

S 429. SPIESS (Mathias). Connecticut Circa 1625: Its Indian
Trails, Villages and Sachemdoms. 29pp, large folding
map, printed wrappers. n.p. (CT Society of Col.
Dames), 1934. $18.00

S 430. SPIESS (Mathias). The Indians of Connecticut. 33pp,
wrappers. CT, 1933. $10.00

S 431. SPINDEN (H. J.). (American Museum of Natural History,
Handbook No. 3, New York, 1917) Ancient Civilizations
of Mexico and Central America. 271pp, 86 photographs
and drawings of hundreds of objects, cloth. $50.00
___Another Copy. 1922, (2d ed.). $40.00
___Another Copy. 1928 (3rd revised ed.). $40.00
___Another Copy. Same. $20.00
___Another Copy. 3rd and revised ed., 5th print.
$25.00

S 432. SPINDEN (H. J.). Indian Symbolism. 18pp, 40 figures,
wrappers. New York, 1931. $20.00

S 433. SPINDEN (H. J.). Maya Art and Civilization. xxxvi,
432pp of text containing 372 figures, plus 74pp of pls
and color frontis, revised and enlarged edition with
added illus, cloth, marbled bds. Falcon Wing Press,
Indian Hills, 1957. $85.00

S434. SPINDEN (H. J.). (Buffalo Society of Natural Sciences, Bulletin, Vol. 14, No. 11, 1928) Maya Inscriptions Dealing with Venus and the Moon. 59pp, illus, wrappers. $35.00

S435. SPINDEN (H. J.). (Memoirs of American Anthropological Assoc., Vol. II, Part 3, Lancaster New Era Printing, 1908) The Nez Perce Indians. pp165-274, 5 pls, bibliography, 17x25.5cm, wrappers. $35.00

S436. SPINDEN (H. J.). (Peabody Museum Papers, Vol. VI, No. IV, 1924) The Reduction of Mayan Dates. 299pp, 4pp photographs, 62 figures, spine chipped, repair to page 175-176. $85.00
____Another Copy. Same. Wrappers, tear to top of spine. $35.00

S437. SPINDEN (H. J.). Songs of the Tewa. 125pp, cloth. Also contains "An Essay on American Indian Poetry" and a appendix with the original Tewa Texts and explanatory notes. Exposition of Indian Tribal Arts, New York, 1933. $90.00
   Campbell: p.232. Saunders: 1978. Weigle: p.213. One of the excellent publications of the Exposition of Indian Tribal Arts which had John Sloan as president and other leading Southwestern artists on the editorial board. (TE)
____Another Copy. Same. Printed bds. $50.00
____Another Copy. Same. $35.00

S438. SPINDEN (H. J.). (Peabody Museum Memoirs, Vol. VI, 1913) A Study of Maya Art, Its Subject Matter and Historical Development. 285pp of text containing 286 figures, 29pp of photographs, fold-out map, cloth. New York, 1970 (reprint). $140.00

S439. SPINDLER (George). (University of California, Publications in Culture and Society, vol. 5, 1955) Sociocultural and Psychological Processes in Menomini Acculturation. 271pp, wrappers. Fine. $45.00

S440. SPINDLER (Louise). (American Anthropological Association, Memoir 91, Menasha, 1962) Menomini Women and Culture Change. 113pp, wrappers. $18.00
____Another Copy. Same. Fine. $15.00
____Another Copy. Same. Good-Very Good. $10.00

S441. SPINDLER (Will H.). Tragedy Strikes at Wounded Knee. 138pp, wrappers. Reprint with additional material. Vermillion, 1972. $10.00

S442. SPLAWN (A. J.). Ka-Mi-Akin. The Last Hero of the Yakimas. 436pp, three quarter calf and bds, stamped in gilt, port., Portland, 1917. $125.00
   Howes: S-838. Author spent over 50 years among the people about whom he wrote and many years gathering information for these excellent historical sketches. The Indian Side of the Yakima Wars of 1855-8. (RMW)
____Another Copy. Same. Light soil, corners bumped. $75.00

___Another Copy. Yakima, WA, 1958 (3rd ed.) 497pp.
                                                       $20.00

___Another Copy. Yakima, 1980, (4th print.) 508pp,
d.j. $20.00

S443. SPOEHR (A.). (Field Museum Anthropology Series, Vol. 33, No. 1, 1941) Camp, Clan, and Kin Among the Cow/Creek Seminole of Florida. 28pp, 1 figure. $16.00

S444. SPOEHR (A.). (Field Museum Anthropology Series, Vol. 33, No. 4, 1947) Changing Kinship Systems, A Study in Acculturation of the Creeks, Cherokee and Choctaw. pp151-235, 13pp illus. $29.00

S445. SPOEHR (A.). (Field Museum Anthropology Series, Vol. 33, No. 3, 1944) The Florida Seminole Camp. pp119-150, 8 figures, 5 full-page photographs. $23.00

S446. SPOEHR (A.). (Field Museum Anthropological Series, Vol. 33, No. 2, 1942) Kinship System of the Seminole. pp29-113, 15pp figures. $39.00

S447. SPOEHR (A.). (Field Museum Anthropological Series, Vol. 27, No. 2, 1940) Notes on Skidi Pawnee Society. pp67-119, 1 figure. $23.00

S448. SPOONER (Walter W.). The Back-Woodsmen; or, Tales of the Border. A Collection of Historical and Authentic Accounts of Early Adventure Among the Indians. 608pp, frontis, illus, pictorial cloth. Cincinnati, Chicago, 1883 (1st ed.). $80.00

S449. SPORES (Ronald). The Mixtec Kings and Their People. xvii, 269pp, 16pp photographs, 4 maps, bibliography, index. Norman, 1967 (1st ed.), d.j. $25.00
Study of the Mixtec Indians of northwest Oaxaca prior to Spanish entry into their lands in 1520 and their life under Spanish rule to 1600.

S450. SPORES (Ronald). (Vanderbilt University Publications in Anthropology, No. 11, Nashville, 1974) Stratigraphic Excavations in the Nochixtlan Valley Oaxaca. 79pp, illus, wrappers. $18.00

S451. SPRADLEY (James P.). Guests Never Leave Hungry: The Autobiography of James Sewid. A Kwakiutl Indian. 310pp, photographs, bibliography, index, autographed by Chief James Sewid. Yale, 1971 (3rd print.) d.j.
                                                     $12.00

S452. SPRAGUE (Marshall). Massacre: The Tragedy at White River. 364pp, photographs, map endpapers, index, bibliography. Ute Indian raid on White River Agency, in 1879. Boston, 1957 (1st ed.). $25.00
___Another Copy. Same. $20.00

S453. SPRANZ (B.). Kunst in Alten Mexico. 46pp, 29pp of photographs, 1 map. Freiburg, 1964. $10.00

S454. SPRATLING (W.). Mas Humano Que Divino, el Pueblo Sonriente del Antiguo Veracruz Retratado Intimamente por Si Mismo. 94pp, 25 full-page sepia and 40 full-page b/w photographs, 11 smaller b/w photographs, map, cloth. Mexico City, 1960. $35.00

S455.   SPRING (Samuel). Sermon Delivered Before the Massachu-
        setts Missionary Society, May 25, 1802, the Annual Re-
        port, and Several Interesting Things Relative to Mis-
        sions. 56pp, plain wrappers, stitched. Newburyport,
        1802. $25.00
            Speech by Red Jacket on the state of the Seneca
        Nations, pp51-56.
S456.   SQUIER (E. G.). (Smithsonian Contributions to Knowl-
        edge, Vol. II, 1851) Aboriginal Monuments of the
        State of New York, Comprising the Results of Original
        Surveys and Exploration With an Illustrative Appendix.
        iv, 188pp, 72 figures, 14pp maps and plans, cloth.
        (One of eight monographs included in this Volume.)
                                                          $165.00
        ____Another Copy. Same. $125.00
        ____Another Copy. Same. Rebound, cloth. $90.00
        ____Another Copy. Same. Original cloth, ex-library.
                                                           $75.00
        ____Another Copy. Above monograph only. $85.00
        ____Another Copy. Above monography only. $60.00
S457.   SQUIER (E. G.) and DAVIS (E. H.). (Smithsonian In-
        Institution Contributions to Knowledge, Vol. 1, Washing-
        ton, 1848, 1st ed.) Ancient Monuments of the Mississippi
        Valley.... 306pp, maps. Howes: S-861. Field: 1480.
        Larned: 588. $165.00
S458.   SQUIER (E. G.). Antiquities of the State of New York:
        Being the Results of Extensive Original Surveys and
        Explorations, With a Supplement on the Antiquities of
        the West. 343pp, 14 full-page pls, 80 engravings on
        wood, cloth. Geo. H. Derby, New York, 1851. $90.00
S459.   SQUIER (E. G.). Nicaragua: Its People, Scenery, Monu-
        ments, and the Proposed Interoceanic Canal. (2 Volumes).
        Vol. 1: xxiv, 424pp. Vol. 2: iv, 3-452pp. Numerous
        folding maps and pls, some are colored, cloth. New
        York, D. Appleton, 1856. $150.00
            Rich in illustrations and descriptions of idols, tem-
        ples, sculptures, utensils and the Indians of Nicaragua.
        Lithography by Sarony and Major, New York.
S460.   SQUIER (E. G.). Peru, Incidents of Travel and Explora-
        tion in the Land of the Incas. 599pp, frontis, numerous
        engravings, decorated cloth, rear hinge started, light
        edge wr. New York, Harper & Bros., 1877 (1st ed.).
                                                          $175.00
S461.   SQUIER (E. G.). Report Upon the Aboriginal Monuments
        of Western New York. pp41-62 in "Proceedings of the
        New York Historical Society," January, 1849, com-
        plete issue, printed wrappers, 622pp total. New York,
        1849. $10.00
S462.   SQUIER (E. G.). The States of Central America. 782pp,
        maps, pls, woodcut illus, cloth. New York, 1856.
                                                           $30.00

S463. STACY-JUDD (Robert B.). The Ancient Mayas: Adventures in the Jungles of Yucatan. 277pp, illus with photographs, no. 435 of 500 copies, inscribed by author.
Los Angeles, 1934. $75.00
___Another Copy. Same. Not signed. $60.00

S464. STAFFORD (Cora E.). Paracas Embroidery: A Study of Peruvian Tapestry Designs. Examination of perfectly embroidered textiles from 429 mummies exhumed at the Paracas site. 4to, New York, 1941 (1st ed.). $85.00

S465. STAGG (Albert). The First Bishop of Sonora. Antonio de los Reyes, O.F.M. 106pp plus index, illus, bibliography. The Franciscan attempting to reform the Indian missions after the Jesuits. Tucson, 1976 (1st ed.).
$10.00

S466. STANDING BEAR (Luther). Land of the Spotted Eagle. 259pp, photographs, drawings. Much on Sioux Indian life in the old days by this Sioux writer. Boston, 1933 (1st ed.). $30.00

S467. STANDING BEAR (Luther). My People the Sioux. 287pp, frontis, illus with drawings and photographs, decorated cloth. Boston, 1928. $60.00
___Another Copy. Same. $60.00
___Another Copy. Same. $45.00
___Another Copy. Same. $45.00
___Another Copy. Boston, New York, 1933. $40.00

S468. STANDS IN TIMBER (John) and LIBERTY (Margot). Cheyenne Memories. 309pp plus index, photographs, maps, bibliography. Fine history by a Northern Cheyenne who was born in 1884 and became self-elected keeper of the oral literature of his people. New Haven, 1967 (1st ed.), d.j. $25.00
___Another Copy. 1969 (2d print.), d.j. $17.00
___Another Copy. 1974, d.j. $35.00

S469. STANLEY (F.). The Apaches of New Mexico 1540-1940. 438pp plus index, author's presentation copy. Pampa, TX, 1962 (1st ed.), chipping and wear to d.j. $45.00

S470. STANLEY (F.). The Jicarilla Apaches of New Mexico 1540-1967. v, 376pp, limited to 500 copies, signed by author, cloth. Pampa, TX, 1967 (1st ed.), d.j. $55.00
___Another Copy. Same. Author's presentation copy.
$50.00
___Another Copy. Same. $45.00

S471. STANLEY (F.). Mescalero Epic. 20pp, wrappers. Nazareth, 1969. Well-written account of a building of a church on the Mescalero Indian Reservation. Limited to 400 copies, signed by author. $10.00

S472. STANLEY (F.). The San Ildefonso, New Mexico, Story. 23pp, signed by author, limited to 400 copies, wrappers. Nazareth, 1969 (1st ed.). $10.00

S473. STANLEY (F.). Satanta and the Kiowas. 377pp, index, photograph, bibliography, presentation copy, signed by

author. Borger, TX, 1968, d.j. Nice. $45.00
___Another Copy. 391pp, frontis, Jim Hess Printers,
Borger, TX, 1968, d.j. $40.00
___Another Copy. Same. Author inscription. $60.00

S474. STANLEY (Henry M.). My Early Travels and Adventures
in America and Asia (2 Volumes). 291pp, 414pp, 2
photogravure portraits, index. Indian conflicts and other materials during the late 1860s. New York, 1895
(1st ed.). $70.00

S475. STANWELL-FLETCHER (John F.). Eskimo: A Phrase
Book and Short Dictionary For the Enlightenment of Mem-
bers of the American Polar Expedition. 2pp, 42pp.
With: Useful Eskimo Words and Phrases. 4pp. Type-
scripts, carbon copies. Phrase book on letterhead:
The American Polar Basin Expedition. Both with signa-
ture of Melville P. Cummin, a member of the expedition.
N.p., n.d. $55.00

S476. STARKEY (Marion L.). The Cherokee Nation. 355pp plus
index, illus, bibliography. New York, 1946 (1st ed.),
d.j. $35.00
___Another Copy. Same. no d.j. $30.00
___Another Copy. Same. Dulled gilt lettering. $30.00

S477. STARR (Emmet). History of the Cherokee Indians and
Their Legends and Folklore. 672pp, photographs, map,
references, index. Howes: S-900. Rader: 2976.
Oklahoma City, OK, 1921 (1st ed.). $125.00

S478. STARR (F.). Catalogue of a Collection of Objects Illustrating the Folklore of Mexico. xv, 132pp of text containing 10 drawings, plus 32pp of photographs, cloth.
Folk-Lore Society, London, 1899. $60.00

S479. STARR (F.). Indians of Southern Mexico, An Ethnographic Album. 32pp of text, plus 151 leaves of photographs. Large oblong folio (10½" x 13"), cloth, limited
to 500 copies, numbered and signed by the author.
Chicago, 1899. $895.00
Palau: 332064. Starr, a noted anthropologist, surveyed the Indians of Puebla, Oaxaca, Morelia, Mexico
City and Tlaxcala and produced this work, considered to
be one of the finest of the genre and a major contribution to the advancement of photo-anthropology.
___Another Copy. Same. $650.00

S480. STARR (F.). In Indian Mexico. A Narrative of Travel
and Labor. x, 425pp of text, and 111pp of photographs,
cloth. Chicago, 1908 (1st ed.). $175.00
___Another Copy. Same. $100.00
___Another Copy. Same. $90.00

S481. STARR (F.). Notes Upon the Ethnography of Southern
Mexico (2 Volumes). Part I: 98pp, 72 photographs.
Part II: 109pp, 52 photographs. Wrappers. Davenport,
1900 and 1902. $80.00

S482. ST. CLAIR (Major Gen. Arthur). A Narrative of the

Manner in Which the Campaign Against the Indians in the
Year One Thousand Seven Hundred and Ninety-One was
Conducted, Under the Command of Major General St.
Clair ... and the Reports of the Committee Appointed to
Inquire into the Causes of the Failure Thereof. 20pp,
272pp, 24pp, subscribers' names and errata leaf. Re-
bound in half-heather, marbled bds. Portrait not is-
sued with this copy (included in some but not all copies
of this edition, Howes: S-24 does not list a portrait).
Philadelphia, 1812. $300.00
    Howes: S-24. Sabin: 75020. Field: 1349. Howes:
    "Attempt to vindicate his surprise and rout by Ohio
    Indians." (RMW)
    ___Another Copy. Same. $250.00
S483. STEARN (E. Wagner) and ALLEN (E.). The Effect of
    Smallpox on the Destiny of the Amerindian. 149pp plus
    index, bibliography, author's presentation copy. Boston,
    1945 (1st ed.), d.j. $10.00
S484. STEARNS (M. L.). Haidah Culture in Custody, the Mas-
    set Band. 335pp, 15 photographs, 6 figures, 45 tables,
    cloth. Seattle, 1981. $38.00
    ___Another Copy. Same. d.j. $25.00
S485. STEDMAN (Raymond Wm.). Shadows of the Indian.
    Stereotypes in American Culture. 273pp plus index,
    illus, bibliography. The projected image of the Ameri-
    can Indian in literature, art and popular culture. Nor-
    man, 1982 (1st ed.), d.j. $25.00
    ___Another Copy. Same. $20.00
S486. STEELE (Phillip). The Last Cherokee Warriors. 111pp,
    illus, map, bibliography. History of Cherokee outlaws
    Zeke Proctor and Ned Christie and their 'war' with the
    U.S. Government and Judge Isaac Parker during the
    1880s and 1890s on the Arkansas-Oklahoma frontier.
    Gretna, LA, 1974 (1st ed.), d.j. $25.00
    ___Another Copy. Same. $15.00
S487. STEELE (William O.). The Cherokee Crown of Tannassy.
    162pp, notes, bibliography, map endpapers. Winston-
    Salem, 1977 (1st ed.), d.j. $10.00
S488. STEELE (William O.). The Wilderness Tattoo. A Narrative
    of Juan Ortiz. 184pp, drawings, bibliography. Ortiz
    accompanied de Narvaez to Florida in 1527, was captured
    and adopted by the Timucuan Indians, joined DeSoto in
    1539 and served as his interpreter until his death in
    1542. New York, 1972 (1st ed.), d.j. $10.00
S489. STEELE (Zadock). The Indian Captive; or, A Narrative
    of the Captivity and Sufferings of Zadock Steele. Re-
    lated by Himself. To Which is Prefixed an Account of
    the Burning of Royalton. 144pp, 12mo, leather cvrd
    bds. Montpelier, VT, for Author, E. P. Walton, Print-
    er, 1818. $250.00
S490. STEEN (Charlie R.). (National Park Service, Archaeological

Research Series No. 9, 1959) Excavations at Tse-Ta'a, Canyon de Chelly National Monument, Arizona. 160pp, 46 figures, principally full-page photographs, wrappers. $30.00

    Another Copy. Same. Folding map. $15.00

S491. STEFANSSON (V.). Das Geheimnis der Eskimos, Vier Jahre im Nordlichsten Kanada. 272pp, 85 photographs, 2 fold-out maps, cloth. Leipzig, 1925. $80.00

S492. STEFANSSON (V.). My Life with the Eskimo. ix, 538pp, many photographic illus, 2 folded maps, original cloth. New York, 1921. $22.00

S493. STEFANSSON (V.) and WISSLER (C.). (Anthropological Papers of American Museum of Natural History, Vol. XIV, Parts I & II, New York, 1919, 1978 reprint) Stefansson-Anderson Arctic Expedition. 483pp, 139 illus, 3 fold-out maps, cloth. $80.00

    The 1908-1912 expedition to the Arctic--under the aegis of the American Museum of Natural History--provided a major advance in the knowledge then available on the Coronation Gulf Eskimo and the MacKenzie Eskimo. The text includes 95 illustrations of several hundred objects of material culture and a special paper by Clark Wissler, "Harpoons and Darts in the Stefansson Collection," which contains 44 illustrations of harpoon heads and darts from Point Hope, Point Barrow District and Franklin Bay District. (EAP)

S494. STEFANSSON (Violet Irwin). Kak, the Copper Eskimo. 253pp, decorated cloth. New York, 1927 (new ed.). $25.00

S495. STEGGERDA (M.). (Carnegie Institute Publication No. 434, 1932) Anthropometry of Adult Maya Indians, A Study of Their Physical and Physiological Characteristics. vi, 113pp, 8pp photographs, 3 maps. $75.00

    Another Copy. Same. $35.00

S496. STEGGERDA (M.). (Carnegie Institution Publication No. 531, New York, 1941, 1st ed.) Maya Indians of Yucatan. 280pp of text, plus 32pp of photographs, 35pp of figures, bibliography, index, errata slip, wrappers. Light wear and soil, hinges reinforced. $50.00

    Another Copy. New York, 1984. Cloth. $95.00

S497. STEINER (Stan). The New Indians. 438pp, illus, index, bibliography, endpaper maps. New York, 1968, d.j. $15.00

    Another Copy. Same. $12.00

    Another Copy. Same. $10.00

S498. STEINER (Stan). Spirit Woman. The Diaries and Paintings of Bonita WaWa Calachaw Nunez. xix, 243pp, color frontis, 37pp of paintings with 8 in color. New York, Harper & Row, 1980 (1st ed.), d.j. $25.00

    Another Copy. Same. $12.00

S499. STENDAHL (A.). Pre-Columbian Art. 32pp, 59

photographs, map. Exhibition Catalogue, Dallas Museum of Fine Arts, Texas State Fair, 1950. $10.00

S500. STENDAHL (A.). Pre-Columbian Art. 32pp, 46 photographs. Exhibition Catalogue, Lowe Gallery, n.d. (c.1955). $10.00

S501. STENDAHL (A.) and PRICE (V.). Pre-Columbian Sculpture. 32pp, 54 photographs. Exhibition Catalogue, La Jolla Art Center, 1956. $10.00

S502. STEPHEN (A. M.). Hopi Journals (2 Volumes). Vol. I: liii, 767pp, 409 drawings, 20 full-page color pls. Vol. II: ix, pp768-1417, figures 410-529, 5 full-page color pls, 10 fold-out maps (maps 5 and 7 are missing), blue linen and gilt cvrs, some rippling and very light water stains on upper and lower margins of Vol. I, otherwise this set of the most important and most comprehensive study ever published on Hopi ceremonies and material culture is in Very Good condition. New York, 1936. $650.00

Alexander M. Stephen's two journals of his late 19th Century travels and research in the Hopi country are one of the benchmark publications in American Indian studies, and represent the most complete study of Hopi culture. These two volumes, brim-filled with illustrations of ceremonies and rituals, masks, dances, and Kachinas, closely examines and illustrates virtually every aspect of Hopi ceremonies. (EAP)
____Another Copy. Same. Front hinge strengthened and small waterstain right corner last 21pp of Vol. 1. $450.00
____Another Copy. New York, 1969 Reprint. Cloth. $225.00

S503. (STEPHEN POWERS). (University of California, Archaeological Research Facility Contributions, No. 28, Berkeley, 1975, 1st ed.) Stephen Powers, California's First Ethnologist and Letters of Stephen Powers to John Wesley Powell Concerning Tribes of California. 94pp, 4to, wrappers. Includes "Life of Stephen Powers" by Susan Park, and "Letters of Stephen Powers" edited by R. F. Heizer. $20.00

S504. STEPHENS (John L.). Incidents of Travel in Central America, Chiapas and Yucatan (2 Volumes). 424pp, 474pp, engravings by Catherwood, foxed, rebound. New York, Harper Bros., 1841 (1st ed.). $150.00
____Another Copy. Same. Original gilt-stamped cloth. $225.00
____Another Copy. Harper Bros., 1848. (2 Volumes). Vol. I: xii, 459pp, 18 pls, 1 folding map, plan. Vol. II: xvi, 478pp, 46 pls, 1 folding map, plan. $135.00
____Another Copy. Harper Bros., 1852. Original decorated cloth. $200.00
____Another Copy. Rutgers University Press (2 Volumes)

346pp, 401pp, cloth backed bds. $20.00
___Another Copy. Rutgers University Press (2 Volumes in 1). $15.00
___Another Copy. Norman, 1973 (2 Volumes). Boxed, edited and introduction by V. Von Hagen. $25.00

S505. STEPHENSON (Mrs. Frederick C.). One Hundred Years of Canadian Methodist Missions, 1824-1924. 255pp, maps, map endpapers, index. Indian missions in the west and British Columbia. Toronto, 1925 (1st ed.). $35.00

S506. STERN (Bernhard). (Contributions to Anthropology, Vol. XVII, Columbia University, New York, 1934) The Lummi Indians of Northwest Washington: The Cycle of Life, Tribal Culture, Legend and Lore. 127pp, 5 pls and map. $75.00
___Another Copy. Same. Cloth. $57.00
___Another Copy. Same. Original cloth. $30.00
___Another Copy. Same. Rebound. $15.00

S507. STERN (Theodore). (American Ethnological Society, Monograph No. 41, Seattle, 1965) The Klamath Tribe. A People and Their Reservation. 365pp, illus. $30.00
___Another Copy. Same. d.j. $25.00
___Another Copy. Same. $22.00
___Another Copy. Same. $20.00

S508. STERN (T.). (American Ethnological Society, Monograph XVII, 1950) The Rubber-Ball Games of the Americas. vii, 122pp, 1pp of photographs, 7 maps. $30.00

S509. STEVENS (Frank E.). The Black Hawk War, Including a Review of Black Hawk's Life. 323pp, index, nearly 300 pls, cloth. Chicago, for Author, 1903 (1st ed.).
$75.00

S510. STEVENS (R. E.) (Editor). Wakefield's History of the Black Hawk War. 224pp, portrait, pls. Caxton Club, Lakeside Press reprint of 1834 edition. Madison. 1976, d.j. $30.00

S511. STEVENSON (James). Ceremonial of Hasjelti Dailjis and Mythical Sand Paintings of the Navajo Indians. pp229-284, drawings, colored pls of sand paintings, newly rebound. From: the 8th Annual Report of Smithsonian Institution, Bureau of American Ethnology, Washington, 1891 (1893). $15.00

S512. STEVENSON (James). Illustrated Catalogue of the Collections Obtained from the Indians of New Mexico and Arizona in 1879. Extracted from Smithsonian Annual Report, Washington, 1883. pp307-465, 350 illus, map, includes several lithographed pls in color of artifacts, rebound in wrappers. $60.00

S513. STEVENSON (James). Illustrated Catalogue of the Collections Obtained from the Pueblos of Zuni, New Mexico, and Walpi, Arizona, in 1891. pp511-606, pls, rebound. Removed from Smithsonian Institute Bureau of American Ethnology Annual Report No. 2, Washington, 1883 (1884). $27.00

S514. STEVENSON (M. C.). The Zuni Indians, Their Mythology, Esoteric Fraternities, and Ceremonies. 634pp of text containing 34 photographs and drawings, plus 139pp of color and b/w photographs and drawings. Cloth. Originally Smithsonian Institute Bureau of American Ethnology Annual Report No. 23, Washington, 1904. Glorieta, 1970 reprint. $95.00

Probably one of the most important and most comprehensive studies ever done on the ceremonies, customs and material culture of the Zuni, this volume has been out of print for years in both editions. The 1985 second reprint brings back into print this essential Southwest volume, with its fascinating text and its myriad of illustrations of ceremonies, dancers, kachinas, masks and other ceremonial objects.

____Another Copy. Same. $50.00

S515. STEWARD (John F.). Lost Maramech and Earliest Chicago. History of the Foxes and Their Downfall Near the Great Village of Maramech. Original Investigations and Discoveries. 390pp, illus, cloth. Chicago, 1903. $45.00

STEWARD (Julian H.). See also BAE Bulletin Nos. 116, 119, 120, 128, 136 and 143.

S516. STEWARD (Julian H.). (Bureau of Ethnology Anthropological Paper 18, Washington, 1941) Archaeological Reconnaissance of Southern Utah. 80pp, pls, text figures, folding map, printed wrappers. Spine fade, else almost fine. $15.00

____Another Copy. Offprint BAE Bulletin 128. $10.00

S517. STEWARD (Julian H.). The Blackfoot. 45pp, 16 illus and 10 pls, some being hand-colored maps, 4to, stiff wrappers. National Park Service, Berkeley, 1934 (2d ed.). $30.00

____Another Copy. Same. $25.00

S518. STEWARD (Julian H.). (University of Utah, Bulletin Vol. 23, No. 7, 1933) Early Inhabitants of Western Utah, Part 1--Mound and House Types. 34pp, pls, figures, maps, wrappers. $20.00

S519. STEWARD (Julian H.). (University of California Publications in American Archaeology and Ethnology, Vol. 33, No. 3, Berkeley, 1933) Ethnology of the Owens Valley Paiute. 108pp, 10pp photographs, 11 figures, 2 maps. $49.00

S520. STEWARD (Julian H.). Handbook of South American Indians (7 Volumes). Over 5,000pp contained in this 7-volume edition, hundreds of illus, cloth. Vol. 1: Marginal Tribes: Southern South America. Vol. 2: Andean Civilizations. Vol. 3: Tropical Forest Tribes. Vol. 4: Caribbean Tribes. Vol. 5: Comparative Ethnology. Vol. 6: Physical Anthropology. Vol. 7: Index. New York, 1963, reprint edition. $150.00

S521. STEWARD (Julian H.). Indian Tribes of Sequoia National

Park Region. 31pp, 2 hand-colored maps, bibliography, 4to, stiff wrappers. National Park Service, Berkeley, 1935 (1st ed.). $25.00

S522. STEWARD (Julian H.). (University of California Publications in American Archaeology and Ethnology, Vol. 24, No. 3, Berkeley, 1929) Petroglyphs of California and Adjoining States. 191pp, 73pp photographs, 92 figures, 49 maps. $87.00

S523. STEWARD (Julian H.). (University of New Mexico, Anthropology Series, Vol. 1, No. 3, Albuquerque, 1936) Pueblo Material Culture in Western Utah. 88pp, 7pp photographs, 15pp drawings. $39.00
___Another Copy. Same. $30.00
___Another Copy. Same. $15.00

S524. STEWART (Dorothy N.). Handbook of Indian Dances: Indian Ceremonial Dances in the Southwest, Vol. I: New Mexico Pueblos. 16pp including seven full-page color serigraphs illustrating the dances, a block-book, hand type-set, printed on pictograph press by author, inscribed and initialed by author, pictorial wrappers. Santa Fe, 1950 (1st ed.). $90.00
___Another Copy. Same. Owner's name. $75.00
___Another Copy. Same. $50.00
___Another Copy. Santa Fe, 1952. $15.00

S525. STEWART (Hilary). Cedar, Tree of Life to the Northwest Coast Indians. 192pp, 52 photographs and 571 drawings, 3 maps. Cloth. Vancouver, 1984. $39.00
From the giant red cedar trees came the raw materials used by the Northwest Coast Indians for their superbly crafted art and artifacts: masks, totem poles, bentwood storage boxes, dugout canoes, massive buildings, baskets, matting, clothing and scores of other objects. This abundantly illustrated book discusses how these objects were made and used, and examines their role in daily and ceremonial life. Heavily researched and containing more than 600 illustrations, this volume is the first major work to examine the use of cedar in Northwest Coast art and artifacts. (EAP)

S526. STEWART (Hilary). Indian Artifacts of the Northwest Coast. 172pp, numerous illus, mostly drawings, some photographs of pre-historic implements. Seattle, 1975. $35.00
From the Tlingit in the north to the Coast Salish in the south, this book spans the broad range of the Northwest Coast, depicting a wealth of stone, bone, antler and shell artifacts of the early Indian cultures.
___Another Copy. Same. d.j. $30.00

S527. STEWART (Hilary). Indian Fishing. Early Methods on the Northwest Coast. 179 double-column pp plus index, photographs, drawings, bibliography, oblong. Seattle, 1977 (1st ed.), d.j. $15.00

S528. STEWART (Hilary). Looking at Indian Art of the Northwest Coast. 111pp, illus, bibliography, index, wrappers. Both modern and traditional art. University of
Washington, Seattle, 1979. $10.00

S529. STEWART (T. Dale). (Field Museum Anthropological
Series, Vol. 31, No. 1, Chicago, 1939, 1st ed.) Anthropometric Observations on the Eskimos and Indians of
Labrador. 160pp plus index and 16 photographic pls,
map, bibliography, wrappers. $10.00

S530. STEWART (T. D.). (Middle American Research. Tulane
University Publication 31, No. 7, 1974) Human Skeletal
Remains from Dzibilchaltun, Yucatan, Mexico, with a
Review of Cranial Deformity Types in the Maya Region.
26pp, 4 tables, 10 figures. $10.00

STIRLING (Matthew). See also BAE Bulletin Nos. 117, 135, 138,
157, 164, 173, 186 and 191.

S531. STIRLING (Matthew and Marion). Archaeological Notes on
Almirante Bay, Bocas del Toro, Panama. pp225-284,
17 photographic pls, printed wrappers. Offprint Smithsonian Anthropological Papers, Washington, 1964.
$10.00

S532. STIRLING (Matthew and Marion). (Bureau of American
Ethnology, Anthropological Papers, No. 73, Washington,
1964) The Archaeology of Taboga, Uraba and Taboguilla Islands, Panama. pp285-348, 31 figures, plus
46pp of photographs, wrappers. $25.00
_____Another Copy. Offprint of same. $10.00

S533. STIRLING (Matthew). Indians of the Americas. 432pp,
many fine color illus and photographs. On Southwest,
Eastern, Northern and Arctic Indians. National Geographic Society, Washington, 1961. $17.00

S534. STIRLING (Matthew). (Smithsonian Miscellaneous Collections, Vol. 97, No. 5, Washington, 1938) Three Pictographic Autobiographies of Sitting Bull. 57pp, illus,
frontis of Sitting Bull from a photograph by Barry,
wrappers. A printing of the Kimball pictographic record
with 55 drawings, the Smith records with 21 drawings
and the Pettinger record with 13 drawings. $50.00
_____Another Copy. Same. $37.00
_____Another Copy. Same. $30.00
_____Another Copy. Same. $27.00

S535. (STOCKBRIDGE). (Senate Report 173, 58:2, Washington,
1904, 1st print.) Stockbridge and Munsee Tribe of
Indians. 39pp, removed. Allotment of lands in Wisconsin, with a review of treaty provisions. $15.00

S536. STODDARD (Amos). Sketches, Historical and Descriptive,
of Louisiana. viii, 172pp, 175-488pp, full leather.
Philadelphia, Mathew Carey, 1812 (1st ed.). $450.00
Howes: S-1021. Sabin: 91928. Field: 1505. Relation of Indians to French, Spanish and English conquerors, antiquities, Indian life and customs, and a

chapter on Indians as descendants of 12th Century Welsh settlers. (RMW)

S537. STOLL (Otto). Etnografia de Guatemala. 258pp, folding map, wrappers. Guatemala, 1958. $25.00

S538. STOLPE (H.). Collected Essays in Ornamental Art. South America. Atlas. 83pp, 16pp of finely executed drawings of clubs from Brazil and Guiana, 4pp of drawings of Peruvian and Chilean 19th Century shirts, 20pp of photographs, leather and bds, large folio (18½"x13"). Stockholm, 1927. $150.00

S539. STOLPE (Joh.). A Look at the Lummis. 28pp, illus, wrappers. Present conditions among this Northwest Coast Indian group. Bellingham, WA, 1972 (1st print. thus). $10.00

S540. STOLTMAN (J.). (Peabody Museum Monographs No. 1, 1974) Groton Plantation, an Archaeological Study of a South Carolina Locality. 308pp, 58 photographs, 35 tables. $15.00

S541. STONE (Doris). (Peabody Museum, Memoirs, Vol. IX, No. 1, 1941) Archaeology of the North Coast of Honduras. 105pp, 97 figures, almost all large photographs of objects. $125.00
____Another Copy. Same. Soiled cvr, chipped and repaired spine. $65.00

S542. STONE (Doris) and BALSER (C.). Arte Precolombino de Costa Rica. 49pp, text in Spanish and English, 22 tipped-in color photographs. Exhibition catalogue, San Jose, 1964. $15.00

S543. STONE (Doris). (Yale University Peabody Museum, Papers, Vol. XXVI, No. 2, Cambridge, 1949) The Boruca of Costa Rica. 50pp, illus. $35.00
____Another Copy. Same. $30.00

S544. STONE (Doris). (Middle American Research Series, Part 1 of Publication No. 8, Tulane University, 1938) Masters in Marble. 70pp, 31 illus, text figures, wrappers. About carved vases from the Ulua Valley, Honduras. $45.00

S545. STONE (Doris). (Peabody Museum, Papers, Vol. XLIII, No. 2, 1962) The Talamancan Tribes of Costa Rica. x, 108pp of text containing 1 map, plus 14pp photographs. $35.00
____Another Copy. Same. Ex-library. $30.00

S546. STONE (Eric). Medicine Among the American Indians. 125pp plus map and indices, photographs, drawings, graphs, bibliography, presentation copy of author, signed first name only. Shows some use. New York, 1932 (1st ed.). $25.00

S547. STONE (Livingston). Notes on the McCloud River Wintu and Selected Excerpts from Alexander T. Taylor's Indianology of California. Edited by Robert F. Heizer. 79pp, 4to, wrappers. Berkeley, 1973 (1st ed.). $15.00

S548. STONE (Martha). At the Sign of Midnight. The Concheros Dance Cult of Mexico. 255pp, b/w and color photographs, drawings, notes, index. Tucson, 1975 (1st ed.) d.j. As new. $20.00

S549. STONE (William L.). The Life and Times of Sa-Go-Ye-Wat-Ha, or Red Jacket. Second edition with index and memoir of the author added. 510pp, 5 pls, limited to 500 copies. Albany, J. Munsell, 1866. $90.00

S550. STONE (William L.). Life of Joseph Brant--Thayendanegea: Including the Border Wars of the American Revolution, and Sketches of the Indian Campaigns of Generals Harmer, St. Clair and Wayne (2 Volumes). Vol. 1: xxxiv, 428pp, lxxiv. Vol. 2: viii, 540pp, lxiv, 8 pls (2 folding), one facsimile, original cloth. New York, G. Dearborn, 1838 (1st ed.). $145.00
___Another Copy. New York, A. V. Blake, 1838, original cloth. Same collation, 2 volumes. $100.00
___Another Copy. Buffalo, Phinney & Co., 1851, original cloth, xxxii, 428pp, lxxiv; viii, 540pp, lxiv, 2 pls, 2 volumes. $60.00

S551. STORDEUR-YDID (D.). Harpons Paleo-Esquimaux de la Region d'Igloolik. 107pp of text containing 25 figures, plus 10pp photographs, wrappers. Paris, 1980. $15.00
___Another Copy. Same. $14.00

S552. STORM (Hyemeyotists). Seven Arrows. 371pp, first book about ancient ways of the plains people by an Indian. New York, 1972 (1st ed.), d.j. $35.00
___Another Copy. Same. $15.00
___Another Copy. Same. $10.00

S553. STORY (D. A.). (Texas Historical Commission, State Building Commission Report 13, Austin, 1968, 1st ed.) Archaeological Investigations at Two Central Texas Gulf Coast Sites. 72pp, illus, pls, maps, bibliography, large 8vo, wrappers. $10.00

S554. STOTT (M.). (National Museum of Man, Mercury Series, Ottawa, 1975) Bella Coola Ceremony and Art. 153pp, 11 illus, 16 pls, 4to, wrappers. $25.00

S555. STOUT (D. B.). San Blas Cuna Acculturation: An Introduction. 124pp, illus, wrappers. New York, 1947. $45.00

S556. STOUT (Joseph). Apache Lightning, the Last Great Battle of the Ojo Calientes. xi, 210pp, photograhic illus, notes, bibliography, index. New York, Oxford, 1974 (1st ed.), d.j. $15.00
___Another Copy. Same. $12.00
___Another Copy. Same. $10.00

S557. STOUTENBURGH (John, Jr.). Dictionary of the American Indian. 459pp, New York, 1940. $20.00
___Another Copy. New York, 1960, d.j. $12.00
___Another Copy. Same. $10.00

S558. STRALEY (W.). Archaic Gleanings. A Study of the

Archaeology of Nuckolls County, Nebraska. 49pp plus 9 pls (folding map), photographic frontis, copy #150 of limited edition, not copyrighted. Nelson, NE, 1909. $25.00

_____Another Copy. Same. #156. $25.00

S559. STRANAHAN (C. T.). (Senate Document 257, 56:1, Washington, 1900) Claims of Nez Perce Indians. 120pp, removed. Indian claims for services rendered as scouts, couriers and messengers under Gen. O. O. Howard during the Nez Perce War of 1877. $50.00

S560. STRATTON (R. B.). Captivity of the Oatman Girls: Being an Interesting Narrative of Life Among the Apache and Mohave Indians. 290pp, 2pp, illus, pls, map. Bit of fraying head and tail of spine, corners. Occasional foxing to contents. Howes: S-1068. New York, 1858. $250.00

_____Another Copy. Same. Original cloth. $75.00

_____Another Copy. Same. Heavy wear and soiling, 2pp glued back in, edge chips, complete copy in fair condition. $50.00

_____Another Copy. Same. No frontis, worn, foxed. Good. $50.00

S561. STREETER (Daniel W.). An Arctic Rodeo. 356pp, photographic illus, map, Smith Sound Eskimos of Greenland. New York, 1929. $30.00

S562. STRICKLAND (Rennard). Fire and the Spirits; Cherokee Law from Clan to Court. 260pp, illus, maps, bibliography, index. Traces Cherokee system of laws from ancient spirit decrees to fusion of tribal law with American law. Provides a brief review of Cherokee history and explains the circumstances surrounding the stages of development of the legal system. Norman, 1975 (1st ed.), d.j. $25.00

_____Another Copy. Same. $20.00

S563. STRONG (Emory). Stone Age in the Great Basin. 274pp, illus, index, glossary, endpaper maps. Portland, 1976. $25.00

Absorbing account of prehistoric Indian culture in Nevada. Profusely illustrated with photographs of archaeological findings.

_____Another Copy. Same. $12.00

S564. STRONG (Emory). Stone Age on the Columbia River. 254pp, 107 illus. Portland, 1959, d.j. $25.00

S565. STRONG (Emory) (Editor). (Oregon Archaeological Society, Portland, 1959) Wakemap Mound: A Stratified Site on the Columbia River. 38pp, illus, wrappers. $15.00

S566. STRONG (James C.). Wah-Kee-Nah and Her People. The Curious Customs, Traditions and Legends of the North American Indians. xiii, 275pp, frontis, gilt stamped pictorial cloth. New York, Putnam, 1893. $60.00

A discussion of many tribes from all areas of the

country, but the chief value is the material covering
the Northwest Coast Indians with whom the author had
much contact from 1850 to 1856.
    ___Another Copy. Same. Later cloth. $48.00
    ___Another Copy. New York, London, 1893, original
decorated cloth, some shelf wear. $60.00
    ___Another Copy. Same. Gilt decorated cloth, ex-
library with markings, bookplate, cardpocket removed.
    $25.00

S567. STRONG (Nathaniel T.). Appeal to the Christian Community on the Condition and Prospects of the New York
Indians.... 65pp, wrappers. Backstrip chipped away.
A Seneca chief speaks out against the tract circulated
by the Society of Friends attempting to revoke the recent treaty concluded between the Seneca and the U.S.
New York, 1841 (1st ed.). $40.00

S568. STRONG (W. D.). (Smithsonian Institution, Miscellaneous
Collections, Vol. 92, No. 14, 1935) Archaeological Investigations in the Bay Islands, Spanish Honduras.
vi, 175pp, 33 photographs, 38 figures. $55.00
    ___Another Copy. Same. $40.00

S569. STRONG (W. D.) and EVANS (C.). Cultural Stratigraphy
in the Viru Valley, Northern Peru. xx, 373pp of text
containing 81 figures, 18 tables, another 29pp of photographs, cloth. New York, 1952. $75.00

S570. STRONG (W. D.). (Field Museum Anthropology Leaflet
No. 24, Chicago, 1926) The Indian Tribes of the Chicago Region. 35pp, 8 pls, wrappers. $20.00

S571. STRONG (W. D.). (Smithsonian Miscellaneous Collections,
Vol. 93, No. 10, Washington, 1935, 1st ed.) An Introduction to Nebraska Archaeology. 315pp plus index and
25 photographic pls, illus, maps in text, bibliography,
wrappers. $20.00

S572. STRONG (W. D.). (Smithsonian Institution Miscellaneous
Collections, Vol. 97, No. 1, 1938) Preliminary Report
on the Smithsonian Institution, Harvard University
Archaeological Expedition to Northwestern Honduras,
1936. v, 126pp of text containing 32 figures and 16pp
of photographs. $35.00

S573. STRONG (W. D.). (University of California Publications
in American Archaeology and Ethnology, Vol. 21, No. 4,
1925) The Uhle Pottery Collection from Ancon. 72pp,
8pp photographs, 1 map, 11 figures. $40.00

S574. STUART (George and Gene). Discovering Man's Past in
the Americas. 211pp, approx 200 color photographs and
50 drawings, cloth. National Geographic Society,
Washington, 1969. $25.00

S575. STUART (George and Gene). The Mysterious Maya.
198pp, 150 photographs. National Geographic Society,
Washington, 1977. $15.00

S576. STUART (W. B.). (National Museum of Canada, Mercury

Series No. 3, 1972) Gambling Music of the Coast Salish Indians. 114pp, 2 figures, 2 tables, wrappers. $10.00

S577. STUBBS (S. A.). Bird's-Eye View of the Pueblos. xviii, 122pp, 20pp of aerial photographs of the pueblos, 22 figures, cloth. Norman, 1950. $34.00
___Another Copy. Same. d.j. $30.00
___Another Copy. Same. $25.00

S578. STUBBS (S. A.) and STALLINGS (W. S., Jr.). The Excavation of Pindi Pueblo, New Mexico. 165pp, 40 pls with multiple illus, 4to, wrappers. Santa Fe, 1953. $45.00

S579. STURTEVANT (W. C.) (General Editor) (DAMAS, D., Editor). Handbook of the North American Indians. Arctic. xvi, 829pp, 618 illus, cloth. Washington, 1984. $57.00
(See Note to following entry.)

S580. STURTEVANT (W. C.) (General Editor) (HELM, J., Editor). Handbook of the North American Indians. Subarctic. 853pp, 526 illus, cloth. Washington, 1981. $48.00
These two publications, part of a set that will eventually number 20 volumes, summarize the cultural (with particular emphasis on material culture) and historic knowledge of Eskimo peoples from pre-historic times to present. The writing, by teams of experts, is exceptionally good, and each of the two volumes is filled with hundreds of figures, including many from archival and old, out of print sources that illustrate several thousand artifacts. (EAP)

S581. STURTEVANT (W. C.). (Yale University Publications in Anthropology, No. 64, New Haven, 1960) The Significance of Ethnological Similarities Between Southeastern North America and the Antilles. 58pp, wrappers. $20.00

S582. SUN BEAR. Buffalo Hearts; A Native American's View of Indian Culture, Religion and History. 128pp, illus, wrappers. Healdsburg, 1970 (1st ed.). $10.00

S583. SUPHAN (R. J.). Oregon Indians II. 543pp, maps, cloth. Garland American Indian Ethnohistory Series, 1974. $35.00

S584. SUPREE (Burton). Bear's Heart: Scenes from the Life of a Cheyenne Artist of 100 Years Ago with Pictures by Himself. 64pp, oblong 4to, illus, full-page color drawings. Philadelphia, 1977 (1st ed.), d.j. $15.00

S585. (SUQUAMISH INDIANS). (Suquamish Museum, 1985) The Eyes of Chief Seattle. 56pp, 17 color and 64 b/w photographs, 1 map. $13.00

S586. SUSNIK (B.). Los Aborigines del Paraguay, IV, Cultura Material. 237pp of text, plus 95pp of b/w and color photographs. Museo Etnografico, Asuncion, 1982. $25.00

S587. SUTTLES (W. P.). Coastal Salish and Western Washington

Indians. I. 569pp, numerous maps, cloth. Garland
American Indian Ethnohistory Series, 1974. $35.00

S588. SUTTLES (W.). (British Columbia Provincial Museum,
Memoir No. 2, 1955) Katzie Ethnographic Notes. And:
The Faith of a Coast Salish Indian. 123pp. $24.00
___Another Copy. 1979. $10.00

S589. SUTTON (George M.). Eskimo Year. 321pp, illus. Norman, 1985 (2d ed.), d.j. $15.00

S590. SWADESH (Mauricio) et al. Diccionario de Elementos del
Maya Yucateco Colonial. 135pp, wrappers. Mexico
1970. $15.00

S591. SWADESH (Mauricio). Elementos del Tarasco Antiguo.
190pp, wrappers. Mexico, 1969. $15.00

S592. SWAN (James G.). (Smithsonian Institution Contributions
to Knowledge, No. 267) The Haidah Indians of Queen
Charlotte's Islands, British Columbia, with a Brief Description of Their Carvings, Tatoo Designs, Etc. 18pp
and 7 pls, with two in color, 4to. Washington, 1879.
$125.00

S593. SWAN (J. G.). (Smithsonian Contributions to Knowledge,
No. 220, Washington, 1870) The Indians of Cape Flattery, at the Entrance to the Strait of Fuca, Washington
Territory. ix, 108pp, 44 drawings of artifacts, first
published study of this Nootka people, later cloth binding. $185.00

S594. SWAN (James G.). The Northwest Coast; or, Three
Years' Residence in Washington Territory. 435pp, 4pp
ads, frontis, folding map, pls, original cloth. New
York, Harper & Bros., 1857 (1st ed.). $185.00
Howes: S-1164. Field: 1526. Very good copy of
this important book on Washington Territory and the
Northwest Coast, containing much information on Indian
life, ceremonies, language and condition. (RMW)

S595. SWAN (Michael). Temples of the Sun and Moon: A Mexican Journey. Illus. London, 1954, d.j. $20.00

SWANTON (John R.). See also BAE Bulletin Nos. 29, 39, 43, 44,
46, 47, 68, 73, 88, 98, 99, 103, 108, 123, 127, 132, 133,
137, 143, 145, 149, 164, 180 and 186.

S596. SWANTON (John R.). (American Ethnological Society, Vol.
III, Leyden, 1912) Haida Songs. With: Tsimshian
Texts by F. Boas. 284pp, cloth. $65.00

S597. SWANTON (John R.). (Smithsonian Miscellaneous Collections, Vol. 85, No. 7, 1931) Modern Square Grounds
Of The Creek Indians. 46pp, 15 figures, 5pp photographs. $23.00
___Another Copy. Same. Wrappers. $20.00

S598. SWANTON (John R.). The Quipu and Peruvian Civilization. pp587-596, printed wrappers. Offprint Smithsonian Anthropological Papers, Washington, 1943.
$10.00

S599. SWANTON (John R.). Social and Religious Beliefs and

Usages of the Chickasaw Indians. Extract from BAE
Annual Report, Washington, 1928. $30.00

S600. SWEET (J. D.). Dances of the Tewa Pueblo Indians. xi,
99pp, 16 color photos, 3 b/w, 1 drawing, 1 map.
Santa Fe, 1985. $15.00

S601. SWEZEY (Sean) and JAMES (Steven R.). (Contributions
of University of California Archaeological Research Facility, No. 23, Berkeley, 1975) Ethnographic Interpretations: 12-13; Socio-Religious Aspects of Resource Management, and Practices of Warfare Among California
Indians. 109pp, 4to, bibliography, map, wrappers.
$15.00

S602. SWINTON (George). Eskimo Sculpture. 224pp, over 150
illus, several in color, text in French and English, oblong 4to, signed by author. Toronto, 1965 (1st ed.)
d.j. $125.00
___Another Copy. Same, no inscription. $100.00

S603. SWINTON (George). Sculpture of the Eskimo. 251pp plus
index, photographs (some in color), map, bibliography.
London, 1972 (1st ed.). $45.00

S604. SYLVESTER (Herbert M.). Indian Wars of New England.
(3 Volumes). 528pp, 625pp, 703pp, indexes. Vol. 2
has "Cleveland," The Arthur H. Clark Co. pasted over
other imprint, original cloth, W. B. Clark, Boston,
1910 (1st ed. thus). $275.00
___Another Copy. Boston, 1910. Waterstains to in-
terior of Vols. 1 and 2 and to spine of Vol. 3. $75.00
___Another Copy. Cleveland, A. H. Clark Co., 1910.
Waterstains to Vol. 1, cvrs soiled, contents sound.
$250.00

S605. SYLVYANUS (G.). (Papers of School of American Archaeology, No. 11, Santa Fe, 1910, 1st ed.) The Correlation
of Maya and Christian Chronology. 12pp, wrappers.
$10.00

-T-

T1. TABIO (E.) and REY (E.). Pre-Historia de Cuba. 280pp,
25 illus, wrappers. Havana, 1966. $35.00

T2. TALBOT (Francis). Saint Among Savages. Life of Isaac
Jogues. 466pp, endpaper maps, cloth, a French Jesuit
born at Orleans in 1607, spent many years in Canada
as a missionary and was killed by the Mohawks in 1646.
New York, 1935. $20.00
___Another Copy. Same. $10.00

T3. TAMARIN (A.) and GLUBOK (S.). Ancient Indians of the
Southwest. 96pp, 64 photographs, written for younger
readers, a fine overview of an early culture. New
York, 1975. $15.00

T4.   TANNER (Clara Lee). Southwest Indian Craft Arts. 202
      double-column pp plus index, many photographs, several
      in color, bibliography, on baskets, textiles, pottery,
      silver, jewelry, kachinas, carving and minor crafts.
      Tucson, 1968 (1st print.). $25.00
      ___Another Copy. Same. $20.00
T5.   TANNER (C. L.). Southwest Indian Painting. xvii, 157pp
      plus 56 pls, illus (42 in color), map endpaper, decorative
      cloth. Tucson, 1957 (1st ed.). $135.00
          This comprehensive and sensitive presentation of In-
      dian easel art from prehistory to the 1970s, limited to
      2,250 copies, provides an in-depth study of 200 Indian
      artists from Arizona and New Mexico tribes. Considered
      to be the best study available on Indian painting of the
      Southwest, this important volume has an excellent, well-
      researched text and great illustrations of the best of
      Southwest Indian painting. (EAP)
      ___Another Copy. Same. $50.00
      ___Another Copy. Tucson, 1973. $70.00
T6.   TANNER (C. L.). Prehistoric Southwestern Craft Arts.
      226pp, 4to, illus, index, maps, bibliography. Tucson,
      1975 (1st ed.), d.j. $22.00
T7.   TANNER (Helen Hornbeck). The Ojibwas, A Critical Bib-
      liography. 78pp, wrappers, lists 275 works on the
      Ojibwas with introductory bibliographical essays. Bloom-
      ington, 1976, (1st ed.). $12.00
      ___Another Copy. Same. $22.00
T8.   TANNER (John). A Narrative of the Captivity and Adven-
      tures of ... During Thirty Years Residence Among the
      Indians in the Interior of North America. xxxiv, 427pp,
      edition of 2,000 copies. Ross and Haines, 1956 (reprint
      of 1830 ed.), d.j. $30.00
T9.   TANTAQUIDGEON (Gladys). (Pennsylvania Historical Com-
      mission, Harrisburg, 1942) A Study of Delaware Indian
      Medicine Practice and Folk Beliefs. 91pp, wrappers.
                                                          $15.00
      ___Another Copy. Same. $12.00
T10. TARAZONA DE GONZALES (S. G.) and BASCO (E. B. K.).
      Atlas Arqueologico del Estado Yucatan (2 Volumes).
      Vol. I: 249pp, 16pp of b/w and 5pp color photographs,
      5pp of site drawings. Vol. II: 36 folio-size (17½ x 13")
      pp, 18pp of maps, cloth. Instituto Nacional de Antro-
      pologia e Historia, Mexico City, 1980. $30.00
T11. TARAZONA DE GONZALES (S. G.). (Colleccion Cientifica
      Arqueologia, No. 62, Instituto Nacional de Antropologia
      e Historia, Mexico City, 1978) Codices Genealogicos,
      Representaciones Arquitectonicas. 65pp, 13pp of color
      photographs, 14 figures, wrappers. $12.00
T12. TATUM (Lawrie). Our Red Brothers and the Peace Policy
      of President Ulysses S. Grant. 366pp, photographs,
      foreword by Richard N. Ellis, reprint of 1899 ed., much

firsthand information on the southern plains Indians.
Howes: T-42. Rader: 3035. Lincoln, 1970, d.j.
$15.00

T13. TAX (Sol). The Civilizations of America. Selected Papers
of the XXIXth International Congress of Americanists.
viii, 328pp (38 papers), 35pp of figures. Chicago,
1951. $40.00

T14. TAX (S.) et al. Heritage of Conquest. 306pp, maps,
bibliography, index. Glencoe, IL, 1952 (1st ed.), d.j.
$15.00

T15. TAX (S.) (Editor). Indian Tribes of Aboriginal America.
(Selected papers of the XXIXth International Congress
of Americanists, held in New York, 1949) x, 410pp,
total of 48 papers, many of them heavily illus, about 60%
deal with Indians from Alaska to the Rio Grande; the rest
deal with Indians of Mesoamerica and South America, cloth.
Chicago, 1952. $57.00
___Another Copy. Same. $50.00

T16. TAX (S.). (Smithsonian Publications of the Institute of
Social Anthropology, No. 16, Washington, 1953) Penny
Capitalism: A Guatemalan Indian Economy. 230pp, folded
maps, wrappers. $25.00
___Another Copy. Same. $15.00
___Another Copy. Same. $15.00

T17. TAXAY (D.). Money of the American Indians and Other
Primitive Currencies of the Americas. 158pp, 31pp
photographs, 6pp drawings. New York, 1970, cloth.
$30.00

T18. TAYLOR (Colin). The Warriors of the Plains. 144pp,
4to, illus, index, bibliography, map endpapers. New
York, 1975 (1st ed.), d.j. $15.00
___Another Copy. Same. $12.00

T19. TAYLOR (Dee). (University of Montana Contributions to
Anthropology, No. 3, Missoula, 1973) Archaeological
Investigations in the Libby Reservoir Area, Northwest
Montana. 140pp, 4to, illus, wrappers. $18.00

TAYLOR (Douglas). See BAE Bulletin No. 119.

T20. TAYLOR (Douglas). The Caribs of Dominica. pp105-159,
6 photographic pls, bibliography, printed, wrappers,
offprint Smithsonian Anthropological Papers, Washington.
1938. $10.00

T21. TAYLOR (Edith). (Southwest Museum Leaflet, No. 20, Los
Angeles, 1947) Mohave Tatooing and Face Painting.
13pp, 16mo, illus, wrappers. $10.00

T22. TAYLOR (Graham). The New Deal and American Indian
Tribalism. The Administration of the Indian Reorganization Act 1934-45. 195pp, notes, bibliography, acknowl-
edgements, index. Lincoln, NE, 1980 (1st ed.), d.j.
$17.00

T23. TAYLOR (H. C.) et al. Coastal Salish and Western Washington Indians III. 422pp, maps, cloth. Garland American Indian Ethnohistory Series, 1974. $40.00

T24. TAYLOR (H. C.). Oregon Indians I. 326pp, maps, cloth. Garland American Indian Ethnohistory Series, 1974. $30.00

T25. TAYLOR (Mrs. H. J.). The Last Survivor. The Story of To-Tu-Ya (Foaming Water). 20, (2)pp, 1/2 cloth, bds. San Francisco, 1932. $15.00

T26. (TAYLOR, James B.). A Narrative of the Horrid Massacre by the Indians, of the wife and children of the Christian Hermit, a resident of Missouri, with a full account of his life and sufferings never before published. 24pp, frontis, bound in later 1/2 leather, Ayer: 214. Imprints Inventory: 280. Howes: N-14. St. Louis, 1840 (1st ed.). $1,500.00

T27. TAYLOR (J. G.). Netsilik Eskimo Material Culture, The Roald Amundsen Collection from King William Island. 173pp, 62 illus, 53 tables, 1 map. Oslo, 1974. $30.00
Obtained between 1903 and 1905 on Amundsen's Gjoa Expedition through the Northwest passage, this collection, the world's largest, of about 1,200 Netsilik objects is housed in the University Ethnographical Museum in Oslo, with small portions of the collection found in the Ethnographical Museum in Gergen and in the National Museum in Denmark. This out of print monograph--the only complete study of the collection--provides a description of the material and illustrates about 150 of its objects. (EAP)

T28. TAYLOR (L. A.). Plants Used as Curatives by Certain Southeastern Tribes. 88pp, wrappers. Botanical Museum, Harvard University, Cambridge, 1940. $45.00

T29. TAYLOR (W. E.). (National Museum of Man, Paper No. 1, Ottawa, 1972) An Archaeological Survey Between Cape Parry and Cambridge Bay, N.W.T., Canada in 1963. 106pp, 15pp photographs. $12.00

T30. TAYLOR (William, Jr.). (American Antiquity, Vol. 33, No. 4, Part 2, 1968) The Arnapik and Tyara Sites: An Archaeological Study of Dorset Culture Origins. 129pp, 27 figures of multiple stone artifacts, wrappers. $35.00
___Another Copy. Same. $18.00
___Another Copy. Same. $15.00

T31. TAYLOR (W. E.) et al. Masterpieces of Indian and Eskimo Art from Canada. 200+ unnumbered pp, text in French and English, b/w and color photographs, wrappers. Paris, 1969 (1st ed.). $30.00

T32. TAYLOR (W. E.). (Museum of Northern Arizona, Bulletin 30, 1958) Two Archaeological Studies in Northern Arizona. 30pp, map. $12.00

T33. TEAKLE (Thomas). The Spirit Lake Massacre. 317pp plus index, notes, references. Ayer Supplement: 124. Iowa City, IA, 1918 (1st ed.). $45.00

T34. TEBBEL (John) and JENNISON (Keith). The American Indian Wars. 320pp, illus, 22pp maps, bibliography, index. New York, 1960. $30.00

___Another Copy. Same. d.j. $12.00

T35. TEBBEL (John). The Compact History of the Indian Wars. 334pp, illus by Gil Walker, cloth. New York, 1966.
$15.00

T36. TEDLOCK (B.). Time and the Highland Maya. vii, 245pp, 32 illus, 4 tables, cloth. Albuquerque, 1982. $40.00
This account of the ritual life of the Quiche Indians of Highland Guatemala offers a rare glimpse at the importance of ancient religious symbols in the day world of the 20th century. There is such a wealth of new material and field data on native religious practices that this study has been called, "...a model of scholarship." This is a highly readable, well-written study that makes a major contribution to Mesoamerican studies. (EAP)
___Another Copy. Soft cover. $18.00

T37. TEDLOCK (Dennis). Popol Vuh. New Translations by Author. 380pp, with map and 26 photographs to illus text. New York, 1985, d.j. $20.00

T38. TEEPLE (J. E.). (Carnegie Institution Contributions to American Archaeology, No. 2, 1930) Maya Astronomy. pp31-115, 19 figures. $45.00

T39. TEICHER (Morton I.). (University of Washington, AES Proceeding, 1960, Seattle, 1960) Windigo Psychosis: A Study of a Relationship between Belief and Behavior Among the Indians of Northeastern Canada. 129pp, wrappers, 2d print. $27.00

T40. TEIT (J. A.). (American Museum of Natural History, Memoirs, Vol. II, Part V, 1906) Lillooet Indians. pp193-300, 38 figures containing drawings of several hundred objects of material culture, rock painting and tattooing, cloth, 8vo. New York, 1975 (reprint). $40.00

T41. TEIT (James). (American Museum of Natural History, Memoirs Vol. II, Anthropology I, 1900 Jesup Expedition, IV) The Thompson Indians of British Columbia. pp165-392, figures, nos. 118-294, folio (11"x14"), wrappers, sml piece lacking, soiled, chipped. $150.00

T42. TEJERO CASTILLO (N.) et al. (Instituto Nacional de Antropologia e Historia, Corpus Antiquitatum Americanensium, Mexico City, 1975) Mexico VIII. Ofrendas Mexicas en el Museum National de Antropologia. 156pp of text in Spanish and English, 50pp photographs.
$12.00

T43. TELLECHEA (Manuel). Compendio Gramatical Para la Inteligencia del Idioma Tarahumar.... Octavo, stiff vellum with ties, full page engraving of a priest giving the "Good Word" to the Indians. Inscribed by author. Mexico, 1826. $900.00
Vinaza: 419. Garcia Icazbalceta; Apuntes: 76. Sabin: 94615. Palau, 329425. Tellechea, a missionary to the Tarahumara Indians in the northern Mexican state

of Chihuahua, includes not only a grammar useful for learning the Tarahumara language but also sermons, dialogues and a catechism for use in converting the Indians. (WR)

T 44. TELLO (J. C.). Antigo Peru. Primera Epoca. 183pp, 116 photographs and drawings of artifacts, 3 fold-out pls, 2 fold-out maps. Lima, 1929. $40.00

T 45. TELLO (J. C.). Arqueologia del Valle de Casma: Culturas Chavin, Santa o Huaylas Yunga y Sub-Chimu. 345pp, illus, folded charts,wrappers. Lima, 1956. $45.00

T 46. TELLO (J. C.). Paracas. Primera Parte. 307pp, 93 full-page (14"x10"), color pls, 143 b/w photographs, 117 figures, cloth. Publicacion del Proyecto 86 del Programa 1941-42 de The Institute of Andean Research de NY. Lima, 1959. $175.00

T 47. TEMPLE (W. C.). (Illinois State Museum Papers Vol. II, Part 2, 1958) Indian Villages of the Illinois Country, Historic Tribes. 218pp, 4 photographs. $27.00

T 48. (TENAYUCA). Tenayuca: Estudio Arqueologico de la Piramide de Este Lugar. Over 200 illus, numerous pls with several in color, folding plans, 4to, wrappers, multiple studies by various authors, including Roque J. Ceballos Novelo, Enrique Juan Palacios. Mexico, 1935. $175.00

T 49. (TEOTIHUACAN). La Poblacion del Valle de Teotihuacan. Introduccion, Sintesis y Conclusiones por Manuel Gamio. 100pp, 66 illus, 4 are folding, folding map, newly rebound, slight water stains to some pp. Mexico, 1922. $125.00

T50. TERADA (K.). Excavations at La Pampa in the North Highlands of Peru, 1975. Report 1 of the Japanese Scientific Expedition to Nuclear America. xii, 323pp, 47 figures plus 129pp of photographs and drawings and 32 tables and charts. Cloth. Tokyo, 1979. $195.00

In order to investigate the origins of culture in the Andean region, a group of Japanese scientists conducted a series of archaeological surveys over a period of nearly two decades. These three large volumes (each is $8\frac{1}{2}$"x 12") (See T-51 and T-52) describe in extraordinary detail the results of several of the excavations done in the 1970s. Each volume--considered to be among the most important on the archaeology of these sites--features descriptions and illustrations of objects excavated layer by layer, and develops a theoretical framework for their significance. (EAP)

T51. TERADA (K.) and ONUKI (Y.). Excavations at Huacaloma in the Cajamarca Valley, Peru, 1979. Report 2 of the Japanese Scientific Expedition to Nuclear America. xiv, 351pp, 68 figures plus 135pp of photographs and drawings and 35 tables, cloth. Tokyo, 1982. $225.00

See T-50.

T52.   TERADA (K.) and ONUKI (Y.). The Formative Period in
the Cajamarca Basin, Peru: Excavations at Huacaloma and
Layzon, 1982. Report 3 of the Japanese Scientific Expedition to Nuclear America. xxii, 491pp, 124 figures
plus 146pp of photographs and drawings and 147 tables,
cloth. Tokyo, 1985. $225.00
See T-50.

T53.   TERMER (F.). (Hamburg Museum fur Volkerkunde, Monographs VIII, 1973) Palo Gordo, Ein Beitrag Zur Archaeo-
gie des Pazifschen Guatemala. 251pp, 144 b/w photographs, 21pp of color pls, 17pp of drawings. $90.00

T54.   TERRELL (John Upton). American Indian Almanac. 495pp,
maps, cloth. New York, 1971. $10.00

T55.   TERRELL (John Upton). Apache Chronicle. 411pp, illus,
index, bibliography, maps. New York, 1972 (1st ed.),
d.j. $15.00
___Another Copy. Same. $12.00

T56.   TERRELL (J. U.). The Arrow and the Cross. A History
of the American Indian and the Missionaries. 253pp,
notes, bibliography. Santa Barbara, 1979 (1st ed.),
d.j. $25.00
___Another Copy. Same. $15.00

T57.   TERRELL (J. U.). Black Robe: The Life of Pierre-Jean
DeSmet, Missionary, Explorer, Pioneer. 381pp, endpaper maps. New York, 1964. $20.00

T58.   TERRELL (J. U.). Indian Women of the Western Morning.
214pp, selected bibliography, index, a comprehensive
study of the Indian women's life in early America. New
York, 1974 (1st print.), d.j. $15.00

T59.   TERRELL (J. U.). The Navajos. The Past and Present of
a Great People. 299pp, map, bibliography, index. New
York, 1970 (1st ed.), d.j. $10.00

T60.   TERRELL (J. U.). The Plains Apache. 227pp plus index,
maps, notes, bibliography, covers some 30 years and the
many different groups that made up the Plains Apaches.
New York, 1975 (1st ed.), d.j. $15.00
___Another Copy. Same. $12.00
___Another Copy. Same. $10.00

T61.   TERRELL (J. U.). Pueblos, Gods and Spaniards. 350pp
plus index, maps, bibliography, explorers and conquis-
tadores up to time of reconquest. New York, 1973 (1st
ed.), d.j. $17.00

T62.   TERRELL (J. U.). Sioux Trail. 213pp. New York, 1974.
                                                       $20.00
___Another Copy. Same. $15.00
___Another Copy. Same. $10.00

T63.   TERRELL (J. U.). Traders of the Western Morning. Commerce in Precolumbian North America. With Introduction
by Carl S. Dentzel. 129pp, frontis, illus with 4 maps.
bibliography, index, cloth. Southwest Museum, Los
Angeles, 1967 (1st ed.). $25.00

T64. (TERRITORY). (House of Representatives Document 509, 59:2, Washington, 1907, 1st print.) Indian Territory-- Forest Reserve. 20pp, large folding color map, removed. $17.00

T65. TERRY (James). Sculptured Anthropoid Ape Heads, Found in or Near the Valley of the John Day River, A Tributary of the Columbia River, Oregon. xv, 5 full-page pls that are lithographed, 4to, cloth. New York, 1891. $45.00

T66. (TETON DAKOTA INDIANS). (House of Representatives Executive Document 96, 42:3, Washington, 1873) Letter from the Secretary of the Interior relative to the condition, location ... of the Teton Dakota. 16pp, removed, wrappers. $23.00

T67. (TEWA BASIN PUEBLOS). Tewa Basin Studies. The Indian Pueblos. Vol. I ... with ... Spanish American Villages, Vol. II (Parts I and II) with ... Physical Surveys. (4 volumes). 124pp, 143pp, 275pp, 156pp, maps, thick quarto, cloth backed limp bds, mimeographed. n.p., 1935. $350.00
   A most impressive, interesting and important work compiled under the auspices of the Indian Land Research Unit of the Office of Indian Affairs, funded by the Federal Emergency Relief Administration. An extensive physical and sociological analysis of the region, volume one treating the Tewa Pueblos as an entity, the second volume (in two parts) treating the Spanish-American village, and the final volume treating the physical aspects of the region, including extensive reference to sheep and cattle raising. Volume one includes a chapter on Tewa pottery, largely about Maria Martinez. (WR)

T68. (TEWA INDIANS). The Tewa World: Space, Time, Being and Becoming in a Pueblo Society. 197pp, 11 figures. Chicago, 1969. $25.00

T69. (TEXAS). (Lower Plains Archaeological Society, Bulletin 1, Midland, 1970, 1st print.) 53pp, maps, illus, bibliography, wrappers, articles include: Man and Flint; Archaeology of Lamb County, Texas, etc. $10.00

T70. (TEXAS). (Lower Plains Archaeological Society, Bulletin 2, Midland, 1972, 1st ed.) 71pp, maps, illus, bibliography, wrappers, articles include: Flake Blades ... W. San Saba County, etc. $10.00

T71. (TEXAS). (Lower Plains Archaeological Society. Bulletin 3, Midland, 1973, 1st ed.) 72pp, maps, illus, bibliography, wrappers. Articles include: Why Kill More Bison...., etc. $10.00

T72. (TEXAS). (Geological Society of America, Bulletin 51, New York, 1940) Pleistocene Artifacts ... Associated Fossils From Bee County, Texas, with: New Pliocene Mastodon. pp1627-1664, pls, figure, wrappers. $12.00

T73. (TEXAS). (Texas Historical Commission, Survey Reports No. 7, Austin, 1970, 1st ed.) Texarkana Reservoir

Enlargement. 92pp, illus, maps, bibliography, large
8vo, wrappers. $12.00

T74. (TEXAS). (Texas Archaeological Society, Bulletin 16,
Abilene, 1945, 1st ed.) 158pp, illus, original wrappers,
8vo, articles include: Mid-Ouachita Pottery; Boat-Shaped
Objects from Val Verde and Bosque Counties; Bone Im-
plement Burial, Collin County, etc. $20.00

T75. (TEXAS). (Texas Archaeological Society, Bulletin 19,
Lubbock, 1948, 1st ed.) 192pp, illus, original wrappers,
8vo, articles include: Merrell Site; McGee Bend Reser-
voir; Archaeological Reconn. in No. Coahuila; Caddoan
Prehistory; Recent Archaeology Research in Oklahoma;
"Gilmore Corridor," etc. $20.00

T76. (TEXAS). (Texas Archaeological Society, Bulletin 28,
Austin, 1957, 1st ed.) 318pp, illus, original wrappers,
8vo, articles include: Early Man Near Lewisville; Williamson County Mound Material; Grace Creek Site; Historic
Indian House in Washington County, etc. $17.00

T77. (TEXAS). (Texas Archaeological Society, Bulletin 29,
Austin, 1958, 1st ed.) 254pp, illus, 8vo, original wrap-
pers, articles include Indian Tribes of Texas; N.E.,
Central, Coastal and Trans-Pecos Texas Archaeology;
Guide to Texas Archaeology Literature, etc. $20.00

T78. (TEXAS). (Texas Archaeological Society, Bulletin 30,
Austin, 1969, 1st ed.) 327pp, illus, 8vo, original wrap-
pers, articles include Indian Grinding Stones of Eastern
Texas; Archaic Material from North America; Devil's
Mouth Site; Coahuiltecan Ethnography, etc. $15.00

T79. (TEXAS). (Texas Archaeological Society, Bulletin 31,
Austin, 1960, 1st ed.) 345pp, illus, original wrappers,
8vo, articles include The Caddoan Area; Val Verde County
Cave Material; Crumley Site, etc. $15.00

T80. (TEXAS). (Texas Archaeological Society, Bulletin 32,
Austin, 1961, 1st ed.) 336pp, illus, 8vo, original wrappers, articles include Terraces of Rio Grande; Coahuiltecan Ethnography; Scored Pottery and Pottery Types of
Texas Coastal Bend; 5 site reports. $15.00

T81. (TEXAS). (Texas Archaeological Society, Bulletin 33,
Austin, 1962, 1st ed.) 256pp, illus, 8vo, original wrappers, articles include Centipede and Damp Cave Excavations; Roark Cave; Langtry Creek Burial Cave; basketry
illus, etc. $15.00

T82. (TEXAS). (Texas Archaeological Society, Bulletin 34,
Austin, 1963, 1st ed.) 220pp, illus, 8vo, original wrap-
pers, articles include North Shore of Corpus Christi
Bay; Youngsport Site; Wolfshead Site; Smithport Landing
Site; Guide to Pottery Sorting and Meaning of Pottery
Types, etc. $15.00

T83. (TEXAS). (Texas Archaeological Society, Bulletin 35,
Austin, 1964, 1st ed.) 258pp, illus, 8vo, original
wrappers, articles include Archaeology of Llano Estacado;

Three Panhandle Sites; Historic Sites in Coastal Southern Texas; Pottery from the Texas Coastal Area, etc.
$15.00

T 84. (TEXAS). (Texas Archaeological Society, Bulletin 36, Austin, 1965, 1st ed.) illus, 8vo, original wrappers, articles include Bipolar Flaking Techniques of Texas and New Mexico; Anderson's Mill, Granite Beach, Clark, Brawley's Cave, Cedar Creek Sites, etc. $15.00

T 85. (TEXAS). (Texas Archaeological Society, Bulletin 37, Dallas, 1967, 1st ed.) 248pp, illus, 8vo, original wrappers, articles include Excavation of Gilbert Site; European Trade Goods and Indian Artifacts, Tobacco Pipes, Tools, etc. $15.00

T 86. (TEXAS). (Texas Archaeological Society, Bulletin 38, Dallas, 1968, 1st ed.) 146pp, illus, 8vo, original wrappers, articles include Cad Mound; A Bibliography of Puebloan Trade Pottery; Paleo Flake Knife; sites, etc.
$12.00

T 87. (TEXAS). (Texas Archaeological Society, Bulletin 39, Dallas, 1968, 1st ed.) 172pp, illus, 8vo, original wrappers, articles include Coral Snake Mound; Acton Site; Paleo-Indian Artifacts, etc. $12.00

T 88. (TEXAS). (Texas Archaeological Society, Bulletin 40, Dallas, 1969, 1st ed.) 282pp, illus, 8vo, original wrappers, articles include Clovis Fluted Point; Two Prehistoric Cemetery Sites; Paleo-Indian Blades; Making Notch Arrow Shafts for Stone Points; etc. $12.00

T 89. (TEXAS). (Texas Archaeological Society, Bulletin 41, Dallas, 1970, 1st ed.) 315pp, illus, 8vo, original wrappers, articles include Whitney Reservoir Area; Berclair Site, etc. $10.00

T 90. (TEXAS). (Texas Archaeological Society, Bulletin 42, Dallas, 1971, 1st ed.) 385pp, illus, 8vo, original wrappers, articles include Prehistoric Settlement of DeCordova Bend Reservoir, Central Texas; Fullen Site; John Pearce Site, etc. $10.00

T 91. (TEXAS). (House of Representatives Miscellaneous Document 142, 41:2, Washington, 1970, 1st print.) Texas-- Indian Depredations. 7pp, removed. $10.00

T 92. (TEXAS). (Texas Historical Commission, Report 23, Austin, 1973, 1st ed.) Zacatecan Missionaries in Texas, 1716-1834. 181pp, illus, pls, maps, bibliography, lrg 8vo, wrappers. $20.00

T 93. (TEXTILES). (University Museum, Philadelphia, 1984) The Gift of Spiderwoman, Southwestern Textiles, the Navaho Tradition. Introduction by J. B. Wheat and P. Hearne. 48pp, 26 full-page color photographs, 6 full and half-page b/w photographs, 1 map. $23.00

T 94. (TEXTILES). Navajo Blankets. Introduction by J. B. Wheat. 56pp, 36 b/w and 4 color photographs--all full page. Melbourne, 1978. $22.00

THALBITZER (William). See also BAE Bulletin No. 40, Part 1.

T95. THALBITZER (W.). (Intro) and HOLTVED (E.) (Editor).
Otto Fabricius' Ethnographical Works. 137pp, 36 figures, objects of material culture from Greenland, 2
fold-out illus. Meddelelser om Gronland, Bd. 140, Nr.
2, Copenhagen, 1962. $57.00

T96. THATCHER (Benjamin B.). Indian Biography: or, An
Historical Account of Those Individuals Who Have Been
Distinguished Among the North American Natives as
Orators, Warriors, Statesmen and Other Remarkable
Characters. (2 Volumes). pp324, 320, frontis of Chief
Red Jacket, 3/4 leather with marbled bds, 12mo.
J & J Harper, New York, 1832 (1st ed.). $100.00
___Another Copy. New York, 1873. $50.00
___Another Copy. Glorieta, 1973, 2 volumes, pp xxiv,
324, x; 320, xi, portrait of Red Jacket. $45.00

T97. THATCHER (B. B.). Tales of the Indians, Being Prominent Passages of History of the North American Indians.... 253pp, frontis, full leather, hinges split on
exterior. Boston, 1831. $25.00

T98. THIERSANT (P. Dabry De). De l'Origine des Indiens du
Nouveau-Monde et Leur Civilisation. 358pp, 7 illus,
4to, ex-library, few pages chipped, lacks frnt cvr.
Paris, 1883 (1st ed.). $65.00

T99. THIRY (Paul and Mary). Eskimo Artifacts Designed For
Use. 337pp, photographs (some in color). Seattle,
1977 (1st ed.), d.j. $35.00

T100. THOMAS (Alfred Barnaby) (Editor). Forgotten Frontiers;
A Study of the Spanish Indian Policy of Don Bautista
de Anza, Governor of New Mexico, 1777-1787. 420pp,
index, bibliography, maps. Norman, 1969, d.j. $25.00
___Another Copy. Same. $20.00
___Another Copy. Same. $15.00

T101. THOMAS (Alfred Barnaby). (Coronado Curato Cent.
Publications, Vol. XI, Albuquerque, 1940, 1st ed.)
The Plains Indians and New Mexico, 1751-1778. A Col-
lection of Documents.... 221pp plus index, bibliography.
Rittenhouse: 570. $100.00

T102. THOMAS (Anthony E.). (American Anthropological Assn,
Anthropology Studies, No. 3, Washington, 1970) Pi-lu-
ye-kin. The Life History of a Nez Perce Indian. 68pp,
4pp, photographs, maps, references, wrappers. $10.00

THOMAS (Cyrus). See also BAE Bulletin Nos. 4, 8, 10, 12, 18
and 44.

T103. THOMAS (Cyrus). The Cherokees in Pre-Columbian Times.
97pp, 16mo, limp cloth. New York, 1890. $20.00

T104. THOMAS (Cyrus). Day Symbols of the Maya Year.
pp199-265, 6 pls of multiple glyphs, taped wrappers,
extracted from BAE 16th Annual Report, Washington,
1897. $20.00
___Another Copy. Same. $12.00

T105.   THOMAS (Cyrus). Introduction to the Study of North
        American Anthropology. xiv, 391pp, some underlining,
        108 photographs and drawings, cloth. Cincinnati, 1903.
                                                    $39.00
T106.   THOMAS (Cyrus). Mayan Calendar System, II. pp197-
        320, original wrappers, separate printing from Smith-
        sonian Institute BAE Annual Report No. 22, Part I,
        Washington, 1904. $22.00
T107.   THOMAS (Cyrus). (In ... Smithsonian Institution Con-
        tributions to North American Ethnology, Vol. V, Wash-
        ington, 1882) A Study of the Manuscript Troano
        (Maya). xxxvii, 234pp, 96 illus, 4 color pls, 4to.
                                                    $100.00
T108.   THOMAS (David). Travels Through the Western Country
        in the Summer of 1816. 320pp, errata, lacks map, full
        leather. Auburn, NY, D. Rumsey, 1819 (1st ed.).
                                                    $75.00
            Field: 1549. "One of the first works first to draw
        attention to the aboriginal monuments of central New
        York." (RMW)
T109.   THOMAS (Davis) and RONNEFELDT (K.) (Editors). People
        of the First Man: Life Among the Plains Indians In
        Their Final Days of Glory. The Firsthand Account of
        Prince Maximilian's Expedition Up The Missouri River
        1833-34. 256pp, illus, map endpapers, 4to. New York,
        1976, d.j. $40.00
        ____Another Copy. Same. $30.00
        ____Another Copy. New York, 1983, People ... The
        Firsthand Account of Prince Maximilian zu Wied, Water-
        colors by Karl Bodmer. 256pp, square 4to, illus, in-
        dex, endpaper maps, d.j. $30.00
T110.   THOMAS (E. H.). Chinook: A History and a Dictionary
        of the Northwest Coast Trade Jargon. 179pp. Port-
        land, 1935. $20.00
        ____Another Copy. Same. $18.00
        ____Another Copy. Portland, 1970, 171pp. $12.00
T111.   THOMAS (H.). Joseph Brant (Thayendanegea): Mohawk
        Indian War Chief. 176pp. New York, 1977. $15.00
T112.   THOMAS (N. D.). (New World Archaeological Foundation,
        Brigham Young University Paper No. 36, 1974) The
        Linguistic, Geographic and Demographic Position of the
        Zoque of Southern Mexico. 52pp, 45 figures. $10.00
T112a. THOMAS (P. J.) Our Centennial Memoir ... San Francisco
        de Assis in its Hundredth Year ... 192pp, 12mo, pls,
        map. San Francisco, 1877. $100.00
            Howes: T-179. Founding of Missions in California
T113.   THOMAS (P. M.). (Middle American Research, Publication
        45, Tulane University, 1981) Prehistoric Maya Settle-
        ment Patterns at Becan, Campeche, Mexico. (2 Vol-
        umes). Vol. I: text. 116pp. Vol. II: Maps, 23
        folding maps, wrappers. $35.00

THOMAS (Robert K.). See BAE Bulletin No. 180.

T114. THOMPSON (Ben W.) (Editor) and PARKS (C.) (Compiler). Who's Who in Indian Relics. No. 4. 412pp, lrg 8vo, ex-library of Congress, photographs (some in color) of collectors and their collections. Kirkwood, MO, 1976 (1st ed.). $35.00

T115. THOMPSON (Ben W.) (Editor) and PARKS (C.) (Compiler). Who's Who in Indian Relics. No. 5. 339pp, lrg 8vo, ex-library of Congress, photographs (some in color) of collectors and their collections. Kirkwood, MO, 1980 (1st ed.). $30.00

T116. THOMPSON (Erwin N.). Modoc War: Its Military History and Topography. 188pp, plus 13 maps with explanatory text, 19 photographs. Sacramento, 1971 (1st ed.).
$17.00

T117. THOMPSON (J.). The North American Indian Collection. 124pp, 226 photographs. Berne, 1977. $50.00
The American Indian art collection of the Berne Historical Museum is not well known, though it contains some extraordinary pieces. A good deal of the collection was acquired in the 18th and 19th centuries, and very little, if any, contact influence can be seen in the bulk of the fine objects that make up this choice collection. There is excellent data and acquisition information given for each of the 319 items, 226 of which are illustrated in very good photographs. (EAP)

T118. THOMPSON (J. E. S.). (Field Museum Anthropological Series, Vol. XVII, No. 3, 1931) Archaeological Investigations in the Southern Cayo District, British Honduras. pp217-362 (some uncut) of text, plus 10pp figures and 28pp of photographs of objects, 1 map.
$30.00
In the Maya ruins in the southern Cayo District (located along the Guatemalan border), excavated in early 1928 by the Marshall Field Expedition, a wealth of material was uncovered. Monuments, votive caches, and burial sites yielded an incredibly rich array of stone, jade and ceramic objects--many of which appear in the photographs in this 55 year old, out of print study, one of the most important to examine the art and archaeology in this area. (EAP)

T119. THOMPSON (J. E. S.). (Field Museum of Natural History, Anthropology Leaflet No. 33, Chicago, 1936) Archaeology of South America. 160pp of text containing 17 figures, plus 12pp of photographs. $40.00
___Another Copy. Same. $25.00

T120. THOMPSON (J. E. S.). (Field Museum, Anthropology Leaflet, 1932) The Civilization of the Mayas. 114pp, 11pp containing approx 100 drawings of objects and designs, 12pp photographs. $25.00
___Another Copy. Chicago, 1953. $15.00

___Another Copy.   Chicago, 1958. $12.00

___Another Copy. $10.00

T121. THOMPSON (J. E. S.). (American Philosophical Society,
       Memoirs, Vol. 93, Philadelphia, 1972) A Commentary on
       the Dresden Codex. 156pp, 45 illus, includes a color
       facsimile of codex, folio, cloth with d.j. $200.00

       ___Another Copy. Same. $175.00

       ___Another Copy. Same. $65.00

T122. THOMPSON (J. E. S.). (Field Museum Publication 241,
       Anthropology Series, Vol. XVII, No. 1, 1927) A Cor-
       relation of the Mayan and European Calendars. 21pp.
                                                          $18.00

T123. THOMPSON (J. E. S.). (Field Museum Anthropological
       Series, Vol. XVII, No. 2, 1930) Ethnology of the Mayas
       of Southern and Central British Honduras. pp27-213
       of text (some uncut) plus 17pp of photographs and 7pp
       of drawings, 1 map. $80.00

       This publication resulted from four visits made in
       1927 and 1928 by the author, one of the leading author-
       ities on the ethnology and archaeology of this region.
       Though not a heavily detailed study, the text, nonethe-
       less provides data, information and conclusions unavail-
       able in any other publication. Long out of print, this
       study's text and very good illustrations make it one of
       the scarcest publications on the Southern Mayas. (EAP)

       ___Another Copy. Same. $85.00

       ___Another Copy. Same. $75.00

T124. THOMPSON (J. E. S.). Maya Archaeologist. xvii, 284pp,
       24 figures, 2 maps, plus 16pp of photographs, cloth.
       Norman, 1963. $35.00

T125. THOMPSON (J. E. S.). (Carnegie Institute, Contributions
       to American Archaeology, No. 11, 1934) Maya Chronol-
       ogy: The Fifteen Tun Glyph. pp244-254, 3 figures.
                                                          $20.00

T126. THOMPSON (J. E. S.). (Carnegie Institute Publication
       No. 589, 1950) Maya Heiroglyphic Writing. xvii,
       347pp, 64pp photographs and drawings, 64pp of de-
       scriptions. $350.00

T127. THOMPSON (J. E. S.). (Civilization of American Indian,
       Vol. 56, Norman, 1960) Maya Hieroglyphic Writing. An
       Introduction. xxiii, 476pp, 64pp of illus, cloth.
       Norman, 1960. $95.00

       ___Another Copy. Norman, 1962 (2d print.), 339
       double-column pp plus index and 64 pls plus explana-
       tory page, bibliography, d.j. $20.00

T128. THOMPSON (J. E. S.). Maya History and Religion. 415pp,
       17 pls. Norman, 1970 (1st ed.). $30.00

       ___Another Copy. Same. $20.00

T129. THOMPSON (J. E. S.). Mexico Before Cortez, An Account
       of the Daily Life, Religion and Ritual of the Aztecs and
       Kindred People. x, 298pp of text, and 33pp of

photographs and drawings, cloth. New York, 1933.
$30.00
___Another Copy. Same. $22.00

T130. THOMPSON (J. E. S.). The Rise and Fall of Maya Civilization. 288pp, illus, cloth. Norman, 1966 (7th
print.) $10.00
___Another Copy. Norman, 1973 (2d ed., enlarged).
$22.00

T131. THOMPSON (J. E. S.). (Carnegie Institution Contribu-
tions to American Archaeology, No. 10, 1934) Sky
Bearers, Colors and Directions in Maya and Mexican
Religion. pp210-242 and 5pp of photographs. $45.00
___Another Copy. Same. $40.00

T132. THOMPSON (L.) and JOSEPH (A.). The Hopi Way.
151pp, 34 full-page photographs, illus cloth cvr.
U.S. Indian Service, Lawrence, 1944. $40.00
___Another Copy. Same. $10.00

T133. THOMPSON (Stith). European Tales Among the North
American Indians: A Study in the Migration of Folk-
tales. 151pp, wrappers. Colorado Springs, 1919.
$25.00

T134. THOMPSON (William). Wigwam Wonder Tales. 156pp,
29 pls by Carl M. Boog, all are full-page, myths were
collected by the author with the assistance of Pliny
Earle Goddard. Myths pertain to Northwest Indians and
beside the pleasure they give in reading, these stories
have high ethnological value. New York, Scribner's,
1919, d.j. $20.00

T135. THOMSON (C.). Ancient Art of the Americas from New
England Collections. 140pp, 145 lrg photographs.
Exhibition catalogue, Museum of Fine Arts, Boston,
1972. $25.00

T136. THOMSON (Charles). Causes of the Alienation of the
Delaware and Shawanese Indians from the British Interest. 184pp, folding map, rebound in cloth, limited to
250 copies. Philadelphia, John Campbell, 1867. $110.00
Field: 1548. Indians cheated out of lands by Governor Thomas Penn, and their response--which was to
massacre as many whites as possible. Originally published in 1759. (RMW)

T137. THORNBROUGH (G.) (Editor). (Indiana Historical Society,
Publications Vol. 21, Indianapolis, 1961) Letter Book
of the Indian Agency at Fort Wayne 1809-15. 272pp,
map, index, ex-library, reproduced from original manuscripts in Clements Library. $15.00
___Another Copy. Same. $10.00

T138. THRAPP (Dan L.). The Conquest of Apacheria. 405pp,
illus, index, bibliography, maps. Norman, 1975, d.j.
$22.00
___Another Copy. Norman, 1967 (1st ed.). $20.00

T139. THRAPP (Dan L.) (Editor, Annotator, Introduction).

Dateline Fort Bowie. Charles Fletcher Lummis Reports on an Apache War. 199pp plus index, photographs, drawings, maps. Norman, 1979 (1st ed.), d.j. $15.00

T140. THRAPP (Dan L.). General Crook and the Sierra Madre Adventure. 187pp plus index, photographs, maps, folding maps in rear pocket, bibliography, the 1883 campaign against the hostile Apaches. Norman, 1972 (1st ed.), d.j. $17.00

T141. THRAPP (Dan L.). (Southwestern Studies Monograph 39, El Paso, 1973, 1st ed.) Juh: An Incredible Indian. 44pp, frontis, map, stiff pictorial wrappers, an important study of this prominent Apache who was a contemporary of Victorio. $20.00

T142. THRAPP (Dan L.). Victorio and the Mimbres Apaches. 393pp, illus, index. New York, 1974 (1st ed.), d.j. $40.00

____Another Copy. Same. $25.00
____Another Copy. Same. $15.00

T143. THWAITES (Reuben Gold) (Editor). Chronicles of Border Warfare, or, a History of the Settlements by the Whites, of Northwestern Virginia, and of the Indian Wars, and Massacres in that Section of the State by Alexander Scott Withers. 447pp, index, cloth. Cincinnati, 1895 (7th impression, new edition). $55.00

T144. THWAITES (R. G.). Early Western Travels 1748-1846. Volume XXV Comprising the Series of Original Paintings by Charles Bodmer to Illustrate Maximilian's Travels. 81 pls, lrg folding map, gilt stamped cloth (40x53cm). Cleveland, A. H. Clark, 1906. $300.00

Bodmer's paintings are the finest depiction of the Indians of the Missouri River Frontier. He was the last white artist to record Mandan Indians before the 1837 smallpox epidemic. (OTB)

T145. THWAITES (R. G.) (Editor). Jesuit Relations, and Allied Documents, 1610-1791: The Original French, Latin and Italian Texts, with English Translations (73 Volumes). 8vo, cloth. Cleveland, 1896-1901, (1st ed.). $1,500.00

The information contained in this set about Jesuit contacts with Indians in New France (America) is both early and extensive. These narratives report on activities of the missionaries among the Indians, Fur Traders and explorers in the earliest period of settlement of North America. They are often crude in style, as might be expected of reports hastily written in Indian lodges and mission houses in the wilderness, but they are the best surviving first-hand reports of marvelous adventures, sacrifices, life among the Indians, dances, culture and war. (RMW)

____Another Set. Complete. Ex-library, original binding with library marks on the spines. One volume has scuffing on spine. $1,100.00

T146.   TIBBLES (Thomas H.). Buckskin and Blanket Days; Mem-
         oirs of a Friend of the Indians: Written in 1905.
         336pp, escaping from the Border Ruffians, Tibbles spent
         a winter as guest of Omaha Indians where he fought the
         Sioux and hunted buffalo. Garden City, 1957 (1st ed.),
         d.j. $20.00
         ___Another Copy. Same. $15.00

T147.   (TIBBLES, Thomas). Ploughed Under. The Story of an
         Indian Chief Told by Himself. 268pp, pictorial cloth.
         New York, 1881. $60.00
         A novel, supposedly by a Sioux chief, "Bright Eyes,"
         but actually by Thomas Tibbles, an Indian Rights activ-
         ist. The novel pleads for a recognition of the injustices
         to Indians. Eberstadt: 112:208. (WR)

T148.   (TIEDKE, K. E.). (Michigan State College Special Bul-
         letin 369, 1951) A Study of the Hannahville Indian
         Community (Menominee County, Michigan). 43pp, illus,
         map, wrappers. $10.00

T149.   TILGHMAN (Zoe A.). Quanah the Eagle of the Comanches.
         196pp, illus by Phoebe Ann White. Oklahoma City,
         1938 (1st ed.), d.j. $85.00

T150.   TILLER (Veronica E.). The Jicarilla Apache Tribe: A
         History, 1846-1970. 265pp, illus, index, maps, bibliog-
         raphy. Lincoln, 1983 (1st ed.) d.j. $25.00
         ___Another Copy. Same. $20.00

T151.   TILLETT (L.) (Collector and Editor). Wind on the Buffalo
         Grass: The Indians' Own Account of the Battle at the
         Little Big Horn River and the Death of Their Life on
         the Plain. xv, 160pp, illus, index, lrg oblong 8vo,
         facsimiles; daily life, 15 eye-witness accounts, aftermath
         --from the Indians' point of view. New York, 1976
         (1st ed.), d.j. $35.00
         ___Another Copy. Same. $40.00
         ___Another Copy. Same. $35.00

T152.   TIMBER (John Stands In). Cheyenne Memories. 330pp,
         illus, index. New Haven, 1969 (2d ed.), d.j. $35.00

T153.   TITIEV (Mischa). (University of Michigan Occasional Con-
         tributions No. 15, 1951) Araucanian Culture in Transi-
         tion. 164pp of text containing 9 figures, 16pp of
         photographs. $25.00

T154.   TITIEV (Mischa). The Hopi Indians of Old Oraibi.
         Change and Continuity. 371pp plus index, photographs,
         pls, notes, unique in that this work contains Titiev's
         diary for his 1933-34 stay, and also shows change over
         a nearly 40-year period. Ann Arbor, 1972 (1st ed.),
         d.j. $25.00

T155.   TITIEV (Mischa). (Papers of Peabody Museum, Vol. XXII,
         No. 1, Cambridge, 1944, 1st ed.) Old Oraibi. A
         Study of the Hopi Indians of Third Mesa. 264 double-
         column pp plus index, photographic frontis, drawings,
         maps, bibliography, rebound in cloth with original

wrappers bound in, pencil lines in margin of some
pages. $30.00

T156. (TLINGIT). (University of Pennsylvania, Museum Journal
       Vol. 20, No. 2, 1929) The Bride of Tongass: A Study
       of the Tlingit Marriage Ceremony. also: Turquois
       Mosaics from Northern Mexico; also: Zapotec Funerary
       Urns. pp113-203, illus. $15.00

T157. TODD (John). The Lost Sister of Wyoming. An Authen-
       tic Narrative. 160pp, 12mo, original cloth. Northhamp-
       ton, Mass., J. H. Butler, 1842 (1st ed.). $95.00
              Field: 1555. Ayer: 297. Centers on the Wyoming,
       Pennsylvania, massacre, especially the story of Frances
       Slocum.

T158. TODKILL (Anas). My Lady Pokahontas. A True Relation
       of Virginia with Notes by John E. Cook. 190pp, cloth.
       Boston, 1888. $18.00

T159. (TOLTEC INDIANS). (Fuentes Para la Historia de Mexico)
       I Historia Tolteca Chichimeca Anales de Quauhtinchan
       Version Preparado y Anotado por Heinrich Berlin en
       Colaboracion con Silvia Rendon. Prologo de Paul
       Kirchhoff. 144pp, plus Codice, 25 pls with explana-
       tions, inscribed by Kirchhoff, wrappers. Mexico, 1947.
                                                                 $75.00

T160. TOMKINS (William). Universal Indian Sign Language of
       the Plains Indians of North America Together with a
       Simplified Method of Study, A List of Words in Most
       General Use, A Codification of Pictographic Symbols of
       the Sioux and Ojibway: A Dictionary of Synonyms, A
       History of Sign Language, Chapters on Smoke Signaling,
       Use of Idioms, Etc., and Other Important Co-Related
       Matter. 96pp, illus, printed self-wrappers. San Diego,
       1929 (4th ed.). $20.00
       ____Another Copy. San Diego, 1941 (8th ed.) 112pp,
       3pp photographs, 47pp drawings. $18.00

TOOKER (Elisabeth). See also BAE Bulletin No. 190.

T161. TOOKER (Elisabeth). Iroquois Ceremonial of Midwinter.
       189pp, illus, map, cloth. Syracuse University Press,
       1970, d.j. $10.00

T162. TOOKER (E.) (Editor). (New York State Museum, Albany,
       1967) Iroquois Culture, History and Prehistory: Pro-
       ceedings of the 1965 Conference on Iroquois Research.
       129pp, illus, wrappers, 2d print. $20.00

T163. TOOKER (William Wallace). (The Algonquian Series, Vol.
       VI, New York, 1901 1st ed.) The Bocootawanaukes or
       the Fire Nation.... 86pp, limited to 250 copies, uncut,
       unopened. $20.00

T164. TOOKER (W. W.). Indian Place-Names on Long Island and
       Islands Adjacent with Their Probable Significations.
       xviii, 314pp, cloth. New York, 1911. $25.00

T165. TORAL (H. C.), et al. (Editors). Arte Ecuatoriano.
       (2 Volumes). Tomo I: 226pp, 190 lrg color photographs

of pre-Columbian art and 15 lrg color photographs of
20th century craft objects. Tomo II: 296pp, 260 lrg
color photographs of architectural objects from 16th century to the present, colonial art and 19th and 20th
century art. Decorated leather cvrs, folio (10½"x14¼"),
leather slipcase. Barcelona, Quito, 1976. $175.00

T166. TORIBIO MEDINA (Jose). Los Aborigenes de Chile.
431pp, illus, wrappers. Santiago, 1952. $125.00

T167. TORRANCE (G.). Native American Parfleche, A Tradition
of Abstract Painting. 36pp, 6 color and 6 b/w photographs, folio, map. Exhibition catalogue, Kansas City
Art Institute, 1984. $14.00
___Another Copy. Same. $12.00

T168. TOSCANO (S.). Arte Precolombino del Occidente de
Mexico. 229pp, 150 full and half-page photographs,
2 full-page color pls, 2 figures. Mexico City, 1946.
$30.00

T169. (TOTEM POLES). (Museum of Canada. Bulletin 119,
1950) Totem Poles (2 Volumes). Vol. I: Totem Poles
According to Crests and Topics. xii, 433pp, 186
photographs. Vol. II: Totem Poles According to Locations. ix, pp435-880, 375 photographs. $285.00

T170. (TOTEM POLES). The Totems of Alaska. 13pp, plus
20 pls, a few small chips to wrappers. 21 tipped in
photographic pls of totems in village scenes. Winter
and Pond were among the best Alaska and Northwest
photographers. Wickersham: 6424. Smith: 10269 (1
location). Juneau, Winter & Pond Co., 1909 (1st ed.).
$90.00

T171. TOTTEN (G. O.). Maya Architecture. 250pp, 114 b/w
and color photographs and drawings (12"x16½") in size,
decorated gilt cloth, repairs to inner hinges. Maya
Press, Washington, 1926. $250.00
___Another Copy. New York, 1977, reprint of 1926
ed., 250pp, 104 pls, 8 color reconstructions, folio
(11"x17"). $75.00

T172. TOUHY (Donald R.) (Editor). Selected Papers from the
14th Great Basin Anthropological Conference. 171pp,
maps, bibliography, 4to, wrappers. Includes Cowboys
& Indians--An Ethnohistorical Portrait of Indian-White
Relations on Ranches in Western Nevada; Western Shoshone of Nevada and U.S. Government 1863-1950; Washo
Internal Diversity and External Relations, etc. Socorro,
1978 (1st ed.). $20.00

T173. TOULOUSE (Joseph H., Jr.). Cremation Among the Indians of New Mexico. pls, printed wrappers, inscribed
by the author to western historian Herbert Brayer.
n.p., 1944. $20.00

T174. TOUSSAINT (Manuel) et al. Planos de la Cuidad de
Mexico. Siglos XVI y XVII: Estudio Historico, Urban-
istico y Bibliograpfico. 200pp, 28 maps and plans, sml

4to, wrappers, includes Codice "Plano en Papel de Maguey" (Postclassic map of Tenochtitlan) and Plano Atribuido a Herman Cortes. Mexico, 1938. $85.00

T175. TOVAR (Antonio). Catalogo de las Lenguas de America del Sur. 406pp, wrappers, extensive bibliography, 3,500 items. Buenos Aires, 1961. $45.00

T176. TOVILLA (Capitan Don Martin Alfonso). Relacion Historica Descriptiva. De las Provincias, de la Nerapaz y de la del Manche. Originally published in 1635. 275pp, Introduction by F. V. Scholes and E. B. Adams, wrappers. Guatemala, 1960. $45.00

T177. TOWLE (M. A.). (Viking Fund Publications in Anthropology, No. 30, 1961) The Ethnobotany of Pre-Columbian Peru. Foreword by G. R. Willey. ix, 180pp, 15pp of photographs and drawings, map, cloth. $40.00
___Another Copy. Same, stiff wrappers. $20.00

T178. TOWNSEND (Charles Wendell) (Editor). Captain Cartwright and His Labrador Journal. 380pp plus index, drawings, bibliography, folding map, introduction by Wilfred T. Grenfell, flecking of cloth, George Cartwright's journal was first published in 1772. Boston 1911 (1st ed., thus). $20.00

T179. TOWNSEND (Earl C.). Birdstones of the North American Indian. xii, 719pp, index, bibliography, 298 pls, some in color, 4to, limited to 750 copies. Indianapolis, for Author, 1959 (1st ed.). $750.00

T180. TOWNSHEND (Charles H.). The Quinnipiack Indians and Their Reservation. 81pp, 14 pls, text illus, 4to, cloth, about tribe which once lived in the New Haven area. New Haven, CT, privately printed, 1900. $60.00

TOZZER (Alfred M.). See also BAE Bulletin No. 74.

T181. TOZZER (Alfred M.). (Archaeological Institute of America, 1907) A Comparative Study of the Mayas and the Lacandones. xxi, 195pp containing 45 figures, plus 28pp of photographs, repairs to frnt cvr and spine, rear cvr chipped. $95.00

T182. TOZZER (A. M.) and ALLEN (G. M.). (Peabody Museum Papers, Vol. 4, No. 3, Cambridge, 1910) Animal Figures in the Maya Codices. pp283-372, 39 pls, wrappers. $45.00
___Another Copy. Same. ex-library, lacks frnt cvr. $35.00

T183. TOZZER (A. M.). (Peabody Museum Papers, Vol. IX, 1921) A Maya Grammar, With Bibliogrpahy of the Works Noted. xvi, 301pp. $45.00

T184. TOZZER (A. M.). (Peabody Museum, Memoirs, Vol. V., No. 3, 1913) A Preliminary Study of the Prehistoric Ruins of Nakum, Guatemala. pp143-201, 53 figures, and 20pp of photographs, 4 fold-out maps and plans, later cloth binding. $165.00

T185. (TRAVEL REPORT). Report and Supplementary Report of

a Visit to Spotted Tail's Tribe of Brule Sioux Indians,
the Yankton and Santee Sioux, Ponkas and the Chippewas of Minnesota. October, 1870. (Wrapper Title).
28pp, wrappers. Philadelphia, 1870. $45.00

T 186. (TREATIES). Acts of the Fourteenth Congress of the
United States Passed at the Second Session. vi, 113pp,
plain contemporary wrappers, some wear with sporadic
light staining, unopened, acts include eight Indian
Treaties. Washington, 1817, (1st ed.). $75.00

T 187. (TREATIES). Acts Passed at the Second Session of the
Twenty-Second Congress of the United States. 124pp,
63pp appendix, 31pp index, original printed wrappers,
contains fourteen Indian treaties and many other acts,
2 sml holes in frnt wrapper not affecting printing, some
wear, unopened. Washington, 1833 (1st ed.). $100.00

T 188. (TREATIES). Acts Passed at the Second Session of the
Twenty-Fourth Congress of the United States. 159pp,
original printed wrappers, some wear, partially unopened, contains Indian treaties and other acts.
Washington, 1837 (1st ed.). $85.00

T 189. (TREATIES). Message from the President of the United
States, Transmitting an Extract from the Occurrences
at Fort Jackson in August, 1814, During the Negotiation of a Treaty with the Indians. 10pp, disbound.
Washington, printed by William A. Davis, 1816. $35.00

T 190. (TREATIES). Survey of Lands for Cheyenne and Arapahoe Indians. Letter from the Secretary of the Interior....
12pp, removed, 1868 treaty with a survey of the lands
granted to them in western Kansas. Washington, 1868.
$65.00

T 191. (TREATIES). Treaties and Agreements of the Chippewa
Indians. 142pp, 4to, wrappers, facsimile reprints of
46 treaties and agreements from 1785 to 1902. Washington, n.d. $15.00
___Another Copy. Same. wrappers. $12.00

T 192. (TREATIES). Treaties and Laws of the Osage Nation, as
Passed to November 26, 1890. 103pp, full calf. Cedar
Vale, KS, 1895. $225.00
Hargrett: 208. Very rare. Compiled by W. S. Fitzpatrick, a member of the State Senate of Kansas, and
later a successful oil man in Oklahoma. The work gives
all treaties with the United States, the Constitution of
the tribe, and the revised criminal laws. Partially interleaved. Hargrett gives no locations. (WR)

T 193. TREGANZA (A. E.). An Archaeological Reconnaissance
of Northeastern Baja California, and Southeastern
California. 13pp, 4pp of figures, reprinted in 1942
from American Antiquity, Vol. 8, No. 2. $12.00

T 194. TREGANZA (A. E.). (University of California Archaeological
Survey Report No. 23, 1954) Fort Ross: A Study in
Historical Archaeology. 26pp and illus, wrappers.
$20.00

T195.   TREGANZA (A. E.). (University of California Archaeologi-
cal Survey Report No. 47, 1959) The Patterson Mound,
A Comparative Analysis of the Archaeology of Site
Ala-328. 92pp and illus. $25.00
T196.   TREGANZA (A. E.) and COOK (S. F.). (University of
California Publications in American Archaeology and
Ethnology, Vol. 40, No. 5, 1950) The Quantitative
Investigation of Indian Mounds. 41pp, wrappers.
$30.00
T197.   TREGANZA (A. E.). (University of California Archaeologi-
cal Survey Report No. 26, 1954) Salvage Archaeology
in Nimbus and Redbank Reservoir Areas, Central Cali-
fornia. 39pp and illus, wrappers. $20.00
T198.   TREGANZA (A. E.). (University of California Archaeologi-
cal Survey Report No. 46, 1959) Salvage Archaeology
in the Trinity Reservoir Area, Northern California Field
Season, 1958. 32pp and illus. $22.00
___Another Copy. Same. wrappers. $10.00
T199.   TREGANZA (A. E.) and BIERMAN (A.). (University of
California Anthropological Records, Vol. 20, No. 2,
1958) The Topanga Culture Final Report on Excava-
tions, 1948. 41pp and illus, stiff wrappers. $20.00
T200.   TRELEASE (Allen W.). Indian Affairs in Colonial New
York: The Seventeenth Century. 379pp, frontis, illus,
index, bibliography, cloth. Cornell University Press,
Ithaca, NY, 1960, d.j. $15.00
T201.   TRENHOLM (Virginia Cole). The Arapahoes, Our People.
372pp, illus, 1 map. Norman, 1970 (1st ed.), d.j.
$26.00
___Another Copy. Same. $20.00
___Another Copy. Same. $25.00
T202.   TRENHOLM (V. C.). The Shoshonis: Sentinels of the
Rockies. 367pp, illus with photographs. Norman,
1964 (1st ed.), d.j. $40.00
___Another Copy. Same. $30.00
___Another Copy. Same. $25.00
T203.   TRIMBORN (H.). Archaologische Studien. In Kordilleren
Boliviens. 76pp, 66 illus. Berlin, 1959. $12.00
T204.   TRIMBORN (H.). Archaologische Studien In Den Kordill-
eren Boliviens III. 182pp, 136 illus. Berlin, 1967.
$35.00
T205.   TROTTER (George A.). From Feather, Blanket and Tee-
pee. The Indians Fight for Equality. 190pp. New
York, 1955. $10.00
T206.   TROYER (Carlos). Indian Music Lecture: The Zuni In-
dians and Their Music, an Address Designed for Read-
ing at Musical Gatherings, Describing the Lives, Cus-
toms, Religions, Occult Practices and the Surprising
Musical Development of the Cliff Dwellers of The South
West. 44pp, portrait, biographical appreciation of
author by Charles Wakefield Cadman, stiff pictorial

wrappers, some soiling and wear. Philadelphia, 1913,
(1st ed.). $35.00
 Saunders: 2003. Almost the entire publication is
devoted to the cultural and religious practices of the
Zuni. The author was a friend of Frank Hamilton
Cushing and interpreted Zuni songs for him. (TE)

T207. TRUESDELL (L.) (Editor). The Indian Population of the
United States and Alaska: 1930. 238pp. Bureau of
the Census, Washington, 1937. $30.00

T208. TRUETTNER (William). The Natural Man Observed: A
Study of Catlin's Indian Gallery. 323pp, over 400 illus
with several full-page color pls, inscribed by author.
Washington, 1979. $125.00
____Another Copy. Same. d.j. $25.00

T209. TRUMBELL (Benjamin). A Compendium of the Indian Wars
of New England. More Particularly such as the Colony
of Connecticut Have Been Concerned and Active In.
Edited by Frederick B. Hartranft. 63pp, 4to, cloth
backed bds, one of 50 copies printed on Kelmscott hand
made paper in an edition of 400 copies, the first publication of the manuscript compiled in 1767. Hartford,
1926. $35.00
____Another Copy. Same, original wrappers. $50.00
____Another Copy. Hartford, 1926, one of 350 copies
printed on Georgian antique paper, 63pp, stiff printed
wrappers. $20.00

T210. TRUMBULL (Henry). History of the Discovery of America; of the Landing of Our Forefathers at Plymouth, and
of Their Most Remarkable Engagements with the Indians
in New-England. 256pp, three-panel color frontis, 2
color pls, original leather rebacked. Boston, J. P.
Peaslee, 1828. $60.00
 Howes: T-370. Sabin: 97196. Field: 1569. Also
covers the Creek and Seminole War, defeat of Generals
Braddock, Harmer and St. Clair, and early Western
settlements. Howes: "A Well-nigh worthless production
of a seventeen year old lad which enjoyed wide favor by
an uncritical public." (RMW)
____Another Copy. Boston, N. C. Barton, 1846, ...A
New Edition.... viii, 1-320pp, color pls, decorated
cloth. $60.00

TRUMBULL (James Hammond). See also BAE Bulletin No. 25.

T211. TRUMBULL (James Hammond). Indian Names of Places,
Etc., In and On the Borders of Connecticut: With
Interpretations of Some of Them. 93pp, cloth. Hart-
ford (privately printed, limited to 250 copies), 1881.
                                                       $25.00

T212. TRUMBULL (J. H.). (Transactions American Philological
Assn, 1872) Notes on 40 Algonkian Versions of the
Lord's Prayer. 116pp, includes Micmac, Delaware, Cree,
Chippeway, versions cover two and a half centuries:

Montagnias, 1632 to the Chippeway New Testament. Hartford, 1873, wrappers. $125.00

TSCHOPIK (Harry, Jr.). See also BAE Bulletin No. 143.

T213. TSCHOPIK (H.). (American Museum of Natural History, Anthropological Papers, Vol. 44, Part 2, 1951) The Aymara of Chucuito, Peru. 1. Magic. pp137-308 containing 11 figures, plus 10pp of photographs, inscribed by author. $60.00

T214. TSCHOPIK (H.). (Smithsonian Institution, Social Anthropology, Publication 5, 1947) Highland Communities of Central Peru, A Regional Survey. viii, 56pp and 16pp of photographs, 2 maps. $25.00
___Another Copy. Same. $15.00
___Another Copy. Same. $10.00

T215. TSCHOPIK (H.). (American Museum of Natural History, Science Guide No. 135, New York, 1952) Indians of the Mongana. 23pp, illus, wrappers, concerning Peru. $10.00

T216. TSCHOPIK (H.). (Peabody Museum Papers, Vol. 17, No. 1, 1941) Navaho Pottery Making, An Inquiry into the Affinities of Navaho Painted Pottery. 101pp, 16pp photographs, 4 figures. $87.00

T217. TSCHOPIK (H.). (Peabody Museum Papers, Vol. XXVII, No. III, 1946) Some Notes on the Archaeology of the Department of Puno, Peru. x, 57pp of text, 34 figures, 10pp photographs. $35.00

T218. TUCK (J. A.). Newfoundland and Labrador Prehistory. 128pp, 28 b/w and 3 color illus of hundreds of objects. National Museum of Man, 1976. $15.00

T219. TUCK (J. A.). Onondaga Iroquois Prehistory. A Study in Settlement Archaeology. 249pp plus index, photographs, drawings, bibliography, site evolution used to interpret the origin and development of Onondaga culture. Syracuse, 1971 (1st ed.), d.j. $15.00

T220. TUCKER (Glenn). Tecumseh. Vision of Glory. 384pp plus index, frontis, maps, bibliography, the biography of one of the greatest Indian leaders of the old frontier. Indianapolis, 1956 (1st ed.), d.j. $25.00
___Another Copy. Same. cloth. $35.00
___Another Copy. Same. $25.00

T221. TUCKER (Sara) (Compiler). (Scientific Papers, Vol. 2, Illinois State Museum, 1942) Indian Villages of the Illinois Country. Part 1, Atlas. xiii, 18pp, 54 map facsimile pls loose in portfolio, bibliography, original wrappers, location of Indian tribes and villages, river courses and the added knowledge of the territory in general during the period of 1671-1830. $75.00
___Another Copy. Same. $100.00

T222. TUGGLE (W. O.). Sham, Ham and Japheth: The Papers of W. O. Tuggle, Comprising His Indian Diary, Sketches and Observations. Edited by Eugene Current-Garcia.

361pp, index, map. Athens, 1973 (1st ed.), d.j.
$25.00

W. O. Tuggle was an agent for the Creek and Yuchi
Indians during the 1870s and 1880s. First half of the
book is devoted to his Indian experiences and includes
his diary of his 1879 trip through the Indian Territory.
___Another Copy. Same. folding sheet of maps of
Creek Nation laid in. $25.00
___Another Copy. Same. cloth. $20.00

T223. TUNNELL (C.). (Texas Historical Commission Special Report No. 18, Austin, 1975, 1st ed.) Fluted Projectile
Points Adair-Steadman Site in Northwestern Texas.
38pp plus maps and pls, bibliography, lrg 8vo, wrappers. $10.00

T224. TUNNELL (C.). (Texas Historical Commission Report No.
30, Austin, 1978, 1st ed.) Gibson Lithic Cache from
Western Texas. 73pp, illus, pls, maps, bibliography,
lrg 8vo, wrappers. $10.00

T225. TUNNELL (C.). (Texas Historical Commission Report No.
6, Austin, 1967, 1st ed.) Archaeological Excavations
at Presidio San Agustin de Ahumada. 116pp, illus, pls,
maps, bibliography, lrg 8vo, wrappers. $10.00

T226. TUNNELL (C.) and JENSEN (Harold P., Jr.). (Texas
Historical Commission Report No. 17, Austin, 1969, 1st
ed.) Archaeological Excavations in Lyndon B. Johnson
State Park, Summer, 1968. 96pp, illus, pls, maps,
bibliography, lrg 8vo, wrappers. $12.00
___Another Copy. Same. $10.00

T227. TUNNELL (C.) and HALLOUF (R.). (Texas Historical
Commission Special Report No. 17, Austin, 1975, 1st
ed.) Cultural Resources in the Canyons of the Rio
Grande. 28pp plus maps and pls, bibliography, lrg 8vo,
wrappers. $10.00

T228. TURK (R.). Scholder/Indians. 126pp, 25 color illus.
Flagstaff, 1978 (2d ed.). $18.00

T229. TURNER (Frederick J.). The Character and Influence
of the Indian Trade in Wisconsin: A Study of the
Trading Post as an Institution. 92pp, cloth. Norman,
1977 (1st ed.), d.j. $10.00

T230. TURNER (G.). Hair Embroidery in Siberia and North
America. 102pp, 16pp of photographs of about 50 embroidered objects of clothing, 26 drawings. Oxford,
1955. $20.00

T231. TURNER (G.). Indians of North America. 270pp, 16mo,
64pp of color illus, 22 b/w drawings, 44 b/w photographs, cloth. Poole, 1979. $18.00

T232. TURNER (Katherine C.). Red Men Calling on the Great
Father. 235pp. Norman, 1951 (1st ed.). $25.00
___Another Copy. Same. $15.00
___Another Copy. Same. $10.00

T233. TURNEY-HIGH (H. H.). (American Anthropological Assn,

Memoirs, No. 56, 1941) Ethnography of the Kutenai.
202pp, 1 map, 8pp photographs. $39.00
___Another Copy. Same. $35.00

T234. TURNEY-HIGH (H. H.). (American Anthropological Assn,
Memoirs, No. 48, 1937) The Flathead Indians of Mon-
tana. 161pp, 1 illus. $25.00
___Another Copy. Same. $12.00

T235. TUSHINGHAM (A. S.). Gold for the Gods. 146pp, 365
figures, 34 in color, an exhibition catalogue of an
exhibition of pre-Inca and Inca gold and artifacts
from Peru. Canada, 1976, d.j. $20.00

T236. TYLEE (Mrs. Arthur F.). The Challenge of Amazon's
Indians. A Story of Missionary Adventure ... Amongst
the Nhambiquara Indians. 92pp, illus, cloth. New
York, 1931. $22.00
___Another Copy. Same. $12.00

T237. TYLOR (Edward B.). Anahuac; or, Mexico and the
Mexicans, Ancient and Modern. xii, 344pp, errata, in-
dex, folding map, several pls, some in color, text illus,
full leather, marbled endpapers. London, Longman,
Green, Longman & Roberts, 1861 (1st ed.). $140.00
      Field: 1582. Contains much information on the
Indians of Mexico, their artifacts and culture.

T238. TYLER (Hamilton A.). Pueblo Animals and Myths.
274pp, maps, bibliography, index, demonstrates the
Indians' naturalistic view of the animals and explains
how they came to be elevated to the status of spirits
and gods. Norman, 1975 (1st ed.), d.j. $25.00
___Another Copy. Same. $15.00

T239. TYLER (H. A.). Pueblo Birds and Myths. 308pp, illus,
index, maps, offers several layers of information on
the very special place of birds in Pueblo life. Norman,
1979, d.j. $20.00
___Another Copy. Same. $15.00

T240. TYLER (H. A.). (Civilization of the American Indian
Vol. 71, Norman, 1964, 1st ed.) Pueblo Gods and
Myths. 300pp plus index, map, bibliography, d.j.
                                                  $25.00

T241. TYLER (S. Lyman). A History of Indian Policy. 321pp
plus index, photographs, art work by Indian students
of the Institute of American Indian Art, maps (some
folding), 1 color map, bibliography, appendices,
wrappers, covers treaties and trade, removal, reservation system, land allotment, tribal reorganization.
Washington, 1973. $10.00

T242. TYRELL (J. W.). Across the Sub-Arctics of Canada: A
Journey of 3,200 Miles by Canoe and Snowshoe Through
the Barren Lands. vi, 7, 270pp, 10 pls, illus, folded
map, original decorated cloth, several chapters on the
Eskimo, customs of the Eskimo, etc. Wm. Briggs,
Toronto, 1897. $75.00

T243.   TYSON (Carl N.).   The Pawnee People.   105pp, 1pp,
        photographs, 1 drawing, 1 color photograph, maps,
        signed by tribal chairman, errata, wrappers, one of
        the Indian Tribal Series.   Phoenix, 1975 (1st ed.).
                                                          $15.00
T244.   TYSON (Job R.).   Discourse on the Surviving Remnant
        of the Indian Race in the United States.   38pp, wrap-
        pers.   Philadelphia, A. Waldie, 1836. $35.00
            Much criticism of Georgia for usurpation of lands
        granted by treaty to the Creek Indians.
        ___Another Copy.   Same. $35.00
T245.   TYLER (Patrick F.).   Historical View of the Progress of
        Discovery on the More Northern Coasts of America,
        With Descriptive Sketches of the Natural History by
        James Wilson.   444pp, 9 engravings, vignette on half
        title page, folding map, 1/2 leather, frnt hinge cracked,
        edge wr, contents very good.   Edinburgh, 1832 (1st
        ed.). $150.00
            Sabin: 97657.   Includes several sections on Indians.

                            -U-

U1.   UBBELOHDE-DOERING (H.).   The Art of Ancient Peru.
        color frontis, 55pp, map, 240 pls, rear cvr warped,
        some staining to upper margin not affecting text or pls.
        New York, 1952. $50.00
U2.   UBBELOHDE-DOERING (H.).   Auf Den Konigsstrassen Der
        Inka, Reisen und Forschungen in Peru.   360pp, 304
        photographs, most of which are full-page, map, cloth.
        Berlin, 1941. $100.00
U3.   UBBELOHDE-DOERING (H.).   Kunst Im Reiche Der Inca.
        300pp, plus an 8pp text in rear pocket, 4 full-page
        color and 240 b/w full-page photographs, 5 drawings,
        map, cloth.   Tubingen, 1952. $80.00
U4.   UBBELOHDE-DOERING (H.).   Old Peruvian Art.   xvii, 64
        pls, 12 in color, included are 29 examples of textiles,
        4to, wrappers w/soiled, chipped d.j.   New York,
        E. Weyhe, 1936. $85.00
        ___Another Copy.   London, 1936, 64pp. $57.00
        ___Another Copy.   London, 1936, abbreviated ed.,
        17pp, xii color pls, 63 illus, wrappers, 4to. $55.00
U5.   UBBELOHDE-DOERING (H.).   On the Royal Highways of
        the Inca.   illus.   New York, 1967, d.j. $65.00
U6.   UBELAKER (D. H.).   (Smithsonian Contributions to Anth-
        ropology, No. 29, Washington, 1981)   The Ayalan
        Cemetery: A Late Integration Period Burial Site on the
        South Coast of Ecuador.   175pp, 119 illus, wrappers.
                                                          $30.00

U7.   UBELAKER (D. H.). (Smithsonian Contributions to Anth-
      ropology No. 18, 1974) Reconstruction of Demographic
      Profiles from Ossuary Skeletal Samples. xi, 79pp, 27
      figures. $14.00
U8.   UHLE (Max). Die Alten Kulturen Perus Im Hinblick Auf
      Die Archaologie und Geschichte Kontinents. 50pp, 20
      figures, wrappers. Berlin, 1935. $20.00
U9.   UHLE (M.) and PUTNAM (E. K.). (Proceedings of the
      Davenport Academy of Sciences, Vol. XIII, 1914) The
      Nazca Pottery of Ancient Peru and the Davenport Col-
      lection of Nazca and other Peruvian Pottery. 46pp of
      text containing 13 photographs and drawings, plus 23pp
      of b/w and 2pp of color photographs, map. $45.00
U10. ULLOM (Judith C.) (Compiler). Folklore of the North
      American Indians. An Annotated Bibliography. 120pp
      plus index, drawings by many artists reproduced from
      books they illustrated listed in this bibliography, 152
      references cited. Washington, 1979 (1st ed.). $15.00
U11. (UMATILLA RESERVATION). (House of Representatives
      Report 387, 48:1, Washington, 1884) ...Providing for
      the Allotment in Severalty to the Indians Residing upon
      the Umatilla Reservation.... 4pp, removed. $10.00
U12. UNDERHILL (Ruth). (American Anthropological Assn,
      Memoirs No. 46, 1936) The Autobiography of a Papago
      Woman. 64pp. $13.00
U13. UNDERHILL (R.). (American Ethnological Society, Mono-
      graphs, XIII and XIV) Ceremonial Patterns in the
      Greater Southwest, also: Factionism in Isleta Pueblo.
      127pp, cloth. New York, 1948. $28.00
      ____Another Copy. Same. $25.00
U14. UNDERHILL (R.). First Penthouse Dwellers of America.
      175pp, 30pp of photographs, cloth. Santa Fe, 1946
      (2d ed., revised, enlarged.) $30.00
      ____Another Copy. Same. $15.00
      ____Another Copy. New York, 1938 (1st ed.), 155pp,
      illus, map endpapers. $25.00
      ____Another Copy. Same. $22.00
U15. UNDERHILL (R.). Hawk Over Whirlpools. (Southwest
      Indian fiction.) New York, 1940. $22.00
U16. UNDERHILL (R.). Here come the Navaho! A History of
      the Largest Indian Tribe in the United States. 285pp,
      163 photographs. Bureau of Indian Affairs, 1953.
                                                        $34.00
      ____Another Copy. Lawrence, 1953, later printing,
      wrappers. $15.00
      ____Another Copy. Same. $10.00
U17. UNDERHILL (R.). Indians of the Pacific Northwest.
      232pp, 115 illus. Bureau of Indian Affairs, 1945,
      1953. $30.00
      ____Another Copy. Bureau of Indian Affairs, 1960.
                                                        $23.00

_____Another Copy. Bureau of Indian Affairs, 1963.
$45.00

U18.   UNDERHILL (R.). Indians of Southern California. 73pp,
37 illus, 1 full-page map of Mission Indian Reservations
in California in 1938. Bureau of Indian Affairs, 1941.
$20.00
_____Another Copy. Same. $15.00
_____Another Copy. U.S. Department of Indian Affairs,
n.d. (c. 1940). $12.00
_____Another Copy. Lawrence, Kansas, n.d., 74pp, lrge
8vo, illus with photographs and drawings by Velino
Herrera, bibliography, wrappers. $22.00

U19.   UNDERHILL (R.). The Navajos. 288pp, illus, index,
maps, bibliography. Norman, 1956 (1st ed.), d.j.
$25.00
_____Another Copy. Same. $25.00
_____Another Copy. Same. lacks d.j. $20.00
_____Another Copy. Norman, 1971, d.j. $22.00

U20.   UNDERHILL (R.). The Northern Paiute Indians of California and Nevada. 72pp, 37 pls. Bureau of Indian Affairs, 1941. $28.00

U21.   UNDERHILL (R.). Papago Indian Religion. vi, 259pp,
cloth. New York, 1946 (1st ed.). $69.00
_____Another Copy. Same. $50.00

U22.   UNDERHILL (R.). The Papago and Pima Indians of Arizona.
68pp, 45 illus, wrappers. U.S. Office of Indian Affairs, 1940. $17.00
_____Another Copy. Bureau of Indian Affairs, 1941,
64pp, 46 illus. $18.00
_____Another Copy. Same. 71pp, 45 illus. $14.00
_____Another Copy. Lawrence, 1965, 71pp, illus, wrap-
pers. $12.00

U23.   UNDERHILL (Ruth). People of the Crimson Evening.
Illus by Velino Herrera. 127pp, wrappers, Sherman Institute, Riverside, 1951. $15.00

U24.   UNDERHILL (Ruth). Pueblo Crafts. 147pp, 102 illus,
wrappers, Bureau of Indian Affairs, Washington, DC,
1944. $30.00
_____Another Copy. Same, Washington, 1965. $15.00
_____Another Copy. Same, Washington, 1944. $12.00
_____Another Copy. Same, Phoenix, 1945. $10.00

U25.   UNDERHILL (Ruth) et al. (American Tribal Religions,
Vol. 4, Flagstaff, 1979, 1st ed.) Rainhouse and Ocean.
Speeches for the Papago Year. 148pp, plus index,
drawings, photographs, map, references, wrappers.
$15.00
_____Another Copy. Same. $10.00
_____Another Copy. Same. $20.00

U26.   UNDERHILL (Ruth). Red Man's America. A History of
Indians in the United States. 369pp, plus index, illus,
bibliography, notes, endpaper maps, maps, Univ. of

Chicago Press, 1953 (1st ed.). $15.00
    Another Copy. Same. $12.00

U27. UNDERHILL (Ruth). Singing for Power. The Song Magic of the Papago Indians of Southern Arizona. 158pp, illus, Berkeley, 1938 (1st ed.). $27.00
    Another Copy. Same, Berkeley, 1976. $15.00

U28. UNDERHILL (Ruth). (U.S. Indian Service, Indian Life and Customs, No. 4, Phoenix, 1946, 1st ed.) Work a Day Life of the Pueblos. 174pp, photographs, drawings, bibliography, cloth. $30.00
    Another Copy. Same. $20.00

U29. UNRAU (William E.). The Emigrant Indians of Kansas; A Critical Bibliography. 78pp, wrappers, lists 187 printed works, Bloomington, 1979 (1st ed.). $15.00
    Another Copy. Same. $10.00

U30. UNRAU (William E.). The Kansa Indians, A History of the Wind People, 1673-1873. 244pp, illus, index, maps, bibliography, Norman, 1971 (1st ed.), d.j. $25.00
    Another Copy. Same. $17.00
    Another Copy. Same. $15.00

U31. UNRAU (William E.). The Kaw People. 104pp, photographs, drawings, maps, bibliography, wrappers, Phoenix, 1975 (1st ed.). $10.00

U32. UPTON (Richard) (Editor). (Montana and the West Series, Vol. I, El Segundo, 1983, 1st ed.) The Indian as a Soldier at Fort Custer, Montana, 1890-1895. Lt. Samuel C. Robertson's First Cavalry Crow Indian Contingent. 148pp, photographs by Goff, drawings by Remington, end-paper maps, appendices, footnotes, bibliography, index, cloth. $27.00
    Another Copy. Same, with d.j. $30.00

U33. (UTAH). (House of Representatives Executive Document 44, 41:2, Washington, DC, 1870, 1st printing) Suppressing Indian Hostilities in Utah. 7pp. Removed. $15.00

U34. (UTAH). (Senate Document 32, 55:1, Washington, DC, 1897, 1st printing) Uintah Indian Reservation. 19pp, folding map. Removed. $20.00

U35. (UTAH). (Senate Document 154, 57:1, Washington, DC, 1902, 1st printing) Uintah Indian Reservation, Utah. 89pp. Removed. $20.00

U36. (UTAH). (House of Representatives Document 671, 57:1, Washington, DC, 1902, 1st printing) Uintah Indian Reservation--Surveys and Examination. 53pp plus 12 photographic pls and 3 folding maps. Removed. $30.00
    Another Copy. Same. $25.00

U37. (UTAH). (Senate Document 159, 58:3, Washington, DC, 1903, 1st printing) Opening of the Uintah Indian Reservation in Utah. 24pp. Removed. $15.00

U38. (UTE). (House of Representatives Executive Document 157, 43:1, Washington, DC, 1874, 1st printing) Condition and Wants of the Ute Indians of Utah: The Pai-utes

of Utah, Northern Arizona, Southern Nevada, and Southeastern California; The Go-Si Utes of Utah and Nevada....
35pp. Removed. $20.00

U39. (UTE). (Senate Executive Document 62, 45:3, Washington,
DC, 1879, 1st printing) Report of the Commission ...
To Make Certain Negotiations with the Ute Indians in ...
Colorado. 61pp, plus 6 maps (4 folding), 40 illus.
Removed. $45.00
Contains detailed report on White River Agency, the
land, rivers, buildings, with agreements and Indian
signers.
___Another Copy. Same. $35.00

U40. (UTE). (House of Representatives Document No. 152,
55:2, Washington, DC, 1897, 1st printing) Supply of
Water for the Southern Ute Indian Reservation. 6pp.
Removed. $15.00

U41. UTLEY (R. M.) and WASHBURN (W. E.). The American
Heritage History of the Indian Wars. 352pp, over 250
illus, several in color, sml 4to, boxed, New York, 1977.
$45.00

U42. UTLEY (Robert M.). The Last Days of the Sioux Nation.
301pp, plus index and photographs, bibliography, New
Haven, 1963 (1st ed.), d.j. $35.00
___Another Copy. Same, New Haven, 1972, d.j. $15.00

-V-

V1. (VACCINATION). (House of Representatives Document No.
82, 22:2, Washington, DC, 1833) Vaccination Problems,
with rolls of Indians by tribe who received the vaccina-
tions. 6pp. Removed. $30.00

V2. VAIL (A. L.). A Memorial of James M. Haworth, Superintendent of United States Indian Schools. 178pp, frontis,
pp 177 and 178 supplied in facsimile, rear endpapers
missing, some interior waterstain, cloth, Kansas City,
1886 (1st ed.). $125.00
Howes: V-3. A hard-to-find book in any condition.
Mr. Haworth was Kiowa Agent in 1873; also supplies
material on Satanta, Big Tree, material on the Comanches,
Cheyennes, etc.

V3. VAIL (Eugene A.). Notice Sur les Indiens de l'Amerique
du Nord. 246pp, folding hand-colored map, 4 hand-
colored pls (after those by Charles Bird King in the
McKenney & Hall "History of the Indian Tribes of North
America."), original printed wrappers bound into 1/2
leather and bds, Paris, Arthus Bertrand, 1840 (1st ed.).
$300.00
Howes: V-7. Field: 1592. Contains a French

version of the great Gallatin "Map of the Indian Tribes
of North America About 1600...," Wheat: 417.
    ___Another Copy. Same, newly rebound. $400.00

V 4.   VAILLANT (G. C.). (American Museum of Natural History,
Science Guide No. 88, 1935, 1940) Artists and Craftsmen in Ancient Central America. 101pp, 154 illus,
wraps. $30.00
    ___Another Copy. Same, New York, 1935. $20.00

V5.   VAILLANT (G. C.). Aztecs of Mexico, Origin, Rise and
Fall of the Aztec Nation. 340pp, 64pp of photographs,
28 figures, cloth, Garden City, NY, 1944. $25.00
    ___Another Copy. Same, New York, 1931. $17.00
    ___Another Copy. Same, New York, 1941. $12.00
    ___Another Copy. Same, London, 1951. $12.00

V 6.   VAILLANT (George C.). (American Museum of Natural History,
Anthropology Papers, Vol. 35, Part II, New York, 1935)
Excavations at El Arbolillo. 279pp, 28 pls of multiple
artifacts, wrappers. $60.00
    ___Another Copy. Same. $50.00

V7.   VAILLANT (S. B. and G. C.). (American Museum of Natural
History, Anthropology Papers, Vol. 35, Part I, 1934)
Excavations at Gualupita. 135pp, 35 figures, mostly
full-page, 6 tables, wrappers. $60.00

V8.   VAILLANT (G. C.). (American Museum of Natural History,
Anthropology Papers, Vol. 32, Part II, New York, 1931)
Excavations at Ticoman. 241pp, 40pp of pls, 18 figures,
6 maps, wrappers. $75.00
    ___Another Copy. Same. $60.00
    ___Another Copy. Same. $50.00

V 9.   VAILLANT (George C.). (American Museum of Natural History,
Anthropology Papers, Vol. 32, Part I, New York, 1931)
Excavations at Zacatenco. 197pp, illus, folding chart,
wrappers. $50.00

V10.   VAILLANT (George C.). Indian Arts in North America.
xiii, 159pp, 96pp of b/w photographs, 1 color pl, New
York, 1939. $135.00
    ___Another Copy. Same. $75.00

V11.   VALARDE (Pablita). Old Father: The Story Teller.
66pp, illus by author, color pls, pictorial cloth, inscribed and signed by author, Globe, 1960 (1st ed.).
   $50.00
    Santa Clara Pueblo legends told to the author by her
grandfather and great-grandfather, illustrated by the
author, one of the foremost Indian artists.

VALCARCEL (Luis E.). See also BAE Bulletin No. 143.

V12.   VALCARCEL (Luis E.). Historia de la Cultura Antigua
del Peru. (2 Volumes). Vol. I: 199pp, 1943, Mexico,
Vol. II: 245pp, 1949, Mexico. Wrappers. $60.00

V13.   VALCARCEL (Luis E.). Indians in Peru. Photographs by
P. Verger. 201pp, 87 full-page photographs, map, cloth,
New York, 1950. $50.00
    ___Another Copy. Same. $35.00

V14. VALKENBURGH (R. V.). Dine Bikeyah. v, 200pp, 19pp
of maps, Office of Indian Affairs, Navajo Service,
Window Rock, 1941. $28.00

V15. VALLE (R. H.). Bibliografia Hernan Cortes. 269pp,
color frontis, limited to 1,000 copies, wraps. $25.00

V16. VAN CAMP (G. R.). Kumeyaay Pottery, Paddle and Anvil
Techniques of Southern California. 123pp, 15pp of
photographs and drawings, 13 tables, 3 maps, wrappers,
Socorro, 1979. $15.00

V17. VAN DEN BRINK (J. H.). The Haida Indians, Cultural
Change Mainly Between 1876-1970. x, 275pp, 5 maps,
cloth, Leiden, 1974. $60.00

V18. VAN DER AA (Pieter). Eerste Shceeps-Togt Ter Verder
Ontdekking Van De West-Indien, Door Jean Dias De
Solis, En Vincent Yanes Pinzon, Gegaan Naar Jukatan
In't Jaar 1506. Engraved title page, plus additional 6pp,
folio (9" x 14"), new endpapers, new marbled bds,
printed paper spine label, Leyden, 1706. $175.00

V19. VANDERWERTH (W. C.) (Compiler). Indian Oratory.
Famous Speeches by Noted Indian Chieftains. 292pp,
illus, bibliography, Norman, 1971 (1st ed.), d.j.
$20.00
___Another Copy. Same. $10.00

V20. VAN DE VELDE (P. and H. R.). (Southwest Museum Pa-
pers, No. 13, Los Angeles, 1939) The Black Pottery of
Cayotepec, Oaxaca, Mexico. 43pp, 30 photographs, 1
figure, wraps. $12.00
___Another Copy. Same. $15.00
___Another Copy. Same. $10.00

V21. VAN EVERY (Dale). Disinherited: The Lost Birthright of
the American Indian. 279pp, bibliography, maps, index,
New York, 1966, d.j. $17.00
___Another Copy. Same. $10.00

V22. VAN KIRK (J. & P.) and SOLIS (Patricia). The World of
Tikal (Guatemala). 98pp, numerous photographs, sml
4to, folding map, text in Spanish and English, guide to
the ruins and environs, St. Petersburg, 1985 (1st ed.).
$30.00

V23. VAN PELT (Garrett). Old Architecture of Southern Mexico.
125pp, over 200 photographs, folio (10" x 14"), original
decorated cloth, Cleveland, 1926 (1st ed.). $85.00

V24. VAN ROEKEL (Gertrude). Jicarilla Apaches. xvii, 86pp,
20pp of photographs, notes, selected readings, San
Antonio, Naylor, 1971 (1st ed.), d.j. $20.00
___Another Copy. Same. $10.00

V25. VAN SERTIMA (Ivan). They Came Before Columbus.
288pp, 40 pls showing artifacts, New York, 1976.
$15.00

VANSTONE (James W.). See also BAE Bulletin No. 199.

V26. VANSTONE (James W.). (Field Museum, Fieldiana Anthropology, Vol. 60, 1970) Akulivikchuk: A 19th Century

Eskimo Village on the Nushagak River, Alaska.   123pp,
14 drawings, 15pp of photographs, wrappers. $20.00
___Another Copy. Same. $25.00
___Another Copy. Same. $20.00

V27.   VANSTONE (J. W.). (Field Museum, Fieldiana Anthropology,
Vol. 54, No. 2, 1968) An Annotated Ethnohistorical
bibliography of the Nushagak River Region, Alaska.
pp149-189, wrappers. $18.00
___Another Copy. Same. $20.00
___Another Copy. Same. $25.00

V28.   VANSTONE (J. W.). (Field Museum, Fieldiana Anthropology,
Vol. 67, Chicago, 1976) The Bruce Collection of Eskimo
Material Culture from Port Clarence, Alaska. 69pp, plus
47 pls, wrappers. $35.00
___Another Copy. Same. $15.00
___Another Copy. Same. $12.00

V29.   VANSTONE (J. W.). Eskimos of the Nushagak River: An
Ethnographic History. 192pp, maps, index, bibliography,
Univ. of Washington, Seattle, 1967 (1st ed.), d.j.
                                                   $30.00
___Another Copy. Same. $15.00

V30.   VANSTONE (J. W.). (Field Museum, Fieldiana Anthropology,
Vol. 70, Chicago, 1978) E. W. Nelson's Notes on the
Indians of the Yukon and Innoko Rivers, Alaska. 80pp,
2 illus, 2 maps, wrappers. $13.00

V31.   VANSTONE (J. W.). (Field Museum, Fieldiana Anthropology,
Vol. 63, No. 2, Chicago, 1972) The First Peary Collec-
tion of Polar Eskimo Material Culture. pp 31-80, maps,
photographs, wrappers. $15.00
___Another Copy. Same. $22.00
___Another Copy. Same. $10.00

V32.   VANSTONE (J. W.). (Field Museum, Fieldiana Anthropology,
Vol. 72, Chicago, 1979) Historic Ingalik Settlements
Along the Yukon, Innoko, and Anvik Rivers, Alaska.
108pp, 6 pls, 5 figures, wrappers. $20.00
___Another Copy. Same. $17.00

V33.   VANSTONE (J. W.). Historic Settlement Patterns in the
Nushagak River Region, Alaska. 149pp, 44 illus, wraps,
Fieldiana Anthropology, Vol. 61, Chicago, 1971. $30.00

V34.   VANSTONE (J. W.). (Field Museum, Fieldiana Anthropology,
Vol. 71, Chicago, 1979) Ingalik Contact Ecology: An
Ethnohistory of the Lower Middle Yukon, 1870-1935.
284pp, 22 full-page photographs, 6 figures, wrappers.
                                                   $30.00
___Another Copy. Same. $35.00

V35.   VANSTONE (J. W.). (Field Museum, Fieldiana Anthropology,
Vol. 62, Chicago, 1972) Nushagak, An Historic Trading
Center in Southwestern Alaska. 93pp, 16 full-page
photographs, 5 figures, 4 tables, wraps. $17.00
___Another Copy. Same. $25.00

V36.   VANSTONE (J. W.). Point Hope: An Eskimo Village in

Transition. Univ. of Washington, Seattle, 1962.
$15.00

V37. VANSTONE (J. W.). (Field Museum, Fieldiana Anthropology,
Vol. 56, No. 43, Chicago, 1968) Tikchik Village. A
Nineteenth Century Riverine Community in Southwestern
Alaska. 158pp, 14 photographs, 19 figures, 4 tables,
wrappers. $17.00
____Another Copy. Same. $30.00

V38. VANSTONE (J. W.) (Editor). (Field Museum, Fieldiana
Anthropology, Vol. 64, Chicago, 1973) V. S. Khrom-
chenko's Coastal Explorations in Southwest Alaska, 1822.
95pp, maps, bibliography, wrappers. $17.00
____Another Copy. Same. $15.00

V39. VANSTONE (J. W.) and TOWNSEND (Joan). (Field Museum,
Fieldiana Anthropology, Vol. 59, Chicago, 1970) Kijik:
An Historic Tanaina Indian Settlement. 202pp, illus,
wrappers. $30.00
____Another Copy. Same. $22.00

V40. VAN ZANTWIJK (R.). The Aztec Arrangement, The Social
History of Pre-Spanish Mexico. xxv, 345pp, 45 illus,
5 maps, cloth, Norman, 1985. $35.00
____Another Copy. Same. $25.00

V41. VARNER (J. G.) and VARNER (J. J.). The Florida of the
Inca: A History of the Adelantado, Hernando de Soto,
Governor and Captain General of the Kingdom of Florida,
and Other Heroic Spanish and Indian Cavaliers, Written
by the Inca, Garcilaso de la Vega. xlv, 655pp, figures,
Univ. of Texas, Austin, 1951, d.j. $45.00

V42. VAUGHN (J. W.). Indian Fights: New Facts on Seven
Encounters. xv, 250pp, pls, maps, bibliography, index,
Fetterman disaster, Cheyenne Fork, Rosebud Campaign,
Reno in the Valley, etc. High Spot: 156. University
of Oklahoma, 1966 (1st ed.), d.j. $20.00

V43. VAUGHN (J. W.). The Reynolds Campaign on Powder River.
xv, 239pp, pls, map, bibliography, index, government
decision to force a final showdown with hostile Indians.
Custer High Spot: 35. University of Oklahoma,
1961 (1st ed.), d.j. $25.00

V44. VAUGHN (J. W.). With Crook on the Rosebud. 9pp,
245pp, pls, map endpapers, bibliography, index.
Custer High Spot: 42. "As for an analysis of the battle of the Rosebud, certainly nothing is ever to surpass
the masterful reconstruction by J. W. Vaughn."
Harrisburg, 1956, (1st ed.), d.j. $30.00

V45. VAZQUEZ GASTELU (Antonio). Arte de Lengua Mexicana....
2pp, 54pp, 1pp, octavo, modern half calf and marbled
bds, some worming at inner gutter of first third of text,
restored, not affecting letterpress, title-leaf remargined
at inner edge, some old, private ownership stamps on
title and a few other leaves. Provenance: A) Marcas
de Fuego of a colonial convent library removed from top

and bottom edges; B) ownership stamp of Nicolas Leon;
C) acquired as duplicate from the John Carter Brown
library. Puebla: por Diego Fernandez Leon, 1726.
$1,800.00

Vinaza: 286. Garcia Icazbalceta Lenguas: 33 (1716
ed.). Medina (Puebla): 361. Pilling: 1412. The fourth
edition of this uncommon and significant work on the language of the Aztecs, "Corregido segun su original por el
Br. D. Antonio de Olmedo y Torre." The first edition
appeared in 1689, with subsequent ones appearing in
1693, 1716, 1726 and later. Vazquez Gastelu, a native
of Puebla, was a professor of the "Mexican Language"
at the Royal College of San Juan and San Pedro. (WR)

V46. VAZQUEZ DE ESPINOSA (Antonio). (Smithsonian Miscellaneous Collections, Vol. 102, Washington, 1942) Description
of the Indies (c.1620) Translated by Charles Upson
Clark. 862pp, wrappers. $75.00

___Another Copy. 1968 reprint, cloth. $85.00

___Another Copy. Washington, 1948, text in Spanish,
wrappers. $60.00

V47. VEGA (P. F.) et al. Guia del Museo de America. 172pp
of text and 33pp of photographs. Madrid, 1965. $20.00

V48. VEILLETTE (J.) and WHITE (G.). Early Indian Churches:
Wooden Frontier Architecture in British Columbia. xx,
195pp, illus, maps, bibliography, lrge 8vo, wrappers,
light wear. University of British Columbia, 1977. $10.00

V49. VELASQUEZ (Pedro). Memoir of an Eventful Expedition in
Central America; Resulting in the Discovery of the Idola-
trous City of Iximaya, in an Unexplored Region; and the
Possession of Two Remarkable Aztec Children.... 35pp,
illus, original wrappers. New York, E. F. Applegate,
1850 (1st ed.). $75.00

Field: 1598. "It is the most circumstantial fiction
which the brain of an advertising agent ever conceived."
Obviously a cornerstone in any collection of Americana.
(RMW)

V50. VELASQUEZ de CARDENAS y LEON (Carlos Celedonio).
Breve Practica, y Regimen Confessonario de Indios, en
Mexicano, y Castellano.... 12ff, 54pp, sml octavo, contemporary limp vellum. Impresso en Mexico: En la Imprenta de la Bibliotheca, Mexicana, 1761. $1,200.00

Medina (Mexico): 4747. Vinaza: 350. Garcia Icazbalceta Lenguas: 79. Palau: 357575. Velasquez was an
ecclesiastical judge in the archbishopric of Mexico City
and an examinador sinodal. He is notable for his role in
conserving the form of the indigenous Mexican language
in his time. The text in this manual for hearing the
confessions of the Indians and doling out penances is in
both Spanish and Nahuatl, the language spoken by more
than half of the Indians in Mexico at the time. (WR)

V51. VENIAMINOV. Gospoda Nashego Iisusa Khrista Evangelie.

(The Gospel of Our Lord Jesus). xiv, 258pp. St.
Petersburg, 1896. $235.00
    The pagination is in Church Slavonic, with several
leaves misnumbered. The individual pages are enclosed
in ornamental frames. The text is in parallel columns in
Russian and Aleutian-Fox. Original tan printed wrappers.
This is the 2d edition of Veniaminov's translation of the
Gospel of St. Matthew in the Aleutian-Fox language.
First printed in Moscow in 1840. Wickersham: 5871.
Pilling: pp.101-103. (EAP)

V52. (VERA CRUZ). Las Ruinas de Cempoala y del Templo del
Tajin. Exploradas por el Director del Museo Nacional de
Arqueologia, Don Francisco del Paso y Troncoso. pp95-
161, plus 56 pls of sites, plans, models, 4to, wrappers.
Museo Nacional, Mexico, 1912. $125.00

V53. VERRILL (A. H.). The American Indian: North, South
and Central America. 485pp, 47pp of photographs, cloth.
New York, 1927. $30.00
    ___Another Copy. Same. $20.00
    ___Another Copy. New York, 1945. $10.00

V54. VERRILL (A. H.). Old Civilizations of the New World.
377pp plus index, photographs, illus, bibliography.
Indianapolis, 1929 (1st ed.). $15.00

V55. VERUT (Dominique). Precolombian Dermatology and Cos-
metology in Mexico. 100pp, 80 color pls. n.p., 1973,
d.j. $60.00

V56. VERWYST (F. Chrysostom). Chippewa Exercises; Being a
Practical Introduction into the Study of the Chippewa
Language. 494pp, complete reprint of 1901 ed.
Minneapolis, 1971. $25.00

V57. VESTAL (Stanley). Happy Hunting Grounds. 220pp, illus
by Frederick Wiggold, signed by author, one of Vestal's
earliest works, gives a comprehensive picture of the life
of the Plains Indian, written as fiction. Rader: 3530.
Chicago, 1928 (1st ed.). $35.00
    ___Another Copy. Same. $30.00

V58. VESTAL (S.). New Sources of Indian History 1850-1891.
351pp, illus, newly rebound, the Ghost Dance, Prairie
Sioux, much original material. Rader: 3533. Norman,
1934 (1st ed.). $50.00

V59. VESTAL (S.). Sitting Bull, Champion of a Sioux; A Biography by.... 366pp, illus, map, bibliography, index.
Boston 1932 (1st ed.). $40.00
    ___Another Copy. Same, gilt dim on spine. $23.00
    ___Another Copy. Norman, 1957 (2d print.), d.j.
$20.00

V60. VESTAL (S.). Warpath and Council Fire. 324pp plus
index, photographs, maps, bibliography, map endpapers,
the Plains Indians' struggle for survival in war and in
diplomacy, 1851-1891. Dustin: 539. New York, 1948,
(1st ed.), d.j. $35.00

      ___Another Copy. Same. lacks d.j. $25.00
      ___Another Copy. Same. Ink inscription. $25.00

V61. VETROMILE (Eugene). The Abnakis and Their History, or Historical Notices on the Aborigines of Acadia. 171pp, pls, other drawings, top 1/2" and lower 1/4" of backstrip chipped away, clippings attached to frnt endpapers. Field: 1602. New York, 1866 (1st ed.). $125.00

V62. VETROMILE (E.). Indian Good Book, Made by Eugene Vetromile, S.J., Indian Patriarch, for the Benefit of the Penobscot, Passamaquoddy, St. John's, Micmac and Other Tribes of the Abnaki Indians ... Old-Town Indian Village and Bangor. (2), 12, (2 errata), 13-586pp, 8 pls, vignette text illus, 16 mo, full calf tooled in gilt, a.e.g., n.p., n.d. (c.1870s). $250.00

      Third edition, enlarged with new material on pp436-586. First published in 1856 (Field: 1601, 2d ed only) Roman Catholic prayer book, including service for mass, catechism, hymns, etc., in various dialects of the Abnaki--Pilling, Algonquian Languages, pp507, see long descriptive notes. The historical introduction and titles are in English. (CLR)

V63. VEYTIA (Mariano). Historia Antigua de Mexico (2 Volumes). pp401, 365, illus, 17 color pls, most are of codices. $125.00

V64. VICTOR (Frances Fuller). The Early Indian Wars of Oregon.... 700pp plus index, newly rebound in cloth with leather label, repaired tear to introduction page, else nice. Howes: V-88. Smith: 10548. Salem, 1894 (1st ed.). $200.00

V65. VIDLER (V.). American Indian Antiques, Arts and Artifacts of the Indians of the Northeast. 156pp, 140 b/w and 6 color photographs. Cranbury, 1976, cloth. $30.00
      ___Another Copy. Same. d.j. $20.00

V66. VIETZEN (Raymond C.). The Immortal Eries. 387, (1)pp, 122 illus, some maps, cloth. Elyria, OH, 1945, d.j. $30.00

V67. VILLACORTA (J. A. and C. A.). Arqueologia Guatemalteca. Tomo I only. 383pp, 300 illus of sites, artifacts, wrappers, tear in cvr. Guatemala, 1930. $125.00

V68. VILLAR (A.). (Carnegie Institution Publication 559, 1945) The Maya of East Quintana Roo. xii, 182pp of text containing 9 figures, 13 tables, plus 6 pp of photographs. $95.00

V69. VILLASENOR (D.). Tapestries in Sand, the Spirit of Indian Sandpainting. 112pp, 16 color illus. Healdsburg, 1963. $12.00
      ___Another Copy. Same. $10.00

V70. VIOLA (H. J.). The Indian Legacy of Charles Bird King. 152pp, illus, plus 16 full-page color portraits, 4to. New York, 1976. $35.00

___Another Copy. Same. $30.00
___Another Copy. Same. d.j. $25.00

V71. VIOLA (Herman). Thomas L. McKenney. Architect of America's Early Indian Policy: 1816-1830. xii, 365pp, frontis, 22pp illus, endpaper maps, notes, bibliography, index. Chicago, Sage-Swallow, 1974, (1st ed.), d.j. $25.00

V72. VIVIAN (Gordon). (National Park Service Archaeological Research Series No. 8, 1964) Gran Quivira: Excavations in a 17th Century Jumano Pueblo. ix, 168pp, illus, 4to, wrappers. $35.00
___Another Copy. Same. $25.00

V73. VIVIAN (G.). (National Park Service Archaeological Research Series No. 5, Washington, 1959) The Hubbard Site and Other Tri-Wall Structures in New Mexico and Colorado. 92pp, 4to, illus, wrappers. $25.00
___Another Copy. Same. $20.00

V74. VIVIAN (G.). (University of New Mexico Publications in Anthropology, No. 13, 1965) The Three-C Site, an Early Pueblo II Ruin in Chaco Canyon, New Mexico. 48pp, 3pp of figures, 6pp photographs. $23.00

V75. VOEGELIN (E. W.). (University of California Anthropological Records, Vol. 2, No. 1, 1938) Tubatulabal Ethnography. 90pp, 6pp of photographs, 14 figures. $39.00

V76. VOGEL (Virgil J.). American Indian Medicine. 583pp, index, bibliography. Norman, 1977, d.j. $30.00
    Shows effect of Indian Medicinal practices on White civilization and discusses Indian theories of disease and methods of combating disease. Also lists Indian drugs that have won acceptance in the "Pharmacopoeia of the United States." (GFH)
___Another Copy. Same. $35.00

V77. VOGEL (V. J.). This Country Was Ours: A Documentary History of the American Indian. 473pp, index, bibliography. New York, Harper, 1972 (1st ed.), d.j. $25.00

VOGET (Fred W.). See also BAE Bulletin Nos. 151 and 180.

V78. VOGET (F. W.). Osage Indians I. 44pp, 4to, maps, cloth. Garland American Indian Ethnohistory Series, 1974. $30.00

V79. VOGT (Evon Z.). Los Zincantecos, un Pueblo Tzotzil de los Altos de Chiapas. 496pp, 16 pp of photographs, 23 figures, cloth. Mexico City, 1966. $22.00

V80. VOGT (E. Z.). (Peabody Museum Papers, Vol. 41, No. 1, Cambridge, 1951) Navaho Veterans: A Study in Changing Values. 227pp, wrappers. $35.00
___Another Copy. Same. $30.00

V81. VOGT (E. Z.) (Editor). People of Rimrock: A Study of Values in Five Cultures. 342pp, illus, index, maps, bibliography. Cambridge, 1967, d.j. $20.00
    Study of Values in a small area of Western New Mexico which contains 5 distinct cultures: Zuni, Navajo,

Spanish-American, Mormon and Texas Homesteaders.
___Another Copy. Cambridge, 1967 (2d print.), d.j.
$10.00

V 82. VOGT (Evon). Zinacantan: A Mayan Community in the
Highlands of Chiapas. illus, Harvard University Press,
1969, d.j. $45.00
___Another Copy. Same. $30.00

V 83. VOGT (Evon) et al. Desarrollo Cultural de los Mayas.
403pp, studies (4 in English) by Vogt, Willey, Proskouriakoff, Graham and others, wrappers. UNAM,
Mexico, 1964. $60.00

V 84. VOLK (Ernest). (Peabody Museum Papers, Vol. 5, 1911)
The Archaeology of the Delaware Valley. xvi, 258pp,
plus 127 pls and maps, wrappers. $160.00

V 85. VOLNEY (C. F.). View of the Climate and Soil of the
United States of America; To Which are Annexed Some
Accounts of Florida, The French Colony on the Scioto,
Certain Canadian Colonies and the Savages or Natives.
xxviii, 446pp, erratum, 2 folding maps, 2 folding pls,
full calf, frnt hng broken. Philadelphia, J. Conrad,
1804 (1st ed.). $225.00
Howes: V-141. Field: 1610. Includes a vocabulary
of the Miami Indians of Indiana and contains many comments on the Indians.

V 86. VON DEN STEINEN (K.). Uter Den Naturvolken Zentral
Brasiliens. Reisechilderung Und Ergebnisse Der Zweiten
Schingu-Expedition, 1887-1888. xvi, 413pp, 153 photographs and drawings, principally of objects of material
culture, 11 full-page pls, marbled and linen bds, illus
frnt cvr. Berlin, 1897. $275.00

V 87. VON EUW (Eric). Corpus of Maya Hieroglyphic Inscriptions, Vol. 5, Part I, Xultun. 62pp, photographs, drawings, maps, folio, wrappers. Steles discovered by Morley, as well as new finds. Cambridge, 1978, (1st ed.).
$15.00

V 88. VON GRAFFENFIED (C.). Eine Sammlung Von Eskimo-
gegenstanden Aus Gambell, St. Lorenzinsel, Alaska
Beschreibender Katalog. pp 383-427, 30 photographs and
drawings, wrappers, offprint, Yearbook, Bern Historical
Museum, 49 and 50, 1969 and 1970. $12.00

V 89. VON HAGEN (Victor Wolfgang). The Ancient Sun Kingdoms
of the Americas, Aztec, Maya, Inca. 608pp plus index,
220 drawings and photographs (a few in color), maps,
bibliography. Cleveland, 1961, d.j. $12.00

V 90. VON HAGEN (V. W.). The Aztec and Maya Papermakers.
120pp, plus 39 pls, frontis which is tipped in pl from the
Dresden Codex, introduction by Dard Hunter. New York,
J. J. Augustin, 1944 (1st trade ed.). $90.00
___Another Copy. Same. waterstain to 1/4 inch to top
of last 50pp, cloth with water spot. $80.00

V 91. VON HAGEN (V. W.). The Desert Kingdoms of Peru.

191pp, 19 color and 118 b/w photographs, 25 drawings, 3 maps, cloth.   New York, 1965. $30.00

V92.   VON HAGEN (V. W.). Ecuador and the Galapagos Islands. 290pp, illus with photographs. Norman, 1949 (1st ed.). $40.00

V93.   VON HAGEN (V. W.). F. Catherwood, Architect-Explorer of Two Worlds. xv, 60pp of text and 32pp of illus, cloth. Barre, 1968. $25.00

V94.   VON HAGEN (V. W.). Frederick Catherwood, Architect. color frontis, 177pp, contains views of ancient monuments in Central America, Chiapas and Yucatan, 16 pls, introduction by Aldous Huxley, inscribed by author. New York, 1950. $50.00
_____Another Copy. Same, cloth. $45.00
_____Another Copy. Same. $30.00
_____Another Copy. second ed. $25.00

V95.   VON HAGEN (V. W.). Highway of the Sun. 314pp plus index, photographs, maps, bibliography, map endpapers, about the Incas. New York, 1955 (1st ed.), d.j.
$12.00

V96.   VON HAGEN (V. W.) (Editor). The Incas of Pedro de Cieza de Leon. 381pp plus index, translated by Harriett DeOnis, illus, bibliography. Norman, 1959, (1st print.), d.j. $15.00

V97.   VON HAGEN (V. W.). (Museum of the American Indian, Notes and Monographs, No. 53, New York, 1943) The Jicaque (Torrupan) Indians of Honduras. 112pp, frontis, wrappers. $45.00
_____Another Copy. Same. $40.00

V98.   VON HAGEN (V. W.). Jungle in the Clouds: A Naturalist's Exploration in the Republic of Honduras. 268pp, color frontis, illus, includes a visit to Copan, ex-library. New York, 1946. $25.00
_____Another Copy. London, 1946. 223pp, 41 illus, endpaper maps. $20.00

V99.   VON HAGEN (V. W.). Maya Explorer: John Lloyd Stephens and the Lost Cities of Central America and Yucatan. 324pp, pls, maps (1 folding), bibliography, index. University of Oklahoma, 1947, (1st print.), d.j.
$15.00
_____Another Copy. Norman, 1948, wear to d.j. $20.00

V100. VON HAGEN (V. W.). Off with Their Heads. 220pp, photographs, folding map, map endpapers, signed by author, eight months with the headhunting Jivaro Indians in Ecuador. New York, 1937, (1st ed.). $17.00

V101. VON HAGEN (V. W.). (Museum of the American Indian, Notes and Monographs, No. 51, New York, 1939) The Tsatchela Indians of Western Ecuador. 79pp, 11pp of photographs, wrappers. $18.00

V102. VON SCHMIDT-PAULI (E.). We Indians. The Passing of a Great Race. Being the Recollections of the Last

of the Great Indian Chiefs, Big Chief White Horse Eagle
(as told to Von schmidt-Pauli). 248pp plus color frontis.
Some rather fantastic material. We learn for example,
that Custer and all his 5000 men were killed at the
Little Big Horn. Dustin: 242. New York, 1931 (1st
ed.), d.j. $30.00
___Another Copy. Same. lacks d.j. $25.00

V103. VON SCHULERSCHOMIG (I.). Werke Indianischer Goldschmiedekunst. 80pp, 41 b/w and 4 color photographs,
bds. Berlin, 1972. $12.00

V104. VON SPIX (Dr. Joh. Bapt.) and VON MARTIUS (C. F.
Phil.). Travels in Brazil, in the Years 1817-1820. (2
Volumes). Vol. 1: xxii, 327pp, 4 engraved pls. Vol.
2: x, 298pp, 5 engraved pls. Rebound in cloth,
ex-library. London, Longman, Hurst, Rees, Orme and
Green, 1824 (1st ed.). $250.00
     Field: 1472. "Very interesting work ... occupied
with minute and, we may be certain, accurate descriptions of the Indians of the pampas and mountains, of
whose physique and customs are illustrative." (RMW)

V105. VON TSCHUDI (Dr. J. J.). Travels in Peru. 354pp,
frontis, plus 1 pl, translated from the German by
Thomasina Ross, original cloth. New York, 1854.
                                                            $90.00

V106. VON WINNING (H.). Anecdotal Sculpture of Ancient West
Mexico. 96pp, 222 b/w and 8 color photographs, 21
drawings. Los Angeles, 1972. $12.00

V107. VON WINNING (H.). Portrayal of Pathological Symptoms
in Pre Columbian Mexico. 81pp, 58 photographs and
drawings, map, wrappers. Pearson Museum, Series No.
87/1, 1987. $25.00

V108. VON WINNING (H.). Pre-Columbian Art of Mexico and
Central America. 388pp, 317 color photographs, 278 b/w
photographs, full leather, buckram slipcase, folio size
special edition limited to 1,800 copies, this copy numbered and inscribed by author. New York, 1968.
                                                           $375.00
___Another Copy. New York, Abrams, 1968, soil to
d.j. $200.00
___Another Copy. Same. $185.00
___Another Copy. New York, Abrams, n.d. (c.1968),
d.j. $175.00

V109. VON WINNING (H.). Shaft Tomb Figures of West Mexico.
xiv, 183pp, 335 illus, 1 color pl. Los Angeles, 1974.
                                                            $20.00

V110. VON WRANGEL (F. P.). Ethnographic Observations on the
Coast Miwok and Pomo by Contre-Admiral F. P. Von
Wrangell and P. Kostromitonov of the Russian Colony,
Ross, in 1839. 20pp, wrappers, translated by Fred
Stross, ethnographic notes by R. F. Heizer, 1974.
                                                            $20.00

V111. VON WUTHENAU (A.). Alt-Amerikanische Tonplastik
(Kunst der Welt). 215pp, 41pp of color and 36pp of
b/w photographs, 29 drawings, map, cloth. Baden-
Baden, 1965. $25.00

V112. VON WUTHENAU (A.). The Art of Terra-Cotta Pottery in
South America. 203pp, 87 pls, 29 figures, ex-library,
some damage to bottom edge of frnt cvr. New York,
1965. $25.00

V113. VON WUTHENAU (A.). Unexpected Faces in Ancient
America, 1500 B.C.-A.D. 1500: The Historical Testimony of Pre-Columbian Artists. 240pp, 120 illus, 16
color pls. New York,1975. $45.00

V114. VOORHIES (B.). (New World Archaeological Foundation,
Brigham Young University, Paper No. 41, 1976) The
Chantuto People: An Archaic Period Society of the
Chiapas Littoral, Mexico. 147pp, 80 figures, 27 tables.
$20.00

V115. VOTH (H. R.). (Field Museum, Publication 157, Anthropological Series, Vol. XI, No. 2, 1912) Brief Miscellaneous Hopi Papers. 149pp, 24pp of photographs and
drawings. $70.00
Six papers describing different aspects of Hopi culture are included in this volume. Four papers deal with
burial customs, the Eagle Cult, the New Year ceremony
and marriage rights on the wedding morning; two papers
deal with Hopi myths.

V116. VOTH (H. R.). (Field Columbian Museum, Publication 100,
Anthropological Series, Vol. VI, No. 3, 1905) Hopi
Proper Names, the Stanley McCormick Expedition. 52pp,
the meanings of hundreds of Hopi proper names are
given including prefixes and suffixes. $38.00

V117. VOTH (H. R.). (Field Museum Publication 156, Anthropological Series, Vol. XI, No. 1, 1912) The Oraibi
Marau Ceremony. 88pp, 33 lvs of photographs w/tissue
guard. $165.00

V118. VOTH (H. R.). (Field Columbia Museum, Publication 97,
Anthropological Series, Vol. VI, No. 2, 1905) Oraibi
Natal Customs and Ceremonies, the Stanley McCormick
Expedition. 21pp, 8 photographs, 1 drawing, the cere-
monies attending the birth and the first twenty days in
the life of a Hopi infant are described. $40.00

V119. VOTH (H. R.). (Field Columbian Museum, Publication 84,
Anthropological Series Vol. VI, No. 1, 1903) The
Oraibi Oaqol Ceremony, the Stanley McCormick Hopi
Expedition. 50pp text, 28pp of photographs, and additional 28pp text explaining the photographs. $95.00
A day by day account of the nine-day ceremony is
provided, based on the author's viewing of the ceremony
on a number of occasions in the late 19th century. The
very good photographs are of dances, dancers and objects of material culture.

V120. VOTH (H. R.). (Field Columbian Museum, Publication 61, Anthropological Series, Vol. III, No. 2, 1901) The Oraibi Powamu Ceremony. pp 63-158, 38 lves of b/w and color drawings and photographs, morocco (worn), marbled endpapers, hngs repaired, pages soiled and some chipped. $65.00

V121. VOTH (H. R.). (Field Columbian Museum, Publication 83, Anthropological Series, Vol. III, No. 4, 1903) The Oraibi Summer Snake Ceremony, the Stanley McCormick Expedition. 224pp, 71pp of photographs, repairs to cvrs. $125.00

In this very detailed account of the Snake Dance, Voth reported virtually every aspect of the ceremony. The photographs, of splendid quality, capture the dance and the ceremony and remain one of the great photographic records of southwest Indian ceremonies.
___Another Copy. Same. Cloth. $100.00

V122. VOTH (H. R.). (Field Columbian Museum, Publications 96, Anthropology Series Vol. 8, Chicago, 1905) The Traditions of the Hopi. vii, 319pp, slightly chipped wrappers, 110 myths collected by author on the Stanley McCormick Expedition. $95.00
___Another Copy. Same. $87.00
___Another Copy. Same. taped wrappers, cvr wrn, contents complete. $75.00
___Another Copy. Millwood, 1973, reprint. $69.00

-W-

W1. WADDELL (J. O.). (Univ. of Arizona Anthropology Papers, No. 12, 1969) Papago Indians at Work. ix, 159pp, 19 figures, wrappers. $15.00
___Another Copy. Same. $10.00

W2. WADE (E. L.) and STRICKLAND (R.). Magic Images: Contemporary Native American Art. 128pp, 139 b/w and 11 color photographs, Norman, 1981. $24.00

W3. WADE (M. H.). Indian Fairy Tales, As Told to the Little Children of the Wigwam. 240pp, 10 full-page drawings, cloth, Boston, 1906. $37.00
___Another Copy. Same. $12.00

W4. WADSWORTH (Beula). Design Motifs of the Pueblo Indians, with Applications in Modern Decorative Arts. 96pp, 190 illus, cloth, San Antonio, 1957. $25.00
___Another Copy. Same, d.j. $20.00

WAGLEY (Charles). See also BAE Bulletin No. 143.

W5. WAGLEY (Charles). (American Anthropological Assoc., Memoir No. 71, Menasha, 1949) The Social and Religious Life of a Guatemalan Village. 150pp, illus, wrappers. $17.00

W6.   WAGLEY (Charles) and GALVAO (Eduardo). The Tenetehara
      Indians of Brazil: A Culture in Transition. Columbia
      Univ. Press, New York, 1949, d.j. $20.00

W7.   WAGNER (Glendolin D.) and ALLEN (W. A.). Blankets and
      Moccasins. 304pp, pls, decorative endpapers, decorated
      cloth, interesting work on the Crows, in part from the
      journals of Allen, Caldwell, 1933 (1st ed.). $75.00
      ___Another Copy. Same. $65.00

W8.   WAGNER (Emile R.) and DUNCAN (L.). La Civilizacion
      Chaco-Santiaguena. 18 of 19 pls present, all pls in color,
      wrappers, Buenos Aires, 1932. $50.00

W9.   WAGNER (Gunter). Yuchi. Separate printing from Volume
      III of Handbook of American Indian Languages. pp
      295-384, wrappers, New York, 1934. $10.00

W10. WAISBARD (Roger and Simone). Masks, Mummies and
      Magicians. A Voyage of Exploration in Pre-Inca Peru.
      176pp, photographs, drawings, map, New York, 1965
      (1st Amer. ed.), d.j. $12.00

W11. WAKEFIELD (John A.). History of the War Between the
      United States and the Sac and Fox Nations of Indians....
      152pp, original muslin over bds, half morocco and cloth
      slipcase, Jacksonville, Illinois, printed by Calvin
      Goudy, 1834. $750.00
          Graff: 4510. Byrd: 213. Howes: W-19. Sabin:
      100978. Streeter Sale: 1449. A scarce and valuable
      account of the Black Hawk War and other Indian troubles
      by a first hand witness, including the account of the
      captivity of the Hall sisters, as related by Sibley Hall.
      Wakefield based his account of the 1827 campaign on
      oral reminiscences and newspaper accounts, but he was
      a participant in the last two campaigns. He served as
      a scout and dispatch bearer and was wounded at the bat-
      tle of Axe River. This is not the first printing of an
      account of the Hall captivity, but that contained in the
      1832 pamphlet was so full of errors that this may be
      noted as the first accurate account, and the first in
      book form. (Wm. Reese Co.)

W12. WAKEFIELD (W. H.). (Univ. of Texas, Texas Archaeologi-
      cal Survey Reports, No. 5, Austin, 1968) Palmetto Bend
      and Choke Canyon Reservoirs, Texas. 43pp, maps,
      pls, bibliography, lrge 8vo, wrappers. $10.00

W13. WALDMAN (C.). Atlas of the North American Indian. xi,
      276pp, 54pp, 21 drawings, 122 two-color maps, cloth,
      New York, 1985. $42.00
          This unusual--perhaps unique--atlas provides a series
      of overviews, organized by subject, of American Indian
      culture and history. There are seven subjects, each of
      which is broken down into sections, accompanied by a
      number of maps that are especially helpful in conveying
      information.
          Included in this fact-filled work are extensive

cross-references and several comprehensive detailed appendices. (AEP)

W14. WALENS (S.). Feasting with Cannibals, An Essay on Kwakiutl Cosmology. 202pp, 14 photographs, of Kwakiutl objects and rituals, cloth, Princeton, 1981. $28.00

W15. WALKER (C. B.). The Mississippi Valley, and Prehistoric Events Giving an Account of the Original Formation of the Great Valley, of its First Inhabitants, the Mound Builders. 784pp, 4 lithographic pls, rebacked in full leather, Burlington, Iowa, 1880. $60.00
____Another Copy. Burlington, 1881. $25.00

W16. WALKER (Cora). Cuatemo: Last of the Aztec Emperors. Illus, Dayton Press, New York, 1934. $50.00
____Another Copy. Same. 348pp, drawings, photographs, maps, errata. $20.00

W17. WALKER (Deward E., Jr.) (Editor). The Emergent Native American. A Reader in Culture Contact. 818pp, bibliography, Boston, 1972 (1st printing), d.j. $20.00

W18. WALKER (Edwin Francis). (Publications of Frederick Webb Hodge Anniversary Publication Fund, Vol. VI, Los Angeles, 1952) Five Prehistoric Archaeological Sites in Los Angeles County, California. 112pp, 49 pls (photographs, charts, drawings), figures, bound in later cloth. $15.00
____Another Copy. Same. $12.00

W19. WALKER (J. R.) and DeMALLIE (R. J.) (Editors). Lakota Society. 223pp, 96 photographs, cloth, Lincoln, 1982. $30.00

W20. WALKER (J. R.), DeMALLIE (R. J.) and JAHNER (E.) (Editors). Lakota Belief and Ritual. 313pp, plus index, photographs, drawings, some in color, bibliography, notes, appendices, Lincoln, 1980 (1st ed.), d.j. $22.00
____Another Copy. Same. $15.00

W21. WALKER (J. R.). (American Museum of Natural History, Anthropology Papers, Vol. 16, 1917) The Sun Dance and Other Ceremonies of the Oglala Division of the Teton Dakota. pp 53-221, 1/4 leather. $75.00
____Another Copy. Disbound, no wrappers. $20.00

W22. WALKER (John). Excavations of the Arkansas Post Branch of the State of Arkansas. 255pp, illus, wraps, National Park Service, Washington, 1971. $15.00

W23. (WALKER RIVER RESERVATION). (Senate Executive Doc. 7, 47:2, Washington, 1882) Message from the President of the United States ... an agreement made by Pah-Ute Indians and granting a right of way to the Carson and Colorado RR Co. through the Walker River Reservation, in Nevada. 5pp. Removed. $10.00

W24. (WALKER RIVER RESERVATION). (House of Representatives Executive Document 15, 48:1, Washington, 1883) Right of Way to the Carson and Colorado RR Co. through Walker River Reservation in Nevada. 7pp. Removed. $10.00

WALKER (Winslow M.). See also BAE Bulletin No. 113.
W25. WALKER (Winslow M.). (Smithsonian Misc. Collections,
Vol. 94, No. 14, Washington, 1935) A Caddo Burial Site
at Natchitoches, Louisiana. 15pp, plus illus, wraps.
$10.00
WALLACE (Anthony F. C.). See also BAE Bulletin Nos. 150 and
180.
W26. WALLACE (Anthony F. C.). The Death and Rebirth of the
Seneca. 384, xi, (1)pp, 15 illus, 2 maps, index, bib-
liography, notes, references, cloth, New York, 1970
(1st ed.), d.j. $25.00
____Another Copy. Same. $12.00
W27. WALLACE (Anthony F. C.) (Editor). Halliday Jackson's
Journal ... the Seneca Indians, 1798-1800. Reprint from
Quarterly Journal of the Pennsylvania Historical Assoc.,
Vol. IXI, No. 2, April, 1952. 55pp, illus, wrappers.
$10.00
W28. WALLACE (Anthony F. C.). King of the Delawares: Teedy-
uscung, 1700-1763. 305pp, endpaper maps, bibliographical
reference, index, cloth, Philadelphia, Univ. of Pennsyl-
vania, 1949 (1st ed.), d.j. $15.00
____Another Copy. Same. $25.00
W29. WALLACE (Ernest) and HOEBEL (E. Adamson). The Com-
anches, Lords of the Southern Plains. 364pp, plus in-
dex, illus, map, bibliography, Norman, 1952 (1st ed.),
d.j. $30.00
____Another Copy. Same. $20.00
____Another Copy. Same. $25.00
____Another Copy. Same, Norman, 1976. $20.00
____Another Copy. Same, Norman, 1982. $12.00
W30. WALLACE (Paul A. W.). Indian Paths of Pennsylvania.
227pp, illus with maps, endpaper maps, index, appendix,
bibliographical notes, Harrisburg, 1965 (1st ed.), d.j.
$30.00
____Another Copy. Same. $35.00
W31. WALLACE (S. E.). The Land of the Pueblos. 285pp, 11
engravings, cloth, New York, 1888. $70.00
____Another Copy. Troy, 1889 (2nd ed.). $35.00
W32. WALLACE (William J.). Desert Foragers and Hunters; In-
dians of the Death Valley Region. 43pp, photographs,
wrappers, Ramona, 1979 (1st ed.). $12.00
____Another Copy. Same. $10.00
W33. WALLACE (William J.). (Southwest Museum Leaflet No.
23, Los Angeles, 1949) Hupa Warfare. 16pp, bibliog-
raphy, wrappers. $10.00
W34. WALLIS (Ethel). God Speaks Navajo. x, 146pp, map, 8pp
of photographs, cloth and bds, New York, 1968 (1st
ed.), d.j. $15.00
Story of Faye Edgerton who was missionary to the
Navajo for nearly half a century and who translated the
New Testament into their language.
____Another Copy. Same. $10.00

W 35. WALLIS (Wilson and Ruth). The Micmac Indians of Eastern
Canada. Illustrations, Univ. of Minnesota, 1955, d.j.
$125.00

W 36. WALTERS (M. H.). Early Days and Indian Ways: Journal
of Madge Hardin Walters. 254pp, illus, Los Angeles,
1956 (1st ed.), d.j. $20.00
Good material on Navajo, Sioux and Blackfoot by one
with a true understanding of the American Indian. Author was a dealer and collector of Navajo rugs, silver
work and other Indian artifacts.

W 37. WALTERS (Paul A. F.). The Cities That Died of Fear.
46pp, illus, the story of the Saline Pueblos, printed
wrappers, n.p., 1931. $20.00

W 38. WALTERS (W. F.). Navajoland: A Journey of Legends.
65pp, illus with drawings, Farmington, for author, 1964.
$28.00

W 39. WALTON (A. T.) et al. After the Buffalo Were Gone, the
Louis Warren Hill, Sr., Collection of Indian Art. 255pp,
20pp of color photographs and 402 b/w photographs, 3
figures, 2 maps, St. Paul, 1985. $35.00
This collection offers a unique contribution to the
scholarship of Indian art in that it documents the effects
of the transition period (roughly 1880-1940) on the art
of an Indian people--in this case, the Blackfeet. In 1952
the collection was divided; half of it was given to the
Museum of the Plains Indian, and the other half was re-
tained by the Northwest Area Foundation. This catalogue
that reunites the collection contains four essays, and illustrates more than 400 objects, most of which are Blackfeet.
(EAP)

W 40. WALTON (George). Fearless and Free. The Seminole War,
1835-1842. 260pp, illus, bibliography, Indianapolis, 1977
(1st ed.). $15.00
_____Another Copy. Same. $10.00

W 41. (WANAMAKER). The Wanamaker Primer on the North American Indian. Hiawatha: Produced in Life. Wanamaker--
Originator. 55, (16)pp, photographs, illus, decorated
bds, sml 8vo, n.p., 1909. $90.00
First section describes history, conditions, and future
of North American Indians, includes a description of the
1908 Wanamaker Expedition. Second section is the poem
"Hiawatha," with photographs, a film of which was produced on the Crow reservation.
_____Another Copy. Same. $60.00

W 42. WARBURTON (Austen D.) and ENDERT (J. F.). Indian
Lore of the North California Coast. 174pp, illus, bibliography, Santa Clara, 1966. $12.00

W 43. WARD (A.). (Center for Anthropological Studies, Contribution No. 1, Albuquerque, 1978) Limited Activity and
Occupation Sites, A Collection of Conference Papers. xii,
214pp, 45 figures, wraps. $28.00

W44. WARD (A.). (Center for Anthropological Studies, Ethnology
Report Series No. 2, Albuquerque, 1980) Navajo Graves.
An Archaeological Reflection of Ethnographic Reality.
viii, 54pp, 10 figures, wraps. $18.00
___Another Copy. Albuquerque, 1986. $15.00
___Another Copy. Same. $12.00

W45. WARD (D. J. H.). Meskwakia and the Meskwaki People
(Tama County, Iowa). 43pp, map, wrappers. $15.00
Reprint from Iowa Journal of History and Politics,
April, 1906. Includes account of lands bought and owned
by these Indians during 1857-1905, with table; list of
names of 342 Meskwakis; phonology of the language, etc.

W46. WARD (D. J. H.). The Problem of the Mounds. 23pp,
includes: history, size of mounds, contents, investigative
methods, wrappers, reprint of Iowa Journal of History
and Politics, for 1905. $10.00

W47. WARD (D. J. H.). Some Iowa Mounds. Reprint from Iowa
Journal of History and Politics, January, 1904. 36pp,
plans, lists and describes mound groups, wraps. $10.00

W48. WARD (Elizabeth). No Dudes, Few Women: Life with a
Navajo Range Rider. xi, 251pp, cloth, Albuquerque,
1951 (1st ed.), d.j. $45.00

W49. WARDELL (Morris L.). A Political History of the Cherokee
Nation, 1838-1907. 370pp, plus index, illus, folding
map, extensive bibliography, Norman, 1938 (1st ed.),
d.j. $50.00
___Another Copy. Norman, 1977, d.j. $20.00

W50. WARDWELL (Allen). The Gold of Ancient America. 148pp,
numerous illus with 8 in color, includes Peru, Colombia,
Ecuador, Panama, Costa Rica, and Mexico; Greenwich,
1968. $35.00

W51. WARDWELL (Allen). Objects of Bright Pride: Northwest
Coast Indian Art from the American Museum of Natural
History. 128pp, map, pls, bibliography, 4to, wraps,
New York, 1978 (1st ed.). $20.00

W52. WARDWELL (Allen). Pre-Columbian Art, Mexico, Mesoamerica, and South America. 24pp, 36 large photographs, Exhibition Catalogue, Gray Gallery, Chicago,
1971. $12.00

W53. WARDWELL (Allen). Yakutat South Indian Art of the
Northwest Coast. 82pp, 110 b/w and 2 color photo-
graphs, wrappers, Art Institute, Chicago, 1964. $30.00
___Another Copy. Same. $25.00

W54. WARE (Eugene F.). The Indian War of 1864--and Personal
Adventures Connected Therewith. 601pp, 30 illus,
cloth, Topeka, 1911 (1st ed.). $85.00
___Another Copy. New York, 1960 (1st ed. thus),
d.j. $40.00
___Another Copy. Same. $20.00
___Another Copy. Same. $30.00

W55. (WARFARE PRACTICES). Scalping and Torture: Warfare

Practices Among the North American Indians. 110pp, illus, bibliography, notes, stiff wraps, collection of three articles, 1906-1941, Ohsweken, Ontario, 1985. $12.00

W56. WARREN (J. Mason). An Account of Two Remarkable Indian Dwarfs Exhibited in Boston Under the Name of Aztec Children. Reprinted from the American Journal of Medical Science, Vol. XX, 17pp, 2 hand-colored pls, wrappers, Boston, J. Wilson & Son, 1851. $125.00

W57. WARREN (William W.). (Collections of the Minnesota Historical Society, Vol. V, St. Paul, 1885, 1st ed.) History of the Ojibway Nation. 535pp, index, cloth. $120.00
____Another Copy. Same. $100.00
____Another Copy. Minneapolis, 1957, d.j. $22.00

W58. WASHBURN (Cephas). Reminiscences of the Indians. viii, 9-236pp, cloth, Richmond, VA, Presbyterian Committee, 1869 (1st ed.). $250.00
Howes: W-127. Field: 1622. Narration of experiences of this early missionary to the Indians, who, like the Jesuits, traveled hundreds of miles to work with the Tribes in their own forest lands. (R. M. Weatherford)

W59. WASHBURN (D. K.) and SAYERS (R.) (Editors). The Elkus Collection. Southwest Indian Art. 222pp, 212 b/w and 27 color photographs, map, San Francisco, 1984. $22.00

W60. WASHBURN (Wilcomb E.). The Indian in America. 296pp, illus, index, maps, New York, 1975 (1st ed.), d.j. $20.00

W61. WASHBURN (Wilcomb E.) Red Man's Land--White Man's Law. A Study of the Past and Present Status of the American Indian. 266pp, plus index, notes, New York, 1971 (1st ed.), d.j. $12.00
____Another Copy. Same, wraps. $10.00

W62. (WASHINGTON TERRITORY). (Senate Executive Document 82, 48:2, Washington, DC, 1885, 1st printing) Agreement With Indians in Washington Territory (Yakima Indian Reservation). 11pp, 4 folding maps. Removed. $25.00

W63. (WASHINGTON TERRITORY). (House of Representatives Executive Document No. 45, 35:1, Washington, DC, 1858, 1st printing) Expenses of the Indian Wars in Washington and Oregon Territories. 16pp. Removed. $20.00

W64. (WASHINGTON TERRITORY). (House of Representatives Document No. 505, 63:2, Washington, DC, 1913, 1st printing) Indian Tuberculosis Sanitarium and Yakima Indian Reservation Project. 20pp, chart. Removed. $22.00

W65. (WASHINGTON TERRITORY). (Senate Executive Document 46, 34:1, Washington, DC, 1856, 1st printing) Indian Disturbances in the Territories of Washington and Oregon. 10pp, report of Isaac Stevens on Indian battles in Seattle, on Puget Sound, The Dalles, etc. Removed. $20.00

W66. (WASHINGTON TERRITORY). (Senate Document 188, 59:2, Washington, DC, 1907, 1st printing) Lower Band of Chinook Indians of the State of Washington. 5pp. Removed. $10.00

W67. (WASHINGTON TERRITORY). (House of Representatives Executive Document 102, 43:1, Washington, DC, 1874, 1st printing) Reservation in the Territory of Washington for the Coeur d'Alene and Other Indian Tribes. 11pp. Removed. $10.00

W68. WASLEY (C.). (American Anthropologist, Vol. 51, No. 4, Part 2, 1949, Memoir No. 71) The Social and Religious Life of a Guatemalan Village. 150pp, 3pp photographs, wrappers. $25.00
___Another Copy. Same. $30.00

W69. WASSEN (S. H.). (Etnologiska Studier. Etnografiska Museet, Goteborg. No. 16, 1949) Contributions to Cuna Ethnography and Some Archaeological Observations from Boquete, Chiriqui, Panama. 192pp, 81 figures, wraps. $25.00

W70. WASSEN (S. H.). (Etnologiska Studier 28--Etnografiska Museet, Goteborg, 1965) Use of Some Specific Kinds of South American Indian Snuff and Related Paraphernalia. 132pp, 58 illus, map, wrappers. $15.00

W71. WATERMAN (T. T.). (Univ. of California Publications in American Archaeology and Ethnology, Vol. 12, No. 7, Berkeley, 1917) Bandelier's Contribution to the Study of Ancient Mexican Social Organizations. pp249-282, wrappers. $20.00

W72. WATERMAN (T. T.). (Univ. of California Publications in American Archaeology and Ethnology, Vol. 11, No. 6, Berkeley, 1916) The Delineation of the Day-Signs in the Aztec Manuscripts. pp 297-398, wrappers. $25.00

W73. WATERMAN (T. T.). North American Indian Dwellings. pp 461-485, pls, wrappers, offprint from Smithsonian Report for 1924, Washington, 1925. $10.00

W74. WATERMAN (T. T.). (Museum of the American Indian, Notes and Monographs, No. 59, New York, 1973) Notes on the Ethnology of the Indians of Puget Sound. 145pp, 35 photographs of baskets, 18 photographs and 13 drawings of objects of material culture, wrappers. $23.00
___Another Copy. Same. $12.00
___Another Copy. Same. $10.00

W75. WATERMAN (T. T.). (Heye Foundation Indian Notes, Vol. 7, No. 2, New York, 1930) The Paraphernalia of the Dawamish, "Spirit Canoe Ceremony." pp 129-276, bound in later cloth. $10.00

W76. WATERMAN (T. T.). (Univ. of California Publications in American Archaeology and Ethnology, Vol. 8, No. 6, Berkeley, 1910) The Religious Practices of the Diegueno Indians. 104pp, 8pp photographs, wraps. $45.00

W77. WATERMAN (T. T.) and COFFIN (G.). (Heye Foundation

Indian Notes and Monographs, New York, 1920) Types
of Canoes on Puget Sound. 45pp, 1 figure, 5pp photographs, 2pp of drawings, wrappers. $25.00
___Another Copy. Same. $30.00

W78. WATERMAN (T. T.) and GREINER (R.). (Heye Foundation Indian Notes and Monographs, New York, 1921)
Indian Houses of Puget Sound. 61pp, pls, figures, bibliography, wrappers. $30.00

W79. WATERMAN (T. T.). The Whaling Equipment of the Makah
Indians. 50pp, plus 8 pls, figures, bibliography, wrappers, Univ. of Washington, 1955. $30.00

W80. WATERS (Frank). Book of the Hopi. 347pp, 4to, illus,
New York, 1964. $40.00
Revelation of the Hopi's historical and religious world-
view of life related by Hopi elders interpreting the hither-
to unknown meaning and functions of their year-long cere-
monial cycle. Large attractive volume, illustrated with
photographs and Hopi color drawings.
___Another Copy. Same, d.j. $30.00
___Another Copy. Same, d.j. $40.00
___Another Copy. New York, 1973, d.j. $45.00

W81. WATERS (Frank). Masked Gods: Navaho and Pueblo Cere-
monialism. 438pp, decorative cloth, Albuquerque,
1950 (1st ed.). $60.00
___Another Copy. Same, d.j. $75.00
___Another Copy. Same, lacks d.j. $62.00
___Another Copy. Same. $50.00
___Another Copy. Chicago, 1951. $25.00

W82. WATERS (Frank). Pumpkin Seed Point. 175pp, drawings,
glossary, observations from three years with the Hopi
while recording Hopi religious traditions and beliefs,
Chicago, 1969 (1st ed.), d.j. $25.00
___Another Copy. Same. $35.00

W83. WATKINS (Frances E.). (Southwest Museum Leaflet No.
16, Los Angeles, n.d.) The Navaho. 47pp, illus,
wrappers. $10.00

W84. WATSON (Don). Cliff Dwellings of the Mesa Verde: A
Story in Pictures. 52pp, illus, stiff printed wraps.
Mesa Verde, n.d., c.1955. $15.00

W85. WATSON (Don). Cliff Palace: The Story of an Ancient
City. 142pp, illus, stiff printed wrappers, Ann Arbor,
1947. $25.00
___Another Copy. Ann Arbor, 1941. $15.00
___Another Copy. Ann Arbor, 1940 (1st ed.). $12.00

W86. WATSON (Don). Indians of the Mesa Verde. v, 188pp,
illus, stiff printed wrappers, Mesa Verde, 1953. $20.00
___Another Copy. Mesa Verde, 1961. $12.00
___Another Copy. Same. $10.00

W87. WATSON (J. B.). (American Anthropologist, Vol. 54, No.
2, Part 2, 1952, Memoir No. 73) Cayua Culture Change:
A Study in Acculturation and Methodology. 144pp,

                    map, plus 4pp of photographs, wraps. $25.00
                    ___Another Copy. Same. $10.00
W88.   WATSON (Virginia). The Princess Pocahontas. 306pp,
                    illus by George Wharton Edwards, some pls in color,
                    cloth with color illus overlay, New York, 1916. $15.00
W89.   WATTS (John S.). Indian Depredations in New Mexico.
                    66pp, wrappers, reprint of a work originally issued in
                    1858, Tucson, 1964. $12.00
W90.   WAUCHOPE (Robert). (Society for American Archaeology,
                    Memoirs No. 21, Salt Lake City, 1966) Archaeological
                    Survey of Northern Georgia. 481pp, illus, wrappers.
                                                                   $35.00
W91.   WAUCHOPE (R.). (Middle American Research. Tulane
                    Univ., Publication No. 14, 1948) Excavations at
                    Zacualpa, Guatemala. 192pp, 25 pls, 79 figures, wraps.
                                                                   $45.00
                    ___Another Copy. Same. $40.00
W92.   WAUCHOPE (Robert). Lost Tribes and Sunken Continents:
                    Myth and Method in the Study of American Indians.
                    155pp, 28 illus, Chicago Univ. Press, 1962, d.j. $12.00
                    ___Another Copy. Same. $10.00
W93.   WAUCHOPE (R.). (Middle American Research. Tulane
                    Univ., Publication 28, No. 1, 1961) Ten Years of Middle
                    American Archaeology: Annotated Bibliography and News
                    Summary, 1948-1957. 106pp, wrappers. $30.00
                    ___Another Copy. Same. $20.00
W94.   WAUCHOPE (R.). They Found the Buried Cities. Explora-
                    tion and Excavation in the American Tropics. 382pp,
                    illus, Univ. of Chicago Press, 1965, d.j. $15.00
W95.   WAX (Murray L.) and BUCHANAN (R. W.) (Editors).
                    Solving "The Indian Problem": The White Man's Burden-
                    some Business. 217pp, plus index, selected bibliography,
                    New York, 1975 (1st ed.), d.j. $12.00
W96.   WEATHERFORD (Mark). Bannock--Paiute War. The Cam-
                    paign and Battles. 93pp, account and analysis of war
                    from official documents, wrappers, Corvallis, 1959
                    (2nd ed.). $85.00
W97.   WEATHERFORD (Mark). Chief Joseph. His Battles--His
                    Retreat. 127pp, account of campaign against Joseph,
                    with roster of Howard's officers, wrappers, very scarce
                    book on the Nez Perce War, Corvallis, 1958 (2nd ed.).
                                                                  $125.00
W98.   WEATHERFORD (Mark). Rogue River Indian War. 103pp,
                    Southwest Oregon, 1850-56. Precipitated by influx of
                    settlers and miners. scarce account, privately printed,
                    n.p., n.d. (Ashland Oregon). c.1959. $75.00
W99.   WEATHERWAX (Paul). Indian Corn in Old America. 245pp,
                    plus index, illus, bibliography, New York, 1954 (1st
                    ed.), d.j. $27.00
W100. WEAVER (M. P.). (Heye Foundation, Indian Notes and
                    Monographs, No. 56, New York, 1967) Tlapacoya Pottery

in the Museum Collection. 48pp, plus 41 photographic pls, maps, drawings, bibliography, wrappers. $10.00

W101. WEAVER (Sally). (National Museum, Publications in Ethnology, No. 4, Ottawa, 1972) Medicine and Politics Among the Grand River Iroquois: A Study of the Non-Conservatives. 182pp, illus, wrappers. $12.00

W102. WEBB (Clarence H.). (Geoscience and Man, Vol. XVII, Louisiana State Univ., Baton Rouge, 1977) The Poverty Point Culture. x, 73pp, illus, maps, figures, bibliography, index, lrge 8vo, wrappers. $10.00

W103. WEBB (Edith Buckland). Indian Life at the Old Mission. 326pp, 4to, illus, maps, bibliography, Lincoln, 1982, d.j. $35.00
_____Another Copy. Same. $30.00

W104. WEBB (Edith). Pigments Used by the Mission Indians of California. 13pp, 4to, wrappers, Washington, 1945. $10.00

W105. WEBB (George). A Pima Remembers. 126pp, wraps, Tucson, 1959 (1st ed.). $12.00

W106. WEBB (Walter Prescott). The Great Plains. 515pp, plus index, illus, maps, bibliographies, Boston, 1931 (1st ed. thus). $15.00

WEBB (William S.). See also BAE Bulletins Nos. 118, 122, and 129.

W107. WEBB (W. S.) and SNOW (C. E.). (Univ. of Kentucky, Reports in Archaeology and Anthropology, Vol. 6, 1945) The Adena People. 369pp, 28 figures, folding map, folding tables, bibliography, 8vo, wrappers. $85.00
_____Another Copy. Knoxville, 1981, cloth, d.j. $25.00
_____Another Copy. Same, lacks d.j. $15.00

W108. WEBB (W. S.), et al. The Adena People, No. 2. xi, 123pp, 29 figures, wrappers, Ohio Historical Society, 1957. $30.00
_____Another Copy. Same. $35.00
_____Another Copy. Same, rebound in cloth. $25.00

W109. WEBB (W. S.) and FUNKHOUSER (W. D.). (Univ. of Kentucky, Reports in Archaeology and Anthropology, Vol. 2, 1932) Archaeological Survey of Kentucky. vi, 463pp, 65 figures, folding map, 72 county maps, bibliography, index, 8vo, original wrappers. $85.00

W110. WEBB (W. S.) and HAAG (W. G.). (Univ. of Kentucky, Reports in Archaeology and Anthropology, Vol. 7, No. 1, 1947) Archaic Sites in McLean County, Kentucky. 46pp, 11 figures, bibliography, 8vo, original wrappers, ex-lib. $25.00

W111. WEBB (W. S.) and HAAG (W. G.). (Univ. of Kentucky, Reports in Archaeology and Anthropology, Vol. 4, No. 1, 1939) The Chiggerville Site: Site I, Ohio County, Kentucky. 62pp, folding plan, 2 folding tables, bibliography, 8vo, original wrappers. $35.00

W112. WEBB (W. S.) and FUNKHOUSER (W. D.). (Univ. of

Kentucky, Reports in Archaeology and Anthropology,
Vol. 3, No. 5, 1937) The Chilton Site in Henry County,
Kentucky. pp 173-206, 34 figures, plan, 8vo, original
wrappers. $25.00

W113. WEBB (W. S.) and HAAG (W. G.). (Univ. of Kentucky,
Reports in Archaeology and Anthropology, Vol. 5, No.
4, 1942) The C. & O. Mounds at Paintsville: Sites jo
2 and jo 9, Johnson County, Kentucky. pp 292-372, 18
figures, bibliography, 8vo, wrappers. $30.00

W114. WEBB (W. S.). (Univ. of Kentucky, Reports in Archaeology and Anthropology, Vol. 5, No. 6, 1943) The
Crigler Mounds Sites Be 20 and Be 27 and the Hartman
Mound Site Be 32, Boone County, Kentucky. pp 500-579,
20 figures (several folding), bibliography, 8vo, original
wrappers. $40.00

W115. WEBB (W. S.) and HAAG (W. G.). (Univ. of Kentucky,
Reports in Archaeology and Anthropology, Vol. 4, No.
2, 1940) Cypress Creek Villages: Sites 11 and 12,
McLeod County, Kentucky. pp 67-110, 27 figures,
bibliography, 8vo, original wrappers. $25.00

W116. WEBB (W. S.) and FUNKHOUSER (W. D.). (Univ. of
Kentucky, Reports in Archaeology and Anthropology,
Vol. 1, No. 6, 1931) The Duncan Site on the Kentucky-
Tennessee Line. pp 417-487, 46 figures, folding map,
8vo, original wrappers. $35.00

W117. WEBB (W. S.) and HAAG (W. G.). (Univ. of Kentucky,
Reports in Archaeology and Anthropology, Vol. 7, No.
2, 1947) The Fisher Site, Fayette County, Kentucky.
pp 47-104, 19 figures, bibliography, 8vo, original
wrappers. $30.00

W118. WEBB (W. S.) and HAAG (W. G.). (Univ. of Kentucky,
Reports in Archaeology and Anthropology, Vol. 4, No.
3, Part I, 1946) Indian Knoll Site Oh 2, Ohio County,
Kentucky. pp 113-365, 58 figures, folding map, bib-
liography, 8vo, original wrappers. $30.00
___Another Copy. Same. $47.00

W119. WEBB (W. S.) and HAAG (W. G.). (Univ. of Kentucky,
Reports in Archaeology and Anthropology, Vol. 4, No.
3, Part 2, 1948) Indian Knoll Skeletons of Site Oh 2,
Ohio County, Kentucky. pp 366-555, 53 figures, folding tables, bibliography, index, 8vo, original wrappers.
$35.00

W120. WEBB (W. S.). (Univ. of Kentucky, Reports in Archaeology and Anthropology, Vol. 8, No. 1, 1952) The Jonathan Creek Village Site 4, Marshall County, Kentucky.
141pp, 54 figures, bibliography, 8vo, original wrappers.
$20.00

W121. WEBB (W. S.) and FUNKHOUSER (W. D.). (Univ. of
Kentucky, Reports in Archaeology and Anthropology,
Vol. 3, No. 1, 1933) The McLeod Bluff Site in
Hickman County, Kentucky. 33pp, 16 figures, 8vo,

original wrappers. $25.00

___Another Copy. Same. $15.00

W122. WEBB (W. S.) and HAAG (W. G.). (Univ. of Kentucky,
Reports in Archaeology and Anthropology, Vol. 5, No.
3, 1941) The Morgan Stone Mound Site 15, Bath County, Kentucky. pp 219-291, 20 figures (2 folding),
bibliography, 8vo, original wrappers. $30.00

W123. WEBB (W. S.) and HAAG (W. G.). (Univ. of Kentucky,
Reports in Archaeology and Anthropology, Vol. 5, No.
2, 1941) Mt. Horeb Earthworks Site I and the Drake
Mound Site II, Fayette County, Kentucky. pp 139-218,
29 figures, folding profile, bibliography, 8vo, original
wrappers. $30.00

W124. WEBB (W. S.) and FUNKHOUSER (W. D.). (Univ. of Kentucky, Reports in Archaeology and Anthropology, Vol.
1, No. 3, 1930) The Page Site in Logan County, Kentucky. pp 117-232, 89 photographs, fold-out map, original wrappers. $32.00

___Another Copy. Same. $15.00

W125. WEBB (W. S.) and FUNKHOUSER (W. D.). (Univ. of Kentucky, Reports in Archaeology and Anthropology, Vol.
3, No. 3, 1935) The Ricketts Site in Montgomery County, Kentucky. pp 71-100, 26 figures, diagram, 8vo,
original wrappers. $25.00

W126. WEBB (W. S.). (Univ. of Kentucky, Reports in Archaeology and Anthropology, Vol. 5, No. 7, 1943) The Riley
Mound Site Be 15 and the Landing Mound Site Be 17,
Boone County, Kentucky. pp 580-697, 30 figures (2
folding), bibliography, index, 8vo, original wrappers.
$30.00

W127. WEBB (W. S.) and FUNKHOUSER (W. D.). (Univ. of Kentucky, Reports in Archaeology and Anthropology, Vol.
3, No. 4, 1936) Rock Shelters in Menifee County, Kentucky. pp 105-167, 24 figures, folding map, bibliography, 8vo, original wrappers. $25.00

___Another Copy. Same. $22.00

W128. WEBB (W. S.) and FUNKHOUSER (W. D.). (Univ. of Kentucky, Reports in Archaeology and Anthropology, Vol.
1, No. 4, 1930) Rock Shelters of Wolfe and Powell Counties, Kentucky. pp 239-306, 50 figures, folding map,
8vo, original wrappers. $35.00

W129. WEBB (W. S.) and FUNKHOUSER (W. D.). (Univ. of Kentucky, Reports in Archaeology and Anthropology, Vol.
1, No. 2, 1929) The So-Called "Ash Caves" in Lee
County, Kentucky. pp 37-112, 62 figures, 8vo, original
wrappers. $30.00

W130. WEBB (W. S.) and FUNKHOUSER (W. D.). (Univ. of Kentucky, Reports in Archaeology and Anthropology, Vol.
1, No. 5, 1931) Tolu Site in Crittenden County, Kentucky. pp 315-410, 80 figures, folding map, 8vo, original wrappers. $35.00

W131. WEBB (W. S.) and FUNKHOUSER (W. D.). (Univ. of Kentucky, Reports in Archaeology and Anthropology, Vol. 1, No. 1, 1929) The Williams Site in Christian County, Kentucky. 29pp, 36 figures, 8vo, original wrappers.
$40.00

W132. WEBB (William) and WEISTEIN (Robert). Dwellers at the Source. Southwestern Indian Photographs by A. C. Vroman, 1895-1904. 213pp, cloth, New York, 1973, d.j.
$25.00

W133. WEBER (R. L.). (Fieldiana, Vol. 62, No. 2, 1978) A Seriation of the Lake Prehistoric Santa Maria Culture of Northwestern Argentina. 50pp, 27 photographs, 30 drawings of urns, 48 drawings of designs, wraps.
$10.00

W134. WEBER (S. A.) and SEAMON (P. D.) (Editors). Havasupai Habitat. A. F. Whiting's Ethnography of a Traditional Indian Culture. xxi, 288pp, 14pp of photographs and drawings, 2 maps, chart, 35 tables, cloth. $35.00
____Another Copy. Same. $25.00

WEDEL (Waldo R.). See also BAE Bulletins Nos. 112, 130, 155, 157, 164, and 174.

W135. WEDEL (W. R.). (U.S. National Museum Bulletin 183, Washington, DC, 1943) Archaeological Investigations in Platte and Clay Counties, Missouri. 284pp, 50 pls of multiple artifacts, wrappers. $45.00
____Another Copy. Same. $38.00
____Another Copy. Same. $20.00

W136. WEDEL (W. R.). (Smithsonian Misc. Collections Vol. 101, No. 3, 1941) Environment and Native Subsistence Economies in the Great Plains. 29pp, 1 figure, 5pp of photographs, wrappers. $18.00

W137. WEDEL (W. R.). Prehistoric Man on the Great Plains. 355pp, 24 pls, Norman, 1961 (1st ed.). $30.00
____Another Copy. Norman, 1978, d.j. $22.00

W138. WEEKS (A. G.). Massasoit of the Wampanoags. 270pp, frontis, wrappers, Massachusetts, 1920. $25.00

W139. WEEMS (John Edward). Death Song. The Last of the Indian Wars. 300pp, plus index, notes, endpaper maps, Garden City, NY, 1976 (1st ed.), d.j. $15.00
____Another Copy. Same. $12.00

W140. WEER (Paul). (Indiana Historical Society Prehistory Research Series, Vol. 1, No. 4, 1938, 1st ed.) Preliminary Notes on the Caddoan Family. pp 111-130, wrappers.
$10.00

W141. WEER (Paul). (Indiana Historical Bulletin, Vol. 14, No. 2, 1937) Preliminary Notes on the Siouan Family. pp 99-120, wrappers. $10.00

WEIANT (C. W.). See BAE Bulletins Nos. 139 and 143.

W142. (WELCH, ANDREW). A Narrative of the Early Days and Remembrances of Oceola Nikkanochee, Prince of Econchatti, A Young Seminole Indian; Son of Econchatti-Mico,

King of the Red Hills, in Florida; With a Brief History
of His Nation, and His Renowned Uncle, Oceola, and
His Parents; and Amusing Tales, Illustrative of Indian
Life in Florida. 5 leaves, 228pp, 3 lithographic pls,
half calf and marbled bds, London, 1841. $750.00
    Decker: 37, 110. Sabin: 56642. This work is at-
tributed to Dr. Andrew Welch, a physician of St. Augustine, later resident in London. It gives the biography
of Oceola's nephew, at that time a youth in Dr. Welch's
care in London, with considerable detail about the
Seminole Wars both from the recollections of the young
man, and presumably the knowledge of the Doctor. The
book also contains, in the appendix, the text of the
Treaty of Moultrie Creek of 1824. The author is attributed with several other works on the Seminole Wars,
including "A Narrative of the Life and Sufferings of
Mrs. Jane Johns," Charleston, 1837. "A Seminole
Tragedy, A Narrative," 1849. (WR)
    ____Another Copy. Modern cloth, London, 1841.
                             $325.00

W143. WELD (Isaac). Travels Through the States of North America, and the Provinces of Upper and Lower Canada,
During the Years 1795, 1796, and 1797. viii, 552pp,
errata, 8 maps (some folding), pls, rebound in cloth,
London, John Stockdale, 1800 (4th ed.). $300.00
    Howes: W-235. Sabin: 102541. The author covers
the natives and fur trade and shows his preference for
Canada over America.

W144. WELLCOME (Henry S.). The Story of Metlakahtla.
xx, 482pp, pls, 1 adv page, about self-supporting
village established by missionary Wm. Duncan among
British Columbia Tsimshean Indians, cloth, London and
New York, 1887. $85.00
    ____Another Copy. Same. $55.00

W145. WELLMAN (Paul I.). Broncho Apache. 303pp, cloth, novel
based upon what is known about Massai, a Chiricahua
Apache who escaped from Geronimo's prison train some-
where east of St. Louis in September of 1886, New
York, 1936 (1st ed.). $50.00

W146. WELLMAN (Paul I.). Death in the Desert: The Fifty
Years War for the Great Southwest. 308pp, illus, folding map, bibliography, index, New York, 1935 (1st ed.).
                             $50.00

W147. WELLMAN (Paul I.). Death on Horseback: Seventy Years
of War for the American West. 484pp, portraits, pls,
maps, bibliography, index, Philadelphia, 1947, d.j.
                             $35.00

W148. WELLMAN (Paul I.). Indian Wars and Warriors. East.
180pp, plus index, illus by Lorence Bjorklund, maps,
for younger readers, but well done, Boston, 1959
(1st ed.), d.j. $10.00

W149. WELLS (O. N.). Salish Weaving, Primitive and Modern.
36pp, 20 b/w and 2 full-page color photographs, 12
drawings, plus several hundred designs displayed, map,
wraps, Sardis, 1969. $15.00

W150. WELSH (Herbert). Civilization Among the Sioux Indians:
Report of a Visit to Some of the Sioux Reservations of
South Dakota and Nebraska. 58pp, map, self-wrappers,
stapled, Philadelphia, 1882. $100.00
Welsh, an official of the Indian Rights Association,
reports on his visit to the Sioux Indian reservations,
and recommends improvements which would protect the
Indians from unscrupulous agents and speculators.

W151. WELSH (Herbert). Crow Creek Reservation, Dakota. Action of the Indian Rights Association, and Opinions of
the Press, West and East, Regarding Its Recent Occupation by White Settlers, Together with the Proclamation
of the President Commanding the Removal of the Settlers
and Restoring of the Lands to the Indians. 45pp, with
two inserts updating the case (8pp), the other (4pp),
wrappers, Philadelphia, 1885 all. $100.00
___Another Copy. Same. $80.00

W152. WELSH (Herbert). Report of a Visit to the Great Sioux
Reserve, Dakota, Made During the Months of May and
June, 1883, in Behalf of the Indian Rights Association.
49pp, stiff wrappers, Germantown, 1883. $100.00

W153. WELSH (William). Report of a Visit to the Sioux and Ponka
Indians on the Missouri River. 36pp, wrappers, Wash-
ington, GPO, 1872. $125.00
___Another Copy. Same. $30.00
___Another Copy. Same. $30.00

W154. WELTFISH (Gene). The Origins of Art. 300pp, drawings, material on the Bakairi Indians of the Amazon,
the Mimbres, California Indians, Indianapolis, 1953
(1st ed.), d.j. $17.00

W155. WENDORF (Fred) et al. (Museum of Northern Arizona,
Bulletin 27, Flagstaff, 1953) Archaeological Studies
in the Petrified Forest National Monument. 200pp, plus
index, photographs, drawings, maps, wrappers. $30.00

W156. WENDORF (F.) et al. The Midland Discovery: A Report
of the Pleistocene Human Remains from Midland, Texas.
viii, 139pp, plus, map, figures, bibliography, index,
Univ. of Texas, 1955 (1st ed.). $15.00

W157. WERNER (Fred H.). The Dull Knife Battle. Doomsday
for the Northern Cheyennes. 119pp, illus, Greely, 1981
(1st ed.). $10.00

W158. WERSTEIN (Irvin). Massacre at Sand Creek. 186pp,
2 maps, index, New York, 1963 (1st ed.), d.j. $17.00

W159. WESLAGER (C. A.). The Delaware Indian Westward Mi-
gration with the Texts of Two Manuscripts (1821-1822)
Responding to General Lewis Cass's Inquiries About
Lenape Culture and Language. 251pp, plus index,

maps, brief bibliography, Wallingford, PA, 1978 (1st
ed.), d.j. $25.00
___Another Copy. Same. $17.00

W160. WEST (George A.). (Bulletin, Public Museum of Milwaukee,
Vol. XVII, 1934, 1st ed.) Tobacco, Pipes and Smoking
Customs of the American Indians. (2 Volumes). Vol.
1: Is text containing history of tobacco use, cultivation,
pipe manufacture, etc., together with an extensive
classification of aboriginal pipes. 477pp. Vol. 2:
Contains 257 pls showing thousands of pipes and their
components. pp 477-994. Also contains figures, 19
maps, bibliography, index, lrge 8vo, bound in protective vinyl cvrs, the author spent almost 50 years studying the subject, here presented. Impressive and very
scarce. $650.00
___Another Copy. Same, wrappers. $225.00

W161. WEST (John). The Substance of a Journal During a Residence at the Red River Colony, British North America;
and Frequent Excursions Among the North-West American
Indians, in the Years 1820, 1821, 1822, 1823. 210pp,
3 illus, bds, inner hinge starting, London, 1824.
                                                             $650.00
___Another Copy. Rebound, ex-lib. $325.00
___Another Copy. Vancouver, 1967. $25.00

W162. WEST (R. C.). (Smithsonian Institute of Social Anthropology, Publication No. 7, 1948) Cultural Geography
of the Modern Tarascan Area. vi. 77pp of text containing 6 figures, 21 maps, and 14pp photographs, wrappers.
                                                             $30.00
___Another Copy. Same. $15.00

W163. WESTHEIM (Paul). Arte Antiguo de Mexico. 248pp, 150
figures, Mexico, 1963 (1st ed.). $50.00

W164. WESTHEIM (Paul). Ideas Fundamentales del Arte Pre-
Hispanico en Mexico. 288pp, 118 figures, 4 color pls,
wrappers, Mexico City, 1957 (1st Spanish ed.). $60.00
___Another Copy. Enlarged ed., 327pp, 158 pls,
Mexico, 1972. $45.00

W165. WESTHEIM (Paul) et al. Prehispanic Mexican Art. 447pp,
225 illus, 193 color pls, 4to, New York, 1972. $90.00

W166. WESTON (Donald). (Michigan Dept. of State Archaeological
Survey Report No. 3, 1974) An Archaeological Survey
of the Proposed Quanicassee Nuclear Power Plant Transmission Line Route. 46pp, wrappers. $10.00

W167. (WEST VIRGINIA). West Virginia Archaeologist, No. 19.
56pp, illus, mostly St. Albans site, points, etc., wraps,
Moundsville, WV, 1966. $15.00

W168. WETHERINGTON (R. K.). (Fort Burgwin Research Center
No. 6, Taos, 1968) Excavations at Pot Creek Pueblo.
104pp, 63 figures, wrappers. $18.00

W169. WETMORE (Ruth Y.). First on the Land: The North
Carolina Indians. 196pp, illus, Winston-Salem, 1974
(1st ed.), d.j. $20.00

W170. WEYER (E.). Jungle Quest. 198pp, 34 illus, New York,
       1955 (1st ed.). $15.00
W171. WEYER (E. M.). (American Museum of Natural History,
       Anthropological Papers, Vol. XXXI, Part IV, New York,
       1930) Archaeological Material from the Village Site at
       Hot Springs, Port Moller, Alaska. pp 239-279, illus,
       bibliography, wrappers. $40.00
W172. WEYER (E. M.). The Eskimos, Their Environment and
       Folkways. 483pp, 17 figures, 4 fold-out maps, cloth,
       New Haven, 1932, Hamden, 1962. $40.00
W173. WHARFIELD (H. B.). Alchesay, Scout with General
       Crook; Sierra Blanca Apache Chief; Friend of Fort
       Apache Whites; Counselor to Indian Agents. 53pp, illus,
       index, wrappers, El Cajon, 1969 (1st ed.). $17.00
W174. WHARFIELD (Col. H. B.). With Scouts and Cavalry at
       Fort Apache. Edited by John A. Carroll. 124pp, illus,
       index, endpaper maps, special autographed leather-
       bound edition of 50 copies, Tucson, 1965 (1st ed.).
                                                              $65.00
       ____Another Copy. Trade edition. $30.00
       ____Another Copy. Same. $28.00
W175. WHARTON (Clarence). Satana. The Great Chief of the
       Kiowas and His People. 239pp, plus index, photographs
       and other illus, Dallas, 1935 (1st ed.), d.j. $60.00
WHEAT (Joe Ben). See also BAE Bulletin No. 154.
W176. WHEAT (Joe Ben). The Addicks Dam Site ... Southeast
       Texas. Offprint, Smithsonian River Basin Survey Pa-
       pers, Washington, 1953. pp 143-242, 19 photographic
       pls, figures, map, bibliography, printed wrappers.
                                                              $10.00
W177. WHEAT (J. B.) et al. Among Ancient Ruins, the Legacy
       of Earl H. Morris. 94pp, 67 photographs, map, wraps,
       Boulder, 1985. $15.00
W178. WHEAT (J. B.). (Univ. of Arizona Bulletin, Vol. XXV,
       No. 3, Tucson, 1954) Crooked Ridge Village. 183pp,
       15pp of photographs, 62 figures, fold-out map, rebound
       in cloth. $30.00
       ____Another Copy. In original wrappers. $20.00
W179. WHEAT (J. B.). (American Anthropological Assoc., Vol.
       57, No. 2, Part 3, Memoir No. 82, 1955) Mogollon Cul-
       ture Prior to A.D. 1000. 242pp, 12 figures, 18 tables,
       wrappers. $23.00
W180. WHEAT (J. B.). (Memoirs of the Society for American
       Archaeology, American Antiquity, Vol. 26, Menasha and
       Salt Lake City, 1972) Olsen-Chubbuck Site: Paleolithic
       Bison Kill. x, 180pp, illus, figures, bibliography,
       wrappers. $15.00
W181. WHEAT (J. B.). Introduction. Patterns and Sources of
       Navajo Weaving. 20pp, 12 b/w and 9 color photographs,
       Salt Lake City, 1976. $10.00
W182. WHEAT (M. M.). Survival Arts of the Primitive Paiutes.
       130pp, 226 photographs, wrappers, Reno, 1967. $12.00

W183. WHEELER (E.) et al. (Garland American Ethnohistory
    Series, 1974) California Indians III, Pitt River Indians;
    Fall River Valley. 362pp, cloth. $30.00
W184. WHEELER (Edward S.). Scheyichbi and the Strand; or,
    Early Days Along the Delaware. With an Account of
    Recent Events at Sea Grove.... 116pp, frontis, illus,
    cloth, Philadelphia, 1876 (1st ed.). $50.00
W185. WHEELER (George M.). (Report Upon United States Geo-
    graphical Surveys West of the One Hundredth Meridian,
    Vol. VII, Washington, DC, GPO, 1879) Archaeology.
    xxi, 497pp, color frontis, 20 pls, map, index, many pls
    of artifacts: Chipped stone implements, stone and iron
    knives, stone vessels, etc., cloth. $75.00
WHEELER (R. P.). See BAE Bulletin No. 185.
W186. WHEELOCK (Eleazar). A Plain and Faithful Narrative of
    the Original Design, Rise, Progress, and Present State
    of the Indian Charity School at Lebanon, in Connecticut.
    55pp, cloth backed bds, facsimile reprint of Boston,
    1763 edition, limited to 125 copies, Rochester, NY, n.d.,
    c.1900. $15.00
W187. WHEELRIGHT (Mary C.). The Myth and Prayers of the
    Great Star Chant and the Myth of the Coyote Chant.
    190pp, edited with commentaries by David P. McAllester.
    22 serigraph color pls by Louie Ewing after sand paint-
    ings recorded by Franc J. Newcomb and others, Navajo
    Religion Series IV, Santa Fe, 1956 (1st ed.). $200.00
W188. WHEELRIGHT (Mary C.) (Editor). (Bulletins of the House
    of Navajo Religion, No. 2, Santa Fe, 1940, 1st ed.)
    Myth of Sontso (Big Star). 13pp, wrappers. $35.00
    _____Another Copy. Same, 1957, revised ed., with
    Coyote Chant added. $15.00
W189. WHEELRIGHT (M. C.) and McALLESTER (D. P.). Texts
    of the Navaho Creation Chants. 38pp, 2 figures, Cam-
    bridge, n.d. $17.00
W190. WHEELRIGHT (M. C.) (Editor). (Bulletins of the House
    of Navajo Religion No. 1, Santa Fe, 1939, 1st ed.)
    Tleji or Yehbechai Myth by Klah Hasteen. 14pp, wraps.
                                                        $40.00
    _____Another Copy. Same, 1948, 2nd printing. $20.00
    _____Another Copy. Same, 1955, 4th printing. $12.00
W191. WHERRY (Joseph H.). Indian Masks and Myths of the
    West. 273pp, illus, cloth, New York, 1969 (1st ed.),
    d.j. $15.00
    _____Another Copy. Same. $12.00
    _____Another Copy. Same. $12.00
W192. WHERRY (Joseph H.). The Totem Pole Indians. 152pp,
    illus, folio, cloth, New York, 1964 (1st ed.), d.j.
                                                        $15.00
W193. WHITE (E. E.). Experiences of a Special Indian Agent.
    Introduction by Edward E. Dale. 340pp, Norman,
    1965, d.j. $12.00

W194.   WHITE (Rev. Henry). Indian Battles: With Incidents in
         the Early History of New England. 427pp, index,
         cloth, New York, 1859. $30.00
W195.   (WHITE, JOHN). The Watercolor Drawings by John White.
         26pp with additional 27 illus, wrappers, includes
         Indians from Eastern U.S., Florida, and Eskimos, New
         York, Morgan Library, 1965. $15.00
W196.   WHITE (John). Pictorum Britanniae Partem Olim Incolenti-
         um Aliquot Icones. Qui Mihi Incolarum Virginiae Icones
         Dedit Pictor.... Folio, 5 full-page prints of Indians
         of America, with accompanying text, disbound, (Frank-
         fort, 1590). $600.00
             The Indians depicted display obvious European qual-
         ities and are shown in typical 16th century heroic poses
         and scenes, complete with European weapons. The
         prints are made to enforce the notion that there were
         resemblances between the inhabitants of ancient Scot-
         land and the Indians of North America.
WHITE (Leslie A.). See also BAE Bulletins nos. 136 and 184.
W197.   WHITE (Leslie A.). The Acoma Indians. Removed from
         Smithsonian Annual Report, No. 47, Washington, 1932.
         pp 17-192, pls, bibliography, rebound. $22.00
W198.   WHITE (L. A.). (Texas Memorial Museum, Bulletin No.
         6, Austin, 1963) The Ethnography and Ethnology of
         Franz Boas. 76pp, pls, bibliography, wrappers. $15.00
W199.   WHITE (L. A.) (Editor). Lewis Henry Morgan: The In-
         dian Journals, 1859-1862. 229pp, over 100 illus, 16
         full-page color pls, 4to, Ann Arbor, 1959. $60.00
         ___Another Copy. Same, d.j. $40.00
W200.   WHITE (L. A.). (American Anthropologist, Vol. 44, No.
         4,Part 2, 1942) The Pueblo of Santa Ana, New Mexico.
         360pp, 54 figures, 7pp of photographs, wraps. $58.00
         ___Another Copy. Same, rebound in cloth. $50.00
W201.   WHITE (L. A.). (American Anthropological Assoc., Mem-
         oirs, No. 38, 1932) The Pueblo of San Felipe. 69pp,
         3pp of photographs, 17 figures, wrappers. $40.00
         ___Another Copy. Same. $35.00
W202.   WHITE (L. A.). (American Anthropological Assoc., Mem-
         oirs, No. 43, 1935) The Pueblo of Santo Domingo.
         210pp, 53 figures, 8 pls, wrappers. $50.00
         ___Another Copy. Same. $60.00
W203.   WHITE (Leslie) and BERNAL (I.). (Instituto Nacional
         Antropologia e Historia, Mexico, 1960) Correspondencia
         de Adolfo Bandelier: La Interpretacion Morgan-
         Bandelier de la Sociedad Azteca/Correspondencia
         Bandelier-Garcia Icazbalceta. 322pp, frontis, wrappers.
                                                              $25.00
         ___Another Copy. Same. $40.00
W204.   WHITE (Lonnie J.). Hostiles and Horse Soldiers. Indian
         Battles and Çampaigns ín the West. 231pp, illus,
         sketch maps, Boulder, 1972 (1st book ed.), d.j. $17.00

W205. WHITE (Lonnie). White Women Captives of Southern Plains
Indians, 1866-1875. 27pp, 4to, good accounts with verbatim descriptions from local newspapers of the day,
separate printing from Journal of the West, wraps,
Los Angeles, 1969. $10.00

W206. WHITE (Raymond). (Univ. of California Publications in
American Archaeology and Ethnology, Vol. 48, No. 2,
Berkeley, 1963) Luiseno Social Organization. 103pp,
map, bibliography, wrappers. $35.00

WHITE (Theodore E.). See BAE Bulletin No. 158.

W207. WHITECOTTON (Joseph W.). The Zeysotecs. Princes,
Priests and Peasants. 332pp, plus index, photographs,
drawings, maps, notes, bibliography, Norman, 1977
(1st ed.), d.j. $15.00

W208. WHITEFORD (A. H.). North American Indian Arts.
160pp, approx. 1,000 color drawings, New York, 1970.
                                                               $12.00

W209. WHITFIELD (Henry). A Further Discovery of the Present
State of the Indians in New England, Concerning the
Progress of the Gospel Among Them. x, 46pp, edition
of 250 copies, wraps, reprint of the fifth Eliot tract,
entitled "Light Appearing," New York, J. Sabin, all
copies initialed by same, 1865. $35.00

W210. WHITFIELD (Henry). Strength Out of Weakness: or, A
Glorious Manifestation of the Further Progress of the
Gospel Among the Indians in New England. 59pp, un-
bound, edition of 250 copies initialed by Mr. Sabin,
New York, Joseph Sabin, 1865 (1st ed. thus). $45.00

W211. WHITING (B. B.). Paiute Sorcery. 110pp, map,
wrappers. $22.00

W212. WHITMAN (W.). The Oto. xvi, 132pp, cloth, New York,
1937. $40.00

W213. WHITMAN (William). The Pueblo Indians of San Ildefonso.
164pp, New York, 1947 (1st ed.), d.j. $25.00

W214. WHITNEY (Caspar). The Flowing Road, Adventures on
the Great Rivers of South America. 319pp, maps, cloth,
Philadelphia, 1912. $10.00

W215. WHITNEY (Harry). Hunting with the Eskimo. The Unique
Record of a Sportsman's Year Among the Northermost
Tribe, the Big Game, the Nature Life, and the Battle
for Existence Through the Long Arctic Night. xiv,
453pp, 8vo, many photographic illus, folding map,
original cloth, New York, 1910. $55.00
     Whitney went to Etah aboard the "Erik" in 1908,
spent the winter, and sledged to Ellesmere Island to
hunt Musk-ox. Much on the Eskimo.
____Another Copy. Same. $50.00

W216. WHITTEN (N. E.). Sacha Runa, Ethnicity and Adaptation
of Ecuadorian Jungle Quichua. xviii, 348pp, 56 photographs, 4 diagrams, 3 maps, cloth, Urbana, 1976.
                                                               $25.00

W217. WHITTEN (N. E.). Sicuanga Runa: The Other Side of Development in Amazonian Ecuador. 314pp, illus, Chicago, 1985. $18.00

W218. WHYMPER (Frederick). Travel and Adventure in the Territory of Alaska, Formerly Russian America. 353pp, folding map, illus, decorated cloth, New York, Harper & Bros., 1869. $90.00
    Wickersham: 6030. Field: 1657. Smith: 10978. Whymper traveled to British Columbia in 1862 and on to Alaska with an expedition in 1865. He visited Sitka, Norton Sound, Kamchatka, Yukon River, and Ft. Yukon. This is one of the earliest books on Alaska and contains much on the natives.
    ___Another Copy. Ann Arbor, 1966. $20.00

W219. WICKE (C. R.). Olmec, An Early Art Style of Pre-Columbian Mexico. xvii, 188pp, 36 photographs and drawings, map, cloth, Tucson, 1971. $30.00

W220. WIESENTHALL (M.). Peru and the Inca Civilization. 95pp, plus index, 194 color photographs, New York, 1978 (1st ed.), d.j. $10.00

W221. WILBERT (J.). Indios de la Region Orinoco Ventuari. 263pp, illus, map, wrappers, Caracas, 1963. $25.00

W222. WILBERT (J.). The Thread of Life: Symbolism of Miniature Art from Ecuador. 112pp, 157 figures, Dumbarton Oaks, No. 12, 1974. $15.00

W223. WILBERT (Johannes). (UCLA Latin American Studies, Vol. 44, Los Angeles, 1978, 1st ed., d.j.) Folk Literature of the Ge Indians (Eastern Brazil). 653pp, index to motifs, glossary, bibliography, map. $35.00

W224. WILBERT (Johannes). (UCLA Latin American Studies, Vol. 15, Los Angeles, 1970, 1st ed., d.j.) Folk Literature of the Warao Indians. Narrative Material and Motif Content. 614pp, motif index, glossary, bibliography, folklore of Indians from the Orinoco Delta of Venezuela and Guyana. $25.00

W225. WILBUR (Marguerite Eyer) (Translator). (Quivira Society Publications, Vol. II, Los Angeles, 1931) The Indian Uprising in Lower California 1734-1737 as Described by Father Sigismundo Taraval. 290pp, plus index, illus, map, limited to 665 copies, wraps. $125.00

WILDER (Carleton Stafford). See BAE Bulletin No. 186.

W226. WILDSCHUT (William) and EWERS (John C.). (Contributions from Museum of the American Indian, Vol. XVI, New York, 1959) Crow Indian Beadwork; A Descriptive and Historical Study. 55pp, b/w and color illus, bibliography, wraps. $17.00
    ___Another Copy. Same. $10.00

W227. WILDSCHUT (Wm.). (Heye Foundation, Museum of the American Indian Contribution, Vol. XVII, New York, 1960) Crow indian Medicine Bundles. 178pp, illus, wraps. $50.00

___Another Copy. Same, 1975. $24.00

___Another Copy. Same, 1975. $25.00

W228. WILGUS (A. C.). Old Civilizations of Inca Land. 141pp, 55 illus, cloth, American Museum of Natural History, New York, 1935, 1972 (reprint). $20.00

W229. WILHELM (Paul). Travels in North America, 1822-1824. Translated by W. Robert Nitske. Edited by Savoie Lottinville. 456pp, illus, index, map, bibliography, Norman, 1973 (1st ed.), d.j. $30.00

Paul Wilhelm, Duke Wurttemberg, traveled up the Missouri in 1823 to Ft. Kiowa in South Dakota. Much of the book concerns the Indians of the Nebraska-Dakota plains, especially the Pawnees and Otoes, also much on the Osage. This is a new translation of the 1835 German text, and the first annotated edition to appear in any language. Illustrated in color and b/w, with paintings by Bodmer, Catlin, McKenney and paintings from the Duke's collection.

W230. WILKE (Philip J.) (Editor). Background to Prehistory of the Yuha Desert Region. 109pp, maps, bibliography, wrappers, Ramona, 1976 (1st ed.). $12.00

___Another Copy. Same. $15.00

___Another Copy. Same. $10.00

W231. WILKE (P. J.). The Cahuilla Indians of the Colorado: Ethnohistory and Prehistory. 79pp, illus, maps, bibliography, 4to, wrappers, Ramona, 1975 (1st ed.).

$20.00

___Another Copy. Same. $15.00

W232. WILKEN (Robert L.). Anselm Weber, O.F.M.: Missionary to the Navaho 1898-1921. xiv, 255pp, illus, map, cloth, Milwaukee, 1955. $30.00

W233. WILKENS (Thurman). Cherokee Tragedy. The Story of the Ridge Family and the Decimation of a People. 382pp, plus index, photographs, drawings, notes, bibliography, endpaper maps, New York, 1970 (1st ed.), d.j. $25.00

W234. WILL (George F.) and HYDE (George E.). Corn Among the Indians of the Upper Missouri. 317pp, plus index, photographs, cloth, reprint of 1917 issue, Lincoln, 1964. $15.00

W235. WILLARD (Mrs. E. S.). Kin-Da-Shon's Wife: An Alaskan Story. 281pp, 6 adv-pp, pls, author sought to record Chilkat Indian life at beginning of White contact, New York, 1892 (1st ed.). $45.00

___Another Copy. Same. $30.00

___Another Copy. Same, inner hinges cracked.

$22.00

W236. WILLARD (Theodore Arthur). City of the Sacred Well. Being a Narrative of the Discoveries and Excavations of Edward Herbert Thompson in the Ancient City of Chichen Itza with Some Discourse on the Culture and

Development of Mayan Civilization. 293pp, illus, maps, cloth, New York, 1926. $45.00

___Another Copy. Same. $30.00

W237. WILLARD (T. A.). The Last Empires of the Itzaes and Mayas. 436pp, plus index, illus, maps, newly rebound, Glendale, 1933 (1st ed.). $20.00

W238. WILLEMS (E.). Buzios Island, A Caicara Community in Southern Brazil. viii, 116pp, 3 drawings, 2 maps, American Ethnological Society, New York, 1952. $25.00

___Another Copy. Same. $20.00

W239. WILLETT (Marinus). A Narrative of the Military Actions of Colonel Marinus Willett, Taken Chiefly from His Own Manuscript. 162pp, portrait, rebound in later cloth, New York, G. & C. & H. Carvill, 1831 (1st ed.).

$225.00

Howes: W-438. Field: 1659. Colonel Willett served on the frontiers of New York during the Revolution and, thus, fought against the Six Nations. (RMW)

W240. WILLETT (William M.). Scenes in the Wilderness: An Authentic Narrative of the Labors and Sufferings of the Moravian Missionaries Among the North American Indians. 208pp, frontis, 12mo, original calf, rebacked in leather, New York, G. Lane & C. B. Tippett, 1847. $45.00

Howes: W-439. Field: 1660. Covers formation of the Moravian Mission, the massacre at Gnadenhutten, missions in Ohio and Pennsylvania. (RMW)

___Another Copy. Same. $60.00

___Another Copy. New York, 1851. $45.00

W241. WILLEY (Benjamin G.). Incidents in White Mountain History: Containing Facts Relating to the Discovery and Settlement of the Mountains, Indian History and Traditions.... 322pp, 4pp ads, illus, original cloth, Boston, N. Noyes, 1856. $75.00

Field: 1661. "Much information on Indian history and Border Warfare."

WILLEY (Gordon R.). See also BAE Bulletins Nos. 143, 155, and 164.

W242. WILLEY (Gordon R.). (Smithsonian Misc. Collections, Vol. 113, 1949) Archaeology of the Florida Gulf Coast. 660pp, 60pp of photographs, 76 figures, 20 maps, 17 tables, wrappers. $125.00

___Another Copy. Ex-lib with markings. $35.00

W243. WILLEY (G. R.). (Peabody Museum Papers, Vol. 64, No. 1, 1972) The Artifacts of Altar de Sacrificios. 275pp, illus, 4to, wrappers. $25.00

W244. WILLEY (G. R.). An Introduction to American Archaeology. (Volume II Only). Vol. II: South America. (Complete). 559pp, numerous illus, 4to (9" x 12"), Englewood Cliffs, 1971. $30.00

W245. WILLEY (G. R.) et al. (Peabody Museum Papers, Vol. 44, Cambridge, 1965) Prehistoric Maya Settlements in the Belize Valley. 589pp, 319 illus to include photographs and drawings, 36 charts, 6 tables, fold-out map in rear pocket, wrappers. $75.00

____Another Copy. Same. $85.00

W246. WILLEY (G. R.). (Viking Fund Publications in Anthropology, No. 23, 1956) Prehistoric Settlement Patterns in the New World. vii, 202pp, wraps. $22.00

W247. WILLEY (G. R.) and McGIMSEY (C. R.). (Peabody Museum Papers, Vol. XLIX, No. 2, 1954) The Mongarillo Culture of Panama. 158pp of text containing 34 figures, 12 tables, plus 33pp of photographs, wrappers. $35.00

____Another Copy. Same. $25.00

W248. WILLIAMS (Anita Alvarez de). (Baja California Series, No. 34, Los Angeles, 1975, 1st ed.) Travelers Among the Cucapa. 161pp, illus, edition of 600 copies, wraps. $25.00

W249. WILLIAMS (A. W.). (Smithsonian Contributions to Anthropology, Vol. 9, 1970) Navajo Political Process. ix, 75pp, 1 figure, 10pp of photographs, wraps. $18.00

____Another Copy. Same. $12.00

____Another Copy. Same. $10.00

W250. WILLIAMS (Clara A.). Ned the Indian. 8 color pls, a classic childrens book, Chicago, 1912 (1st ed.), d.j. $20.00

W251. WILLIAMS (Rev. Eleazer). Life of Te-Ho-Ra-Gwa-Ne-Gen, Alias Thomas Williams, A Chief of the Caughnawaga Tribe of Indians in Canada. 91pp, cloth, some cracking of brittle leaves, one leaf taped at hinge, one is loose, edition of 200 copies, Albany, J. Munsell, 1859 (1st ed.). $65.00

Howes: W-451. Sabin note: 104213. Field: 1670. Howes: "Biography of the son of Eunice Williams--the Deerfield captive of 1704--prominent in New York's border wars and the unquestionable father of the biographer, the unscrupulous 'Lost Dauphin' Pretender."

____Another Copy. 1859, 1st ed., same collation, rebound, ex-lib copy. $45.00

W252. WILLIAMS (G. D.). (Peabody Museum Papers, Vol. XIII, No. I, 1931) Maya-Spanish Crosses in Yucatan. xiv, 256pp, 47pp of photographs and tables, wrappers. $50.00

W253. WILLIAMS (John). The Redeemed Captive Returning to Zion, or a Faithful History of Remarkable Occurrences in the Captivity and Deliverance of Mr. John Williams. 248pp, 12mo, original calf, leather label, Greenfield, Mass., T. Dickman, 1800 (6th ed.). $145.00

Field: 1672. Ayer, Supplement 1, 137. Howes: W-461. "One of the most famous and most popular captivity narratives. Williams, a Harvard graduate, in charge of the Church at Greenfield when it was attacked by Indians in 1703, was taken, with others, to Canada,

his wife and two of his children being Tomahawked on
the way. As a powerful picture of Indian Cruelty,
ranks next to the Toelandson captivity narrative."
___Another Copy. Springfield, Mass., 1908, 212pp,
16mo, frontis. $25.00

W254. WILLIAMS (S.) and BRAIN (J. P.). (Peabody Museum
Papers, Vol. 74, 1983) Excavations at the Lake George
Site, Yazoo County, Mississippi, 1958-1960. xviii,
483pp, 349 figures, wrappers. $80.00

W255. WILLIAMS (S.). (Peabody Museum Papers, Vol. LVII,
1968) The Waring Papers, The Collected Works of Antonio J. Waring, Jr. xviii, 345pp, 90 figures, 26 tables,
wrappers, $58.00

W256. WILLIAMS (Stephen W.). A Biographical Memoir of the
Rev. John Williams, First Minister of Deerfield, Massachusetts, with a Slight Sketch of Ancient Deerfield, and
an Account of the Indian Wars in that Place and Vicinity.
127pp, original cloth backed bds, Greenfield, Mass.,
C. J. J. Ingersol, 1837 (1st ed.). $100.00
Howes: W-486. Field: 1674. Also contains an appendix with the journal of John Williams kept during his
captivity.

W257. WILLIAMS (Walter L.). The Spirit and the Flesh: Sexual
Diversity in American Indian Culture. 344pp, Boston,
1986. $22.00

W258. WILLIAMSON (Thomas S.). Josuwa, Qa Wayacopi Kin, Qa
Rute, Ohanyanpi Qon Oyakapi Wowapi Kin. 81 double-
column pp, full leather, the books of Joshua, Judges
and Ruth in Sioux, New York, 1875 (1st ed.). $125.00

WILLIS (Bailey). See BAE Bulletin No. 52.

W259. WILLOUGHBY (Charles C.). (Peabody Museum Papers,
Vol. XI, No. 1, 1924) Indian Burial Place at Winthrop,
Massachusetts. 37pp, 4pls, 20 illus, with notes on the
skeletal remains by Earnest A. Hooton, printed wraps.
                                                           $20.00

W260. WILLOYA (William). Warriors of the Rainbow; Strange
and Prophetic Dreams of the Indian Peoples. 94pp, color
illus by Indian artists, wrappers, Healdsburg, 1962
(1st ed.). $10.00

W261. WILLSON (R. W.). (Peabody Museum Papers, Vol. VI,
No. 3, 1924) Astronomical Notes on the Maya Codices.
46pp of text containing 6 figures and 5 tables, plus 9pp
of photographs, wrappers. $60.00

W262. WILSON (Charles Banks) (Editor). Indians of Eastern
Oklahoma Including Quapaw Agency Indians. 43,
(1)pp, notes, wrappers, Afton, Oklahoma, 1956. $15.00

W263. WILSON (Dorothy D.). Bright Eyes: The Story of Sus-
ette La Flesche, An Omaha Indian. 396pp, bibliography,
index, New York, 1974 (1st ed.), d.j. $14.00
___Another Copy. Same. $15.00
___Another Copy. Same. $17.00
___Another Copy. Same. $10.00

W264.   WILSON (E.). North American Indian Designs. 130pp,
        102pp of drawings of designs and objects, cloth, British
        Museum, 1984. $15.00
W265.   WILSON (Elijah Nicholas). Among the Shoshones. 222pp,
        illus, Salt Lake City, 1910 (1st ed.). $100.00
        ___Another Copy. Same, inner hinges cracked.
                                                             $65.00
WILSON (Elsie A.). See BAE Bulletin No. 143.
W266.   WILSON (Gilbert). (American Museum of Natural History,
        Anthropology Papers, Vol. XXX, No. IV, New York,
        1928) Hidatsa Eagle Trapping. 138pp, wrappers.
                                                             $30.00
        ___Another Copy. Same. $17.00
W267.   WILSON (G. L.). (American Museum of Natural History,
        Anthropological Papers, Vol. XXXXIII, Part V, New
        York, 1934) The Hidatsa Earthlodge. 78pp, 45 illus,
        9 fold-out drawings in rear pocket, wrappers. $30.00
W268.   WILSON (Gilbert). (American Museum of Natural History,
        Anthropology Papers, Vol. XV, No. II, New York, 1924)
        The Horse and Dog in Hidatsa Culture. 176pp, wraps.
                                                             $30.00
W269.   WILSON (Herbert Earl). The Lore and Lure of Yosemite;
        The Indians, Their Customs, Legends and Beliefs; Big
        Trees, Geology and the Story of Yosemite. 135pp, illus,
        bds, San Francisco, 1926. $25.00
        ___Another Copy. Los Angeles, 1931. $20.00
W270.   WILSON (Marcius). American History: Comprising His-
        torical Sketches of the Indian Tribes; A Description of
        American Antiquities, with an Inquiry into Their Origin
        and the Origin of the Indian Tribes; History of the
        United States, with Appendices Showing Its Connection
        with European History; History of the Present British
        Provinces; History of Mexico; and History of Texas,
        Brought Down to the Time of Its Admission into the
        American Union. 672pp, maps, embossed cloth, worn
        lacking rear cvr, foxing,contents complete, Cincinnati,
        1847 (2nd ed.). $40.00
W271.   WILSON (Raymond). Ohiyesa, Charles Eastman, Santee
        Sioux. 206pp, plus index, photographs, notes, bibliog-
        raphy, Urbana, 1983 (1st ed.), d.j. $15.00
W272.   WILSON (Thomas). (Lord Bishop of Sodar and Man) The
        Knowledge and Practice of Christianity Made Easy to the
        Meanest Capacities: or, An Essay Towards an Instruc-
        tion for the Indians ... Together with Directions and
        Prayer. (8), (4), (36), 270pp, 16mo, full calf, hinges
        tender, London, J. Osborn, 1743 (3rd ed.). $85.00
        ___Another Copy. Same. $65.00
W273.   WILTSEY (Norman). Brave Warriors. 379pp, frontis por-
        trait, 36pp of photographs, bibliography, index, Cald-
        well, 1963 (1st ed.), d.j. $25.00
        ___Another Copy. Caldwell, 1964. $15.00

W274. WIMBERLY (S.) and NEWMAN (M. T.). (Univ. of Alabama, Geological Survey of Alabama, Museum Papers No. 36, 1960) Indian Pottery from Clarke County and Mobile County.... 262pp, pls, folding tables, bibliography, wraps. $22.00

W275. WIMBERLY (S.) and TOURTELOT (H. A.). (Univ. of Alabama, Geological Survey of Alabama, Museum Papers No. 19, 1941) The Mcquorquodale Mound: A Manifestation of the Hopewellian Phase.... x, 42pp, figures. bibliography, index, wrappers. $17.00

W276. (WIMER, JAMES). Events in Indian History, Beginning with an Account of the Origin of the American Indians, and Early Settlements in North America. 633pp, 8 folding lithographed pls (by Sinclair's Lithography, Philadelphia), full calf, Lancaster, G. Hills & Co., 1841 (1st ed.). $200.00

Field: 511. Howes: W-548. Contains many of the Classic Indian Captivities.

___Another Copy. Same. $75.00

W277. WINCHELL (Newton H.). The Aborigines of Minnesota. A Report Based on Collection of Jacob Browner and on Field Surveys and Notes of Alfred Hill and Theodore Lewis. xiv, 761pp, 36 half-tone pls, 642 figures, 26 fold-out inserts, leather and linen cvr, St. Paul, Minnesota Historical Society, 1911. $395.00

___Another Copy. Same, gilt stamped half morocco. $150.00

W278. WINCHELL (Newton H.). (Collections of Minnesota Historical Society, Vol. XVI, Part I, St. Paul, 1913) The Weathering of Aboriginal Stone Artifacts. 186pp, 19 pls, 20 figures, cloth. $30.00

___Another Copy. Same. $50.00

W279. WINGER (O.). The Lost Sister Among the Miamis. 143pp, 7pp, photographs, drawings, maps, account of Frances Slocum's captivity with the Miamis, Elgin, Illinois, 1936 (1st printing). $25.00

W280. WINGERT (P. S.). American Indian Sculpture, A Study of the Northwest Coast. xii, 144pp, 7 drawings, 2 maps, 76pp of photographs, cloth, New York, 1949. $125.00

W281. WINGERT (P. S.). Prehistoric Stone Sculpture of the Pacific Northwest. 60pp, 41 lrge photographs of stone sculptures, wraps, Portland Art Museum, 1952. $30.00

W282. (WINNEBAGO). (House of Representatives Executive Document 50, 38:1, Washington, 1864, 1st printing) Winnebago Indians: Pre-emptors on Home Reservation. 66pp. Removed. $20.00

W283. (WINNEBAGO INDIANS). Rejoinder to the Defence Published by Simon Cameron, February 6th, 1855, to the Charges Made Against Him as Commissioner to Carry into Effect the Treaty with the Half-Breed Winnebago

Indians; Also, Public Document ... to the Members of
the Senate and House of Representatives of Pennsylvania,
and All Others Whom it May Concern. xvi, 72pp,
printed wrappers, n.p., n.d. $275.00
    In 1838 Cameron was appointed commissioner to settle
certain claims of the Winnebago Indians and caused a
scandal by altering claims through paying claims on his
own bank, thereby earning himself extra funds and the
title "The Great Winnebago Chief." The first part of
this pamphlet (pp.iii-xvi) contains letters from many
eminent men supporting Cameron's conduct as the Commissioner. The HR Document which follows in the second
part (pp.1-72) is a compilation of letters condemning
his actions as fraudulent and calling for severe retribu-
tion. (WR)

W284. WINSHIP (George P.). The Cambridge Press 1638-1692.
A Reexamination of the Bay Psalm Book and the Eliot
Indian Bible. ix, 385pp, facsimiles, 2 original leaves
inserted, index, half leather and cloth, printed by the
Lakeside Press, Philadelphia, Univ. of Pennsylvania,
1945 (1st ed.). $575.00
    This edition contains an original leaf from John
Eliot's "Holy Bible," 1661-63, and Thomas Morton's
"New England's Memorial," 1669.

W285. WINSHIP (G. P.). The Coronado Expedition, 1540-1542.
Extracted from BAE Annual Report No. 14, Part I, 1896.
pp 329-624, 47 illus, rebound in buckram. $85.00
    Another Copy. Same, cloth. $65.00

W286. WINSHIP (George P.). The Eliot Indian Tracts. (4),
18pp, wrappers, "Reprinted with additions, from Bibliographical Essays ...," Cambridge, Mass., 1925 (1st
separate printing). $30.00

W287. WINSLOW (Ola E.). John Eliot. "Apostle to the Indians."
218pp, plus index, photographs, bibliography, Boston,
1968 (1st ed.), d.j. $10.00

W288. WINTEMBERG (W. J.). (National Museum of Canada Annual
Report for 1929, Bulletin No. 67, 1931) Distinguishing
Characteristics of Algonkian and Iroquoian Cultures.
pp 65-126, 15 pls, wraps. $25.00

W289. (WINTER, GEORGE). The Journals and Indian Paintings
of George Winter, 1837-1839. 208pp, index, 30 pls with
24 in color, 4to, Indianapolis, Indiana Historical Society,
1948 (1st ed.). $75.00
    Another Copy. Same. $50.00

W290. WISE (Jennings C.). The Red Man in the New World
Drama. A Politico-Legal Study with a Pageantry of
American Indian History. 628pp, frontis, illus, index,
cloth, Washington, DC, 1931. $35.00
    Another Copy. Same. $30.00

W291. WISSLER (Clark). The American Indian, An Introduction
to the Anthropology of the New World. 495pp, 82 illus,

fold-out map, cloth, New York, 1922. $28.00

___Another Copy. Same. $25.00

___Another Copy. Same. $20.00

W292. WISSLER (Clark). (American Museum of Natural History, Anthropology Papers, Vol. XXIX, Part I, New York, 1927) Distribution of Moccasin Decorations Among the Plains Tribes. 21pp, drawings, wrappers. $25.00

W293. WISSLER (Clark). (American Museum of Natural History, Guide Leaflet No. 50, New York, 1919) Indian Beadwork. 31pp, 20 pls, figures, wrappers. $25.00

W294. WISSLER (Clark). Indian Cavalcade; or, Life on the Indian Reservation. 351, (19)pp, illus, cloth, New York, 1938. $25.00

___Another Copy. Same. $20.00

W295. WISSLER (Clark). (American Museum of Natural History, Handbook Series no. 1, New York, 1927) Indians on the Plains. 172pp, 55 illus, cloth. $40.00

___Another Copy. New York, 1941. $30.00

___Another Copy. New York, 1912. (North American Indians on the Plains). $35.00

___Another Copy. New York, 1930. $20,00

W296. WISSLER (Clark). Indians of the United States. Four Centuries of Their History and Culture. 319pp, index, 18pp of photographs, cloth, 1940 (1st ed.). $25.00

___Another Copy. New York, 1941. $22.00

___Another Copy. New York, 1940. $17.00

W297. WISSLER (Clark). Medicine Among the American Indians. Reprint of Volume 1, No. 1, of Ciba Symposia. 35pp, illus, wrappers, Ramona, 1980. $15.00

___Another Copy. Same. $10.00

___Another Copy. Same. $10.00

W298. WISSLER (Clark). (American Museum of Natural History, Anthropological Papers, Vol. XI, Part I, 1912) Societies and Ceremonial Associations in the Oglala Division of the Teton-Dakota. 99pp, 9 figures, wrappers. $47.00

W299. WISSLER (Clark) (Editor). (American Museum of Natural History, Anthropology Papers, Vol. XI, New York, 1912-16. 1975 Reprint) Societies of the Plains Indians. 1,039pp, 101 illus, cloth. $135.00

This definitive volume on Plains Indian Societies and rituals contains thirteen separate papers--written by Wissler, Lowie, Goddard, Skinner and Murie--that were published from 1912 to 1916. By the time these papers were published, many of the societies had ceased to hold meetings and many of the rituals were no longer performed. Thus, the field research, which sought out surviving members of the societies and participants in the rituals, provided the last opportunity to acquire eyewitness accounts of what occurred at ceremonies no longer performed and in societies no longer in existence. (EAP)

W300. WISSLER (Clark). (American Museum of Natural History,
Anthropology Papers, Vol. XVI, Part III, New York,
1918) The Sun Dance of the Blackfoot Indians. pp
225-270, wraps. $12.00
___Another Copy. Same. $25.00
W301. WITHERS (Alexander S.). Chronicles of Border Warfare;
or, A History of the Settlement by the Whites, of
North-Western Virginia: And of the Indian Wars and
Massacres.... 320pp, adv. leaf, original full calf,
Clarksburg, Virginia, Joseph Israel, 1831 (1st ed.).
$275.00
Howes: W-601. Field: 1690. "Of this scarce book,
very few copies are complete or in good condition....
The author took much pains to be authentic, and his
chronicles are considered by Western Antiquarians, to
form the best collection of frontier life and Indian War-
fare, that has been printed."
___Another Copy. Cincinnati, Robert Clarke, 1895,
green cloth, xx, 447pp, portrait, ex-lib copy. $90.00
___Another Copy. Parsons Advocate, n.d., c.1960s,
227pp, pictorial wrappers. $35.00
W302. WITHERSPOON (G.). Language and Art in the Navajo
Universe. xviii, 214pp, 8 photographs, 24 figures,
cloth, Ann Arbor, 1977, 1982. $30.00
W303. WITT (Shirley) and STEINER (Stan). The Way: An
Anthropology of American Indian Literature. 261pp,
New York, 1972 (1st ed.). $25.00
WITTHOFT (John). See also BAE Bulletin No. 180.
W304. WITTHOFT (John) et al. Metallurgy of the Tlingi, Dene,
and Eskimo. 17 photographs of knives, masks, and
boxes, wrappers, Philadelphia, 1969. $10.00
W305. WHITTLESEY (Charles). Descriptions of Ancient Works in
Ohio. 20pp, 7 pls, 4to, removed from Smithsonian Con-
tributions of Knowledge, Washington, 1850. $35.00
W306. (WIYOT, YUROK, COMANCHES). Two Nineteenth Century
Ethnographic Documents on the Wiyot and Yurok of
Northwestern California and the Comanches of New Mexico
and Texas. 53pp, 4to, illus, bibliography, wrappers,
Berkeley, 1973 (1st ed.). $25.00
First half devoted to material on the Indians of Klamath
River and Humboldt Bay area of California. Last 27
pages devoted to "Ethnographic Information on the
Comanches Gathered from the Mouth of a Trapper Who
Was Their Prisoner for 13 Years" by Leon de Cessac.
Edited by T. R. Hester and Translated by Fred H.
Stross. (GFH)
W307. WOLCOTT (H. F.). A Kwakiutl Village and School. 132pp,
illus, map, wrappers, New York, 1967 (1st ed.).
$10.00
___Another Copy. Same. $20.00
W308. WOLF (Carolyn) and FOLK (Karen R.). Indians of North

and South America: A Bibliography Based on the Collection at the Willard E. Yager Library--Museum, Hartwick College, Oneonta, NY. 576pp, checklist of over 4,200 titles, indexed by title, series, and subject, Metuchen, NJ, 1977. $15.00

W309. WOLFART (H. C.). (American Philosophical Society, Vol. 63, Part 5, Philadelphia, 1973) Plains Cree: A Grammatical Study. 90pp, 4to, wrappers. $35.00

W310. WOLFART (H. C.) and CARROLL (J. F.). Meet Cree: A Guide to the Language. xx, 116pp, bibliography, wraps, Univ. of Alberta Press, 1981 (new, revised ed.). $15.00

W311. WOLFF (Werner). Dechiffrement de l'Ecriture Maya et Traduction des Codices. (2 Volumes). Vol. I: Text, 308pp. Vol. II: Plate Volume, 13 pls, plus 96 illus. Wrappers, Geuthner, Paris, 1938. $175.00

W312. WOOD (Erskine). Days with Chief Joseph, Diary, Recollections and Photographs. 40pp, illus, wrappers, recollections of a 14-year-old boy who visited Chief Joseph at his home in Nespelem, Washington; Portland, 1970. $10.00

W313. WOOD (Mary L.). Life Against the Land; A Short History of the Pueblo Indians. 40pp, illus, wrappers, Leadville, 1974 (1st ed.). $10.00

W314. WOOD (Nancy). Hollering Sun (The Indians of Taos Pueblo). 92 unnumbered pp, photographs by Myron Wood, Taos Indian thoughts in verse form, New York, 1972 (1st ed.), d.j. $23.00
___Another Copy. Same. $15.00
___Another Copy. Same, signed. $25.00

W315. WOOD (Nancy). The Man Who Gave Thunder to the Earth. A Taos Way of Seeing and Understanding. 165pp, New York, 1976 (1st ed.), d.j. $15.00

W316. WOOD (Nancy). War Cry on a Prayer Feather. Prose and Poetry of the Ute Indians. 108pp, portraits and photographs, New York, 1979 (1st ed.). $15.00

W317. WOOD (Nancy). When Buffalo Free the Mountains. The Survival of America's Ute Indians. 293pp, photographs, Garden City, NY, 1980 (1st ed.), d.j. $22.00
___Another Copy. Same. $15.00
___Another Copy. Same. $15.00

W318. WOOD (Norman B.). Lives of Famous Indian Chiefs: From Cofachigui, the Indian Princess, and Powhatan; Down to and Including Chief Joseph and Geronimo. 771pp, thk 8vo, red cloth with silver lettering and decorations, 77 illus, Aurora, Illinois, American Indian Historical Publishing co., 1906 (1st ed.). $40.00

Several western Indian Chiefs including Quanah Parker, with an account of the captivity of his mother, Cynthia Ann Parker. 77 illustrations, many of Indian Chiefs, and most of these photographs are credited to D. F. Barry.

WOOD (W. Raymond). See also BAE Bulletins Nos. 176, 189, and 198.

W319. WOOD (W. Raymond). (Smithsonian Contributions to Anthropology, No. 15, 1971) Biesterfeldt: A Post-Contact Coalescent Site on the Northeastern Plains. xiv, 108pp, 20pp of photographs, 16 figures, wrappers. $22.00
___Another Copy. Same. $20.00
___Another Copy. Same. $17.00

W320. WOOD (W. R.). (Plains Anthropologist, Vol. 10, No. 28, Lincoln, 1965) The Redbird Focus and the Problem of Ponca Prehistory. pp 79-145, illus, maps, wraps. $12.00

W321. WOODALL (J. Ned). (Southern Methodist University Contributions in Anthropology, No. 3, Dallas, 1969) Archaeological Excavations in the Toledo Bend Reservoir, 1966. 93pp, photographs of artifacts, limited to 600 copies, wrappers. $10.00

W322. WOODBURY (G.). (Univ. of Texas, Anthropology Papers Series, Bulletin Vol. 1, No. 5, 1937) Notes ... Skeletal Remains of Texas; Also Other Articles. 39pp, illus, bibliography, 8vo, wrappers. $10.00

W323. WOODBURY (R.). Alfred V. Kidder. 200pp, illus, short biography, selected writings, selected bibliography, wrappers, New York, Columbia Univ., 1973. $10.00

W324. WOODBURY (R. B.). (Memoirs of the Society for American Archaeology, American Antiquity, Vol. 17, Menasha and Salt Lake City, 1961) Prehistoric Agriculture at Point of Pines, Arizona. xiv, 48pp, illus, figures, bibliography, wrappers. $10.00

W325. WOODBURY (R. B.). (Peabody Museum Papers, Vol. 34, Reports of the Awatovi Expedition No. 6, Cambridge, 1954) Prehistoric Stone Implements of Northwestern Arizona. 240pp, 4to, 27 collotype illus of multiple artifacts, wrappers. $50.00

W326. WOODBURY (R. B.) and TRIK (A. S.). The Ruins of Zaculeu Guatemala. (2 Volumes). Vol. I: xviii, 324pp, 168 figures, 2 fold-out maps in rear pocket. Vol. II: vi, pp 325-466, 3pp of color and 120pp of b/w photographs, 4pp of drawings. Decorated gilt cloth, United Fruit Co., Richmond, 1953. $85.00

W327. WOODCOCK (George). Peoples of the Coast, the Indians of the Pacific Northwest. 223pp, photographic illus with some in color, bibliography, index, Indiana Univ., Bloomington, 1977 (1st ed.), d.j. $30.00

W328. WOODRUFF (Janette). Indian Oasis. 325pp, portrait frontis, illus, about author's Indian service with the Crows, Paiutes and Papagos as told the Cecil Dryden, cloth, Caldwell, 1939 (1st ed.). $25.00
___Another Copy. Same, with d.j. $35.00

W329. WOODS (Samuel). (H. R. Executive Document 51, 31:1, Washington, 1850, 1st printing) Pembina Settlement.

Report of Major Wood (sic), Relative to His Expedition
to ... and the Condition of Affairs on the North-Western
Frontier of the Territory of Minnesota. 55pp, folding
map, self wraps. $80.00

WOODWARD (Arthur). See also BAE Bulletin No. 166.

W330. WOODWARD (Arthur). (Museum of Northern Arizona, Bulletin No. 14, Flagstaff, 1938, 1st ed.) A Brief History
of Navajo Silversmithing. 78pp, illus, field notes by
Richard Van Valkenburgh, wrappers. $45.00
___Another Copy. Flagstaff, 1946, 2nd ed., 84pp,
15pp photographs, cloth. $30.00
___Another Copy. Same, rebound in paper wraps.
$20.00

W331. WOODWARD (Arthur). (Oregon Archaeology Society,
Publication No. 2, Portland, 1965) Indian Trade Goods.
38pp, photographs, bibliography, wrappers. $10.00

W332. WOODWARD (Ashbel). Wampum, a Paper Presented to the
Numismatic and Antiquarian Society of Philadelphia.
61pp, full red calf, original wraps bound in, Albany,
J. Munsell, 1878. $45.00

W333. WOODWARD (Grace Steele). The Cherokees. 359pp, illus,
cloth, Norman, 1963 (1st ed.), d.j. $35.00
___Another Copy. Same. $25.00

W334. WOODWARD (Grace Steele). Pocahontas. 215pp, plus in-
dex, illus, color frontis, bibliography, endpaper maps,
Norman, 1969 (1st ed.), d.j. $15.00
___Another Copy. Same. $15.00
___Another Copy. Norman, 1970, d.j. $12.00

W335. WOODWORTH (Ellis). The Godly See. A True Story of
Hi-a-wat-ha. 44pp, part two-color printing, wrappers,
Syracuse, 1900 (1st ed.). $20.00

W336. WOOLSEY (A. M.). (Univ. of Texas--Publications, Vol.
3, No. 2, Austin, 1938) Additional Lake Buchanan
Sites, and Other Articles. 153pp, maps, pls, figures,
bibliography, site and artifact photographs, lrge 8vo,
wrappers. $35.00

WOOLWORTH (Alan R.). See BAE Bulletins Nos. 176 and 189.

W337. WORCESTER (Donald E.). The Apaches, Eagles of the
Southwest. 389pp, illus, index, maps, bibliography,
Norman, 1979 (1st ed.), d.j. $30.00
___Another Copy. Same. $25.00

W338. WORCESTER (Donald E.). Forked Tongues and Broken
Treaties. 464pp, plus index, photographs, maps,
bibliography, Caldwell, 1975 (1st ed.), d.j. $30.00
___Another Copy. Same. $25.00
___Another Copy. Same. $20.00

W339. (WORCESTER, SAMUEL). New Echota Letters: Contributions of Samuel A. Worcester to the "Cherokee Phoenix."
Edited by Jack Frederick Kilpatrick. 130pp, square
8vo, bibliography, Dallas, 1968 (1st ed.), d.j. $25.00
The letters appeared in "The Cherokee Phoenix,"

printed in what now is Oklahoma, from 1828 to 1832. Worcester championed the Cherokees and was much against the unfeeling policies being carried out by the government. Letters show not only how he served the Cherokee Nation, but also how he went to prison for doing so. (GFH)

W340. WORMINGTON (H. M.). Ancient Man in North America. 198pp, illus, cloth, Denver, 1949 (3rd ed., revised). $40.00
_____Another Copy. Denver, 1957, 4th ed., xviii, 322pp, 72 photographs, drawings, maps. $25.00
_____Another Copy. Same. $12.00

W341. WORMINGTON (H. M.). Prehistoric Indians of the South- west. 191pp, 58 illus, Denver Museum of Natural His- tory, cloth, 1947. $20.00
_____Another Copy. Same, wrappers. $15.00
_____Another Copy. Denver, 1959, cloth, d.j. $10.00
_____Another Copy. Same. $15.00

W342. WORMINGTON (H. M.). (Denver Museum of Natural His- tory, Proceedings No. 1, Denver, 1955, 1st ed.) A Reappraisal of the Fremont Culture. (12), 200pp, pls, figures, maps, bibliography, wrappers. $22.00

W343. WORMINGTON (H. M.). (Denver Museum of Natural His- tory, Denver, 1951) The Story of Pueblo Pottery. 61pp, 57 photographs, wrappers. $17.00

W344. WORSLEY (Israel). A View of the American Indians; Their General Character, Customs, Language, Public Festivals, Religious Rites, and Traditions, Shewing Them to be the Descendants of the Ten Tribes of Israel. 185pp, half morocco and bds, London, 1828. $250.00

W345. (WPA--New Mexico). Indian Lands in New Mexico ... New Mexico State Planning Board. (37), 208pp, numer- ous folding maps, tables, thk quarto, printed wraps, Santa Fe, 1936. $40.00

W346. WREN (Christopher). A Study of North Appalachian In- dian Pottery. Republished from Vol. XIII, Proceedings of the Wyoming Historical and Geological Society. 101pp, 31 pls, text figures, cloth, Wilkes-Barre, 1914. $35.00

W347. (WRIGHT, ASHER). Gaa Nah Shoh Ne De O Waah Sao Nyoh Gwah Na Wen Ni Yuh. 136pp, later cloth, Seneca Mission Press, 1843. $200.00
Sabin: 105546. Pilling, Iroquoian, p.176. Pilling: "Hymns in the Seneca Language, prefaced with Wright's method of writing Seneca." (RMW)

W348. WRIGHT (Barton). Hopi Material Culture. Artifacts Gathered by H. R. Voth in the Fred Harvey Collection. 127pp, photographs, bibliography, wrappers, Flagstaff, 1979 (1st ed.). $40.00
_____Another Copy. Same. $25.00
_____Another Copy. Same, rebound in cloth. $30.00

W349. WRIGHT (Barton). Kachinas, A Hopi Artist's Documentary.

262pp, oblong 4to, illus, index, Flagstaff, 1980, d.j.
$45.00

Barton Wright, the recognized authority on Kachinas, presents detailed commentary on 237 Kachina paintings. The paintings are all by Hopi Cliff Bahnimptewa and are produced in full color.

____Another Copy. Flagstaff, 1973, 1st ed. d.j.
$45.00

____Another Copy. Same. $45.00

W350. WRIGHT (Barton). Kachinas of the Zuni. xiv, 151pp, 53 full-page and half-page color drawings of more than 200 Kachinas, cloth, Flagstaff, 1985. $60.00

The importance of the Zuni Kachina Cult is explored in this study, the first new information to be published on Zuni Kachinas in over half a century. Described are the quadrennial ceremonies, annual performances, traditional dances, and curing rites associated with Zuni culture. Each participant Kachina or society figure is described or illustrated by Duane Dishta, a Zuni artist. (EAP)

____Another Copy. Same. $45.00

W351. WRIGHT (B.). Pueblo Cultures. 67pp, 35pp of photographs of dances, altars, artifacts. Iconography of religions, wrappers, Section x, fasc. 4, Leiden, 1986.
$68.00

W352. WRIGHT (Barton). Pueblo Shields from the Fred Harvey Fine Art Collection. 96pp, illus, bibliography, Flagstaff, 1976 (1st ed.), d.j. $25.00

Full account of the history and construction of handheld shields of the Puebloan cultures of Arizona and New Mexico by the Curator of the Museum of Northern Arizona. Illustrated with photographs and drawings.

____Another Copy. Same. $30.00

____Another Copy. Same. $25.00

W353. WRIGHT (B.). The Unchanging Hopi. An Artist's Interpretation in Scratchboard Drawings and Text. 109pp, illus with drawings, Flagstaff, 1975 (1st ed.), d.j.
$15.00

W354. WRIGHT (D.). Winnipeg Collects, Inuit Art from Private Collections. 48pp, 32pp of photographs, wraps, Winnipeg Art Gallery, 1987. $15.00

WRIGHT (Fred Eugene). See BAE Bulletin No. 52.

W355. WRIGHT (G. D.). (New York State Archaeological Association, Occasional Papers, No. 4, Rochester, 1963) The Neutral Indians: A Source Book. 95pp, map, bibliography, gathers nearly all original source material on these Indians, located between and "neutral" in wars between Hurons and Iroquois, early maps listed. $20.00

W356. WRIGHT (G. Frederick). The Ice Age in North America and Its Bearing Upon the Antiquity of Man. 648pp, 14pp publishers ads, 4 maps, map of Alaska in color,

148 photographs, line drawings, pictorial frnt cvr, lrge 8vo, New York, 1902. $30.00

W357. WRIGHT (J. Leitch). William Augustus Bowles, Director General of the Creek Nation. 211pp, frontis, index, map, bibliography, Athens, 1967 (1st ed.), d.j. $25.00

___Another Copy. Same. $20.00

W358. WRIGHT (Margaret Nickelson). The History and Hallmarks of Hopi Silversmithing. Hopi Silver. 100pp, plus index, photographs, drawings by Barton Wright, glossary, bibliography, map, wrappers, Flagstaff, 1972 (1st ed.). $10.00

___Another Copy. Same. $15.00

W359. WRIGHT (M.). A Guide to the Indian Tribes of Oklahoma. 300pp, illus, bibliography, maps, Norman, 1951 (1st ed.). $20.00

___Another Copy. Same. $15.00

W360. WRIGHT (Robert C.). Indian Masonry. 123pp, frontis, original decorated bds, torn along spine edge, Ann Arbor, 1907. $35.00

Discusses world-wide Masonic Signs and their pur- ported use by the Ojibwa and other tribes in healing rites.

___Another Copy. Same, rebound. $30.00

W361. WUERTELE (Elizabeth). (Univ. of California Archaeological Research Contributions No. 26, Berkeley, 1975) Biblio- graphical History of California Anthropological Research, 1850-1917. 116pp, 4to, lists hundreds of works on California archaeology and ethnology, wrappers. $25.00

___Another Copy. Same. $20.00

W362. (WYANDOTT). (Senate Executive Document 77, 41:2, Washington, 1870, 1st printing) Wyandott Indian Claims. 55pp. Removed. $15.00

W363. (WYANDOTT). (House of Representatives Executive Docu- ment 83, 41:3, Washington, 1871, 1st printing) Claims for Property Taken from Them by Whites. 7pp. Re- moved. $10.00

W364. WYKOFF (Don G.). The Horton Site Revisited. 1967 Excavations at SQ-11, Sequoyah County, Oklahoma. 190pp, photographs, drawings, references, wrappers, Norman, 1970 (1st ed.). $10.00

W365. WYCKOFF (L. L.). (Museum of the American Indian, Notes and Monographs, No. 58, New York, 1971) A Suggested Nicaraguan Pottery Sequence Based on the Museum Collection. 88pp, 26pp of photographs, 15pp of drawings, wraps. $15.00

___Another Copy. Same. $12.00

___Another Copy. Same. $10.00

W366. WYLLIS (Andrew IV) and STUART (George) et al. (Middle American Research, Publication 31, Tulane Univ., 1975) Archaeological Investigation of the Yucatan Peninsula.

247 illus, several color pls, includes Gruta De Chac, Dzibilchaltun, Rio Bec area, Cancun, wrappers. $60.00

W367. WYMAN (Anne). (Southwest Museum Leaflet No. 1, Los Angeles, n.d.) Cornhusk Bags of the Nez Perce Indians. 6pp, illus, brief work with photographic pls of two examples of Nez Perce bags, wrappers. $10.00

W368. WYMAN (L. C.) et al. Beautyway: A Navaho Ceremonial. 218pp, 7 b/w and 16 full-page color reproductions of sandpaintings; booklet in rear pocket: "The Myth of Beautyway in Navaho Language." The myths are recorded and translated by Father Berard Haile, with a variant myth recorded by Maud Oakes, New York, 1957. $98.00

___Another Copy. Same. $35.00

W369. WYMAN (L. C.). Blessingway, With Three Versions of the Myth Recorded and Translated from the Navajo by Fr. Berard Haile, O.F.M. xviii, 660pp, 29 figures, 4 tables, cloth, Tucson, 1970. $30.00

W370. WYMAN (L. C.) and HARRIS (S. K.). The Ethnobotany of the Kayenta Navaho. 66pp, wrappers. $17.00

W371. WYMAN (L. C.). The Mountainway of the Navajo, with a Myth of the Female Branch Recorded and Translated by Father Berard Haile. xv, 271pp, frontis, illus of 32 Mountainway Sandpaintings, reference, index, Tucson, Univ. of Arizona, 1975 (1st ed.), d.j. $20.00

W372. WYMAN (L. C.) and KLUCKHOHN (C.). (American Anthropological Association, Memoir No. 50, 1938) Navaho Classification of Their Song Ceremonials. 38pp, wrappers. $24.00

___Another Copy. Same. $17.00

W373. WYMAN (L. C.) and BAILEY (F. L.). (Univ. of New Mexico Publications in Anthropology, No. 12, 1964) Navaho Indian Ethnoentomology. 158pp, 50 drawings of figures found in sandpaintings, map, wraps. $27.00

W374. WYMAN (L. C.). Navaho Sand Painting. 88pp, 21 photographs, Taylor Museum, Colorado Springs, 1960, 1971. $25.00

W375. WYMAN (L. C.) and BAILEY (Flora L.). (Univ. of New Mexico Bulletin, Vol. 4, No. 2, 1943) Navaho Upward-Reaching Way: Objective Behavior, Rationale and Sanction. 47pp, wrappers. $20.00

___Another Copy. Same. $12.00

W376. WYMAN (L. C.). (Museum of Navajo Ceremonial Art, Santa Fe, 1965, 1973) The Red Antway of the Navajo. 238pp of text, plus 58 b/w and color photographs, wrappers. $18.00

W377. WYMAN (L. C.). (Univ. of New Mexico Publications in Anthropology, No. 7, 1952) The Sandpaintings of the Kayenta Navaho, An Analysis of the Louisa Wade Wetherill Collection. 120pp, 49 figures, wrappers. $40.00

W378. WYMAN (L. C.). (Smithsonian Contributions to Anthropology,

Vol. 13, 1970) Sandpainting of the Navaho Shootingway
and the Walcott Collection. 114pp, 1 color and 44 b/w
photographs, cloth. $40.00
___Another Copy. Same. $35.00
___Another Copy. Same. $35.00
___Another Copy. Same. $25.00

W379. WYMAN (L. C.). Southwest Indian Drypainting. xxiii,
320pp, illus, including 32 color pls, 2 double-page
maps, notes, bibliography, index, Santa Fe, School of
American Research, 1983 (1st ed.), d.j. $45.00
___Another Copy. Same. $35.00
___Another Copy. Same. $28.00

W380. WYTH (John). Graphic Sketches from Old and Authentic
Works, Illustrating the Costume, Habits, and Character,
of the Aborigines of America. 18pp, plus 24 full-page
pls, each with explanatory text, adv. leaf for part 2
(never published), original cloth, New York, J. & H. G.
Langley, 1841 (1st ed.). $300.00
Sabin: 103094. Field: 1701. Very scarce book,
the first in a projected series of views of the natives
and the country, each part to include about 50 plates
and maps. Contains the first printing in America of
John White's illustration of North American Indians, the
first drawings ever done of these natives. (RMW)

-Y-

Y1. YAGER (W. E.). Orite of Adequentaga: The Journal of
Johannes Van Dyk, 1634-1635. Edited by Roland Hill.
185pp, illus, privately printed, wrappers, about travels
in Mohawk country, cvr loose, Walton, New York, 1953.
$35.00

Y2. (YAKIMA). (Senate Executive Document No. 67, 53:2,
Washington, DC, 1894) Yakima Indians--Agreement.
41pp, folding color map of Indian lands. Removed.
$30.00

Y3. (YAKIMA). The Yakimas. Treaty Centennial 1855-1955.
64pp, illus, map, decorated wrappers, Yakima, Washington, 1955 (1st ed.). $15.00
Tribal history published by authority of Yakima
Tribal Council. Tribal photographs.

Y4. (YANKTON). (Senate Executive Document No. 55, 57:1,
Washington, DC, 1901) Title of Yankton Indians to the
Pipestone Reservation in Minnesota. A Dispute over
sacred Pipestone quarries. 8pp. Removed. $10.00

Y5. YANOVSKY (E.). (U.S. Dept. of Agriculture, Misc. Publication No. 237, 1936) Food Plants of the North American Indians. 84pp, wrappers. $35.00

Y6.   (YAQUI INDIANS). Studies of the Yaqui Indians of Sonora,
        Mexico. 142pp, wrappers, Lubbock, 1936. $30.00
Y7.   YARROW (H. C.). Introduction to the Study of Mortuary
        Customs Among the North American Indians. 114pp,
        4to, index, half leather, bds, marbled end-papers,
        covers burial in mounds, boxes, canoes, plus dances,
        etc. Washington, DC, GPO, 1880 (1st ed.). $45.00
Y8.   YATES (L. G.). Charm Stones, the So-Called "Plummets"
        or "Sinkers" of California. Offprint from Bulletin No.
        2, Santa Barbara Society of Natural History for Year
        1890. 16pp plus 31 illus, ex-lib, wrappers. $35.00
Y9.   YAVA (Albert). Big Falling Snow. A Tewa-Hopi Indian's
        Life and Times and the History and Traditions of His
        People. 179pp, plus index, photographs, endpaper maps,
        New York, 1978 (1st ed.). $12.00
Y10. YAWGER (Rose). The Indian and the Pioneer. An Histori-
        cal Study. Volume I only (Vocabulary). 189pp, frontis,
        9 pls, t.e.g., Syracuse, NY, C. W. Bardeen, 1893
        (1st ed.). $45.00
Y11. YENNE (B.) and GARRATT (S.). Pictorial History of the
        North American Indian. 192pp, approx 140pp of color
        and b/w photographs, 15pp of drawings, 12pp of maps,
        New York, 1984. $20.00
        ____Another Copy. Same, d.j. $15.00
Y12. YOUNG (Calvin M.). Little Turtle (Me-She-Kin-No-Quah).
        The Great Chief of the Miami Indian Nation: With a Sketch
        of His Life Together with That of Wm. Wells and Some
        Noted Descendants. 249pp, illus with photographs, many
        of artifacts taken from Little Turtle's grave, Fort Wayne,
        1956 (reprint of 1917 ed.). $25.00
Y13. YOUNG (Egerton R.). Algonquin Indian Tales. 258pp,
        photographs, drawings by J. E. Laughlin, New York,
        1903 (1st ed.). $30.00
Y14. YOUNG (Egerton R.). By Canoe and Dog Train Among the
        Cree and Saulteaux Indians. xvi, 267pp, frontis, illus,
        pictorial cloth, New York, Eaton and Mains, n.d.,
        c.1899. $15.00
Y15. YOUNG (Egerton R.). On the Indian Trail: Stories of
        Missionary Work Among the Cree and Saulteaux Indians.
        214pp, 10 pls, original decorated cloth, 10pp of ads,
        New York, 1897. $15.00
Y16. YOUNG (Egerton R.). Oowikapun or How the Gospel Reached
        the Nelson River Indians. 240pp, pls, decorative cloth,
        historical fiction about Northwest Indians, New York,
        1896. $35.00
        ____Another Copy. Same, New York, 1894. $40.00
        ____Another Copy. Same, New York, 1894. $20.00
Y17. YOUNG (Jon Nathan). The Pottery Jewels of Joseph Lone-
        wolf. 59 unnumbered pp, many full color illus, wrappers,
        Scottsdale, 1975 (1st ed.). $12.00
Y18. YOUNG (Mary Elizabeth). Redskins, Ruffleshirts, and

Rednecks: Indian Allotments in Alabama and Mississippi, 1830-1860. 217pp, 8 pls, 6 tables, 17 maps, 2 graphs, index, bibliography, Norman, 1961 (1st ed.), d.j.

$30.00

____Another Copy. Same. $15.00

Y19. YOUNG (P.) and HOWE (J.) (Editors). (Univ. of Oregon Anthropological Papers No. 9, 1976) Ritual and Symbol in Native Central America. vi, 141pp, 8 figures, wrappers. $15.00

Y20. YOUNG (Robert W.) (Editor). The Navaho Yearbook. (6th Report). 353pp, photographs, maps, wrappers, Window Rock, 1957. $10.00

Y21. YOUNG (Robert W.) (Editor). The Navaho Yearbook. (7th Report). 401pp, charts, tables, photographs, maps, wrappers, Window Rock, 1958. $10.00

Y22. YOUNG (Robert W.). The Ramah Navahos. Tl'ohchiniji Dine Keedahat'inii Baa Hane' Son of Former Many Bends. 34pp (text in Navaho and English), Navaho Historical Series No. 1, Haskell Institute, 1967. $15.00

Y23. YOUNG (Robert W.). The Role of the Navajo in the Southwestern Drama. 94pp, photographs, maps, bibliography, wrappers, Gallup, 1968 (1st ed.). $10.00

Y24. YOUNG (Robert W.) and MORGAN (William). (U.S. Bureau of Indian Affairs, Navajo Historical Series No. 3, Phoenix, 1954) Navajo Historical Selections. Selected, Edited and Translated from the Navajo. 209pp, 4to, printed wrappers. $20.00

____Another Copy. Same. $15.00

____Another Copy. Same. $12.00

Y25. YOUNG (Thomas). Narrative of a Residence on the Mosquito Shore, During the Years 1839, 1840, and 1841. iv, 172pp, 24pp ads, 3 full-page pls, later cloth, London, Smith, Elder and Co., 1842 (1st ed.). $100.00

Field: 1705. The author spent three years in the Mosquito Kingdom and relates much information about the savage tribes of the interior, who delighted in martyring missionaries who traveled among them.

Y26. (YUMA). (Senate Executive Document No. 68, 53:2, Washington, DC, 1894) Yuma Indians: Agreement with.... 32pp, plus 2 folding maps of the Reserve in San Diego County, California. Removed. $35.00

-Z-

Z1. ZAPATER (Horacio). Los Aborigenes Chilenos a Traves de Cronistas y Viajeros. 142pp, wrappers, Santiago de Chile, 1973. $25.00

Z2. ZAVALA (M.). Gramatica Maya. Edicion Facsimilar, Hecha.

por Jose Diaz-Bolio. 94pp, wrappers, Merida, 1974 (reprint of 1896 ed.). $25.00

___Another Copy. Same. $15.00

Z3.   ZAVALA (M.) and MEDINA (A.). Vocabulario Espanol-Maya. 72pp, wrappers, Edicion Facsimilar, Merida, 1975 (reprint of 1898 ed.). $15.00

Z4.   ZEISBERGER (David). A Collection of Hymns, for the Use of the Delaware Christian Indians, of the Missions of the United Brethren, in North America. (8), 305, (3)pp, full leather, edited by Abraham Luckenbach, contains Zeisberger's 1802 dedication, hinges loose, Bethlehem, J. & W. Held, 1847. $150.00

Z5.   ZEISBERGER (David). Indian Dictionary: English, German, Iroquois--The Onondaga; and Algonquin--The Delaware. vi, 236pp, 4to, cloth, Cambridge, Mass., J. Wilson & Son, 1887. $150.00

___Another Copy. Same. $150.00

___Another Copy. Same, rebound in heavy linen. $95.00

Z6.   (ZEISBERGER, DAVID). David Zeisberger's History of the North American Indians. Edited by Archer Butler Hulbert and William N. Schwarze. Printed for Ohio Archaeological and Historical Society, Quarterly Publication Vol. XIX, January & April, 1910, Nos. 1 & 2. 189pp including notes, index, wraps. $50.00

___Another Copy. Same. $40.00

___Another Copy. Same. $50.00

Z7.   ZEISBERGER (David) and DU PONCEAU (Peter Stephen). Grammar of the Language of the Lenni Lenape or Delaware Indians. Translated from the German Manuscript by Peter Du Ponceau with a Preface and Notes by the Translator. 188pp, errata, original wraps, Philadelphia, James Kay, Jr., 1827. $150.00

Zeisberger was a missionary who worked for many years among the Lenape and his works remain a prime source for not only language but religion and history. The translator, Du Ponceau, was one of the first linguists to analyze the structure and relationship of American Indian languages to one another.

Z8.   ZENGEL (M. S.) et al. The Art of Ancient and Modern Latin America, Selections from Public and Private Collections in the United States. 228pp, 137 photographs--almost all full-page, New Orleans, 1968. $12.00

Z9.   ZENIL (Alfonso M.). (Instituto Nacional de Antropologia e Historia, Mexico, 1971) Monolitos Olmecas y Otros en el Museo de la Universidad de Veracruz. 53pp, 71 pls, in portfolio with ties, text in English and Spanish, wrappers. $35.00

Z10. ZENIL (Alfonso M.). The Olmec Tradition. 82pp, 49 photographs--mostly full-page, Houston, 1963. $10.00

Z11. ZERRIES (O.). Indianer Vom Amazonas, Kunst und Handwerk der Indianer des Tropischen Sudamerika. 160pp, 6 full-page color and 26 half and full-page b/w photographs, 30 drawings, map, wraps, Munich, 1960. $40.00

Z12. ZERRIES (Otto). Wild-Und Buschgeister in Sudamerika. 401pp, illus, map, wrappers, Wiesbaden, 1954. $30.00

Z13. ZIELINSKI (John M.). Mesquakie and Proud of It. 110pp, 2pp of ads, photographs, drawings by Leonard Young Bear, map, wrappers, Kalona, IA, 1976 (1st ed.).
$10.00

Z14. ZIMMERMAN (Arthur Franklin). Francisco de Toledo. Fifth Viceroy of Peru, 1569-1581. 300pp, plus index, bibliography, endpaper maps, much on the relations with the Incas, Caldwell, 1938 (1st ed.). $12.00
___Another Copy. Same. $25.00
___Another Copy. Same. $18.00

Z15. ZIMMERMAN (Charles Leroy). White Eagle, Chief of the Poncas. 273pp, photographs, maps, drawings, endpaper maps, society and history of the Poncas before and after removal, cloth, n.p., 1941 (1st ed.). $60.00

Z16. ZITKALA-SA (Gertrude Bonnin). Old Indian Legends Retold. 165pp, drawings by Angel de Cora, Iktomi and other stories from Sioux folklore, Boston, 1901 (1st ed.).
$10.00

Z17. ZOLBROD (P. G.). Dine Bahane, The Navajo Creation Story. xi, 431pp, cloth, Albuquerque, 1984. $35.00
___Another Copy. Same. $40.00

Z18. ZOLLA (Elemire). The Writer and the Shaman. A Morphology of the American Indian. 299pp, plus index, notes, New York, 1973 (1st ed.), d.j. $25.00
The character of the Indian in American literature as perceived by Whites from the colonial days to the present, discussing many authors such as Grinnell, Mabel Luhan, D. H. Lawrence, Mary Austin, Oliver LaFarge, Mari Sandoz, etc.
___Another Copy. Same. $12.00
___Another Copy. Same. $15.00

Z19. ZORITA (Alonso de). Life and Labor in Ancient Mexico. The Brief and Summary Relation of the Lords of New Spain. 328pp, illus, maps, translated and with an introduction by Benjamin Keen. Cloth, New Brunswick, 1971, d.j. $15.00
This edition, the first in English, is a study both of Aztec social and economic organization and of the post-conquest relations of Spaniards and Indians written by a Spanish Judge who served in the Indies in the mid-1500s.
___Another Copy. Same. $25.00

Z20. (ZUNI). The Zunis: Self Portrayals by the Zuni People. 245pp, 46 stories from oral literature of the Zunis of New Mexico, Albuquerque, 1972. $20.00
___Another Copy. Same. $28.00

Z21.   zu WIED (Prince Maximilian) and BODMER (Karl). People of
       the First Man, Life Among the Plains Indians in Their
       Final Days of Glory.   256pp, 67 b/w and 86 color draw-
       ings, cloth, New York, 1976, 1982. $35.00
           In 1883, Prince Maximillian of Germany and the artist
       Karl Bodmer traveled some 5,000 miles along the Missouri
       River. This account of their expedition is important for
       a number of reasons--not the least of which is Bodmer's
       magnificent water colors (most are full-page or larger)
       that provide a wondrous record of the people, ceremonial
       activities, and material culture of many plains tribes,
       including the Mandan, Blackfoot, Cree and Sioux. Maxi-
       millian's monumental narrative has long been regarded
       as one of the classics of early Western exploration. (EAP)

Massachusett S405
Mattamuskeet G36
Maya B116, B363, B419, B464, B561-B568, B641, B662,
    B742-B744, B755, C38, C64, C73, C117, C222, C314,
    C319-C321, C385, C409, C498, C501, C504, D61,
    D73, D74, D80-D83, D183, E30, E31, E66, F106,
    F146, G10, G11, G17, G18, G40, G81, G94, G105,
    G107, G150, G164, G174, G179, H57, H130, H131,
    H193, H194, H223, I55, I56, I61, J100, J135, J136,
    K105, K159, K168, K247, K251, L108, L129, L131,
    L132, L218, L223, L232, L240, M68, M77, M143,
    M256-M265, M269-M271, M296, M338, M347, M396,
    M410, M477, M478, M480-M482, M499, N10, N103,
    O1, O10, P10, P11, P99, P109, P227, P281, R28,
    R30, R158, R160, R173-R178, R234-R236, S1, S2,
    S8, S66, S68, S80, S371, S409, S433, S434, S436,
    S438, S463, S496, S575, S605, T36, T38, T104,
    T106, T107, T113, T118, T120, T121-T128, T130, T131,
    T171, T181-T183, V68, V82, V83, V87, V89, V90,
    V99, W236, W237, W245, W252, W261, W311
Mazahua I59
Menomini-Menominee B17, B154, H305, K31, M312,
    M313, N81, O123, P278, S276, S280, S285, S439,
    S440
Meskwakis W45
Mesquakie-Musquakie M99, O125
Miami A141, D306, H145, H454, V85
Micmac L62, L121, T212, V62, W35
Millcayac D154
Mimbrenos K1, N44, P71, P201
Mimmac G258
Mingo C296, H2
Miskito B158, Y25
Mistassini R197, R198, S398
Miwok B351, B376, G86, H179, M272, V110
Mixtec D100, D278, D289, S329, S449
Modoc B350, C515, F162, L18, M281, M379, M417-M419,
    M525, O78, P75, R52, R123, T116
Mogollon H124, H125, J60, L114, M183, M187, M190,
    M193, M195, W179
Mohave-Mojave B227, D157, G213, K206-K209, K222,
    M91, O14, S136, S210, S273, S560, T21
Mohawk G191, G206, H212, H453, K86, M421, M466,
    O7, P205, R145, T111, Y1
Mohegan B46, H150, M532, P83, P84
Moki H390
Mongarillo W247
Monlaki G163
Montagnais-Naskapi B175, K64, L55, M362, M535,
    S398, S400, T212
Montauk O9